READING BETWEEN THE LINES
Toward an Understanding of Current Social Problems

THIRD EDITION

Amanda Konradi
Ohio University

Martha Schmidt
The University of Akron

Boston   Burr Ridge, IL   Dubuque, IA   Madison, WI   New York   San Francisco   St. Louis
Bangkok   Bogotá   Caracas   Kuala Lumpur   Lisbon   London   Madrid   Mexico City
Milan   Montreal   New Delhi   Santiago   Seoul   Singapore   Sydney   Taipei   Toronto

Higher Education

READING BETWEEN THE LINES: TOWARD AN UNDERSTANDING OF CURRENT
SOCIAL PROBLEMS, THIRD EDITION
Published by McGraw-Hill, a business unit of The McGraw-Hill Companies, Inc., 1221
Avenue of the Americas, New York, NY 10020. Copyright © 2004 by The McGraw-Hill
Companies, Inc. All rights reserved. Previous editions © 2001, 1998 by Mayfield Publishing
Company. No part of this publication may be reproduced or distributed in any form or by
any means, or stored in a database or retrieval system, without the prior written consent of
The McGraw-Hill Companies, Inc., including, but not limited to, any network or other
electronic storage or transmission, or broadcast for distance learning.
Some ancillaries, including electronic and print components, may not be available
to customers outside the United States.

2 3 4 5 6 7 8 9 0 FGR/FGR 0 9 8 7 6 5 4 3

Editor-in-chief: *Thalia Dorwick*
Publisher: *Phil Butcher*
Sponsoring editor: *Carolyn Henderson Meier*
Marketing manager: *Dan Loch*
Production services manager: *Jennifer Mills*
Production service: *Hockett Editorial Service*
Manuscript editor: *Sheryl Rose*
Art director: *Jeanne M. Schreiber*
Design manager: *Cassandra Chu*
Cover designer: *Joan Greenfield*
Interior designer: *Jenny El-Shamy*
Art manager: *Robin Mouat*
Production supervisor: *Rich Devitto*

The text was set in 10/12 Book Antiqua by Graphic Arts Center and printed on acid-free,
45# New Era Matte by Quebecor World, Fairfield.

Cover images: Barbara Penoyau/Getty Images/PhotoDisc and Amos Morgan/Getty
Images/PhotoDisc

Library of Congress Cataloging-in-Publication Data

Reading between the lines: toward an understanding of current social problems / [edited
  by] Amanda Konradi, Martha Schmidt.—3rd ed.
      p. cm.
    ISBN 0-07-282152-3
    1. Social problems. I. Konradi, Amanda, II. Schmidt, Martha (Martha A.)

HN17.R43 2004
361.1–dc21

                                                                2003051217

www.mhhe.com

A.K. — To Andrei Konradi and Normal Juliet Wikler who inspired me to think critically and read between the lines.

M.S. — To Edna Ruth Geiger Schmidt for demonstrating the power of unconditional love and unfailing determination.

Brief Contents

Contents

Chapter 5: Race and Ethnicity   179

Chapter 6: Gender and Sexuality   256

SECTION III: SOCIAL PROBLEMS AND SOCIAL INSTITUTIONS   308

Chapter 7: Work   308

Chapter 8: Family 368

Chapter 9: Education   428

Chapter 10: The Criminal Justice System   481

Chapter 11: Illness and Health Care   563

Chapter 12: The Environment   608

Chapter 13: Global Politics, Terrorism, and War   645

Preface

We have found that teaching social problems courses frequently poses several dilemmas for sociology instructors. Typically, a course in social problems is offered as a general education course without prerequisites. Students therefore often lack even the most basic sociological concepts with which to analyze the material. They tend to resort to popular psychological explanations for human behavior—most of which they have received from talk shows, magazines, self-help books, or dinner-table conversations. Those students who have taken an introductory sociology course often find that social problems courses fail to reinforce the concepts that are central to the sociological imagination. Still beginners, these students are not analytically sophisticated enough to tease out theoretical connections by themselves. Social problems courses can easily turn into classes that require students to memorize facts and figures but which do not offer the theoretical tools to understand and explain the problems of daily social life.

As our book title suggests, we believe that a central goal of any social problems course is to encourage students to think critically about problems. We want our students to read between the lines of the explanations and remedies currently offered as truths by journalists and politicians. We want students to question their own perceptions and beliefs about social problems as well as those portrayed in the larger culture around them. With this book, we seek to provide students with the sociological tools to understand not just the problems themselves but also the politics of social problems debates.

THE THIRD EDITION

In the preceding two editions of this text, we focused on providing students with a conceptual framework for understanding social problems and presenting accessible readings that enable an integrated race, class, and gender analysis. In addition to including twenty new readings in this third edition, we have expanded our introduction and coverage of topics. Specifically, we have

- expanded chapter introductions to enhance the ability of students and instructors to use *Reading Between the Lines* as the sole textbook in a social problems course,
- added a new chapter on global politics, terrorism, and war,
- added material covering a variety of new topics, such as the death penalty, religion, militarism, and the micro aspects of inequality,
- expanded our coverage of social construction and introduced the conceptual ideas of claims and claims makers,
- presented the contributions that a feminist perspective can add to each of the four theoretical approaches, and
- added a reading to our framing chapter, "Thinking About Social Problems," that explicitly addresses how symbolic interactionist research is relevant to the analysis of inequality.

ORGANIZATION

This third edition is somewhat reorganized. This book now consists of thirteen chapters presented in three sections.

Section I, "Toward an Understanding of Current Social Problems," includes Chapters

1 and 2, "A Conceptual Tool Kit" and "Thinking About Social Problems." Together these two chapters provide a conceptual framework for reading the selections in the rest of the book. Chapter 1 discusses how sociologists approach the analysis of social problems, and Chapter 2 presents five pieces in which sociologists discuss the kinds of questions that should guide examination of social life. Each reading also provides concrete examples that illustrate how the author uses the questions to uncover something unique about social problems. Together and separately, the readings provide models of the sociological imagination.

Section II, "Social Problems and Inequality," includes Chapters 3–6. Section II introduces students to three dominant systems of oppression in American society and explains how they independently and collectively contribute to inequality in our society. The section will help students understand how we come to recognize macro and micro aspects of economic, race, and gender inequality and how race, class, and gender are relevant social categories. In addition to the standard learning tools featured in every chapter, each chapter in Section II contains an introduction that discusses key terminology, theoretical perspectives, and general statistics related to the problem, as well as how the four conceptual frameworks apply to the problem, how the readings tie to the conceptual frameworks, and the key arguments of each reading.

Section III, "Social Problems and Social Institutions," contains the remaining seven chapters of this book. Readings in this section focus on problems as a product of the routine workings of various organizations with which Americans have almost daily contact (such as places of work or education) or those whose aim is to ameliorate the problems of society (such as the criminal justice system and health care facilities). Readings in this section also highlight the ways that interconnections of the institu-

tional processes of governments and corporations contribute to global problems of environmental degradation, terrorism, and warfare. The readings also focus on the ordinary or unexamined ways that people carry out their lives and duties as members of families, workplaces, or educational institutions. These chapters reflect how structural inequalities of class, race, and gender are perpetuated through the repetition of individual behaviors in the varied domains of daily life. The chapters in Section III are structured similarly to those in Section II, but do not introduce new key terms. We hope that as students read Sections II and III, their understanding of the different kinds of conceptual analysis outlined in this introduction will be clarified and reinforced.

PEDAGOGICAL AIDS

Working together, the authors and the editors have developed a format for the text that supports the goal of a readable, practical, and attractive text. Always striving to help students master the material, we have added a number of new features to the chapters:

- Learning objectives at the beginning provide students with guidance about what conceptual information they should draw from the readings.

- Key terms discussed in the chapter introduction are reiterated toward the end.

- Focusing Questions, which appear at the end of chapter introductions, direct students to read with reference to the big picture. Questions for Discussion, which appear immediately following each reading, push students to draw out the main conceptual issues. Questions for Debate, at the end of chapters, encourage students to draw connections between the readings and to weigh the value of the different theoretical perspectives.

- The Social Web section presents Internet Web sites where students can find additional empirical information and information about activism relevant to the chapter topic.

- Perspectives on the Problem and Connecting the Perspectives, two short discussions which show how the four conceptual frameworks apply to each problem and how each reading ties to the conceptual frameworks, consistently reinforce the theoretical focus of the book.

SUPPLEMENTS PACKAGE

With the assistance of Carolyn Wood, we expanded the Instructor's Manual of the second edition. The updated manual, which we think instructors will find helpful, whether using this book as the major source of readings for a course or as a companion to another textbook, includes a test bank, suggestions for classroom activities and assignments, and visual aids to help instructors prepare lectures. Please contact your McGraw-Hill sales representative for more information.

IN APPRECIATION

With each edition of this book we become indebted to more colleagues and friends for telling us about their favorite articles, offering editorial advice, and giving us emotional support. We are deeply grateful to Diane Ciekawy, Woody Doane, Glenn Doston, Kathryn Feltey, Mary Beth Krouse, Matthew Lee, Patricia Martin, Josie Mendez Negrete, Barry Ochrach, Pamela Roby, Bob Sheak, Barbara Ellen Smith, Nancy Tatarek, Verta Taylor, Lynet Uttal, Miriam Wallace, and John Zipp. We are also indebted to Cheryl Kennedy and Carolyn Spurlock in the department of sociology at Ohio University for providing support for this project. And we thank Carolyn Wood for proofreading. Amanda also thanks Bob Capuzzo, Kristin Mazzio, Laura Nadeau, and Jennifer Waligura, for providing exceptional care to her children and enabling her to work on this project.

Many academic reviewers have provided exceptionally useful feedback on earlier editions of this book that assisted us in developing this edition. We thank:

Deborah Abowitz, Bucknell University

Jacqueline Bergdahl, Wright State University

Dean Braa, Western Oregon State University

Robert Carothers, Kent State University

Martha Copp, East Tennessee State University

Kathryn J. Fox, University of Vermont

Jim Jones, Mississippi State University

Martha O. Loustaunau, New Mexico State University

Yvonne D. Newsome, Agnes Scott College

Susan M. Ross, Lycoming College

Martha Shockey, St. Ambrose University

John R. Stratton, University of Iowa

Renée T. White, Central Connecticut State University

Your thoughtful reviews have made this a better book, and we are deeply grateful. In addition to our formal reviewers, four graduate student instructors at Ohio University—Rebecca Dolinsky, Pamela Hunt, Christopher Newton, and Roberta Roberson—have provided invaluable feedback on using the book.

We would like to thank our first editor, Serina Beauparlant at Mayfield Publishing Company, for inspiring us to pursue this book and Carolyn Henderson Meier and her staff at McGraw-Hill for helping us develop the pedagogical aspects of this edition. Finally, we thank the production team at McGraw-Hill for tying it all together—especially Rachel Youngman of Hockett Editorial Service, Sheryl Rose, Cassandra Chu, and Jen Mills.

SECTION I
Toward an Understanding of Current Social Problems

Chapter 1
A Conceptual Toolkit

Learning Objectives

By the end of this chapter you should be able to:

- Describe what it means to approach social problems subjectively and objectively.
- Recognize the four theoretical frameworks.
- Identify the difference between macro features of society (social systems and institutions) and micro features of society (interaction).
- Explain the value of a feminist approach to social problems.
- Explore aspects of your own life experience from a micro and macro perspective.

Angela's Story

To say that Memorial Day in the Mississippi Delta is hot is like saying the cars racing around the track in Indianapolis five hundred miles to the north go fast. The thick trousers and long sleeves that Angela wore might have been appropriate for spring in the Midwest, but here they were nearly unbearable. Still, she was glad to have these clothes. She had borrowed them, an old purse, and shoes that were a full size too small, and hoped she would look good enough to convince the hotel manager that she was employable. She had never held a job. Marriage and motherhood had filled up her years since she was a teenager. The clothes had achieved the desired result, and she was told to report for her job as a hostess the following morning. Maybe it had been the clothes, or perhaps her missing teeth, swollen wrist, and look of absolute despair that had convinced her new boss how much she needed a job.

Angela had finally found the nerve to leave her husband, Tom. On a night four months earlier, he had beaten her so savagely she had been convinced he would kill her. After she left, she had been afraid to stay in town. Her husband was, after all, a police officer, and he knew the city better than she did. So she had boarded a southbound train with her six sons and headed for family, safety, and a new life.

This new life was hard, harder than she had ever imagined. Just getting herself and her kids out of the train station in this new city had proved a challenge. Her aunt had agreed to let the family move in with her,

1

but all Angela had was an address. She had no ride, no money, and no friends. She wandered the streets until she spotted a pleasant-looking young woman getting into a car. Angela mustered her courage and begged the woman to take her to her new home. It took a while to find the house. It was, it turned out, literally on the wrong side of the tracks, directly in the shadow of a large pharmaceutical factory, in a neighborhood where most White people didn't venture. The house was built in the "shotgun" style common to Southern homes—long and narrow, each room added piecemeal on the back of the preceding room, so that if you fired a shotgun through the front door, the bullet would pass through each room and exit through the back door. The house leaned, the roof was held together with tar paper, and the windows were rotting and had been nailed shut for fear of burglars. There was no air conditioning. A toilet sat on the front porch.

Over the next few months, daily survival proved to be a daunting task. Her aunt had Alzheimer's disease, and Angela was frightened to leave her alone with the children. Her cousin finally agreed to watch the children if Angela could find work. Neither woman had enough money to feed all those kids, and Angela refused to go to the welfare office. She feared that welfare workers would attempt to locate her husband to pay child support; that meant he would know where she was hiding. She tried begging on the street with her children, which proved to be a disaster. She didn't know that in this city beggars were required to pay twenty-five dollars for a panhandler's license. The police arrested her, and she spent the night in jail. After that, she tried selling the only thing she felt she owned outright—her body. But after every "trick" she cried, wondering if she had traded in one abusive life for another.

Still, her children seemed happier than they had been in a long time. Her oldest boys, twin 16-year-olds, had made the honor roll in school. They both wanted to be pastors, and the family joked about the "twin ministries" in their midst. She always lectured her sons about the importance of doing their schoolwork. Angela herself couldn't read, and she told her children she didn't want their lives to turn out the way hers had. She warned them to stay away from the crack cocaine being sold on the sidewalks where they played.

Angela's 7-year-old, her baby, worried her the most. Two years earlier he had been run down by a hit-and-run driver. The hospital's chaplain had had the unfortunate duty of informing Angela that her darling boy was dead on arrival in the emergency room. Ten minutes later, the chaplain rushed back to tell her that his heart had been restarted and declared that a miracle had occurred. For six weeks the boy lay in a coma. During this time, Angela's husband became increasingly violent and eventually stabbed Angela's identical twin sister. Despite her sister's injury and outrage, Angela had felt she couldn't leave Tom. Every bit of her strength was devoted to her ailing son.

Now, two years later, the boy still suffered from epilepsy. Most of the time the seizures could be controlled with daily medication. The drugs were expensive, though, and when the prescription bottle was nearly empty, Angela would turn to hustling. Yet, when she saw her son happy, coming out of the depression that had haunted him for months, it all seemed worth it.

Now she had a job, and the future was looking brighter. She still needed to panhandle a little, enough for food, medicine, and bus fare to work. She befriended a woman who gave her clothes and bought food for the family. Her new employer was teaching her to read. The worry never left her heart, and sleep never came easily—still, maybe now she had a chance.

. . .

Angela's story is the story of social problems in American society today. She is the person, the name, the life behind the headlines that daily announce the problems plaguing our society. The politicians, the analysts, and the "film-at-eleven" teasers that interrupt our nightly television viewing often neglect to say that social problems are about people—people whose daily lives are affected by forces beyond their control. The big issues—power, poverty, welfare reform, racism, sexism, health care, crime, education, and the environment—are all played out in the minute details of Angela's life. Social problems are not just numbers, speculative theories, and political proposals. They are fundamentally about people's everyday lives.

Reading Between the Lines

Popular culture today abounds with images, messages, and warnings about social problems. Talk shows, self-help manuals, magazines, radio shock-jocks, political pundits, and televangelists all caution us about the dangers lurking within our society, offer their versions of what went wrong, and sell us their answers of what must be done to fix it. These analyses are typically oversimplified portrayals of very complex problems, frequently misguided and misinformed, and often just plain wrong.

If you are new to sociology, you are undoubtedly already immersed in information and beliefs about the causes, consequences, and cures of social problems. You may find the challenge of sorting through these messages and weeding out the faulty explanations and misguided solutions to be a daunting task. At times, you may feel that you have been presented with a smorgasbord of facts and figures that offers you little guidance in truly understanding social problems. Developing a sociological imagination can help us all to examine social problems, whether we are students, scholars, policy makers, or just citizens who want to make informed choices. As instructors of social problems, we find the process of challenging students to think sociologically about social problems to be stimulating, rewarding, and even fun.

We created this book with several goals in mind. First, we want to introduce you to the scope of conditions currently considered to be social problems by sociologists and to acquaint you with different conceptual approaches to the study of social problems. Second, we want to provide you with the tools to read between the lines of all of the messages we receive in the popular culture, to analyze social problems critically, and to understand the politics of the social problems debates. We challenge you to question your own assumptions about what constitutes social reality and how the everyday world operates. Finally, we want to demonstrate that social problems are interconnected and that every individual living in our society is in some way implicated in current social problems.

An analysis of social problems requires attention to three principal areas:

1. the ways social life and cultural beliefs are organized by world and state economies and political systems, and by class, race, and gender
2. the ways that individuals, making decisions within the realm of opportunities and options available to them, reproduce and sometimes challenge patterns of inequality

3. the ways that conditions and issues come to be widely accepted as social problems

Perspectives and Assumptions

Sociologists can approach the study of social problems in very different ways. The perspectives and assumptions that we hold can profoundly shape what questions we ask about social problems, the explanations and conclusions we reach about them, and, ultimately, the solutions we offer to remedy problems. In this section, we will describe some of the most common approaches that sociologists currently use to examine social problems. The approaches we describe here are not mutually exclusive, because each emphasizes a different aspect of social life. We would like you to think of this discussion as a sort of "tool kit," from which you can select what you think are the best tools for critically analyzing social problems.

One significant distinction in the way sociologists approach social problems is whether they are interested in explaining an objective reality or how human subjects come to believe that there is an objective reality (subjective analysis). Sociologists engaged in **objective analysis** all accept social problems as real conditions that can be measured, explained, and, we hope, solved. They may have vastly different views on the causes and cures of social problems, but they all agree that social problems exist independently of what people think about them and cause very real suffering in people's everyday lives. Sociologists who pursue **subjective analysis** all believe that human behaviors, traits, or social conditions become "problems" through a collective process of definition. Put another way, social problems are **social constructions** that exist as a result of human efforts to pin negative labels on human behaviors, traits, or social conditions. If a community does not see a human behavior, trait, or condition as problematic, it seeks no solution, even if someone is in pain. In the sections below we will discuss objective and subjective analysis of social problems in more detail.

Objective Analysis of Social Problems
Micro and Macro Exploration

To begin our discussion, let's return to the story of Angela. One way to look at her story is to examine the larger social forces shaping her life that are beyond her control. We might, for example, look at the lack of opportunities available to Angela to financially support herself and her children. How do current welfare policies constrain her ability to receive aid? Why are there so few social supports available to women who want to leave their battering husbands? Why is our current system of health care so expensive that Angela turns to prostitution in order to buy medicine for her gravely ill son? What are the ways that city developers have abandoned her predominantly Black neighborhood, except as the ideal location for industries no one wants to live near? Sociologists who ask these kinds of questions are engaged in **macro analysis** of social problems. These sociologists are concerned with identifying the larger social structures and enduring features of society—economic, political, educational, or legal—that constrain the opportunities available to people.

Another way to examine the social problems shaping Angela's life is to find out how she negotiates the world around her; that is, we might focus on the choices she makes and the ways she responds to particular conditions. For example, we might look at why she left her abusive husband when she did. Or we could try to understand the skills she has developed to survive life on the streets or the ways she copes with the continual threat of arrest. How does she deal with having to choose prostitution in order to buy food and medicine for her family? What is life like for a woman who is trying to raise children on her own and hold a job when she can't read? Sociologists who ask these kinds of questions are engaged in **micro analysis.** They look at how individuals interact with one another to create their daily reality. What do social problems mean to people and how do they cope with them? Additionally, micro analysis involves exploring how people perpetuate social problems through their interactions. When individuals beat up their wives or children, hurl racist insults at people, or deny them jobs because of the way they look, they are contributing to social problems.

To sum up, macro analysis involves asking questions about how enduring social processes in societies give structure to daily life; micro analysis involves asking questions about how individuals with specific attributes and different group affiliations negotiate situations. One really needs to explore both the large forces external to individuals and individuals' ways of making decisions and engaging one another to grasp the nature of social problems in our world.

Objective Theoretical and Conceptual Frameworks

Another set of conceptual tools available to us for use in objective analysis are the different theories that sociologists use to examine social problems: conflict theory, functionalist theory, and symbolic interactionism. Sociologists looking at social life through the lenses of conflict theory and functionalist theory tend to ask macro questions. Sociologists looking at life through the lens of symbolic interactionism tend to ask micro questions.

One of the most common approaches scholars of social problems take is **conflict theory.** The key assumption of this theory is

that inequality is endemic to our modern society, and social groups with greater status are in a constant state of struggle with social groups with lesser status. Those with greater status use their power to preserve their positions of privilege; those with less status seek to alter the balance of power and gain access to opportunities and resources. The primary means the powerful use to maintain their positions are exerting their control over social institutions and decision-making processes and controlling access to resources such as the media, the legislature, the courts, and the economy. Individuals and groups who have little money and little political clout have little power to change an unjust system and thus fewer options available to them.

Sociologists who explore how social conflict and inequality contribute to social problems differ in what they believe is the most fundamental social inequality. Some argue that it is the economic system, but others argue that it is race, gender, or even sexuality. However, all would agree that enduring social practices that structure our lives are not neutral; some individuals and groups benefit from them while others suffer. From a conflict perspective, the study of social problems entails identifying the ways that power differences between groups and individuals result in social conditions that cause psychic or physical suffering.

Conflict theorists would argue that the social problems that shape Angela's life result from the lack of economic, political, and social opportunities available to her as a poor, African American woman. The behaviors she engages in that are deemed socially inappropriate—prostitution and begging—are, in fact, the result of having very few economic options. Sociologists using conflict theory might explain the absurdity of requiring the poorest people in society to pay twenty-five dollars for a panhandling license as a way to deal with the "problem" of street beggars without actually addressing the economic conditions of their city.

Conflict theorists might also analyze Angela's story by focusing on the trap in which poor people often find themselves. The way for Angela to get out of poverty is to find a well-paying job, yet there are virtually no jobs in her area. She must rely on an inadequate system of public transportation to look for work elsewhere. She must also have clothing that is suitable for employment, yet without a paycheck to purchase those clothes, she must borrow or beg. She needs to work to provide medicine for her son, yet the minimum-wage job that she can find offers no medical benefits. If she takes time away from her job to take her child to a free clinic, she risks being fired. All these factors exist within an economic system in which even the middle class is struggling, and in which it is nearly impossible for the poor to find employment with wages that can support a family. Conflict theorists would not see Angela as a victim in this system. Rather, they would likely see her as a woman making the best decisions she can, given her limited options.

The conflict perspective in sociology traces back to Karl Marx's mid-nineteenth-century analysis of class relations in the developing European capitalist economy. Jane Addams's, Charlotte Perkins Gilman's, and Alice Paul's research on urban social problems in Chicago and W. E. B. DuBois's analyses of the causes and consequences of racial inequality in American society are early-twentieth-century exemplars of analyses of power in the United States. C. Wright Mills is best known for popularizing the conflict approach in the United States in the 1950s and 1960s. He is credited with developing the concept of the "sociological imagination" and providing powerful critiques of American institutions that demonstrated that a "power elite" had great control over the government and economy. Since the 1960s, many feminist sociologists have taken up this general perspective to expose the patriarchal nature of American society.

In this book, readings informed by conflict theory appear in every chapter. For example, it shapes Donald Barlett and James Steele's investigation of corporate welfare, John Isbister's exploration of worldwide poverty, Barbara Ehrenreich and Frances Fox Piven's examination of the effects of welfare reform in an economy where jobs are increasingly scarce, Grace Chang's research on the formation and implementation of immigration policy, Kathleen Blee's analysis of how the Ku Klux Klan recruits and retains members, Diane McEachern and her colleagues' analysis of domestic violence among the Navajo, Jonathan Kozol's analysis of the inequalities in public education, Steven Manning's description of corporate involvement in schools, Barry Yeoman's analysis of the prison industrial complex, John Lamberth's analysis of racial bias in traffic apprehensions, and Ken Silverstein's documentation of how financial concerns shape the development of new drugs.

Sociologists who use **functionalist theory** to analyze social problems also focus on large social structures. Whereas sociologists using conflict theory stress the importance of power in understanding social conditions, sociologists looking through the lens of functionalist theory focus on how problems are related to a breakdown in social organization. Functionalist theory proposes (1) that societies evolve, (2) that human groups and individuals have needs that must be fulfilled, and (3) that all institutions within the social structure of a society must be integrated to fill the needs adequately. Under conditions of slow change, the institutions of the society function well, they are able to evolve so that their integration is maintained, and the majority of people's needs are met. However, when a society changes rapidly, the enduring social processes that give structure to daily life—institutions—often do not readjust quickly enough to meet many human needs. Until the gap between people's needs and the ability of the social structure to meet those needs is closed, social problems occur and people suffer physically and psychologically.

Through the lens of functionalist theory, a sociologist would likely view Angela's plight as a result of a breakdown of social organizations. What prevented social organizations (church groups, social service agencies, the legal system) from taking care of Angela when her husband abused her? What formal or informal social supports are needed for Angela to replace her husband's income? How do panhandling and prostitution function as economic safety nets for the poor, catching them from falling into starvation or homelessness? Do middle-class people have other kinds of economic safety nets—like assistance from family members—that poor people don't have?

Functionalist analysis of society traces back to 1893 when Émile Durkheim published an analysis of how the division of labor in a society produces social cohesion. His work was published in French and translated into English in 1933. Professors at the University of Chicago investigated Durkheim's central idea that problems in society emerged from the breakdown of social organization. These researchers argued that the amount of poverty, crime, violence, and drug use had risen in Chicago because waves of immigrants were not integrated into the institutional structures of the city. Robert Park, Ernst Burgess, and Louis Wirth are credited with developing the Chicago School of sociology and with making the study of social problems central to American sociology.

Currently, the counterintuitive quality of functionalist theory is widely appreciated by sociologists of social problems. Beginning with the functionalist assumption that all enduring aspects of society serve a social purpose, sociologists turn our common wisdom on its head. By showing how social problems experienced as psychically or physically painful by some provide benefits to others, they help us identify resistance to proposed social policies. By showing that behaviors we may label as deviant (and in fact criminalize) actually sustain individuals and communities, they can help us see why eradication efforts tend to fail and, maybe, push us to rethink them.

In this book, a variety of readings are informed by functionalist theory. William Julius Wilson argues that ghetto-related behavior is an adaptation to lack of opportunity and lack of institutional supports. Amy Caiazza examines how violence against women affects the long-term health of impoverished societies and the world, with an eye toward modifying U.S. foreign policy. Martin Jankowski explores how gangs are positively integrated in their communities and the needs they fill. Edward Kain puts the "nuclear" family form in historic context, clarifying that it is a recent adaptation to the relatively prosperous circumstances of the middle class. Lillian Rubin explains how the institutions of work and family have failed to compensate for recent rapid changes in the economy, leaving families' needs unmet. Kristin Luker exposes how teenage girls' decisions to become parents are responsive to both lack of institutional supports and their poverty.

Symbolic interactionism is a third approach that some sociologists use in looking at social problems. Whereas analysis using conflict theory and functionalist theory involve examining social structures, symbolic interactionist analysis involves exploring the micro level. The symbolic interactionist perspective posits that enduring social relations exist because of the consistent ways that people interact every day. Thus, sociologists using this perspective focus on the ways that individuals create social reality through their daily interactions. They study how individual lines of action become interwoven, forming the processes that give structure to our lives.

Through the lens of symbolic interaction, social inequality, which is the basis of social problems, is produced and reproduced through the repetition of individual behaviors that set others apart. This contrasts with the central assumption of both conflict and functionalist theories, that social problems are caused by larger social forces or enduring practices that transcend individuals.

Sociologists using the symbolic interactionist perspective argue that we are often unaware of how our behavior creates or perpetuates inequality because we do not tend to analyze our everyday assumptions. We want to believe that our behavior is free from bias. However, we need not be personally biased to reproduce inequality. When we conform our behavior to the enduring social practices of our society and interpret and apply rules to specific situations in accord with past practices, we reproduce inequalities inherent in the rules. Sociologists using the symbolic interactionist perspective focus on understanding how individuals and groups give meaning to situations, interpret the behaviors of other people in them, and form their own behavior in response. They seek to expose the implicit assumptions and unspoken worldviews that guide actions that result in inequalities of various kinds.

For interactionists, shifts in viewpoint are necessary, if not entirely sufficient, to eliminate social problems. Resolving social problems requires altering how people interact both consciously and unconsciously in all arenas of social life: family, government, work, recreation, criminal justice, health care, and so on. It is a matter of getting individuals to challenge the customary ways of doing things and to question the behaviors they use to preserve their sense of self.

Looking at Angela's life through the lens of symbolic interactionism would involve looking at her beliefs and behaviors and those of the people she encounters to understand how they shape her life. Sociologists using this perspective might look at how her husband's perception of his social role gave him a reason to beat his wife. They might examine whether her children perceive their lives to be more stable in a situation where there is violence or lack of income. They would ask how the police view Angela when they see her panhandling. Do they see her as a poor woman trying to get economic resources, or as immoral, mentally ill, or criminal? Likewise, they would ask how the people from whom Angela tries to beg see her and respond to her. Is she in need of help and worthy of a handout, a personal threat to their safety, to blame for her own problems? Should she be the recipient of snide remarks, walked around at a distance, or simply ignored?

Herbert Blumer is credited with coining the term *symbolic interaction* in 1969. However, the roots of this sociological perspective (Blumer refused to call it a theory) trace back to the University of Chicago as well. There, George Herbert Mead and W. I. Thomas developed a framework for thinking about the development of the self in relation to society and for making a connection between worldview and action. Two women, Jane Addams and Jessie Taft, provided early symbolic interactionist accounts of the gendering of men's and women's worlds (in 1910 and 1915, respectively). In the 1960s, Howard Becker made a major contribution to the study of social problems by developing a theory of labeling that explained how deviants were created by social institutions.

This book presents a variety of readings that address symbolic interactionist questions. Michael Schwalbe and colleagues explain the generic processes in face-to-face interactions that are the basis of much inequality. Kevin Bales looks at the interpretive frameworks that promote slavery within the global economy. Kathryn Edin and Laura Lein explore how single mothers make ends meet on a welfare check. Barbara Perry shows how nonwhites use violence to "do race" and maintain social boundaries, group privileges, and racial hierarchies. Scott Coltrane describes how a couple must redefine themselves in order to reorganize their family roles. Gillian Dunne explores how lesbian parents reconfigure caring and earning responsibilities that are generally allocated on the basis of gender in heterosexual unions. Nancy Naples documents how women's definitions of motherhood vary by class and race, such that those most separated from the middle-class "domestic ideal" see political activism as mothering work. Myra Sadker and David Sadker depict how teachers in many small and subtle ways reassert gender norms and unconsciously reproduce inequality in their classrooms. William S. Lofquist and Amanda Konradi use the lens of symbolic interaction to expose how culturally embedded narrative frameworks shape legal actors' behavior and justice outcomes in the trial process. Finally, Daniel Chambliss and Carol A. Heimer and Lisa Staffen document how patients and their parents are affected by the worldviews of the hospital staff.

Subjective Analysis of Social Problems

Sociologists using a social constructionist approach seek to understand how particular conditions and issues come to be widely accepted as problematic. They argue that no universal condition or issue is inherently bad. Rather, they see that conditions are labeled as bad by humans, so that conditions seen as problems vary from culture to culture and across time. A good example of this is the pain that children experience as a result of being hit by adults. Fifty years ago, beating a child was considered to be an acceptable and even necessary form of discipline; today it is considered to be abuse and is labeled a criminal act. Likewise, spanking a child remains controversial within parenting, educational, psychological, and medical circles today. Does spanking constitute physical abuse, and is it therefore a criminal act, or is it an effective and harmless means of normal discipline?

Social constructionists are not only concerned with *whether* a condition is defined as a social problem. They are also focused on the ways that beliefs about the nature of a particular problem—including its causes, its effects, and the characteristics of the people affected by it—come to be widely accepted. In short, they ask *how* a problem is defined. To define a condition as a problem is to demand a solution. How a problem is defined shapes what solutions are proposed. The goal for social constructionists is to discover who is involved in labeling a particular condition or issue as a problem, who benefits from this process, and who benefits from particular policies designed to address social problems. Social constructionists often demonstrate that societal recognition of conditions as problems is not tied to measurable increases or decreases in specific conditions.

Sociologists interested in social construction make a distinction between **claims** about social problems—assertions about the positive or negative aspects of a situation, condition, or attribute—and **claims makers**—those who seek to impose a particular definition of reality. Although a complete understanding of the emergence of a social problem requires attention to both, sociologists usually focus their research on either the rhetoric or the politics of the debate. Some sociologists examine the types of claims and counterclaims that are central to giving an undesirable condition a typical face, and how horror stories and attention grabbers are used to engage the emotions and the moral involvement of the public. Rhetorical idioms—forms of argument central to our culture—that sociologists have uncovered as the basis for much claims making include loss, endangerment, entitlement, misinformation, and calamity.

Other sociologists look at how different claims makers organize groups that are able to exert their power and interest through available public forums. They analyze the claims-making process in its historical context. That is, they explore how particular ways of framing the problem resonate with other social debates in the past and the present. They document how particular claims gain authority through their association with particular public individuals like visible leaders and celebrities. In the process, they also often expose the lack of an empirical basis for claims that sway public opinion. Sociologists interested in the politics of claims making also examine how social problems become formalized through legislation, whether a legislated solution leads to a significant reduction in the problem, and when and how new claims-making efforts emerge in response to governmental failure to eradicate problems.

The constructionist approach to social problems does not provide answers about the causes of harmful conditions nor does it offer solutions. However, it is a very important perspective because constructionist studies provide information about why some problems are allowed to languish and others become the focus of valuable resources. In addition, constructionist studies reveal arguments and strategies that have been effective in bringing social problems to the attention of the general public and can serve as a guide for those interested in social change.

Sociologists looking at Angela through the lens of social construction would not deny that Angela suffers. Yet, they would focus their research on how the social policies that affect her life are based on certain assumptions about what is morally bad, harmful, and worthy of public concern. Many people would call Angela's family "broken," and many policy makers would argue that so-called "broken homes" are responsible for our social ills. Yet poor women historically have had to deal with raising children on their own, because slavery, the labor market, or warfare separated husbands and fathers from their families. A sociologist interested in the rhetoric of claims making would ask what particular representations of poor women lead the public to accept the idea that they are unworthy. A sociologist interested in the politics of claims making would look at why poor women like Angela are now seen as the cause, rather than the result, of social problems, which social actors have made claims about the negative traits of poor women, and what broader social conditions give their claims resonance.

In 1941, Richard Fuller and Richard Myers made the first proposal that social problems were the result of collective action. They argued that social problems follow a typical career: When a threat is posed to a group or to a group's values, they take action, mobilize others, and eventually succeed in bringing about action that affirms their values. In their 1977 book, *Constructing Social Problems,* Malcolm Spector and John I. Kitsusi stated definitively that claims makers create social problems. Spector and Kitsusi were influenced by the development of ethnomethodology in sociology and by Peter Berger and Thomas Luckman's analysis of the social construction of reality. Since the 1980s, the number of constructionist accounts of social problems has mushroomed, ranging from how coffee has been constructed as a social problem to the "discovery" of child abuse to the emergence of stalking laws.

This book contains a variety of readings that explore the social construction of social problems. For example, Barbara Katz Rothman explores how medical expertise is produced and the rise of genetics as a meaningful explanation in medicine. Joshua Gamson explores why talk shows are seen as "trash" television. Nathan Glazer provides a social constructionist analysis of how the U.S. Census has played a significant role in reifying racial categories and racial divisions in the U.S. Jieli Li discusses how Asian Americans' problems have gone unnoticed because of the construction of an image of Asians as model citizens. Gloria Steinem provides a constructionist analysis of media coverage of the recent mass murders in high schools. Judith Lorber evaluates the evidence supporting constructionist and alternative explanations for sexuality. Kristin Luker examines the timing of social construction of the problem of teen pregnancy. Steven Donziger exposes how increases in the number and severity of criminal laws reflect fears rather than actual changes in crime rates. Robert Lifton and Greg Mitchell examine how the reasonability and legitimacy of the death penalty is sustained in the U.S., in spite of international rejection of this sanction. Valerie Kuletz identifies how Native Americans' perspectives were overlooked in the creation of nuclear policy that directly affected the region in which they lived.

At the end of this introduction you will find a summary chart that connects each reading to a theoretical perspective: Conflict Theory, Functionalist Theory, Symbolic Interaction, and Social Construction.

Feminist Concerns and Analysis

In the past three decades, sociologists operating from a **feminist perspective** have substantially shifted some of the debates about social problems. These sociologists argue that gender inequality is fundamental in our society. Many believe that gender inequality is even more basic than economic inequality and that problems based on gender inequality cut across all spheres of social life. They point out many social problems in the arenas of life we typically think of as "private" and far removed from the economy and politics: the family, home, sexual relationships, and even our bodies. Feminist sociologists have brought concerns about gender inequality to bear on research conducted using all of the four theoretical perspectives discussed above: conflict theory, functionalism, symbolic interaction, and social construction. They have criticized broad social policy initiatives that don't take into account the different social expectations placed on women and men and the added burden of gender discrimination that women face. In addition, feminist researchers have argued strongly for the need to examine the ways that race, gender, and class inequalities combine to contribute to social problems.

Some feminist sociologists explore micro analysis and symbolic interactionist concerns, focusing on what gender differences mean to individuals and the ways that people perpetuate gender inequality. These might look at how the men who insisted that Angela have sex with them in return for money perpetuate the cultural view of women as sexual objects. They might also look at what being a woman, a wife, and a mother means to Angela and how the cultural expectations of these roles collide in her life. For example, to be a good mother means providing food and health care for her children, yet to do these things, she has to turn to prostitution, which makes her a "bad" woman in the eyes of many people.

Other feminist sociologists pursue macro research and adopt functionalist or conflict perspectives to look at how inequalities based on gender, race, and class are built into our social structures. These scholars focus on the ways poverty disproportionately affects women and racial minorities, especially Hispanic and African American women. Statistics show that regardless of the job Angela is able to secure, her earning potential will be substantially less than her husband's. In addition, the primary financial, emotional, and caretaking responsibilities of raising children continue to fall on women in this culture. Angela is doomed to poverty because she has six children to raise. Realistically, the best way for her to economically support her children is to marry and again become financially dependent on a man's income. Thus, the social institutions in the United States keep her from gaining economic or social independence.

Finally, sociologists undertake feminist constructionist analysis. They look specifically at how assumptions about gender and sexuality are features of claims. They also analyze how men claims makers stand to gain power relative to women by creating new categories of deviant behavior that fall within women's predominant sphere of responsibilities. Or they examine the conditions that lead to women's success in raising public awareness of spousal battery, the construction of shelters for battered women, and the passage of the federal Violence Against Women Act.

Examples of feminist analyses in this book include the readings by Patricia Hill Collins, Grace Chang, Ruth Sidel, Barbara Ehrenreich and Frances Fox Piven, Kathryn Edin and Laura Lein, Kathleen Blee, all those in Chapters 6 and 8, Barbara Ehrenreich, Arlie Russell Hochschild, Barbara Reskin, Myra Sadker and David Sadker, Amanda Konradi, Carol Heimer and Lisa Staffen, and Joshua Goldstein.

The Politics of Sociological Analysis

In this book, we present you with a sociological way of seeing. It may feel liberating, because it helps you put vague impressions into words. Or it may feel foreign, because it makes you question your "commonsense" view of the world. It may even feel uncomfortable, because it makes you question your place in the world. The fact that sociologists' ways of representing society—making an image of it or imagining it—evoke strong emotions speaks to its political quality. It exposes a reality that many would prefer not to notice. To the extent that sociologists focus on social structure and the patterning of behavior and not on individual choices, their work is often characterized as "liberal" or "left wing" by nonsociologists. Likewise, to the extent that sociologists examine the construction of reality and ask students to rethink what they accept as real, they frequently are charged with radicalism. This use of labels to dismiss sociological analysis is unfortunate. A thorough examination of a phenomenon (social or otherwise) requires that researchers consider how items under investigation are defined. To understand an individual's behavioral choices requires that her or his life be placed in a broader social context and demands an examination of why her or his so-called personal troubles are or are not recognized as public concerns.

To label sociological analyses as "leftist" and "radical" and to dismiss them on that basis often reflects the discomfort that individual readers experience over the demands of critical thinking about their place in society. A sociological perspective requires us to recognize: (1) that the opportunities available to some people are not available to others, and that those of us who "have" may have at the expense of others (whether or not the conditions leading to such inequality are of our own making); and (2) that we are implicated daily in the creation of social problems if we continue to carry out many organizational and institutional practices that we were raised to view as neutral. In short, social problems belong to all of us, not just those who experience harm directly as a result of them. Therefore, we must alter our own behavior for many social problems to be ameliorated. This is a heavy message and a hard reality to face. However, dismissing sociological analyses as "political dogma" because they force us to question ourselves and others will not make social problems go away.

As the editors of this book, responsible for its form and content, we are also involved in the political process of defining what social problems are and who has valid ways of explaining them and providing solutions to them. It could not be otherwise. We try in this introduction to give you a sense of how we made the choices that resulted in this product, so that you may also critically evaluate this book in its entirety.

How This Book Is Organized

We have included the selections in this book based on several criteria. Foremost, they represent current writings in the major social problems on which we focus. We believe that you will find the authors' arguments straightforward and clear and the data accessible, even if you do not have previous training in sociology. Some pieces not written by sociologists are included because the authors tell an important story with sociological insights. Several selections that focus on social policy are included because they illustrate how different ways of viewing social problems lead to different solutions. We believe that, because social problems are inherently political, no one group should be allowed to define the scope of social problems presented to students. Thus, we have included pieces by authors of varied races and genders so you can read about the perspectives of subordinate, as well as dominant, group members. In the summary chart on pages 16 to 18, we have placed the readings in relation to the theoretical perspectives.

We have organized this book into thirteen chapters and three sections. Section I, "Toward an Understanding of Current Social Problems," includes this introduction and the next chapter, "Thinking About Social Problems." Together these two chapters provide a conceptual framework for reading the selections in the rest of the book. Section II, "Social Problems and Inequality," includes Chapters 3–6. Section II introduces you to three dominant systems of oppression in American society and explains how they independently and collectively contribute to inequality in our society. It illustrates macro and micro aspects of the production of economic, race, and gender inequality and will help you understand how we come to recognize race, class, and gender as relevant social categories. Each chapter in Section II begins with an introduction that provides a table of contents, learning objectives, a discussion about theoretical perspectives on the problem, a discussion providing some general statistics, short discussions that show how the four conceptual frameworks apply to this problem and how the readings tie to the conceptual frameworks, summaries of the readings that highlight the key arguments of each reading, and some focusing questions to help you pull the important issues from the readings. Following each reading, you will find discussion questions. At the end of each chapter you will find a list of key terms introduced in the chapter, information about Internet Web sites relevant to the topic, and questions for debate.

Section III, "Social Problems and Social Institutions," contains the remaining seven chapters of this book. Readings in this section focus on problems as a product of the routine workings of various organizations with which Americans have almost daily contact (such as places of work or education) or those whose aim is to ameliorate the problems of society (such as the criminal justice system and health care facilities). The readings also focus on the ordinary or unexamined ways that people carry out their lives and duties as members of families, workplaces, or educational settings. These chapters reflect how structural inequalities of class, race, and gender are perpetuated through the repetition of individual behaviors in the varied domains of daily life. The introductions in Section III are similar to those in Section II, but do not introduce new key terms. We hope that as you read Sections II and III, your understanding of the different kinds of conceptual analysis outlined in this introduction will be clarified and reinforced.

How to Use This Book

We encourage you to read this book with a pencil in your hand. Talk to the authors in the margins. Think about and answer the questions we pose at the beginning and end of the chapters and at the end of each reading. Try to develop the ability to identify when different approaches are being used to explain social problems and to examine how our social world is constructed.

Above all else, we encourage you to raise questions regarding the definitions, approaches, issues, and solutions that are a part of any discussion about social problems. Take intellectual risks. Question your own previously held beliefs. Question those of your colleagues or classmates. Question the perspectives of the various authors presented in this book and the overall perspectives that we have proposed here. Question the views of your professor, your congressional representative, your family, and your friends. Argue, debate, and discuss. And always be like the five-year-old child who must continuously ask, "But why?"

KEY TERMS

objective analysis
subjective analysis
social construction
macro analysis
micro analysis
conflict theory
functionalist theory
symbolic interactionism
claims
claims makers
feminist perspective

THE SOCIAL WEB

A variety of sociologically related professional organizations are concerned with analysis of social problems and policy.

- The Society for the Study of Social Problems focuses on understanding and ameliorating social problems. The SSSP Web site can be found at itc.utk.edu/sssp.
- The Association for Humanist Sociology can be found at www.humanistsoc.org.

- The Society for the Psychological Study of Social Issues supports interactionist research into social inequality. Its Web site can be found at www.spssi.org.
- The American Sociological Association Web site can be found at www.asanet.org.

QUESTIONS FOR DEBATE

1. You might begin with this brief exercise. Turn a piece of paper sideways and make four columns. In the first column, make a list of ten issues or conditions that immediately come to your mind as social problems. In the second column, note the reasons why you believe they are social problems (for example, the number of people affected, the seriousness of harm caused by the problems, or your personal experience with them). In the third column, jot down what you presently perceive to be their causes, and in the fourth column record any solutions that immediately come to your mind. Now compare your list to the list of someone else in the class. What do the similarities and differences of the lists reflect?

2. If we can measure the physical and psychological impact of social problems, why do we need the social constructionist perspective?

3. Think about the social problem at the top of your list (see Question 1 above). Is it something that many others also seem to be concerned about? What can you say about its construction as something worthy of concern?

4. What might someone looking at social problems from a feminist perspective say about the three social problems at the top of your list?

SUMMARY CHART—CONNECTING PERSPECTIVES

Reading	Author	Title	Conflict Theory	Functionalist Theory	Symbolic Interactionism	Social Constructionism
1	C. Wright Mills	The Sociological Imagination	X			
2	Patricia Hill Collins	Toward a New Vision: Race, Class, and Gender as Categories of Analysis and Connection	X			
3	Michael Schwalbe et al.	The Reproduction of Inequality: Interactionist Analysis			X	
4	Barbara Katz Rothman	The Limits of Science in Understanding Who We Are				X
5	Joshua Gamson	Why I Love Trash	X			X
6	William Greider	One World, Ready or Not: The Manic Logic of Global Capitalism	X			
7	George Ritzer	Enchanting a Disenchanted World: Revolutionizing the Means of Consumption	X			
8	Donald L. Barlett and James B. Steele	Corporate Welfare	X			
9	Kevin Bales	The Social Psychology of Modern Slavery	X		X	
10	Grace Chang	Disposable Domestics: Immigrant Women in the Global Economy	X			
11	John Isbister	A World of Poverty	X	X		
12	William Julius Wilson	Ghetto-Related Behavior and the Structure of Opportunity				X
13	Ruth Sidel	The Enemy Within	X			
14	Barbara Ehrenreich and Frances Fox Piven	Without a Safety Net	X			
15	Kathryn Edin and Laura Lein	Making Ends Meet on a Welfare Check			X	
16	Nathan Glazer	American Diversity and the 2000 Census				X
17	Jieli Li	Exploring Asian Americans: The Myth of the "Model Minority" and the Reality of Their Lives				X
18	Christopher Jencks and Meredith Phillips	The Black-White Test Score Gap	X			
19	Kathleen Blee	The Place of Women Inside Organized Racism	X			
20	Barbara Perry	Beyond Black and White: Ethnoviolence Between Oppressed Groups			X	
21	Gloria Steinem	Supremacy Crimes				
22	Amy Caiazza	Why Gender Matters: Women, Militarism, and Violence		X		X
23	Diane McEachern, Marlene Van Winkel, and Sue Steiner	Domestic Violence Among the Navajo: A Legacy of Colonization	X			

SUMMARY CHART—CONNECTING PERSPECTIVES

Reading	Author	Title	Conflict Theory	Functionalist Theory	Symbolic Interactionism	Social Constructionism
24	Judith Lorber	Embattled Terrain				X
25	Scott Coltrane	Family Mar: Fatherhood, Housework, and Gender Equity			X	X
26	Jill Andresky Fraser	White-Collar Sweatshop	X			
27	Arlie Russell Hochschild	The Time Bind: When Work Becomes Home and Home Becomes Work				X
28	Barbara Ehrenreich	Nickel and Dimed: On (Not) Getting By in America			X	
29	Martin Sanchez Jankowski	Gang Business: Making Ends Meet		X		
30	Barbara Reskin	The Effects of Affirmative Action on Other Stakeholders				
31	Edward L. Kain	The Myth of Family Decline		X		
32	Lillian B. Rubin	Families on the Fault Line: America's Working Class Speaks About the Family, the Economy, Race, and Ethnicity		X		
33	Gillian A. Dunne	Lesbians Blurring the Boundaries and Transforming the Meaning of Parenthood and Kinship			X	
34	Nancy A. Naples	Activist Mothering, Community Caretaking, and Civic Work			X	
35	Kristin Luker	Dubious Conception: The Politics of Teenage Pregnancy		X		
36	Jonathan Kozol	Savage Inequalities: Children in America's Schools	X			
37	Steven Manning	How Corporations Are Buying Their Way into America's Classrooms	X			
38	Myra Sadker and David Sadker	Missing in Interaction			X	
39	Joe R. Feagin, Hernán Vera, and Nikitah Imani	Confronting White Students: The Whiteness of University Spaces				X
40	James W. Fraser	Religion and Public Education in a Multicultural America				X
41	Steven R. Donziger	Crime and Policy				X
42	Barry Yeoman	Steel Town Lockdown	X			
43	Robert Jay Lifton and Greg Mitchell	Who Owns Death?				X
44	John Lamberth	DWB Is Not a Crime: The Numbers Show That Police Unfairly and Unconstitutionally Pull Over More Cars Driven by Blacks	X			
45	William S. Lofquist	Whodunit? An Examination of the Production of Wrongful Convictions			X	

(continued)

SUMMARY CHART—CONNECTING PERSPECTIVES

(continued)

Reading	Author	Title	Conflict Theory	Functionalist Theory	Symbolic Interactionism	Social Constructionism
46	Amanda Konradi	"I Don't Have to Be Afraid of You": Rape Survivors' Emotion Management in Court			X	
47	Robert A. Hanneman	Your Money or Your Life: Access to Medical Care as a Social Problem	X			
48	Ken Silverstein	Millions for Viagra, Pennies for Diseases of the Poor	X			
49	Joshua Wolf Shenk	An Old City Seeks a New Model				X
50	Daniel F. Chambliss	The Patient as Object			X	
51	Carol A. Heimer and Lisa R. Staffen	The Social Organization of Responsibility in the Hospital and the Home			X	
52	Michael T. Klare	Resource Wars: The New Landscape of Global Conflict	X			
53	Bob Burtman	Open Season on Open Space	X			X
54	Valerie L. Kuletz	Mapping the Nuclear Landscape				
55	Paul Hawken	Natural Capitalism		X		
56	Joseph S. Nye	Why the World's Only Superpower Can't Go It Alone		X		
57	Chip Pitts and Jennifer Holmes	Liberty vs. PATRIOTism				X
58	Joshua S. Goldstein	Conquests: Sex and Rape in Wartime	X		X	
59	David Lamb	The Painful Art of Reconciliation				

Chapter 2
Thinking About Social Problems

Learning Objectives

By the end of this chapter you should be able to:

- Recognize the unique sociological perspective advocated by each of the authors.
- Describe what we can gain by studying the subjective and objective nature of problems.
- Explain what we can learn about social problems by studying macro features of society—social systems and institutions—and micro features of society—interaction.
- Identify how social construction is a feature of all social problems.

Connecting the Perspectives

What is unique about a sociological approach to the study of social life? How does it differ from common sense? What can I get out of working to develop an ability to see as a sociologist? What can I get out of studying social problems sociologically? These are all fair questions. For this chapter, we have selected five readings that seek to answer them. The first three readings approach social problems from an objective perspective. That is, the authors set aside the question of how we come to understand specific phenomena as problematic and focus on explaining the phenomena. C. Wright Mills explains what he thinks it means to see the world as a sociologist and what the average person can gain from cultivating an ability to analyze social structures and to place his or her life experience in historical context. Mills also makes a key distinction between individuals' troubles and social issues, providing a good working definition of social problems. Patricia Hill Collins, author of the second reading, is oriented to the same concerns about social change that drive Mills's writing. However, she advocates developing a structural analysis of social life that is attentive to race and gender as well as class and economics. She argues further for developing a sociologically informed politics that transcends the cleavages in our society caused by our different experiences with race, gender, and class. Michael Schwalbe and colleagues focus our attention on the everyday behavior that produces the race, gender, and class inequalities central to Collins's analysis. Drawing on a wide range of interactionist studies, they show that similar kinds of group practices found across social contexts produce a variety of forms of inequality. The fourth and fifth readings are concerned with the subjective nature of social problems and the important social forums through which deviance, deficiency, and undesirability are established. Barbara Katz Rothman discusses how technology plays a role in the construction of our evolutionary history, illness, and our futures. Joshua Gamson raises questions about the role of media in social life and the people who spend their time critiquing it.

The authors of these five readings make strong statements about the questions sociologists should ask and the kinds of data that are relevant to answer them. They also provide good illustrations. We encourage you to view these pieces as models of sociological reasoning that can guide your own thinking about social problems, specifically about the matters raised in Chapters 3–13.

Reading Summaries

In "The Sociological Imagination," C. Wright Mills argues that the unique contribution of the discipline of sociology is not a specific method for studying social life, but a way of thinking or seeing that places individuals and their problems in social–historic context. This reading, which is taken from a longer book by the same name, is one of the most quoted pieces of twentieth-century sociological writing.

Mills begins with the observation that we tend to experience our lives in terms of the daily face-to-face interactions we have in our jobs, our education, our social organizations, and our immediate communities. What we need, he argues, is to learn the ability to see the world we inhabit in terms of large-scale economic and political relationships and institutions (stable practices/social arrangements and associated interpretive frameworks). We need to learn to see that the society we inhabit, our daily routines, and we ourselves (who we are, what we like, and what we do) are products of history. For example, Mills notes that war, not personal ambition, turns insurance salesmen into rocket launchers. Today, the closure of automobile plants, not personal ambition, turns welders into the unemployed and stay-at-home mothers into minimum-wage fast-food employees. Mills maintains that we must learn to recognize that the well-being we enjoy and the troubles we endure are the products of large forces that cause sweeping change and that leave some of our social institutions in opposition. Mills argues that we must also think big when we think about history: beyond our personal genealogies, beyond the history of our state and our nation to the world. When we think in these terms, for example, we will recognize that our fate is tied both to the decisions of CEOs in global corporations and to the labor actions of home health care workers in Detroit or rug makers in Pakistan. We will also recognize that our "personal troubles" are "public issues," matters of relevance to a broader sector of society. When we become aware of all the other people who are situated similarly to ourselves, Mills argues, we can understand our own experiences and make reasonable predictions about our futures.

Mills suggests that good analysis of a society or any social group focuses on three kinds of questions. The first kind of question concerns the structure of the society or group: discovering how the society or group is organized, what its component parts are, how the organization is different from other ways of maintaining social order, and how each component contributes to the long-term continuity and change of the society or group. The second kind of question looks at the place of the society or group in all of known human history and in the present historical period. The third kind asks, (1) what are the main attributes of women and men that are most successful in the present historic period and will be the most successful in the future? and (2) what are the group and societal processes of selection and formation, liberation and repression, sensitization and desensitization that produce a common human nature characteristic of the historic period? The **sociological imagination** is the ability to keep these questions in mind and shift among them, looking at the big political picture and then looking at the psychology of individuals and making connections between them. The sociological imagination is the ability to consider the single family and its financial concerns and make connections to the budget of the United States, or to consider the admissions practices of your university or college and make connections to the semiliterate strawberry picker in Watsonville, California. The sociological imagination is the ability to think in terms of the intimacy of dating practices and in terms of the impersonal nature of the global economy and finance capital, and to draw connections between them.

What are social problems? Toward the end of his answer to this question, Mills makes a useful distinction between personal troubles and public issues. **Personal troubles** are specific to individuals and their immediate personal relationships. They are character or personality related. **Public Issues** are related to the interpenetration and overlap of institutions—widespread and long-term practices that organize the various aspects of social life: production, reproduction, leisure, consumption, government, residency, and so forth. They are structural matters because they transcend the individuals they affect and tie the present to the past and future. The purpose of the sociological study of social problems is to increase our understanding of conditions of individual psychic and physical suffering as products of specific institutional relationships. It is also to discover whether proposed solutions to conditions identified as problems will resolve their underlying structural causes, serve as Band-Aids, or create additional institutional contradictions. Finally, the sociological study of social problems could move you beyond the feelings of anxiety and apathy that Mills identifies as psychologically central to our age.

Two questions drive Patricia Hill Collins's discussion: How can we find another way to conceptualize race, gender, and class so that we can use them more productively as analytic categories? How can we transcend the cleavages in our society caused by our different experiences with race, gender, and class so as to form diverse working groups that are necessary for achieving social change? Beginning with the empirical reality of inequality in the United States, Collins argues for a sociological perspective that recognizes race, class, and gender as social relationships through which individuals are connected. Viewed from this perspective, race, class, and gender are not things that belong to individuals but descriptors of the individual's status relative to others. Race, sociologically, is the privileged position of the white CEO and the disadvantaged position of the African American, Latina American, and Asian American factory or service worker. Gender, sociologically, is the privileged position of the husband who comes home and puts his feet up and the disadvantaged position of his wife who returns from work to make dinner, wash the clothes, and put the kids to bed. Race and gender, in this view, are achieved through social practice. Thinking in terms of Mills, the value of this relational perspective to the study of social problems is that it connects the psychic and physical suffering of some to their subordination and, in turn, to the psychic and physical health of advantaged others.

Collins warns us that few people are exclusively victims or oppressors of others. Multiple systems of oppression—race, class, gender, age, sex—overlap and interlock such that African American men and African American women have different experiences. Likewise, some African Americans have class privilege relative to poor

Whites. The key is not for sociologists to figure out how oppression adds up but rather to sort out how individuals may experience their oppressions differently in a variety of social contexts. Thinking in terms of Mills's set of questions about what kinds of persons prevail in the current historic period, Collins argues that sociologists need to assume that all contexts are raced, classed, and gendered and analyze how they matter, separately and together, for the individuals within the contexts.

Toward the end of developing an integrative analysis of social life, Collins directs us to think about three dimensions through which race, class, and gender oppression can be analyzed. The **institutional dimension of oppression** refers to how the ordinary way of doing things in schools, businesses, the workplace, government agencies, and places of worship systematically assign greater advantages and privileges to those who already have advantages and privileges and limit access and opportunity of those who are subordinate. The **symbolic dimension of oppression** is constituted of socially recognized explanatory structures, which can include law, medicine, science, and psychology, that are used to provide reasonable accounts for the existing patterns of race, class, and gender inequality. The **individual dimension of oppression** refers to the ways in which our experiences of racial, gender, and class domination and subordination become part of our biographies and of our reflexive ways of approaching new situations.

In the final section of the reading, Collins tackles the matter of achieving social change, a serious concern for those who study social problems. Her first suggestion is that we all focus on owning our privileges and our power and getting ourselves beyond voyeuristic, passive interest in the experiences of subordinated groups. This is applicable to the classroom. Specifically, White students and male students should not sit back and wait to be "taught" about the lived experience of racial and gender oppression by their racial-ethnic minority or women peers. Whites and men should become involved in exploring how they may contribute to or be advantaged by the maintenance of racial and gender inequality and related social problems. Collins's second suggestion is that instead of forming identity groups, individuals should form diverse workgroups focused on common causes. Recognizing that we are all differently situated in the matrix of social relations, it is more useful to focus on problem solving, knowing that we each bring different strengths to the table because of our lived experiences. This too is applicable to your college education. Ask peers in this class (or any other) who are of another gender, race, and class to be your study partners. Collins's final suggestion concerns people who are both privileged and oppressed developing within themselves the capacity to be empathetic, to take a real interest in the facts of other people's lives as individuals and as groups. Developing an ability to be empathetic is something we do at varying speeds, but creating opportunities for it to happen certainly can facilitate it. You can speed the process along by continuing discussions that start in your classroom with others in the laundry room, in recreation areas, in your student union, and over the lunch table.

Michael Schwalbe and colleagues note that a lot has been said about what kinds of inequalities exist and how large the gaps are between groups, but little has been done to explain how inequality is created and reproduced. In order to determine if there are common patterns of interaction that cut across contexts and produce the consistent relations of domination and subordination we know as gender, race, and class, they reviewed a wide range of qualitative research.

In these studies of symbolically cohesive social worlds and face-to-face interaction they identify four "generic processes": **othering, subordinate adaptation, boundary maintenance** and **emotion management.**

Othering is the invention of categories and human traits relevant to them with the intent to mark members associated with the new category as inferior. Othering can be done explicitly to oppress members of a group, but also consists of powerful people helping each other maintain an impression of competence relative to those with less. Subordinated people also sometimes appropriate the classification schemes of the powerful and mark people of their kind as legitimate outcasts.

Unequal conditions lead those who are deprived to develop means to cope with deprivation. Whether the adaptations are intended to resist the inequality or not, they typically contribute in some way to the reproduction of subordination. Some subordinates accept less power in relationships that provide them with feelings of self-worth. Others accept general control in exchange for freedom from interference in a limited realm. Subordinates also collaborate to form groups that provide alternate means to make a living and alternate ladders to social status. These subcultures provide means for members to achieve some material success, but these means often limit individuals' chances to enter the mainstream culture. The subculture may also achieve group solidarity by discouraging members from making contacts with dominant group members that could lead to upward mobility. A final subordinate adaptation is acquiescence, simply accepting one's position of inequality. This takes the form of either working on the edge of the culture or dropping out.

Elites also preserve their privileges and power by explicitly cooperating to limit others' access to valuable resources. This is largely achieved institutionally. Class boundaries are maintained through state laws and traditions that construct families as clearly defined social units. The parents in the families then pass on their advantages only to their own biological or adopted children. Teachers reinforce class and gender divisions among their students. These practices ensure that only some individuals gain the cultural capital necessary to compete for elite positions in the economy and to move unself-consciously in elite social situations. Elites also maintain their position by controlling access to networks necessary to gain information and through which rewards are disbursed and deals are negotiated. Finally, violence is used to maintain boundaries when ideological and spatial separations fail.

Emotion management involves the production of appropriate amounts and types of feelings. In order to maintain a system of inequality, anger, resentment, and despair among the subordinates must be redirected or limited. Likewise, sympathetic feelings by the privileged for those subordinated must be minimized. Appropriate feeling displays are achieved through ways of talking and writing that impose rules about what can be said and how it can be said. Technological discussions of war, for example, eliminate consideration of pain and death experienced by the enemy or one's own soldiers. The way events and information are framed can also evoke specific emotions aimed toward producing mass public support for governmental actions. Individuals also acquire habits of interpretation and emotion that work as a result of being socialized into the broader American culture and specific organizational contexts. Service workers learn to suppress emotional displays that contradict the interests of their employer. Men learn to devalue their own and others' emotions, not to be empathetic to women, and to deny their own feelings of fear. Organizations also script events so as to achieve emotional solidarity among members of a group. This type of scripting is intended to elide inequality.

Schwalbe and colleagues argue that in order to create hierarchies, programs of boundary maintenance, othering, and emotion management are necessary. Thus, we might consider race, class, and gender as routine ways of thinking, speaking, and acting used by some to exploit and dominate others. In this book you will find many readings that document the reproduction of inequality. For example, Kathryn Edin and Laura Lein discuss how mothers on welfare adapt to their marginal economic circumstances, limiting their upward mobility. Kathleen Blee describes how women in racist organizations create a supportive emotional context to nurture recruits' identification with the group and to foster feelings of solidarity among all members. Barbara Perry shows how violent boundary maintenance on the part of members of oppressed groups to achieve privilege in fact furthers the system of racial inequality in the U.S. Myra and David Sadker show how elementary school teachers contribute to future gender inequality among their students. Amanda Konradi discusses how rape survivors manage their emotions in the courtroom in order to resist further oppression.

Barbara Katz Rothman wants us to consider the role of science in constructing reality. She is specifically concerned with how the technologies associated with genetics shape our understanding of the past, present, and future. She argues that while genetic screening and testing can tell us the nature of an individual's chromosomal makeup, it frequently cannot tell us whether an individual will have some specific trait and rarely can tell us how the individual will experience the trait. When a scientist looks at an individual who has some specific trait and reasons backwards about its genetic basis, the scientist is making a **deterministic argument,** not providing an explanation. Rothman argues that we must recognize both the limitations of science to provide us with explanations and the limited value of the predictions it does produce. Rothman explains that scientific predictions are value laden and, in certain social contexts, it may be unreasonable to make them. Whether the source of the label is science or something else, the social consequences of being labeled deviant are the same: stigma, discrimination, and disadvantage.

Scientists have managed to sidestep public evaluation of the ethical and moral implications of their work by directing attention to the technological complexity of the research process. The public is told they cannot comment until they understand how the work is done. Rothman argues that while bioethicists could in theory bring moral analysis to scientific research, they do not. Funded through research grants, they serve primarily the needs of scientists. They translate scientific jargon to the public, but do not work to make the public's concerns intelligible to scientists. In short, they protect the power of scientists to define reality. However, Rothman believes that the public is capable of evaluating the morality of scientific technologies in spite of a lack of technical expertise. She argues that the public must not acquiesce to scientific claims of authority. We must recognize our right to ask what the social implications are for new technologies and our right to draw lines that limit the scientific enterprise. Otherwise, we will play little part in the construction of our future.

Although individuals experience social problems as psychically and physically painful, their status as matters of public concern is gained largely through media exposure. Public awareness of some problems, like drunken driving, result from focused campaigning by organized groups like Mothers Against Drunk Driving (MADD). In a calculated way, MADD used television, radio, and print media to slowly raise public consciousness that danger exists on the road. School violence, on the other hand, leaped into public consciousness when the shootings at Columbine High School received high-profile coverage. What types of concerns are given coverage on television and radio, in print, or on the Internet, and whom these media represent as authorities on particular subjects are matters of analysis for sociologists of social problems.

Joshua Gamson is interested in the role that the media play in the making and unmaking of our realities. He is specifically concerned with how media can alter relations of power between the members of dominant and subordinate groups. In Gamson's reading, taken from *Freaks Talk Back,* his topic is "trash TV"—daytime talk shows. Gamson analyzes the debates about the content of these shows: the arguments made by those who see them as dangerous and those who see them as liberating. He also assesses what the people who make the arguments have to gain from their versions of reality— their versions of what talk shows "really are"—becoming widely accepted. This approach to media is another example of social constructionist analysis.

Gamson makes the case that talk shows both blur and reassert distinctions among people. Talk shows provide a public forum for people who are expected to hide themselves and their behaviors; however, the forum presents them as oddities and treats their concerns as entertainment. Talk shows destabilize the "normal," which gives members of a society a sense of place, including their rightful sense of superiority to others. By focusing on matters of sexuality, talk shows also cross a social boundary and put the spotlight on typically private matters. This boundary crashing forces societal conversations about the nature and future of the public sphere. Finally, talk shows attach lower-class status to those who cross the lines between public and private and normal and abnormal.

Focusing Questions

To focus your reading of the selections in Section I, we urge you to keep the following four questions in mind: How does this approach get beyond the individual to the social and structural aspects of society? How does this approach build on the ones I read previously? What questions does this author say I should ask about social life? What would it mean to look at my life through this lens?

1

THE SOCIOLOGICAL IMAGINATION
C. WRIGHT MILLS

Nowadays men often feel that their private lives are a series of traps. They sense that within their everyday worlds, they cannot overcome their troubles, and in this feeling, they are often quite correct: What ordinary men are directly aware of and what they try to do are bounded by the private orbits in which they live; their visions and their powers are limited to the close-up scenes of job, family, neighborhood; in other milieux, they move vicariously and remain spectators. And the more aware they become, however vaguely, of ambitions and of threats which transcend their immediate locales, the more trapped they seem to feel.

Underlying this sense of being trapped are seemingly impersonal changes in the very structure of continent-wide societies. The facts of contemporary history are also facts about the success and the failure of individual men and women. When a society is industrialized, a peasant becomes a worker; a feudal lord is liquidated or becomes a businessman. When classes rise or fall, a man is employed or unemployed; when the rate of investment goes up or down, a man takes new heart or goes broke. When wars happen, an insurance salesman becomes a rocket launcher; a store clerk, a radar man; a wife lives alone; a child grows up without a father. Neither the life of an individual nor the history of a society can be understood without understanding both.

Yet men do not usually define the troubles they endure in terms of historical change and institutional contradiction. The well-being they enjoy, they do not usually impute to the big ups and downs of the societies in which they live. Seldom aware of the intricate connection between the patterns of their own lives and the course of world history, ordinary men do not usually know what this connection means for the kinds of men they are becoming and for the kinds of history-making in which they might take part. They do not possess the quality of mind essential to grasp the interplay of man and society, of biography and history, of self and world. They cannot cope with their personal troubles in such ways as to control the structural transformations that usually lie behind them. . . .

The history that now affects every man is world history. Within this scene and this period, in the course of a single generation, one sixth of mankind is transformed from all that is feudal and backward into all that is modern, advanced, and fearful. Political colonies are freed; new and less visible forms of imperialism installed. Revolutions occur; men feel the intimate grip of new kinds of authority. Totalitarian societies rise, and are smashed to bits—or succeed fabulously. After two centuries of ascendancy, capitalism is shown up as only one way to make society into an industrial apparatus. After two centuries of hope, even formal democracy is restricted to a quite small portion of mankind. Everywhere in the underdeveloped world, ancient ways of life are broken up and vague expectations become urgent demands. Everywhere in the overdeveloped world, the means of authority and of violence become total in scope and bureaucratic in form. Humanity itself now lies before us, the super-nation at either pole concentrating its most co-ordinated and massive efforts upon the preparation of World War Three.

The very shaping of history now outpaces the ability of men to orient themselves in accordance with cherished values. And which values? Even when they do not panic, men often sense that older ways of feeling and thinking have collapsed and that newer beginnings are ambiguous to the point of moral stasis. Is it any wonder that ordinary men feel they cannot cope with the larger worlds with which they are so suddenly confronted? That they cannot understand the meaning of their epoch for their own lives? That—in defense of selfhood—they become morally insensible, trying to remain altogether private men? Is it any wonder that they come to be possessed by a sense of the trap?

It is not only information that they need in this Age of Fact, information often dominates their attention and overwhelms their capacities to assimilate it. It is not only the skills of reason that they need—although their struggles to acquire these often exhaust their limited moral energy.

What they need, and what they feel they need, is a quality of mind that will help them to use information and to develop reason in order to achieve lucid summations of what is going on in the world and of what may be happening within themselves. It is this quality, I am going to contend, that journalists and scholars, artists and publics, scientists and editors are coming to expect of what may be called the sociological imagination.

1

The sociological imagination enables its possessor to understand the larger historical scene in terms of its meaning for the inner life and the external career of a variety of individuals. It enables him to take into account how individuals, in the welter of their daily experience, often become falsely conscious of their social positions. Within that welter, the framework of modern society is sought, and within that framework the psychologies of a variety of men and women are formulated. By such means the personal uneasiness of individuals is focused upon explicit troubles and the indifference of publics is transformed into involvement with public issues.

The first fruit of this imagination—and the first lesson of the social science that embodies it—is the idea that the individual can understand his own experience and gauge his own fate only by locating himself within his period, that he can know his own chances in life only by becoming aware of those of all individuals in his circumstances. In many ways it is a terrible lesson; in many ways a magnificent one. We do not know the limits of man's capacities for supreme effort or willing degradation, for agony or glee, for pleasurable brutality or the sweetness of reason. But in our time we have come to know that the limits of 'human nature' are frighteningly broad. We have come to know that every individual lives, from one generation to the next, in some society; that he lives out a biography, and that he lives it out within some historical sequence. By the fact of his living he contributes, however minutely, to the shaping of this society and to the course of its history, even as he is made by society and by its historical push and shove.

The sociological imagination enables us to grasp history and biography and the relations between the two within society. That is its task and its promise. To recognize this task and this promise is the mark of the classic social analyst. . . .

No social study that does not come back to the problems of biography, of history and of their intersections within a society has completed its intellectual journey. Whatever the specific problems of the classic social analysts, however limited or however broad the features of social reality they have examined, those who have been imaginatively aware of the promise of their work have consistently asked three sorts of questions:

1. What is the structure of this particular society as a whole? What are its essential components, and how are they related to one another? How does it differ from other varieties of social order? Within it, what is the meaning of any particular feature for its continuance and for its change?
2. Where does this society stand in human history? What are the mechanics by which it is changing? What is its place within and its meaning for the development of humanity as a whole? How does any particular feature we are examining affect, and how is it affected by, the historical period in which it moves? And this period—what are its essential features? How does it differ from other periods? What are its characteristic ways of history-making?
3. What varieties of men and women now prevail in this society and in this period? And what varieties are coming to prevail? In what ways are they selected and formed, liberated and repressed, made sensitive and blunted? What kinds of 'human nature' are revealed in

the conduct and character we observe in this society in this period? And what is the meaning for 'human nature' of each and every feature of the society we are examining?

Whether the point of interest is a great power state or a minor literary mood, a family, a prison, a creed—these are the kinds of questions the best social analysts have asked. They are the intellectual pivots of classic studies of man in society—and they are the questions inevitably raised by any mind possessing the sociological imagination. For that imagination is the capacity to shift from one perspective to another—from the political to the psychological; from examination of a single family to comparative assessment of the national budgets of the world; from the theological school to the military establishment; from considerations of an oil industry to studies of contemporary poetry. It is the capacity to range from the most impersonal and remote transformations to the most intimate features of the human self—and to see the relations between the two. Back of its use there is always the urge to know the social and historical meaning of the individual in the society and in the period in which he has his quality and his being. . . .

2

Perhaps the most fruitful distinction with which the sociological imagination works is between 'the personal troubles of milieu' and 'the public issues of social structure.' This distinction is an essential tool of the sociological imagination and a feature of all classic work in social science.

Troubles occur within the character of the individual and within the range of his immediate relations with others; they have to do with his self and with those limited areas of social life of which he is directly and personally aware. Accordingly, the statement and the resolution of troubles properly lie within the individual as a biographical entity and within the scope of his immediate milieu—the social setting that is directly open to his personal experience and to some extent his willful activity. A trouble is a private matter: values cherished by an individual are felt by him to be threatened.

Issues have to do with matters that transcend these local environments of the individual and the range of his inner life. They have to do with the organization of many such milieux into the institutions of an historical society as a whole, with the ways in which various milieux overlap and interpenetrate to form the larger structure of social and historical life. An issue is a public matter: some value cherished by publics is felt to be threatened. Often there is a debate about what that value really is and about what it is that really threatens it. This debate is often without focus if only because it is the very nature of an issue, unlike even widespread trouble, that it cannot very well be defined in terms of the immediate and everyday environments of ordinary men. An issue, in fact, often involves a crisis in institutional arrangements, and often too it involves what Marxists call 'contradictions' or 'antagonisms.'

In these terms, consider unemployment. When, in a city of 100,000, only one man is unemployed, that is his personal trouble, and for its relief we properly look to the character of the man, his skills, and his immediate opportunities. But when in a nation of 50 million employees, 15 million men are unemployed, that is an issue, and we may not hope to find its solution within the range of opportunities open to any one individual. The very structure of opportunities has collapsed. Both the correct statement of the problem and the range of possible solutions require us to consider the economic and political institutions of the society, and not merely the personal situation and character of a scatter of individuals.

Consider war. The personal problem of war, when it occurs, may be how to survive it or how to die in it with honor; how to make money out of it; how to climb into the higher safety of the military apparatus; or how to contribute to the war's termination. In short, according to one's values, to find a set of milieux and within it to survive the war or make one's death in it meaningful. But the structural issues of war have to do with its causes; with what types of men it throws up into command; with its effects, upon economic and political, family and religious institutions, with the unorganized irresponsibility of a world of nation-states.

Consider marriage. Inside a marriage a man and a woman may experience personal troubles, but when the divorce rate during the first four years of marriage is 250 out of every 1,000 attempts, this is an indication of a structural issue having to do with the institutions of marriage and the family and other institutions that bear upon them.

Or consider the metropolis—the horrible, beautiful, ugly, magnificent sprawl of the great city. For many upper-class people, the personal solution to 'the problem of the city' is to have an apartment with private garage under it in the heart of the city, and forty miles out, a house on a hundred acres of private land. In these two controlled environments—with a small staff at each end and a private helicopter connection—most people could solve many of the problems of personal milieux caused by the facts of the city. But all this, however splendid, does not solve the public issues that the structural fact of the city poses. What should be done with this wonderful monstrosity? Break it all up into scattered units, combining residence and work? Refurbish it as it stands? Or, after evacuation, dynamite it and build new cities according to new plans in new places? What should those plans be? And who is to decide and to accomplish whatever choice is made? These are structural issues; to confront them and to solve them requires us to consider political and economic issues that affect innumerable milieux.

In so far as an economy is so arranged that slumps occur, the problem of unemployment becomes incapable of personal solution. In so far as war is inherent in the nation-state system and in the uneven industrialization of the world, the ordinary individual in his restricted milieu will be powerless—with or without psychiatric aid—to solve the troubles this system or lack of system imposes upon him. In so far as the family as an institution turns women into darling little slaves and men into their chief providers and unweaned dependents, the problem of a satisfactory marriage remains incapable of purely private solution. In so far as the overdeveloped megalopolis and the overdeveloped automobile are built-in features of the overdeveloped society, the issues of urban living will not be solved by personal ingenuity and private wealth.

What we experience in various and specific milieux, I have noted, is often caused by structural changes. Accordingly, to understand the changes of many personal milieux we are required to look beyond them. And the number and variety of such structural changes increase as the institutions within which we live become more embracing and more intricately connected with one another. To be aware of the idea of social structure and to use it with sensibility is to be capable of tracing such linkages among a great variety of milieux. To be able to do that is to possess the sociological imagination.

3

What are the major issues for publics and the key troubles of private individuals in our time? To formulate issues and troubles, we must ask what values are cherished yet threatened, and what values are cherished and supported, by the characterizing trends of our period. In the case both of threat and of support we must ask what salient contradictions of structure may be involved.

When people cherish some set of values and do not feel any threat to them, they experience *well-being*. When they cherish values but *do* feel them to be threatened, they experience a crisis—either as a personal trouble or as a public issue. And if all their values seem involved, they feel the total threat of panic.

But suppose people are neither aware of any cherished values nor experience any threat? That is the experience of *indifference*, which, if it seems to involve all their values, becomes apathy. Suppose, finally, they are unaware of any cherished values, but still are very much aware of a threat? That is the experience of *uneasiness*, of anxiety, which, if it is total enough, becomes a deadly unspecified malaise.

Ours is a time of uneasiness and indifference—not yet formulated in such ways as to permit the work of reason and the play of sensibility. Instead of troubles—defined in terms of values and threats—there is often the misery of vague uneasiness; instead of explicit issues there is often merely the beat feeling that all is somehow not right. Neither the values threatened nor whatever threatens them has been stated; in short, they have not been carried to the point of decision. Much less have they been formulated as problems of social science. . . .

It is true, as psychoanalysts continually point out, that people do often have 'the increasing sense of being moved by obscure forces within themselves which they are unable to define.' But it is *not* true, as Ernest Jones asserted, that 'man's chief enemy and danger is his own unruly nature and the dark forces pent up within him.' On the contrary: 'Man's chief danger' today lies in the unruly forces of contemporary society itself, with its alienating methods of production, its enveloping techniques of political domination, its international anarchy—in a word, its pervasive transformations of the very 'nature' of man and the conditions and aims of his life.

It is now the social scientist's foremost political and intellectual task—for here the two coincide—to make clear the elements of contemporary uneasiness and indifference. It is the central demand made upon him by other cultural workmen—by physical scientists and artists, by the intellectual community in general. It is because of this task and these demands, I believe, that the social sciences are becoming the common denominator of our cultural period, and the sociological imagination our most needed quality of mind. . . .

QUESTIONS FOR DISCUSSION

1. What varieties of men and women now prevail in this society?
2. What seem to be the widely recognized public issues in our society?
3. Can you provide some examples of how your personal biography reflects larger historic trends in American society or even the world?

2

TOWARD A NEW VISION

Race, Class, and Gender as Categories of Analysis and Connection

PATRICIA HILL COLLINS

The true focus of revolutionary change is never merely the oppressive situations which we seek to escape, but that piece of the oppressor which is planted deep within each of us.

—AUDRE LORDE
Sister Outsider, 123

Collins, Patricia Hill. Fall 1998. "Toward a New Vision: Race, Class, and Gender as Categories of Analysis and Connection." *Race, Sex, & Class,* vol. 1, no. 1. Reprinted with permission of the publisher.

Audre Lorde's statement raises a troublesome issue for scholars and activists working for social change. While many of us have little difficulty assessing our own victimization within some major system of oppression, whether it be by race, social class, religion, sexual orientation, ethnicity, age or gender, we typically fail to see how our thoughts and actions uphold someone else's subordination. Thus, white feminists routinely point with confidence to their oppression as women but resist seeing how much their white skin privileges them. African-Americans who possess eloquent analyses of racism often persist in viewing poor White women as symbols of white power. The radical left fares little better. "If only people of color and women could see their true class interests," they argue, "class solidarity would eliminate racism and sexism." In essence, each group identifies the type of oppression with which it feels most comfortable as being fundamental and classifies all other types as being of lesser importance.

Oppression is full of such contradictions. Errors in political judgment that we make concerning how we teach our courses, what we tell our children, and which organizations are worthy of our time, talents and financial support flow smoothly from errors in theoretical analysis about the nature of oppression and activism. Once we realize that there are few pure victims or oppressors, and that each one of us derives varying amounts of penalty and privilege from the multiple systems of oppression that frame our lives, then we will be in a position to see the need for new ways of thought and action.

To get at that "piece of the oppressor which is planted deep within each of us," we need at least two things. First, we need new visions of what oppression is, new categories of analysis that are inclusive of race, class, and gender as distinctive yet interlocking structures of oppression. Adhering to a stance of comparing and ranking oppressions—the proverbial, "I'm more oppressed than you"—locks us all into a dangerous dance of competing for attention, resources, and theoretical supremacy. Instead, I suggest that we examine our different experiences within the more fundamental relationship of domination and subordination. To focus on the particular arrangements that race or class or gender take in our time and place without seeing these structures as

sometimes parallel and sometimes interlocking dimensions of the more fundamental relationship of domination and subordination may temporarily ease our consciences. But while such thinking may lead to short term social reforms, it is simply inadequate for the task of bringing about long term social transformation.

While race, class and gender as categories of analysis are essential in helping us understand the structural bases of domination and subordination, new ways of thinking that are not accompanied by new ways of acting offer incomplete prospects for change. To get at that "piece of the oppressor which is planted deep within each of us," we also need to change our daily behavior. Currently, we are all enmeshed in a complex web of problematic relationships that grant our mirror images full human subjectivity while stereotyping and objectifying those most different than ourselves. We often assume that the people we work with, teach, send our children to school with, and sit next to . . . will act and feel in prescribed ways because they belong to given race, social class or gender categories. These judgments by category must be replaced with fully human relationships that transcend the legitimate differences created by race, class and gender as categories of analysis. We require new categories of connection, new visions of what our relationships with one another can be. . . .

[This discussion] addresses this need for new patterns of thought and action. I focus on two basic questions. First, how can we reconceptualize race, class and gender as categories of analysis? Second, how can we transcend the barriers created by our experiences with race, class and gender oppression in order to build the types of coalitions essential for social exchange? To address these questions I contend that we must acquire both new theories of how race, class and gender have shaped the experiences not just of women of color, but of all groups. Moreover, we must see the connections between these categories of analysis and the personal issues in our everyday lives, particularly our scholarship, our teaching and our relationships with our colleagues and students. As Audre Lorde points out, change starts with self, and relationships that we have with those around us must always be the primary site for social change.

How Can We Reconceptualize Race, Class and Gender as Categories of Analysis?

To me, we must shift our discourse away from additive analyses of oppression (Spelman 1982; Collins 1989). Such approaches are typically based on two key premises. First, they depend on either/or, dichotomous thinking. Persons, things and ideas are conceptualized in terms of their opposites. For example. Black/White, man/woman, thought/feeling, and fact/opinion are defined in oppositional terms. Thought and feeling are not seen as two different and interconnected ways of approaching truth that can coexist in scholarship and teaching. Instead, feeling is defined as antithetical to reason, as its opposite. In spite of the fact that we all have "both/and" identities (I am both a college professor and a mother—I don't stop being a mother when I drop my child off at school, or forget everything I learned while scrubbing the toilet), we persist in trying to classify each other in either/or categories. I live each day as an African-American woman—a race/gender specific experience. And I am not alone. Everyone has a race/gender/class specific identity. Either/or, dichotomous thinking is especially troublesome when applied to theories of oppression because every individual must be classified as being either oppressed or not oppressed. The both/and position of simultaneously being

oppressed and oppressor becomes conceptually impossible.

A second premise of additive analyses of oppression is that these dichotomous differences must be ranked. One side of the dichotomy is typically labeled dominant and the other subordinate. Thus, Whites rule Blacks, men are deemed superior to women, and reason is seen as being preferable to emotion. Applying this premise to discussions of oppression leads to the assumption that oppression can be quantified, and that some groups are oppressed more than others. I am frequently asked, "Which has been most oppressive to you, your status as a Black person or your status as a woman?" What I am really being asked to do is divide myself into little boxes and rank my various statuses. If I experience oppression as a both/and phenomenon, why should I analyze it any differently?

Additive analyses of oppression rest squarely on the twin pillars of either/or thinking and the necessity to quantify and rank all relationships in order to know where one stands. Such approaches typically see African-American women as being more oppressed than everyone else because the majority of Black women experience the negative effects of race, class and gender oppression simultaneously. In essence, if you add together separate oppressions, you are left with a grand oppression greater than the sum of its parts.

I am not denying that specific groups experience oppression more harshly than others—lynching is certainly objectively worse than being held up as a sex object. But we must be careful not to confuse this issue of the saliency of one type of oppression in people's lives with a theoretical stance positing the interlocking nature of oppression. Race, class and gender may all structure a situation but may not be equally visible and/or important in people's self-definitions. In certain contexts, such as the antebellum American South and contemporary South America, racial oppression is more visibly salient, while in other contexts, such as Haiti, El Salvador and Nicaragua, social class oppression may be more apparent. For middle class White women, gender may assume experiential primacy unavailable to poor Hispanic women struggling with the ongoing issues of low paid jobs and the frustrations of the welfare bureaucracy. This recognition that one category may have salience over another for a given time and place does not minimize the theoretical importance of assuming that race, class and gender as categories of analysis structure all relationships.

In order to move toward new visions of what oppression is, I think that we need to ask new questions. How are relationships of domination and subordination structured and maintained in the American political economy? How do race, class and gender function as parallel and interlocking systems that shape this basic relationship of domination and subordination? Questions such as these promise to move us away from futile theoretical struggles concerned with ranking oppressions and towards analyses that assume race, class and gender are all present in any given setting, even if one appears more visible and salient than the others. Our task becomes redefined as one of reconceptualizing oppression by uncovering the connections among race, class and gender as categories of analysis.

1. Institutional Dimension of Oppression

Sandra Harding's contention that gender oppression is structured along three main dimensions—the institutional, the symbolic, and the individual—offers a useful model for a more comprehensive analysis encompassing race, class and gender oppression (Harding 1986). Systemic relationships of domination and subordination structured through social institutions such as schools, businesses, hospitals, the work place, and government agencies represent the institutional dimension of oppression. Racism, sexism and elitism all have concrete institutional locations. Even though the workings of the institutional dimension of oppression are often obscured with ideologies claiming equality of opportunity, in actuality, race, class and gender place Asian-American women, Native American men, White men, African-American women, and other groups in distinct institutional niches with varying degrees of penalty and privilege.

Even though I realize that many . . . would not share this assumption, let us assume that the institutions of American society discriminate, whether by design or by accident. While many of us are familiar with how race, gender and class operate separately to structure inequality, I want to focus on how these three systems interlock in structuring the institutional dimension of oppression. To get at the interlocking nature of race, class and gender, I want you to think about the antebellum plantation as a guiding metaphor for a variety of American social institutions. Even though slavery is typically analyzed as a racist institution, and occasionally as a class institution, I suggest that slavery was a race, class, gender specific institution. Removing any one piece from our analysis diminishes our understanding of the true nature of relations of domination and subordination under slavery.

Slavery was a profoundly patriarchal institution. It rested on the dual tenets of White male authority and White male property, a joining of the political and the economic within the institution of the family. Heterosexism was assumed and all Whites were expected to marry. Control over affluent White women's sexuality remained key to slavery's survival because property was to be passed on to the legitimate heirs of the slave owner. Ensuring affluent White women's virginity and chastity was deeply intertwined with maintenance of property relations.

Under slavery, we see varying levels of institutional protection given to affluent White women, working class and poor White women, and enslaved African women. Poor White women enjoyed few of the protections held out to their upper class sisters. Moreover, the devalued status of Black women was key in keeping all White women in their assigned places. Controlling Black women's fertility was also key to the continuation of slavery, for children born to slave mothers themselves were slaves.

African-American women shared the devalued status of chattel with their husbands, fathers and sons. Racism stripped Blacks as a group of legal rights, education, and control over their own persons. African-Americans could be whipped, branded, sold, or killed, not because they were poor, or because they were women, but because they were Black. Racism ensured that Blacks would continue to serve Whites and suffer economic exploitation at the hands of all Whites.

So we have a very interesting chain of command on the plantation—the affluent White master as the reigning patriarch, his White wife helpmate to serve him, help him manage his property and bring up his heirs, his faithful servants whose production and reproduction were tied to the requirements of the capitalist political economy, and largely propertyless, working class White men and women watching from afar. In essence, the foundations for the contemporary roles of elite White women, poor Black women, working class White men, and a series of other groups can be seen in stark

relief in this fundamental American social institution. While Blacks experienced the most harsh treatment under slavery, and thus made slavery clearly visible as a racist institution, race, class and gender interlocked in structuring slavery's systemic organization of domination and subordination.

Even today, the plantation remains a compelling metaphor for institutional oppression. Certainly the actual conditions of oppression are not as severe now as they were then. To argue, as some do, that things have not changed all that much denigrates the achievements of those who struggled for social change before us. But the basic relationships among Black men, Black women, elite White women, elite White men, working class White men and working class White women as groups remain essentially intact.

A brief analysis of key American social institutions most controlled by elite White men should convince us of the interlocking nature of race, class and gender in structuring the institutional dimension of oppression. For example, if you are from an American college or university, is your campus a modern plantation? Who controls your university's political economy? Are elite White men over-represented among the upper administrators and trustees controlling your university's finances and policies? Are elite White men being joined by growing numbers of elite White women helpmates? What kinds of people are in your classrooms grooming the next generation who will occupy these and other decision-making positions? Who are the support staff that produce the mass mailings, order the supplies, fix the leaky pipes? Do African-Americans, Hispanics or other people of color form the majority of the invisible workers who feed you, wash your dishes, and clean up your offices and libraries after everyone else has gone home?

If your college is anything like mine, you know the answers to these questions. You may be affiliated with an institution that has Hispanic women as vice-presidents for finance, or substantial numbers of Black men among the faculty. If so, you are fortunate. Much more typical are colleges where a modified version of the plantation as a metaphor for the institutional dimension of oppression survives.

2. The Symbolic Dimension of Oppression

Widespread, societally-sanctioned ideologies used to justify relations of domination and subordination comprise the symbolic dimension of oppression. Central to this process is the use of stereotypical or controlling images of diverse race, class and gender groups. In order to assess the power of this dimension of oppression, I want you to make a list, either on paper or in your head, of "masculine" and "feminine" characteristics. If your list is anything like that compiled by most people, it reflects some variation of the following:

Masculine	Feminine
aggressive	passive
leader	follower
rational	emotional
strong	weak
intellectual	physical

Not only does this list reflect either/or dichotomous thinking and the need to rank both sides of the dichotomy, but ask yourself exactly which men and women you had in mind when compiling these characteristics. This list applies almost exclusively to middle class White men and women. The allegedly "masculine" qualities that you probably listed are only acceptable when exhibited by elite White men, or when used by Black and Hispanic men against each other

or against women of color. Aggressive Black and Hispanic men are seen as dangerous, not powerful, and are often penalized when they exhibit any of the allegedly "masculine" characteristics. Working class and poor White men fare slightly better and are also denied the allegedly "masculine" symbols of leadership, intellectual competence, and human rationality. Women of color and working class and poor White women are also not represented in this list, for they have never had the luxury of being "ladies." What appear to be universal categories representing all men and women instead are unmasked as being applicable to only a small group.

It is important to see how the symbolic images applied to different race, class and gender groups interact in maintaining systems of domination and subordination. If I were to ask you to repeat the same assignment, only this time, by making separate lists for Black men, Black women, Hispanic women and Hispanic men, I suspect that your gender symbolism would be quite different. In comparing all of the lists, you might begin to see the interdependence of symbols applied to all groups. For example, the elevated images of White womanhood need devalued images of Black womanhood in order to maintain credibility.

While the above exercise reveals the interlocking nature of race, class and gender in structuring the symbolic dimension of oppression, part of its importance lies in demonstrating how race, class and gender pervade a wide range of what appears to be universal language. Attending to diversity in our scholarship, in our teaching, and in our daily lives provides a new angle of vision on interpretations of reality thought to be natural, normal and "true." Moreover, viewing images of masculinity and femininity as universal gender symbolism, rather than as symbolic images that are race, class and gender specific, renders the experiences of people of color and of non-privileged

White women and men invisible. One way to dehumanize an individual or a group is to deny the reality of their experiences. So when we refuse to deal with race or class because they do not appear to be directly relevant to gender, we are actually becoming part of some one else's problem.

Assuming that everyone is affected differently by the same interlocking set of symbolic images allows us to move forward toward new analyses. Women of color and White women have different relationships to White male authority and this difference explains the distinct gender symbolism applied to both groups. Black women encounter controlling images such as the mammy, the matriarch, the mule and the whore, that encourage others to reject us as fully human people. Ironically, the negative nature of these images simultaneously encourages us to reject them. In contrast, White women are offered seductive images, those that promise to reward them for supporting the status quo. And yet seductive images can be equally controlling. Consider, for example, the views of Nancy White, a 73-year-old Black woman, concerning images of rejection and seduction:

> My mother used to say that the black woman is the white man's mule and the White woman is his dog. Now, she said that to say this: we do the heavy work and get beat whether we do it well or not. But the white woman is closer to the master and he pats them on the head and lets them sleep in the house, but he ain't gon' treat neither one like he was dealing with a person (Gwaltney, 148).

Both sets of images stimulate particular political stances. By broadening the analysis beyond the confines of race, we can see the varying levels of rejection and seduction available to each of us due to our race, class and gender identity. Each of us lives with an allotted portion of institutional privilege and penalty, and with varying levels of rejection and seduction inherent in the symbolic images applied to us. This is the context in which we make our choices. Taken together, the institutional and symbolic dimensions of oppression create a structural backdrop against which all of us live our lives.

3. The Individual Dimension of Oppression

Whether we benefit or not, we all live within institutions that reproduce race, class and gender oppression. Even if we never have any contact with members of other race, class and gender groups, we all encounter images of these groups and are exposed to the symbolic meanings attached to those images. On this dimension of oppression, our individual biographies vary tremendously. As a result of our institutional and symbolic statuses, all of our choices became political acts.

Each of us must come to terms with the multiple ways in which race, class and gender as categories of analysis frame our individual biographies. I have lived my entire life as an African-American woman from a working class family and this basic fact has had a profound impact on my personal biography. Imagine how different your life might be if you had been born Black, or White, or poor, or of a different race/class/gender group than the one with which you are most familiar. The institutional treatment you would have received and the symbolic meanings attached to your very existence might differ dramatically from what you now consider to be natural, normal and part of everyday life. You might be the same, but your personal biography might have been quite different.

I believe that each of us carries around the cumulative effect of our lives within multiple structures of oppression. If you want to see how much you have been affected by this whole thing, I ask you one simple question—who are your close friends? Who are the people with whom you can share your hopes, dreams, vulnerabilities, fears and victories? Do they look like you? If they are all the same, circumstance may be the cause. For the first seven years of my life I saw only low income Black people. My friends from those years reflected the composition of my community. But now that I am an adult, can the defense of circumstance explain the patterns of people that I trust as my friends and colleagues? When given other alternatives, if my friends and colleagues reflect the homogeneity of one race, class and gender group, then these categories of analysis have indeed become barriers to connection.

I am not suggesting that people are doomed to follow the paths laid out for them by race, class and gender as categories of analysis. While these three structures certainly frame my opportunity structure, I as an individual always have the choice of accepting things as they are, or trying to change them. As Nikki Giovanni points out, "we've got to live in the real world. If we don't like the world we're living in, change it. And if we can't change it, we change ourselves. We can do something" (Tate 1983, 68). While a piece of the oppressor may be planted deep within each of us, we each have the choice of accepting that piece or challenging it as part of the "true focus, of revolutionary change."

How Can We Transcend the Barriers Created by Our Experiences with Race, Class and Gender Oppression in Order to Build the Types of Coalitions Essential for Social Change?

Reconceptualizing oppression and seeing the barriers created by race, class and gen-

der as interlocking categories of analysis is a vital first step. But we must transcend these barriers by moving toward race, class and gender as categories of connection, by building relationships and coalitions that will bring about social change. What are some of the issues involved in doing this?

1. Differences in Power and Privilege

First, we must recognize that our differing experiences with oppression create problems in the relationships among us. Each of us lives within a system that vests us with varying levels of power and privilege. These differences in power, whether structured along axes of race, class, gender, age or sexual orientation, frame our relationships. African-American writer June Jordan describes her discomfort on a Caribbean vacation with Olive, the Black woman who cleaned her room:

> . . . even though both "Olive" and "I" live inside a conflict neither one of us created, and even though both of us therefore hurt inside that conflict, I may be one of the monsters she needs to eliminate from her universe and, in a sense, she may be one of the monsters in mine (1985, 47).

Differences in power constrain our ability to connect with one another even when we think we are engaged in dialogue across differences. Let me give you an example. One year, the students in my course "Sociology of the Black Community" got into a heated discussion about the reasons for the upsurge of racial incidents on college campuses. Black students complained vehemently about the apathy and resistance they felt most White students expressed about examining their own racism. Mark, a White male student, found their comments particularly unsettling. After claiming that all the Black people he had ever known had expressed no such beliefs to him, he questioned how representative the view points of his fellow students actually were. When pushed further, Mark revealed that he had participated in conversations over the years with the Black domestic worker employed by his family. Since she had never expressed such strong feelings about White racism, Mark was genuinely shocked by class discussions. Ask yourselves whether that domestic worker was in a position to speak freely. Would it have been wise for her to do so in a situation where the power between the two parties was so unequal?

In extreme cases, members of privileged groups can erase the very presence of the less privileged. When I first moved to Cincinnati, my family and I went on a picnic at a local park. Picnicking next to us was a family of White Appalachians. When I went to push my daughter on the swings, several of the children came over. They had missing, yellowed and broken teeth, they wore old clothing and their poverty was evident. I was shocked. Growing up in a large eastern city, I had never seen such awful poverty among Whites. The segregated neighborhoods in which I grew up made White poverty all but invisible. More importantly, the privileges attached to my newly acquired social class position allowed me to ignore and minimize the poverty among Whites that I did encounter. My reactions to those children made me realize how confining phrases such as "well, at least they're not Black," had become for me. In learning to grant human subjectivity to the Black victims of poverty, I had simultaneously learned to deny White victims of poverty. By applying categories of race to the objective conditions confronting me, I was quantifying and ranking oppressions and missing the very real suffering which, in fact, is the real issue.

One common pattern of relationships across differences in power is one that I label "voyeurism." From the perspective of the privileged, the lives of people of color, of the poor, and of women are interesting for their entertainment value. The privileged become voyeurs, passive onlookers who do not relate to the less powerful, but who are interested in seeing how the "different" live. Over the years, I have heard numerous African-American students complain about professors who never call on them except when a so-called Black issue is being discussed. The students' interest in discussing race or qualifications for doing so appear unimportant to the professor's efforts to use Black students' experiences as stories to make the material come alive for the White student audience. Asking Black students to perform on cue and provide a Black experience for their White classmates can be seen as voyeurism at its worst.

Members of subordinate groups do not willingly participate in such exchanges but often do so because members of dominant groups control the institutional and symbolic apparatuses of oppression. Racial/ethnic groups, women, and the poor have never had the luxury of being voyeurs of the lives of the privileged. Our ability to survive in hostile settings has hinged on our ability to learn intricate details about the behavior and world view of the powerful and adjust our behavior accordingly. I need only point to the difference in perception of those men and women in abusive relationships. Where men can view their girlfriends and wives as sex objects, helpmates and a collection of stereotypes, categories of voyeurism—women must be attuned to every nuance of their partners' behavior. Are women "naturally" better in relating to people with more power than themselves, or have circumstances mandated that men and women develop different skills? . . .

Coming from a tradition where most relationships across difference are squarely rooted in relations of domination and subordination, we have much less experience relating to people as different but equal. The classroom is potentially one powerful and safe space where dialogues among individuals of unequal power relationships can occur. The relationship between Mark, the student in my class, and the domestic worker is typical of a whole series of relationships that people have when they relate across differences in power and privilege. The relationship among Mark and his classmates represents the power of the classroom to minimize those differences so that people of different levels of power can use race, class and gender as categories of analysis in order to generate meaningful dialogues. In this case, the classroom equalized racial difference so that Black students who normally felt silenced spoke out. White students like Mark, generally unaware of how they had been privileged by their whiteness, lost that privilege in the classroom and thus became open to genuine dialogue. . . .

2. Coalitions Around Common Causes

A second issue in building relationships and coalitions essential for social change concerns knowing the real reasons for coalition. Just what brings people together? One powerful catalyst fostering group solidarity is the presence of a common enemy. African-American, Hispanic, Asian-American, and women's studies all share the common intellectual heritage of challenging what passes for certified knowledge in the academy. But politically expedient relationships and coalitions like these are fragile because, as June Jordan points out:

> It occurs to me that much organizational grief could be avoided if people understood that partnership in misery does not necessarily provide for partnership for change: When we get the monsters off our backs all of us may want to run in very different directions (1985, 47).

Sharing a common cause assists individuals and groups in maintaining relationships that transcend their differences. Building effective coalitions involves struggling to hear one another and developing empathy for each other's points of view. The coalitions that I have been involved in that lasted and that worked have been those where commitment to a specific issue mandated collaboration as the best strategy for addressing the issue at hand.

Several years ago, master's degree in hand, I chose to teach in an inner city, parochial school in danger of closing. The money was awful, the conditions were poor, but the need was great. In my job, I had to work with a range of individuals who, on the surface, had very little in common. We had White nuns, Black middle class graduate students, Blacks from the "community," some of whom had been incarcerated and/or were affiliated with a range of federal anti-poverty programs. Parents formed another part of this community, Harvard faculty another, and a few well-meaning White liberals from Colorado were sprinkled in for good measure.

As you might imagine, tension was high. Initially, our differences seemed insurmountable. But as time passed, we found a common bond that we each brought to the school. In spite of profound differences in our personal biographies, differences that in other settings would have hampered our ability to relate to one another, we found that we were all deeply committed to the education of Black children. By learning to value each other's commitment and by recognizing that we each had different skills that were essential to actualizing that commitment, we built an effective coalition around a common cause. Our school was successful, and the children we taught benefited from the diversity we offered them.

. . . None of us alone has a comprehensive vision of how race, class and gender operate as categories of analysis or how they might be used as categories of connection. Our personal biographies offer us partial views. Few of us can manage to study race, class and gender simultaneously. Instead, we each know more about some dimensions of this larger story and less about others. . . . Just as the members of the school had special skills to offer to the task of building the school, we have areas of specialization and expertise, whether scholarly, theoretical, pedagogical or within areas of race, class or gender. We do not all have to do the same thing in the same way. Instead, we must support each other's efforts, realizing that they are all part of the larger enterprise of bringing about social change.

3. Building Empathy

A third issue involved in building the types of relationships and coalitions essential for social change concerns the issue of individual accountability. Race, class and gender oppression form the structural backdrop against which we frame our relationships— these are the forces that encourage us to substitute voyeurism . . . for fully human relationships. But while we may not have created this situation, we are each responsible for making individual, personal choices concerning which elements of race, class and gender oppression we will accept and which we will work to change.

One essential component of this accountability involves developing empathy for the experiences of individuals and groups different than ourselves. Empathy begins with taking an interest in the facts of other people's lives, both as individuals and

as groups. If you care about me, you should want to know not only the details of my personal biography but a sense of how race, class and gender as categories of analysis created the institutional and symbolic backdrop for my personal biography. How can you hope to assess my character without knowing the details of the circumstances I face?

Moreover, by taking a theoretical stance that we have all been affected by race, class and gender as categories of analysis that have structured our treatment, we open up possibilities for using those same constructs as categories of connection in building empathy. For example, I have a good White woman friend with whom I share common interests and beliefs. But we know that our racial differences have provided us with different experiences. So we talk about them. We do not assume that because I am Black, race has only affected me and not her or that because I am a Black woman, race neutralizes the effect of gender in my life while accenting it in hers. We take those same categories of analysis that have created cleavages in our lives, in this case, categories of race and gender, and use them as categories of connection in building empathy for each other's experiences.

Finding common causes and building empathy is difficult, no matter which side of privilege we inhabit. Building empathy from the dominant side of privilege is difficult, simply because individuals from privileged backgrounds are not encouraged to do so. For example, in order for those of you who are White to develop empathy for the experiences of people of color, you must grapple with how your white skin has privileged you. This is difficult to do, because it not only entails the intellectual process of seeing how whiteness is elevated in institutions and symbols, but it also involves the often painful process of seeing how your whiteness has shaped your personal biography. Intellectual stances against the institutional and symbolic dimensions of racism are generally easier to maintain than sustained self-reflection about how racism has shaped all of our individual biographies. Were and are your fathers, uncles, and grandfathers really more capable than mine, or can their accomplishments be explained in part by the racism members of my family experienced? Did your mothers stand silently by and watch all this happen? More importantly, how have they passed on the benefits of their whiteness to you?

These are difficult questions, and I have tremendous respect for my colleagues and students who are trying to answer them. Since there is no compelling reason to examine the source and meaning of one's own privilege, I know that those who do so have freely chosen this stance. They are making conscious efforts to root out the piece of the oppressor planted within them. To me, they are entitled to the support of people of color in their efforts. Men who declare themselves feminists, members of the middle class who ally themselves with anti-poverty struggles, heterosexuals who support gays and lesbians, are all trying to grow, and their efforts place them far ahead of the majority who never think of engaging in such important struggles.

Building empathy from the subordinate side of privilege is also difficult, but for different reasons. Members of subordinate groups are understandably reluctant to abandon a basic mistrust of members of powerful groups because this basic mistrust has traditionally been central to their survival. As a Black woman, it would be foolish for me to assume that White women, or Black men, or White men or any other group with a history of exploiting African-American women have my best interests at heart. These groups enjoy varying amounts of privilege over me and therefore I must

carefully watch them and be prepared for a relation of domination and subordination.

Like the privileged, members of subordinate groups must also work toward replacing judgments by category with new ways of thinking and acting. Refusing to do so stifles prospects for effective coalition and social change. Let me use another example from my own experiences. When I was an undergraduate, I had little time or patience for the theorizing of the privileged. My initial years at a private, elite institution were difficult, not because the coursework was challenging (it was, but that wasn't what distracted me) or because I had to work while my classmates lived on family allowances (I was used to work). The adjustment was difficult because I was surrounded by so many people who took their privilege for granted. Most of them felt entitled to their wealth. That astounded me.

I remember one incident of watching a White woman down the hall in my dormitory try to pick out which sweater to wear. The sweaters were piled up on her bed in all the colors of the rainbow, sweater after sweater. She asked my advice in a way that let me know that choosing a sweater was one of the most important decisions she had to make on a daily basis. Standing knee-deep in her sweaters, I realized how different our lives were. She did not have to worry about maintaining a solid academic average so that she could receive financial aid. Because she was in the majority, she was not treated as a representative of her race. She did not have to consider how her classroom comments or basic existence on campus contributed to the treatment her group would receive. Her allowance protected her from having to work, so she was free to spend her time studying, partying, or in her case, worrying about which sweater to wear. The degree of inequality in our lives and her unquestioned sense of entitlement concerning that inequality offended me. For a while, I categorized all affluent White women as being superficial, arrogant, overly concerned with material possessions, and part of my problem. But had I continued to classify people in this way, I would have missed out on making some very good friends whose discomfort with their inherited or acquired social class privileges pushed them to examine their position.

Since I opened with the words of Audre Lorde, it seems appropriate to close with another of her ideas. . . .

> Each of us is called upon to take a stand. So in these days ahead, as we examine ourselves and each other, our works, our fears, our differences, our sisterhood and survivals, I urge you to tackle what is most difficult for us all, self-scrutiny of our complacencies, the idea that since each of us believes she is on the side of right, she need not examine her position (1985).

I urge you to examine your position.

REFERENCES

Collins, Patricia Hill. 1989. "The Social Construction of Black Feminist Thought." *Signs.* Summer 1989.

Gwaltney, John Langston. 1980. *Drylongso: A Self-Portrait of Black America.* New York: Vintage.

Harding, Sandra. 1986. *The Science Question in Feminism.* Ithaca, New York: Cornell University Press.

Jordan, June. 1985. *On Call: Political Essays.* Boston: South End Press.

Lorde, Audre. 1984. *Sister Outsider.* Trumansberg, New York: The Crossing Press.

———. 1985 "Sisterhood and Survival." Keynote address, conference on the Black Woman Writer and the Diaspora, Michigan State University.

Spelman, Elizabeth. 1982. "Theories of Race and Gender: The Erasure of Black Women." *Quest* 5:36–38.

Tate, Claudia, ed. 1983. *Black Women Writers at Work.* New York: Continuum.

QUESTIONS FOR DISCUSSION

1. How is thinking of race, class, and gender as systems of oppression different from viewing them as personal attributes of individuals?
2. Do you agree with Collins's comparison of the race, class, and gender relations on a plantation under slavery with the race, class, and gender relations at a contemporary university?
3. Why does Collins argue that ranking oppressions is counterproductive?
4. What do you as a student have to do to avoid "voyeurism" in your college experience?
5. What are the issues around which you are most likely to work in coalition with people of other races, genders, and classes?

3

THE REPRODUCTION OF INEQUALITY
Interactionist Analysis[*]

MICHAEL SCHWALBE   •   SANDRA GODWIN   •   DAPHNE HOLDEN   •   DOUGLAS SCHROCK
SHEALY THOMPSON   •   MICHELE WOLKOMIR

Abstract

The study of inequality has been largely defined as the study of its measurable extent, degree, and consequences. It is no less important, however, to understand the interactive processes through which inequalities are created and reproduced in concrete settings. The qualitative research that bears on understanding these processes has not yet been consolidated, and thus its theoretical value remains unrealized. In this article we inductively derive from the literature a sensitizing theory of the generic processes through which inequality is reproduced. The major processes that we identify are othering, subordinate adaptation, boundary maintenance, and emotion management. We argue that conceiving the reproduction of inequality in terms of these generic processes can resolve theoretical problems concerning the connection between local action and extra-local inequalities, and concerning the nature of inequality itself.

Sociologists have traditionally asked three questions about inequality: What kind of inequalities exist? How large are these inequalities? and How are these inequalities created and reproduced? Answers to the first two questions can be found in a vast literature on inequalities in income, wealth, status, political power, health, and other resources. It is fair to say that we know a great deal about patterns of resource distribution both across and within social groups. Yet without answers to the third question our knowledge remains documentary. To *explain* inequality requires attention to the processes that produce and perpetuate it.

Such processes can be studied in various ways. Historical data can reveal process, or at least provide an empirical basis from which to infer it. Quantitative analyses of changes in resource distribution over time can also provide a basis for testing and refining ideas about process. Alternatively, process can be examined directly, through qualitative research. Many qualitative studies have in fact looked at how inequality is reproduced (see Horowitz 1997 for a review). . . . In this article we analytically consolidate this body of qualitative work, deriving from it a conceptual scheme that can take us far toward answering that third question about inequality. . . .

We take inequality to be endemic to and pervasive in late capitalist societies (our

From Michael Schwalbe et al., "Generic Processes in the Reproduction of Inequality: An Interactionist Analysis" in *Social Forces*, December 2000, 79 (2): 419–452. Reprinted by permission of University of North Carolina Press.

[*]The authors thank Gary Alan Fine, Sherryl Kleinman, Patricia Yancey Martin, Jim Thomas, and Christine Williams for helpful comments on an earlier version of this article. Direct correspondence to Michael Schwalbe, Department of Sociology, North Carolina State University, Raleigh, NC 27695-8107. E-mail: michael_schwalbe@ncsu.edu.

main concern here). We ask, How is this inequality reproduced?—and then seek answers in terms of the generic processes out of which inequality emerges or is sustained. To call these processes "generic" does not imply that they are unaffected by context. It means, rather, that they occur in multiple contexts wherein social actors face similar or analogous problems. The precise form a process takes in any given setting is a matter for empirical determination. Managers and mushroomers may build trust in different ways, using the resources they have at hand, but there is still a generic process of "building trust" that can be studied and analyzed, with the goal of understanding its occurrence more generally.

The Qualitative Literature as Data for Inductive Analysis

While our theoretical orientation is symbolic interactionist, much qualitative work does not wear this label. What matters for our purposes, however, is not the label but whether the work in question can tell us something useful about (1) what happens in face-to-face interaction, such that a form of inequality is the result; (2) how symbols and meanings are created and used to sustain the patterns of interaction that lead to inequality; or (3) how inequality itself is perceived, experienced, and reacted to, such that it is either reproduced or resisted. These concerns are, in effect, the criteria we used to select the studies we examined. We have not reviewed every qualitative study that bears on some issue related to inequality. Rather, we focused on studies compatible with interactionist principles, and which also could be interpreted as showing how disparities in power, status, suffering, or reward are created and reproduced. . . .

Our analysis of the literature leads us to propose that four generic processes are

central to the reproduction of inequality: *othering, subordinate adaptation, boundary maintenance,* and *emotion management*—each of which in turn comprises several subprocesses. We argue that these transsituationally occurring processes, as revealed in a diverse body of qualitative research, are the key forms of joint action through which inequalities are reproduced in small groups, complex organizations, communities, and societies. In the final section of the paper we consider how a focus on generic processes can resolve theoretical problems concerning the connection between local action and extra-local inequalities, and concerning the nature of inequality itself.

Othering

The term *othering* has come to refer to the process whereby a dominant group defines into existence an inferior group (Fine 1994). This process entails the invention of categories and of ideas about what marks people as belonging to these categories.[1] From an interactionist perspective, othering is a form of collective identity work (Hadden & Lester 1978; Snow & Anderson 1987; Schwalbe & Mason-Schrock 1996) aimed at creating and/or reproducing inequality. The literature suggests that othering can take at least three forms: (1) oppressive othering; (2) implicit othering by the creation of powerful virtual selves; and (3) defensive othering among subordinates. In each case, meanings are created that shape consciousness and behavior, such that inequality is directly or indirectly reproduced.

Oppressive Othering

Oppressive othering occurs when one group seeks advantage by defining another group as morally and/or intellectually inferior. Perhaps the clearest examples are racial classification schemes. Social historians and historical sociologists have shown how elites in Europe and America used such schemes to claim superiority vis-à-vis peoples in Africa, Asia, and the New World, and later to prevent working-class solidarity in North America (Allen 1994; Brown 1993; Omi & Winant 1986; Roediger 1991). Qualitative research has examined how these schemes are used, intentionally or inadvertently, in ways that reproduce inequality in the present.

Blee (1996), for example, shows how Klan women used racial ideologies to make sense of apparent differences between people, create scapegoats, build community among themselves, and maintain feelings of superiority. Frankenberg (1993) shows how even whites who disavowed racism used a discourse of race that makes *whiteness* invisible, effectively defining whites as the standard group and thus implicitly defining Others as exotic and different (see also Gallagher 1995). Rollins (1985) shows how middle/upper-middle-class white women defined the women of color whom they employed to do domestic work as irresponsible, childlike, and happy to serve (see also Romero 1992). Oppressive othering, these studies suggest, commonly entails the overt or subtle assertion of *difference as deficit*.

Othering can also create patterns of interaction that reaffirm a dominant group's ideology of difference. For example, Holden's (1997) study of a homeless shelter shows how the mostly white, middle-class volunteers deflected residents' complaints by defining them as ungrateful, "having an attitude," or "in need of rules," and thereby evoked angry responses that were taken as further proof that the residents were at fault. The inequalities (both within and outside the shelter) that gave rise to the residents' complaints were thus obscured. Anderson (1990) shows how young black men who adopt the "urban predator" pose as a matter of style, self-assertion, or self-protection are then treated by whites in ways that lead to tense encounters—thus affirming, for whites, the dangerousness they stereotypically attribute to black males (see also Vander Ven 1998).

Oppressive othering can also take the form of turning subordinates into commodities. For example, Rogers (1995; see also Kunda 1992) shows how "temps" are defined by full-time employees as unambitious and incompetent, and thus not to be taken seriously as co-workers. In this we see old-fashioned stereotyping. What Rogers also shows is how the owners of temp agencies abet the problem by encouraging temp workers to change their names, voices, and job histories to appear suited for various work assignments. This demand for fakery creates a trap: if temps do not misrepresent themselves, they risk being cut off from assignments; if they do, their chances for a full-time job with an employer who has been duped are slim. Temporary workers experience this situation as profoundly alienating, and thus seldom work to their full capacity—in turn making it likely that they will remain marginally-employed Others.

The symbolic tools used to accomplish oppressive othering include not only classification schemes but *identity codes,* which are the rules of performance and interpretation whereby members of a group know what kind of self is signified by certain words, deeds, and dress (Schwalbe & Mason-Schrock 1996:125–27). To know the code is to know how to elicit the imputation of possessing a desired kind of self. Oppressive othering entails the creation of identity codes that make it impossible for members of a subjugated group to signify fully creditable selves. A code that treats a male body and Caucasian features as signs of competence peremptorily discredits those with female bodies and African features. Equally insidious are identity codes that define the adaptive or dissident behaviors of subordinates as signs of inferior selves—thus turning acts of resistance into evidence that subordination is deserved and inequality is legitimate.

Creating Powerful Virtual Selves

Inequality is reproduced by identity work that upholds the dramaturgical fronts of the powerful. These fronts obscure discrediting backstage realities, create powerful virtual (i.e., imputed) selves, and implicitly create inferior Others. The impression that elites possess powerful, worthy selves—no matter the reality—can induce feelings of trust, awe, and/or fear that help to legitimate inequality and deter dissent (cf. Della Fave 1980; Wolf 1986).[2]

This kind of identity work is typically done by elites or would-be elites. For example, Jackall (1988) shows how corporate managers tried to foster impressions of competence and trustworthiness, so as to appear destined for top executive positions. Gillespie (1980) shows how the wives of politicians enact the role of "public wife" to create the impression that their husbands are strong, moral, and deserving of election. In his analysis of the presidency, Hall (1979) shows how candidates shape their public performances to elicit imputations of strength and masculinity. Similarly, Haas and Shaffir (1977) show how medical students learn to fashion a "cloak of competence" to legitimate their status as physicians.

The creation of powerful virtual selves depends on more than the dramaturgical skill of individuals. Wealth is typically needed to acquire that skill (a form of cultural capital), along with material signs of competence and power. Wealth can also buy the image-making services of PR firms, media doctors, and speech writers. Cooper-

ation is important, too. Elites typically engage in mutually supportive facework that serves to maintain, vis-à-vis subordinate groups, a collective impression of competence and trustworthiness.[3] The general (and long-recognized) principle here is that an unequal distribution of wealth and power generates an unequal distribution of ability to shape symbolic realities, including powerful virtual selves. . . .

Defensive Othering Among Subordinates

Defensive othering is identity work done by those seeking membership in a dominant group, or by those seeking to deflect the stigma they experience as members of a subordinate group. When homeless men disparage other homeless men as "lazy bums," they practice a kind of defensive othering (Snow & Anderson 1987). A similar process occurs in the workplace, as Padavic (1991) shows, when some women join men in disdaining other women whom the men define as unattractive. Field (1994) likewise shows how some Irish immigrants distance themselves from those whose behavior feeds the stereotype of the rowdy Irish drunk. The process, in each case, involves accepting the legitimacy of a devalued identity imposed by the dominant group, but then saying, in effect, "There are indeed Others to whom this applies, but it does not apply to me." . . .

Though defensive othering is an adaptive reaction, it nonetheless aids the reproduction of inequality. When members of subordinate groups seek safety or advantage by othering those in their own group, the belief system that supports the dominant group's claim to superiority is reinforced. Subordinate solidarity is also undermined. Thus when some subordinates break solidarity and seek to fashion powerful, or at least creditable, selves by embracing and enforcing the identity code of the dominant group, they inadvertently aid the reproduction of a larger system of inequality.

Subordinate Adaptation

Qualitative studies of oppressive situations often highlight the strategies that people use to cope with the deprivations of subordinate status. We do not claim that all such strategies merely reproduce inequality. Some coping strategies might be largely reproductive in their consequences; others resist inequality or seek to abolish it. What qualitative research shows, however, is that most strategies of adaptation have dual consequences, challenging some inequalities while reproducing others. Exactly what consequences follow from any particular strategy is, of course, an empirical matter. Our point is that subordinates' adaptations to inequality play an essential part in its reproduction. We see three types of adaptations implicit in the literature: (1) trading power for patronage; (2) forming alternative subcultures; (3) hustling or dropping out.

Trading Power for Patronage

One way to adapt to subordinate status is to accept it, while seeking ways to derive compensatory benefits from relationships with members of the dominant group. Stombler and Martin (1994) give us the example of women who seek status and feelings of self-worth by becoming "little sisters" for fraternity men who, in actuality, objectify the women as sexual mascots. Similarly, Yount (1991) shows how women coal miners felt compelled to accept men's sexist "compliments," because, as women in traditionally male jobs, they wanted affirmation of their femininity. In these cases, members of a subordinate gender group accept practices that demean and disempower them in exchange for a degree of approval and protection. . . .

Subordinates may try to sustain these symbiotic relationships by using the same imagery that the dominant group uses to legitimate inequality. For example, Ronai and Ellis (1989) show how strippers enhance their earnings by performing in ways that feed men's sexual fantasies. Ronai and Ellis argue that in doing this, strippers use the gender order to con men into paying more for their performances (cf. Frank 1998). While this strategy may pay off for the women who use it, the larger consequence is reproduction of the sexist imagery that helps to sustain the subordination of women in general. What is situationally adaptive for some members of a subordinate group thus can be disadvantageous, on the whole, for other members of the same group.

Power can also be traded for autonomy—the bargain often made by working-class men. Instead of challenging management for control of the labor process, working-class men often accept less control in exchange for the satisfaction of being free from the indignity of close supervision (Cherry 1974; Schwalbe 1985; Hodson 1991).[4] This bargain reproduces class inequality by preserving managerial control of the labor process. It also reinforces an element of gender ideology that links manhood to control. Even if "control" is largely an illusion, men are still encouraged to stake their feelings of worth on having it, and thus may strive for it in domestic and political realms as well.

Forming Alternative Subcultures

Adaptation to subordinate status can be individual (trying to scam one's way through the system) or collective. In the latter case, people who share a subordinate status vis-à-vis the dominant group(s) collaborate to create alternative prestige hierarchies, forms of power, and ways to make a living (cf. Hughes 1958:49–55). Qualitative research has examined the origins, content, and consequences of a number of these alternative subcultures. These studies show how collective adaptation strategies can be simultaneously subversive and reproductive of inequality.

For example, Bourgois (1995) shows how the urban drug trade offers a path to status and economic success for young men who have no chance for industrial work, nor the cultural capital to break into middle-class service jobs (see also Adler & Adler 1983). Similarly, Anderson (1990) shows how the lack of good jobs in the inner city leads to the creation of a subculture wherein young men achieve status through violence and sexual prowess, while young women achieve it by having babies and outfitting them in fashionable clothes (see also Jacobs 1994). These signs of status—money, might, sexuality, consumer goods—are echoes of the dominant culture, the alternative culture providing other ways to achieve them.

The problem, however, is that conflict with the dominant culture tends to make success within the alternative culture tenuous, both economically and psychologically. As Bourgois, Anderson, and others (MacLeod [1987] 1995) have shown, even those who do well by the standards of the street tend to acquire habits and create situations (drug addiction, lack of education, multiple dependents, criminal records) that are debilitating and risky, and diminish chances for mainstream success, even in the form of stable working-class employment. As this pattern unfolds, members of dominant groups may also perceive that their stereotypes of subordinate Others as stupid, violent, irresponsible, and licentious are largely true. . . .

The need for subgroup solidarity in the face of a hostile dominant culture can perpetuate inequality when members of subordinate groups discourage "collaboration with the enemy" by individuals seeking upward mobility for themselves. For example, black students who try hard to please their teachers may be reined-in by peers who accuse them of "acting white" (Fordham & Ogbu 1986). Working-class men may show a similar disdain, or at least ambivalence, toward efforts to achieve middle-class status (Halle 1984; Fantasia 1988; Sennett & Cobb 1972). Inequality is thus perpetuated by discouraging individual striving.[5]

Adaptive subcultures have a reproductive effect in part because they allow psychic needs to be met, despite subordination. For example, Burawoy (1979) shows how machine operators turned a piece-rate pay system into a satisfying game of "making out," in which workers competed to see who could earn the most with the least effort. Similarly, Paules (1991) shows how waitresses created a workplace culture that gave them autonomy and space for self-assertion vis-à-vis customers and managers. Similar patterns of subculture building by organizational subordinates have been noted in schools (Becker et al. [1961] 1977), prisons (Ward & Kassebaum 1965), and the military (Shibutani 1978). Organizational elites often tolerate or even encourage the formation of such adaptive subcultures, since they function to mitigate overt resistance and to stabilize relations of inequality.

Hustling or Dropping Out

The modal adaptation to inequality is acquiescence: accepting one's place within existing hierarchies of status, power, and wealth—while trying to make that place reasonably comfortable. This sort of adaptation implies acceptance of conventional goals and means of achieving them (as per Merton 1967; see also Becker 1995 on the "power of inertia"). Another possibility, however, is to work the margins of the system, looking for a niche within which one can hustle for a living. By "hustling" we mean economic activity that is officially considered illegal or dishonest.

The study of groups that survive by hustling has been a staple tradition for qualitative sociologists. From classic studies of gangs (Short & Strodtbeck 1965) to contemporary studies of Gypsies (Kephart 1987), fortune tellers (Boles, Davis, & Tatro 1983), and drug dealers (Adler 1985), qualitative research has shown how members of subordinate groups, rather than challenge the system or push their way into the mainstream, organize to exploit it from the edge. Usually this means exploiting those who are more vulnerable—the jobless, the elderly, the uneducated, the addicted. This kind of hustling exploits the human fallout from extra-local inequalities, and in turn helps to reproduce those inequalities by further debilitating the already weak.

"Dropping out" is another response to inequality that might, though need not always, reproduce it. Individual dropping out—out of school, out of the corporate rat race, out of political involvement—is part of what we are referring to. Certainly the withdrawal of participation by people who are fed up with powerlessness and disrespect has the effect of allowing things to go on as they are. What qualitative sociologists have looked at more closely, however, is collective dropping out, that is, the formation of counter-cultural groups. . . .

Do such groups promote change or retard it? Certainly the withdrawal of dissident energy from the mainstream does little to threaten existing hierarchies. Counter-cultural groups may also strive to reject one form of inequality, yet internally reproduce other inequalities present in the dominant culture (Brown 1992; Kleinman 1996). Then again, even fringe and separatist groups that engage in no overt political action can foster change by modeling its possibility. Whether such groups inspire or, through withdrawal, impede change, depends, of course, on the historical context. Our point is that a holistic view of the process through which inequality is reproduced must take into account adaptations that involve dropping out, as well as fitting in.

Boundary Maintenance

Preserving inequality requires maintaining boundaries between dominant and subordinate groups. These boundaries can be symbolic, interactional, spatial, or all of these. By preserving these boundaries, dominant groups protect the material and cultural capital they have acquired and upon which they rely to preserve their dominance. In plainer terms, the reproduction of inequality depends on elites cooperating to limit Others' access to valued resources.

Most boundary maintenance is accomplished institutionally. Schools, governments, police forces, banks, and work organizations can be seen as functioning, in part, to maintain boundaries between stratified groups. It is often easier, however, to document the boundary-maintaining *results* of institutional action than to see how these results are produced. Qualitative research can help us to see how these results arise out of face-to-face interaction. The processes we discern in this regard are: (1) transmitting cultural capital; (2) controlling network access; and (3) the use of violence or the threat thereof.

Transmitting Cultural Capital

"Cultural capital" refers to the knowledge, skills, habits, values, and tastes that are acquired in the course of socialization, and which can be turned to one's advantage in particular social settings (Bourdieu 1977). Everyone acquires cultural capital; but not everyone acquires the kind that is useful and valued in middle-, upper-middle-, and upper-class circles. Any privileged group can keep subordinates out by limiting access to the requisite cultural capital. Without the right cultural capital, one simply cannot make connections, interact competently, or be taken seriously in certain places. A group's boundaries can thus be maintained by regulating access to the cultural capital one needs to get in.

Families are the primary settings in which cultural capital is transmitted. This ensures selectivity in the transmission of cultural capital, since families are strictly-bounded social units. The state-enforced laws and traditions governing membership in families are the principal means whereby social class boundaries are maintained through the selective transmission of cultural and material capital (Allen 1987). The ideology of competitive individualism also imposes a moral imperative on parents—especially middle- and upper-middle-class parents, whose class standing depends on earned income rather than durable wealth—to make sure that their children acquire as much cultural capital as possible, so as to avoid a fall into the working class (Ehrenreich 1989; Hays 1996; Kohn 1969).

Schools are also key institutions for transmitting cultural capital. Getting in to schools in which valued cultural capital can be acquired requires knowhow and money (Cookson & Persell 1985). Even presuming entry, the cultural capital a student brings to school will limit what is acquired there. Students from lower- and working-class backgrounds often have difficulty getting their middle-class teachers to respect them and recognize their capabilities (Rosenbaum 1976; Luttrell 1997). School then comes to be experienced as a hostile, or at least inhospitable, place, making academic success even less likely. Social distance between teachers and students, combined with middle-class cultural hegemony in the schools, can thus engender an interactive

process—often occurring beneath the conscious awareness of teachers and students—that nearly ensures an unequal distribution of the cultural capital potentially available in school.

Qualitative studies of schools also suggest how inequality can be reproduced when teachers reinforce what seem like innocuous boundaries between "natural" social groups. Thorne's (1993) ethnography of an elementary school shows how this occurs in regard to gender. While boys and girls engage in their own territorial "boundary work," teachers abet this process of marking gender divisions by establishing separate play areas for boys and girls, encouraging boys and girls to play different games, rewarding different kinds of behaviors, and assigning different kinds of tasks.[6] We suggest, following Lever (1978), that such boundary work has the result, over the long haul of a school career, of selectively transmitting to boys the kinds of habits and skills that are likely to be rewarded in the job market and the corporation.

Cultural capital is also assessed and acquired in workplaces. Knowing how to play golf, for instance; or how to make the right kind of small talk at parties, may open doors to acquiring more resources that can be turned to one's further advantage. A similar process can be seen in trade unions. Getting an apprenticeship may hinge not simply on having adequate qualifying skills, but on having an inside sponsor, the right ethnic surname, and a zest for football. What this suggests is that inter-group boundaries are often maintained by the use of social markers that are largely invisible to non-gatekeepers.

What matters for reproducing inequality is the transmission of cultural capital that is valued by those who control access to jobs, pay, and positions of status and power. Subordinates are kept out, and privilege preserved, by selectively transmitting valued cultural capital to those who are, by birth or display of special aptitude, deemed worthy of having it. This process reproduces inequality not only through the unequal distribution of resources, but by legitimating hierarchy. Because it can be hard to see how cultural capital is transmitted in families and schools, and even harder to see how it is "cashed in" in closed circles, the unequal distribution of wealth, power, and status can come to look as if it corresponds to a natural distribution of ability (Bourdieu 1984).

Controlling Network Access

The processes of selectively transmitting cultural capital and controlling network access overlap. Access to networks is controlled, in part, by selectively transmitting cultural capital; without the right credentials, it may be impossible to break into a network. But cultural capital per se does not guarantee access to elite networks *within* a group. Within a group, everyone may have roughly the same stocks of cultural capital. Inequality within the group may then be reproduced by controlling access to the key networks through which information is traded, decisions and deals are made, and rewards are disbursed.

Traweek's (1988) ethnographic study of physicists shows how networks are crucial to the reproduction of inequality in this field of science. Traweek shows how the directors of a few prominent research labs form a network through which post-docs are given, grants awarded, and people defined as stars or drones. What goes on in this network determines, in short, the fates of people's careers. Members of the elite network also effectively choose who will succeed them. Women who manage to break into the predominantly male *world* of high-energy particle physicists suffer, Traweek's analysis shows, because of their exclusion from key *networks*.

Access can also be regulated by subordinate actors in a network. For example, Ostrander's (1984) study of upper-class women shows how their volunteer work created opportunities to form political and business alliances between families (see also Daniels 1988; Lamont 1992). Moreover, as these women interacted on the boards of various civic organizations, they were able to assess newcomers to the community and determine if they had the right stuff—money, credentials, manners, and politics—to be admitted to the circle of local elites. In this way, the women not only helped to control network access, they also helped to reproduce the patriarchal authority of their husbands and fathers, who controlled family wealth and businesses.

Jackall's (1988) study of corporate managers shows how access to top networks depended on making one's peers and bosses feel comfortable. Having the right cultural capital was crucial for inducing such comfort; but, as Jackall shows, it was consistent behavior—keeping secrets (or sharing them appropriately), not selling out one's allies or boss, looking like a winner and avoiding blame for failures—that mattered for *staying* in the network. As in the world of physics, these networks were the means through which promotion decisions were made, projects approved, blame assigned, and elite succession accomplished. To be cut out of a network was to lose influence and power, and to have one's fate sealed. . . .

The Threat and Use of Violence

To focus solely on the selective transmission of cultural capital and the control of network access would suggest that the reproduction of inequality is more genteel than it is. Boundaries are indeed maintained, perhaps most effectively and efficiently on a daily basis, through ideological and spatial separations. People can nonetheless get "out of place" when inequalities become too much to bear. Violence—the application of damaging force to human bodies—may then be necessary, from the standpoint of elites, to protect their power and privilege, and to ensure that boundaries do not break down.

What has qualitative research shown about how violence, or the threat thereof, is used to maintain boundaries? In one sense, not much. Most studies of violence by political and economic elites have been done by journalists and historians (e.g., Colby & Dennett 1995; James 1996). Qualitative sociologists have tended to study violence by nonelite members of dominant groups (e.g., Athens 1997). A number of studies have shown how men use violence and threats to control the social lives of their female partners (Denzin 1984; Ferraro & Johnson 1983; Jones 1993). Other studies have shown how men cooperate in their use of degrading remarks, sexual bribery, and restriction of knowledge to keep women in place at work (Padavic 1991; Tallichet 1995; Yount 1991). Gardner (1995) shows that many of these same forms of inhibiting harassment occur in public as well. The effect of these forms of action, whether it is physical or verbal, is to limit women's access to people and places from which might be acquired the resources needed to challenge men for power (see also Chafe 1977).[7]

Violence can also function ideologically to maintain boundaries. When the capacity to enact violence is valorized within a culture, it becomes a criterion by which to decide who qualifies for membership in dominant or elite groups. . . .

Emotion Management

All social arrangements consist of people doing things together in recurrent, orderly ways. Essential to maintaining these patterns of action are patterns of feeling. There

must be, if not feelings of satisfaction, then feelings of complacency or resignation; there must be fear of change or of being punished for protest; and there must not be too much sympathy for the oppressed or too much anger toward elites. Sustaining a system of inequality, one that generates destabilizing feelings of anger, resentment, sympathy, and despair, requires that emotions be managed. . . .

. . . Inequality is reproduced as emotions are subtly shaped by symbolic and material culture. . . . We consider how emotions are managed by (1) regulating discourse; (2) conditioning emotional subjectivity; and (3) scripting mass events.

Regulating Discourse

Discourse is more than talk and writing; it is a way of talking and writing. To regulate discourse is to impose a set of formal or informal rules about what can be said, how it can be said, and who can say what to whom (Potter & Wetherell 1987). A courtroom is at one extreme in regard to degree of formal regulation; a barroom at the other. Inasmuch as language is the principal means by which we express, manage, and conjure emotions, to regulate discourse is to regulate emotion. The ultimate consequence is a regulation of action.

Cohn's (1987) study of the "technostrategic" language of defense intellectuals provides an example of how a form of discourse can mute potentially inhibiting emotions. Cohn reports that technostrategic discourse strictly avoids reference to human pain and suffering, and instead uses the abstract and dispassionate language of strikes, counter-strikes, megatonnage, and megadeaths. Given the rules of this discourse, to speak of pain and suffering is to discredit one's self as a "soft-headed activist instead of an expert" (708). We see here a form of discourse being used as an emotional anesthetic that allows technical experts to more efficiently serve the interests of political and military elites.

Corporate managers, as Jackall (1988) shows, use a similar rationalist discourse when making decisions that will hurt people (cf. Maccoby 1976). This discourse helps corporate managers stay focused on profits, even taking pride in their ability to make tough decisions that are "best for the company." In this case, corporate elites use a form of discourse—a language of efficiencies, returns, and fiduciary responsibilities—that keeps compassion at bay and facilitates the pursuit of narrow economic interests. As in the world of defense intellectuals, the privileged discourse of corporate managers can also be used to exclude or discredit those who are unable or unwilling to engage in it.

Discourse can be regulated to simultaneously quell some emotions and evoke others. This is most apparent in wartime, when political and military elites try to regulate the national discourse in ways that arouse and sustain enthusiasm for mass violence, while provoking hatred for enemy leaders and decreased sympathy for civilians on the other side. In the case of war, discourse must be regulated institutionally, via the mass media. This is accomplished by describing events, if they are described at all, in the frames preferred by elites (Gamson & Modigliani 1989), and by excluding dissident voices that might, by using alternative language and frames, evoke resistant emotions in the citizenry.

When a form of discourse is established as standard practice, it becomes a powerful tool for reproducing inequality, because it can serve not only to regulate thought and emotion, but also to identify Others and thus to maintain boundaries as well. Those who wish to belong to the dominant group, or who simply want to be heard, may feel compelled to use the master's linguistic tools. Hegemonic discourses are not, however, eternal. As Wasielewski (1985) suggests, discourses that deny expression to the pain and anger of the oppressed create a powerful emotional tension, which in turn fosters the emergence of charismatic leaders. Such leaders catalyze change by articulating what is repressed and linking the resolution of repressed feelings to dissident action. All hegemonic discourses may thus carry within them the seeds of their own destruction.

Conditioning Emotional Subjectivity

A basic tenet of symbolic interactionism is that people act toward things based on the meanings they learn to give to things (Blumer 1969). We take this idea to apply to emotion as well: people's feelings toward things—other people, situations, events, objects—depend on the meanings they learn to give to those things. Emotion thus depends, first of all, on interpretation. It also depends, however, on self-awareness of arousal and what is then done, cognitively or interactively, to manage that arousal. An individual's acquired *habits* of interpretation and of emotion work are what we mean by conditioned emotional subjectivity.

Qualitative research in the sociology of emotions shows how emotional subjectivity can be conditioned in ways that reproduce inequality. A classic example is Hochschild's (1983) study of flight attendants and bill collectors. Hochschild shows how employers train these workers to respond emotionally to people and situations in ways that allow business to get done. Flight attendants learn how to avoid getting angry by picturing obnoxious passengers as cranky children. Bill collectors learn how to quash their feelings of sympathy for people who fall behind on their payments. What these and many other service jobs demand, Hochschild says, is not craft skill but skill at managing one's own emotions and the emotions of others—in ways that serve an employer's interests (see also Hall 1993; Leidner 1993).

Employers in service industries have a clear interest in conditioning workers' emotional subjectivity. Teaching workers to be efficient performers of emotional labor is part of the process whereby employers try to extract more value from labor than is returned to workers in the form of wages. Conditioning workers' emotional subjectivity—making emotional labor a matter of habit—is thus an important part of reproducing economic inequality. In the case of Hochschild's female flight attendants, something more is going on. When employers teach them not to be angered by the sexist behavior of male passengers, flight attendants are compelled to collude in the reproduction of gender inequality.

Scully and Marolla's (1984) study of convicted rapists suggests another link between sexism, discourse, and emotional conditioning. Scully and Marolla examined the accounts rapists used to excuse and justify their behavior. Some men justified their acts by claiming that their victims were seducers, that their victims enjoyed it, or that she said "no" but meant "yes." Other men excused themselves by claiming that they were drunk, stoned, or mentally distressed during the crime. A common feature of these accounts is that they preclude appreciation for the victim's fear, pain, and suffering. The men thus avoid empathizing or sympathizing with their victims.

The significance of Scully and Marolla's study is underscored by two points. One is that many of the men, in describing their crimes, told of using the same accounts to facilitate their action. These accounts functioned, in other words, as legitimations that allowed the men to act on violent impulses aimed at women. A second point is that the rapists' excuses and justifications are commonplace, familiar to any adult raised in U.S. culture. We see these accounts as elements of a wider sexist discourse that, on the one hand, devalues women's subjectivity and, at the same time, conditions men's subjectivity in a way that diminishes empathy with women, and thus facilitates action that perpetuates male supremacy.

Emotional subjectivity must be similarly conditioned to enable mass violence. Armies and police forces would be feckless if it were not possible to condition individuals to suppress feelings of empathy for those whom they are ordered to batter or kill. Individuals must thus be taught how to put aside inhibiting feelings—fear as well as empathy—and do what they are told. Some theorists have argued that this kind of conditioning is a defining feature of hegemonic masculinity (Connell 1995; Seidler 1991; Schwalbe 1992). Part of learning to be a man, the argument goes, is learning to devalue emotions—not only the emotions of those who might become targets of violence, but one's own emotions as well, because if one's own emotions are seen as unimportant, or as signs of weakness, then it becomes easier to despise those who show emotion or value it.

The flip side to the conditioning of masculine emotional subjectivity is the creation of femininity, as both a complementary form of conditioning and a set of adaptive practices. As a complementary form of conditioning, conventional femininity involves learning not only to value others' emotions (men's in particular), but often to value them more highly than one's own (Miller 1976; Bartky 1990). It may also entail conditioning one's self to accept as normal the feelings that are attendant to subordination.[8] Femininity can also be seen as a subcultural adaptation that consists of practices for managing the emotions of men (cf. Janeway 1980). This suggests, as a general principle, that the smooth reproduction of inequality depends as much on subordinates managing the emotions of dominants, as vice versa.

Scripting Mass Events

Humans are self-reflective, fraught with conflicting feelings, and capable of reconditioning themselves. These qualities create a problem in that emotional subjectivity cannot be so firmly conditioned that it can be taken for granted as a stable determinant of conformist behavior. Those who have an interest in preserving the status quo must therefore find ways both to reaffirm the desired conditioning, and, at extraordinary times, induce desired emotions in masses of people. Elite shaping of public discourse, we have already suggested, is part of how this is done. Another way is through the scripting of emotion-inducing events. . . .

When we refer to the "scripting" of emotion-inducing events, we mean their orchestration to bring about an intended emotional result. Zurcher gives us two examples. In one case, he analyzes what might be called the macroscripting of a college football game (Zurcher 1982). He examines the set of activities—practices, press conferences, facility preparation, rallies—leading up to the game, the timing of these activities, the defining of the game's importance, the feeling rules invoked, and the interaction on the day of the game to show how this organization produces a powerful emotional experience for thousands of people. In another case, Zurcher (1985) analyzes a war game and shows how the event is scripted and orchestrated by military leaders to generate enthusiasm for practice killing. . . .

Scripted events that inspire feelings of solidarity at the level of the "race," the firm, or the nation, reproduce inequality by encouraging subordinates to ignore inequality and embrace the dominant regime. Mass political rallies, wars, parades, and national celebrations are spectacular examples. The same social technology of emotion management is used on smaller scales. For example, Schwalbe (1996) shows how the leaders of men's movement gatherings artfully combined simple acts—decorating a room with totemic objects, burning incense, playing ethereal music, drumming, chanting, invoking spirits, and excluding women—to induce a feeling of emotional communion that compelled men to ignore political conflicts, social class differences, and sexist behavior by other men. Other studies have shown how organizational leaders likewise script meetings to manage emotions in ways that deflect challenges to existing hierarchies (e.g., Kleinman 1996: 63–89; Kunda 1992).[9]

The practices of regulating discourse, conditioning emotional subjectivity, and scripting events clearly overlap. Events are always organized by using some form of discourse, which is likely to be reinforced by the event itself. Events also have socializing effects on their organizers and participants. Moreover, the kinds of emotional responses that events can induce depend on prior conditioning. No one of these practices can ensure the reproduction of inequality; rather, as we see them, they are all necessary to the process, and are most powerful when organized to be mutually reinforcing. These same methods of emotion inducement can also be used, of course, to incite dissident behavior; thus, under the right conditions, they are as essential to producing change as they are to reproducing the status quo.

Implications

. . .

Inequality as Condition, Process, and Experience

Some argue that we should combine quantitative information about the conditions under which people act with qualitative analyses of how people cope with deprivation. But even this can leave us with a static view of inequality. What is missing is an analysis of the *relationships* that arise between those who seek, or seek to preserve, an unequal share of resources, power, and privilege for themselves, and those who resist or adapt. Our formulation identifies the generic processes through which these relationships of domination and subordination are created and maintained. We see these processes not merely as generic, in the sense of occurring in multiple contexts, but as essential and generative.

Suppose, for example, that one wished to create a hierarchy of wealth, status, and power based on the familiar notion of "race." To do so would *require* a program of othering, boundary maintenance, and emotion management. Subordinates would also have to find ways to adapt, or the arrangement would collapse. Similarly, inequalities typically identified as having to do with class, gender, and sexuality depend for their reproduction on some combination of these same processes. The implication, to put it another way, is that these processes are what give rise to the forms of inequality we commonly know as "race," "class," "gender," and so on. We would thus claim that some generic processes are more important than others, because they are *generative of* patterns and conditions that are significantly consequential for large numbers of people.[10]

Getting at these processes requires bracketing certain labor-saving reifications. "Race," "class," and "gender," for example, though often used as explanatory variables, are merely labels for routinized forms of thought, speech, and action through which some people attempt to dominate and exploit others. Just as gender has been recognized as a form of doing (West & Zimmerman 1987), we would argue that race and class must also be examined as they are constituted by particular forms of thought, speech, and action that create and maintain relations of domination and subordination.

Instead of asking, for example, What effect does race have on income?—as if we knew what "race" is and that it is the same everywhere—we would ask, How do people think, feel, and interact here, such that some material or felt inequality is a result, whether intended or not? Or, instead of presuming to know what "gender" is and that gender inequality will be obvious if present, we might study the beliefs and practices that seem to constitute gender in a setting, and then try to discern the consequences of these beliefs and practices. Class, too, can be approached as a situated construction, accomplished through people's daily efforts to make a living; through struggles between workers and employers to control the labor process and the disposition of the surplus; and through cooperation among elites to control business, finance, and government. . . .

NOTES

1. Michelle Fine (1994) argues that social scientific research is often implicated in the process of othering. When researchers define a group or type of people as objects of curiosity and targets of study, the unconscious subtext may be that "these people are interesting because they are different from us." To focus attention on a group in this way—that is, from the implicit standpoint of the dominant culture—is, in effect, to contribute to their continued othering.

2. Subordinates may also engage in a kind of silent othering aimed at deflating the impressive virtual selves that dominants try to create. For example, Pierce (1995) describes how paralegals defined their overly demanding bosses as "immature children" who needed a lot of hand-holding. This kind of cognitive coping strategy makes interaction more bearable for subordinates, but at the same time allows oppressive patterns of interaction to persist.

3. It might seem that the Clinton sexual misconduct debacle, commonly called the "Monica Lewinsky affair," is an example of elites failing to do face-work for one of their own. Attacks on Clinton's character can be seen, however, as self-serving attempts by elites to signify a concern for morality, and thus to reinforce the illusion of elite virtue. Focusing on Clinton as an individual also functions to avoid bringing into question the system that put him in office.

4. It is not only working-class men who trade power for autonomy. Paules's (1991) study of waitresses shows working-class women doing much the same thing. There are, however, reasons to expect this kind of adaptive strategy to vary by gender. Men may be more inclined to seek autonomy because they are less economically and physically vulnerable than women, and because they are taught to see autonomy as a sign of manhood.

5. Individual striving for upward mobility does not, of course, threaten the system against which subordinates are reacting. In fact, *individual* striving is encouraged because it protects the larger system of inequality by making collective protest unlikely. Allowing a limited amount of upward mobility also serves to legitimate inequality by implying that the system allows the truly gifted to get ahead, and that those who remain at the bottom belong there because of their lesser merits.

6. Van Ausdale and Feagin (1996) show how young children use racial categorization schemes to do an analogous kind of boundary work.

7. In a study of Appalachian women, Gagne (1992) shows how a lack of reproductive freedom, sexist stereotypes about women, lack of transportation, lack of job opportunities, and ideologies that legitimated violence made women vulnerable to violence and allowed men to use it with near impunity. Gagne's study reminds us that the effectiveness of violence as a means of social control depends on the context in which it is used.

8. Bartky (1990:42–44, 63–82) argues that part of socialization into femininity is learning to take pleasure in practices that have the consequence of reinforcing women's subordination. DeVault's (1991) study of women's work in feeding families can be interpreted as showing how socialization into femininity equips and conditions women to create meaning and satisfaction in activities that pose no threat to male supremacy.

9. Scripting can also be seen as a form of work-process rationalization. Leidner's (1993) studies of fast-food workers show how employers routinize not only manual tasks but also the interactions that workers are supposed to have with customers. The goal of this scripting, Leidner suggests, is to regulate the emotions of workers and customers, so as to make the outcomes of these interactions predictable and profitable.

10. Giddens (1979, 1984) treats the tacit rules that guide interaction as generative of structure, in much the way that the rules of grammar are generative of well-formed, meaningful sentences. Somewhat differently, we presuppose the existence of an interaction order (Goffman 1983) and treat generic social processes as generative of types of experiences and relationships, in much the way that the rules of scholarship are generative of different kinds of literary experiences than the rules of poetry.

REFERENCES

Adler, Peter. 1985. *Wheeling and Dealing: An Ethnography of an Upper-Level Drug Dealing and Smuggling Community.* Columbia University Press.

Adler, Patricia, and Peter Adler. 1983. "Shifts and Oscillation in Deviant Careers: The Case of Upper-Level Dealers and Smugglers." *Social Problems* 31:195–207.

Allen, Michael Patrick. 1987. *The Founding Fortunes.* E.P. Dutton.

Allen, Theodore. 1994. *The Invention of the White Race.* Verso.

Anderson, Elijah. 1990. *Streetwise: Race, Class, and Change in an Urban Community.* University of Chicago Press.

Athens, Lonnie. 1997. *Violent Criminal Acts and Actors Revisited.* University of Illinois Press.

Bartky, Sandra. 1990. *Femininity and Domination.* Routledge.

Becker, Howard S. 1995. "The Power of Inertia." *Qualitative Sociology* 18:301–309.

Becker, Howard, Blanche Geer, Everett Hughes, and Anselm Strauss. [1961] 1977. *Boys in White: Student Culture in Medical School.* Transaction.

Blee, Katherine. 1996. "Becoming a Racist: Women in Contemporary Ku Klux Klan and Neo-Nazi Groups." *Gender and Society* 10:680–702.

Blumer, Herbert. 1969. *Symbolic Interactionism.* Prentice-Hall.

Boles, Jacqueline, Phillip Davis, and Charlotte Tatro. 1983. "False Pretense and Deviant Exploitation: Fortunetelling as a Con." *Deviant Behavior* 4:375–94.

Bourdieu, Pierre. 1977. "Cultural Reproduction and Social Reproduction." Pp. 487–511 in *Power and Ideology in Education,* edited by Jerome Karabel and A.H. Halsey. Oxford University Press.

———. 1984. *Distinction.* Harvard University Press.

Bourgois, Phillipe. 1995. *In Search of Respect: Selling Crack in El Barrio.* Cambridge University Press.

Burawoy, Michael. 1979. *Manufacturing Consent.* University of Chicago Press.

Brown, Elaine. 1992. *A Taste of Power: A Black Woman's Story.* Pantheon.

Brown, Richard H. 1993. "Cultural Representation and Ideological Domination." *Social Forces* 71:657–76.

Chafe, William. 1977. *Women and Equality: Changing Patterns in American Culture.* Oxford University Press.

Cohn, Carol. 1987. "Sex and Death in the Rational World of Defense Intellectuals." *Signs* 12:687–718.

Colby, Gerard, with Dennett, Charlotte. 1995. *Thy Will Be Done.* Harper Collins.

Connell, Robert. 1995. *Masculinities.* University of California Press.

Cookson, Peter, and Persell, Caroline. 1985. *Preparing for Power.* Basic Books.

Daniels, Arlene. 1988. *Invisible Careers.* University of Chicago Press.

Della Fave, L. Richard. 1980. "The Meek Shall Not Inherit the Earth: Self-Evaluation and the Legitimacy of Stratification." *American Sociological Review* 45:955–71.

Denzin, Norman K. 1984. "Toward a Phenomenology of Domestic Family Violence." *American Journal of Sociology* 90:483–513.

DeVault, Marjorie. 1991. *Feeding the Family.* University of Chicago Press.

Ehrenreich, Barbara. 1989. *Fear of Falling.* Pantheon.

Fantasia, Rick. 1988. *Cultures of Solidarity.* University of California Press.

Ferraro, Kathleen, and Johnson, John M. 1983. "How Women Experience Battering: The Process of Victimization." *Social Problems* 30:325–39.

Field, Stephanie J. 1994. "Becoming Irish: Personal Identity Construction among First-Generation Irish Immigrants." *Symbolic Interaction* 17:431–52.

Fine, Michelle. 1994. "Working the Hyphens: Reinventing Self and Other in Qualitative Research." Pp. 70–82 in *Handbook of Qualitative Research,* edited by Norman K. Denzin and Y. Lincoln. Sage.

Fordham, S., and J. Ogbu. 1986. "Black Students' School Success: Coping with the 'Burden of Acting White.' " *Urban Review* 18:176–206.

Frank, Katherine. 1998. "The Production of Identity and the Negotiation of Intimacy in a 'Gentleman's Club.' " *Sexualities* 1:175–201.

Frankenberg, Ruth. 1993. *The Social Construction of Whiteness.* University of Minnesota Press.

Gagne, Patricia. 1992. "Appalachian Women: Violence and Social Control." *Journal of Contemporary Ethnography* 20:387–415.

Gallagher, Charles. 1995. "White Reconstruction in the University." *Socialist Review* 24:165–87.

Gamson, William, and Andre Modigliani. 1989. "Media Discourse and Public Opinion on Nuclear Power: A Constructionist Approach." *American Journal of Sociology* 95:1–37.

Gardner, Carol Brooks. 1995. *Passing By: Gender and Public Harassment.* Temple University Press.

Giddens, Anthony. 1979. *Central Problems in Social Theory.* University of California Press.

———. 1984. *The Constitution of Society: Outline of the Theory of Structuration.* University of California Press.

Gillespie, Joanna. 1980. "The Phenomenon of the Public Wife: An Exercise in Goffman's Impression Management." *Symbolic Interaction* 3:109–25.

Goffman, Erving. 1983. "The Interaction Order." *American Sociological Review* 48:1–17.

Haas, Jack, and William Shaffir. 1977. "The Professionalization of Medical Students: Developing Competence and a Cloak of Competence." *Symbolic Interaction* 1:71–88.

Hadden, Stuart, and Marilyn Lester. 1978. "Talking Identity: The Production of 'Self' in Interaction." *Human Studies* 1:331–56.

Hall, Elaine. 1993. "Waitering/Waitressing: Engendering the Work of Table Servers." *Gender and Society* 7:329–46.

Hall, Peter. 1979. "The Presidency and Impression Management." *Studies in Symbolic Interaction* 2:283–305.

Halle, David. 1984. *America's Working Man.* University of Chicago Press.

Hays, Sharon. 1996. *The Cultural Contradictions of Motherhood.* Yale University Press.

Hochschild, Arlie. 1983. *The Managed Heart.* University of California Press.

Holden, Daphne. 1997. "On Equal Ground: Sustaining Virtue Among Volunteers in a Homeless Shelter." *Journal of Contemporary Ethnography* 26:117–45.

Horowitz, Ruth. 1997. "Barriers and Bridges to Class Mobility and Formation: Ethnographies of Stratification." *Sociological Methods and Research* 25:495–538.

Hughes, Everett C. 1958. *Men and Their Work.* Free Press.

Jackall, Robert. 1988. *Moral Mazes: The World of Corporate Managers.* Oxford University Press.

Jacobs, Janet L. 1994. "Gender, Race, Class, and the Trend Toward Early Motherhood: A Feminist Analysis of Teen Mothers in Contemporary Society." *Journal of Contemporary Ethnography* 22:442–62.

James, Joy. 1996. *Resisting Street Violence: Radicalism, Candor, and Race in U.S. Culture.* University of Minnesota Press.

Janeway, Elizabeth. 1980. *Powers of the Weak.* Knopf.

Jones, Rachel K. 1993. "Female Victim Perceptions of the Causes of Male Spouse Abuse." *Sociological Inquiry* 63:351–61.

Kephart, William M. 1987. *Extraordinary Groups: An Examination of Unconventional Life-Styles.* St. Martin's.

Kleinman, Sherryl. 1996. *Opposing Ambitions: Gender and Identity in an Alternative Organization.* University of Chicago Press.

Kohn, Melvin. 1969. *Class and Conformity.* Dorsey.

Kunda, Gideon. 1992. *Engineering Culture.* Temple University Press.

Lamont, Michele. 1992. *Money, Morals, and Manners.* University of Chicago Press.

Leidner, Robin. 1993. *Fast Food, Fast Talk: Service Work and the Routinization of Everyday Life.* University of California Press.

Lever, Janet. 1978. "Sex Differences in the Complexity of Children's Play and Games." *American Sociological Review* 43:471–83.

Luttrell, Wendy. 1997. *Schoolsmart and Motherwise: Working-Class Women's Identity and Schooling.* Routledge.

Maccoby, Michael. 1976. *The Gamesman.* Bantam.

MacLeod, Jay. [1987] 1995. *Ain't No Makin' It.* 2d ed. Westview.

Merton, Robert K. 1967. *Social Theory and Social Structure.* Free Press.

Miller, Jean Baker. 1976. *Toward a New Psychology of Women.* Beacon.

Omi, Michael, and Howard Winant. 1986. *Racial Formation in the United States.* Routledge & Kegan Paul.

Ostrander, Susan. 1984. *Women of the Upper Class.* Temple University Press.

Padavic, Irene. 1991. "The Re-Creation of Gender in a Male Workplace." *Symbolic Interaction* 14:279–94.

Paules, Greta. 1991. *Dishing It Out: Power and Resistance Among Waitresses in a New Jersey Restaurant.* Temple University Press.

Pierce, Jennifer. 1995. *Gender Trials.* University of California Press.

Potter, J., and M. Wetherell. 1987. *Discourse and Social Psychology.* Sage.

Roediger, David. 1991. *The Wages of Whiteness: Race and the Making of the American Working Class.* Verso.

Rogers, Jackie K. 1995. "Just a Temp: Experience and Structure of Alienation in Temporary Clerical Employment." *Work and Occupations* 22:137–66.

Rollins, Judith. 1985. *Between Women: Domestics and Their Employers.* Temple University Press.

Romero, Mary. 1992. *Maid in the U.S.A.* Routledge.

Ronai, Carol Rambo, and Carolyn Ellis. 1989. "Turn-Ons for Money." *Journal of Contemporary Ethnography* 18:271–98.

Rosenbaum, James E. 1976. *Making Inequality.* Wiley & Sons.

Schwalbe, Michael. 1992. "Male Supremacy and the Narrowing of the Moral Self." *Berkeley Journal of Sociology* 37:29–54.

——— 1996. *Unlocking the Iron Cage: The Men's Movement, Gender Politics, and American Culture.* Oxford University Press.

Schwalbe, Michael, and Douglas Mason-Schrock. 1996. "Identity Work as Group Process." Pp. 13–47 in *Advances in Group Processes,* Vol. 13, edited by Barry Markovsky, Michael Lovaglia, and R. Simon. JAI Press.

Scully, Diane, and Joseph Marolla. 1984. "Convicted Rapists' Vocabularies of Motive: Excuses and Justification." *Social Problems* 31:530–44.

Seidler, Victor. 1991. *Recreating Sexual Politics.* Routledge.

Sennett, Richard, and Jonathan Cobb. 1972. *The Hidden Injuries of Class.* Vintage.

Shibutani, Tamotsu. 1978. *The Derelicts of Company K.* Jossey-Bass.

Short, James, and Fred Strodtbeck. 1965. *Group Processes and Gang Delinquency.* University of Chicago Press.

Snow, David, and Leon Anderson. 1987. "Identity Work among the Homeless: The Verbal Construction and Avowal of Personal Identities." *American Journal of Sociology* 92:1336–71.

Stombler, Mindy, and Patricia Yancey Martin. 1994. "Bringing Women In, Keeping Women Down: Fraternity 'Little Sister' Organizations." *Journal of Contemporary Ethnography* 23:150–84.

Tallichet, Suzanne E. 1995. "Gendered Relations in the Mines and the Division of Labor Underground." *Gender and Society* 9:697–711.

Thorne, Barrie. 1993. *Gender Play: Girls and Boys in School.* Rutgers University Press.

Traweek, Sharon. 1988. *Beamtimes and Lifetimes.* Harvard University Press.

Van Ausdale, Debra, and Joe Feagin. 1996. "Using Racial and Ethnic Concepts: The Critical Case of Very Young Children." *American Sociological Review* 61:779–93.

Vander Ven, Thomas M. 1998. "Fear of Victimization and the Interactional Construction of Harassment in a Latino Neighborhood." *Journal of Contemporary Ethnography* 27:374–98.

Ward, David A.C., and Gene Kassebaum. 1965. *Women's Prison: Sex and Social Structure.* Aldine.

Wasielewski, Patricia. 1985. "The Emotional Basis of Charisma." *Symbolic Interaction* 8:202–222.

West, Candace, and Sarah Fenstermaker. 1995. "Doing Difference." *Gender and Society* 9:8–37.

West, Candace, and Don Zimmerman. 1987. "Doing Gender." *Gender and Society* 1:125–51.

Wolf, Charlotte. 1986. "Legitimation of Oppression: Response and Reflexivity." *Symbolic Interaction* 9:217–34.

Yount, Kristen R. 1991. "Ladies, Flirts, and Tomboys: Strategies for Managing Sexual Harassment in an Underground Coal Mine." *Journal of Contemporary Ethnography* 19:396–422.

Zurcher, Louis. 1982. "The Staging of Emotion: A Dramaturgical Analysis." *Symbolic Interaction* 5:1–22.

———. 1985. "The War Game: Organizational Scripting and the Expression of Emotion." *Symbolic Interaction* 8:191–206.

QUESTIONS FOR DISCUSSION

1. What do Schwalbe and colleagues mean by "generic" processes?

2. How do practices of Othering, subordinate adaptation, boundary maintenance, and emotion management operate to support each other?

3. Can you think of examples of each of the generic processes outlined by Schwalbe and colleagues in your own daily life?

4. Have you ever sought to resist some sort of inequality and realized that your efforts in fact sustained it?

4

GENETICS MAPS AND HUMAN IMAGINATIONS
The Limits of Science in Understanding Who We Are

BARBARA KATZ ROTHMAN

It is important to understand how far from perfect the predictive nature of genetic information is. And it is just as important to understand how far genetics is from control: in that way too, genetics is a lot like the weather reports.

But it is also important to recognize that genetic information, made available to us through genetic screening and testing, does offer some information, some predictability. Sometimes the prediction does approach the absolute: some versions of genes are lethal. If a baby inherits one of these forms of a gene, it simply won't survive. Most of the time the predictions are far more erratic, best expressed as probabilities: a 30 percent chance of type I diabetes; a 50 percent lifetime chance of ovarian cancer.

Genetic screening or testing starts with the gene, the genotype, and then makes predictions, however vague or specific, about the phenotype. These predictions—inaccurate, incomplete, uncertain as they are—open up the enormous quandaries of contemporary bioethics. But we also use genetics the other way around: this outcome, this phenotype, implies something about the genotype. This is most usually called "genetic determinism," saying that something—a physical trait, a characteristic, a skill, a disability—is caused by genes.

Genetics, as we use it, is a way of understanding life, "human nature," behavior, being in the world. But genetics is also a way of shutting our eyes to understanding. Genetics is also a way of avoiding explanations.

Saying "it's genetic" is like throwing your hands up in the air; it's a fatalistic, deterministic "explanation" that is no explanation at all.

When my oldest kid, Daniel, was in first grade, he came home all excited about a science experiment that they had done in school. He very carefully set it up for us in the kitchen, measuring baking soda and vinegar and creating quite a little flurry of activity in a glass jar. And when my husband and I admired all of this, and asked him, "So Danny, how does that work?" he answered, shrugging his shoulders, "I don't know—it's science!"

That is science-as-magic. Most of the time that kind of story presents a lesson about the necessity of understanding science better. We are continually told that if we understood science better, we wouldn't have foolish fears and superstitions. We wouldn't fear crazy science fiction scenarios because we would understand that science is no danger to us. For all of my working life in the sociology of biomedical technology, what I've heard continually from the scientists and the doctors and the technicians is that to know them is to love them: if only you understood what we are doing, you would appreciate our work.

But genetics itself has a science-as-magic quality. For all practical purposes the study of genetics often works like a surprisingly accurate and very sophisticated tea-leaf reading. One of my favorite cartoons shows a turbanned "Madame Rosa" replacing the "Fortune Teller" sign in her front window with one that says "Geneticist." For many of the "gene for" something-or-others that we've been hearing and reading so much about, they haven't even found the gene itself. They've found a marker, an indication that somewhere in that neighborhood on the chromosome there must be such a gene because people who share that marker share some illness, condition or phenomenon. It's a prediction, and it might work fairly well in some cases, but it is in no way an explanation.

In science as in life, prediction does not actually depend on explanation. Danny could predict a pretty good show in the jar for us, without any kind of explanation of why vinegar and baking soda would do that. All the livelong day we rely on predictions that we can't always explain. Part of that is because of the role of technology in our lives: nobody has the time or the energy to understand all of it. Some of it you just use, predicting that the alarm clock will work, the freezer will freeze the ice cubes yet again, the plane will stay up in the air. That is the appeal of those "how things work" books—we take an awful lot for granted in the world of technology. But there are other kinds of predictions we make, predictions that we cannot necessarily explain. Something happens that I know my sister will find funny and my mother will not. Can I explain that? Not in any meaningful way, just by saying it happened that way before and so it will happen that way again. It's the "kind of thing" my sister finds funny and my mother not. Why? What in their history, psyche (genes?)?

Because the technology involved in the tea-leaf reading of genetics is so incredibly complicated, the essentially primitive nature of the predictions may elude us. This struck me forcefully some years back when I visited a lab where prenatal diagnosis was done. They worked with aspirated amniotic fluid, the water in the womb suctioned out with a needle. Cells from the fetus float in that water. Those cells were cultured, and then magnified and photographed. The next part of the process was cutting out the individual chromosomes and pasting them in size order on a piece of paper, counting how many pairs there were and seeing if there were any extras. Literally—cutting and pasting and counting. If there were three 21st chromosomes the fetus could be diagnosed as having Down syndrome. Three 18th chromosomes and the fetus had, by definition, the condition known as trisomy 18.

I'm not belittling how complicated it is to get to the cut-and-paste portion of the diagnosis. Suffice it to say that up until the mid-1950s geneticists thought there were 48 rather than 46 chromosomes. So it is a complicated technological feat to photograph, enlarge and count those chromosomes. But it is not an explanation. To diagnose, to predict Down syndrome is not to explain Down syndrome. And to predict the fact of Down syndrome is not to predict the experience of Down syndrome. One fetus so diagnosed is not strong enough to survive the pregnancy; another is born with grave physical and mental handicaps and dies very young; and another grows up well and strong and stars in a television show.

Even where genetics does offer understanding and explanation, that doesn't necessarily improve the predictions. . . . Sickle-cell anemia is understood thoroughly, from the single misspelled base pair in the DNA through to the misshapen red blood cells clogging the capillaries, and still they cannot predict which person will be severely and which mildly affected by the disease.

So what genetics has to offer us is prediction, with greater or lesser accuracy and greater or lesser specificity. Prediction is a concept that you and I are familiar with. We can have ideas about predictions—legitimate ideas, backed by solid values we hold firmly and dearly—that are not dependent on the particular technology in use. Judgments about the worth, value and danger of genetic predictions do not require an understanding of the science underlying the prediction. Moral authority does not rest on technical authority.

A person might claim that this is not a good historical moment to predict the future sexual orientation of a male fetus. And that claim, that belief, that value judgment is not dependent on the technology. Tell me you can do it with a brain scan in utero, with fetal cells withdrawn from amniotic fluid, or by playing Judy Garland tapes at the pregnant belly. One's judgment about whether or not this is a good kind of prediction to be making doesn't depend on the technology that does the predicting, and it certainly doesn't depend on one's ability to understand the technology.

This seems so obvious, so clear to me. And yet we permit ourselves, over and over again, to be intimidated by the technology, by the science of it all. I've attended countless conferences on genetics, biotechnology, ethical issues in genetics, and the like. And virtually every one of them starts with a scientist explaining the technology. The lights go down, the slides go up on the screen, and the technological razzle-dazzle begins. Then, and only then, is the discussion opened up to "ethical" or "social" concerns.

The technical presentation is supposed to open up the discussion, but what it does is silence people. People want to talk about the moral and ethical concerns they have, they want to talk about the consequences of these new technologies in their lives and the lives of their children. They want to talk about how this work might change the world, for better or for worse, and how we might control it. They want to talk about what the technology means in their lives, and instead they're told they have to understand the technology before they can judge it.

. . .

When I go to a genetics conference to discuss the bioethical issues involved in, for example, finding the "gay gene," and the meeting starts with the geneticist explaining how he did his research, how he ran those gels, how the science and technology of it all works—that too shapes the discussion that follows. We don't discuss "Should you do this?"; we discuss "How did you do this?" We don't discuss "Do we want to know if there is a way of predicting sexual orientation?"; we discuss how well we can predict sexual orientation.

Is research into human genetics fundamentally a social, political and ethical concern, with some technological obstacles? Or is it fundamentally a technological concern, with some social, political and ethical obstacles? The official American version has been the latter: three billion dollars of funding goes to the technical work, and 3 percent is tithed for "ethical, legal and social implications (ELSI)." Arthur Caplan, a prominent bioethicist, has called ELSI the full-employment act for bioethicists. It came about as the response of James Watson, co-describer of the double helix and first director of the Human Genome Project, to the ethical questions being raised at a press conference. ELSI, the cash cow for ethics, stands in an inherently contradictory position: a statement that those concerns are being taken seriously, and a statement that they are not to be taken seriously enough to interfere with the project.

Bioethics generally, and ELSI specifically, ends up in the middle, between biomedical science and research on the one hand, and the concerns of the public on the other. But with all the power and the big money in the hands of the science, bioethics becomes a translator, sometimes an apologist, sometimes an enabler, of scientific "progress.". . .

Bioethics has become its own kind of technical language, its own form of mystification. Mystification is a political tool: making something complicated is a way of disempowering people. I'm a sociology professor; I get paid to read. I can afford to take a couple of years and read in genetics and bioethics. Most people probably cannot do that; they have other things to do. But the conclusion that I have come to, from all of that technical reading in genetics and in bioethics, is that you don't need the technical understanding to make the moral judgments.

A group of sociologists in Scotland came to the same conclusion. They ran focus groups of lay people on ethical issues in genetics. They concluded, "Technical competence was neither relevant nor important to the majority of participants in our study: they discussed issues without need to display technical competence. When technical issues were mentioned, the accuracy of the knowledge was irrelevant to the point being made." They gave an example of a group discussion in a working-class area of Edinburgh: "They are going a little far. If they want to go an' investigate the DNA system and find oot that OK somebody's gay because there is a little slip-up in the XY hormone, we can do an injection and fix that, or a kid's going to be born mongoloid, rather than abort we may be able to find a way that we can actually sort the gene oot. We are getting to the part with genetic engineering if somebody is going to get a deformed child then they just get rid of it and say 'right the next one that you produce will be.' "

This person is completely wrong on every technical point going. XY isn't a hormone; mongoloid isn't the current word and it's not a "gene" to be "sorted out." And so what? The question that the person is rais-

ing is about drawing moral lines, about drawing lines and going too far. Again, you or I may or may not agree with him, just as we may or may not agree with the far more sophisticated language the theologians used. But moral authority does not rest on technical authority: the concerns that are being raised, including the concerns that you personally may feel, are in and of themselves worth discussing.

Genetics, as a science, as a practice and as an ideology, is offering us a great deal. But we have to decide if we want what it has to offer. Those decisions are not technical matters. The technology of it all *is* overwhelming. Keep bandying about terms like "alleles," "RFLPS," "clines," "22Qlocus," and most of us are left in the dust. Promise a cure for cancer, an end to human suffering, and it's hard to argue. As sociologist Troy Duster puts it, "Technical complexities of vanguard research in molecular biology and the promises of success incline us to go limp before such scientific know-how."

We cannot afford to go limp. We'll be carried off to places we might very well choose not to go.

. . .

Questions for Discussion

1. Why does Rothman argue that genetics can also constitute "a way of avoiding explanations"?
2. Why might it not be a good historical moment to use genetics to make certain predictions?
3. How has your life been shaped by medical technology, including genetics?
4. As described by Rothman, what are the differences between explanation, prediction, and understanding provided by genetics?

5

WHY I LOVE TRASH

JOSHUA GAMSON

One can only imagine what this constant attention to the fringes of society, to those who break rules, is doing to our society's ability to define and constrain deviance. One thing seems fairly certain: law-abiding, privacy-loving, ordinary people who have had reasonably happy childhoods and are satisfied with their lives, probably won't get to tell their stories on Phil, Sally, or Oprah. . . . Television talk shows are not interested in adequately reflecting or representing social reality, but in highlighting and trivializing its underside for fun and profit.

> —PROFESSORS VICKI ABT AND MEL SEESHOLTZ[1]

Nobody wants to watch anything that's smarmy or tabloid or silly or unseemly— except the audience.

> —TALK SHOW HOST SALLY JESSY RAPHAEL[2]

Doesn't she look like a weird, scary drag queen?

> —FILMMAKER GREGG ARAKI,
> on talk show host Sally Jessy Raphael[3]

Let's begin here: talk shows are bad for you, so bad you could catch a cold. Turn them off, a women's magazine suggested in 1995, and turn on Mother Teresa, since watching her "caring feelings" radiate from the screen, according to psychologist Dr. David McClelland of Harvard,

has been shown to raise the level of an antibody that fights colds. "It stands to reason," reasons the *First* magazine writer, "that viewing threatening, confrontational images could create an opposite reaction." In fact, given that talk shows "create feelings of frustration" and fear, "shatter our trust and faith" in our expectations of people's behavior, and "give us a false perception of reality," it is perhaps best to watch game shows or soaps while nursing that cold. Watching daytime talk shows could conceivably send you into a decline into pathologies of all sorts: scared, angry, disgusted, convinced that you are abnormal for not fitting in with the "cast of misfits and perverts," susceptible to both perversion and more colds.

While the Mother Teresa versus Jerry Springer matchup is out there enough to be camp, the hand-wringing it represents is only an exaggerated version of the many criticisms and political rallying cries aimed at talk shows over the last few years. Experts of all sorts can be found issuing warnings about talk show dangers. Before bringing out Dr. McClelland, for instance, the *First* article quotes George Gerbner, dean emeritus of the Annenberg School for Communication ("These shows are virtually destroying the goodness of America"), Harvard psychiatrist Alvin Poussaint ("It does not bode well for the future generation of young people growing up on a steady diet of this drivel"), and Fred Strassberger, once chair of the media task force of the American Psychological Association ("It's now becoming alarmingly clear that talk shows are adding greatly to the fear, tensions and stress in our society"); later, TV critic Tom Shales joins in ("These shows are portraying Americans as shallow monsters"), along with psychologist Robert Simmermon ("cruel exploitation of people's deepest wounds to entertain viewers who could very well wind up believing such aberrant behavior is normal").[4] Goodness, normality, and stability, if we buy these arguments, are all threatened by the drivel, exploitation, and monstrosities of daytime TV talk shows.

One person's trash, though, is another person's gold mine. Sure, I sometimes hate these shows. What's not to hate? They can be among the most shrill, mean, embarrassing, fingernails-on-the-blackboard, one-note, pointless jabber. But I can't help it, I love them just the same. In part, I love them because they are so peculiar, so American, filled with fun stuff like "relationship experts" (who are not actually required to have any credentialed expertise; it's almost enough just to declare "I'm a people person") and huge emotions, and hosts who wear their hypocrisies on their tailored sleeves, shedding tears for the people whose secrets they extract for profit while attacking them for revealing secrets on national television, riling up their guests and then scolding them for being so malicious. Silly as they can be, daytime TV talk shows are filled with information about the American environment in which they take root, in which expertise and authenticity and rationality are increasingly problematic, and in which the lines between public and private are shifting so strangely. And they embody that information with Barnumesque gusto. I like what talk shows make us think about.

But there's more to my affinity. Although you might not know it from looking at me, and although in many ways my behaviors and tastes are embarrassingly conventional—a good story, a comfortable pair of jeans, hugs—I identify with the misfits,

monsters, trash, and perverts. From that perspective, talk shows look rather different. If you are lesbian, bisexual, gay, or transgendered, watching daytime TV talk shows is pretty spooky. (Indeed, it must be unnerving and exciting for pretty much anyone whose behavior or identity does not conform to the dominant conventions of goodness, decency, and normality.) While you might get a few minutes on national news every once in a while, or a spot on a sitcom looking normal as can be, almost everywhere else in media culture you are either unwelcome, written by somebody else, or heavily edited.

On television talk shows, you are more than welcome. You are begged and coached and asked to tell, tell, tell, in an absurd, hyper enactment of what Michel Foucault called the "incitement to discourse," that incessant modern demand that we voice every this-and-that of sexuality.[5] Here you are testifying, dating, getting laughs, being made over, screaming, performing, crying, not just talking but talking back, and you are doing these things in front of millions of people. The last few years have seen shows on "lipstick lesbians," gay teens, gay cops, lesbian cops, cross-dressing hookers, transsexual call girls, gay and lesbian gang members, straight go-go dancers pretending to be gay, people who want their relatives to stop cross-dressing, lesbian and gay comedians, gay people in love with straight ones, women who love gay men, same-sex marriage, drag queen makeovers, drag kings, same-sex sexual harassment, homophobia, lesbian mothers, gay twins, gay beauty pageants, transsexual beauty pageants, people who are fired for not being gay, gay men reuniting with their high school sweethearts, bisexual teens, bisexual couples, bisexuals in general, gays in the military, same-sex crushes, hermaphrodites, boys who want to be girls, female-to-male transsexuals, male-to-female transsexuals and their boyfriends, and gay talk shows—to mention just a few. Watching all this, be it tap-dancing drag queens or married gay bodybuilders or self-possessed bisexual teenagers, I sometimes get choked up. For people whose life experience is so heavily tilted toward invisibility, whose nonconformity, even when it looks very much like conformity, discredits them and disenfranchises them, daytime TV talk shows are a big shot of visibility and media accreditation. It looks, for a moment, like you own this place.

Indeed, listening closely to the perspectives and experiences of sex and gender nonconformists—people who live, in one way or another, outside the boundaries of heterosexual norms and gender conventions—sheds a different kind of light on talk shows.[6] Dangers begin to look like opportunities, spotlights start to feel like they're burning your flesh. Exploiting the need for visibility and voice, talk shows provide them, in distorted but real, hollow but gratifying, ways. They have much to tell about those needs and those contradictions, about the weird and changing public sphere in which people are talking. Just as important for my purposes, talk shows shed a different kind of light on sex and gender conformity. They are spots not only of visibility but of the subsequent redrawing of the lines between the normal and the abnormal. They are, in a very real sense, battlegrounds over what sexuality and gender can be in this country: in them we can see most clearly the kinds of strategies, casualties, and wounds involved, and we can think most clearly about what winning these kinds of battles might really mean. These battles over media space allow us to get a grip on the ways sex and gender conformity is filtered through the daily interactions between commercial cultural industries and those making their lives within and around media culture. I watch talk shows for a laugh and a jolt of recognition, but also for what they can tell me about a society that funnels such large questions—indeed, that funnels entire *populations* nearly wholesale—into the small, loopy spectacle of daytime talk.

Defecating in Public

It is a long, twisted road that takes us toward insight, but the controversy over the talk show genre in general—a genre itself largely composed of controversy and conflict—is a promising first step. On the one side, cultural critics, both popular and scholarly, point adamantly toward the dangers of exploitation, voyeurism, pseudo-therapy, and the "defining down" of deviance, in which the strange and unacceptable are made to seem ordinary and fine. On the other side, defenders both within and outside the television industry argue that talk shows are democracy at work—flawed democracy but democracy nonetheless—giving voice to the socially marginalized and ordinary folks, providing rowdy commonsense counterpoints to elite authority in mass-mediated culture. Beneath each position, and in the space between them, is a piece of the puzzle with which this book is playing.

The list of dangers is well worth considering. There is, to begin with, concern for the people who go on the shows, who are offered and accept a deal with the devil. They are manipulated, sometimes lied to, seduced, used, and discarded; pick 'em up in a limo, producers joke, send 'em home in a cab. They are sometimes set up and surprised—"ambushed," as critics like to call it—which can be extremely damaging, even to the point of triggering lawsuits and murderous impulses, as in the case of Scott Amedure, who revealed his secret crush for Jonathan Schmitz on a never-aired *Jenny Jones Show,* including his fantasy of tying Schmitz up in a hammock and spraying him with whipped cream and champagne. Amedure was murdered several days later by

Schmitz, who, after receiving an anonymous love note, went to his admirer's trailer home near Detroit and shot him at close range with a 12-gauge shotgun. Schmitz complained that the show had set him up to be humiliated. "There was no ambush," a spokeswoman for *Jenny Jones* owner Warner Brothers said; "that's not our style." Amedure, Schmitz proclaimed, had "fucked me on national TV."[7]

Although most survive without bodily harm, guests often do considerable damage to themselves and others. They are offered airfare and a hotel room in New York, Los Angeles, or Chicago, a bit of television exposure, a shot of attention and a microphone, some free "therapy." In exchange, guests publicly air their relationship troubles, deep secrets, and intimate life experiences, usually in the manners most likely to grab ratings: exaggerated, loud, simplified, and so on. Even more disturbing, perhaps, it is those who typically do not feel entitled to speak, or who cannot afford or imagine therapy, who are most vulnerable to the seduction of television. This is, critics suggest, not a great deal for the guests, since telling problems and secrets in front of millions of people is a poor substitute for actually working them out. Not to mention, critics often add, a bit undignified. "Therapy is not a spectator sport," says sociologist and talk show critic-at-large Vicki Abt. Telling secrets on television is "like defecating in public."[8]

While it is worth challenging the equation of talking and defecating, all this, we will see, is basically the case. But it is also the easy part: talk shows are show business, and it is their mission to exploit. They commodify and use talkers to build an entertainment product, which is then used to attract audiences, who then are sold to advertisers, which results in a profit for the producers. Exploitation thus ought to be the starting point for analysis and not, as it so often is, its conclusion. The puzzling thing is not the logic of commercial television,

which is well documented, well understood, and extremely powerful, but why so many people, many of them fully aware of what's expected of them on a talk show, make the deal. . . .

Critics are even more troubled by the general social effects of talk shows. Here and there, a critic from the Left, such as Jill Nelson writing in *The Nation,* assails the casting of "a few pathological individuals" as representatives of a population, distracting from social, political, and economic conditions in favor of stereotypes such as "stupid, sex-addicted, dependent, babymakers, with an occasional castrating bitch thrown in" (women of all colors) and "violent predators out to get you with their penis, their gun, or both" (young black men).[9] More commonly, though, critics make the related argument that talk shows indulge voyeuristic tendencies that, while perhaps offering the opportunity to feel superior, are ugly. *"Exploitation, voyeurism, peeping Toms, freak shows,* all come to mind in attempting to characterize these happenings,"* write Vicki Abt and Mel Seesholtz, for instance.[10] . . . These "fairground-style freak shows" are just a modern-day version of throwing Christians to the lions, psychologists Heaton and Wilson assert: in place of Christians we have "the emotionally wounded or the socially outcast," in place of lions are "psychic demons," in place of blood there is psychological damage, in place of crowds yelling "Kill, kill, kill!" we have crowds yelling "Why don't you cut his balls off?"[11] . . . Talk shows are pruriently addictive, the argument goes, like rubbernecking at car wrecks: daytime talk shows are to public information what pornography is to sexual intimacy.

The lines are drawn so starkly: between Christians and Romans, between "deviant and dysfunctional types" and "some folks," the guests and "us," between "the fringes of society, those who break rules" and "law-abiding, privacy-loving, ordinary people who have had reasonably happy childhoods and are satisfied with their lives." These are important lines, and plainly political ones, and the ones critics most fiercely act to protect. And as one who falls both within and outside the lines, I find the confidence with which critics draw them in need of as much careful consideration as the genre's alarming exploitations.

In fact, the lines of difference and normality are the centerpiece of the arguments against talk shows: talk shows, critics repeat over and over, redefine deviance and abnormality, and this is not a good thing. "The lines between what is bizarre and alarming and what is typical and inconsequential are blurred," point out psychologists Heaton and Wilson; talk shows "exaggerate abnormality" by suggesting that "certain problems are more common than they are, thus exaggerating their frequency," and by embellishing "the symptoms and outcomes of problems, thus exaggerating their consequences." Viewers are left with images of "drag queens getting makeovers and transsexuals' surprising transformations blended together with normal adolescent development."[12] Kurtz, himself a regular on political talk shows, is a little less clinical in his assessment: "This is more than just harmless diversion. It is, all too often, a televised exercise in defining deviancy down. By parading the sickest, the weirdest, the most painfully afflicted before an audience of millions, these shows bombard us with sleaze to the point of numbness. The abnormal becomes ordinary, the pathetic merely another pause in our daily channel surfing."[13]

This boundary between the normal and the abnormal, tightly linked to those between decent and vulgar, sacred and profane, healthy and unhealthy, and moral and immoral, is the key not only for critics in journalism, but for those in politics as well. "This is the world turned upside down," former secretary of education William Bennett complained of daytime talk.[14] "We've forgotten that civilization depends on keeping some of this stuff under wraps."[15] . . .

The interesting thing here is not just that talk shows are seen as a threat to norms and normality—they are indeed just that, and the fight is often between those who think this is a good thing and those who think it is not—but just who threatens whom here, who is "us" and who is "them." Sexual nonconformists are only the most obvious specter. Consider the common strategy of listing topics to demonstrate the degraded status of talk shows: "Maury Povich has done women who leave husbands for other women, student-teacher affairs, and a woman who says she was gang-raped at fourteen. Geraldo Rivera has done transsexuals and their families, teen prostitutes, mud-wrestling women, swinging sexual suicide, power dykes, girls impregnated by their stepfathers, serial killers, kids who kill, and battered women who kill."[16] One need not deny the prurience and sensationalism of talk shows to see the connections being made by critics. Serial killers and bisexual women, transsexuals and mud wrestlers, dykes and battered women: "the sickest, the weirdest, the most painfully afflicted." New York *Daily News* columnist Linda Stasi, not shy about telling us what she really thinks, provides a further, complicating hint of the threatening categories: talk shows, she says, have become "a vast, scary wasteland where the dregs of society—sociopaths, perverts, uneducated lazy scum who abuse their children and sleep with anyone who'll have them—become stars for fifteen minutes."[17] That list is a typical and fascinating mix: perverts and those lacking education, lazy people and people who have a lot of sex. . . .

The "dregs of society" argument, in fact, almost always lumps together indecency, sexual difference, lack of education, and social class—though class is typically coded as "uneducated" or "inarticulate," or, when linked to race, as "trash" or "urban." . . . The examples continue, but after even just a taste the equations start to come clear: uneducated is lazy is sex-loving is sexually perverted is non-middle-class is soulless losers.

Puzzle pieces begin to emerge from these criticisms. How exactly do poverty and lack of education, sex and gender nonconformity, and race come to be lumped together and condemned as monstrosities? What are we to make of these equations? Are they the result of exploitative programming that scripts and markets weird people most of "us" wouldn't talk to in a supermarket, selling the middle-class audience its own superiority? Are they the result of willful distortions by guardians of middle-class morality and culture, part and parcel of the ongoing "culture wars" in the United States? Are they, as defenders of the genre suggest, the result of a democratization process that threatens those who are used to the privilege of owning and defining public discourse?

The Chatter of the Dispossessed

Audiences and participants sit in a circular form and—this is the only TV format in which this happens—speak out, sometimes without being called on. They yell at each other, disagree with experts, and come to no authoritative conclusions. There is something exhilarating about watching people who are usually invisible—because of class, race, gender, status—having their say and, often, being wholly disrespectful of their "betters."
—*Professor Elayne Rapping*[18]

As long as they speak the King's English, we say it's OK. But then you get someone who isn't wealthy, who doesn't have title or position, and they come on and talk about something that's important to them—all of a sudden we call that trash.
—*Talk show host Jerry Springer*[19]

Just as exploitation is an obvious component of talk shows, so is democratization. Where critics choose one Greco-Roman analogy, defenders tout another. In place of the Christian-eating spectacle, they see, although not always so simply, a democratic forum. Where critics see "freaks" and "trash," defenders see "have-nots" and "common people." These are important counterpoints, and raise important questions suppressed by critics, of voice, visibility, and inclusion. But this line of thinking, too, on its own tends to run in an unhelpful direction, simplifying the conditions of visibility, the distortions of voice, and the restrictions on inclusion that daytime talk involves. Just because people are talking back does not mean we are witnessing democratic impulses and effects.

It is easy enough to discern the elitism in criticisms of talk shows, or any other popular genre, and defenders of talk shows from within the industry push up against it with a defense of the masses, painting themselves as both defenders of free speech and friends of the common folk.[20] . . .

This populist defense of talk shows, familiar from arguments about popular culture in general, is taken many steps beyond the shoulder-shrugging "it's a free country" line. Talk shows, defenders claim, give voice to common folks and visibility to invisible folks, and it is this characteristic that elicits such hostility. Indeed, Donahue and others assert, the talk show genre was and is a "revolutionary" one. "It's called democracy," Donahue argues, "but [before my program] there were no shows that—every day, let just folks stand up and say what-for. I'm proud of the democracy of the show."[21] . . . When the excluded become included, there is always a fight. The nastiness of critics toward talk shows, the argument goes, is simply a veiled anxiety about cultural democratization—and especially about the assertive, rowdy space taken on talk shows by usually silent classes of people. . . . "Do you ever call a Congressman trash?" asks Jerry Springer. "It's a euphemism for trailer park, minorities, space between their teeth. We all know it. They don't want to hear about them, they don't want to see them."[22] Springer argues that he is giving unpopular people "access to the airwaves" ("as if embarrassing them before millions," snorts Howard Kurtz, "were some kind of public service").[23] Princess Di with bulimia is news on *20/20* with Barbara Walters, Yale-educated host Richard Bey complains, but his own show—which, on the day I attended, included a "freeloader" named Rob lying on his back on a spinning "Wheel of Torture" while his dorm-mates poured buckets of paint and baked beans on him— is trash. "They don't think these people deserve to be heard or seen," he suggests, taking a sort of working-person's-hero pose. "Mine is a working class audience. It's very representative of America."[24] . . .

Indeed, daytime talk, as a woman-oriented genre, is arguably rooted in social movement–generated changes of the sixties and seventies, especially those pushed by feminism. Defenders point to the genre's predominantly female audience, and in particular to its feminist-inspired reworking of what counts as legitimate public discussion, as evidence that it is a genre of "empowerment." Most significantly, TV talk is built on a radical departure from what has traditionally been seen to belong in the public sphere: drawing on "the personal is political" charge of feminism, talk shows move personal lives to the forefront of public discussion. Their popularity . . . [is] a symptom of "a transformation in the nature of the political," and "the means of expression of these new areas of political struggle are quite different from those of formal politics."[25] Talk shows, such arguments suggest, are politics by other means. . . .

Previously silenced people speaking in their own voices, spaces for "alternative epistemologies" opening up, common sense

battling the politics and ideology of traditional elites, political arenas expanding, "epic dislocations" and rethinking of social categories: these would all seem to be significant, healthy contributions of the talk show genre to democratic practice. Indeed, it would seem, talk shows, even if they aren't exactly good for you, are at least good for us—especially those of us with an investment in social change. Yet even setting aside the tendency to romanticize "the masses" and the near gibberish of claims such as "*The Oprah Winfrey Show* functions as a new bildungsroman that charts the irritant in the system through an endless narrative of discomfort" and so forth,[26] something seems a bit fishy here. If you have ever actually watched a few hours of talk shows, they seem about as much about democracy as *The Price Is Right* is about mathematics. Sniffing around this territory more closely, digging through some of its assumptions, clarifies further where we have to go.

Two claims in particular hide within the defenses of talk shows, even the critical defenses: that talk shows "give voice" and that they operate as some kind of "forum." Pushing at them a little uncovers more interesting questions. It is certainly true that, more than anywhere else on television, talk shows invite people to speak for themselves. But do people on daytime talk really wind up speaking in a voice that they and others recognize as somehow authentically their own? How do the medium and the genre structure the "voices" that come out? What sorts of speaking voices are available, and in what ways are they distorted? How could we even tell a "real" voice from a "false" one? Second, there is the question of the "forum." It is certainly true that talk shows come closer than anywhere else on American television to providing a means for a wide range of people, credentialed but especially not so credentialed, to converse about all sorts of things. But is daytime talk really a forum, a set of conversations? How do the production and programming strategies shape the capacity for discussion, and the content of conversation? If . . . talk shows are simultaneously spectacle and conversation,[27] what is the relationship here between the circus and the symposium, and what is the political significance of their combination?

It is tempting to choose sides in all of this, and often I do. Depending on my mood, I might be annoyed by the paternalistic moralizing critics and tout defiant perversity, or I might find myself overwhelmed by the willful, wasteful stupidity of TV talk and recommend V-chip brain implants. But I have now gone a different route, guided by the Big Issues running through the talk show debates and by my own gnawing ambivalence, both as scholar and as just a guy.

What critics and defenders, both inside my brain and outside of it, agree upon is that talk shows are consumed with blurring old distinctions (while often reaffirming them), with making differences harder to tell (while often asserting them with ease): the deviant isn't readily distinguished from the regular person, class stereotypes melt into the hard realities on which they rest, what belongs in private suddenly seems to belong in front of everybody, airing dirty laundry looks much like coming clean. Talk shows wreak special havoc with the "public sphere," moving private stuff into a public spotlight, arousing all sorts of questions about what the public sphere can, does, and should look like.[28] In doing so, they mess with the "normal," giving hours of play and often considerable sympathy to stigmatized populations, behaviors, and identities, and at least partly muddying the waters of normality. And since those brought into the public sphere of TV talk are increasingly distant from the white middle-class guests of earlier years, talk shows wind up attaching class difference to the crossing of public/private and normal/abnormal divides. It is around this stirred pot, in which

humdrum and freaky, off-limits and common property, high status and low, sane and crazed, all brew together, that the anxious flies swarm. . . .

NOTES

1. Vicki Abt and Mel Seesholtz, "The Shameless World of Phil, Sally, and Oprah: Television Talk Shows and the Deconstructing of Society," *Journal of Popular Culture* 28, no. 1 (1994): 211.
2. Howard Kurtz, *Hot Air: All Talk, All the Time* (New York: Times Books, 1996), 52.
3. In *The Advocate,* December 12, 1995, 12.
4. Ruth Bonapace et al., "Is It Time to Turn Off Talk TV?" *First,* June 12, 1995, 90–94.
5. Michel Foucault, *The History of Sexuality,* volume 1 (New York: Vintage, 1990), chapter 1. Readers familiar with Foucault's work will notice his general influence on this book as a whole, in his observations that modern sexuality is organized not around a principle of repression, but through "the wide dispersion of devices that were invented for speaking about it, for having it be spoken about, for inducing it to speak of itself, for listening, recording, transcribing, and redistributing what is said about it" (34); in his questioning of whether increased speech about sexuality offers possibilities for liberation, or rather its reverse; and in his observation that contemporary power operates largely by delineating the normal from the abnormal in myriad ways, most prominently by making visible and stigmatizing the "abnormal." On this sort of "normalizing" power, see also Michel Foucault, *Discipline and Punish* (New York: Vintage, 1979). (For an extension of Foucault's ideas to lesbian and gay politics, see Mark Blasius, *Gay and Lesbian Politics: Sexuality and the Emergence of a New Ethic* [Philadelphia: Temple University Press, 1994], and to AIDS politics, see Joshua Gamson, "Silence, Death, and the Invisible Enemy: AIDS Activism and Social Movement 'Newness,'" *Social Problems* 36, no. 4 [1989]: 351–67.) Foucault was, in the end, perhaps more pessimistic than I, and not especially interested in the mass media as one of the many "regimes of truth" ferreting out sexuality and making it "speak of itself," but I am clearly indebted to basic insights of his writing.
6. Although I use other terms as well (gay, lesbian, bisexual, and transgender; queer;

sexual minorities), I work primarily with the somewhat awkward *sex and gender nonconformity* because it calls attention to the social and relational aspects of sex and gender statuses. "Minority" implies a fixed, unchanging shared characteristic, and "gay or lesbian" tends also to imply an essential, stable kind of self; "sex and gender nonconformist" serves as a reminder that sex and gender identities are constructed with reference to, and through exclusion of, those with identities tagged as deviant. I do not mean to suggest that nonconformity is embraced by all lesbians, gays, transgenders, and bisexuals, only that it is their status as outsiders to heterosexual or traditional gender norms, not some innate difference, that is socially relevant.

I use the term *transgender* to encompass the range of people whose presentation, entity, or behavior involves crossing from one gender to another: transsexuals (who live or seek to live in the gender "opposite" to that assigned to them at birth, and typically change their bodies through surgery and/or hormone treatment) and cross-dressers (who change their gender presentation for periods of time, but usually live at least part-time in the gender assigned to them at birth), including drag queens and transvestites.

7. Chris Bull and John Gallagher, "Talked to Death," *Advocate,* April 18, 1995, 20–22; Michelangelo Signorile, "The *Jenny Jones* Murder: What Really Happened?" *OUT,* June 1995, 26–29, 142–46; Michelle Green, "Fatal Attraction," *People,* March 27, 1995, 40–44.
8. In Janice Kaplan, "Are Talk Shows out of Control?" *TV Guide,* April 1, 1995, 12.
9. Jill Nelson, "Talk Is Cheap," *The Nation,* June 5, 1995, 801.
10. Abt and Seesholtz, 206.
11. Jeanne Albronda Heaton and Nona Leigh Wilson, *Tuning In Trouble: Talk TV's Destructive Impact on Mental Health* (San Francisco: Jossey-Bass, 1995), 127–28.
12. Heaton and Wilson, 131–32, 163.
13. Kurtz, 63.
14. In Empower America, "Press Conference" (Washington, DC: Federal Document Clearing House, October 26, 1995).
15. In Maureen Dowd, "Talk Is Cheap," *New York Times,* October 26, 1995, A25.
16. Kurtz, 52.
17. In Kurtz, 67.
18. Elayne Rapping, "Daytime Inquiries," *Progressive,* October 1991, 37.
19. In Joe Chidley, "Taking In the Trash," *McClean's,* February 19, 1996, 53.
20. For a historical and theoretical treatment of criticisms of mass culture, see Patrick Brantlinger, *Bread and Circuses: Theories of Mass Culture as Social Decay* (New York: Cornell University Press, 1985); for a discussion of the vexed relationship between intellectuals and popular culture, see Andrew Ross, *No Respect: Intellectuals and Popular Culture* (New York: Routledge, 1989).
21. ABC News, *Nightline* ("Phil Donahue"), January 26, 1996.
22. In Mark Schone, "Talked Out," *Spin,* May 1996, 74.
23. Kurtz, 61.
24. In Schone, 74.
25. Carpignano et al., 51.
26. Gloria Jean Masciarotte, "C'mon, Girl: Oprah Winfrey and the Discourse of Feminine Talk," *Genders,* no. 11 (1991): 83.
27. Wayne Munson, *All Talk: The Talkshow in Media Culture* (Philadelphia: Temple University Press, 1994).
28. This moving around of public-private boundaries (and other social boundaries) is also a more general effect of new media technologies, as Joshua Meyrowitz argues in *No Sense of Place: The Impact of Electronic Media on Social Behavior* (New York: Oxford University Press, 1985).

QUESTIONS FOR DISCUSSION

1. In what ways do talk shows construct social problems? How do they shape the ways we think about problems?
2. Why have talk shows become such a popular venue for public discussion about social problems?
3. Do you agree with the perspective that talk shows are a "democratizing" force in the ways problems are discussed? Or do talk shows represent a trivializing of problems?

KEY TERMS

sociological imagination
personal troubles
public issues
institutional dimension of oppression
symbolic dimension of oppression
individual dimension of oppression
othering
subordinate adaptation
boundary maintenance
emotion management
deterministic argument

THE SOCIAL WEB

A variety of resources can provide you with national-level data on social problems. We suggest that you begin your search with the following two:

- FedStats is the gateway to statistics from more than 100 U.S. government agencies. We recommend you start with topic links A to Z and Mapstats. See www.fedstats.gov.
- The U.S. Census Bureau Web site also supplies a wealth of information arranged by topic and alphabetically. See www.census.gov.

We also suggest you explore the role of the media in the construction of social problems through the following two sites:

- Accuracy in Media is a nonprofit, grassroots citizens' watchdog of the news media that critiques botched and bungled news stories and sets the record straight on important issues that have received slanted coverage. See www.aim.org.
- The *Adbusters* magazine Web site has many examples of creative resistance to advertising, including spoof ads, a jammers gallery, and stickers: adbusters.org/creativeresistance.

QUESTIONS FOR DEBATE

1. Do you agree with the statement made by William Bennett about talk shows—"this is the world turned upside down"?
2. What might Schwalbe and colleagues have to say about talk shows?
3. Do C. Wright Mills and Patricia Hill Collins generally agree on how we should understand our social world and experiences?
4. What troubles in your own college life are also social issues?
5. How do differences in power and privilege constrain our ability to connect with one another?

Chapter 3
Power, Capitalism, and Globalization

Contents

Learning Objectives

By the end of this chapter you should be able to:

- Recognize how these authors use one or more of the major perspectives to analyze the global and U.S. economies.

- Explore how economic inequality is shaped by inequalities of race, class, and gender.

- Describe various consequences of globalization and capitalism.

- Analyze how individuals contribute to economic inequality through their everyday behavior.

- Explain how social systems and institutions perpetuate economic inequality.

Defining the Problem

We use Chapter 3, "Power, Capitalism, and Globalization" as a starting point for looking at how various systems of inequalities are structured. The readings in this chapter all address the ways that the economy is linked with power and inequality. Specifically, they analyze the **economic disparity**—the gap between rich and poor—that results from a capitalist system. **Capitalism** is composed of three essential dimensions: private property, a free market, and the goal of profit. With profit as their driving motivation, corporations compete to maximize their control of the market by driving smaller firms out of business. As companies grow they acquire more economic and political power. Their leaders have the ability to influence social policies such as tax laws, environmental legislation, antitrust regulations, and fair labor practices, all to increase their economic advantage. Capitalism is inherently a system of inequality that supercedes the abilities, desire, and needs of individuals. It is a system that many sociologists see as the most fundamental way inequality is structured.

The consequences of a capitalist economy are no longer confined to a few nations. **Globalization** refers to the process by which capitalism has become a worldwide system. The business of doing business does not happen within the confines of national boundaries. The largest corporations in the world operate in many countries at the same time. These **multinational corporations** may be headquartered in one country, obtain necessary resources in another, manufacture components in a third, assemble a product in a fourth, all while marketing products in numerous other nations.

Technology has given information and communication abilities to individuals around the world. It has also allowed multinational corporations to operate continuously across the globe, despite borders and time zones, in ways that increase their profits. Wired and wireless technologies have given corporations increased mobility to go wherever labor and valued resources are cheapest. Check the tags sewn into the clothing you wear. You may read that your T-shirt was made in Sri Lanka, Indonesia, China, or Thailand. These countries—and many others—are typically poor. They frequently have no laws mandating a living wage, safe working conditions, or restrictions on child labor. They often have no regulations that restrict air or water pollution or that limit the disposal of hazardous waste.

Sociologists are concerned with the consequences of the increasing globalization of capitalism. These effects can be seen in the power that wealthy individuals and corporations have within the United States and around the world. Sociologists also study the effects of globalization on people in other cultures. This system has resulted in increased exploitation of labor, especially the work of women and children—commonly resulting in outright slavery. Globalization has also produced environmental degradation and the depletion of many resources. It has resulted in an enormous gap between rich and poor nations and people. Finally, many sociologists examine the ways

that the United States has "exported" its own culture throughout the world, resulting in the degradation of the values and norms of other cultures.

Scope of the Problem

Most sociologists agree that the economic system is the most fundamental cause of social problems. Fifty years ago, C. Wright Mills, a famous American sociologist and conflict theorist, used the term **power elite** to describe the overlap between economic, governmental, and military institutions. He argued that power in the United States is concentrated in the hands of a small group of elites who operate within these three institutions to increase their own power base.

Each year, *Forbes* magazine profiles the superwealthy that constitute Mills's notion of the power elite. Known as "the *Forbes* 400," the names of the wealthiest 400 Americans appear on this list of the elites' elites.[1] Just to get on the bottom of the *Forbes* 400 list in 2001, one needed a net worth of $600 million, up from $500 million in 1998. In 1984, only twelve billionaires were on the list. By 2001 the wealthiest 256 Americans (two-thirds of the list) were billionaires. The twenty-five wealthiest individuals in the United States together are worth well over one-third of a trillion dollars. Within the past three decades, economic power has become increasingly concentrated in the hands of a few superwealthy individuals and corporations; two-thirds of the wealth in the United States is owned by 10 percent of the population.

One of the major consequences of the wealth of the United States being controlled by relatively few people is the ability of the power elite to influence politics, public policy, and resources. Despite efforts at campaign finance reform, the 2001–2002 election

---

[1]*Forbes* Magazine, www.forbes.com, August 6, 2002.

cycle saw a record-breaking increase in the amount of money donated by businesses to the two major political parties.[2] Within the first six months of 2001 alone, nearly $99 million was donated to national political parties. The industries that gave the most money included securities and investments, telecommunications, insurance, pharmaceuticals, tobacco, banks, and lawyers. Although labor unions were also significant donors, businesses gave more than eleven times the amount unions contributed. Many wealthy corporations donated to both political parties; this ensures that no matter which political party is in power, the interests of these industries will be served.

This is not to suggest that these super-wealthy do not do good things for people and their communities. Many businesses and elite individuals engage in philanthropic work. Yet the job of business is not to ensure a quality of life for workers or to promote a decent quality of life within communities or nations. The first task of the corporate world is to make a profit.

The incredible wealth of the "superrich" Americans can also be seen on a global level. The wealthiest twenty-five individuals in the world together are worth nearly half of a trillion dollars, more than the total gross domestic product of India, the second most populated nation in the world.

There is also tremendous economic disparity between rich and poor nations.[3] The United States is by far the wealthiest nation in the world, with a gross domestic product of nearly $10 trillion. Japan, the second wealthiest nation, has a gross domestic product of less than one-half that amount.

The wealth of the United States is greater than that of 175 other countries *combined!*

The poverty experienced by other nations has a profound impact on the lives of people around the globe. In the poorest 50 countries, people have an average annual income of less that $500 U.S. Millions of poor men, women, and children are forced to work in hazardous and exploitive conditions.[4] At least 20 million people are bonded laborers and many more are forced into slavery. Children are especially vulnerable victims of forced labor. According to the International Labour Organization 179 million children—1 in every 8—are working in harsh conditions; 8.5 million children are forced into slavery, prostitution, or military organizations.

Perspectives on the Problem

Sociologists using a *conflict* perspective on globalization would study how the system operates to benefit the economic and political power of a relatively few nations, corporations, and individuals. A sociologist using a *functionalist* perspective would examine whether the global system of capitalism promotes an efficient way to produce and distribute goods and services. A functionalist would likely see the exportation of American values as the inevitable result of a well-ordered economic system. A sociologist using a *symbolic interactionist* perspective would explore how individuals in the United States and in other nations are affected by the global system of capitalism and how people perpetuate economic and political inequality through their everyday actions. *Social constructionists* would analyze how elite nations and corporations have the ability to promote ideas that make nations and individuals believe that inequality ei-

---

[2]Common Cause, "Life of the Party: A New Soft Money Study from Common Cause," www.commoncause.org, August 13, 2002.

[3]World Bank, *World Development Indicators* database, April 2002.

[4]Anti-Slavery, Child Labour Programme, www. antislavery.org.

ther does not exist or is necessary. A social constructionist would also be interested in the ways that nations, organizations, and individuals challenge the prevailing beliefs about capitalism and inequality.

Connecting the Perspectives

In this section's readings, the authors all see the forces of capitalism growing increasingly global and believe the interests of the rich and powerful are being served in the current economic system. William Greider uses a conflict perspective to examine the ways that the enormous yet nameless and faceless capitalist forces control production throughout the world, significantly reducing the power of individual governments. Also using a conflict approach, George Ritzer takes a slightly different view of global capitalism. Rather than looking at the production of goods, he explores the consequences of global marketing and consumption of goods for indigenous cultures. Donald Barlett and James Steele use a conflict perspective to examine wealth and power in the United States, focusing on the huge number of tax dollars spent each year to support major corporations. Kevin Bales takes an interactionist approach to look at the ways that slavery is promoted within the global economy. He explores how enslaved individuals contribute to their own exploitation and why they see no way out of the system. Finally, Grace Chang uses a conflict approach to analyze how the global economy interacts with commonly held beliefs about race and immigration policies to contribute to the economic exploitation of immigrant women in the United States.

Reading Summaries

In "One World, Ready or Not," Greider argues that "the storm upon us" is the devastation brought about by the ways that capitalism has become global—ways that are unprecedented in human history. The massive force of our global economy provides opportunities for some while creating a drastic system of inequality extending throughout the world. The powers of organized labor and individual governments have been weakened by the growing influence of multinational corporations. Greider argues that the immense economic and political power of multinational corporations is even beginning to supersede traditional nationalistic and ethnic boundaries. Within the "one world" Greider describes, our borders are becoming less relevant as economic forces, larger than the force of any one nation, affect the economies of all nations and their people. The power of global capitalism is beyond the control of any one individual, government, or corporation. Thus, although the benefits of the global economy fall to multinational corporations, any individual corporation is vulnerable to the immense forces of global capitalism.

As you read Greider's argument, think about they ways that your own state, community, or family has been affected by the global economy. Perhaps a factory has been closed down in a nearby city and relocated to another country where labor is cheap and government regulation of industry is lax. Perhaps a family member has been "downsized" as large companies merge and eliminate a portion of their workforce. What are the consequences of these changes?

In "Enchanting a Disenchanted World," Ritzer also recognizes the significance of global economic forces, but he focuses on the implications of mass consumption. Americans are engaging in **hyperconsumerism** that represents a new form of capitalist control. People are increasingly encouraged to go into debt—primarily through loans and credit cards—to purchase expensive products they really don't need. The American obsession with buying goods and services is shaping consumption patterns worldwide. The forces of global capitalism that concern Greider are resulting in a global marketplace for American products. Everything from Barbie dolls to Coca-Cola to McDonald's and the Hard Rock Café is being exported to nations around the world at staggering rates.

The increasingly Americanized global marketplace has serious repercussions. Nike shoes and Gap clothing do more than cover bodies, Pizza Hut and Planet Hollywood do more than fill stomachs, and Disney does more than make children laugh. These distinctly American products and services also promote American culture. They reflect American values such as speed, winning, popularity, and wealth. Ritzer warns that the increased presence of these goods presents a "profound threat" to indigenous cultural products and practices of countries around the world. Not only does the trend toward hyperconsumerism threaten to standardize practices around the world, it also has an effect on the utilization of natural and human resources and contributes to the degradation of the environment.

America's economic policies—including taxation, industry deregulation, and trade practices—have all combined to benefit the wealthy and powerful at the expense of the middle class and the poor. In "Corporate Welfare," Donald L. Barlett and James B. Steele document the ways that corporations or industries receive special economic benefits from federal, state, and local governments. These benefits, in the forms of tax exemptions, loans, grants, and subsidies, total billions of dollars each year. Additionally, economic advantages are granted to the wealthiest corporations. The annual amount the federal government spends on welfare programs for corporations far exceeds the amount spent on welfare for the nation's poor—and that does not include the amount spent at state and local levels. Yet the people

residing in the states and municipalities that grant corporate benefits gain very little from this allocation of tax dollars. Jobs, especially those that offer sufficient wages, are rarely created to the extent that businesses and industries promise to officials. Nationally, the corporations who have received the largest benefits have in fact eliminated more jobs than they have created. Barlett and Steele argue that despite its drawbacks to the American public, corporate welfare will continue to flourish to benefit the wealthy and powerful for as long as it is permitted.

In "The Social Psychology of Modern Slavery," Kevin Bales examines one of the most heinous consequences of the global economy for the world's poorest individuals. Contrary to popular belief in the United States, the institution of **slavery** is flourishing worldwide. Millions of impoverished men, women, and children are forced by violence or the threat of violence into slave labor. Bales argues that, although it has evolved since the United States outlawed it in the nineteenth century, slavery is still both persistent and widespread. The cost of owning a human being today is cheaper, making slaves more expendable to their owners. Slavery is produced and maintained outside the realm of laws that prohibit it. The trafficking of women and children for prostitution, sweatshops, or domestic labor has become a major component of organized crime in Europe, Asia, South America, and Africa.

Bales takes an interactionist approach to explore why and how slavery is perpetuated. While acknowledging that people may have no economic options other than bonded servitude, Bales argues that many slaves contribute psychologically to their own exploitation. Laborers are manipulated into believing that the system of slavery cannot be changed and that their economic conditions would be worsened if they were to fight against slaveholders. Moreover, many children, especially girls, are culturally socialized into obedience and submission, making them prime targets for sexual exploitation and abuse. Bales calls for more research on ending slavery and rehabilitating victims of coerced labor to both physical and psychological freedom.

In "Disposable Domestics: The New Employable Mothers," Chang shows that shifts in the global economy and changes in recent U.S. immigration policies have contributed significantly to the oppressive conditions facing undocumented Mexican women working in the United States. She argues that, beginning in the 1970s, declining economic conditions in Mexico and other Central American countries led women to cross the southern border of the United States illegally to look for unskilled positions in agriculture and other areas. In 1986, Congress passed the Immigration Reform and Control Act (IRCA), which prohibited employers from hiring undocumented workers and allowed illegal immigrants to file for amnesty to gain the status of legal residents. The IRCA also included two exclusions intended to limit the welfare rolls.

Because the Immigration and Naturalization Services (INS) interpreted the new laws stringently, many immigrant women who were eligible for amnesty did not apply. This means that they did not have adequate means to support their children financially. As a result, many of these women were driven into the underground economy where they repeated a long-established pattern: poor women of color providing child care and domestic help to economically more privileged White women. Because of their position in the race–class structure, these White women benefited from the situation whether or not they realized it. Chang uses a feminist perspective to analyze the implications of a system in which, in order to hold professional middle-class jobs, privileged women hire poor, illegal immigrants to provide care for their children.

FOCUSING QUESTIONS

While you are reading Chapter 3, keep the following questions in mind: Does the system of economic inequality on both global and national levels serve as a starting point for understanding other forms of inequality? Can the unequal distribution of power that marks all social problems be traced to economic structures, or are other forms of inequality—especially those based on race and gender—more fundamental? How do institutions and people together create the structure of economic inequality? Finally, how might the economic system be altered to ameliorate economic inequality? Can the system of global capitalism be made more just, or must the system be completely dismantled in order to end economic suffering?

6

ONE WORLD, READY OR NOT
The Manic Logic of Global Capitalism

WILLIAM GREIDER

Imagine a wondrous new machine, strong and supple, a machine that reaps as it destroys. It is huge and mobile, something like the machines of modern agriculture but vastly more complicated and powerful. Think of this awesome machine running over open terrain and ignoring familiar boundaries. It plows across fields and fencerows with a fierce momentum that is exhilarating to behold and also frightening. As it goes, the machine throws off enormous mows of wealth and bounty while it leaves behind great furrows of wreckage.

Now imagine that there are skillful hands on board, but no one is at the wheel. In fact, this machine has no wheel nor any internal governor to control the speed and direction. It is sustained by its own forward motion, guided mainly by its own appetites. And it is accelerating.

The machine is modern capitalism driven by the imperatives of global industrial revolution. The metaphor is imperfect, but it offers a simplified way to visualize what is dauntingly complex and abstract and impossibly diffuse—the drama of a free-running economic system that is reordering the world.

The logic of commerce and capital has overpowered the inertia of politics and launched an epoch of great social transfor-mations. Settled facts of material life are being revised for rich and poor nations alike. Social understandings that were formed by the hard political struggles of the twentieth century are put in doubt. Old verities about the rank ordering of nations are revised and a new map of the world is gradually being drawn. These great changes sweep over the affairs of mere governments and destabilize the established political orders in both advanced and primitive societies. Everything seems new and strange. Nothing seems certain.

Economic revolution, similar to the impulse of political revolution, liberates masses of people and at the same time projects new aspects of tyranny. Old worlds are destroyed and new ones emerge. The past is upended and new social values are created alongside the fabulous new wealth. Marvelous inventions are made plentiful. Great fortunes are accumulated. Millions of peasants find ways to escape from muddy poverty.

Yet masses of people are also tangibly deprived of their claims to self-sufficiency, the independent means of sustaining hearth and home. People and communities, even nations, find themselves losing control over their own destinies, ensnared by the revolutionary demands of commerce.

The great paradox of this economic revolution is that its new technologies enable people and nations to take sudden leaps into modernity, while at the same time they promote the renewal of once-forbidden barbarisms. Amid the newness of things, exploitation of the weak by the strong also flourishes again.

The present economic revolution, like revolutions of the past, is fueled by invention and human ingenuity and a universal aspiration to build and accumulate. But it is also driven by a palpable sense of insecurity. No one can be said to control the energies of unfettered capital, not important governments or financiers, not dictators or democrats.

And, in the race to the future, no one dares to fall a step behind, not nations or major corporations. Even the most effective leaders of business and finance share in the uncertainty, knowing as they do that the uncompromising dynamics can someday turn on the revolutionaries themselves.

As history confirms, every revolution gradually accumulates its own tensions and instabilities, the unresolved contradictions that deepen and eventually lead it to falter or break down. Likewise, this revolution is steadily creating the predicate for its own collapse. The imperatives driving enterprise and finance and leading to great social transformations reveal, in turn, the inherent contradictions that are also propelling the world toward some new version of breakdown, the prospect of an economic or political cataclysm of unknowable dimensions.

Our wondrous machine, with all its great power and creativity, appears to be running out of control toward some sort of abyss. Amid revolutionary fervor, such warnings may sound far-fetched and, as history tells us, usually go unheeded until one day, sometimes quite suddenly, they are confirmed by reality.

. . .

Before the machine can be understood, one must first be able to see it. The daunting shape and scope of the global system are usually described by opaque statistics from business and economics, but only the most sophisticated can grasp the explosive dynamics in those numbers. To visualize this great drama in its full dimensions, one must also see the people.

When I visited Bangkok, in Thailand, the newspapers were preoccupied with the melancholy saga of Honey, a work elephant who was severely injured when a truck sideswiped her on the highway. As doctors tried to mend the elephant's smashed hip, contributions poured in from heartsick citizens, including the king. Elephants have been the emblem of Thai culture for at least seven centuries, but are now gradually dying out. Honey's death prompted editorial reflections on the price of prosperity.

The new national symbol of Thailand, one could say, is the traffic jam. Bangkok's are the worst in Asia, citizens remark with an air of disgusted pride. Their daily commuting routines are the longest in developing Asia, and Thais manipulate schedules endlessly to try to avoid the hours of steaming in tropical congestions of cars. The problem is that Thais are buying cars much faster than the government is building a modern transportation system. Thailand may emerge as Toyota's biggest overseas market aside from the United States.[1]

In Poland, the newly chartered Warsaw Stock Exchange was under way in a stately old pre-Communist building on Aleje Jeroszolimskie. Trading was quite thin since only two dozen companies had their shares listed and Poles were already experiencing the turbulence of Adam Smith's *niewidzialna ręka rynku,* "the invisible hand of the market." Stock prices rose fabulously in 1993, and many of the pioneer investors became instantly wealthy, zloty millionaires, at least on paper. The stock market crashed the following spring. As shares fell 40 to 70 percent in ten days, the Polish traders adopted the style of gallows humor familiar to mature financial markets around the world. Watching stocks plunge 27 percent in a single day, a broker observed: "The Warsaw Stock Exchange still awaits its first suicide."[2]

The lobby of Warsaw's Victoria Intercontinental Hotel, a favorite of foreign business travelers, was filled with hopeful plungers. Each morning Polish entrepreneurs would spread their business prospectuses across the broad coffee tables and sit back, a bit fidgety, while visiting investors from Frankfurt or New York or Milan inspected the numbers.

On the city's industrial outskirts, meanwhile, workers at the Huta Luchini steelworks were on strike. They closed down the mill to demand a share of the ownership. These steelworkers had once been revolutionaries themselves, among the militant members of Solidarity, the free trade union that arose to confront the Polish Communist regime in the early 1980s and had campaigned for the autonomy of workers and enterprises organized on principles of self-management. The Warsaw steelworks is now owned by an Italian conglomerate.

In China, as the November days turned crisp and cold, the citizens of Beijing shopped at sidewalk markets for the traditional supplies of winter cabbage. High, squared-off mounds of cabbages attended by merchants in blue smocks with white kerchiefs on their heads were stacked at street corners along Chang An—Avenue of Eternal Peace—the mainstem boulevard. Farmers hauled cabbages into the city every day, stacked on trucks, bicycle-powered wagons and overloaded handcarts. The ritual reflects a national memory of poverty and famine. Every autumn a family acquires its store of winter cabbages as insurance against the ancient threat of scarcity. One can see the cabbages hanging atop communal walls or outside apartment windows, their outer leaves blackened by Beijing's sooty air.

Meanwhile, traffic on the boulevard was abruptly interrupted to make way for a caravan of important personages—a fleet of limousines and police escorts racing down the center lanes, with blue lights flashing. It was Jean Chrétien, the Canadian prime minister, and a trade delegation from Ottawa and the provinces. Kohl, Mitterrand, Major, Balladur, Bentsen, Brown, Christopher—visiting political leaders from the most advanced economies, statesmen seeking contracts for home companies and access to China's explosive market, have become a commonplace.

As usual, McDonald's was already there, selling burgers to consumers. From Kuala Lumpur to Moscow, the company acts like an advanced scout for the global revolution, somehow able to detect the emergence of disposable incomes before other firms see it. Chinese buy their winter cabbages and also fast food. McDonald's measures its market potential with numbers like these: In the United States, there is a McDonald's restaurant for every 29,000 Americans. In China, despite rapid expansion, there is one McDonald's for every 40 million Chinese.

In Tokyo, the Sony Corporation, an authentic symbol of Japan's manufacturing excellence, is on the verge of becoming an un-Japanese company. The human resources manager, Yasunori Kirihara, lamented the prospect but explained it as an inevitable consequence of global economic integration. At present, he said, Sony's employees are split roughly fifty-fifty between Japanese and foreigners. As Sony continues to relocate its factories elsewhere, from Southeast Asia to Mexico, the substantial majority of its workforce, about 60 percent, will soon be outside Japan.

A new Japanese word, *kudoka,* has been popularized in business and political circles to describe this phenomenon. *Kudoka,* I was told, did not exist in the language before the 1980s. Its meaning should be familiar to American industrial workers who have seen their manufacturing jobs disappear. In English, it means "hollowing out."

In Everett, Washington, just north of Seattle, workers on the assembly line for Boeing's new 777, the company's latest addition to its line of large-body aircraft, gossiped that they might be shut down by the earthquake in Kobe, Japan. The main body section of the "Triple Seven," as Boeing people call their new plane, is manufactured by Mitsubishi Heavy Industries, though its plant, as it turned out, was not damaged by the quake. The 777 is a brilliant expression of America's productive prowess in advanced technologies, but the aircraft is manufactured, piece by piece, in twelve different countries.

As these scattered glimpses suggest, the symptoms of upheaval can be found most anywhere, since people in distant places are now connected by powerful strands of the same marketplace. The convergence has no fixed center, no reliable boundaries or settled outcomes. As enterprise opens up new territories, the maps keep changing—changing so rapidly that it has already become commonplace to speak of "one world" markets for everything from cars to capital. The earth's diverse societies are being rearranged and united in complicated ways by global capitalism. The idea evokes benumbed resignation among many. The complexity of it overwhelms. The enormity makes people feel small and helpless.

The essence of this industrial revolution, like others before it, is that commerce and finance have leapt inventively beyond the existing order and existing consciousness of peoples and societies. The global system of trade and production is fast constructing a new functional reality for most everyone's life, a new order based upon its own dynamics and not confined by the traditional social understandings. People may wish to turn away from that fact, but there is essentially no place to hide, not if one lives in any of the industrialized nations.

The only option people really have is to catch up with the reality. The only way to escape a sense of helplessness is to confront this new world on its own terms and try to understand its larger implications. The actual system, as we shall see, does not conform to the economic theory it presumes to follow. Nor are people and nations actually powerless to influence its behavior, as conventional wisdom asserts. But people and nations may restore a sense of control over their own destinies only if they are willing to face the complexity, only by grasping the operating imperatives that drive the global system and the full scope of human consequences that it yields.

Grasping the meaning of this new order requires one to set aside reflexive national loyalties in order to see the system whole. I have tried at least to do that. Above all, I avoid the standard nationalist complaints (most often aimed at Japan) that preoccupy so many books about the global economy, especially books written by Americans. (While I have tried to stand outside national identity and see things in a spirit of universality, I do not imagine for a moment that I succeeded fully. Like most people, I am bound by culture and personal experience, by limitations of language and native biases, to one nation.)

The usual question—is America winning or losing?—can be disposed of quickly. The answer is yes. America is winning, and yes, it is losing. Some sectors of Americans are triumphant and other sectors are devastated, but not in equal measures. The same rough answer applies in differing degrees throughout most of the world, especially among the wealthiest nations—Germany, France or Britain, even Japan.

Books that nominate one country or another as "the winner" of global competition have a very short shelf life since these things change so rapidly. In 1992, a best-selling author heralded Europe, led by Germany, as the likely champion for its superior economic system; eighteen months later Europe and Germany were mired in gloomy forecasts from their own business leaders, complaining about their failure to keep up with American flexibility. Likewise, the United States has been written off and revived a number of times. Even Japan, so wealthy that many thought it had already won the race, is now experiencing its own tangible crisis of self-doubt.[3]

The obsession with nations in competition misses the point of what is happening: The global economy divides every society into new camps of conflicting economic interests. It undermines every nation's ability to maintain social cohesion. It mocks the assumption of shared political values that supposedly unite people in the nation-state.

That is the fundamental reason politics has become so muddled in the leading capitalist democracies. In recent years voters have turned on established parties and leaders, sometimes quite brutally, in the United States, Canada, Italy, France, Sweden and Japan, to name the most spectacular cases. Nor is there any ideological consistency to these voter rebellions. Socialists were tossed out in socialist Sweden, then restored to power a few years later. In a single election, the Conservative Party of Canada was reduced from governing majority to a remnant of two parliamentary seats. The business party that ruled Japan without interruption for four decades, the Liberal Democrats, was ousted by dissident reformers, then regained power in an unstable coalition of its own, this time led by a socialist.

Deeper political instability lies ahead for these societies because the global economy has put a different political question on the table: What exactly is the national interest in these new circumstances? No elected

government in the richest countries, neither right nor left, has produced a definition that convinces its own electorate. Indeed, some important governments, clinging to the inherited postwar orthodoxy, are pursuing economic strategies that arguably do injury to majorities of their own citizens. This reflects not only the heavy hand of defunct theory, but also that insecure politicians do not know what else to do.

Political confusion in the dominant economies is set against a fundamental countervailing reality: For most people living in most parts of the world, the global economy began in 1492. In their history, the centuries of conquest and economic colonization were integral to the rise of industrial capitalism in Europe and North America, but the returns were never really shared with them. Books by Americans proclaiming "one world" may seem quite precious and self-centered to those people. For them, the global economy long ago consigned most regions of the world to lowly status as commodity producers—the hewers and haulers, the rubber tappers, tin miners and cane cutters. What William Faulkner said of the American South applies as well to those colonialized nations that used to be known as the Third World: the past is never dead, it is not even past. (The global economy has a language problem: The old labels for categories of nations are confused or obsolete. "Third World," a condescending term coined for the Cold War, is now meaningless. Even the "West" is useless if it is meant to designate the advanced economies, since Japan is among them and booming Asia lies west of the United States, not east. We are reduced to cruder terms like rich and poor nations, advanced and primitive economies.)

From the perspective of most of these countries, the present industrial revolution is a rare opening in history, a chance to get out from under. Some of them are succeeding, climbing rapidly in wealth and establishing at least a fragile basis for national self-sufficiency. Dozens of others are trying to do the same. All of them approach the present with deep historical skepticism, the memory of how many times their aspirations were thwarted by the leading economic powers, how many previous openings turned out to be illusory.

When all the larger economic and political questions are exhausted, the heaviest legacy of this new "one world" may be the psychological blow to national arrogance. Americans reflexively think of themselves as without any real peers. Number One. In their own racialist ways so do the Japanese and the Germans. Tribal assumptions of inherited superiority are embedded in the cultures of the French and Chinese and Muslims, among many others. These folk illusions are now under vigorous assault, contradicted by the emerging economic reality.

During my travels I experienced certain small epiphanies: The amazement of watching a great modern industrial factory at work. The anguish of encountering exploited young people, peasant children turned into low-wage industrial workers, struggling to understand their own condition. The simple delight any tourist feels at glimpsing the weird variety of human life and also the underlying sameness.

The most powerful moments, however, were the recurring experiences of witnessing poor people who dwell in marginal backwaters doing industrial work of the most advanced order. People of color, people who are black, yellow, red, brown, who exist in surroundings of primitive scarcity, are making complex things of world-class quality, mastering modern technologies that used to be confined to a select few. The tools of advanced civilization are being shared with other tribes. Multinational corporations, awesomely powerful and imperiously aloof, are the ironic vehicle for accomplishing this generous act of history.

The confident presumption that certain high-caliber work can be done only by certain people (mainly, it is assumed, by well-educated white people in a few chosen countries) is mistaken. Observing these scenes of industrial activity, I thought first of the explosive implications for the future of work and prosperity in the advanced economies, including America. The portents are stark and threatening. Yet the meaning also has to be understood in the broader sweep of human history. Watching former peasants making high-tech goods for the global market, I eventually reached a simpler, more nourishing understanding. Of course, I thought. People are capable, everywhere in the world.

Is it conceivable that commerce, pursuing narrow self-interested ends, might accomplish what idealistic politics has never been able to achieve—defeating stubborn ideas of racial superiority? I returned from my travels imagining it might someday be possible. Certainly, enormous conflicts lie ahead for the peoples of the world, political and economic collisions, possibly including the violence of wars between rival economies. Nevertheless, the process of globalization is visibly dismantling enduring stereotypes of race and culture, ancient assumptions of supremacy. This transformation will someday be understood as the most radical dimension of the revolution.

. . .

The raw energies of the global system, its power of excitement, can be glimpsed in the daily headlines about important business deals. Anheuser-Busch buys a stake in Kirin, Japan's biggest brewery, also a 5 percent share of China's Tsingtao, then acquires

10 percent of Antarctica, the leading beer of Brazil. Siemens of Germany forms a partnership with Skoda Plzen to manufacture steam turbines in the Czech Republic. Volvo opens an assembly line near Xian, China, with Chinese machinists making Swedish tour buses. Switzerland's Roche bids $5.3 billion for the U.S. pharmaceutical Syntex, while Smith-Kline Beecham buys another American company for $2.3 billion. NEC, the Japanese electronics giant, agrees to collaborate with Samsung, the Korean multinational, to make DRAM memory chips, probably at a plant in Portugal, to supply the $5 billion European market.

The problem, of course, is that the stories are too diverse and plentiful to make the motivating principles very clear. As the announcements of new ventures accumulate in breathtaking number, the effect is like the blur of a major blizzard. IBM announces quarterly losses of $8 billion and plans to cut 35,000 jobs. Bausch & Lomb begins making contact lenses and Ray-Ban sunglasses in India. Colgate-Palmolive opens a toothbrush factory in Colombia. AT&T forms an alliance with the national telephone companies of Sweden, Switzerland and the Netherlands; its American rival MCI pairs off with British Telecommunications.

Coca-Cola returns to Vietnam, this time without the U.S. military forces. Toyota picks Kentucky to make automobiles, BMW picks South Carolina, Mercedes picks Alabama. Ford and General Motors hope the Chinese government will pick them to make cars in China.[4]

John F. Welch Jr., CEO of General Electric and widely admired for hard-headed corporate strategies, has warned fellow executives not to be lulled by self-congratulations or press clippings about how American companies have regained an edge over foreign competitors. "Things are going to get tougher," he predicted in mid-1994. "The shakeouts will be more brutal. The pace of change more rapid." What lies ahead, Welch said, is "a hurricane."[5]

The accumulating evidence supports this warning. After two decades of dramatic changes the revolutionary pressures are not abating or leveling off into familiar patterns. The dynamics appear to be accelerating. What is the nature of the storm upon us? A new structure of power is gradually emerging in the world, forcing great changes everywhere it asserts itself. The broad dimensions are defined by a baseline of unsettling facts:

1. During the last generation the world's 500 largest multinational corporations have grown sevenfold in sales. Yet the worldwide employment of these global firms has remained virtually flat since the early 1970s, hovering around 26 million people. The major multinationals grew in sales from $721 billion in 1971 to $5.2 trillion in 1991, claiming a steadily growing share of commerce (one third of all manufacturing exports, three fourths of commodity trade, four fifths of the trade in technology and management services). Yet the human labor required for each unit of their output is diminished dramatically.

While this galaxy of major global firms grew in size, its center of gravity also shifted. America's flagship companies, from du Pont and IBM to GE and General Motors, were the modern progenitors of globalized manufacturing after World War II, but the United States has lost its dominance. In 1971, 280 of the largest 500 multinationals were American-based. By 1991, the United States had only 157 on the list.

Europe's largest companies surpassed America's in number and sales volume during the last half of the 1980s. By 1991, Europe had 168 of the largest 500. Japan, meanwhile, had risen in twenty years from 53 to 119. A few important multinational corporations have even emerged in countries that were once very poor—Korea, Taiwan, even Thailand. The corporate girth of nations is gradually dispersing, leveling out.[6]

2. The basic mechanism of globalization—companies investing capital in foreign countries, buying existing assets or building new factories—has accelerated explosively during the last fifteen years. The volume of foreign direct investment nearly quadrupled during the 1980s, reaching $2 trillion in the 1990s. The largest portion of that capital flow, about 25 percent, actually went into the United States during the 1980s, reversing the historic pattern. The United States became a debtor nation and sold off domestic assets to foreign investors; Japanese auto companies, among others, prudently located assembly plants in the States.[7]

Direct investing across borders cooled off for several years amid the major recessions of the early 1990s, but as it resumed the heaviest flows of capital were aimed in a different direction—building new production in the so-called emerging markets of Asia and selected nations in Latin America and Eastern Europe. Indeed, another historic relationship seemed broken: the utter dependence of poor nations on the prosperous. This time around, while the advanced economies remained stagnant or mired in recession, a league of poorer economies was enjoying a spectacular investment boom.

The growth of transnational corporate investments, the steady dispersal of production elements across many nations, has nearly obliterated the traditional understanding of trade. Though many of them know better, economists and politicians continue to portray the global trading system in terms that the public can understand—that is, as a collection of nations buying and selling things to each other. However, as the volume of world trade has grown, the traditional role of national markets is increasingly eclipsed by an alternative system: Trade generated within the multinational companies themselves as they export and import among their own foreign-based subsidiaries.

According to one scholarly estimate, more than 40 percent of U.S. exports and nearly 50 percent of its imports are actually goods that travel not in the open marketplace, but through these intrafirm channels. A U.S. computer company ships design components to its assembly plant in Malaysia, then distributes the finished hardware back to the United States and to other buyers in Asia and Europe. A typical Japanese plant located in America "imports" most of its components from its parent corporation and allied suppliers, then "exports" products back to the parent in Japan or sister affiliates in other countries.[8]

All of this intrafirm traffic is counted in the national trade statistics, but national identities are increasingly irrelevant to the buyers and sellers. Nation-to-nation trade flows are driven more and more by the proprietary strategies of the multinational corporations organizing their own diversified production, less and less by traditional concepts of comparative advantage among nations or the economic policies of home governments.

The shifting content of trade has led many leading governments, including the one in Washington, to embrace a strategy that might confound some citizens (if it were explained to them clearly) because it seems to offend nationalist intuition. The governments are actively promoting the dispersal of capital investment and production to foreign locations on the assumption that this will lead to increased exports for home-based production (and more jobs for domestic workers). As the flagship multinationals make more things overseas, they will presumably ship more homemade goods to their overseas affiliates. That, anyway, is the logic governments embrace.

3. Finance capital—the trading of stocks, bonds, currencies and more exotic forms of financial paper—has accelerated its movements around the world at an astonishing pace. International bank loans more than quadrupled from 1980 to 1991, reaching $3.6 trillion. Global bond financing expanded likewise. Cross-border stockholdings in the so-called Triad—Europe, Japan and the United States—nearly doubled during a few years in the late 1980s.

The global exchange markets in national currencies—swapping dollars for yen or deutschemarks for francs or scores of other such trades—are moving faster still. Foreign-exchange trading totaled more than $1.2 trillion a day by the early 1990s, compared to only $640 billion a day as recently as 1989. Since financial traders usually move in and out of different currencies in order to buy or sell a nation's stocks or bonds, this furious pace of currency exchange reflects the magnifying presence of borderless finance.

The entire global volume of publicly traded financial assets (about $24 trillion) turns over every twenty-four days. The International Monetary Fund, which attempts to monitor such matters, claims that this quickening pace is unexceptional since, it points out, the trading in U.S. government bonds is even faster. The entire traded volume of U.S. Treasury debt ($2.6 trillion) turns over every eight days.[9]

Despite the staggering volume the financial trading across borders is mostly transacted by a very small community: the world's largest thirty to fifty banks and a handful of major brokerages that do the actual trades on behalf of investor clients— wealthy individuals and the various pools of private capital, smaller banks and broker-

ages, pension funds, mutual funds and so on—as well as the banks' own portfolios.

As the volume has swelled, the global financial markets have become much more powerful—and much more erratic. Sentiment and prices can shift suddenly and sharply, cascading losses across innocent bystanders like the multinational corporations that depend on predictable currency values for their cross-border trade or national governments that watch helplessly as global finance raises their domestic interest rates or devalues their currencies. "Crisis" has become an overworked word. Market economists speak more politely of "disturbances." These are the decisive breaks in prices that occur when global investors suddenly lose confidence in one investment sector or an entire country and abruptly shift huge amounts of capital elsewhere, quick as the electronic impulses of modern banking.

To make sense out of these bewildering facts, it helps to think of the global system in cruder terms, as a galaxy of four broad, competing power blocs—each losing or gaining influence over events. The biggest, most obvious loser in these terms is labor, both the organized union workers and wage earners in general. Wages are both rising and falling around the world, but workers at both ends of the global economy have lost substantial control over their labor markets and the terms of employment. "Now capital has wings," as New York financier Robert A. Johnson explained succinctly. "Capital can deal with twenty labor markets at once and pick and choose among them. Labor is fixed in one place. So power has shifted."

National governments, likewise, have lost ground on the whole, partly because many have retreated from trying to exercise their power over commerce and finance, implicitly ceding to the revolutionary spirit. In the advanced economies, most governments have become mere salesmen, promoting the fortunes of their own multinationals in the hope that this will provide a core prosperity that keeps everyone afloat. The clearest evidence that this strategy is not working is the condition of labor markets in the wealthiest nations: either mass unemployment or declining real wages (nominal pay adjusted for inflation), and, in some cases, both of these deleterious effects.

The more subtle evidence of the dilemma of leading governments is their deteriorating fiscal condition: most are threatened by rising, seemingly permanent budget deficits and accumulating debt. The swollen fiscal deficits of the United States are the largest in size, but far from the worst in relative terms. The general fiscal crisis of rich nations is driven by the same fundamental—disappointing economic growth that, year after year, fails to generate the tax revenues needed to keep up with the public obligations established in more prosperous times. The modern welfare state, the social protections that rich nations enacted to ameliorate the harsh inequalities of industrial capitalism, is now in peril. Some would say it is already obsolete.

Ironically, the governments of developing countries, at least the most successful ones, are less enthralled by the global system's theory and rhetoric and more willing to impose their own terms on capital and trade. Given their own historical memory, poor countries attempt, if they can, to bargain within the system—making nationalistic trade-offs with global firms and investors. Some succeed; many are overwhelmed.

The multinational corporations are, collectively, the muscle and brains of this new system, the engineers who are designing the brilliant networks of new relationships. It is their success at globalization that has inevitably weakened labor and degraded the control of governments. Some smart organizations are even reconfiguring themselves into what business futurists have dubbed

"the virtual corporation," a quick-witted company so dispersed that it resembles the ganglia of a nervous system, a brain attached to many distant nodes but without much bodily substance at the center.[10]

Despite their supple strengths the great multinationals are, one by one, insecure themselves. Even the most muscular industrial giants are quite vulnerable if they fail to adapt to the imperatives of reducing costs and improving rates of return. Critics who focus on the awesome size and sprawl of the global corporations find this point difficult to accept, but the executives of Volkswagen, GM, Volvo, IBM, Eastman Kodak and Pan American Airlines can attest to it. Those well-known firms, among many others, have experienced the harsh consequences of straying from the path of revolution. Their stocks were hammered, their managements ousted, tens of thousands of employees discarded. Behind corporate facades, the anxiety is genuine.

The Robespierre of this revolution is finance capital. Its principles are transparent and pure: maximizing the return on capital without regard to national identity or political and social consequences. Global finance collectively acts as the disinterested enforcer of these imperatives, like a Committee of Public Safety presiding over the Terror (though historians would note that Robespierre's revolutionaries pursued the opposite objective of reducing the great inequalities of wealth).

Financial investors monitor and punish corporations or whole industrial sectors if their returns weaken. Finance disciplines governments or even entire regions of the globe if those places appear to be creating impediments to profitable enterprise or unpleasant surprises for capital. If this sounds dictatorial, the global financiers also adhere to their own rough version of egalitarian values: they will turn on anyone, even their own home country's industry and government, if the defense of free capital seems to require it.

As the Jacobins learned during the French Revolution, it is the most zealous, principled advocates of new values who are ultimately most at risk in a revolutionary environment. Master financiers seem to appreciate this, too. George Soros, the Hungarian-American billionaire who became fabulously wealthy by grasping the new principles of global investing before others, often emphasizes his own fallibility. In early 1994, when Soros got things wrong, he lost $600 million during two days of brisk disturbance in global bond markets. When Robespierre got things wrong, he was guillotined before a cheering mob in the Place de la Révolution.

Even the most powerful players—titans of finance or the multinationals regularly demonized in popular lore—are themselves dwarfed by the system and subject to its harsh, overwhelming consequences. To describe the power structure of the global system does not imply that anyone is in charge of the revolution. The revolution runs itself. This point is critical to understanding its anarchic energies and oblivious disregard for parochial victims or, for that matter, the seeming impotence of enterprises themselves to control things. This revolution is following historical patterns of behavior that industrial capitalism has reiterated across the centuries—an explosive cycle of renewal, migration and destruction that is typically ignited by human invention.

NOTES

Author's Note: As these notes reflect, I have relied on many diverse sources, but none was more valuable than the *Financial Times* of London. The *Financial Times* provides an authoritative snapshot of action in the global economy every day, with superb reporting and analysis, much more comprehensive than anything published in the United States.

1. The elephant population of Thailand has declined to 1,975 in the wild and 2,938 domesticated animals, according to Rodney Tasker, *Far Eastern Economic Review,* April 29, 1993. Daily commuting time in Thailand is the longest in Asia, according to a survey of affluent consumers: *Far Eastern Economic Review,* August 27, 1992. Thai auto sales and traffic jams: Victor Mallet, *Financial Times,* November 27, 1993.

2. The Warsaw stock market crash: *Warsaw Voice,* April 24, 1994.

3. Economist Lester Thurow wrote as recently as 1992: "History and human nature tells us that it will be far easier for the Americans and the Japanese to avoid doing what they must do if they are to win. Future historians will record that the twenty-first century belonged to the House of Europe!" *Head to Head: Coming Economic Battles Among Japan, Europe, and America* (New York: Morrow, 1992).

4. Anheuser-Busch: *Financial Times,* June 29 and July 30, 1993, and February 23, 1995; Siemens: *Financial Times,* July 21, 1993; Taiwan Aerospace: *Financial Times,* July 24, 1993; drug company mergers: *Financial Times,* May 4, 1994; NEC-Samsung: *Financial Times,* February 7, 1995; IBM losses: *Wall Street Journal,* July 28, 1993; Bausch & Lomb, Colgate-Palmolive: *Wall Street Journal,* August 4, 1993; AT&T: *Financial Times,* June 24, 1994; Coca-Cola: *Financial Times,* July 22, 1993.

5. John F. Welch Jr., *Wall Street Journal,* June 21, 1994.

6. The 500 largest global firms are described in *Multinationals and the National Interest: Playing by Different Rules,* Office of Technology Assessment, U.S. Congress, September 1993. American firms still dominate among the largest, accounting for 7 of the 20 biggest multinationals, as ranked by foreign assets.

   The top 20 are, in order: Royal Dutch Shell (UK/Netherlands), Ford, GM, Exxon, IBM (U.S.), British Petroleum (UK), Asea Brown Boveri (Switzerland/Sweden), Nestlé (Switzerland), Philips Electronics (Netherlands), Mobil (U.S.), Unilever (UK, Netherlands), Matsushita Electric (Japan), Fiat (Italy), Siemens (Germany), Sony (Japan), Volkswagen (Germany), Elf Aquitaine (France), Mitsubishi (Japan), GE and du Pont (U.S.). Cited in "World Investment Report 1993: Transnational Corporations and Integrated International Production," United Nations, from *Financial Times,* July 21, 1993.

7. *Multinationals and the National Interest*, OTA. The biggest owners of the $2 trillion in foreign productive assets continue to be U.S. firms, with a total of $474 billion, followed by Britain, $259 billion, and Japan, $251 billion: *Financial Times*, July 21, 1993.

8. The intrafirm trade patterns vary from country to country. For Japanese manufacturing, 51 percent of all exports from affiliates were to the parent companies or other sister affiliates in 1989, according to John H. Dunning, *Multinational Enterprises and the Global Economy* (Reading, MA: Addison-Wesley, 1993).

9. Bank lending growth is from the annual reports of the Bank for International Settlements. Other financial data is from "International Capital Markets, Part I," International Monetary Fund, 1993.

10. William H. Davidow and Michael S. Malone, *The Virtual Corporation: Structuring and Revitalizing the Corporation for the 21st Century* (New York: HarperCollins, 1992).

QUESTIONS FOR DISCUSSION

1. Are there opportunities created by the increasing power of the global economy?
2. How does Greider's argument shift the ways that we think about the power of individual governments versus the power of larger economic structures?
3. How do we consider solutions to economic inequality when the processes of global capitalism are so massive and beyond individual or government control?

7

ENCHANTING A DISENCHANTED WORLD
Revolutionizing the Means of Consumption

GEORGE RITZER

American society is now better characterized by consumption than production. That is, as more and more basic production is taking place in other nations, especially in developing nations, consumption has assumed center stage in American society. Although advertising has certainly proliferated enormously, other mechanisms for controlling consumers can be identified. The new means of consumption are the most important of these controls. Their development after World War II supplemented the efforts, begun in the 1920s in advertising, to control consumers. People are lured to the cathedrals of consumption by the fantasies they promise to fulfill and then kept there by a variety of rewards and constraints. The idea is to keep people at the business of consumption. This is nowhere clearer than in the case of credit cards, which lure people into consumption by easy credit and then entice them into still further consumption by offers of "payment holidays," new cards, and increased credit limits. The beauty of all of this, at least from the point of view of those who profit from the existing system, is that people are kept in the workplace and on the job by the need to pay the monthly minimums on their credit card accounts and, more generally, to support their consumption habits.

The Economy

There are, of course, many other factors involved in the growth of the new means of consumption. The booming economy—especially the dramatic expansion in the 1990s, as reflected in the startling upturn in the stock market and a minuscule unemployment rate—has left large numbers of people with unprecedented amounts of disposable income. For such people, consumption, especially shopping, has become a major form of recreation. Increasingly, many people have the time to spend their large incomes. For example, many are retiring earlier even as their life expectancy is increasing. The result is many years of the life cycle in which the focus, to a large extent, is on consumption. And because of the booming economy, an increasing number of retirees have the wherewithal to be active consumers.

The growth of the new means of consumption also has been fueled by the increasing reality that corporations, including those that own the new means of consumption, are driven by the stock market in which it is not good enough to maintain a high level of profitability; profits must show a substantial increase from one year (or even quarter) to the next. This creates a continually expanding need to lure people into the marketplace more frequently and more actively and to keep them there longer. Old customers need to be retained and new customers recruited. The new means of

consumption offer more new goods and services in increasingly fantastic settings, an irresistible combination to many people. The new means of consumption both lure more people out of their homes to consume *and* allow them to consume more even while they are at home. The fantastic settings represent key sites where more of people's resources are extracted *and* more of their future income is captured as credit card or other consumer debt.

There is a confluence of interests: People want, or at least are led to think that they want, all of those goods and services. The new means of consumption require consumers to want those things and in increasing quantities. The same is true of manufacturers. Bankers and the executives of credit card companies also have vested interests in increased consumption because that means rising debt and growing income from servicing that debt. . . .

There is little question that the United States is increasingly characterized by what now could be termed *hyperconsumption*,[1] and that most Americans are increasingly obsessed by consumption.[2] According to Juliet B. Schor, Americans spend three or four times as much time shopping as Western Europeans. Of the total land area of the United States, about 4 billion square feet is devoted to shopping centers, which works out to sixteen square feet of shopping area per capita. And most important, "The average American is consuming, in total, more than twice as much as he or she did forty years ago."[3] On a per capita basis, Americans are apt to consume more of virtually everything than people in most, if not all, other nations of the world. Examples include television sets, VCRs, computers, microwave ovens, automobiles and the energy needed to keep them running. In the realm of services, Americans are the world leaders in the consumption of medical, psychiatric, legal, and accounting services. It is not just that they consume more of everything, but more varieties of most things are available to, and used by, American consumers than those of most other nations. To take just one example, the number of toys on the shelves of Toys 'R Us often stuns visitors to the United States. (As we will see, Americans are eager to see the rest of the world join them in hyperconsumption.)

At its broadest level, hyperconsumption[4] is a highly democratic form of consumption involving the vast majority of the population. The amount of money available to individuals for consumption varies enormously, but virtually everyone today is a consumer to some degree. The poor have fewer resources than the rich, most ethnic and racial minority groups have much less to spend than members of the majority, children fewer means than adults, and so on, but all are enmeshed in the consumer culture. Even those who live on the streets survive off the discards and charity of that wildly affluent culture.[5] This is not to deny the immense impact of factors such as race, class, gender, and so forth on consumption . . . but it is virtually impossible for anyone in the United States today to avoid being deeply involved in, or at least touched by, the culture of consumption.

Those with lots of resources may buy high-priced originals, and those with modest means may buy inexpensive imitations, but all are buying. Beyond the purchase of luxury goods (or cheap simulations of them), everyone must consume the basics (food, for example) needed to survive, although here, too, there is likely to be great variation in the prices paid for, and the quality of, the goods obtained. America is characterized by mass consumption because all but a handful of the population is actively involved in one way or another as consumers. The mass character of consumption also means that the occupations of large numbers of people are implicated in the culture of consumption. Many millions of people work in fast food restaurants, shopping malls, superstores, gambling casinos, cruise ships, and the like.[6]

There is yet another sense that mass consumption is characteristic of American society: People are apt to spend most, if not all, of their available resources on consumer goods and services. In fact, in many cases it is no longer enough to spend all available resources, one is enticed to go deeply and increasingly into debt.[7] Various data support this contention. For example, the rate of personal savings as a percentage of disposable income dropped from 6.2 percent in 1992 to 3.8 percent in 1997.[8] Only slightly more than half of all American households indicated in 1995 that they had any savings at all. Those in the world's other advanced economies manage to save two to three times what Americans save.[9] Conversely, Americans are far more likely to be in debt, and the average level of indebtedness is much greater. Huge and ever-increasing sums of money are owed on home mortgages, car loans, and credit card balances.[10] Many find themselves unable to repay their debts as reflected, for example, in the increases in credit card delinquencies and bankruptcies.[11]

Within a few decades, the United States has gone from a society that emphasized personal savings to one that focuses on debt. Banks have, to a large degree, shifted from the business of inducing people to save to luring them into debt. In 1997 Americans received 3.1 *billion* pieces of mail imploring them to sign up for a credit card.[12] The profits from servicing debt, especially credit card debt, are much higher than those derived from savings. Easy and extensive credit has played a key role in making America's modern mass consumer society possible and that, especially in the form of credit cards, is being exported to many parts of the world. . . .

Changing the Way Others Consume

The new means of consumption are being rapidly and aggressively exported. However, in many places around the world speed, efficiency, a do-it-yourself mentality and limited interaction are devalued. Those in other nations are led to consume more and more like Americans. In many countries this poses a profound threat to indigenous culture. At the minimum, it poses the danger of a global standardization and homogenization as more people around the world consume in the primarily American new means of consumption and obtain goods in much the same way Americans do. It also involves increased consumption around the world and threats derived from that to global resources, the environment, and so on.

Although we will focus on the exportation of the new American means of consumption to the rest of the world, it goes without saying that there is a simultaneous exportation of American-style products and the lifestyle they bring with them. Even if they are manufactured elsewhere, these products (Nike® shoes is a good example) reflect American culture and have American logos. Mattel® is scheduled to introduce in Japan a line of clothing fashioned after the attire of its iconic Barbie doll. The company is relying on the fact that the Barbie doll itself is already beloved in Japan. Said one young Japanese woman: "I'm incredibly happy that the Barbie brand is coming . . . I will buy some for sure."[13]

How America consumes is likely to have a profound impact (these days quite quickly) on most other developed nations. This is the case in part because American-based corporations are intent on, and aggressive about, exporting American consumer goods and the American way of consuming them. In most of the world's developed nations (and in many less developed ones)

potential customers are bombarded by American products and advertisements. (I see this process as better described by the term *Americanization* than *globalization*;[14] the latter would indicate more of a multidirectional relationship among many nations.[15]) Many of those being assailed in these ways are far from hostile to the blitz. Indeed, all indications are, at least in the realm of consumption, that the days of the "ugly American" are long past. Judging by their popularity and proliferation, virtually every new incursion of American goods and services and the American way of consumption appears quite welcome.[16]

In fact, many people from around the world travel to the United States to shop in the new means of consumption and to purchase American goods:

> Strolling past the Saks Off Fifth outlet, Dress Barn and a camera store in the vast corridors of the Potomac Mills discount mall in Dale City, Va., three college students from France smiled with anticipation as they spotted a shop that sold athletic wear.
>
> When they emerged with their purchases, including the New York Yankees baseball caps that were high on their list, one student . . . said, "Now that we've seen the tourist sights, we can go home."[17]

It is little wonder that the American cathedrals of consumption are so eager to export the American way of consuming.

The current worldwide acceptance and popularity of American cathedrals of consumption stands in stark contrast to, for example, the situation in the 1940s, when a major commotion took place in France over the threat posed by the exportation of Coca-Cola® to the wine-loving French cafe culture. Quite a bit of heat was generated over what came to be known as "Coca-colonization."[18] In the end, Coca-Cola gained a foothold in France that led neither to the disappearance of that nation's beloved cafes nor the wines consumed in them and virtually everywhere else in France, but the initial reaction was telling.

Although much of the world now seems enamored of the American way of consuming, that is not to say that controversy has completely disappeared. For example, a similar, albeit less heated, version of the "Coca-colonization" debate occurred over the opening of Euro Disney outside Paris. As a result of adverse publicity stemming from the "McLibel" trial in London,[19] McDonald's has become a prime target of a number of health, environmental, and other groups.[20] There have also been periodic objections to the opening of McDonald's in, for example, the older parts of the world's great cities.[21] Although such protests continue to occur, in the main they are quite muted and are overwhelmed by the evidence of wide-scale acceptance of, indeed excitement over, American consumer exports.

Although the aggressive exporting of American consumer culture is one factor in its worldwide acceptance, another key is the absence, with the fall of Communism, of any viable worldwide alternative to the American model. Whatever its problems in practice, Communism served as an alternative world–historical model around which people could rally against American capitalism and its model of consumption.[22] Today, all that remains for those opposed to these things is opposition based on local considerations. Such local forms of resistance to the American mode of consumption are apt to continue in some locations, but they are not likely to offer a serious impediment.

Much of the worldwide opposition to American economic practices has focused on the exportation of American production theories and methods. Although the exportation of the American mode of production certainly continues, it is increasingly being supplanted in importance by the exportation of the American way of consuming. This parallels a similar shift within the United States.

A Growing International Presence

There is much data to support the idea that the new means of consumption are a growing international presence. Take the case of McDonald's. In 1991, a little more than a quarter of its restaurants were outside the United States; by 1996, more than 40 percent of its sites were overseas. In 1991, McDonald's restaurants were found in 59 nations; by 1996, they were in 101 nations. The percentage of overseas outlets will continue to grow (about 80 percent of new restaurants in 1997 were built outside the United States). System-wide sales increased from $12.4 billion in 1986 to $31.8 billion in 1996. Less than a third of system-wide sales came from outside the United States in 1986, but in 1996 that proportion had grown to nearly one-half, with sales in the United States (approximately $16 billion) exceeding international sales by less than 1 billion dollars.[23] One observer offered a broader perspective on the exportation of the American means of consumption:

> Tool around Australia: the regional malls sprouting along its highways look more than a bit familiar. Walk Brazil's streets: a sign says Chocolate, but the store feels like Ann Taylor, the R. L. Polo store mimics Ralph Lauren and Bill Brothers bears a strong resemblance to Brooks Brothers. Tour Bangkok: the Big C Superstores are the image of Wal-Marts.[24]

Examples of the influence of the American means of consumption on other cultures are legion:

- Canada has been invaded by superstores and almost all other new means of consumption. Said a consultant, "We haven't seen the end of the U.S. invasion."[25]

- Israel has now acquired a McDonald's, but it also has Domino's and Kenny Rogers' Roasters®. Then there is the Gap, Tower Records®, Hard Rock Cafe, and most recently Planet Hollywood.[26]

- Among many other American new means of consumption, home shopping TV has recently come to Russia.[27]

- A second American-style shopping center (the first had opened three weeks earlier), Polus Center, opened in Budapest, Hungary, in late 1996. Lines were long and people waited half an hour to enter the stores. Five percent of the city's population, 100,000 people, showed up for the mall's first weekend. The mall includes 100 stores, a multiplex movie theater, a skating rink, and nineteen bars and restaurants. The anchor of the mall is a huge "hypermarket" combining a supermarket and a discount center. Similar malls are under construction throughout central and eastern Europe—Czech Republic, Poland, Slovakia, Romania, Ukraine, and Croatia. Said a teenager working in his family's clothing store in the Polus Center, "Finally, we have something really Western in this boring country."[28]

- Wal-Mart and Sam's Club arrived in China in late 1996, and several other superstores are there as well, although these stores have done little more than establish a beachhead. They must adapt to a variety of differences between China and the United States. For example, the Chinese typically live in small apartments, which "means that huge American-sized packages and cases are out; smaller, compact sizes are in."[29] Customers usually walk or bike to the store, which limits what they can carry home with them.

- Japan is seen as ripe for American-style shopping malls.[30] The largest of the current malls is small by American standards (seventy-nine mainly small shops and thirteen restaurants). One mall developer predicts that there will be fifty to sixty malls in Japan within the next two decades. Because of high prices at home, the Japanese spend large sums of money outside the country. This is seen as an indication that the Japanese consumer is sensitive to price and would be attracted to American-style innovations such as malls and discount stores.[31]

- In Hanoi, Vietnam, "Baskin-Robbins is here and expanding. TGI Friday and Kentucky Fried Chicken are scheduled to open their first outlets in Ho Chi Minh City next year. And McDonald's is reportedly on the way."[32] In the former Saigon, now Ho Chi Minh City, there is the Saigon Superbowl with its thirty-two-lane bowling alley, huge video arcade, eight-table billiard parlor, food courts featuring burgers and fries, twenty-plus store shopping mall featuring Baskin-Robbins® ice cream, as well as children and elders riding "the escalator over and over, amazed at the contraption."[33] The mall came to Ho Chi Minh City even before McDonald's, which opened in 1998.

- In Argentina and Brazil, a half-dozen water parks and amusement parks are under construction at a cost of about $1.5 billion. Large cities are being surrounded by shopping malls complete with multiplex movie theaters and game centers of various types. Theme restaurants such as Planet Hollywood are expanding, as are indigenous varieties such as Rock in Rio Cafe®. Said one developer, "Entertainment has graduated from a secondary theme to a central one in Latin America . . . We've learned you can make money from showing people a good time."[34] These developers are drawing on American models and American expertise.

- For their part, American developers are eager for new Latin American markets. Already, a major amusement park is within a two-and-a-half hour drive of *every* major American city. There is fear of a shakeout in the overdeveloped theme-restaurant market and similar problems confront other types of entertainment centers, and hence the attraction of the underserved Latin American market.[35]

- In Paris, "The Champs-Élysées is now an American mall, complete with Disney Store and Planet Hollywood."[36] And that grand boulevard has long had McDonald's and Burger King. More shocking is what has happened to Saint Germain des Prés. Once a quaint neighborhood known for its book shops and cafes, it is now being invaded by international shops such as Louis Vuitton, Georgio Armani, Dior, and Cartier. "It didn't matter that these companies were French (or Italian), they're still mega-corporations that are proud to have the same exact product on shopping streets in Hong Kong, Beverly Hills, Monte Carlo, Tokyo, London, New York, Bal Harbour and the other side of the Seine."[37] They are joining other less elegant chains such as Benetton®, Body Shop®, and the Gap, which are already there. Although locals are generally opposed to the luxury shops, they quietly whisper that, "It's better than McDonald's."[38]

- England already looks increasingly like the United States, at least as far as its means of consumption are concerned:

  West Thurrock is probably the greatest bastion of American shopping culture in Great Britain.

  There are familiar names, now recognizable to most Brits, such as Burger King and Toys 'R Us. There's a giant American-style supermarket.

And farther along the service road is something more unusual for Britain: a gargantuan, thoroughly American mall called Lakeside Shopping Centre, which offers a range of department stores, scores of smaller shops, parking for 12,000 cars, and the requisite food court with quick-service cuisine from many lands.

But it is the latest American-bred addition to this shopping tract that has brought national attention to modest West Thurrock: "Costco . . . arrived here late last year, opening the first warehouse membership club in Britain amid an onslaught of media fanfare."[39]

Not satisfied, a large factory outlet developer is looking into various sites in England, largely because its American tenants such as Nike and the Gap see European expansion as key to their continued growth.[40] For their part, the English are attracted to the American discounters for a very good reason—the high cost of American products in England.[41]

Many in other parts of the world not only are accepting of the new means of consumption but are producing their own variants that they are eager to export to the United States. For example, in Latin America, the Rock in Rio Cafe has clearly taken a lead from American theme restaurants with its "entry by monorail, walls with projected imagery that changes the decor, and an indoor fireworks show every night."[42] Its developer eventually plans to turn the tables and export his theme restaurant to the United States: "Why import something American when we can do it better ourselves. . . . After all, you can export as much as you import in today's world."[43]

There was a time when American production was the envy of the world, and others were eager to emulate its structures and methods. Today, it is more America's new means of consumption that virtually every nation around the world covets. Although there are certainly foreign precursors of many of these means, there is something quintessentially American about McDonald's, Disney, Wal-Mart, and the Flamingo Hotel, and also about their respective founders Ray Kroc, Walt Disney, Sam Walton, and Bugsy Siegel.

However, although the largely American cathedrals of consumption have made in-roads in many parts of the world, it is important to remember that other nations retain means of consumption that are distinctly their own. Tokyo has fast food restaurants, large discount stores, and department stores, but it also has a profusion of small shops and innumerable automatic vending machines "that dispense not only soft drinks and cigarettes, but also beer and liquor, socks, ties, women's stockings, coffee, hot noodles, magazines and . . . unbelievably, flowers and engagement rings."[44]

Critics of the Trend

It is abundantly clear that many welcome the invasion of the largely American new means of consumption, but there are critics of this trend and especially its homogenizing impact:

> This view that the culture of consumerism is a type of generic culture . . . is buttressed by the spread of huge shopping centers. Remarkably alike in design and in content, these free-market temples sell the same clothes (Levis, Nike), serve the same food (Pizza Hut, McDonald's, Taco Bell) and show the same movies. From Santiago to Rio de Janeiro, Bogota and Mexico City, these centers in effect allow people to travel without leaving home and to feel at home even when traveling.[45]

The area around Kruger National Park in South Africa has a casino linked to a shopping mall. Considerable attention is being devoted to developing this area to attract more tourists, but the head of the tourist agency is obviously aware of the dangers of American-style development:

> The most successful or enduring cultural happenings internationally are not staged Disney-type events, with tourists as a spectator audience and with locals as actors. . . . They are living festivals such as the running of the bulls in Pamplona, the Carnival in Rio and Easter in Jerusalem . . .
>
> What better way . . . than to assist in the creation of ways for tourists to actually engage with living cultures by bringing travellers into our townships, villages and kraals. Why give them Disney when you can give them authentic Africa?[46]

There is no question that this exportation of the American means of consumption to the rest of the world involves a process of Americanization. There is a danger of backlash here, but McDonald's among others has sought to be "glocal"—that is, integrate the global with the local.[47] (This is also true of the Disney parks in Tokyo and outside Paris.[48]) McDonald's does this by using many local owners and by adapting its products to each local environment.[49] A good example is the McDonald's in Delhi, India. Given the Indian deification of the cow, this McDonald's sells the "Maharaja Mac" made from 100 percent mutton. Also on the menu because of the large number of vegetarians in India are "Vegetable McNuggets." Nonetheless, McDonald's has had opposition, especially from animal rights activists, one of whom said, "I am against McDonald's because they are the chief killers of cows in the world. . . . We don't need cow killers in India."[50]

In sum, there has been an explosion of the largely American new means of consumption not only in the United States, but in many other parts of the world. They have brought with them many undoubted benefits such as lower prices and a cornucopia of consumer goods unheard of in human history. They have also brought a series of potential drawbacks not the least of which is the fact that people throughout the United States, and increasingly throughout the rest of the world, have become voracious consumers.

NOTES

1. Rosalind Williams. *Dream Worlds: Mass Consumption in Late Nineteenth-Century France.* Berkeley: University of California Press, 1982.
2. Americans are not the only ones obsessed with consumption. For a discussion of the Japanese case, see John Clammer. *Contemporary Urban Japan: A Sociology of Consumption.* Oxford: Blackwell, 1997.
3. Juliet B. Schor. *The Overworked American: The Unexpected Decline of Leisure.* New York: Basic Books, 1991, p. 109.
4 Clammer also uses the term *hyperconsumption* to describe contemporary Japanese consumption; see John Clammer. *Contemporary Urban Japan: A Sociology of Consumption.* Oxford: Routledge, 1997, p. 54.
5. Stephen E. Lankenau. *Native Sons: A Social Exploration of Panhandling,* Doctoral Dissertation, College Park, MD, 1997.
6. Given this focus on consumption, I have opted not to discuss the situation confronting the millions of people who work in or on behalf of the cathedrals of consumption. This is an important issue, worthy of a book of its own.
7. Robert Manning and Brett Williams. *Credit Card Nation: America's Dangerous Addiction to Consumer Debt.* New York: Basic Books, 1996.
8. Robert J. Samuelson. "Shades of the 1920s?" *Washington Post,* April 22, 1998, p. A23.
9. Juliet B. Schor. *The Overspent American: Upscaling, Downshifting, and the New Consumer.* New York: Basic Books, 1998, p. 20.
10. George Ritzer. *Expressing America: A Critique of the Global Credit Card Society.* Thousand Oaks, CA: Pine Forge Press, 1995.
11. The Japanese have managed to engage in hyperconsumption while remaining largely opposed to debt and reliant on a cash economy. See John Clammer. *Contemporary Urban Japan: A Sociology of Consumption.* Oxford: Routledge, 1997.
12. Jacob N. Schlesinger. "Are Lenders Letting Optimism Go Too Far?" *Wall Street Journal,* April 20, 1998, p. A1.
13. Kevin Sullivan. "Barbie Doll: Japan's New Look." *Washington Post,* December 16, 1996, p. A20.
14. George Ritzer. *The McDonaldization Thesis: Explorations and Extensions.* London: Sage, 1998.
15. I am taking a position that is opposed by most globalization theorists as well as Featherstone, who argues against this idea and who sees a shift away from the United States in particular and the West in general. See Mike Featherstone. *Consumer Culture and Postmodernism.* London: Sage, 1991, pp. 127, 142.
16. However, there are limits to this, as Mars Inc. candy makers discovered in Russia, where its America-oriented ads, as well as a general return to "Russianness," led to a backlash and renewed interest in "real Russian chocolate." See Christian Caryl. "We Will Bury You . . . with a Snickers Bar." *U.S. News and World Report,* January 26, 1998, pp. 50, 52; see also Daniel Williams. "Advertisers Cash in on Things Russian." *Washington Post,* June 12, 1998, p. A16.
17. Edwin McDowell. "Bazaar; Megamalls; Dropping in to Shop." *The Orange County Register,* August 4, 1996, p. D4.
18. Richard F. Kuisel. *Seducing the French: The Dilemma of Americanization.* Berkeley: University of California Press, 1993.
19. John Vidal. *Counter Culture vs. Burger Culture.* London: Macmillan, 1997.
20. McDonald's sued two members of Greenpeace for passing out leaflets critical of the company. The trial ran for more than two years, becoming the longest running trial in the history of Great Britain. The judge's decision in mid-1997 was generally seen as a partial and pyrrhic victory for McDonald's. The case became the rallying cry for a large number of individuals and groups critical of McDonald's on a wide variety of grounds.
21. Jane Perlez. "A McDonald's? Not in Their Medieval Square." *New York Times,* May 23, 1994, p. A4.

22. Of course, with capitalism now triumphant throughout virtually the entire world, the conditions (e.g., hyperexploitation) may be being put into place to allow for the reemergence of a radical alternative to capitalism.

23. McDonald's Corp. *The Annual: McDonald's Corporation Annual Report.* Chicago: Author, 1996.

24. Judith H. Dobrzynski. "The American Way." *New York Times,* April 6, 1997, section 6, p. 79ff.

25. Jim Fox. "Category Killers Mount Major Canadian Invasion; US Retailers in Canada." *Discount Store News,* vol. 34, July 17, 1995, p. 44ff.

26. David Horovitz. "Big Macs Challenge the Cuisine of the Kibbutz." *The Irish Times,* July 21, 1995, p. 8.

27. Michael Freeman. "Cubicov Zirconiumich: US-Produced Russian Home Shopping Show 'TV Style'." *Mediaweek,* vol. 5, June 5, 1995, p. 12ff.

28. Robert Muraskin. "Hungary to Shop, American Style." *Washington Post,* November 29, 1996, p. B12.

29. Keith B. Richburg. "Attention, Shenzen Shoppers!" *Washington Post,* February 12, 1997, p. C14.

30. As well as theme parks: In addition to DisneySea now under construction, Universal Studios will build a new park in Western Japan. See Mary Jordan. "Universal Studios to Build a Theme Park in Japan." *Washington Post,* May 10, 1998, p. A26.

31. Sandra Sugawara. "D.C. Developer Sounds the Call of the Supermall for Japan." *Washington Post-Real Estate,* August 3, 1996, pp. E1, E4.

32. Mai Hoang. "The Americanization of Vietnam." *Washington Post,* May 11, 1997, p. A25.

33. Kevin Sullivan. "Saigon Goes to the Superbowl: American-Style Mall Draws Young, Newly Affluent Vietnamese." *Washington Post,* June 6, 1997, p. A29.

34. Jonathan Friedland. "Can Yanks Export Good Times to Latins?" *Wall Street Journal,* March 6, 1997, p. A11.

35. Jonathan Friedland. "Can Yanks Export Good Times to Latins?" *Wall Street Journal,* March 6, 1997, p. A11.

36. Dana Thomas. "La Mall Epoque." *Washington Post,* January 3, 1997, p. D6.

37. Dana Thomas. "La Mall Epoque." *Washington Post,* January 3, 1997, p. D6.

38. Dana Thomas. "La Mall Epoque." *Washington Post,* January 3, 1997, p. D6.

39. Jeff Kaye. "Invasion of the Discounters: American-Style Bargain Shopping Comes to the United Kingdom." *Los Angeles Times,* May 8, 1994, p. D1ff.

40. Peter Jones. "Factory Outlet Shopping Centres and Planning Issues." *International Journal of Retail & Distribution Management,* vol. 23, January 1995, p. 12ff.

41. Jeff Kaye. "Invasion of the Discounters: American-Style Bargain Shopping Comes to the United Kingdom." *Los Angeles Times,* May 8, 1994, p. D1ff.

42. Jonathan Friedland. "Can Yanks Export Good Times to Latins?" *Wall Street Journal,* March 6, 1997, p. A11.

43. Jonathan Friedland. "Can Yanks Export Good Times to Latins?" *Wall Street Journal,* March 6, 1997, p. A11.

44. John Clammer. *Contemporary Urban Japan: A Sociology of Consumption.* Oxford: Routledge 1997, p. 72.

45. Gabriel Escobar and Anne Swardson. "From Language to Literature, a New Guiding Lite." *Washington Post,* September 5, 1995, p. A1ff.

46. Justin Arenstein. "Tourism Boom Expected for Mpumalanga." *Africa News,* May 27, 1997.

47. James L. Watson (ed.). *Golden Arches East: McDonald's in East Asia.* Stanford, CA: Stanford University Press, 1997.

48. Mary Yoko Branne. "'Bwana Mickey': Constructing Cultural Consumption at Tokyo Disneyland," in Joseph Tobin (ed.). *Remade in Japan: Everyday Life and Consumer Taste in a Changing Society.* New Haven: Yale University Press, 1992, pp. 216–234; John Van Maanen. "Displacing Disney: Some Notes on the Flow of Culture." *Qualitative Sociology 15* (1992):5–35.

49. Thomas L. Friedman. "Big Mac II." *New York Times,* December 11, 1996, p. A21.

50. Kenneth J. Cooper. "It's Lamb Burger, Not Hamburger, at Beefless McDonald's in New Delhi." *Washington Post,* November 4, 1996, p. A14.

QUESTIONS FOR DISCUSSION

1. What are the consequences of "hyperconsumerism" for U.S. citizens?

(continued)

(continued)
2. What are the effects of "exporting American goods and the American way of consuming them" to other nations? Are there cultural, as well as economic, impacts on people in these countries?

3. Many critics believe that the increased exportation of American products and corporations, such as Coca-Cola, McDonald's, and Toys 'R Us, represents a form of cultural imperialism. Do you agree with this perspective?

8
_____

CORPORATE WELFARE

DONALD L. BARLETT • JAMES B. STEELE

How would you like to pay only a quarter of the real estate taxes you owe on your home? And buy everything for the next 10 years without spending a single penny in sales tax? Keep a chunk of your paycheck free of income taxes? Have the city in which you live lend you money at rates cheaper than any bank charges? Then have the same city install free water and sewer lines to your house, offer you a perpetual discount on utility bills—and top it all off by landscaping your front yard at no charge?

Fat chance. You can't get any of that, of course. But if you live almost anywhere in America, all around you are taxpayers getting deals like this. These taxpayers are called corporations, and their deals are usually trumpeted as "economic development" or "public-private partnerships." But a better name is corporate welfare. It's a game in which governments large and small subsidize corporations large and small, usually at

the expense of another state or town and almost always at the expense of individual and other corporate taxpayers.

Two years after Congress reduced welfare for individuals and families, this other kind of welfare continues to expand, penetrating every corner of the American economy. It has turned politicians into bribery specialists, and smart business people into con artists. And most surprising of all, it has rarely created any new jobs.

While corporate welfare has attracted critics from both the left and the right, there is no uniform definition. By [our] definition, it is this: any action by local, state or federal government that gives a corporation or an entire industry a benefit not offered to others. It can be an outright subsidy, a grant, real estate, a low-interest loan or a government service. It can also be a tax break—a credit, exemption, deferral or deduction, or a tax rate lower than the one others pay.

The rationale to curtail traditional welfare programs, such as Aid to Families with Dependent Children and food stamps, and to impose a lifetime limit on the amount of aid received, was compelling: the old system didn't work. It was unfair, destroyed incentive, perpetuated dependence and distorted the economy. An 18-month . . . investigation has found that the same indictment, almost to the word, applies to corporate welfare. In some ways, it represents pork-barrel legislation of the worst order. The difference, of course, is that instead of rewarding the poor, it rewards the powerful.

And it rewards them handsomely. The federal government alone shells out $125 billion a year in corporate welfare, this in the midst of one of the more robust economic periods in the nation's history. Indeed, thus far in the 1990s, corporate profits have totaled $45 trillion—a sum equal to the cumulative paychecks of 50 million working Americans who earned less than $25,000 a year, for those eight years.

That makes the federal government America's biggest sugar daddy, dispensing a range of giveaways from tax abatements to price supports for sugar itself. Companies get government money to advertise their products; to help build new plants, offices and stores; and to train their workers. They sell their goods to foreign buyers that make the acquisitions with tax dollars supplied by the U.S. government; engage in foreign transactions that are insured by the government; and are excused from paying a portion of their income tax if they sell products overseas. They pocket lucrative government contracts to carry out ordinary business operations, and government grants to conduct research that will improve their profit margins. They are extended partial tax immunity if they locate in certain geographical areas, and they may write off as business expenses some of the perks enjoyed by their top executives.

The justification for much of this welfare is that the U.S. government is creating jobs. Over the past six years, Congress appropriated $5 billion to run the Export-Import Bank of the United States, which subsidizes companies that sell goods abroad. James A. Harmon, president and chairman, puts it this way: "American workers . . . have higher-quality, better-paying jobs, thanks to Exim-bank's financing." But the numbers at the bank's five biggest beneficiaries—AT&T, Bechtel, Boeing, General Electric and McDonnell Douglas (now a part of Boeing)—tell another story. At these companies, which have accounted for about 40% of all loans, grants and long-term guarantees in this decade, overall employment has fallen 38%, as more than a third of a million jobs have disappeared.

The picture is much the same at the state and local level, where a different kind of feeding frenzy is taking place. Politicians stumble over one another in the rush to arrange special deals for select corporations, fueling a growing economic war among the states. The result is that states keep throwing money at companies that in many cases are not serious about moving anyway. The companies are certainly not reluctant to take the money, though, which is available if they simply utter the word relocation. And why not? Corporate executives, after all, have a fiduciary duty to squeeze every dollar they can from every locality waving blandishments in their face.

State and local governments now give corporations money to move from one city to another—even from one building to another—and tax credits for hiring new employees. They supply funds to train workers or pay part of their wages while they are in training, and provide scientific and engineering assistance to solve workplace technical problems. They repave existing roads and build new ones. They lend money at bargain-basement interest rates to erect plants or buy equipment. They excuse corporations from paying sales and property taxes and relieve them from taxes on investment income.

There are no reasonably accurate estimates on the amount of money states shovel out. That's because few want you to know.

Some say they maintain no records. Some say they don't know where the files are. Some say the information is not public. All that's certain is that the figure is in the many billions of dollars each year—and it is growing, when measured against the subsidy per job.

In 1989 Illinois gave $240 million in economic incentives to Sears, Roebuck & Co. to keep its corporate headquarters and 5,400 workers in the state by moving from Chicago to suburban Hoffman Estates. That amounted to a subsidy of $44,000 for each job.

In 1991 Indiana gave $451 million in economic incentives to United Airlines to build an aircraft-maintenance facility that would employ as many as 6,300 people. Subsidy: $72,000 for each job.

In 1993 Alabama gave $253 million in economic incentives to Mercedes-Benz to build an automobile-assembly plant near Tuscaloosa and employ 1,500 workers. Subsidy: $169,000 for each job.

And in 1997 Pennsylvania gave $307 million in economic incentives to Kvaerner ASA, a Norwegian global engineering and construction company, to open a shipyard at the former Philadelphia Naval Shipyard and employ 950 people. Subsidy: $323,000 for each job.

This kind of arithmetic seldom adds up. Let's say the Philadelphia job pays $50,000. And each new worker pays $6,700 in local and state taxes. That means it will take nearly a half-century of tax collections from each individual to earn back the money granted to create his or her job. And that assumes all 950 workers will be recruited from outside Philadelphia and will relocate in the city, rather than move from existing jobs within the city, where they are already paying taxes.

All this is in service of a system that may produce jobs in one city or state, thus fostering the illusion of an uptick in employment. But it does not create more jobs in the nation as a whole. Market forces do that, and that's why 10 million jobs have been created since 1990. But most of those jobs have been created by small- and medium-size companies, from high-tech startups to franchised cleaning services. Fortune 500 companies, on the other hand, have erased more jobs than they have created this past decade, and yet they are the biggest beneficiaries of corporate welfare.

To be sure, some economic incentives are handed out for a seemingly worthwhile public purpose. The tax breaks that companies receive to locate in inner cities come to mind. Without them, companies might not invest in those neighborhoods. However well intended, these subsidies rarely produce lasting results. They may provide short-term jobs but not long-term employment. And in the end, the costs outweigh any benefits.

And what are those costs? The equivalent of nearly two weekly paychecks from every working man and woman in America—extra money that would stay in their pockets if it didn't go to support some business venture or another.

If corporate welfare is an unproductive end game, why does it keep growing in a period of intensive government cost cutting? For starters, it has good p.r. and an army of bureaucrats working to expand it. A corporate-welfare bureaucracy of an estimated 11,000 organizations and agencies has grown up, with access to city halls, statehouses, the Capitol and the White House. They conduct seminars, conferences and training sessions. They have their own trade associations. They publish their own journals and newsletters. They create attractive websites on the Internet. And they never call it "welfare." They call it "economic incentives" or "empowerment zones" or "enterprise zones."

Whatever the name, the result is the same. Some companies receive public services at reduced rates, while all others pay the full cost. Some companies are excused from paying all or a portion of their taxes due, while all others must pay the full amount imposed by law. Some companies receive grants, low-interest loans and other subsidies, while all others must fend for themselves.

In the end, that's corporate welfare's greatest flaw. It's unfair. One role of government is to help ensure a level playing field for people and businesses. Corporate welfare does just the opposite. It tilts the playing field in favor of the largest or the most politically influential or most aggressive businesses. In the next story, and those that follow in the coming weeks, you will meet the beneficiaries of corporate welfare—and the people who pay for it.

States at War

Arkansas
Ever Try to Drink a Potato Chip?

The water in Evansville, Ark., stinks—literally.

The town sits smack atop a geological formation where sulfur, natural gas and other petroleum products mingle with the groundwater. The result is a nasty mix that is unusable to residents. Many of the town's wells are also contaminated with potentially deadly *E. coli* pollutants. So a commodity most Americans take for granted simply does not exist in Evansville. "My five-year-old daughter doesn't know what it's like to get water out of a faucet," says resident Helen Martin. For the past five years, 200 families in this hamlet in the northwestern part of the state have sought $750,000 from the Arkansas Economic Development Commission for a new water system. Sorry, comes the reply, there is no money in the budget.

City water in Jonesboro, Ark., doesn't stink. In fact, even wastewater flowing out

of the big, new Frito-Lay plant there runs through an expanded treatment facility in order to minimize environmental problems. That expansion was part of a multimillion-dollar incentive package the AEDC gave Frito-Lay to lure the company to Jonesboro. Frito-Lay is not exactly needy. It is a profitable subsidiary of PepsiCo Inc., the giant soft-drink and snack-food company, that had sales of $20.9 billion in 1997.

Evansville is one of the minor casualties in the war among the states over jobs. Money is lavished on would-be employers even at the expense of some citizens' basic needs. But in the minds of state politicians and economic developers, this is a small price to pay. From a purely economic point of view, they are dead wrong. But economics and politics are seldom a rational mix.

Jonesboro got its plant after the community and state agreed to enlarge the sewage-treatment facility and provide an array of other economic incentives. Exactly how much aid was pumped into Frito-Lay to build the plant is not easy to find out. A Frito-Lay representative said the information was "proprietary." An AEDC representative, Michaela Johnson, was equally secretive, saying, "That whole project's confidential. We can't divulge that."

Based on reports published when Jonesboro was recruiting Frito-Lay, and on more recent information obtained from other sources, [we] estimate the value of the Frito-Lay aid package at more than $10 million. And that is in addition to $104.7 million in industrial-development revenue bonds issued by the city of Jonesboro to build and equip the potato-chip plant. The other incentives include the 140-acre plant site, a rail spur, road improvements, a construction grant, tax credits for new employees and a 20% discount on sewer bills for the next 15 years. That sewage-treatment plant, by the way, cost $7 million and is large enough to accommodate a second city the size of

Jonesboro (pop. 50,000). So for each of the 165 workers at the plant, the government has invested $61,000—which is a lot of chips.

Lynn Markley, a spokeswoman for Frito-Lay, says the company selects the general region where it wants to locate a new plant. It then prepares a sort of shopping list of requirements for the facility and contacts states about incentives.

"When we need to . . . build a plant, say, in Jonesboro, [we] look at a 150-mile radius to the center of the market; says Markley. "We knew we needed a plant in the Tennessee-Arkansas-Missouri area. So with very detailed information, we contacted those states and gave them very specific details on what we needed . . . [And] based on that, the states compete."

Meanwhile, in Evansville the campaign for clean water goes on, and the citizens cope as best they can. Says Janie Watkins who along with her husband runs the town's only grocery store: "If we take a bath, we don't wash clothes. If we wash clothes, you can't take a bath. Most people get a bath every day. We can't . . . You get [a bath] every two days or three days, you're lucky."

Christina Seward, mother of three small children, says her boys love to drink water "But I don't have to tell them not to drink this water," she says. "The taste, the dirt—you wouldn't want to drink it. You put water in a glass, and you can see the dirt settle to the bottom. We don't know what's in it—we just know it's not safe."

Indeed, the Sewards' well was tested by the Arkansas Department of Health in 1996 and found to be contaminated with particles of fecal matter "too numerous to count." The Sewards use well water only to wash clothes, but not light-colored articles. The water turns "white things yellow," says Seward.

In order to drink, cook, bathe and wash, residents haul bottled water from nearby towns or load up on barrels from natural springs in the hills above Evansville. Since their campaign for water began, residents have appealed repeatedly to the state to provide a share of the $1.5 million project. "We've done everything they wanted us to do," says Kaye Trentham, who operates K.T's Café. "But we still don't have water."

The Evansvilles of America are growing in number as the job wars intensify. Since the 1980s, states have added one economic-incentive program after another to retain existing corporations and lure new ones. Even states that once refused to compete are reversing course. North Carolina, which had long shunned big-ticket deals, abruptly shifted gears last summer and enacted the Economic Opportunity Act of 1998. The first two beneficiaries:

- Federal Express, the global delivery service with headquarters in Memphis, Tenn., that had 1997 revenues of $11.5 billion, will receive $115 million in state tax concessions and other economic benefits to build a hub at Greensboro, N.C.
- Nucor, a company based in Charlotte, N.C., that operates steel mills in half a dozen states and had 1997 revenues of $4.2 billion, will receive $155 million in state economic assistance to build a mini-steel mill in Hertford County in the northeastern corner of the state.

Why has North Carolina joined in the great scramble to give away incentives? The same reason all the other combatants are in it: jobs. Or at least job announcements. As John Hood, president of the John Locke Foundation (a Raleigh, N.C., public policy institute that advocates individual liberty, a free-market economy and limited government), put it, "Creating jobs is not the goal of these [economic-incentive] programs. The goal of these programs is to create job announcements."

And create them they do.

Said David N. Dinkins (then mayor of New York City) in October 1993, on $31 million in incentives awarded to Kidder, Peabody Group Inc.: "The decision by Kidder, Peabody demonstrates in dramatic fashion that our job-retention strategies are working."

Said Jim Rout, mayor of Tennessee's Shelby County (where Memphis is located), in July 1995, on more than $20 million in incentives given to Birmingham Steel Corp.: "These are not expenses—they're investments. These kinds of investments will pay off . . . It represents skilled, well-paying jobs."

Said Frank O'Bannon, Governor of Indiana, in March 1997, on a $1.7 million tax abatement to Crown Equipment Corp. for a plant in Greencastle, Ind.: "With at least 200 good-paying new jobs, this expansion will be an important addition not only to Putnam County's economy but to all of west-central Indiana."

Said Christine Todd Whitman, Governor of New Jersey, in May 1997, on millions of dollars passed around to four large businesses under the state's new Business Employment Incentive Program: "This is what the BEIP was meant to do, create jobs and increase opportunities for New Jersey families . . . This is . . . a red-letter day for jobs [in New Jersey]."

Don't believe it.

Jobs are created, of course, by the American economy—not by this process.

[Our] investigation has established that almost without exception, local and state politicians have doled out tens of billions of taxpayer dollars to businesses that are in fact eliminating rather than creating jobs. Some of the money has gone to prop up individual companies and avoid the consolidation within industries that an unfettered market would bring about. Some has been pumped into profitable companies, making them more profitable. Some has been

awarded to companies that have threatened to move if they don't get it. Some has been diverted to businesses that local politicians have somehow divined will be more successful than their competitors. And last, some has gone to entire industries that are shrinking.

Witness a $300,000 grant to Anchor Glass Container Corp. last year, described by Pennsylvania Governor Tom Ridge's administration as part of an effort "to retain 275 existing jobs" at the firm's Connellsville, Pa., plant.

Retain 275 jobs?

A decade earlier, in 1987, Anchor Glass employed 9,900 people nationwide—about 1,000 of them in Pennsylvania. By the time the company began seeking economic incentives, more than half the work force had vanished as employment plunged to 4,500. Two plants were closed in Pennsylvania. And just a few months earlier, the Connellsville plant had completed another round of layoffs, bringing the total for the year to 200. The company was telling the state all it needed to know about what kind of future it saw in Connellsville.

Cities go to extremes to keep jobs in the manufacturing sector, partially because they pay more than most service jobs. Here is how Edward G. Rendell, mayor of Philadelphia, explained why last year $307 million in local and state economic incentives in addition to $119 million in federal aid was being given to Kvaerner ASA, Europe's largest shipbuilder: "Those are good, honest jobs that pay a living wage and significant benefits. Jobs you can build a family on."

True enough. But Rendell cannot reverse the tide of economic forces. And no industry is a better example of the futility of subsidies than American shipbuilding. It has not been a vital U.S. business for decades. Yet surplus shipyards continue to be kept alive by subsidies from local and state governments, the federal government and sometimes all three. Without this aid, consolidation would have occurred long ago—as it has in virtually every other field, from defense to banking. Avondale Industries in New Orleans, for example, first went on the corporate-welfare rolls in the 1930s, when the state waived payment of personal property taxes. It's still on the dole today. Over the past decade, Avondale has been excused from paying $8 million in property taxes alone.

Nebraska
The Job Is Meaty; The Pay Is Not

Not long ago, the state of Nebraska created an authority to dispense corporate welfare. It's called the Nebraska Quality Jobs Board. So what does the board consider a "quality job"?

Well, when do you want to go to the bathroom? In the morning or the afternoon? Pick one or the other. Not both. That is your choice at Nebraska Beef Ltd., an Omaha beef-packing company and jobs-board beneficiary. Listen to a young Mexican worker— he has taken a few days off at the suggestion of a supervisor, who noted that immigration agents were coming to the plant to inspect citizenship papers. Listen as the worker describes his daily routine on the factory floor, where he wields a 6-in. knife, slashing carcasses on an assembly line that never slows:

"We tell the [supervisors], 'Hey, I want to use the rest room.' [They say,] 'O.K., 10 minutes. Go now.' [That's] only once a day [you can go] . . . I have to think if I can go drink some water because I know I'm going to have to go use the rest room." He continues: "We start at 6 o'clock in the morning. But I got there at 5 o'clock to just get ready, drink my coffee, work my steel . . . If we work 10 hours, they give us a break at 2:30. If we was going to go nine hours, they don't give us no break."

Nebraska Beef is the entity that got the breaks. The jobs board awarded the company an estimated $7.5 million in tax credits in 1996, as well as a laundry list of other benefits. The award was all the more curious because the company had started work on its new plant before the board even existed. Other aid has pushed the total value of giveaways to Nebraska Beef to between $24 million and $31 million.

An exact total is not available, since the state refuses to disclose the amount of taxpayer funds for this or any other approved project. But Nebraska does say that the tax credits were extended under programs that "could substantially reduce or even eliminate [a] company's tax liability."

When state lawmakers created the jobs board in 1995, they had in mind "major business expansion and relocation projects needed to stimulate the growth of populations and create better jobs for the citizens of Nebraska."

At Nebraska Beef, many of the workers are not citizens, in part because even hard-working Nebraskans aren't likely to come running for jobs that start at about $8 an hour for such grueling labor. Nebraska Beef employees can count on a raise of 25¢ an hour every year they stay on the job, which means that in two years, a butcher is making $8.50. That is $17,680 a year for a 40-hr. week, about $1,200 above the poverty level for a family of four.

Not surprisingly, Nebraska Beef goes through employees the way it does carcasses: at one point, 50% of the workers who completed state training for their jobs were gone within 10 months. A review by the state auditor of public accounts showed that Nebraska Beef had used at least a million dollars in state funds in one year to train workers who eventually left their jobs. The audit noted dryly, "It would appear the number of employees no longer employed with the company and amount of money spent for job training on these individuals was not in the best interest of the state of Nebraska." . . .

New York
When Factories Become
Fixer-Uppers

Defenders of economic incentives like to say that safeguards can be built into the law, so that if companies fail to deliver on the promised number of jobs, they can be required to pay back the taxes that have been canceled. If you believe that, it might be worth pondering the story of ABB Instrumentation Inc. in Rochester, N.Y. The company, which makes industrial instruments, is a subsidiary of ABB Asea Brown Boveri Ltd., the giant Swiss and Swedish conglomerate with interests in power generation, transmission and distribution.

In 1991, ABB applied to the County of Monroe Industrial Development Agency, requesting tax breaks and other incentives to move from its aging downtown Rochester location into a new building in a suburban industrial park. The company explained that its plant, built in 1906, was in a "declining industrial neighborhood on the west side of Rochester." ABB said there had been "no significant cost improvements or modernization . . . since 1950," which threatened its "ability to compete in a tightening world market." In short, neither ABB nor its predecessor had spent money updating the plant.

Nonetheless, the company was quite blunt about what it would do if economic aid was not forthcoming: relocate to Ohio, or England, or even Mexico or Venezuela. Only then did COMIDA agree to issue $21 million in industrial revenue bonds, with ABB using the proceeds to erect a new building. COMIDA excused the company from paying sales tax on materials to construct the plant. And it waived a chunk of

ABB's real estate taxes for 10 years. Overall, the tax breaks were worth about $5 million.

To secure a real estate–tax abatement, a company is required by Monroe County to guarantee that it will create 25 new jobs. If it fails to do so, it must refund a portion of the reduced taxes. ABB promised to boost employment at the new facility from 723 workers in the first year to 819 by the third. Instead, even before moving into its new building, the company began cutbacks. By December 1996, ABB reported that its work force totaled just 393. In short, rather than creating the 25 positions required by the county, ABB eliminated 426 real and projected jobs.

Then ABB cried poverty, telling the development agency, "If you rescind the tax exemption, we'll owe $1.2 million in taxes, which we can't afford."

To date, Monroe County has waived collection. Thus, a division of a multinational company—which had sales of $31 billion last year—received some $26 million in tax breaks and economic aid. For what? To eliminate 426 jobs.

After failing to keep a facility up to date, a company claims a plant is "archaic" and threatens to close it unless government officials come up with incentives to help pay for modernization. That is what happened in Louisville, Ky., where a much larger conglomerate, General Electric Co., said that to meet profit goals, its plant had to be modernized—with taxpayer dollars. This from a company that appears at the top of the lists of the "best managed" corporations in America, whose revenue last year reached $91 billion and whose earnings topped $8 billion.

GE, which over the years had failed to update a washing-machine factory in Louisville—described as an "obsolete facility" that is "just one step above archaic"—threatened to close it unless state and local governments helped subsidize its modernization and 7,000 hourly employees agreed to cost-cutting work rules.

Faced with this threat, Kentucky officials hired Coopers & Lybrand, an accounting and consulting firm, to conduct a study—paid for by GE—on whether the company really intended to turn out the lights. The answer Coopers & Lybrand came up with: yes.

It is not clear why the state of Kentucky believed it was the responsibility of taxpayers to improve GE's profit margins. Nevertheless, in 1993, Kentucky granted $19 million in income tax breaks over 10 years to the washing-machine factory in GE's sprawling Appliance Park complex. The city of Louisville and Jefferson County kicked in an additional $1 million.

The tax break notwithstanding, employment in Appliance Park continues to fall. Last February, GE announced that over the next two years, 1,500 jobs would be eliminated as range and dryer production is phased out and moved to Georgia, where wages are lower, and Mexico, where wages are much lower. Today 6,200 people work in Appliance Park—down 72% from a high of 22,250 in 1973. . . .

Alabama
Singing Lessons from an
Auto Company

There was no question that like UPS, Mercedes-Benz was going to build a plant someplace in this country. First of all, the U.S. is an important market for Mercedes; second, wages and more flexible work schedules make manufacturing costs lower here than in Europe.

Lower than Mercedes-Benz ever imagined. Alabama taxpayers essentially built and equipped a new plant for the company in the tiny town of Vance, a few miles east of Tuscaloosa. Mercedes received a package of incentives that totaled $253 million in value. For example, Alabama acquired and developed the plant site in Vance for $60 million. It used National Guard troops to clear the land and spent $77.5 million on utility improvements and roads.

The Mercedes-Benz plant illustrates a fundamental principle of corporate welfare: everyone else pays for economic incentives—either with higher taxes, fewer services or both.

To understand this, go to the Vance Elementary School, located a football field or two from the plant. Of course, you cannot actually see the school building. That is because it is surrounded by portable classrooms—17 in all. They are being added at the rate of two a year. Inside the school, the results of crowding 540 pupils (expected to be 700 to 800 within the next two years) into a building designed for 290 are readily apparent—a marked contrast with the roominess of the $30 million training school the state built for Mercedes. Throughout the school day, students stand in line to take their turn in one of the six tiny rest rooms serviced by a septic system, which produces its own unpleasant consequences on occasion, since the septic tanks were also built for 290 pupils. That contrasts with the new sewer lines the state laid for Mercedes. Then there is the cafeteria. Because of the overcrowding, lunch starts at 10:30 A.M.—soon to be 10:15—not long after many pupils ate breakfast. Last there is the safety issue. Vance and other schools in the area are in the middle of tornado alley. Whenever a tornado watch is sounded, the portable classrooms are emptied, and pupils are shepherded into classrooms in the main building.

To be sure, Mercedes is not responsible for all these deficiencies. Alabama traditionally has ranked near the bottom of the 50 states when it comes to education. But the presence of Mercedes has not added anything, except more students.

Nevertheless, at the elementary school, principal David Thompson is an unabashed Benz booster. When the school needed extra buses to transport pupils to the ballet, Thompson said, Mercedes provided them. And when the car company learned the school was mounting a production of *Hansel and Gretel,* it dispatched several of its expats to help the pupils learn German songs. The experience made a lasting impression on the students. As Thompson put it, "They couldn't tell you your multiplication tables if you asked them. If you say, 'What's 9 times 7?', they probably have already forgotten it. But they can still sing those songs in German."

Ohio
Does GM Mean General Movers?

Given the money politicians are willing to spend, it is no wonder companies have made their assets portable—game pieces that can be moved around the board of economic development. General Motors Corp. has played the game like a champion, a classic example of a company that has secured hundreds of millions of dollars in corporate welfare at the same time that it has eliminated thousands of jobs. And, according to business analysts, GM has to eliminate 50,000 more jobs if it wants to survive the next century.

In effect, the company is in the process of auctioning its surviving jobs to the highest bidders in the communities where it does business. Here's how it works: during the summer of 1997, GM let it be known that it was considering a $355 million expansion of an assembly plant in Moraine, Ohio, to build sport-utility vehicles. The decision would hinge on the size of tax breaks granted by the city government. After all,

two other cities with GM truck plants— Shreveport, La., and Linden, N.J.—were vying for the new facility. At least that is what GM officials hinted to Moraine officials. And that is what the local newspaper, the Dayton *Daily News,* duly reported.

There was one problem. The story GM floated was not true. Company executives later apologized for any misunderstanding. Erroneous claims aside, Moraine agreed to exempt General Motors from taxes on $355 million worth of machinery, equipment and inventory for 10 years and to excuse the company from real estate taxes for 15 years on the planned $65 million building.

So how much did GM save? Moraine city officials will not say, but county officials estimate GM is off the hook for $30 million in real estate and personal property taxes. GM also put the touch on the county economic-development authority for a cash grant of $1 million.

GM extracted the concessions at a time when the company's profits for 1995 and 1996 totaled $11.8 billion. To put that figure in context, it would be enough money to run the West Carrollton schools, where most Moraine children attend classes, for the next 400 years. As 1997 gave way to 1998, GM dangled the possibility of yet another plant before the Moraine city fathers, and they jumped. This time the tax relief amounts to an estimated $28 million—or about $156,000 for each of the 180 new jobs to be created.

One final twist: Moraine employees will be hired under a new, three-tiered wage scale, with workers starting at about $9 an hour. Once upon a time, the starting wage for such jobs was in the double digits. Nonetheless, Mayor Roger Matheny said that "this offers us job security and lets us know GM is going to be here for a long while."

Not necessarily. Other communities have showered tax breaks on GM and its partners, assuming they would create or at least retain jobs. They were wrong. Volvo-GM closed a jointly owned plant (GM was the minority partner) in Orrville, Ohio, in 1996—just seven years after the county cut property and inventory taxes in half. Some 400 jobs were lost. The two automakers moved operations to Pulaski County, Va., where millions of dollars more in economic incentives awaited.

In 1984 and 1988, Ypsilanti Township, Mich., granted 12-year tax abatements on $250 million worth of new equipment and machinery that GM installed in its Willow Run assembly plant. On its application for the second tax abatement, GM said no new jobs would be created but 4,900 existing jobs "will be retained as a result of the project." A GM executive reaffirmed the company's commitment at a township board meeting.

But in February 1992, GM announced it intended to close Willow Run and move production to Arlington, Texas, where it got a better deal. The township countered with a lawsuit, charging that the tax abatements created a binding obligation. A local judge agreed, accusing GM of "having lulled" the people of Ypsilanti and then trying to skip town. The state court of appeals reversed the decision and concluded that "hyperbole and puffery" in seeking tax breaks "does not necessarily create a promise." . . .

GM executives say they merely do what everyone else does. Moreover, they say, local and state governments often come calling on them. As a GM official explained, when Saturn was conceived, it was a clean sheet, a new type of plant representing a huge investment. Once it became publicly known what GM was planning, he said, "we received proposals from every state in the union except Hawaii and Alaska. We had file cabinets full of material from every state . . . Every one had to be responded to. It took on a life of its own."

Yet there had to be states that knew GM could not build there just for logistical reasons, he said. Nevertheless, government officials submitted formal proposals so they could tell their constituents they had at least tried. "[A politician] always wants to be perceived as someone who tried to bring home the bacon, even if the bacon doesn't arrive."

And that is where the real blame for corporate welfare rests.

As Ohio state senator Charles Horn, a persistent critic of tax abatements, put it when commenting on concessions granted GM, "We know companies are manipulative, but it's the nature of business to go after every dollar that's legally available. Don't place the blame on the company; place the blame on government. This is government's folly."

QUESTIONS FOR DISCUSSION

1. How widespread is the practice of corporate welfare? Can you offer other examples from your own state or community?
2. How do states compete with one another for corporate business? What are the effects of this competition?
3. Think about commonly held attitudes about welfare to poor individuals. Are attitudes toward corporate welfare different? Why or why not?

9

THE SOCIAL PSYCHOLOGY OF MODERN SLAVERY
KEVIN BALES

For Meera, the revolution began with a single rupee. When a social worker came across Meera's unmapped village in the hills of Uttar Pradesh in India three years ago, he found that the entire population was in hereditary debt bondage. It could have been in the time of their grandfathers or great-grandfathers—few in the village could remember—but at some point in their past, the families had pledged themselves to unpaid labor in return for loans of money. The debt passed down through the generations. Children as young as five years old worked in quarry pits, making sand by crushing stones with hammers. Dust, flying rock chips and heavy loads had left many villagers with silicosis and injured eyes or backs.

Calling together some of the women, the social worker proposed a radical plan. If groups of 10 women agreed to set aside a single rupee a week from the tiny sums the moneylenders gave them to buy rice, he would provide seed money and keep the funds safe. Meera and nine others formed the first group. The rupees slowly mounted up. After three months, the group had enough to pay off the loan against which Meera was bonded. She began earning money for her work, which greatly increased the amount she could contribute to the group. In another two months, another woman was freed; the following month, a third came out of bondage.

At that point, the other members, seeing that freedom was possible, simply renounced their debts and declared themselves free. The moneylenders quickly moved against them, threatening them and driving them from the quarries. But the women were able to find jobs in other quarries. New groups followed their example. The social worker has taken me to the village twice, and on my second visit, all its inhabitants were free and all their children in school.

Less than 100 kilometers away, the land turns flat and fertile. Debt bondage is common there, too. When I met Baldev in 1997, he was plowing. His master called him "my halvaha," meaning "my bonded plowman." Two years later I met Baldev again and learned that because of a windfall from a relative, he had freed himself from debt. But he had not freed himself from bondage. He told me:

> After my wife received this money, we paid off our debt and were free to do whatever we wanted. But I was worried all the time—what if one of the children got sick? What if our crop failed? What if the government wanted some money? Since we no longer belonged to the landlord, we didn't get food every day as before. Finally, I went to the landlord and asked him to take me back. I didn't have to borrow any money, but he agreed to let me be his halvaha again. Now I don't worry so much; I know what to do.

Lacking any preparation for freedom, Baldev reenrolled in slavery. Without financial or emotional support, his accidental emancipation didn't last. Although he may not bequeath any debt to his children, his family is visibly worse off than unbonded villagers in the same region.

To many people, it comes as a surprise that debt bondage and other forms of slavery persist into the 21st century. Every country, after all, has made it illegal to own and exercise total control over another human being. And yet there are people like Baldev who remain enslaved—by my estimate, which is based on a compilation of reports from governments and nongovernmental organizations, perhaps 27 million of them around the world. If slaveholders no longer own slaves in a legal sense, how can they still exercise so much control that freed slaves sometimes deliver themselves back into bondage? This is just one of the puzzles that make slavery the greatest challenge faced by the social sciences today. Despite being among the oldest and most persistent forms of human relationships, found in most societies at one time or another, slavery is little understood. Although historians have built up a sizable literature on antebellum American slavery, other types have barely been studied. It is as if our understanding of all arachnids were based on clues left by a single species of extinct spider. In our present state of ignorance, we have little hope of truly eradicating slavery, of making sure that Meera, rather than Baldev, becomes the model.

The New Slavery

Researchers do know that slavery is both evolving and increasing in raw numbers. Like spiders, it permeates our world, typically hidden in the dark spaces of the economy. Over the past few years, journalists and activists have documented numerous examples. Human trafficking—the involuntary smuggling of people between countries, often by organized crime—has become a huge concern, especially in Europe and Southeast Asia. Many people, lured by economic opportunities, pay smugglers to slip them across borders but then find themselves sold to sweatshops, brothels or domestic service to pay for their passage; others are kidnapped and smuggled against their will. In certain areas, notably Brazil and West Africa, laborers have been enticed into signing contracts and then taken to remote plantations and prevented from leaving. In parts of South Asia and North Africa, slavery is a millennia-old tradition that has never truly ended.

The plight of these people has drawn the attention of governments and organizations as diverse as the Vatican, the United Nations, the International Organization for Migration, and Amnesty International. Two years ago the U.S. government established a central coordinating office to deal with human trafficking. Academic researchers are beginning to conduct intensive studies. The anecdotal and journalistic approach is slowly transforming into the more rigorous inquiry of social science. For example, Urs Peter Ruf of the University of Bielefeld in Germany has documented the evolution of master-slave relations in modern Mauritania. Louise Brown of the University of Birmingham in England has studied women forced into prostitution in Asia. David Kyle of the University of California at Davis and Rey Koslowski of Rutgers University have explored human smuggling. I have posited a theory of global slavery and tested it through case studies in five countries.

A common question is why these practices should be called slavery rather than just another form of superexploitation. The answer is simple. Throughout history, slavery has meant a loss of free will and choice backed up by violence, sometimes exercised by the slaveholder, sometimes by elements of the state. That is exactly what other researchers and I have observed. Granted, workers at the bottom of the economic ladder have few options to begin with, but at some point on the continuum of exploitation, even those options are lost. These workers are unable to walk away.

Human suffering comes in various guises, yet slavery has a distinctive horror that is evident to those of us who have seen it in the flesh. Even when it does not involve beating or other physical torture, it brings about a psychological degradation that often renders victims unable to function in the outside world. "I've worked in prisons and with cases of domestic violence," says Sydney Lytton, an American psychiatrist who has counseled freed slaves. "This is worse."

Although each of the manifestations of slavery has unique local characteristics, one of the aims of social scientists is to understand their universal features, so that therapies developed in one place can be applied elsewhere. Foremost among these commonalities is the basic economic equation. In 1850 an agricultural slave cost $1,500 in Alabama (around $30,000 in today's dollars). The equivalent laborer can be had for around $100 today. That payment might be made as part of a "loan" or as a "fee" to a trafficker. A young woman in Southeast Asia or eastern Europe might be sold several times, through a series of brokers and pimps, before she ends up in a brothel.

One should not read too much into these specific dollar amounts, because what the slaveholder purchases is somewhat different in each case. The basic point is that forced labor represents a much smaller percentage of business expenses than it used to. It took 20 years of labor for an antebellum American slave to repay his or her purchase price and maintenance costs; today it takes two years for a bonded laborer in South Asia to do the same. This fall in price has altered not only the profitability of slavery but also the relationship between slave and master. The expensive slave of the past was a protected investment; today's slave is a cheap and disposable input to low-level production. The slaveholder has little incentive to provide health care or to take care of slaves who are past their prime.

Several trends could account for this shift. The world's population has tripled since World War II, producing a glut of potential slaves. Meanwhile the economic transformation of the developing world has, whatever its benefits, included the loss of community and social safety nets, matched by the erection of vast shantytowns. But the vulnerability of large numbers of people does not make them slaves; for that, you need violence. The key factor in the persistence of slavery is the weak rule of law in many regions. Widespread corruption of government and police allows violence to be used with impunity even when slavery is nominally illegal.

Free Your Mind Instead

A second commonality among different forms of slavery is the psychological manipulation they all involve. The widely held conception of a slave is someone in chains who would escape if given half a chance or who simply does not know better. But Meera's and Baldev's stories, among numerous others, suggest that this view is naive. In my experience, slaves often know that their enslavement is illegal. Force, violence and psychological coercion have convinced them to accept it. When slaves begin to accept their role and identify with their master, constant physical bondage becomes unnecessary. They come to perceive their situation not as a deliberate action taken to harm them in particular but as part of the normal, if regrettable, scheme of things.

One young woman I met in northeastern Thailand, Siri, has a typical story. A woman approached her parents, offered to find their 14-year-old daughter a job, and advanced them 50,000 baht (at the time, about $2,000) against her future income. The broker transferred Siri to a low-end brothel for twice that sum. When she tried to escape, her debt was doubled again. She was told to repay it, as well as a monthly rent of 30,000 baht, from her earnings of 100 baht per customer.

Siri had little idea what it meant to be a prostitute. Her initiation took the form of assault and rape. Shattered, the teenager had to find a way to carry on with life. In the world in which she lived, there were only those with total power and those with no power. Reward and punishment came from a single source, the pimp. Young women in Siri's position often find building a relationship with the pimp to be a good survival strategy. Although pimps are thugs, they do not rely solely on violence. They are adept at fostering insecurity and dependence.

Cultural norms have prepared these young women for control and compliance. A girl will be told how her parents will suffer if she does not cooperate and work hard, how the debt is on her shoulders and must be repaid. Thai sex roles are clearly defined, and women are expected to be retiring, nonassertive and obedient—as the women are repeatedly reminded. The pimps also cite religion. The young women are encouraged to believe that they must have committed terrible sins in a past life to deserve their enslavement and abuse. They are urged to accept this karmic debt, to come to terms with it and to reconcile themselves to their fate.

To live in slavery, the young women often redefine their bondage as a duty or a job or a form of penance. To accept their role and the pimp's, they must try to diminish their view of themselves as victims who have been wronged. They must begin to see their enslavement from the point of view of the slaveholder. At the time of my visit, the women in Siri's brothel were at various stages in this process of submission. Some were even allowed to visit their families during holidays, for they always came back.

A similar psychology operates in a different form of slavery, one that involves domestic servants that African and Asian diplomats and business executives have brought with them to Europe and North America. As an employee of the Committee against Modern Slavery, Cristina Talens worked for several years to free and rehabilitate domestic slaves who had been brought to Paris. She told me that liberating the body was much easier than freeing the mind:

> In spite of the violence, and the living and working conditions, people in slavery have their own mental integrity and their own mechanisms for surviving. Some may actually like different aspects of their life, perhaps the security or their understanding of the order of things. When you disrupt this order, suddenly everything is confused. Some of the women who were freed have attempted suicide. It is easy to assume that this happened because of the abuse they had lived through. But for some of these women, slavery had been the major psychological building block in their lives. When that was destroyed, the meaning of their life was like a bit of paper crushed up and thrown away. They were told: "No, this is not the way it is supposed to be. Start all over again." It was as though their life had no meaning.

Plausible Deniability

The psychology of the slave is mirrored by that of the slaveholder. Slavery is not a simple matter of one person holding another by force; it is an insidious mutual dependence that is remarkably difficult for slaveholder as well as slave to break out of. Branding the slaveholder as pure evil may in some way comfort us, but maintaining that definition becomes difficult when one meets actual slave masters.

Almost all the slaveholders I have met and interviewed in Pakistan, India, Brazil and Mauritania were family men who thought of themselves simply as business-men. Pillars of the local community, they were well rewarded financially, well inte-grated socially, and well connected legally and politically. Their slaveholding was not seen as a social handicap except, possibly, by "outsiders" who, they felt, misunder-stood the local customs of business and labor.

How is it that such nice men do such bad things? A government official in Baldev's district who held bonded workers was frank about his slaveholding:

> Of course I have bonded laborers: I'm a landlord. I keep them and their families, and they work for me. When they aren't in the fields, I have them doing the household work washing clothes, cook-ing, cleaning, making repairs, every-thing. After all, they are from the Kohl caste; that's what they do, work for Vaisyas like me. I give them food and a little land to work. They've also bor-rowed money, so I have to make sure that they stay on my land till it is paid back. They will work on my farm till it is all paid back. I don't care how old they get; you can't just give money away!
>
> After all, there is nothing wrong in keeping bonded labor. They benefit from the system, and so do I. Even if agriculture is completely mechanized, I'll still keep my bonded laborers. You see, the way we do it, I am like a father to these workers. It is a father-son rela-tionship; I protect them and guide them. Of course, sometimes I have to discipline them as well, just as a father would.

Other slaveholders also have told me that their slaves are like their children, that they need close control and care. They make the argument of tradition: because the practice has been going on for so long, it must be the natural order of things. For oth-ers, it is a simple question of priorities: they say that enslaving people is unfortunate but that their own family's welfare depends on it. Often slaveholders have interposed many layers of management between themselves and the slaves. They purposely deny them-selves the knowledge of what they are do-ing and thus the responsibility for it.

Forty Acres and a Mule

All this points to the need for a highly de-veloped system of rehabilitation for freed slaves and slaveholders alike. Physical free-dom is not enough. When slaves were emancipated in the U.S. in 1865, the govern-ment enacted no such rehabilitation. Gen-eral William Tecumseh Sherman's promise to give each former slave "forty acres and a mule" never materialized. The result was four million people dumped into a shattered economy without resources and with few legal protections. It can be argued that America is still suffering from this liberation without rehabilitation.

Human-rights worker Vivek Pandit of the Vidhayak Sansad organization in India has been liberating bonded laborers for more than 20 years. He is adamant that real liberation takes place in the mind, that phys-ical freedom isn't enough—as was the case with Baldev. Conversely, mental freedom can bring about physical freedom—as it did for Meera.

Pandit's organization has devised a program of education that prepares former bonded laborers for a life of freedom. They are taught basic science to promote their curiosity and attention to detail; role-playing to stimulate problem solving; and games to develop strategic thinking and teamwork. This training comes after a challenging public dialogue in which the laborer recounts and renounces his or her bondage. The renunciation is recorded and read out in the village. "When the ex-slave has fixed his thumbprint to this public document," Pandit says, "they can't go back."

Several models of liberation and rehabilitation are currently being field-tested. . . . The experience of these programs suggests that a combination of economic support, counseling and education can lead to stable, sustainable freedom. This kind of work is still in its early stages, though. No systematic evaluations of these programs have been carried out. No social scientist has explored a master-slave relationship in depth.

Slave economics are another puzzle. How can would-be liberators crack the dark economy and trace the slave-made products to our homes? Why are such large numbers of people being trafficked across continents, how many of these people really are enslaved, and why are these flows apparently increasing? What is the impact of this workforce on national economies? What are the links among the traffic in people, drugs and guns?

Studying bondage can be socially and politically controversial. Researchers in the field face numerous ethical dilemmas, and clarity and objectivity are all the more difficult to achieve when individuals and governments seek to conceal what they are doing. If there is good news, it is the growing recognition of the problem. The plight of enslaved child workers has drawn significantly increased funding, and new partnerships between antislavery organizations and industries that use slave-made commodities provide an innovative model for abolition. But if our figures are correct, only a small fraction of slaves are reached and freed every year. Our ignorance of their hidden world is vast.

QUESTIONS FOR DISCUSSION

1. What are the characteristics of contemporary slavery?
2. How do slaveholders maintain their control over slaves?
3. Why are slave rehabilitation programs necessary?

10

DISPOSABLE DOMESTICS
Immigrant Women Workers in the Global Economy

GRACE CHANG

The nomination of Zoë Baird for US Attorney General in 1993 forced a confession that provoked a public uproar: Baird admitted to employing two undocumented Peruvian immigrants, as a baby-sitter and a driver, in clear violation of the immigration law prohibiting the hiring of "illegal" aliens. Responses to Baird's disclosure indicate that her "crime" is a pervasive phenomenon.[1] Deborah Sontag reported in the *New York Times* that two-career, middle-class families employing so-called illegal immigrants to do child care and domestic work is so common that employment agencies routinely recommend undocumented immigrants to their clients. As the director of one Manhattan nanny agency said, "It's just a reality of life that without the illegal girls, there wouldn't be any nannies, and the mommies would have to stay home and mind their own kids."[2] Another agency's director said bluntly, "It all comes down to money. . . . The reason that people hire immigrants without papers is that they're looking to save. If they want legal, they can get it, but it costs."[3] According to a survey of 18 New York agencies, "illegal" workers earned as little as $175 a week and "legal" workers as much as $600.[4]

Thus, the uproar surrounding Baird was not so much a response to the discovery that some people flouted the law by employing

undocumented workers. This was hardly news. Rather, the public outcry was a reflection of resentment that this practice was so easily accessible to the more privileged classes while other working-class working mothers struggled to find any child care. As one critic of Baird commented, "I don't think it's fair. I raised my kids while I was working. I worked days. My husband worked nights at the post office. Our in-laws filled in when they had to."[5] Another woman pointed out: "Average working mothers don't make nearly what she makes, and yet we are obligated to follow the law."[6]

What was conspicuously absent from most of the commentary on the Baird controversy was concern for the plight of the undocumented workers themselves. Two other news stories involving immigrant women working in private households appeared in a California newspaper the same time Baird's situation was making headlines across the nation; yet these stories did not receive comparable attention. The first of these involved Claudia Garate, who immigrated from Chile at age 19 in order to take a job as an au pair for a professional couple. Garate testified before the state Labor Commissioner in Sonoma County that she slept on the floor and worked on call twenty-four hours a day, seven days a week as a maid, baby-sitter, cook, and gardener for $50 a month. Garate's employers held on to her visa and passport and withheld her pay for 13 months, claiming they would deposit it in a bank account for her. The second case involved Maria de Jesus Ramos Hernandez, who left her three children in Mexico to work as a housekeeper in California. Once here, her employer repeatedly raped her, telling her that he had paid her way here and would have her jailed if she did not submit to him.[7]

Evidence indicates that while Garate's and Hernandez's cases may have been extreme, abuse of undocumented women working in private households is not uncommon. Lina Avidan, then–program director for the San Francisco–based Coalition for Immigrant and Refugee Rights and Services (CIRRS), said, "I have clients who work . . . seven days a week, doing child care from 6 a.m. to 10 p.m. [for] $200 a month. Clearly, they are working in the homes of the wealthy and they're not even getting minimum wage."[8] A 1991 CIRRS survey of Chinese, Filipina, and Latina undocumented women in the San Francisco Bay area revealed that the majority (58 percent) of the employed undocumented Latinas surveyed held jobs in housecleaning and in-home care of children or the elderly, while the remainder worked in service jobs or factories. They were usually earning between $250 and $500 per month. Forty percent of these women were supporting between one and three people on these wages, while 38 percent were supporting between four and six.[9] Members of *Mujeres Unidas y Activas* (MUA), a support group for Latina immigrant domestic workers, report that they commonly endure conditions approaching slavery or indentured servitude.[10] . . .

Taken together, these accounts indicate that middle-class households often make exploitative use of immigrant women to do child care and domestic work. They also suggest the advances of many middle-class white women in the workforce have been largely predicated on the exploitation of poor, immigrant women. While middle- and upper-class women entrust their children and homes to undocumented immigrant women, the immigrant women often must leave their own children to work. Some leave their children with family in their home countries, hoping to earn enough to return or send money back to them.[11] Thus, middle- and upper-class women are readily able to find "affordable" care for their children at the expense of poor immigrant women and their children. The employment of undocumented women in dead-end, low-wage, temporary service jobs makes it possible for middle- and upper-class women to pursue salaried jobs and not have to contend with the "second shift" when they come home.

A predictable outgrowth of the Baird controversy has been the proposal that the existing Immigration Reform and Control Act (IRCA) be changed so that household employers are exempted from the prohibition against hiring "illegal" immigrants, or that household workers are given special visas.[12] If the law were changed to meet this "popular demand," it would only serve to legitimize the exploitation of thousands of undocumented immigrants. These proposals raise the specter of a counterpart in private household work to some of the most brutally exploited contract laborers used in agriculture: "disposable nannies" who may be dumped once babies become older or newer immigrants can be found who are willing to work for even lower wages.

The Immigration and Naturalization Service (INS), through its execution of IRCA, has continued to fulfill the historical role of the state in using immigration and welfare policies to maintain women of color as a super-exploitable, low-wage labor force.[13] A historical example is the use of "employable mother" rules by many states from the 1940s through 1960s to deny black mothers benefits, thereby coercing them to perform agricultural and domestic work. In implementing current immigration policy, the INS has continued this pattern. The INS's execution of IRCA, denying legalization to undocumented women whose citizen children have received public assistance, channels these women into and maintains them in the secondary labor force, private household work, and institutional service work.

The Immigration Reform and Control Act of 1986: A Compromise

The Immigration Reform and Control Act of 1986 emerged after nearly a decade of debate in Congress and in the public domain about what impact immigration, particularly "illegal" immigration, had on the US economy. The act had two main objectives that were contradictory: to reduce the number of undocumented immigrants and to provide rights and the chance to legalize to those undocumented immigrants who had already lived and worked in the country. Unable to reconcile these conflicting impulses, Congress incorporated a number of provisions into the law as concessions to various interest groups. First, to discourage illegal immigration, the law established employer sanctions against those who knowingly employed undocumented immigrants. Second, to provide rights and protections to undocumented persons, the amnesty program offered those who could prove they had lived in the country "illegally" since at least 1982 the chance to apply for temporary resident status. Finally, in response to the concerns of growers about how the law might affect the availability of agricultural labor, Congress created three special classes of those who could enter the country or gain residency as agricultural workers.[14]

Some of the most heated debate surrounding IRCA centered around the issue of whether immigrants generally contribute to or deplete from the public coffers. This debate led lawmakers to include in IRCA provisions governing whether those perceived as potentially welfare dependent should be able to gain residency and whether "legalized persons" should be allowed to receive certain entitlements. The virtual hysteria that has arisen around protecting public revenues and guarding against the growth of a population of welfare dependents undoubtedly influenced the inclusion of two provisions of IRCA, the public-charge exclusion and the five-year bar, to restrict aliens' access to social services and public benefits. . . .

The Five-Year Bar from Federal Assistance

The amnesty program represented a recognition, at least on the part of some lawmakers, that thousands of undocumented aliens had lived in the United States, worked, and contributed to the American economy for years without ever enjoying the rights of those recognized as full, "legitimate" members of the society.[15] The remarks of one representative suggest that some lawmakers hoped to bring relief to the undocumented through IRCA: "We will be bringing people out of a shadow economy, people will be paying taxes, people will be coming out into the sunshine, there will not be the abuse of workers, employers will not be able to provide poor-quality jobs for people, they will not be able to oppress people."[16] Of course, not all lawmakers had such generous intentions in mind in formulating IRCA. Many were more concerned with protecting public resources for "native" Americans than with protecting the rights of the undocumented. The perception of immigrants as welfare burdens fueled fears that the amnesty program would create a tremendous, immediate strain on social service funds.[17] In direct response to these concerns, Congress included in IRCA a provision barring legalization applicants from most federal assistance programs, including AFDC, food stamps, and certain forms of Medicaid. The bar period extends for five years from the time someone applies for temporary residency.[18]

The Public-Charge Ground of Exclusion and the Special Rule

In addition to the five-year bar, a provision of immigration law dating back to 1882 was retained in IRCA to guard against the expected welfare drain by newly legalized aliens. This provision, excluding those "likely to become a public charge," is used to identify those who might be unable to support themselves because of some physical or mental limitation.[19] Prior to IRCA, all aliens applying for an immigrant visa were subject to a test to determine whether they were likely to be able to earn a living in the United States. This test considers factors such as the applicant's age, health, past and current income, education, and job skills. Past receipt of public benefits is considered a significant but not determinative factor. The traditional test gives applicants one way of overcoming the public-charge ground of exclusion, even if they have received public benefits, if they can show that they are currently employed or able to provide for themselves and their families.[20]

Under IRCA, Congress established a "special rule" providing a second test for legalization applicants unable to pass the traditional test.[21] This test examines the alien's recent past and requires the applicant to have a history of employment that demonstrates self-support without receipt of public cash assistance.[22] This history of employment need not be continuous, thus allowing for periods of unemployment and seasonal or migrant labor.[23] Congressional testimony

indicates that Congress created the "special rule" with the intent of liberalizing the public-charge standard or providing a second means of overcoming this standard.[24] Specifically, it was made with the recognition that many of the undocumented are "working poor," unlikely to become dependent on public benefits despite their low incomes.[25]

The amnesty, five-year bar, and public-charge provisions of IRCA were formulated in the face of a wide spectrum of views on what rights and benefits should be extended to immigrants. IRCA represented an uneasy compromise of these views and the task of implementing IRCA was left to the discretion of the INS. In executing IRCA, the INS has applied more restrictive interpretations of the law. For example, Congress intended to open eligibility for legalization to large numbers of people, including those who were low-income, with the "special rule."[26] But the INS did not utilize the "special rule" properly and instead implemented its own interpretations of the law, which were not consistent with Congress's liberalizing intent. The result of this practice was that many undocumented women who had received public assistance for their children were wrongfully denied amnesty.

The Case of *Zambrano v. INS*

The INS's implementation of IRCA, particularly its application of the law to undocumented women, has been challenged in the case *Zambrano v. INS*. The class-action suit was filed in the Ninth Circuit in April 1988 on behalf of a group of plaintiffs who were mostly women with dependents and the class they represent.[27] The complaint against the INS, filed by California Rural Legal Assistance (CRLA), the National Immigration Law Center (NILC), and San Mateo County Legal Aid (SMCLA), co-counsel for the plaintiffs, made two claims: that the INS's practices contradicted the congressional intent in passing IRCA and that these practices discriminated against and imposed extreme hardship on undocumented women with children.[28] In August 1988, the NILC and SMCLA withdrew from the case and the Mexican American Legal Defense and Education Foundation (MALDEF) joined CRLA as co-counsel. The declarations of two of the plaintiffs, Marta Zambrano and Maria C., illustrate how the INS's execution of the amnesty and public-charge provisions of IRCA adversely affected undocumented women with children and obstructed their chances of obtaining better working and living conditions.[29]

Marta Zambrano, whose name the case assumed, was a Mexican citizen who had lived continuously in the United States since 1979. Marta had four children with US citizenship, ages eight, six, four, and three, at the time of her declaration in 1988. Between 1979 and 1983, she worked in a factory, picked cauliflower, and did many kinds of work in the fields, even while she had two small children. She only began receiving AFDC for her children in 1983, when she became pregnant with her third child and her common-law husband left her because she refused to have an abortion.[30]

Marta first heard about the amnesty program in 1986 on the radio and through friends. She went to a program at her church for information and was told that she could not receive AFDC for her children if she wanted to legalize. She also heard on the radio and from her friends that people who received welfare were not eligible for legalization. Convinced that she would not qualify, Zambrano did not pursue an amnesty application. Only at the urging of an attorney did she file her application on May 4, 1988, the latest possible date. In June 1988, she was interviewed by the INS and informed that her application was denied because her children had received AFDC.[31]

Marta received AFDC for her US-citizen children because their natural fathers contributed no support to the family. Since 1986, Marta sought work but was refused in many instances because she did not have work authorization, which she could only obtain through legalization. Potential employers turned Marta away from work in the fields and as a dishwasher and housecleaner. Even when Marta obtained part-time work, she did not earn enough money to cover living expenses and child care.[32]

Anna R. was less fortunate than Marta Zambrano in that she never even applied for amnesty. She was a citizen of El Salvador and had lived in California since 1981. She had four children, two of whom were US citizens. Shortly after IRCA was passed, Anna began preparing to apply for amnesty by gathering necessary documents. In January 1988, Anna was abandoned by the father of her children. At that time she was unable to find full-time employment without work authorization and applied for AFDC for her children, who had US citizenship. She also began working as a housekeeper, one day per week for three different employers. She earned about $400 per month and received no support from her children's father.[33]

Anna heard from the radio, television, and her relatives that receiving welfare would disqualify her from legalization. Thus she did not apply before the May 4, 1988, deadline, as she had intended to since 1986. Had she been informed that the receipt of AFDC by her US-citizen children should not disqualify her from legalization, she would have applied and would otherwise have been eligible.[34]

The other plaintiffs reported similar circumstances and obstacles to legalization. Each of the women had children, some or all of whom were US citizens. Those who received AFDC payments had received them only for US-citizen children, who were fully entitled to these benefits. Most of the women had some work history and, if unemployed at the time of applying for amnesty, would have presumably returned to the workforce when their family circumstances and child-care needs allowed. Some were employed at the time, but their incomes were insufficient to provide for them and their dependents without supplementary AFDC benefits. One received Supplemental Security Income (SSI) payments on behalf of her child, who had cerebral palsy.[35]

These women represent an entire class of people adversely affected by the improper INS practices. The plaintiffs contended that they are among the many thousands of undocumented persons to whom Congress intended to offer an opportunity to become citizens.[36] Yet they have been impeded from obtaining legal status and its benefits (such as work authorization) either through outright denial by the INS or because they were discouraged from applying based on information about the INS's improper practices. The complaint against the INS presented two claims, only the first of which has been addressed by the Court.

First Claim: The INS Has Violated IRCA

The complaint filed against the INS in April 1988 alleged that INS policies and procedures were "in contradiction of the plain meaning of IRCA and Congressional intent."[37] The INS applied its own "Proof of Financial Responsibility" (PFR) regulations, which the plaintiffs maintained were more restrictive than intended in the liberalized standards created under IRCA.[38] The PFR regulations attributed public benefits received by an amnesty applicant's dependents to the applicant. As revealed in the declarations of the plaintiffs, this included AFDC received by children who were fully entitled to these benefits as US citizens. The INS's use of these regulations resulted in the denial of amnesty to applicants who would otherwise have been eligible under IRCA's liberalized standards, such as the "special rule."[39]

The US District Court for the Eastern District of California addressed the first claim in the *Zambrano* case on July 31, 1989. After a thorough review of the INS regulations, the IRCA statute, and the legislative history surrounding its passage, Judge Edward Garcia issued a partial summary judgment and a permanent injunction on the INS regulations. The INS was ordered to reopen the cases of those who had been adversely affected by the regulations. This included two classes of people: first, those who filed applications on time but were denied as "likely to become a public charge" under the invalidated regulations, and second, those who were eligible for legalization but had not applied because they were discouraged by information about the INS's prior practices.[40] The INS was ordered to accept amnesty applications until December 31, 1989, for this second class of people.[41]

The INS appealed the July 1989 decision on a number of grounds.[42] The INS first appealed it in the Ninth Circuit Court of Appeals.[43] In February 1992, the court ruled against the INS, and the INS subsequently filed a writ of certiorari to the US Supreme Court in November 1992.[44] If the Supreme Court does take up the case, it could remand it to the lower courts to decide the remaining issues, such as the second claim made against the INS.

Second Claim: The INS's Regulations Discriminate on the Basis of Sex

A second claim made against the INS was the charge that the INS regulations are discriminatory on the basis of sex and thus violate the equal protection clause.[45] The complaint asserted that the effect of the INS's regulations and procedures was that "legalization under IRCA [was] not made available or [was] made available on an unequal basis [with men] to substantial numbers of women."[46] Certainly, the declarations of the plaintiffs indicated that the INS's practices resulted in the wrongful denial of amnesty to many women whose children received AFDC or other benefits. Moreover, it was estimated that at least 4,000 potential women applicants chose not to apply for amnesty in California alone because they were discouraged by information about the INS's regulations.[47]

Diane Bessette, who acted as a legalization counselor for Catholic Community Services in Sacramento, has called attention to a third group of women for whom the INS regulations have posed inhumane choices. These women have managed to qualify for temporary resident status but must again overcome the INS's public-charge exclusion practices when they apply for permanent residency. Under the five-year bar, a legalization applicant must not receive certain public benefits after applying for temporary residency to maintain his or her application in good standing. He or she must choose between continuing to receive public assistance for his or her dependents or losing this means of support to complete the legalization process.[48] Because many single women with children cannot survive without the assistance, Bessette points out, many will be forced to forego adjusting to permanent residency.[49] In other words, these women face a double bind. Without legal status and its concomitant work authorization, they cannot find employment at adequate wages. Without adequate wages, they must provide for their children by some means, but they sacrifice the chance to gain legal status for themselves if they receive aid for their children as supplements to these wages.

One woman who made a declaration in the *Zambrano* case revealed that she became homeless because she gave up public assistance to apply for amnesty.[50] Others who "choose" illegal status or are denied amnesty will most likely suffer unemployment or employment in exploitative circumstances because they lack work authorization.[51] Rather than bringing these women "out of the shadows," the law has served to condemn them and their children to marginal working and living conditions. Perhaps one of the gravest consequences of the INS regulations has been to perpetuate the feminization of poverty among undocumented immigrants.

A number of recent studies indicate that undocumented persons, particularly women, have become or remain part of an underclass despite the generous potentials of the amnesty program.[52] First, undocumented women have been confined to employment in the secondary sector and often remain in highly exploitative work conditions for fear of losing their chances to legalize. The CIRRS survey revealed that undocumented women suffer many forms of worker exploitation, including not being paid for work, being paid lower wages than documented coworkers, and sexual harassment. . . .

Second, these women earn incomes far below the poverty level; yet they underutilize public assistance and social services to which they or their children are fully entitled, fearing that they will jeopardize their legalization applications. A study conducted in 1989 by the Comprehensive Adult Student Assessment System (CASAS) found that newly legalized persons used services and benefits at very low rates, "probably lower than for the [California] population as a whole." Two factors need to be considered to see how the improper INS regulations may have affected these rates: first, the family profiles of the respondents, and, second, the proper IRCA regulations regarding amnesty applicants' rights to public assistance and services. Of those who participated in the survey, approximately 43 percent of the families had at least one child born in the US. This implies that for almost half of the survey participants, at least one family member should not have been restricted by his/her immigration status, by IRCA's five-year bar, or by public-charge concerns. AFDC, the program that raised complications most often in the *Zambrano* case, is restricted by the five-year bar for legalization applicants and is a cash assistance program. Therefore, it is only available to the citizen children of newly legalized persons, but receipt of these benefits should only be attributed to the children themselves, not their parents. Yet fewer than one percent (0.9 percent) of families that entered the country prior to 1982 reported receiving AFDC benefits at the time of the survey. . . .

Moreover, these studies indicate that the INS has contributed to both of these patterns by its improper practices and its failure to publicize the proper regulations regarding amnesty and the public-charge exclusion. The INS failed to publicize accurate information about the amended regulations, even after they were permanently enjoined under the 1989 order. While the INS claimed that "clarification memos" were issued in 1987 and 1988, the court rejected these claims, pointing out that they were never disseminated to the public.[53] . . .

The evidence certainly supports the second claim made in *Zambrano v. INS* that the INS has "acted knowing and intending that the direct effect of their actions is to exclude or burden substantial numbers of women."[54] For several reasons, the plaintiffs' attorneys did not have the opportunity to pursue this second claim. Earlier, they attempted to show that a large percentage of those persons who have been denied under the improper regulations are single women with children, but the INS refused to comply with discovery orders that would allow them to compile statistics demonstrating this pattern.[55] Stephen Rosenbaum of CRLA, co-counsel for the plaintiffs, commented

that sexual discrimination is extremely difficult to prove; the INS's noncompliance with the discovery orders certainly contributed to this difficulty. Rosenbaum also said that the plaintiffs did not pursue this claim because the first claim, charging the INS's statutory violations, was deemed stronger.[56]

Nevertheless, the evidence clearly suggests that the INS's practices discriminate largely against women. In fact, one could argue that the second claim could be expanded to charge that the INS's actions constitute not only sexual but racial discrimination as well. Through these actions, the INS has performed its historical role in regulating the labor of immigrant women for local business interests in manufacturing and agriculture and for middle-class households seeking child care and domestic workers.[57] Thus, it could be established that the INS indeed acted "knowing and intending" that the effects of its practices would be to exclude many women so that they would need to seek or remain in low-wage employment. . . .

Debating Motherhood

On May 7, 1998, a full ten years after the *Zambrano* class-action suit was filed against the INS, the Ninth Circuit Court of Appeals dismissed the case from Superior Court.[58] This transpired after the INS had tried repeatedly to appeal to both the Ninth Circuit Court of Appeals and to the Supreme Court with no success, then ultimately resorted to trying to achieve its goals through the legislative process. Congress enacted, as part of the Illegal Immigration Reform and Immigrant Responsibility Act (IIRIRA) of 1996, section 377, which stipulated that the courts' jurisdiction over legalization matters would be limited to cases in which people had filed their applications or had attempted to file but were rejected by the INS. The stipulation was also made retroactive such that it applied to the *Zambrano* case. Subsequently, the INS filed another motion and succeeded in having the prior orders vacated and the case dismissed based on the new law's retroactivity.[59]

As Pauline Gee of California Rural Legal Assistance, co-counsel for the plaintiffs in *Zambrano,* said: "INS went to Congress because it couldn't win in the courts and had Senator Simpson, as his last act before retiring, pass this statute." Vibiana Andrade of the Mexican American Legal Defense and Education Fund, also co-counsel for the plaintiffs, commented: "Congress can do all kinds of things. In immigration law, it has unfettered discretion to do so. It has been a really frustrating ten-year fight." Andrade said it was particularly maddening that throughout the court battle the INS never contested the rulings against the agency, that it had implemented the law improperly, and that it had violated IRCA in applying its own public-charge standards. Instead, the INS reduced the case to a jurisdiction issue and ultimately won on the grounds that these matters should not be within the courts' discretionary powers.[60]

The *Zambrano* litigation brought important results for tens of thousands of immigrant families seeking to legalize their status. Under the early *Zambrano* rulings and injunctions, many people who had been denied or prevented from obtaining legal status because of the INS's improper public-charge standard implementation were able to have their legalization applications reconsidered or to file late applications for amnesty or work authorization.[61] However, the ultimate dismissal and the lengthy wait for this disappointing final outcome brought extreme hardship for many immigrant women and their children. Ten years represents a long period in many innocent children's lives—for some perhaps the bulk of their childhoods—during which time their mothers' lack of work authorization or legal

immigration status meant that the entire family lived in poverty, in "the shadows," and at the service of dominant society.

Moreover, after the *Zambrano* case was dismissed, applications were considered only from those who could prove that they were "front desked"—that is, that they had tried to apply for amnesty but were turned away from even submitting an application at an agency office on the basis of the incorrect INS regulations.[62] Andrade argues that this is extremely unfair as it fails to address those who had not attempted to file applications because they had heard they would not be eligible if they had received public benefits or services. Andrade and co-counsel had argued that these people formed the largest group of plaintiffs in *Zambrano,* and that the INS contributed to these people's declining to apply by publicizing misinformation on the radio and television.

A year after the *Zambrano* case dismissal, the federal government made a long-overdue clarification of the public-charge provisions. This new guidance, issued May 25, 1999, defines "public charge" as a person who cannot support herself or himself without depending on cash assistance such as Temporary Aid to Needy Families, SSI, or General Assistance for income, or who needs long-term institutional care. The guidance emphasizes that the INS should look at many factors to determine if an applicant is likely to become a public charge in the future, and it cannot make its decision based solely on receipt of cash assistance in the past. Instead, it must consider all of the following factors: age, health, income, family size, education, and skills. The California Immigrant Welfare Collaborative, a coalition of immigrant rights organizations providing outreach and education around the issue, recommends that applicants who have received welfare in the past highlight information such as current employment or the availability of support from family members in the country during their INS interviews.[63]

The new INS guidance also clarifies that the use of Medi-Cal, Healthy Families (a new health-insurance program in California for children ages one to nineteen with family incomes at or below 200 percent of the federal poverty level), or other health services by an applicant or family members will not affect her or his immigration status unless it is for long-term care. Nor will the use of food stamps, WIC (Women, Infants, and Children aid), public housing, or other noncash programs by an applicant or family members. Finally, the use of cash assistance by an applicant's children or other family members is not grounds to refuse entry (or re-entry) to the United States or to deny permanent residency or citizenship unless it is the applicant's family's only income.

It is important to understand that the 1999 INS guidance issued on the public-charge standard was not a change but a clarification of the existing law as it should have been implemented originally. Ironically, the INS guidance cites the *Zambrano* case in the clarification.[64] Throughout the *Zambrano* litigation, the INS never disputed that its regulations and practices contradicted IRCA, nor did it rush to issue corrections to its improper regulations even once they were enjoined. This lends credibility to the argument that the public-charge provisions were not only misinterpreted or improperly implemented by the INS but perhaps deliberately obscured. These INS practices rendered immigrants, particularly those with dependents, more exploitable in the labor market. Moreover, they facilitated US employers' abilities to extract cheap labor from these women and at the same time allow the state to evade responsibility for the welfare of resident and citizen children.

The case of the Latina mothers in *Zambrano* highlights the need for a demysti-fication of immigrant women as welfare dependent and a recognition that they are working mothers, often single heads of households, who benefit US capital and society at large through grossly undercompensated productive and reproductive labor, for other people's families as well as their own. At the very least, women should be offered a means to gain work authorization, permanent residence, or citizenship. The fact that in raising their own children, they, too, provide a service in nurturing future adult citizens should not be obscured by ideologies casting their children as somehow less worthy. . . .

NOTES

1. The *San Francisco Chronicle* reported that, although no precise figures exist, "experts believe a large percentage of the estimated 3 million undocumented workers now residing in the United States are employed in child-care and domestic work." See "Hiring of Aliens Is a Widespread Practice," *San Francisco Chronicle,* January 15, 1993, p. A-6.
2. Deborah Sontag, "Increasingly, Two-Career Family Means Illegal Immigrant Help," *New York Times,* January 24, 1993, p. A-13.
3. Sontag, "Increasingly, Two-Career Family Means Illegal Immigrant Help," p. A-13.
4. Sontag, "Increasingly, Two-Career Family Means Illegal Immigrant Help," p. A-13.
5. Felicity Barringer, "What Many Say About Baird: What She Did Wasn't Right," *New York Times,* January 22, 1993, p. A-1.
6. Barringer, "What Many Say About Baird," p. A-10.
7. Carla Marinucci, "Immigrant Abuse: 'Slavery, Pure and Simple,'" *San Francisco Examiner,* January 10, 1993, pp. A-1, A-8.
8. Marinucci, "Immigrant Abuse."
9. Chris Hogeland and Karen Rosen, "Dreams Lost, Dreams Found: Undocumented Women in the Land of Opportunity" (San Francisco: Coalition for Immigrant and Refugee Rights and Services, Immigrant Women's Task Force, 1991), pp. 10–11.
10. Carla Marinucci, "Silence Shields Abuse of Immigrant Women," *San Francisco Examiner,* January 11, 1993, pp. A-1, A-10.

11. The CIRRS report suggested that the availability of "underground" service jobs for women in housecleaning, child care, and the garment industry encourages women to migrate alone or without families. As one respondent, Rosa, explained: "I am very worried because we left the children with my parents, who are very old. We have not been able to send money home as planned because everything costs so much here." See Hogeland and Rosen, "Dreams Lost, Dreams Found," p. 5.

12. Interview with Warren Leiden, executive director of AILA, Washington, DC, March 22, 1993; interview with Lina Avidan, program director of CIRRS, San Francisco, March 15, 1993. Several proposals for a visa for "home care workers" (i.e., domestic workers, child-care workers, and home-health aides) emerged in response to the Zoë Baird affair.

13. The arguments in this chapter build on socialist feminist theory proposing that the welfare state mediates the conflicting demands for female home and market labor by subsidizing some women to remain home in order to reproduce and maintain the labor force while channeling others into low-wage work.

14. Undocumented workers who worked for 90 days in agriculture between May 1985 and May 1986 could gain temporary legal resident status as special agricultural workers (SAWs). If the SAW pool dropped below sufficient numbers, additional workers could be admitted as replenishment agricultural workers (RAWs). Finally, the category of nonimmigrant, temporary agricultural workers (H-2As) was maintained so that growers could obtain laborers if they were unable to find legal resident or citizen workers. Those entering under this type of visa are presumed to be here temporarily without the intention to remain. Immigration Reform Task Force, "Report from the States on the State Legalization Impact Assistance Grant Program" (Washington, DC: American Public Welfare Association, May 1989), pp. 1, 28–30. See also Leonard Dinnerstein and David M. Reimers, *Ethnic Americans* (New York: Harper & Row Publishers, 1988), pp. 103–106, for an overview of IRCA and its origins.

15. In a report of the House Judiciary Committee, the plight of the undocumented was aptly described: "These people live in fear, afraid to seek help when their rights are violated, when they are victimized by criminals, employers or landlords, or when they become ill." House of Representatives Report No. 682 (I), 99th Congress, 2nd Session (1986), cited in *California Rural Legal Assistance (CRLA) v. Legal Services Corporation (LSC)*, No. 89-16734., DC No. CV-89-1850-SAW, Opinion, October 26, 1990, p. 13299.

16. Congressional Record H10596-7 (daily edition, October 15, 1986), cited in *CRLA v. LSC*, p. 13299.

17. A Senate Judiciary Committee report states: "The Committee notes the concern expressed by state and local governments regarding the potential fiscal impact arising from participation in public assistance programs by the legalized population. This concern is related to the experience . . . with refugee populations, whose dependence on special Federal entitlement programs has reached 70 percent in the past year, thereby thwarting the primary intent of the . . . program, which is to encourage economic self-sufficiency among refugees." Report of the Committee on the Judiciary on S. 2222, Senate Report No. 485, 97th Congress, 2nd Session, (Washington, DC: Government Printing Office, June 1982), p. 49.

18. Charles Wheeler, "Alien Eligibility for Public Benefits," *Immigrants' Rights Manual of the National Immigration Law Center* (September 1990), pp. 11–45.

19. Charles Wheeler and Beth Zacovic, "The Public Charge Ground of Exclusion for Legalization Applicants," *Interpreter Releases* 64:35 (September 14, 1987), p. 1046.

20. Wheeler, "Alien Eligibility for Public Benefits," pp. 11–48.

21. Wheeler and Zacovic, "The Public Charge Ground of Exclusion," p. 1047.

22. 8 USC section 1255a (d) (B)(iii). "Public cash assistance" includes only those programs that provide monetary assistance, not in-kind benefits such as food stamps or medical services. See Wheeler, "Alien Eligibility," pp. 11–49.

23. Wheeler, "Alien Eligibility," pp. 11–49.

24. Wheeler and Zacovic, "The Public Charge Ground," p. 1047.

25. Wheeler and Zacovic, "The Public Charge Ground," p. 1047. Also see L. Chavez and R. Rumbaut et al., *The Politics of Migrant Health Care* (San Diego: University of California, August 1985). This study estimated that

30 to 40 percent of undocumented persons had incomes below the federal poverty level guidelines, although more than 90 percent of these men and 64 percent of these women were employed. Thus, a large proportion of legalization applicants might be viewed as potential public charges, solely on the basis of their low incomes. With the "special rule," Congress tried to prevent the use of income as the sole criterion for determining the excludability or admissibility of applicants such as these.

26. Wheeler and Zacovic, "The Public Charge Ground," p. 1047.
27. The Ninth Circuit includes Alaska, Arizona, California, Guam, Hawaii, Idaho, the Mariana Islands, Montana, Nevada, Oregon, and Washington.
28. Second Amended Complaint, *Zambrano v. INS,* Civ. No. S-88-455 EJG/EM (E.D. Cal. August 26, 1988), pp. 18–19.
29. The only named male plaintiff was himself temporarily disabled by kidney failure and received county General Assistance while undergoing treatment and therapy.
30. Second Amended Complaint, pp. 3–5.
31. Second Amended Complaint, pp. 3–5.
32. Second Amended Complaint, pp. 3–5.
33. Second Amended Complaint, pp. 10–11.
34. Second Amended Complaint, pp. 10–11.
35. Second Amended Complaint, pp. 3–11.
36. Second Amended Complaint, p. 2.
37. Second Amended Complaint, p. 2.
38. Second Amended Complaint, p. 18.
39. Second Amended Complaint, p. 19.
40. Order Granting Plaintiffs' Motions for Partial Summary Judgment, Permanent Injunction and Redefinition of Class, *Zambrano v. INS,* Civ. No. S-88-455 EJG/EM (E.D. Cal. July 31, 1989), pp. 8–19.
41. Order Granting Plaintiffs' Motions, p. 19.
42. First, INS challenged the order to review the cases of those class-two members who applied for amnesty under the extended deadline. Second, INS contended that the courts do not have jurisdiction over this matter, arguing that the plaintiffs should be required to exhaust the administrative remedies before gaining judicial review. This jurisdictional issue was raised by INS in the *Zambrano* case as well as in a number of other cases involving the legalization program (e.g., *Ayuda v. Thornburgh, Catholic Social Services v. Barr, LULAC v. INS,* and *Perales v. Thornburgh*). Third, INS has contended that plaintiffs'

counsel should not have access to the names of the class-one members. (This information was conveyed to me in interviews with Susan Drake, lawyer, National Immigration Law Center, October 1990, and Stephen Rosenbaum, lawyer, California Rural Legal Assistance, November 25, 1991.)
43. *Zambrano v. INS* (972 F2d 1122), 9th Cir., 1992.
44. Petition for certiorari pending, *INS v. Zambrano* 92-849, 61 USLW 3404 (1992).
45. Second Amended Complaint, p. 19.
46. Second Amended Complaint, p. 19.
47. Declaration of Beth Zacovic, Legal Aid attorney, at *Zambrano v. INS.* Civ. No. S-88-455 EJG-EM (E.D. Cal. May 17, 1988). Zacovic obtained these statistics in an interview with a legislative analyst for Los Angeles County in April 1988; cited in Diane Bessette, "Getting Left Behind: The Impact of the 1986 Immigration Reform and Control Act Amnesty Program on Single Women With Children," *Hastings International and Comparative Law Review* 13: 2 (Winter 1990), p. 301.
48. Bessette, "Getting Left Behind," p. 300.
49. Bessette, "Getting Left Behind," p. 303.
50. Declaration of Mavis Anderson, cited in Bessette, "Getting Left Behind," p. 304.
51. Bessette, "Getting Left Behind," 302.
52. I use the term *underclass* here as I would the term *underdeveloped nation* to indicate a group of people that has been marginalized or deliberately deprived of the means to achieve economic autonomy and political power.
53. Order, pp. 5–6.
54. Second Amended Complaint, p. 19.
55. Bessette, "Getting Left Behind," p. 300.
56. Interview with Stephen Rosenbaum, lawyer, California Rural Legal Assistance, November 25, 1991.
57. In this chapter, I draw on socialist feminist theory, which proposes that the state regulates the labor of women through welfare policy. Internal colonialist theory proposes that the state regulates the labor of immigrants through immigration policy. This is achieved through immigration policies that allow for the importation or "recruitment" of foreign labor and through policies that deny these laborers the rights of citizens, thus rendering them more easily exploitable. For a more extensive discussion of this topic, see note 15 above and Mario Barrera, *Race and Class in the Southwest: A Theory of Racial Inequality* (Notre Dame, IN: University of Notre Dame Press, 1979), especially pp. 116–22.

58. The National Immigration Law Center in Los Angeles is providing a service to advise those previously eligible to apply for work authorization under *Zambrano* to investigate other possibilities for legalization.
59. Interviews with Pauline Gee and Vibiana Andrade, November 1999; "Memorandum of Points and Authorities in Support of Plaintiffs' Motion for Award of Reasonable Attorneys' Fees Under Equal Access to Justice Act," *Zambrano v. INS*, US District Court, Eastern District of California, August 10, 1998, pp. 7–11.
60. Moreover, Andrade explained that the broader impact of IIRIRA has been devastating for immigrant rights, as it drastically limits the Court's jurisdiction in immigration and deportation matters. See also Anthony Lewis, "The Mills of Cruelty," *New York Times*, December 14, 1999, p. A-31, on efforts to modify IIRIRA in order to restore immigration judges' discretion or some process by which a deportation can be stayed in cases of extreme hardship or cruelty.
61. Approximately 25,000 members of Class 1 benefited from the preliminary and permanent injunctions by having their legalization applications reopened and considered under the correct, more favorable standards. Most Class 1 members were able to legalize their immigration status because of the *Zambrano* lawsuit. At least 11,000 Class 2 members received the right to file late applications because INS had failed to publicize the "clarification memos" with the correct public-charge standards. See "Memorandum of Points and Authorities," pp. 10–12.
62. Interview with Sheila Neville, lawyer, National Immigration Law Center, Los Angeles, November 1999.
63. California Immigrant Welfare Collaborative, "New INS Guidance on Public Charge: When Is It Safe to Use Public Benefits?," May 25, 1999. Available through National Immigration Law Center at 213-639-3900.
64. Interview with Vibiana Andrade, November 18, 1999.

QUESTIONS FOR DISCUSSION

1. If the "super-exploitation" of Latinas is driven by broad economic shifts and changes in government policy as Chang argues, these forces should affect others besides White women and women of color. Can you identify the ways that men, White or Latino, also benefit from the described pattern of exploitation?
2. Would the bad working conditions Chang described have occurred if Whites did not at some level accept the premise that Latinas are racially inferior?
3. Are the seeds of future racial inequality being sown when the children of Latinas who are U.S. citizens by birth are relegated to lives of poverty because they belong to a racial minority?

KEY TERMS

economic disparity
capitalism
globalization
multinational corporations
power elite
hyperconsumerism
slavery

THE SOCIAL WEB

- *Forbes* magazine publishes an extensive report on superwealthy Americans: www.forbes.com.
- Explore what can be done to eliminate slavery: www.antislavery.org.
- The Central Intelligence Agency of the United States has published a report on the exploitation of women's slave labor entitled "International Trafficking in Women to the United States: A Contemporary Manifestation of Slavery and Organized Crime," by Amy O'Neill Richard: www.usinfo.state.gov/topical/global/traffic/report/homepage.htm.
- Take *U.S. News'* virtual tour of Bill Gates's $63 million, 66,000-square-foot home: www.usnews.com/usnews/nycu/tech/billgate/gatehigh.htm.

QUESTIONS FOR DEBATE

1. What are the structural and cultural effects of globalization? What kinds of social problems result from each?
2. How has the United States benefited from the resources of other nations? Is globalization functional for the U.S. at the expense of other countries?
3. Does the U.S. have a responsibility to assist impoverished countries?
4. Do you think globalization is a good thing? Why or why not?

Chapter 4
Poverty

Contents

Learning Objectives

By the end of this chapter you should be able to:

- Recognize how these authors use one or more of the major perspectives to analyze poverty.
- Explore how poverty is shaped by inequalities of gender and race.
- Identify the ways that poverty is socially constructed.
- Describe various consequences of poverty.
- Analyze how individuals contribute to poverty through their everyday behavior.
- Explain how social systems and institutions perpetuate poverty.

Defining the Problem

Although the term *poverty* is a fairly common one in discussions about social problems in the United States, the actual definition of poverty is widely debated. The definition of poverty that is used has important implications for those who make economic and social policies and for those who receive welfare services. Sociologists generally regard **absolute poverty** as a condition in which individuals do not have the most fundamental resources to meet their survival needs. People living in absolute poverty may lack necessary food, water, clothing, or shelter. Their children are likely to be malnourished, and they do not have access to basic health care. Absolute poverty is a standard of minimum sufficiency. It allows us to discuss poverty on a worldwide basis. Absolute poverty is likely to be common in underdeveloped nations. In these countries, premature death rates are high, illiteracy is widespread, and, as we discussed in the introduction to Chapter 2, children are frequently used as a cheap source of labor in sweatshop conditions. Governments provide few safety nets to ensure the well-being of families. This is the most severe form of poverty.

Relative poverty is a term sociologists use to describe people whose survival needs may be met but who are nonetheless poor. These individuals experience a great deal of economic insecurity. They have few options for the goods and services that are considered necessary for a good quality of life, such as housing, education, and health care. Although most of the people living in relative poverty in the U.S. are working, they are nevertheless **underemployed.** They have low-wage jobs, and their incomes fall well below the country's median household income. Relative poverty is a useful concept because it refers to measuring poverty in a specific context. It allows us to measure the number of people who experience a substandard of living relative to others who live in the same country. For example, poor people in the United States do not experience the extreme poverty, such as lack of clean drinking water or the threat of starvation, that the poor in other nations do. However, they experience a compromised life with more limited options when compared to many other Americans.

The **poverty threshold** is the standard used by the U.S. government to measure the rate of poverty in our nation and to determine eligibility for many services. In 2000, the poverty threshold for a family of three was an income of $13,738. Most sociologists believe that this figure is an arbitrary number that does not adequately reflect the income required to achieve a decent standard of living. It is calculated using the cost of a basic diet for a year and multiplying by 3 (assuming the poor spend one-third of their income on food). Many scholars would argue for a relative poverty threshold that is roughly one-half of the median family income, or $25,445.

Scope of the Problem

Following a drastic increase in the 1980s, poverty in the United States began declining in the mid-1990s. In 2000, more than 32 million people fell below the poverty threshold. The **poverty rate** is the percent of the population whose total income falls at or below the poverty threshold. The poverty rate in 2000 was 11.3 percent, representing a decline in the poverty rate from 12.7 percent (35 million people) in 1998.[1]

Poverty is most severely experienced in inner cities. Whereas the suburbs had a poverty rate of 7.8 percent, more than 16 percent of people living in central cities lived in poverty. The South is the poorest region in the country, although nationwide poverty rates vary widely, from 6.3 percent in New Hampshire to 18.7 percent in New Mexico.

Although nearly half of Americans living in poverty are White, racial minorities are disproportionately affected by poverty. Whereas 7.5 percent of non-Hispanic Whites were living in poverty in 2000, the poverty rate for Hispanics was 21.2 percent. The rate for Asian Americans was 10.7 percent. Twenty-two percent (1 in 5) of Black Americans are living in poverty. These numbers are disturbingly high. Still, they represent the lowest poverty level for minorities since 1959, the earliest year for which these statistics are available.

Gender also significantly affects the experience of poverty. Most people who live in poverty are women and their children. Nearly one-fourth of single-mother families live in poverty. Gender, race, and family type are interwoven; less than 5 percent of White married-couple families live below the poverty threshold, but one-fifth of White single-mother families do. Twenty percent of Asian and 34 percent of Black and Hispanic single-mother families live in poverty.

By far, the group most affected by poverty globally, as well as in the United States, is children. More than 16 percent (more than 11 million) of children in the U.S. live in poverty. The child poverty rate in the U.S. is two to three times higher than in other industrialized nations. Eight percent (2 million) of our nation's children under age 6 live in extreme poverty; their families' income falls below one-half of the poverty threshold.[2]

Perspectives on the Problem

Sociologists who study poverty do so from a variety of perspectives. Some take a *macro* approach, looking at the large economic processes and forces that cause poverty both

---

[1] U.S. Census Bureau, *Current Population Survey,* March 2000 and 2001.

[2] "Low-Income Children in the United States: A Brief Demographic Profile," National Center for Children in Poverty, September 2002.

globally and within specific countries or regions. For example, a sociologist using a *conflict* perspective is likely to examine the ways that policies related to poverty benefit wealthy individuals and nations. They are likely to explore whether specific social policies increase or decrease poverty rates. A sociologist using a *functionalist* perspective would examine the ways that poverty is beneficial to the capitalist system by, for example, ensuring that there is always a reserve pool of available workers during times of economic expansion. Other sociologists use a *micro*-level analysis to examine the consequences of poverty for the people whose lives are most drastically affected. Many scholars who use an *interactionist* approach explore the consequences of welfare policies on individuals. They believe that poverty, which most profoundly affects racial minority groups, women, and children, can be understood only within the complex matrix of race, class, and gender. Finally, while sociologists agree that poverty is an objective condition that has serious consequences for people's lives, *social constructionists* focus on the ways that cultural discourse about poverty constructs how the poor are viewed and treated.

Connecting the Perspectives

The readings in this section represent these varied approaches to studying poverty. John Isbister uses a conflict perspective to examine poverty on a global level, arguing that wealthy nations have a responsibility to assist poor ones. William Julius Wilson looks at the structural causes of poverty in the United States, especially as they affect the African American community. Using a functionalist perspective, he explores how the breakdown of social support structures in inner cities undermines individual families' ability to cope. Ruth Sidel uses a social constructionist approach to explore cultural discourse about the poor. She argues that poor

women have become the scapegoats for many social problems in the United States. Taking a conflict perspective, Barbara Ehrenreich and Frances Fox Piven examine the effects of welfare reform in an economy where jobs are increasingly scarce. Finally, Kathryn Edin and Laura Lein use an interactionist approach to look at the effects of welfare on the lives of single mothers and the difficulties they face in trying to survive on welfare benefits.

Reading Summaries

In "A World of Poverty," Isbister explores the causes and consequences of poverty on a global level. So-called **Third World** nations have a multitude of languages, religions, and cultural ways of life. The characteristics these nations share that transcends other differences is the fact that, relative to **First World** nations, they experience widespread poverty. The consequences of such pervasive poverty are great. People in these nations are more likely to have ongoing, severe health problems, be poorly educated, experience childhood malnutrition, and die prematurely.

According to Isbister, developed nations are, to a great degree, responsible for the poverty in poor countries. The economic gap between rich and poor nations is staggering. This gap is produced by the relationship between wealthy and impoverished countries. Rich nations have been able to accumulate wealth by exploiting the resources, labor, and environments of poor nations. Thus, individuals who live in First World countries like the United States share responsibility for global poverty. The wealthy always obtain privileges at the expense of the poor, and Isbister argues that the same can be said of the global economic system.

In "Ghetto-Related Behavior and the Structure of Opportunity," Wilson focuses on the intersections between poverty and race in the United States. He specifically examines structured inequality in urban ghettos, and points out that the opportunities available for African Americans in inner-city neighborhoods are extremely limited. Jobs are scarce, housing is inadequate, and educational opportunities are deficient. Additionally, the resources available in other communities, such as transportation and job information networks, are lacking. Thus "circumstances generally taken for granted in middle-class society are often major obstacles that must be overcome in the inner-city ghetto." Wilson maintains that these factors severely constrain the choices that individuals living in these neighborhoods can make. Without the employment-based culture and opportunities that other citizens have, some ghetto residents turn to drugs, crime, and gang activity. This behavior, in turn, contributes to a level of violence and fear that affects all ghetto residents, and people become more socially isolated from one another as a matter of survival. Yet this isolation also contributes to the loss of social resources, which, in turn, perpetuates the loss of opportunity for all ghetto residents.

Wilson has been criticized by some sociologists for taking a **culture of poverty** approach that focuses on the traits poor people have acquired that contribute to their own impoverishment. Yet Wilson is clear to point out that ghetto conditions result from an inadequate economy that has all but abandoned inner-city neighborhoods. He blames the lack of employment opportunities for the levels of crimes, drug abuse, and violence that make up much of life in urban ghettos. These are not ghetto-*specific* problems; that is, they are found in middle-class neighborhoods as well. Rather, these behaviors are ghetto-*related*, appearing more commonly in areas that have more poverty and fewer jobs.

In "The Enemy Within," Sidel analyzes the ways our culture views the poor as morally deficient, sexually irresponsible, and socially deviant. Although most poor people in the United States are not dependent on welfare, poverty has become equated with welfare. Sidel discusses how numerous myths about welfare recipients contribute to a climate that dehumanizes the poor, especially poor mothers. The derision with which our culture views mothers on welfare turns poor women, especially poor African American women, into "folk devils" who are "the ultimate outsiders" in American society. Thus, Sidel argues, "mother-only families are being blamed for virtually all of the ills affecting American society."

Why does American society hate the poor for being poor? Sidel argues that in a post–Cold War era, we have no distinct enemies outside U.S. borders. Thus, welfare recipients have become the new enemy. Moreover, as the average wages for Americans stagnate while the income of the super-rich grows to unprecedented levels, the poor increasingly take the blame for the economic troubles of middle-class Americans. Just as we are diverted by a magician's sleight of hand, we are encouraged to focus the gaze of our discontent on the poor instead of on the elites who benefit from economic restructuring. In blaming welfare mothers for both their own plight and our economic anxieties, we perpetuate the belief that poverty is caused by the lack of individual achievement. Therefore, we do not acknowledge the ways that economic inequality is structured in the United States.

In "Without a Safety Net," Barbara Ehrenreich and Frances Fox Piven examine the consequences of welfare reform. During the 1990s, the U.S. stock market performed well, and unemployment and poverty rates decreased. Welfare reform became a popular political issue. The new welfare reform, called **Temporary Aid to Needy Families (TANF),** was premised upon the idea that people on welfare simply had to be forced to go to work. It also set strict time limits on assistance. Policy makers assumed that jobs were plentiful and that families could be supported above the poverty threshold if only people went to work.

According to Ehrenreich and Piven, welfare reform was shortsighted and misguided. The minimum-wage jobs that welfare recipients were likely to get did not pay enough to lift families out of poverty. Moreover, the late 1990s saw a downturn in the economy; even low-wage service jobs began to disappear. This occurred precisely at the time when many welfare recipients reached their five-year time limit for assistance. Welfare rolls are dropping, yet families are not able to get along without it. Instead, many people are finding themselves trying to eke out an existence in poverty without the traditional safety net provided by a secure welfare system.

Edin and Lein look specifically at policies and practices of the welfare system. "Making Ends Meet on a Welfare Check" presents the results of their study of welfare recipients to determine how effective programs are in meeting the needs of America's poor families. They found that even the minimal costs of maintaining a family with young children, including housing, utilities, food, clothing, transportation, and education, far exceeded the benefits mothers were receiving from the government. Despite the widespread public belief that welfare is a generous system that provides amply for its recipients, Edin and Lein describe the extreme difficulties in making ends meet on welfare. Only one woman (out of 214 mothers) spent only what she received in welfare. This left her with such little money that her child often went hungry and inadequately clothed. The women's experiences described in this reading represent a stark contrast to the public attitudes about welfare that Sidel discusses. Edin and Lein show us that surviving on welfare takes planning, hard work, and a lot of luck.

FOCUSING QUESTIONS

As you read through the articles in Chapter 4, consider the following questions: How is poverty a structural problem that is created and sustained by social forces beyond poor people's control? Why do we hold such negative views toward the poor in American society? Finally, think about the social policies aimed at preventing poverty. Do they help or punish poor people? Who benefits from recent reforms? What policies do you think would be truly effective for eliminating poverty?

11

A WORLD OF POVERTY

JOHN ISBISTER

A poverty curtain has descended right across the face of our world, dividing it materially and philosophically into two different worlds, two separate planets, two unequal humanities—one embarrassingly rich and the other desperately poor.

—MAHBUB UL HAQ,
The Poverty Curtain

"And what about the people of your household?" he asked Akuebue.
"They were quiet when I left them. There was no sickness, only hunger."

—CHINUA ACHEBE,
Arrow of God

The third world today covers most of the globe. It embraces countless cultures, religions, traditions, and ways of life. Its achievements are monumental. Yet there is a single characteristic that pervades the third world, distinguishing it from the industrialized countries: widespread poverty. Not everyone in the third world is poor: there are middle-class strata as well as pockets of luxury. There are productive factories and sparkling computer centers. But the *favela* dwellers, the peasants, the underemployed, and many of the industrial workers of the third world subsist at standards of living that are low to the point of incomprehension for people living in the industrialized world.

Poverty has many dimensions. It can be thought of as an absolute condition or as relative. Absolute poverty is a standard of living so pressing that it brings with it life-threatening malnutrition and disease. The United Nations Development Program (UNDP) has estimated the number of people in absolute poverty in the world in several different ways. The most obvious criterion is simply a lack of income. Using a poverty line of a dollar a day, the UNDP estimates that about 1.3 billion people, or one-third of the population in the developing world, are poor.[1]

Lack of income is only the beginning of an understanding of poverty, however. The UNDP has developed a capability poverty measure (CPM), measuring the lack of three basic capabilities: (1) the capability to be well nourished, measured by the proportion of children under the age of five who are underweight; (2) the capability for healthy reproduction, measured by the proportion of births unattended by trained health personnel; and (3) the capability to be educated, measured by female illiteracy. This measure of basic opportunity puts particular emphasis on the status of women. Use of the capability criterion yields a higher estimate of poverty in the third world than does the income criterion: about 37 percent of the population, or 1.6 billion people. Other attributes of poverty exist, including being disabled, lacking adequate housing, having poor health and dying prematurely, having to put children in employment, having to accept demeaning or low-status work, and having food security for only a few months

Isbister, John. 1998. "A World of Poverty." In *Promises Not Kept*. 4th ed. West Hartford, CT: Kumarian Press. Reprinted with permission from the publisher.

TABLE 1   Poverty in Selected Countries (mid-1990s)

Country	*Percentage of Population That Is Income Poor*	*Percentage of Population That Is Capability Poor*
Bangladesh	47.5	76.9
India	25.4	61.5
Pakistan	34.0	60.8
Guinea-Bissau	49.0	56.6
Morocco	13.1	49.7
Uganda	55.0	45.9
Indonesia	16.7	42.3
Ghana	35.9	39.3
Kenya	37.0	33.8
Tunisia	14.1	29.9
Peru	32.0	25.7
Zimbabwe	25.5	22.3
Thailand	21.8	21.1
Sri Lanka	22.4	19.3
China	10.9	17.5
Venezuela	31.3	15.2

Source: United Nations Development Program, *Human Development Report 1996* (New York: Oxford University Press, 1996), 27. Reprinted with permission from the publisher.

a year.[2] The condition of being poor is complicated, and the dividing line between the poor and the near-poor is inexact. Clearly, however, the prevalence of poverty in the world is massive. Table 1 contains the UNDP estimates of both income poverty and capability poverty in the mid-1990s. The countries are listed in order of the capability index, with the poorest at the top.

Whatever criterion is used, about one-third of the third world's population lives in poverty. In Africa, the proportion is closer to one-half. More than 70 percent of the world's poor are Asians.[3] Most of the poor—over three-quarters—live in rural areas, according to UNDP estimates. In spite of the fact that they grow crops, they endure monotonous, unbalanced diets; inadequate caloric intake; and malnutrition. They have lower health standards than urban people and have less access to clean water and sanitation facilities. They suffer the diseases of the undernourished. At each age their prob-

ability of dying is higher than that among the rest of the population.

Poverty is not restricted to this most desperate stratum of human beings, however. A great deal of the world's poverty should be thought of in relative terms—that is, poverty is a relationship. One thinks of oneself as poor only if others are rich and one's poverty is measured against that richness. The surviving Pygmies of the Congo's rain forest live at a subsistence level and suffer from diseases that have been eliminated elsewhere, but they do not think of themselves as poor. They live in a self-contained society, hunting and gathering as their ancestors did for centuries, in harmony with the forest and its spirits. But Mauwa Funidi, the librarian of Kisangani, who actually has access to more goods and services than the Pygmies do, is desperately poor.

Poverty in this relative sense is found in every country in the world. In the United States, millions of people live in a poverty that is frightening, scandalous, and unfamiliar to almost all who surround them. Most receive income that is much greater than that of the typical person in Asia or Africa, but this does not mean that their poverty is any less real. The homeless living on the sidewalks in central cities or in temporary shelters, single parents in slum housing, the unemployed who have exhausted their resources, former farmers who ran into debt before losing their patrimonies to foreclosure—these are some of the faces of poverty in one of the world's richest countries. What poverty really means is the inability to make choices. A family of four in the United States with $8,000 annual income is completely constrained in its choices and deeply impoverished, but in the world's low-income countries, where the average income per person was the equivalent of $430 in 1995,[4] a family of four with $8,000 would be privileged.

The *third world* and *poverty* are both terms of relationship. The third world is the world dominated, the world excluded from power. The poor are the people on the bottom, the people denied the benefits of the society in which they live.

The differences in income that exist in today's world are staggering. In Switzerland in 1995, the average income per person was the equivalent of U.S.$40,630; in the United States, the figure was $26,980. In the poorest forty-nine countries, with more than half of the world's population, the average income was $430, 1.6 percent of the typical U.S. income and just 1 percent of Switzerland's.[5] . . .

This is the overwhelming truth about the world we inhabit: the gap between the richness of the developed countries and the poverty of the third world is so huge that it is almost beyond our understanding. How can one imagine living for a whole year on the money one now spends in just one month? It would not be a matter of "belt tightening"; it would be a totally different and devastating life. In the United States, Canada, or Britain, an ordinary family with one working parent typically lives in a house or an apartment with several bedrooms, a living room, a kitchen, at least one bathroom, running water, and a heating system. The family has a car, quite a lot of clothes, a radio, a television set, some books, and enough extra money to eat out from time to time, go to the movies, and take a vacation. The family members are generally in good health, and if they are not they have access to modern medical technology, the expense of which is often insured. Described this way, it does not seem like a great deal. But for Mauwa, Domitila, Shahhat, Rigoberta, and the Mossi people, it is a universe apart. It is not quite as incomprehensible to them as their situation is to us, since Western popular culture—movies, magazines, and television—has swept into most corners of the world and created some impressions of middle-class life in the industrialized world. It is so distinct from their situations as to be absolutely unattainable, however.

Among the poor of the world, a family typically shares one room—and in rural areas, the room may provide shelter for farm animals as well. The family members do not have enough good food to eat. They usually (but not always) have enough to prevent starvation, but they suffer from dietary deficiencies of both calories and particular nutrients. They have few clothes, no private cars, no vacations, and no money to spend on things beyond necessities. They experience perpetual insecurity because they hardly ever have savings sufficient to tide the family over during bad times. Above all, they are threatened by bad health—high infant mortality, less than full physical development of children, susceptibility to disease, uncertain life spans.

The pattern is far from uniform—every conceivable variation exists in the third world, as in the developed world. No variation, however, can conceal the basic fact of overwhelming poverty throughout much of Asia, the Middle East, Africa, and Latin America: the almost unclothed people living in the streets of Calcutta and Bombay, the gaunt herders of central Africa whose fertile plains are slowly but inexorably eroding into desert, the peasants of northeastern Brazil driven from their homes by drought and landowners, the bark-clothed peasants of Mozambique fleeing from war zones.

One feature shared by all the world's poor is insecurity. When times are good—when the rains fall, when the market price is high—the family can be fed and a few improvements made to the dwelling. Bad luck may strike at any time, though, and wipe out the chance for survival itself. When times are bad in Africa, in India, in China, thousands starve to death. The consciousness of imminent disaster, a fear of what the future will bring, has been found by social scientists to be pervasive among the world's poor, and for good reason.

The poverty of the third world is not "traditional"; it is not an ancient way of life. The traditional cultures of the third world are rich and various, and they are closer to the surface of everyday life than traditions usually are in the industrialized world, where they have been suppressed. The old folkways of the third world have little to do with poverty. The great religions of the third world—Hinduism, Buddhism, Islam—are not apologies for poverty; they are integral worldviews that bind the generations together. The philosophies and customs that developed over the millennia led to a sense of belonging, not a sense of exclusion. Scattered throughout the world are some significant groups of people living in completely traditional ways much as their ancestors did—for example, in the rain forests of Africa, New Guinea, and some parts of the

Philippines. In learning about them we can discern something about the common heritage of the human race.

The way that these traditional people live is not, however, typical of the widespread poverty that mars the face of the globe. The endless urban slums are not traditional; they are recent. The population explosion that magnifies the number of poor and threatens the very survival of the globe is a phenomenon of the last century, not of time immemorial. The poor laborers in the tobacco, cocoa, banana, cotton, rubber, and sugar fields are not obeying traditional cultural imperatives; they are producing export crops for sale in the prosperous markets of the United States and Europe. . . .

Poverty is never shared equally, even in the poorest countries. Every society has some rich, some middle income, and some poor, and the relative size of the income gap between the rich and the poor varies greatly among countries. One should not think that because India, for example, had an average income of $340 in 1995 that all Indians enjoyed that modest income. The majority of Indians had less than $340 a year, and a substantial number of Indians had very much less. Correspondingly, middle-class and wealthy Indians commanded a great deal more of the country's economic resources.

The distribution of income among different groups has been surveyed in a number of the world's poor countries, although it must be conceded that the data are suspect. The surveys have been taken in different years, using different concepts and statistical methods, and with differing degrees of accuracy. Consequently, international comparisons are perilous. Nevertheless, the latest available data appear to confirm what has sometimes been called the Kuznets curve: as countries' average incomes rise from the very poorest levels, income distribution first becomes unequal, then more equal.[6] Put differently, it appears that when economic growth takes place in poor countries, it does not usually improve the status of the poorest; rather, it raises the rewards of upper-income groups and leaves the poor further behind. Only after a certain level of economic development has occurred can the poor share in its fruits. . . .

Poverty is not shared equally by the sexes. Women have access to less health care than men. They receive less schooling; consequently, their illiteracy rates are higher. They perform work that is more tedious and of lower status than men's work, and they receive less compensation. They usually work longer hours because, in addition to their work outside the home, they are almost always solely responsible for all the work inside the home. . . .

The poor are undernourished and malnourished—with less caloric intake and less protein and vitamin intake than they need. As a consequence, many of their children do not achieve full physical and mental development. In a survey for the period 1989–95, the World Bank found that between one-quarter and two-thirds of children under the age of five in the poorest countries of the third world were malnourished. The proportion for China was 17 percent, but the proportions for Bangladesh and India were 84 and 63 percent, respectively.[7]

The poor are susceptible to disease and premature mortality at much higher rates than are the people of richer countries. The third world has actually seen dramatic improvements in health and longevity over the last fifty years, as the benefits of public health and sanitation measures have been extended throughout the world. Yet large differences still exist between developed and developing countries.

Disease is far more prevalent in the third world than in the rich countries. Surveys in Latin America and Africa have shown that fully 90 percent of the people studied were infested with some form of parasite. In Peru, for example, 113 out of 122

men sampled in the armed forces had parasitic infections. Ninety percent of people in an area of East Africa were found to have beef tapeworms. The prevalence of tropical diseases such as hookworm, bilharzia, filariasis, and schistosomiasis is almost universal in some areas.[8] These diseases are typically associated with pain and loss of strength, and sometimes with early mortality. The UNDP estimates that about a fifth of the people in the third world lack access to any primary health care services.[9]

Illiteracy is widespread in the third world. Although schooling has expanded rapidly in the last several decades, one-quarter of the men and fully one-half of the women are still unable to read or write. Between 900 million and 1 billion people are illiterate, three-quarters of them in the five largest Asian countries.[10]

These are the bare facts about living standards in the third world—low average incomes, substantial numbers of people living in the direst and most life-threatening poverty, and an incredible gap between the poor countries and the economically developed countries. It would not be correct to call this situation a crisis, because it persists from year to year. It is a tragedy. . . .

The Betrayal of Responsibility

The people in the rich countries bear some responsibility for the poverty of the third world. There are two dimensions to this responsibility. First is a difficult set of questions related to causality: How did the economic progress of the rich countries help or hurt the prospects of the poor? How did the empires of the rich impact the lives of the poor? How are the policies of the rich today affecting the standards of living of the third world? These complex questions are addressed in subsequent chapters.

There is a much simpler dimension to the responsibility of the rich, however, a dimension completely independent of one's answers to the questions in the previous paragraph. Living in a world of obscene inequality, the privileged have a moral responsibility to do what they can to improve the lot of the less privileged. This responsibility arises from the common humanity of all people; we are a single species. It is a responsibility recognized by most ethical and religious systems. It is a responsibility urged upon the rich by spokespeople of the world's poor in countless conferences and forums. It is a responsibility willingly embraced by many people and institutions in the rich countries. Taken as a whole, however, and with those honorable exceptions, the rich countries have rejected and betrayed their responsibility to the third world.

The evidence that the rich do not recognize their responsibility to the world's poor is everywhere. When the agenda before the U.S. government is to cut its budgetary deficit, the most vulnerable items include foreign aid, because it has only a weak domestic constituency. When Americans were considering the desirability of a North American Free Trade Agreement (among Mexico, Canada, and the United States), almost all the debate centered on the advantages and disadvantages of the pact for American citizens; the welfare of the Mexicans was ignored or considered irrelevant. Americans have been loath to intervene in Bosnia, Rwanda, and Zaire, when intervention in those countries could have saved the lives of civilians. Closer to home, "welfare reform" in the United States has come to mean not providing more generously for the disadvantaged but providing more stringently and punitively.

Perhaps the rich avoid grappling with the inequity on the planet and their responsibility for it because a full understanding would seriously threaten the sense they have of themselves. Most people in North America and western Europe do not think of themselves as rich beyond imagination,

and certainly not as oppressors. On the contrary, they see themselves as comfortable, perhaps, but still struggling to make ends meet; as financially insecure, but hoping to do a bit better in the future. Most see themselves in the position of the little guy, fighting for some advantage against forces that are more powerful.

In their own societies and daily lives, that kind of an attitude makes sense, but from a global perspective, it is nonsense. Most Americans, for example, live lives of incredible luxury compared with almost everyone in the third world. There are exceptions—the poor in the North, the rich in the South—but not many. If Americans and Europeans were to think of themselves in this sort of global context, as constituting the world's privileged, they might then face painful questions relating to their responsibilities. They might have to ask themselves: Where does their responsibility lie? Does their material comfort require others to be poor? Are they making world poverty worse, or are they part of the solution? Should they try to be part of the solution? What solutions might there be? Will an attack on world poverty require sacrifices from them? What kind of sacrifices?

These are questions that most people in the developed world would prefer to avoid. It is stretching an analogy only a bit to recall the "good Germans" of the 1930s and 1940s who knew nothing about the Holocaust being perpetrated by the regime to which they gave loyalty because they did not want to know. If people today know nothing about the hunger and disease of India, Congo, Cambodia, and Honduras (to say nothing of south-central Los Angeles), it is in large measure because they would prefer not to, because the knowledge would powerfully threaten their rather complacent sense of themselves. If they turn their backs on the majority of the world's population and address only their own problems, it is because it would be shocking and dangerous to do otherwise.

The privileged are turning their backs. Most people in the developed countries, having achieved a comfortable standard of living, are largely oblivious to the fate of the world's majority and to their own responsibility for that fate.

One should not overstate the argument. People in the rich countries cannot solve the problems of the poor countries by themselves. The destiny of the third world is in the hands of its people, to make of it what they will. It is they who will determine their future, not North Americans or Europeans. To think otherwise is to perpetuate a peculiarly modern form of cultural imperialism, to conceive of the rich as puppet masters, manipulating the strings that make the rest of the world dance. They do not.

There is plenty of responsibility to go around for the predicament of the world's poor, and third world leaders can claim a lot of it. Military regimes have attacked their own people, protected the exploiters of their own poor, and squandered billions on armaments. Nationalist leaders have wasted resources on flashy, self-serving projects. Voices of the needy have been squelched. The principal drama of the third world rests in the third world, among its own people.

Still the prosperous countries and their institutions—their governments, armed forces, corporations, voluntary associations—powerfully affect the constraints within which the third world must determine its future. Having played a central role in the creation of the world's inequities, they could allow themselves to be used constructively. They will not help by being missionaries, by trying to bring the ideology of free markets or even democratic institutions to the third world. The people of the poor countries will do that well or badly by themselves, and there is not much that the rich can do about it. Their responsibility is to reform their own institutions, to lend a hand

that is open and not clenched, to be helpful and not harmful to the world's poor. This is a task that is achievable and is also respectful of the third world, not manipulative.

NOTES

1. United Nations Development Program, *Human Development Report 1997* (New York: Oxford University Press, 1996), 27.
2. Robert Chambers, *Whose Reality Counts? Putting the First Last* (London: Intermediate Technology Publications, 1997), cited in UNDP, *Human Development Report 1997*, 17. The UNDP has used a number of separate measures of poverty to develop a human poverty index, which it employs in addition to the income measure and the capability measure.
3. UNDP, *Human Development Report 1997*, 27.
4. World Bank, *World Development Report 1997* (New York: Oxford University Press, 1997), table 1.
5. World Bank, *World Development Report 1997*, table 1.
6. World Bank, *World Development Report 1997*, table 5.
7. World Bank, *World Development Report 1997*, table 6.
8. See Andrew M. Kamarck, *The Tropics and Economic Development: A Provocative Inquiry into the Poverty of Nations* (Baltimore: Johns Hopkins University Press, 1973), chap. 7.
9. UNDP, *Human Development Report 1997*.
10. UNDP, *Human Development Report 1997*.

QUESTIONS FOR DISCUSSION

1. Isbister claims that "poverty is a relationship." What does this mean? What are the implications of thinking about poverty as a relationship?
2. According to Isbister, who is responsible for global poverty? What are the various ways that wealthy countries share responsibility for poverty? Do you agree with Isbister's perspective?

12

GHETTO-RELATED BEHAVIOR
AND THE STRUCTURE OF OPPORTUNITY
WILLIAM JULIUS WILSON

Seven out of eight people residing in ghettos in metropolitan areas in 1990 were minority group members, most of them African-Americans.

As we shall soon see, the residents of these jobless black poverty areas face certain social constraints on the choices they can make in their daily lives. These constraints, combined with restricted opportunities in the larger society, lead to ghetto-related behavior and attitudes—that is, behavior and attitudes that are found more frequently in ghetto neighborhoods than in neighborhoods that feature even modest levels of poverty and local employment. Ghetto-related behavior and attitudes often reinforce the economic marginality of the residents of jobless ghettos.

I choose the term "ghetto-related" as opposed to "ghetto-specific" so as to make the following point: Although many of the behaviors to be described and analyzed here are rooted in circumstances that are unique to inner-city ghettos (for example, extremely high rates of concentrated joblessness and poverty), they are fairly widespread in the larger society. In other words, these behaviors are not unique to ghettos, as the term "ghetto-specific" would imply; rather they occur with greater frequency in the ghetto.

. . .

Neighborhoods that offer few legitimate employment opportunities, inadequate job information networks, and poor schools lead to the disappearance of work. That is, where jobs are scarce, where people rarely, if ever, have the opportunity to help their friends and neighbors find jobs, and where there is a disruptive or degraded school life purporting to prepare youngsters for eventual participation in the workforce, many people eventually lose their feeling of connectedness to work in the formal economy; they no longer expect work to be a regular, and regulating, force in their lives. In the case of young people, they may grow up in an environment that lacks the idea of work as a central experience of adult life—they have little or no labor-force attachment. These circumstances also increase the likelihood that the residents will rely on illegitimate sources of income, thereby further weakening their attachment to the legitimate labor market.

On the other hand, many inner-city ghetto residents who maintain a connection with the formal labor market—that is, who continue to be employed mostly in low-wage jobs—are, in effect, working against all odds. They somehow manage to work steadily despite the lack of work-support networks (car pools, informal job information networks), institutions (good schools and training programs), and systems (child care and transportation) that most of the employed population in this country rely on. Moreover, the travel costs, child care costs, and other employment-related expenses consume a significant portion of their already meager incomes. In other words, in order to fully appreciate the problems of employment experienced by inner-city ghetto workers, one has to understand that there is both a unique reality of work and a culture of work (see sections that follow).

Accordingly, as we examine the adaptations and responses of ghetto residents to persistent joblessness in this chapter, it should be emphasized that the disappearance of work in many inner-city neighborhoods is the function of a number of factors beyond their control. Too often, as reflected in the current public policy debates on welfare reform, the discussion of behavior and social responsibility fails to mention the structural underpinnings of poverty and welfare. The focus is mainly on the shortcomings of individuals and families and not on the structural and social changes in the society at large that have made life so miserable for many inner-city ghetto residents or that have produced certain unique responses and behavior patterns over time.

Given the current policy debates that tend to assign blame and attribute failure to personal shortcomings, these are the points that the reader should keep in mind as I discuss the responses and adaptations to chronic subordination, including those that have evolved into cultural patterns. The social action—including behavior, habits, skills, styles, orientations, attitudes—discussed in this chapter ought not to be analyzed as if it were unrelated to the broader structure of opportunities and constraints that have evolved over time. This is not to argue that individuals and groups lack the freedom to make their own choices, engage in certain conduct, and develop certain styles and orientations, but it is to say that these decisions and actions occur within a context of constraints and opportunities that are drastically different from those present in middle-class society.

Many inner-city ghetto residents clearly see the social and cultural effects of living in high-jobless and impoverished neighborhoods. A 17-year-old black male who works part-time, attends college, and resides in a ghetto poverty neighborhood on the West Side stated:

> Well, basically, I feel that if you are raised in a neighborhood and all you see is negative things, then you are going to be negative because you don't see anything positive. . . . Guys and black males see drug dealers on the corner and they see fancy cars and flashy money and they figure: "Hey, if I get into drugs I can be like him."

A 25-year-old West Side father of two who works two jobs to make ends meet presented a similar point of view about some inner-city black males:

> They try to find easier routes, uh, and had been conditioned over a period of time to just be lazy, so to speak. Uh, motivation nonexistent, you know, and the society that they're affiliated with really don't advocate hard work and struggle to meet your goals such as education and stuff like that. And they see what's around 'em and they follow that same pattern, you know. The society says: "Well, you can sell dope. You can do this. You can do that." A lot of 'em even got to the point where they can accept a few years in jail, uh, as a result of what they might do. . . . They don't see nobody getting up early in the morning, going to work or going to school all the time. The guys they—they be with don't do that . . . 'cause that's the crowd that you choose—well, that's been presented to you by your neighborhood.

Describing how children from troubled neighborhoods get into drugs and alcohol, an unemployed black male who lives in a poor suburb south of Chicago stated:

> They're in an environment where if you don't get high you're square. You know what I'm saying? If you don't get high some kind of way or another . . . and then, you know, kids are gonna emulate what they come up under. . . . I've watched a couple of generations—I've been here since '61. I watched kids, I saw their fathers ruined, and I seen 'em grow up and do the very same thing. . . . The children, they don't have any means of recreation whatsoever out here, other than their backyards, the streets, nothing. . . . The only way it can be intervened if the child has something outside the house to go to, because it is—just go by the environment of the house, he's destined to be an alcoholic or a drug addict.

Some of the respondents relate the problems facing children to the limited opportunity structure in high-jobless neighborhoods. "There's less opportunities over here: it's no jobs. The kids aren't in school, you know, they're not getting any education, there's a lot of drugs on the streets. So, you know, wrong environment, bad associations," reported a 40-year-old mother of six who lives in a ghetto poverty tract on the South Side.

> So you have to be in some kind of environment where the kids are more, you know, ready to go to school to get an education instead of, you know, droppin' out to sell drugs because they see their friends, on the corner, makin' money: they got a pocket fulla money, you know. They got kids walkin' around here that's ten years old selling drugs.

In recent years, the process of inner-city neighborhood deterioration has been clearly related to the growth of the inner-city drug industry. The decline of legitimate employment opportunities among inner-city residents increases the incentive to sell drugs. When asked the best way to get ahead in Chicago, a 29-year-old unmarried, employed cook and dishwasher from a poor black neighborhood in which only one in four adults was employed in 1990 stated: "I hate to say it, but it, it look to me dealin' drugs, 'cause these guys make money out there. This is wrong, but, you know, uh—they make a lot of money, fast."

A 35-year-old unemployed male from a nearby neighborhood with a comparable jobless rate emphatically justified his involvement in drug trafficking:

> And what am I doing now? I'm a cocaine dealer—'cause I can't get a decent-ass job. So, what other choices do I have? I have to feed my family . . . do I work? I work. See, don't . . . bring me that bullshit. I been working since I was fifteen years old. I had to work to take care of my mother and father and my sisters. See, so can't, can't nobody bring me that bullshit about I ain't looking for no job.

The presence of high levels of drug activity in a neighborhood is indicative of problems of social organization. High rates of joblessness trigger other problems in the neighborhood that adversely affect social organization, including drug trafficking, crime, and gang violence.

In our 1993 survey of two high-jobless neighborhoods on Chicago's South Side respondents revealed that the increase in drug trafficking heightened feelings that their neighborhoods had become more dangerous. As a consequence, many residents retreated to the safety of their homes. "More people are dying and being killed," reported one respondent. "There are many drugs sold here every day. It's unsafe and you can't even go out of your house because of being afraid of being shot." Another stated, "I stay home a lot. Streets are dangerous. Killings are terrible. Drugs make people crazy." Similar sentiments were voiced by other residents who felt trapped. One put it this way: "It's scary to see these people. I'm afraid to go outside. I know people who go to work and leave the music on all day and night."

It is important to emphasize that the norms and actions within the drug industry in ghetto neighborhoods can also affect the behavior of those who have no direct involvement. For example, the widespread possession of guns among drug dealers, and therefore the increased availability of weapons in the neighborhood, prompts others to arm themselves. Some acquire weapons for self-protection, others for settling disputes that have nothing to do with drugs, and still others for the simple purpose of gaining respect from peers and acquaintances in the neighborhood. A National Institute of Justice survey of 758 male students in ten inner-city public high schools in California, Illinois, New Jersey, and Louisiana revealed that "22 percent of the students possess guns," 12 percent carry them all or most of the time, and "another 23 percent carry guns now and then." Within this survey the students revealed that the primary reason for their most recent gun acquisition was self-protection.

Neighborhoods that feature higher levels of social organization—that is, neighborhoods that integrate the adults by means of an extensive set of obligations, expectations, and social networks—are in a better position to control and supervise the activities and behavior of children. Youngsters know they will be held accountable for their individual and group action; at the same time, they know they can rely on neighborhood adults for support and guidance. In terms of levels of social organization, black working-

and middle-class neighborhoods in Chicago stand in sharp contrast to the new poverty neighborhoods. Data from the 1989–90 survey reveal that in addition to much lower levels of perceived unemployment than in the poor neighborhoods, black working- and middle-class neighborhoods also have much higher levels of perceived social control and cohesion, organizational services, and social support.

The connectedness and stability of social networks in strong neighborhoods transcend the household because the neighborhood adults have the potential to observe, report on, and discuss the behavior of the children in different circumstances. These networks reinforce the discipline the child receives in the home, because other adults in the neighborhood assume responsibility for maintaining a standard of public or social behavior even on the part of children who are not their own. As Frank Furstenberg put it, "Ordinary parents are likely to have more success when they reside in communities where the burden of raising children is seen as a collective responsibility and where strong institutions sustain the efforts of parents."

The norms and supervision imposed on children are most effective when they reflect what James S. Coleman has called "intergenerational closure"—that is, the overlapping of youth and adult social networks in a neighborhood. Intergenerational closure is exhibited in those neighborhoods where most parents know not only their children's friends but the parents of those friends as well. As a general rule, adolescents seem to benefit directly from the exchange of resources produced by their parents' social integration with others in the neighborhood.

Nonetheless, social integration may not be beneficial to adolescents who live in neighborhoods characterized by high levels of individual and family involvement in aberrant behavior. "Although we tend to think of social integration as a desirable endpoint," state Laurence Steinberg and his colleagues, "its desirability depends on the nature of the people that integration brings one into contact with. There are many communities in contemporary America in which it may be more adaptive for parents to be socially isolated than socially integrated. Indeed, some of Frank Furstenberg's recent work on family life in the inner city of Philadelphia suggest that social isolation is often deliberately practiced as an adaptive strategy by many parents living in dangerous neighborhoods."

Despite being socially integrated, the residents in Chicago's ghetto neighborhoods shared a feeling that they had little informal social control over children in their environment. A primary reason is the absence of a strong organizational capacity or an institutional resource base that would provide an extra layer of social organization in their neighborhoods. It is easier for parents to control the behavior of the children in their neighborhoods when there exists a strong institutional resource base, when the links between community institutions such as churches, schools, political organizations, businesses, and civic clubs are strong. The higher the density and stability of formal organizations, the less that illicit activities such as drug trafficking, crime, prostitution, and gang formation can take root in the neighborhood. A weak institutional resource base is what distinguishes high-jobless inner-city neighborhoods from stable middle-class and working-class areas. As one resident of a high-jobless neighborhood on the South Side of Chicago put it, "Our children, you know, seems to be more at risk than any other children there is, because there's no library for them to go to. There's not a center they can go to, there's no field house that they can go into. There's nothing. There's nothing at all."

Parents in high-jobless neighborhoods have a much more difficult task of controlling the behavior of their adolescents, of preventing them from getting involved in activities detrimental to pro-social development. Given the lack of organizational capacity and weak institutional base, some parents choose to protect their children by isolating them from activities in the neighborhood, including the avoidance of contact and interaction with neighborhood families. Wherever possible, and often with great difficulty considering the problems of transportation and limited financial resources, they attempt to establish contact and cultivate relations with individuals, families, and institutions outside the neighborhood, such as church groups, schools, and community recreation programs.

In short, social isolation deprives inner-city residents not only of conventional role models, whose strong presence once buffered the effects of neighborhood joblessness, but also of the social resources (including social contacts) provided by mainstream social networks that facilitate social and economic advancement in a modern industrial society. This form of social isolation also contributes to the formation and crystallization of ghetto-related cultural traits and behaviors, a subject to which I now turn.

. . .

"Culture" may be defined as the sharing of modes of behavior and outlook within a community. The study of culture involves an analysis of how culture is transmitted from generation to generation and the way in which it is sustained through social interaction in the community. To act according to one's culture—either through forms of nonverbal action, including engaging in or refraining from certain conduct, or in the verbal expression of opinions or attitudes concerning norms, values, or beliefs—is to follow one's inclinations as they have been developed by influence or learning from other members of the community that one belongs to or identifies with.

All communities within the broader society share common modes of behavior and outlook. However, the extent to which communities differ with respect to outlook and behavior depends in part on the degree of the group's social isolation from the broader society, the material assets or resources they control, the benefits and privileges they derive from these resources, the cultural experiences they have accumulated as a consequence of historical and existing economic and political arrangements, and the influence they wield because of those arrangements.

Despite the overwhelming poverty, black residents in inner-city ghetto neighborhoods verbally reinforce, rather than undermine, the basic American values pertaining to individual initiative. For example, the large survey of the UPFLS found that nearly all the black respondents felt that plain hard work is either very important or somewhat important for getting ahead. Indeed, fewer than 3 percent of the black respondents from ghetto poverty census tracts denied the importance of plain hard work for getting ahead in society, and 66 percent expressed the view that it is very important.

Nonetheless, given the constraints and limited opportunities facing people in inner-city neighborhoods, it is altogether reasonable to assume that many of those who subscribe to these values will, in the final analysis, find it difficult to live up to them. Circumstances generally taken for granted in middle-class society are often major obstacles that must be overcome in the inner-city ghetto. Take, for example, the case of a 29-year-old black male from a high-jobless neighborhood on the South Side who is employed in a job without the fringe bene-

fits most workers associate with stable employment, such as paid sick leave. His situation is described in the field notes prepared by a member of the UPFLS research team.

Clifford is a 29-year-old black male who quit school in eleventh grade and currently works night-shifts (from 7 P.M. to 5 A.M.) as a "dishwasher and assistant cook" in a western suburb of Chicago. He has lived in the city for 16 years and in his present neighborhood for two years. He resides with his mother, a homemaker of 52, his sister of 23, a younger sister of 18, and a little brother of 12. Clifford has never been married and has no children. While he was raised partly on welfare support, he has never received public aid himself.

Clifford has been working for several years as a dishwasher for different employers. He now cooks, mops, and washes dishes for $4.85 an hour. He has held this job since February of 1985 without taking a single day of vacation. His supervisor has made it crystal clear to him that he is expendable and that if he takes too much (that is, any) vacation, they will not keep him. On the day of the interview, he had had a molar pulled and was in great pain (partly due to the fact that, not having any money and having already borrowed cash to pay for the extraction, he could not buy the prescribed pain-killers); yet he was . . . reluctant to call his boss and ask for an evening off.

When I asked if he expects to find a better job soon, he laughed: "I don't know: this is up to the employers, if they wanta hire me." Should he find one, it would be "somethin' in the restaurant business, hospital, or maybe a hotel or somethin', doing dishes."

He has not taken any steps to get further education or training, mainly because his work schedule and lack of resources make such planning quasi-impossible. Yet he clearly would like to get more so he "can better [himself] in life," he says, as he tucks his shirt under his armpits, strokes his belly, yawns as he lays stretched out on the couch. . . . With his present wage, he cannot save any money ("You can't, uh [chuckles], I be right back to my next day. You can't. Don't make enough").

There are many individuals in the inner-city ghetto like Clifford, people who struggle against the odds at great individual sacrifice to live up to mainstream norms and ideas of acceptability. For example, a woman in one of the new poverty neighborhoods on the South Side described her husband's financial struggles:

My husband, he's worked in the community. He's 33. He's worked at One Stop since he was 15. And right now, he's one of the highest paid—he's a butcher—he's one of the highest paid butchers in One Stop. For the 17—almost 18—years that he's been there, he's only making nine dollars an hour. And he's begged and fought and scrapped and sued and everything else for the low pay he gets. And he takes so much. Sometimes he come home and he'd sit home and he'd just cry. And he'd say, "If it weren't for my kids and my family, I'd quit." You know, it's bad, 'cuz he won't get into drugs, selling it, you know, he ain't into drug using. He's the kind of man, he want to work hard and feel good about that he came home. He say that it feels bad sometime to see this 15-year-old boy drivin' down the street with a new car. He saying, "I can't even

pay my car note. And I worry about them comin' to get my car."

There are many people in the inner-city ghetto (like Clifford and the butcher) who are working hard under extremely difficult circumstances to make a go of it. Some are able to maintain their employment only under considerable strain, while others, because of the very nature of their economic circumstances, are sometimes compelled to act in ghetto-related ways—for example, existing for a period of time without a steady job or pursuing illegitimate means of income. They may strongly agree with mainstream judgments of unacceptable behavior and yet feel utterly constrained by their circumstances, forced sometimes to act in ways that violate mainstream norms. Outsiders may observe their overt behavior and erroneously assume that they regard this illegitimate income as rightful.

Thus, in some cases, ghetto-related behavior may not reflect internalized values at all. People are simply adapting to difficult circumstances. In addition to constraints associated with limited access to organizational channels of privilege and influence, there are also constraints on the choices they can make because they lack access to mainstream sources of information needed to make responsible and helpful decisions. For example, research conducted in a Chicago inner-city high school suggested that many of the seniors had attainable goals and could have made a successful post–high school transition had they received adequate information, guidance, and resources. In addition, every counselor at this high school reported that he or she did not have sufficient informational materials, time, and training needed to provide students with effective career counseling.

Individuals in the inner-city ghetto can hardly avoid exposure to many kinds of recurrent and open ghetto-related behavior in the daily interactions and contacts with the people of their community. They therefore have the opportunity to familiarize themselves with a range and combination of modes of behavior that include elements of both the mainstream and the ghetto. The degree of exposure to culturally transmitted modes of behavior in any given milieu depends in large measure on the individual's involvement in or choice of social networks, including networks of friends and kin. Through cultural transmission, individuals develop a cultural repertoire that includes discrete elements that are relevant to a variety of respective situations. For example, jobless individuals who receive cultural transmissions that grow out of lack of steady employment may find some of the transmitted elements, such as street-corner panhandling, quite relevant to their situation. This, as Ulf Hannerz points out, is why some elements of culture should be seen as *situationally adaptive*—that is, they provide members of a group with models of behavior that apply to situations specific to that community.

As Hannerz also notes, however, not all aspects of cultural transmission involve rational decisions as to which aspects of a person's cultural repertoire are relevant in a given situation. There is also the phenomenon of accidental or nonconscious cultural transmission—also called transmission by precept—whereby a person's exposure to certain attitudes and actions is so frequent that they become part of his or her own outlook and therefore do not, in many cases, involve selective application to a given situation. The cultural sharing exemplified in role modeling epitomizes this process. "When a mode of behavior is encountered frequently and in many different persons," it is more likely to be transmitted by precept. Ghetto-related practices involving

overt emphasis on sexuality, idleness, and public drinking "do not go free of denunciation" in inner-city ghetto neighborhoods. But the failure of forces of social organization allow these practices to occur much more frequently there than in middle-class society, so the transmission of these modes of behavior by precept, as in role modeling, is more easily facilitated.

Skills, habits, and styles are often shaped by the frequency at which they are found in their own community. As Dr. Deborah Prothrow-Stith so clearly shows in her book, *Deadly Consequences,* youngsters in inner-city ghetto neighborhoods are more likely than other children to see violence as a way of life. They are likely to witness violent acts and to have role models who do not adequately control their own violent impulses or restrain their own anger. Accidental cultural transmission can also be seen in the development and crystallization of outlooks or beliefs that grow out of the common experiences of many different people. Elijah Anderson points out that receiving respect from peers, acquaintances, and strangers has become highly valued among inner-city adolescents, who have increasingly been denied status in mainstream terms. Respect is often granted when one is carrying and willing to use an assault weapon. Accordingly, given the ready availability of firearms, knives, and other weapons, adolescents' experiments with aggressive behavior often have deadly consequences.

In short, regardless of the mode of cultural transmission, ghetto-related behaviors often represent particular cultural adaptations to the systematic blockage of opportunities in the environment of the inner city and the society as a whole. These adaptations are reflected in habits, skills, styles, and attitudes that are shaped over time.

QUESTIONS FOR
DISCUSSION

1. Do you agree with the emphasis that Wilson places on ghetto culture?
2. Do you find his argument linking cultural problems with the structural lack of opportunities to be convincing?

3. Are there ways that Wilson's discussion of drugs and other crimes can be seen as functionalist, or do you think Wilson is writing more directly from a conflict approach?

13

THE ENEMY WITHIN
RUTH SIDEL

> *Conflict between groups is, of course, nothing new. What may be new in Western Christian tradition . . . is how the use of Satan to represent one's enemies lends to conflict a specific kind of moral and religious interpretation, in which "we" are God's people and "they" are God's enemies, and ours as well.*
>
> —ELAINE PAGELS,
> *The Origin of Satan*

They are despised, denigrated, ostracized from mainstream society. In earlier times, they were known as the "dangerous classes"; today they are labeled the "underclass." They are pictured as virtually irredeemable, lazy, dependent, living off the hard-earned money of others. They

are poor single mothers. They are welfare recipients. They are the enemy within.

The demonizing of poor single mothers has been an integral part of the recent onslaught on the safety net, meager and inadequate as it is, that has existed in the United States since the passage of the Social Security Act of 1935. Poor mothers have been deemed unworthy, the "undeserving poor"; nearly 15 million welfare recipients have been painted with one brush, have been relegated to that area in society that is beyond the pale. Systematic stereotyping and stigmatizing of "welfare mothers" was necessary in order to dehumanize them in the eyes of other Americans before the harsh and tenuous lifeline of Aid to Families with Dependent Children (AFDC) and the other bare-bones social programs could be shredded. The implicit and often explicit message is: If welfare recipients are so unworthy, perhaps such harsh treatment, such punishment, is warranted, even necessary, in order to modify their social and reproductive behavior. Perhaps, it has been said, removing cash and other benefits, forcing mothers to work even at dead-end jobs for poverty wages, and denying aid to children of teenagers and to additional babies born while the mother is receiving AFDC is the only way to deal with this "deviant" and "irresponsible" group. Many politicians claim that they are promoting these Draconian measures against the poor as a form of "tough love," "for their own good." These cuts in assistance and services may be painful at first, this reasoning goes, and some suggest that this current generation of poor parents may have to be written off, but in the long run these harsh measures will enable the next generation to "stand on their own two feet." Congress, the tough but responsible parent, will force the poor, as though they were rebellious adolescents, to shape up, to reform their delinquent ways.

Just over a decade ago, social scientist Charles Murray, author of *Losing Ground: American Social Policy 1950–1980,* articulated the values, priorities, and underlying agenda of America's war against the poor:

> Some people are better than others. They deserve more of society's rewards, of which money is only one small part. A principal function of social policy is to make sure they have the opportunity to reap those rewards. Government cannot identify the worthy, but it can protect a society in which the worthy can identify themselves.

Thus the government legitimizes the existing social hierarchy and safeguards the affluence and lifestyles of those whom Murray deems "better," and more "worthy." Murray continues by proposing an "ambitious thought experiment":

> . . . scrapping the entire federal welfare and income-support structure for working-age persons, including AFDC,

Medicaid, Food Stamps, Unemployment Insurance, Worker's Compensation, subsidized housing, disability insurance, and the rest. It would leave the working-aged person with no recourse whatsoever except the job market, family members, friends, and public or private locally funded services. It is the Alexandrian solution: cut the knot, for there is no way to untie it.

It is noteworthy that the only "knots" being "cut" in the mid-1990s are those that afford some protection to the poor. Now, there is virtually no discussion of dismantling Unemployment Insurance, Worker's Compensation, or disability insurance, programs that provide help in times of need for a broad spectrum of Americans, not just the poor. In current efforts to move toward balancing the federal budget, there is considerable discussion about cutting Medicaid (the health program that serves the poor), Medicare (the health program that serves the elderly), education, health research, and environmental protection. But while debate rages on about how and how much to cut these programs, the beneficiaries have not been denigrated and made into pariahs. In the discussion about Medicare, older people have not been disparaged; in debate about cutting money for education, children have not been demonized. Only when the discussion moves to the drastic reduction in support of programs that primarily help poor women and their children are the recipients portrayed as fundamentally different from mainstream Americans.

The rhetoric that has accompanied and paved the way for the continuing assault on programs for poor women and children was fueled by a pledge made by then-candidate Bill Clinton during the 1992 presidential campaign. After a Clinton speechwriter consulted with political pollsters and felt that the issue would resonate with voters, the decision was made to call for stronger measures in dealing with welfare. Consequently, Mr. Clinton first stated his now-famous phrase in a speech at Georgetown University on October 23, 1991: "In a Clinton Administration, we're going to put an end to welfare as we know it." As Senator Daniel Patrick Moynihan, Democrat from New York, has stated, "The Republicans took him at his word" and went much further. But the only real way to end welfare as we know it, Moynihan continues, is "just to dump the children on the streets." And indeed that is exactly what is happening.

Today as AFDC is being decimated and other programs that serve the poor are threatened by cutbacks, the litany of criticism against poor single women is relentless. Mother-only families are being blamed for virtually all of the ills afflicting American society. Out-of-wedlock births have been blamed for the "breakdown of the family," for the crime rate, drug and alcohol addiction, poverty, illiteracy, homelessness, poor school performance, and the rending of the social fabric. The labeling of some citizens as "dependent"—that is, dependent on social welfare programs rather than on spouses, parents, or other family members, or other more acceptable federal programs—indiscriminately discredits an entire group of women and children without regard to their character or their specific work and/or family history. Whether they are receiving benefits because they had a child outside of marriage or because they are separated, divorced, or widowed, or because the father of their children deserted them, welfare recipients have been labeled as being part of a "culture of illegitimacy"; moreover, some legislators have gone so far as to equate illegitimacy with promiscuity. As the political tide has rapidly turned against the poor, particularly poor women, rhetoric has escalated to previously unimagined levels of hyperbole and vitriol. At a 1994 news con-

ference called by the Mainstream Forum, a group of centrist and conservative House Democrats affiliated with the Democratic Leadership Council (the political organization President Clinton helped found and headed when he was governor of Arkansas), Representative Nathan Deal, a Georgia Democrat, declared that welfare was dead. He went on to state, "The stench from its decaying carcass has filled the nostrils of every American."

This scathing stereotyping and stigmatizing of poor mothers has severe consequences for them, for their children, and for the society as a whole. As sociologist Erving Goffman has pointed out,

> By definition, of course, we believe the person with a stigma is not quite human. On this assumption we exercise varieties of discrimination, through which we effectively, if often unthinkingly, reduce his life chances. We construct a stigma-theory, an ideology to explain his inferiority and account for the danger he represents. . . .

The very words that are being used tell us what to think and how to feel. Poor women are characterized by their "dependence," an absolute negative, a polar opposite of that valued American characteristic, "independence." This label presumes that *they* are "dependent," that *they* passively rely on the government for their day-to-day needs while *we*, the rest of us, are "independent," "pull ourselves up by our bootstraps," are out there "on our own." These designations leave no room for the considerable variation and complexity that characterize most people's lives, for the fact that virtually all of us are in varying degrees dependent on others and on societal supports during our adult lives—that many of us have been recipients of financial or other kinds of help from family members, that many have been helped by inheritance, by assistance in finding (and sometimes keeping) a job, by tax deductions for mortgage payments, or the federal subsidy of farm prices, or by programs such as Medicare or Unemployment Compensation or disability assistance.

Dividing people into "us" and "them" is facilitated by the resurrection of terms such as "illegitimacy," that encourage the shaming and denigration of mothers and their out-of-wedlock children. It is far easier to refuse aid to "them," to people who engage in disgraceful, stigmatizing behavior than to people who seem like "us." David Boaz, executive vice-president of the Cato Institute, a libertarian organization, even hopes to resurrect the term "bastard": "We've made it possible for a teenage girl to survive with no husband and no job. That used to be very difficult. If we had more stigma and lower benefits, might we end up with 100,000 bastards every year rather than a million children born to alternative families?"

Poor, single mothers, particularly AFDC recipients, are being portrayed as the ultimate outsiders—marginalized as nonworkers in a society that claims belief in the work ethic, marginalized as single parents in a society that holds the two-parent, heterosexual family as the desired norm, and marginalized as poor people in a society that worships success and material rewards.

Perhaps the most dehumanizing and degrading references to welfare recipients occurred on the floor of the House of Representatives on March 24, 1995, during the debate on a bill that would cut $69 billion in spending on social welfare programs over the next five years. Welfare recipients were compared to animals by two Republican members of the House. Representative John L. Mica of Florida held up a sign that said, DON'T FEED THE ALLIGATORS. He explained, "We post these warnings because unnatural feeding and artificial care create dependency. When dependency sets in, these otherwise able alligators can no longer survive on their own." Mica then noted that while "people are not alligators . . . we've upset the natural order. We've created a system of dependency."

The most commonly held myths that legitimize putting impoverished women and children "outdoors" are that young women have children out of wedlock primarily to receive AFDC and need to be punished and resocialized to make them more responsible; that women receiving welfare have numerous children either because of their promiscuity or in order to increase their benefits; that AFDC provides ample benefits, enough for recipients to live quite comfortable lives; that recipients want to be "idlers," and are mired in a "culture of dependency," and therefore resist joining the paid labor force; and that AFDC recipients are overwhelmingly African-American.

The facts are considerably different from these myths:

- Virtually all studies indicate that over four-fifths of teenage pregnancies are unintended;

- The average number of children in families on welfare is two;

- From 1975 to 1994, the average AFDC benefit per family, measured in constant dollars, *dropped by 37 percent and in no state do welfare benefits plus food stamps bring recipient families up to the federally designated but grossly inadequate poverty line;*

- Seventy-one percent of adult AFDC recipients have recent work histories, and almost half of the families who leave welfare do so to work; and

- While black families are indeed proportionately overrepresented on the welfare rolls, in 1992 they comprised 37.2 percent of all AFDC cases while whites comprised 38.9 percent.

The persistence of these myths about welfare recipients and the resistance of policy makers to the facts despite their repeated reiteration by experts in the field of social welfare is noteworthy. It appears that the United States *needs* to have someone to blame, people to hate, a group to rally against. For nearly a half-century, Americans had a clear-cut enemy—communism. Throughout the Cold War, there existed an ideology we could despise, countries to fear, foreign leaders to demonize. We had external villains whom we could blame for many of the world's ills and whom we could identify as evil in order to define ourselves as good. There were enough countries under the banners of communism and socialism so that if the United States suddenly took a more accepting view of one—as Americans did toward China following the 1972 visit of Richard Nixon—there were always other countries on whom we could project our fear and animosity. With the worldwide breakdown of so-called communist countries (with the exception of Cuba and North Korea), who would be the enemy now? Whom could we distrust and despise? Who would be the devil that in comparison would make us feel righteous and worthy? Who would be the "them" to help us to feel more truly "us"?

Furthermore, over the past decade and a half we have seen two dramatic economic shifts within the United States—shifts that have had significant impact on the social and economic well-being and on the collective psyche of many Americans and that have placed in jeopardy the achievement of the American Dream for millions of Americans. The first has been a massive concentration of wealth and income in the hands of the richest among us. In 1977, the highest fifth of all households received 44 percent of total national income, the middle three-fifths received 51.8 percent, while the lowest fifth received 4.2 percent. By 1993, the in-come of the highest fifth rose to 48.2 percent, the highest percentage of income on record for that group; the income of the middle three-fifths dropped to 48.2 percent, the lowest share on record; and the bottom fifth received only 3.6 percent, also the lowest share ever recorded. Over the same decade and a half, the income of the top 5 percent rose from 16.8 percent to 20 percent. According to Kevin Phillips, author of *Arrogant Capital: Washington, Wall Street, and the Frustration of American Politics,* "the 100,000 American families in the top tenth of one percent enjoy by far and away the greatest wealth and income gains in the 1980s," but despite their enormous affluence, "the Clinton tax increases of 1993 did not concentrate on the high-income, high-political-influence, investment-dollar rich, the people making $4 million or $17 million a year." There is consequently a greater gap in income today between rich and poor than at any time since such data have been collected and, as Phillips points out, those profiting the most are the top tenth of one percent.

If we examine differences in wealth among the U.S. population, we see an even more dramatic differential. In 1989, the top one-half of one percent (the "super-rich") owned 31.4 percent of total household wealth, an increase of five percentage points since 1983. Moreover, the top 20 percent of the population owned 84.6 percent of total wealth. Since one-fifth of Americans owned 84.6 percent of total wealth, the remaining four-fifths owned only 15.4 percent. More specifically, the top one-half of one percent owned nearly twice as much wealth (31.4 percent) as the bottom 80 percent of all Americans (15.4 percent)! Preliminary estimates indicate that between 1989 and 1992, 68 percent of the increase in total household wealth went to the richest one percent—an even greater gain than during the 1980s. According to economist Edward Wolff,

As a result, the concentration of wealth reached a postwar high in 1992, the latest year for which data are available. If these trends continue, the super-rich will pull ahead of other Americans at an even faster pace in the 1990s than they did in the '80s.

While the rich have become significantly richer both in terms of income and wealth, not only have the poor lost ground but the working class and many in the middle class have lost ground as well. If we examine education and income, we find that between 1979 and 1989 the real average hourly wages of male high school dropouts declined 18 percent and the income of female dropouts declined nearly 12 percent. Income declined substantially (nearly 13 percent for males and over 3 percent for females) for high school graduates as well. Males with one to three years of college also experienced a significant decline in income (over 8 percent) while females with the same amount of education saw their income rise slightly (nearly 4 percent). Only when workers had completed four years of college did both men and women realize an increase in income over the decade of the 1980s—for men a bare rise of 0.2 percent and for women a significant increase of 12.6 percent. The real advantages accrued to workers with postgraduate training—nearly 10 percent for males and nearly 13 percent for females. However, as companies have downsized and restructured during the 1980s, millions of blue- and white-collar workers have been laid off and have had to scramble for whatever employment they could find—be it full-time or part-time. An estimated 3 million workers have been laid off between 1989 and 1995 as corporate profits have soared. Many workers have found it necessary to piece together two or more part-time jobs in order to earn anything like their original salaries and many have been unable to obtain work that provides income even approximating their previous salaries.

Moreover, as manufacturers have transferred semi-skilled work out of the country since the 1960s and 1970s, during the 1990s skilled white-collar jobs are increasingly being sent to other countries as well, where the work is being done at a fraction of the cost by educated locals. Texas Instruments, for example, is designing sophisticated computer chips in India; Motorola recently set up equipment design and computer programming centers in China, India, Singapore, Hong Kong, Taiwan, and Australia.

Not only have millions of Americans lost jobs, income, status, and, in some cases, their roles as workers and earners, but millions of families have seen their neighborhoods deteriorate; the quality of schools, public transportation, health care, and other services decline. They have seen crime rates and their feelings of physical insecurity rise, and their overall quality of life plummet. Whom can they blame? I suggest that during the past fifteen years when the working class and the middle class were losing ground, a period during which the rich and "truly rich" were increasing their income and their share of the nation's wealth to what many consider obscene levels, we have seen a strategy on the part of many politicians, policy makers, and conservative thinkers to encourage the middle and working classes to blame their losses on the poor and the powerless, particularly women and people of color, rather than on the rich and powerful.

In branding all welfare recipients "dependent," "lazy," or "rotten mothers," we are singling out an entire group of people and declaring them deviant because of their economic status at a particular moment in time. If we narrow the designated group to poor, single welfare recipients, we are adding marital status to economic status and thereby declaring those particular traits central to their character, to their functioning in society. We are, in effect, stating that those details of a person's life "reflect the kind of person [s]he 'really' is." She could be a conscientious, caring mother, a loving daughter, a hardworking student, a pious churchgoer, a loyal friend, and a concerned neighbor, but the details of her life by which we as a society are judging her and finding her wanting are her current economic status and whether or not she has participated in a marriage ceremony. The designations "dependent," "lazy," and "rotten mothers" are assumed to characterize all welfare recipients—particularly those who have never been married. They are generalizations assumed to be true of an entire group of people, regardless of their personal characteristics and circumstances. Major policy decisions are therefore being made on the basis of massive stereotyping. In other words, false assumptions about millions of poor women are being encoded into a social policy that will affect the lives and the life chances of these women and their children for years, possibly decades to come.

The irrationality and arbitrary quality of these judgments raise questions about the value and meaning to a society of branding an individual—or an entire category of people—as outside the norms or boundaries of that society. Erikson, citing the work of French sociologist Emile Durkheim, discusses how forms of deviance "may actually perform a needed service to society by drawing people together in a common posture of anger and indignation" so that they then "develop a tighter bond of solidarity than existed before." Moreover, defining deviance and designating certain individuals who have crossed the line as outcasts stipulates the boundaries of behavior for others in the society. In some sense, the boundaries a society sets create the deviants in that society. In a country such as Sweden where births to unmarried women are far more common and accepted than in the United States, these mothers are not designated deviant and ostracized from mainstream society. In the United States, however, the opprobrium associated with "illegitimacy" is once again causing those who have a child outside of marriage to be labeled deviant and, indeed, in Toni Morrison's words, to be "put outdoors."

Are welfare mothers today's folk devils? They surely have been "stripped of all favorable characteristics and imparted with exclusively negative ones," and they are surely being blamed for much of what is wrong in American society. And, of course, the subtext, often but not always unspoken, is the myth that most of these poor, single, child-bearing women are black. Even if one asks a sociology class, most of whom are themselves members of minority groups, "From what racial background are most AFDC recipients?" the answer invariably is that most of them are African-American. This image of the poor, inexorably intertwined with the long-standing baggage of racist ideology, facilitates their being perceived as folk devils. As anthropologist Leith Mullings has stated, "Women of color, and particularly African-American women, are the focus of well-elaborated, strongly held . . . ideologies concerning race, class, and gender." She goes on to state that "the images, representations, and symbols that form ideologies often have complex meanings and associations that are not easily or readily articulated, making them difficult to challenge."

Historically, African-American women have been described on the one hand by the image of " 'Mammy,' the religious, loyal, motherly slave. . . ." and, on the other hand, by the image of " 'Jezebel,' the sexually aggressive, provocative woman governed entirely by libido." As Mullings states, this Mammy/Jezebel stereotype is a variation of the widespread madonna/whore dualism but the issue of race adds an even more pernicious element to the classic stereotype. The view of African-Americans as a different species, what Mullings and others have termed the "otherness of race," has "justified the attribution of excessive sexuality." That "sexuality continues to be a major theme in the discourse about race" assures that it is also a major theme in the discourse about poor women. Moreover, the Mammy image, so prevalent through the first half of the twentieth century and memorialized in popular culture by the film *Gone With the Wind*, has been replaced, according to Mullings, by the image of the "emasculating matriarch." Therefore, whether through overt sexuality or through control within the family that supposedly robs black men of their authority and power, black women are portrayed as deviant and as the primary cause of the problems within the black family and within the black community.

Patricia Hill Collins, author of *Black Feminist Thought: Knowledge, Consciousness, and the Politics of Empowerment*, analyzes the ways in which these deeply rooted images of black women underlie and buttress the harsh treatment of poor women over the past two decades and particularly during the 1990s:

> Portraying African-American women as matriarchs allows the dominant group to blame Black women for the success or failure of Black children. Assuming that Black poverty is passed on intergenerationally via value transmission in families, an elite white male standpoint suggests that Black children lack the attention and care allegedly lavished on white, middle-class children and that this deficiency seriously retards Black children's achievement. Such a view diverts attention from the political and economic inequality affecting Black mothers and children and suggests that anyone

can rise from poverty if he or she only received good values at home. Those African-Americans who remain poor are blamed for their own victimization.

The problems the United States should be addressing as we move into the next century are widespread poverty amidst incredible affluence, massive hopelessness and alienation among those who feel outside of the boundaries of the society, and a deeply felt despair among the poor and the working class that is increasingly expressed through violence. There is no question that the welfare system in particular and the society in general have not addressed these issues and, in fact, have exacerbated them— not through generosity but through miserliness, not through the coddling of recipients but through their humiliation, not through making poor people dependent on a panoply of services but rather by not providing the essential education, job training, child care, health care, and, perhaps most important, jobs by which families can support themselves at a decent standard of living. The central problem American society must deal with is not the character of poor women and the structure of the welfare system; the central problem is poverty, the multiplicity of ways that it is embedded in the structure of American society, and the need to find real ways of altering that fundamental structure in order to truly help people move into mainstream society. We must recognize that people are not poor due to character defects but rather that the poverty that plagues so many Americans has been socially constructed and therefore must be dealt with by fundamental economic and social change.

Before dealing directly with exactly who are the poor in America, the nature of the welfare system, the current dismantling of Aid to Families with Dependent Children and other programs essential to those who are most in need, and the impact of these changes on poor women and children, let us examine the broader assault on single-parent families of which the war on poor women and children is the central component. Single parenthood (which must be seen as a code phrase for *female* single parenthood since the vast majority of single parents are mothers) has over the past few years been defined, in Stan Cohen's words, as a "threat to societal values" and indeed social policy and "the way society conceives itself" are being dramatically changed. What is the nature of this assault on single mothers and what are the repercussions for single parents, for their children, and for American society as a whole?

QUESTIONS FOR DISCUSSION

1. Can you identify other commonly held beliefs about the poor that Sidel does not mention?
2. What are the images of the poor that we frequently see in popular media?
3. How does gender shape myths of the poor?
4. Can you use the arguments presented in Section II to explain why current welfare reform focuses on reducing aid to the poor?

14

WITHOUT A SAFETY NET
BARBARA EHRENREICH • FRANCES FOX PIVEN

Just four years ago, Kimberly Hill was a poster child for welfare reform. A tall, strikingly attractive mother of two, she had been on welfare off and on for several years until, in 1995, a caseworker urged her to get computer training. Her first job—for which she rated a mention in a 1998 *San Francisco Chronicle* story titled "Firms Find Talent Among Disabled, Welfare Recipients"—was no prize. "People knew I was off welfare," she told us, "and they treated me like I had the plague." Hired as an administrative assistant, she found herself being

asked to clean the rest room. She got luckier with her next job, at a staffing agency, where, after a series of promotions, she was earning $65,000 a year. Then, on December 20, 2001, just as the recession became official, she was laid off.

Hill meets us at Starbucks because she doesn't think the neighborhood where she lives is a good place for us to be wandering around. She is confident and direct, but admits to feeling the stress of being out of work. She has found one part-time office job and is about to add another, but neither offers health insurance. We ask if she would go back on welfare if things got bad enough. "No," she says, thrusting her chin out for emphasis. "It's too horrible, a horrible experience—demeaning."

Reprinted with permission from *Mother Jones,* May/June 2002: 35. Copyright © 2002 by Foundation for National Progress.

Beverly Ransom was another welfare-to-work success story. We met her in Miami's Liberty City—site of the 1980 riot—at the storefront office of Low Income Families Fighting Together, a community organization that works for welfare rights and affordable housing. A bright-eyed, straight-backed woman of 50, with gray hair pulled back into a small ponytail, she speaks with pride about the catering job she found after years on welfare. But lately the work has fallen off; the catering companies that used to give her more work than she could handle just haven't been calling anymore. "Catering is based on tourism," she says. "Last year at this time I had so much work I had to beg for days off. Now I need food stamps." She gets $118 a week from unemployment insurance, but rent for herself and her children, who are 12 and 14, is $500 a month. Her biggest fear is that she'll end up in a shelter: "What do I do? My kids are at an age where they would be traumatized."

In 1996, when welfare reform was enacted, a recession seemed about as likely as the destruction of the World Trade Center by a handful of men armed with box cutters. The assumptions behind welfare reform were, one, that a job could lift a family out of poverty and, two, that there would always be enough jobs for anyone plucky enough to go out and land one. The first assumption was shaky from the start; women leaving welfare ended up earning an average of less than $8 an hour, hardly enough to support a family. Now the second assumption has crumbled as well: More than 2 million people lost their jobs last year, and single mothers have been especially hard hit. According to the Federal Bureau of Labor Statistics, the employment rate of women who head families fell far more sharply last fall than overall employment, by three percentage points in just three months.

There is, of course, a venerable New Deal program to protect laid-off workers—unemployment insurance—but it is, perversely enough, designed to offer the least help to those who need it the most. People in temporary, part-time, or very low-wage jobs—the kind most often available to someone leaving welfare—often don't qualify for benefits. According to the Economic Policy Institute, about 70 percent of former welfare recipients who have lost their jobs during the current recession are not eligible for unemployment.

In the past, poor single mothers had their own form of unemployment insurance—welfare. Contrary to the stereotype, most welfare recipients worked, at least intermittently, falling back on public assistance when a child got sick or a car broke down. But in their zeal to save the poor from their supposed sins of laziness, irresponsibility, and promiscuity, the reformers entirely overlooked the role of welfare as a safety net for working mothers. Temporary Aid to Needy Families (TANF), which is what the new version of welfare is called, has just one aim: to push the poor into the job market to become "self-sufficient." Whatever sense this made in the boom years when welfare reform was devised, it makes none now. As a poster at an East Harlem community organization put it, the acronym has come to stand for "Torture and Abuse of Needy Families."

Of course, pre-reform welfare was never adequate: Grants were low (an average of $550 a month nationwide), and recipients were routinely hassled and humiliated by the bureaucracy. Still, under the old system, if you were demonstrably poor and had children to support, you were entitled to cash assistance. The new system, legislated in 1996 with the passage of the Personal Responsibility and Work Opportunity Reconciliation Act, ended that entitlement. The law set strict time limits on assistance (no more than five years in a lifetime for most people), encouraged private companies to bid on contracts to administer welfare, and gave states wide discretion to cut people from the rolls.

Under the current system, someone who applies for welfare is lucky to get any benefits. More likely, the family will be "diverted"—sent to a food bank, told to apply for child support from an absentee parent, or assigned to a training program designed to keep them searching for a job. Those who make it through this process may see their benefits cut for any of a multitude of infractions (including, in some cases, having a child who regularly skips school).

These practices, often characterized as part of an effort to endow the poor with "self-esteem," have been extremely effective—at least at cutting the welfare rolls. A report by the National Campaign for Jobs and Income Support shows that welfare caseloads rose as unemployment went up in the recession of 1990–1991, but that this time, caseloads actually fell in 14 of the 47 states where unemployment rose between March and December 2001. In Wisconsin, the state that pioneered a particularly draconian version of welfare reform under the leadership of former governor and current Health and Human Services Secretary Tommy Thompson, unemployment rose by 0.6 percentage points during the same period, but the welfare rolls just kept on dropping—by 29 percentage points. And changes now being debated could make the program even less accessible to poor families: . . . the Bush administration is pushing measures that would make benefits more difficult to get, and even harder to keep.

So what do you do when there are few jobs available and the safety net lies in tatters? We talked to former welfare recipients who recently lost their jobs in five states— New York, Oregon, California, Florida, and Illinois. Some had already exhausted their five-year lifetime benefit limit; others remained potentially eligible for welfare.

None of them were having much luck. While the media tends to focus on displaced dot-commers and laid-off Enron executives, these women represent the hidden underside of the recession. In the scary new world of post-welfare America, their experience has been like that of someone who looks out an airplane window on a bright, clear day and sees nothing at all below.

Janet Cook is one of the many who have gone from welfare to work to nothing in a few short years. We talked to her by phone at a residential motel in Portland, Oregon, where she was paying more than $300 a week for the single room she shared with her husband and their four children. Cook, who is in her late 30s, held a job with a truck manufacturer for six years until she was laid off last April. Her husband is a construction worker, and they used to live in the houses that his company was working on, moving on as each was completed. Then, last fall, the company relocated to another city, and the couple decided to stay rather than yank their kids out of school. With no jobs in sight and their savings soon eaten up by the motel bills, there was nothing to do but apply for welfare.

It's "murder to get through the process," Cook says. "You have to be flat broke so you can't function. They want you to land a job, so they make you wait. They don't give you cash for the first two weeks. The first week they make you attend a job workshop. The second week is job search. If you miss one hour, you start over for the whole two weeks." On the day we spoke to her, the family was leaving the motel and moving to a shelter. (Cook ultimately did get benefits, but not until a Legal Aid attorney intervened on her behalf.)

All of the former welfare recipients we interviewed described the maze of obstacles that now lies between a needy family and even a paltry amount of cash assistance—a set of hurdles far more daunting than the pre-reform bureaucracy. There are long lines in welfare centers with waits, one New York woman told us, of up to nine hours. In a Latino neighborhood, there may be no Spanish-speaking caseworker on duty. In the 1960s, a federal regulation required that welfare offices accept oral applications. Now, you may have to fill out the same form three times, just to save the agency photocopying expenses.

"They close your case for any small thing now," reports Dulce Severino, a mother of two who lives in Brooklyn. "You can't speak to a social worker—you have to wait a whole day to see them. And they speak badly to people when they finally see them. There are ugly words, almost fights with the social workers." Another Brooklyn woman reports that "some days there are almost riots"—and there really would be, she believes, if it weren't for the heavy police presence inside the welfare centers.

Applicants who aren't turned away at the welfare office often face another obstacle—the private companies that increasingly contract with states and municipalities to administer welfare programs. The 1996 law allows governments to contract with churches and community groups, but most contracts have gone to such distinctly non-faith-based entities as Maximus, Unisys, and Lockheed Martin. Some companies specialize in "job readiness" services; others do everything from conducting interviews to determining recipients' eligibility, often under contracts that reward them for any funds they do not spend.

Sharon Bush, a mother of four who lives in the East New York section of Brooklyn, applied for welfare in November after medical problems forced her to quit her job. After she filled out the paperwork, two caseworkers paid her a visit to investigate her claim; next, she was sent to Curtis and Associates, a private, for-profit job placement firm. There she was given a lengthy test,

shown to a desk with a phone, and told to start cold-calling companies in search of a job. "They don't help, they don't provide contacts," she says. "Meanwhile there are all these people sitting there, waiting, who need back rent." She would have to report to Curtis, she was told, from 9:30 to 4:30 daily for four weeks. In the meantime she'd receive some emergency assistance—a total of $156.60.

The sheer hassle of "reformed" welfare is enough to discourage many people from even applying. But the best-known and most clear-cut way that TANF keeps the rolls down is through the five-year lifetime limit on benefits. The clock started ticking with the passage of the welfare reform law in 1996, with the consequence that 120,000 families exhausted their benefits just as the recession hit in 2001. Dulce Severino's family is one of them, although she has worked most of the time since 1992, packing clothes in the sweatshop factories that have sprung up in her Brooklyn neighborhood of Bushwick. Because her earnings were so low— her best wage was $5.15 an hour—Severino received a welfare wage supplement, so the clock on her lifetime limit was running even as she worked. If she had been paid better, she would still be eligible for welfare today.

For women without work or welfare, "luxuries" like nonemergency medical care are the first things to go. Nicey Jenkins of Liberty City took computer training to get off welfare, but ended up working at McDonald's instead. She has given up on paying her credit card bills: "I can't give them anything. I can't make the minimum payment." Another woman we met in Liberty City has declared bankruptcy. Each woman we talked to mentioned family as a major source of support—the grown son who picks up the phone bill, the sisters who offer to babysit, the boyfriend who pitches in for the rent. Without her family, Jenkins says, "I would have killed myself."

Mostly, though, people talked about the daily challenge of putting food on the table. Beverly Ransom reports that "sometimes we have breakfast for dinner. . . . A lot of the times I skip the meal because I can go without. My first priority is my kids. I say, 'I'm not hungry right now.'" Nicey Jenkins buys boiling meats—like neck bones—and serves them over rice. Sometimes, to please her kids, she makes fake fast food: "We have 'KFC night,' 'Taco Bell night.' It works when they're young."

All across the country, the dangerous combination of recession and a damaged safety net is driving families to soup kitchens, food pantries, and shelters. A U.S. Conference of Mayors survey on hunger and homelessness in major cities showed that [in 2001,] requests for emergency food assistance rose by an average of 23 percent, while requests for shelter increased by 13 percent. Another national survey of food pantry and soup kitchen users found that almost 40 percent had been cut off from welfare benefits within the past two years. Data gathered by Food for Survival, one of New York City's largest food-pantry groups, indicate that 1 in 5 New Yorkers—a total of 1.5 million people—use emergency food assistance at least once a year; a majority of those receiving such help for the first time are single mothers who say that what they most need is a job.

Even before the recession struck, welfare reform was hardly the "resounding success" President Bush called it this spring. To be sure, it was easy, at least in the boom years, to earn more in a job than the meager cash allowances welfare offered. But as critics of reform have repeatedly pointed out, the $7 and $8 an hour averaged by former welfare recipients was about $6 short of what the Economic Policy Institute calculates a family of three needs for a minimally adequate, bare-bones budget. It was in the boom year of 2000 that the nation's largest

network of food banks, America's Second Harvest, reported "a torrent of need that we cannot meet," with many local charities blaming the rising demand for their services on welfare reform and insufficient wages. Milwaukee, a city whose widely publicized "W-2" program makes it the veritable capital of welfare reform, saw dramatic increases in the use of food pantries and emergency shelters through the late '90s.

No small part of the pre-recession misery of the poor was due to the states' Scrooge-like administration of TANF. In a number of states recipients are not told that they might be eligible for food stamps and Medicaid—a key benefit, since many low-wage jobs don't offer health insurance—even after they leave welfare. Nor have the states reliably provided the promised support, especially child care subsidies, for women making the transition from welfare to work. You might start leaving your children with a child care provider only to find out that your subsidy had never made its way through the bureaucratic maze. One woman, whose story we learned from Eastern Michigan University researcher Valerie Polakow, took her four-year-old to work with her because the promised child care subsidy had not materialized. Her employer fired her for showing up with the child; then, in a neat Catch-22, TANF threatened her with reduced benefits for losing her job.

And there seems to be little inclination among politicians to fix such problems in this year's overhaul of TANF. State and local governments, knowing that they'll be left with providing emergency services as women who can't find a job are cut from the rolls, want more flexibility in extending benefits. Some Democrats in Congress are arguing for more spending on child care. But no one expects fundamental changes to the 1996 reform and its premise—that the job market holds all the answers, in good times and bad.

With six years' hindsight, it's hard to fathom why no one, back in 1996, seems to have thought ahead to a time when jobs would be in short supply and millions of Americans might sorely need cash assistance. We talked to Mary Jo Bane, a Harvard professor who left her post as the Clinton administration's Assistant Secretary for Children and Families in 1996 to protest the direction of reform. "People mumbled about it," she says, "but the economy was so good then. . . ." David Ellwood, who along with Bane co-chaired Clinton's welfare reform task force and who also teaches at Harvard, told us, "Many people thought about the possibility of a downturn. The real question is why the people who drafted the bill, and signed it, willfully didn't."

Part of the answer may lie in the peculiar economic euphoria of the mid- and late '90s, when bearishness began to seem unpatriotic and prosperity looked like a permanent entitlement. The emphasis, even among liberals, was on "making work pay" and expanding benefits such as child care and the Earned Income Tax Credit, which provides low-income working families with up to $4,000 a year in cash. Hardly anyone, welfare recipients included, wanted to see welfare-as-we-knew-it restored.

But the main problem, says Ellwood, was sheer irresponsibility—the very flaw the reformers aimed to eliminate among welfare recipients. "There was just enormous pressure to reduce welfare, and the attitude toward a possible economic downturn was basically, 'We'll cross that bridge when we come to it.' " According to Ellwood, Clinton believed the money that states saved as a result of welfare reform could be used to help people in case of a recession; he did not foresee that a downturn would find states strapped for funds and eagerly slashing programs like Medicaid and child care.

The result has been that America entered its most recent recession as defenseless as if we had to face a terrorist attack without firefighters or emergency rescue workers. The safety net that sustained millions of the poor through previous downturns, however inadequately, has been torn to shreds.

We could see the current crisis, whose effects on unemployment will persist long after the recession technically ends, as an opportunity for genuine reform—including meaningful assistance for those who cannot find work, and reliable help, such as child care, for those who can. But instead, the Bush administration and Congress, like the welfare reformers who preceded them, seem poised to look the other way.

QUESTIONS FOR DISCUSSION

1. What are the consequences of welfare reform for poor families?
2. Why do we hold such negative attitudes toward welfare recipients?
3. What happens when our social "safety nets" disappear?

15

MAKING ENDS MEET ON A WELFARE CHECK
KATHRYN EDIN • LAURA LEIN

Along Minnesota's Highway 72—which runs between the Canadian border town of Rainy River and Bemidji, Minnesota—a large, crudely lettered billboard greets the southbound traveler:

> WELCOME TO MINNESOTA
> LAND OF 10,000 TAXES
> BUT WELFARE PAYS GOOD

Antiwelfare sentiment is common among Minnesotans, who live in a state with high personal income taxes and cash welfare benefits substantially above the national median. . . . But even in southern states, where cash welfare benefits are very low and taxes modest, citizens are likely to denigrate welfare. In 1990, about 40 percent of respondents in each region told interviewers from the National Opinion Research Center that the United States spends too much on welfare.[1] In 1994, another nationally representative survey found that 65 percent of Americans believed welfare spending was too high (Blendon et al. 1995).

Legislators recognize welfare's unpopularity. In the first half of the 1990s, several states cut benefits, and all let their value lag behind inflation. In addition, most states applied for federal waivers to experiment with benefit limitations or sanctions not allowed by the old federal rules. Some states estab-

lished a "family cap," which denied additional cash to mothers who had another child while receiving welfare. In other states, mothers whose children were truant from school lost a portion of their cash grant. Furthermore, under the new federal rules, all states must limit the amount of time a mother spends on welfare to five years.

Public dissatisfaction with welfare persists despite the fact that cash benefits to welfare recipients have declined by more than 40 percent in real terms since the mid-1970s (Blank 1994, 179). The reasons for the continuing public discontent throughout this period are complex, but probably rest on the widespread belief that the federal welfare entitlement perpetuated laziness and promiscuity (Bobo and Smith 1994; Page and Shapiro 1992).[2] Lazy women had babies to get money from the welfare system, the story went, and then let lazy boyfriends share their beds and live off their benefits. These lazy and immoral adults then raised lazy and immoral children, creating a vicious cycle of dependency.

Those who have promoted this view include the news media and talk show hosts, but social scientists also have contributed. The most widely known "scientific" argument was developed by Charles Murray, who in 1984 claimed that welfare actually makes the poor worse off. Federal welfare became too generous during the 1960s and 1970s, Murray argued, and began to reward unwed motherhood and indolence over marriage and jobs (Murray 1984). Social scientists spent much of the late 1980s attempt-

Edin, Kathryn and Laura Lein. 1997. "Making Ends Meet on a Welfare Check." Pp. 20–59 in *Making Ends Meet: How Single Mothers Survive Welfare and Low-Wage Work.* New York: Russell Sage Foundation. © 1997 Russell Sage Foundation, New York, N.Y. with permission from the publisher.

ing to discover whether Murray was right. Typically, economists judged the merits of the claim by estimating the disincentive effects of more or less generous state welfare benefits on work (for a review of this literature, see Moffitt 1992). Other researchers attempted to measure the effect of varying state benefits on marriage, divorce, and remarriage (Bane and Ellwood 1994).

The task we set for ourselves in this chapter is a more fundamental one. In order to assess whether any welfare program is too generous, one must compare its benefits to the cost of living faced by that program's recipients. An obvious starting point is to ask how much families headed by single mothers spend each month to make ends meet, and how that income compares with what they receive from welfare.

How Much Do Welfare-Reliant Mothers Spend?

In 1992, Donna Carson, a forty-year-old African American mother of two living in San Antonio, characterized herself as "ambitious and determined." She had spent most of her adult life playing by the rules. After high school graduation, she got a job and got married. She conceived her first child at age twenty-five, but her husband left before the child was born. Soon after her son's birth, she arranged for her mother to take care of him and went back to work. Because she did not have to pay for child care, her wages from her nurse's aide job combined with the child support she received from her ex-husband were enough to pay the bills. Ten years later, when she turned thirty-six, she had a second child. This time she was not married to the father. Carson's mother was willing to watch this child as well, so again she returned to work. Shortly there-

after, Carson's father's diabetes worsened and both of his legs were amputated. Her mother was overwhelmed by the tragedy and checked herself into a psychiatric hospital, leaving Carson to care for her two children and her disabled father alone. Seeing no other way out, she quit her job and turned to welfare. . . .

Three years later, when we were talking with her, Carson was still on welfare, and her budget was tight. Her typical monthly expenditures were about $920 a month. One-third of that amount went to rent and utilities, another third went to food, and the rest went to cover her children's clothing, their school supplies, her transportation, and all the other things the family needed. Her combined monthly benefits from AFDC and food stamps, however, came to only $477.

Some months, she received a "pass through" child support payment of $50 from the father of her first child, who was legally obligated to pay. Although this payment did not reduce her . . . benefits, her food stamps did go down by about $15 every time she received it. The father of her second child bypassed the formal child support system and paid her $60 directly each month. To get the rest of the money she needed, Carson took care of a working neighbor's child during the day. This neighbor could pay only $100 a month, but gave her the money in cash so that Carson's welfare caseworker could not detect the earnings and reduce her check. She got the rest of the money she needed from her father, who paid her $250 in cash each month to care for him.

Though Carson had more personal tragedy than most, her budget was similar to that of most other welfare recipients we talked with. . . . Our respondents averaged $213 a month on housing, $262 on food, $336 on other necessary expenses, and $64 on items that were arguably not essential—a total of $876 for an average family of 3.17 people.[3]

Housing Expenses

The housing expenses of welfare-reliant families varied substantially. This variation depended on whether recipients paid market rent, had a housing subsidy in a public housing project or a private building . . . or shared housing with a relative or friend. Donna Carson paid market rent, which in San Antonio was quite low but still higher than what most mothers pay in subsidized units. However, apartments that meet the physical criteria required for Section 8 tended to be in neighborhoods with less access to public transportation than the neighborhoods where housing projects were generally located, so these families usually had to maintain an automobile. Consequently, while public housing and Section 8 residents paid roughly the same amount for housing, Section 8 families spent far more for transportation.

In most cases, the welfare-reliant families who shared housing with a friend or relative were able to split the rent, utilities, telephone bill, and other household expenses. Thus, their expenses for rent and these other items were relatively low. About half of those who shared housing lived with one or both parents. The other half lived with siblings or friends. Mothers who lived with a parent usually made only token contributions toward the rent and took some portion of the responsibility for utilities and household maintenance. Most lived with their parents precisely because they could not afford to maintain their own households. Those who lived with a sibling or friend usually paid half of the household expenses. Sometimes, however, mothers "rented" only a portion of the living space (a single room, for example) and paid only a quarter or a third of the household costs.[4]

Food Expenses

Food expenditures averaged $262 a month for the welfare-reliant families we interviewed. This means that these mothers spent $19 per person on food in a typical week. This amount is nearly identical to the federal government's cheap food plan (the "thrifty food budget"), which uses as its base what poor mothers bought for their families in the 1950s and adjusts the prices in that "basket" for inflation each year (Ruggles 1990; Schwarz and Volgy 1992). The average weekly food stamp allotment for the families we interviewed, however, was slightly lower than this amount—$16 per person. . . . This meant that the average mother had to cover $40 of food expenses each month with income from some source other than food stamps.[5]

Food stamp benefits also varied with family income, including cash welfare. In the lowest . . . benefit states, therefore, families could receive up to $292 a month in food stamps for a family of three, or $21 per person per week in 1991, and families in these sites who reported no outside income received this maximum. Most found it sufficient to cover the bulk of their food expenditures. Families in states that paid more generous welfare benefits received roughly 30 cents less in food stamps for each additional dollar in cash welfare benefits. Because of this, hardly anyone who lived outside the South could pay their food bills with food stamps alone.[6] In San Antonio, food stamps covered 99 percent of respondents' average food expenditures; in Charleston, 88 percent; in Chicago, 80 percent; and in high-benefit Boston, only 65 percent.

Other Expenses

Besides housing and food, clothing took the next biggest bite out of the average family's monthly budget, followed by transportation, laundry and toiletries, telephone charges, medical expenses, baby care, and appliance and furniture costs. On average, welfare-reliant mothers spent $69 a month on clothing. This means that the mothers with whom we spoke typically purchased $261 worth of shoes, coats, and other apparel for each family member in a year.[7] Most of this was for their children, since children continually grow out of their clothing.

Welfare-reliant mothers employed a number of strategies to contain their clothing expenditures. Virtually all purchased some of their clothing at thrift or second-hand stores, and most scoured neighborhood yard sales. During our interviews, many mothers proudly showed us their second-hand buys: a barely worn pair of name-brand jeans or a winter coat that was practically new and only a bit too small. A mother's largest expense in the clothing category was for children's shoes. Children not only went through two or more pairs of shoes a year, but shoes in children's sizes and in good condition were seldom available at neighborhood thrift stores. Winter coats, hats, mittens, and boots were also expensive, and most children grew out of them every other winter. Thus in the winter months, clothing needs could become an added hardship. One mother told us,

> In the winter months, I have had to keep my children at home on the really cold days because I didn't have warm enough clothes to dress them. I have learned to swallow my pride, though, and go to the second-hand shops and try to get the right kind of winter clothes for the boys.

The welfare-reliant mothers we interviewed felt that second-hand clothing was acceptable for younger children, whose peers were still largely unconcerned with appearance. One mother told us,

For shopping I go to yard sales and the Salvation Army for Jay's clothes. Fortunately, he isn't the type of kid who always has to have Nike sneakers or he won't go to school. I get him K-Mart ones, or I go to the used clothes store [on] Belmont [Avenue]. I probably spend $200 a season on new clothes for him, but some of those he can wear from season to season.

Other mothers reported that their older children—especially high school boys—felt they could not maintain their self-respect or the respect of their peers while wearing K-Mart shoes to school. Some mothers felt that if they did not purchase name-brand sneakers, an athletic jacket, or other popular items for their teenagers, their children might be lured into criminal activity so they could buy these items themselves:

> My boy, he sees these kids that sell drugs. They can afford to buy these [tennis shoes] and he can't. So I have my little side-job and [I buy them for him]. You got to do it to keep them away from drugs, from the streets.

One mother told us that in order to buy her child a $50 pair of tennis shoes, she ate only one meal a day for a month. The savings in her food bill were enough to cover the purchase of the shoes. Most mothers in her neighborhood did not feel it was necessary to go hungry to meet their children's clothing needs, because they could generate the extra cash in other ways. . . .

Mothers who bought new clothing generally had to put the clothing on layaway. They paid a small portion of the purchase price each month. Some others found professional shoplifters who would note the children's sizes, shoplift the clothing, and sell it for a fraction of the ticket price to the mother.

Transportation cost the average welfare-reliant family $62 a month. Families living in Charleston (where there was little access to public transportation) and families living outside central cities spent more because they had to maintain automobiles or pay for taxis. At the time of our interviews, welfare rules limited the value of a family's automobile to $2,500. This meant that mothers had older cars, which generally required more frequent repair and got poorer gas mileage. All of the states we studied had mandatory insurance laws, and respondents told us that minimum insurance coverage cost at least $40 a month. In addition, Chicago and metropolitan Boston required that families purchase city stickers to park on the street, and South Carolina taxed the value of a family's car each year.

Although mothers who had access to public transportation spent less than those mothers who maintained cars, bus and subway transportation cost the average mother who used it more than $60 a month. Few mothers lived in areas where they could walk to the laundromat or the grocery store. In neighborhoods that provided these amenities, rents were higher. Since few mothers could afford child care, a shopping trip required that mothers bring their children with them and pay the bus or subway fares for the older children as well (younger children often ride free).

Laundry, toiletries, and cleaning supplies also constituted a significant proportion of monthly expenses. Some mothers washed their clothing in the bathtub and let it air-dry in their apartment or outside. This was a time-consuming task, however, and mothers complained that their clothes did not get as clean as machine-washed clothing. A few mothers owned or rented their own washers and dryers, but most used local laundromats. Because most families' clothing stock was slim (for example, two or three pairs of pants for each person was typical), mothers usually washed their clothing once each week or more. Laundromat prices varied, but mothers seldom spent less than

$6 for coin machines each time they visited the laundromat, for roughly three loads.

All told, the welfare-reliant mothers had to spend $23 in a typical month to wash and dry their clothing and an additional $29 on toiletries and cleaning supplies. Food stamps could not be used to purchase toiletries or cleaning supplies, so mothers had to pay for sponges, cleaning fluids, dishwashing liquid, hand and laundry soap, bleach, toilet paper, hair care products, deodorant, disposable razors, and feminine products with cash.

Ninety-two percent of our sample had telephone service for at least part of the year. On average, families spent $31 monthly on telephone charges. Twenty-six percent of the welfare recipients had their phone disconnected at least once during the past year because of nonpayment. When mothers ran short of money, they were usually more willing to do without a phone than to neglect rent, utilities, food, clothing, transportation, or other essentials. Basic service charges also varied widely by site. In San Antonio, where basic local service cost about $12 a month, families spent only $18 a month for phone-related costs. In all other sites, comparable service ranged from $20 to $25 a month, and families spent much more. These costs included not only charges for local and long-distance calls but connection and reconnection charges as well. Although not strictly necessary for a family's material well-being, mothers without telephones had a difficult time maintaining contact with welfare caseworkers and their children's schools. It was also more difficult to apply for jobs because prospective employers could not reach them to set up an interview. Some solved this dilemma by sharing a phone with a neighbor; messages left with neighbors, however, were not always promptly forwarded.

Medicaid, the government's health insurance program for low-income families, offered free emergency care and routine physician care. All the households in our welfare-reliant sample were covered by Medicaid. Over-the-counter medicines and other medical services, however, were not covered and constituted another $18 of the average welfare-reliant mother's monthly budget. These expenses included routine drugstore costs, such as those for pain relievers, cough syrup, adhesive bandages, vitamin tablets, or other medicines families frequently used. In addition, few state Medicaid programs pay for prescription birth control pills, abortions, antidepressants, or other mental health drugs. Nor do most Medicaid plans pay for dental care, except for emergency oral surgery.

Diapers and other baby care products cost an average welfare-reliant family $18 a month (37 percent of the welfare recipients in our sample had babies in diapers). Welfare-reliant mothers with infants and young toddlers typically received formula, milk, eggs, and cheese from WIC (Women's, Infants', and Children's nutritional program). Most mothers told us, however, that they were usually one or two cans short of formula each month and had to purchase them at the grocery store. In addition, WIC does not provide disposable diapers, which constituted roughly 80 percent of the cash welfare-reliant mothers had to spend on baby care. Only a tiny minority of the mothers we interviewed used cloth diapers; although cheaper than disposables, cloth diapering was not practicable for mothers who relied on laundromats. In addition, mothers who used cloth diapers reported substantial upfront costs (they had to buy the diapers), and these mothers spent substantially more for laundry supplies than other mothers. Mothers also averaged $14 a month on school-related expenses and $7 a month on child care.

Appliances and furniture cost the typical family another $17 a month. Generally mothers purchased both new and used furniture and appliances with installment pay-

ments. Because they could not get bank credit, these mothers would often arrange credit at local thrift shops and "rent-to-own" furniture stores. Although local thrift stores did not generally apply finance charges to mothers' purchases (they usually held the item until it was fully paid for), rent-to-own furniture stores did. Because the latter stores charged very high interest rates and allowed long repayment periods, mothers sometimes ended up paying two to three times the actual value of the item. Meanwhile, mothers who missed a payment could have the furniture repossessed, losing whatever equity they had built up.

Miscellaneous items in the families' budgets included check cashing fees and fees for money orders, debt service, burial insurance . . . and haircuts. These items totaled $47 in the average month.

Nonessentials

Entertainment cost the typical family $20 each month and was usually limited to video rentals; occasionally it included movies, trips to amusement parks, and travel (mothers sometimes sent their children to relatives during the summer). Mothers spent an average of $22 for cigarettes and alcohol each month, mostly on cigarettes. Mothers seldom bought their own alcohol, and those who drank depended on boyfriends, friends, and family members to pay for their drinks. This was also true for most mothers who used marijuana or other drugs. In addition, mothers spent an average of $3 a month for the lottery, $6 a month for cable television, and $13 a month to eat out. All told, the typical welfare-reliant family spent $64 a month on these nonnecessary items, or about 7 percent of their total budget.[8] Although not physical necessities, the items met crucial psychological needs.

Although the mothers in our sample worried about day-to-day material survival, most saw survival as having broader "psychological" and "social" dimensions. One mother commented:

> You know, we live in such a materialistic world. Our welfare babies have needs and wants too. They see other kids going to the circus, having toys and stuff like that. You gotta do what you gotta do to make your kid feel normal. There is no way you can deprive your child.

This woman's statement captures a common sentiment among the welfare recipients we interviewed: children need to have an occasional treat, and mothers who refuse them may deprive their offspring of normalcy. Even among Mexican American mothers in San Antonio, who spent less than any of the other welfare-reliant mothers, one family in six paid a small monthly fee for a basic cable subscription. These mothers told us they saw the cable subscription as a cheap way of keeping their kids off the streets and out of trouble.

The mothers themselves needed an occasional boost too. Many reported that by spending small amounts on soda pop, cosmetics, cigarettes, alcohol, or the lottery, they avoided feeling like they were "completely on the bottom," or that their lives were "completely hopeless." When we asked respondents if they could do without them, they replied that these items gave them some measure of self-respect, and without them they would lose hope of bettering their situations:

> I never buy for myself, only for my son. Well, I take that back. I allow myself two of what I guess you would call luxuries. Well, I guess three. First, I buy soda pop. I do not eat meals hardly ever, but I always have to have a can of Pepsi in my hand. I drink Pepsi nonstop. My boyfriend, he buys it for me by the case 'cause he knows how much I like it, and I guess it's the pop that gives me my

energy for dealing with my son—you know, the sugar and caffeine and stuff.
>
> And then I treat myself to the cigarettes. Without the smoking, I would just worry all the time about how we was going to eat and would never relax. I feel like I deserve some little pleasure, you know, and so those cigarettes keep me up, keep me feeling that things aren't so bad.
>
> And the other thing is, I buy my cosmetics. I mean, I go around feeling so low all the time, and the makeup makes me feel, you know, better about myself. I feel like I'm not so poor when I can buy myself some cosmetics at the discount house.

The few respondents who spent money on alcohol reported similar sentiments:

> Oh, sometimes, you know, just to relax or somethin', I just go out and have a few. And when I'm really low, I sometimes go out and tie one on, if you know what I mean. Sometimes I think I'll go crazy all day in the house if I can't get out once in a while. I just couldn't take it.

Although few mothers played the lottery with any regularity, those who did also viewed it as a sort of escape:

> I just can't afford not to buy some tickets when the pot gets real big. I sometimes buy five tickets if I can afford it. I like to plan what I'm going to do with it, you know, fantasize and stuff—dream of what it would be like to own nice things and such.

. . .

"It's Just Not Enough"

How far did benefits go toward meeting the needs of welfare-reliant families? All 214 of our welfare-reliant respondents reported that their combined benefits ran out long before the month was over. One mother told us: "I don't ever pay off all my bills so there isn't ever anything left over. As soon as I get my check, it's gone and I don't have anything left." Another respondent said:

> What you have to live off isn't enough. Me myself, I just got back on and I had been off for about six years because I was working. But [I had some health problems and needed some medical insurance so] I had to get back on the program. It's just not enough. You just can't live off it especially with three kids or two kids. It is impossible, the things you have to do to last you until the next month. Me myself, I get $380 [in cash] for three kids [plus food stamps]. The rent I pay is just impossible plus my other little bills.

Only a handful of the welfare-reliant mothers with whom we spoke came close to meeting their expenses with combined welfare benefits, and only one got by on these benefits alone. When mothers received their check, they prioritized their expenses, usually paying for housing (rent, electricity, gas) and purchasing food before attending to their other bills. After housing and food, the typical family had $90 left to pay for their other expenses: clothing, transportation, laundry, school supplies, furniture and appliances, over-the-counter medicines and toiletries, haircuts, telephone calls, and items such as diapers and routine dental care. . . .

One mother in eight came within $50 of covering her expenditures with her welfare benefits. As a group, these twenty-six mothers were unusual in several ways. First, all of them received subsidized housing or shared housing costs with a friend or relative. Second, half of them received substantial in-kind assistance from a variety of community organizations (in some cases, between twenty and thirty organizations per family over the course of a year) and

from their families and friends. Third, half sold most of their food stamps for cash. They then got their food from community organizations and purchased almost all their other necessities from neighborhood fences who sold stolen groceries, clothing, and toiletries at cut-rate prices. Our best guess is that in the absence of these strategies, these mothers would have had to spend between $200 and $300 more a month to keep their families together.

Only one of our 214 mothers—an extremely frugal, publicly housed Boston-area resident—was able to meet her expenses with her welfare benefits. She made ends meet because she lived in an unusually generous state and spent nothing whatsoever on entertainment, alcohol, cigarettes, or the lottery; nothing on child care; nothing on school supplies (what the school did not provide, her son did not get); and nothing on furniture or appliances (she scavenged broken-down furniture from alleys). She spent nothing on transportation, since all her friends lived in the projects and she walked nearly everywhere she needed to go. She also spent very little on laundry because she washed clothes in the bathtub and let them air-dry. She spent little on clothing because she purchased the majority of the family's clothes (the few there were) at thrift stores. Finally, she spent nothing for Christmas, birthdays, or any other special occasion. No other respondent in *any* site made ends meet on so little. Since her child frequently went hungry, had only one change of clothes, and often missed school because he lacked adequate winter clothing, several of this woman's neighbors (whom we interviewed) had reported her to child protective services for neglect. . . .

Surviving on Welfare

Americans have long worried that welfare benefits are too generous. Many hear about high rates of out-of-wedlock births among the poor and conclude that welfare contributes to the problem. A more fundamental question is how do individual welfare recipients actually use the government support they receive. What standard of living do welfare benefits afford single mothers?

We have attempted to answer this question by interviewing 214 welfare-reliant mothers about what they spent to keep their families together. We also examined the level of welfare benefits available to the mothers. We found that for most welfare-reliant mothers food and shelter alone cost almost as much as these mothers received from the government. For more than one-third, food and housing costs exceeded their cash benefits, leaving no extra money for uncovered medical care, clothing, and other household expenses. When we added the costs of other necessities to the mothers' budgets, it was evident that virtually all welfare-reliant mothers experienced a wide gap between what they could get from welfare and what they needed to support their families. In fact, with only one exception, we met no welfare mother who was making ends meet on her government check alone. Mothers filled the gap through reported and unreported work and through handouts from family, friends, and agencies. . . . Finally, we asked the difficult question of whether welfare-reliant mothers' expenditures were truly necessary. We found that our mothers' budgets were far below the household budgets collected by the Consumer Expenditure Survey in 1991 for single-parent families. Our welfare-reliant mothers also spent less than the lowest income group the CES interviewed. Our conclusion is that the vast majority of our welfare-reliant mothers' expenses were at the very low end of widely shared national consumption norms.

Despite spending far more than their welfare benefits, many of the families we interviewed experienced serious material hardship. Variations in benefit levels had real consequences for welfare-reliant single mothers and their children. Lower benefits substantially increased material hardship as did having larger families. Life on welfare, it seems, was an exceedingly tenuous affair.[9] An articulate Chicago respondent put it this way:

> I don't understand why [Public Aid is] punishing people who are poor if you want to mainstream them. If indeed, the idea is to segregate, to be biased, to create a widening gap between the haves and the have-nots, then the welfare system is working. If it is to provide basic needs, not just the financial but psychological and social needs of every human being, then the system fails miserably.

NOTES

1. In 1994, 49 percent of Americans thought that welfare programs discouraged people from working, and two-thirds believed that welfare encouraged women to have more children than they would have had if welfare were not available (Blendon and others 1995).
2. These responses were gathered during the center's General Social Survey.
3. Due to rounding, these estimates do not total $876.
4. We did not include any teenage mothers living at home. Mothers under age eighteen constitute only a tiny portion of all mothers on the welfare rolls (U.S. House of Representatives 1995, table 10-27). We did interview seventeen teenage mothers and found that they paid almost none of their own bills because most of them lived rent-free with their mothers while they tried to finish school. Therefore, these teenage mothers could not construct a household budget.
5. Nor could families with housing subsidies, disability income, or reported outside income buy all of their food with food stamps.
6. There is a reduction in food stamp benefits as cash benefits rise.
7. $(69/3.17) \times 12$
8. In terms of nonnecessary spending, more than a third of families spent nothing whatsoever on entertainment during the previous year, two-thirds never ate out; nearly half had spent nothing on cigarettes or alcohol during the

year; and four-fifths had gone without cable television.

9. Whereas Charles Murray portrayed an overly generous welfare system that kept the poor in poverty because it rewarded their indolence, mothers saw welfare as a stingy and punishing system that placed them and their children in a desperate economic predicament.

REFERENCES

Bane, Mary Jo and David T. Ellwood. 1994. *Welfare Realities: From Rhetoric to Reform*. Cambridge, MA: Harvard University Press.

Blank, Rebecca M. 1994. "The Employment Strategy: Public Policies to Increase Work and Earnings." In *Confronting Poverty*, edited by Sheldon H. Danziger, Gary D. Sandefur, and Daniel H. Weinberg. Cambridge, MA: Harvard University Press; New York: Russell Sage Foundation.

Blendon, Robert J., Drew E. Altman, John Benson, Mollyann Brodie, Matt James, and Gerry Chervinsky. 1995. "The Public and the Welfare Reform Debate." *Archives of Pediatric and Adolescent Medicine* 149:1065–1069.

Bobo, Lawrence and Ryan A. Smith. 1994. "Antipoverty Policy, Affirmative Action, and Racial Attitudes." In *Confronting Poverty*, edited by Sheldon H. Danziger, Gary D. Sandefur, and Daniel H. Weinberg. Cambridge, MA: Harvard University Press; New York: Russell Sage Foundation.

Moffitt, Robert. 1992. "Incentive Effects of the U.S. Welfare System: A Review." *Journal of Economic Literature* 30 (March):1–61.

Murray, Charles A. 1984. *Losing Ground: American Social Policy*. New York: Basic Books.

———. 1993. "Welfare and the Family: The U.S. Experience." *Journal of Labor Economics* 11:S224–S262.

Page, Benjamin I. and Robert Y. Shapiro. 1992. *The Rational Public: Fifty Years of Trends in America's Policy Preferences*. Chicago: University of Chicago Press.

Ruggles, Patricia. 1990. *Drawing the Line: Alternative Poverty Measures and Their Implications.* Washington, D.C.: Urban Institute Press.

Schwarz, John E. and Thomas J. Volgy. 1992. "Social Support for Self-Reliance: The Politics of Making Work Pay." *American Prospect* 9 (Spring):67–73.

U.S. House of Representatives, Committee on Ways and Means. 1995. Overview of Entitlement Programs (Green Book). Washington: U.S. Government Printing Office.

QUESTIONS FOR DISCUSSION

1. What are the difficulties of making ends meet on welfare that are not obvious to people who have never been poor?

2. Some of the mothers Edin and Lein interviewed purchased goods or services that might be considered unessential by many policy makers (such as telephone service, cable TV service, and brand-name shoes). Why did these women consider such expenditures necessary?

3. How do public attitudes about welfare differ from the reality of these women's lives? Why do you think there is such a gap between welfare policies and the needs of poor mothers?

KEY TERMS

absolute poverty
relative poverty
underemployment
poverty threshold
poverty rate
Third World
First World
culture of poverty
Temporary Aid to Needy Families (TANF)

THE SOCIAL WEB

- The Institute for Research on Poverty publishes numerous reports related to poverty, services, and welfare: www.ssc.wisc.edu/irp.
- National Public Radio and American Radio Works have co-produced an extensive report on child poverty, "The Forgotten Fourteen Million," by John Biewan: www.americanradioworks.org/features/14_million.
- For information on homelessness, go to the Web site of the National Coalition for the Homeless: www.nationalhomeless.org.

QUESTIONS FOR DEBATE

1. Do wealthy nations and individuals benefit from the existence of poverty? Do they have a responsibility to help poor people and countries?
2. What are the structural factors that contribute to poverty in American society?
3. What changes have to occur in order for poverty to be eliminated? What are the obstacles to those changes happening?
4. Is the current system of welfare a good one? Why or why not? What changes would you recommend in the welfare system?

Chapter 5
Race and Ethnicity

Contents

Learning Objectives

By the end of this chapter you will be able to:

- Recognize how the authors use one or
  more of the major perspectives to explore
  race, ethnicity and racism.

- Explore how racial and ethnic inequality
  is shaped by class inequalities and gender.

- Identify the ways that race and ethnicity
  are socially constructed.

- Describe various consequences of racial
  and ethnic inequality and racism.

- Analyze how individuals contribute to
  racial and ethnic inequality and the oppression of non-Whites through their
  everyday behavior.

- Explain how social systems and institutions perpetuate racial and ethnic inequality and racism.

Defining the Problem

Sociologists generally use the term **race** to
refer to groups of people who share physical
traits, such as stature, skin color, and facial
features. Presently, racial categories recognized in official governmental documents
include White, Black, American Indian or
Alaskan Native (Eskimo and Aleut), Asian,
Native Hawaiian and Pacific Islander. **Ethnicity,** in contrast, refers to cultural differences that set groups apart from each other:
shared rituals, meaning systems, languages,
and frequently religions. Ethnicity and race
can overlap, as demonstrated by the existence of Hispanic Whites and Hispanic non-
Whites. Racial and ethnic inequality are
persistent features of American society, such
that the life chances for Whites of European
origin—access to good employment, income, health care, governmental supports,
and so forth—are better than for other
groups. **Racism** is a concept sociologists use
to explain the social conditions and human
actions that lead to the persistence of racial
inequality.

Sociologists of social problems view
**race, ethnicity, and racism as social con-
structions.** Simply put, both the "natural"
groupings that we recognize between races
and the ways we conceptualize unacceptable
inequality are social products and are subject
to change. Race is "a concept which signifies
and symbolizes social conflicts and interests
by referring to different types of human bodies."[1] This constructionist way of conceptualizing race focuses attention on the social
activities that involve meaning-making over
time. It focuses attention on how the relative
economic and political power of groups of
people and the specific struggles in which
they are involved determine what comes to

---

[1]Michael Omni and Howard Winant. "Racial Formation," in *Racial Formation in the United States: From the
1960s to the 1990s* (New York: Routledge, 1994), 53–76.

count as race within a society. If we define race in this way, then it can be understood as a **structural** not individual, **feature of society.** Race is not within a person, but rests in the meaning given to characteristics of that person. There is no evidence that race has a biological basis (chromosomal or hormonal). Genetic similarities cannot be demonstrated on the basis of their physical characteristics. In sum, sociologists believe that it is not that individual people have a race, but rather that race is a way of thinking that is embedded in social practices.

Sociologists tend to agree that race is something that Americans notice and act on all the time. We make interpretations about people and situations on the basis of skin color, facial features, clothing, and so forth. However, we have varied degrees of awareness about our reliance on race as a meaningful social category. Whites, who infrequently experience racial discrimination, tend to be unaware of the importance of race in their own and others' thinking in comparison to Blacks, Hispanics, Asians, and other people of color. This experience of not "seeing" race allows Whites not to see the privileges associated with being White in a society organized around race. It is only through a reflective effort that many Whites become aware of their **racial privilege.** In "White Privilege and Male Privilege," Peggy McIntosh, a White English professor, reflects on coming to terms with the social advantages she has relative to non-Whites:

> My schooling gave me no training in seeing myself as an oppressor, as an unfairly advantaged person, or as a participant in a damaged culture. I was taught to see myself as an individual whose moral state depended on her moral will. . . . After frustration with men who would not recognize male privilege, I decided to work on myself at least by identifying some of the daily effects of

white privilege on my life. . . . I can if I wish arrange to be in the company of people of my race most of the time. I can avoid spending time with people whom I was trained to mistrust and who have learned to mistrust my kind or me. If I should need to move, I can be pretty sure of renting or purchasing housing in an area which I can afford and in which I want to live. . . . I can be sure that my children will be given curricular materials that testify to the existence of their race. . . . I can be casual about whether or not to listen to another woman's voice in a group in which she is the only member of her race. . . . I do not have to educate my children to be aware of systemic racism for their own daily physical protection. . . . I can speak to a powerful male group without putting my race on trial. . . . I am never asked to speak for all the people of my racial group. . . . I can choose blemish cover or bandages in "flesh" color and have them more or less match my skin.[2]

Sociologists currently recognize two key causes of racial inequality: the acts of individuals—**individual racism**—and governmental and social practices that systematically disadvantage one group relative to another—**institutional racism.** Individuals can perpetrate racist acts intentionally, driven by hostility toward a particular group, or unintentionally, making decisions on the basis of stereotypes. Today, institutional racism is often unintentional, but it is the result of explicit historical efforts to control and limit non-Whites and non-Europeans. From the beginning of the na-

---

[2] Peggy McIntosh, "White Privilege and Male Privilege: A Personal Account of Coming to See Correspondences Through Work in Women's Studies," Working Paper 189, Wellesley College Center for Research on Women, Wellesley, MA, 1988.

tion, the U.S. government and the country's social and economic leadership defined and enforced norms and role relationships that were racially distinct. White legislators and leaders gave racial minorities a limited set of roles, all of which were subordinate relative to the positions mapped out for white Europeans. More than 200 years have passed, a civil rights movement has matured, and federal and state legislation now grant Blacks citizenship, the right to vote, and full civil rights, and prohibit governmental discrimination on the basis of race. The majority of Americans now believe that members of different races should be treated equally. However, the basis for decision making in many areas of life—such as qualifications for employment, advancement, compensation, loans, mortgages, entry into college—have not been systematically scrutinized. Well-intentioned decision makers—employers, loan officers, admissions officers—continue to carry out practices created to achieve an unequal effect, and they produce that result. Knowles and Prewitt provide a good illustration of individual and institutional racism:

> The murder by K.K.K. members and law enforcement officials of three civil rights workers in Mississippi was an act of individual racism. That the sovereign state of Mississippi refused to indict the killers was institutional racism. The individual act of racist bigots went unpunished in Mississippi because of policies, precedents, and practices that are an integral part of the state's legal institutions. A store clerk who suspects that black children in his store are there to steal candy but white children are there to purchase candy, and who treats the children differently, the blacks as probable delinquents and the whites as probable customers, also illustrates individual racism. Unlike the Mississippi murders, the store clerk is not a bigot and may not even consider himself prejudiced, but his behavior is shaped by racial stereotypes which have been part of his unconscious since childhood. A university admissions policy which provides for entrance only to students who score high on tests designed primarily for white suburban high schools necessarily excludes black ghetto-educated students. Unlike the legal policies of Mississippi, the university admission criteria are not intended to be racist, but the university is pursuing a course which perpetuates institutional racism. The difference, then, between individual and institutional racism is not a difference in intent or of visibility. Both the individual act of racism and the racist institutional policy may occur without the presence of conscious bigotry, and both may be masked intentionally or innocently.[3]

The institutional form of discrimination is less visible than individual discrimination, yet it is devastating because social institutions are interrelated and the racial inequality is cumulative. For example, disadvantage in hiring reduces one's ability to secure a solid income. This, in turn, limits one's access to health insurance, limits the number of places one can live, limits one's children's access to a good school district, and so forth.

Although sociologists agree that racial inequality is a product of individual and institutional racism, what we should treat as a problem is a contested issue among the American public. The explanation that racial inequality stems from the intentional acts of hostile individuals is more palatable to many

---

[3]Louis Knowles and Kenneth Prewitt, eds., "Institutional and Ideological Roots of Racism," in *Institutional Racism in America* (Englewood Cliffs, NJ: Prentice-Hall, 1969), 4–5.

Whites. They cling to this construction of the problem because they are uncomfortable with the culpability and accountability implied by institutional definitions. Whites who only recognize the existence of individual racism, and especially its intentional form, see the road to racial equality as color blindness (paying no attention to race). This **color-blind** approach is preferred by some people of color as well. Other Americans who experience daily racial subordination argue that sociologists haven't gone far enough in describing institutional racism. They believe that we need to broaden our analysis to encompass organizational cultures. They argue that we should seek to eliminate a **racist atmosphere**—the persistence of verbal and interpersonal behaviors in workplaces, schools, medical establishments, and so forth, that make Whites (the majority culture) feel secure and minorities insecure.[4]

All social problems researchers concerned with the objective analysis of racial and ethnic inequality seek to explain the empirical reality that resources and opportunities are not evenly distributed among individuals who fall into different socially recognized racial and ethnic categories, that Whites as a group appear to do better than members of other groups, and that many Blacks appear to be members of a permanent underclass. Covering the range of substantive specializations within sociology, they document the disproportionate burdens experienced by non-Whites in terms of their lack of access to employment, health care, and education and their overexposure to the criminal justice system and to environmental toxins. Macro analysts focus on how the reality of group difference is cemented through cultural and institutional means. They explore how the media, gov-

ernment, family, education, and other institutions continuously focus on race as important and define the limits of appropriate independent and collaborative behavior for Whites and non-Whites. Micro analysts analyze how individual members of society come to accept the social parameters for behavior as "real" and how their day-to-day behavior preserves the subordinate place of Blacks and other non-Whites relative to Whites. Sociologists working from both macro and micro perspectives study how racial inequality is preserved with and without physical force and coercion.

Scope of the Problem

Who lives in the United States? The U.S. Census conducted in April 2000 yielded the following population distribution for those listing one race: 75.1 percent White, 12.3 percent Black, 0.9 percent American Indian or Alaskan Native (Eskimo and Aleut), 3.6 percent Asian, 0.1 percent Native Hawaiian or Pacific Islander, and 5.5 percent other. An additional 2.4 percent of the population listed two or more races, and 12.5 percent of the entire population identify themselves as being of Hispanic origin.[5] The United States is expected to become progressively more multicultural over the next 50 years.[6] Some of the change will be due to immigration, but most of it will result from the increased fertility of specific groups. The start of the shift can be seen when population data from 1980 and 1999 are compared. The percentages of children who are black, non-

---

[4]Bob Blauner, *Black Lives, White Lives: Three Decades of Race Relations in America* (Berkeley, CA: University of California Press, 1989).

[5]Census Brief, "Overview of Race and Hispanic Origin," U.S. Bureau of the Census, March 2001.

[6]"Resident Population of the United States: Middle Series Projections, 2001–2005, by Sex, Race, and Hispanic Origin, with Median Age" and "Resident Population of the United States: Middle Series Projections, 2035–2050, by Sex, Race, and Hispanic Origin, with Median Age" (Washington, D.C.: U.S. Bureau of the Census, Population Estimates Program).

Hispanic, and American Indian/Alaskan Native remained stable between 1980 and 1999; however, the percentage of White non-Hispanic children declined between 1980 and 1999 from 74 percent to 65 percent, and the percentage of Asian/Pacific Islander children rose from 2 percent to 4 percent. By 2020, the Census Bureau projects that more than 20 percent of the children in the United States will be of Hispanic origin and 6 percent will be Asian/Pacific Islander.[7]

Race, however, is not simply an issue of demographic composition, it is a matter of how group membership matters to individuals' life chances. Are racial-ethnic groups gaining access to opportunities in proportion to their representation in the population? Do all racial-ethnic groups have the same likelihood of living to a ripe old age? Do majority and minority members of society have contact with each other, such that they can draw on experience rather than stereotypes? Using these kinds of questions as the basis for further consideration, most sociologists agree that in the contemporary United States racial inequality is a social problem of monumental proportions. Consider the following indicators of health, educational attainment, employment, income, and segregation.

The overall infant mortality rate for the United States in 1999 was 705.6 deaths before age 1 per 100,000 live births. However, the mortality rate of Black infants was 1,455.8, compared to 576.8 for Whites. Blacks had more than double the White rate of infant deaths due to complications of pregnancy, labor, and delivery (159.1 vs. 53.8), diseases of the circulatory system (29.9 vs. 14.4), diseases of the respiratory system (41.6 vs. 12.6), and accidents (41.6 vs. 17.9).[8]

The mortality rate for children ages 1–4 also varied with race. Although it has continued to drop for young Black children since 1980, their rate remained almost twice that for White children of comparable age. Young Asian/Pacific Islander children continued to have the lowest death rates.[9] The mortality rate for adolescents (15–19 years old) in 1999, 70 deaths per 100,000, continued to drop from that of 1980. However, the death rate remained substantially higher for Black boys than for White and Hispanic boys, and the primary cause of death differed as well. Firearms were the leading cause of death for Black and Hispanic adolescent boys; car accidents were the leading cause of death for White and Asian/Pacific Islander boys and all adolescent girls.[10] Inequities of violent victimization extend into the adult population. In 1999, 16.2 Blacks 12 years or older per 100,000 in the population were likely to experience serious violence compared to 8.7 Whites per 100,000. Blacks in the same age range were six times more likely to be murdered than Whites.[11]

Educational attainment varies by race as well. In 2000, 88.4 percent of the White non-Hispanic population 25 years old or older had completed high school; 78.9 percent of non-Hispanic Blacks and 57 percent of Hispanics had done so. An additional 28.1 percent of the White population 25 years old or older had completed four or more years of college, compared to only 16.6 percent of the Black and 10.6 percent of the Hispanic population.[12] Projections for 2028 suggest increases in high school graduation across the board for all groups of native-born women

---

[7]"America's Children 2000" (Washington, D.C.: U.S. Bureau of the Census, Population Estimates and Projections), www.childstats.gov/ac2000/poptxt.asp.

[8]*National Vital Statistics,* report 49 (8) (September 21, 2001).

[9]"America's Children 2000."

[10]Ibid.

[11]Bureau of Justice Statistics, U.S. Department of Justice.

[12]"Table A-2, Percent of People 25 Years Old and Over Who Have Completed High School or College, by Race, Hispanic Origin and Sex: Selected Years 1940–2000" (Washington, D.C.: U.S. Bureau of the Census).

and men. Estimates of college graduation among the native-born population suggest a slight drop for White men, a substantial increase for Black men, and a slight increase for Hispanic men. Comparable projections for women show increases in college graduation rates for all groups, with the greatest increase among Hispanic women.[13]

Labor force participation, unemployment, and earnings differ by race and gender. Although unemployment rates were down across the board, blacks remained a bit more and Hispanics a bit less than twice as likely as Whites to be unemployed.[14] In 2000, the labor force participation of Black men continued to be lower than that of White and Hispanic men across all age groups. However, labor force participation of Black women was higher than that of White women and Hispanic women. Only Hispanic teenage girls worked as much as their White and Black counterparts.[15]

Educational attainment predicts access to more skilled, higher status, and higher paid positions, and median full-time earnings for Whites, Blacks, and Hispanics reflect the disparities in educational attainment described above. In 2000, the median full-time earnings for Black men and Hispanic men were 75.2 percent and 61.9 percent, respectively, of the median earnings of White men. In the same period, the median full-time earnings for Black women and Hispanic women were 85.8 percent and 72.8 percent, respectively, of the median earnings of White women.[16] These 2000 figures show a decrease in the earnings gap between Black and White men, but an increase in the earnings gap between White and other women.

How consumer groups spend their money is another indicator of their status. Fewer Blacks than non-Blacks live in dwellings they own. Consequently, Blacks spend more on housing (29 percent) than do non-Blacks (25 percent). Black consumers also spend a greater percentage of their income on food eaten at home and less on health care and entertainment than non-Black consumers. Hispanics (separated from Blacks and non-Blacks) have similar spending patterns as blacks.[17]

Different kinds of measures show that residential segregation remains high in the United States, and Whites and minority group members are likely to have little daily contact. Evenness measures "compare the spatial distributions of different groups" and show that Whites, Blacks, Hispanics, and Asians are unevenly distributed through city neighborhoods. This unevenness cuts across geographic regions and is found in large and small metropolitan areas. Concentration measures show that Blacks, Asians, and Hispanics, in declining order, live in more densely populated geographic areas than Whites. Centralization measures show that Blacks tend to live closer to the center of cities than other racial groups. Clustering measures show that Blacks, Hispanics, and Asians tend to live closer to members of their own race than to others.[18]

---

[13]Jennifer Cheesman Day and Kurt J. Bauman, "Have We Reached the Top? Educational Attainment Projections of the U.S. Population," Working paper 43, Population Division, U.S. Bureau of the Census, May 2000.

[14]"Overview of Report on the American Workforce 2001" (Washington, D.C.: Bureau of Labor Statistics, U.S. Department of Labor).

[15]Ibid.

[16]Ibid.

[17]Ibid.

[18]Roderick J. Harrison and Daniel H. Weinberg, "Residential Segregation Definitions, Excerpted from Racial and Ethnic Segregation: 1990" (Washington, D.C.: U.S. Bureau of the Census), www.census.gov/hhes/ www.housing/resseg/def, revised February 3, 1999. "Residential Segregation Summary Tables" Washington, D.C.: U.S. Bureau of the Census), www.census.gov/ hhes/www/housing/resseg/sumtabs, revised February 3, 1999.

Are White children who have little or no contact with Black, Hispanic, or Asian children prepared to deal with them as equals in adulthood?

Perspectives on the Problem

Sociologists using a *conflict perspective* would explore how those with power use race and ethnicity—ideas—as tools to help retain their position. They would study how Whites benefit and Blacks, Hispanics, Asians, and others are damaged by the majority belief that race is a natural trait. A sociologist using a *functionalist perspective* on race would look at whether the institutions of society meet the needs of all racial groups and support their integration into the social fabric. A sociologist using a *symbolic interactionist perspective* would examine how Whites and non-Whites enact their identities on a daily basis. She or he would explore how mundane activities recreate inequalities that already exist. A sociologist using a *social constructionist perspective* would examine the historical specificity of our ideas about race and how these ideas reflect shifting racial and economic dynamics in our society.

Connecting the Perspectives

Taking a historical view, Nathan Glazer provides a social constructionist analysis of how the U.S. census has played a significant role in reifying racial categories and racial divisions. Turning to the present, Jieli Li examines how the media have constructed an Asian "model minority" and how this relatively recent racial stereotype obscures real differences among ethnic groups and very real social problems. Christopher Jencks and Meredith Phillips take up the concerns of the conflict perspective in examining how access to institutions of higher education, and upward mobility generally, is tied to widely used tests that are not free of bias.

Bringing feminism to bear on the conflict perspective, Kathleen Blee documents how the maintenance of traditional gender roles within racist organizations, such as the Ku Klux Klan, supports the organization's success in recruiting and retaining members. Finally, adopting a symbolic interactionist perspective, Barbara Perry shows how non-Whites use violence to "do race" and maintain social boundaries, group privileges, and racial hierarchies.

Reading Summaries

Nathan Glazer writes about the role of government data collection—in the form of the U.S. census—in creating and preserving racial divisions. He examines documenting practices from 1787 to the present and is concerned with changes in the way the census catalogs race and the range of classifications used. He observes that the 2000 census cataloged race in more detail than education, income, housing status, and so forth. Glazer argues that although initial categorization by race was undoubtedly motivated by White othering, it now reflects other forces. Recording information about race in detail is in large part a product of the requirements of litigation under civil rights and voting rights acts. Detailed racial statistics are the only means through which discrimination can be proven in court. In addition, the current attention to detail reflects the increased power of non-White ethnic groups who are interested in using census data to secure greater access to resources. For example, the official census minority of "Hispanic" reflects the political pressure exerted by Mexican Americans in the 1970s to create a census category to replace "Spanish Surname" that would encompass Mexicans, Puerto Ricans, and Cubans. Glazer urges us not to reify the census and to avoid using only official census categories, which are the basis of most analyses of residential segregation, as our only barometer of change. Instead, he asks that we consider other social indicators that were once, but no longer are, parts of the census. In particular, he asks us to assess racial integration and assimilation on the basis of rates of intermarriage.

Is there a successful minority group in the United States after which all immigrant and minority groups should pattern themselves? In "Exploring Asian Americans," Jieli Li seeks to determine if there is empirical evidence to support the assertion that Asian Americans are such a "model minority." He systematically explores the assumptions that underlie five myths about Asian Americans and reviews the available published research. Li concludes that there is very little support for the myths that Asian Americans, as a group, are faring well, that they have reached the level of education and earnings obtained by whites, that they are successful entrepreneurs who hold managerial positions, that they are academic whiz kids, or that they don't have any problems. He argues that continued propagation of these myths in the media and continued public acceptance of them allows serious social problems of unemployment, exploitation, poverty, illiteracy, and racial discrimination to fester.

Christopher Jencks and Meredith Phillips explore the consistent gap between Whites' and Blacks' scores on vocabulary, reading, and mathematics tests and tests that theoretically measure scholastic aptitude and intelligence. Pointing to the importance of these kinds of tests in determining access to higher education, employment, and ultimately earnings, the authors argue that we should seek to identify the causes of the gap and act to reduce it. They point out that focusing on improving the quality of applicants for college and employment po-

sitions will allow politically unpopular racial preference programs to be phased out.

Jencks and Phillips dispute claims that the test score gap is a result of a deficient Black culture or simply an expression of income inequality between Blacks and Whites, something that educators cannot easily influence. They suggest that there may be value in two newer theories to which educators could respond. The first proposes that membership in a castelike minority leads to an oppositional culture that downgrades majority emblems of success (like education). Thus, Black children fear acting in ways that are identified as White, for example, pursuing success in school, because their peers may view them as attempting to separate from their cultural group. The second theory, drawn from the work of Claude Steele, proposes that in order to avoid discomfort, we seek to avoid situations in which we will be stereotyped. Schools present a high stereotype threat for many Black children; thus they do not invest in an academic identity or in behaviors oriented to academic success.

In the second section of the reading, Jencks and Phillips review five possible biases in cognitive tests and discuss why only two—labeling bias and selection system bias—are of serious concern. They also assess whether there is evidence to support the view that the test score gap is more hereditary than environmental. To do this, they review the few studies that have compared the success of adopted Black children raised in White and Black homes in the United States and studies of racially mixed children raised in Germany. They conclude that there is little evidence that innate ability plays a large role in the gap. This reading concludes with an assessment of what schools can do to reduce the gap, more detailed discussions of how much fear of acting white and stereotype threat might contribute to the gap, and how we can explain more of the gap.

In "The Place of Women Inside Organized Racism" Kathleen Blee details what she has learned through face-to-face interviews with thirty-four women who were members of the Ku Klux Klan, or neo-Nazi, White power skinhead, or Christian Identity groups. She explains how their participation in familial, social, and operative roles is vital to the long-term existence of these hate organizations. In their familial roles, racist women bear the next generation of potential members and ensure they are socialized into the subculture. They teach children racist beliefs, ensure a consistency of message through selective play-dates and home schooling, and provide children with opportunities to play adult roles at rallies. In addition, racist women sustain fictive-kin relations with other group families and support the movement through their consumption choices. In their social roles, racist women ensure that racist events have positive entertainment value for all participants. They also recruit new members and mentor new women recruits, teaching them skills essential for self-sufficiency: sewing, cooking, and first aid. As informal leaders, racist women nurture and sustain the commitment of others to the group, providing the foundation that is necessary for an intergenerational racist movement. They also distribute political literature and participate in paramilitary activities.

Barbara Perry offers a preliminary analysis of minority-on-minority hate crime in "Beyond Black and White" to contribute to the development of a truly multicultural analysis of U.S. race relations. Using a symbolic interactionist perspective, she examines how hate crime can be understood as a means for members of a group to sustain cohesion, demarcate group boundaries, main-tain status hierarchies, and assert group dominance within them. Perry argues that many minority group members feel they are competing with each other for the favors of the White majority. Rather than identify themselves as commonly oppressed by the majority group, they seek to assign blame for their relatively unequal positions. Minority-on-minority hate crime occurs when minority group members accept hegemonic ideologies of White racial superiority and seek to "disempower the competition" through violence.

Perry provides two case studies to support her argument. She describes how blacks' acceptance of common stereotypes of Koreans and other Asian Americans as immigrants and outsiders leads them to see individuals who open businesses in Black communities as jumping to the head of the line. Viewing only their relationship as consumers versus Asian entrepreneurs in their communities and not the Asian entrepreneurs' relationship to Whites, Blacks do not recognize that these Asian businesspeople are oppressed; they have been shut out of White markets. Asian entrepreneurs' efforts to assimilate and advance independent of their Black neighbors, a result of their own internalized biases against Blacks, ratifies Blacks' perceptions. Hate crime is one means Blacks use to fight the perceived injustice of being exploited by an unworthy oppressor. Violence directed at "successful" Asian entrepreneurs is a means for Blacks to assert the preferred place of the native-born population, to take Asians down a notch, and to punish them for their apparent assimilation. Perry explains the basis for Black animosity and violence toward the Jewish population in a parallel manner. She concludes that hate crimes directed from one minority to another ultimately serve the interests of the White majority.

FOCUSING QUESTIONS

Glazer, Li, Jencks and Phillips, Blee, and Perry approach the problem of explaining contemporary racial inequality and conflict from different directions. To focus your reading of these selections, keep the following questions in mind: What evidence do you have from your own experience that race is a social construct? How is racial inequality a structural problem? How do institutions and the acts of individuals contribute to the persistence of racial inequality? How are gender and class inequalities related to those of race? What do the arguments made by the authors mean for you as a person of a particular race?

16

AMERICAN DIVERSITY AND THE 2000 CENSUS

NATHAN GLAZER

The 2000 census, on which the Census Bureau started issuing reports in March and April of 2001, reflected, in its structure and its results, the two enduring themes of American racial and ethnic diversity, present since the origins of American society in the English colonies of the Atlantic coast: first, the continued presence of what appears to be an almost permanent lower caste composed of the black race; and second, the ongoing process of immigration of races and peoples from all quarters of the globe, who seem, within a few generations, to merge into a common American people.

To make two such large generalizations is admittedly a bold move. Undoubtedly, as further data from the census is released, we will have evidence of the continuing progress of American blacks in education, occupational diversity, and income. We will have grounds for arguing that the effects of integration into a common people can be seen, at long last, among American blacks. And when it comes to the new waves of immigration of the past few decades, some will question whether the process of assimilation and incorporation, which has swallowed up so many groups and races and religions into a common American people, will continue to work its effects on the new groups now gathered together under the terms "Hispanic" and "Asian." Yet I believe it can be argued that this large distinction in the processes of assimilation and integration that has persisted during the three- or four-century history of American diversity—the distinction between blacks and others—still shows itself, and still poses some of the most difficult questions for American society.

From *Public Interest,* Summer 2000: 3–18. Reprinted by permission of Nathan Glazer.

The First Census

The distinction makes itself evident in the very history and structure of the census, and in the character of the data that it first presents to the public today. In the first census of 1790, required for purposes of apportionment by the U.S. Constitution adopted in 1787, the separation between blacks and whites was already made. Indeed, that separation was itself foreshadowed by the Constitution, which, in a famous compromise, decreed that "Representatives . . . shall be apportioned among the several states . . . according to their respective numbers, which shall be determined by adding to the whole number of free persons . . . three-fifths of all other persons." Those "other persons" were slaves. The "three-fifths" was a compromise between excluding all slaves for purposes of apportionment (which would have reduced the weight of the Southern slave states in the union) or counting them simply as persons (which would have given the slave states too great weight).

The census could have fulfilled the requirements of the Constitution by counting only slaves. But what was to be done with free blacks? There were, even then, free blacks, but their civil status was sharply below that of whites. It was apparently decided that they could not be simply numbered among the "free persons" referred to in the Constitution but had to be clearly distinguished from whites. So the first census went beyond the Constitution: It counted "free white males and females" as one category, "slaves" as another, but then added a category of "all other free persons." The count of "other persons"—slaves—and "all other free persons"—free blacks—produced the total number of blacks. Thus from the beginning, white could be differentiated from black. That has remained the most enduring distinction in the U.S. census.

In that first census, following the apportionment provision of the Constitution, "Indians not taxed" were also excluded. Over time, this simple scheme has been extended to cover other races and ethnic groups as they entered the new nation through immigration, to a degree which is possibly unique among national censuses, and which we will explore below. But the census begins crucially with the distinction between white and black. As Clara Rodriguez writes in her book *Changing Race:*

> Between the drafting of the Constitution of 1787 and the taking of the first census in 1790, the term *white* became an explicit part of [the free population]. . . . Theoretically, those in political charge could have chosen another definition for the [free population]. . . . They could have chosen "free English-speaking males over sixteen" or "free males of Christian descent" or "of European descent." But they chose color. Having named the central category "white" gave a centrality and power to color that has continued throughout the history of the census.

But of course this reflected the centrality of the black-white distinction in American society and the American mind. Rodriguez goes on to note that on occasion in the pre–Civil War censuses "aliens and foreigners not naturalized," separately numbered, are combined in one table with native whites and citizens in a table of "total white." "In the 1850 census, the category 'free whites' is changed to simply 'whites,' which suggests by this time it was evident that all the people in this category were free."

The Color Line

Color—race—has since been elaborated to a remarkable degree in the U.S. census. The most striking aspect of the American census of 2000—as of the few before—is that the short form, which goes to all American households, consists mostly of questions on race and "Hispanicity." Two large questions ask for the respondent's race, and whether the respondent is of "Spanish/Hispanic" origin, and both go into considerable detail in trying to determine just what race, and just what kind of "Hispanic," the respondent is. The race question lists many possibilities to choose from, including, to begin with, "white" and "black," and going on to "Indian (Amer.)," with an additional request to list the name of the tribe, "Eskimo," or "Aleut." And then under the general heading "Asian or Pacific Islander (API)," it lists as separate choices Chinese, Filipino, Hawaiian, Korean, Vietnamese, Japanese, Asian Indian, Samoan, Guamanian, "Other API," and finally "Other race (print name)." In the 2000 census, it was possible for the first time for the respondent to check more than one race. This change was made after an extended discussion in the 1990s about how to account for those with parents of different race, who wanted to check off both, or perhaps more than two.

The question on whether one is Spanish/Hispanic also goes on to list a range of possibilities: "Mexican, Mexican-Am. [for "American"], or Chicano" (to account for the fact that Mexican Americans choose different terms to describe themselves), "Puerto Rican," "Cuban," and "other Spanish/Hispanic," with again the request to write in one group. In the 1990 census, a host of examples—"Argentinean, Colombian, Dominican, Nicaraguan, Salvadoran, Spaniard, and so on," was offered.

The observant and conscientious citizen may note that many other matters of interest to the census and the polity—whether one is of foreign birth or not, a citizen or not, and one's education, occupation, income, housing status, etc.—are all relegated to the long form, which goes to a large sample of citizens. And he may also ask why the census pays such great and meticulous attention to race and ethnicity (or rather one kind of ethnicity, that of Spanish-Hispanic background).

Many answers, going back to the first census of 1790, and before that, to the Constitution that prescribed a regular decennial census, and before that, to the first arrival of black slaves in the English colonies in the early seventeenth century, are available to explain why the first statistics the census makes available today, along with the raw number of the population in each state and locality, are those describing race and ethnicity. But there is also an immediate and proximate answer of much more recent currency: Congress requires that ethnic and racial statistics be available within a year of the census for the purpose of redrawing the boundaries of congressional districts, and the other electoral districts for state legislative assemblies, and for city and county elected officials.

Ethnic and racial statistics have become so significant for redistricting because of the Civil Rights Act of 1964, the Voting Rights Acts of 1965, and the latter's amendments of 1970, 1975, and 1982. Admittedly, these acts, which simply proscribe discrimination on the basis of race and national background, did not necessarily require such detailed statistics to check on the presence of discrimination in various spheres of life and, in particular, in the free exercise and effect of the vote. But the course of the law has been to use statistical tests to determine whether there is discrimination. The right enshrined in the Voting Rights statute, to the free exercise of the vote, has been extended through litigation and administrative and judicial rule-making to cover rights to the drawing of congressional and other district boundaries in such a way as to protect or enhance the ability of minority groups, blacks in particular, but others too, to elect representatives of their own group. If blacks are to be protected from discrimination, interpreted as the creation of voting districts that enhance the power of blacks to choose a black representative, if they are so inclined, then detailed statistics of how a race is distributed are necessary.

That is why the first statistics that come out of the census are those that make it possible to redraw district lines immediately on the basis of the new census, and for various groups to challenge the new district lines if they are aggrieved. "Growing minority groups will likely face lawsuits over redistricting," reads one news headline in the *Wall Street Journal,* with the subtitle, "One California assemblyman says his caucus 'will sue' regardless of the rationale for redrawing districts." The story tells us:

> Here in Orange County [California], . . . a dozen Latino officials last week huddled in a spartan conference room over a map of Southern California as Art Montez, felt-tipped marker in hand, lopped the city of Westminster off the state's 68th Assembly District. Westminster's large population of conservative whites makes it "impossible for a minority candidate to win there," Mr. Montez, a political activist and school board member, explained to the group.

But this is only the beginning of a struggle that will move through the state legislature and almost inevitably to the Department of Justice and the federal courts, where the racial and ethnic statistics and the role they have played in drawing up new districts will be carefully examined and disputed. For those with the responsibility of drawing up the new districts—the state legislatures primarily—the central concern is generally the maximization of the number of representatives of the party in power in the state legislature. A second concern is to maintain for the incumbents of the favored

party district boundaries that secure their return. But overlaying these historic political reasons for drawing district lines, which courts accept in some measure as legitimate, is a new imperative, the protection of minority groups.

The Four "Official" Minorities

"Portrait of a Nation" is the title of a major story on the first results of the census in the *New York Times,* and it is accompanied by elaborate colored maps. The colors provide information on the distribution of the minority population—blacks, Hispanics, Asians, American Indians.

To explain how these have become *the* American minorities—to the exclusion of many other possible minorities—and why their numbers and distribution are in every newspaper report considered the most important information to look for in the census, would require a précis of American history. It is hardly necessary to explain why blacks are the first of the minority groups. They have been a significant presence in the United States and its predecessor colonies from the beginning. Our greatest national trauma—the Civil War—was directly occasioned by the problem of black slavery, and the most significant amendments to the Constitution became part of that quasi-sacred document in order to deal with the consequences of black slavery.

American Indians were there even before the beginning but were considered outside the society and polity unless they individually entered into non–Indian-American society, as many have, through intermarriage and assimilation. Their status has changed over time, from outside the polity as semi-sovereign foreign nations, to subjects almost without rights, to a population confined on reservations, to one that now increasingly becomes part of the society. Indeed, today, to be able to claim an American-Indian heritage is a plus for one's social status. This is too complex a history to be reviewed here. There is good reason to maintain a separate count of Indians, though there are great complexities in doing so.

"Hispanics," too, were there from before the beginning, if we take into account the Spaniards and Creoles moving up from Mexico who had already established colonial settlements in northern Mexico—what is now the Southwest of the United States—before the first English colonists had established permanent settlements on the Atlantic coast. Of course, they were not "Hispanics" then. Two hundred and fifty years later, this mixed population became part of the United States as a result of the annexation of the northern part of Mexico after the Mexican-American war. But it contained then a small population of Mexicans and Indians, and interestingly enough, despite the sense of racial difference felt by the Anglo-Americans, and despite the prejudice against Mexicans, they were not differentiated in the census as a separate group until 1930. Until then, one presumes, they were "white." In that year, Clara Rodriguez notes, a census publication, responding to the increase in immigration from Mexico as a result of the revolutionary wars and troubles of the 1920s, reported that "persons of Mexican birth or parentage who were not definitely reported as white or Indian were designated Mexican" and included in "other races." In 1940, this policy was changed, and Mexicans became white again. By 1950, added to the growing number of Mexicans in the Southwest, as a result of immigration in the previous decades, was a large number of Puerto Ricans in New York City, migrants from the island of Puerto Rico, which had been annexed after the Spanish-American War of 1898. In that census year, the two were combined in the census—along with smaller numbers of other groups—into a "Spanish-surnamed" group.

In the wake of Castro's victory in Cuba, a third large group of Latin Americans emigrated to the United States. Whether or not one could make a single meaningful category out of Mexicans, Puerto Ricans, and Cubans, separated as they are by culture, history, and to some extent by racial characteristics, they were so combined, with a host of other Spanish-speaking groups, into a "Hispanic" category in the census of 1970. The creation of the category was a response to political pressure from Mexican Americans. It now includes large numbers of Nicaraguans, Guatemalans, Salvadorans, Dominicans, Colombians, Ecuadorians, and others fleeing the political and economic troubles of their homelands.

Racial and ethnic groups are conventionally described today as "constructed," but it is worth noting that this "construction" is not simply the result of white determinations—it is also the result of group insistence, at least to some degree. As Peter Skerry tells us in his book *Counting on the Census:*

> The finalized questionnaires for the 1970 census were already at the printers when a Mexican American member of the U.S. Interagency Committee on Mexican American affairs demanded that a specific Hispanic-origin question be included. . . . Over the opposition of Census Bureau officials, who argued against inclusion of an untested question so late in the process, [President] Nixon ordered the secretary of commerce and the census director to add the question.

And so "Hispanics" were born. The pressure to maintain the category, with all its subdistinctions, persists. The distinguished demographer Stanley Lieberson has written about a well-intentioned intervention at a conference preparatory to the 1990 census:

I naively suggested that there was no reason to have an Hispanic question separate from the ethnic ancestry question [an ancestry question has been part of the long form since 1980] since the former . . . could be classified as a subpart of the latter. Several participants from prominent Hispanic organizations were furious at such a proposal. They were furious, by the way, not at me (just a naive academic), rather it was in the form of a warning to census personnel of the consequences that would follow were this proposal to be taken seriously.

The last of the four minorities distinguished in the census is the "Asian," a creation—or construction—that has as complex a history as that of the Hispanic. Chinese and Japanese individuals were undoubtedly present in the United States before they were first listed as "races" in 1870—by then there was a substantial population of Chinese in California, and they were already the subject of racist legislation. In 1930, "Filipino," "Hindu" [sic], and "Korean" were added as separate races, and it became the pattern to add a new "race" for each Asian immigrant group as it became numerous. Eventually, we have the complex category of "Asian and Pacific Islander" (API), with all its listed subgroups.

As in the case of the Mexicans, the initial discrimination that made each of these a separate group was undoubtedly racist and reflected a sense of white superiority. The Asian groups were all subjected to discriminatory legislation. One could be naturalized as a citizen only if one were "white" (or, after the Civil War, black). All sorts of restrictions, from land ownership to the pursuit of certain professions or occupations, were imposed on them by various states because they were noncitizens. But Asian immigrants were denied because of race the right of becoming citizens. These groups

were indeed nonwhite, but their separate classification was more than a matter of keeping neat statistics. An identity was being selected for a group felt to be inferior. This identity may well have been the one the members of the group would have chosen, but it was not they who decided they should be numbered aside from the dominant whites.

In more recent decades, the power to name and describe has shifted: The groups themselves, or those who speak for them, now shape how they are to be described, named, differentiated, and counted. And the political and administrative process bends to their desires. Why do we distinguish so many subgroups among the "Asian and Pacific Islanders"? There is a separate story for each category. But note one account by Peter Skerry from the political history of the census: The Census Bureau tried to simplify and shorten the Asian and Pacific Islander question for the 1990 census. Congressman Robert Matsui introduced legislation "in which the formatting of the API race question was spelled out, even to the point of stipulating that 'Taiwanese' be one of the subgroups. . . . It was only President Reagan's pocket veto that blocked this extraordinary degree of Congressional involvement in what is ordinarily considered the technical side of questionnaire design."

A Melting Pot?

These then are the four "official" minorities, though no law names these and only these as minorities. But what has happened then to all those others once considered "minorities," ethnic groups that were in the first quarter of the twentieth century in the eye of public attention because of the recency of their immigration, their lower social and economic status, and the concern that they could not be assimilated? Immigration was largely cut off by law in the 1920s because of these concerns. The United States has been a country of immigration since its origins, and by some measures the immigration of the first two decades of the twentieth century was much greater than the immigration of the last three decades, which has swelled the numbers of the new minorities. Had one picked up a book on American minorities and race relations in the 1950s, Jews might have been presented as the typical minority: Much of the social theory and social psychology on minority status was formulated with the position of Jews in mind. Jews were a major element in the mass immigration that preceded the present one, from the 1880s to the 1920s. Other major components of this immigration were Italians, Poles, Hungarians, Czechs, Slovaks, Slovenes, Croats, Serbs, Greeks, Armenians, Lebanese, Syrians, and many other peoples of Eastern and Southern Europe and the Near East. Are they no longer included in the story of American minorities?

One can go further back and ask, what has happened to the Irish, the Germans, the Swedes, Norwegians, and Danes, and the host of immigrants who came earlier and were also once sharply distinguished as separate groups, different from the founding group, the English? Does not the story of American diversity include all these too? How has the palette become restricted to the four minorities that play so large a role in the current census?

The simple answer is that integration and assimilation reduce over time the differences that distinguish one group from another, or from the original settler group, what Tocqueville called the "Anglo-Americans." We have no good term for this group. WASP ("White Anglo-Saxon Protestant") has been used in recent decades, ironically or derisively, for the founding element and their descendants. But aside from the necessity to distinguish such a group histor-

ically, no term is currently really necessary: Immigrants merge in two or three generations into a common American people, and ethnic distinctions become less and less meaningful. Ethnicity becomes symbolic, a matter of choice, to be noted on the basis of name or some other signifier on occasion, of little matter for most of one's life.

At one time, the census distinguished the foreign-born by place of birth, and the foreign-born parents of the native-born by place of birth, permitting us to track ethnic groups (somewhat uncertainly, owing to the lack of fit between ethnicity and national boundaries) for two generations. The rest of the population was classed as natives of native parentage, not further distinguishable, at least in the census, on the basis of their ethnicity. In 1980, the question on birthplace of parents was dropped, to the distress of sociologists and students of ethnicity. A new question on "ancestry" was added, which, in theory, would permit us to connect people to ethnic groups in the third generation and beyond. But the amount of mixture among groups, through marriage, is today such that the answers to the ancestry question, if one is not an immigrant or the child of an immigrant with a clear sense of ancestry, are not helpful in distinguishing an ethnic group much beyond the second generation. The answers then become so variable, so dependent on cues from the census itself—such as the examples the census form gives to the respondent regarding what is intended by the term "ancestry," which is by no means clear to many people—as to be hardly meaningful. It is a question that permits some 40 million Americans, seven times the population of Ireland, to declare that they are of "Irish" ancestry.

There are indeed differences of some significance based on ethnicity among the native white population, and sometimes these become evident—when home countries are involved in conflict, for example—

or even paramount. This is particularly evident for Jews, who are marked not only as a religion . . . but also by ethnicity. . . . The exceptional history that resulted in the killing of most of the Jews of Europe, and the creation of a regularly imperiled state of Israel, ties Jews to their past and to their co-religionists abroad much more than other ethnic groups. They are not to be found in any census count—they are not a "race" and not even, for the census, an "ancestry," even though that answer would make sense for most Jews.

Sociologists and political scientists can plumb for differences among the native white population, and they will find not insignificant differences in income, occupation, political orientation, and so on. Jews, for example, are exceptional among "whites" for their regular overwhelming support for Democrats. Indeed, the differences among native whites, ethnically distinguished, may be greater than those among the official minority groups or between any of them and the native white population. Yet from the point of view of public opinion and official notice, these differences are not significant. The ethnic groups of the great immigrations of the nineteenth and early twentieth century have sunk below the horizon of official attention. They have merged into the "white" population, become integrated and assimilated, and only emerge as a special interest on occasion, stimulated by a conflict or crisis involving the home country.

"Whiteness Theory"

Recently, this somewhat benign view of American history, one in which immigrant groups steadily assimilate to, and become part of, the common American people, has been challenged by historians who argue that this was a strictly limited process, available only to whites, and, further, that many of those who were eventually included as full Americans had to overcome a presumption that they were not "really" white. In other words, race is crucial, both at its beginning and, by implication, throughout American history, for full inclusion. To take one powerful and clear statement of this position:

> The saga of European immigration has long been held up as proof of the openness of American society, the benign and absorptive powers of American capitalism, and the robust health of American democracy. "Ethnic inclusion," "ethnic mobility," and "ethnic assimilation" on the European model set the standard upon which "America," as an ideal, is presumed to *work;* they provide the normative experience against which others are measured. But this pretty story suddenly fades once one recognizes how crucial Europeans' racial status as "free white persons" was to their gaining entrance in the first place; how profoundly dependent their racial inclusion was upon the racial exclusion of others; how racially accented the native resistance was even to *their* inclusion for something over half a century. [Matthew Frye Jacobsen, in *Whiteness of a Different Color*]

The implication of this point of view is that the present minorities as commonly understood exist not only because of the recency of their immigration but primarily because of color: They are not white. Their ability to become full and equal participants in American society is thereby limited because of America's racist character.

But I believe these "whiteness theorists" are wrong. The racist character of the past is clear, and a degree of racism in the present is also evident, despite radical changes in public opinion and major changes in law and legal enforcement. But there has been a striking and irreversible change between the

1920s—when immigration from Eastern and Southern Europe was sharply reduced and immigration from Asia was banned entirely—and the postwar decades and, in particular, the period since the 1960s. Public institutions and significant private institutions today may only take account of race for the purpose of benefiting minorities.

The whiteness theorists may have a story to tell about the past, but it is one that has limited bearing on the present. The new immigrant groups are for the most part distinguished by race or quasi-racial characteristics from the population of European white origin. Yet it seems likely they progress pretty much at the same rate, affected by the same factors—their education and skills, their occupations, the areas of the country in which they settle, and the like—as the European immigrants of the past.

They merge into the common population at the same rate too. We will soon have analyses of marriages between persons of different race and ethnicity, to the extent the census makes possible, but we already know that the number and percentage of intermarriages between persons from the minorities and the majority has grown greatly in recent decades. One analysis of the 1990 census, reported by David T. Canon in his *Race, Redistricting and Representation,* shows that "for married people between the ages of twenty-five and thirty-four, 70 percent of Asian women and 39 percent of Hispanic women have white [sic] husbands." But only 2 percent of black women in the same age group were married to white men. The theme of black difference contrasted with the intermixture and merger of other groups is clearly sounded in these and other statistics.

The End of "Race"?

The first studies conducted by independent analysts of the 2000 census statistics brought up sharply the degree to which blacks are still distinguished from other minorities or subgroups in the United States by residential segregation. "Analysis of Census Finds Segregation Along with Diversity," reads one headline. "Segregation" in this analysis is measured by the diversity of census tracts, as experienced by the "average" person of a given group or race. The average white person lives in a tract that is 80 percent white, down from 85 percent in 1990; the average black person lives in a tract that is 51 percent black, down from 56 percent in 1990; the average Hispanic is less "segregated" by this measure—his tract is 45 percent Hispanic, and increased from 43 percent in 1990. But one may explain this degree of segregation and its rise since 1990 by the huge increase, based on immigration, much of it illegal, of the Hispanic population. The average Asian lives in a tract that is not particularly Asian—18 percent, as against 15 percent in 1990. This rise reflects to some degree the 50 percent increase of the Asian population, mostly through immigration, in the decade.

Local reporting focused on the relative proportions of the minority groups in each community, and also on the degree of segregation. Integration proceeds, but slowly. There are black census tracts in Boston with almost no whites and white tracts with almost no blacks. We calculate these figures every census, as if watching a fever report. The overall picture is that the segregation of blacks is great, the segregation of Hispanic groups, despite the recency of their immigration and their foreign tongue, is rather less, and little segregation is noted among Asians.

The big news of the census was that "Hispanics" had for the first time surpassed blacks in number, but that was only the case if one excluded from the black population those individuals who had chosen the race "black" along with another race. Hispanics rose to 35.3 million, a 61 percent increase in

10 years; blacks rose by about 16 percent to 34.7 million, or 36.4 million if one added those who chose more than one race. Blacks are 12.3 percent of the population, about the same percentage they have maintained for the past century. The increase in Hispanics was much greater than expected: It was generally agreed that one reason for this increase was a larger number of illegal immigrants than had been previously calculated, 9 million according to one demographer instead of 7, perhaps as much as 11 million according to another demographer.

Making the comparison between the two largest minorities was complicated by the fact that respondents could choose more than one race for the first time, and 7 million did so. Analysis of these mixed-race choices, even reporting on them, is not easy. A reporter writes: "Five percent of blacks, 6 percent of Hispanics, 14 percent of Asians and 2.5 percent of whites identified themselves as multi-racial." But why are these multi-race choosers labeled "black" or "Asian"? Is the "one drop" rule once used by the southern states operating here? If someone chooses "American Indian" and another race, do we include that person in the count of American Indians? If we do, that would increase the number of American Indians by more than 50 percent. The Office of Management and Budget oversees the race and ethnic statistics compiled by federal agencies, and it has determined that for their purposes (affirmative-action monitoring and the like) all multi-race choosers who chose white and a minority race are to be counted as being part of the minority, a decision that has pleased minority advocates. But does it reflect how these individuals see themselves?

The mixed-race choices complicate the issue of choosing a base on which to measure the progress of, or possible discrimination against, minorities, an important step in affirmative action programs. That is the reason some minority leaders opposed allowing the mixed-race option. If the base becomes smaller, the degree of discrimination that one may claim in noting how many members of the group have attained this or that position is reduced.

Now that the option exists, it is clear many are eager to choose two or even more races. Among blacks there seems to be less willingness to choose two races than among Asians and American Indians—perhaps because it may be seen as something like race betrayal. But it is noteworthy that younger persons more often choose two races than older ones. If one creates a combined black group by putting together blacks with those who choose black as one of the races they tick off, 2.3 percent of this combined group 50 years of age or older turn out to be multi-race choosers, but 8.1 percent of those 17 and younger choose more than one race. But those who choose the option of black-white are still quite few—fewer in number than those who choose white-other ("other" in the racial category means Hispanic), or white-Asian, or white-American Indian.

When the statistics of intermarriage are analyzed, one can be sure there will be a considerable rise in white-black marriages since 1990, even if the percentage of such intermarriages is considerably less than white-Asian or Hispanic–non-Hispanic marriages. Blacks are still more segregated, more separated, in residence than other minority groups. They are more sharply defined in their consciousness as separate: History has made them so. But even among blacks, one sees the process of assimilation and integration, as measured by choice of race and by intermarriage, at work. By the census of 2010 or 2020, these processes will be further advanced. Indeed, one may perhaps look forward to a time when our complex system of racial and ethnic counting is made so confusing by the number of possible choices, singular and multiple, that the whole scheme is abandoned. Many Americans hope so.

17

EXPLORING ASIAN AMERICANS
The Myth of the "Model Minority" and the Reality of Their Lives

JIELI LI

There is a myth revolving around Asian Americans in the United States. Many Americans are led to believe that Asian Americans fare well as higher achievers in education and social status. The myth of the "model minority" first surfaced in the mid-1960s when William Petersen published his article "Success Story, Japanese American Style" in *New York Times Magazine* on January 9, 1966. By the early 1980s, the myth became more entrenched in American society as *Newsweek* (6 December 1982) had a cover story to applaud Asian Americans as a "Model Minority" that have achieved success despite their suffering from prejudice

and discrimination. The author wrote, "Asian Americans now enjoy the nation's highest median family income: $22,075 a year compared with $20,840 for whites, and . . . the industrious Asians believe they are contributing a needed shot of some vanishing American values: thrift, strong family ties, sacrifice for the children" (p. 39). *Time* (31 August 1987) continued to praise Asian American businessmen as successful entrepreneurs, and Asian American youths as academic "whiz kids," especially in math and sciences.

The image of model minority created by the media has generated a popular belief that Asian Americans are no longer the disadvantaged . . . and the discrimination and prejudice are things of the past. While Asian Americans' relative accomplishments should not be denied by any means, the myth associated with the "model minority" thesis is questionable in its validity. In short,

Li, Jieli. 1999. "Exploring Asian Americans: The Myth of the 'Model Minority' and the Reality of Their Lives." Pp. 134–41 in *Perspectives in Social Problems*, edited by Robert P. McNamara. St. Paul, MN: Coursewise. Copyright © 1999 Jieli Li, Ohio University. Reprinted by permission.

it is misleading in many ways and does not reflect the reality of Asian American lives.

Myth 1: "Asian Americans as an Ethnic Group Are Generally Faring Well."

It has been a long tradition in American society that the people of Asian descent are referred to as "Asian Americans." As such, they tend to be labeled indiscriminately as "all faring well." Lowe (1991) and Trueba et al. (1993) argue that it is misleading to lump together Asians as a single homogeneous ethnic group, for Asian immigrants came from different parts of Asia such as Mainland China, Japan, Taiwan, Hong Kong, Singapore, the Philippines, Korea, Thailand, Vietnam, Laos, Indonesia, Malaysia, and so on. These groups are a collection of diverse people with distinct linguistic, cultural, and social backgrounds. For example, Asian Indians come from different cultural traditions than Chinese, Japanese, and Koreans. Southeastern Asian cultures can also be distinguished in many ways from those of East Asia. In addition, the Asian population in the United States varies substantially in terms of region of residence, educational levels, occupational levels, generations in the United States, recency of immigration, and proficiency of English.

The 1993 U.S. Bureau of the Census data indicate that there is a wide variation in education attainment among American Asian groups with Asian Indians the highest and Southeast Asians among the lowest. Thus, Asian Americans vary accordingly in socioeconomic status, with some occupying high-paying jobs and some low-paying jobs. However, statistics on family earnings can be misleading if not differentiated between native-born and foreign-born Asians. Socioeconomic differences are found to exist between native-born Asians and foreign-born Asians. For example, there is a big earnings gap between Japanese Americans, almost three-quarters native born and Vietnamese, recently new arrivals (Hsia 1988, p. 180). Chinese Americans are similarly polarized into two groups, with the native-born more established and newcomers struggling at the bottom of society. Even for the new arrivals, the Asian immigrants range from well-educated professionals and business people to poorly educated and penniless refugees. Barringer et al. (1993) found that there is a huge difference in terms of human and economic resources between the Taiwanese and Hmong immigrants. The former are mostly well-educated professionals while the latter are refugees. Hence, the myth about the homogeneity of Asian Americans is a misperception that largely overlooks cultural and socioeconomic differences that exist among Asian American groups.

Myth 2: "Asian Americans Have Reached and Even Surpassed Educational and Earnings Parities with Whites."

What consistently favors the "model minority" thesis is the statistical data on higher educational attainment among Asian Americans—the percentage of educational level is higher for Asian Americans than those for whites and other minority groups. The 1994 U.S. Census indicates that the percentage of Asian Americans having graduated from college (42%) is well above that of whites (23%). Two factors may contribute to this high percentage. First, as compared to other Asian subgroups, native-born Japanese and Chinese Americans are more educated and professional, and the data that were used to support the model minority thesis were primarily collected from these two groups (Lyman 1974, p. 119). Second, there has been a constant influx of immigrants from Asia since 1965, generally viewed as a "brain drain." Most of the Asian immigrants, especially those from East Asian countries and Asian India, were either educated professionals in their home countries or students who came to the United States for advanced degrees and later decided to stay permanently. For example, between 1988 and 1990, Asians accounted for over half the number of professional immigrants admitted to the United States from all over the world (Kanjanapan 1995). This demographic movement reversed the pre-1965 pattern of older Asian immigrants, who generally had low educational attainment and low socioeconomic status.

However, statistics focusing only on educational level without taking into account economic returns to education [are] misleading. Although Asian Americans have higher educational attainments, the economic returns to their education are low. Asian professionals are overrepresented in technical careers such as engineering, and underrepresented in law, medicine, teaching, and administration. Even in the same industries, Asian immigrants received earnings far below those of whites (Chan 1991). When they have a comparable income, they usually earned it by acquiring more education and by working more hours. Asian professionals are mostly found in entry-level and mid-level technical-oriented positions. Li (1980) points out that native- and foreign-born Asian Americans have experienced, in one way or another an overqualification for occupations or an underemployment of their education. If all things are considered equal, many Asian Americans achieve less than their white counterparts.

Roos (1977) compares Japanese Americans with whites. Taking into consideration means of income, education, and income adjusted for age and school years completed, he concluded that Japanese Americans had not yet reached earnings parity with whites despite that Japanese Americans had higher average education than whites. Thus, his findings indicate that education did not close the gap between native-born Japanese Americans and white earnings.

Hirschman and Wong (1981) found that with educational level considered equal, Asian Americans, especially those foreign-born Asians, receive earnings far below those of whites. Even though native-born Japanese, Chinese, and Filipino males achieved average income equivalent to or higher than white males, parity of earnings is not commensurate with education and occupation between whites and Asians. As Espiritu (1997) observes, "in 1990, highly educated Asian American men who worked full time, full year, earned about 10% less than white men—even though the former were much more likely to have a graduate degree" (p. 67). Hurh and Kim (1989) employ a theoretical approach of equity to challenge the conventional type of measurement of the Asian American success. They suggest that the reward and the cost index should be added in an empirical analysis to compare Asian ethnic groups with whites and other minority groups in terms of cost or investment and reward or achievement. They select six factors in a regression analysis of individual earnings: (1) the age of workers; (2) educational attainment; (3) prestige score for the worker's occupation; (4) mean income of the worker's state; (5) number of weeks worked; and (6) number of hours worked. The comparison is made among ethnic groups between individual original and adjusted earnings (Table 1). Adjusted earnings refer to the earnings that would be received by a member of each group, if the person has the same level of education, occupational prestige, and number of hours worked. Their findings, as measured by uneven ratio,

TABLE 1 **Original and Adjusted Individual Earnings, and Earnings Ratio of Whites, Asians, and Non-Asian Minority Groups (1980)**

	Original Earnings (Dollars)	Adjusted Earnings (Dollars)	Ratio	Sample Size
Non-Asian Groups				
Whites	16,822	16,822	1	54,656
American Indians	10,449	13,255	.79	358
Mexicans	11,009	13,967	.83	2,321
Puerto Ricans	10,820	15,799	.94	421
Blacks	10,586	13,484	.80	5,716
Asian Groups (Native-born)				
Japanese	17,905	16,046	.95	8,668
Chinese	16,324	15,675	.93	3,385
Filipinos	12,566	15,401	.92	1,991
Koreans				
Asian Indians				
Vietnamese				
Asian Groups (Foreign-born)				
Japanese	19,939	17,857	1.06	2,515
Chinese	14,689	12,402	.74	9,306
Filipinos	14,988	15,056	.89	7,440
Koreans	15,985	14,017	.83	3,488
Asian Indians	20,112	14,283	.85	5,666
Vietnamese	9,309	11,423	.68	2,712

Source: Hurh and Kim (1989: 522–533)

indicate that while whites and Asians are equal in the cost of investment, Asians achieve less than whites; and although the level of achievement of some Asians may be equal to that of whites, the cost of achievement is higher for Asians than for whites. Their findings also indicate that the earnings ratio of foreign-born Asians (except Japanese whose high earning ratio is more related to Japan's export market than [the] U.S labor market [Nee and Sanders 1985]) [is] no better than that of non-Asian minorities, such as black and Mexican Americans.

Related to the issue is the myth associated with statistical data showing that the annual family income is higher for Asian Americans than for whites. Again, the data is misleading because it overlooks a number of significant variables. A careful examina-

tion of the existing data points in the other direction. The 1980 U.S. Census shows that although the mean annual family income of Asians is relatively higher than that of whites, mean annual individual earnings are relatively lower for Asians than for whites. . . . In their study, Gardner et al. (1985) point out that poverty rates of Southeast Asian refugee groups are higher than those of any other minority group in America. For example, the percentage of families living below poverty level is 35.1 for Vietnamese, compared to 26.5 for blacks. Rumbaut and Ima (1988) indicate that about 90 percent of Hmong families have incomes below the poverty level. The 1994 U.S. Census further reports that while there is a higher percentage of Asians who have an annual family income of $50,000 or more than that of whites, the percentage of Asian Americans living below the poverty level is also higher than whites.

There are reasons for what seems to be contradicting figures. (1) Higher median incomes for Asian families are largely due to a greater number of workers per family, which helps to increase the higher family income. The 1980 U.S. Census shows that 63 percent of Asian Americans families had two or more paid workers and 17 percent had three or more, as compared to 55 percent and 12 percent for whites. Chun (1980) suggests that a more accurate measurement index of group comparison for household income should include the number of hours worked and the number of wage earners per household, and that Asian Americans' high income may [be] attributed to "longer work hours or sacrificed weekends." (2) The size of the Asian family is traditionally larger than that of the white family. The average household size is 3.1 for Chinese, 2.7 for Japanese, 3.6 for Filipino, 3.4 for Korean, 2.9 for Asian Indians, and 4.4 for Vietnamese, as compared to 2.7 for whites (Gardner et al. 1985). (3) Most Asians are concentrated in metropolitan areas such as Los Angeles, San Francisco, New York, and Hawaii, where the cost of living is higher than the national average (Woodrum 1984; Takaki 1993).

Family income statistics can be misleading when applied to the foreign born and particularly for recent immigrants and refugees. There is a high percentage of Asian Americans, post–1965, who do not have higher educational attainments. The 1990 U.S. Census indicates that over 22 percent of Asian Americans twenty-five years and older have less than a high school degree, and about 90 percent of these people are immigrants. The 1993 U.S. Census also indicates that there is a high percentage of Asian Americans who have difficulty speaking English. Their upward mobility is severely restricted by these disadvantages.

The median income for those with limited English ranges from $15,000 to $20,000, and the median income for those with limited English and low level of education is usually less than $10,000 for a full-time job (Ong and Hee 1994). Southeast Asian refugees, particularly those who arrived after 1978, constitute a large portion of this disadvantaged Asian population. This Asian American group suffers the most, compared to other minority groups in the United States. They have the highest percentages of low educational levels (64%) and of English deficiency (55%), and the highest rates of unemployment (33% for males, 58% for females) and of welfare dependency (Ong and Umemoto 1994). Among them, about 10 percent of Vietnamese and 16 percent of Cambodians and Laotians are extremely poor with annual incomes of only $6,307, well below the poverty level (Ong 1993). Espiritu (1997) comments that "these statistics call attention to the danger of lumping all Asian groups together because Southeast Asians—and other disadvantaged groups—do not share in the relatively favorable socioeconomic outcomes attributed to the 'average' Asian American" (p. 72).

Myth 3: "Asian Americans Are Successful Entrepreneurs Who Have Occupied More Managerial Positions."

The myth relating to the success image of Asian American entrepreneurs holding more managerial positions is misleading. Most Asian American "managers" are self-employed instead of working in larger firms. The growing number of Asian American–owned businesses in the 1970s and 1980s, primarily used to uphold the myth, only indicates Asian immigrants' own solution to social barriers created by labor market discrimination. According to a survey conducted in 1988 by Fawcett and Gardner (1994), nearly half of the Korean male entrepreneurs were college educated, but most of them are unable to find a job consistent with their education and qualifications. The problems of labor underemployment have turned many Asians toward self-employment, with Koreans being concentrated in the businesses of grocery, dry-cleaning, whole-sale and retail sales, and fast-food services; Chinese in garment factories, restaurants, and gift shops; and Cambodians in the doughnut business (Espiritu 1997).

Those small businesses are heavily clustered in their ethnic communities. With limited capital, they compete in highly risky, marginally profitable businesses such as small grocery markets, garment workshops, and restaurants (Bonacich and Jung 1982). Contrary to the myth, few of those small business owners are able to gain upward social mobility. The majority of these businesses have earned low profits, and chances for bankruptcy are high. Taking Southeast Asian Americans as an example, Espiritu (1997) points out that in 1990, 18 out of 20 businesses failed during their first-year [of] operations. Even for those that survive, they heavily depend on unpaid or minimally paid labor of family members or relatives and on staying open long hours. According to the survey of Ong and Hee (1994), about 42 percent of Asian American business owners work more than 50 hours a week and 26 percent work more than 60 hours per week. Moreover, three-quarters of Asian American businesses do not hire a single employee from outside.

Hurh and Kim (1984), in their study of Korean Americans in the Los Angeles area, found that many of those small businesses are primarily Mom and Pop stores with few or no paid employees and low profit. Gold (1994) describes those small Asian American businesses, like ones owned by Vietnamese Americans, as "exploiting themselves to maintain marginal or undercapitalized enterprises" (p. 212). Chan (1991) critically commented that a sign of success in Asian American entrepreneurship is "a disguised form of cheap labor: [they] work long hours, and many of them could not stay afloat were it not for the unpaid labor they extract from their spouses, children, and other relatives" (pp. 169–170).

The problems that Asian entrepreneurs have encountered reflect a structural inequality of American society. Many scholars point out that the American economy is divided into a core and peripheral sectors with [the] labor market being split into a primary and secondary market. The primary market is located in the core economic sector in which workers have higher earnings and better working conditions, while the secondary market in the peripheral sector is characterized by low-paying jobs and worse working conditions. Socioeconomic mobility is restricted by this split labor market in which workers are distributed on the basis of race, ethnicity, gender, and nativity, rather than according to education, work experience, or other kinds of human capital (Chan 1991).

Even for those few Asians who work in [the] primary labor market and occupy managerial positions, they are facing a barrier of [a] "glass ceiling," through which "top management positions can only be seen, but not reached" (Takaki 1989). According to Takaki, the data collected in 1988 indicate that there were only 8 percent of Asian Americans with real "managerial" jobs, compared to 12 percent for all other groups in the United States. Asians were generally absent from positions of executive leadership in American corporations, despite that they were highly educated.

Arguing against the model minority thesis, Bonacich and Jung (1982) describe Asian Americans as a "middleman minority." As assimilated "outsiders," they are constrained by structural arrangements of society, surviving by occupying certain "occupational niches" that are non- or less competitive with the dominant ethnic group. Even in those competitive occupations, Asian Americans are unable to receive the same returns on their education and reach earnings parity with the majority group. Viewed from this perspective, . . . they are blocked from advancing into positions of authority or decision-making power. The U.S. Commission on Civil Rights (1992) admits that there exists a "glass ceiling" blocking the promotion of Asians to senior-level or top management positions in various sectors of mainstream economy.

Myth 4: "Asian American Youth Are 'Whiz Kids.'"

The evidence indicates that not all Asian American students do well in school. They vary in their experiences of academic achievement and attitude toward school work. In her field study, Lee (1996) examined the variability of Asian American students at Academic High School and found that despite some Asian students who are at the top of academic rankings, there are many low achieving Asian American students. In one of the schools she examined, during the 1988–89 school year, "fifteen Asian students were deselected from Academic due to weak academic performance and sent back to their neighborhood schools. Of the eighteen students in the class of 1989 who were deemed ineligible to graduate with their class, three (16%) were Asian" (p. 56). There was also a high proportion of Vietnamese-born youths who were neither at school nor in the labor force (Gardner et al. 1985). Trueba, Cheng, and Ima (1993) challenge the stereotypic notions of the academic success of Asian youth and discuss a large number of at-risk students from Asian

backgrounds—Pacific Islander families, as well as Southeast Asian refugee families. They point out that the academic failure of those students is more associated with socioeconomic structure than culture.

Lee (1996) found that contrary to the popular belief that Asian students are culturally motivated to achieve success, some Asian students, especially recent arrivals, did not regard school as the key to success in society and resisted any behavior that motivated academic success. These students have troubles with the rules required for academic success such as regular attendance, doing homework, and so on. However, the academic problems those Asian students have encountered have been largely overlooked due to the label that Asian students have few problems with assimilation.

As one Asian American student commented:

> They [whites] will have stereotypes, like we're smart. . . . They are so wrong, not everyone is smart. They expect you to be this and that and when you're not. . . . (shook her head) And sometimes you tend to be what they expect you to be and you just lose your identity. . . . just lose being yourself. Become part of what . . . What someone else want[s] you to be. And it's really awkward too! When you get bad grades, people look at you really strangely because you are sort of distorting the way they see an Asian. It makes you feel really awkward if you don't fit the stereotype. (Lee 1996, p. 59)

Myth 5: "Asian Americans Don't Seem to Have Any Problems."

Associated with the myth of model minority is the popular belief that Asian Americans do not . . . have any problems. . . . As Kou

(1979) points out, Asian Americans have less visibility in positions of institutional power and in political influence, as compared with other minority groups. Despite some recent efforts, there remains a slow progress in Asian American political participation. As a result, Asian Americans are generally excluded from public discourse of government policy. In the minds of most Americans, Asians are not the same as other minority groups. Minorities like African Americans, Latinos, and Native Americans are the "real" ones that need welfare assistance because they, unlike Asians, are experiencing disproportionate levels of poverty and educational underachievement.

Asian Americans do have the same problems as other minority groups. These problems are little known because "Asian Americans find themselves all lumped together and their diversity as groups is overlooked. Groups that are not doing well, such as unemployed Hmong, the Downtown Chinese, the elderly Japanese, the old Filipino farm laborers have been rendered invisible" (Takaki 1989, pp. 477–478). Chinatowns may illustrate the lives of the poor population of American Chinese and Asian American groups. The glitter of the neon signs disguises the poverty among the aged, the unemployed, and newly arrived immigrants. The people in inner-city Chinatowns suffer from deteriorating housing conditions, inadequate health care, poor working environment, and a rising crime rate—almost all the social problems that can be found in any low-income areas of American cities. For example, in the 1970s when the media was vigorously praising Asian American success, in San Francisco "inner-city Chinatown unemployment was almost double the citywide average, and two thirds of the housing stock was substandard, and tuberculosis rates were six times the national average" (Kitano and Daniels 1995, p. 52).

Low wages and exploitation are prevalent in ethnic enclaves as its economy usually operates outside the mainstream economy and labor market. Workers in garment sweatshops and restaurants often worked seventy hours a week but received much less than minimum wage and had no labor union or job security (Kwong 1987, p. 66). Kinkead (1992) calls those Asian Americans who live on the margin of American society "prisoners of Chinatown," where federal assistance is hardly available. Language barriers and unfamiliarity with the American system shut these people out of the rest of society and at the same time conceal the problems from the public. "To be out of sight is also to be without social services," Takaki observes. "Thinking Asian Americans have succeeded, government officials have sometimes denied funding for social service programs designed to help Asian Americans learn English and find employment" (Takaki 1989, p. 478).

Indeed, the image of "model minority" hurts rather than benefits Asian groups. The stereotypes of Asian Americans have caused social ignorance of the poverty, unemployment, illiteracy, and other social ills. As a result, they are denied social services they badly need to cope with those problems. For instance, many educational institutions adopt unwritten quotas to restrict the enrollment of qualified Asian American students, and some institutions even fail to consider Asian Americans as a minority who deserve the same treatment as other minorities. Additionally, the federal and state assistance to the development of small businesses often excludes Asian Americans as an eligible minority.

In addition, the stereotype has done more harm than good to interracial relationships between Asian Americans and other minorities. According to Chun (1980) and Osajima (1988), labeling Asians as a "model minority," as it emerged in the midst of civil rights movements, served a political purpose of turning public attention away from the racial tensions of American society. By praising Asian Americans, the proponents of the model minority thesis sent a political message to other minorities that they should model their behavior after Asian Americans rather than spending their time protesting inequality. If Asian Americans can make it on their own, the failure of other minority groups would be their own fault. In this sense, this model is a disservice to the community.

Asian Americans are one of the fastest growing minorities. As in the past, many people still view them as if they are all alike . . . and made it on their own in an adopted country. In a comment on this misperception, I. M. Pei, the renowned Chinese-American architect, said that "people must realize that there really isn't such a thing as an Asian-American. . . . There are Chinese, Koreans, Japanese, Vietnamese, Indians and so forth. So many different cultures. So many different experiences. We need to understand their differences and complexities, their success and failures" (*The New York Times Magazine*, November 30, 1986). While the image of Asian Americans remains more myth than reality, this reality needs to be further explored to reveal the diverse socioeconomic experiences of different Asian American groups in American society.

REFERENCES

Barringer, Hebert, Robert W. Gardner, and Michael J. Levin. 1993. *Asian and Pacific Islanders in the United States.* New York: Russell Sage Foundation.

Bonacich, Edna, and Tae Hwan Jung. 1982. "A Portrait of Korean Small Business in Los Angeles, 1977." Pp. 75–98 in *Koreans in Los Angeles: Prospects and Promises,* edited by Eui-Young Yu, Earl H. Phillip, and Eun Sik Yang. Los Angeles: Koryo Research Institute and Center for Korean-American and Korean Studies, California State University.

Chan, Sucheng. 1991. *Asian Americans: An Interpretive History.* Boston, MA: Twayne Publishers.

Chun, Ki-Taek. 1980. "The Myth of Asian American Success and Its Educational Ramifications." *IRCD Bulletin* (a publication of the Institute for Urban and Minority Education, Teachers College, Columbia University) 15(1):1–12.

Espiritu, Y. L. 1997. *Asian American Women and Men: Labor, Laws, and Love.* Thousand Oaks, CA: Sage.

Fawcett, J. T. and R. W. Gardner. (1994). "Asian Immigrant Entrepreneurs and Non-entrepreneurs: A Comparative Study of Recent Korean and Filipino Immigrants," *Population and Environment,* 15:211–38.

Gardner, R.W., B. Robey, and P Smith. 1985. "Asian American: Growth, Change and Diversity." *Population Bulletin* 40(4):1–44.

Gold, S. 1994. "Chinese Vietnamese Entrepreneurs in California." Pp. 196–266 in *The New Asian Immigration in Los Angeles and Global Restructuring,* edited by P. Ong, E. Bonacich, and L. Cheng. Philadelphia: Temple University Press.

Hirschman, Charles and Morrison G. Wong. 1981. "Trends in Socioeconomic Achievement among Immigrant and Native-Born Asian-Americans, 1960–1976," *The Sociological Quarterly* 22 (Autumn):495–514.

Hsia, Jayjia. 1988. *Asian Americans in Higher Education and at Work.* Hillsdale, NJ: Lawrence Erlbaum Associates.

Hurh, Won Moo and Kwang Chung Kim. 1989. "The 'Success' Image of Asian Americans: Its Validity, and Its Practical and Theoretical Implications." *Ethnic and Racial Studies* 12(2):512–38.

———. 1984. *Korean Immigrants in America: A Structural Analysis of Ethnic Confinement and Adhesive Adaptation.* Madson, NJ: Fairleigh Dickinson University Press.

Kanjanapan, W. 1995. "The Immigration of Asian Professionals to the United States: 1988–1990." *International Migration Review* 29:7–32.

Kinkead, Gwen. 1992. *Chinatown: A Portrait of a Closed Society.* New York: HarperCollins.

Kitano, Harry H. L. and Roger Daniels. 1995. *Asian Americans: Emerging Minorities.* 2nd ed. Englewood Cliffs, NJ: Prentice-Hall.

Kou, Wen H. 1979. "On the Study of Asian-Americans: Its Current State and Agenda." *Sociological Quarterly* 20:279–90.

Kwong, Peter. 1987. *The New Chinatown.* New York: Hill & Wong.

Lee, Stacey J. 1996. *Unraveling the "Model Minority" Stereotype: Listening to Asian American Youth.* New York: Columbia University, Teachers College Press.

Li, Angelina H. 1980. *Labor Utilization and the Assimilation of Asian Americans.* Springfield, VA: National Technical Information Service, U.S. Department of Commerce.

Lowe, L. 1991. "Heterogeneity Hybridity, Multiplicity: Marking Asian American Differences." *Diaspora* 1(1):24–44.

Lyman, Stanford M. 1974. *Chinese Americans.* New York: Random House.

Nee, Victor and Jimy Sanders. 1985. "The Road to Parity: Determinants of the Socioeconomic Achievements of Asian Americans." *Ethnic and Racial Studies* 8(1):75–93.

Ong, P. 1993. *Beyond Asian American Poverty: Community Economic Development Policies and Strategies.* Los Angeles, CA: LEAP, UCLA, Asian American Studies Center.

Ong, P. and S. Hee. 1994. "Economic Diversity." Pp. 165–89 in *The State of Asian Pacific America: Economic Diversity, Issues, and Policies,* edited by P. Ong. Los Angeles, CA: LEAP, UCLA, Asian American Center.

Ong, P. and K. Umemoto. 1994. "Life and Work in the Inner-City." Pp. 87–112 in *The State of Asian Pacific America: Economic Diversity, Issues, and Policies,* edited by P. Ong. Los Angeles, CA: LEAP, UCLA, Asian American Center.

Osajima, Keith. 1988. "Asian Americans as the Model Minority: An Analysis of the Popular Press Image in the 1960s and 1980s," Pp. 165–74 in *Reflections on Shattered Windows: Promises and Prospects for Asian American Studies,* edited by Okihiro et al. Pullman: Washington State University Press.

Roos, P. A. 1977. *Questioning the Stereotypes: Differentials in Income Attainment of Japanese, Mexican-Americans, and Anglos in California.* Rockville, MD: National Institute of Mental Health (DHEW).

Rumbaut, R. G. and K. Ima. 1988. *The Adaptation of Southwest Asian Refugee Youth: A Comparative Study.* Washington, D.C.: U.S. Office of Refugee Resettlement.

Takaki, Ronald. 1989. *Strangers from a Different Shore: A History of Asian Americans.* Boston: Little, Brown.

———. 1993. *A Different Mirror: A History of Multicultural America.* Boston: Little, Brown.

Trueba, Henry T., Li Rong Lilly Cheng, and Kenji Ima. 1993. *Myth or Reality: Adaptive Strategies of Asian Americans in California.* Washington D.C.: The Falmer Press.

U.S. Commission on Civil Rights. 1992. "Civil Rights Issues Facing Asian Americans in the 1990s." Washington D.C.: U.S. Government Printing Office, February, pp. 131–36.

Woodrum, Eric. 1984. "An Assessment of Japanese American Assimilation, Pluralism, and Subordination," *American Journal of Sociology* 87(2):157–69.

QUESTIONS FOR DISCUSSION

1. Why is "Asian" a controversial racial designation?
2. How does the social construction of the model minority work against the successful extension of social policies to people who need them?
3. Which model minority myth associated with Asian Americans is most problematic?
4. How does the ideology of a model minority result in structural consequences? Consider, for example, college admissions policies, affirmative action programs, and immigration policy.

18

THE BLACK–WHITE TEST SCORE GAP

CHRISTOPHER JENCKS • MEREDITH PHILLIPS

African Americans currently score lower than European Americans on vocabulary, reading, and mathematics tests, as well as on tests that claim to measure scholastic aptitude and intelligence.[1] This gap appears before children enter kindergarten (Figure 1), and it persists into adulthood. It has narrowed since 1970, but the typical American black still scores below 75 percent of American whites on most standardized tests.[2] On some tests the typical American black scores below more than 85 percent of whites.[3]

The black–white test score gap does not appear to be an inevitable fact of nature. It is true that the gap shrinks only a little when black and white children attend the same schools. It is also true that the gap shrinks only a little when black and white families have the same amount of schooling, the same income, and the same wealth. But despite endless speculation, no one has found genetic evidence indicating that blacks have less innate intellectual ability than whites. Thus while it is clear that eliminating the test score gap would require enormous effort by both blacks and whites and would probably take more than one generation, we believe it can be done. This conviction rests mainly on three facts:

• *When black or mixed-race children are raised in white rather than black homes, their preadolescent test scores rise dramatically.* Black

adoptees' scores seem to fall in adolescence, but this is what we would expect if, as seems likely, their social and cultural environment comes to resemble that of other black adolescents and becomes less like that of the average white adolescent. . . .

• *Even nonverbal IQ scores are sensitive to environmental change.* Scores on nonverbal IQ tests have risen dramatically throughout the world since the 1930s.[4] The average white scored higher on the Stanford-Binet in 1978 than 82 percent of whites who took the test in 1932.[5] Such findings reinforce the implications of adoption studies: large environmental changes can have a large impact on test performance.

• *Black–white differences in academic achievement have also narrowed throughout the twentieth century.* The best trend data come from the National Assessment of Educational Progress (NAEP), which has been testing seventeen-year-olds since 1971 and has repeated many of the same items year after year. Figure 2 shows that the black–white reading gap narrowed from 1.25 standard deviations in 1971 to 0.69 standard deviations in 1996. The math gap fell from 1.33 to 0.89 standard deviations.[6] When MinHsiung Huang and Robert Hauser analyzed vocabulary scores for adults born between 1909 and 1969, the black–white gap also narrowed by half.

In a country as racially polarized as the United States, no single change taken in isolation could possibly eliminate the entire

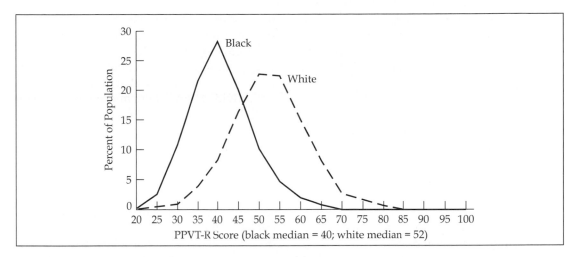

FIGURE 1 Vocabulary Scores for Black and White Three- and Four-Year-Olds, 1986–94. (*Source:* National Longitudinal Survey of Youth Child Data, 1986–94. Black N = 1,134; white N = 2,071. Figure is based on black and white three- and four-year-olds in the Children of the National Longitudinal Survey of Youth (CNLSY) data set who took the Peabody Picture Vocabulary Test-Revised (PPVT-R). The test is the standardized residual, coded to a mean of 50 and a standard deviation of 10, from a weighted regression of children's raw scores on their age in months, age in months squared, and year-of-testing dummies. . . .)

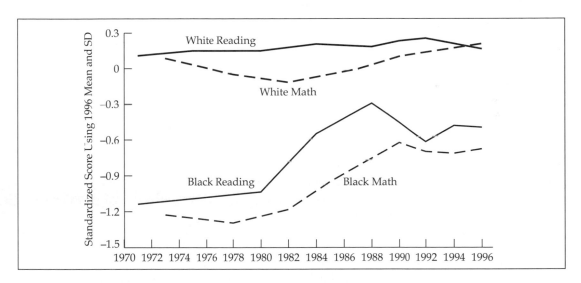

FIGURE 2 NAEP Reading and Mathematics Scores for Black and White Seventeen-Year-Olds, 1971–96. (*Source:* National Assessment of Educational Progress. Tests in all years are in a common metric and have been rescaled so that the 1996 population mean is zero and the 1996 standard deviation is 1.00.)

legacy of slavery and Jim Crow or usher in an era of full racial equality. But if racial equality is America's goal, reducing the black–white test score gap would probably do more to promote this goal than any other strategy that commands broad political support. Reducing the test score gap is probably both necessary and sufficient for substantially reducing racial inequality in educational attainment and earnings. Changes in education and earnings would in turn help reduce racial differences in crime, health, and family structure, although we do not know how large these effects would be. . . .

The best recent data on test scores and earnings come from the National Longitudinal Survey of Youth (NLSY), which gave the Armed Services Vocational Aptitude Battery to a national sample of young people in 1980.[7] Among employed men who were 31 to 36 years old in 1993, blacks earned 67.5 percent of what whites earned, a modest but significant improvement over the situation in 1964.[8] The big change occurred among blacks with test scores near or above the white average. Among men who scored between the 30th and 49th percentiles nationally, black earnings rose from 62 to 84 percent of the white average. Among men who scored above the 50th percentile, black earnings rose from 65 to 96 percent of the white average. . . . In this new world, raising black workers' test scores looks far more important than it did in the 1960s. . . .

Some skeptics have argued that scores on tests of this kind are really just proxies for family background. As we shall see, family background does affect test performance. But even when biological siblings are raised in the same family, their test scores hardly ever correlate more than 0.5. Among children who have been adopted, the correlation falls to around half that level.[9] The claim that test scores are only a proxy for family background is therefore false. Furthermore, test score differences between siblings raised in the same family have sizable effects on their educational attainment and earnings.[10] Thus while it is true that eliminating the black–white test score gap would not fully reduce

the black–white earnings gap . . . the effect would surely be substantial.

Reducing the black–white test score gap would reduce racial disparities in educational attainment as well as in earnings. The nationwide High School and Beyond survey tested twelfth-graders in 1982 and followed them up in 1992, when they were in their late twenties. At the time of the followup only 13.3 percent of the blacks had earned a B.A., compared with 30 percent of the non-Hispanic whites. Many observers blame this disparity on black parents' inability to pay college bills, black students' lack of motivation, or the hostility that black students encounter on predominantly white college campuses. All these factors probably play some role. Nonetheless, Figure 3 shows that when we compare blacks and whites with the same twelfth grade test scores, blacks are *more* likely than whites to complete college. Once we equalize test scores, High School and Beyond blacks' 16.7 point disadvantage in college graduation rates turns into a 5.9 point advantage.[11]

Eliminating racial differences in test performance would also allow colleges, professional schools, and employers to phase out the racial preferences that have caused so much political trouble over the past generation. If selective colleges based their admission decisions solely on applicants' predicted college grades, their undergraduate enrollment would currently be 96 or 97 percent white and Asian. To avoid this, almost all selective colleges and professional schools admit African Americans and Hispanics whom they would not admit if they were white. Racial preferences of this kind are politically unpopular.[12] If selective colleges could achieve racial diversity without making race an explicit factor in their admission decisions, blacks would do better in college and whites would nurse fewer political grudges.

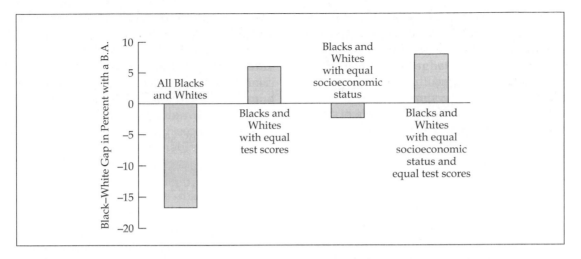

FIGURE 3 Gap in Eventual College Graduation Rates among Blacks and Whites Who Were in Twelfth Grade in 1982, Controlling Socioeconomic Status and Test Scores, 1992 (*Source:* Authors' tabulations from High School and Beyond 1992 followup. Test score is the sum of vocabulary, reading, and math scores. Socioeconomic status includes parents' income, occupation, schooling, possessions in the home, marital status, number of siblings, urbanism, and region. The standard error for black–white gap is about 2.5 percentage points.)

Advocates of racial equality might be more willing to accept our argument that narrowing the test score gap is crucial to achieving their goals if they believed that narrowing the gap was really feasible. But pessimism about this has become almost universal. In the 1960s, racial egalitarians routinely blamed the test score gap on the combined effects of black poverty, racial segregation, and inadequate funding for black schools. That analysis implied obvious solutions: raise black children's family income, desegregate their schools, and equalize spending on schools that remain racially segregated. All these steps still look useful, but none has made as much difference as optimists expected in the early 1960s.

- The number of affluent black parents has grown substantially since the 1960s, but their children's test scores still lag far behind those of white children from equally affluent families. Income inequality between blacks and whites appears to play

some role in the test score gap, but it is quite small.

- Most southern schools desegregated in the early 1970s, and southern black nine-year-olds' reading scores seem to have risen as a result. . . . Even today, black third-graders in predominantly white schools read better than initially similar blacks who have attended predominantly black schools. But large racial differences in reading skills persist even in desegregated schools, and a school's racial mix does not seem to have much effect on changes in reading scores after sixth grade or on math scores at any age.[13]

- Despite glaring economic inequalities between a few rich suburbs and nearby central cities, the average black child and the average white child now live in school districts that spend almost exactly the same amount per pupil.[14] Black and white schools also have the same average number of teachers per pupil, the same pay scales, and teachers with almost the same amount of formal education and teaching experience.[15] The most important resource difference between black and white schools seems to be that teachers in black schools have lower test scores than teachers in white schools. This is partly because black schools have more black teachers and partly because white teachers in black schools have unusually low scores. . . .

For all these reasons, the number of people who think they know how to eliminate racial differences in test performance has shrunk steadily since the mid-1960s. While many people still think the traditional liberal remedies would help, few now believe they would suffice.

Demoralization among liberals has given new legitimacy to conservative explanations for the test score gap. From an empirical viewpoint, however, the traditional conservative explanations are no more appealing than their liberal counterparts. These explanations fall into three overlapping categories: the culture of poverty, the scarcity of two-parent black families, and genes.

- In the 1960s and 1970s, many conservatives blamed blacks' problems on a culture of poverty that rejected school achievement, the work ethic, and the two-parent family in favor of instant gratification and episodic violence. In the 1980s, conservatives (as well as some liberals) characterized the "black underclass" in similar terms. But this description only fits a tiny fraction of the black population. It certainly cannot explain why children from affluent black families have much lower test scores than their white counterparts.
- Conservatives invoke the decline of the family to explain social problems almost as frequently as liberals invoke poverty. But once we control a mother's family background, test scores, and years of schooling, whether she is married has even less effect on her children's test scores than whether she is poor. . . .

- Scientists have not yet identified most of the genes that affect test performance, so we have no direct genetic evidence regarding innate cognitive differences between blacks and whites. But we have accumulated a fair amount of indirect evidence since 1970. Most of it suggests that whether children live in a "black" or "white" environment has far more impact on their test performance than the number of Africans or Europeans in their family tree. . . .

Taken as a whole, then, what we have characterized as the "traditional" explanations for the black–white test score gap do not take us very far. This has led some people to dismiss the gap as unimportant, arguing that the tests are culturally biased and do not measure skills that matter in the real world. Few scholars who spend time looking at quantitative data accept either of these arguments, so they have had to look for new explanations of the gap. These new explanations can mostly be grouped under two overlapping headings: culture and schooling.

In the late 1960s and early 1970s, many blacks and some whites dismissed cultural explanations of the test score gap as an effort to put down blacks for not thinking and acting like upper-middle-class whites. Since then, cultural explanations have enjoyed a slow but steady revival. In 1978 the Nigerian anthropologist John Ogbu suggested that caste-like minorities throughout the world tended to do poorly in school, even when they were visually indistinguishable from the majority.[16] Later, Ogbu argued that because blacks had such limited opportunities in America, they developed an "oppositional" culture that equated academic success with "acting white."[17] By linking black culture directly to oppression, Ogbu made it much easier for liberals to talk about cultural differences. Jeff Howard and Ray Hammond added another important strand to this argument when they suggested that academic competence developed partly through competition, and that "rumors of inferiority" made blacks reluctant to compete academically.[18] More recently, Claude Steele has argued that people of all races avoid situations in which they expect others to have negative stereotypes about them, even when they know that the stereotype does not apply. According to Steele, many black students "disidentify" with school because constructing a personal identity based on academic competence entails a commitment to dealing with such stereotypes on a daily basis.[19]

Social scientists' thinking about "school effects" has also changed since the late 1960s. The 1966 Coleman Report and subsequent "production function" studies convinced most economists and quantitative sociologists that school resources had little impact on achievement.[20] Since 1990, however, new statistical methods, new data, and a handful of genuine experiments have suggested that additional resources may in fact have sizable effects on student achievement. The idea that resources matter cannot in itself explain the black–white achievement gap, because most school resources are now fairly equally distributed between blacks and whites. But certain crucial resources, such as teachers with high test scores, are still unequally distributed. And other resources, such as small classes and teachers with high expectations, may help blacks more than whites. . . . The idea that resources matter also suggests that "compensatory" spending on black schools could be valuable, at least if the money were used to cut class size and implement policies that have been shown to help. . . .

Test Bias

Many blacks and some whites believe that all cognitive tests are racially biased. . . . Christopher Jencks discusses five possible varieties of racial bias in testing. He concludes that two of the five constitute serious problems and that three are probably of minor importance.

Labeling Bias

What Jencks calls "labeling bias" arises when a test claims to measure one thing but really measures something else. This is a major problem when tests claim to measure either intelligence or aptitude, because these terms are widely used to describe innate "potential" as well as developed abilities. The notion that intelligence and aptitude are innate seems to be especially salient in discussions of racial differences. Thus, the statement that "blacks are less intelligent than whites" is widely understood as a statement about innate differences. Yet almost all psychologists now agree that intelligence tests measure developed rather than innate abilities, and that people's developed abilities depend on their environment as well as their genes. Even psychologists who believe that racial differences in test performance are to some extent innate agree that intelligence tests overstate the difference one would observe if blacks and whites grew up in identical environments. Intelligence tests therefore constitute a racially biased estimate of innate ability, which is what nonpsychologists often mean by the word "intelligence." Test designers cannot eliminate this bias by changing the content of intelligence tests. The only way to eliminate it is to change the tests' labels so as to emphasize the fact that they measure developed rather than innate skills and abilities.

Content Bias

"Content bias" arises when a test contains questions that favor one group over another. Suppose, for example, that black and white children spoke mutually unintelligible versions of English. A test given in white English would then underestimate black children's skills and vice versa. . . . If one takes a standard vocabulary test and winnows out words with unusually large black–white differences, for example, the black–white gap does not shrink much. Likewise, if one compares black children to slightly younger white children, blacks and whites find the same words easy and difficult. Nor is the black–white gap on tests that measure familiarity with the content of American culture consistently larger than the gap on nonverbal tests that do not measure familiarity with any particular culture. Because the racial gap in children's test performance is not confined to items that measure exposure to white language, culture, or behavior but is dramatically reduced when black children are raised in white homes, Jencks suggests that it may reflect differences in the way blacks and whites are taught to deal with what they do not know and in the emphasis they put on learning new cognitive skills.

Methodological Bias

Methodological bias arises when we assess mastery of some skill or body of information in a way that underestimates the competence of one group relative to another. Methodological bias would be important if, say, having black rather than white testers changed the relative standing of black and white test takers. That does not appear to be the case. There is some evidence that describing a test in different ways can affect different groups' relative performance, but we do not yet know how general this is. . . .

Prediction Bias

A generation ago many egalitarians argued that using the SAT to screen applicants for selective colleges was unfair to blacks because tests of this kind underestimated black applicants' academic potential. For most colleges, academic potential means undergraduate grades. Almost all colleges have found that when they compare black and white undergraduates who enter with the same SAT scores, blacks earn *lower* grades than whites, not just in their first year but throughout their college careers. . . . Likewise, when firms compare black and white workers with the same test scores, blacks usually get slightly lower ratings from their supervisors and also do a little worse on more objective measures of job performance.[21] In psychological parlance, this means that tests like the SAT do not suffer from "prediction bias."

Selection System Bias

The test score gap between black and white job applicants has traditionally averaged about one standard deviation. When employers do not screen workers, the performance gap is likely to be much smaller— typically more like two-fifths of a standard deviation.[22] The reason for this discrepancy is not that blacks perform better than whites with the same test scores. The reason is that test scores explain only 10 to 20 percent of the variation in job performance, and blacks are far less disadvantaged on the noncognitive determinants of job performance than on the cognitive ones.

Because blacks perform no better on the job than whites with similar scores, many people assume that using tests to select workers is racially fair. But if racial fairness means that blacks and whites who could do a job equally well must have an equal chance of getting the job, a selection system that emphasizes test scores is almost always unfair to most blacks (and to everyone else with low test scores). Imagine a company that has 600 applicants for 100 openings. Half the applicants are black and half are white. If the firm hires all applicants as temporary workers and retains those who perform best on the job, and if the performance gap between blacks and whites averages 0.4 standard deviations, about 36 blacks will get permanent jobs. If the firm selects the 100 applicants with the highest scores, about 13 blacks will get permanent jobs.[23] Jencks argues that the first outcome should be our yardstick for defining racial fairness. Using this yardstick, the second system is clearly biased against blacks. In effect, Jencks says, the second system forces blacks to pay for the fact that social scientists have unusually good measures of a trait on which blacks are unusually disadvantaged.

The Heredity–Environment Controversy

When the U.S. Army launched the world's first large-scale mental testing program in 1917, it found that whites scored substantially higher than blacks. Biological determinists immediately cited these findings as evidence that whites had more innate ability than blacks, but cultural determinists quickly challenged this interpretation. By the late 1930s most social scientists seem to have been convinced that either genetic or cultural factors could explain the gap. Neither side had a convincing way of separating the effects of heredity from the effects of culture, so the debate was an empirical standoff.

After 1945 the horrors of the Holocaust made all genetic explanations of human differences politically suspect. Once the U.S.

Supreme Court declared de jure racial segregation unconstitutional in 1954, genetic explanations of racial differences became doubly suspect because they were identified with southern resistance to desegregation. As a result, environmentalism remained hegemonic throughout the 1960s. Then in 1969 Arthur Jensen published an article in the *Harvard Educational Review* arguing that educational programs for disadvantaged children initiated as part of the War on Poverty had failed, and that the black–white test score gap probably had a substantial genetic component.[24] Jensen's argument went roughly as follows:

- Most of the variation in white IQ scores is genetic.[25]
- No one has advanced a plausible environmental explanation for the black–white gap.
- Therefore it is more reasonable to assume that part of the black–white gap is genetic than to assume it is entirely environmental.

Jensen's article created such a furor that psychologists once again began looking for evidence that bore directly on the question of whether racial differences in test performance were partly innate. . . .

Two small studies have tried to compare genetically similar children raised in black and white families. Elsie Moore found that black children adopted by white parents had IQ scores 13.5 points higher than black children adopted by black parents.[26] Lee Willerman and his colleagues compared children with a black mother and a white father to children with a white mother and a black father. The cleanest comparison is for mixed-race children who lived only with their mother. Mixed-race children who lived with a white mother scored 11 points higher than mixed-race children who lived with a black mother.[27] Since the black–white IQ gap averaged about 15 points at the time these two studies were done, they imply that about four-fifths of that gap was traceable to family-related factors (including schools and neighborhoods).[28]

A better-known study dealt with black and mixed-race children adopted by white parents in Minnesota. The mixed-race children were adopted earlier in life and had higher IQ scores than the children with two black parents. When the 29 black children were first tested, they scored at least ten points higher than the norm for black children, presumably because they had more favorable home environments than most black children.[29] When these children were retested in their late teens or twenties, their IQ scores had dropped and were no longer very different from those of Northern blacks raised in black families.[30] The most obvious explanation for this drop is that the adoptees had moved out of their white adoptive parents' homes into less favorable environments.[31] But because the study did not cover black or mixed-race children adopted by black parents, it does not seem to us to provide strong evidence on either side of the heredity–environment debate.

Racially Mixed Children

Race is not a well-defined biological category. It is a social category, whose biological correlates vary geographically and historically. America has traditionally classified people as black using the "one drop" rule, under which anyone with known black ancestors is black. As a result, people are often treated as black even though they have a lot of European ancestors. If blacks with a lot of European ancestors had the same test scores as those with no European ancestors, we could safely conclude that the black–white test score gap was a by-product of social classification rather than heredity. But when we find that light-skinned blacks score

higher than dark-skinned blacks, we cannot rule out the possibility that this difference is environmental. Light skin has traditionally been a social asset for black Americans, and the correlation between light skin and test performance could reflect this fact. To get around this problem, we need less visible genetic markers. Two studies have used blood markers to estimate the percentage of Europeans in a black child's family tree. Neither study found a correlation between the number of "European" blood markers and IQ.[32]

Although racially mixed children are culturally black in America, and are almost always raised by black parents in black communities, this is not true everywhere. Klaus Eyferth studied the illegitimate children of black and white soldiers stationed in Germany as part of the army of occupation after World War II. All these children were raised by their German mothers.[33] There was considerable prejudice against blacks in Germany at the time, and any child of a German mother who looked black was also presumed to be illegitimate, which carried additional stigma. But mixed-race German children did not attend predominantly black schools, live in black neighborhoods, or (presumably) have predominantly black (or mixed-race) friends. When Eyferth gave these children a German version of the Wechsler IQ test, children with black fathers and white fathers had almost identical scores.[34]

Taken in isolation, none of these studies would carry much weight. The samples are small, and the comparisons could be distorted by unmeasured genetic or environmental influences. . . . We read these studies as supporting three tentative conclusions:

- When "black" genes are not visible to the naked eye and are not associated with membership in a black community, they do not have much effect on young children's test scores.

- Growing up in an African-American rather than a European-American family substantially reduces a young child's test performance.
- When black Americans raised in white families reach adolescence, their test scores fall.

These studies do not prove that blacks and whites would have exactly the same test scores if they were raised in the same environment and treated the same way. But we find it hard to see how anyone reading these studies with an open mind could conclude that innate ability played a *large* role in the black–white gap.[35]

What Can Schools Do?

Instead of asking whether schools cause the black–white test score gap, Ronald Ferguson asks what they can do to reduce it. . . . His survey of the evidence leads him to five conclusions.

- Teachers have lower expectations for blacks than for whites.
- Teachers' expectations have more impact on black students' performance than on white students' performance.
- Teachers expect less of blacks than of whites because black students' past performance and behavior have been worse. Ferguson finds no evidence that teachers' expectations differ by race when they are asked to assess children who have performed equally well and behaved equally well in the past.
- By basing their expectations on children's past performance and behavior, teachers perpetuate racial disparities in achievement.
- Exhorting teachers to have more faith in black children's potential is unlikely to change their expectations. But professional development programs in which teachers actually see disadvantaged black children performing at a high level can make a difference.

. . . Ferguson reviews school policies that might help reduce the black–white test score gap. A substantial number of randomized experiments suggest that smaller classes raise test scores.[36] The largest of these studies is the Tennessee class-size experiment, which covered 6,572 children in 76 schools. It found that cutting class size by a third between kindergarten and third grade (from about 23 to about 15) raised both reading and math scores by about a third of a standard deviation for blacks and by a sixth of a standard deviation for whites. After children moved to larger classes in fourth grade, the benefits associated with having been in smaller classes began to diminish, especially for blacks. But the benefits were still sizable at the end of the seventh grade, which is the last year for which we currently have data.[37]

History is never as tidy as a randomized experiment, but the historical record seems consistent with the hypothesis that reducing class size raises reading scores. Averaged across all grade levels, the pupil–teacher ratio fell from 26:1 in the early 1960s to 17:1 in the early 1990s. About half the extra teachers were used to cut the number of students in regular classrooms. The size of the average class therefore fell from 29 in 1961 to 24 in 1991.[38] Ferguson finds that changes in the pupil–teacher ratio predict changes in the black–white reading gap among NAEP nine-year-olds quite well. . . . The pupil–teacher ratio fell substantially in the 1970s. Both black and white nine-year-olds' reading scores rose during this period, but blacks' scores rose more, which is what the Tennessee results would predict. Unfortunately, nine-year-olds' math scores did not rise in tandem with their reading scores.

Black nine-year-olds' math scores rose only a little during the 1970s, and white nine-year-olds' math scores hardly changed at all.[39] Perhaps the impact of smaller classes on math scores was offset by other countervailing influences, such as a less demanding curriculum.

Counting the number of teachers in a school is easier than measuring their competence. Ferguson argues that a teacher's test score is the best readily available indicator of the teacher's ability to raise children's test scores. No one has done randomized experiments to see whether hiring teachers with higher test scores improves student achievement, but a large body of nonexperimental research by Ferguson and others suggests that high-scoring teachers are more effective. Ferguson therefore concludes that using competency exams to screen out low-scoring teachers will help children in the long run. Screening out teachers with low scores should benefit blacks even more than whites, because black children are now considerably more likely than whites to have teachers with low scores. But competency exams will not do much to raise students' test scores unless the passing score is high enough to eliminate a substantial fraction of potential teachers. At present, few states or school districts set the cut point on competency tests very high.

Unfortunately, raising the passing score on teacher competency exams will also reduce the percentage of blacks who qualify for teaching jobs. This is a major political problem. It may also be a pedagogic problem, since Ferguson finds some evidence that black children learn more from black teachers. But this evidence is far weaker and less consistent than the evidence that teachers with high test scores will raise black children's scores.

School desegregation can also raise black children's achievement under some circumstances. The findings of David Griss-mer and his colleagues strongly suggest that desegregation raised southern black nine-year-olds' test scores in the 1970s. In a study covering the early 1990s, Meredith Phillips also found that attending a whiter school probably had a positive effect on black students' reading scores in the early grades. But she found less evidence that the racial mix of middle schools and high schools affected reading scores. Nor did a school's racial mix have a consistent influence on black students' math scores.[40] Since racially mixed schools have higher-scoring teachers, and since we often assume that teachers in racially mixed schools have higher expectations for their students, this finding is puzzling.

One common hypothesis about why black children derive such modest benefits from attending what seem to be better schools is that racially mixed schools track black students into classrooms where their classmates are mostly black and their teachers expect very little. Ability grouping is obviously a contentious issue even in racially homogeneous schools. Students in low-ability classes usually cover less material than those in mixed-ability classes, but covering less material does not necessarily mean that students learn less. Ability grouping is supposed to increase the odds that slower learners get instruction appropriate to their skills. If that happened, slow learners could be better off.

Public debates about ability grouping seldom pay much attention to empirical evidence about its impact, perhaps because the evidence does not fit either side's preconceptions. Ferguson's review suggests that assigning children to separate classrooms on the basis of their presumed ability has no significant effect, positive or negative, on the test scores of children in the middle or bottom third of the distribution. This kind of grouping may help high-scoring students a little, but if so the effect is very small.[41] Assigning students to heterogeneous classrooms and then grouping them by ability *within* a heterogeneous classroom appears to increase math achievement for all children, but there have been only a handful of randomized experiments with this kind of grouping, so it is hard to be sure.[42] The impact of ability grouping on reading skills is apparently unknown. Research on this subject is now mostly qualitative. Only one experimental study of ability grouping and test performance has been conducted since 1974.

At the high school level, black and white students are almost equally likely to say they are in the college preparatory program, but white students are substantially more likely to take academically demanding classes, such as second-year algebra, geometry, or Advanced Placement courses of various kinds. Ferguson finds that class assignments depend on students' previous grades, test scores, and socioeconomic background, but not on their race per se. We do not know *how* socioeconomic background affects course assignments. High-SES parents may encourage their children to take more demanding courses even when their children's test scores or grades are marginal. High-SES parents may also pressure schools to let their children take such courses. It would be a mistake to fault schools for letting high-SES students take demanding courses, however. Instead, we should probably fault schools for not pushing more low-SES students into such courses.

Fear of "Acting White"

An influential 1986 article by Signithia Fordham and John Ogbu drew attention to the fact that academically successful black adolescents often said their classmates disparaged them for "acting white." Some black students also reported that they had stopped working hard in order to avoid such taunts. Since 1986 many successful black adults have also reported such experiences. So have other ethnographers. Indeed, this explanation for blacks' academic problems has become part of American folklore and is often repeated in the mass media. Philip Cook and Jens Ludwig were apparently the first scholars to test such claims quantitatively with national data.[43] . . .

If black students were less committed to academic success than white students, we would expect blacks to do less homework and skip school more often. Cook and Ludwig find that few students, black or white, do much homework. The median black, like the median white, spends between two and four hours a week doing homework outside school. The hardest-working whites do more homework than the hardest-working blacks, but even for these students the difference is not huge: 14 percent of white tenth-graders report spending more than ten hours a week on homework, compared with 10 percent of blacks. When it comes to skipping school, racial differences are negligible.

Cook and Ludwig also investigate the social costs of academic success for blacks and whites. They do not challenge Fordham and Ogbu's claim that working hard or getting good grades can lead to charges of racial disloyalty. But white students who work hard are also taunted as "nerds" and "geeks." Black students' fear of "acting white" can only exacerbate the black–white test score gap if academic success has higher social costs for blacks than for whites, or if blacks are more responsive than whites to such social costs. Since Fordham and Ogbu studied an all-black high school, they could not investigate these issues.

In 1990 the National Education Longitudinal Survey (NELS) asked tenth-graders whether they had been physically threatened at school, whether they often felt put down by other students in their classes, whether other students thought of them as popular, whether other students thought of them as part of the "leading crowd," and whether they were popular with the opposite sex. Cook and Ludwig use these measures to assess the social consequences of getting A's in math and of being a member of the student honor society. Their analysis yields two findings.

- Getting A's in math is almost unrelated to being threatened, feeling put down by other students, and feeling unpopular. Honor society members appear to feel *less* threatened and *more* popular than other students.
- The social costs and benefits of academic success are about the same for blacks and whites. Where racial differences do arise, blacks usually benefit slightly more than whites from academic success.

Cook and Ludwig's findings suggest that while academic success can have social costs, it also has benefits. If schools can reduce the costs or increase the benefits, student achievement is likely to improve. Judging by Cook and Ludwig's findings, however, the improvement would be as large for whites as for blacks. If that were the case, the racial disparity in academic achievement would not change much.

Ferguson challenges these conclusions. . . . He agrees that fear of acting white probably plays a minor role in *creating* the black–white test score gap that we observe in American high schools, but it may nonetheless be an important obstacle to *reducing* the gap. Ferguson compares American high schools to a mile-long race in which two competitors are nearing the end of the course. They are separated by forty yards. Both are jogging. Neither is out of breath. Observing this scene, we could ask why the black runner was behind. But we could also ask why the black runner was not trying to catch up. The "acting white" hypothesis does not seem to explain why black

high school students are behind their white classmates. But it may well explain why they are not making more effort to catch up.

"Stereotype Threat"

Claude Steele and Joshua Aronson argue that academically successful blacks worry about the possibility that getting a low score on a test will confirm the stereotype that blacks are not academically talented. This kind of anxiety, they argue, can actually impair successful blacks' performance. They ran a series of ingenious experiments in which a white experimenter gave Stanford undergraduates a test composed of difficult verbal questions from the Graduate Record Exam. Black students made substantially more mistakes when they were asked to record their race before taking the test. Blacks also made more mistakes when they were told that the test measured "verbal reasoning ability" than when they were told that the study focused on "psychological factors involved in solving verbal problems." White students' performance did not depend on the way the experimenter described the test or on whether they recorded their race.

Steele and Aronson's findings strongly suggest that anxiety about racial stereotypes and intellectual competence can sometimes depress able black students' test performance. But their findings do not tell us how general this phenomenon is. Steele believes that what he calls "stereotype threat" is mainly a problem for blacks who have an emotional investment in seeing themselves as good students.[44] He also believes that it helps explain why so many black students "disidentify" with school.[45] We do not yet know whether stereotype threat affects the amount of time black students spend studying or how much they learn when they study. But we do have some indirect evidence.

Steele believes that "remedial" programs for black undergraduates can exacerbate stereotype threat and depress blacks' academic performance. Working with colleagues at the University of Michigan, he initiated an alternative program for a random sample of all students entering in the early 1990s. This program described itself as *more* demanding than the normal first-year curriculum. It seems to have boosted black students' undergraduate grades not just while they were in the program but afterwards.[46] This outcome suggests that the best way to improve black undergraduates' performance may be to treat them like everyone else and expect more than we do now. This may also be the best way to counter the perception that blacks are less intelligent than whites—a perception that has faded over the past twenty years but is still widespread.[47] Ferguson's review of research on teachers' expectations suggests that this logic also applies to younger black students.

Can We Explain More of the Gap?

The evidence summarized above shows that traditional explanations for the black–white test score gap do not work very well. . . .

Our best guess is that successful new theories about the causes of the black–white gap will differ from traditional theories in at least three ways:

- Instead of looking at families' economic and educational resources, successful theories will probably pay more attention to the way family members and friends interact with one another and with the outside world. A good explanation of why white four-year-olds have bigger vocabularies than black four-year-olds is likely to focus on how much parents talk to their children, how they deal with their children's questions, and how they react when their children either learn or fail to learn something, not on how much money the parents have in the bank.[48]

- Instead of looking mainly for resource differences between predominantly black and predominantly white schools, successful theories will probably pay more attention to the way black and white children respond to the same classroom experiences, such as having a teacher of a different race or having a teacher with low expectations for students who read below grade level.

- Instead of trying to trace the black–white test score gap to economic or demographic influences, successful theories will probably have to pay more attention to psychological and cultural differences that are harder to describe accurately and therefore easy to exaggerate. Collecting accurate data on such differences would require a massive investment of effort, perhaps comparable to what psychologists invested in developing cognitive tests during the first half of the twentieth century. It would also require far closer cooperation between psychologists, ethnographers, and survey researchers than one ordinarily sees in academic life.

NOTES

1. We are indebted to Karl Alexander, William Dickens, Ronald Ferguson, James Flynn, Frank Furstenberg, Arthur Goldberger, Tom Kane, David Levine, Jens Ludwig, Richard Nisbett, Jane Mansbridge, Susan Mayer, Claude Steele, and Karolyn Tyson for helpful criticisms of earlier drafts. But we did not make all the changes they suggested, and they are in no way responsible for our conclusions.

2. These statistics also imply, of course, that a lot of blacks score above a lot of whites. If the black and white distributions are normal and have the same standard deviation, and if the black–white gap is one (black or white) standard deviation, then when we compare a randomly selected black to a randomly

selected white, the black will score higher than the white about 24 percent of the time. If the black–white gap is 0.75 rather than 1.00 standard deviations, a randomly selected black will score higher than a randomly selected white about 30 percent of the time.

3. Although this book concentrates on the black–white gap, similar issues arise when we compare either Hispanics or Native Americans to whites or Asians. We have concentrated on the black–white gap because far more is known about test performance among blacks and whites than among other groups. This reflects the fact that white American scholars have traditionally been more concerned about the plight of blacks than about the plight of other minorities, as well as the fact that blacks were (until recently) far more numerous than Native Americans, Asians, or even Hispanics.

4. Flynn (1987); Neisser (1998).

5. The 1932–78 comparison for whites is derived from Flynn (1984), who shows that IQ scores rose by roughly 13.8 points between 1931–33 and 1976–80. Tuddenham (1948) reported an equally dramatic improvement in the test performance of American soldiers between World War I and World War II. Since the trend found by Flynn appears to have been roughly linear, the net increase between 1917 and 1978 was probably close to 18 points (1.2 standard deviations). Flynn (personal communication) reports that restandardization of the Wechsler intelligence tests shows a further increase in mean IQ since 1978.

6. The standardized black–white gap always looks larger in NAEP than in other surveys, because NAEP reports standard deviations that have been corrected for measurement error. In addition, the standard deviation of seventeen-year-olds' reading and math scores has fallen over time, making the pre-1996 gaps look larger than they would if they were expressed in contemporary standard deviations. Five other major national surveys of high school seniors conducted since 1965 also show black–white convergence . . ., as do surveys of younger children. . . .

7. Almost all members of Cutright's sample took a version of the AFQT that included equal numbers of questions on vocabulary, arithmetic, and spatial relations. The Armed Services Vocational Aptitude Battery (ASVAB) did not include a spatial relations test, so we could not exactly reproduce the 1950–53 AFQT. To approximate the 1950–53 test we summed men's scores on the ASVAB tests of word knowledge, numerical operations, and mechanical reasoning. Our results did not change appreciably when we used other ASVAB tests instead.

8. To match Cutright's sample, we selected men who took the ASVAB between the ages of 18 and 23. Cutright had no data on whether respondents were Hispanic. We treated Hispanics as white, but our results hardly changed when we dropped Hispanics. Cutright's data were limited to men who worked in jobs covered by social security in 1964, whereas our NLSY sample covered all men of the relevant age.

9. See Jencks and others (1972, appendix A); Loehlin (1980); and Cherny and Cardon (1994).

10. Korenman and Winship (forthcoming).

11. The results shown in Figure 3 do not change if we use years of schooling rather than college graduation as the dependent variable. Similar results can be found in samples dating back to the early 1960s, so they are not attributable to affirmative action. Affirmative action mainly affects *where* blacks go to college, not *whether* they go.

12. Proposition 209 banned racial preferences in California's public institutions but did not cover private institutions. The Fifth Circuit's *Hopwood v. State of Texas* decision banned such preferences in both public and private institutions throughout Texas, Louisiana, and Mississippi. The U.S. Supreme Court refused to review *Hopwood,* so it does not apply elsewhere in the United States. Should the Supreme Court endorse the *Hopwood* principle in the future, it would cover both public and private institutions throughout the nation.

13. Phillips (1997) found that a 10 point increase in the percentage of white students was associated with a .027 standard deviation increment in third-grade reading scores, holding "true" first-grade scores constant. Attending a 90 percent white school rather than an all-black school could therefore raise third-grade reading scores by .243 standard deviations. The estimated effect was smaller in later elementary grades and often changed signs. For math the effects were smaller than for reading and changed sign in high school.

14. Tabulations by William Evans show that the average black student lived in a district that

spent $5,387 in 1992, while the average white student lived in a district that spent $5,397. In 1972 the figures (in 1992 dollars) were $3,261 for blacks and $3,397 for whites. These estimates come from a file that matches expenditure data collected by the Census of Governments in 1972, 1982, and 1992 with demographic data on Census tracts in 1970, 1980, and 1990. A few districts cannot be matched. For details on the samples see Evans, Murray, and Schwab (1997).

15. On salaries, teacher training, and teacher experience, see Boozer, Krueger, and Wolkon (1992, p. 299). Boozer, Krueger, and Wolkon's data cover secondary schools. Because most teachers prefer high-scoring students, and experienced teachers get preference in assignments, we would expect blacks to get less experienced teachers than whites in the same high school. We have not seen comparable recent data on elementary schools. For earlier data see Coleman and others (1966) and Mosteller and Moynihan (1972).

16. Ogbu (1978).

17. Ogbu (1986); Fordham and Ogbu (1986).

18. Howard and Hammond (1985).

19. Steele (1992, 1997).

20. Coleman and others (1966); Mosteller and Moynihan (1972); Jencks and others (1972); and Hanushek (1989).

21. Hartigan and Wigdor (1989); and Wigdor and Green (1991).

22. A test score gap of 1 SD implies a job performance gap of 0.4 SDs if the correlation between test scores and performance is 0.4 or—more realistically—if the correlation between test scores and performance is 0.25 and the gap between blacks and whites with the same test score averages 0.15 SDs (Hartigan and Wigdor, 1989).

23. In the test score case the black mean is -0.5 SDs and the white mean is $+0.5$ SDs. If the within-race SDs are equal, they are both $(1 - 0.5^2)^{0.5} = 0.866$. If the cutpoint is set at $+1$ SD, blacks must be $1.5/0.866 = 1.73$ SDs above the black mean, whereas whites must be only $0.5/0.866 = 0.577$ SDs above the white mean. The selection rates are then 4.2 percent for blacks and 28.3 percent for whites. Blacks will therefore get $4.2/(28.3 + 4.2) = 13$ percent of the jobs. In the case of temporary workers the black mean is -0.2 SDs, the white mean is $+0.2$ SDs, and the within-race SDs are 0.98, so blacks must be $1.2/.98 = 1.22$ SDs above the black mean and

whites must be $0.8/.98 = 0.816$ SDs above the white mean. The selection rates are then 11.1 percent for blacks and 20.8 percent for whites, so blacks get $11.1/(11.1 + 20.8) = 36$ percent of jobs.

24. Jensen (1969).

25. Based on his estimates of the correlations between twins reared together and apart, adopted siblings, and other kinds of relatives, Jensen suggested that 80 percent of the variance in white children's test scores was traceable to genetic differences. More recent estimates usually put the percentage between 30 and 70 percent (Jencks and others, 1972, appendix A; Plomin and DeFries, 1980; Rao and others, 1982; and Chipuer, Rovine, and Plomin, 1990). We regard 50 percent as a reasonable middle-of-the-road estimate for white children. Recent work (summarized in Plomin and Petrill, 1997) suggests that genes explain more of the variance in adults' scores than in children's scores, perhaps because adults are in a better position to choose environments compatible with their genetic propensities.

26. Moore (1986) studied 23 white and 23 black families. The sample included 20 biracial children and 26 all-black children. In black families the 6 biracial children scored 2.8 points higher than the 17 all-black children. In white families the 14 biracial children scored 1.5 points lower than the 9 all-black children.

27. Willerman, Naylor, and Myrianthopoulos (1974) studied 129 four-year-olds, 101 of whom were raised by a white mother and 28 of whom were raised by a black mother. Among the married mothers the 50 children raised by a white mother and a black father had mean IQs of 104.7, while the 17 children raised by a black mother and a white father had mean IQs of 96.4. Among single mothers, who provide a cleaner comparison of the effects of growing up in a "white" rather than a "black" environment, the 51 children raised by a white mother had mean IQs of 99, while the 11 children raised by a black mother had mean IQs of 88. The mixed-race children raised by black and white mothers presumably had about the same mixture of "African" and "European" genes, but the parents may have been subject to different forms of genetic selection relative to others in their racial group.

28. Children raised by, say, black and white single mothers usually grow up in different

neighborhoods and attend different schools. Nonetheless, black children raised by white parents are unlikely to have exactly the same overall environment as white children raised by the same parents. We do not know how white parents treat their black and white children, but there could be important differences favoring either group. We do know that teachers often treat black and white children somewhat differently . . . and strangers are even more likely to do so. In addition, black and white children see themselves somewhat differently and may choose different environments as a result.

29. Most adoptees were first tested between the ages of four and sixteen. Weinberg, Scarr, and Waldman (1992, table 2) report data indicating that at the time of initial testing IQ scores averaged 97 for adoptees known to have had two black parents ($N = 29$), 109 for adoptees known to have had one black and one white parent ($N = 68$), and 109 for adoptees with a black mother and a father of unknown race ($N = 33$). The IQ gap between all-black and mixed-race children was much larger in the Minnesota study than in other studies (Moore, 1986; see also Flynn, 1980, on Eyferth).

30. Weinberg, Scarr, and Waldman (1992) report data suggesting that when the Minnesota adoptees were retested, the IQ means were 89 for black adoptees ($N = 21$), 99 for mixed-race adoptees ($N = 55$), and 99 for those whose father's race was unknown ($N = 25$). Adjusting for changes in test norms makes the decline about 2 points larger (Waldman, personal communication, August 6, 1997).

31. It is also conceivable that genetic differences between blacks and whites become more important in adolescence. McCartney and others' (1990) meta-analysis of twin studies suggests that the relative importance of home environment falls in adolescence and that the relative importance of genes increases. Thus if black adoptees had average test scores prior to adolescence because the negative effects of their genes were offset by the positive effects of their adoptive homes, and if their home environment exerted less influence after they reached adolescence, their test scores might fall.

32. Loehlin, Vandenberg, and Osborne (1973) and Scarr and others (1977). These studies would be more convincing if blood group classification were more reliable. With today's technology it should be possible to classify children more accurately along the European-versus-African ancestry continuum, but conducting such a study would be politically difficult.

33. The most detailed summary of this study in English is found in Flynn (1980). Eyferth sampled roughly 5 percent ($N = 181$) of the children known to have been fathered by black French and American soldiers between 1945 and 1953. He then constructed a matched sample of 83 children fathered by white soldiers. The two samples were matched only on characteristics of the mother and location, not characteristics of the father, which were largely unknown. Eighty percent of the black fathers were American and 20 percent were French Africans. Flynn reports that in the U.S. army of occupation the black–white gap on the Army General Classification Test (a predecessor of the AFQT) was about four-fifths that in the general population.

34. The means were 96.5 for mixed-race children and 97.2 for all-white children. The sampling error of this difference is about 4 points.

35. Skeptics may wonder whether other experts read this literature the way we do. That question is not easy to answer. Snyderman and Rothman (1987) asked a sample of over 1,000 psychologists, sociologists, and educational researchers. "Which of the following best characterizes your opinion of the heritability of the black–white differences in IQ?" Of the 661 "experts" who returned a questionnaire, 14 percent declined to answer this particular question, 24 percent said the data were insufficient to support a reasonable opinion, 1 percent thought the gap was "due entirely to genetic variation," 15 percent thought it was "due entirely to environmental variation," and 45 percent thought it was "a product of both genetic and environmental variation." It is not clear how many of those who gave the "both" response would accept our conclusion that genes do not play a *large* role in the black–white gap. Nor is it clear how many of Snyderman and Rothman's respondents had read the research that Nisbett reviews.

36. Glass and others (1982).

37. Mosteller (1995). For a far more skeptical view see Hanushek (1998).

38. Lewitt and Baker (1997).

39. Both black and white nine-year-olds' math scores did rise after 1982, but class size has not changed much since the late 1970s.

40. Phillips (1997).

41. In a review limited to randomized experiments, Mosteller, Light, and Sachs (1996) found ten studies covering 2,641 students that compared heterogeneous classrooms to classrooms tracked on the basis of estimated ability or past achievement ("XYZ grouping"). Averaged across all students, the mean difference in achievement between the two methods was exactly zero. There was some evidence that the least skilled students learned less and that the most skilled students learned more under XYZ grouping, but this difference was not statistically significant.

42. Mosteller, Light, and Sachs (1996) found only three experimental studies that compared the effect of ability grouping within heterogeneous classrooms with the effect of ungrouped heterogeneous classrooms.

43. For a more recent analysis along the same lines see Ainsworth-Darnell and Downey (forthcoming).

44. Frederick Vars and William Bowen's finding . . . that grade disparities between black and white undergraduates increase as their SAT scores increase is consistent with the hypothesis that stereotype threat is more of a problem among high-achieving blacks.

45. Osborne (forthcoming) presents evidence that the correlation between high school grades and self-esteem falls during the high school years for blacks but not whites.

46. Steele and others (1997).

47. The 1990 General Social Survey (GSS) asked respondents to rate various groups on a scale that ran from 1 ("unintelligent") to 7 ("intelligent"). Among white respondents, 31 percent gave blacks a score of 3 or less, 16 percent gave southern whites a score of 3 or less, and 6 percent gave all whites a score of 3 or less. We do not know how these ratings have changed over time, but we do have trend data on a related question. Since 1977 the GSS has repeatedly asked respondents why blacks have worse jobs, income, and housing than whites. One possible answer is that "most blacks have less inborn ability to learn." In 1977, 26 percent of whites agreed that this was one possible explanation for black poverty. By 1994, just before the publication of *The Bell Curve*, only 14 percent agreed. In 1996, only 10 percent agreed. This question almost certainly understates the percentage of whites who entertain doubts about blacks' intellectual ability. To begin with, Americans are far more likely to blame poverty on laziness than stupidity, and the GSS shows that this pattern holds for black poverty as well. This means that even whites who doubt blacks' intellectual ability may not think this is an important factor in explaining black poverty. In addition, some whites probably think blacks are unintelligent for environmental reasons, and others are probably reluctant to report politically incorrect views. Nonetheless, we believe the downward trend is real. We are indebted to Joseph Swingle for analyzing the GSS for us.

48. See, for example, Hart and Risley (1992).

REFERENCES

Ainsworth-Darnell, James and Douglas Downey. Forthcoming. "Assessing the Oppositional Explanation for Racial/Ethnic Differences in School Performance." *American Sociological Review*.

Boozer, Michael, Alan Krueger, and Shari Wolkon. 1992. "Race and School Quality since *Brown* v. *Board of Education.*" *Brookings Papers on Economic Activity (Microeconomics):* 269–326.

Cherny, Stacey and Lon Cardon. 1994. "General Cognitive Ability." In *Nature and Nurture in Middle Childhood,* edited by John DeFries, Robert Plomin, and David Fulker. Oxford: Blackwell.

Chipuer, Heather, Michael Rovine, and Robert Plomin. 1990. "LISREL Modeling: Genetic and Environmental Influences on IQ Revisited." *Intelligence* 14(1):11–29.

Coleman, James, and others. 1966. *Equality of Educational Opportunity.* Department of Health, Education, and Welfare.

Evans, William N., Sheila Murray, and Robert Schwab. 1997. "School Houses, Court Houses, and State Houses after Serrano." *Journal of Policy Analysis and Management* 16 (January):10–31.

Flynn, James. 1980. *Race, IQ, and Jensen.* London: Routledge and Kegan Paul.

———. 1984. "The Mean IQ of Americans: Massive Gains 1932 to 1978." *Psychological Bulletin* 95(1):29–51.

———. 1987. "Massive IQ Gains in 14 Nations: What IQ Tests Really Measure." *Psychological Bulletin* 101(2):171–91.

Fordham, Signithia and John Ogbu. 1986. "Black Students' School Success: Coping with the 'Burden of Acting White.'" *Urban Review* 18(3):176–206.

Glass, Gene, and others. 1982. *School Class Size.* Beverly Hills: Sage Publications.

Hanushek, Eric. 1989. "The Impact of Differential Expenditures on School Performance." *Educational Researcher* 18(4):45–51.

———. 1998. "The Evidence on Class Size," occasional paper 98-1. University of Rochester, W. Allen Wallis Institute of Political Economy.

Hartigan, John and Alexandra Wigdor, eds. 1989. *Fairness in Employment Testing: Validity Generalization, Minority Issues, and the General Aptitude Test Battery.* Washington: National Academy Press.

Howard, Jeff and Ray Hammond. 1985. "Rumors of Inferiority." *New Republic,* September 9:18–23.

Jencks, Christopher, and others. 1972. *Inequality: A Reassessment of the Effect of Family and Schooling in America.* Basic Books.

Jensen, Arthur. 1969. "How Much Can We Boost IQ and Scholastic Achievement?" *Harvard Educational Review* 39:1–123.

Korenman, Sanders and Christopher Winship. Forthcoming. "A Reanalysis of *The Bell Curve.* Intelligence, Family Background, and Schooling." In *Meritocracy and Society,* edited by Steven Durlauf and Samuel Bowles. Princeton University Press.

Lewitt, Eugene and Linda Schumann Baker. 1997. "Class Size." *Future of Children* 7(3):112–21.

Loehlin, John. 1980. "Recent Adoption Studies of IQ." *Human Genetics* 55:297–302.

Loehlin, John, Steven Vandenberg, and R. T. Osborne. 1973. "Blood Group Genes and Negro-White Ability Differences." *Behavior Genetics* 3:263–70.

McCartney, Kathleen, Monica Harris, and Frank Bernieri. 1990. "Growing Up and Growing Apart: A Developmental Meta-Analysis of Twin Studies." *Psychological Bulletin* 107(2): 226–37.

Moore, Elsie. 1986. "Family Socialization and IQ Test Performance of Traditionally and Transracially Adopted Black Children." *Developmental Psychology* 22(3):317–26.

Mosteller, Frederick. 1995. "The Tennessee Study of Class Size in the Early Grades." *Future of Children* 5(2):113–27.

Mosteller, Frederick and Daniel P. Moynihan, eds. 1972. *On Equality of Educational Opportunity.* Random House.

Mosteller, Frederick, Richard Light, and Jason Sachs. 1996. "Sustained Inquiry in Education: Lessons from Skill Grouping and Class Size." *Harvard Educational Review* 66(4):797–842.

Neisser, Ulrich, ed. 1998. *The Rising Curve: Long-Term Gains in IQ and Related Measures.* Washington: American Psychological Association.

Ogbu, John. 1978. *Minority Education and Caste: The American System in Cross-Cultural Perspective.* Academic Press.

———. 1986. "The Consequences of the American Caste System." Pp. 19–56 in *The School Achievement of Minority Children: New Perspectives,* edited by Ulrich Neisser. Hillsdale, NJ: Erlbaum.

Osborne, Jason. Forthcoming. "Race and Academic Disidentification." *Journal of Educational Psychology.*

Phillips, Meredith. 1997. "Does School Segregation Explain Why African Americans and Latinos Score Lower Than Whites on Academic Achievement Tests?" Paper prepared for the annual meeting of the American Sociological Association.

Plomin, Robert and John DeFries. 1980. "Genetics and Intelligence: Recent Data." *Intelligence* 4:15–24.

Plomin, Robert and Stephen Petrill. 1997. "Genetics and Intelligence: What's New?" *Intelligence* 24(1):53–77.

Rao, D. C., and others. 1982. "Path Analysis under Generalized Assortative Mating." *Genetical Research* 39:187–98.

Scarr, Sandra, and others. 1977. "Absence of a Relationship between Degree of White Ancestry and Intellectual Skills Within a Black Population." *Human Genetics* 39:69–86.

Snyderman, Mark and Stanley Rothman. 1987. "Survey of Expert Opinion on Intelligence and Aptitude Testing." *American Psychologist* 42(2):137–44.

Steele, Claude. 1992. "Race and the Schooling of Black Americans." *Atlantic Monthly,* April: 68–78.

———. 1997. "A Threat in the Air: How Stereotypes Shape Intellectual Identity and Performance." *American Psychologist* 52(6):613–29.

Steele, Claude, and others. 1997. "African American College Achievement: A 'Wise' Intervention." Stanford University Department of Psychology.

Tuddenham, Reed. 1948. "Soldier Intelligence in World Wars I and II." *American Psychologist* 3:54–56.

Weinberg, Richard, Sandra Scarr, and Irwin Waldman. 1992. "The Minnesota Transracial Adoption Study: A Follow-Up of IQ Performance at Adolescence." *Intelligence* 16: 117–35.

Wigdor, Alexandra and Bert Green, eds. 1991. *Performance Assessment in the Workplace,* vol. 1. Washington: National Academy Press.

Willerman, Lee, Alfred Naylor, and Ntinos Myrianthopoulos. 1974. "Intellectual Development
of Children from Interracial Matings: Performance in Infancy and at 4 Years." *Behavior Genetics* 4(1):83–90.

QUESTIONS FOR DISCUSSION

1. What is the strongest argument for developing social policies to reduce the
test score gap between Blacks and
Whites?

2. How do recent cultural explanations of
the test score gap (fear of acting White
and stereotype threat) differ from traditional explanations?

3. Why do Jencks and Phillips conclude
that only two problems of racial bias in
cognitive tests are serious?

4. How do the results of studies of the test
scores of racially mixed children demonstrate that race is socially constructed?

5. Are Ferguson's proposals, which are
summarized by Jencks and Phillips,
racist?

19

THE PLACE OF WOMEN
Inside Organized Racism

KATHLEEN M. BLEE

Deep in rural Pennsylvania, eighteen young women gathered on an out-door stage to be photographed for the cover of their group's newsletter giving a collective Nazi salute at the 1992 Annual Aryan Festival. Some held babies. One of them spoke for the group, announcing that white Aryan women were now ready to do battle with ZOG (the Zionist-occupied gov-ernment) and its white traitor supporters and that the threat of neither imprisonment nor death could deter them from this mission.[1]

That same year, the Aryan Women's League (AWL) published a eulogy to a woman they characterized as "epitomiz[ing] Aryan womanhood." They extolled her "legacy of absolute loyalty to her husband, her children, and her Race, which she served all her life." Particularly noted was her deepening racist involvement over her forty-five years of political activism, which began in her young adulthood. First a Girl Scout leader and Republican Party activist, she later worked on behalf of American Independent Party presidential candidate George Wallace; she then married a mid-western Klan leader. Her political career culminated when she became the Klan's state secretary and, during her husband's imprisonment and in defiance of federal authorities, operator of a racist publishing house.[2]

These two vignettes of racist activism are quite different, but both present women in familial as well as racial roles. Women are mothers of babies; women are politically supportive wives who parade the vilest form of racism. To those victimized and disgusted by organized racism, such images are frightening and confusing. They suggest that women's family-oriented activities not only can expand to a politics of caretaking, justice, and resistance to capitalism, colonialism, and imperialism, such as that displayed by the Argentinean Mothers of the Plaza de Mayo or by mothers involved in environmental justice movements in the United States, but also can become deeply entangled with reactionary and bigoted interests. These images highlight women's familial concerns being used to support agendas of racial supremacy.[3] . . .

As racist groups reach out to recruit women, it is increasingly important to examine their gender-specific appeals. How does the racist movement reconcile its desire for women as members with its historically deep masculinist emphasis? What roles do women play in racist groups and how are these changing? Might issues of gender become a weak spot in organized racism, a point of tension between its strategic need for unity and growth and its ideological commitment to a male-dominated racial struggle? . . .

Women in Racist Groups

Women's activities in organized racism differ considerably across groups. In general, Christian Identity and Klan groups tend to emphasize women's familial and social roles, while women in some white power skinhead and other neo-Nazi groups are involved in more direct action, playing what I term "operative" roles. But these distinctions are often blurred. Groups overlap in their memberships and women move between groups. Even groups that share a similar racist philosophy vary in their treatment of women members, reflecting their different histories, their leaders' ideas, and their balance of male and female members. In general, the roles of racist women fall into three categories: familial, social, and operative.

Familial Roles

The most common activities for women in organized racism are racial elaborations of the domestic roles to which women are traditionally assigned.[4] Racist activist women are expected to assume tasks associated with creating and nurturing a racist family. Because some segments of organized racism, especially Ku Klux Klan groups, emphasize that organized racism is "like a family," the scope of those tasks is not clear. Sometimes, the racist family is invoked to refer to women's responsibilities to their husbands and children. At other times, it denotes women's obligation to sustain a collective "family" of organized racists. Many racist leaders try to create a familial atmosphere by stitching together political and recreational activities that promote loyalty and commitment among their followers. As Robert Miles of Aryan Nations told one reporter, "No one who joins these circles is ever without family. Each of us is the father and the mother, the brother and the sister of every white child who's within our ranks."[5]

Nearly every Klanswoman I interviewed partly framed her discussion of organized racism in terms of family, claiming that organized racism promoted "family-like" qualities of caring and mutual responsibility among its members. Although, as I show later, many Klanswomen have specific criticisms of their groups, on an abstract level they insist that the Klan's ideal follows a family model. "Everyone's real supportive and, naturally you're going to have your little arguments here and there, but . . . basically, they're all real supportive, just like a big family," concluded a Klanswoman. An Aryan supremacist claimed that her racist colleagues were "part of my life, like family." A Nazi said that the thing she liked best in the group was "the camaraderie and the sense we get of having an extended family. The kinship we feel is probably the most important thing to all involved." Another claimed that "the unity between people who live so far apart is amazing. It is its own family." A southern woman made a Klan rally sound like a family reunion: "We'd all be together. The guys would play football. And it was like a big family, togetherness. It was the perfect utopia." Just as threats and conspiracies are understood by racist women largely in terms of their impact on immediate family and on daily life, so too the "virtue" of being in a racist group is often expressed in terms of its impact on self and family. A member of a violent Aryan group summarized how she felt about the group by saying, "It's given me more purpose and commitment in my life and I think it's helped me get closer to . . . my family, my friends. It's strengthened bonds of commitment."

The family sought by the racist community is more than just a metaphor. European fascism was built on existing cultural practices and norms, including those that governed family life.[6] Similarly, modern organized racism is based in part on familial expectations and ideologies, however distorted.[7] This invocation of family life also enables those within the racist movement to draw on codes of behavior and understandings by which personal relationships are fashioned and judged. As they learn to understand organized racism in terms of familial qualities, recruits to racist groups apply their expectations of familial relationships to those within racist groups. For some members, this analogy is positive, bolster-

ing their commitment to organized racism. But for others, including many women, the equation of family life and racist group life exposes painful conflicts. Women whose experience in racist groups does not measure up to idealized portraits of family life—those who find racist groups oppressively male-dominated or male leaders patronizing or dismissive of women—feel cheated and resentful. Others find that the emphasis on family life contradicts the demand that they sever relationships with family members outside the racist movement.

Families are expected to serve as platforms for racist recruitment efforts. Modern neo-Nazi and some Klan groups enlist women and adolescent girls, hoping to absorb entire families. In a Nazi publication a reporter described a rally to which "many brought their families. Loving fathers and mothers watched their children play all across the compound with the pure Aryan children from other families. I saw with my own eyes what we all are working so hard to achieve in microcosm. A pure White nation made up of happy, successful White families working and playing together under the protection of the Swastika."[8] A Klan leader commented that "you couldn't join the Klan unless your whole family came in at the same time. It was truly a family of families."[9]

In most racist groups, women are expected to mother their immediate families as well as the larger racist "family." Except in a few racist skinhead and neo-Nazi groups, women racists are told to fulfill their obligations to male intimates and to the racist movement by bearing Aryan babies. Cautioning racist men that "selecting a proper mate is the only way to give us the possibility in life to improve the heritary [*sic*] makeup of the coming generation," racist groups make it clear that racial obligation includes racial procreation. Such pronouncements are particularly frequent in Christian Identity and neo-Nazi groups that emphasize long-term planning for a racist future. This maternal responsibility is made explicit in the recruiting efforts of some groups that seek to win the "birth-rate war" by enlisting race-conscious white Aryan women who will give birth to a large number of children.[10]

In reality, the childbearing patterns and expectations of racist activist women are more mixed than the glorification of fertility in racist propaganda might suggest. On the one hand, several women I interviewed spoke with enthusiasm about their potential or actual contributions to increasing the white population, including one neo-Nazi who described being in a racist recruitment video "pregnant and strolling down the street with my baby and [being] so proud." Similarly, a skingirl interviewed by sociologist Mark Hamm commented that "what people don't know is that the [skinhead group] are strong into family values and strong antidrug. There are 11 women in our group and 8 are pregnant. This is the most important way we can carry on with the white power tradition."[11] An eighteen-year-old woman interviewed by a reporter at an Aryan Fest prided herself on supporting the white movement even before she had her own babies by contributing toward movement drives for "cribs, baby clothes, [and] diapers" for "white families starting out."[12]

On the other hand, many women in my study who were childless at the time of their interview expressed a desire to have no more than three or four children. Although a few predicted vaguely that they would have "a big white family" or that they wanted "as many [children] as possible," most were like a neo-Nazi who alluded to pressure in the movement to have many babies, commenting that she would have "of course more than the typical one or two that the women of today want" but insisting that she was "not really aiming for ten either." A skinhead said that she supported the idea of having a lot of children—"at least four"—but that she was not willing to begin having babies until she and her boyfriend were financially and geographically stable and "prepared to raise our children in a decent environment." Another, an aspiring racist, told a reporter that the emphasis on babies—the insistence of male skinhead leaders that "the purpose of intercourse is to have as many white Christian babies as possible"—made her and her girlfriends reluctant to pursue their involvement in the racist movement.[13] Women with children and those older than thirty tended to be the most conservative in their childbearing goals. Most claimed that they did not want any additional children beyond the one or two they already had. One Klanswoman lowered her voice as she confided, "My husband wanted seven kids. I had two. I don't want any more." A skinhead, pregnant with her first child, concluded that she would have "only as many [children] as we can afford. I wouldn't want to deprive children of what they need just to have more." Some women even elaborated medical steps they had taken to ensure that they would not again become pregnant.

Racist women are also held responsible for socializing their children into racial and religious bigotry. They often provide verbal instruction in the norms of racist living, such as direct admonitions "to stay away from nigger children"; sometimes their cautions are more indirect. For example, a skinhead mother recounted a conversation she had had with her elementary school-aged daughter, a story oddly preceded by the mother's assurance that "I don't push her to believe any beliefs." "My daughter understands," the mother insisted. "She knows she's a special person. . . . It's the little things, [like] when she didn't know what a black kid was, I explained that she's different because of color, to let her know that she shouldn't be involved with nonwhite."

The children are ushered into a world of racial and religious hatred at a very early age. Homes are strewn with drawings, photos, flyers, videos, and pamphlets filled with vicious lies and threats against racial and religious enemies. In one house, a child's high chair featured a hand-scrawled swastika on the back. In another, children's crayons lay on flyers denouncing Jews as inhuman. Still others displayed pictures of lynchings on living room walls or newspaper clippings about the bombing of the Oklahoma City federal building on refrigerator doors. Male leaders of racist groups, too, are involved in efforts to socialize youths as racist activists. A particularly pernicious means of targeting the very young is the racist comic book, like the *New World Order Comix* published by the National Alliance and distributed by skinhead groups.

Children have easy entry into the spectacle of organized racism. Toddlers learn that Jews are the offspring of Satan. Their older siblings learn to call nonwhites "mud people" as readily as other children learn the names of video games. From birth, some Klan children are installed in a "Klan Kid Korp," preparing them for a life of racist activism.[14] Garbed in miniature Klan robes and flaunting imitation torches and guns, they are introduced to racist activism as fun and frolic. One woman told me, "At night, the lighting of the crosses, that is a big to-do. The men, of course, were in the front lines, the women were there, and there were lots of children, too, lots of children running around and they were just so happy." Racist women extend this socializing further, creating networks of like-minded families in which their children can find assurance that their views are correct, even typical. Some children of racist families attend Aryan-only schools, where they can find white supremacist friends. Others are home-schooled, a method that almost all racist groups promote if not require to prevent children from becoming "double-minded"

as they learn different racial values at home and in school (even in Christian schools.)[15]

Some children are assigned minor tasks in racist groups; thus, in one Klan chapter "the kids fold the pamphlets and put them in plastic bags and then take them at night and throw them onto lawns." They also are prompted to secure children in other white supremacist groups as pen pals, an effort intended to deepen their racist identity and create a network of future activists. One such letter, credited to "Jessica," age six and in the first grade, starts out with the neutral statement that she likes "to skate and play with my best friend," but it ends with a message that seems to have been fed to her by an adult: "I love the white race and I want to keep my race alive." Similarly, "Kimberly," a thirteen-year-old, describes her "red hair" and her interests in "TV, roller blades, talking on the phone" and then adds, "I am proud to be white." Writings purportedly by racial activist children, though perhaps actually penned by adults, are found both in newsletters aimed at the young (e.g., *Little Aryan Warrior's*) and in propaganda issued from adult women's racist groups. An eight-year-old girl asks other children, "Are you tired of . . . [s]itting on your butt, watching the Cosby Show? Letting other kids make fun of you? Then do something about it NOW!"[16] A twelve-year-old girl is presented as the author of a poem titled "Being White Is Not a Crime," which reads in part:

> White and proud
> That's what I am
> Storming the streets
> Getting rid of the trash.
> What's wrong with knowing
> your race is strong?[17]

. . . But socialization from adult relatives is not the only or even the most likely route into adult racist activism. More than half of the women I interviewed had no immediate or extended family members who were racist activists or held strongly racist views. Some women insisted, in the words of one, that their parents "secretly agreed" with their racist views or might be "closet racists," but many admitted that their parents' racial views were much opposed to their own; their mothers, fathers, or both "believed that everyone's equal" and even had played some small part in civil rights or other progressive movements. One said her father was victimized by the Klan when he was sexually involved with a non-white woman, another that "my parents would have a massive stroke if they found out that I was a racist." Only logical contortions enabled one skinhead to reconcile her views with her upbringing: "The whole time I was young I was taught that racism was awful, that you just weren't racist, you just didn't judge someone on the basis of skin color. And I still believe that way. . . . I don't care about skin color. It's just that I don't agree with multiculturalism and I know that race mixing hurts society." . . .

A less obvious but also important role played by women racists within the family pertains to their control of family consumption. Just as some progressive movements have struggled to politicize consumers' choices,[18] so too racist groups try to channel the money they spend into sympathetic hands. Some urge their members to boycott products certified as kosher.[19] Several women I interviewed claimed to avoid these foods, though most could not identify the symbols that marked rabbinical endorsement (a recent inventory of such symbols posted on a white supremacist women's group Internet webpage may increase their awareness). Other groups encourage the bartering or trading of goods and services among racist activists and support vendors who sell racial paraphernalia.

At least a few women use their positions in racist groups, or those of their husbands, to benefit from racist purchasing. Some try to support themselves through their racist activities. A widow of a prominent racist activist sells "Aryan crafts"; Aryans, her advertisements claim, should buy from her rather than purchasing goods from major corporations ("who knows where the money is spent!") or frequenting "the mud [i.e., minority] infested, Jewish inspired shopping malls."[20] Another woman runs an enterprise called "Cathie's Celtic Corner," and yet another hawks racist gear in ads in racist magazines.[21] One woman sells "hand crafted N.S. [National Socialism] banners" along with Viking statues, etched glass, and other wares.[22]

Social Roles

Women also must act as the social facilitators of racist groups, an expectation nearly as deep-seated as that making them responsible for bearing white children and raising them as racists. The importance of this role has grown in recent years as racists have sought to increase the longevity of their groups.[23] When social ties are strengthened, members who have individual identities as racist activists come to view themselves as part of a larger social movement, developing a "collective identity" of racist activism. In describing an "incubation period during which new collective identities are formed . . . in submerged social networks out of view of the public eye,"[24] the sociologist Carol Mueller captures how social networks among its members support organized racism. Social ties . . . strongly influence people to join racist movements; in addition, as members of racist groups come to know each other in social as well as activist settings, they reinforce one another's commitment to the goals of organized racism. They create the "oppositional subculture" by which organized racism is sustained over time.[25]

Racist groups have proven remarkably successful in structuring the social lives of their adherents around movement activities. When I asked racist women how much of their socializing takes place with others in the racist movement, their estimates ranged from 50 to 100 percent, with most guessing 85 to 90 percent. As a Klanswoman told me, "Once you get into the Klan, it becomes your whole family, all your socializing, all your parties." Racist women give a variety of explanations for their predilection to spend free time among fellow racists. These include mutual protection ("a lot of people like us are afraid we will be hunted"; "we look out for one another when one is in trouble") and loyalty ("I'm totally secure in my trust in everyone in [her group]"). They also cite reinforcement of their beliefs ("I like being with people who share my beliefs"; "you do not need to defend your beliefs to anyone because they already share your views"), lack of access to other sets of friends ("when I decided I was going to be a skinhead, I lost a lot of friends, but I gained friendships I can count on"), and a perceived need for rapid and accurate sources of information ("everyone just updates on events that I should know about that are excluded from normal papers"). It is women who are responsible for making racist group life work, for creating rallies and meetings that leave people with a positive feeling. They often succeed; a skinhead remembered that her first Klan rally "was just like a big reception; it was a lot of fun." A neo-Nazi similarly recalled being surprised to find that a racist event was "kind of like a big powwow or something. There was no cross burnings or screaming."

A flyer advertising a neo-Nazi event promises a day of fellowship and racist learning, along with a social time of music and meals at a local banquet hall—meals served, of course, by "the ladies." Such gendered division of labor is common among racist groups; thus, for the social hour following a strategy meeting at the Aryan Nations' racist compound in Idaho, a sixty-year-old woman played the organ and baked cookies.[26] Although women remain in charge of providing meals for racist events in many groups, some leaders deny that such gender-specific assignments demonstrate women's marginality to racist operations. In the *Aryan Research Fellowship Newsletter*'s report on the Aryan Nations Youth Conference, a spokesman for the group claimed that women prepared meals on-site only to protect the gathered male racists, who otherwise would have had to buy meals in town (where they might fall into the hands of local police or antiracist activists).[27]

The emphasis on survivalism and self-sufficiency in the racist movement may heighten this gendered division of labor in the future.[28] One racist women's group sees its responsibility as "first aid, child safety, [and organizing an] emergency information guide, maternity clothes exchange, Aryan Alphabet Coloring book, Aryan Parent's Newsletter, [racist] P.O.W. art collection and fund."[29] Christian Identity women are organized as "White Nurses," preparing to heal the broken bodies of Aryan (male) combatants in the coming race war.[30] Another group defines women's roles in the racist movement as midwifery, child care, and survival cooking.[31] Barb, an Aryan supremacist, instructs new women recruits that "woman's big responsibility is to be ready to fight to raise children (no drop off day camps), and be ready to offer other women a shoulder to cry on. Many young women today didn't have a parent to teach them to cook from scratch (even the generation past had that problem and turned to TV dinners); to hand sew, and now women must learn it themselves and teach their children." The wife of a prominent Aryan supremacist—whom one racist skinhead woman described to me, without intended irony, as "like Donna Reed . . . a very nice, wonderful, matronly woman"—Barb is a model racist social facilitator. Her role is doggedly maternal, coaching younger skin-girls "how to make our men happy and the importance of being good parents, and make sure we're eating nutritionally, and does anyone need vitamins?" At the racist compound where she lived, this model homemaker would "have us stay and make muffins and coffee and bring them out to our men [but] she'd go through the roof if a man stepped in our flowers 'cause she had these gardens all around the place."[32]

Acting as social facilitators, women are central to efforts to create links between organized racist groups and outsiders. Indeed, women's greater participation and visibility in the racist movement are probably responsible for making it more accessible to mainstream populations. Because women seem incongruous in organized racism, they lend an air of placidity to racist gatherings and seem to lessen the threat that such groups pose. Women holding babies, schooling children, or serving chicken at buffet tables can to some degree "normalize" racial politics. A journalist recounts: "I see a Nazi sitting with a latte at an outdoor bistro table. This Nazi has no swastikas, no tattoos, no combat fatigues. Instead, she has a chic red bob, blue tinted sunglasses and a small son. If I hadn't seen her heil the Nazis at noon, I would only see a pretty mother in her early 20s enjoying the late evening sun."[33] Racist women acknowledge their role in this effort, noting that their involvement helps racist groups convey a sense of the ordinariness of racist activism; in the words of one woman, they "portray a positive image [of] honor and integrity."[34] After several members of his group appeared on a TV talk show, one male racist leader commented: "the women did quite well, dressing modestly, using proper makeup and proper arguments. The men should have stayed at home."[35]

Racist women also take more deliberate steps to gain entree to mainstream populations, seeking connections with sympathetic outsiders and attempting to recruit new members into the movement; they act as the racist equivalents of what, in her study of the African American civil rights movement, Belinda Robnett calls "bridge leaders."[36] A Nazi group declares its members "advocates [of] a community form of activism" and urges them to get out and meet people, so that they might show by example "the society that we would like to see." In so doing, "we will do much to break the image that the Zionist controlled news-media portrays about white nationalists." Among the varieties of community involvement suggested are "running for public office, engaging in business, and generally acting as responsible citizens, all while being openly known as National Socialists."[37]

Many neo-Nazi and Klan groups practice some form of community "outreach." One woman described the work of women in her group on behalf of animal protection, which they support as an affirmation of "mother nature" against the masculine "cowardly excuse for power called 'sport killing,' . . . the need in their pitiful lives to establish a sense of dominance." Some go further, claiming environmentalism and animal rights as issues for white racist activists since "it is not necessary to carry on a race if there is not a world to live in."[38] Such efforts, along with programs in self-education, first aid, and survival cooking, are described by a member as "projects that bring respect in the community so *they*'ll listen."[39]

Racist women understand that groups of women who seem innocuous can attract people into racist politics. They are fully aware that most people enter the racist movement through personal contacts with existing members, and they work to create the opportunities that make such recruitment possible. Bible study groups bring ordinary women into contact with hard-core racists. Animal rights turn into Aryan rights. One recruit told of attending a women's meeting billed as a Christian apocalyptic "preparation for end times"; she thought that "it would be boring—but it turned out to be excellent and exciting, with all the women who participated (and most did) taking part and exchanging ideas, really great." Although she expressed disappointment that "many things listed were not covered in depth due to time running down," the list of topics shows a strategic mixture of fundamentalist Christianity, self-sufficiency, and racism, with lessons on women in Scriptures, home birthing, healing with herbs, and homeschooling tucked between workshops on "how to use the system" and revelations about domestic spy satellites and secret inoculations with microscopic "transformers" meant to "track our people."[40] Perhaps the greatest threat posed by modern organized racism is seen not in the highly visible parades of middle-aged Klan members, who inevitably are far outnumbered by anti-Klan demonstrators, but in the mundane advertisements for toddler car seats and Aryan cookbooks that appear in white power newsletters and on Aryan electronic bulletin boards.

Operative Roles

The operative roles taken by women in organized racism range from routine clerical tasks to informal (and, very occasionally, formal) leadership and paramilitary activities.[41] Most racist groups allow women to take part in public activities, though such participation is less common in Christian Identity and some Klan groups.

Women are found as formal leaders in only a handful of groups, but they often exercise informal leadership. Recognizing women's importance as informal leaders challenges the common assumption that all racist leaders are men.[42] That erroneous impression is created by the extreme difficulty of gathering information about the racist movement: most scholars and journalists rely on the public statements of self-appointed racist spokesmen like David Duke. Moreover, the ostentatious organizational titles that racist men customarily bestow on each other—Grand Dragon, Imperial Wizard, Commander—misleadingly imply a hierarchical structure of authority. Though their titles suggest that they command the obedience of hundreds of followers, these men may in fact enjoy little more than token allegiance from a handful of marginally committed group members. Conversely, those who actually lead racist groups may have no titles.

If we focus on the practices of leadership rather than on self-enhancing claims or titles, the picture we see is different and more complex. "Leadership," in the sense of providing group cohesion, mediating conflict, developing political strategies, and nurturing collective identity, often is concentrated in the middle and less visible layers of racist organizations. These leaders, though not always women, are the right-wing equivalent of what the anthropologist Karen Brodkin Sacks terms "centerwomen": those who maintain and strengthen social groups.[43] Racist centerwomen command racist groups very differently than do male racist leaders. Men's leadership in racist groups typically is described as manipulative, distant from followers, and simultaneously contemptuous of racist group members and dependent on their adoration and respect for self-aggrandizement.[44] In contrast, women's informal racist leadership is more elusive, indirect, and personal. It may also be more effective and more dangerous. One woman noted that the male leaders "think of me as being all for people on their side. That's how they look at it, too. 'On our side.' (Laughs) No, no complexities involved, right. They think of me as one of them, but yet not one of them. I know they have a hard time accepting me the way I am." Another distinguished herself from male leaders by noting, "I don't go for titles or offices or anything. I don't care about them." And a third downplayed her influence in the organization, saying that she was interested only in "routing the sociopaths out of the movement."

One way of exploring such differences in racist leadership style is suggested by Dick Anthony and Thomas Robbins's distinction between "norm-rejecting" and "norm-affirming" religious groups.[45] Norm-rejecting groups, like male racist leaders, favor heroic uniqueness and individual enlightenment over conventional behavior. Norm-affirming groups, in contrast, are formed around strong beliefs and strict rules. Women racist leaders who operate in the fashion of norm-affirming groups may be able to nurture more sustained commitment to their groups, to have more success in recruiting new members, and to be less likely to alienate potential recruits. As one woman recounts of members of her group: "The girls look up to me. They're still going to dress their way, the way they do and I only suggest. I suggest you don't have your hair this way [she used her hand to demonstrate the very short hair of 'skinheads']. I suggest you grow your hair out. . . . If there's a little bit of hair you get along in the world much better." Another notes the problems faced by young recruits, which need to be addressed by older members such as herself: "[Her group]'s gonna have to work on these young people. And show exactly what's gonna happen, that you're all right."

Priscilla, a Klanswoman who declined to describe herself as a leader because she had no official title, but who nonetheless admitted that her work was vital to her group, similarly nurtured activism. She recounted her efforts to gently persuade recruits to attend public marches, an escalation of their engagement that entails greater personal danger and risk of exposure than do private rallies or meetings. While male leaders make harsh demands, insisting that recruits risk everything for the movement, Priscilla uses a subtler and more personal appeal. "I've been on rallies. I've been on marches," she informs me. "All they have to do is send a flyer and I will have everybody show up. That makes me feel good because they respect me that much. I don't tell them, 'Hey, you have to take your last dime and spend it on gas and starve to death to get there.' . . . I'm not like that. I'd say, 'Hey, it'd be great to have you.'"

Several women, in describing recruitment efforts, make it clear that they are practicing leadership indirectly and through social ties. One tells me, "I have a way of speaking in grocery stores, department stores. I approach people out of the blue, not as a [racist group] person. But if they look at something, I make a comment and that leads into something else. 'Cause they get into a conversation with me and then I try to explain some things. I don't bring up [her group] or nothing. No, I don't do that. But I try to educate them, I try to throw out little things that might make them think." Other women dismiss their male comrades' attempts to thrust racist literature and flyers into the hands of potential recruits as "ineffective."[46] One woman insists that her low-key approach is more productive, especially for recruiting women: "I'd say, 'Come over. We'll get together, we'll talk, we'll have some fun.' I mean, we have picnics where all the kids play together, all the women get together. We cook our meals, you know. We sit around, we talk about how the kids are progressing, what they want in their lifetime, in their lifestyle."

Women's informal leadership does not stop with recruitment. Racist women also play an important part in creating the social community of racism and in easing new recruits into that social world. A white supremacist tells of her efforts to guide young women in the practices of racist activism: "I've got girls that tell me, 'Lookit, I got a new tattoo,' and I'm, like, 'That's nothing to be proud of, that's stupid. It'll poison your blood and when the race war comes you can't give blood. . . . Don't go out and get tattoos and shave your head 'cause nobody's gonna listen to that.' To me I think they're a lot better if they get themselves an education, a steady job, a nice place to live, than think about having tattoos." Such instruction in daily life as a racial activist suggests a form of leadership quite different from that provided by the battle-worn male warrior glorified in racist literature. Women like this white supremacist mediate between the proclaimed goals of racist groups (for example, to foment a race war) and the actions that bolster such goals. When she instructs "her" girls to avoid tattoos and shaved heads and to pursue education and jobs, she is creating an organizational space in which complex personal identities can be configured as personal and collective identities of racist activism. Perhaps even more frightening, she is attempting to make possible something heretofore unknown: a long-term and intergenerational racist movement. In nudging her young charges to become more effective and dedicated racist activists, this middle-aged woman illustrates how women's practices of informal leadership can secure racist goals.

Women's operative roles in organized racism are not limited to private acts of leadership. At least some women participate fully in direct action. A Norwegian racist women's group, Valkyria, uses a paramilitary approach to organize against prostitution and pornography. Its members take part in strategy meetings with men and train with weapons.[47] Terrorist actions by women racists, though still uncommon in the United States, are on the rise.[48] Among the women I interviewed, about one-third reported that they had been arrested for violent acts in connection with racist activism, usually for assault; more than three-quarters claimed to have been in a physical fight with members of minority groups.[49] One woman, notorious for her public role at the helm of a major Nazi group, proudly described her physical prowess on behalf of white supremacy in a 1994 interview with *Mademoiselle*. As the "three-year reigning champion" of the hammer toss, she and her husband-to-be, the male champion, won the honor of "getting to light the ceremonial swastika"— a startling outcome for the daughter of wealthy parents who had earlier studied photography at the Art Institute in Chicago.[50]

Women's public activism can serve strategic goals for racist groups. When racists confront antiracist protestors, the participation of women can discourage retaliation. A journalist watching a Nazi "flag parade" in Idaho observed: "Three young women with babies in strollers salute the Nazis. Immediately, they are surrounded by screaming protesters. One young Nazi mother cradles a baby in one hand and uses the other to punch a young man repeatedly in the face until he is bloody. A young Nazi man who is with her stands back and lets her be the warrior. The strategy works: The man who has been beaten will not hit a woman."[51]

Women usually take operative roles that are less public. Some work to support racist prisoners. A number of racist publications carry letters purporting to be from the wives and families of men imprisoned for racist activities, decrying the conditions in which their menfolk are forced to live or lamenting their difficulties in visiting the prison. In a typical example, the wife of a man apparently imprisoned for racist terrorism writes:

Our life changed dramatically . . . when my husband was arrested, stood trial, and was convicted . . . we were expecting the birth of our son. . . . After our son's birth, I relocated to where we now live, and became a welfare recipient. What a colossal nightmare! [My husband] got moved . . . farther and farther away from us and deeper and deeper into the more violent penitentiaries. Our visits stopped as the costs of visiting were way out of sight. . . . [Then] people found out and some support began coming in. From that time on, two groups have sent regular support and best wishes, one group was you [Bounties Bestowing . . . Blessings Bequeathed] folks.[52]

. . . Most of women's—and men's—actions in racist groups are more mundane, although not inconsequential. The women I interviewed described hours spent photocopying literature, making flyers, distributing propaganda, spraying racist graffiti on buildings and highways, writing to current and potential racist activists, promoting and managing white power bands, stamping public library books with racist messages and phone line numbers, and tucking racist literature under windshield wipers and house welcome mats, in grocery bags, and in racks of restaurant menus. Others work the Internet, seeing it as a way for racist women of all ages and levels of experience to recruit others "without ever leaving home or taking away from their families."[53] These actions are largely ineffectual as means of recruiting new members to the racist movement, but they help spread a message of intimidation to the potential targets of racist groups.

In her study of women in the late-twentieth-century Italian underground, Luisa Passerini observes that "the discovery of a specific female identity—beyond the illusory mimicking of male models, in the organization and in the armed struggle—comes later than the fundamental decision to get involved."[54] Those in modern organized racism have no specific female identity as yet. Women's roles are in flux, neither submissive (as tradition demands of women) nor clearly activist (as racist propaganda suggests). But we should not see women in today's organized racism as simply mimicking male models. Their experiences in organized racism, no less than those of men, are highly gender-specific. Women enter racist groups because of contacts and issues that reflect their places as women in the larger society. And once inside organized racism, women find themselves pushed to follow several and sometimes conflicting paths: to shape the racial family, to bolster its social networks, and to assert themselves as leaders and activists. . . .

NOTES

1. "White Women Practice Unity," *Aryan Action Line*, no. 2 (winter 1992): I.
2. Untitled item in "Aryan Women's League" file, Anti-Defamation League of B'nai B'rith, New York.
3. The classic discussion of maternalism in politics is Sara Ruddick, *Maternal Thinking: Toward a Politics of Peace* (New York: Ballantine, 1989); see esp. 231. The essays in Alexis Jetter, Annelise Orleck, and Diana Taylor, eds., *The Politics of Motherhood: Activist Voices from Left to Right* (Hanover, N.H.: University Press of New England, 1997), broaden the treatment of maternalist political practices. See also Virginia Shapiro, *The Political Integration of Women: Roles, Socialization, and Politics* (Urbana: University of Illinois Press, 1984), 152, 182.
4. Feminist scholars have argued that a number of social movements organize women on the basis of a "female consciousness" grounded not in feminism but in the commonality of women's tasks. See Temma Kaplan, "Female Consciousness and Collective Action: The Case of Barcelona, 1910–1918," *Signs* 7 (1982):

545–66; see also Nancy F. Cott, "What's in a Name? The Limits of 'Social Feminism'; or, Expanding the Vocabulary of Women's History," *Journal of American History* 76 (1989): 809–29.

5. Robert Miles is quoted in "Bigotry or Brotherhood?" a special report by the *Spokane Spokesman Review–Spokesman Chronicle,* December 31, 1986.

6. Mabel Berezin, *Making the Fascist Self: The Political Culture of Interwar Italy* (Ithaca, N.Y.: Cornell University Press, 1997), 69.

7. Conflicting stances toward families and family life have also characterized extremist right-wing movements of the past, which at once sought to appropriate families and to reshape them. For example, the propaganda (though not the practice) of the 1920s Ku Klux Klan strongly emphasized the need to transform white Christian family life along racist lines, particularly by punishing philandering husbands. The modern racist movement shows little interest in such reshaping of personal or family life despite some pressure from racist activist women to do so.

8. NSDAP/AO, *The New Order,* September–October 1994, 2.

9. From testimony of Robert E. Miles, given in the 1988 Ft. Smith, Arkansas, trial of white supremacists for sedition; in "Extremist" file, Anti-Defamation League.

10. *Viking Viewpoint: Truth and Honor,* no. 16 (1993).

11. Skingirl quoted in Mark S. Hamm, *American Skinheads: The Criminology and Control of Hate Crimes* (Westport, Conn.: Praeger, 1994), 180.

12. Quoted in *New York Daily News,* July 27, 1993; clipping in Anti-Defamation League files.

13. Quoted in *New York Daily News,* July 27, 1993; clipping in Anti-Defamation League files.

14. "Klan Kid Korp," in *Prescript of the Order of the * of the **** (distributed by Knights of the Ku Klux Klan, ca. 1997), 15.

15. "Special Information for Homeschoolers" (distributed by Scriptures for America, ca. 1996).

16. *WAR* 8.2 (ca. 1989): 6.

17. *White Sisters* II (1992).

18. Kathleen M. Blee, "Family Patterns and the Politicization of Consumption Relations," *Sociological Spectrum* 5 (1985): 295–316; Dana Frank, *Purchasing Power: Consumer Organizing, Gender, and the Seattle Labor Movement, 1919–1929* (New York: Cambridge University Press, 1994).

19. For example, see "Kosher Racket Revealed: Secret Jewish Tax on Gentiles" (pamphlet distributed by an anonymous racist group, ca. 1991).

20. Advertisement for Debbie's Crafts in *Race and Reason* (ca. 1995); see also "Aryan Women's League: Crafts, Products, and Informational Services" (flyer distributed by the Aryan Women's League, ca. 1994).

21. See the "Aryan Women's League" file, clippings ca. 1993, Anti-Defamation League.

22. *Valkyrie Voice,* no. 2 (ca. 1997).

23. On the importance of social ties in organizing and maintaining social movements, see, for example, Donatella della Porta, *Social Movements, Political Violence, and the State: A Comparative Analysis of Italy and Germany* (Cambridge: Cambridge University Press, 1995); Nigel Fielding, *The National Front* (London: Routledge and Kegan Paul, 1981); Martha Crenshaw, "Theories of Terrorism: Instrumental and Organizational Approaches," in *Inside Terrorist Organizations,* ed. David C. Rapoport (New York: Columbia University Press, 1988), 13–31; Mary G. Harris, *Cholas: Latino Girls and Gangs* (New York: AMS Press, 1988); Suzanne Staggenborg, "Social Movement Communities and Cycles of Protest: The Emergence and Maintenance of a Local Women's Movement," *Social Problems* 45 (1998): 180–204; Mark Chesler and Richard Schmuch, "Participant Observation in a Super-Patriot Discussion Group," *Journal of Social Issues* 19 (1963): 18–30; Elizabeth T. Buhmann, "Rethinking the Problem of Girls in Gangs," unpublished paper, Office of the Attorney General of the State of Texas (Austin, 1992); Anne Campbell, "Self-Definition by Rejection: The Case of Gang Girls," *Social Problems* 34 (1987): 451–66; Angela McRobbie and Jenny Garber, "Girls and Subcultures," in *Resistance through Rituals: Youth Subcultures in Post-war Britain,* ed. Stuart Hall and Tony Jefferson (New York: Holmes and Meier, 1976), 208–22; and Carl S. Taylor, *Dangerous Society* (East Lansing: Michigan State University Press, 1990).

24. Carol Mueller, "Conflict Networks and the Origins of Women's Liberation," in Laraña, Johnston, and Gusfield, *New Social Movements: From Ideology to Identity,* 237.

25. See Hank Johnston, Enrique Laraña, and Joseph R. Gusfield, "Identities, Grievances, and New Social Movements," in Laraña, Johnston, and Gusfield, *New Social Movements,* 24,

and Crenshaw, "Theories of Terrorism." See also Caroline Kelly and Sara Breinlinge, *The Social Psychology of Collective Action: Identity, Injustice, and Gender* (London: Taylor and Francis, 1996), 80, 134.

26. "Preaching a Gospel of Hate," *Chicago Tribune,* May 23, 1985.

27. "Report on the Aryan Nations Youth Conference," *Aryan Research Fellowship Newsletter,* June–August 1990, 8–12.

28. Self-sufficiency is not a new idea within organized racism. The Aryan Knights of the Ku Klux Klan of Pennsylvania in the early 1970s claimed to offer its members benefits that ranged from "places to stay as you travel" to "mechanics, blood banks, and . . . AAA benefits." Bill Sickles, letter of April 8, 1972, in "Aryan Knights, Export PA" file, Special Collections, Howard-Tilton Memorial Library, Tulane University.

29. Aryan Women flyer, ca. 1992.

30. Floyd Cochran, "Sisterhood of Hate" (pamphlet, privately published, 1993); posted at (www.evnetwork.org/sister.html) (accessed January 2001).

31. See Les Back, Michael Keith, and John Solomos, "Racism on the Internet: Mapping Neo-Fascist Subcultures in Cyberspace," in Kaplan and Bjørgo, *Nation and Race,* 73–101.

32. "Report on the Aryan Nations Youth Conference."

33. Amy Benfer, "Salon Mothers Who Think: Nazi Family Values," *Salon.com,* July 15, 1999 (www.salon.com/mwt/hot/1999/07/15/aryan_compound/index.html) (accessed January 2001).

34. "Report on the Aryan Nations Youth Conference."

35. "Aryan Update" phone line, May 25, 1993.

36. Belinda Robnett, *How Long? How Long? African-American Women in the Struggle for Civil Rights* (New York: Oxford University Press, 1997), 17–32. On ties between members of organized social movements and those in their larger environment, see Clarence Y. H. Lo, "Communities of Challengers in Social Movement Theory," in *Frontiers in Social Movement Theory,* ed. Aldon D. Morris and Carol McClurg Mueller (New Haven: Yale University Press, 1992), 229.

37. *NSV [National Socialist Vanguard] Report* 5.2 (April/June 1987).

38. White Aryan Resistance, hate line transcription, October 10, 1989; see also "Earth First," *WAR* 8.2 (1989): 8.

39. "Earth First," *WAR* 8.2 (1989): 8.

40. "Report on the Aryan Nations Youth Conference."

41. See June Preston, "Women Emerging as White Supremacist Leaders," Reuters News Service article, September 12, 1999.

42. For example, Jessie Daniels overlooks the informal leadership of women when she asserts that "white women are primarily valuable to the movement for two qualities: their reproductive abilities and sexual attractiveness"; see *White Lies: Race, Class, Gender, and Sexuality in White Supremacist Discourse* (New York: Routledge, 1997), 57.

43. Karen Brodkin Sacks, "What's a Life Story Got to Do with It?" in *Interpreting Women's Lives: Feminist Theory and Personal Narrative,* ed. Personal Narratives Group (Bloomington: Indiana University Press, 1989), 85–95. See also Susan D. Rose, "Women Warriors: The Negotiation of Gender in a Charismatic Community," *Sociological Analysis* 48 (1987): 245–58. On the development of collective identity, see Johnston, Laraña, and Gusfield, "Identities," and Hank Johnston and Bert Klandermans, "The Cultural Analysis of Social Movements," in *Social Movements and Culture,* ed. Hank Johnston and Bert Klandermans (Minneapolis: University of Minnesota Press, 1995), 3–24. On mediation as leadership, see Luisa Passerini, *Fascism in Popular Memory: The Cultural Experience of the Turin Working Class,* trans. Robert Lumley and Jude Bloomfield (Cambridge: Cambridge University Press, 1987), 139.

44. For example, see Ezekiel, *Racist Mind,* 61–148.

45. Dick Anthony and Thomas Robbins, "Religious Totalism, Violence, and Exemplary Dualism: Beyond the Extrinsic Model," in *Millennialism and Violence,* ed. Michael Barkun (London: Frank Cass, 1996), 10–50.

46. See *The Record: North Jersey's Intelligence Report,* August 26, 1993, and "Loveland Man Heads Nazi Group," *Greeley Tribune,* February 15, 1993; both clippings in the collection of the Anti-Defamation League.

47. Katrine Fangen, "Living Out Our Ethnic Instincts: Ideological Beliefs among Right-Wing Activists in Norway," in Kaplan and Bjørgo, *Nation and Race,* 202–30.

48. See "Cookbooks and Combat Boots," *Klanwatch Intelligence Report* 56 (1991). There is little literature on women as terrorists. Two important studies are Richard G. Braungart

and Margaret M. Braungart, "From Protest to Terrorism: The Case of SDS and the Weathermen," in della Porta, *Social Movements and Violence,* 45–78, and Gilda Zwerman, "Mothering on the Lam: Politics, Gender Fantasies, and Maternal Thinking in Women Associated with Armed, Clandestine Organizations in the United States," *Feminist Review,* no. 47 (summer 1994): 33–56. A more superficial account is Daniel E. Georges-Abeyie, "Women as Terrorists," in *Perspectives on Terrorism,* ed. Lawrence Zelic Freeman and Yonah Alexander (Wilmington, Del.: Scholarly Resources, 1983), 71–84.

49. Despite such violent activities, the stereotype of racist women as merely the sexual chattel of men persists. In their introduction to *Racist Violence in Europe,* the collection of essays they edited, Tore Bjørgo and Rob White insist that "female activists in racist and other right-wing groups tend to be assigned to non-fighting and subordinate roles" (11). Women in gangs are similarly either ignored or sexualized in research and journalism, though feminist studies find that gang girls, while still quite dependent on boys, have been steadily gaining independence. See Karen A. Joe and Meda Chesney-Lind, " 'Just Every Mother's Angel': An Analysis of Gender and Ethnic Variations in Youth Gang Membership," *Gender and Society* 9 (1995): 412, and Meda Chesney-Lind, Randall G. Shelden, and Karen A. Joe, "Girls, Delinquency, and Gang Membership," in *Gangs in America,* ed. C. Ronald Huff, 2nd ed. (Thousand Oaks, Calif.: Sage, 1996), 185–204.

50. Farai Chideya, "Women Who Love to Hate," *Mademoiselle,* August 1994, 134–37, 186.
51. Benfer, "Nazi Family Values."
52. "Bounties Bestowing . . . Blessings Bequeathed" (ca. 1996), n.p.; see also "The Jubilee's 'Captive Christian Penfriends Correspondence List,' " December 1994, n.p.
53. Lisa Turner of Church of the Creator, cited in *Poisoning the Web: Hatred Online* (New York: Anti-Defamation League, 1999), 48.
54. Luisa Passerini, "Lacerations in the Memory: Women in the Italian Underground Organizations," in della Porta, *Social Movements and Violence,* 193.

QUESTIONS FOR DISCUSSION

1. How are women's traditional roles key to the development of an intergenerational racist movement?
2. Why does Blee see informal "centerwoman" leadership as extremely dangerous?
3. How is being racist a learned behavior?
4. Do you feel confident that you could spot a member of an organized racist movement? What does your answer suggest in terms of developing an effective response to this social movement?

20

BEYOND BLACK AND WHITE
Ethnoviolence Between Oppressed Groups

BARBARA PERRY

Abstract

It is ironic that at the same time that policy makers, scholars and commentators point to the increasing diversity of the United States, they stubbornly persist in collapsing racial and cultural relations into a black-white binary. If we are to make sense of the current state of racial and cultural conflict, it is imperative that we broaden our understanding to recognize the United States for what it is: a multicultural, multiracial and multiethnic community, characterized by multiple and cross-cutting coalitions and cleavages. It is particularly important to acknowledge this in our conversations about hate crime, where minority on minority violence is not unheard of. Two recent conflicts highlight this often overlooked reality: the Crown Heights, NY violence between blacks and Jews in 1991; and the black-Asian-Hispanic conflicts which exploded in the Los Angeles riots of 1992. While obviously signs of the long-standing tensions among and between these similarly marginalized groups, these incidents represent efforts to negotiate identity and place in the United States. These events—and others like them—present the actors with opportunities to do difference through violence.

This paper explores the phenomenon of intercultural violence among and between oppressed groups. This task is made difficult by the lack of literature in this area. Thus what follows is a preliminary analysis, in which I have drawn from the fields of anthropology (e.g., Herdt, 1997; Almaguer, 1995), social work (e.g., Greene), and cultural studies (e.g., West, 1993, 1994; Hooks, 1992, 1994, 1995). Specifically, I argue that minority on minority hate crime can be understood as a resource for 'doing difference'. However, this bias-motivated violence is played out within the broader context of white, male, heterosexual supremacy. Consequently, violence between oppressed groups is an attempt to sustain identity, and to attain some semblance of dominance on the part of groups who may otherwise be marginalized. As a test of my proposition, I will examine . . . illustrative sets of relationships: African American–Asian American; Jewish–African American. . . .

Doing Difference, Doing Hate Crime

Race, gender, sexuality, and all those dimensions of difference which shape our social world, represent what West & Fenstermaker (1987, 1993) refer to as 'ongoing accomplishments' (see also Messerschmidt, 1993, 1997). Difference and identity are created through conscious, reflective pursuit and must be established and re-established under varied conditions. In other words, identity-construction is an activity concerned with "managing situated conduct" (West & Zimmerman, 1987: 127), according to socially normative expectations of what constitutes the 'essence' of one's race or gender, for example.

The construction of identity is an interactional accomplishment by which actors perform their 'manliness' or 'womanliness', their 'whiteness' or 'blackness' or 'Asianness'. They do so with an eye to how their behavior will be interpreted or evaluated by others. Central to this conceptualization is the notion of 'accountability'. At all times, in all situations, actors are concerned with whether their behavior *will be seen to be* in accordance with approved standards for their assigned identity. Consequently,

> To the extent that members of society know their actions are accountable, they will design their actions in relation to how they might be seen and described by others (West & Fenstermaker, 1987: 25).

Since this enactment is situated within existing relations of power, the conduct will generally repeat and thus support those relations (Winant, 1997, 1998). Conventional culture is consumed with ensuring our awareness of and commitment to traditional notions of gender, sexuality, race, and so on. Movies, advertising, the legal order, even the organization of department stores take for granted the *essential* differences between groups noted earlier. It is in this context that we are continually expected to 'account' for our gendered behavior, for example.

Within the essentialist understanding of identities, there is very little space for ambiguity, or crossing the boundaries between categories of difference. Speaking of gender, specifically, West & Zimmerman (1987: 136) contend that

> A person engaged in virtually any activity may be held accountable for performance of that activity as a *woman* or a *man,* and their incumbency in one or the other sex category can be used to legitimate or discredit their other activities.

In other words, accountability involves the assessment of behavior as either conforming or deviating from culturally normative standards. Whenever we 'do difference'—which is a recurring effort—we leave ourselves open to reward or censure. So it is that we are discouraged from the "attempt to cross the line, to transgress, desert or quit" (Bourdieu, cited in Fine, 1997: 58).

To the extent that individuals or groups 'perform' in a way that corresponds to the 'mythical norm' or in ways that correspond to normative conceptions of one's identity construct, they are held to be doing difference appropriately (Messerschmidt, 1997). In so doing, they uphold the boundaries that separate them from the Other, and ultimately the social relations of power. Conversely, when individuals or groups cross those boundaries, when they fail to perform their identity in normative ways, they are held to be doing difference inappropriately, and thereby leave themselves open to censure. . . .

. . . It is in this context that hate crime emerges as a resource for doing difference, and punishing those who do difference inappropriately.

To summarize: when we do difference, when we engage in the process of identity formation, we do so within the confines of structural and institutional norms. In so doing—to the extent that we conform to normative conceptions of identity—we reinforce the structural order. However, not everyone always performs 'appropriately'. Frequently, we construct our gender, or race, or sexuality in ways that in fact challenge or threaten socio-cultural arrangements. We step out of line, cross sacred boundaries, or forget our 'place'. It is in such a context that hate crime often emerges as a means of responding to the threats. The tensions between actors may culminate in violent efforts to reassert the dominance of one, and realign the relative positions of both.

Moreover, it is important to keep in mind that identity is shaped relationally.

Both the perpetrator and the victim of hate are continually engaged in the process of constructing their identities:

> . . . it is not only the racist or sexist who constructs difference, but the victim of each or both who seeks to create difference as well. At times, the 'victim' has done so in response to the racism and/or sexism in the society in order to survive, but at other times movements made up of these 'victims' have sought to redefine difference as part of a struggle for power and personhood (Rothenberg, 1992; 48).

Such alternative constructions of difference challenge the carefully molded perceptions of about how the world should be, and what each person's or each group's place is in that world. When confronted with such novelties, one means by which to 'put things right' is through violence. Consequently, hate crime provides a context in which the perpetrator can reassert his/her identity, and at the same time, punish the victim(s) for the individual or collective performance for his/her identity. In other words, hate-motivated violence is used to sustain or create the privilege of one group, and to police the boundaries between groups by reminding the Other of his/her 'place'. Perpetrators thus recreate their own masculinity, or blackness, while punishing the victims for their deviant identity performance.

Hate crime, then, is a forceful illustration of what it is to engage in situated conduct. The interactions between groups provide a context in which both compete for the privilege to define difference in ways that either perpetuate or reconfigure hierarchies of social power. Simultaneous and oppositional efforts to do difference set up tensions in which the act of victimization co-constructs the victim and perpetrator. This confrontation is informed by the broader cultural and political arrangements which "allocate rights, privilege and prestige according to biological or social characteristics" (Sheffield, 1995: 438). Perpetrators attempt to reaffirm their collective identity, their access to resources and privilege, while at the same time limiting the opportunities of the victims to express their own needs. The performance of hate violence, then, confirms the 'natural' relations of difference.

Can We All Get Along?

The same diversity that threatens the white majority—and thus underlies hate crime—similarly causes ruptures and discomfort among and between this nation's oppressed groups. These ruptures ultimately revolve around identity and recognition. Yet such struggles for recognition take place on different terms viz. oppressed groups, as opposed to those involving white-minority relations. The white majority excludes or marginalizes subordinate groups. However, within the politics of interethnic conflicts, there emerges an opportunity to acquire or sustain recognition. . . .

One way to overcome, indeed overturn, this negation is to extrapolate the 'rules of the game' to the context of subordinate ethnic conflict, to mark another as 'different, marked, inferior'. Only in this way can the subordinate establish some semblance of dominance, demanding of other oppressed groups that which is not forthcoming from the hegemonic majority. Punished, repressed and reprimanded for asserting their ethnic identity within view of the majority culture, members of subordinate groups can opt to engage in hate crime as an alternative resource for constructing their identities.

Consequently, minority on minority violence can be viewed within the framework of 'doing difference' (West & Zimmerman, 1987; West & Fenstermaker, 1995; Messerschmidt, 1993) since it too revolves around hierarchical conflict. Interethnic violence among and between subordinate groups "becomes a 'field of possibilities' for transcending class and race discrimination," i.e. a critical resource for doing race, in particular (Messerschmidt, 1993: 103). But it is important to interpret such violence within the master narrative of white, heterosexual, masculine hegemony. That is, minority on minority hate crime is not only about Korean–African American conflict, or African American–Jewish conflict. Rather, it is about how these tensions play out in the context of relations of racial/ethnic/gender subordination. As Ikemoto (1995: 307) contends, "If you experience racism as one marginalized by it, then you may use racism to explain your relationship with other groups and their members." Even in their relationships with one another, members of subordinate groups are "dependent on the will and leftovers of a dominant group" (Ikemoto, 1995: 308). Ultimately, hegemonic constructions of race or gender identity infuse the experiences and interactions of subordinate groups as well.

One might expect the common experiences and marginality of oppressed groups to provide the basis for solidarity rather than division. It is not unreasonable to suppose that they might recognize and exploit their common hardships. Gay men and lesbians share with recent immigrants and native-born racial minorities discrimination, harassment, and violent victimization. All are subject to ongoing daily patterns of (mis)treatment which seek to maintain their inferior status.

In practice, what emerges is not always a shared commitment to racial or gender justice, but instead shared antagonisms and hostilities directed toward one another. Their rage at their continued disempowerment is misdirected downwards or sideways toward those who are similarly victimized, rather than upwards toward those who seek to exploit the cleavages. The 1992 Los Angeles riots were a clear illustration of this tendency, representing as they did

> . . . a multi-racial, trans-class, and largely male display of justified social rage. For all its ugly xenophobic resentment, its air of adolescent carnival, and its downright barbaric behavior, it signified the sense of powerlessness in American society (West, 1993: 255).

Ironically, the common 'powerlessness' becomes the basis for conflict rather than community. Even in Los Angeles, the combatants generally attacked one another, rather than posing any direct threat to their white oppressors.

Evidence of these divisions is apparent in opinion polls which illustrate the negative perceptions which oppressed groups hold of one another (Oliver & Johnson, 1984). There are chilling parallels between dominant and subordinate groups' readings of other minority groups. In fact, hegemonic systems of meaning construction are reproduced in the context of interethnic relations. Oliver & Johnson (1984) summarize research findings of interethnic antagonisms manifest in perceptions of power accruing to other minority groups, of unfair employment competition, and negative stereotyping. Similarly, Holmes (1994: B8) reports the findings of a national poll commissioned by the National Conference of Christians and Jews. The results suggest strongly that blacks, Asians and Hispanics generally hold even more negative views of one another than do whites. Forty-six percent of Hispanics and 42% of blacks saw Asians as "unscrupulous, crafty and devious in business." Sixty-eight percent of Asians and 49% of blacks agreed that Hispanics "tend to have bigger families than they are able to support." Thirty-one percent of Asians and 28%

of Hispanics believed that blacks "want to live on welfare."

These findings are indicative of the hostilities between groups. Yet they are also indicative of the extent to which dominant world views permeate all members of society. They reinforce the assertion that the society of the United States is grounded in constantly shifting hierarchies of oppression. In other words, they 'revealed the power of racist rhetoric between politically, economically, and culturally disadvantaged groups' (Chun, 1996: 3). Perhaps we should not have expected solidarity after all. Subordinate groups are not immune to the power of hegemonic ideologies. They too are a crucial part of the audience, having listened to, observed and lived within the structures of inequality. . . .

Even immigrants arrive here with pre-packaged ideas of how race and gender operate in the United States, having been 'informed' by American media outlets world-wide. This is especially important in understanding the relationship between African Americans and other minority groups. White supremacy is re-inscribed in the hostility with which other people of color greet blacks in this country:

> In race talk, the move into mainstream America always means buying into the notion of American blacks as the real aliens. Whatever the ethnicity or nationality of the immigrant, his nemesis is understood to be African American . . . Often people of color . . . hold black people responsible for the hostility they encounter from whites. It is as though they see blacks as acting in a manner that makes things hard for everybody else (hooks, 1995: 198–199).

This is what distinguishes minority relations from majority-minority relations: the sense that all Others are in competition for the favors of the white majority; they are in

a struggle to assign blame for their relative positions of inferiority. The struggle for economic, political and cultural empowerment becomes a struggle to disempower 'the competition', through violence if necessary.

What follows is an exploratory attempt to make sense of intercultural violence between and among subordinate groups. I have chosen to explore two illustrative sets of relationships in order to focus my discussion. The group and inter-group dynamics explored here cross lines of race, ethnicity, class, gender and sexuality. The salience of each of these components differs, of course, from situation to situation, and from group to group. The cases I have chosen provide insight into very different patterns and relationships which nonetheless share common themes. Consequently, I examine hate-motivated violence among and between: African Americans and Asians; and Jews and African Americans. . . .

African American–Asian Conflict

The black and Hispanic victimization of Korean shop-owners in the aftermath of the Rodney King verdict illustrates the potential for violence when subordinate groups—especially those with a long history in the United States—are threatened by what is perceived as the empowerment of another oppressed group. Nowhere is the racial animus between blacks and Asians more apparent than in the low-income, predominantly black communities where so many Koreans have established 'mom-and-pop' businesses. As newcomers to the United States, Korean employment opportunities are often blocked by language, educational and, of course, racial barriers. They turn instead to self- and family-employment in the retail trade. In cities like New York, Los Angeles and Atlanta, upwards of 30% of Koreans are small business owners. In this role, they assume the role of commercial 'middle-men' between corporations reluctant to locate in the inner city, and their low-income, non-white clientele. The entrepreneurial stance adopted by Koreans is not welcomed by the African Americans inhabiting these communities. Quite the contrary: from the perspective of African Americans, Koreans are 'foreign' interlopers who have, first of all, forced out black business owners, and secondly, engaged in exploitive practices:

> In the space of a few years, the Korean newcomers have come to own most of the grocery shops, the shops selling wine and spirits, and the delicatessens in the predominantly black areas where they have settled and gone into business. In the process, they have become the target of angry protests and even violence by the black residents (Jo, 1992: 398).

In this light, Koreans are seen to have "jumped the queue" in the struggle for political and economic opportunities tantamount to success. This makes them vulnerable to the opprobrium and resentment of the oppressed communities they serve. This is clear in the response of one black youth asked in a television interview to explain the looting: "Because we hate 'em. Everybody hates them" (Frontline, April 27, 1993).

This racial animosity springs from a number of sources within the context of both African American and Asian American's efforts to construct their racial identities. Like all other members of United States society, each of these groups perceives the other through the lens of cultural mythologies. Asians see African Americans as criminals, as welfare cheats, as threats to their economic and physical well-being. African Americans see Asians as 'perpetual foreigners', as unsavory business people. These tendencies are exacerbated by ongoing media coverage which highlights the ten-

sions rather than efforts at reconciliation. This was the case in the context of the 1990 boycott of Korean businesses in Flatbush, N.Y., where the media coverage was deemed to be "inflammatory and polarizing" and "overly simplistic and in some cases blatantly racist" (U.S. Commission on Civil Rights, 1992: 37). And it was also the case in the treatment of the Los Angeles riots in 1992, in which the mainstream media contributed to the animosity by

> . . . spotlighting tensions between African Americans and Koreans above all efforts to work together . . . (and) by exploiting racist stereotypes of Koreans as unfathomable aliens, this time wielding guns on rooftops and allegedly firing wildly into crowds (Kim, 1993: 221).

Such divisive mechanisms encourage blacks and Asians to adopt an oppositional stance relative to one another—they are portrayed as inevitable enemies rather than allies. And unfortunately, they all too often accept these externalized interpretations of their relationship, as evidenced by their long-term animosities. Jo (1992) catalogs the charges and countercharges levied by blacks and Asians as each group attempts to construct itself as the wronged party. Korean shop-owners in particular are said to be rude, exploitive, unwilling to hire blacks, and unfairly advantaged by government programs. African Americans are said to be unwilling to co-operate or understand, unreliable workers, criminal threats and unfairly advantaged by government programs (see also McClain & Stewart, 1995).

Black hostility toward Asian shop-owners has apparently inspired anti-Asian violence, as a means of recouping their lost prominence in the community. A seven-block black neighborhood in Washington, D.C. has seen nine fire-bombings of Korean businesses since 1984. In Los Angeles, more than 20 Korean shop-owners have been killed in black communities since 1990. During the Los Angeles riots, 300 Chinese businesses were looted and burned; in all, 40% of the businesses lost were Asian owned (Cho, 1993). Moreover, anti-Asian violence and harassment are endemic in these communities (U.S. Commission on Civil Rights, 1992).

In large measure, black perpetrators of anti-Asian hate crime are reacting to the particular way in which Asian Americans construct their racial identity in the context of a white supremacist culture. Asians' assigned roles as 'middle-men' are taken as a sign of their 'preferred status' in United States society. They are held accountable—and found guilty—as illegitimate interlopers, who entered 'the game' very late, yet nonetheless managed to vault over the heads of native-born African Americans. The 'appropriate' place of Asian immigrants—according to native-born African Americans—is at the end of the queue. In contrast, they are perceived to have relatively little problem in assimilating into the mainstream relative to the historical experiences of blacks. In spite of the fact that they are racially and ethnically 'not white', Asians are *seen to be* readily accepted by the white community. A community worker interviewed by Jo (1992: 405) declaimed that "Koreans think that they are white!"

The dual image of Asians as middlemen and as the model minority further divides them from African Americans. Freer (1994: 191) attributes the hostility of blacks toward Asians to the perception that Asian Americans collectively attain the American dream at the expense of black success. Asians' efforts to assimilate and advance are taken as arrogance that must be met with hostility, even violence. Perhaps even more than the dominant white culture, African American inner city poor are threatened by the apparent success of Asian Americans. In addition to the economic competition represented by the latter is the competition for place and status relative to the white power structure. Asian Americans are exploitable as a wedge against native-born blacks who are told to look to Asians as an indication that the American dream is open to all, *if only you are willing to work for it.* Korean shopowners, Chinese entrepreneurs, and Japanese executives are held up as models of the potential for assimilation and advancement—with the implied message that African Americans just don't work hard enough. To the extent that Asian Americans are seen to enact this role, they are met with the hostility of blacks who do not fare well in the implied comparison. Consequently, Asians become caught between the racism of whites and the racialized resentment of blacks:

> The model minority myth plays a key role in establishing a racial hierarchy which denies the oppression of Asian Americans while simultaneously legitimizing the oppression of other racial minorities and poor whites (Chang, 1995: 329).

Violence is a readily available outlet for this misdirected hostility. It is a means of empowerment for blacks who see themselves losing ground relative to newly arrived immigrants—losing ground, that is, in economic, political and cultural terms. In light of the impoverishment and structural unemployment of so many black youths, in particular, alternative mechanisms for empowerment are rare. Consequently, violence directed towards Asian Americans is a simultaneous effort to reclaim some of this loss in status, while seeking to remind Asians of their appropriate place in the racialized pecking order.

Jews and African Americans

Joshua Price poignantly expresses one source of inter-group hostility among oppressed groups when he states that "Although Jewish, I understand myself as an almost-insider to Anglo culture in the United States" (cited in Lugones & Price, 1995: 113). He is not alone in seeing himself and American Jews as 'almost insiders', quite like Asians. And this provokes anger toward what many perceive as a 'privileged minority'. Price further admits to complicity in white dominance, in exchange for inclusion in their ranks. He too is asked—and often agrees—"to maintain solidarity and loyalty—often in order to break, exclude, violate, exploit and deny those people who are outside the inner circle" (Lugones & Price, 1995: 113). Much like African Americans throughout their history in the United States, Jews experience a 'double consciousness' described by Du Bois as the simultaneous construction of identity within the context of both dominant and subordinate cultures. Understandably, this causes insecurity and discomfort all around. Cornel West (1994: 111) also speaks to this uneasy positioning of Jews relative to subordinate blacks and dominant whites when he observes that

> The images of black activists yelling "Where's Hitler when we need him?" and "Heil Hitler," juxtaposed with those of David Duke celebrating Hitler's birthday seem to feed a single line of intolerance burning on both ends of the American candle, that threatens to consume us all.

More so even than Asians, American Jews occupy a paradoxical position in the racialized hierarchy of power and place. And, more so than Asians, they are seen as co-conspirators in the plot to maintain the subordination of blacks. Consequently, they are held accountable by black Americans to a construction of racial identity that is seen as oppositional and threatening. To an alarming extent in some quarters, Jews are held to be complicit in the formation and maintenance of a racialized hierarchy which subor-

dinates blacks. Anti-Semitic violence then becomes a mechanism for transcending racial domination, and an important resource for constructing relational identities.

This uneasy relationship between blacks and Jews has a lengthy history, punctuated by periods of conciliation. In many ways, black anti-Semitism has paralleled that of the white Christian majority. Nineteenth-century religious teachings portrayed Jews as protagonists, as in black catechisms, for example:

Q. Who killed Jesus?
A. The wicked Jews.
Q. The wicked Jews grew angry with our Savior, and what did they do to Him?
A. They crucified Him.

Similar sentiments are expressed in many black spirituals of the time, which make such claims as "Virgin Mary had one son, The cruel Jews had him hung" (Dinnerstein, 1994: 198). As often as not, prejudices grounded in religious teachings were accompanied by secular stereotypes which further vilified the 'wicked Jews' as greedy, insatiable and conniving in their quest for wealth. A turn-of-the-century article in *Colored America* insisted that Jews were

> . . . parasitical and predatory rather than conservatory and constructive in tendencies—preying upon and devouring the substance of others (cited in Dinnerstein, 1994: 199).

Little has changed in this century. Black Americans still share with white Americans the perception of Jews as Christ killers, predators and greedy financiers:

> This is part of the way racism works—it is easier to scapegoat Jews . . . than to target larger structures of white supremacy. . . . It is a distortion of reality to act as though any form of black anti-Semitism, however virulent, exists in isolation from the anti-Semitism that is

learned whenever anyone absorbs without question the values of mainstream white culture (hooks, 1995: 210).

Yet the relationship between blacks and Jews in the United States retains its own specificity in light of the relative economic and political positions of the two groups. On the one hand, both are 'not white' and therefore outsiders. But Jews are both 'not white' and 'white', or at least 'almost white'. By virtue of the latter, they are also insiders, sharing the white skin privilege—something African Americans can never accomplish.

In this vein, West (1993) identifies the predominant cultural and structural dynamics which condition relations between blacks and Jews, and which set the stage for interethnic violence. First, he contends, black anti-Semitism reflects black anti-whitism. Jewish complicity in the politics and economics of racism in the United States is seen to reinforce the subordination of the nation's black community. There is a sense among some blacks that Jews could only become 'white' in America because of the existence of blacks. Thus, Jewish-black relationships reproduce broader white-black relationships of power which assume a paternalistic, often exploitive face, in that they

> . . . have almost always been as philanthropist to recipient, shopkeeper to customer, landlord to tenant, employer to employee, teacher to student, welfare worker to client, and so forth (Dinnerstein, 1994: 224).

The perceived role of Jews in the continued oppression of black America is taken as a sign of betrayal between 'natural allies'. West (1994) holds that blacks have heightened expectations of Jews in light of the similarity of their historical experiences of oppression, and earlier coalitions around civil rights. Blacks and Jews alike have experienced (at different times and places) enslavement, ghettoization, subjugation, diaspora and violence. In light of these similarities, then, black Americans are embittered by the perception that their allies have become their enemies. As evidence of this betrayal, they point to Jewish resistance to affirmative action and state social security provisions, for example. In a dialogic paper, Pogrebin & Hutchinson (1994: 219) declare:

> Now we often march in opposite directions or face each other across an abyss. Now our two communities clash regularly over issues of power, priorities, competitive oppression and conflicting self-interest.

This sense of betrayal is enhanced by the corresponding fear that Jews, like Asians, like Hispanics, like all other subordinate groups, have vaulted past African Americans in economic and political strength. The result is a case of "underdog resentment and envy directed at another underdog who has 'made it' in American society" (West, 1994: 151). Jewish appeals to the aforementioned similarity of oppression, then, ring hollow in the ears of African Americans who have been surpassed in power, left behind by Jewish success. Moreover, whatever measure of success achieved by Jews is seen as a further evidence of Jews as co-conspirators in white racism. It is success won, not through effort and initiative, but by white nepotism.

While the social and economic malaise of black Americans provides the background for black anti-Semitism, the Nation of Islam in recent years has provided its public forum. The rhetoric of Islam—as preached by such leaders as Farrakhan and Muhammad, for example—provides a menu of ideologies which co-construct blacks as the chosen people and Jews as the worst of all 'white Devils'. Just as white supremacist groups condition and encourage hate motivated sentiment and activity, so too does the anti-Semitism of Farrakhan and Muhammad. Jews are to be blamed for alcohol and drug abuse in black communities, for negative stereotypes of blacks in entertainment media, for black poverty. *The Secret Relationship Between Blacks and Jews* provides much of the fodder for this virulence, holding Jews accountable for slavery and black genocide in general. Muhammad's and Farrakhan's frequent references to 'Jew York City', 'Jewnited Nations' and 'Columbia Jewniversity' highlight the perception of the breadth of Jewish control and manipulation. In a recent interview, Farrakhan exploits the image of Jews as usurious leeches:

> In the '20s, '30s and '40s, up into the '50s, the Jews were the primary merchants in the black community. Wherever we were, there they were. What was their role? We bought food from them; we bought clothing from them; we bought furniture from them; we rented from them . . . Sucking the lifeblood from our own community (Farrakhan, 1996: 53).

In the context of the structural and cultural relationship between blacks and Jews, interethnic violence persists as a resource for the establishment and reestablishment of racial and ethnic identity. This is especially important for poor African American youth who lack access to alternative means by which to compete with Jews. Resentment toward Jewish progress is manifest in bias-motivated harassment and victimization which enhances that status of the perpetrator(s), while seeking to disempower the victim(s). It attests to the group alliance of the perpetrators, and especially to their 'insider' status. Conversely, it reconstructs the Jewish victims as perpetual 'outsiders'. This is a curious—but important—inversion of the groups' relative positionality in the broader culture, where blacks are always the out-

siders, while Jews are seen to travel the boundaries between insider and outsider at will. This is at the heart of what Steele (1994: 180) refers to as the 'unseen problem' between blacks and Jews: the "presumption by the larger society that we make up a brotherhood of outsiders . . . and we fight against each other to prove it wrong, to show that we have no such brotherhood."

These dynamics were readily apparent in the violence that followed the death of Gavin Cato in Crown Heights, N.Y. The long-simmering antagonism toward the neighborhood's Hasidic Jews boiled over into a week of violence, which included the stabbing death of Yankel Rosenbaum. Here, too, the black community espied evidence of preferential treatment and white racism, as when Hasidim were accompanied by police escorts, or allowed to organize street patrols which harassed black community members. In response, spurred by Cato's death, blacks sought to preserve both the geographical and racialized boundaries between themselves and the 'Other' by violence, harassment and vandalism accompanied by exclusionary messages that included "Heil Hitler" and "Get the Jews Out."

For the black community of Crown Heights, the Hasidim were "out of place" both in geographical and political terms. They had betrayed their 'allies' by siding with the white majority. Consequently, the killing of Cato lit a fuse that had long laid in wait. His death provided the context and the motive for black demonstrations of racial solidarity, even across ethnic groups (e.g., Haitians, Jamaicans).

To humiliate, devalue and victimize the identifiable 'white Jewish devil' is to simultaneously proclaim the positive collective identity of the African American, very much in contrast to the negative identity generally assigned blacks in this culture. It is, moreover, a means of distancing oneself from the

Other. Anti-Semitic violence reinforces the differences rather than the similarities between these two differently oppressed groups. It reasserts the particular and unique suffering of blacks in the United States. There is a certain resentment toward the Jewish assumption of share oppression. The language and activities of anti-Semitism make that resentment clear (Lester, 1994: 172). . . .

Conclusion: Building Bridges

These preliminary remarks were intended to draw attention to the reality of intercultural violence among and between oppressed groups. I have suggested that such intercultural violence may be seen as efforts to police boundaries between groups, thereby enhancing the solidarity and privilege of the perpetrator's reference community, and simultaneously minimizing the power of the victim group. Deprived of the unobstructed right to enact a forceful identity within view of the majority culture, members of subordinate groups may turn to hate crime as an alternative resource for constructing their collective identities. Disempowered economically, socially and politically, minority groups struggle between themselves for ascendancy, often in violent and repressive ways.

The irony of this particular manifestation of identity construction is that the perpetrator and the victim have often experienced a similarity (but not sameness) of oppression. In other words, blacks, Jews, Asians, and others not explicitly noted herein have all suffered various degrees of discrimination and victimization. Yet rather than acknowledging this and forming coalitions, they have often resorted to conflict among themselves. Freer (1994: 174) provides an apt summary:

Competition for scarce resources is akin to metaphorical competition over a single slice of an entire pie. Too often the fight between two individuals, or in this case groups, over that single slice detracts from any efforts to enlarge the pie itself, or to question the distribution scheme in the first place.

Contending minority groups have so internalized the dominant aspects of white masculine supremacy that this is the only lens through which they can view one another. In such a context, it becomes difficult to imagine how the 'pie' might otherwise be shaped and shared.

Consequently, the interethnic alliances necessary to minimize interethnic violence rest on practices that empower all minority groups in such a way as to lift all together, rather than some at the expense of others. In other words, such strategies must be "transformative rather than simply effective in reducing tensions or addressing particular problems." . . . Energies must be devoted to the identification and acknowledgement of what these communities share rather than what divides them. All too often this will mean recognizing the common economic, political, and social oppressions that have historically threatened minority groups in the United States. For example, while the Los Angeles riots of 1992 revealed the multiple fractures among and between minority groups, it was also a pivotal point for the mobilization of inter-ethnic coalitions. Unlike any prior urban 'race riot', the events leading up to and following the Los Angeles made visible the antipathy of white citizenry and public officials toward all minority groups. Consequently, they renewed and gave birth to an array of—albeit tenuous—coalitions, such as the Multicultural Collaborative. It is of course unfortunate that it took such a tragic series of events to inspire this co-operation; nonetheless, these organizations suggest models for future collaboration that crosses racial, ethnic, gender and class lines. If a city so fraught with conflict and violence can engender inter-group collaboration, then coalitions elsewhere must not be inconceivable. Moreover, coalition building can go far in establishing a dynamic of identity construction that is less competitive, less of a zero-sum game.

Successful transformation also requires that scholars and activists consistently look "beyond black and white" to recognize the layers of inter-racial and inter-ethnic relationships that characterize the contemporary United States. Changing demographics and shifting power bases demand that we widen our understanding of difference in this country. Both inter- and intra-group cleavages attest to the complexity of ethnic relations as we enter the twenty-first century. Consequently, "a serious effort must be made to incorporate the histories and contemporary experiences of people of color between the two poles of Black and white on the racial spectrum" (Cho, 1993: 207). Moreover, as argued herein, this incorporation must move beyond even the inclusion of diverse racial identities to account for the experiences of those whose identities are simultaneously grounded in gender and class categories, since 'doing difference' subsumes multiple identities.

Acknowledgments

The author wishes to thank Alex Alvarez for his thoughtful feedback and advice, and an anonymous reviewer for *Sociology of Crime, Law and Deviance*.

REFERENCES

Almaguer, T. (1995). Chicano Men: A Cartography of Homosexual Identity and Behavior. In: M. Kimmel & M. Messner (Eds), *Men's Lives* (pp. 418–431). Boston, MA: Allyn and Bacon.

Chang, R. (1995). Toward an Asian American Legal Scholarship: Critical Race Theory, Post-Structuralism and Narrative Space. In: R. Delgado (Ed.), *Critical Race Theory* (pp. 322–336). Philadelphia PA: Temple University Press.

Cho, S. (1993). Korean Americans vs. African Americans: Conflict and Construction. In: R. Gooding-Williams (Ed.), *Reading Rodney King, Reading Urban Uprisings* (pp. 196–211). New York, NY: Routledge.

Chun, Je. (1996). Color of Racism. *WE Magazine* (online), www.asiandir.com/we.march96/color.html.

Dinnerstein, L. (1994). *Anti-Semitism in America.* New York, NY: Oxford University Press.

Farrakhan, L. (1996). Black Muslims Are Telling the Truth About Jews. In: P. Winters (Ed.), *Race Relations: Opposing Viewpoints* (pp. 50–54). San Diego, CA: Greenhaven Press.

Fine, M. (1997). Witnessing Whiteness. In: M. Fine, L. Weis, L. Powell, & L. Mun Wong (Eds), *Off-White: Readings on Race, Power and Society* (pp. 57–65). New York, NY: Routledge.

Freer, R. (1994). Black-Korean Conflict. In: M. Baldassare (Ed.), *The Los Angeles Riots* (pp. 175–203). Boulder, CO: Westview.

Frontline (1993). *Is LA Burning?*

Greene, B. (1997). Ethnic Minority Lesbians and Gay Men: Mental Health and Treatment Issues. In: B. Greene (Ed.), *Ethnic and Cultural Diversity Among Lesbians and Gay Men* (pp. 216–239). Thousand Oaks, CA: Sage.

Herdt, G. (1997). *Same Sex, Different Cultures.* Boulder, CO: Westview.

Holmes, S. (1994). Survey Finds Minorities Resent One Another Almost as Much as They Do Whites. *New York Times*, B8.

Hooks, B. (1995). *Killing Rage.* New York, NY: Henry Holt and Co.

Hooks, B. (1994). *Outlaw Culture.* New York, NY: Routledge.

Hooks, B. (1992). *Black Looks.* Boston MA: South End Press.

Ikemoto, L. (1995). Traces of the Master Narrative in the Story of African American/Korean American Conflict: How We Constructed Los Angeles. In: R. Delgado (Ed.), *Critical Race Theory* (pp. 305–315). Philadelphia, PA: Temple University Press.

Jo, M. H. (1992). Korean Merchants in the Black Community: Prejudice Among the Victims of

Prejudice. *Ethnic and Racial Studies, 15*(3), 395–411.

Kim, E. (1993). Home Is Where the *Han* Is: A Korean American Perspective on the Los Angeles Upheavals. In: R. Gooding-Williams (Ed.), *Reading Rodney King, Reading Urban Uprisings* (pp. 215–235). New York, NY: Routledge.

Lester, J. (1994). The Lives People Live. In: P. Berman (Ed.), *Blacks and Jews: Alliances and Arguments* (pp. 164–177). New York, NY: Delta.

Lugones, M., & Price, J. (1995). Dominant Culture: El Deseo por un Alma Pobre. In: D. Harris (Ed.), *Multiculturalism from the Margins* (pp. 103–128). Westport, CT: Bergin and Garvey.

McClain, P., & Stuart, J. (1995). *Can We All Get Along? Racial and Ethnic Minorities in American Politics.* Boulder, CO: Westview.

Messerschmidt, J. (1997). *Crime as Structured Action.* Thousand Oaks, CA: Sage.

Messerschmidt, J. (1993). *Masculinities and Crime.* Lanham, MD: Rowman & Littlefield.

Oliver, M., & Johnson, J. (1984). Interethnic Conflict in an Urban Ghetto: The Case of Blacks and Latinos in Los Angeles. *Research in Social Movements, Conflict and Change, 6,* 57–94.

Pogrebin, L. C., & Hutchinson, E. O. (1994). A Dialogue on Black-Jewish Relations. In: F. Pincus & H. Ehrlich (Eds), *Race and Ethnic Conflict* (pp. 219–226). Boulder, CO: Westview.

Rothenberg, P. (1992). The Construction, Deconstruction and Reconstruction of Difference. In: R. Baird & S. Rosenbaum (Eds), *Bigotry, Prejudice and Hatred* (pp. 47–64). Buffalo, NY: Prometheus Books.

Sheffield, C. (1995). Hate Violence. In: P. Rothenberg (Ed.), *Race, Class and Gender in the United States* (pp. 432–441). New York, NY: St. Martin's Press.

Steele, S. (1994). Breaking Our Bond of Shame. In: P. Berman (Ed.), *Blacks and Jews: Alliances and Arguments* (pp. 178–180). New York, NY: Delta.

United States Commission on Civil Rights (1992). *Civil Rights Issues Facing Asian Americans in the 1990s.*

West, C., & Fenstermaker, S. (1995). Doing Difference. *Gender and Society, 9*(1), 8–37.

West, C., & Fenstermaker, S. (1993). Power, Inequality and the Accomplishment of Gender: An Ethnomethodological View. In: Paula England (Ed.), *Theory on Gender/Feminism on Theory* (pp. 151–174). New York, NY: Aldine de Gruyter.

West, C., & Zimmerman, D. (1987). Doing Gender. *Gender and Society, 1*(2), 125–151.

West, C. (1994). *Race Matters.* New York, NY: Vintage Books.

West, C. (1993). Learning to Talk Race. In: R. Gooding-Williams (Ed.), *Reading Rodney King, Reading Urban Uprisings* (pp. 255–260). New York, NY: Routledge.

Winant, H. (1998). Racial Dualism at Century's End. In: W. Lubiano (Ed.), *The House That Race Built* (pp. 87–115). New York, NY: Vintage.

Winant, H. (1997). Where Culture Meets Structure: Race in the 1990s. In: D. Kendall (Ed.), *Race, Class and Gender in a Diverse Society* (pp. 26–38). Boston, MA: Allyn and Bacon.

QUESTIONS FOR DISCUSSION

1. How do you "do race" or "do difference"? To what extent are you aware of acting to preserve group privilege?
2. Are the causes of violence directed against Asians and Jews similar or different?

KEY TERMS

race
ethnicity
racism
race, ethnicity, and racism as social constructions
race as a structural feature of society
racial privilege
individual racism

institutional racism
color blindness
racist atmosphere

THE SOCIAL WEB

- The Southern Poverty Law Center began as a small civil rights law firm in 1971. Now it is internationally known for its tolerance education program, its legal victories against white supremacist groups, its tracking of hate groups, and its sponsorship of the Civil Rights Memorial: www.splcenter.org.
- INCITE! Women of Color Against Violence is a national activist organization of radical feminists of color, advancing a movement to end violence against women of color and their communities through direct action, critical dialogue, and grassroots organizing: www.incite-national.org.
- The Crosspoint is the Net's biggest collection of links in the field of human rights, antiracism, refugees, women's rights, antifacism, Shoan, and so on. The Crosspoint also lists links to Jewish organizations, migrant organizations, and others. The Crosspoint was built and is being maintained by the Magenta foundation in Amsterdam, The Netherlands. Magenta was founded in 1992 after the violent racist attacks on migrants in Germany: www.magenta.nl/crosspoint.
- The American Civil Liberties Union's mission is to fight civil liberties violations wherever and whenever they occur. In particular, the ACLU focuses on extending rights to those segments of the population that have traditionally been denied them. An extensive study of racial profiling can be found at www.aclu.org/profiling.
- Artists Against Racism is a registered, Canadian-based nonprofit organization that produces national and International educational projects for youth. AAR teaches that regardless of one's religion, ethnicity, nationality, or skin color, we are all one people. Through AAR, artists reach out as role models to youth via video and radio public service announcements, subway and outdoor billboards, school posters, music magazine ads, and more: www.artistsagainstracism.org.

QUESTIONS FOR DEBATE

1. Explain how racist violence by whites against non-Whites and by non-White ethnic groups against each other is gendered. Put another way, how do racist hate crimes rest on hegemonic ideas of gender?
2. Is socialization into a subculture the necessary *and* sufficient element for racist organizations to exist, or only a necessary element?
3. Do you agree with Barbara Perry's analysis that Asians are damaged by the perception that they have assimilated? Which other author would agree with you?

Chapter 6
Gender and Sexuality

Contents

Learning Objectives

By the end of this chapter you should be able to:

- Recognize how the authors use one or more of the major perspectives to explore gender and sexuality.
- Explore how gender inequality is shaped by inequalities of race and class.
- Identify the ways that gender and heterosexuality are socially constructed.
- Describe various consequences of gender inequality and heterosexism.
- Analyze how individuals contribute to gender inequality and the oppression of gays and lesbians through their everyday behavior.
- Explain how social systems and institutions perpetuate gender inequality and heterosexism.

Defining the Problem

Sociologists of social problems view **gender and sexuality as social constructions.** Simply put, the "natural" differences that we recognize between men and women and between heterosexuals and homosexuals are socially achieved. They are ideas and related patterns of behavior that are fostered through all manner of cultural means that exist separate from women's and men's bodies. **Masculinity, femininity,** and sexuality are subjective ideal behavior patterns for individuals who are socially identified as women and men. Traditional ideals of masculinity direct men to be heterosexual, independent, aggressive, unemotional, and dominant in their relations with women. Traditional ideals of femininity direct women to be heterosexual, dependent, passive, emotional, and subservient and supportive in their relations with men. The media, government, family, education, and other institutions are social forums in which the appropriate scope of behavior for women and men is continuously defined. When institutions promote a narrow, traditional scope of action for women and men, they promote **sexism** and **homophobia**—discrimination against women and against gays and lesbians. From the social constructionist view, ridding society of gendered inequality requires scrutiny of the ideals institutions foster and whom these ideals benefit.

All social problems researchers concerned with an objective analysis of gender seek to explain the empirical reality that women and men generally share different behavioral patterns, women and men generally do not have the same social status, and women are generally subordinate to men. Sociologists conceptualize gender in three dominant ways.[1] One perspective is that

[1]Barbara Risman, "Gender as Structure," in *Gender Vertigo: American Families in Transition* (New Haven: Yale University Press, 1998), 13–31.

gendered "selves" produce masculine and feminine behaviors. Simply put, your chromosomal composition preordains a tendency for you to behave in masculine or feminine ways, *or* your very early childhood socialization sets your gender identity within you. As an adult you act as you are, biologically or socially, a woman or a man. From a gendered selves perspective, inequality stems from the different values placed on what women and men do, and it persists from generation to generation because neither chromosomes nor socialization patterns change. In this view of gender, there are two ways to achieve greater equality. First, efforts should be made to value men's and women's different contributions to society in a more equal way. Second, if behavioral differences are due to socialization, efforts can be made to raise boys and girls in a more similar way.

There are two very problematic features of this gendered selves approach. It assumes stability of gender and personality traits throughout life. It also assumes much greater differences between women and men than among women and among men.

A second explanation of gender difference and inequality is that **social structure** (as opposed to biology or individual learning) creates **gendered behavior.** Simply put, in any context, your behavior is shaped by your social position. Those on top behave like leaders and bosses, those below behave like followers and assistants. Men and women *appear* to be different because they happen to be in different structural locations that demand different behaviors from them. Men typically hold organizational and institutional positions at work and in the family that demand aggression, for example. Women typically work in supportive organizational and institutional positions. Thus, according to this perspective, if you put a woman in a position typically held by a man, she will behave in a masculine way; and if you put a man in a position held by a woman, he will behave in a feminine way. Equality (particularly economic equality), according to this perspective, will be achieved by giving women access to positions from which they have been excluded.

A fundamental flaw in this structural explanation of gender is that it neglects the idea that the work world to which women aspire is itself gendered. Women and men never experience identical structural conditions in organizations and never will, because women are always seen *as women* and men are always seen *as men.* As long as gender exists as a culturally ingrained way of marking people, the gender and sexuality of the person in the location will matter.

A third perspective is that **"doing" gender** reproduces inequality. Being labeled as a member of a sex category (man or woman) makes you morally accountable for behavior consistent with other members of that group. Women and men are expected to "do" gender—to behave recognizably as women or as men—to facilitate interaction. Because maleness and femaleness are generally viewed as natural and normal, "doing" gender means behaving in ways that reestablish the existing differences and inequalities between men and women. It is not that we have stable male and female personality traits; rather, we are all responding to the same social expectations and are mostly acting to conform, and we are supporting and/or sanctioning the gender performances of others. Thus, in order to be recognized as men, men act bossy, aggressive, and unemotional. In order to be recognized as women, women follow orders, act acquiescent, and display emotion. If greater equality is to be achieved, we have to broaden our social notions of what is acceptable for men and women and individually reflect on what motivates our actions.

There are two serious weaknesses in this way of conceptualizing gender. First, it places too little emphasis on the ways that contexts shape the choices available to women and men. That is, it doesn't recognize that more and less "doing" gender is demanded by different situations. Second, it places too little emphasis on women's and men's attachment to a gender identity and on how that attachment guides interactional choices.

The weaknesses of each perspective mean that we must use all three. We must appreciate that gender is built into social life via socialization, institutional organization, and interaction. We must recognize that these different aspects of gender are reinforcing, such that even people who do not choose to live gendered lives or to support male dominance find themselves doing so as a result of the logic of the choices available to them.

Scope of the Problem

A review of statistics concerning women's and men's places in government, business, the military, and law enforcement, and their patterns of victimization and right to be free from discrimination based on sexual orientation demonstrates the existence of gender inequality.

Men dominate the government. Only twenty-nine women have served in the president's cabinet or in cabinet-level positions since the nation's founding, a mere 4.9 percent. In the current cabinet, only three of twelve positions are held by women.[2] In 2002, men held 86.2 percent of Senate seats, 87 percent of the seats in the House, 78 percent of the sitting U.S. Supreme Court, 72.3 percent of elected state executive positions (governors, lieutenant governors, attorney generals, and key commissioners), 77.4 per-

cent of state legislative seats, and were mayors of 85 percent of the 100 largest U.S. cities.[3]

Business ownership is also concentrated in the hands of men. The 1997 U.S. Bureau of the Census survey of women business owners found that 26 percent of nonfarm businesses were owned solely by women and only an additional 17 percent were owned equally by women and men. The firms owned by women, defined as privately held companies of which women own at least 51 percent, were smaller and earned less on average than the firms owned by men. Average 1997 receipts for firms owned by women were $151,100; for jointly owned firms, $259,200; and for firms owned by men $582,500.[4]

Gender disparity in income is pervasive. In 2000, the median weekly earnings for full-time women wage and salary workers were 76 percent of men's ($511 vs. $672). The **gendered earnings disparity** (gap) exists in managerial and specialty occupations with the highest median weekly earnings as well as in lower income positions. Women and men working for an hourly wage in 2000 earned $9.57 and $11.36, respectively, for each hour worked.[5] Instead of increases in experience and education decreasing the earnings gap, they widen it.[6] In 2000, median weekly earnings for men who were high school graduates were $415 and for women,

[2]"Snapshots of Current Political Leadership," The Whitehouse Project, www.thewhitehouseproject.org/becomeleader/snapshotswomen.html accessed June 18, 2002.

[3]"Women in Elective Office 2002 Fact Sheet Summaries," Center for American Women and Politics, Eagleton Institute for Politics—Rutgers, the State University of New Jersey, www.rci.rutgers.edu/~cawp/facts/cawpfs.html, accessed June 26, 2002.

[4]"Women Owned Businesses: 1997," Census Brief: Survey of Women Owned Business Enterprises (Washington, D.C.: U.S. Bureau of the Census, October 2001).

[5]"Highlights of Women's Earnings in 2001," Report 960 (Washington, D.C.: Bureau of Labor Statistics, Department of Labor, May 2002).

[6]Why We Still Care about the Gender Gap," National Partnership for Women and Families, www.nationalpartnership.org, accessed June 18, 2002.

$314 (75.6 percent of men's). Median weekly earnings for men who were college graduates were $1,082 and for women, $784 (72 percent of men's). The gendered earnings disparity cuts across race too, but also varies. Women's proportion of men's earnings was less among Whites (75.2 percent) than among Blacks (87.1 percent) and Hispanics (88 percent).[7]

Women are underrepresented in positions of honor and authority in the military, law enforcement, and the judiciary. In 2002, women constituted 14 percent of the armed forces. They had gained access to all branches of the military; however, they were restricted from "combat" posts in each branch of the service (about 88 percent of posts are open to women). Women made up 3 percent of the top category of officers (brigadier and general), 31 percent of the lieutenant and colonel level, and 66 percent of the lowest tier of officers.[8]

Women held a minority (12.7 percent) of all sworn law enforcement positions in 2001. Women of color held 4.8 percent of them. In small agencies, fewer sworn women worked (8.1 percent), and practically no women of color (1.2 percent). Women's access to command positions also varies by agency size: Women hold 7.3 percent and 3.4 percent of top command positions in large and small agencies, respectively, although 55.9 percent of large agencies and 97.4 percent of small agencies reported no women in top command positions.[9]

In spite of women and racial-ethnic minorities comprising almost 40 percent and 20 percent, respectively, of persons now having earned law degrees, most criminal policy makers and judges making the decisions about what the constitution requires are predominately White men. As of July 2001, women made up 22.2 percent of supreme court justices, 20.1 percent of circuit court judges, 19.2 percent of district court judges and 26.3 percent of justices of state courts of last resort.[10]

Men are more likely than women to be victims of violent crime; however, the gender gap is closing. The National Crime Victimization Survey (NCVS) conducted in 2000 shows that 32.9 of every 1,000 men and boys older than 12 were victims of violent crime, compared to 23.2 of every 1,000 women and girls older than 12. This contrasts to 68.0 men and 31.4 women per 1,000 in 1973 and 57.6 men and 32.0 women per 1,000 in 1990. Men are more likely to be victimized by strangers, and women are more likely to be victimized by someone they know, an intimate, a friend, or an acquaintance. Women are the majority of victims of intimate violence: In 1998 they were 72 percent of the murder victims and 85 percent of the battery victims of intimates. Six in ten women who were sexually assaulted in 2000 reported their assailant was an intimate. These gendered patterns of violation are consistent across race and ethnicity.[11]

The status of legal protections that pertain to sexuality in 2002 demonstrated the inequality gays and lesbians experience. Twenty-seven states and the District of Columbia prohibited hate crimes based on the victim's sexual orientation. However, only twelve states and the District of Columbia explicitly protected the right of all persons

---

[7]"Highlights of Women's Earnings in 2001."

[8]Helena Carreiras, "Gender Integration in the Armed Forces: A Cross National Comparison of Policies and Practices in NATO Countries." NATO working paper, June 5, 2002.

[9]Kim Lonsway et al., "Equality Denied: The Status of Women in Policing: 2001." National Center for Women in Policing, Feminist Majority Foundation, April 2002.

[10]"A Current Glance at Women in the Law," American Bar Association, Commission on Women in the Profession, www.abanet.org/women/home.

[11]Bureau of Justice Statistics, U.S. Department of Justice.

to be free from discrimination on the basis of their sexual orientation. Three states (Delaware, Montana, and South Carolina) continued to exclude same-sex partners from the protection of domestic violence statutes. Fifteen states allowed consenting adults to be prosecuted for freely expressing themselves sexually in a private setting.[12]

Perspectives on the Problem

Sociologists using a *conflict perspective* would explore how those with power use gender, an idea, as a tool to help retain their position. They would study how heterosexual men benefit and women and gays are damaged by the majority belief that heterosexual masculinity is a natural trait. A sociologist using a *functionalist perspective* on gender would look at whether the roles and behaviors of women and men in a society were well integrated to contribute to the long-term success of the society. A sociologist using a *symbolic interactionist* perspective would examine how women and men enact their identities on a daily basis. She or he would explore how the mundane activities of sharing household chores, taking care of children, and going on dates recreate inequalities that already exist. A sociologist using a *social constructionist perspective* would examine the historical specificity of our ideas about how men and women should behave and how these ideas reflect shifting racial and economic dynamics in our society.

Connecting the Perspectives

We chose the readings in this section to highlight these four ways of thinking about gender while also keeping you focused on race, class, and sexuality. Gloria Steinem provides a constructionist analysis of media coverage of the recent mass murders in high

schools. Amy Caiazza examines how violence against women affects the long-term health of impoverished societies and the world, with an eye toward modifying U.S. foreign policy. Diane McEachern and colleagues adopt a conflict perspective and explore how women battery among Navajos is a product of U.S. military domination and a calculated obliteration of the Navajos' cultural practices. Judith Lorber evaluates the evidence supporting constructionist and alternative explanations for sexuality. Scott Coltrane examines how parenting behavior is a matter of "doing" gender and explores some of the obstacles couples face in making changes in the way they divide child care and housework.

Reading Summaries

Steinem directs us to the obvious in "Supremacy Crimes": The recent killings in high schools, and in fact most solo cases of mass murder, have been done by white heterosexual (and homophobic) men. The recent mass media coverage does not acknowledge this and, thus, ignores the contribution that a particular conception of masculinity makes to deadly violence. What we as a society have to contend with, she argues, is the creation of a class of individuals who believe themselves entitled to superiority and who believe that a manly response to frustration is violent behavior. Moreover, Steinem suggests we should recognize that in being blind to the gendering of this particular violence, the media reinforce the ideological hegemony of the problematic masculinity.

In "Why Gender Matters: Women, Militarism, and Violence," Caiazza argues that efforts to fight terrorism should recognize how violence directed at women affects their capacity to perform their vital roles as parents. Caiazza proposes that economic instability in a culture that devalues women results in women becoming targets of men's frustrations. When violation of women be-

---

[12]National Gay and Lesbian Task Force, Washington, D.C., www.ngltf.org.

comes an accepted and ingrained part of a society, it reduces women's participation in society, symbolically ratifies their status as second-class citizens, and limits their ability to meet their children's needs. Violence directed toward women thus leads to greater economic insecurity.

Economically insecure women act to protect their children. Some women accept cultural norms of violence, orient themselves toward militarism and terror, engage in direct acts of violence, support adult men who are violent, and, most importantly, socialize their children into radicalism. Each generation of children who learn that violence is acceptable becomes the next generation of militants and potential terrorists who may direct it outwardly. Other women, who recognize that violence contributes to their economic insecurity, work for peace. This is especially the case if they make the connection between the economic well-being of their own children and all children. It is through the activism of such women that the cycle of generational violence might be broken. Thus, Caiazza argues, the government should focus foreign policy on reducing the threat of violence in poor women's lives and strengthening their capacity to care for their families. Enabling women to be successful in meeting their familial obligations while resisting militarism is necessary to produce a generation of children who also eschew violence.

Caiazza adopts a functionalist perspective in this article. Consider this more abstract statement of her argument. She proposes that economic instability leads to men perpetrating behavior that in the short term controls women, but in the long term is dysfunctional for the entire society, because it undermines women's capacity to meet their children's needs. Thus violence ultimately leads toward a continued breakdown in social organization. When women follow the dictates of the culture and orient to violence to achieve some stability, it rein-

forces the cultural ideology but does nothing to alter the economic conditions. Violence breeds more violence. Only through intervention that helps fill the gap between women's needs and the lack of supportive social institutions can we produce stable and peaceful countries.

In "Domestic Violence Among the Navajo: A Legacy of Colonization," McEachern and colleagues describe how gender statuses in the Navajo culture changed and woman battery emerged as a result of White interference in Navajo social and legal institutions. Prior to 1883, women were socially and legally equal to men, extracting power from the communal ownership of land, from their position as the individuals from whom possessions were inherited, and from their right to participate in public decision making. In this earlier period, the authors argue, there is extremely little documented evidence of violence directed at women. In those cases in which the battery of women or children is documented, it is treated as a cultural aberration, not an acceptable behavior for a Navajo man.

In 1883, the federal government began to erode the institutional supports for women's power. As a result of forced changes, a new generation of abusive men emerged. Now, the authors argue, domestic violence is a growing problem for the Navajo. Reporting is hampered, battered women's ability to leave dangerous situations is hampered, intervention by police in ongoing abuse is difficult, and the time officers can devote to cases is limited. Lack of temporary housing and medical resources make helping battered Navajo women leave violent situations a time-consuming proposition. Certainly *something* needs to be done to reduce violence and provide victims with appropriate support. Because the violence Navajo women experience from Navajo men is a product of White patriarchal culture, the authors argue, it will not be eradicated by further external intervention.

Rather, the solution must come from critical reflection by the Navajos themselves.

In "Embattled Terrain," Judith Lorber explores the ways that feminists think about gender and sexuality: as stable, almost "essential" features of individuals and as a product of socialization and social context. In essence, she weighs the approaches discussed in the introduction of the chapter in relation to a specific issue. Lorber challenges the idea that sexuality is essential, that it follows from biology and gender. She points out that although at least four sexual identities exist in our culture—heterosexual man, heterosexual woman, lesbian, and gay—many individuals do not fit neatly in these categories. Women and men who identify as heterosexual report histories of same-sex activity; men who identify as gay and women who identify as lesbian report histories of heterosexual contact. Biology does not consistently trump socially constructed gender. Children who are born with ambiguous genitalia that are "corrected" shortly after birth enact sexualities consistent with both their chromosomal sex and their social gender. Transgendered men and women, individuals who live and pass as members of the opposite gender, further demonstrate that gender is a social status. According to Lorber, either/or (dichotomous) thinking about sexuality maintains the existing social structure and the authority of heterosexually identified men in positions of authority.

When the social nature of sexuality is ignored, whether it be in acts of violence in high schools, in gang rapes in fraternities, or in the freely chosen lives of transgendered men, an important political dimension of society goes unrecognized.

Coltrane is interested in the well-documented persistence of a traditional division of labor in the home, which inordinately burdens women despite their increased paid employment. In "Family Man: Fatherhood, Housework, and Gender Equity," he explores the difficulties of changing this pattern by closely examining how one couple, Gary and Susan Carter, arrived at a system of sharing child care. By analyzing the struggle behind a "success story" we come to a greater appreciation for the ways that societal ideas about women's and men's appropriate roles (what sociologists call gender ideology) structure individual decisions and behavior. The Carters decided to each work part-time in order to facilitate splitting parenting responsibility for their children. They found, however, that their efforts were hindered by their own and other people's assumptions. Coltrane argues that altering patterns of gender inequality requires the commitment of both men and women to change gender ideology. The Carters' story shows that to change traditional family relations fundamentally, the parties involved must seriously question cultural assumptions about what it means to be a man or a woman.

Focusing Questions

Each of the authors in Chapter 6 approaches the problem of explaining contemporary gender inequality from a different direction. To focus your reading of these selections, keep the following questions in mind: How is gender inequality a structural problem? How do institutions and the acts of individuals contribute to the persistence of gender inequality? How are class and race inequalities related to those of gender? What do the arguments made by the authors mean for you as a person of a particular gender and sexual orientation?

21

SUPREMACY CRIMES
GLORIA STEINEM

You've seen the ocean of television coverage, you've read the headlines: "How to Spot a Troubled Kid," "Twisted Teens," "When Teens Fall Apart."

After the slaughter in Colorado that inspired those phrases, dozens of copycat threats were reported in the same generalized way: "Junior high students charged with conspiracy to kill students and teachers" (in Texas); "Five honor students overheard planning a June graduation bombing" (in New York); "More than 100 minor threats reported statewide" (in Pennsylvania). In response, the White House held an emergency strategy session titled "Children, Violence, and Responsibility." Nonetheless, another attack was soon reported: "Youth With 2 Guns Shoots 6 at Georgia School."

I don't know about you, but I've been talking back to the television set, waiting for someone to tell us the obvious: it's not "youth," "our children," or "our teens." It's our sons—and "our" can usually be read as "white," "middle class," and "heterosexual."

We know that hate crimes, violent and otherwise, are overwhelmingly committed by white men who are apparently straight. The same is true for an even higher percentage of impersonal, resentment-driven, mass killings like those in Colorado; the sort committed for no economic or rational gain except the need to say, "I'm superior because I can kill." Think of Charles Starkweather,

who reported feeling powerful and serene after murdering ten women and men in the 1950s; or the shooter who climbed the University of Texas Tower in 1966, raining down death to gain celebrity. Think of the engineering student at the University of Montreal who resented females' ability to study that subject, and so shot to death 14 women students in 1989, while saying, "I'm against feminism." Think of nearly all those who have killed impersonally in the workplace, the post office, McDonald's.

White males—usually intelligent, middle class, and heterosexual, or trying desperately to appear so—also account for virtually all the serial, sexually motivated, sadistic killings, those characterized by stalking, imprisoning, torturing, and "owning" victims in death. Think of Edmund Kemper, who began killing animals, then murdered his grandparents, yet was released to sexually torture and dismember college students and other young women until he himself decided he "didn't want to kill *all* the coeds in the world." Or David Berkowitz, the Son of Sam, who murdered *some* women in order to feel in control of *all* women. Or consider Ted Bundy, the charming, snobbish young would-be lawyer who tortured and murdered as many as 40 women, usually beautiful students who were symbols of the economic class he longed to join. As for John Wayne Gacy, he was obsessed with maintaining the public mask of masculinity, and so hid his homosexuality by killing and burying men and boys with whom he had had sex.

Steinem, Gloria. 1999. "Another Crime Is Hiding in Plain Sight." *Ms.* August/September, pp. 45–47. Reprinted with permission from the publisher.

These "senseless" killings begin to seem less mysterious when you consider that they were committed disproportionately by white, non-poor males, the group most likely to become hooked on the drug of superiority. It's a drug pushed by a male-dominant culture that presents dominance as a natural right; a racist hierarchy that falsely elevates whiteness; a materialist society that equates superiority with possessions, and a homophobic one that empowers only one form of sexuality.

As Elliott Leyton reports in *Hunting Humans: The Rise of the Modern Multiple Murderer*, these killers see their behavior as "an appropriate—even 'manly'—response to the frustrations and disappointments that are a normal part of life." In other words, it's not their life experiences that are the problem, it's the impossible expectation of dominance to which they've become addicted.

This is not about blame. This is about causation. If anything, ending the massive cultural cover-up of supremacy crimes should make heroes out of boys and men who reject violence, especially those who reject the notion of superiority altogether. Even if one believes in a biogenetic component of male aggression, the very existence of gentle men proves that socialization can override it.

Nor is this about attributing such crimes to a single cause. Addiction to the drug of supremacy is not their only root, just the deepest and most ignored one. Additional reasons why this country has such a high rate of violence include the plentiful guns that make killing seem as unreal as a video game; male violence in the media that desensitizes viewers in much the same way that combat killers are desensitized in training; affluence that allows maximum access to violence-as-entertainment; a national history of genocide and slavery; the romanticizing of frontier violence and organized crime; not to mention extremes of wealth and poverty and the illusion that both are deserved.

But it is truly remarkable, given the relative reasons for anger at injustice in this country, that white, non-poor men have a near-monopoly on multiple killings of strangers, whether serial and sadistic or mass and random. How can we ignore this obvious fact? Others may kill to improve their own condition—in self-defense, or for money or drugs; to eliminate enemies; to declare turf in drive-by shootings; even for a jacket or a pair of sneakers—but white males addicted to supremacy kill even when it worsens their condition or ends in suicide.

. . .

Men of color and females are capable of serial and mass killing, and commit just enough to prove it. Think of Colin Ferguson, the crazed black man on the Long Island Railroad, or Wayne Williams, the young black man in Atlanta who kidnapped and killed black boys, apparently to conceal his homosexuality. Think of Aileen Carol Wuornos, the white prostitute in Florida who killed abusive johns "in self-defense," or Waneta Hoyt, the upstate New York woman who strangled her five infant children between 1965 and 1971, disguising their cause of death as sudden infant death syndrome. Such crimes are rare enough to leave a haunting refrain of disbelief as evoked in Pat Parker's poem "jonestown": "Black folks do not / Black folks do not / Black folks do not commit suicide." And yet they did.

Nonetheless, the proportion of serial killings that are not committed by white males is about the same as the proportion of anorexics who are not female. Yet we discuss the gender, race, and class components of anorexia, but not the role of the same factors in producing epidemics among the powerful.

The reasons are buried deep in the culture, so invisible that only by reversing our assumptions can we reveal them.

Suppose, for instance, that young black males—or any other men of color—had carried out the slaughter in Colorado. Would the media reports be so willing to describe the murderers as "our children"? Would there be so little discussion about the boys' race? Would experts be calling the motive a mystery, or condemning the high school cliques for making those young men feel like "outsiders"? Would there be the same empathy for parents who gave the murderers luxurious homes, expensive cars, even rescued them from brushes with the law? Would there be as much attention to generalized causes, such as the dangers of violent video games and recipes for bombs on the Internet?

As for the victims, if racial identities had been reversed, would racism remain so little discussed? In fact, the killers themselves said they were targeting blacks and athletes. They used a racial epithet, shot a black male student in the head, and then laughed over the fact that they could see his brain. What if *that* had been reversed?

What if these two young murderers, who were called "fags" by some of the jocks at Columbine High School, actually had been gay? Would they have got the same sympathy for being gay-baited? What if they had been lovers? Would we hear as little about their sexuality as we now do, even though only their own homophobia could have given the word "fag" such power to humiliate them?

Take one more leap of the imagination: suppose these killings had been planned and executed by young women—of any race, sexuality, or class. Would the media still be so disinterested in the role played by gender-

conditioning? Would journalists assume that female murderers had suffered from being shut out of access to power in high school, so much so that they were pushed beyond their limits? What if dozens, even hundreds of young women around the country had made imitative threats—as young men have done—expressing admiration for a well-planned massacre and promising to do the same? Would we be discussing their youth more than their gender, as is the case so far with these male killers?

I think we begin to see that our national self-examination is ignoring something fundamental, precisely because it's like the air we breathe: the white male factor, the middle-class and heterosexual one, and the promise of superiority it carries. Yet this denial is self-defeating—to say the least. We will never reduce the number of violent Americans, from bullies to killers, without challenging the assumptions on which masculinity is based: that males are superior to females, that they must find a place in a male hierarchy, and that the ability to dominate *someone* is so important that even a mere insult can justify lethal revenge. There are plenty of studies to support this view. As Dr. James Gilligan concluded in *Violence: Reflections on a National Epidemic,* "If humanity is to evolve beyond the propensity toward violence . . . then it can only do so by recognizing the extent to which the patriarchal code of honor and shame generates and obligates male violence."

I think the way out can only be found through a deeper reversal: just as we as a society have begun to raise our daughters more like our sons—more like whole people—we must begin to raise our sons more like our daughters—that is, to value empathy as well as hierarchy; to measure success by other people's welfare as well as their own.

But first, we have to admit and name the truth about supremacy crimes.

QUESTIONS FOR
DISCUSSION

1. What, if anything, do we gain by labeling the high school murders in Colorado and Georgia "supremacy crimes"?

2. Why have the media not focused on the male gender and the heterosexuality of the majority of mass killers in U.S. history?

22

WHY GENDER MATTERS
Women, Militarism, and Violence

AMY CAIAZZA

Ever since the Taliban claimed victory and sovereignty over Afghanistan in 1997, it has waged war against Afghan women. The Taliban's radical fundamentalist form of *sharia*, Islamic rule, banned women's education, activism, and even physical presence in Afghan society. Women have been beaten and put to death for violating these rules. Under a system of legalized hatred for women, women are subject to increasing, so-called "private" forms of violence, including rape and domestic violence, with little recourse (Human Rights Watch 2001). Arab and other Muslim feminists in Pakistan, Bangladesh, Malaysia, India, and Turkey have publically criticized and taken organized action against the Taliban's and others' use of religion and state power to repress women (Afkhami 1995; see websites for the Revolutionary Association of Women in Afghanistan and Women Living Under Muslim Law). In the United States, the Feminist Majority and other women's advocates have repeatedly called attention to the Taliban's antiwomen activities.

Until recently, few Americans paid attention to the Taliban's actions. Men and women on the left and the right dismissed Taliban policies as culturally specific, or as an internal political situation in which the United States or the United Nations had no stake (in contrast, there was global uproar over the destruction of Buddhist statues by the Taliban; Pollitt 2001). In our ignorance of Islam, the Arab world, other Muslim societies, and Afghan society in particular, most Americans assumed that Afghan women never enjoyed independence or autonomy. In fact, there was an Afghan women's movement as early as the 1920s. By the

From "Why Gender Matters in Understanding September 11: Women, Militarism, and Violence" by Amy Caiazza. Reprinted with permission of Institute for Women's Policy Research (IWPR), Washington D.C., 2001.

1970s, two decades before the Taliban, Afghan women benefited from relatively high levels of education and leadership in Afghanistan.

Perhaps our collective neglect of the treatment of women in Afghanistan was a missed opportunity to foresee or even prevent the events of September 11, 2001. Societies that condone and even promote violence against women have shown over and over again that they tend to be violent in other ways as well. Even if we dismiss the claim that women's rights are central to human rights, there are centuries of evidence that physical, political, and economic violence against women is a harbinger of other forms of violence. Few societies that are plagued by it are otherwise peaceful.

The United States should pay particular attention to women when attempting to counteract terrorism and encourage more peaceful and democratic political systems in Afghanistan and throughout the world. In our foreign and domestic policies, we should look at both the victims and perpetrators of violence and terrorism. We should pay particularly close attention to the work of those who are effective opponents of violence against women. By doing so, we are more likely to address the root causes of terrorism and violence at home and in the wider world.

This chapter analyzes women's roles as victims, supporters, and opponents of violence, terrorism, and militarism and proposes policy recommendations from its findings. It outlines important links between economic development, violence, women's activism, and peace-building efforts. Economic instability, combined with patriarchal views of women's roles, breeds conditions that lead to violence against women and undermine their capacity to build peaceful societies. In turn, violence against women heightens economic instability—as a result it sows the seeds of other forms of violence committed worldwide by

men. In reaction, women sometimes resort to violence themselves, although more often they become activists for peace. Understanding why and when women fight for peace—and including them in peace building efforts—is crucial to guaranteeing higher levels of peace and security throughout the world.

Women as Victims of Militarism and Violence

"What has happened to us—our properties have been damaged, our bodies have been damaged. Everything—our life has absolutely changed. . . . The spirit has been damaged."

—MOZAMBICAN WOMAN AND
VICTIM OF CIVIL WAR
(quoted in Turshen 2001, 60)

Where institutionalized violence and terrorism exist, women are often singled out as targets. Like men, they are victims, innocent bystanders, loved ones of victims, or refugees displaced by war. Because men are more likely to be involved in violence as soldiers and militants, women are more often displaced by their absence. The U.N. Human Rights Commission reports that two thirds of all people who have been turned into refugees in recent years have been women and their dependent children. Women are also targeted directly through deliberate murder, rape, and injury. In Christian, Muslim, and Buddhist societies, especially in modern ethnic and religious conflicts, male fighters have used rape to impregnate "enemy" women as a form of genocide. Terrorists' sperm "dirties" an ethnic line, and raped women may be rejected by their own societies. Such rape tactics are also designed to demoralize enemy men (Stiglmayer 1994; Turshen 2001). The recent genocidal movements in the former Yugoslavia and Rwanda saw rape used as a method of terror on a grand scale (Human Rights Watch 1996; Stiglmayer 1994).

Even in relatively peaceful societies like the United States, women are targets of violent acts such as rape and domestic violence. Elected officials, judges, and public policies in many states ignore or dismiss the right to freedom from violence as impractically complicated to enforce. Such acts of violence are often treated as private matters with little public consequence. But this purportedly "private" form of violence has important political ramifications. It stops women from being involved in their communities, and it reinforces the notion that they are second-class citizens (Caiazza 2001; Caiazza and Hartmann 2001; Enloe 1993; Sapiro 1993). This kind of violence is a form of daily terrorism against women as a class of citizens (Fineman and Mykitiuk 1994).

Whenever women are the victims of violence that goes unaddressed socially or politically, their victimization indicates that violence is an official, popular, and acceptable strategy for achieving political, social, or economic power. Violence is self-perpetuating: sons watch and do; daughters watch and submit and often do. In the United States, neglected and abused children are nearly twice as likely to commit crimes and be arrested as are other children (Harvard School of Public Health, Division of Public Health Practice, Violence Prevention Programs 2001). Similarly, men who beat, rape, or kill women are likely to be violent in other areas of their lives. They are likely to abuse children and to use violence to achieve a variety of goals in addition to subordinating women, such as achieving political power (Friedman 1994). Simply stated, violence against women and other forms of violence are inextricably linked.

In addition, where violence against women is particularly endemic or ignored, women are often less able to care for their families, thanks to their increased physical and, often, economic insecurity. This, in turn, contributes to insecurity and instability in society as a whole (Friedman 1994). Where violence of any sort is an acceptable strategy for achieving power, societal instability only encourages its further use.

Finally, even without considering violence per se, "non-violent" forms of repressing women's rights also contribute to a country's economic and political instability. Across the globe, when women have more rights and equality, national standards of living also rise—life expectancy is higher, incomes and education levels are higher, and birthrates are lower. As countries more fully include women in political, economic, and social rights, standards of living improve as well (Crossette 2001). A country with little violence, but relatively few opportunities for gender equality, is unlikely to achieve high levels of economic and political development.

Women as Terrorists and Supporters of Militarism

"Violence is the only way to answer violence!"
—GUDRUN ENSSLIN, FEMALE LEADER OF GERMANY'S 1970S BAADER-MEINHOF GANG (quoted in Huffman 1999)

Women are not only passive victims of terrorism and violence. Some women, although a relatively small number, participate in or encourage terrorism. Women have committed acts of terrorism, including suicide bombings, in India, Palestine, and other countries. In one of the few cases when a world leader was killed during an act of terrorism, a woman assassinated India's Rajiv Gandhi in 1991. In Norway, a right-wing group has a "women's wing" of terrorists

(Fangen 1997). In the United States, there has been a deliberate policy by the KKK's male leadership to recruit women as racist activists (Blee 1992).

But it is men who comprise the overwhelming majority of individuals who practice terrorism. In part, this is because of sexist and patriarchal norms that preclude women from militaristic action and limit their public or activist roles. Since many terrorist groups are rooted in diverse religious fundamentalist or right-wing ideologies, their male leaders often refuse to let women assume men's traditional roles as soldiers, terrorists, martyrs, or so-called freedom fighters. Their terrorist actions are often justified as defending a social order that is dependent on women's "purity" and requires the exclusion of women from many facets of public life.

Some women take part in terrorism when there are few perceived outlets for gender equality. Frustrated with a lack of outlets for their public activism, women turn to the kinds of strategies that many alienated groups have adopted: to fight against mainstream political institutions using extreme tactics (Fangen 1997).

When not playing the role of terrorists directly, some women support men's militancy in their traditional roles as mothers by nurturing families committed to militarist or terrorist causes (Ibanez 2001). In many societies, women have been traditionally charged with passing on the cultural norms and expectations of their communities to sons and daughters. When those norms include the use of violence for political ends, women encourage the radicalism and militaristic self-sacrifice that lead to terrorist acts. Notably, women's roles perpetuating these values are not unique to nongovernmental terrorist groups: the values of "feminine sacrifice," in which mothers give their sons to militarist causes, are promoted by many military policymakers who would

loathe being compared with terrorists (Enloe 2000a).

Women's support for militarism has been a resource that sustains both terrorist and formal military conflict. Such support can bring moral weight to militarist movements and encourage involvement in them. In some cases, women are moved to provide active logistical support for militarism and terrorism (i.e., by feeding and clothing militants, delivering messages, and providing other resources). Women have played all these roles prominently in recent decades in areas as diverse as El Salvador, Nicaragua, Northern Ireland, Palestine, and Israel (see Hammami 1997; Sharoni 1997 and 2001).

For many women, participating in and supporting (though rarely planning) acts of terrorism are ways to "protect" their families, homes, and communities. As mothers and wives, many women accept their traditional roles as protectors of their husbands' and children's well-being. In times and places of violent conflict, political disjuncture, and economic insecurity, women may feel unable to do so. *When women live in oppressed or alienated communities, they may also have few formal ways to work for political change. Being allowed inside small, elected, secret terrorist organizations may allow some women to see themselves as fighting for the promise of a more just and stable way of life* (Hammami 1997; Ibanez 2001).

Men's support of and participation in terrorist or militarist activities can also stem from a desire to bring about justice in the face of economic or political insecurity. However, their goals and aspirations are justified more often by the rhetoric of building a society based on religious or political ideals than in explicitly protecting or bettering the lives of their children and families. These "private" concerns are considered women's realm. And, because of traditional gender roles, women approach these concerns through different activities than men.

Women as Peacemakers

"[We should] cease to be silent . . . protest against those who bear the responsibility for this cursed war . . . [and not] relinquish the struggle until our sons come home."
—SHOSHANA SHMUELI, FOUNDER OF THE ISRAELI PARENTS AGAINST SILENCE (quoted in Sharoni 1997, 152)

Not all women who react to terrorism or militarism support it. In many cases, women respond by becoming activists for peace. Again, they often do so because they accept their traditional responsibilities for guaranteeing their families' private social, economic, and physical well-being, but feel unable to fulfill them. They are moved to fight the circumstances, including conditions of violence, causing their uncertainty. They hope to build a society that will allow them to ensure their families' safety. In the Middle East, Latin America, and Northern Ireland, for example, women have fought state-sponsored and non-state-sponsored terrorism through their activism (Aretxaga 1997; Fisher 1989; Sharoni 1997). Their efforts are not based on an inherently "feminine" predisposition toward peace but result from their desire to fulfill their traditional responsibilities as mothers and wives.

In many cases, women act on behalf of peace because they moved from wanting to protect only their own families to protecting all children. At some point, they recognize that to address their own political and economic insecurity, they need to address a larger set of conditions facing their communities (Fisher 1989). In Russia, Israel, Serbia, Italy, and Spain, mothers have come together to protest militarism precisely because they first felt a need to protect their children. They have resorted to protests and other highly visible and disruptive tactics in the absence of democratic mechanisms for change. In part, because they have the moral weight of motherhood behind them, they have, at times, been very effective (Caiazza forthcoming).

Many women's peace movements demand greater accountability and more responsiveness from their governments and other institutions. They become activists for democracy. Because their activism is often rooted in their family roles, when women activists are included in building a country's democratic systems and civil society, they are also more likely to prioritize policies that focus on building the well-being of families and overall systems of social welfare. This, in turn, can lead to more economic stability and political security.

Policy Recommendations: Counteracting Terrorism by Addressing Women's Concerns

Throughout the world, violence and radicalism are associated with political and economic disjuncture, alienation, and dysfunction. Men and women who become terrorists do so because they see few alternatives for pursuing political change. They are frustrated by their economic and political insecurity. They have little trust in government or other institutions. As a result, they turn to movements that promise them justice, power, and access to resources. These movements are often rooted in a desire to return to a more conservative culture and win greater independence from Western hegemony. In many cases, they are based on extremist right- or left-wing ideas. The men and women involved in them see violence as a justified, or even the only, way to achieve their goals. These conditions politicize both men and women—both in support of and against militarism.

For women, radicalism often stems from a desire to protect their homes and communities in times of economic and political insecurity. They turn to political movements that promise safety, better living conditions, and broader economic opportunities, as well as political or religious justice.

These conclusions point to a set of policy implications that the United States and other industrialized democracies should heed if they hope to encourage democracy throughout the world. These recommendations encompass a long-term strategy for developing women's rights as a tool for building global peace and security.

• U.S. international policy should unequivocally oppose violence against women and regimes that condone it. Efforts to combat it should be as central to our evaluations of democracy as competitive elections and universal suffrage.

While direct and indirect violence against women exists in virtually every country, we should not ignore it as incidental to other forms of violence. In most countries marked by political violence, violence against women is particularly rampant. Often, political institutions in those countries treat women as second-class citizens by denying them the right to participate fully in all aspects of society. They officially or unofficially encourage violence against them. U.S. policy should use every available economic and diplomatic means to vigorously oppose these regimes.

As part of its program to fight violence against women, U.S. policy should provide women with the resources that allow them to escape violent situations and achieve individual autonomy. Such efforts can include providing educational and health care assistance to women, through legislation and policies like the Afghan Women and Children Relief Act of 2001, introduced in the U.S. Congress in November of 2001. This legislation would provide such assistance

through local institutions and nongovernmental organizations, particularly women's organizations, as much as possible (Feminist Majority 2001).

Turning a blind eye to violence against women—at home and abroad—also needs to be publicly recognized as a sign that violence is an acceptable part of a society that undermines a country's stability. The seeds of terrorism are sown in violence against women and the repression of women's rights.

• Women need to be included as equal partners in implementing political and economic development. U.S. foreign policy should make women's involvement in democratization central to its international aid programs.

Women's concerns need to be taken seriously and incorporated into development policies. As the United States and other countries pursue policies encouraging development, they should make including indigenous women's voices a top priority, not an afterthought.

Incorporating women into development efforts offers many positive outcomes in addition to improving women's status. Because of women's central roles in caring for their families, and women activists' resulting focus on social welfare, including women's perspectives can also encourage more stability, growth, and well-being. Empowering women to take part in political processes can be a successful way to encourage democracy and stability (Enloe 2000b).

Policies requiring women's participation in nation- and peace-building would mandate that any government established in Afghanistan with U.S. assistance respect and guarantee women's rights; design reconstruction programs to give women and girls access to health care, education, and other social welfare resources; and distribute humanitarian assistance equitably. These policies should be central to U.S. development programs worldwide.

• As counter-movements to terrorism, women's peace movements should be especially encouraged and targeted for financial aid under U.S. foreign policies. They should also be specifically incorporated into reconstruction efforts supported by the United States.

Women's peace movements have been effective agents of change in many settings where terrorism and military conflict are rampant. They draw attention to the consequences of militarism on a community's families, and they bring moral weight to arguments for peace. In many settings, they could provide the basis for large-scale efforts to counter terrorist organizations. But, as currently constituted, these movements are usually small and have few resources to mobilize women and demand attention from terrorist organizations or governments. More investment in these movements by U.S. international aid efforts would encourage peace around the world.

Because women's peace movements have been so effective, and because of women's clear stake in peacemaking processes, in October of 2001 the U.N Security Council adopted a resolution (#1325) formally calling on peace officials in the United Nations, NATO, and other official organizations to explicitly include women in negotiations for ceasefires and post-war reconstruction. The United States should wholeheartedly support this recommendation in the implementation of both international and U.S. peace and development programs. In some of its programs—including its grants to grassroots women's and refugees' organizations in Afghanistan and Pakistan starting in 1997—it has already done so. These efforts should be widened and continued.

• In the long term, U.S. foreign policy and international organizations should place a higher priority on programs to encourage economic and political development, especially in the most authoritarian and impoverished countries. These programs are among the most likely to increase levels of security among men and women and address the conditions that encourage terrorism.

Economic and political development efforts can diminish many of the national and international hatreds that currently plague the world. They can create more obvious opportunities for men and women to promote change through less violent means and to achieve economic success. Perhaps most importantly, they can also make it easier for women and men to protect their families—economically, politically, and physically. As a result, they can alleviate some of the pressures that inspire men and women to take up arms and/or engage in terrorist activity.

In combating terrorism, the United States and other governments should rely on more than traditional intelligence and counter-terrorism strategies. Overall, total spending on U.S. foreign economic aid is currently about three times spending on military aid. But in the tense and highly militarized countries of the Middle East, U.S. military aid outstrips economic aid by about 50 percent (U.S. Department of Commerce, Bureau of the Census 2000). We should spend at least equal efforts and resources encouraging effective economic development around the world, especially in this region. Investing more in economic aid, especially in the Middle East, could partially counterbalance our image as a country that funds violence by supplying military arms; it would also address some of the root causes of terrorism.

NOTE

This paper was . . . supported by a grant from the Ford Foundation. Dr. Caiazza is a Study Director at the Institute for Women's Policy Research. . . . Thanks go to Cynthia Enloe of Clark University as well as Barbara Gault, Heidi Hartmann, Vicky Lovell, and Linda Silberg of IWPR for their comments on earlier drafts of this paper.

REFERENCES

Afkhami, Mahnaz. 1995. *Faith and Freedom: Women's Human Rights in the Muslim World (Gender, Culture, and Politics in the Middle East)*. Syracuse: Syracuse University Press.

Aretxaga, B. 1997. *Shattering Silence: Women, Nationalism, and Political Subjectivity in Northern Ireland*. Princeton: Princeton University Press.

Blee, Kathleen. 1992. *Women of the Klan: Racism and Gender in the 1920s*. Berkeley: University of California Press.

Caiazza, Amy. 2001. "Women's Community Involvement: The Effects of Money, Safety, Parenthood, and Friends." Research-in-Brief. Washington, DC: Institute for Women's Policy Research.

Caiazza, Amy. Forthcoming. *Mothers and Soldiers: Men's and Women's Organizing in 1990s Russia*. New York: Routledge.

Caiazza, Amy, and Heidi Hartmann. 2001. "Gender and Civic Engagement." Paper presented to the working group on Work, Family, Democracy, organized by the Johnson Foundation and the Harvard School of Public Health. June (Milwaukee, WI).

Crossette, Barbara. 2001. "Living in a World without Women." *The New York Times*, November 4. Available at website: www.nytimes.com. Accessed November 2001.

Enloe, Cynthia. 1993. *The Morning After: Sexual Politics at the End of the Cold War*. Berkeley: University of California Press.

Enloe, Cynthia. 2000a. *Maneuvers: The International Politics of Militarizing Women's Lives*. Berkeley: University of California Press.

Enloe, Cynthia. 2000b. "Masculinity as Foreign Policy Issue." *Foreign Policy in Focus*, vol. 5, issue 36. Washington, DC: Institute for Policy Studies.

Fangen, Katrine. 1997. "Separate or Equal? The Emergence of an All-Female Group in Norway's Rightist Underground." *Terrorism and Political Violence* 9 (3): 122–64.

Feminist Majority. 2001. "Senate to Consider Bill for Afghan Women." *Feminist Daily News Wire*, November 2, 2001.

Fineman, Martha Albertson, and Roxanne Mykitiuk. 1994. *The Public Nature of Private Violence: The Discovery of Domestic Abuse*. New York: Routledge.

Fisher, Jo. 1989. *Mothers of the Disappeared*. London: Zed Books.

Friedman, Sara Ann. 1994. *Creating Violence-Free Families: A Symposium Summary Report*, New York. 23–25 May 1994. New York: Baha'i International Community, United Nations Development Fund for Women, and United Nations Children Fund.

Hammami, Rema. 1997. "Palestinian Motherhood on the West Bank and Gaza Strip." In Alexis Jetter, Annelise Orleck, and Diana Taylor, eds., *The Politics of Motherhood: Activist Voices from Left to Right*, 161–8. Hanover: University Press of New England.

Harvard School of Public Health, Division of Public Health Practice, Violence Prevention Programs. 2001. "Violence Statistics." Webpage available at www.hsph.harvard.edu/php/VPP/peace.html.

Huffman, Richard. 1999. "Gudrun Ensslin." Available at website www.baader-meinhof.com/who/terrorists/bmgang/ensslingudrun.html. Accessed October 2001.

Human Rights Watch. 1996. *Shattered Lives: Sexual Violence during the Rwandan Genocide and Its Aftermath*. New York: Human Rights Watch.

Human Rights Watch. 2001. *Afghanistan: Humanity Denied, Systematic Violations of Women's Rights in Afghanistan*. New York: Human Rights Watch.

Ibanez, Ana Cristina. 2001. "El Salvador: War and Untold Stories—Women Guerrillas." In Caroline O.N. Moser and Fiona C. Clark, eds., *Victims, Perpetrators, or Actors? Gender, Armed Conflict, and Political Violence*, 117–39. London: Zed Books.

Politt, Katha. 2001. "Where Are the Women?: Subject to Debate." *The Nation*, October 22. Available at website www.thenation.com. Accessed November 2001.

Sapiro, Virginia. 1993. "'Private' Coercion and Democratic Theory: The Case of Gender-Based Violence." In George E. Marcus and Russell L. Hanson, eds., *Reconsidering the Democratic Public*, 427–50. University Park, PA: Pennsylvania State University Press.

Sharoni, Simona. 1997. "Israeli Women Organizing for Peace." In *The Politics of Motherhood: Activist Voices from Left to Right*, ed. Alexis Jetter, Annelise Orleck, and Diana Taylor, 144–60. Hanover, NH: University Press of New England.

Sharoni, Simona. 2001. "Rethinking Women's Struggles in Israel-Palestine and in the North

of Ireland." In Caroline O. N. Moser and Fiona
C. Clark, eds., *Victims, Perpetrators, or Actors?
Gender, Armed Conflict, and Political Violence,*
85–98. London: Zed Books.

Stiglmayer, Alexandra, ed. 1994. *Mass Rape: The
War against Women in Bosnia-Herzegovina.* Lincoln, NE: University of Nebraska Press.

Turshen, Meredith. 2001. "The Political Economy
of Rape: An Analysis of Systematic Rape and
Sexual Abuse of Women during Armed Conflict in Africa." In Caroline O. N. Moser and
Fiona C. Clark, eds., *Victims, Perpetrators, or Actors? Gender, Armed Conflict, and Political Violence,* 55–68. London: Zed Books.

U.S. Department of Commerce, Bureau of the
Census. 2000. *Statistical Abstract of the United
States: 2000.* Washington, DC: Government
Printing Office.

QUESTIONS FOR DISCUSSION

1. How are women's traditional roles key to the development of both radicalism and peace?
2. What obstacles do you perceive to making women's political and economic rights part of foreign policy?
3. Caiazza argues that ideology gets in the way of seeing "private" violence directed toward women in other parts of the world as important. Does a similar gender ideology also limit the public response to violence against women in the United States?
4. How is the toleration of the oppression of women functional for terrorists?

23

DOMESTIC VIOLENCE AMONG THE NAVAJO
A Legacy of Colonization

DIANE MCEACHERN • MARLENE VAN WINKLE • SUE STEINER

The history of colonization has dramatically shaped the experience of many Native people with regard to gender relationships. Among one native community in the Philippines, the Ibaloi, when women are asked what makes a good husband, three areas are mentioned frequently. Women say a good husband is a man who does not drink, does not hit his wife, and is someone who works hard in the field. According to these same women, this set of standards is not "traditional" because there was a time when alcohol consumption and family violence were not part of village life. Alcohol abuse and domestic violence are, to them, part of the "price you have to pay" and "a woman's cross to bear" since the advent of economic and religious colonization. These two statements refer to economic and religious influences that stem from the colonization of the Philippines by both Spain and later the United States.

One forum for the discussion of these and other issues pertinent to Native peoples was the 1987 International Indigenous Peoples Conference sponsored by the Philippine National movement. A Native American delegate from a U.S. reservation commented on his profound experience in one of the remote mountain villages he had visited while in the Philippines. He told the participants that although he was from halfway around the world, he felt more at home in the village with tribal Bontoc people than he did in the nearby "border" town near his reservation home in the United States. While he did not speak the Bontoc language, the culture of the people and the manner in which he, as a visitor, was treated overwhelmed him with a sensation of home. The conference contained and generated a rich energy as indigenous group delegates from all over the world assessed the "price" they were all paying for the subjugation of their communities to Western, and more specifically, the United States global power.

As do native women in the Philippines, Native American women from a variety of tribes within the United States also bear the brunt of colliding cultures and government colonial policies. This reading presents an exploratory analysis of domestic violence among Navajo Indians of the Southwest United States, with a focus on the Western Navajo Reservation in Arizona. Specific attention is paid to the effects of colonization, the clash between Native American and mainstream American culture, and the effects of living in an isolated rural area.

Information for the paper was gathered through the authors' experiences as social work practitioners working in the area of domestic violence and working with Native Peoples, and through ethnographic research conducted among Navajo men and women in Northeastern Arizona. The authors interviewed community leaders, social service providers, and women who had experienced domestic violence. The latter were contacted through the authors' personal networks and the network of service providers. Interviews were conducted by one of the authors who is a member of the Navajo community. This fluid research methodology is essential, given the cultural-based reluctance to discuss domestic violence that is common among the Navajo, as well as the Navajo community's discomfort with outsiders.

Domestic Violence

Although women have been beaten within the confines and privacy of their intimate relationships throughout historical record it wasn't until the late 1980s that the Surgeon General of the United States identified domestic violence as the number one public health problem for women. It remains the leading cause of injuries to women ages 15–44. These injuries are more common than muggings, auto accidents, and cancer deaths combined (Dwyer, Smokowski, Bricout, & Wodarski, 1995). The historical context within which battering has developed is that of male domination within and outside the family unit. Throughout most of Western European history, the patriarchal family was directly supported by the laws and practices of the larger society. That historical legacy was brought to the United States and continues to influence the dominant social structure. The patriarchal family predates capitalist society, and so does violence against women within it. . . .

Pre-capitalist and early capitalist patriarchal authority was based on the father's control of "his" household, which was the focus of daily life and productive activity for everyone. In Western Europe, marriage laws explicitly recognized the family as the domain of the husband, forced women to conform to the man's will, and punished men and women unequally for infractions of marriage vows (Dobash & Dobash, 1979).

In their historical overview of wife beating, Dobash and Dobash (1979) note that, "through the seventeenth, eighteenth, and nineteenth centuries, there was little objection within the community to a man's using force against his wife as long as he did not exceed certain tacit limits" (p. 42). It is this historical reality that is relevant to exploring the development of domestic violence among Native Americans in general, and within the Navajo Nation, more specifically.

Domestic Violence Among Native Americans

Working with Native Americans requires the ability to collapse the past and present into a current reality. Time often takes on a different meaning, with the past feeling like a part of the present. Given this cultural reality, it is impossible to explore a present situation without exploring its historical context. While Native American women come from a diversity of tribal and cultural backgrounds, they share similar experiences and legacies of rapid social change. Much of this change can be directly linked to European colonization, disease decimation from European contact, Christian missionizing, and relocations to "less desirable" geographic areas and/or boarding schools. Although domestic violence is an issue which dates back throughout history among European populations, most scholars of Native American cultures believe that domestic violence is a relatively recent phenomenon which coincides with the advent of colonial rule and the subjugation of Native Americans. As one Navajo woman put it, "A lot of women are having trouble with their husbands. The only model the men have is the macho white man. They try to copy him and

Navajo women object" (Shepardson, 1982, p. 101).

There seems to be relatively little information about Native cultures regarding violence against women prior to European contact. What is known is that in most Native American societies men's and women's roles were delineated in such a way that violence against women among their own groups did not seem to be a common and regular practice (Allen, 1986; Neithammer, 1977; Wagner, 1988). For example, among Iroquois women, there was recognition that, ". . . As an Indian woman I was free. I owned my own home, my person, the work of my own hands. I was better as an Indian woman than under white law" (Fletcher, 1888, p. 2). Traditionally, within Navajo culture, women shared equal rights with men, and sometimes enjoyed superior authority and importance. Navajo common law reflected these values through women's property ownership and control, the mother's determinative role in tracing ancestry, and married couples' practice of residing with the wife's family. Some cultures treat women as property, or their culture's law retains vestiges of the notion that women are property. Navajo common law used property and ownership concepts in a different way: "In marriage, . . . a man becomes property of a woman, a woman property of a man" (Zion & Zion, 1993, p. 35). In this way, Navajo common law conceived the reciprocal relations of a man and woman as an interdependent bond. Women's equal status and dignity are reinforced by Navajo literature, which details Navajo women's important work and essential role in society. Their greatest deity, Changing Woman, who is also Mother Earth, symbolizes women's social importance.

In their study of rape and Navajo traditional response to it, Zion and White (1986) could not locate sources which clearly defined early Navajo rape customs. They concluded that rape was relatively absent from early Navajo society. Similarly, they found that the available literature seems to indicate that domestic violence and child abuse were known but were an aberration. Native American scholar Paula Gunn Allen (1986) contends that the crime of domestic violence is caused by economic dislocation, the destruction of traditional institutions, and the introduction of individualism and the individualistic norms of paternalism and patriarchal rule. These new concepts were mandated and forced upon the Native American community in a variety of ways, some of which are described below.

Prior to 1883, marriage practices, divorce, and inheritance were strongholds of women's power within the tribe. Divorce could be enacted by women simply by removing the husband's belongings from the home. Wealth such as animals, the home, and possessions in the family passed through the mother to her daughters. In 1883, the Commissioner of Indian Affairs introduced the Court of Indian Offenses for Indian reservations, where some of the "new" crimes included traditional marriage practices, traditional divorce, and traditional inheritance (Zion & Zion, 1993). The resulting regulations changed the power balance between men and women. The federal government also thought that the best way to "civilize" Indians was to turn them into farmers with exclusive rights to a fixed area of land. The federal government, through the Dawes Act of 1886, required the allotment of Indian lands. These allotments were made to men and not women, further eroding Native American women's power. One of the theories behind the Dawes Act was that individual land ownership would "restore" manhood to Indian men (Deutsch, 1991). The allotment system "was intended to transform Indians who lived under varied kin systems into male-headed, monogamous nuclear families," either ignoring or

attacking Indian concepts of family (Scharff, 1991, p. 64).

Another destructive innovation was the adoption of the strong, male leader—"the head man." U.S. government leaders insisted that the Navajos select male leaders (Underhill, 1956). Navajo women had enjoyed a strong role in the public decisions of Navajo clan groups. They lost their ability to participate in decisions made by male leaders given absolute power. Thus, alien law and government destroyed traditional relationships and concentrated power in the hands of male leaders. Without the institutionalized protection of Navajo common law, Navajo women suffered. In this way, non-Indian paternalism and patriarchy were introduced to Navajos. Navajo men learned several Anglo "traditions" including robbing women of economic and political power and wife-beating.

The use of boarding schools is another powerful instituted practice that is repeatedly mentioned when talking with Native Americans about the issues facing them today. Between 1850 and 1950, the federal government practiced widespread systematic removal of Indian children from their families and communities and placed them into state- and church-run boarding schools. This was to become known as "the boarding school era." The boarding school was an important component of the efforts to destroy tribal cultures. For many people these schools were a traumatic experience that included physical, sexual and emotional abuse. The federal government implemented coordinated efforts to eradicate each tribe's religion, identity, language, and social organization. The effects of these destructive efforts still reverberate at many levels including the family. Away from their families, prohibited from speaking their languages and practicing their traditions, generations of Indian children grew up in institutions that widely used corporal punishment as a means of "socialization" (Brown, 1971). . . .

Interviews conducted by the authors often included mention of the boarding schools. One Navajo man, a traditional counselor, was asked to give his view of domestic violence. He began recounting an incident that happened to him when he was going to a boarding school. He spoke of the harsh treatment he and other children received. He told of priests who sexually abused boys and how cruel some of the teachers were. He then went further back in history and talked about why hogans are constructed in the shape they are. He said that a hogan represents the center of the family and community and it is round to replicate the body of a pregnant woman. The logs used in construction represent her hands clasped around her belly. He explained that "home is wherever woman is." At first we tried to ask about domestic violence in other ways to try and get him to say something about the present situation but each time he would refer back to boarding school times. To this man, domestic violence was not defined merely in terms of abuse occurring within the home, but more broadly as that which was done to Native Americans through the use of boarding schools.

Domestic Violence Among the Navajo

The Navajo Nation is the largest and most populous American Indian nation with over 250,000 members. Spanning Arizona, New Mexico and Utah, the Navajo Nation encompasses 17.5 million acres—and is larger than the states of Connecticut, Delaware, Maryland, Massachusetts and Rhode Island combined. The 1990 Census reports that the percentage of Navajos living below the poverty level was approximately 56 percent as compared to approximately 13 percent for the United States. The average annual per capita income of the Navajo people was $4,106 compared to the U.S. average of $19,082 in 1990. Navajo unemployment ranges from 36 percent to over 50 percent seasonally. Navajo Nation President Albert A. Hale (1996) further describes conditions on the Reservation:

> . . . many of these conditions can be attributed to a lack of infrastructure which itself is directly related to the failure of the federal government to live up to its trust and treaty responsibilities. For example, the Navajo reservation has 2,000 miles of paved roads while West Virginia, which is roughly equivalent in size, has over 18,000 miles. Similarly, the vast majority of Navajo homes lack electricity, running water and telephones, or all of the above. (p. 4)

Domestic violence is a growing problem on the Navajo reservation, and it is particularly difficult in Western Navajo. Western Navajo has a varied topography, generally mountainous with deep canyon lands. For every dirt road there is a corresponding footpath and many families live miles from other families. The largest town in the area is Tuba City with a population of 8,000. Although Western Navajo has the second highest population and covers one-third of the total reservation land area, it has the fewest services for women and children victims of domestic violence. Without a phone, money, and transportation, and with miles between houses, a Navajo woman faces a formidable challenge in attempting to leave a violent partner. People on the reservation live in geographically rural areas with long distances between services. This further complicates the issue of family violence. Rural populations are generally not large enough to support specialized services, and transportation is a perennial problem. There is a high lack of awareness of services, or knowledge as to whether a battered woman's shelter could, in fact, provide emergency transport. There is no phone service to many households. Specific to reservation life, if a woman wants to leave her abusive partner, she may need to leave the reservation. This means leaving her family network. Often, she will not be able to find work in the nearby border towns and returning to the reservation and the perpetrator becomes the lesser of two evils, especially when her children are involved.

Perpetrators of domestic violence have a sense of how to maintain control over their victims. They know that phones, money and transportation can be vital links to a woman's ability to escape to safety. Many of the conditions that exist within the Navajo Nation in general, and in the Western Navajo more specifically, exacerbate the problem of domestic violence, and limit a woman's opportunities to leave violent situations. The following anecdotes, with details changed to preserve anonymity, are representative of stories heard often from women on the reservation, and express many of the dilemmas a Navajo woman faces:

> May, a Navajo woman, dropped her husband off at the trading post on the Navajo Reservation so he could unload hay. As she drove off she became stuck in mud. As a result, she was late in returning to pick up her husband. In a rage, he hit her repeatedly in front of the children while they were in the trading post parking lot. During the attack, the three young children screamed for him to stop. Badly beaten, with a serious eye injury, the woman fled and walked for hours in the snow until she came to a home where she was allowed to stay the night. There was no telephone, and with

the severe shortage of Navajo police she might not have gotten assistance from them. The next day, she again set off on foot until she came to another house where the family had a car and gas and was able to drive her 50 miles to the hospital so she could have her eye treated.

A Navajo woman was severely beaten by her husband in her home. Her children ran from the house to get help from relatives about a half mile down the road. A relative notified police officers and requested an ambulance. The ambulance arrived first, but the paramedics found that the road to the home was too muddy for the ambulance to get through. The paramedics began to walk through the mud to the house, and were eventually picked up by police officers whose vehicle was able to make it through the mud. The woman was severely hurt, and was taken from her home by the paramedics in the police vehicle, which became stuck in the mud while leaving the house. The vehicle was eventually freed from the mud, and the woman taken to a hospital. Unfortunately, the length of time that it took the police and paramedics to arrive allowed the husband to flee, and the delays meant that a great deal of time passed before the woman was able to get medical attention.

Sometime in 1991, Sara was beaten by her husband, Ned. They are Navajo and live with their two toddlers and baby on the Navajo Reservation. Ned had been drinking when he began hitting and screaming at Sara. Ned kept a gun in the house and had threatened to kill Sara a number of times. She decided to take the beating and hope that he would soon pass out so she could escape with the children. They did not own a phone, there was no cash in the house, and the car was not running.

Ned soon passed out and Sara, experiencing back pain, extensive bruises and a swollen eye, gathered her children and left the house. She carried the baby while the two toddlers walked beside her. It was summer and as the heat began pressing on the day, Sara and the children walked two miles on a dirt path to a main road which was also unpaved. She then hitched a ride 10 miles to the Trading Post, a small store located in most Chapter House areas. No one was around so she walked a mile to the Chapter House office building. There was a phone there but, as is common, it was broken. As luck would have it, a police officer drove by and Sara flagged him down. It was rare good fortune because there are only 5 police officers patrolling the 4,100 square mile area. The officer drove her and her exhausted children 50 miles to a relay point. Another police officer picked her up and took her to the nearest shelter which was 100 miles away. The shelter was full. They found another shelter in a nearby town outside the reservation with space. By that time it was about 8 o'clock at night. Sara and the children eventually returned to Ned.

Contradictions Within Law Enforcement

"Equality of rights under the law shall not be denied or abridged by the Navajo Nation on account of sex . . ." so reads the Navajo Nation Bill of Rights. What U.S. women could not get passed before the national government, Navajo women were accorded outright. Yet due to the various conditions outlined previously, it is difficult for law enforcement to be of much assistance to women who are being battered in their homes.

The small town of Kayenta, in Western Navajo, has just five officers patrolling 4,100 square miles. The officers are responsible for 15,270 people. Police in this endless horizon of red rock formations and valleys aren't unlike those in other rural, poor districts around the nation. For Navajo officers, however, the task is compounded by the reservation's horrifying host of social ills: unemployment, alcoholism, suicide and murder rates multiple times the national average. It is particularly challenging for police in this area. In the past nine years, three officers were murdered on the job, one committed suicide and another was jailed for killing his wife (Boorstein, 1997). Navajo police chief Leonard Butler noted the changes for police, saying, "When I started in 1971, a lot of our time was taken up with livestock being shot or windmill disputes. Now, in one week I've got two fatal accidents, one suicide and five people killed. There are times when you don't want to go to work anymore."

Navajo officers mirror their community. Alcohol and drug abuse, divorce, domestic violence or suicide seem to touch nearly every life. Often they blame the victim in domestic violence disputes, saying she must have done something to bring on the abuse. In this way they conform to the attitude of many law officers in the U.S. For all of these reasons, some Navajo women are concerned that in domestic violence situations, help from law enforcement officers may not be readily available.

Directions for Intervention

In July 1993, the Navajo Nation enacted the Domestic Abuse Prevention Act. This act states that domestic violence is a crime, specifies that protection is to be provided for all populations, outlines services for victims, and specifies penalties for perpetrators.

The Resolution of the Navajo Nation Council (CJY-52-93) accompanying the act states:

1. Domestic violence is occurring on the Navajo Nation in epidemic proportions. Many Navajo persons are beaten, harassed, threatened or otherwise subjected to abuse within the domestic setting; and
2. Domestic violence has a lasting detrimental effect on the individuals who directly experience the abuse and on their children, who carry memories of violence with them into their adult lives and may themselves become violent and abusive.

This legislation demonstrates the Navajo Nation's commitment to addressing the issue of domestic violence, and provides a strong foundation on which interventive efforts can be built. Discussions with Navajo women suggest a possible direction for intervention which deserves further attention. Within many Native cultures when a breakup happened as a result of abuse, the woman who left was viewed as honorable for having the respect and dignity to leave a destructive relationship behind. She did not have to fear retaliation or terrorism. The husband recognized her right to make her own choices and if he could not respect this, the tribe intervened to ensure her safety and teach him proper behavior (Balzer et al. 1993). Navajo women with whom we spoke no longer feel that they would be respected in that way. One woman described her deep shame and embarrassment when her partner abused her. She was extremely afraid of her partner and tried to keep the problems hidden for as long as she could until he almost killed her.

There are women who have been victims and have been able to leave their abusers and get help. One of those women who was interviewed on the reservation said that she saw a connection between women battering and subjugation in other forms. She described how these acts of violence have the same dynamics as those of the invasion of one country by another; the master over slave, the colonization of native people, and Western men's subjugation of women. This suggests that an interventive approach that might prove effective with Navajo women could be built on the work of Brazilian educator Paulo Freire (1970). Freire writes about peasants, and how they can use liberating education to overcome depression and transform their situations. The descriptions of the oppressed peasants fit victims of domestic violence quite well. He describes the peasants as people who feel that they do not know things, that they do not know how to change things, that distrust themselves, and that are very self-deprecating. "So often do they hear that they are good for nothing, know nothing and are incapable of learning anything—that they are sick, lazy, and unproductive—that in the end they become convinced of their own unfitness" (p. 45). This leaves them believing that they do not know how and that they are unable to change their current situations.

Freire stresses that to overcome oppression and to leave oppressive situations, reflection is essential. We must reflect on our situation, before we can act to change it. He points out the importance of gaining a critical awareness of oppression through dialogue and what he calls "liberating education." Liberating education means not talking at people, not explaining to people, but dialoguing with them. It means helping them to develop a critical consciousness by having conversations with others who are in a similar situation, or have been in a similar situation. This can be done through dialogue groups, where women can come together to explore their lives, and to make connections between their situations and the bigger picture. To do this we must first trust that these women are capable of looking critically at their lives, and capable of reason and reflection. We must also trust that they have the answers and must find them through conversation and struggle with others. This means abandoning our efforts to tell Navajo women in battering situations what they must do, and instead supporting them in their development of a critical consciousness gained through dialogue.

Freire's work may also suggest a direction to take with Navajo batterers. Freire stresses that those who are oppressed emulate their oppressor, and become emotionally dependent. This leads them to take out their frustrations on others who are oppressed around them.

> The peasant is a dependent. He can't say what he wants. Before he discovers his dependence, he suffers. He lets off steam at home, where he shouts at his children, beats them, and despairs. He complains about his wife and thinks everything is dreadful. He doesn't let off steam with the boss because he thinks the boss is a superior being. Lots of times, the peasant gives vent to his sorrows by drinking. (Freire, 1970, p. 47)

Some of the violence of Navajo men toward their female partners may be a result of their own oppression. These men can be helped to understand how the various forms of oppression are related, and how their oppression by the dominant society is resulting in their taking their frustration out at home. Dialogue groups with the male batterers, that focus on consciousness raising and their experience as Native American men in an Anglo-dominated society, can help them better understand themselves and their actions. Dialogue groups could also help them develop more appropriate options for handling their anger and frustration.

Interventions based on Freire's work on liberating education are culturally relevant for the Navajo given the Navajo's experience of colonization and oppression. Freire's model was developed with South American peasants, many of whom, like the Navajo, were living in rural, generally isolated areas. They had also experienced years of colonization and oppression, and extreme poverty. Use of Freire's model also seems appropriate given that it is an intervention that does not require outsiders to come in and try to "fix" the problem for those living on the reservation, as has been tried by Anglos for many years.

Years of colonization have left their mark on members of the Navajo Nation. The Navajo Nation exists within a climate of institutionalized violence, where some of their traditional values of equality and harmony have been broken down. This has led to an increase in family violence. Poverty and a lack of infrastructure and social services exacerbate the problems that Navajo women face when trying to leave violence in their homes. Future research must continue to document the prevalence and severity of the problem of domestic violence on the Navajo reservation, and culturally relevant interventions must be developed and evaluated.

REFERENCES

Allen, Paula Gunn. 1986. *The Sacred Hoop: Recovering the Feminine in American Indian Traditions.* Boston: Beacon Press.

Balzer, R., G. James, L. LaPrarie, and T. Olson. 1993. *Mending the Sacred Circle: Coming Back to Where We Began.* Duluth, MN.

Boorstein, M. 1997, February 24. "Lonely, deadly police work." *Arizona Republic*, p. 1.

Brown, D. 1971. *Bury My Heart at Wounded Knee.* New York: Holt, Reinhart, & Winston.

Deutsch, S. 1991. "Coming Together, Coming Apart—Women's History and the West." *Montana Magazine of Western History* 41:58–60.

Dobash, E. and R. Dobash. 1979. *Violence Against Wives: A Case Against the Patriarchy.* New York: The Free Press.

Dwyer, D., P. Smokowski, J. Bricout, and J. Wodarski. 1995. "Domestic Violence Research: Theoretical and Practical Implications for Social Work." *Clinical Social Work Journal* 23:185–98.

Fletcher, Alice. 1888. *Report of the International Council of Women.* Washington, DC: Darby Printer.

Freire, P. 1970. *Pedagogy of the Oppressed.* New York: Continuum Publishing Co.

Hale, A. 1996. The Navajo Nation Report. Office of the President and Vice President, The Navajo Nation.

Neithammer, C. 1977. *Daughters of the Earth: The Lives and Legends of American Indian Women.* New York: Macmillan.

Scharff, M. 1991. "Gender and Western History: Is Anybody Home on the Range?" *Montana Magazine of West History* 41:62–65.

Shepardson, M. 1982. "The Status of Navajo Women." *American Indian Quarterly* 6.

Underhill, R. 1956. *Navajos.* Norman, OK: University of Oklahoma.

Wagner, S. 1988. "The Root of Oppression Is the Loss of Memory: The Iroquois and the Early Feminist Vision." Paper delivered at the 1988 Champlain Valley Historical Symposium. Plattsburgh, New York.

Zion, J. and M. White. 1986. "The Use of Navajo Custom in Dealing with Rape." In Indian Health Service (ed.) *Final Report: A Case Study of Family Violence in Four Native American Communities.* Washington, DC: Department of Health and Human Services.

Zion, J. and B. Zion. 1993. "Hozho's Sokee—Stay Together Nicely: Domestic Violence Under Navajo Common Law." *Arizona State Law Journal* 25.

QUESTIONS FOR DISCUSSION

1. How does this analysis of battery among the Navajo support a social constructionist analysis of gender?
2. How does this analysis of battery among the Navajo support a structural understanding of gender?
3. Having undermined the institutional supports for Navajo women—their social authority and their rights to land—does the federal government have a responsibility to make services available to battered Navajo women? If so, what does the government need to do?
4. Is the increasing level of violence on the Navajo reservation a sign of cultural assimilation into the American mainstream?

24

EMBATTLED TERRAIN

JUDITH LORBER

Gender is not a homogeneous category, but involves status, identity, and display. *Gender status*—being

From "Embattled Terrain" by Judith Lorber in *Revisioning Gender* edited by Myra Marx Ferree, Judith Lorber, and Beth Hess (Eds.). Copyright © 1999. Reprinted by permission of Alta Mira Press.

taken as a man or a woman—in Western society implies dominance and assertiveness. *Gender identity*—the sense of self as a man or a woman, which can have various sexual identifications—presents interaction and legal issues. *Gender display*—being feminine versus being masculine according to late-twentieth-century postindustrial norms and expectations—involves sexualized behavior and appearance. *Sexuality* involves desired and actual sexual attraction, emotions, and fantasies, not just behavior. A *sexual identity* involves self-identification and a lifestyle; a *sexual status* involves social recognition of the identity (Klein, Sepekoff, and Wolf 1985; Person 1980). In the past decade, bisexuals and transgenders have become recognized social categories along with gays and lesbians, but the boundaries and definitions of each group, as well as their relationships to gender and sexual identity, transgression, and politics, present fascinating theoretical and conceptual issues (Bornstein 1994; Bristow and Wilson 1993; Garber 1992, 1995; Tucker 1995).

In the following analysis of the feminist discourse on gender and sexuality, I will argue that one side of these debates construes gender statuses, identities, and displays as both binary and stable, almost "essential," whereas the other sees them as derived from socialization and social context and thus potentially both multiple and fluid. Although these contrasting views are often implicit, they have political implications for feminist stances on sexuality. . . .

The following discussion of heterosexuality and transgendering examines the theoretical assumptions on gender and sexuality in the different feminist perspectives and the consequent political outcomes. . . .

Lesbigays, Transgenders, and Queers: Who's Who?

The feminist sex wars of the 1980s (Ferguson et al. 1984; Vance 1984) have not disappeared, but they have been superseded somewhat by the current arguments over bisexuality and transgendering. Framed by similar theories of gender and sexuality as essential or socially constructed, the issues

here are the stability of sexual choice, the boundaries of sexual identities, and the politics of transgression (Gamson 1995, 1998; McIntosh 1993; Wilson 1993).

Fifty years ago, Kinsey used a seven-point scale to place people on a heterosexual–homosexual continuum of sexuality, from all male–female sexual acts to all male–male or all female–female (Kinsey, Pomeroy, and Martin 1948; Kinsey et al. 1953). What was revolutionary at the time were Kinsey's statistics showing that a significant proportion of Americans fell into the middle ranges of the scale: They had engaged in both heterosexual and homosexual sex. Yet no one seemed to pay much attention to what we now call bisexuality. All the rhetoric was in terms of binary sexual identities—heterosexual or homosexual.

With the advent of the women's and the homosexual rights movements of the 1970s, it became clear that sexuality is gendered and that there are at least four sexual identities: heterosexual women and men, and lesbians and gays. The new nomenclature for homosexuals reflected the political and lifestyle split between lesbians and gays (McIntosh 1993; Taylor and Whittier 1992). Lesbian idealization of emotionally intimate sexuality and coupling was congruent with the feminist valorization of women's nurturant and expressive qualities. In contrast, the gay movement's pre-AIDS political stance called for liberation through anonymous and promiscuous sexual acts, almost a caricature of conventional masculine sexuality. Each type of sexual behavior could be attributed to female–male differences (sexuality as biology) or to choice and commitment (sexuality as socially constructed). Given that there are many gay men in long-term coupled relationships, often raising children (Weston 1991), and that there are lesbians who enjoy sadomasochistic sex and multiple partners (Hollibaugh and Moraga 1983), the evidence would seem to be on the side of a socially constructed sexual orientation rather than intrinsic male–female characteristics.

However, the debate over the origins and stability of homosexuality continues among sexologists and psychiatrists (Docter 1988; Green and Money 1969; Stoller 1985; Walters and Ross 1986) and among gays and lesbians writing about themselves (Abelove, Barale, and Halperin 1993; Bristow and Wilson 1993; Greenberg 1988; Kitzinger 1987; Stein 1992; Whisman 1996). Studies of *bisexuality* (serial or simultaneous same- and cross-sex sexual relationships) have shown how difficult it is to document the conventional sexual categories empirically (Klein and Wolf 1985; Rust 1995; Tucker 1995). Are we talking about desire, preference, identity, or social status? Sexual identities—heterosexual, homosexual, bisexual—are responses not just to psychic input but also to social and cultural strictures and pressures from family and friends. Because Western culture now constructs sexuality dichotomously (Laqueur 1990), many people whose sexual inclinations and experiences are bisexual are forced to choose between a heterosexual and homosexual identity as their "real" self.

Rust's (1992, 1993) research on bisexual and lesbian sexual identity found that 90 percent of the self identified lesbians who answered her questionnaire had heterosexual relationships, 43 percent after coming out as lesbians, but these were discounted; what counted for these lesbians were their current relationships. The women who identified themselves as bisexual, in contrast, put more emphasis on their sexual attraction to both women and men. Assuming that all self-identified gay men and lesbians have exclusively same-sex partners not only renders invisible the complexities of sexuality but can also have disastrous health outcomes, as has been found in the spread of HIV infection and AIDS among lesbians (Goldstein 1995).

Gender shapes bisexual relationships as much as it does those that are heterosexual and homosexual. One early study found great variations in feelings and behavior within a small sample of bisexuals, but although gender was irrelevant to their choice of partner, sexual scripting was not only gendered, but quite conventional, with both women and men saying that women partners were more emotionally attuned and men partners more physically sexual (Weinberg, Williams, and Pryor 1994). The authors say that this gender-typing is paradoxical:

> In a group that often sets itself against societal norms, we were surprised to discover that bisexual respondents organized their sexual preferences along the lines of traditional gender stereotypes. As with heterosexuals and homosexuals, gender is the building material from which they put together their sexuality. Unlike these groups, however, the edifice built is not restricted to one gender. (p. 57)

Rust (1995) found that her bisexual respondents spoke of being attracted to another person because of particular personality characteristics, ways of behaving, interests, intellect, looks, style. The physical sex, sexual orientation, masculinity, femininity, and gender markers are just the beginning set of parameters, and they might differ for a quick sexual encounter, a romantic liaison, a long-term relationship. Rather than comparing categories of gender or sexuality, researchers might want to compare types of relationships.

As for group identification, gender and sexuality can play out in many ways (Connell 1992). Sedgwick (1990) notes that some homosexuals (e.g., gay drag queens and butch lesbians) want to cross into the other gender's social space, whereas for others (e.g., macho gay men and lesbian separatists), "it is instead the most natural thing in the world that people of the same gender, people grouped under the single most determinative diacritical mark of social organization, people whose economic, institutional, emotional, physical needs and knowledges may have so much in common, should bond together also on the axis of sexual desire" (p. 87).

The issues of gender identification and display that Sedgwick raises are even more problematized by transgenders—transsexuals, transvestites, and hermaphrodites. Transsexuals are individuals with cross-gender identification; some pass as members of the desired gender more or less permanently through cross-dressing and renaming, while others undergo medicalized sex change (hormones and surgery) and change their legal and marital status as well (Bolin 1988; Morris 1975). Although the initial medical research on transsexuals (Green and Money 1969) accepted their insistence that they had believed they belonged in the opposite gender from early childhood (indeed, that was a condition for the surgery), stories began to emerge of the deliberate use of their mothers' hormones by boys and other manipulations of the medical teams (Garfinkel 1967:285–88). And it was also startling to those believing in clear-cut sex and sexual categorization to find that there are transsexuals who are homosexual in desire and behavior, both before and after surgery (Bolin 1988; Feinbloom et al. 1976).

Hermaphrodites and pseudohermaphrodites are people born with ambiguous genitalia or hormonal input (Fausto-Sterling 1993). In the Dominican Republic, there has been a genetic phenomenon in which children who looked female at birth and were brought up as girls produced male hormones at puberty. Their genitalia masculinized, their voices deepened, and they developed a male physical appearance (Imperato-McGinley et al. 1979). Most gradually changed to men's social roles—working

outside the home, marrying, and becoming heads of households. Not all those who lived as men had fully functioning genitalia, and all were sterile. Some researchers who studied these pseudohermaphrodites claim that those who decided they would adopt men's identities and social roles despite having been raised as girls "appear to challenge both the theory of the immutability of gender identity after three or four years of age and the sex of rearing as the major factor in determining male-gender identity" (Imperato-McGinley et al. 1979:1236). They stress the effects of the hormonal input and secondary male sex characteristics at puberty. Others question whether the pseudohermaphrodites were reared unambiguously as girls, given their somewhat abnormal genitalia at birth, arguing that the community recognized and had names for a third sex category (Herdt 1990). At puberty, although virilization was not total, it provided the opportunity for the choice of the more attractive social role. In Papua New Guinea, many of these children were identified by experienced midwives at birth and reared anticipatorily as boys (Herdt 1990; Herdt and Davidson 1988). They went through boys' rituals as they grew up, but their identity as adult men was stigmatized; because of their small penises, they did not allow themselves to be fellated by adolescent boys, which made them fully men in that culture.

In Westernized countries, "clarifying" surgery has usually been done right after birth on children born with ambiguous genitalia to support an unambiguous gender categorization (Kessler 1990, 1998). In the past few years, there has been an intersex movement in protest against what is felt to be genital mutilation and the ruin of future sexual pleasure (Angier 1996; Cowley 1997). The sexual potentialities of true hermaphrodites with male and female genitalia who are not surgically altered can be gleaned from Fausto-Sterling's (1993) account of

Emma, who was born in 1937 with a penis-like clitoris as well as a vagina. Raised as a girl, Emma used her penis in sexual relationships with women, and her vagina in sexual relations with her husband. She refused to have vaginal closure and to live as a man because it would have meant a divorce and her having to get a job. Emma's gender identity was that of a woman; she was physiologically bisexed, and thus able to be heterosexual in her sexual relations with her husband as well as with her women lovers.

Transvestism, or cross-dressing, is a familiar phenomenon in many societies throughout history, with many combinations and permutations of gender and sexual display, identity, and social status (Epstein and Straus 1991; Kates 1995; Nanda 1990; Williams 1986). In Western societies, women have dressed as men to work in nontraditional jobs, join the military, or enter other places where women are not allowed (Wheelwright 1989; Woodhouse 1989). Others cross-dress for performances (drag queens and kings), for parties and parades, for sexual pleasure, and just for kicks (Ekins 1997; Garber 1992). The two types of gender display—passing and transgressive—have totally different implications for gender identity and gender politics.

Passing both normalizes and disrupts conventional gender categories. Those who construct their gender against their sex assignment, whether through cross-dressing or surgical alteration of genitalia, reaffirm the conventional categories of man and woman, typically dressing conservatively and making their genitalia congruent with their outward gender display. Against this almost essentialist perspective, their own behavior sabotages the essentiality of the categories; in Garber's (1992) words, anyone who passes successfully (by crossing any boundaries) possesses "extraordinary power . . . to disrupt, expose, and challenge, putting in question the very notion of the 'original' and of stable identity" (p. 16). But only if they "unmask." Transgenders who pass as normal women or men achieve a successful transformation, but their achievement (and the gender resistance it entails) must remain a secret. As Gagné and Tewksbury (1998) say of their transgendered respondents:

> The need to come to terms with and publicly proclaim an alternative gender identity outweighed the fear of rejection and desire for self-preservation. But the need to avoid social erasure compelled a complete (even if temporary) transformation. For most, identity achievement entailed the public expression of gender in ways that reflected an internalized sense of self, not one externally imposed upon them. Often this required enacting the gender of the "opposite" sex/gender category, the only known possibility available. (p. 86; see also Gagné, Tewksbury, and McGaughey 1997)

Queers openly subvert binary gender and sexual categories through their deliberate mixtures of clothing, makeup, jewelry, hairstyles, and behavior. Transgression—queering—is their goal. By not constructing gender and sexuality in expected ways, they make visible, . . . the performativity on which the whole gender order depends. In their self-presentation, mixtures of partners in relationships, nonconventional combinations of housemates, and in-your-face political acts and cultural performances, they are saying to heterosexuals, "Get over it" and "Get used to it" (Warner 1993). Yet the more outrageous the behavior, the more the boundaries get drawn between "them" and "us" (Gamson 1998).

Despite the attempts of queer theorists to include lesbians, gays, bisexuals, transgenders, and hermaphrodites under one transgressive category, they themselves have broken up into multiple groups with different political goals. Lesbians, gays, and bisexuals are grouping under the rubric "lesbigay" in academic centers, and there is a *Journal of Gay, Lesbian, and Bisexual Identity,* which was started in 1996. Their agenda is the decentering of heterosexuality and the expansion of sexual possibilities. Nonetheless, there is still uneasiness between lesbians and bisexuals over the politics of identity, because the political stance of those lesbians and gays who argue that homosexuality is not a matter of choice is undermined by bisexual behavior and politics (McIntosh 1993; Rust 1995).

Transsexuals and transvestites now often call themselves transgenders. Although cross-dressing is a standard phase on the road to sex-change surgery, many transvestites do not even want to change their gender, let alone their genitalia. Ekins (1997) distinguishes three patterns among men—those related to sex ("body femaling"), sexuality ("erotic femaling"), and role behavior ("gender femaling"). Hermaphrodites are in an even more anomalous position. They can choose to live as men or women, but if they do not have "clarifying" surgery, their genitalia will not match their gender status. Even if they do have surgery, they are usually infertile. Although there has been some shared activism with groups opposing female genital mutilation (but not around infertility), for the most part hermaphrodites feel they don't fit in with any other gender, sex, or sexual group. It is not surprising that they have developed their own identity politics with a separate organization, Intersex Society of North America, which publishes a journal on the Internet, *Hermaphrodites with Attitude* (see also Angier 1996).

The double identity of belonging and not belonging to a category of stigmatized people has created hostility toward transsexuals and transgenders among some feminists and toward bisexual women among some lesbians. As Raymond (1979) says in arguing that male-to-female transsexuals are not women:

> We know that we are women who are born with female chromosomes and anatomy, and that whether or not we were socialized to be so-called normal women, patriarchy has treated and will treat us like women. Transsexuals have not had this same history. No man can have the history of being born and located in this culture as a woman. He can have the history of *wishing* to be a woman and of *acting* like a woman, but this gender experience is that of a transsexual, not of a woman. Surgery may confer the artifacts of outward and inward female organs but it cannot confer the history of being born a woman in this society. (p. 114; for a response, see Stone 1991)

On lesbian politics and bisexuality, Rust (1995) says: "Lesbians have become invested in a gender-based definition of lesbianism. Bisexuals, by challenging both dichotomous gender and dichotomous sexuality, challenge the very existence of lesbianism" (p. 59).

In sum, the content of the transgressions (gender status, sexual behavior, sexual identity, appearance, genitalia) and the divisions between those who want to pass as normal women and men and those who are open gender rebels make it theoretically and politically impossible to speak of "transgenders" as a unified category. This fragmentation of identity groups and their conflicting agendas undermine the possibilities for unified political action. As Gamson (1995) says, "In the contemporary American political environment, clear identity categories are both necessary and dangerous distortions, and moves to both fix and unfix them are reasonable" (p. 401). Without a political agenda for change, transgressiveness soon loses its sting:

> We transgress in order to insist that we are there, that we exist, and to place a distance between ourselves and the dominant culture. But we have to go further—we have to have an idea of how things could be different, otherwise transgression ends in mere posturing. In other words, transgression on its own leads eventually to entropy, unless we carry within us some idea of transformation. It is therefore not transgression that should be our watchword, but transformation. (Wilson 1993, 116)

(In)conclusion

In this chapter, I have shown that the feminist differences over heterosexuality, and multiple sexualities are to a great extent based on contrasting theories of gender. One gender perspective relies on clear and dichotomous categories of women and men with different sexual needs and behavior. In the contrasting perspective, gender is one of the social statuses that intersect with all the socially significant statuses, especially race and ethnicity, social class, sexual orientation, and age.

AUTHOR'S NOTE

Parts of this chapter are adapted from *Paradoxes of Gender* (Yale University Press, 1994). I thank Myra and Beth for their editing, and Carolle Charles, Maren Lockwood Carden, Susan Farrell, Eileen Moran, and Barbara Katz Rothman for their astute comments on this chapter.

REFERENCES

Abelove, Henry, Michèle Aina Barale, and David M. Halperin, eds. 1993. *The Lesbian and Gay Studies Reader*. New York: Routledge.

Angier, Natalie. 1996. "Intersexual Healing: An Anomaly Finds a Group." *New York Times*, February 4, Week in Review, p. 14.

Bolin, Anne. 1988. *In Search of Eve: Transsexual Rites of Passage*. South Hadley, MA: Bergin & Garvey.

Bornstein, Kate. 1994. *Gender Outlaw: On Men, Women, and the Rest of Us*. New York: Vintage.

Bristow, Joseph and Angelia R. Wilson, eds. 1993. *Activating Theory: Lesbian, Gay, and Bisexual Politics*. London: Lawrence & Wishart.

Connell, R. W. 1992. "A Very Straight Gay: Masculinity, Homosexual Experience, and Gender." *American Sociological Review* 57:735–51.

Cowley, Geoffrey. 1997. "Gender Limbo." *Newsweek*, May 19, pp. 64–66.

Docter, Richard F. 1988. *Transvestites and Transsexuals: Toward a Theory of Cross-Gender Behavior*. New York: Plenum.

Ekins, Richard. 1997. *Male Femaling: A Grounded Theory Approach to Cross-Dressing and Sex-Changing*. New York: Routledge.

Epstein, Julia and Kristina Straus, eds. 1991. *Body Guards: The Cultural Politics of Gender Ambiguity*. New York: Routledge.

Fausto-Sterling, Anne. 1993. "The Five Sexes: Why Male and Female Are Not Enough." *Sciences* (March–April):20–25.

Feinbloom, Deborah Heller, Michael Fleming, Valerie Kijewski, and Margo P. Schulter. 1976. "Lesbian/Feminist Orientation among Male-to-Female Transsexuals." *Journal of Homosexuality* 2(1):59–71.

Ferguson, Ann, Ilene Philipson, Irene Diamond, Lee Quinby, Carole S. Vance, and Ann Barr Snitow. 1984. "Forum: The Feminist Sexuality Debates." *Signs* 10:106–35.

Gagné, Patricia and Richard Tewksbury. 1998. "Conformity Pressures and Gender Resistance among Transgendered Individuals." *Social Problems* 45:81–101.

Gagné, Patricia, Richard Tewksbury, and Deanna McGaughey. 1997. "Coming Out and Crossing Over: Identity Formation and Proclamation in a Transgender Community." *Gender & Society* 11:478–508.

Gamson; Joshua G. 1995. "Must Identity Movements Self-Destruct? A Queer Dilemma." *Social Problems* 42:390–407.

———. 1998. "Publicity Traps: Television Talk Shows and Lesbian, Gay, Bisexual, and Transgender Visibility." *Sexualities* 1:11–41.

Garber, Marjorie. 1992. *Vested Interests: Cross-Dressing and Cultural Anxiety*. New York: Routledge.

———. 1995. *Vice Versa: Bisexuality and the Eroticism of Everyday Life*. New York: Simon & Schuster.

Garfinkel, Harold. 1967. *Studies in Ethnomethodology*. Englewood Cliffs, NJ: Prentice-Hall.

Goldstein, Nancy. 1995. "Lesbians and the Medical Profession: HIV/AIDS and the Pursuit of Visibility." *Women's Studies* 24: 531–52.

Green, Richard and John Money, eds. 1969. *Transsexualism and Sex Reassignment*. Baltimore: Johns Hopkins University Press.

Greenberg, David F. 1988. *The Construction of Homosexuality*. Chicago: University of Chicago Press.

Herdt, Gilbert. 1990. "Mistaken Gender: 5α-Reductase Hermaphroditism and Biological Reductionism in Sexual Identity Reconsidered." *American Anthropologist* 92:433–46.

Herdt, Gilbert and Julian Davidson. 1988. "The Sambia 'Turnim-man': Sociocultural and Clinical Aspects of Gender Formation in Male Pseudohermaphrodites with 5α-Reductase Deficiency in Papua, New Guinea." *Archives of Sexual Behavior* 17:33–56.

Hollibaugh, Amber and Cherrie Moraga. 1983. "What We're Rollin' Around in Bed With: Sexual Silences in Feminism." Pp. 394–405 in *Powers of Desire: The Politics of Sexuality*, edited by Ann Snitow, Christine Stansell, and Sharon Thompson. New York: Monthly Review Press.

Imperato-McGinley, Julianne, Ralph E. Peterson, Teofilo Gautier, and Erasmo Sturla. 1979. "Androgens and the Evolution of Male-Gender Identity among Male Pseudohermaphrodites with 5a-Reductase Deficiency." *New England Journal of Medicine* 300:1233–37.

Kates, Gary. 1995. *Monsieur d'Eon Is a Woman: A Tale of Political Intrigue and Sexual Masquerade*. New York: Basic Books.

Kessler, Suzanne J. 1990. "The Medical Construction of Gender: Case Management of Intersexed Infants." *Signs* 16:3–26.

———. 1998. *Lessons from the Intersexed*. New Brunswick, NJ: Rutgers University Press.

Kinsey A. C., W. B. Pomeroy, and C. E. Martin. 1948. *Sexual Behavior in the Human Male*. Philadelphia: W. B. Saunders.

Kinsey, A. C., W. B. Pomeroy, C. E. Martin, and P. H. Gebhard. 1953. *Sexual Behavior in the Human Female*. Philadelphia: W. B. Saunders.

Kitzinger, Celia. 1987. *The Social Construction of Lesbianism*. Newbury Park, CA: Sage.

Klein, Fritz, Barry Sepekoff, and Timothy J. Wolf. 1985. "Sexual Orientation: A Multi-variable Dynamic Process." *Journal of Homosexuality* 11, (1–2):35–49.

Klein, Fritz and Timothy J. Wolf, eds. 1985. *Two Lives to Lead: Bisexuality in Men and Women*. New York: Harrington Park.

Laqueur, Thomas. 1990. *Making Sex: Body and Gender from the Greeks to Freud*. Cambridge, MA: Harvard University Press.

McIntosh, Mary. 1993. "Queer Theory and the War of the Sexes." Pp. 30–52 in *Activating Theory: Lesbian, Gay, and Bisexual Politics*, edited by Joseph Bristow and Angelia R. Wilson. London: Lawrence & Wishart.

Morris, Jan. 1975. *Conundrum*. New York: Signet.

Nanda, Serena. 1990. *Neither Man or Woman: The Hijiras of India*. Belmont, CA: Wadsworth.

Person, Ethel Spector. 1980. "Sexuality as the Mainstay of Identity: Psychoanalytic Perspectives." *Signs* 5:605–30.

Raymond, Janice G. 1979. *The Transsexual Empire: The Making of the She-male*. Boston: Beacon.

Rust, Paula. 1992. "The Politics of Sexual Identity: Attraction and Behavior among Lesbian and Bisexual Women." *Social Problems* 39: 366–86.

———. 1993. "'Coming Out' in the Age of Social Constructionism: Sexual Identity Formation among Lesbian and Bisexual Women." *Gender & Society* 7:50–77.

———. 1995. *Bisexuality and the Challenge to Lesbian Politics: Sex, Loyalty, and Revolution*. New York: New York University Press.

Sedgwick, Eve Kosofsky. 1990. *Epistemology of the Closet*. Berkeley: University of California Press.

Stein, Edward, ed. 1992. *Forms of Desire: Sexual Orientation and the Social Constructionist Debate*. New York: Routledge.

Stoller, Robert J. 1985. *Presentations of Gender*. New Haven, CT: Yale University Press.

Stone, Sandy. 1991. "The *Empire* Strikes Back: A Posttranssexual Manifesto." Pp. 280–304 in *Body Guards: The Cultural Politics of Gender Ambiguity*, edited by Julia Epstein and Kristina Straus. New York: Routledge.

Taylor, Verta and Nancy E. Whittier. 1992. "Collective Identity in Social Movement Communities: Lesbian Feminist Mobilization." Pp. 104–29 in *Frontiers in Social Movement Theory*, edited by Aldon Morris and Carol McClurg Muellen. New Haven, CT: Yale University Press.

Tucker, Naomi, ed. 1995. *Bisexual Politics: Theories, Queries, and Visions*. New York: Harrington Park.

Vance, Carole S., ed. 1984. *Pleasure and Danger: Exploring Female Sexuality*. Boston: Routledge & Kegan Paul.

Walters, William W. A. and Michael W. Ross. 1986. *Transsexualism and Sex Reassignment.* Oxford: Oxford University Press.

Warner, Michael, ed. 1993. *Fear of a Queer Planet: Queer Politics and Social Theory.* Minneapolis: University of Minneapolis Press.

Weinberg, Martin S., Colin J. Williams, and Douglas W. Pryor. 1994. *Dual Attraction: Understanding Bisexuality.* New York: Oxford University Press.

Weston, Kathleen M. 1991. *Families We Choose: Lesbians, Gays, Kinship.* New York: Columbia University Press.

Wheelwright, Julie. 1989. *Amazons and Military Maids: Women Who Cross-Dressed in Pursuit of Life, Liberty and Happiness.* London: Pandora.

Whisman, Vera. 1996. *Queer by Choice: Lesbians, Gay Men and the Politics of Difference.* New York: Routledge.

Williams, Walter L. 1986. *The Spirit and the Flesh: Sexual Diversity in American Indian Culture.* Boston: Beacon.

Wilson, Elizabeth. 1993. "Is Transgression Transgressive?" Pp. 107–17 in *Activating Theory: Lesbian, Gay, and Bisexual Politics,* edited by Joseph Bristow and Angelia R. Wilson. London: Lawrence & Wishart.

Woodhouse, Annie. 1989. *Fantastic Women: Sex, Gender, and Transvestism.* New Brunswick, NJ: Rutgers University Press.

QUESTIONS FOR DISCUSSION

1. How do political goals manifest themselves in performances of sexuality?
2. Can we understand the breadth of human sexuality when we rely on dichotomous categories of men and women? Is a perspective of gender as a social status more useful?

25

FAMILY MAN
Fatherhood, Housework, and Gender Equity

SCOTT COLTRANE

Why Study Men in Families?

Men's involvement in families, or lack of it, is a relatively new topic of concern for researchers and is part of a renewed interest in women's lives led by feminist scholars. My interest in these issues coincided with my own children's births over a decade ago. Unsatisfied with a peripheral role in their upbringing, I changed jobs several times, and eventually returned to graduate school to study sociology. While at the University of California, I studied with Nancy Chodorow, who recently had written *The Reproduction of Mothering,* an influential book on why women mother (and coincidentally, why men do not). Her complex neo-Freudian theory

From *Family Man: Fatherhood, Housework, and Gender Equity* by Scott Coltrane. Copyright © 1996 by Oxford University Press, Inc. Used by permission of Oxford University Press, Inc.

placed much emphasis on the establishment of gender identity within families where mothers do all the child care. She described an unconscious process wherein male children compensate for a deep and painful sense of betrayal by the mother through their rejection of things feminine, including the feminine parts of their own psyches.[1]

Superficially, my own case seemed to contradict Chodorow's theory, insofar as I was raised by a nurturing stay-at-home mother and a distant breadwinner father. If the capacity and motivation for nurturing children is dependent on early childhood experience, then why was I, having been raised almost exclusively by my mother, so interested in being a nurturing caregiver to my own kids? With further study, I learned that Chodorow was suggesting that the capacity for nurturing exists in both boys and girls as a result of early experiences with a parent— usually the mother. It's just that men tend to suppress and devalue the soft and vulnerable parts of their psyches in an unconscious effort to maintain a firm sense of masculinity. But that sense of oppositional masculinity seemed so fragile and insecure to me that it appeared to be an oppressive trap. From my own experiences of personal growth as a child care worker in college, I wondered if caring for children might not provide other men with opportunities for fuller emotional lives. Could men reclaim a more complete sense of manhood that was not based on rejecting the softer or more "feminine" sides of themselves? That question led me on a search for the reasons why men might be drawn to caring for their children and into the realm of the sociology and social psychology of gender and families.

I was impressed by Chodorow's idea that gender socialization and the formation of masculine and feminine selves, with accompanying patterns of gender inequality in the larger society, were perpetuated through the organization of parenting. I be-

came interested in the social forces that promoted men's assumption of family work and began to study the potential outcomes of involved fathering. I soon discovered that scholars had paid scant attention to fathers before the 1970s. Most psychologists and sociologists had assumed that fathers were peripheral to family functioning, even if their presence was usually deemed desirable. More recently, researchers have begun to help us understand how fathers directly and indirectly influence children and other family members, and how men's family involvements intersect with other aspects of their lives.[2] The few studies that have been conducted with men who are highly involved with their children suggest that fathers can "mother" in the sense that they can interact with and care for infants much like women do. What's more, the children of fathers who share responsibility for the everyday details of their upbringing tend to exhibit enhanced intellectual, cognitive, social, and emotional skills.[3] But a puzzle remains. Despite the potential payoffs of fathers taking a more active role in the family, large-scale surveys still show that most men avoid doing routine child care or housework. What's going on? Why is family work obligatory for women and mothers, yet still optional for men?

Regrettably, most of the popular books on men's changing family roles don't move us very far in answering these questions. With only a few exceptions, books on American fathers have been naively optimistic or bitterly reactionary.[4] In books like *Daddy's Home* and *Good Morning, Merry Sunshine,* we learned the intimate details of what it feels like for a reporter to take a leave of absence from his newspaper job to care for his infant daughter—lampooned in the comic strip *Doonesbury.*[5] We also have a few books by psychologists and social workers who present personal accounts from nurturing fathers struggling to become single parents or attempting to share parenting with their wives.[6] Although these advocates of the "new father" give us a glimpse into the inner lives of nurturing men and provide some useful advice to men who want to care for children, their analyses typically leave women out altogether. By focusing only on the men, and by ignoring most of the larger social, political, and economic contexts and consequences of their actions, these authors fail to give us a complete picture of men's family roles.[7] At the other end of the spectrum, we have men's authors like Robert Bly, who tell us to toughen up and reconnect with our absent fathers through all-male initiation rites.[8] These reactionary approaches are best understood as a backlash against women's modestly expanding opportunities.[9]

Family Life and Social Change

Looking back over the past few decades in the United States, we see rapid shifts in women's employment and slower, though still significant, shifts in men's family roles. Although the everyday routines of family life appear to be timeless and natural (as well as somewhat trivial), they reveal and foreshadow some of the most dramatic social changes of this century.[10] In 1960, hardly anyone questioned why women did nearly all of the child care and housework. Most women were not employed and three out of four mothers were housewives. During the 1970s, more women entered the labor force, and some began to question why they should continue to do all the domestic chores. Researchers conducting studies in the 1970s were surprised to find that men were still doing little around the house or with children, even when their wives were working outside the home.[11] In the 1980s, about half of mothers with children under 18 had entered the paid labor force, and many observers continued to expect the division of household labor to equalize. Some slight shifts in the allocation of domestic responsibilities did occur during the early 1980s, with women putting in fewer hours than they had a decade earlier. As researchers like Arlie Hochschild documented, however, wives in two-job families continued to remain responsible for the *second shift* of raising children and running households.[12] Has anything changed since the 1980s? Yes and no. Mothers continue to enter the labor force in record numbers and women still do most of the family work. Nevertheless, important economic and social transformations are under way that will have profound implications for men's involvement in families.

Reluctant Pioneers

Gary and Susan Carter would not strike most people as radical innovators or social pioneers. In dress, appearance, and demeanor, they are virtually indistinguishable from other couples in this quiet neighborhood of young families on the edge of suburbia.[13] The landscape is dotted with trees, swing sets, and horse corrals, and Gary Carter's pickup truck with knobby tires and lumber racks sits in the driveway of their ranch style house. Gary is a 34-year-old building contractor who has worked in construction since he graduated from high school in a neighboring town. He looks and acts like most of his "hang-loose" carpenter buddies; walrus mustache, healthy tanned face, casual Hawaiian shirt, and a ready smile. Susan Carter recently earned a master's degree in psychology and has been working toward certification as a marriage counselor and divorce mediator. She, too, blends in with her co-workers, though her dress and demeanor are more reserved than Gary's. They have two children, eight-year-old Jennifer, and five-year-old Jason.

For the past four years, Gary and Susan have been sharing the routine care of Jennifer and Jason while they work part-time at their jobs. This is an increasingly common pattern among parents with preschool-aged children. Thirty percent of fathers and over 40 percent of mothers with children under five now work non-day shifts, allowing them to share the care of their children. When the mother works part-time or a non-day shift, the father is now the most common child-care provider for the children.[14] This is the case in the Carter family.

Why Did They Share?

The reasons Gary and Susan gave for sharing child care and employment were typical of those heard from other parents I interviewed. Most said they were simply focusing on what was good for the kids and what was economically feasible. Like many fathers, Gary talked about wanting to "bond" with his kids but worried about earning enough money to support his family. He and Susan worked out an arrangement where they both worked about half time, though both felt that it was a constant struggle to balance their work and family commitments.

Although Gary had been financially successful as a carpenter and contractor, he came to realize that having two earners in the household could be a kind of insurance policy for him and for the family.

> From the business standpoint, it started looking down. We were coming off a real unstable economy and it was long-term guess work for me. I wanted to be realistic about it: the next bad times I wanted help financially. So that, at least, was one of my trade-offs. The other thing is that, physically, construction is real hard on the body and, I figured I could last longer if I worked three days

a week, although it's real tough when everyone else is building five or even seven days a week.

As a result of adopting a three-day work week, Gary lost some contracting jobs, was forced to rely exclusively on self-employment, and reduced his income by almost half. Nevertheless, he rationalized his short work week by comparing himself to his contractor buddies who never saw their families and to a few whose marriages "went sour" because they were never home. Gary also admitted that he was motivated to share child care and employment because of his commitment to his wife, Susan. After years of talk and schooling, Gary had come to realize that Susan's desire to become a counselor was not just a passing fancy, but was necessary to her happiness.

Susan wanted to pursue a fulfilling career of her own and talked about feeling limited when she had been the only one with the children on a regular basis. She was adamant in her support for women and men choosing their own paths in life: "People should be whatever and whoever they want and need to be." She referred to women who were forced to be only housewives and men who were forced to be sole breadwinners as "halves." For Susan, the only way for both spouses to become "whole" was to share the family work and the paid work: for mother and father simultaneously to be homemakers and breadwinners.

A major impetus for the Carters' sharing was a belief that many would call "conservative" or "old fashioned." Both Gary and Susan believed strongly that their kids should not be left with "strangers" during the day; that children needed to be with their parents on a regular basis. Gary talked about people abusing child care by "dumping the kids there for ten hours a day" and vowed that he would never do that. He admitted it was difficult to forgo regular contracting work to perform child care, but he called his time with his children "precious." When I asked him how it felt to know that he could be earning many times what it would cost to pay a child-care worker to care for his children, he answered, "I wouldn't trade this time with the kids for anything." Saying "they're only small once," he commented that within the year they would both be in school until 2:00 P.M. every day and that he would "gradually get my work time back." Similarly, Susan commented that she felt her children could have "handled day care just fine," but that she preferred that they be with her or with their father. She made a point of mentioning that many parents had no choice but to rely on day care, but she felt that children fared better in their own parents' care. She attributed their ability to avoid using outside child care to the flexibility of her and Gary's schedules and their strong commitment to be with their kids.

Ambivalent Reactions

The reactions that Susan and Gary got from most of the people around them were discouraging. Their decision to share breadwinning and homemaking was described as "a little odd" by many friends, and Gary commented that many friends "bet against" them. Gary also felt that Susan's parents, though usually silent, thought less of him because he had relinquished the sole provider role. Gary was seen as less of a man because he cut back on his time at work, and Susan's "maternal instinct" was called into question because she left the kids with Gary rather than "allowing" him to go to work. Gary and Susan also reported ambivalent reactions from neighbors and co-workers, even if most never mentioned the subject directly. According to Gary, most simply "scratched their heads in disbelief."

In discussing how others reacted to their situation, Susan suggested there was a "profound lack of understanding" about their efforts at sharing paid work and family work: "They either don't believe it, or they do believe it and it changes how they relate to us. People are really threatened. Reactions were negative for a really long time, and it took a track record before it started getting more positive." After they initiated their sharing routine, Gary was likely to be at school meetings or other child-centered activities where numerous mothers were present. He soon discovered that most mothers were reluctant to believe he really performed a full range of family work.

> At first they'd ask me, "Is this your day off?" And I'd say, "If it's the day off for me, why isn't it the day off for you?" They'd say, "Well, I work 24 hours a day!" And I'd say, "Yeah, right, I got my wash done and hung out, and the beds made, and the shopping done." It would take the mother a couple of times to realize that I really did that stuff.

After repeated contact, however, some mothers began to include Gary in their conversations and occasionally approached him for advice about how to deal with a problem child, usually a son. Gary also reported that he received more attention than he deserved simply for watching his own children. More than Susan, his actions were noticed and praised, even though he considered her the more adept parent. Susan commented, "I can bust my butt at that school, and all he has to do is show up in the parking lot and everybody's all ga-ga over him."

When couples like the Carters share family work and paid work, you might expect that the wife would get similar attention and praise for assuming half of the breadwinner role. Not so, according to Susan. Reactions to her career ambitions were mostly mixed, and she said Gary's parents did not readily accept her as a co-provider.

> In the beginning there was a real strong sense that I was in the space of Gary's economic duty. That came from his parents pretty strongly. The only way that they have been able to come to grips with this in any fashion is because Gary has also been financially successful. If he had decided, you know, "Outside work is not for me, I'm going to stay home with the kids and she's going to work," I think there would have been a whole lot more flak than there was. I think it's because he did both and was successful that it was okay.

Although others in their circle of friends were more supportive of their efforts, Susan reported that many still couldn't quite figure out what was going on with them.

> It's funny because we both talked about child care plans in terms of, "well you have to ask Gary—that's his day with the kids" or "you better check it out with Susan because the kids will be with her." At school, especially, a lot of people thought we were divorced and were sharing these kids, you know, since we were rarely together because the other person was always at work. So it got to be sort of a joke, "Are you guys really together or are you not?"

Others reported that they admired Susan and Gary's arrangements, but couldn't understand how they ever got there. The reactions the Carters received are similar to reactions other role sharing-couples have reported.[15] Social networks of close-by friends and relatives can easily discourage couples from raising children and doing housework differently from their own parents.

According to Susan, most people assumed it was her fault that Gary was "sacrificing" his career, and since she was still in training and not yet making much money, she felt especially vulnerable to attack. Friends and co-workers saw his contracting business as a huge success and couldn't understand how he could give up that earning potential to "babysit." Susan commented, "I became the bad guy in a lot of circles, and it took Gary a long time to convince people that he really wanted it this way." When I last talked to the Carters, the children were about ready to attend school every day, but Gary still had no plans to go back to work full time. Susan reported that most people had "finally gotten it" that Gary wasn't just going along with her demands, but that he was now fully committed to sharing the family work with her.

Sharing the Worry of Child Care

One of the most interesting findings about families that share child care is that the men go through some personal and emotional changes as they perform more of the mundane child-tending tasks. These changes are not the same for all men, but, for many, the process of routine caregiving fosters more intimate relationships with their children and provides them with opportunities for developing emotional sensitivities. In the Carter family, most of the child care tasks were shared about equally—including awakening their two children, helping them dress, bathing them, putting them to bed, supervising them, disciplining them, chauffeuring them, taking them to the doctor, caring for them when they were sick, arranging for babysitters, playing with them, and planning outings for them. When they began sharing the daily chores associated with raising children, they found that the experience initiated some subtle changes in Gary and the marriage.

Gary began by talking about some initial difficulties he had in watching his children. In the beginning, when he was "on duty," he had some trouble accepting that "just" being with the kids was important work.

> It was real hard to learn to sit down and hold them when they were sick. I had to keep telling myself that this is important, you need to be here with them doing nothing. (laughs) Which is the feeling I had—I'm not doing anything—but I was. Eventually those things really paid off with the trust the kids developed in me.

Not only did Gary learn how to "really be there" with the kids, but he also learned how to anticipate potential problems. For example, he talked about how his level of concern for child safety was heightened after he rearranged his work schedule to do half of the parenting.

> There's a difference in being at the park with the kids since we went on this schedule. Before it was, like, "Sure jump off the jungle bars. Go for it!" But when you're totally responsible for them, and you know if they sprained an ankle or something, you have to pick up the slack, it's like you have more investment in the kid, and you don't want to see them hurt, and you don't want to see them crying. I find myself being a lot more cautious with them.

Although Susan initiated the child-care sharing plan, she was surprised by Gary's developing competence as a parent. Gary came to the marriage with little knowledge of child development and limited expertise as a caregiver. Nevertheless, Susan described how Gary began to notice subtle cues from the children as a result of being with them on a regular basis. She saw some changes in him that she had not anticipated, and her reaction to sharing the nurturing role with him was sometimes mixed. In part, this was because he became more sensitive and caring than she had expected, and his newfound skills intruded on her previous monopoly over the attentive and intuitive parts of parenting.

> I used to worry about the kids a lot more. I would say in the last year it's evened itself out quite a bit. That was an interesting kind of thing in sharing that started to happen that I hadn't anticipated. I suppose when you go into this your expectations about what will happen—that you won't take your kids to day care, that they'll be with their dad, and they'll get certain things from their dad and won't that be nice, and he won't have to worry about his hours—but then when it starts creeping into other areas that you didn't have any way of knowing it was going to have an impact on. When he began to raise issues about the kids or check in on them at school when they were sick or troubled, I thought, "Where did he get the intuitive sense to know what needed to be done? It wasn't there before." A whole lot of visible things happened.

Talking about Gary's parenting, Susan made it clear that she had to take some risks in the beginning to trust him with the kids. At first, his parenting style was all rough and tumble play and wild excitement, but it didn't take long for him to figure out that there were many other ways that he could interact with the children. Eventually, he developed a full range of parenting skills, including clear limit setting, frequent talks, anticipating needs, and enjoying quiet times. Susan's ability to "let go" and not hover over Gary when he was with the children contributed to his developing competence as an everyday father. Susan summed up her current attitude about Gary's parenting by saying, "I trust him totally with the kids, I don't have to worry about it at all."

The transformation that Gary underwent was significant to all members of the Carter family, but perhaps most of all to Gary himself. He commented that being a father was the top priority in his life right now, and that when people asked him what he did, he would reply "I'm a father." He focused on how the details of caring for Jennifer and Jason had helped him establish a special bond with them. Like many involved fathers I interviewed, Gary said that after he was "on duty" with the kids for a day or more, they would call for him in the middle of the night (rather than their mother). He noted that everyday child care could be a drudgery, but that it led to a sense of fulfillment when he could comfort them after a nightmare or after some other emotional crisis: "It's a good feeling to really know your kids and to have them trust you."

Susan reflected on how Gary had recently even come to share some of her characteristic reactions about leaving the kids. It used to be that when they went away for a weekend before they started splitting the child care, she would have a difficult time leaving the children, and would feel guilty about it. At those times, Gary used to give Susan a "hard time" by saying things like "Good grief, you go away once a year for two days and you can't even have a good time!" After spending significant amounts of routine time with the children for about a year and half, however, the tables turned. Susan reported that when they tried to go away for a weekend, "He was really antsy about leaving the kids. He had a really hard time saying goodbye."

Even though Gary began to interact with the children in a style that was more sensitive than his earlier behavior, he reminded me that the way he took care of the kids was "like a man." For instance, he talked about enjoying being playful with the kids, and loved going on spontaneous adventures with them. This he attributed to a basic difference in parenting styles between men and women.

> For some reason, I really feel that women aren't that flexible with kids. And men seem to be able to say, "Okay if you want to go to the beach, grab your suits and a towel and let's go." Like I'll grab some snacks (laughs)—gotta have food—and we're off. With women, it's like you can't do it without making a big chore out of it: you've gotta plan it all out and take a few changes of clothes, and all this extra stuff, and by the time you get in the car, it's all packed down and it's this big production. I like being able to do that with the kids—just grab a couple of things and go.

Susan also commented that Gary was able to provide the children with a type of love and care that balanced her parenting style. "I've always been the one who's worried about them physically and mentally. Gary tends to be with them, you know, just however they are. It's sort of a more open naive approach, just accepting, which is really nice for the kids." Susan described herself as tending to worry about the "business stuff"—like practicing piano regularly and making sure their homework was done right. About herself, she said, "I don't play as well with them in terms of just getting into whatever they want to do. He's really good at that." She went on to praise his ability to "really be with them," rather than focusing on what else they should be doing or what needed to be done next.

Gary and Susan had worked out a division of child-care labor that left more of the fun activities to Gary. I wondered what impact this might have on their relations with each other and with the children and how they felt about it. Whereas Susan explained this division on the basis of personality differences, Gary relied on assumed genetic differences between men and women. Like the other couples I interviewed, the Carters were continually negotiating unique arrangements that fit their specific personalities and drew on their notions of the way things should be. Since most people gain a profound sense of purpose and belonging from their family membership, and because their family identities are tied up with what they do for the family, negotiations over who does what often carry symbolic meanings far beyond the surface content of the tasks involved.

In the Carter household, Susan justified the expense of her training, the hours away from her children, and Gary's forgone earnings, because they enhanced her future earning potential. Perhaps to allay some guilt, she also mentioned that she and her husband played different roles as parents and that her children would benefit from having both of them intimately involved in their upbringing. She was grateful that Gary was able to assume many of the hours of child care and she appreciated that he was now sharing some of the worry. On balance, she did not feel that her role with the children had been displaced: "I'm still the mom." Gary agreed that Susan had a special and irreplaceable relationship with the children and gave her credit for being the "better communicator." He still relied on her occasionally to solve sibling disputes or to help him talk through an issue so that he could figure out his feelings. The child care was the easy part, according to the Carters, for that is what motivated their attempts at sharing in the first place. For housework, on the other hand, things did not evolve quite so effortlessly.

Sharing the Burden of Housework

Like most women in America today, Susan Carter reported that she had to frequently instruct and remind Gary before he began to notice and take care of the basics of running a home.

> Initially, when it all started out, I think part of him felt like he was doing me a big favor, that he was making this all possible for me. Bottom line was: if I got home and the house was trashed, dinner wasn't made, and the kids were filthy, then it would be easier for me to take my kids to day care somewhere, so that when I went and picked them up they would have been fed and the house would still be clean. All I'd have to do is bring them home, give them a bath, and put them to bed. So I said, "There's a missing piece here, maybe it's time to talk about what it is you do all day when you're at home with the kids." For a long time it was, "Well, I do the kids." "Well, okay, you can only do so much of that and there's other things that have to get done." It took a good year for us to fine tune the fact that the wash still had to get done, the dishes still needed to be cleaned up, meals still had to be made; that if we really wanted this to work so that when I got home from work I could have some good time with the kids too, other things needed to be accomplished during the day.

Gary acknowledged that it took him some time to notice what needed doing, and said that there were still disagreements about cleaning standards and timetables. He described himself as "more relaxed about clutter," and said that Susan's housecleaning standards were higher than his. He claimed that "when I get into a cleaning mode, I clean better than she does," but also admitted that she cleaned more consistently. Susan agreed, sort of.

Like most couples I interviewed, Gary's and Susan's descriptions of their task allocation, and their explanations for how their division of labor evolved, differed somewhat.

Each spouse sorted cards listing household and child care tasks into five piles according to who most often performed them. Although the overall portrayal of task allocation was fairly similar for both spouses, husbands tended to claim more credit than their wives were willing to grant them. By averaging the responses between spouses, I came up with a middle-ground estimate of who did what for 64 routine household chores.[16]

In the case of the Carters, Susan did more of the housecleaning, including dusting, mopping, tidying, and cleaning bathrooms. Nevertheless, Gary did more of the vacuuming, and tasks like sweeping and making beds tended to be shared about equally. Susan was rated as doing slightly more of the total kitchen work, and more of the menu planning and shopping, but tasks like making breakfast, cooking dinner, washing dishes, and wiping counters were shared about equally with Gary. While the Carters rated Susan as doing more of the ironing and mending, both spouses mentioned that Gary did some of the ironing, and both rated the time-consuming task of laundry as equally shared. Thus, when it comes to the most frequent and repetitive housework tasks like cooking, washing, and vacuuming, we can see that the Carters shared more than most couples, though their sharing was not an even 50–50 division. During the interviews, when Susan was asked what she liked best about Gary's housework, she replied, "That he does half of it."

Unlike most couples we interviewed, the Carters also shared many of the outside chores and other miscellaneous household and family tasks. For instance, while Gary was more likely to fix something on a broken car, Susan was more likely to wash the cars and take care of routine auto maintenance, such as arranging for periodic tune-ups. Susan did more general yard work and gardening, but Gary mowed the lawn.

Susan paid the bills and handled the taxes, but both took care of insurance and investments. Also unlike most couples we interviewed, the Carters were equally likely to perform "kinkeeping"—writing, phoning, and visiting relatives or friends—as well as initiating and planning couple dates and social get-togethers.

How did these task divisions come about? Was it an easy process or a constant struggle? According to Susan, it took months, and sometimes years of effort to reallocate the household chores in this manner, but once they had a system in place they gained more appreciation for what the other had to do. For instance, Gary talked about how assuming more responsibility for housework motivated him to encourage Susan to buy whatever she needed to make housecleaning easier.

> It was real interesting when I started doing more housework. Being in construction, when I needed a tool, I bought the tool. If I needed to work on a table saw, I went out and bought a good table saw. And I really realized—and I think I enjoyed it—that when most women buy a house cleaning tool or whatever, I mean, like when they go to buy an iron, they shop and shop and get the $5.95 model. I mean it's the cheapest thing they can get. But when I vacuum floors, I looked at this piece of shit, I mean I can't vacuum the floor with this and feel good about it. It's not doing a good job. So I got a good vacuum system. If I'm going to vacuum, I'm going to vacuum right. So I have more appreciation for the details of house cleaning. When I clean the tubs, I want something that is going to clean the tubs; I don't want to work extra hard. You know, I have a special kind of sponge to use for cleaning the tubs. So I have more of an appreciation for what she had to do. I

tell her, "If you know of something that is going to make it easier, let's get it."

One of my colleagues who was reading interview excerpts commented that Gary's attitude toward housework was a bit on the macho side. Nevertheless, his comments show he was redefining housework in terms he could understand and accept. He was starting to "own" it. Housekeeping and child care often remain within the province of the wife, even if the husband begins to help out by performing some tasks. If the wife is always making lists for the husband and must continually remind him to do chores, she retains responsibility for being the household manager. In some areas, the Carters had begun to transcend such manager-helper dynamics. Gary began to assume full responsibility for the tasks that were mutually designated as primarily his. Rather than being forced to accept lower standards in return for "help," Susan Carter was quite satisfied with Gary's efforts, at least on the two chores mentioned above. For vacuuming and cleaning the tubs, he may even have increased the previous standards in the Carter household. Significantly, Gary Carter tackled them in a fashion that was comfortable for him—"using the right tool for the job."

The Impacts of Sharing on the Marriage

The Carters also demonstrate how sharing the family work can affect the husband–wife relationship. Just as Susan observed that Gary had become more sensitive since he began doing more child care, Gary talked about changes in Susan since she had gone back to school and was now committed to pursuing her career.

Ya know, it's hard to relate to the other side until you're there. I would come home and be dead tired and probably cranky, and when the phone rang and I had business, when I was on the phone it was [very animated] "Oh hi! How are you doing?" and when I put the phone down I was cranky again. It was funny the other day she did the same thing. She came home kind of down and out and somebody she had to perk up for was on the phone and I just kind of laughed and said, "Yeah, you've got that phone voice down too." It's hard not to worry about that, but I can accept it more because I've been there.

Such convergence of experience between spouses can have a beneficial impact on marriages, but it can also raise some uncomfortable feelings. Because it was previously "her job" to be the sensitive and intuitive one, Susan was occasionally ambivalent about Gary's developing intuition and his growing worry about the kids. At times it seemed as though Gary was ambivalent about Susan's commitment to her career, in part because he worried that she would become too involved outside the family. He talked about how switching to their split schedule was followed by "better talk around the dinner table," yet he sometimes expressed concern and dismay over how much of Susan's time and emotional energy her outside work was consuming.

Gary was eager to have Susan become a co-provider and the two were in the process of working out what future job sharing would mean in terms of their individual careers, their feelings of self worth, and their division of family labor. Gary hoped that when Susan started making more money they could hire someone to help once a week with the housecleaning. Susan talked at length about their shifting parenting and career issues, with each person alternately supporting and questioning what the other was doing.

Gary knows how wrapped up in his career he was when he decided to do this with me, and [as] he sees me doing more and more in my career he worries that I'm becoming like he was, that somehow I'm backing out of the family thing. . . . He sees that I'm physically not there as much for the kids and he wonders if maybe it's because I'm putting too much into my work. But nothing occupies my thoughts more than my kids. . . . So we both have a whole lot of concerns of not knowing why or how we're going to do this now. On the one hand, he's beginning to feel like maybe he doesn't want to keep building anymore, but on the other hand, he knows he's good enough, he can still do it. So I'm saying, "If I'm going to be making a fair amount of money, you go do what you want to do, or do something else." It's not like I want to be the total financial provider either—I would never want to take the role that he had, it didn't look like much fun. So now we're talking about how it is that we're going to do this in the future and it may open up some new possibilities.

Thus, while Gary was generally perceived as having made the greater financial sacrifice in the past, Susan was now approaching a position where she would provide some financial cushion and might even be able to give Gary more flexibility in his future career options.

The Carters were not forging a new balance between work and family because they were following some abstract political goals or dogmatic notions of gender justice. They were responding to an unstable economic climate and trying to raise their kids the way they thought was right. Because their actions were alternately scripted and improvised, and because each partner was continually adjusting to the other, their balancing

act of shared parenting and economic providing resembled a kind of dance. When they went into their marriage, they both assumed that Susan would be the only one to stay home with the children. Neither entered it thinking they should share everything or try to create some egalitarian new-age gender-blending. In fact, they still disagree about the value of feminism and the women's movement. When asked if women were disadvantaged in our society, Gary answered with a simple "No." For emphasis, he added that he would definitely hire a woman contractor "but only if she was competent." Susan described herself as "no women's libber" in college, but explained that she was exposed to various ideas about sexism and gradually accepted a pro-feminist perspective.

The Impacts of Sharing on the Children

Despite their different attitudes toward feminism, after they gave birth to their first child, Gary and Susan Carter agreed that their daughter Jennifer should be able to do whatever she wanted. Susan commented,

She was a real bright kid and Gary was proud of her, and it didn't matter that she was a girl. Coming from that place of pride, having people say to him "Weren't you disappointed you didn't have a son?" He'd look at them like, "What's that supposed to mean?" So he had some new awareness about it too, but they aren't anything like what mine are. Still, they seem to translate into the same kind of values and behavior.

Thus, although Gary did not embrace the political ideals that Susan did, nor use a language of disadvantage to talk about gender relations, he encouraged his daughter to set high goals for herself. In addition, he waxed eloquent when he talked about his kindergarten son's future capacities for fathering. The way he saw it, with a real-life involved father as a role model, Jason was "way ahead of the game" and would easily be able to handle the nurturing aspects of parenting when he grew up and had kids of his own.

Susan also had high hopes for her children, but since she was still somewhat ambivalent about the future fate of feminism, she worried that she was setting her children up for disappointment. In discussing how sharing parenting with Gary might affect her children, she mentioned some positive aspects, but focused on her fear that she might be encouraging unrealistic expectations in her children.

> I think it has the potential of making their lives more fulfilling. Jennifer's very nurturing and could do that number, but she also has a real strong drive and she's bright and she ought to do something else in her life too. I think she's going to have a different picture about it than I did, and I worry that if she goes about looking for a mate who's going to be able to share in all that, chances are she's not going to find one; or if she gets a mate thinking she can make that happen, chances are it won't. My concern is that they'll go out there and they'll meet people that won't play by the new rules. It's not fair because it's really my fight. I worry about Jason, too; that I've laid this on him. I have these values that I really believe in, and I raise him to be kind and gentle, but then I send him out there into a tough world, unarmed. Poor kid.

Susan's worries about her children's future prospects raise some interesting issues. Recent research confirms her suggestion that involved fathering does have an impact on children's attitudes about gender.[17] In one study at the University of Michigan, Norma Radin and her colleagues compared children raised in families where couples shared parenting with children raised in more conventional families. Parents and children from various family types were interviewed and given a battery of psychological tests in 1977, when the children were preschoolers (3–5 years old). The parents were interviewed again in 1981, when the children were between 7 and 9 years old. In 1988, the researchers interviewed the children again (when they were 14–16 years old), asking about their views on future employment and family plans. Teenagers raised in families with greater father participation when the children were preschoolers, and those with greater father participation when children were aged 7 to 9, held less traditional views. Teens whose fathers had been involved in routine child care expressed more approval for spouses working full time and sharing childrearing and were more negative about only husbands working with wives staying home to care for the kids. Teens raised almost exclusively by mothers, not surprisingly, had expectations for traditional parenting arrangements themselves.[18]

Although the Michigan researchers confirmed Susan Carter's hunch that her children would have higher expectations for sharing employment, housekeeping, and childrearing with a future spouse, they came to a different conclusion. Instead of worrying about the children raised in shared parenting families, they questioned the ability of children in conventional mother-does-it-all families to adapt to the changing realities of family life. It's likely that children from Ozzie and Harriet type families will be the ones with unrealistic expectations. With almost two-thirds of teenagers expected to be in two-earner families when they become parents, those with attitudes more favorable to sharing paid and unpaid work may be better prepared for the future. The gender flexibility of the shared parenting kids, along with the other benefits of having two involved parents, are likely to outweigh the negative impacts of high expectations for egalitarian relationships.

There is ample evidence that times are changing. Mothers are increasingly likely to be employed when they are pregnant, shortly after they give birth, and throughout their children's school years. Both men and women are waiting longer to have children and having fewer of them. Some women are beginning to make nearly as much money as men, and divorce continues to be common. Given these projections, it makes sense that men and women should divide the care of their homes and children more equally than they have in the past.

Nostalgia for the Past and Dreams for the Future

Recent defenders of "traditional family values" include Dan Quayle who ridiculed TV's Murphy Brown for deciding to have a baby without a husband, and Phyllis Schlafly, who tells married women to quit their jobs and devote their time to tending husbands, children, and homes.[19] This public rhetoric uses idyllic images of bygone days to argue for a return to "family values," but most critics agree that the underlying message is that we should reinstate old-style paternal authority. Popular feminist authors tend to focus on the potential benefits of an emerging democracy within families, contrasting recent developments with trenchant critiques of the patriarchal roots of "traditional" family practices.[20] Similar debates are played out in the pages of scholarly journals, as academics either celebrate or lament recent changes in American family life.[21]

Arguments about the state of American families and the future of family life frequently take on mythical proportions far beyond the facts at hand.[22] Often the debates are more about the relative power of men versus women, locals versus newcomers, whites versus blacks, or middle class versus working class. It's difficult to separate underlying political and social issues from the emotional heartstrings that such debates set resonating with uncanny frequency.

Throughout the past century, public fears about the demise of the family have surfaced with annoying regularity. Politicians and religious leaders tend to fan the flames of controversy in an effort to further their own agendas. Appeals to a bygone era regularly capture our attention and reinforce idyllic images from the past, however unrealistic. No one wants to argue with cultural icons like "mom and apple pie" or "good ol' dad." Unfortunately, mythical images of The Family and public displays of hand wringing rarely move us close to understanding the changes and challenges faced by today's families.

If, like the Carters, fathers began to act like mothers by nurturing children, and mothers began to act like fathers by being breadwinners, what would happen? Would the family go extinct? You might think so, if you took political and religious fundamentalist rhetoric seriously, but this scenario is very unlikely. People today are just as concerned about raising happy and healthy children as they ever were, perhaps even more so, since society's problems are publicized more widely. With politicians lamenting the breakdown of "family values" and TV comedies offering similarly unrealistic images of family life, it is difficult to decide what is really happening to The American Family. Talking about The Family (with a capital T) obscures the fact that families have always varied from place to place and from time to time. There has always been a rich diversity of family types, it's just that the forms they take, and what people do within them, may be changing faster now than at other times in our recent history.

In our nostalgia for a mythical past, we tend to envision an ideal family that transcends time and place. In reality, families are very specific forms of human organization that continually evolve and change as they respond to various pushes and pulls. Since we all grew up in families, we have strong feelings about various family members, carry at least a few family-related emotional scars or unresolved issues, and tend to cling to romantic images of family life. In short, it is extremely hard to talk about family life or family changes objectively. The ideological baggage we bring to discussions about how families are, or should be, is so personally biased and emotionally charged that we probably would do better to drop any pretense of pure objectivity. Although we can never fully transcend our biases, we can draw on the available family research to help us understand what changes are underway and where they might lead.

NOTES

1. Nancy Chodorow, *The Reproduction of Mothering: Psychoanalysis and the Sociology of Gender* (Berkeley: University of California Press, 1978); See also Dorothy Dinnerstein, *The Mermaid and the Minotaur: Sexual Arrangements and Human Malaise* (New York: Harper & Row, 1976).

2. For reviews of research on fathers by psychologists, see Ross Parke, *Fathers* (Cambridge, MA: Harvard University Press, 1981); Michael Lamb, *The Role of the Father in Child Development* (New York: Wiley, 1981); and Henry B. Biller, *Fathers and Families: Paternal Factors in Child Development* (Westport, CT: Auburn House, 1993). For recent sociological studies of fathers, see Kathleen Gerson, *No Man's Land: Men's Changing Commitments to Family and Work* (New York: Basic Books, 1993); Shirley M. H. Hanson and Frederick W. Bozett (eds.), *Dimensions of Fatherhood* (Beverly Hills, CA: Sage, 1985); Jane C. Hood (ed.), *Men, Work, and Family* (Newbury Park, CA: Sage, 1993); Robert A. Lewis and Robert E. Salt (eds.), *Men in Families* (Beverly Hills, CA: Sage, 1986); William Marsiglio (ed.), *Fatherhood: Contemporary Theory, Research, and Social Policy* (Newbury Park, 1995). For an excellent history of U.S. fatherhood, see Robert L. Griswold, *Fatherhood in America* (New York: Basic Books, 1993).

3. Kyle Pruett, *The Nurturing Father* (New York: Warner, 1987); Norma Radin, "Caregiving Fathers in Intact Families," *Merrill-Palmer Quarterly* 27 (1981): 489–514; Norma Radin, "The Influence of Fathers upon Sons and Daughters and Implications for School Social Work," *Social Work in Education* 8 (1986): 77–91; Barbara Risman, "Can Men Mother?" in B. Risman and P. Schwartz (eds.), *Gender in Intimate Relationships* (Belmont: CA: Wadsworth, 1989); E. Williams, N. Radin, and T. Allegro, "Children of Highly Involved Fathers: An 11-Year Follow-up" (University of Michigan, Ann Arbor, 1991), cited in *Babies and Briefcases,* Hearings before the Select Committee on Children, Youth, and Families, House of Representatives, One Hundred Second Congress, First Session, June 11, 1991, U.S. Government Printing Office, Washington DC, pp. 78–85.

4. For exceptions to this pattern, see Griswold, *Fatherhood in America,* Gerson, *No Man's Land,* and others listed in note 2.

5. Mike Clary, *Daddy's Home* (New York: Seaview Books, 1982); Bob Greene, *Good Morning, Merry Sunshine: A Father's Journal of His Child's First Year* (New York: Atheneum, 1984); Gary B. Trudeau, *Doonsbury* (Universal Press Syndicate, 1985).

6. Pruett, *The Nurturing Father*; Geoffrey Greif, *The Daddy Track and the Single Father* (Lexington, MA: Lexington Books, 1985). For an account of middle-age sons longing for contact with their fathers, see Samuel Osherson, *Finding Our Fathers: The Unfinished Business of Manhood* (New York: Free Press, 1986).

7. For a more nuanced and critical look at shared parenting from a practicing feminist therapist, see Diane Ehrensaft, *Parenting Together* (New York: Free Press, 1987).

8. Robert Bly, *Iron John: A Book About Men* (Reading, MA: Addison-Wesley, 1990).

9. On the subject of men's reactionary responses to women's modest gains, see Scott Coltrane and Neal Hickman, "The Rhetoric of Rights and Needs: Moral Discourse in the

Reform of Child Custody and Child Support Laws," *Social Problems* 39 (1992): 40–61; and Susan Faludi, *Backlash: The Undeclared War Against American Women* (New York: Crown, 1991).

10. For a review of historical trends and social forces affecting family life, see Randall Collins and Scott Coltrane, *Sociology of Marriage and the Family: Gender, Love, and Property,* 4th ed. (Chicago: Nelson Hall, 1995); Robert Griswold, *Fatherhood in America* (New York: Basic, 1993); Steven Mintz and Susan Kellog, *Domestic Revolutions: A Social History of American Family Life* (New York: Free Press, 1988); Joseph Pleck, "American Fathering in Historical Perspective," in Michael S. Kimmel (ed.), *Changing Men: New Directions in Research on Men and Masculinity* (Newbury Park, CA: Sage, 1987), pp. 83–97.

11. See Joanne Miller and Howard Garrison, "Sex Roles: The Division of Labor at Home and in the Workplace," *Annual Review of Sociology* 8 (1982): 237–262; Alexander Szalai (ed.), *The Use of Time: Daily Activities of Urban and Suburban Populations in Twelve Countries* (The Hague: Mouton, 1972); Kathryn E. Walker and Margaret E. Woods, *Time Use: A Measure of Household Production of Family Goods and Services* (Washington, DC: American Home Economics Association, 1972).

12. Arlie Hochschild with Anne Machung, *The Second Shift: Working Parents and the Revolution at Home* (New York: Viking, 1989).

13. Informants have been given pseudonyms to protect their identities. Interviews were conducted individually with each spouse. Subsequent follow-up interviews were conducted with some couples on a return visit to their home. (See Chapters 3 to 5.)

14. O'Connell, *Where's Papa?*

15. See Elizabeth Bott, *Family and Social Network* (New York: Free Press, 1957); Scott Coltrane, "Social Networks and Men's Family Roles," *Men's Studies Review* 8 (1991): 8–15; Laura Lein, "Male Participation in Home Life," *Family Coordinator* 28 (1979): 489–495; Dave Riley, "Network Influences on Father Involvement in Childrearing," in Cochran et al. (eds.), *Extending Families* (Cambridge: Cambridge University Press, 1991).

16. For a more complete description of the interview and card sort methodology employed in the case studies, see Coltrane, "Household Labor and the Routine Production of Gender," *Social Problems* 36 (1989): 473–490.

17. Ross D. Parke, "Fathers and Families," in M. Bornstein (ed.), *Handbook of Parenting* (Hillsdale, NJ: Erlbaum, in press).

18. Williams, Radin, and Allegro, *Children of Involved Fathers.*

19. For examples, see Phyllis Schlafly, *The Power of the Christian Woman* (Cincinnati: Stanford Publishing, 1981); George Gilder, *Sexual Suicide* (Quadrangle, 1973); Rush Limbaugh, *The Way Things Ought to Be* (New York: Pocket Books, 1992).

20. See, for example, Letty Pogrebin, *Family Politics: Love and Power on an Intimate Frontier* (New York: McGraw-Hill, 1983); Barbara Ehrenreich, *The Hearts of Men: American Dreams and the Flight from Commitment* (New York: Anchor, 1984).

21. See, for example, David Popenoe, "American Family Decline, 1960–1990: A Review and Appraisal," *Journal of Marriage and the Family* 55 (1993): 527–542; Norval Glenn, "A Plea for Objective Assessment of the Notion of Family Decline," *Journal of Marriage and the Family* 55 (1993): 542–544; Judith Stacey, "Good Riddance to The Family: A Response to David Popenoe," *Journal of Marriage and the Family* 55 (1993): 545–547; Philip Cowan, "The Sky Is Falling, But Popenoe's Analysis Won't Help Us Do Anything About It," *Journal of Marriage and the Family* 55 (1993): 548–553; and David Popenoe, "The National Family Wars," *Journal of Marriage and the Family* 55 (1993): 553–555.

22. For insightful analyses of such processes, see Stephanie Coontz, *The Way We Never Were: American Families and the Nostalgia Trap* (New York: Basic Books, 1992) and Arlene Skolnick, *Embattled Paradise: The American Family in an Age of Uncertainty* (New York: Basic Books, 1991). For a contrasting view, see David Blankenhorn, *Fatherless America: Confronting Our Most Urgent Social Problem* (New York: Basic Books, 1995).

QUESTIONS FOR DISCUSSION

1. What are the difficulties that women and men face in trying to change traditional gender-based patterns of expectations and behaviors?

2. Why do such changes require a fundamental shift of gender ideology within
this culture?
3. Think of the ways that you or members of your family have attempted

to change gender-based expectations.
What problems have you encountered?
4. What are the rewards of making such
changes?

KEY TERMS

gender as social construction
sexuality as social construction
masculinity
femininity
sexism
homophobia
gendered selves
gendered behavior
doing gender
gendered earnings disparity

THE SOCIAL WEB

- The Feminist Majority Foundation, founded in 1987 is a research and activist organization dedicated to women's equality, reproductive health, and nonviolence: www.feminist.org/welcome/index.html.
- Institute for Women's Policy Research publishes a very useful report on the status of women in the U.S.: www.iwpr.org/states/home.html.
- Gendergap is a watchdog site that tracks women's access to sites of power, relative to men's: www.Gendergap.com.
- The National Sexual Violence Resource Center supplies information about the management and care of victims of sexual assault: www.nsvrc.org.
- Tracy's Passion Page is an individual, but highly respected, effort to tackle the issue of women's access to the military: www.tracy-liz.net/country/militarywoman/milwoman.htm.

QUESTIONS FOR DEBATE

1. Gloria Steinem says, "It's not their [men's] life experiences that are the problem, it's the impossible expectation of dominance to which they've become addicted." Do you agree?
2. What are some examples that show your own gender identity is socially constructed or fixed?
3. Are there clear boundaries of sexual identity? Why or why not?
4. What recommendations would you make to combat domestic violence? What obstacles do you see to putting them into practice?
5. Should treatment of women be a consideration in U.S. foreign policy?

SECTION III
Social Problems and Social Institutions

Chapter 7
Work

Contents

Learning Objectives

By the end of this chapter you should be able to:

- Recognize how these authors use one or more of the major perspectives to analyze work.
- Explore how workplace inequality is shaped by inequalities of race, class, and gender.
- Describe various consequences of the changing definition of work.
- Analyze how individuals contribute to workplace inequality through their everyday behavior.
- Explain how social systems and institutions perpetuate workers' inequality.

Defining the Problem

Work is a fundamental institution that is central to our financial, physical, and psychological well-being. Our work can be vital to our sense of self and level of happiness. The jobs that we hold—our working conditions, wages, sense of job security, and the appreciation that we feel as workers—profoundly shape our quality of life. Yet workplaces are not neutral settings. The basic patterns of inequality that are embedded in other social institutions are played out in employment patterns and conditions. Our jobs, in fact, are often the places where we are most likely to encounter the effects of the massive economic forces discussed in Chapter 3. The changing economic structure and the pressure of global capitalism affect our working lives.

Some sociologists of social problems take a macro approach to studying work. They focus on the structural aspects of work and how the institution of work fits with other major social institutions like the economy, politics, and education. They are likely to look at patterns of employment, unemployment, and wage scales. Often these researchers look at underemployment. In this condition workers do not earn adequate wages to meet their basic needs for health and well-being. Other sociologists using a macro approach study occupations and professions. They may examine the social status of numerous occupations (for example, a physician has a higher social status than a nurse, who in turn has a higher status than a plumber). These researchers look at patterns of education and wages as they relate to occupational status. They may also look at the ways that occupations are segregated according to gender and race. Other sociologists examine the role of unions in the workplace. They look at the ability of unions to organize workers, increase wages, and improve working conditions. They may also explore the reasons for the current decline in union membership and the consequences of this decline for workers' wages and job security.

Other social problems investigators use a micro approach to study work. They are likely to look at the problems people encounter in their everyday work lives. They may study the kinds of tasks people are expected to do and how managers treat employees. Some focus on the subservient demeanor that employees are expected to assume and the tools that management uses (e.g., drug screening, personality tests, lie detector tests) to maintain control over workers. They may look at the consequences of these conditions on workers' sense of self, work, and well-being. Many workers find that there are also emotional expectations that accompany their jobs. People in service-oriented professions, such as flight attendants and nurses, are expected to present themselves on the job in a way that communicates emotional traits like compassion, friendliness, and happiness. They are also expected to manage the emotions of the people with whom they interact on the job. This intense emotion work can affect how people perceive their public and private emotional lives. Other researchers using a micro perspective explore the meaning of work for people's sense of self-fulfillment. They look at how the role of worker interacts with other roles in peoples lives and differences in that process based on gender and social class. These researchers frequently focus on how people, especially women, cope with the dual competing demands of work and family.

Other researchers focus on the physical conditions in which workers are required to operate. They investigate the occupations with high rates of work-related injuries and illnesses. Typically, these are occupations characterized by low wages. They are often jobs that do not offer health care insurance or sick leave. Some of these researchers look at the long-term consequences of these jobs on people's health; others look at the response of employers, as well as state and federal officials, in dealing with workplace hazards.

Scope of the Problem

In 2002, 135 million people were employed in the United States, representing 63 percent of the total population older than age 16.[1] Unemployment was low; yet the 5.7 percent rate still represents 8.2 million individuals who were out of work. Another 1.4 million people were "marginally attached" to the labor force. These are people who wanted jobs and had looked for work within the previous twelve months, but were not officially counted among the unemployed.

Unemployment varies greatly across racial groups. While 5.1 percent of Whites were jobless, the unemployment rates for Hispanics and Blacks were 7.8 percent and 9.8 percent, respectively.

---

[1]"News: Employment Situation Summary: October 2002." Bureau of Labor Statistics, U.S. Department of Labor.

Median earnings for the 9.8 million full-time wage and salaried workers in the United States in 2002 were $605 per week;[2] median annual income for full-time employees was $31,460. Wages varied with education. Full-time workers older than age 24 who had not completed high school earned a median wage of $388 weekly, compared to high school graduates' median weekly wages of $534. College graduates earned significantly more at $944 per week.

Full-time income varies greatly according to gender. Women's median full-time income in 2002 was $528 per week, amounting to 78 percent of men's median weekly income of $676. In managerial and professional specialty occupations, women earned on average only 70.5 percent of men's earnings. Even among the most educated workers (those with advanced or professional degrees), women earned less than men. The highest 10 percent of women workers earned $1,834 per week, amounting to 68 percent of the weekly $2,682 earned by their male counterparts. Within racial categories, gender inequality was highest among Whites. In 2002, Black women earned 89.3 percent of Black men's wages, and Hispanic women made 90.5 percent of Hispanic men's wages.

This is not because gender inequality is greater in the White community. It is because on average White women and Black and Hispanic women and men all earn less than White males. Wage disparities are great across racial categories. In 2002, all full-time Hispanic and Black workers earned median weekly wages of $421 and $485, respectively. In other words, Hispanic and Black workers earned 68 and 78 percent, respectively, of the wages of White workers. Race and gender considered together further illustrate the nature of wage disparity in the United States. Black men who worked full-time in 2002 earned 73 percent of median wages for White men. Black women's earnings are 83 percent of White women's wages. Black women earned, on average, 65 percent of White men's wages.

Paid holidays and vacation days are the most common type of employee benefit offered in the private sector.[3] One-half of workers in the private sector are provided with medical insurance benefits. Only 26 percent of workers have long-term disability insurance coverage. Slightly less than half of private sector workers receive retirement benefits. Both public and private sector workers (in companies of fifty or more employees) are eligible for the Family and Medical Leave Act (FMLA). This act allows employees up to twelve weeks of unpaid leave each year to address immediate family needs such as the birth, adoption, or foster care of a child or the serious illness of a spouse, child, or parent. Because this law mandates only unpaid leave, it is more likely to benefit families with higher incomes.

In 2001, 16.28 million workers were members of labor unions.[4] Wages for union members are higher than for other workers in most occupational groups. In 2001, the median weekly wage for union members was on average 25 percent higher in 12 major occupational groups than the wage for nonunion full-time workers. Union workers are more likely to have health care benefits and pension plans (79 percent) than their nonunion counterparts (44 percent). Union members are also more likely to have job security than nonunion workers. Despite

---

[2]"Usual Weekly Earnings of Full-Time Wage and Salary Workers: Third Quarter 2002" (USDL 02-599). Bureau of Labor Statistics, U.S. Department of Labor.

[3]"Employee Benefits in Private Industry, 2000" (USDL 02-389). Bureau of Labor Statistics, U.S. Department of Labor.

[4]Data obtained from "Union Difference," published on the Web site of the AFL-CIO.

the many benefits of labor unions to workers, they represent a declining proportion of workers. In 2001, 13.5 percent of the American labor force belonged to unions, a decline from nearly 15 percent in 1995.

Between 1999 and 2001, nearly 10 million workers were displaced, an increase of more than 2 million in the workers who were displaced between 1997 and 1999.[5] Nearly half of these displacements were the result of plant closings or moves. Most workers found another job fairly quickly, although 22 percent of them remained unemployed, and 14 percent left the labor force. More than half of the workers who were reemployed were working for lower wages in their new jobs. Three in ten of these workers had to take more than a 20 percent reduction in their wages.

Although work is a basic part of our lives, America's workplaces can be dangerous. Between 1996 and 2001, 36,369 workers in the United States died as a result of workplace injuries.[6] The most deadly industries were construction, transportation, and services. In 2000, 5.7 million workers were injured or contracted work-related illnesses, constituting 6.1 percent of all full-time workers.[7] That same year, 2.8 million cases of sick or injured workers involved lost workdays. Most injuries involved motor vehicle or machinery accidents. Our workplaces can also be violent places. Every week, twenty workers are murdered on the job; homicide is the second leading cause of death on the job and the leading cause of death on the job for workers younger than age 18.[8] Most of these homicides are committed in the course of a robbery. An additional one million workers are assaulted on the job each year. Forty-eight percent of those assaults are committed by a health care patient.

Perspectives on the Problem

Sociologists using a *conflict* perspective would explore how occupational patterns, wage scales, and employment conditions perpetuate the capitalist system of inequality. They would also examine race and gender bias in patterns of employee hirings, firings, wages, and promotions. Sociologists using a *functionalist* approach to study work would look at how patterns of employment, unemployment, and wage systems help to maintain a well-balanced economy. They also examine the gaps between the kinds of jobs that employers need to have filled and the education and skill levels of potential workers. Sociologists who use an *interactionist* approach would look at the meaning of work in people's lives. They would also examine the problems that people encounter in their everyday workplaces. Finally sociologists using a *social constructionist* perspective would look at how the nature of work is constructed by employers, employees, policy makers, and the general public.

Connecting the Perspectives

The readings in this section take a variety of approaches to studying work. Jill Andresky Fraser takes a social constructionist approach in studying how work is redefined in traditionally white-collar jobs. Using a conflict perspective, Arlie Hochschild explores gender differences in work, arguing that

[5]"Worker Displacement, 1999–2001" (USDL 02-483). Bureau of Labor Statistics, U.S. Department of Labor.

[6]"Census of Fatal Occupational Injuries, 2001." Bureau of Labor Statistics in cooperation with state and federal agencies, U.S. Department of Labor.

[7]"Workplace Injuries and Illnesses in 2000" (USDL 01-472). Bureau of Labor Statistics, U.S. Department of Labor.

[8]"Violence in the Workplace Fact Sheet, June 1997." National Institute for Occupational Safety and Health, U.S. Department of Health and Human Services.

men and women see the workplace in general—and manage family and work specifically—in very different ways. Barbara Ehrenreich conducts a symbolic interactionist analysis of the problems associated with low-wage employment by spending several months trying to economically, physically, and emotionally survive working in low-wage service-sector jobs. Martin Sanchez Jankowski presents an intriguing view of work by marginalized individuals. Using a functionalist perspective, he analyzes the ways that members of street gangs perceive their activities as worthwhile work in their communities. Finally, Barbara Reskin takes a social constructionist approach to look at how public policies affect work and commerce. She analyzes socially constructed images of affirmative action programs and explores the data that suggest these images are false.

Reading Summaries

In "White-Collar Sweatshop," Fraser uses a social constructionist perspective to examine the changing nature of the world of professional, white-collar work in the United States. Once considered the dream jobs for the country's educated workforce, these jobs have become bastions of overwork, job insecurity, and increasing stress. White-collar workers are being asked to do more with fewer resources and are continuously reminded that their jobs are not secure. According to Fraser, America's corporations have embarked on a public relations campaign to justify these "sweatshop" conditions. Corporate CEOs publish books and articles that portray the world of business as mean and heartless. They often use the language of welfare to promote a picture of corporate life that makes workers expendable. In this genre of CEO literature, treating workers badly is portrayed as both necessary and a good thing: winning the "war"—

maximizing profits—is the only goal an executive officer should have. Yet Fraser points out that while CEOs are justifying eliminating jobs and placing higher demands on workers, their own salaries have skyrocketed to degrees never before seen in American business.

America's corporations are not just trying to sell the rightness of this new way of doing business to the general public. Fraser argues that they are also trying to convince workers that their own poor treatment is justified. White-collar workers have been inundated with workshops, seminars, and support groups that are supposedly designed to promote teamwork, motivation, and self-esteem. These "feel-good" programs focus on improving the emotional state of workers, without addressing the demands of longer work hours, diminished pay, and the threat of layoffs. Yet Fraser contends that these attempts to construct the corporate workplace often backfire, leaving many workers frustrated and angry at their employers.

Our next reading discusses gender differences in the workplace. In "The Time Bind: When Work Becomes Home and Home Becomes Work," Hochschild looks at the different ways that women and men deal with the conflicts between work and family demands. She interviews workers at "Amerco," a company well known for its "family-friendly" policies, such as flex-time and job-sharing options. Hochschild discovers that Amerco's employees do not take full advantage of these policies and continue to work longer hours than ever before. Why do workers choose to stay in the workplace when they have the option to be at home with their families?

Hochschild concludes that the assumption that people would rather be at home with their families than at work is incorrect. The difficulties of combining work and family responsibilities can be overwhelming, especially for women. When women leave work, they typically find themselves going home to a "second shift" of child care, housework, and the everyday management of family life. The home is thus not a peaceful place of respite and relaxation. For many women, it is where the most stress and hardest work await them. The women in Hochschild's study report that work is the place where they feel valued and respected. It is also frequently where women have the best social support systems—where they have friends and can laugh. Hochschild acknowledges the level of worker anxiety over potential unemployment. However, she argues that families are also unstable. With "increasing numbers of people . . . getting their 'pink slips' at home," women and men often find solace at work.

In "Nickel-and-Dimed: On (Not) Getting By in America," Ehrenreich examines the world of temporary employment. Ehrenreich decides to give up her professional middle-class life (temporarily) and seek employment in the low-wage workforce that women moving off welfare must also enter. This reading is a fascinating, often painful, account of the struggles she encounters while simply trying to make it in the minimum-wage labor market. Ehrenreich quickly learns that she must work two jobs in order to make ends meet. Her microlevel analysis shows the insecurities and indignities that characterize this type of employment. Many aspects of low-wage work surprise Ehrenreich, including the constant reconfiguration of finances that she must do based on the weekly uncertainty of her income. Ehrenreich shows that the life faced by those who are leaving welfare for employment is defined by exhausting work and wages too low to live on comfortably.

In "Gang Business: Making Ends Meet," Jankowski approaches the study of gangs from a functionalist theoretical perspective not often taken by investigators of crime in urban areas. He seeks to understand how gangs are similar to, rather than different from, the more conventional social organizations in society. He examines the ways that gangs are integrated into the web of life in their communities. His provocative findings are based on interviews with and observations of Irish, Puerto Rican, African American, Dominican, and Chicano gangs in large cities in different parts of the United States.

Jankowski argues that it is a myth that gangs are parasitic on communities and that gang members are the least-fit members of society. Instead, he argues that gang members share the same entrepreneurial spirit that drives successful corporate business leaders. They are competitive, driven to accumulate profit through business ventures, and seek status. Although gangs provide many illegal goods to their neighborhoods—most notably alcohol, drugs, and guns—and provide illegal forms of recreation—gambling, numbers, or cock fights—they also provide to the community services they perceive as needed. They offer "protection" for individuals and businesses in the absence of a police presence and "demolition" services to tenants faced with unacceptable living conditions. In short, gangs are a resource that the community can rely on if force is necessary.

The gangs' business decisions also demonstrate that they recognize an obligation to the community, Jankowski asserts. Gang members refuse to demolish property in their own communities if it will leave their neighbors homeless or possibly lead to their deaths. In order to protect the women in the community, they refuse to become involved in local prostitution. Gangs also operate marginally profitable legal businesses like grocery stores or auto repair shops and occasionally refurbish buildings and rent them cheaply. This community orientation maintains the legitimacy of the gang. Jankowski argues that gangs provide an outlet for motivated youths who believe in the American dream and are tolerated by communities because they fill real needs.

Our final reading examines the ways that public policy can affect workplace patterns of inequality. In "The Effects of Affirmative Action on Other Stakeholders," Reskin explores the arguments against affirmative action policies. Opponents of affirmative action frequently argue that such programs promote reverse discrimination against White males in job hiring and promotions. They also assert that affirmative action is too expensive for U.S. businesses because it decreases productivity, reduces systems of merit, and treats employees unfairly. Policy makers often use these arguments to justify proposals to dismantle affirmative action programs.

Reskin examines available data to determine if affirmative action has resulted in reverse discrimination and to explore the economic impact of such policies on American commerce. She concludes that true cases of reverse discrimination are extremely rare and that affirmative action programs have not resulted in the hiring and promotion of unqualified workers. Moreover, heads of the major U.S. corporations support affirmative action practices, indicating that hiring practices, levels of productivity, and stock values have all increased with these programs. Reskin explores the gap between the public's perceptions of affirmative action policies and the realities of these policies put into practice. She argues that affirmative action opponents use the media to construct the idea that such programs amount to nothing more than unfair quota systems—a perception that is far from the patterns that employment data reveal.

FOCUSING QUESTIONS

Consider the following questions as you read this chapter: In what ways does the workplace reflect patterns and problems of the larger economic structure? How are patterns of racial and gender inequality embedded in the labor force in the United States? Think about your own work experiences. What was the worst job you ever had? What aspects of the job made it so bad? What was your best job? What does work mean to your sense of self?

26

WHITE-COLLAR SWEATSHOP
JILL ANDRESKY FRASER

Has there never been a better time to work in corporate America?

A new business-world order exists, spawned and nurtured by tumultuous changes during the 1980s and 1990s. By the dawn of the twenty-first century, the United States could boast of remarkably low unemployment, high corporate profits, and labor markets so tight that signing bonuses were reported to be almost common for everyone from new college graduates to teachers and even civil servants.[1] "In some parts of the country, just about anyone who can breathe and is ambulatory has a job—and in some cases, they'll make exceptions," was the way one Conference Board economist put it.[2]

Although wild stock swings suggested that the extraordinary bull market of the past two decades might finally be exhausted, the prolonged years of buoyant equity growth had yielded enormous sums of capital, ripe for investment in America's business future. By the turn of the millennium, the United States' economy was in uncharted heady waters, with venture capital investments, initial public offerings, and stock price-to-earnings ratios all at record levels, and almost every week, it seemed, another off-the-charts corporate merger guaranteed to create a new global superpower. Although some industries were experiencing painful contractions, many others were thriving.

Within this environment, one might assume that the rewards and challenges of work would likewise be unparalleled, especially for the United States' skilled and experienced white-collar workforce, nearly 80 million men and women strong.[3] Yet behind the era's high-flying statistics are dismal workplace realities that many readers . . . will recognize all too well from their own lives.

Overwork is epidemic, for men and women whose job demands keep increasing, not because of career advances but because of a corporate environment that has depended upon *squeezing*, . . . more and more work out of fewer people with fewer resources. For today's white-collar staffers, the balanced and secure nine to five work lives of their parents' generation belongs to a utopian past, as they struggle to fulfill job demands that require them to work after dinner and during lunch hours, . . . or on Saturdays and Sundays, in between the innings of their children's Little League games, during summer or winter vacations, while waiting on line at movie theaters, driving their cars virtually anywhere, or on countless other occasions as well. Signs of round-the-clock overwork are inescapable; during a late August afternoon ride in a rented pedal boat, after a game of miniature golf, my family and I shared a Long Island pond with a woman who was peddling her two young daughters around, all the while speaking to her office via cell phone. . . .

. . .

Corporate America's campaign to replace postwar employment practices with ever more demanding, stressful, and unrewarding workplace conditions has been fought, in large part, on the public relations front. It's been a two-pronged effort: to minimize the fallout from negative changes among a company's current employees, retirees, and laid-off personnel; and to offer a long-term rationale for change, despite its costs, to the larger community of institutional investors, government lawmakers and regulators, and potential employees and business partners.

It has been an effort to incubate a cultural revolution, as one corporation after another has attempted to reeducate Americans about the world of work and the rationale behind—indeed, inevitability of—harsh new changes. So long as the stock market soared and the U.S. economy looked unstoppable during the 1990s, contemporary business leaders were as successful in winning converts as their paternalistic counterparts were half a century ago.

But nothing lasts forever in the business world. As financial conditions became more volatile near the turn of the millennium, the limits to corporate America's spin campaign became clearer. After nearly two decades of deteriorating work conditions, many white-collar men and women no longer trusted their employers—no matter what strategies public relations and management consultants concocted—nor did they care about much of anything besides their prospects for "jumping ship" to a better corporate position or retiring as quickly as possible. With the value of most large-corporate stocks in a slump, the sales pitch for "sweatshop" management practices had apparently lost its effectiveness among investors as well.

"Selling" the White-Collar Sweatshop

When it has come to proselytizing for the new work-world order, few have been as aggressive or outspoken as Albert J. Dunlap, the once-revered, recently reviled chief executive and corporate turn-around artist whose best-selling 1996 memoir was entitled, with perfect accuracy, *Mean Business*. Dunlap ranks as one of the most fascinating of contemporary business figures, in large part because his spectacular rise and fall as a business icon reveals so much about the allure, as well as limitations, of current harsh management techniques.

Some personal background is important in understanding his success as a business "evangelist." After early stints elsewhere, Dunlap assumed the chairmanship of Scott Paper Company in 1994, at a time when that firm was losing nearly $300 million a year. His nineteen-month tenure there quickly became the stuff of 1990s business legend: he fired 11,200 people, one third of the company's workforce, drove its stock price up by 225 percent, and sold off Scott to a competitor, netting himself a $100 million paycheck in the process.

"The term 'to Dunlap' has become a verb in the business lexicon," he gloated after that sale, explaining that his very name had become a synonym for "eliminating everything that is not the best."[4] Many agreed: within the large-corporate and investment communities, Dunlap's knack for tying the leanest and meanest of management strategies to exceptional stock market results—without any apologies along the way—amounted to proof incontrovertible that his was the formula for success in the harsh and competitive global economy.

As "Chainsaw Al"'s career progressed, he went on to terminate about 50 percent of the staffers at Sunbeam, where he next signed on as CEO. There he managed to drive up the company's stock price by nearly 60 percent in one single day, just by *announcing* his agreement to take the helm. But the chief executive's aura of infallibility faded after he wound up getting "dunlapped" himself in 1998, amid signs that his cuts had decimated Sunbeam's infrastructure and product lines while failing to achieve significant financial improvements or to position the company for future profitability and growth.[5]

Regardless of its author's tarnished stature, *Mean Business* remains one of the classics of the current, hugely popular genre of books by CEOs: a not-too-surprising offshoot of the United States' equity-obsessed culture, in which the ability to keep a company's stock shares rising is viewed by some as little short of genius. One could speculate endlessly about the psychological subtext behind America's chief executives' compulsion to reinvent themselves as the contemporary business world's version of philosopher-kings. . . .

The compulsion to reinterpret the world for the rest of us has motivated quite a few business executives in a similar direction. Often, their philosophies rest upon a "sweatshop" vision of the workplace: a corporate environment in which there is little security, predictability, or even human kindness. Instead of these old creature comforts, readers are offered a scenario for corporate success which typically runs along these lines: If they (our visionary corporate leaders) and we (their fortunate employees) all work as hard as we can, to the utmost of our capabilities, *every single moment of every single day,* we all may thrive—at least for a while—in a new economy that is difficult and demanding, but potentially rewarding.

Dunlap, who liked to compare himself to Rambo, explained in *Mean Business* that "the harsh reality of business life is that what works today won't even be satisfac-

tory tomorrow. The predators are out there, circling, trying to stare you down, waiting for any sign of weakness, ready to pounce and make you their next meal."[6]

In his universe, there is one basic message: Business is battle and any employee who cannot cope is, or should be, cannon fodder. When it comes to younger workers (who have yet to be tested under this kind of fire), successful executives (who may share similar aggressive tendencies), and well-heeled investors (who tend to assess the corporate world primarily in terms of its stock-price swings), such management machismo has won plenty of adherents during the past decade or so. Thus, Dunlap's philosophical treatise has continued to draw rave reviews, even after his success at Scott Paper was eclipsed by his later failure at Sunbeam. . . .

Corporate leaders are far from the only people who have taken pen to paper during the past decade or so in an effort to convince the American public of the benefits of tight fiscal controls, tough management styles, and ever-higher performance standards. But these days few books by consultants or other business experts carry the weight of those by successful CEOs, who in the current economic climate come close to attaining the celebrity stature of star athletes.

"I believe in the value of paranoia," wrote another corporate superstar, Intel's then chief executive Andrew S. Grove, in his *Only the Paranoid Survive.* "Business success contains the seeds of its own destruction. The more successful you are, the more people want a chunk of your business and then another chunk and then another until there is nothing left. I believe that the prime responsibility of a manager is to guard constantly against other people's attacks and to inculcate this guardian attitude in the people under his or her management."[7]

Elsewhere, Grove invoked a Darwinian vision of the workplace in which an individual's career success and failure were determined by the corporation's instinctive quest for survival (which, like that of any species, is viewed as utterly natural and beyond morality). "Do people seem to be 'losing it' around you?" he asked. "Think about it. You and your management have both been selected by the evolutionary forces of your business to be at the top of your organization. Your genes were right for the original business. But if key aspects of the business shift around you, the very process of genetic selection that got you and your associates where you are might retard your ability to recognize the new trends."[8]

In the business world sketched out by CEO-writers like these, the workplace changes that have taken place during the 1980s and 1990s were unequivocally good and inevitably necessary, and, above all else, produced results. Irrelevant was the impact of these changes upon corporate men and women who were forced to accommodate heavier workloads, constantly increasing productivity demands, greater intrusions of work upon home life, diminished job security, and reduced financial rewards.

Within this publishing genre, the justification for all lies squarely in one place: the U.S. stock market. That was a message plenty of people were willing to accept at face value, at least while the bull market soared.

The Tougher Sell: Executive Compensation

Corporate America's spin-masters have had far less success in persuading people to accept another key element of the new business-world order: skyrocketing executive compensation levels.

During the 1980s and most especially the 1990s, chief-executive pay reached levels so astronomically high as to raise questions among employees and investors alike about the degree to which the nation's corporate leaders were willing to live by their own lean-and-mean creed. According to one study, the annual compensation of chief executives of large corporations (which typically included salary, bonuses, and stock grants and options) rose from an average of $1.8 million back in 1990 to $10.6 million in 1998, an increase of about 490 percent in less than a decade. This occurred during a period in which many people's paychecks barely kept up with inflation; countless others, with careers disrupted by corporate downsizings or mergers, actually lost financial ground as they spent retirement savings, sold homes, or accepted lower-paying jobs in order to meet their household obligations.[9] . . .

It's hard to imagine how anyone could justify these outrageous paychecks, and few have tried. GE's Jack Welch, who earned $150 million in the three years between 1996 and 1998, responded to a question from a shareholder at the company's annual meeting by simply quipping, "Sure, I'm one of the fat cats. In fact, I'm the fattest cat because I'm lucky enough to have this job."[10]

The disparity that developed during these past two decades between executive reward and employee cutbacks was little short of breathtaking. Back in 1978, the leaders of America's major corporations earned just under 30 times the pay of their average workers. Just seventeen years later, they earned more than 115 times as much. Indeed, by 1997 the Economic Policy Institute calculated that the average business leader worked just half a week in order to bring home as much as his or her typical employee managed to earn over the entire year.[11] According to one *BusinessWeek* report, subtitled "Even Executives Are Wincing at Executive Pay," three of every four people surveyed believe that the top staffers of large corporations simply were paid too much.[12]

For most men and women, the conclusion seemed unavoidable; during the United States' recent boom, the CEOs of large corporations received a disproportionate share of the goodies while imposing the bulk of the economic recovery's cost upon their employees. No wonder that was a tough message for even the most public-relations-oriented of business leaders to sell to the American public.

For many of today's white-collar workers, plagued by overwork, deteriorating benefits, and much too much stress, the boss's salary has become an irritant they just cannot overlook. "You hear comments about Sandy Weill *all the time*," one Citigroup staffer told me in disgust, referring to the company's chairman. "He becomes the voodoo doll here." In 1998 Weill earned $167 million at a time when the bank planned to cut 5 percent of its workforce while reducing 401K, pension, and other benefits.[13] . . .

Given these levels of inequity, it's not surprising that executive compensation has surfaced as a symbol—among a growing, if loose, coalition of white-collar workers, union activists, investors, muck-raking journalists, and legislators—of something rotten in today's business universe. . . .

An analysis of executive compensation trends reveals a clear pattern: those business leaders willing to make harsh human-resources-related cuts in the interest of boosting the bottom line (and presumably the stock price) are often well rewarded for their efforts. Xerox gave its chairman and chief executive officer, Paul Allaire, a 51 percent raise in bonus and salary (to about $7.5 million) during 1997 and then announced plans early in 1998 to eliminate nine thousand jobs, or about 10 percent of its workforce.[14]

For all those corporate staffers whose work lives have worsened thanks to such management dictates as "Keep raising the bar" and "There's no free ride," another trend has been galling: the United States' top executives simply do not seem to be held to the same inflexibly high standards as they are. At Warnaco—which lost $32 million after taxes during 1998—its chairman, Linda J. Wachner, earned a total compensation package (including options) estimated at $73.4 million.[15] Apple Computer lost nearly $2 billion under the seventeen-month leadership of Gilbert F. Amelio; the CEO still received $2 million in salary and bonus, as well as a severance payment of $6.7 million.[16] . . .

The Inside Spin

There's another side to the corporate campaign to win Americans' allegiance to the demanding new world of work: internal public relations.

During the 1980s and 1990s, many large corporations launched workplace seminars, support groups, and a host of other programs that, whether explicitly or not, aimed to reeducate their current or soon-to-be-former employees about the necessities and virtues of harsh corporate changes. Typically combining New Age techniques with an evangelical thrust, these initiatives seldom focused simply upon helping staffers adjust. They aimed to win pumped-up, motivated converts who would be ready to perform and thrive under the most grueling and even hostile of business conditions.

The theory behind them might have made sense, but internal public relations initiatives have frequently backfired, adding fuel to feelings of cynicism or anger among overworked, insecure, stressed-out employees. NYNEX's "Winning Ways" program, a company-wide initiative that was conducted during the mid-1990s, is illustrative. Its objective was to nurture a new mentality among the struggling company's employees—the mentality of a winner. William C. Ferguson, the retired chief executive of

NYNEX, described Winning Ways as promoting "the key behaviors and attitudes that help us exceed customer expectations and win in the marketplace. These behaviors start with integrity and leadership."[17]

Although NYNEX had thrived in the early years after the AT&T divestiture, by the 1990s the company seemed to be on an unstoppable downhill roll, thanks to a costly and divisive union strike, the expenditure of hundreds of millions of dollars on a series of failed acquisitions, and the gradual layoff of more than 20 percent of the workforce. In retrospect, this employee program seems to have been part of a "holding pattern" by the company's top executives, who spent these years floundering between one ineffective management initiative after another, only to finally resolve their problems through what was billed as a "merger of equals" (but basically boiled down to a takeover of NYNEX by the thriving Bell Atlantic).

I learned about Winning Ways from a group of mid-level employees I interviewed during my research. They and their peers made no bones about their contempt for it, using a company-wide nickname to dismiss it: "Whining Ways." They viewed the seminar as yet another consultant-designed time-waster—part of a pattern which suggested to them that top management was clueless about the company's future direction as well as out of touch with everyone below the executive suite.

"First it was 'Quality,' " sneered Bobby, an M.B.A. by training, who had joined the telecommunications company during the early 1980s as part of its large administrative staff. "There were *billions* of consultants. Lots of training. A lot of it was common sense. Then after 'quality' started costing so much, they phased it down. Then it went to 'Winning Ways.' That was the new world— where they would make you feel good about yourself while they were feeling good about letting you go."

To the NYNEX staffers I interviewed, Winning Ways was little more than an inept attempt to pull the wool over their eyes: to boost their self-esteem with some "touchy-feely" exercises, as Bobby termed them, during a troubled corporate era in which intelligent men and women could not help recognizing that there were plenty of reasons to lose confidence in the company's future, as well as their own.

Attendance was mandatory. "It was required of us. It was absolutely required. You had to sign that you had gone," complained Joan, a computer technician. "There were things like pictures that could either be an old woman or a young woman. The point was, things are different depending upon how you see them. And both points are valid," she drew the sentence out, as if she were in a kindergarten class repeating a lesson from her teacher.

"There'd be six of us sitting at a table, working on puzzle pieces. They were all mixed up. We could only do the puzzle if we worked together." She paused, then said, "It was completely useless for us. Afterwards, my boss suggested we have group meetings. *That* was the only difference."

For Bobby, it was his memory of the group "jump" that still drove him to distraction, long after it had taken place. "We spent three whole days together, off-site, dressed-down. You were required to go. One exercise was, how many different ways can you jump around the room?" So he and his colleagues jumped—on one leg, on both legs, with their hands in the air, with one hand covering an eye. They jumped and they jumped and they jumped some more. "Then the leaders would say things like, 'Look at how creative you are, how many different ways you can figure out to manage to jump around the room.' And we all did it," Bobby told me, his voice laced with contempt for everyone in the room, including himself. "We all did it."

The NYNEX seminar sent him into a spiral of self-disgust while generating even more powerful negative emotions toward his employer; yet the focus of "Winning Ways" was to feel upbeat, no matter what was going on within the corporation or the business world at large. "They'd bring up family big-time. Realize what you have: your family, your career—but *not* your job," Bobby pointed out. While everyone was thinking those good thoughts, soft music played in the background.

His voice faded away for a while as he recalled the scene to himself. "People would sit there and say, 'We can't believe we're doing this.' After all," he concluded, "at the end of day you've got a company that provides poor service, that is not well managed, and that is totally hostage to its union situation. They're spending money on things like this that are just fluff. That's the cynicism. That's the irony."

It's tough to quantify how much of the many billions of dollars spent each year on management consultants has paid for misguided internal PR efforts like these. But the landscape of corporate America has been littered in recent years with countless costly and ineffective counterparts to NYNEX's Winning Ways program: tiny testaments to the difficulty of brainwashing intelligent men and women into believing that they are better off than they once were within today's harsh new world of work.

Phillip was a veteran of the process. He had spent years in the marketing division of a chain of radio stations that went through a series of corporate mergers. Job conditions worsened each time his company got sold. One set of new corporate parents after another "kept cutting costs, cutting costs," he recalled. "They'd want a 10 percent decrease in the expense budget, but for sales to be increased by 10 percent or so. Then the next year, they'd say, cut it again by 10 percent and push up sales by another 10 percent."

In a pattern that has become all too predictable within the United States' large corporations, consultants were soon brought in to run employee motivational seminars. "I remember one set of meetings along the way," he told me, "when we had to all get together and stand up in front of the group and say what we were feeling. Our manager told us, 'We're going to talk about our feelings—there's a new openness here.' Some of us even started crying. We were really expressing our hopes."

That was only the beginning. "Then we had to get into a circle. Hold hands. Close our eyes. There were two different circles moving in two different directions. Then when the circle stopped moving, you had to fall backwards and trust that the person who was behind you would catch you. Then there was another exercise with boards and cinder blocks. The only way you could get across was if people would share their boards with you."

Since the program coincided loosely with a corporate era in which layoffs were rampant and other cutbacks continued, participants were dubious, to put it mildly, about the company's motives. With attendance mandatory and a clear corporate line to follow, this feel-good-fest was viewed by many people as yet another turn in their work lives over which they had no control.

The "spider webs" were a good example. "They tied up ropes between two trees so that it looked like a web," explained Phillip. "You literally had to lie on the ground and hold yourself stiff and be passed through the ropes. You had to hope that someone on the other side would catch you." He paused, as if searching for the right way to describe the experience. "This was the most uncomfortable thing for professional men and women. A lot of us," he confided, "felt uncomfortable, embarrassed, reluctant to play the games. But they kept at it. It was almost like it was designed to break you down. I think it was a way of humiliating us." He paused again. "If we would have been kept at our jobs, it would be one thing. But many people were fired anyway."

For Phillip, the equivalent of NYNEX's group "jumps" were the mandatory water sports. "There were dump tanks. We had to participate in that too. They gave everybody squirt guns and there were all these executives running around squirting each other. You felt you were under a microscope. One person refused to do it. I felt," he recalled, "if I don't squirt, will I be gone too?" Again, a pause. "In the end, plenty of people wound up getting fired—the squirters and the nonsquirters. What did it matter?"

The Public Relations Backlash

There was a pattern to the metaphors that people chose when describing their employers' internal public relations campaigns. "It's Orwellian," was a theme I heard repeatedly as men and women recounted the various ways that companies tried to convince them that bad things were really good. "It's like Vietnam," was another popular refrain (typically among people whose employers liked to deny that layoffs were really layoffs). One man went so far as to compare conditions at NYNEX to those in the Stalinist Soviet Union, since he felt that nothing the company told its employees could be trusted.

Clearly the public relations pitches were misfiring. White-collar workers particularly loathed the linguistic maneuvers that corporations relied upon to distance themselves from the human repercussions of their actions. Thus, layoffs were termed "releases of resources" by Bank of America, "career-change opportunities" by Clifford of Vermont, "schedule adjustments" by Stouffer Foods Corporation, and "elimination of employment security policy" by Pacific Bell.

AT&T opted for a *Star Wars*-like phrase: "force management program." Bell Labs was notable during the nineties if only because its euphemism for downsizing hinted at something a bit closer to reality: "involuntary separation from payroll."[18]

Employee "reward" programs were often another enormous source of discontent. Since top executives usually aimed to control financial expenditures, at least when it came to people outside the executive suite, the popular trend was toward nonmonetary rewards. The theory behind them served the corporation's interests, if not the employee's: if you pay people a bonus to reward hard work, they will come to expect it and eventually stop working harder—so the safest course is never to get started. (Fortunately for top executives, their compensation packages weren't expected to produce the same result, although it's hard to know why not.) Investors and management consultants loved nonmonetary programs like these, since they had no impact on the company's bottom line.

But rather than bonding white-collar staffers closer to their employers, these initiatives nurtured widespread cynicism and resentment. "The company set up a 'Way to Go' program that recognized the very best ass-kissers," recalled "Keffo," a contributor to the Internet magazine *Temp Slave*. "It was all mucky-muck bullshit created to perpetuate the myth that the company cared about its workers. Of course, none of these workers ever got something real, like a raise in pay."[19]

Like the wolf in grandmother's clothing, motivational programs often boiled down to new and different corporate strategies to overwork staffers. Bank of America, one of the most notorious practitioners of layoffs and cutbacks during the past decade, came up with a noteworthy example in 1999, when it developed a program offering employees the chance to "adopt an A.T.M." machine.

This was not a profit-making venture for the employees; instead, bank volunteers were given the chance to clean an automatic teller machine and its surrounding area so long as they did so on their own time after work and without extra pay. The benefits from such adoptions were, presumably, lower janitorial costs for the bank and, perhaps, happier customers; it's hard to imagine much in the way of extra gratification for already busy staffers, who likely had more than enough cleaning tasks already waiting for them at home. More than 2,800 of the bank's 158,000 staffers signed up, perhaps because they hoped the extra work would shelter them whenever the next round of corporate cutbacks came along. Fortunately, California's state labor commissioner interceded, informing the bank that the program violated "basic precepts of wage and hour law."[20]

Without being quite so blatant, other programs have created new work for corporate staffers while pretending to add meaning to their lives. One popular, if often ineffective, internal spin technique links employee-motivation efforts with charitable activities. The corporate payoff includes plenty of positive buzz among lawmakers, potential investors, and the general populace. Staffers—whose regular workloads typically don't get reduced when "volunteer" assignments are layered on top—wind up with more job stress as they struggle to cope.

At HarperCollins, Annette (who worked in the publicity department) participated in the company's "Visions and Values" program. She and a group of colleagues from various job categories and departments were assigned to paint a facility owned by a nonprofit organization. It was not a matter of choice. "It was done very diplomatically, but you were given the sense, politely, that this was expected of you. So you did it."

The experience was anything but rewarding, she recalled. "It was a farce, really. We made a mess of it—after all, we weren't painters. We didn't know how to be careful and we didn't want to be doing this in the first place. I actually felt sorry for the people whose rooms we were painting." From Annette's vantage point, the only employee "bonding" that took place among the group's members was a kind of "reverse bonding, because we all felt so cynical about the whole process. After all, we had no choice about doing this. It only made our work lives harder, because we had to do this during the workweek and then find time during evenings or weekends to catch up on all the jobs we still needed to do."

She paused, then concluded, "All that 'Visions and Values' was about was making the company look good to the outside world. And that was a joke," she added, "because they really didn't give a s——— about anything but profit." Soon after her participation, in fact, HarperCollins made headlines because of a company-wide layoff.[21]

But despite the time and money that has been spent upon Visions and Values, Winning Ways, and countless variations on their ill-conceived management themes, corporate America's internal spin campaign was far from successful during the 1990s. That's not too surprising, perhaps: it's easier for chief executives to sway readers with their aggressive certainties and stock market prowess than it is for employers to convince their white-collar staffers that all the changes they *know* have made work life worse are really just plain great after all. And within the ranks of workforce distrust and discontent—as well as popular resentment over excessive executive compensation levels—may come, finally, an effort to halt "sweat-shop" corporate trends and to restore a more equitable balance to the twenty-first-century workplace.

NOTES

1. Louis Uchitelle, "Signing Bonus Now a Fixture Farther Down the Job Ladder," *New York Times,* June 10, 1998, A1.
2. Nina Munk, "The New Organization Man," *Fortune,* March 16, 1998 (on-line edition).
3. The Bureau of Labor Statistics (BLS) reports that in 1999 the average total size of the U.S. workforce was 133,488,000. Figuring out exactly how many of those workers fit the category "white-collar" isn't simple: the term itself is no longer officially in use, since the United States changed its job-category terminology with the Census of 1980. The BLS's last recorded use of the term was in 1982, when it reported 53,470,000 white-collar workers, out of a total 99,526,000-person workforce. For the purposes of this book, it makes sense to combine two large job categories currently tracked by the bureau: managerial and professional specialty, of which there were 40,467,000, and technical, sales, and administrative support, at 38,921,000, as of 1999.
4. Albert J. Dunlap with Bob Andelman, *Mean Business: How I Save Bad Companies and Make Good Companies Great* (New York: Times Business, 1996), 31.
5. John A. Byrne, "Chainsaw," *BusinessWeek,* October 18, 1999, 128–49; James R. Hagerty and Martha Brannigan, "Inside Sunbeam, Raindrops Mar Dunlap's Parade," *Wall Street Journal,* May 22, 1998, B1; Martha Brannigan and Joann S. Lublin, "Dunlap Faces a Fight over His Severance Pay," *Wall Street Journal,* June 16, 1998, B1.
6. Dunlap, ix.
7. Andrew S. Grove, *Only the Paranoid Survive: How to Exploit the Crisis Points That Challenge Every Company and Career* (New York: Currency, Doubleday, 1996), 3.
8. Grove, 108.
9. John Cassidy, "Wall Street Follies," *The New Yorker,* September 13, 1999, 32. Cassidy cited statistics from a study jointly published by the Insitute for Policy Studies and the advocacy group United for a Fair Economy.
10. Jennifer Reingold, "Executive Pay," *BusinessWeek,* April 27, 1997, 59; Jennifer Reingold, "Executive Pay," *BusinessWeek,* April 20, 1998, 65; Jennifer Reingold, "Executive Pay," *BusinessWeek,* April 19, 1999, 72; William M. Carley, "GE Chairman Defends Pay, Stresses Quality," *Wall Street Journal,* April 24, 1997, A4.
11. Lawrence Mishel, Jared Bernstein, and John Schmitt, *The State of Working America, 1998–1999* (Ithaca, N.Y.: ILR Press, 1999), 211.
12. Jennifer Reingold with Amy Borrus, "Even Executives Are Wincing at Executive Pay," *BusinessWeek,* May 12, 1997, 40.
13. Reingold, April 19, 1999, 72; Paul Beckett, "Citigroup Makes Move to Change Pension Benefits," *Wall Street Journal,* April 2, 1999, A4; Matt Murray, "Citigroup Expecting to Chop 8,000 Jobs," *Wall Street Journal,* September 13, 1998, A3.
14. Raju Narisetti, "Xerox's Chief Has Rise of 51% in Salary, Bonus," *Wall Street Journal,* April 10, 1998, B7.
15. Cassidy.
16. Jim Carlton, "Apple Paid Ex-CEO $9.2 Million After Ouster," *Wall Street Journal,* December 8, 1997, B10.
17. William C. Ferguson, "Ethical Foundations," *Executive Excellence,* vol. 14, no. 6 (June 1997): 15–16.
18. Cited from William Lutz's *The New Doublespeak,* in Steven Levy, "Work Is Hell: Why Dilbert Is No Joke," *Newsweek,* August 12, 1996, 57.
19. Jeff Kelly, ed., *The Best of Temp Slave!* (Madison, Wis.: Garrett County Press, 1997), 21.
20. Jeffrey L. Seglin, "The Right Thing: Playing It the Company Way, After Hours," *New York Times,* February 20, 2000, section 3, 4.
21. Doreen Carvajal, "$270 Million HarperCollins Charge Is Set," *New York Times,* August 5, 1997, D1.

QUESTIONS FOR DISCUSSION

1. What are the "sweatshop" conditions in which white-collar workers increasingly have to operate?
2. What are the techniques that CEOs use to justify their treatment of workers?
3. What are the implications of Andresky Fraser's argument for the ways that we think about work?

27

THE TIME BIND
When Work Becomes Home and Home Becomes Work

ARLIE RUSSELL HOCHSCHILD

If working parents are "deciding" to work full time and longer, what experiences at home and work might be influencing them to do so? When I first began this research, I assumed that home was "home" and work was "work"—that each was a stationary rock beneath the moving feet of working parents. I assumed as well that each stood in distinct opposition to the other. In a family, love and commitment loom large as ends in themselves and are not means to any further end. As an Amerco parent put it, "I work to live; I don't live to work." However difficult family life may be at times, we usually feel family ties offer an irreplaceable connection to generations past and future. Family is our personal embrace with history.

Jobs, on the other hand, earn money that, to most of us, serves as the means to other ends. To be sure, jobs can also allow us to develop skills or friendships, and to be part of a larger work community. But we seldom envision the workplace as somewhere workers would freely choose to spend their time. If in the American imagination the family has a touch of the sacred, the realm of work seems profane.

In addition, I assumed, as many of us do, that compared to the workplace, home is a more pleasant place to be. This is after all one

reason why employers pay workers to work and don't pay them to stay home. The very word "work" suggests to most of us something unpleasant, involuntary, even coerced.

If the purpose and nature of family and work differ so drastically in our minds, it seemed reasonable to assume that people's emotional experiences of the two spheres would differ profoundly, too. In *Haven in a Heartless World,* the social historian Christopher Lasch drew a picture of family as a "haven" where workers sought refuge from the cruel world of work. Painting in broad strokes, we might imagine a picture like this: At the end of a long day, a weary worker opens his front door and calls out, "Hi, Honey! I'm home!" He takes off his uniform, puts on a bathrobe, opens a beer, picks up the paper, and exhales. Whatever its strains, home is where he's relaxed, most himself. At home, he feels that people know him, understand him, appreciate him for who he really is. At home, he is safe.

At work, our worker is "on call," ready to report at a moment's notice, working flat out to get back to the customer right away. He feels "like a number." If he doesn't watch out, he can take the fall for somebody else's mistakes. This, then, is Lasch's "heartless world," an image best captured long ago in Charlie Chaplin's satirical *Modern Times.* In that film, Charlie acts the part of a hapless factory hand on an automated assembly line moving so fast that when he takes a moment to scratch his nose, he falls desperately behind. Dwarfed by the inhuman scale of the workplace, pressured by the line's relentless pace, Charlie quickly loses his humanity, goes mad, climbs into the giant machine that runs the conveyor belt, and becomes a machine part himself.

It was just such images of home and work that were challenged in one of my first interviews at Amerco. Linda Avery, a friendly thirty-eight-year-old mother of two daughters, is a shift supervisor at the Demco Plant, ten miles down the valley from Amerco headquarters. Her husband, Bill, is a technician in the same plant. Linda and Bill share the care of her sixteen-year-old daughter from a previous marriage and their two-year-old by working opposite shifts, as a full fifth of American working parents do. "Bill works the 7 A.M. to 3 P.M. shift while I watch the baby," Linda explained. "Then I work the 3 P.M. to 11 P.M. shift and he watches the baby. My older daughter works at Walgreens after school."

When we first met in the factory's breakroom over a couple of Cokes, Linda was in blue jeans and a pink jersey, her hair pulled back in a long blond ponytail. She wore no makeup, and her manner was purposeful and direct. She was working overtime, and so I began by asking whether Amerco required the overtime, or whether she volunteered for it. "Oh, I put in for it," she replied with a low chuckle. But, I wondered aloud, wouldn't she and her husband like to have more time at home together, finances and company policy permitting. Linda took off her safety glasses, rubbed her whole face, folded her arms, resting her elbows on the table, and approached the question by describing her life at home:

> I walk in the door and the minute I turn the key in the lock my older daughter is there. Granted, she needs somebody to talk to about her day. . . . The baby is still up. She should have been in bed two hours ago and that upsets me. The

dishes are piled in the sink. My daughter comes right up to the door and complains about anything her stepfather said or did, and she wants to talk about her job. My husband is in the other room hollering to my daughter, "Tracy, I don't *ever* get any time to talk to your mother, because you're always monopolizing her time before I even get a chance!" They all come at me at once.

To Linda, her home was not a place to relax. It was another workplace. Her description of the urgency of demands and the unarbitrated quarrels that awaited her homecoming contrasted with her account of arriving at her job as a shift supervisor:

> I usually come to work early just to get away from the house. I get there at 2:30 P.M., and people are there waiting. We sit. We talk. We joke. I let them know what's going on, who has to be where, what changes I've made for the shift that day. We sit there and chit-chat for five or ten minutes. There's laughing, joking, fun. My coworkers aren't putting me down for any reason. Everything is done with humor and fun from beginning to end, though it can get stressful when a machine malfunctions.

For Linda, home had become work and work had become home. Somehow, the two worlds had been reversed. Indeed, Linda felt she could only get relief from the "work" of being at home by going to the "home" of work. As she explained,

> My husband's a great help watching our baby. But as far as doing housework or even taking the baby when I'm at home, no. He figures he works five days a week; *he's* not going to come home and clean. But he doesn't stop to think that I work *seven* days a week. Why should I have to come home and do the housework without help from anybody else?

My husband and I have been through this over and over again. Even if he would just pick up from the kitchen table and stack the dishes for me, that would make a big difference. He does nothing. On his weekends off, I have to provide a sitter for the baby so he can go fishing. When I have a day off, I have the baby all day long without a break. He'll help out if I'm not here, but the minute I am, all the work at home is mine.

With a light laugh, she continued, "So I take a lot of overtime. The more I get out of the house, the better I am. It's a terrible thing to say, but that's the way I feel." Linda said this not in the manner of a new discovery, a reluctant confession, or collusion between two working mothers—"Don't you just want to get away sometimes?"—but in a matter-of-fact way. This was the way life was.

Bill, who was fifty-six when I first met him, had three grown children from a contentious first marriage. He told me he felt he had already "put in his time" to raise them and now was at a stage of life in which he wanted to enjoy himself. Yet when he came home afternoons he had to "babysit for Linda."

In a previous era, men regularly escaped the house for the bar, the fishing hole, the golf course, the pool hall, or, often enough, the sweet joy of work. Today, as one of the women who make up 45 percent of the American workforce, Linda Avery, overloaded and feeling unfairly treated at home, was escaping to work, too. Nowadays, men and women both may leave unwashed dishes, unresolved quarrels, crying tots, testy teenagers, and unresponsive mates behind to arrive at work early and call out, "Hi, fellas, I'm here!"

Linda would have loved a warm welcome from her family when she returned from work, a reward for her day of labors at the plant. At a minimum, she would have

liked to relax, at least for a little while. But that was hard to do because Bill, on *his* second shift at home, would nap and watch television instead of engaging the children. The more Bill slacked off on his shift at home, the more Linda felt robbed of rest when she was there. The more anxious the children were, or the messier the house was when she walked in the door, the more Linda felt she was simply returning to the task of making up for being gone.

For his part, Bill recalled that Linda had wanted a new baby more than he had. So now that they were the parents of a small child, Bill reasoned, looking after the baby should also be more Linda's responsibility. Caring for a two-year-old after working a regular job was hard enough. Incredibly, Linda wanted him to do more. That was her problem though, not his. He had "earned his stripes" with his first set of children.

Early Saturday mornings, while Linda and the kids were rustling about the house, Bill would get up, put his fishing gear and a six-pack of beer into his old Ford truck, and climb into the driver's seat. "Man, I slam that truck door shut, frraaammm!, and I'm ready to go! I figure I *earned* that time."

Both Linda and Bill felt the need for time off, to relax, to have fun, to feel free, but they had not agreed that it was Bill who needed a break more than Linda. Bill simply climbed in his truck and took his free time. This irritated Linda because she felt he *took* it at her expense. Largely in response to her resentment, Linda grabbed what she also called "free time"—at work.

Neither Linda nor Bill Avery wanted more time at home, not as things were arranged. Whatever images they may have carried in their heads about what family and work should be like, the Averys did not feel their actual home was a haven or that work was a heartless world.

Where did Linda feel most relaxed? She laughed more, joked more, listened to more interesting stories while on break at the factory than at home. Working the 3 P.M. to 11 P.M. shift, her hours off didn't coincide with those of her mother or older sister who worked in town, nor with those of her close friends and neighbors. But even if they had, she would have felt that the true center of her social world was her plant, not her neighborhood. The social life that once might have surrounded her at home she now found at work. The sense of being part of a lively, larger, ongoing community—that too, was at work. In an emergency, Linda told me, she would sacrifice everything for her family. But in the meantime, the everyday "emergencies" she most wanted to attend to, that challenged rather than exhausted her, were those she encountered at the factory. Frankly, life there was more fun.

How do Linda and Bill Avery fit into the broader picture of American family and work life? Psychologist Reed Larson and his colleagues studied the daily emotional experiences of mothers and fathers in fifty-five two-parent Chicago families with children in the fifth to eighth grades. Some of the mothers cared for children at home, some worked part time, others full time, while all the fathers in the study worked full time. Each participant wore a pager for a week, and whenever they were beeped by the research team, each wrote down how he or she felt: "happy, unhappy, cheerful-irritable, friendly-angry." The researchers found that men and women reported a similar range of emotional states across the week. But fathers reported more "positive emotional states" at home; mothers, more positive emotional states at work. This held true for every social class. Fathers like Bill Avery relaxed more at home; while mothers like Linda Avery did more housework there. Larson suggests that "because women are constantly on call to the needs of other family members, they are less able to relax at home in the way men do." Wives were typi-

cally in better moods than their husbands at home only when they were eating or engaging in "family transport." They were in worse moods when they were doing "child-related activities" or "socializing" there. Men and women each felt most at ease when involved in tasks they felt less obliged to do, Larson reports. For women, this meant first shift work; for men, second.

A recent study of working mothers made another significant discovery. Problems at home tend to upset women more deeply than problems at work. The study found that women were most deeply affected by family stress—and were more likely to be made depressed or physically ill by it—even when stress at the workplace was greater. For women, current research on stress does not support the common view of home as a sanctuary and work as a "jungle." However hectic their lives, women who do paid work, researchers have consistently found, feel less depressed, think better of themselves, and are more satisfied with life than women who don't do paid work. One study reported that, paradoxically, women who work feel more valued at home than women who stay home.

In sum, then, women who work outside the home have better physical and mental health than those who do not, and not simply because healthier women go to work. Paid work, the psychologist Grace Baruch argues, "offers such benefits as challenge, control, structure, positive feedback, self-esteem . . . and social ties." Reed Larson's study found, for example, that women were no more likely than men to see coworkers as friendly, but when women made friendly contact it was far more likely to lift their spirits.

As a woman quoted by Baruch put it, "A job is to a woman as a wife is to a man."

For Linda Avery self-satisfaction, well-being, high spirits, and work were inextricably linked. It was mainly at work, she commented, that she felt really good about herself. As a supervisor, she saw her job as helping people, and those she helped appreciated her. She mused,

> I'm a good mom at home, but I'm a better mom at work. At home, I get into fights with Tracy when she comes home late. I want her to apply to a junior college; but she's not interested, and I get frustrated with her, because I want so much for her. At work, I think I'm better at seeing the other person's point of view. People come to me a lot, because I'm good at helping them.

Often relations at work seemed more manageable. The "children" Linda Avery helped at work were older and better able to articulate their problems than her own children. The plant where she worked was clean and pleasant. She knew everyone on the line she supervised. Indeed, all the workers knew each other, and some were even related by blood, marriage, or, odd as it may sound, by divorce. One coworker complained bitterly that a friend of her husband's ex-wife was keeping track of how much overtime she worked in order to help this ex-wife make a case for increasing the amount of his child support. Workers sometimes carried such hostilities generated at home into the workplace. Yet despite the common assumption that relations at work are emotionally limited, meaningful friendships often blossom. When Linda Avery joined coworkers for a mug of beer at a nearby bar after work to gossip about the "spy" who was tracking the deadbeat dad's new wife's overtime, she was among real friends: Research shows that work friends can be as important as family members in helping both men and women cope with the blows of life. The gerontologist Andrew Sharlach studied how middle-aged people in Los Angeles dealt with the death of a parent. He found that 73 percent of the women

in the sample, and 64 percent of the men, responded that work was a "helpful resource" in coping with a mother's death.

Amerco regularly reinforced the family-like ties of coworkers by holding recognition ceremonies honoring particular workers or entire self-managed production teams. The company would decorate a section of the factory and serve food and drink. The production teams, too, had regular get-togethers. The halls of Amerco were hung with plaques praising workers for recent accomplishments. Such recognition luncheons, department gatherings, and, particularly in the ranks of clerical and factory workers, exchange of birthday gifts were fairly common workday events.

At its white-collar offices, Amerco was even more involved in shaping the emotional culture of the workplace and fostering an environment of trust and cooperation in order to bring out everyone's best. At the middle and top levels of the company, employees were invited to periodic "career development seminars" on personal relations at work. The centerpiece of Amerco's personal-relations culture was a "vision" speech that the CEO had given called "Valuing the Individual," a message repeated in speeches, memorialized in company brochures, and discussed with great seriousness throughout the upper reaches of the company. In essence, the message was a parental reminder to respect others. Similarly, in a new-age recasting of an old business slogan ("The customer is always right"), Amerco proposed that its workers "Value the internal customer." This meant: Be as polite and considerate to your coworkers as you would be to Amerco customers. "Value the internal customer" extended to coworkers the slogan "Delight the customer." Don't just work with your coworkers, delight them.

"Employee empowerment," "valuing diversity," and "work-family balance"—

these catchphrases, too, spoke to a moral aspect of work life. Though ultimately tied to financial gain, such exhortations—and the policies that followed from them—made workers feel the company was concerned with people, not just money. In many ways, the workplace appeared to be a site of benign social engineering where workers came to feel appreciated, honored, and liked. On the other hand, how many recognition ceremonies for competent performance were going on at home? Who was valuing the internal customer there?

After thirty years with Amerco, Bill Avery felt, if anything, overqualified for his job, and he had a recognition plaque from the company to prove it. But when his toddler got into his fishing gear and he blew up at her and she started yelling, he felt impotent in the face of her rageful screams—and nobody was there to back him up. When his teenage stepdaughter reminded him that she saw him, not as an honorable patriarch, but as an infantile competitor for her mother's attention, he felt humiliated. At such moments, he says, he had to resist the impulse to reach for the whiskey he had given up five years earlier.

Other fathers with whom I talked were less open and self-critical about such feelings, but in one way or another many said that they felt more confident they could "get the job done" at work than at home. As one human resource specialist at Amerco reflected,

> We used to joke about the old "Mother of the Year Award." That doesn't exist anymore. Now, we don't know a meaningful way to reward a parent. At work, we get paid and promoted for doing well. At home, when you're doing the right thing, chances are your kids are giving you hell for it.

If a family gives its members anything, we assume it is surely a sense of belonging to an ongoing community. In its engineered corporate cultures, capitalism has rediscovered communal ties and is using them to build its new version of capitalism. Many Amerco employees spoke warmly, happily, and seriously of "belonging to the Amerco family," and everywhere there were visible symbols of this belonging. While some married people have dispensed with their wedding rings, people proudly wore their "Total Quality" pins or "High Performance Team" tee-shirts, symbols of their loyalty to the company and of its loyalty to them. In my interviews, I heard little about festive reunions of extended families, while throughout the year, employees flocked to the many company-sponsored ritual gatherings.

In this new model of family and work life, a tired parent flees a world of unresolved quarrels and unwashed laundry for the reliable orderliness, harmony, and managed cheer of work. The emotional magnets beneath home and workplace are in the process of being reversed. In truth, there are many versions of this reversal going on, some more far-reaching than others. Some people find in work a respite from the emotional tangles at home. Others virtually marry their work, investing it with an emotional significance once reserved for family, while hesitating to trust loved ones at home. If Linda and Bill Avery were not yet at that point, their situation was troubling enough, and by no means restricted to a small group. Overall, this "reversal" was a predominant pattern in about a fifth of Amerco families, and an important theme in over half of them.

We may be seeing here a trend in modern life destined to affect us all. To be sure, few people feel totally secure either at work or at home. In the last fifteen years, massive waves of downsizing have reduced the security workers feel even in the most apparently stable workplaces. At the same time, a rising divorce rate has reduced the security they feel at home. Although both Linda and

Bill felt their marriage was strong, over the course of their lives, each had changed relationships more often than they had changed jobs. Bill had worked steadily for Amerco for thirty years, but he had been married twice; and in the years between marriages, he had lived with two women and dated several more. Nationwide, half the people who marry eventually divorce, most within the first seven years of marriage. Three-quarters of divorced men and two-thirds of divorced women remarry, but remarried couples are more likely than those in first marriages to divorce. Couples who only live together are even more likely to break up than couples who marry. Increasing numbers of people are getting their "pink slips" at home. Work may become their rock.

QUESTIONS FOR DISCUSSION

1. Why do so many people feel that the work environment is more pleasurable and offers greater levels of personal satisfaction than the family environment?
2. How do the demands of managing families and jobs affect the women in Hochschild's study?
3. Think about your own experiences of work. Have you ever found your job to be more satisfying than your home life? Why or why not?

28

NICKEL-AND-DIMED
On (Not) Getting By in America

BARBARA EHRENREICH

At the beginning of June 1998 I leave behind everything that normally soothes the ego and sustains the body—home, career, companion, reputation, ATM card—for a plunge into the low-wage workforce. There, I become another, occupationally much diminished "Barbara Ehrenreich"—depicted on job-application forms as a divorced homemaker whose sole

Ehrenreich, Barbara, 1999. "Nickel-and-Dimed: On (Not) Getting By in America." First appeared in *Harpers Magazine*, pp. 37–52. Copyright © 1999 by Barbara Ehrenreich. Reprinted by permission of International Creative Management, Inc.

work experience consists of housekeeping in a few private homes. I am terrified, at the beginning, of being unmasked for what I am: a middle-class journalist setting out to explore the world that welfare mothers are entering, at the rate of approximately 50,000 a month, as welfare reform kicks in. Happily, though, my fears turn out to be entirely unwarranted: during a month of poverty and toil, my name goes unnoticed and for the most part unuttered. In this parallel universe where my father never got out of the mines and I never got through college, I am "baby," "honey," "blondie," and, most commonly, "girl."

My first task is to find a place to live. I figure that if I can earn $7 an hour—which, from the want ads, seems doable—I can afford to spend $500 on rent, or maybe, with severe economies, $600. In the Key West area, where I live, this pretty much confines me to flophouses and trailer homes—like the one, a pleasing fifteen-minute drive from town, that has no air-conditioning, no screens, no fans, no television, and, by way of diversion, only the challenge of evading the landlord's Doberman pinscher. The big problem with this place, though, is the rent, which at $675 a month is well beyond my reach. All right, Key West is expensive. But so is New York City, or the Bay Area, or Jackson Hole, or Telluride, or Boston, or any other place where tourists and the wealthy compete for living space with the people who clean their toilets and fry their hash browns.[1] Still, it is a shock to realize that "trailer trash" has become, for me, a demographic category to aspire to.

So I decide to make the common trade-off between affordability and convenience, and go for a $500-a-month efficiency thirty miles up a two-lane highway from the employment opportunities of Key West, meaning forty-five minutes if there's no road construction and I don't get caught behind some sun-dazed Canadian tourists. I hate the drive, along a roadside studded with white crosses commemorating the more effective head-on collisions, but it's a sweet little place—a cabin, more or less, set in the swampy back yard of the converted mobile home where my landlord, an affable TV repairman, lives with his bartender girlfriend. Anthropologically speaking, a bustling trailer park would be preferable, but here I have a gleaming white floor and a firm mattress, and the few resident bugs are easily vanquished.

Besides, I am not doing this for the anthropology. My aim is nothing so mistily subjective as to "experience poverty" or find out how it "really feels" to be a long-term low-wage worker. I've had enough unchosen encounters with poverty and the world of low-wage work to know it's not a place you want to visit for touristic purposes; it just smells too much like fear. And with all my real-life assets—bank account, IRA, health insurance, multiroom home—waiting indulgently in the background, I am, of course, thoroughly insulated from the terrors that afflict the genuinely poor.

No, this is a purely objective, scientific sort of mission. The humanitarian rationale for welfare reform—as opposed to the more punitive and stingy impulses that may actually have motivated it—is that work will lift poor women out of poverty while simultaneously inflating their self-esteem and hence their future value in the labor market. Thus, whatever the hassles involved in finding child care, transportation, etc., the transition from welfare to work will end happily, in greater prosperity for all. Now there are many problems with this comforting prediction, such as the fact that the economy will inevitably undergo a downturn, eliminating many jobs. Even without a downturn, the influx of a million former welfare recipients into the low-wage labor market could depress wages by as much as 11.9 percent, according to the Economic Policy Institute (EPI) in Washington, D.C.

But is it really possible to make a living on the kinds of jobs currently available to unskilled people? Mathematically, the answer is no, as can be shown by taking $6 to $7 an hour, perhaps subtracting a dollar or two an hour for child care, multiplying by 160 hours a month, and comparing the result to the prevailing rents. According to the National Coalition for the Homeless, for example, in 1998 it took, on average nationwide, an hourly wage of $8.89 to afford a one-bedroom apartment, and the Preamble Center for Public Policy estimates that the odds against a typical welfare recipient's landing a job at such a "living wage" are about 97 to 1. If these numbers are right, low-wage work is not a solution to poverty and possibly not even to homelessness.

It may seem excessive to put this proposition to an experimental test. As certain family members keep unhelpfully reminding me, the viability of low-wage work could be tested, after a fashion, without ever leaving my study. I could just pay myself $7 an hour for eight hours a day, charge myself for room and board, and total up the numbers after a month. Why leave the people and work that I love? But I am an experimental scientist by training. In that business, you don't just sit at a desk and theorize; you plunge into the everyday chaos of nature, where surprises lurk in the most mundane measurements. Maybe, when I got into it, I would discover some hidden economies in the world of the low-wage worker. After all, if 30 percent of the workforce toils for less than $8 an hour, according to the EPI, they may have found some tricks as yet unknown to me. Maybe—who knows?—I would even be able to detect in myself the bracing psychological effects of getting out of the house, as promised by the welfare wonks at places like the Heritage Foundation. Or, on the other hand, maybe there would be unexpected costs—physical, mental, or financial—to throw off all my calculations. Ideally, I should do this with two small children in tow, that being the welfare average, but mine are grown and no one is willing to lend me theirs for a month-long vacation in penury. So this is not the perfect experiment, just a test of the best possible case: an unencumbered woman, smart and even strong, attempting to live more or less off the land. . . .

Three days go by . . . and, to my chagrin, no one out of the approximately twenty places I've applied calls me for an interview. I had been vain enough to worry about coming across as too educated for the jobs I sought, but no one even seems interested in finding out how overqualified I am. Only later will I realize that the want ads are not a reliable measure of the actual jobs available at any particular time. They are . . . the employers' insurance policy against the relentless turnover of the low-wage workforce. Most of the big hotels run ads almost continually, just to build a supply of applicants to replace the current workers as they drift away or are fired, so finding a job is just a matter of being at the right place at the right time and flexible enough to take whatever is being offered that day. This finally happens to me at one of the big discount hotel chains, where I go, as usual, for housekeeping and am sent, instead, to try out as a waitress at the attached "family restaurant," a dismal spot with a counter and about thirty tables that looks out on a parking garage and features such tempting fare as "Pollish [sic] sausage and BBQ sauce" on 95-degree days. Phillip, the dapper young West Indian who introduces himself as the manager, interviews me with about as much enthusiasm as if he were a clerk processing me for Medicare, the principal questions being what shifts can I work and when can I start. I mutter something about being woefully out of practice as a waitress, but he's already on to the uniform: I'm to show up tomorrow wearing black slacks and black shoes; he'll provide the rust-colored polo shirt with HEARTHSIDE embroidered on it, though I might want to wear my own shirt to get to work, ha ha. At the word "tomorrow," something between fear and indignation rises in my chest. I want to say, "Thank you for your time, sir, but this is just an experiment, you know, not my actual life."

. . .

So begins my career at the Hearthside, I shall call it, one small profit center within a global discount hotel chain, where for two weeks I work from 2:00 till 10:00 P.M. for

$2.43 an hour plus tips.[2] In some futile bid for gentility, the management has barred employees from using the front door, so my first day I enter through the kitchen, where a red-faced man with shoulder-length blond hair is throwing frozen steaks against the wall and yelling, "Fuck this shit!" "That's just Jack," explains Gail, the wiry middle-aged waitress who is assigned to train me. "He's on the rag again"—a condition occasioned, in this instance, by the fact that the cook on the morning shift had forgotten to thaw out the steaks. For the next eight hours, I run after the agile Gail, absorbing bits of instruction along with fragments of personal tragedy. All food must be trayed, and the reason she's so tired today is that she woke up in a cold sweat thinking of her boyfriend, who killed himself recently in an upstate prison. No refills on lemonade. And the reason he was in prison is that a few DUIs caught up with him, that's all, could have happened to anyone. Carry the creamers to the table in a monkey bowl, never in your hand. And after he was gone she spent several months living in her truck, peeing in a plastic pee bottle and reading by candlelight at night, but you can't live in a truck in the summer, since you need to have the windows down, which means anything can get in, from mosquitoes on up.

At least Gail puts to rest any fears I had of appearing overqualified. From the first day on, I find that of all the things I have left behind, such as home and identity, what I miss the most is competence. Not that I have ever felt utterly competent in the writing business, in which one day's success augurs nothing at all for the next. But in my writing life, I at least have some notion of procedure: do the research, make the outline, rough out a draft, etc. As a server, though, I am beset by requests like bees: more iced tea here, ketchup over there, a to-go box for table fourteen, and where are the high chairs, anyway? Of the twenty-seven tables, up to six are usually mine at any time, though on slow afternoons or if Gail is off, I sometimes have the whole place to myself. There is the touch-screen computer-ordering system to master, which is, I suppose, meant to minimize server-cook contact, but in practice requires constant verbal fine-tuning: "That's gravy on the mashed, okay? None on the meatloaf," and so forth—while the cook scowls as if I were inventing these refinements just to torment him. Plus, something I had forgotten in the years since I was eighteen: about a third of a server's job is "side work" that's invisible to customers—sweeping, scrubbing, slicing, refilling, and restocking. If it isn't all done, every little bit of it, you're going to face the 6:00 P.M. dinner rush defenseless and probably go down in flames. I screw up dozens of times at the beginning, sustained in my shame entirely by Gail's support—"It's okay, baby, everyone does that sometime"—because, to my total surprise and despite the scientific detachment I am doing my best to maintain, I care. . . .

When I wake up at 4:00 A.M. in my own cold sweat, I am not thinking about the writing deadlines I'm neglecting; I'm thinking about the table whose order I screwed up so that one of the boys didn't get his kiddie meal until the rest of the family had moved on to their Key Lime pies. That's the other powerful motivation I hadn't expected—the customers, or "patients," as I can't help thinking of them on account of the mysterious vulnerability that seems to have left them temporarily unable to feed themselves. After a few days at the Hearthside, I feel the service ethic kick in like a shot of oxytocin, the nurturance hormone. The plurality of my customers are hard-working locals—truck drivers, construction workers, even housekeepers from the attached hotel—and I want them to have the closest to a "fine dining" experience that the grubby circumstances will allow. No "you guys" for me; everyone over twelve is "sir" or "ma'am." I ply them with iced tea and coffee refills; I return, mid-meal, to inquire how everything is; I doll up their salads with chopped raw mushrooms, summer squash slices, or whatever bits of produce I can find that have survived their sojourn in the cold-storage room mold-free. . . .

Sometimes I play with the fantasy that I am a princess who, in penance for some tiny transgression, has undertaken to feed each of her subjects by hand. But the non-princesses working with me are just as indulgent, even when this means flouting management rules—concerning, for example, the number of croutons that can go on a salad (six). "Put on all you want," Gail whispers, "as long as Stu isn't looking." She dips into her own tip money to buy biscuits and gravy for an out-of-work mechanic who's used up all his money on dental surgery, inspiring me to pick up the tab for his milk and pie. Maybe the same high levels of agape can be found throughout the "hospitality industry." I remember the poster decorating one of the apartments I looked at, which said "If you seek happiness for yourself you will never find it. Only when you seek happiness for others will it come to you," or words to that effect—an odd sentiment, it seemed to me at the time, to find in the dank one-room basement apartment of a bellhop at the Best Western. At the Hearthside, we utilize whatever bits of autonomy we have to ply our customers with the illicit calories that signal our love. It is our job as servers to assemble the salads and desserts, pouring the dressings and squirting the whipped cream. We also control the number of butter patties our customers get and the amount of sour cream on their baked potatoes. So if you wonder why Americans are so obese, consider the fact that waitresses both express their humanity and earn their tips through the covert distribution of fats.

Ten days into it, this is beginning to look like a livable lifestyle. I like Gail, who is "looking at fifty" but moves so fast she can alight in one place and then another without apparently being anywhere between them. I clown around with Lionel, the teenage Haitian busboy, and catch a few fragments of conversation with Joan, the svelte fortyish hostess and militant feminist who is the only one of us who dares to tell Jack to shut the fuck up. I even warm up to Jack when, on a slow night and to make up for a particularly unwarranted attack on my abilities, or so I imagine, he tells me about his glory days as a young man at "coronary school"—or do you say "culinary"?—in Brooklyn, where he dated a knock-out Puerto Rican chick and learned everything there is to know about food. I finish up at 10:00 or 10:30, depending on how much side work I've been able to get done during the shift, and cruise home to the tapes I snatched up at random when I left my real home—Marianne Faithfull, Tracy Chapman, Enigma, King Sunny Ade, the Violent Femmes—just drained enough for the music to set my cranium resonating but hardly dead. Midnight snack is Wheat Thins and Monterey Jack, accompanied by cheap white wine on ice and whatever AMC has to offer. To bed by 1:30 or 2:00, up at 9:00 or 10:00, read for an hour while my uniform whirls around in the landlord's washing machine, and then it's another eight hours spent following Mao's central instruction, as laid out in the Little Red Book, which was: Serve the people.

. . .

I could drift along like this, in some dreamy proletarian idyll, except for two things. One is management. If I have kept this subject on the margins thus far it is because I still flinch to think that I spent all those weeks under the surveillance of men (and later women) whose job it was to monitor my behavior for signs of sloth, theft, drug abuse, or worse. Not that managers and especially "assistant managers" in low-wage settings like this are exactly the class enemy. In the restaurant business, they are mostly former cooks or servers, still capable of pinch-hitting in the kitchen or on the floor, just as in hotels they are likely to be former clerks, and paid a salary of only about $400 a week. But everyone knows they have crossed over to the other side, which is, crudely put, corporate as opposed to human. Cooks want to prepare tasty meals; servers want to serve them graciously; but managers are there for only one reason—to make sure that money is made for some theoretical entity that exists far away in Chicago or New York, if a corporation can be said to have a physical existence at all. Reflecting on her career, Gail tells me ruefully that she had sworn, years ago, never to work for a corporation again. "They don't cut you no slack. You give and you give, and they take."

Managers can sit—for hours at a time if they want—but it's their job to see that no one else ever does, even when there's nothing to do, and this is why, for servers, slow times can be as exhausting as rushes. You start dragging out each little chore, because if the manager on duty catches you in an idle moment, he will give you something far nastier to do. So I wipe, I clean, I consolidate ketchup bottles and recheck the cheesecake supply, even tour the tables to make sure the customer evaluation forms are all standing perkily in their places—wondering all the time how many calories I burn in these strictly theatrical exercises. When, on a particularly dead afternoon, Stu finds me glancing at a *USA Today* a customer has left behind, he assigns me to vacuum the entire floor with the broken vacuum cleaner that has a handle only two feet long, and the only way to do that without incurring orthopedic damage is to proceed from spot to spot on your knees. . . .

The other problem, in addition to the less-than-nurturing management style, is that this job shows no sign of being financially viable. You might imagine, from a comfortable distance, that people who live, year in and year out, on $6 to $10 an hour have discovered some survival stratagems unknown to the middle class. But no. It's not hard to get my co-workers to talk about their living situations, because housing, in almost every case, is the principal source of disruption in their lives, the first thing they fill you in on when they arrive for their shifts. After a week, I have compiled the following survey:

- Gail is sharing a room in a well-known downtown flophouse for which she and a roommate pay about $250 a week. Her roommate, a male friend, has begun hitting on her, driving her nuts, but the rent would be impossible alone.

- Claude, the Haitian cook, is desperate to get out of the two-room apartment he shares with his girlfriend and two other, unrelated, people. As far as I can determine, the other Haitian men (most of whom only speak Creole) live in similarly crowded situations.

- Annette, a twenty-year-old server who is six months pregnant and has been abandoned by her boyfriend, lives with her mother, a postal clerk.

- Marianne and her boyfriend are paying $170 a week for a one-person trailer.

- Jack, who is, at $10 an hour, the wealthiest of us, lives in the trailer he owns, paying only the $400-a-month lot fee.

- The other white cook, Andy, lives on his dry-docked boat, which, as far as I can tell from his loving descriptions, can't be more than twenty feet long. He offers to take me out on it, once it's repaired, but the offer comes with inquiries as to my marital status, so I do not follow up on it.

- Tina and her husband are paying $60 a night for a double room in a Days Inn. This is because they have no car and the Days Inn is within walking distance of the Hearthside. When Marianne, one of the breakfast servers, is tossed out of her trailer for subletting (which is against the trailer-park rules), she leaves her boyfriend and moves in with Tina and her husband.

- Joan, who had fooled me with her numerous and tasteful outfits (hostesses wear their own clothes), lives in a van she parks behind a shopping center at night and showers in Tina's motel room. The clothes are from thrift shops.[3]

. . .

It strikes me, in my middle-class solipsism, that there is gross improvidence in some of these arrangements. When Gail and I are wrapping silverware in napkins—the only task for which we are permitted to sit—she tells me she is thinking of escaping from her roommate by moving into the Days Inn herself. I am astounded: How can she even think of paying between $40 and $60 a day? But if I was afraid of sounding like a social worker, I come out just sounding like a fool. She squints at me in disbelief, "And where am I supposed to get a month's rent and a month's deposit for an apartment?" I'd been feeling pretty smug about my $500 efficiency, but of course it was made possible only by the $1,300 I had allotted myself for start-up costs when I began my low-wage life: $1,000 for the first month's rent and deposit, $100 for initial groceries and cash in my pocket, $200 stuffed away for emergencies. In poverty, as in certain propositions in physics, starting conditions are everything.

There are no secret economies that nourish the poor; on the contrary, there are a host of special costs. If you can't put up the two months' rent you need to secure an apartment, you end up paying through the nose for a room by the week. If you have only a room, with a hot plate at best, you can't save by cooking up huge lentil stews that can be frozen for the week ahead. You eat fast food, or the hot dogs and styrofoam cups of soup that can be microwaved in a convenience store. If you have no money for health insurance—and the Hearthside's niggardly plan kicks in only after three months—you go without routine care or prescription drugs and end up paying the price. Gail, for example, was fine until she ran out of money for estrogen pills. She is supposed to be on the company plan by now, but they claim to have lost her application form and need to begin the paperwork all over again. So she spends $9 per migraine pill to control the headaches she wouldn't have, she insists, if her estrogen supplements were covered. Similarly, Marianne's boyfriend lost his job as a roofer because he missed so much time after getting a cut on his foot for which he couldn't afford the prescribed antibiotic.

My own situation, when I sit down to assess it after two weeks of work, would not be much better if this were my actual life. The seductive thing about waitressing is that you don't have to wait for payday to feel a few bills in your pocket, and my tips usually cover meals and gas, plus something left over to stuff into the kitchen drawer I use as a bank. But as the tourist business slows in the summer heat, I sometimes leave work with only $20 in tips (the gross is higher, but servers share about 15 percent of their tips with the busboys and bartenders). With wages included, this amounts to about the minimum wage of $5.15 an hour. Although the sum in the drawer is piling up, at the present rate of accumulation it will be more than a hundred dollars short of my rent when the end of the month comes around. Nor can I see any expenses to cut. True, I haven't gone the lentil-stew route yet, but that's because I don't have a large cooking pot, pot holders, or a ladle to stir with (which cost about $30 at

Kmart, less at thrift stores), not to mention onions, carrots, and the indispensable bay leaf. I do make my lunch almost every day—usually some slow-burning, high-protein combo like frozen chicken patties with melted cheese on top and canned pinto beans on the side. Dinner is at the Hearthside, which offers its employees a choice of BLT, fish sandwich, or hamburger for only $2. The burger lasts longest, especially if it's heaped with gut-puckering jalapeños, but by midnight my stomach is growling again.

So unless I want to start using my car as a residence, I have to find a second, or alternative, job. I call all the hotels where I filled out housekeeping applications weeks ago—the Hyatt, Holiday Inn, Econo Lodge, Hojo's, Best Western, plus a half dozen or so locally run guesthouses. Nothing. Then I start making the rounds again, wasting whole mornings waiting for some assistant manager to show up, even dipping into places so creepy that the front-desk clerk greets you from behind bulletproof glass and sells pints of liquor over the counter. But either someone has exposed my real-life housekeeping habits—which are, shall we say, mellow—or I am at the wrong end of some infallible ethnic equation: most, but by no means all, of the working housekeepers I see on my job searches are African Americans, Spanish-speaking, or immigrants from the Central European post-Communist world, whereas servers are almost invariably white and monolingually English-speaking. When I finally get a positive response, I have been identified once again as server material. Jerry's, which is part of a well-known national family restaurant chain and physically attached here to another budget hotel chain, is ready to use me at once. The prospect is both exciting and terrifying, because, with about the same number of tables and counter seats, Jerry's attracts three or four times the volume of customers as the gloomy old Hearthside.

. . .

Picture a fat person's hell, and I don't mean a place with no food. Instead there is everything you might eat if eating had no bodily consequences—cheese fries, chicken-fried steaks, fudge-laden desserts—only here every bite must be paid for, one way or another, in human discomfort. The kitchen is a cavern, a stomach leading to the lower intestine that is the garbage and dishwashing area, from which issue bizarre smells combining the edible and the offal: creamy carrion, pizza barf, and that unique and enigmatic Jerry's scent—citrus fart. The floor is slick with spills, forcing us to walk through the kitchen with tiny steps like a person in leg irons. . . . Sinks everywhere are clogged with scraps of lettuce, decomposing lemon wedges, waterlogged toast crusts. Put your hand down on any counter and you risk being stuck to it by the film of ancient syrup spills, and this is unfortunate, because hands are utensils here, used for scooping up lettuce onto salad plates, lifting out pie slices, and even moving hash browns from one plate to another. The regulation poster in the single unisex restroom admonishes us to wash our hands thoroughly and even offers instructions for doing so, but there is always some vital substance missing—soap, paper towels, toilet paper—and I never find all three at once. You learn to stuff your pockets with napkins before going in there, and too bad about the customers, who must eat, though they don't realize this, almost literally out of our hands.

The break room typifies the whole situation: there is none, because there are no breaks at Jerry's. For six to eight hours in a row, you never sit except to pee. Actually, there are three folding chairs at a table immediately adjacent to the bathroom, but hardly anyone ever sits here, in the very rectum of the gastro-architectural system. Rather, the function of the peritoilet area is to house the ashtrays in which servers and dishwashers leave their cigarettes burning at all times, like votive candles, so that they don't have to waste time lighting up again when they dash back for a puff. Almost everyone smokes as if his or her pulmonary well-being depended on it—the multinational mélange of cooks, the Czech dishwashers, the servers, who are all American natives—creating an atmosphere in which oxygen is only an occasional pollutant. My first morning at Jerry's, when the hypoglycemic shakes set in, I complain to one of my fellow servers that I don't understand how she can go so long without food. "Well, I don't understand how you can go so long without a cigarette," she responds in a tone of reproach—because work is what you do for others; smoking is what you do for yourself. I don't know why the antismoking crusaders have never grasped the element of defiant self-nurturance that makes the habit so endearing to its victims—as if, in the American workplace, the only thing people have to call their own is the tumors they are nourishing and the spare moments they devote to feeding them.

Now, the Industrial Revolution is not an easy transition, especially when you have to zip through it in just a couple of days. I have gone from craft work straight into the factory, from the air-conditioned morgue of the Hearthside directly into the flames. Customers arrive in human waves, sometimes disgorged fifty at a time from their tour buses, peckish and whiny. Instead of two "girls" on the floor at once, there can be as many as six of us running around in our brilliant pink-and-orange Hawaiian shirts. Conversations, either with customers or fellow employees, seldom last more than twenty seconds at a time. On my first day, in fact, I am hurt by my sister servers' coldness. My mentor for the day is an emotionally uninflected twenty-three-year-old, and the others, who gossip a little among themselves about the real reason someone is out sick today and the size of the bail bond someone else has had to pay, ignore me completely. On my second day, I find out why. "Well, it's good to see you again," one of them says in greeting. "Hardly anyone comes back after the first day." I feel powerfully vindicated—a survivor—but it would take a long time, probably months, before I could hope to be accepted into this sorority.

I start out with the beautiful, heroic idea of handling the two jobs at once, and for two days I almost do it: the breakfast/lunch shift at Jerry's, which goes till 2:00, arriving at the Hearthside at 2:10, and attempting to hold out until 10:00. In the ten minutes between jobs, I pick up a spicy chicken sandwich at the Wendy's drive-through window, gobble it down in the car, and change from khaki slacks to black, from Hawaiian to rust polo. There is a problem, though. When during the 3:00 to 4:00 P.M. dead time I finally sit down to wrap silver, my flesh seems to bond to the seat. I try to refuel with a purloined cup of soup, as I've seen Gail and Joan do dozens of times, but a manager catches me and hisses "No eating!" though there's not a customer around to be offended by the sight of food making contact with a server's lips. So I tell Gail I'm going to quit, and she hugs me and says she might just follow me to Jerry's herself.

But the chances of this are minuscule. She has left the flophouse and her annoying roommate and is back to living in her beat-up old truck. But guess what? she reports to me excitedly later that evening: Phillip has given her permission to park overnight in the hotel parking lot, as long as she keeps out of sight, and the parking lot should be totally safe, since it's patrolled by a hotel security guard! With the Hearthside offering benefits like that, how could anyone think of leaving. . . .

I start tossing back drugstore-brand ibuprofen pills as if they were vitamin C, four before each shift, because an old mouse-related repetitive-stress injury in my upper back has come back to full-spasm strength, thanks to the tray carrying. In my ordinary life, this level of disability might justify a day of ice packs and stretching. Here I comfort myself with the Aleve commercial in which the cute blue-collar guy asks: If you quit after working four hours, what would your boss say? And the not-so-cute blue-collar guy, who's lugging a metal beam on his back, answers: He'd fire me, that's what. But fortunately, the commercial tells us, we workers can exert the same kind of authority over our painkillers that our bosses exert over us. If Tylenol doesn't want to work for more than four hours, you just fire its ass and switch to Aleve. . . .

. . .

Management at Jerry's is generally calmer and more "professional" than at the Hearthside, with two exceptions. One is Joy, a plump, blowsy woman in her early thirties, who once kindly devoted several minutes to instructing me in the correct one-handed method of carrying trays but whose moods change disconcertingly from shift to shift and even within one. Then there's B.J., a.k.a. B.J.-the-bitch, whose contribution is to stand by the kitchen counter and yell, "Nita, your order's up, move it!" or, "Barbara, didn't you see you've got another table out there? Come on, girl!" Among other things, she is hated for having replaced the whipped-cream squirt cans with big plastic whipped-cream-filled baggies that have to be squeezed with both hands—because, reportedly, she saw or thought she saw employees trying to inhale the propellant gas from the squirt cans, in the hope that it might be nitrous oxide. On my third night, she pulls me aside abruptly and brings her face so close that it looks as if she's planning to butt me with her forehead. But instead of saying, "You're fired," she

says, "You're doing fine." The only trouble is I'm spending time chatting with customers: "That's how they're getting you." Furthermore I am letting them "run me," which means harassment by sequential demands: you bring the ketchup and, they decide they want extra Thousand Island; you bring that and they announce they now need a side of fries; and so on into distraction. Finally she tells me not to take her wrong. She tries to say things in a nice way, but you get into a mode, you know, because everything has to move so fast.[4]

I mumble thanks for the advice, feeling like I've just been stripped naked by the crazed enforcer of some ancient sumptuary law: No chatting for you, girl. No fancy service ethic allowed for the serfs. Chatting with customers is for the beautiful young college-educated servers in the downtown carpaccio joints, the kids who can make $70 to $100 a night. What had I been thinking? My job is to move orders from tables to kitchen and then trays from kitchen to tables. Customers are, in fact, the major obstacle to the smooth transformation of information into food and food into money—they are, in short, the enemy. And the painful thing is that I'm beginning to see it this way myself. There are the traditional asshole types—frat boys who down multiple Buds and then make a fuss because the steaks are so emaciated and the fries so sparse—as well as the variously impaired—due to age, diabetes, or literacy issues—who require patient nutritional counseling. The worst, for some reason, are the Visible Christians—like the ten-person table, all jolly and sanctified after Sunday-night service, who run me mercilessly and then leave me $1 on a $92 bill. Or the guy with the crucifixion T-shirt (SOMEONE TO LOOK UP TO) who complains that his baked potato is too hard and his iced tea too icy (I cheerfully fix both) and leaves no tip. As a general rule, people wearing crosses or WWJD? (What

Would Jesus Do?) buttons look at us disapprovingly no matter what we do, as if they were confusing waitressing with Mary Magdalene's original profession.

I make friends, over time, with the other "girls" who work my shift: Nita, the tattooed twenty-something who taunts us by going around saying brightly, "Have we started making money yet?" Ellen, whose teenage son cooks on the graveyard shift and who once managed a restaurant in Massachusetts but won't try out for management here because she prefers being a "common worker" and not "ordering people around." Easy-going fiftyish Lucy, with the raucous laugh, who limps toward the end of the shift because of something that has gone wrong with her leg, the exact nature of which cannot be determined without health insurance. We talk about the usual girl things—men, children, and the sinister allure of Jerry's chocolate peanut-butter cream pie—though no one, I notice, ever brings up anything potentially expensive, like shopping or movies. As at the Hearthside, the only recreation ever referred to is partying, which requires little more than some beer, a joint, and a few close friends. Still, no one here is homeless, or cops to it anyway, thanks usually to a working husband or boyfriend. All in all, we form a reliable mutual-support group: If one of us is feeling sick or overwhelmed, another one will "bev" a table or even carry trays for her. If one of us is off sneaking a cigarette or a pee,[5] the others will do their best to conceal her absence from the enforcers of corporate rationality.

But my saving human connection—my oxytocin receptor, as it were—is George, the nineteen-year-old, fresh-off-the-boat Czech dishwasher. We get to talking when he asks me, tortuously, how much cigarettes cost at Jerry's. I do my best to explain that they cost over a dollar more here than at a regular store and suggest that he just take one from the half-filled packs that are always lying around on the break table. But that would be unthinkable. Except for the one tiny earring signaling his allegiance to some vaguely alternative point of view, George is a perfect straight arrow—crew-cut, hardworking, and hungry for eye contact. "Czech Republic," I ask, "or Slovakia?" and he seems delighted that I know the difference. "Václav Havel," I try. "Velvet Revolution, Frank Zappa?" "Yes, yes, 1989," he says, and I realize we are talking about history.

My project is to teach George English. "How are you today, George?" I say at the start of each shift. "I am good, and how are you today, Barbara?" I learn that he is not paid by Jerry's but by the "agent" who shipped him over—$5 an hour, with the agent getting the dollar or so difference between that and what Jerry's pays dishwashers. I learn also that he shares an apartment with a crowd of other Czech "dishers," as he calls them, and that he cannot sleep until one of them goes off for his shift, leaving a vacant bed. We are having one of our ESL sessions late one afternoon when B.J. catches us at it and orders "Joseph" to take up the rubber mats on the floor near the dishwashing sinks and mop underneath. "I thought your name was George," I say loud enough for B.J. to hear as she strides off back to the counter. Is she embarrassed? Maybe a little, because she greets me back at the counter with "George, Joseph—there are so many of them!" I say nothing, neither nodding nor smiling, and for this I am punished later when I think I am ready to go and she announces that I need to roll fifty more sets of silverware and isn't it time I mixed up a fresh four-gallon batch of blue-cheese dressing? May you grow old in this place, B.J., is the curse I beam out at her when I am finally permitted to leave. May the syrup spills glue your feet to the floor.

I make the decision to move closer to Key West. First, because of the drive. Second and third, also because of the drive: gas is eating up $4 to $5 a day, and although Jerry's is as high-volume as you can get, the tips average only 10 percent, and not just for a newbie like me. Between the base pay of $2.15 an hour and the obligation to share tips with the busboys and dishwashers, we're averaging only about $7.50 an hour. Then there is the $30 I had to spend on the regulation tan slacks worn by Jerry's servers—a setback it could take weeks to absorb. (I had combed the town's two downscale department stores hoping for something cheaper but decided in the end that these marked-down Dockers, originally $49, were more likely to survive a daily washing.) Of my fellow servers, everyone who lacks a working husband or boyfriend seems to have a second job: Nita does something at a computer eight hours a day; another welds. Without the forty-five-minute commute, I can picture myself working two jobs and having the time to shower between them.

So I take the $500 deposit I have coming from my landlord, the $400 I have earned toward the next month's rent, plus the $200 reserved for emergencies, and use the $1,100 to pay the rent and deposit on trailer number 46 in the Overseas Trailer Park, a mile from the cluster of budget hotels that constitute Key West's version of an industrial park. Number 46 is about eight feet in width and shaped like a barbell inside, with a narrow region—because of the sink and the stove—separating the bedroom from what might optimistically be called the "living" area, with its two-person table and half-sized couch. The bathroom is so small my knees rub against the shower stall when I sit on the toilet, and you can't just leap out of the bed, you have to climb down to the foot of it in order to find a patch of floor space to stand on. Outside, I am within a few yards of a liquor store, a bar that advertises "free beer tomorrow," a convenience store, and a

Burger King—but no supermarket or, alas, laundromat. By reputation, the Overseas park is a nest of crime and crack, and I am hoping at least for some vibrant, multicultural street life. But desolation rules night and day, except for a thin stream of pedestrian traffic heading for their jobs at the Sheraton or 7-Eleven. There are not exactly people here but what amounts to canned labor, being preserved from the heat between shifts. . . .

When my month-long plunge into poverty is almost over, I finally land my dream job—housekeeping. I do this by walking into the personnel office of the only place I figure I might have some credibility, the hotel attached to Jerry's, and confiding urgently that I have to have a second job if I am to pay my rent and, no, it couldn't be front-desk clerk. "All right," the personnel lady fairly spits, "So it's housekeeping," and she marches me back to meet Maria, the housekeeping manager, a tiny, frenetic Hispanic woman who greets me as "babe" and hands me a pamphlet emphasizing the need for a positive attitude. The hours are nine in the morning till whenever, the pay is $6.10 an hour, and there's one week of vacation a year. I don't have to ask about health insurance once I meet Carlotta, the middle-aged African-American woman who will be training me. Carla, as she tells me to call her, is missing all of her top front teeth.

. . .

On that first day of housekeeping and last day of my entire project—although I don't yet know it's the last—Carla is in a foul mood. We have been given nineteen rooms to clean, most of them "checkouts," as opposed to "stayovers," that require the whole enchilada of bedstripping, vacuuming, and bathroom-scrubbing. When one of the rooms that had been listed as a stay-over turns out to be a checkout, Carla calls Maria to complain, but of course to no avail. "So make up the motherfucker," Carla orders me, and I do the beds while she sloshes around the bathroom. For four hours without a break I strip and remake beds, taking about four and a half minutes per queen-sized bed, which I could get down to three if there were any reason to. We try to avoid vacuuming by picking up the larger specks by hand, but often there is nothing to do but drag the monstrous vacuum cleaner—it weighs about thirty pounds—off our cart and try to wrestle it around the floor. Sometimes Carla hands me the squirt bottle of "BAM" (an acronym for something that begins, ominously, with "butyric"; the rest has been worn off the label) and lets me do the bathrooms. No service ethic challenges me here to new heights of performance. I just concentrate on removing the pubic hairs from the bathtubs, or at least the dark ones that I can see.

I had looked forward to the breaking-and-entering aspect of cleaning the stay-overs, the chance to examine the secret, physical existence of strangers. But the contents of the rooms are always banal and surprisingly neat—zipped up shaving kits, shoes lined up against the wall (there are no closets), flyers for snorkeling trips, maybe an empty wine bottle or two. It is the TV that keeps us going, from *Jerry* to *Sully* to *Hawaii Five-O* and then on to the soaps. If there's something especially arresting, like "Won't Take No for an Answer" on *Jerry,* we sit down on the edge of a bed and giggle for a moment as if this were a pajama party instead of a terminally dead-end job. The soaps are the best, and Carla turns the volume up full blast so that she won't miss anything from the bathroom or while the vacuum is on. In room 503, Marcia confronts Jeff about Lauren. In 505, Lauren taunts poor cuckolded Marcia. In 511, Helen offers Amanda $10,000 to stop seeing Eric, prompting Carla to emerge from the bathroom to study Amanda's troubled face:

"You take it, girl," she advises. "I would for sure."

The tourists' rooms that we clean and, beyond them, the far more expensively appointed interiors in the soaps, begin after a while to merge. We have entered a better world—a world of comfort where every day is a day off, waiting to be filled up with sexual intrigue. We, however, are only gate-crashers in this fantasy, forced to pay for our presence with backaches and perpetual thirst. The mirrors, and there are far too many of them in hotel rooms, contain the kind of person you would normally find pushing a shopping cart down a city street—bedraggled, dressed in a damp hotel polo shirt two sizes too large, and with sweat dribbling down her chin like drool. I am enormously relieved when Carla announces a half-hour meal break, but my appetite fades when I see that the bag of hot-dog rolls she has been carrying around on our cart is not trash salvaged from a checkout but what she has brought for her lunch.

When I request permission to leave at about 3:30, another housekeeper warns me that no one has so far succeeded in combining housekeeping at the hotel with serving at Jerry's: "Some kid did it once for five days, and you're no kid." With that helpful information in mind, I rush back to number 46, down four Advils (the name brand this time), shower, stooping to fit into the stall, and attempt to compose myself for the oncoming shift. So much for what Marx termed the "reproduction of labor power," meaning the things a worker has to do just so she'll be ready to work again. The only unforeseen obstacle to the smooth transition from job to job is that my tan Jerry's slacks, which had looked reasonably clean by 40-watt bulb last night when I handwashed my Hawaiian shirt, prove by daylight to be mottled with ketchup and ranch-dressing stains. I spend most of my hour-long break between jobs attempting to remove the edible portions with a sponge and then drying the slacks over the hood of my car in the sun.

I can do this two-job thing, is my theory, if I can drink enough caffeine and avoid getting distracted by George's ever more obvious suffering.[6] . . . Our chirpy little conversations had continued. But the last couple of shifts he's been listless and unshaven, and tonight he looks like the ghost we all know him to be, with dark half-moons hanging from his eyes. At one point, when I am briefly immobilized by the task of filling little paper cups with sour cream for baked potatoes, he comes over and looks as if he'd like to explore the limits of our shared vocabulary, but I am called to the floor for a table. I resolve to give him all my tips that night and to hell with the experiment in low-wage money management. At eight, Ellen and I grab a snack together standing at the mephitic end of the kitchen counter, but I can only manage two or three mozzarella sticks and lunch had been a mere handful of McNuggets. I am not tired at all, I assure myself, though it may be that there is simply no more "I" left to do the tiredness monitoring. What I would see, if I were more alert to the situation, is that the forces of destruction are already massing against me. There is only one cook on duty, a young man named Jesus ("Hay-Sue," that is) and he is new to the job. And there is Joy, who shows up to take over in the middle of the shift, wearing high heels and a long, clingy white dress and fuming as if she'd just been stood up in some cocktail bar.

Then it comes, the perfect storm. Four of my tables fill up at once. Four tables is nothing for me now, but only so long as they are obligingly staggered. As I bev table 27, tables 25, 28, and 24 are watching enviously. As I bev 25, 24 glowers because their bevs haven't even been ordered. Twenty-eight is four yuppyish types, meaning everything on the side and agonizing instructions as to

the chicken Caesars. Twenty-five is a middle-aged black couple, who complain, with some justice, that the iced tea isn't fresh and the tabletop is sticky. But table 24 is the meteorological event of the century: ten British tourists who seem to have made the decision to absorb the American experience entirely by mouth. Here everyone has at least two drinks—iced tea and milk shake, Michelob and water (with lemon slice, please)—and a huge promiscuous orgy of breakfast specials, mozz sticks, chicken strips, quesadillas, burgers with cheese and without, sides of hash browns with cheddar, with onions, with gravy, seasoned fries, plain fries, banana splits. Poor Jesus! Poor me! Because when I arrive with their first tray of food—after three prior trips just to refill bevs—Princess Di refuses to eat her chicken strips with her pancake-and-sausage special, since, as she now reveals, the strips were meant to be an appetizer. Maybe the others would have accepted their meals, but Di, who is deep into her third Michelob, insists that everything else go back while they work on their "starters." Meanwhile, the yuppies are waving me down for more decaf and the black couple looks ready to summon the NAACP.

Much of what happened next is lost in the fog of war. Jesus starts going under. The little printer on the counter in front of him is spewing out orders faster than he can rip them off, much less produce the meals. Even the invincible Ellen is ashen from stress. I bring table 24 their reheated main courses, which they immediately reject as either too cold or fossilized by the microwave. When I return to the kitchen with their trays (three trays in three trips), Joy confronts me with arms akimbo: "What is this?" She means the food—the plates of rejected pancakes, hash browns in assorted flavors, toasts, burgers, sausages, eggs. "Uh, scrambled with cheddar," I try, "and that's . . ." "NO," she screams in my face. "Is it a traditional, a super-scramble, an eye-opener?" I pretend to study my check for a clue, but entropy has been up to its tricks, not only on the plates but in my head, and I have to admit that the original order is beyond reconstruction. "You don't know an eye-opener from a traditional?" she demands in outrage. All I know, in fact, is that my legs have lost interest in the current venture and have announced their intention to fold. I am saved by a yuppie (mercifully not one of mine) who chooses this moment to charge into the kitchen to bellow that his food is twenty-five minutes late. Joy screams at him to get the hell out of her kitchen, please, and then turns on Jesus in a fury, hurling an empty tray across the room for emphasis.

I leave. I don't walk out, I just leave. I don't finish my side work or pick up my credit-card tips, if any, at the cash register or, of course, ask Joy's permission to go. And the surprising thing is that you *can* walk out without permission, that the door opens, that the thick tropical night air parts to let me pass, that my car is still parked where I left it. There is no vindication in this exit, no fuck-you surge of relief, just an overwhelming, dank sense of failure pressing down on me and the entire parking lot. I had gone into this venture in the spirit of science, to test a mathematical proposition, but somewhere along the line, in the tunnel vision imposed by long shifts and relentless concentration, it became a test of myself, and clearly I have failed. Not only had I flamed out as a housekeeper/server, I had even forgotten to give George my tips, and, for reasons perhaps best known to hardworking, generous people like Gail and Ellen, this hurts. I don't cry, but I am in a position to realize, for the first time in many years, that the tear ducts are still there, and still capable of doing their job.

. . .

When I moved out of the trailer park, I gave the key to number 46 to Gail and arranged for my deposit to be transferred to her. She told me that Joan is still living in her van and that Stu had been fired from the Hearthside. I never found out what happened to George.

In one month, l had earned approximately $1,040 and spent $517 on food, gas, toiletries, laundry, phone, and utilities. If I had remained in my $500 efficiency, I would have been able to pay the rent and have $22 left over (which is $78 less than the cash I had in my pocket at the start of the month). During this time I bought no clothing except for the required slacks and no prescription drugs or medical care (I did finally buy some vitamin B to compensate for the lack of vegetables in my diet). Perhaps I could have saved a little on food if I had gotten to a supermarket more often, instead of convenience stores, but it should be noted that I lost almost four pounds in four weeks, on a diet weighted heavily toward burgers and fries.

How former welfare recipients and single mothers will (and do) survive in the low-wage workforce, I cannot imagine. Maybe they will figure out how to condense their lives—including child-raising, laundry, romance, and meals—into the couple of hours between fulltime jobs. Maybe they will take up residence in their vehicles, if they have one. All I know is that I couldn't hold two jobs and I couldn't make enough money to live on with one. And I had advantages unthinkable to many of the long-term poor—health, stamina, a working car, and no children to care for and support. Certainly nothing in my experience contradicts the conclusion of Kathryn Edin and Laura Lein, in their recent book *Making Ends Meet: How Single Mothers Survive Welfare and Low-Wage Work,* that low-wage work actually involves more hardship and deprivation than life at the mercy of the welfare state. In the coming months and years, economic conditions for the working poor are bound to worsen, even without the almost inevitable recession. As mentioned earlier, the influx of former welfare recipients into the low-skilled workforce will have a depressing effect on both wages and the number of jobs available. A general economic downturn will only enhance these effects, and the working poor will of course be facing it without the slight, but nonetheless often saving, protection of welfare as a backup.

The thinking behind welfare reform was that even the humblest jobs are morally uplifting and psychologically buoying. In reality they are likely to be fraught with insult and stress. But I did discover one redeeming feature of the most abject low-wage work—the camaraderie of people who are, in almost all cases, far too smart and funny and caring for the work they do and the wages they're paid. The hope, of course, is that someday these people will come to know what they're worth, and take appropriate action.

NOTES

1. According to the Department of Housing and Urban Development, the "fair-market rent" for an efficiency is $551 here in Monroe County, Florida. A comparable rent in the five boroughs of New York City is $704; in San Francisco, $713; and in the heart of Silicon Valley, $808. The fair-market rent for an area is defined as the amount that would be needed to pay rent plus utilities for "privately owned, decent, safe, and sanitary rental housing of a modest (non-luxury) nature with suitable amenities."

2. According to the Fair Labor Standards Act, employers are not required to pay "tipped employees," such as restaurant servers, more than $2.13 an hour in direct wages. However, if the sum of tips plus $2.13 an hour falls below the minimum wage, or $5.15 an hour, the employer is required to make up the difference. This fact was not mentioned by man-

agers or otherwise publicized at either of the restaurants where I worked.

3. I could find no statistics on the number of employed people living in cars or vans, but according to the National Coalition for the Homeless's 1997 report "Myths and Facts About Homelessness," nearly one in five homeless people (in twenty-nine cities across the nation) is employed in a full- or part-time job.

4. In *Workers in a Lean World: Unions in the International Economy* (Verso, 1997), Kim Moody cites studies finding an increase in stress-related workplace injuries and illness between the mid-1980s and the early 1990s. He argues that rising stress levels reflect a new system of "management by stress," in which workers in a variety of industries are being squeezed to extract maximum productivity, to the detriment of their health.

5. Until April 1998, there was no federally mandated right to bathroom breaks. According to Marc Linder and Ingrid Nygaard, authors of *Void Where Prohibited: Rest Breaks and the Right to Urinate on Company Time* (Cornell University Press, 1997), "The right to rest and void at work is not high on the list of social or political causes supported by professional or executive employees, who enjoy personal workplace liberties that millions of factory workers can only daydream about. . . . While we were dismayed to discover that workers lacked an acknowledged legal right to void at work, [the workers] were amazed by outsiders' naive belief that their employers would permit them to perform this basic bodily function when necessary. . . . A factory worker, not allowed a break for six-hour stretches, voided into pads worn inside her uniform; and a kindergarten teacher in a school without aides had to take all twenty children with her to the bathroom and line them up outside the stall door when she voided."

6. In 1996, the number of persons holding two or more jobs averaged 7.8 million, or 6.2 percent of the workforce. It was about the same rate for men and for women (6.1 versus 6.2), though the kinds of jobs differ by gender. About two-thirds of multiple jobholders work one job full-time and the other part-time. Only a heroic minority—4 percent of men and 2 percent of women—work two full-time jobs simultaneously. (From John F. Stinson Jr., "New Data on Multiple Jobholding Available from the CPS," in the *Monthly Labor Review*, March 1997.)

QUESTIONS FOR DISCUSSION

1. What were the unexpected difficulties that Ehrenreich encountered in her low-wage work experience?
2. What factors keep low-wage workers stuck in the low-wage system of employment?

3. What are the implications of this low-wage system on the economy as a whole? Why does this system represent for its workers "not getting by in America"?

29

GANG BUSINESS
Making Ends Meet

MARTIN SANCHEZ JANKOWSKI

Cunning and deceit will serve a man better than force to rise from a base condition to great fortune.

—NICCOLÒ MACHIAVELLI,
The Discourses (1517?)

If there is one theme that dominates most studies of gangs, it is that gangs are collectives of individuals who are social parasites, and that they are parasitic not only because they lack the skills to be productive members of society but, more important, because they lack the values, particularly the work ethic, that would guide them to be productive members of society.[1] However, one of the most striking factors I observed was how much the entre-

preneurial spirit, which most Americans believe is the core of their productive culture, was a driving force in the worldview and behavior of gang members.[2] If entrepreneurial spirit denotes the desire to organize and manage business interests toward some end that results in the accumulation of capital, broadly defined, nearly all the gang members that I studied possessed, in varying degrees, five attributes that are either entrepreneurial in character or that reinforce entrepreneurial behavior.

The first of these entrepreneurial attitudes is competitiveness. Most gang members I spoke with expressed a strong sense of self-competence and a drive to compete with others. They believed in themselves as capable of achieving some level of economic success and saw competition as part of human nature and an opportunity to prove one's self-worth. This belief in oneself often

From *Islands in the Street* by Martin Sanchez Jankowski. Copyright © 1991. Reprinted by permission of The Regents of the University of California and the University of California Press.

took on a dogmatic character, especially for those individuals who had lost in some form of economic competition. The losers always had ready excuses that placed the blame on something other than their own personal inadequacy, thereby artificially reinforcing their feelings of competence in the face of defeat.[3]

Gang members' sense of competitiveness also reflected their general worldview that life operates under Social Darwinist principles. In the economic realm, they believed there is no ethical code that regulates business ventures, and this attitude exempted them from moral constraints on individual economic-oriented action.[4] The views of Danny provide a good example of this Social Darwinist outlook. Danny was a twenty-year-old Irish gang member from Boston:

> I don't worry about whether something is fair or not when I'm making a business deal. There is nothing fair or unfair, you just go about your business of trying to make a buck, and if someone feels you took advantage of him, he has only himself to blame. If someone took advantage of me, I wouldn't sit around bellyaching about it, I'd just go and try to get some of my money back. One just has to ask around here [the neighborhood] and you'd find that nobody expects that every time you're going to make a business deal, that it will be fair—you know, that the other guy is not going to be fair, hell, he is trying to make money, not trying to be fair. This is the way those big business assholes operate too! The whole thing [the system] operates this way.

The second entrepreneurial attribute I observed is the desire and drive to accumulate money and material possessions. Karl Marx, of course, described this desire as the "profit motive" and attributed it primarily

to the bourgeoisie.[5] There is a profit-motive element to the entrepreneurial values of gang members, but it differs significantly from Marx's analysis of the desire to accumulate material and capital for their own sake, largely divorced from the desire to improve one's own material condition. Nor is gang members' ambition to accumulate material possessions related to a need for achievement, which the psychologist David McClelland identifies as more central to entrepreneurial behavior in certain individuals than the profit motive per se.[6] Rather, the entrepreneurial activity of gang members is predicated on their more basic understanding of what money can buy.[7] The ambition to accumulate capital and material possessions is related, in its initial stages (which can last for a considerable number of years), to the desire to improve the comfort of everyday living and the quality of leisure time.

This desire, of course, is shared by most people who live in low-income neighborhoods. Some of them resign themselves to the belief that they will never be able to secure their desires. Others attempt to improve their life situation by using various "incremental approaches," such as working in those jobs that are made available to them and saving their money, or attempting to learn higher-level occupational skills. In contrast, the entrepreneurs of low-income neighborhoods, especially those in gangs, attempt to improve their lives by becoming involved in a business venture, or a series of ventures, that has the potential to create large changes in their own or their family's socioeconomic condition.

The third attribute of entrepreneurial behavior prevalent in gangs is status-seeking. Mirroring the dominant values of the larger society, most gang members attempt to achieve some form of status with the acquisition of possessions. However, most of them cannot attain a high degree of status by accumulation alone. To merit high status among peers and in the community, gang members must try, although most will be unsuccessful, to accumulate a large number of possessions and be willing to share them. Once gang members have accumulated sufficient material possessions to provide themselves with a relative level of comfort or leisure above the minimal, they begin to seek the increase in status that generosity affords. (For philanthropic purposes, accumulating cash is preferable to accumulating possessions, because the more money one has, the more flexibility one has in giving away possessions.)

The fourth entrepreneurial attribute one finds among gang members is the ability to plan. Gang members spend an impressive amount of time planning activities that will bring them fortune and fame, or, at least, plenty of spending money in the short term. At their grandest, these plans have the character of dreams, but as the accounts of renowned business tycoons show, having big dreams has always been a hallmark of entrepreneurial endeavors.[8] At the other end of the spectrum are short-range plans (also called small scams) that members try to pull on one another, usually to secure a loan.

Gang members also engage in intermediary and long-range planning. A typical intermediary plan might concern modest efforts to steal some type of merchandise from warehouses, homes, or businesses. Because most of the sites they select are equipped with security systems, a more elaborate plan involving more time is needed than is the case for those internal gang scams just described. Long-range planning and organization, sometimes quite elaborate, are, as other studies have reported, at times executed with remarkable precision.[9]

Finally, the fifth entrepreneurial attribute common among gang members is the ability to undertake risks. Generally, young gang members (nine to fifteen years of age) do not understand risk as part of a risk-reward calculus, and for this age group, risk-taking is nearly always pursued for itself, as an element of what Thrasher calls the "sport motive,"[10] the desire to test oneself. As gang members get older, they gradually develop a more sophisticated understanding of risk-taking, realizing that a certain amount of risk is necessary to secure desired goals. Now they attempt to calculate the risk factors involved for nearly every venture, measuring the risk to their physical well-being, money, and freedom. Just like mainstream businessmen, they discover that risk tends to increase proportionally to the level of innovation undertaken to secure a particular financial objective. Most of these older gang members are willing to assume risks commensurate with the subjective "value" of their designated target, but they will not assume risks just for the sake of risk-taking.

Economic Activity: Accumulating

With a few exceptions, nearly all the literature on gangs focuses on their economic delinquency.[11] This is a very misleading picture, however, for although gangs operate primarily in illegal markets, they also are involved in legal markets. Of the thirty-seven gangs observed in the present study, twenty-seven generated some percentage of their revenues through legitimate business activity. It is true that gangs do more of their business activity in the illegal markets, but none of them wants to be exclusively active in these markets.[12]

In the illegal market, gangs concentrate their economic activities primarily in goods, services, and recreation. In the area of goods, gangs have been heavily involved in accumulating and selling drugs, liquor, and various stolen products such as guns, auto parts, and assorted electronic equipment.

These goods are sometimes bought and sold with the gang acting as the wholesaler and/or retailer. At other times, the gang actually produces the goods it sells. For example, while most gangs buy drugs or alcohol and retail them, a few gangs manufacture and market homemade drugs and moonshine liquor. Two gangs (one African-American and one Irish) in this study had purchased stills and sold their moonshine to people on the street, most of whom were derelicts, and to high school kids too young to buy liquor legally.[13] Three other gangs (two Puerto Rican and one Dominican) made a moonshine liquor from fermented fruit and sold it almost exclusively to teenagers. Both types of moonshine were very high in alcohol, always above one hundred proof. While sales of this liquor were not of the magnitude to create fortunes, these projects were quite surprisingly capable of generating substantial amounts of revenue.

The biggest money-maker and the one product nearly every gang tries to market is illegal drugs.[14] The position of the gang within the illegal drug market varies among gangs and between cities. In New York, the size of the gang and how long it has been in existence have a great deal to do with whether it will have access to drug suppliers. The older and larger gangs are able to buy drugs from suppliers and act as wholesalers to pushers. They shun acting as pushers (the lowest level of drug sales) themselves because there are greater risks and little, if any, commensurate increase in profit. In addition, because heroin use is forbidden within most gangs, the gang leaders prefer to establish attitudes oriented to the sale rather than the consumption of drugs within the organization. In the past, when the supply was controlled by the Italian Mafia, it was difficult for gangs to gain access to the quantity of drug supplies necessary to make a profit marketing them. In the past ten years, though, the Mafia has given way (in terms of drug supply) to African-American, Puerto Rican, and Mexican syndicates.[15] In addition, with the increased popularity of cocaine in New York, the African-American, Puerto Rican, and Dominican syndicates' connections to Latin American sources of cocaine supply rival, and in many cases surpass, those of Mafia figures.[16] With better access to supplies, gangs in New York have been able to establish a business attitude toward drugs and to capitalize on the opportunities that drugs now afford them.

Some gangs have developed alternative sources of supply. They do so in two ways. Some, particularly the Chicano gangs, have sought out pharmacies where an employee can be paid off to steal pills for the gang to sell on the street.[17] Other gangs, particularly in New York, but also some in Los Angeles, have established "drug mills" to produce synthetic drugs such as LSD (or more recently crack cocaine) for sale on the street. The more sophisticated drug mills, which are controlled by various organized crime families, manufacture a whole line of drugs for sale, including cut heroin, but gangs are almost never involved in them. Those gangs that have established a production facility for generating drugs, no matter how crude it may be, generate sizeable sums of money. Whether a gang is able to establish a sophisticated production and distribution system for drug sales depends on the sophistication of the gang organization and the amount of capital available for start-up purposes.

Stolen guns are another popular and profitable product. Gangs sometimes steal guns and then redistribute them, but most often they buy them from wholesale gun peddlers and then resell them. Sometimes the gangs will buy up a small number of shotguns and then cut the barrel and stock down to about 13 to 15 inches in length and then sell them as "easily concealable." A prospective buyer can get whatever gun he wants if he is willing to pay the going price. In the present study, the Irish gangs have been, commercially speaking, the most involved with guns, often moving relatively large shipments, ranging from sawed-off shotguns to fully automatic rifles and pistols of the most sophisticated types.[18] It was reported that these guns were being moved, with the help of the Irish social clubs, to the Catholics of Northern Ireland for their struggle with the Protestants there. No matter what the destination, rather large sums of money were paid to the Irish gangs for their efforts in acquiring the weapons or in helping move them. Although all the gangs studied were involved in the sale of illegal guns, illegal gun sales constituted a larger proportion of the economic activities of Irish gangs than they did for the others.

Gangs in all three cities were also involved in the selling of car parts. All the parts sold were stolen, some stolen to fill special orders from customers and others stolen and reworked in members' home garages into customized parts for resale. Business was briskest in Los Angeles, where there is a large market, especially among the low-rider clientele, for customized auto parts.[19] The amount of money made from stolen auto parts varies according to the area, whether or not the gang has an agent to whom to sell the parts, and the types of parts sold. On the whole, revenues from stolen auto parts are not nearly as high as those from selling illegal drugs, guns, or liquor, and so less time is devoted by gangs to this activity.

Gangs' business activities also include a number of services, the three most common being protection, demolition (usually arson), and indirect participation in prostitution. Protection is the most common service, both because there is a demand for it in the low-income areas in which gangs operate and because the gangs find it the easiest

service to deliver, since it requires little in the way of resources or training. Gangs offer both personal and business protection. Nearly all the gangs had developed a fee schedule according to the type of protection desired. Most, but certainly not all, of the protection services offered by the gangs in this study involved extortion. Usually the gang would go into a store and ask the owner if he felt he needed protection from being robbed. Since it was clear what was being suggested, the owner usually said yes and asked how much it would cost him. When dealing with naive owners, those who did not speak English very well or did not know American ghetto customs, or with owners who flatly resisted their services, the gang would take time to educate or persuade them to retain its services. In the case of the immigrants (most of whom were Asian or Near Eastern), the gang members would begin by explaining the situation, but usually such owners did not understand, and so the gang would demonstrate its point by sending members into the store to steal. Another tactic was to pay a dope addict to go in and rob the store. After such an incident occurred, the gang would return and ask the owner if he now needed protection. If he refused, the tactics were repeated, and almost all the owners were finally convinced. However, for those owners who understood and resisted from the start, more aggressive tactics were used, such as destruction of their premises or harassment of patrons. More often than not, continued pressure brought the desired result. However, it should be noted that in the vast majority of cases, no coercion was needed, because store owners in high-crime areas were, more often than not, happy to receive protection. As one owner said to me: "I would need to hire a protection company anyway, and frankly the gang provides much more protection than they could ever do."

Gangs also offer their services as enforcers to clients who need punishment administered to a third party. Small-time hustlers or loan sharks, for example, hired some gangs to administer physical coercion to borrowers delinquent in their repayments. More recently one gang offered and apparently was hired by a foreign government to undertake terrorist acts against the government and people of the United States.[20] Although that was an extreme case, nearly all gangs seek enforcement contracts because the fee is usually high, few resources have to be committed, and relatively little in the way of planning (compared to other projects) is needed.

The permanent elimination of or damage to property is another service gangs offer. This more often than not involves arson, and the buildings hit are commonly dilapidated. The gangs' clients are either landlords who want to torch the building to get the insurance money or residents who are so frustrated by the landlord's unwillingness to provide the most basic services that they ask the gang to retaliate. In both cases, there is usually much preliminary discussion of the project within the gang. These service jobs require a good deal of discussion and planning because there is the potential to hurt someone living in the building or to create enormous hardship if people have no alternative place to live, and the gang will do almost anything to avoid injuring people in its community. The gangs of New York have had the most business along these lines, particularly in the South Bronx, but arson is a service offered in Detroit, Chicago, and Philadelphia as well. As one gang leader from the Bronx said:

You just don't bomb or torch any building that someone wants down. You got to find out who lives there, if they got another place to go, if they would be for takin' out the building and if they'd be OK with the folks [law enforcement authorities]. Then you got to get organized to get everybody out and sometimes that ain't many people and sometimes it is. If there is lots of people in the building, we'd just pass [refuse] on the job . . . now if we can work all these things out, we take the job and we deliver either a skeleton [outer walls are standing, but nothing else] or a cremation [just ashes].

Many potential clients know that a gang will refuse to burn down a building in its neighborhood if some type of harm will come to residents of its community, and so they contract with a gang from another area to do the job. Such incidents always ignite a war not only between the affected gangs but also between the communities. Take the example of the Hornets, a gang from one borough in New York that had contracted to set on fire a building in another borough. Although no one was killed in the fire, a few people were slightly burned, and of course everyone who lived in the building became homeless. At the request of a number of residents, the Vandals, a gang from the affected area, began to investigate and found out who had contracted to torch the building and which gang had been responsible. Then, at the request of an overwhelming majority of the community, the Vandals retaliated by burning down a building in the culprit gang's community. Hipper, a twenty-year-old member of the Vandals, said:

We got to protect our community, they depend on us and they want us to do something so this [the burning of an apartment building in the neighborhood] don't happen again . . . we be torchin' one of their buildings. I hope this don't hurt anybody, but if we don't do this, they be back hurting the people in our community and we definitely don't be letting that happen!

This is an excellent example of the bond that exists between the community and the gang. There is the understanding, then, among the community that the gang is a resource that can be counted on, particularly in situations where some form of force is necessary. Likewise, the gang knows that its legitimacy and existence are tied to being integrated in and responsible to community needs.

Prostitution is one illegal service in which gangs do not, for the most part, become directly involved. Gangs will accept the job of protecting pimps and their women for a fee (fifteen, or 40 percent, of the gangs in this study had), and in this way they become indirectly associated with the prostitution business. Yet they generally avoid direct involvement because they feel protective of the females in their communities, and their organizations are wary of being accused by neighborhood residents of exposing female members of the community to the dangers associated with prostitution.

The last type of illegal economic activity in which all of the gangs in the present study were involved has to do with providing recreation. Some gangs establish numbers games in their neighborhoods. One New York gang had rented what had been a small Chinese food take-out place and was running numbers from the back where the kitchen had once been. (When I first observed the place, I thought it was a Chinese take-out and even proposed we get some quick food from it, which met with much laughter from the members of the gang I was with.) This gang became so successful that it opened up two other numbers establishments. One had been a pizza place (and was made to look as though it still served

pizza slices); the other was a small variety store, which still functioned in that capacity, but also housed the numbers game in the back rooms.

Setting up gambling rooms is another aspect of the recreation business. Eleven of the gangs (or 30 percent) rented small storefronts, bought tables and chairs, and ran poker and/or domino games. The gang would assume the role of the "house," receiving a commission for each game played. Some of the gangs bought slot machines and placed them in their gambling rooms. Five (or 14 percent) of the gangs had as many as fifteen machines available for use.

Finally, ten gangs (27 percent), primarily those with Latino members, rented old buildings and converted them to accommodate cockfights. The gang would charge each cock owner a fee for entering his bird and an entrance fee for each patron. All of these ventures could, at various times, generate significant amounts of capital. The exact amount would depend on how often they were closed by the police and how well the gang managed the competition in its marketplace.

Turning to the legal economic activities undertaken by gangs, I observed that two ran "mom and pop" stores that sold groceries, candy, and soft drinks. Three gangs had taken over abandoned apartment buildings, renovated them, and rented them very cheaply—not simply because the accommodations were rather stark, but also because the gang wanted to help the less fortunate members of its community. The gangs also used these buildings to house members who had nowhere else to live. Undertaken and governed by social as much as economic concerns, these apartment ventures did not generate much income.

Interestingly, the finances of these legal activities were quite tenuous. The gangs that operated small grocery stores experienced periodic failures during which the stores had to be closed until enough money could be acquired (from other sources) to either pay the increased rent, rebuild shelf stock, or make necessary repairs. For those gangs who operated apartment buildings, in every case observed, the absence of a deed to the building or the land forced the gang to relinquish its holdings to either the city or a new landlord who wanted to build some new structure. Though there was a plentiful supply of abandoned buildings, most gangs lost interest in the renovation-and-rental business because such projects always created a crisis in their capital flow, which in turn precipitated internal bickering and conflict.

Other legal economic activities undertaken by the gangs I studied were automobile and motorcycle repair shops, car parts (quasi junk yards), fruit stands, and hair shops (both barber and styling). However, most of these ventures contributed only very modest revenues to the gangs' treasuries. Furthermore, the gang leadership had difficulty keeping most of the legal economic activities functioning because the rank and file were, by and large, not terribly enthusiastic about such activities. Rank-and-file resistance to most of these activities was of three sorts: members did not want to commit regularly scheduled time to any specific ongoing operation; members felt that the legal activities involved considerable overhead costs that lowered the profit rate; and members calculated that the time required to realize a large profit was far too long when compared to illegal economic activity. Thus, when such projects were promoted by the gang leadership and undertaken by the rank and file, they were done under the rubric of community service aid projects. The comments of Pin, a nineteen-year-old African-American gang member

from New York, are representative of this general position of legal economic activity:

> No, I don't go for those deals where we [the gang] run some kind of hotel out of an old building or run some repair shop or something like that. When you do that you can't make no money, or if you do make something it so small and takes so long to get it that it's just a waste of our [the gang's] money. But when the leadership brings it up as a possibility, well, sometimes I vote for it because I figure you got to help the community, many of them [people in the community] say they sort of depend on our help in one way or another, so I always say this is one way to help the community and me and the brothers go along with it. But everybody knows you can't make no money on shit like this.

NOTES

1. Nearly all studies of gangs incorporate this theme into their analysis. . . . *Delinquency and Opportunity,* which argues that many delinquents have the same values as other members of American society. However, even Cloward and Ohlin incorporate some of the conventional argument by accepting the premise that gang members' skills to compete in the larger society have been retarded by a lack of opportunity.

2. See Charles Sabel, *Work and Politics* (Cambridge: Cambridge University Press, 1987), pp. 1–30, on the importance of worldviews in affecting the behavior of individuals in industrial organizations and politics.

3. David Matza mentions a comparable tendency among delinquents to deny guilt associated with wrongdoing when he discusses the delinquent's belief that he is nearly always the victim of a "bum rap" (see Matza, *Delinquency and Drift* [New Brunswick, NJ: Transaction Books], pp. 108–10).

4. I use the term *economic oriented action* the way Weber does: "Action will be said to be

'economical oriented' so far as, according to its subjective meaning, it is concerned with the satisfaction of a desire for 'utilities' (*Nutzleistung*)" (Weber, *Economy and Society,* 1:63).

5. See Karl Marx, *The Economic and Philosophical Manuscripts of 1844,* 4th rev. ed., (Moscow: Progress Publishers, 1974), p. 38.

6. See David C. McClelland, *The Achieving Society* (New York: Free Press, 1961), pp. 233–37.

7. See Lee Rainwater, *What Money Buys: Inequality and the Social Meanings of Income* (New York: Basic Books, 1974). Also see Richard P. Coleman and Lee Rainwater, *Social Standing in America: New Dimensions of Class* (New York: Basic Books, 1978), pp. 29–45.

8. See the accounts of successful entrepreneurs from poor families who dreamed of grandeur and became America's most renowned business tycoons in Matthew Josephson, *The Robber Barons: The Great American Capitalists 1861–1901* (New York: Harcourt, Brace & World, 1962), especially the chapter entitled "What Young Men Dream," pp. 32–49.

9. See Thrasher, *The Gang,* pp. 198–200.

10. Ibid., p. 86.

11. Both the theoretical and empirical literature focus on the gang's criminal activity. For theoretical discussions, see Kornhauser, *Social Sources of Delinquency,* pp. 51–61. For empirical studies, see nearly all of the classic and contemporary work on gangs. A sample of this literature would include Thrasher, *The Gang*; Herman Schwendinger and Julia Schwendinger, *Adolescent Subcultures and Delinquency* (New York: Praeger, 1985); Cloward and Ohlin, *Delinquency and Opportunity.* Two exceptions are Horowitz, *Honor and the American Dream,* and Vigil, *Barrio Gangs.*

12. There are two factors that have encouraged gangs to be more active in illegal markets. First, gangs, like organized crime syndicates, attempt to become active in many economic activities that are legal. However, because so much of the legal market is controlled by groups that have established themselves in strategic positions (because they entered that market a considerable time in the past), gangs have found it difficult at best to successfully penetrate many legal markets. Further, there are financial incentives that have encouraged gangs to operate in the illegal market. These include the fact that costs are relatively low, and while personal risk (in terms of being incarcerated and/or physically hurt) is rather high, high demand along with high risk can produce greater profit margins. Despite the fact that these two factors have encouraged gangs to be more active in the illegal market, it is important to emphasize that nearly all the gangs studied attempted to, and many did, conduct business in the legal market as well.

13. The Schwendingers indicate that "youthful tastes regulate the flow of goods and services in the [adolescent] market" and gangs do take advantage of these tastes.

14. See Fagan, "Social Organization of Drug Use and Drug Dealing among Urban Gangs," pp. 633–67; and Jerome H. Skolnick, *Forum: The Social Structure of Street Drug Dealing* (Sacramento: Bureau of Criminal Statistics/Office of the Attorney General, 1989).

15. See Francis A. J. Ianni, *Black Mafia: Ethnic Succession in Organized Crime* (New York: Simon & Schuster, 1974). Also see Moore, *Homeboys,* pp. 86–92, 114–16.

16. See Peter Lupsha and K. Schlegel, "The Political Economy of Drug Trafficking: The Herrera Organization (Mexico and the United States)" (Paper Presented at the Latin American Studies Association, Philadelphia, 1979).

17. This paying off of employees for drug supplies began, according to Joan Moore, in Los Angeles in the 1940s and 1950s.

18. These gangs can procure fully automatic M-16s, Ingrams, and Uzis.

19. Low riders are people, nearly all of whom are of Mexican descent, who drive customized older automobiles (1950s and 1960s models are preferred), one of the characteristics being that the springs for each wheel are cut away so that the car rides very low to the ground. Some of these cars have hydraulic systems that can be inflated at the flip of a switch so that the car can ride low to the ground at one moment and at the normal level the next. For a discussion of the importance of customized automobiles in Los Angeles, especially among Chicano youth, see Schwendinger and Schwendinger, *Adolescent Subcultures and Delinquency,* pp. 234–45.

20. The El Rukn gang in Chicago was recently indicted and convicted of contracting with the Libyan government to carry out terrorist acts within the United States. See *Chicago Tribune*, 3, 4, 6, 7 November 1987.

REFERENCES

Horowitz, Ruth. *Honor and the American Dream: Culture and Identity in a Chicano Community.* New Brunswick: Rutgers University Press, 1983.

Kornhauser, Ruth Rosner. *Social Sources of Delinquency: An Appraisal of Analytic Models.* Chicago: University of Chicago Press, 1978.

Thrasher, Frederic. *The Gang: A Study of 1303 Gangs in Chicago.* Chicago: University of Chicago Press, 1928.

Vigil, James Diego. *Barrio Gangs: Street Life and Identity in Southern California.* Austin: University of Texas Press, 1988.

Weber, Max. *Economy and Society: An Outline of Interpretive Sociology.* Edited by Guenther Roth and Claus Wittich. Berkeley: University of California Press, 1978.

QUESTIONS FOR DISCUSSION

1. If cities provided more opportunities to poor people in the areas in which gangs operate and provided higher levels of enforcement, would gangs continue to exist?

2. Are the communities in which gangs are tolerated unique, or do all communities accept some illegal behaviors because the gangs are functional?

30

THE EFFECTS OF AFFIRMATIVE ACTION ON OTHER STAKEHOLDERS

BARBARA RESKIN

Affirmative action policies and practices reduce job discrimination against minorities and white women, although their effects have not been large. Some critics charge that affirmative action's positive effects have been offset by its negative effects on white men, on productivity, and on the merit system. The research examined in this chapter shows that affirmative action rarely entails reverse discrimination, and neither hampers business productivity nor unduly increases the costs of doing business. Both theoretical and empirical research suggest that it enhances productivity by encouraging employment practices that better utilize workers' skills.

Reverse Discrimination

For many people, the most troubling aspect of affirmative action is that it may discriminate against majority-group members

(Lynch 1997). According to 1994 surveys, 70 to 80 percent of whites believed that affirmative action sometimes discriminates against whites (Steeh and Krysan 1996, p. 139). Men are more likely to believe that a woman will get a job or promotion over an equally or more qualified man than they are to believe that a man will get a promotion over an equally or more qualified woman (Davis and Smith 1996). In short, many whites, especially white men, feel that they are vulnerable to reverse discrimination (Bobo and Kluegel 1993). When asked whether African Americans or whites were at greater risk of discrimination at work, respondents named whites over African Americans by a margin of two to one (Steeh and Krysan 1996, p. 140). In addition, 39 percent of respondents to a 1997 *New York Times*/CBS News poll said that whites losing out because of affirmative action was a bigger problem than African Americans losing out because of discrimination (Verhovek 1997, p. 32).

Several kinds of evidence indicate that whites' fears of reverse discrimination are exaggerated. Reverse discrimination is rare both in absolute terms and relative to conventional discrimination.[1] The most direct evidence for this conclusion comes from employment-audit studies: On every measured outcome, African-American men were much more likely than white men to experience discrimination, and Latinos were more likely than non-Hispanic men to experience discrimination (Heckman and Siegelman 1993, p. 218). Statistics on the numbers and outcomes of complaints of employment discrimination also suggest that reverse discrimination is rare.

According to national surveys, relatively few whites have experienced reverse discrimination. Only 5 to 12 percent of whites believe that their race has cost them a job or promotion, compared to 36 percent of African Americans (Steeh and Krysan 1996,

pp. 139–40). Of 4,025 Los Angeles workers, 45 percent of African Americans and 16 percent of Latinos said that they had been refused a job because of their race, and 16 percent of African Americans and 8 percent of Latinos reported that they had been discriminated against in terms of pay or a promotion (Bobo and Suh 1996, table 1). In contrast, of the 80 whites surveyed, less than 3 percent had ever experienced discrimination in pay or promotion, and only one mentioned reverse discrimination. Nonetheless, two-thirds to four-fifths of whites (but just one-quarter of African Americans) surveyed in the 1990s thought it likely that less qualified African Americans won jobs or promotions over more qualified whites (Taylor 1994a; Davis and Smith 1994; Steeh and Krysan 1996, p.139).[2]

Alfred Blumrosen's (1996, pp. 5–6) exhaustive review of discrimination complaints filed with the Equal Employment Opportunity Commission offers additional evidence that reverse discrimination is rare. Of the 451,442 discrimination complaints filed with the EEOC between 1987 and 1994, only 4 percent charged reverse discrimination (see also Norton 1996, pp. 44–5).[3] Of the 2,189 discrimination cases that federal appellate courts decided between 1965 and 1985, less than 5 percent charged employers with reverse discrimination (Burnstein 1991, p. 518).

Statistics on the more than 3,000 cases that reached district and appeals courts between 1990 and 1994 show an even lower incidence of reverse-discrimination charges: Less than 2 percent charged reverse discrimination (U.S. Department of Labor, Employment Standards Administration n.d., p. 3). The small number of reverse discrimination complaints by white men does not appear to stem from their reluctance to file complaints: They filed more than 80 percent of the age discrimination complaints that the EEOC received in 1994. Instead, as former

EEOC chair Eleanor Holmes Norton (1996, p. 45) suggested, white men presumably complain most about the kind of discrimination that they experience most and least about discrimination they rarely encounter.

Allegations of reverse discrimination are less likely than conventional discrimination cases to be supported by evidence. Of the approximately 7,000 reverse-discrimination complaints filed with the EEOC in 1994, the EEOC found only 28 credible (Crosby and Herzberger 1996, p. 55). Indeed, U.S. district and appellate courts dismissed almost all the reverse-discrimination cases they heard between 1990 and 1994 as lacking merit.

Although rare, reverse discrimination does occur. District and appellate courts found seven employers guilty of reverse discrimination in the early 1990s (all involved voluntary affirmative action programs), and a few federal contractors have engaged in reverse discrimination, according to the Office of Federal Contract Compliance Program's (OFCCP) director for Region II (Stephanopoulos and Edley 1995, section 6.3).[4]

The actions and reports of federal contractors are inconsistent with the belief that goals are *de facto* quotas that lead inevitably to reverse discrimination. In the first place, the fact that contractors rarely meet their goals means that they do not view them as quotas (Leonard 1990, p. 56). Second, only 2 percent of 641 federal contractors the OFCCP surveyed in 1994 complained that the agency required quotas or reverse discrimination (Stephanopoulos and Edley 1995, section 6.3).

How can we reconcile the enormous gulf between whites' perceptions that they are likely to lose jobs or promotions because of affirmative action and the small risk of this happening? The white men who brought reverse discrimination suits presumably concluded that their employers' choices of women or minorities could not have been based on merit, because men are accustomed to being selected for customarily male jobs (*New York Times*, March 31, 1995).[5] Most majority-group members who have not had a first-hand experience of competing unsuccessfully with a minority man or woman or a white woman cite media reports as the source of their impression that affirmative action prompts employers to favor minorities and women (Hochschild 1995, pp. 144, 308).[6] It seems likely that politicians' and the media's emphasis on "quotas" has distorted the public's understanding of what is required and permitted in the name of affirmative action (Entman 1997). It is also likely that the public does not distinguish affirmative action in employment from affirmative action in education which may include preferences or in the awarding of contracts which have included set-asides.

Affirmative Action and American Commerce

Does affirmative action curb productivity, as some critics have charged? On the one hand, affirmative action could impede productivity if it forces employers to hire or promote marginally qualified and unqualified workers, or it the paperwork associated with affirmative action programs is burdensome. On the other hand, employers who assign workers to jobs based on their qualifications rather than their sex or race should make more efficient use of workers' abilities and hence should be more productive than those who use discriminatory employment practices (Becker 1971; Leonard 1984c; Donohue 1986). Affirmative action could also increase profitability by introducing varied points of view or helping firms broaden their markets (Cox and Blake 1991; Watson, Kumar, and Michaelsen 1993).

Effects on Productivity

There is no evidence that affirmative action reduces productivity or that workers hired under affirmative action are less qualified than other workers. In the first place, affirmative action plans that compromise valid educational and job requirements are illegal. Hiring unqualified workers or choosing a less qualified person over a more qualified one because of their race or sex is illegal and is not condoned in the name of affirmative action (U.S. Department of Labor, Employment Standards Administration n.d., p. 2). Second, to the extent that affirmative action gives women and minority men access to jobs that more fully exploit their productive capacity, their productivity and that of their employers should increase.

Although many Americans believe that affirmative action means that less qualified persons are hired and promoted (Verhovek 1997, p. 32), the evidence does not bear this out. According to a study of more than 3,000 workers hired in entry-level jobs in a cross-section of firms in Atlanta, Boston, Detroit, and Los Angeles, the performance evaluations of women and minorities hired under affirmative action did not differ from those of white men or female or minority workers for whom affirmative action played no role in hiring (Holzer and Neumark 1998). In addition, Columbus, Ohio, female and minority police officers hired under an affirmative action consent decree performed as well as white men (Kern 1996). Of nearly 300 corporate executives surveyed in 1979, 72 percent believed that minority hiring did not impair productivity (*Wall Street Journal* 1979); 41 percent of CEOs surveyed in 1995 said affir-

mative action improved corporate productivity (Crosby and Herzberger 1996, p. 86).[7]

Of the handful of studies that address the effect of affirmative action on productivity, none suggests a negative affect on the employment of women or minorities on productivity. First, the increasing representation of female and minority male workers between 1966 and 1977 and between 1984 and 1988 did not affect firms' productivity (Leonard 1984c; Conrad 1995). Second, in the context of policing, the proportion of minority or female officers are unrelated to measures of departments' effectiveness (Lovrich, Steel, and Hood 1986, p. 70; Steel and Lovrich 1987, p. 67). Third, according to a sophisticated analysis of 1990 data on establishments' and workers' characteristics, there is no relationship between firms employment of women and their productivity in smaller plants, but in plants with more market power (and hence the capacity to discriminate), the more women plants employed, the better the firms' performance (Hellerstein, Neumark, and Troske 1998).

Studies assessing the effect of firms' racial makeup on their profits also show no effects of affirmative action on productivity. An analysis of 100 of Chicago's largest firms over a 13-year period found no statistically significant relationship between the firms' share of minority workers and their profit margins or return on equity (McMillen 1995). This absence of an association is inconsistent with companies using lower standards when hiring African American employees. Finally, according to a study that compared the market performance of the 100 firms with best and worst records of hiring and promoting women and minorities, the former averaged an 18-percent return on investments, whereas the latter's average returns were below 8 percent (Glass Ceiling Commission 1995, pp. 14, 61).[8]

Costs to Business

Estimates of the price tag of affirmative action range from a low of hundreds of millions of dollars to a high of $26 billion (Brimelow and Spencer 1993).[9] More realistic estimates put enforcement and compliance costs at about $1.9 billion (Leonard 1994, p. 34; Conrad 1995, pp. 37–8). According to Andrew Brimmer (1995, p. 12), former Governor of the Federal Reserve Board, the inefficient use of African Americans' productive capacity (as indicated by their education, training, and experience) costs the economy 70 times this much: about $138 billion annually, which is about 2.15 percent of the gross national product. Adding the cost of sex discrimination against white women would substantially increase the estimated cost of discrimination because white women outnumber African American men and women in the labor force by about three to one. The more affirmative action reduces race and sex discrimination, the lower its costs relative to the savings it engenders.

The affirmative action that the federal executive order requires of federal contractors adds to their paperwork. Companies with at least $50,000 in federal contracts that employ at least 50 employees must provide written affirmative action plans that include goals and timetables, based on an annual analysis of their utilization of their labor pool. They must also provide specified information to the OFCCP and keep detailed records on the composition of their jobs and job applicants by race and sex. In response to an OFCCP survey soliciting their criticisms of the program, about one in eight federal contractors complained about the paperwork burden (Stephanopoulos and Edley 1995, section 6.3). Keeping the records required by the OFCCP encourages the bureaucratization of human resource practices.

As noted, informal employment practices, while cheaper in the short run, are also more subject to discriminatory bias and hence cost firms efficiency. Thus, implicit in the logic of the OFCCP's requirements is the recognition that formalizing personnel practices helps to reduce discrimination.

Business Support

U.S. business has supported affirmative action for at least 15 years. The Reagan administration's efforts to curtail the contract compliance program in the early 1980s drew strong opposition from the corporate sector (Bureau of National Affairs 1986a). Among the groups that went on record as opposing cutbacks in federal affirmative action programs was the National Association of Manufacturers, a major organization of US. employers (*The San Diego Union-Tribune* 1995, p. AA-2). All but six of 128 heads of major corporations indicated that they would retain their affirmative action plans if the federal government ended affirmation action (Noble 1986, p.114). A 1996 survey showed similar levels of corporate support for affirmative action: 94 percent of CEOs surveyed said that affirmative action had improved their hiring procedures, 53 percent said it had improved marketing, and—as noted above—41 percent said it had improved productivity (Crosby and Herzberger 1996, p. 86). The business community's favorable stance toward affirmative action is also seen in the jump in stock prices for firms recognized by the OFCCP for their effective affirmative action programs (Wright et al. 1995, p. 281).

Perhaps the most telling sign of business support for affirmative action is the diffusion of affirmative action practices from federal contractors to noncontractors. As noncontractors have recognized the efficiency or market payoffs associated with more objective employment practices and a more diverse workforce, many have voluntarily implemented some affirmative action practices (Fisher 1985).

Affirmative Action and Other Stakeholders

The consequences of affirmative action reach beyond workers and employers by increasing the pools of skilled minority and female workers. When affirmative action prompts employers to hire minorities or women for positions that serve the public, it can bring services to communities that would otherwise be underserved. For example, African-American and Hispanic physicians are more likely than whites and Anglos to practice in minority communities (Kormaromy et al. 1996). Graduates of the Medical School at the University of California at San Diego who were admitted under a special admissions program were more likely to serve inner-city and rural communities and saw more poor patients than those admitted under the regular procedures (Penn, Russell, and Simon 1986).

Women's and minorities' employment in nontraditional jobs also raises the aspirations of other members of excluded groups by providing role models and by signaling that jobs are open to them. Some minorities and women do not pursue jobs or promotions because they expect to encounter discrimination (Mayhew 1968, p. 313). By reducing the perception that discriminatory barriers block access to certain lines of work, affirmative action curtails this self-selection (Reskin and Roos 1990, p. 305). In addition, the economic gains provided by better jobs permit beneficiaries to invest in the education of the next generation.

Affirmative Action, Meritocracy, and Fairness

Affirmative action troubles some Americans for the same reasons discrimination does: They see it as unfair and inconsistent with meritocracy (Nacoste 1990). The evidence summarized above indicates that employers very rarely use quotas and that affirmative action does not lead to the employment of unqualified workers. We know too that many employers implement affirmative action by expanding their recruiting efforts, by providing additional training, and by formalizing human resource practices to eliminate bias. By eliminating cronyism, drawing on wider talent pools, and providing for due process, these practices are fairer to all workers than conventional business practices (*Harvard Law Review* 1989, pp. 668–70; Dobbin et al. 1993, pp. 401–6). After all, managers who judge minority and female workers by their race or sex instead of their performance may judge white workers by arbitrary standards as well (Rand 1996, p. 72).

Available research does not address how often employers take into account race and gender in choosing among equally qualified applicants. Although the courts have forbidden race- and gender-conscious practices in layoffs, they have allowed employers to take into account race or gender in selecting among qualified applicants in order to remedy the consequences of having previously excluded certain groups from some jobs. Such programs trouble some Americans, as we can see from the research evidence presented in the next section.

Americans' Views
of Affirmative Action

The passage of the 1996 California Civil Rights Initiative, which barred this state from engaging in affirmative action, has been interpreted as signaling mounting public opposition to affirmative action. In reality, whites, and African Americans views of affirmative action are both more nuanced and more positive than the California election result suggests. People's responses to opinion polls depend largely on how pollsters characterize affirmative action (Kravitz et al. 1997).[10] About 70 percent of Americans support affirmative action programs that pollsters describe as not involving "quotas" or "preferences" (Steeh and Krysan 1996, pp. 132, 134; Entman 1997, p. 37). Like a red flag, the term "quota" also triggers strong negative reactions. This happens because people view quotas as inconsistent with merit-based hiring and because quotas provoke fear of unfairly losing a job or promotion by members of groups that are not covered by affirmative action. As a result, most whites and African Americans oppose quotas (Hobo and Kluegel, 1993; Steeh and Krysan 1996, pp. 132–3, 148).

A casual reading of newspaper reports indicates considerable instability in Americans' attitudes toward affirmative action and a fair amount of opposition to affirmative action. For example, fewer than one in eight Americans surveyed in a 1995 Gallup poll approved of affirmative action programs that involve hiring quotas, and only 40 to 50 percent of Americans endorsed affirmative action programs designed to give African Americans or women preferential treatment (Moore 1995). However, polls that show low levels of support for affirmative action in the workplace typically ask about practices that are illegal and hence rare in actual affirmative action programs (Kravitz

et al. 1997, p. xi). When pollsters ask about affirmative action in general or about the practices that actual affirmative action programs include, the majority of whites and African Americans are supportive.

In national polls conduct in the mid-1990s, about 70 percent of respondents endorsed affirmative action either as currently practiced or with reforms (Entman 1997, p. 37). For example, almost three-quarters of the respondents to a 1995 Gallup poll approved of employers using outreach efforts to recruit qualified minorities and women (Steeh and Krysan 1996, pp. 132, 134). Most whites and African Americans support such practices as targeted recruitment, open advertising, monitoring diversity, job training, and educational assistance designed to allow minorities to compete as individuals (e.g., training programs). More than three out of four white respondents and 85 percent of African-American respondents to a 1991 Harris survey agreed that "as long as there are no rigid quotas, it makes sense to give special training and advice to women and minorities so that they can perform better on the job" (Bobo and Kluegel 1993; Bruno 1995, p. 24).

We do not know how Americans feel about the kinds of race- or gender-conscious affirmative action that EEOC guidelines and Supreme Court rulings allow. When asked about "preferential hiring," most Americans disapprove. For example, only one-sixth to one-fifth of respondents surveyed during the 1990s favored the preferential hiring and promotion of African Americans because of past discrimination (about 10 to 17 percent of whites and about half to three-quarters of African Americans; Steeh and Krysan 1996, pp. 146–7). Just one survey phrased the question so that it approximately corresponded to what race- and gender-conscious affirmative action entails: giving a preference to a woman or minority over an equally qualified white man. Three-quarters of respondents did not view this practice as discriminatory (Roper Center for Public Opinion 1995).

Overall, the public is less concerned with affirmative action than media accounts would have us believe (Entman 1997). For example, respondents to a 1996 *Wall Street Journal*/NBC News poll ranked affirmative action second to last in importance out of 16 issues.[11] As Robert Entman (1997) argued, the media's framing of affirmative action as controversial exaggerates white opposition to and public discord over it.

In sum, the polls reveal that the majority of whites and African Americans have supported affirmative action since the early 1970s. Most Americans support the affirmative action procedures that employers actually use such as taking extra efforts to find and recruit minorities and women. The broadest support is for practices that expand the applicant pool, but ignore race or gender in the selection process. Thus, Americans' first choice is enhancing equal opportunity without using race- or gender-conscious mechanisms. What most Americans oppose is quotas, an employment remedy that courts impose only under exceptional circumstances. Thus, the kinds of affirmative action practices most Americans support are in synch with what most affirmative action employers do.

Conclusion

Some critics charge that any positive effects of affirmative action come at too high a price. However, the evidence suggests that the predominant effects of affirmative action on American enterprise are neutral, and some are positive. Contrary to popular opinion, reverse discrimination is rare. Workers for whom affirmative action was a hiring consideration are no less productive than other workers. There is no evidence

that affirmative action impairs productivity, and there is some evidence that, when properly implemented, affirmative action increases firms' efficiency by rationalizing their business practices. These neutral to positive effects of affirmative action contribute to the broad support it enjoys in corporate America. The affirmative action practices that appear to be most common—such as special training programs or efforts to expand recruitment pools (Bureau of National Affairs 1986)—have the support of the majority of whites and people of color.

Although most affirmative action practices are neutral with respect to race and gender (e.g., eliminating subjectivity from evaluation systems), some employers take into account race and sex as "plus factors" in choosing among qualified candidates in order to reduce imbalances stemming from their past employment practices. Race- and gender-conscious practices are legal if they are part of court-ordered or voluntary affirmative action programs designed to correct a serious imbalance resulting from past exclusionary practices and as long as they are properly structured so that they do not unnecessarily or permanently limit the opportunities of groups not protected under affirmative action. At least one in four Americans oppose such race- and gender-conscious practices. More generally, any departure from strict reliance on merit troubles some Americans. Others favor taking into account group membership in order to eradicate America's occupational caste system, enhance equal opportunity, and strengthen the U.S. democracy (Steinberg 1995).

The tension between affirmative action and merit is the inevitable result of the conflict between our national values and what actually occurs in the nation's workplaces. As long as discrimination is more pervasive than affirmative action, it is the real threat to meritocracy. But because no one will join the debate on behalf of discrimination, we end up with the illusion of a struggle between affirmative action and merit.

NOTES

1. Lynch's (1989, p. 53) search for white male Southern Californians who saw themselves as victims of reverse discrimination turned up only 32 men.
2. Younger whites, those from more privileged backgrounds, and those from areas with larger black populations—especially black populations who were relatively well off—were most likely to believe that blacks benefited from preferential treatment (Taylor 1994b).
3. Two percent were by white men charging sex, race, or national origin discrimination (three-quarters of these charged sex discrimination), and 1.8 percent were by white women charging race discrimination (Blumrosen 1996, p. 5).
4. In the early years of affirmative action, some federal contractors implemented quotas; since then the OFCCP has made considerable effort to ensure that contractors understand that quotas are illegal.
5. Occupational segregation by sex, race, and ethnicity no doubt contribute to this perception by reinforcing the notion that one's sex, color, or ethnicity is naturally related to the ability to perform a particular job.
6. The disproportionate number of court-ordered interventions to curtail race and sex discrimination in cities' police and fire departments (Martin 1991) and the large number of court challenges by white men (Bureau of National Affairs 1995, pp. 5–12) probably contributed to the public's impression that hiring quotas are common.
7. No data were provided on the proportion who believed that affirmative action hampered productivity.
8. Although firms' stock prices fall after the media report a discrimination suit, they rebound within a few days (Hersch 1991; Wright et al. 1995).
9. The $26 billion estimate includes the budgets of the OFCCP, the EEOC, other federal agencies' affirmative action-related activities, and private firms' compliance costs estimated at $20 million for each million of public funds budgeted for enforcement (Brimelow and Spencer 1993). Arguably, the EEOC's budget—indeed all enforcement costs—should be chalked up to the cost of discrimination, not the cost of affirmative action.
10. Several factors affect Americans' response to surveys about affirmative action in the workplace: whether their employer practices affirmative action (Taylor 1995), their own conception of what affirmative action means (one-third of white respondents to a 1995 CBS/*New York Times* poll acknowledged that they were not sure what affirmative action is; Steeh and Krysan 1996, p.129), whether the question also asks about affirmative action in education, whether the question asks about race- or sex-based affirmative action (although contractors are also obliged to provide affirmative action for Vietnam-era veterans and disabled persons, these groups are invisible in opinion polls), the respondents' own race and sex, the reasons respondents think racial inequality exists, and their level of racial prejudice (Bobo and Kluegel 1993). For full reviews, see Steeh and Krysan (1996) and Kravitz et al. (1997).
11. Only 1 percent of respondents named affirmative action as the most important problem our country faces (Entman 1997, p. 38).

REFERENCES

Becker, Gary S. 1971. *A Theory of Discrimination.* 2d ed. Chicago, IL: University of Chicago Press.

Blumrosen, Alfred W. 1996. *Declaration.* Statement submitted to the Supreme Court of California in Response to Proposition 209, September 26.

Bobo, Lawrence and James R. Kluegel. 1993. "Opposition to Race Targeting." *American Sociological Review* 58:443–64.

Bobo, Larry and Susan A. Suh. 1996. "Surveying Racial Discrimination: Analyses from a Multi-Ethnic Labor Market." Working Paper No. 75, Russell Sage Foundation, New York

Brimelow, Peter and Leslie Spencer. 1993. "When Quotas Replace Merit, Everybody Suffers." *Forbes,* February 15, pp. 80–102.

Brimmer, Andrew F. 1995. "The Economic Cost of Discrimination against Black Americans." Pp. 11—29 in *Economic Perspectives on Affirmative Action,* edited by M.C. Simms. Washington, DC: Joint Center for Political and Economic Studies.

Bruno, Andorra. 1995. *Affirmative Action in Employment.* CRS Report for Congress. Washington, DC: Congressional Research Service.

Bureau of National Affairs. 1986. *Affirmative Action Today: A Legal and Political Analysis. A BNA Special Report.* Washington, DC: The Bureau of National Affairs.

———. 1995. *Affirmative Action after Adarand: A Legal, Regulatory, Legislative Outlook.* Washington, DC: The Bureau of National Affairs.

Burnstein, Paul. 1991. "Reverse Discrimination Cases In the Federal Courts: Mobilization by a Countermovement." *Sociological Quarterly* 32:511–28.

Conrad, Cecilia. 1995. "The Economic Cost of Affirmative Action." Pp. 33–53 in *Economic Perspectives on Affirmative Action,* edited by M. C. Simms. Washington, DC: Joint Center for Political and Economic Studies.

Cox, Taylor H. and Stacy Blake. 1991. "Managing Cultural Diversity: Implications for Organizational Competitiveness." *Academy of Management Executive* 5:45–56.

Crosby, Faye J. and Sharon D. Herzberger. 1996. "For Affirmative Action." Pp. 3–109 in *Affirmative Action: Pros and Cons of Policy and Practice,* edited by R. J. Simon. Washington, DC: American University Press.

Davis, James A. and Tom W. Smith. 1994. *General Social Survey* [MRDF]. Chicago IL: National Opinion Research Center [producer, distributor].

———. 1996. *General Social Survey* [MRDF]. Chicago IL: National Opinion Research Center [producer, distributor].

Dobbin, Frank, John Sutton, John Meyer, and W. Richard Scott. 1993. "Equal Opportunity Law and the Construction of Internal Labor Markets." *American Journal of Sociology* 99:396–427.

Donohue, John J. 1986. "Is Title VII Efficient?" *University of Pennsylvania Law Review* 134:1411–31.

Entman, Robert M. 1997. "Manufacturing Discord: Media in the Affirmative Action Debate." *Press/Politics* 2:32–51.

Fisher, Ann B. 1985. "Businessmen Like to Hire by the Numbers." *Fortune Magazine,* September 16, pp. 26, 28–30.

Glass Ceiling Commission. See U.S. Department of Labor, Office of Federal Contract Compliance Programs, Glass Ceiling Commission.

Harvard Lain Review. 1989. "Rethinking Weber: The Business Response to Affirmative Action." *Harvard Law Review* 102:658–71.

Heckman, James J. and Peter Siegelman. 1993. "The Urban Institute Audit Studies: Their Methods and Findings." Pp. 187–229 in *Clear and Convincing Evidence: Measurement of Discrimination in America,* edited by M. Fix and R. J. Struyk. Washington. DC: The Urban Institute.

Hellerstein, Judith K., David Neumark, and Kenneth R. Troske. 1998. "Market Forces and Sex Discrimination." Department of Sociology, University of Maryland, College Park. Unpublished manuscript.

Hersch, Joni. 1991. "Equal Employment Opportunity Law and Firm Profitability." *Journal of Human Resources* 26:139–53.

Hochschild, Jennifer. 1995. *Facing Up to the American Dream.* Princeton, NJ: Princeton University Press.

Holzer, Harry J. and David Neumark. Forthcoming 1998. "Are Affirmative Action Hires Less Qualified? Evidence from Employer-Employee Data on New Hires." *Journal of Labor Economics.*

Kern, Leesa. 1996. "Hiring and Seniority: Issues in Policing the Post-Judicial Intervention Period." Department of Sociology, Ohio State University, Columbus, OH: Unpublished manuscript.

Kormaromy, Miriam, Kevin Grumbach, Michael Drake, Karen Vranizan, Nicole Lurie, Dennis Keane, and Andrew Bindman. 1996. "The Role of Black and Hispanic Physicians in Providing Health Care in Underserved Populations." *New England Journal of Medicine* 334:1305–10.

Kravitz, David A., David A. Harrison, Marlene E. Turner, Edward L. Levine, Wanda Chaves, Michael T. Brannick, Donna L. Denning, Craig J. Russell, and Maureen A. Conrad. 1997. *Affirmative Action: A Review of Psychological and Behavioral Research.* Bowling Green, OH: Society for Industrial and Organizational Psychology.

Leonard, Jonathan S. 1984c. "Anti-Discrimination or Reverse Discrimination: The Impact of Changing Demographics, Title VII, and Affirmative Action on Productivity" *Journal of Human Resources* 19:145–74.

———. 1990. "The Impact of Affirmative Action Regulation and Equal Employment Law on Black Employment." *Journal of Economic Perspectives* 4:47–63.

———. 1994. "Use of Enforcement Techniques in Eliminating Glass Ceiling Barriers." Report to the Glass Ceiling Commission, April, U.S. Department of Labor, Washington, DC.

Lovrich, Nicholas P., Brent S. Steel, and David Hood. 1986. "Equity versus Productivity: Affirmative Action and Municipal Police Services." *Public Productivity Review* 39:61–72.

Lynch, Frederick R. 1989. *Invisible Victims: White Males and the Crisis of Affirmative Action.* New York: Greenwood.

———. 1997. *The Diversity Machine: The Drive to Change the White Male Workplace.* New York: Free Press.

Martin, Susan E. 1991. "The Effectiveness of Affirmative Action: The Case of Women in Policing." *Justice Quarterly* 8:489–504.

Mayhew, Leon. 1968. *Law and Equal Opportunity: A Study of Massachusetts Commission against Discrimination.* Cambridge, MA: Harvard University Press.

McMillen, Liz. 1995. "[Affirmative Action] Policies Said to Help Companies Hire Qualified Workers at No Extra Cost." *Chronicle of Higher Education,* November 17, p. A7.

Moore, David W. 1995. "Americans Today Are Dubious about Affirmative Action." *The Gallup Poll Monthly.* March, pp. 36–8.

Nacoste, Rupert Barnes. 1990. "Sources of Stigma: Analyzing the Psychology of Affirmative Action." *Law & Policy* 12:175–95.

New York Times. 1995. "Reverse Discrimination Complaints Rare, Labor Study Reports." *New York Times,* March 31, p. A23.

Noble, Kenneth. 1986. "Employers Are Split on Affirmative Goals." *New York Times,* March 3, p. B4.

Norton, Elenor Holmes. 1996. "Affirmative Action in the Workplace." Pp. 39–48 in *The Affirmative Action Debate,* edited by G. Curry. Reading, MA: Addison-Wesley.

Penn, Nolan E., Perry J. Russell, and Harold J. Simon. 1986. "Affirmative Action at Work: A Survey of Graduates of the University of California at San Diego Medical School." *American Journal of Public Health* 76:1144–46.

Rand, A. Barry. 1996. "Diversity in Corporate America." Pp. 65–76 in *The Affirmative Action Debate,* edited by G. Curry. Reading, MA: Addison-Wesley.

Reskin, Barbara F. and Patricia Roos. 1990. *Job Queues, Gender Queues.* Philadelphia, PA: Temple University Press.

Roper Center for Public Opinion. 1995. *Poll Database:* Question ID USGALLUP.95MRW1.R32 [MRDF]. Storrs, CT: Roper Center for Public Opinion [producer, distributor].

San Diego Union-Tribune. 1995. "Groups at Odds over Affirmative Action Revisions." *San Diego Union-Tribune,* September 13, p. AA-2.

Steeh, Charlotte, and Maria Krysan. 1996. "The Polls—Trends: Affirmative Action and the Public, 1970–1995." *Public Opinion Quarterly* 60:128–58.

Steel, Brent S. and Nicholas P. Lovrich. 1987. "Equality and Efficiency Tradeoffs in Affirmative Action—Real or Imagined? The Case of Women in Policing." *Social Science Journal* 24:53–70.

Steinberg, Steven. 1995. *Turning Back: Retreat from Racial Justice in American Thought.* Boston, MA: Beacon.

Stephanopoulos, George and Christopher Edley, Jr. 1995. "Affirmative Action Review." Report to the President, Washington. DC.

Taylor, Marylee C. 1994a. "Beliefs about the Preferential Hiring of Black Applicants: Sure It Happens, But I've Never Seen It." Pennsylvania State University, University Park, PA. Unpublished manuscript.

———. 1994b. "Impact of Affirmative Action on Beneficiary Groups: Evidence from the 1990 General Social Survey." *Basic and Applied Social Psychology* 15:143–78.

———. 1995. "White Backlash to Workplace Affirmative Action: Peril or Myth?" *Social Forces* 73:1385–1414.

U.S. Department of Labor, Employment Standards Administration, Office of Federal Contract Compliance Programs [cited as OFCCP]. n.d. "The Rhetoric and the Reality about Federal Affirmative Action at the OFCCP." Washington, DC: US. Department of Labor.

U.S. Department of Labor, Office of Federal Contract Compliance Programs, Glass Ceiling Commission. 1995. *Good for Business: Making Full Use of the Nation's Human Capital/The Environmental Scar.* Washington, DC: U.S. Government Printing Office.

Verhovek, Sam Howe. 1997. "In Poll, Americans Reject Means but Not Ends of Racial Diversity." *New York Times,* December 14, pp. 1, 32.

Wall Street Journal. 1979. "Labor Letter: A Special News Report on People and Their Jobs in Offices, Fields, and Factories: Affirmative Action Is Accepted by Most Corporate Chiefs." *Wall Street Journal,* April 3, p. 1.

Watson, Warren E., Kamalesh Kumar, and Larry K. Michaelsen. 1993. "Cultural Diversity's Impact on Interaction Process and Performance: Comparing Homogeneous and Diverse Task Groups." *Academy of Management Journal* 36:590–602.

Wright, Peter, Stephen P. Ferris, Janine S. Hiller, and Mark Kroll. 1995. "Competitiveness through Management of Diversity: Effects on

Stock Price Valuation." *Academy of Management Journal* 38:272–87.

Stock Price Valuation." *Academy of Management Journal* 38:272–87.

QUESTIONS FOR DISCUSSION

1. The evidence that Reskin has cited shows that very little reverse discrimination results from affirmative action. Yet many policy makers use the reverse discrimination charge to justify eliminating affirmative action programs. Why do you think this is so?

2. What are the ways that affirmative action increases productivity?

3. What are the ways that claimsmakers for and against affirmative action have constructed this issue? Why is the question of affirmative action so controversial in this country?

THE SOCIAL WEB

- 9to5, National Association of Working Women is a national, grassroots-membership organization that strengthens women's ability to work for economic justice. Founded in 1973, 9to5 has activists in more than 200 cities and members in every state: www.9to5.org.
- The AFL-CIO Web site contains useful information on unionization, occupational health and safety concerns, and issues of balancing work and family: www.afl-cio.org.
- The American Civil Liberties Union offers information on workplace rights, workers' rights to privacy, and rights regarding mandatory workplace drug testing: www.aclu.org.

QUESTIONS FOR DEBATE

1. What are the stresses that all workers encounter at their jobs? Do low-wage workers have additional issues they must cope with?

2. What effects have affirmative action programs had in changing gender- and race-based discrimination in the workplace? What would happen if affirmative action programs were eliminated?

3. Do women and men view the dual responsibilities of work and family in the same ways? What are the consequences of gender differences in attitudes toward the demands of work and family?

4. What do people need to have a productive workplace that contributes to their sense of well-being and self-esteem?

Chapter 8
Family

Contents

Learning Objectives

By the end of this chapter you should be able to:

- Recognize how the authors use one or more of the major perspectives to explore families.
- Explore how family problems are shaped by inequalities of race, gender, and class.
- Identify the ways that the family is socially constructed.
- Describe various consequences of family problems.
- Analyze how individuals contribute to family problems through their everyday behavior.
- Explain how social systems and institutions perpetuate family problems.

Defining the Problem

For humans, "family" is a fundamental aspect of who we are and a resource for accomplishing our lives. Our families are a reference point through which we feel and are connected to the larger social body. American families encompass relationships of biological, legal, and fictive kinship, linking biological and adoptive parents, grandparents, aunts, uncles, cousins, and friends.

Sociologists view the family as an institution—both a pattern of behaviors that people do with and for each other and a set of cultural expectations about what should be done and by whom. Generally speaking, family practices and cultural expectations both are concerned with providing adequate economic, social, and emotional support to ensure the health and welfare of all individuals and the socialization of children.

Sociologists have discovered that over time there is some consistency in the ways that families form and the roles that members take, but that new ways of forming stable, supportive economic and social relationships are always emerging. However, sociologists have also discovered that the cultural ideas about what should be done and by whom are often inconsistent with the diversity of family forms and practices that exist and that are developing. This means that only some collections of individuals in mutually supportive relationships are recognized as families and receive support from their individual neighbors, coworkers, classmates, and through social institutions such as government, religion, education, work, and law.

One approach sociologists take to family problems is to examine the social construction of the ideal type. They seek to determine who benefits from a widely held American belief that a family should be only a legally married heterosexual couple and their biological offspring. They expose the contradictions between this family ideal and the real practice of family, showing that the ideal form is not the statistically most common behavior pattern. Some investigators seek to understand whether non-normative forms of family that successfully meet members' social and economic needs can be models for future practice. Others explore whether providing governmental support and social acceptance of groups of people that function as family units will allow the needs of the most number of people to be met.

Other social problems investigators explore whether the forms of family that are emerging serve the needs of the individuals in them and the larger social body. Some focus on individuals' choices and concern themselves with understanding why people form families "prematurely"—have children before they can easily take on the social obligations of economic and social support. Often these investigators are concerned with youths, who have not finished their education and secured stable employment, and single women, who have limited earning power and lack a partner to bear some of the burden. Others ask whether certain collections of individuals who can provide economic support, but fall outside the culturally sanctioned normative forms, can effectively integrate children into society. They explore whether children of divorced parents, stepparents, gay and lesbian parents, and so forth develop differently from children nurtured within the idealized form (heterosexual two-parent family).

Other social problems investigators examine the difficulties that all kinds of families have in the current social and economic context. They examine whether the institutionalized behavior patterns and the division of labor between the adults, which are intended to meet the economic and social needs of all members, can do so. Of particu-

lar concern to these sociologists is the way that the gendered division of labor in the typical heterosexual family articulates with the shift of women into paid work, the decline of real wages, the global economy, and the current governmental social safety net. They note that even idealized families may not be able to meet the needs of all members. They argue that inadequate socialization of the next generation—as indicated by rates of truancy and delinquency—and family breakdown—as indicated by rates of separation and divorce—may occur when women are pulled into the labor force and social perceptions that mothers are primarily responsible for children's welfare do not change. These investigators point out that some family problems can't be solved without directing action toward the economy and altering hegemonic conceptions of gender and women's and men's social roles. A variety of data provide us with a basis for exploring the social problems of the American family.

Scope of the Problem

Government statistics show that families form in many ways other than the socially constructed ideal: a legal marriage. However, they also show a great deal of stability in family formation through marriage over the past fifty years.[1] The U.S. marriage rate peaked at 11.1 per 1,000 in the population in 1965 and dropped to a low of 8.5 per 1,000 in 1991. For the past decade, it has remained near the low point. In 1979, legal dissolution of families peaked with a high of 5.3 divorces per 1,000 marriages, but for the last

---

[1]The federally funded collection of detailed state-by-state data on marriage and divorce by the Centers for Disease Control/National Center for Health Statistics was suspended in 1996 due to budgetary considerations. These statistics are taken from the "Monthly Vital Statistics Reports."

twenty years it has been near the 4.0 rate recorded in 2001.[2]

Based on data collected in 1995, the National Center for Health Statistics reports that 75 percent of women in the U.S. have been married and 50 percent have cohabitated by age 30. Although the cohabitations break up at a greater rate than first marriages, both the length of marriages and the length of cohabitations depend on the same things. Particularly predictive of the success of both unions are the woman's age at the time the union forms, whether she was raised in an intact two-parent family, whether religion is important to her, her family income, and whether she resides in a community in which rates of male unemployment and poverty are low.[3]

In 1980, 77 percent of all children in the U.S. lived with two parents; by 1999, only 68 percent did. In 1999, 23 percent of children lived only with their mothers, 4 percent only with their fathers, and 4 percent with an adult nonparent. Racial/ethnic differences are substantial in living arrangements. In 1999, 35 percent of Black children, 68 percent of Hispanic children, and 77 percent of White children lived with two parents. Research conducted in the 1990s shows that close to 90 percent of the children living with two parents lived with their biological or adoptive parents. However, close to 3 percent of the biological or adoptive parent couples were unmarried. Some were heterosexual couples, some were homosexual couples.[4]

Despite the existence of long-term gay and lesbian unions and the rise of social ceremonies of commitment, only one state, Vermont, allows and recognizes civil commitments of both gays and lesbians. In 1996, the federal government acted explicitly to eliminate the legal equalization of unions of both homosexuals and heterosexuals, passing the Federal Defense of Marriage Act. The FDMA barred legally married same-gender couples from receiving the federal economic protections afforded opposite-gender couples. As of June 2001, thirty-five states had passed similar laws banning same-gender marriage, which also limited homosexuals' access to social supports disbursed by the state.[5]

State limitations on who may form families through adoption or foster parenting of children reflect idealized notions of family that are not demonstrably related to the capacity of adults to emotionally, socially, or economically provide for children. Thus, the inequality experienced by gays and lesbians under state and federal law extends to their children. The children born and raised *within* gay and lesbian unions cannot count on both of the adults who love and support them being able to make legal decisions pertaining to their welfare, because in forty-seven states gay and lesbian partners of biological parents may not adopt their partners' children.[6]

---

[2] We must be mindful that these divorce figures (and those on cohabitation) are based on voluntary reports made to the federal government and do not include information for California, Colorado, Indiana, and Louisiana. "America's Children 2000," Forum on Child and Family Statistics, www.childstats.gov.

[3] Matthew Bramlett and William Mosher, "Cohabitation, Marriage, Divorce and Remarriage in the United States," National Center for Health Statistics, U.S. Department of Health and Human Services, Centers for Disease Control, Series 23, No. 22, 2002.

[4] "America's Children 2000."

---

[5] "Same-Sex Marriage Laws in the U.S., June 2002," National Gay and Lesbian Taskforce, Washington, D.C. www.ngltf.org.

[6] Only in California, Connecticut, and Vermont do state statutes allow children to legally have two gay or lesbian parents. Existing law has been interpreted to allow gay stepparent adoptions by appellate courts in four states (Illinois, Massachusetts, New York, New Jersey) and the District of Columbia, and lower courts in fifteen states. However, appellate courts in four states (Colorado, Nebraska, Ohio, Wisconsin) have ruled against such adoptions. In the twenty-four remaining states, lesbians' and gays' legal status is not legally determined. "Second-Parent/Stepparent Adoption in the U.S.—June 2002," National Gay and Lesbian Taskforce, Washington, D.C., www.ngltf.org.

Utah also prohibits adoption by anyone in a nonmarital sexual relationship, and several other states only allow single adults who are heterosexual to adopt or provide foster care.[7] Such restrictions on family formation stand in stark contrast to the number of children awaiting adoption or stable foster care situations.

In September of 1999, 581,000 children were in foster care.[8] Their ages ranged from younger than a year to older than nineteen; their average age was 9.9 years. Only 4 percent were in preadoptive placements; an additional 26 percent were living with relatives. The rest could be found in foster family homes (47 percent), group homes (8 percent), institutions (10 percent), and supervised independent living situations (1 percent). The remaining 4 percent were runaways or in trial home placements. Children in foster care had an average stay of thirty-two months and a median stay of twenty months. Fully 17 percent had experienced five or more years of foster placement. In comparison to their representation in the population, non-Hispanic Blacks (39 percent of placements) and Hispanics (17 percent of placements) were over-represented in the foster care population.

In the fiscal year ending September 1999, 46,000 children were adopted from foster care placements. Half were girls and half boys, with a mean age of 6.9 years. Almost half were five years old or younger; only 17 percent were 11 years old or older. At the end of that same fiscal year, 127,000 children remained in foster care awaiting adoption. The mean time children had been awaiting adoption was forty-four months, with 25 percent waiting more than five years (sixty months).

Single women who give birth to children have long been the object of social concern. Overall, there has been a long-term rise in the nonmarital birth rate between 1960 and the present. It is linked to an increase in the number of women of child-bearing age who are unmarried, an increase in cohabiting relationships, and a decline in pregnancy-induced marriage.[9] However, the number of "children raising children" is in decline. In 2001, the teen birth rate fell for the tenth straight year, to 45.9 births per 1,000 females 15–19 years old. This decade-long decline is a substantial 26 percent. Among younger teens, 15–17 years old, the drop has been greater than among older teens, 18–19, who are legally adults: 35 percent vs. 20 percent, respectively.[10]

The decline in teen births is attributable to changes in sexual behavior. In the past decade, the percentage of high school students who reported having sexual intercourse declined and rates of contraceptive use increased.[11] The percentage of teen boys who were sexually active (having reported sexual intercourse in the last three months) declined steadily between 1990 and 1997; the percentage of teen girls who were sexually active rose and then fell during the same time period. There are racial and ethnic differences among teens' sexual activity and contraceptive use. The number of Black and White teens who had ever had

[7]"Adoption and Foster Care Laws in the U.S., July 2002," National Gay and Lesbian Taskforce, Washington, D.C., www.ngltf.org.

[8]Information in this and the subsequent paragraph are taken from "Adoption and Foster Care Analysis and Reporting System Fact Sheet, Interim FY 1999 Estimates as of June 2001," U.S. Department of Health and Human Services, Administration on Children, Youth and Families, Children's Bureau, June 2001.

[9]"America's Children 2000," www.childstats.gov.

[10]"HHS Report Shows Teen Birth Rate Falls to New Record Low in 2001," National Center for Health Statistics, Department of Health and Human Services, Centers for Disease Control, June 6, 2002.

[11]Kaiser Family Foundation, "Teen Sexual Activity Fact Sheet," Kaiser Family Foundation, Menlo Park, CA, August 2000.

intercourse declined between 1988 and 1995, but it rose among Hispanic teens.[12]

Eighty-two percent of White teens, 68 percent of black teens, and 58 percent of Hispanic teens reported using contraceptives when they had intercourse for the first time. Young Black women were more likely to be taking oral contraceptives at first intercourse (15 percent) than whites (8 percent) or Hispanics (3 percent). More young Whites used condoms (71 percent) than Blacks (48 percent) or Hispanics (50 percent). Despite increased use of contraceptives at the beginning of teens' sex lives, fewer reported using contraceptives when they most recently had sexual intercourse. Between 1988 and 1995, only Black teens reported increased use of contraceptives.[13]

The majority of adults work, thus access to good-quality child care is a significant family concern. The first-ever Census Bureau analysis of child-care providers shows that, in 1997, 21 percent of 19.6 million preschoolers were taken care of by grandparents while their parents worked or attended school.[14] The vast majority of the grandparents (85 percent) were not paid for their care work. The remainder of the children received care from their fathers (17 percent), day-care centers (12 percent), other relatives (9 percent), family day-care providers (7 percent), and nursery schools/preschools (6 percent). The financial burden of child care is not equal among families; the percent of families' monthly income spent on child care decreases with increases in income. Poor families devote roughly 20 percent of their budget to child care, compared to non-poor families who devote 7 percent. Families in which mothers are employed spend more on the care of their children than families in which mothers are unemployed ($70/week compared to $50/week).

As outlined in the readings on poverty, many families cannot meet their needs without governmental assistance. For example, in 2002, the federal government estimated that nationally 19,325,272 individuals participated in food stamp programs in the prior twelve months. This was an increase of 12 percent from the prior year. Average monthly participation of households in fiscal year 2001 was 7,446,836. This was substantially lower than the 1997 figure of 9,454,705, but higher than the 2001 figure of 7,333,580.[15]

Perspectives on the Problem

Sociologists using a *conflict perspective* are concerned with how cultural ideals and social policy reflect the power dynamics in our society. They would explore how maintaining the idea that families are and should be formed around a heterosexual union, based on a gendered division of labor, and independently responsible for care and socialization of children serves to maintain the capitalist economic system. They would also study how heterosexual men benefit and women and gays are damaged by the majority belief that the capacity to nurture children is a natural trait. A sociologist using a *functionalist perspective* to study the family would look at whether the division of labor in the family and governmental, religious, and other social supports were well integrated to contribute to the long-term success of the society. A sociologist using a

---

[12]Elizabeth Terry and Jennifer Manlove, "Trends in Sexual Activity and Contraceptive Use Among Teens Research Brief." Washington, D.C.: Child Trends, accessed August 2002.

[13]Ibid.

[14]Statistics in this paragraph are taken from "Who's Minding the Kids? Grandparents Leading Child-Care Providers, Census Bureau Reports," U.S. Department of Commerce News, August 1, 2002.

[15]U.S. Department of Agriculture, Participation data tables accessed August 14, 2002.

symbolic interactionist perspective would examine how people act on their understanding of family to provide economic and social support for their partners and any children. They would explore how individuals' particular perceptions of the boundaries of their family and their acceptance of particular social roles shape the way that they approach the mundane activities of sharing household chores and taking care of children, thus either recreating or challenging social inequalities that already exist. A sociologist using a *social constructionist perspective* would examine the historical specificity of our ideas about family and how particular interest groups are able to influence what sorts of families are recognized in social policy.

Connecting the Perspectives

Edward Kain provides us with a long view on the family unit in the U.S. He shows us how our social constructions of family are inconsistent with the historic record. Using a functionalist perspective, Lillian Rubin explores the current dilemmas of working-class families, accounting for their racial/ethnic differences. Gillian Dunne adopts a symbolic interactionist perspective to explore how lesbian parents reconfigure caring and earning responsibilities that are generally allocated on the basis of gender in heterosexual unions. Nancy Naples also adopts an interactionist perspective to uncover how working-class women of color come to hold a much broader notion of "mothering" than exists within traditional constructions of the family. She shows how this broad understanding of women's work can lead individuals into political action, yielding improvements in the quality of life for more than their own immediate biological families. Finally, Kristin Luker examines the social construction of the problem of teen pregnancy and critically evaluates the

policy in place to solve it. She also addresses the classist, racist, and sexist nature of debates about family problems.

Reading Summaries

In "The Myth of Family Decline," Kain asserts that people who claim the American family is "in decline" or "in crisis" are comparing the range of family forms they see now to an idealized middle-class family unit composed of two parents, children, and possibly grandparents. In reality, Kain points out, the nuclear family unit never was the predominant family form throughout American history. Data show that over the last 150 years many children lived with a single parent or in poverty for some part of their lives. Many of the indicators that sociologists associate with family dysfunction (such as divorce, single heads of households, and poverty) are less prevalent now than at other times in history. Nostalgia for the mythic nuclear family persists, Kain maintains, because Americans are unaware of the real history of the American family.

Kain uses a macro-level analysis of the family to document the typical forms taken by families in different time periods. His understanding of the causes of social problems is most consistent with functionalist theory. Kain argues that the institution of the family is not in crisis. In fact, he points out, if we take a long historic view, we can see that the family has been slowly evolving to meet the changing needs of its members in the new postindustrial economy. In short, the diverse family forms we currently see should be recognized as adaptive responses to real shifts in societal conditions. According to Kain, current political activity to rectify a "decline" in the American family is based on an idealization of a past that never was.

Unlike Kain, Rubin maintains that the working-class family is, in fact, in crisis. In

"Families on the Fault Line," she argues that recent economic downturns and the economic trends discussed in Section II have forced both parents in working-class families to seek employment. Yet, unlike dual-income middle- and upper-class couples, they find that their income is frequently insufficient to cover the cost of quality child care. The solutions of working-class couples to the child-care problem take many forms, but all have potential drawbacks.

Rubin also explores the extent to which the beliefs of working-class men and women make them more or less able to adapt to changing economic conditions. She reports that the husband's age and race both predict the amount of conflict a couple has over the division of household labor and child care because these two attributes correlate closely with belief in traditional gender ideology. Additionally, the general public has failed to see the real shift in women's responsibilities and thus continues to support ways of organizing social life that assume women's responsibilities are primarily in the home. Rubin argues that our social institutions have not developed ways to support the immediate needs of working-class families. Husbands and wives have been forced to individually invent solutions to a common problem, sometimes adapting in ways that hurt themselves and their children.

Gillian Dunne returns to the question: What is a family? For Kain, a family can still be a family if it functions to meet the needs of its members. However, Kain, Rubin, Naples, and Luker implicitly assume that a family is a unit including a man, a woman, and children. They identify the problems of the family and seek solutions without making a problem of the central heterosexual assumption. Dunne shifts the lens on the family and asks, What do partnerships formed by two women committed to each other and their children look like? How do these families

form, and how do the adults divide up the responsibility of meeting each other's and the children's social and economic needs?

Dunne's research is motivated by the observation that although the majority of women are members of the paid workforce, parenting is still structured around gender. The typical division of labor in heterosexual families results in women being responsible for the bulk of hands-on care and men being responsible for generating income. Families organized in this way place a priority on building the male parent's (father's) career, often at the expense of the employed woman's (mother's). This "traditional" organization rests on both the perception that women have a superior biological capacity to nurture children and on the statistical reality that the average man earns more than the average women. Dunne notes that, expecting conflict between career and family, some heterosexual women choose not to become parents. She questions whether gendered specialization is the most efficient and effective way to run a household.

Dunne presents two case studies to represent what she learned from face-to-face interviews with thirty-seven cohabitating lesbian couples with dependent children. She chose to study them because the lack of gender difference in their relationships would require them to organize their parenting around something other than gender. She found that when heterosexual assumptions were not operative, the biological aspect of motherhood did not determine who became the primary wage earner. The decision to bear children was based on desire for the experience, fertility, and capacity to move both careers to a point of financial stability. Once children arrived, the nonbiological parent was regularly involved in all aspects of nurturing, and the biological parent was equally likely to be involved in wage earning. The definition of *mother* was constantly under negotiation. Biological fathers were involved in parenting arrangements to varying degrees and provided nurturing ("mothering") rather than financial support. Dunne concludes that visible lesbian parents draw into question the naturalness of heterosexual practice.

Naples's reading, "Activist Mothering, Community Caretaking, and Civic Work," challenges two widely accepted ideas about mothers' role in the family. Her work undermines the belief that women's caretaking behavior is somehow tied to their biology or hormones. It also questions the belief that "good" mothering requires primarily directing one's attention to the physical and psychological health of children in one's immediate care.

In this reading, based on lengthy face-to-face interviews, Naples shows that many women who have experienced racial, gender, and class oppression hold a broader notion of mothering than members of the White upper class. White women who are protected by class and race privileges may see their mothering responsibilities lying in the sphere of the home and devote themselves to enhancing the quality of this haven from the public world for their mates and offspring. Alternatively, women who observe the structural limits on their own children's lives, who have struggled for their own economic survival, who have been socialized into community work in early childhood, or who have been part of church or civic organizations do not draw hard lines between their biological family and the public sphere. They adopt an "activist" notion of mothering that is public and change oriented. "Good mothering" in their view involves "all actions including social activism that addresses the needs of their children and community." They believe that good mothering is focused on changing the circumstances within which their children will mature, securing economic and social justice for their entire community.

This alternative perception of mothering allows nonparents to claim a legitimate role in the care of children within a community, which has the potential effect of increasing the number of people looking out for children's welfare at any given time. This perception of the family as extending into the community also encourages people to literally open their homes to others, increasing the resource base of the entire community and providing a more stable safety net for children. But American society is not set up to facilitate social change. When activist mothering involves women with children in community work and the paid labor force, Naples finds that they face the same difficulties as Rubin's working-class mothers. The public world is not set up for them to combine work and family. Ironically, they may have to sacrifice close contact with their own children in order to better conditions in the community.

Luker undertakes two projects in "Dubious Conceptions." First, following the logic of social construction, she exposes how the approaches to teenage pregnancy proposed by liberal and conservative claims makers are tied to ideological positions rather than based on a thorough analysis of objective data. Because they make incorrect assumptions about why teens become pregnant, the policies of both groups fall far short of solving the problem. Luker's second project is to develop an analysis of teen pregnancy and policy initiatives from interview data that capture the perspectives of pregnant teenagers. Like Rubin, she believes that microanalysis must be coupled with an understanding of the macrostructures that constrain an individual's options. Thus, she argues that it is essential to examine the motivations of teens who become pregnant in the context of the social and economic conditions in which they live.

Luker argues that teenage pregnancy does not cause poverty, but rather that poverty causes teenage pregnancy. Girls do not have babies and then become poor. Instead, those poor teens who perceive that their opportunities to become full participants in society are severely limited have babies. The economic restructuring of society has particularly disenfranchised young urban teens, and the pregnancy rate is, accordingly, a symptom of the extent to which they are excluded from the "American dream." In the absence of opportunities to become employed and rise out of poverty, girls choose to have babies to assume a positive role in society (mother), to demonstrate responsibility, and to have an incentive to succeed. In short, teens choose to have children in order to change their lives. Luker argues that as long as poor teens feel that they risk little by having children because they do not have better alternatives, they will choose to have children.

FOCUSING QUESTIONS

The following questions are intended to guide your reading of the selections in this chapter: How do Kain, Rubin, Naples, and Luker tie changes in the economic and political structure of American society to changes in individual family units? How do Rubin, Dunne, Naples, and Luker show that the perpetuation of specific ways of thinking about race and gender contributes to social problems faced by different families? After reading Kain, consider: What is the quality of the data that the authors provide to support their claims about the causes and solutions of social problems? Finally, what do the arguments made by the authors mean for you as a person of a particular gender, race, class, and sexual orientation?

31

THE MYTH OF FAMILY DECLINE

EDWARD L. KAIN

Almost daily, the headlines scream out yet another message that seems to indicate the family is on its deathbed in modern America. News magazines include stories on unprecedented rates of divorce, frightening reports of elderly Americans (seemingly forgotten by their family and society) being mistreated and neglected in nursing homes, and children being raised in single-parent families. The evening news talks about the majority of mothers working outside the home and of social movements supporting concerns as diverse as abortion rights and homosexual freedom. All these issues seem to signal that the basic institution in our society is threatened.

These challenges to the family have been met sometimes with dismay and sometimes with resignation, but in recent years they have also been met with counterattacks led by groups rallying around a battle cry for a return to the traditional family of the past. It appears that the war has begun. Those fighting in the trenches, however, are not at all certain of the outcome because there are many separate battles being waged at once.

This . . . is an attempt to step back from the apparent battleground of the closing decades of the twentieth century and evaluate the health of the family in the United States from a broader perspective—one that places current family life within the context of social change. Families do not exist in a vacuum, and we cannot begin to understand the quality of family life in the last decade of the twentieth century unless it is placed within historical and social context. What were American families like in the past? How have families been changing over the past century? What types of family patterns can we expect to see over the next several decades?

Unfortunately, the task of placing family life within a broader context is an assignment with many dangers. Because most of us were born into families and have spent most of our lives in the context of our own family structures, we all have some sense that we are knowledgeable on the topic of family life. It is somewhat difficult to step back from our personal experience and evaluate the institution of the family with objectivity.

To understand families in the present or the future, we must understand families in the past. We cannot possibly assess the health of family life as we near the twenty-first century unless we place it within a broader span of historical time. As individuals and as a culture, however, Americans tend not to think of contemporary issues in historical perspective. This is true not only of popular accounts of family life, but also of the work done by many family scholars as well. Like Rip Van Winkle who awoke to a world vastly different than that to which he was accustomed, we often look upon contemporary family life with dismay. Our world is changing rapidly, and many of these changes seem to challenge our very conception of family life. We long for a return to traditional values and the traditional family structure that we remember from the past.

This dismay at the current state of affairs and desire to return to the past is what I have come to label the "myth of family decline." Our image of families in the past is often based on myth rather than reality. For the past three decades, work by historians, demographers, and sociologists has begun to paint a new picture of the history of family life. Using innovative methods to explore church, family, and civil records, these researchers have discovered patterns of family experience that stand in stark contrast to the images many of us have held about the traditional family.[1]

As an illustration of this point, take the following quiz, which asks a few basic questions about family life both in the past and the present.

A Brief Quiz on Families and Change
in the United States

---

1. Which of the following years had the highest divorce rate in the United States?
   (A) 1935
   (B) 1945
   (C) 1955
   (D) 1965
2. T F Because of the rapid rise in the divorce rate, children are much more likely to live in a single-parent household than they were a century ago.
3. T F In the past, most families lived in three-generation households. It is now much less likely for this to occur, since grandparents are put

into nursing homes instead of cared for in the home.

4. What proportion of women worked outside the home in 1900?
   (A) one in fifty
   (B) one in twenty
   (C) one in ten
   (D) one in five

5. T F Over the past one hundred years, fewer and fewer people have been getting married, so the number of single people has been increasing.

6. T F The high incidence of female-headed households among black families today can be traced to the impact of slavery on family life as well as to the disruption of two-parent, nuclear families among black Americans during the time of Emancipation.

7. What is the most common household type in the United States today?
   (A) a single-parent family with one adult wage earner
   (B) a two-parent family with one adult male wage earner
   (C) a two-parent family with two adult wage earners

8. T F Very few families live below the poverty line (as officially defined by the federal government) for extended periods of time (five consecutive years).

Before I give the results to this quiz, there are two things to keep in mind: First, don't be upset if you did not score very well. I have given this quiz to hundreds of students and professionals, and the typical result is that scores are extremely low. In fact, when I gave the quiz at a conference attended only by professionals who specialize in working with and teaching about family life, most of the questions were answered incorrectly by a majority of the group! Rather than being a statement about the quality of professionals in the area of family, this reflects the tendency of our culture to ignore the past and to base opinions about our basic social institutions (family, education, economy, religion, and government) on a cultural image that often is greatly at variance with reality.

Second, I want to suggest that each of these questions illustrates a basic point. . . . Now, for the answers to the quiz:

Question 1. **Which of the following years had the highest divorce rate in the United States?: (A) 1935; (B) 1945; (C) 1955; (D) 1965.** The correct answer to this question is B. No, that is not a typographical error in the book; the correct answer is 1945. Most people are very surprised that the correct answer is not 1965. "Isn't it true that divorce rates have been rising throughout the century?" they ask. This response clearly illustrates one of the first central points . . . : *We seldom have a historical understanding of family life or of the impact of specific historical events on the functioning of families.* The divorce rates in this country reached a historical peak at the end of World War II. Several explanations have been given for this: First, it is likely that a number of couples married hurriedly after relatively short courtships when the man was about to be sent off to war. Second, the stress of separation may have resulted in the development of other relationships for both the women at home and the men who were away. Third, both spouses may have changed considerably during the war years. The man who returned home from the battlefields may not have been the boy who left, and the woman at home may not have been the same girl whom he had courted and married. While it is true that divorce rates in this country consistently increased from 1950 through 1980, they did not match the peak of 1945 until the mid-1970s.[2]

Question 2. (True or False) **Because of the rapid rise in the divorce rate, children are** much more likely to live in a single-parent household than they were a century ago. This statement is false. Most people do not realize the profound effects on family life that have resulted from rapid declines in the mortality rate since the turn of the century. While divorce has increased throughout this century, the drastic decline in the number of parents who die at an early age (leaving widows, widowers, and orphans behind) more than offsets the increase in single-parent households that results from marital disruption caused by divorce.[3] This question reflects a second basic principle . . . : *If an adequate understanding of family change is to be developed, we must look not only at data from the past but also at the relationships between different types of changes affecting family life.*

Question 3. (True or False) **In the past, most families lived in three-generation households. It is now much less likely for this to occur, since grandparents are put into nursing homes instead of cared for in the home.** This statement is false for a number of reasons. One of the most important findings of the new family history has been a challenge to the idea that the rise of the modern nuclear family (the family including only two parents and their children) is linked to industrialization and is a result of that process. Peter Laslett[4] and others have demonstrated that, at least in England, the nuclear family was the dominant form of household long before the advent of industrialization. Laslett makes a strong argument for the continuity of family life over time, and suggests that in a number of ways the family in the "world we have lost" was much as it is today. This illustrates a third central point . . . : *When we have actual data about family life in the past, it often presents a picture of family life that is drastically different from the image that is common in popular mythology.*

In fairness, I must say that Laslett's work is a reaction to most contemporary theories of the family, which ignore the importance of historical time. Unfortunately Laslett's approach has been criticized for ignoring the dynamic nature of the family as a group. Just as the institution of the family has changed over historical time, individual families change over the family cycle. Subsequent work has suggested that while at any point in time most families in preindustrial Europe may have been nuclear in structure, if families are traced over their development cycle, many of them are extended for brief periods while the elder parents are still alive.[5]

Even if everyone wanted to spend part of their family cycle in a three-generation household, however, it still would not be possible for many families. First, only *one* of the children and his or her family typically lived with the elderly parents, so in every family there would be a number of siblings who would live in nuclear households. In addition, the elder generation seldom survived long enough to spend much time in a three-generation household.

Question 4. **What proportion of women worked outside the home in 1900?: (A) one in fifty; (B) one in twenty; (C) one in ten; (D) one in five.** If you chose answer D, you are right. Yes, fully one in five women worked outside the home in paid occupations at the turn of the century.[6] Many were employed as domestic servants and in agriculture. Others worked in textile mills and in teaching positions. Still others were employed in the new clerical sector, which was expanding as our country moved further into the industrial age. . . .

Most people are surprised that the female labor force participation rate was that high. We tend to have an image that women only started working outside the home during World War II, and that they returned home when the war ended. The rise of female labor force participation is often seen as a recent event linked to the women's movement of the 1960s. Certainly there has been an increase in the number of women working outside the home since 1950. In reality, however, the rate of female labor force participation has been rising relatively consistently since the late nineteenth century. This points to a fourth principle . . . : *Most of the changes occurring in families in the United States are not revolutionary but evolutionary—they are changes that have been happening gradually over a long period of time, and they do not represent a radical change from patterns in the past.*

Question 5. (True or False) **Over the past one hundred years, fewer and fewer people have been getting married, so the number of single people has been increasing.** The correct answer to this question is false. (By now you are probably catching on to the idea that your first guess may have been wrong.) Both the popular press and sociological research in recent years has focused on the increase in singlehood.[7] This increase, however, has only been happening since 1950, a period when more people married than any other time in all of American history. In essence, there was no place for the rate of singlehood to go but up. If a longer historical view is taken, it becomes clear that the rates of singlehood today are still lower than they were a century ago. This reflects a fifth basic point . . . : *When we do include history in our conceptions of family life, we tend to focus only on recent history and remain blind to the broader picture of social change and continuity in family life.*

Question 6. (True or False) **The high incidence of female-headed households among black families today can be traced to the impact of slavery on family life as well as to the disruption of two-parent, nuclear families among black Americans during the time of Emancipation.** This statement is false. While the reasons for the high incidence of single-parent, female-headed households among black Americans today may be complex, they cannot be traced to a legacy developed from the period of slavery and Emancipation. In a series of careful studies, Herbert G. Gutman[8] shows that between 1855 and 1880 as many as 90 percent of black households contained both a husband and wife or just a father with children. The matriarchal household was common neither among antebellum free blacks, nor among black families after Emancipation. The continuing myths about the causes and implications of the structure of black families illustrate another central point . . . : *Historical causes may be built into current explanation of family life, but unless data are used to examine the validity of these historical explanations, our understanding of the relationship between historical events and family life may be seriously flawed.* I might add to this statement the general observation that when groups that are not white, male, or middle-class are concerned, our historical understanding is usually less sophisticated and more often incorrect. The new family history has involved more attention to issues of race, class, and gender—much to the benefit of our understanding of family life in the past.

Question 7. **What is the most common household type in the United States today?: (A) a single-parent family with one adult wage earner; (B) a two-parent family with one adult male wage earner; (C) a two-parent family with two adult wage earners.** This question turns from the history of family life to the contemporary family in the United States. Like the questions on the history of the family, it illustrates that we may have misconceptions about families in contemporary America. The correct answer is C. By far the most common type of household in the United States today is one in which both adults work outside the home.[9] This illustrates that *no matter what* *family life was like in the past, in the contemporary United States the so-called traditional family is a distinct minority.*

Question 8. (True or False) **Very few families live below the poverty line (as officially defined by the federal government) for extended periods of time (five consecutive years).** The statement in question 8 is true. Research using data from the Panel Study of Income Dynamics at the University of Michigan illustrates clearly that a very small percentage of families remain consistently below the poverty line (approximately 4 percent).[10] Rather, families move in and out of poverty as wage earners lose a job, are rehired, a divorce occurs, or additional children are born, changing the stresses upon the family budget. This clearly points to the fact that *our conceptions of the family as a static institution are inadequate, and we must think of families as dynamic groups that change over the lifetimes of the individuals who are involved.*

. . .

. . . Many of these new findings in family history and family sociology have taken quite some time to find their way into textbooks in the social sciences—and even longer to reach the popular consciousness. Most of us still carry images of a mythic extended family of domestic bliss within our minds. It is important, however, to base our decisions about political issues related to families on reality rather than myth.

Partly because of the American tendency to romanticize the past, and partly because of the many changes in family life that seem so evident during the past several decades, it is common for social analysts to conclude that the family is, indeed, in trouble. Analyses that predict the demise of the family have come from both ends of the political spectrum. On the radical side, Christopher Lasch has suggested that the

family is a failure as a "haven in the heartless world" of industrial capitalism, and he paints a gloomy picture about the future prospects of any improvement.[11] According to Lasch, the family is supposed to shield its members from the harsh realities of working life in modern society, and it has failed in this task.

Similarly, the New Evangelical Right fears that the traditional family is in serious danger. Groups like the Moral Majority preach against the sins of modern times and demand that we return to the core American values of the traditional family. The forces of the New Right have supported a variety of types of legislation that attempt to embody these so-called traditional values into the legal structure. Most notable among these attempts was the Family Protection Act, first introduced in September of 1979 by Senator Paul Laxalt. Later versions of the Family Protection Act were introduced to the House by Representative Hansen of Idaho and Representative Smith of Alabama in 1981, and Senator Jepsen of Iowa introduced a revised version to the Senate in June of the same year.[12] I have more fully discussed some of the provisions of the Family Protection Act elsewhere, and a full explication is not necessary here.[13] In essence, the goal of the legislation was to reinforce what is defined as the traditional family—based upon a mythical vision of peaceful family life under patriarchal rule, in which the husband is the breadwinner and the wife is in the home raising the children.

While certainly the most comprehensive in scope, the Family Protection Act is not the only example of attempts in the 1980s to enshrine what is perceived as the traditional family in the laws of the land. Perhaps the most visible example has been the introduction of various versions of a Human Life Amendment, which would ban or limit legal abortion. All these measures can be seen as an attempt to shore up what is perceived as the crumbling foundation of the central institution of any society—the family.

Not everyone, however, agrees with the assessment that the modern family is in trouble. Some, such as Harvard sociologist Mary Jo Bane, argue that while families are changing, they are still vigorous and "here to stay."[14] Bane provides convincing evidence that ties between grandparents and grandchildren and between parents and children have, if anything, become stronger in recent times, rather than weaker.

One reason that the debate about the health of the family is such an important concern is the rapid rate of social change in our society. Changes in our culture create many social problems, as adjustments in some parts of the culture lag behind. William F. Ogburn's concept of cultural lag provides a useful tool for evaluating this problem.[15] As we have moved in the space of a century from an agricultural economy to a postindustrial society, our social institutions have had difficulty keeping up with the massive shifts generated by technological change. The resulting social problems are at the core of many of the political controversies seen today at the national level, including civil rights for people of color, women's rights, and homosexual rights.

Not surprisingly, many of these controversies center on the family: abortion and reproductive rights; homosexuality; the changing roles of women and men; daycare; and comparable worth (the idea that men and women should receive equal pay for jobs that are similar in content, not only for jobs that have the same job title). Because the family is a key institution in any society, and because the transition from agriculture to industry transforms the basic relationships between economic production and family life, many of the cultural lags demanding attention today are reflected in these national political issues.

Unfortunately, as is clear . . . , we are often blind to the realities of family life in the past. Our cultural images of family life in past times are difficult to change, even when data indicate the images are much more myth than reality. Like Rip Van Winkle, we long for a return to the good old days, when life was much simpler and times were happier. . . .

NOTES

1. See, for example, John Demos, *A Little Commonwealth: Family Life in Plymouth Colony* (New York: Oxford University Press, 1970); John Demos and Sarane Spence Boocock (eds.), *Turning Points: Historical and Sociological Essays on the Family* (Chicago: The University of Chicago Press, 1978); Michael Gorden (ed.), *The American Family in Social-Historical Perspective*, 3rd ed. (New York: St. Martin's Press, 1983); Philip Greven, *Four Generations: Population, Land, and Family in Colonial Andover, Massachusetts* (Ithaca: Cornell University Press, 1970); Herbert Gutman, *The Black Family in Slavery and Freedom* (New York: Pantheon, 1976); Kenneth A. Lockridge, *A New England Town: The First Hundred Years* (New York: W. W. Norton & Company, 1970); and Theodore K. Rabb and Robert I. Rotberg (eds.), *The Family in History: Interdisciplinary Essays* (New York: Harper & Row, 1970).

2. For more complete data on trends in marriage, divorce, and remarriage, see Andrew Cherlin, *Marriage, Divorce, Remarriage* (Cambridge, MA: Harvard University Press, 1981).

3. See Peter Uhlenberg, "Death and the Family," *Journal of Family History* 5 (1980):313–20.

4. See Peter Laslett, *The World We Have Lost*, 2nd ed. (New York: Charles Scribner's Sons, 1971).

5. See Lutz Berkner, "The Stem Family and the Developmental Cycle of the Peasant Household: An 18th-Century Austrian Example," *American Historical Review* LXXVII (1972): 398–418.

6. Historical data on female labor force participation in the United States can be found in a number of sources. See, for example, *The Statistical History of the United States from Colonial Times to the Present* (New York: Basic Books, 1976) and United States Bureau of the Census, *The Historical Statistics of the United States*

from Colonial Times to 1970, Bicentennial Edition (Washington, DC: Government Printing Office, 1975).

7. See, for example, Peter Stein, *Single* (Englewood Cliffs, NJ: Prentice-Hall, 1976). The best example of media coverage on singlehood is the flurry of popular articles that quickly appeared after a 1986 study was released projecting the rate of marriage among college-educated women. Both *Newsweek* ("The Marriage Crunch: If You're a Single Woman, Here Are Your Chances of Getting Married," June 2, 1986) and *People* ("Are These Old Maids? A Harvard-Yale Study Says That Most Single Women Over 35 Can Forget About Marriage," March 31, 1986) carried extensive cover stories examining the plight of single women. Little mention is made of where these patterns fit in historical perspective.

8. See Herbert G. Gutman, *The Black Family in Slavery and Freedom* (New York: Pantheon, 1976).

9. See George Masnick and Mary Jo Bane, *The Nation's Families: 1960–1990* (Boston: Auburn Publishing, 1980).

10. Data from the important research resulting from the Michigan Panel of Income Dynamics can be found in a number of volumes, such as Greg J. Duncan and James N. Morgan (eds.), *Five Thousand American Families—Patterns of Economic Progress* (Ann Arbor, MI: Institute for Social Research, 1979).

11. See Christopher Lasch, *Haven in a Heartless World: The Family Besieged* (New York: Basic Books, 1977).

12. For different versions of this legislation, see The Family Protection Act bill H.R. 311. 1981; The Family Protection Act bill H.R. 3955. 1981; The Family Protection Act bill S. 1378. 1981; and The Family Protection Act bill S. 1808, 1979.

13. See Edward L. Kain, "The Federal Government Should Not Foster Legislation Relating to the Family," in Harold Feldman and Andrea Purrot, *Human Sexuality: Contemporary Controversies* (Beverly Hills: Sage, 1984).

14. See Mary Jo Bane, *Here to Stay: American Families in the Twentieth Century* (New York: Basic Books, 1976).

15. See William F. Ogburn, "Cultural Lag as Theory" in Otis Dudley Duncan, *William F. Ogburn on Culture and Social Change* (Chicago: University of Chicago Press, 1964).

QUESTIONS FOR DISCUSSION

1. Determine whether your view of the American family is based in mythology by doing your own historic analysis. Write down what you know about the previous four generations of your family—call your parents or grandparents for information, if necessary. Were all the generations organized in the same way? Were all the generations the same size?

2. Can you relate any shifts in family form to broader economic changes in society?

32

FAMILIES ON THE FAULT LINE
America's Working Class Speaks
About the Family, the Economy, Race, and Ethnicity

LILLIAN B. RUBIN

Not surprisingly, there are generational differences in what fuels the conflict around the division of labor in families. For the older couples—those who grew up in a different time, whose marriages started with another set of ground rules—the struggle is not simply around how much men do or about whether they take responsibility for the daily tasks of living without being pushed, prodded, and reminded. That's the overt manifestation of the discord, the trigger that starts the fight. But the noise of the explosion when it comes serves to conceal the more fundamental issue underlying the dissension: legitimacy. What does she have a *right* to expect? "What do I know about doing stuff around the house?" asks Frank Moreno, a forty-eight-year-old foreman in a warehouse. "I wasn't brought up like that. My pop, he never did one damn thing, and my mother never complained. It was her job; she did it and kept quiet. Besides, I work my ass off every day. Isn't that enough?"

For younger couples, those under forty, the problem is somewhat different. The men may complain about the expectation that they'll participate more fully in the care and feeding of the family, but talk to them about it quietly and they'll usually admit that it's not really unfair, given that their wives also work outside the home. In these homes, the issue between husband and wife isn't only who does what. That's there, and it's a source of more or less conflict, depending upon what the men actually do and how forceful their wives are in their demands. But in most of these families there's at least a verbal consensus that men *ought* to participate in the tasks of daily life. Which raises the next and perhaps more difficult issue in contest between them: Who feels responsible for getting the tasks done? Who regards them as a duty, and for whom are they an option? On this, tradition rules.

Even in families where husbands now share many of the tasks, their wives still bear full responsibility for the organization of family life. A man may help cook the meal these days, but a woman is most likely to be the one who has planned it. He may take the children to child care, but she virtually always has had to arrange it. It's she also who is accountable for the emotional life of the family, for monitoring the emotional temperature of its members and making the necessary corrections. It's this need to be responsible for it all that often feels as burdensome as the tasks themselves. "It's not just doing all the stuff that needs doing," explains Maria Jankowicz, a white twenty-eight-year-old assembler in an electronics factory. "It's worrying all the time about everything and always having to arrange everything, you know what I mean. It's like I run the whole show. If I don't stay on top of it all, things fall apart because nobody else is going to do it. The kids can't and Nick, well, forget it," she concludes angrily.

If, regardless of age, life stage, or verbal consensus, women usually still carry the greatest share of the household burdens, why is it important to notice that younger men grant legitimacy to their wives' demands and older men generally do not? Because men who believe their wives have a right to expect their participation tend to suffer guilt and discomfort when they don't live up to those expectations. And no one lives comfortably with guilt.

It's possible, of course, that the men who speak of guilt and rights are only trying to impress me by mouthing the politically correct words. But even if true, they display a sensitivity to the issue that's missing from the men who don't speak those words. For words are more than just words. They embody ideas; they are the symbols that give meaning to our thoughts; they shape our consciousness. New ideas come to us on the wings of words. It's words that bring those ideas to life, that allow us to see possibilities unrecognized before we gave them words. Indeed, without words, there is no conscious thought, no possibility for the kind of self-reflection that lights the path of change.[1]

True, there's often a long way between word and deed. But the man who feels guilty when he disappoints his wife's expectations has a different consciousness than the one who doesn't—a difference that usually makes for at least some small change in his behavior. Although the emergence of this changing male consciousness is visible in all the racial groups in this study, there also are differences among them that are worthy of comment.

Virtually all the men do some work inside the family—tending the children, washing dishes, running the vacuum, going to the market. And they generally also re-main responsible for those tasks that have always been traditionally male—mowing the lawn, shoveling the snow, fixing the car, cleaning the garage, doing repairs around the house. Among the white families in this study, 16 percent of the men share the family work relatively equally, almost always those who live in families where they and their wives work different shifts or where the men are unemployed. "What choice do I have?" asks Don Bartlett, a thirty-year-old white handyman who works days while his wife is on the swing shift. "I'm the only one here, so I do what's got to be done."

Asian and Latino men of all ages, however, tend to operate more often on the old male model, even when they work different shifts or are unemployed, a finding that puzzled me at first. Why, I wondered, did I find only two Asian men and one Latino who are real partners in the work of the family? Aren't these men subject to the same social and personal pressures others experience?

The answer is both yes and no. The pressures are there but, depending upon where they live, there's more or less support for resisting them. The Latino and Asian men who live in ethnic neighborhoods—settings where they are embedded in an intergenerational community and where the language and culture of the home country is kept alive by a steady stream of new immigrants—find strong support for clinging to the old ways. Therefore, change comes much more slowly in those families. The men who live outside the ethnic quarter are freer from the mandates and constraints of these often tight-knit communities, therefore are more responsive to the winds of change in the larger society.

These distinctions notwithstanding, it's clear that Asian and Latino men generally participate least in the work of the household and are the least likely to believe they have much responsibility there beyond bringing home a paycheck. "Taking care of the house and kids is my wife's job, that's all," says Joe Gomez flatly.

"A Chinese man mopping a floor? I've never seen it yet," says Amy Lee angrily. Her husband, Dennis, trying to make a joke of the conflict with his wife, says with a smile, "In Chinese families men don't do floors and windows. I help with the dishes sometimes if she needs me to or," he laughs, "if she screams loud enough. The rest, well, it's pretty much her job."

The commonly held stereotype about black men abandoning women and children, however, doesn't square with the families in this study. In fact, black men are the most likely to be real participants in the daily life of the family and are more intimately involved in raising their children than any of the others. True, the men's family work load doesn't always match their wives', and the women are articulate in their complaints about this. Nevertheless, compared to their white, Asian, or Latino counterparts, the black families look like models of egalitarianism.

Nearly three-quarters of the men in the African-American families in this study do a substantial amount of the cooking, cleaning, and child care, sometimes even more than their wives. All explain it by saying one version or another of: "I just figure it's my job, too." Which simply says what is, without explaining how it came to be that way.

To understand that, we have to look at family histories that tell the story of generations of African-American women who could find work and men who could not, and to the family culture that grew from this difficult and painful reality. "My mother worked six days a week cleaning other people's houses, and my father was an ordinary laborer, when he could find work, which wasn't very often," explains thirty-two-year-old Troy Payne, a black waiter and father of two children. "So he was home a lot more than she was, and he'd do what he had to

around the house. The kids all had to do their share, too. It seemed only fair, I guess."

Difficult as the conflict around the division of labor is, it's only one of the many issues that have become flash points in family life since mother went to work. Most important, perhaps, is the question: Who will care for the children? For the lack of decent, affordable facilities for the care of the children creates unbearable problems and tensions for these working-class families.

It's hardly news that child care is an enormous headache and expense for all two-job families. In many professional middle-class families, where the child-care bill can be $1,500–2,000 a month, it competes with the mortgage payment as the biggest single monthly expenditure. Problematic as this may be, however, these families are the lucky ones when compared to working-class families, many of whom don't earn much more than the cost of child care in these upper middle-class families. Even the families in this study at the highest end of the earnings scale, those who earn $42,000 a year, can't dream of such costly arrangements.

For most working-class families, therefore, child care often is patched together in ways that leave parents anxious and children in jeopardy. "Care for the little ones, that's a real big problem," says Beverly Waldov, a thirty-year-old white mother of three children, the youngest two, products of a second marriage, under three years old. "My oldest girl is nine, so she's not such a problem. I hate the idea of her being a latchkey kid, but what can I do? We don't even have the money to put the little ones in one of those good day-care places, so I don't have any choice with her. She's just *got* to be able to take care of herself after school," she says, her words a contest between anxiety and hope.

"We have a kind of complicated arrangement for the little kids. Two days a week, my mom takes care of them. We pay her, but at least I don't have to worry when they're with her; I know it's fine. But she works the rest of the time, so the other days we take them to this woman's house. It's the best we can afford, but it's not great because she keeps too many kids, and I know they don't get good attention. Especially the little one; she's just a baby, you know." She pauses and looks away, anguished. "She's so clingy when I bring her home; she can't let go of me, like nobody's paid her any mind all day. But it's not like I have a choice. We barely make it now; if I stop working, we'd be in real trouble."

Even such makeshift solutions don't work for many families. Some speak of being unable to afford day care at all. "We couldn't pay our bills if we had to pay for somebody to take care of the kids."

Some say they're unwilling to leave the children in the care of strangers. "I just don't believe someone else should be raising our kids, that's all."

Some have tried a variety of child-care arrangements, only to have them fail in a moment of need. "We tried a whole bunch of things, and maybe they work for a little while," says Faye Ensey, a black twenty-eight-year-old office worker. "But what happens when your kid gets sick? Or when the baby sitter's kids get sick? I lost two jobs in a row because my kids kept getting sick and I couldn't go to work. Or else I couldn't take my little one to the baby sitter because her kids were sick. They finally fired me for absenteeism. I didn't really blame them, but it felt terrible anyway. It's such a hassle, I sometimes think I'd be glad to just stay home. But we can't afford for me not to work, so we had to figure out something else."

For such families, that "something else" is the decision to take jobs on different shifts—a decision made by one-fifth of the families in this study. With one working days and the other on swing or graveyard,

one parent is home with the children at all times. "We were getting along okay before Daryl junior was born, because Shona, my daughter, was getting on. You know, she didn't need somebody with her all the time, so we could both work days," explains Daryl Adams, a black thirty-year-old postal clerk with a ten-year-old daughter and a nine-month-old son. "I used to work the early shift—seven to three—so I'd get home a little bit after she got here. It worked out okay. But then this here big surprise came along." He stops, smiles down fondly at his young son and runs his hand over his nearly bald head.

"Now between the two of us working, we don't make enough money to pay for child care and have anything left over, so this is the only way we can manage. Besides, both of us, Alesha and me, we think it's better for one of us to be here, not just for the baby, for my daughter, too. She's growing up and, you know, I think maybe they need even more watching than when they were younger. She's coming to the time when she could get into all kinds of trouble if we're not here to put the brakes on."

But the cost such arrangements exact on marriage can be very high. When I asked these husbands and wives when they have time to talk, more often than not I got a look of annoyance at a question that, on its face, seemed stupid to them. "Talk? How can we talk when we hardly see each other?" "Talk? What's that?" "Talk? Ha, that's a joke."

Mostly, conversation is limited to the logistics that take place at shift-changing time when children and chores are handed off from one to the other. With children dancing around underfoot, the incoming parent gets a quick summary of the day's or night's events, a list of reminders about things to be done, perhaps about what's cooking in the pot on the stove. "Sometimes when I'm coming home and it's been a hard day, I think: Wouldn't it be wonderful if I could just sit down with Leon for half an hour and we could have a quiet beer together?" thirty-one-year-old Emma Guerrero, a Latina baker, says wistfully.

But it's not to be. If the arriving spouse gets home early enough, there may be an hour when both are there together. But with the pressures of the workday fresh for one and awaiting the other, and with children clamoring for parental attention, this isn't a promising moment for any serious conversation.

Some of the luckier couples work different shifts on the same days, so they're home together on weekends. But even in these families there's so little time for normal family life that there's hardly any room for anyone or anything outside.

For those whose days off don't match, the problems of sustaining both the couple relationship and family life are magnified enormously. "The last two years have been hell for us," says thirty-five-year-old Tina Mulvaney, a white mother of two teenagers. "My son got into bad company and had some trouble, so Mike and I decided one of us had to be home. But we can't make it without my check, so I can't quit.

"Mike drives a cab and I work in a hospital, so we figured one of us could transfer to nights. We talked it over and decided it would be best if I was here during the day and he was here at night. He controls the kids, especially my son, better than I do. When he lays down the law, they listen." She interrupts her narrative to reflect on the difficulty of raising children. "You know, when they were little, I used to think about how much easier it would be when they got older. But now I see it's not true; that's when you really have to begin to worry about them. This is when they need someone to be here all the time to make sure they stay out of trouble."

She stops again, this time fighting tears, then takes up where she left off. "So now

Mike works days and I work graveyard. I hate it, but it's the only answer; at least this way somebody's here all the time. I get home about 8:30 in the morning. The kids and Mike are gone. It's the best time of the day because it's the only time I have a little quiet here. I clean up the house a little, do the shopping and the laundry and whatever, then I go to sleep for a couple of hours until the kids come home from school.

"Mike gets home at five; we eat; then he takes over for the night, and I go back to sleep for another couple of hours. I try to get up by 9 so we can all have a little time together, but I'm so tired that I don't make it a lot of times. And by 10, he's sleeping because he has to be up by 6 in the morning. So if I don't get up, we hardly see each other at all. Mike's here on weekends, but I'm not. Right now I have Tuesday and Wednesday off. I keep hoping for a Monday–Friday shift, but it's what everybody wants, and I don't have the seniority yet. It's hard, very hard; there's no time to live or anything," she concludes with a listless sigh.

Even in families where wife and husband work the same shift, there's less time for leisure pursuits and social activities than ever before, not just because both parents work full-time but also because people work longer hours now than they did twenty years ago.[2] Two decades ago, weekends saw occasional family outings, Friday-evening bowling, a Saturday trip to the shopping mall, a Sunday with extended family, once in a while an evening out without the children. In summer, when the children weren't in school, a week night might find the family paying a short visit to a friend, a relative, or a neighbor. Now almost everyone I speak with complains that it's hard to find time for even these occasional outings. Instead, most off-work hours are spent trying to catch up with the dozens of family and household tasks that were left undone during the regular work week. When they aren't doing chores, parents guiltily try to do in two days a week what usually takes seven—that is, to establish a sense of family life for themselves and their children.

"Leisure," snorts Peter Pittman, a twenty-eight-year-old African-American father of two, married six years. "With both of us working like we do, there's no time for anything. We got two little kids; I commute better than an hour each way to my job. Then we live here for half rent because I take care of the place for the landlord. So if somebody's got a complaint, I've got to take care of it, you know, fix it myself or get the landlord to get somebody out to do it if I can't. Most things I can do myself, but it takes time. I sometimes wonder what this life's all about, because this sure ain't what I call living. We don't go anyplace; we don't do anything; Christ, we hardly have time to go to the toilet. There's always some damn thing that's waiting that you've got to do."

Clearly, such complaints aren't unique to the working class. The pressures of time, the impoverishment of social life, the anxieties about child care, the fear that children will live in a world of increasing scarcity, the threat of divorce—all these are part of family life today, regardless of class. Nevertheless, there are important differences between those in the higher reaches of the class structure and the families of the working class. The simple fact that middle-class families have more discretionary income is enough to make a big difference in the quality of their social life. For they generally have enough money to pay for a baby-sitter once in a while so that parents can have some time to themselves; enough, too, for a family vacation, for tickets to a concert, a play, or a movie. At $7.50 a ticket in a New York or San Francisco movie house, a working-class couple will settle for a $3.00 rental that the whole family can watch together.

Finding time and energy for sex is also a problem, one that's obviously an issue for two-job families of any class. But it's harder to resolve in working-class families because they have so few resources with which to buy some time and privacy for themselves. Ask about their sex lives and you'll be met with an angry, "What's that?" or a wistful, "I wish." When it happens, it is, as one woman put it, "on the run"—a situation that's particularly unsatisfactory for most women. For them, the pleasure of sex is related to the whole of the interaction—to a sense of intimacy and connection, to at least a few relaxed, loving moments. When they can't have these, they're likely to avoid sex altogether—a situation the men find equally unsatisfactory.

"Sex?" asks Lisa Scranton, a white twenty-nine-year-old mother of three who feigns a puzzled frown, as if she doesn't quite know the meaning of the word. "Oh yeah, that; I remember now," she says, her lips smiling, her eyes sad. "At the beginning, when we first got together, it was WOW, real hot, great. But after a while it cools down, doesn't it? Right now, it's down the toilet. I wonder, does it happen to everybody like that?" she asks dejectedly.

"I guess the worst is when you work different shifts like we do and you get to see each other maybe six minutes a day. There's no time for sex. Sometimes we try to steal a few minutes for yourselves but, I don't know, I can't get into it that way. He can. You know how men are; they can do it any time. Give them two minutes, and they can get off. But it takes me time; I mean, I like to feel close, and you can't do that in three minutes. And there's the kids; they're right here all the time. I don't want to do it if it means being interrupted. Then he gets mad, so sometimes I do. But it's a problem, a real problem."

The men aren't content with these quick sexual exchanges either. But for them it's generally better than no sex at all, while for the women it's often the other way around.

"You want to talk about sex, huh?" asks Lisa's husband, Chuck, his voice crackling with anger. "Yeah, I don't mind; it's fine, only I got nothing to talk about. Far as I'm concerned, that's one of the things I found out about marriage. You get married, you give up sex. We hardly ever do it anymore, and when we do, it's like she's doing me a favor.

"Christ, I know the way we've got to do things now isn't great," he protests, running a hand through his hair agitatedly. "We don't see each other but a few minutes a day, but I don't see why we can't take five and have a little fun in the sack. Sure, I like it better when we've got more time, too. But for her, if it can't be perfect, she gets all wound and uptight and it's like . . ." He stops, groping for words, then explodes, "It's like screwing a cold fish."

She isn't just a "cold fish," however. The problems they face are deeper than that. For once such conflicts arise, spontaneity takes flight and sex becomes a problem that needs attention rather than a time out for pleasure and renewal. Between times, therefore, he's busy calculating how much time has passed: "It's been over two weeks"; nursing his wounds: "I don't want to have to beg her"; feeling deprived and angry: "I don't know why I got married." When they finally do come together, he's disappointed. How could it be otherwise, given the mix of feelings he brings to the bed with him—the frustration and anger, the humiliation of feeling he has to beg her, the wounded sense of manhood.

Meanwhile, she, too, is preoccupied with sex, not with thoughts of pleasure but with figuring out how much time she has before, as she puts it, "he walks around with his mouth stuck out. I know I'm in real big trouble if we don't do it once a week. So I make sure we do, even if I don't want to." She doesn't say those words to him, of course. But he knows. And it's precisely this, the knowledge that she's servicing him

rather than desiring him that's so hard for him to take.

The sexual arena is one of the most common places to find a "his and her" marriage—one marriage, two different sex lives.[3] Each partner has a different story to tell; each is convinced that his or her version is the real one. A husband says mournfully, "I'm lucky if we get to make love once a week." His wife reports with irritation, "It's two, sometimes three times a week." It's impossible to know whose account is closest to the reality. And it's irrelevant. If that's what they were after, they could keep tabs and get it straight. But facts and feelings are often at war in family life. And nowhere does right or wrong, true or false count for less than in their sexual interactions. It isn't that people arbitrarily distort the truth. They simply report their experience, and it's feeling, not fact, that dominates that experience; feeling, not fact, that is their truth.

But it's also true that, especially for women, the difference in frequency of sexual desire can be a response—sometimes conscious, sometimes not—to other conflicts in the marriage. It isn't that men never withhold sex as a weapon in the family wars, only that they're much more likely than women to be able to split sex from emotion, to feel their anger and still experience sexual desire. For a man, too, a sexual connection with his wife can relieve the pressures and tensions of the day, can make him feel whole again, even if they've barely spoken a word to each other.

For a woman it's different. What happens—or, more likely, what doesn't happen—in the kitchen, the living room, and the laundry room profoundly affects what's possible in the bedroom. When she feels distant, unconnected, angry; when her pressured life leaves her feeling fragmented; when she hasn't had a real conversation with her husband for a couple of days, sex is very far from either her mind or her loins. "I run around busy all the time, and he just sits there, so by the time we go to bed, I'm too tired," explains Linda Bloodworth, a white thirty-one-year-old telephone operator.

"Do you think your lack of sexual response has something to do with your anger at your husband's refusal to participate more fully in the household?" I ask.

Her eyes smoldering, her voice tight, she snaps, "No, I'm just tired, that's all." Then noticing something in my response, she adds, "I know what you're thinking; I saw that look. But really, I don't think it's *because* I'm angry; I really am tired. I have to admit, though, that I tell him if he helped more, maybe I wouldn't be so tired all the time. And," she adds defiantly, "maybe I wouldn't be."

Some couples, of course, manage their sexual relationship with greater ease. Often that's because they have less conflict in other areas of living. But whether they accommodate well or poorly, for all two-job families, sex requires a level of attention and concern that leaves most people wanting much of the time. "It's a problem, and I tell you, it has to be well planned," explains thirty-four-year-old Dan Stolman, a black construction worker. "But we manage okay; we make dates or try to slip it in when the baby's asleep and my daughter's out with a friend or something. I don't mean things are great in that department. I'm not always satisfied and neither is Lorraine. But what can you do? We try to do the best we can. Sex isn't all there is to a marriage, you know. We get along really well, so that makes up for a lot.

"What I really miss is that we don't ever make love anymore. I mean, we have sex like I said, but we don't have the kind of time you need to make love. We talk about getting away for an overnight by ourselves once in a while. Lorraine's mother would come watch the kids if we asked her; the problem is we don't have any extra cash to spare right now."

Time and money—precious commodities in short supply. These are the twin plagues of family life, the missing ingredi-

ents that combine to create families that are both frantic and fragile. Yet there's no mystery about what would alleviate the crisis that now threatens to engulf them: A job that pays a living wage, quality child-care facilities at rates people can pay, health care for all, parental leave, flexible work schedules, decent and affordable housing, a shorter work week so that parents and children have time to spend together, tax breaks for those in need rather than for those in greed, to mention just a few. These are the policies we need to put in place if we're to have any hope of making our families stable and healthy.

What we have, instead, are families in which mother goes to work to relieve financial distress, only to find that time takes its place next to money as a source of strain, tension, and conflict. Time for the children, time for the couple's relationship, time for self, time for social life—none of it easily available for anyone in two-job families, not even for the children, who are hurried along at every step of the way.[4] And money! Never enough, not for the clothes children need, not for the doctor's bill, not for a vacation, not even for the kind of child care that would allow parents to go to work in peace. But large as these problems loom in the lives of working-class families, difficult as they are to manage, they pale beside those they face when unemployment strikes, especially if it's father who loses his job.

NOTES

1. See Daniel Stern, *The Interpersonal World of the Infant* (New York: Basic Books, 1985), who argues that a child's capacity for self-reflection coincides with the development of language.
2. For an excellent analysis of the increasing amount of time Americans spend at work and the consequences to family and social life, see Juliet B. Schor, *The Overworked American* (New York: Basic Books, 1992). See also Carmen Sirianni and Andrea Walsh, "Through the Prism of Time: Temporal Structures in Postindustrial America," in Alan Wolfe, ed., *America at Century's End* (Berkeley: University of California

Press, 1991), for their discussion of the "time famine."

3. For the origin of the term "his and her marriage," see Jessie Bernard, *The Future of Marriage* (New York: Bantam Books, 1973).

4. David Elkind, *The Hurried Child* (New York: Addison-Wesley, 1981).

QUESTIONS FOR DISCUSSION

1. In what ways does the economy force families to invent solutions to everyday family problems, such as child care and housework? How are these solutions shaped by gender ideology?

2. Are there problems faced by working-class families that middle-class families don't experience?

3. Lack of social supports—specifically, decent affordable child care, flexible work schedules, and parental leave— contribute to the psychic suffering of families. Given Rubin's perspective, do you think that the lack of these supports is a social problem?

33

LESBIANS BLURRING THE BOUNDARIES AND TRANSFORMING THE MEANING OF PARENTHOOD AND KINSHIP

GILLIAN A. DUNNE

The extension of educational and employment opportunities for women, together with widening experience of the "plastic" nature of sexualities (Giddens 1992, 57), has enabled increasing numbers of Western women to construct independent identities and lifestyles beyond traditional marriage, motherhood, and indeed, heterosexuality (Dunne 1997). As contemporary women's identities expand to incorporate the expectations and activities that have been traditionally associated with masculinity, there has not been an equivalent shift of male identity, let alone practice, into the traditional

domains of women. Exceptions not withstanding (Blaisure and Allen 1995; Doucet 1995; Ehrensaft 1987; VanEvery 1995), a distinctly asymmetrical division of labor remains the majority pattern (Berk 1985; Brannen and Moss 1991; Ferri and Smith 1996; Gregson and Lowe 1995; Hochschild 1989). The intransigent nature of the gender division of labor means that women continue to perform the bulk of domestic work and that mothers bear the brunt of the social and economic penalties associated with caring for children. Men's relative freedom from the time constraints and labor associated with the home and parenting enables them to be more single-minded in the pursuit of employment opportunities and retain their labor market advantages.

From *Gender & Society*, 2000, 14(1):11–35, Copyright © 2000 by Sage Publications, Inc. Reprinted by permission of Sage Publications, Inc.

The perceived contradiction between employment success and motherhood has led to a growth in the numbers of women opting into a paid-working life and out of motherhood (Campbell 1985, 5–8; Morell 1994, 11). Changing patterns of household and family formation have stimulated debates in Europe and North America as to whether there has been a decline in the importance of kinship and family life (Popeno 1988; Scott 1997). Given the way that motherhood represents a core signifier of femininity, and the powerful social pressure on married couples to have children, academic interest is turning to voluntary childlessness (Campbell 1985; Abshoff and Hird 1998; McAllister and Clarke 1998; Morell 1994). . . .

While contemporary women begin to see the demands of motherhood as conflicting with their newly won bid for autonomy, there has been a recent shift in attitudes toward parenting among the lesbian population. A rising awareness of alternatives to heterosexual reproduction has led to the growing recognition that their sexuality does not preclude the possibility of lesbian and gay people having children. In Britain and in the United States, we are witnessing the early stages of a "gayby" boom, a situation wherein lesbian women and gay men are opting into parenthood in increasing numbers. . . .

. . . I argue that an attentiveness to the gender dynamic of sexuality illuminates additional challenges that arise when women combine with women to rear children—the possibility of showing what can be achieved when gender different as a fundamental structuring principle in interpersonal relationships is minimized (see Dunne 1997, 1998a). I suggest a complex and contradictory situation for lesbians who have opted into motherhood via donor insemination. By embracing motherhood, lesbians are making their lives "intelligible" to others—their quest to become parents is often enthu-siastically supported by family and heterosexual friends. However, their sexuality both necessitates and facilitates the redefinition of the boundaries, meaning, and content of parenthood. When women parent together, the absence of the logic of polarization to inform gender scripts, and their parity in the gender hierarchy, means that, to borrow Juliet's words, "We have to make it up as we go along." Their similarities as women insist on high levels of reflexivity and enable the construction of more egalitarian approaches to financing and caring for children. In this way, some of the more negative social consequences of motherhood can be transformed. Although not unique in their achievements, nor assured of their success, women parenting with women have a head start over heterosexual couples because of their structural similarities and the way that egalitarianism is in the interests of both partners.[1] . . .

The Lesbian Household Project

The Lesbian Household Project draws on the experience of 37 cohabiting lesbian couples with dependent children.[2] It is a detailed investigation of the allocation of work and parenting responsibilities between women that aims to provide empirically grounded theoretical insights into divisions of labor more generally. Using a snowball technique, the sample was recruited from across England through a wide range of different sources. The only selection criterion was that partners be living together with at least one dependent child: All who contacted me agreed to participate and were interviewed. . . . There is no reason to assume that the sample is particularly unrepresentative, especially in relation to couples who have experienced donor insemination.

A number of methods, both qualitative and quantitative, innovative and conventional, were used to illuminate respondents' employment, domestic, and caring strategies (see Dunne 1999). After the completion of a background questionnaire, both joint and individual in-depth interviews were carried out, time-use diary data were collected, and participants were contacted again two years after first contact. . . .

Parenting Circumstances

The sample includes 8 households where children were from a previous marriage, 1 household where the children were adopted, and 28 (75 percent) where they had been conceived by donor insemination. In the majority of households (60 percent), there was at least one child younger than five; and in 40 percent of households, co-parents were also biological mothers of older, dependent, or nondependent children. The research revealed a fairly unique and important opportunity for women parenting together—the possibility of detaching motherhood from its biological roots through the experience of social motherhood. Interestingly, 15 women in the study expressed a long-standing desire to mother as a social experience but a strong reluctance to experience motherhood biologically. These women had often taken responsibility for siblings in their families of origin and for the children of others usually featured in their lives and occupational choices. This social-biological separation also meant that motherhood is not necessarily ruled out for women who have fertility problems. Parenting was depicted as jointly shared in 30 households (80 percent). As we will see in the three case studies, in contrast to men who share mothering (Ehrensaft 1987) yet remain happy with the identity of father, the singularity and exclusivity of the identity of mother represented a major problem for women parenting together. . . .

Lesbian motherhood undermines a core signifier of heterosexuality and challenges heterosexual monopoly of and norms for parenting. The social hostility toward those parents and children who transgress the sanctity of heterosexual reproduction is such that the decision to become a mother by donor insemination can never be easily made. Typically, respondents described a lengthy period of soul-searching and planning preceding the arrival of children. For some, this process lasted as long as seven years. Unlike most women, they had to question their motives for wanting children, to critique dominant ideas about what constitutes a "good" mother and family, and to think about the implications of bringing up children in a wider society intolerant of difference. Informing this process was much research—reading the numerous self-help books that are available on lesbian parenting, watching videos on the topic, and attending discussion groups. . . . For respondents in partnerships, a central part of this process was the exploration of expectations in relation to parenting, for example, attitudes to discipline, schooling, and if and how far responsibilities would be shared. Key considerations related to employment situations. Respondents did not expect or desire a traditional division of labor, and thus timing was often influenced by their preference to integrate child care and income generation. In the meanwhile, potential donors were contacted. Respondents described a fairly lengthy process of negotiation with donors that focused on establishing a mutuality in parenting expectations and, if he was previously unknown to the couple, getting to know each other and developing confidence. While recognizing the generosity of potential donors, some were rejected because of personality clashes or concerns about motives, but more usually, rejection was because a donor wanted too much or too little involvement.

Men featured in the lives of most of the children, and it was not unusual for donors to have regular contact with their offspring (40 percent of households); in three households, fathers were actively co-parenting. This involvement was usually justified in terms of providing children with the opportunity to "normalize" their family arrangements by being able to talk to peers about doing things with father. Donors were usually gay men—and all male co-parents were gay. This preference appeared to be based on three main assumptions. First was the respondents' perceptions of gay men as representing more aware, acceptable, and positive forms of masculinity. Their desire to involve men (donors or other male friends) in the lives of children, particularly boys, was often described as being about counteracting dominant stereotypes of masculinity. Second, because of the particularities of gay men's lifestyles, respondents believed that they would be less likely to renege on agreements. Third, they thought that should a dispute arise, a heterosexual donor (particularly if he were married) had greater access to formal power to change arrangements in relation to access and custody. That none expressed any serious difficulties in relation to father and/or donor involvement attests to the value of the careful negotiation of expectations before the arrival of children. It also says much about the integrity and generosity of the men concerned, although it must be noted that most had preschool-age children, and conflicts of interests may come as the children mature.

In situations where children had been conceived in a previous marriage or heterosexual relationship, there was more diversity and conflict regarding fathers' involvement. In several cases, the father had unsuccessfully contested custody on the grounds of the mother's lesbianism. Indeed, two had appeared on daytime television arguing that their ex-wives' sexuality conflicted with their capacity to be good mothers. There were also examples of good relations between mothers and ex-husbands. While there were several examples of fathers having lost contact with their children, in most cases, respondents suggested that the child or children has more quality time with their fathers after divorce than before. Despite tensions and possible conflict between mothers and ex-husbands, these respondents suggested that they worked hard to maintain their children's relationships with the fathers. Thus, ironically, in this group as well as in the donor insemination group of parents, there are examples of highly productive models of cooperation between women and men in parenting.

The role of fathers and/or donors and other male friends in children's lives reminds us that lesbian parenting does not occur in a social vacuum. While generally hostile to the idea of the privatized nuclear family, respondents were keen to establish more extended family networks of friends and kin. Often, respondents described the arrival of children as bringing them closer to or helping repair difficult relations with their families of origin. Typically, they described a wide circle of friends (lesbian "aunties," gay "uncles," and heterosexual friends) and kin supporting their parenting.

I now want to illustrate some of these themes by drawing on the voices of respondents in two partnerships where parenting was shared and where men were involved.

. . .

Thelma and Louise's Story

I think we go about things in our own way, we don't have the role definition. We get the best of both worlds really. We get to continue along the road with our careers and also to spend time as a family and to enjoy the time with the children. Disadvantages? We could earn more money I suppose if we worked full-time, but then it takes away the point of having children I would say. (Thelma).[3]

It was not unusual for both partners to have experienced biological motherhood as the result of donor insemination while in their relationship. At the time of first contact, four couples were in this situation (this number had risen to seven at the follow-up stage two years later). In these households, children were brought up as siblings, and parenting was equally shared. The experiences of Thelma and Louise are not atypical of mothers in this situation. They have been living together for seven years in an apartment that they own in inner-city Manchester. They have two daughters, Polly, age four, and Stef, age two. Thelma works in desktop publishing, and Louise is a teacher. Like many in the sample, Thelma and Louise operationalize shared parenting by reducing their paid employment to half-time. They both wanted to have children; their decisions about timing and who would go first were shaped by emotional and practical considerations. Thelma needed to build up sufficient clientele to enable self-employment from home, and Louise wanted to gain more secure employment.

Louise: I was a year younger and I wasn't really sorted out work-wise and you were.

Thelma: There were very pragmatic as well as emotional reasons for why I should go first. It was when I started freelancing at this place and then I ended up freelancing because I got pregnant. But that seemed okay anyway. . . . I mean it was alright to take a break. I knew that I could get work.

Louise: And I hadn't got there. And there was time to save up as well. During that time we managed to save up quite a lot,

to get over the small baby time. Before getting out to work again.

By the time Louise was pregnant, two years after Thelma, she was in a much stronger position at work, having undergone retraining. She had secured a permanent position in teaching and, after maternity leave, arranged a job share with a friend. Like women more generally, respondents' careers had rarely progressed in a planned linear manner. Instead, their job histories have a more organic quality (see Dunne 1997)—moving across occupations and in and out of education or training. However, in contrast to married women more generally, where the gender division of labor supports the anticipation of financial dependence on husbands when children are young (Mansfield and Collard 1988), an important consideration in the timing of the arrival of children for most biological mothers in this study was the achievement of certain employment aims that would enable greater financial security and allow time to enjoy the children. Their gender parity and this approach to paid employment meant that there were not major earning differentials between partners. This helps to explain why respondents have greater scope in operationalizing shared caregiving, as their options had not been foreclosed by earlier decisions. Although both partners' working part-time brings a reduced standard of living, it also brings the advantage, as Thelma remarks, of enabling both to continue in their careers.

After several miscarriages with an earlier donor, Thelma finally got pregnant. Again, they used their friendship networks to locate a donor who then took on a "kindly uncle" role.

Louise: He was just living with a friend of ours, it was just brilliant.

Thelma: Yeah, and ended up being a really good friend as well. . . . I got pregnant the first go really.

Interviewer: And then did you have any views on how much involvement he should have?

Thelma: I think we both wanted a known father and yes, if they wanted some involvement, that was fine. The clearly defined lines were, we're the parents of the children—or of the child at that time—and so any kind of parenting decisions would always be ours.

Interviewer: And what will Polly call her donor?

Thelma: His name—and she calls him Daddy Paul. So I mean she doesn't ever really call him Daddy. Either she calls him Paul or Daddy Paul.

Louise: He is a bit like an uncle [to them both] she'd see now and again, you know, he'd be like this kindly uncle figure, who'd take her to the pics and take her to the zoo and that kind of thing. Give her treats.

They originally planned that Paul would be the donor for Louise; however, there were difficulties in conception, so a new donor was found. Hugh, a gay friend of Thelma's brother, who was temporarily living in England, agreed. While Thelma and Louise both wanted to experience motherhood biologically, they viewed parenting as shared, and this situation was legally recognized in their gaining of a joint parental responsibility order.

Louise: We don't just happen to have a relationship and happen to have two children. We always thought joint, that's why the court thing was important to us. They are sisters and I defy anybody to question that. That's very important to us and we also made it clear that if we ever split up, if I depart with Stef into the horizon and Thelma with Polly, that we have joint care for them.

. . . Their interpretation of shared parenting brought them up against the limitations of language to describe a social mother's relationship to a child.

Thelma: They both call us Mum.

Louise: It started off that you were going to be Mum and I was going to be Louise, and then coming up to me giving birth to Stef, it just got a bit kind of funny, so we thought it's not really going to work any more because if they're sisters how come?—it just all didn't work, so now we're both Mums. And they just call us Mum.

Thelma: Stef says Mummy Louise or Mummy Thelma.

Louise: And Polly mostly calls us Louise and Thelma doesn't she?

Thelma: Yeah she does. She calls us both Mum when she wants to, but mostly she calls us by our names.

Louise: The last couple of years she's started calling me Mum.

Some of the immensity of the creative project in which lesbians engage is revealed in the tensions in the last two extracts and in the next. While they describe the children as having two mothers, Louise reminds us of the contingent nature of this. The rule of biological connection is unquestioned in the assumption that in the event of a breakup each will depart into the horizon with her own child. This next extract illustrates other practical difficulties faced by the couple as they engage with the wider society.

Louise: It's a lot easier now because we've both had a child. I don't think I had any role models in terms of being a nonbiological mum. There's a thing that if you want to be acknowledged as a parent, you just had to "come out." It's the only way to explain that you're a parent. And even that is a very hard way to explain you're a parent. My inner circle at work would know and it's funny—I nearly wrote it down one day—because it was just like some days I'd be a parent and some days I wasn't. So it would depend on what day of the week it was and who I was talking to. I think I made it harder for us by me not being called Mum [in the early stages]. Because as soon as people found out you weren't the mum, then they'd just—it was like "who the hell are you then?"

Such is the power of ideas about the singularity and the exclusivity of the identity of "Mum" in a social world structured by heterosexual norms that polarize parenting along lines of gender. Respondents had a store of both amusing and uncomfortable stories about other people's confusions about who was the mother of the child or children or the status of social mothers.

. . . The family has interesting and extensive kinship networks. The children have two fathers. Paul was not out to his elderly parents so they did not know about his child. However, Hugh, who comes to England several times a year to see them, had told his mother.

Louise: I think Hugh was terrified of telling his mother—he's an only child—had a very close relationship with his mother and he was terrified of telling her. And she was absolutely delighted with it—"I'm the *children's* grandmother"—she's Stef's grandmother biologically, but she's also Polly's socially. So she's just been this incredible grandmother.
Thelma: Paul's parents don't know. His parents are quite old, they're in their late eighties and they don't know he's gay and I don't think he'd ever tell them. So for him that one's a secret. But his sister knows.
Louise: I think we'd be more worried by it, but I just guess by the time the kids are old enough—I think you've got to start coming out very confidently once you've kids, you can't be messing around really. And it would worry me I think if—if Paul explained to them [the children], that he's

not been able to tell his parents. I'm just hoping that by the time it comes up, they won't be around any more.

This discussion illustrates several important themes that featured across the sample. First, respondents were keen to avoid keeping secrets from their children about their conception. Second, they articulated high levels of positivity about being lesbian[4]— this was seen as essential for supporting their children in their dealings with the outside world. Third, all expressed the desire to have their social bonds recognized by friends and kin as being equivalent to blood ties. Finally, kinship was calculated in a remarkable variety of ways. Kin appeared highly flexible in this, with countless examples like Hugh's mother. This next discussion illustrates respondents' strength of feelings with respect to recognition.

Louise: And family that we see, all of them without exception treat both children equally. That's the deal basically, they're not allowed to pick and choose.
Thelma: It was the same with Grandma. . . . Part of the deal was that Stef and Polly are sisters and if she took one of them, then she had to, by definition, take on the other.
Louise: We were quite assertive with her—and that's why I'm not seeing my dad, it's because he's still kind of learning to do that, until he really gets his head around it. He can't just send one of them a present and not the other. Actually it looks like he's getting there, doesn't he? He's just about cracked it. . . . My sister, when Polly was born, my sister just said I'm auntie [name], without any—obviously she isn't biologically, but in all senses of the word, she is.
Interviewer: And they wouldn't distinguish between the children?
Louise: No. Nobody who we see regularly would. Even school and things like

that—Stef is Polly's sister. . . . the kind of entry through schools is if you're a sibling and that's kind of a high priority and Stef has entry into that school now, because she's Polly's sister. Although biologically they're nothing.

Without exception, respondents believed that they approached and experienced parenting in ways that were very different from the heterosexual norm. They were redefining the meaning and content of motherhood, extending its boundaries to incorporate the activities that are usually dichotomized as mother and father. Going against prevailing norms was never without difficulties and disappointments. In joint and individual interviews, respondents usually singled out the ability and commitment to communicate as crucial. They spoke of arrangements being constantly subject to negotiation and the need to check in regularly with each other so that routines that may lead to taking the other for granted could be rethought and sources of conflict discussed.

Bonnie and Claudia's Story

We've had a lot of interest and a certain amount of envy from a lot of heterosexual couples who had babies at the same time, because they just haven't had the breaks that we've had from the baby. They've had breaks, but they've felt guilty, whereas we don't particularly feel guilty because we know that Peter's with Philip and they both want to be together. (Claudia)

In three partnerships, donors were actively co-parenting from separate households—becoming a "junior partner in the parenting team" as one father described himself. In two cases, the father's parenting was legally recognized in a joint residency order. Bonnie, Claudia, and Philip share the care of Peter, age two. Bonnie and Claudia have lived together for nine years in a terraced house in inner-city Bristol. Bonnie, Peter's biological mother, works full-time in adult education, and Claudia has a half-time teaching post. They describe and contrast their feelings about wanting to have children:

Claudia: Well, I think it was something that I was looking for when I was looking for a relationship. So I think it was a more immediate thing for me. You were interested in principle. And I knew the father—this is Philip—although not with the view to having children. So you got to know him after we met really. And then the subject came up.

Bonnie: I think for you it had always been like a lifelong thing.

Claudia: I always wanted a baby. I wanted us to have about two.

Bonnie: She was just obsessed with babies, weren't you? Whereas, I wasn't really like that, I come from a big family and I like having lots of people around me. It was more for me that I didn't want to have *not* had children. It's different, because I didn't want to look back and think, Oh Christ, I didn't have any children. But I tend to get very caught up in whatever I'm doing, and I was busy doing my job and having this relationship and our friends. So in a way it was Claudia's enthusiasm and sense of urgency about it that actually pushed us to making a decision, taking some action. And the only reason I ended up having the baby was that Claudia had a whole series of fertility problems. We just always decided, didn't we, that if one of us had a problem the other one would.

Their experience illustrates another fairly unique advantage for women who want to become mothers in a lesbian relationship—if one partner has fertility problems, the other may agree to go through the pregnancy instead. There were three other examples of partners swapping for this reason, and several others expressed their willingness to do so. As mentioned earlier, I was struck by the fact that many respondents desired to be mothers but felt reluctant to experience motherhood biologically. As there is no reason to believe that this feeling is confined to the lesbian population, it must pose a real dilemma for some heterosexual women. The advantage of the possibility of detaching motherhood from biology via social motherhood in lesbian relationships helps explain why co-parenting is so eagerly embraced—there were several examples of women who had advertised their desire to meet other lesbians, specifically mentioning a preference for women with children.

In their negotiations with Philip over the four years that preceded the birth of Peter, they came to the decision that he would be an actively involved father.

Claudia: Philip wanted a child, and he, I think, was also looking for a kind of extended family relationship, wasn't he?—with us and the children. But he also wants his freedom, I suppose, his lifestyle, a lot of which he needs not to have children around for. Yes, so it fits in the sense that what we get is time without Peter, to have a relationship that needs its own sort of nurturing and stuff, and he gets special time with Peter and a real bonding. I mean he's seen Peter every day since he's been born. So he has become part of the family, hasn't he?—in a sense, or we've become part of his. But we live in two separate homes. People sometimes don't realize that.

Claudia's words alert us to another underlying reason for respondents' confidence in fathers and/or donors retaining a more minor role in children's lives—routine child care does not usually fit in with the lifestyles of most men, gay or heterosexual. The masculine model of employment that governs ideas of job commitment and what constitutes a valuable worker is based on the assumption that employees are free from the constraints of child care.

After extended maternity leave, Bonnie returned to her successful career in adult education. At this point, Claudia, despite being the higher earner, reduced her employment hours to half-time so that she could become Peter's main caregiver. Men's superior earnings are often described by egalitarian-minded heterosexual couples as ruling out opportunities for shared parenting (Doucet 1995; Ehrensaft 1987). However, women parenting together, without access to ideologies that polarize parenting responsibilities, bring fresh insights to this impasse, which supports gender inequalities.

Bonnie: We started in a completely different place [from heterosexual couples]. I think we feel it's just much easier to be cooperative and to be more creative in the way that we share out paid work and domestic work, because that's how we look at it. We're constantly chatting about it, aren't we, over the weeks, and saying, "How does it feel now? Are you still thinking about staying on part-time?" and we've talked about what it would be like if I went part-time as well, and could we manage on less money?
Claudia: Yes, and I think the thing that's part of the advantage is that in a conventional setup, although it may be easier to start with, everyone knowing what they are supposed to be doing, but the men don't know their children so they miss out. . . . I'm having a balanced life really.
Bonnie: I think that's why we've got the space to enjoy our child in a way that a lot of heterosexuals perhaps don't. It's so easy to fall in—the man earns slightly more so it makes sense for him to do the

paid work, and women have babies anyway. Because we could potentially each have had the child it's all in the melting pot. Nothing is fixed.

Claudia: And I don't think a lot of women [enjoy mothering]. They think they're going to, but they get isolated and devalued, and lose their self-confidence and self-esteem.

It was not unusual to find the higher earner in a partnership reducing her hours of employment to share care or become the main caregiver. In contradiction to the dictates of rational economic models, this was often justified on the grounds that a person in a higher paid or higher status occupation has more power and may be less penalized for time out than someone in a more marginal position (Dunne 1998a). I would argue that their rationale (like the part-time/part-time solution) can actually make good long-term financial sense. It also illuminates masculine assumptions in relation to value—the idea that market work is superior to caring.

As in the vast majority of households (Dunne 1998a), routine domestic work was fairly evenly divided between Claudia and Bonnie. Their guiding principle was that "neither should be running around after the other." Like most respondents, they spoke of the advantage of the absence of gender scripts guiding who should do what (see Dunne 1998b).

Bonnie: Well, I think one of the main advantages [of being in a lesbian relationship] for me is that unlike heterosexual couples there are no assumptions about how we are going to divide things up and how we're going to cope. Because I know that it's perfectly possible for heterosexuals to do things differently and some share tasks more than others and all the rest of it. But they're still all the time having to work against these kind of very dominant set of assumptions about how

things should be done in heterosexual households, whereas we don't have that.

For heterosexual couples, gender difference not only shapes contributions but provides a lens through which they are judged (Baxter and Western 1998; Berk 1985; Dunne 1998b).

Peter goes to a private nursery three days a week (the costs are shared with Philip), and the rest of his care is divided between Claudia, Bonnie, and Philip.

Bonnie: Philip lives in the next street, and so he can just come round every day after work or pick Peter up from nursery and bring him back and do his tea, bath and things, and then we'll roll in about 6:30 or whenever, or sometimes one of us is here anyway.

Claudia: Yes, we try to work that one of us is always at home, either with him or working at home. . . . Quite often there's days when we both have to commute, so Philip usually covers. . . . He's the only one of us who works locally and he's got a bleep [beeper] as part of his job and it's ideal because the nursery can call at any time if there's an emergency.

Interviewer: It strikes me you've got the most ideal situation!

Bonnie: Yes, we think so! [laughing] We're the envy of the mother and toddler group.

Their experience with Philip provides a radical alternative model of cooperative parenting between women and men, based on a consensual nonsexual relationship with a father who is interested in being actively involved in his child's life. In effect, Philip is prepared to engage in mothering,[5] and in doing so, he shares some of the social penalties associated with this activity—all three parents collaborate in balancing the demands of employment and child care, and the result is the lessening of its overall impact. While Bonnie and Claudia were aware that it was difficult to keep Philip abreast of everyday decision making, they were keen to involve him in major ones. This seemed to work well in practice.

Bonnie: [It's worked] extremely well. We keep being surprised. I mean we keep thinking . . . we're going to have a fundamental disagreement about something. But I don't think there has been really.

In this discussion, we can see some of the risks associated with involving biological fathers in children's lives—the potential for disagreement and conflict. While respondents generally seemed to have exercised high levels of control in relation to the terms and conditions of donor access to children, and arrangements were working well, the gradual extension of legal rights to biological fathers (see Smart and Neale 1999) increases the mothers' dependence on the integrity of these men.

Again, finding the right words to describe their parenting relationship was difficult. Bonnie expresses a common feminist critique of the label *mummy*, which is hostile to ways that it can be employed to subsume other aspects of a woman's identity.

Bonnie: I've always been quite keen that Peter should know what our names are anyway. I think there's something completely depersonalizing about the way women sit around and talk about a child's mummy as if she's got no identity. It's fine if there's a baby in the room and it's your child, but everyone will say, "Ask Mummy, tell Mummy." But you become this amorphous mummy to everybody. All women are sort of mummy, they don't have their own identity. So I've been quite keen that he should grow up knowing that people have roles and names, and that you should be able to distinguish between the two.

Yet, her radicalism is tempered by her recognition and desire to celebrate her special connection with the child, and she becomes swayed by arguments for the best interests of the child.

Bonnie: But I also feel completely contradictory, that there is something very special emotionally about having your own mummy.
Claudia: And then Philip had very strong feelings about it all, didn't he? He'd always been clear that he wanted to be Daddy, and while we went on holiday together last summer, he made it very clear that he thought that in some sense you needed to be recognized as Peter's mother, that that was important, an important thing in terms of what the relationship meant, and that it would be wrong to deny Bonnie that. . . . Yes, he [also thought] that Peter would, if we started him calling both of us Mummy, sooner or later he'd be ridiculed by some of the other children, and then he would have a terrible conflict of loyalties, does he go with the crowd or does he protect us? And that we shouldn't put him in that position. So we went for Mummy, Daddy and Claudia. And then he started calling me Mummy anyway. But now he calls me Addie. [laughter]

This Mummy, Daddy, and Claudia configuration that then evolved into Claudia being called Mummy or the nickname Addie is potentially very undermining of the co-mother. Other couples specifically avoided involving biological fathers to this extent because of such complications of status and role. Claudia's confidence in her relationship with Peter was affirmed through her experience of mothering as main caregiver and, hopefully, by their capacity to be aware of the issues, as the discussion above appears to indicate. Philip's desire for recognition as Daddy is at one level less problematic. He earns this validation through his active involvement in parenting, and because he is not attempting to share fatherhood with a partner, there are no additional complications in relation to exclusion. However, the gender dynamics of this are interesting. While much of the social aspect of Philip's parenting involves the activities of mothering, he is content with the identity of dad. Conversely, in common with the rest of the sample, rather than draw upon dominant polarized heterosexual frameworks—mother/father—respondents extend the meaning of motherhood to include so-called fathering activities such as breadwinning. This raises the wider question, What exactly is a father?

Once again, their parenting is supported by a complex network of kin who have been encouraged to recognize and act upon social as well as biological ties. As they map out the main people supporting their parenting, Bonnie and Claudia discuss the input of kin:

Bonnie: That's my sister Holly and her partner Vickie, who is dyke as well, which is very nice, and they live round the corner as well. So in a sense they are part of our community, very much so, and Vickie was around for the birth. So they lead a different sort of lifestyle in the sense that they haven't got any children, so they're definitely sort of aunts that come in and do babysitting and things. They're sort of busy but they're important, and we promote the relationship actually, don't we?

Interviewer: What about Philip's parents? Do they have any . . . ?

Bonnie: Yes, there's Philip's mum and dad. They see him two or three times a year—it's only been a year and a half, but they've made a lot of effort. They came down just after his birth.

It is no simple act, however, for extended family to claim kinship ties in these nontra-ditional situations that require coming to terms with a relative's sexuality. While part of being lesbian and gay is about learning how to come out to self and others, I think we have given scant attention to the work involved when heterosexual family members, particularly elderly parents, claim kinship ties that require coming out on behalf of others. For Philip's parents, it was easier for them to explain his entry into fatherhood to other family members by inventing a complicated story about Philip and Bonnie being or having been lovers.

Claudia: They told all their family that Bonnie and Philip have a kind of relationship.

Bonnie: His parents lied, basically.

Claudia: [The story being that] They're not living together any more because Bonnie is already living with this other woman who is a nurse and has got a mortgage and it would be too complicated to change things.

Bonnie: They absolutely want Peter to be their grandson and they love that, and I think in their own head they're dealing with it, they're very nice to us both, aren't they? They send us joint cards and progress reports.

Claudia: We even slept in a double bed in their house once.

Bonnie: Yes, they accept it, you can see, on one level. But obviously they can't fully accept it, they can't tell their friends. So that's how that goes.

As Claudia had been adopted, her family was used to the complexity of kinship relations.

Claudia: [My family is] all interested and very supportive but there's no one nearby to pop in. . . . They all only see him about twice a year. Family get-togethers, isn't it?

Bonnie: And you made an effort to go and visit and show Peter off.

Claudia's biological parents were described as treating Peter similarly to their other grandchildren, all of whom receive scant attention. Interestingly, in the case of her adoptive parents, in common with many other respondents, the arrival of children helped rebuild bridges after earlier estrangement over issues of sexuality.

Claudia: Well, [my adoptive parents] have much more difficulty with me being a lesbian than my parents do. And they've virtually rejected me really. Not immediately when I came out but later on. And then [my adoptive mother], since she found out that I was trying to get pregnant, has been completely supportive. I think [my adoptive father] finds it more difficult.

Interviewer: And she thinks of Peter as your son?

Claudia: Yes. And she describes herself as his adoptive grandmother.

Bonnie's mother could see distinct advantages in her daughter's parenting arrangements:

> My mum is Peter's grandmother. She's very, very involved with Peter, totally supportive of this relationship, and thinks that—why hadn't anyone ever mentioned it before? It seems a great way to bring up children. Having brought seven children up without the help of my father, she now thinks it's wonderful not only to have a supportive woman partner but a father involved who lives up the road. It's great. Peter sees more of his father than most children probably do. So she's good.

Aside from a wide circle of friends, Bonnie, Claudia, and Philip had support from parents and siblings, with their son Peter looking forward to presents from four sets of grandparents.

Conclusion

These two stories illustrate many common themes that emerged across the sample, particularly the creativity and cooperation that appear to characterize much of the parenting experience of lesbian couples. I have focused on the involvement of fathers and/or donors and on the complexity of kinship to show how like and unlike these families are to other sorts of family formations. I could equally have looked at the important friendship networks that supported their parenting, the presence of lesbian aunties and heterosexual friends. Lesbian families are usually extended families, supported by elaborate networks of friends and kin.

In common with single lesbian mothers in the United States (Lewin 1993, 9), kin occupy an important place in respondents' accounts of their social interaction. My focus on couples in shared parenting situations reveals other interesting dimensions of kinship: the complexity of these relations and the importance respondents placed on having nonbiogenetic ties recognized and validated by family of origin. Demanding recognition of kinship ties in a same-sex context represents an extremely radical departure from the economy of sexual difference underpinning conceptions of kinship more generally (see Butler 1990, 38–43). Considerable effort was involved in achieving this end by all parties. One reason for their usual success in this respect, I believe, is that the presence of children helps make intelligible a lifestyle that can appear strange and "other" to heterosexual observers. This is supported, I think, by the way that often quite strained or difficult relationships between respondents and their parents were transformed as daughters became mothers and their parents became grandparents. Many respondents experienced high levels of enthusiastic support from heterosexual friends in their quest to become, and their experience of being, parents.

Regardless of whether parenting was shared, mothering was usually carried out in a context where mothers experienced a great deal of practical and emotional support from their partners, where routine domestic responsibilities were fairly evenly shared, and where there was a mutual recognition of a woman's right to an identity beyond the home. Beyond the confines of heterosexuality, they had greater scope to challenge the connections between biological and social motherhood and fatherhood. By deprivileging the biological as signifier of motherhood (although this appears to be contingent on the relationship remaining intact) and the capacity to mother, many were actively engaged in extending the meaning, content, and consequence of mothering to include both partners (or even fathers) on equal terms.

Lesbians opting into motherhood in a hostile world have to engage in an extended period of planning: Nothing can be taken for granted. The pleasure they experienced in spending time with their children and the high value they attached to mothering are often reflected in the employment strategies of both parents. Thus, biological motherhood was a poor predictor of differences in income and employment hours within partnerships. They were advantaged by their structural similarities as women and their positioning outside conventionality. In resolving the contradiction between time for children and the need to generate income, their options had not usually been foreclosed by earlier employment choices shaped by the anticipation and/or experience of a gender division of labor (Dunne 1997, 2000). They consequently have greater scope to operationalize their egalitarian ideals in relation to parenting. The high

value they attached to nurturing, together with their desire to be fair to each other, meant that within reason they were prepared to experience a reduced standard of living (see Dunne 1998a). Their views about what constitutes shared parenting were less distorted by ideologies that dichotomized parenting along lines of gender in such a way that men can be seen and see themselves as involved fathers when they are largely absent from the home (Baxter and Western 1998, Ferri and Smith 1996). Consequently, their solution to the contradiction was to integrate mothering and breadwinning.

In their everyday lives of nurturing, housework, and breadwinning, respondents provide viable alternative models for parenting beyond heterosexuality. While our focus is on lesbian partners, anecdotal evidence suggests that lesbians are also founding parenting partnerships on the basis of friendship—with gay men or other lesbians. By finding a way around the reproductive limitations of their sexuality, they experience their position as gatekeepers between children and biological fathers in an unusual way. Ironically, we find examples of highly productive models of cooperation between women and men in bringing up children. Unhampered by the constraints of heterosexuality, they can choose to include men on the basis of the qualities they can bring into children's lives. It is no accident, I believe, that respondents usually chose to involve gay men. These men were seen as representing more acceptable forms of masculinity, and their sexuality barred them from some of the legal rights that have been extended to heterosexual fathers.

Their positioning outside conventionality and the similarities they share as women enable and indeed insist upon the redefinition of the meaning and content of motherhood. Thus, when choosing to opt into motherhood, they are anticipating something very different from the heterosexual norm. Some felt that their gender parity and commitment to egalitarianism enabled a conscious recognition and articulation of the power that was perceived to derive from the actual bodily experience of creating another human being. Within the gender context that frames their arrangements, they felt safe to identify and celebrate this special biological and psychological connectedness with a child because it did not ultimately lead to polarization within the partnership in relation to access to other sources of social reward.

At one level, motherhood bridges the gap between the known and the unknown. It represents a common currency where we can predict the routines, pleasures, and concerns of parents, and sexuality can be sidelined. At another level, however, we have seen that their experience of motherhood seems quite different from that of most heterosexual mothers. Importantly, by building bridges in this way, friends, colleagues, and extended family bear witness to these differences, and their experience reflects back into the lives of others. These alternative reference points may help to reinforce women's confidence in their critique of conventional assumptions shaping heterosexual practice. . . . My concern is that in our contemporary preoccupation with . . . exotic and exciting aspects of sexual radicalism, we ignore the challenge that ordinary lesbian women and gay men pose to the status quo through their prioritization of egalitarian ideals. Central to the reproduction of the social order (institutional heterosexuality, gender inequality) are ideological processes that reify and legitimize current arrangements by rendering invisible or stigmatizing alternatives. The visibility of lesbian parents in the mainstream as they negotiate with schools, health workers, neighbors, employers and coworkers, and heterosexual parents

helps to make intelligible the unimaginable to others. They create a cognitive dissonance that may enable others to evaluate and move beyond the taken-for-grantedness of heterosexuality. As women together, they renegotiate the boundaries, meaning, and content of parenthood. By doing so, they undermine much of the logic shaping conventional divisions of labor, for example, that specialization is the most efficient and effective way to finance and run a household and care for children, that prioritizing the career of the higher earner makes long-term financial sense, and that biological motherhood is the precursor of the capacity to mother. They challenge conventional wisdom by showing the viability of parenting beyond the confines of heterosexuality. Rather than being incorporated into the mainstream as honorary heterosexuals, by building bridges between the known and the unknown, their lives represent, I believe, a fundamental challenge to the foundation of the gender order.

NOTES

Author's note: I would like to dedicate this article to the memory of Linda Edwards, who graciously shared her story of mothering with me during the last few days of her struggle with breast cancer. Her courage and humanity were an inspiration throughout the study. My thanks to all participants in the Lesbian Household Project and to the following for their helpful comments on this article: Shirley Prendergast, Nina Hallowell, Ginny Morrow, Shelley Sclater, Beth Schneider, and the anonymous reviewers, particularly the one who raved!

1. Both VanEvery (1995) and Ehrensaft (1987, 20) mention that women are the driving force in the quest to achieve and maintain egalitarianism. Both comment on the extent to which structural factors, such as men's superior earnings, and wider social expectations mediate success in this respect.
2. I am grateful to the Economic and Social Research Council for funding this recently completed three-year project (reference number R00023 4649).

3. To maintain confidentiality, the names of participants and their children and their geographical location and occupations have been changed. To give some sense of their employment circumstances, I have assigned similar kinds of occupations.
4. I was struck by the almost unanimous confidence of the sample in their sexuality—respondents saw their lesbian identity as a great source of advantage. Their identification as lesbian rather than gay was also evidence of their usually feminist inclinations. In a previous life history study of lesbians who were generally not mothers (Dunne 1997), there were more examples of ambiguity in this respect. I suspect respondents' self-assurance is related to a combination of factors including historical period, being in fulfilling relationships, their achievement of motherhood, and the process of soul-searching that preceded this.
5. Silva (1996) draws a useful distinction between motherhood, a uniquely female experience, and mothering, which, although usually a female practice, can be performed by either gender.

REFERENCES

Abshoff, K., and M. Hird. 1998. Subverting the feminine: The case of child-free women. Paper presented at the Annual Meeting of the British Sociological Association, University of Edinburgh.

Baxter, J., and M. Western. 1998. Satisfaction with housework: Examining the paradox. *Sociology* 1:101–20.

Berk, S. F. 1985. *The gender factory: The apportionment of work in American households.* New York: Plenum.

Blaisure, K., and K. Allen. 1995. Feminists and the ideology and practice of marital equality. *Journal of Marriage and the Family* 57:5–19.

Brannen, J., and P. Moss. 1991. *Managing mothers: Dual earner households after maternity leave.* London: Unwin Hyman.

Butler, J. 1990. *Gender trouble: Feminism and the subversion of identity.* New York: Routledge.

Campbell, E. 1985. *The childless marriage.* London: Tavistock.

Doucet, A. 1995. Gender equality, gender difference and care. Ph.D. diss., Cambridge University, Cambridge, UK.

Dunne, G. A. 1997. *Lesbian lifestyles: Women's work and the politics of sexuality.* London: MacMillan.

———. 1998a. "Pioneers behind our own front doors": Towards new models in the organization of work in partnerships. *Work Employment and Society* 12(2):273–95.

———. 1998b. A passion for "sameness"? Sexuality and gender accountability. In *The new family?* edited by E. Silva and C. Smart. London: Sage.

———. 1999. Balancing acts: On the salience of sexuality for understanding the gendering of work and family-life opportunities. In *Women and work: The age of post-feminism?* edited by L. Sperling and M. Owen. Aldershot, UK: Ashgate.

———. 2000. Lesbians as authentic workers? Institutional heterosexuality and the reproduction of gender inequalities. *Sexualities.* In press.

Ehrensaft, D. 1987. *Parenting together: Men and women sharing the care of the children.* New York: Free Press.

Ferri, E., and K. Smith. 1996. *Parenting in the 1990s.* London: Family Policy Studies Center.

Giddens, Anthony. 1992. *The transformation of intimacy.* Cambridge, MA: Polity.

Gregson, N., and M. Lowe. 1995. *Servicing the middle-classes: Class, gender and waged domestic labor.* London: Routledge.

Hochschild, A. R. 1989. *The second shift.* New York: Avon.

Lewin, E. 1993. *Lesbian mothers.* Ithaca, NY: Cornell University Press.

Mansfield, P., and J. Collard. 1988. *The beginning of the rest of your life: A portrait of newly wed marriage.* London: MacMillan.

McAllister, F., and L. Clarke. 1998. *Childless by choice: A study of childlessness in Britain.* London: Family Policy Studies Centre.

Morell, C. 1994. *Unwomanly conduct.* London: Routledge.

Popeno, D. 1988. *Disturbing the nest: Family change and decline in modern societies.* New York: Aldine.

Scott, J. 1997. Changing households in Britain: Do families still matter? *Sociological Review* 45(4):591–620.

Silva, E. 1996. The transformation of mothering. In *Good enough mothering?* edited by E. Silva and C. Smart. London: Routledge.

Smart, C., and B. Neale. 1999. *Family fragments.* Cambridge, MA: Polity.

VanEvery, J. 1995. *Heterosexual women changing the family: Refusing to be a "wife."* London: Taylor Francis.

1. Given that the structural similarity of lesbian women in the economy contributed to their flexible division of labor, would you expect to find a greater egalitarianism in parenting behavior among heterosexual women and men parents with jobs of similar status and pay?

2. Which are more of a challenge to the dominant ideology of family in the United States: the lesbian parents Dunne studied or the women Naples found (see Reading 34) extending mothering into activism?
3. What can men gain from openness to the lesbian models of parenting?

34

ACTIVIST MOTHERING, COMMUNITY CARETAKING, AND CIVIC WORK

NANCY A. NAPLES

Puerto Rican community worker Nina Reyes's political engagement on the Lower East Side of Manhattan spanned a period of thirty years. During this time, Nina said she was involved in any and all community actions that affected her local community. From struggles for improved sanitation to child care to voter registration to elder care, Nina's trajectory as a community worker illustrates the theme . . . of doing "just what needed to be done" to fight the problems associated with poverty in the urban United States.

Nina moved from Puerto Rico to the Lower East Side with her family when she was ten years old. Raised by her grandmother who worked as a janitor, Nina cred-

its her grandmother "for all my values and ideals because she guided me to be . . . the best I can." Nina met her husband in high school, married, and went right to work as a secretary in a downtown Manhattan law firm. She became active with her husband through the local settlement house and together they developed a new community-based organization designed to advocate for the issues confronting local residents. She first explained that they felt a need to establish the organization as a response to the infusion of funds, new programs, and "strangers" into the Lower East Side as a result of the War on Poverty. As Nina recalled, "When the antipoverty programs came, they all came in one shot, and nobody knew what was going on. See, a whole bunch of strangers were coming into the community that nobody knew. So that's why we became involved."

Nina also emphasized another event that triggered her community work career. In relating her community work history she was reminded of her response to the sanitation strike that occurred during the same year the antipoverty programs were funded and described it as a key event in her initiation as a community worker.[1] She recalled:

> I will never forget how we got involved. Remember the sanitation strike? We got involved when we saw our community becoming a disaster. We got to the point that we rented a truck and picked up the garbage in the street. I had one child at the time, 1964. We used to take our daughter everywhere we went.

Not surprisingly, as a mother of three children, day care became the next major campaign to draw her political energies. Throughout the early part of the 1960s, Nina undertook community work as an unpaid activity while working full time in an office in downtown Manhattan. When the War on Poverty was declared, she found community-based employment in a day care program funded through the EOA. Nina next became involved in a campaign to register Puerto Rican voters while she also worked to expand day care availability for residents of the Lower East Side. She translated her political engagement in the community into paid community work but remained active in campaigns that went beyond her job definition. She continued to emphasize the importance of voter registration and was active in several local elections.

Nina and her husband played important leadership roles in the community organization they helped to create until the early 1980s, when, she reported, it was besieged by internal conflicts and a type of "dirty tricks" politics. She explained why they resigned from the organization: "The leadership was changing, and there was too much politics, too much dirty tricks. And

when it comes to that I don't want to deal with it. I don't like when you have to do harm to somebody to help somebody else." . . .

Nina expressed her frustration with the increased problems in her community since the 1970s and the persistent cutback of funds to support community work programs. When I asked her how she remained committed to community work despite the difficulties, Nina interpreted her lifelong commitment through her deep personal awareness of how racism circumscribed the opportunities of the poor—a response given by most of the African American and Latina resident community workers.

> How do I keep it alive? Because I see the hurt. It's like something that bothers me, and I must say it. You know all these stores, Japanese stores, Korean stores, what I see there is mostly people from Mexico [working in them], and those people work! And when I see them, for some reason I see my father, when my father came to this country. That he had to work so hard for so little money. . . . My father was very good with numbers. . . . When he came here he went and worked in farms in Philadelphia. And then he moved to New York, and he worked in supermarkets like that, driving the deliveries and all that. When, just because he didn't have that knowledge of English he had to work for so minimal, low pay. My father was a very smart man. . . . My father loved poetry. My father read poetry, and he loved to read. . . . He couldn't do more in his life because of the oppression that we live in. And every time I see these Mexican people, it breaks my heart. And I see my father.

Because she had witnessed her father fighting such oppressive forces, Nina was especially concerned about the treatment of

Latino immigrants and was highly critical of California governor Pete Wilson's attacks against Mexican immigrants who, she exclaimed, "are being taken advantage of." With a heightened awareness of the problems faced by immigrants to this country, Nina said she reached out to "newcomers" in her neighborhood and attempted to introduce them to the programs designed to help them learn English, continue their education, or secure food and shelter.

This form of community caretaking was a consistent theme that appeared throughout the oral narratives of the resident community workers and comprises a central component of activist mothering. The notion of activist mothering also highlights how political activism formed a central component of the community workers' motherwork and community caretaking. As a sociological concept, the term captures the ways in which politics, mothering, and labor comprised mutually constitutive spheres of social life for the community workers. It serves to counter traditional constructions of politics as limited to electoral politics or membership in social movement organizations as well as constructions of motherwork and reproductive labor that neglect women's political activism on behalf of their families and communities. . . .

For example, the notion of activist mothering draws attention to the caretaking activities of women who do not have children of their own and who conceive of their community work as mothering.[2] For the resident community workers, paid work formed one component of their mothering practices just as mothering practices formed one component of their paid labor. The notion of activist mothering also draws attention to the caretaking work of women who do not have children of their own and who conceive of their community work as mothering activity. . . .

Defining "Activist Mothering"

I did not begin this research with an interest in mothering per se, although I did wish to examine how mothering activities contributed to, or inhibited, political participation. As I reexamined the activists' personal narratives, I recognized how a broadened definition of mothering was woven in and through their paid and unpaid community work which in turn was infused with political activism. The traditional definition of mothering—nurturing work with children who are biologically or legally related and cared for within the confines of a bounded family unit—failed to capture the community workers' activities and self-perceptions of their motherwork. The term "activist mothering," generated through close reading and rereading of the narratives, better expresses the complex ways the resident community workers, especially the African American women and Latinas, made sense of their own activities.

Activist mothering not only involves nurturing work for those outside one's kinship group, but also encompasses a broad definition of actual mothering practices. The community workers defined "good mothering" to comprise all actions, including social activism, that addressed the needs of their children and community—variously defined as their racial–ethnic group, low-income people, or members of a particular neighborhood. In addition to testifying before public officials, all the resident community workers participated in public protests and demonstrations for improved community services, increased resources, and expansion of community control. Ann Robinson, for example, described her involvement in protests to improve health care, public education, child care, and social services for those residing in her Manhattan neighborhood. Resident community workers who did not have children also viewed their relationship to their communities as one of caretaker. Since most of the resident community workers shared the same race and class background and grew up in the same neighborhoods as those on whose behalf they worked, they saw themselves as beneficiaries of their community work efforts as well.

All the resident community workers with children said that, for the most part, a large portion of their community work derived from concern for their children's well-being. The four African American women and three Puerto Rican women who did not have children traced their motivations for community work to a variety of social problems manifest in their communities and viewed their activism as community caretaking more than politics. The term "activist mothering" highlights the community workers' gendered conceptualization of activism on behalf of their communities, often defined beyond the confines of their families, households, and neighborhoods. Central to their constructions of "community" was a convergence of racial–ethnic identification and class affiliation.

Activist mothering includes self-conscious struggles against racism, sexism, and poverty. Racial discrimination was one of the consistent themes expressed by all the African American and Puerto Rican community workers, and struggles against racism formed a basic undercurrent for most of their community work. Similarity between Latina and African American community workers also emanated from their social location in low-income communities. As residents of poor communities, many of the women described how the deteriorating conditions as well as the inadequate education and health services that threatened their children's growth and development fostered an ongoing commitment to community work. Their own mothers helped interpret experiences with racism and classism and instilled in their daughters a belief in their ability to overcome these obstacles. . . . Fathers also contributed to the cross-generational continuity of activist mothering. Therefore, the conceptualization of activist mothering challenges essentialist interpretations of mothering practices.

Literature discussing women of color's activism further highlights the ways that racism and a commitment to fight for social justice infuses their political analyses and political practices.[3] Women of color as activist mothers, especially those living in poor neighborhoods, must fight against discrimination and the oppressive institutions that shape their daily lives and, consequently, as mothers they model strategies of resistance for their children. For example, African American women's struggle against racism infuses their mothering practices inside and outside their "homeplace."[4] Lessons carved out of the experiences of "everyday racism" contribute to mothering practices include "handing down the knowledge of racism from generation to generation."[5] Referring to this practice in her discussion of homeplace as "a site of resistance," bell hooks (1990, 46) explains: "Working to create a homeplace that affirmed our beings, our blackness, our love for one another was necessary resistance." hooks argues that "any attempt to critically assess the role of black women in liberation struggle must examine the way political concern about the impact of racism shaped black women's thinking, their sense of home, and their modes of parenting" (p. 46).

Patricia Hill Collins (1990) describes the broad-based nature of mothering in the African American community and highlights the work of community "othermothers" who help build community institutions and fight for the welfare of their neighbors.

She argues that the activities of othermothers who form part of the extended kinship networks in the African American community pave the way for the political activism of community othermothers. According to Collins (1991a, 129), "[a] substantial portion of African American women's status in African American communities stems not only from their roles as mothers in their own families but from their contributions as community othermothers to black community development as well." Collins (1991a) and Stanlie James (1993), among others, argue that African and African American women exemplify this tradition of othermothering and community othermothering that can be found in a variety of places and across time.[6] However, these patterns are not natural expressions of a black woman's social or cultural identity. Rather, as analysis of women's community work demonstrates, they are developed in dynamic relationship with particular historic conditions and transmitted through self-conscious socialization practices and political struggles. For example, as Collins and James both point out, African and African American women pass down cultural traditions as well as survival and resistance strategies from one generation to another (also see K. Scott 1991).

Whiteness cushioned the four European American resident community workers from facing the dynamics of racial oppression until they became active in community-based struggles. For one of the four women, such recognition never materialized. Harriet Towers of Philadelphia did not see racism as a problem in her community work and defined the neighborhood in which she worked as "an integrated one," adding, "I've never been prejudiced myself. I could always work with most everyone." When pressed on this point, she insisted that she always got along with everyone, regardless of race. However, early awareness of class inequality and poverty was central to the narratives of all four white women who were living in low-income neighborhoods when President Johnson launched the War on Poverty. Grace Reynolds of Philadelphia described her childhood as one totally defined by struggles for economic survival. Her mother died when she was young. Her father was a laborer, and the family was very poor. Her involvement in the antipoverty programs was her first political activity. Brenda Rivers said she first recognized the need to become active at the community level when, as a new mother, she moved from a small rural town to Philadelphia. Brenda, a mother of a biracial child, stressed antiracism campaigns as well as struggles against the causes of symptoms of poverty in her geographic community.

Like many of the women of color, white community workers Harriet Towers and Teresa Fraser both described how the political education they received from their parents influenced their commitment to community work. Harriet reported that although her mother was ill most of her life, she was active in the church. Her father, who was a corrections officer, "tried to do everything he could" to help the prisoners. She saw his work with prisoners as an early role model for her commitment to community work.

These four white women's motivations for community work as briefly presented here illustrate four of the processes by which political awareness is raised and political commitment is shaped: fighting to improve the quality of their own children's lives (Brenda Rivers and Teresa Fraser); struggling for economic survival (Grace Reynolds); early childhood socialization (Teresa Fraser and Harriet Towers); and church or civic organizational experiences (Harriet Towers). Most resident African American women and Latina community workers interviewed . . . described all four of these patterns when discussing their motivation to participate in community-based struggles for social and economic justice. . . .

Negotiating Community Work and Family-Based Labor

. . . A broadened definition of mothering . . . infused the community work of the women in this study. For many, this continued the activist mothering practices they witnessed as children in their parents' home. The fusing of community work and family-based labor frequently meant opening their homes to those in need. Ethel Pearls of Philadelphia described how she invited young people, especially those with children, who had no other place to live or who were having difficulties in their own homes to stay with her and her family. By 1984 when I interviewed her, Ethel's children were grown and out of the house. She continued to offer her home to others even after she was laid off from her paid community work position. She explained: "They always tell me I had a household of people and if anybody just doesn't have anywhere to stay, they come here." Ethel introduced me to a young woman staying in her house and related:

> She's trying to find someplace to stay. I got bedrooms, so until she gets herself straightened out, she and her baby [are] here. I could never have a fancy house, I guess, but my house is usable. Some people have homes that aren't liveable. . . . I don't have anything fancy. I couldn't because everybody just comes along sometimes and just want to talk, and I don't want to say to them: "Don't sit there." . . . I'm 60 years old now, and God has been good to me. I don't think I've lost anything by trying to help.

. . . Historians of the African American family point out the importance of resource sharing for the survival of low-income people, and personal testimony from my research reveals the continuity of this practice among low-income women in contemporary urban neighborhoods.[7] This practice is not limited to the African American community. The Latinas I interviewed were also taught the importance of sharing resources with others in their community, a practice they took into their own activist mothering.

The intricate relationship between community work and family-based labor also generated tension between a worker's caretaking responsibilities for her own children and her caretaking work in the community. Some of the women expressed regret that the extensive hours they spent on community work took them away from their own children. Pat Martell of the Lower East Side, for example, grieved the time she lost with her children, especially her youngest child. Her husband had a steady blue-collar job when she started as an unpaid community worker outside the home. Pat was subsequently offered a paid community work position in a local CAP. After she accepted the position, she became "so involved in what was going on in the community" that she was unable to spend much time with her two children. She gave birth to another child while working for the CAP. With the support of her daughter's aunt who babysat for her during the day, Pat continued community work. She recalled:

> The youngest one, I was working up until the doctor put me in the hospital a week before she was born, and I went back to work when she was three weeks old. I kind of regret that. . . . She's been raised well, though. And her aunt—I don't know what I'd do without her— took care of her. She's okay, but I've missed a lot. I've missed so much. I look at her sometimes, and I think, my God, she's ten years old and I don't really

know her. . . . We haven't done a lot of things and that's on my conscience right now.

Pat's story again illustrates the blurring between family-based labor and community work as well as the contradictions that result from the overlapping demands. The paid community work position quickly became vital to the economic survival of Pat's family. Her husband lost his job as a skilled laborer and accepted employment as a driver, a position that paid little. The salary from community work helped to keep her family just above the poverty line. Through her community work, Pat provided needed income for her family while she remained actively involved in improving their quality of life in other ways; however, it also meant that she had less time to spend with her children. Her dilemma haunts all mothers who must find a way to secure their family's economic and emotional well-being. Fortunately, the resident community workers were situated within an extensive network of othermothers who assisted them with child care and supported their community work. All of the community workers with children mentioned the importance of other women who helped them negotiate the competing demands of unpaid and paid community work and parental responsibilities.

Tensions between family-based labor and community work increased further when paid work took the worker from her home community. A total of three African American women and three Latinas accepted higher paying positions outside their communities. Five of these six women had children. They encountered two of the most common difficulties faced by employed women with children—the lack of quality child care and the inflexibility of employers who refused to recognize the childcare needs of their employees. As a single parent, Maria Calero could not live with the uncertainties and low pay of neighborhood-based community work. She accepted a "professional" position in a city agency. She recalled:

> I had no day care for my son. . . . Finally, I found day care on the Upper West Side [of Manhattan]. . . . I would take two buses to be at the day care at a quarter to nine in the morning. My boss then had a real position about feminists and would say . . . that I had to be a professional, that my circumstances were of no importance to him. I had to be at my job at nine o'clock in the morning so whether [my son] was clinging or not, I had to leave [him].

Maria expressed much sadness over the pain that this abrupt process of separation caused her son each morning. She believed that this experience had a lifelong negative impact on her son which she could never repair.

Despite the difficulty balancing parenting responsibilities and paid employment in a citywide agency, Maria explained how this work experience enhanced her sense of personal and political power. Yet she also said that it took her away from the original enthusiasm that motivated her community work. In her desire to increase her family's economic resources and advance her professional career, she "became uninspired in the job" and increasingly alienated from her personal goals. Her experience of alienation affected how she related to her children. She felt that the position she accepted in order to increase her ability to support her family directly interfered with her emotional and physical availability to her three children.

In contrast, East Harlem community worker Josephine Card shifted her site of work from noncommunity-based factory work to community work. This shift enabled her to remain more involved in the care of her seven children. She left this position as a school aide when her youngest child was born but continued unpaid community work. Through this work, she learned about the antipoverty programs and applied for a paid position. She accepted a job as an assistant supervisor in the CAP in her neighborhood and was promoted to supervisor three months later. The community work position that Josephine accepted was "only a few blocks away" from her home. Her previous jobs as a factory worker, cashier, and school aide did not offer her the same challenge that the community work position provided. She gained a wide range of additional experiences. She designed programs, provided direct services to her community, spoke in public, and, "at one point," supervised a staff of twelve. For Josephine, the community-based work enhanced her availability to her children as well as increased her self-esteem.

Community work activities of women living and working in low-income communities loosened the supposed boundary between home and community in other ways. In addition to the long hours required by community work, the lack of financial security was another source of stress for the worker and her family. Salaries were often withheld when the organizations ran into funding difficulties. For the most part, salaries were low and increases, rare, or at best, inconsequential. Since the community workers seldom distinguished between their unpaid and paid community work, those who were able to accept the uncertainties of community-based employment often continued working without pay during times of financial crises. Carmen Hernandez, a mother of six, laughed when she told me that she made more money working in a downtown Manhattan office when she was eighteen than as a community worker with twenty years' experience. When she was offered a job in 1977, which would provide a large increase in salary, she turned it down because she didn't want to leave the community. Not only did she decline a higher paying position outside the community, she also resigned from her paid position to become a voting member of the agency's board of directors. During most of the 1970s, she juggled her unpaid community work with college, family responsibilities, and the delicatessen she opened to replace her paid community work position. She was busy an average of twelve hours a day. Sometimes she thought:

> Gee, I must be really crazy, because I have some real fantastic skills, and I don't want to go nowhere else. 'Cause I've had several good job offers. . . . I'll never be rich. I'm comfortable. I'm happy. So I really don't think I want any more than that. As long as I'm happy!

Carmen said her decision to stay active in her community and to situate her paid employment there gave her the chance to be closer to her five children. She valued the opportunity to watch them grow, to get to know their friends, and to be available to them. Overall, the community workers' activist mothering had contradictory effects on their children's lives. On the one hand, their activism often took them away from their families and many women described the frustration they felt when they did not have enough time to spend with their children. On the other hand, their activism also improved their children's health care and education as well as provided a foundation for upward mobility, paving the way for their college education, among other opportunities. However, some children experienced reprisals and other forms of discrimination because of their mothers' activism. . . . Yet, by educating their children on the political organization of their social world and modeling activist mothering, some community workers also contributed to their children's commitment to work on behalf of their defined communities. . . .

Conclusion

The contradictions that arose from the community resident workers' negotiation of family-based labor, unpaid community work, and paid work expose how the so-called separate spheres of social life are braided in and through the social relations of community. Most of the resident community workers viewed both their unpaid and paid work as caretaking or nurturing work despite the radical political activities involved. Their involvement in social protests, public speaking, and advocacy as well as grantwriting, budgeting, and other administrative tasks were viewed as a part of a larger struggle—namely, doing "just what needed to be done" to secure economic and social justice for their communities. The dialectical relationship between the dominant discourse on the political and the community workers' practice of community caretaking contributed to a unique form of community-based political activity that differs profoundly from the civic work of middle- and upper-income men and women who volunteer for not-for-profit associations.[8]

The resident community workers also challenged traditional notions of gender and mothering in their work and served as models for their children as well as others in their community. All of the women interviewed said they held onto a strong sense of their personal power and, for many, the example given by other activist mothers helped strengthen their belief, already established by their own mothers, in their power to effect change in their communities. As funds were withdrawn from their organizations and problems within their communities increased, many of the resident workers drew comfort from the help they could offer other residents. Shifting focus from processes of collective action to individual service was an effective way for the resident community workers to remain committed to the work under increasingly harsh economic and political conditions, although it also contributed to a process of depoliticization. For many, this shift in emphasis was an adaptive response to the increasingly conservative political environment as well as a result of the control placed on them by government funding agencies.

The resident workers grew up with a consciousness of discrimination and injustice that further fueled their commitment and informed their political analyses. Dynamics of racism and classism were particularly salient in the narratives of the African American and Latina community workers. However, analyses of sexism and their relationship to feminism were complicated by the ways in which patterns of race and class shaped the community workers' political praxis, and their perceptions of, and direct experience with, the Women's Movement.

NOTES

1. In December of 1963, nineteen hundred members of Local 813 of the International Brotherhood of Teamsters went on strike. The strike affected removal of refuse from commercial establishments like restaurants and other large businesses. The first day was marked by some violence between the strikers and owner-operators who continued to pick up garbage (Apple 1963). An accord was reached after four days (Stetson 1963).

2. Maternalist politics were used by many middle-class women of the later part of the 1800s and early 1900s to justify their movement into the political or public sphere. Seth Koven and Sonya Michel (1993, 4) define maternalism as "ideologies and discourses that exalted women's capacity to mother and applied to society as a whole the values they attached to the role: care, nurturance, and morality." Maternalist claims were frequently made on the behalf of others—children, working women, immigrants, the poor. In contrast, activist mothers defined themselves as members of the communities they sought to help, thus breaking with the class and racial–ethnic divisions

that often limited maternalist politics of earlier eras. See Molly Ladd-Taylor 1994; Gwendolyn Mink 1995. Furthermore, as this study demonstrates, these women were often already active in the so-called public realm of their neighborhoods as a consequence of their engagement with welfare or health care bureaucracies, housing projects, or neighborhood watch groups, and therefore, they did not need an explicit ideology to justify further involvement. Yet appeals to their identities as mothers and community caretakers did circumscribe their self-presentation as political actors thus limiting their efficacy in the formal political arena.

3. Latinas, Native American women, and Asian American women have well-established traditions of community-based work designed to defend and enhance the quality of life within their communities. See, e.g., Acosta-Belen 1986; Allen 1986, 1995; Glenn 1986; Glenn, Chang, and Forcey 1994; Gluck et al. 1997; Green 1990; Hewitt 1990; Sanchez-Ayendez 1995; Torres 1986.

4. hooks 1990, 41. Also see, e.g., Gilkes 1988; Moraga 1981; Rollins 1995; K. Scott 1991.

5. Essed 1990, 144; also see Carothers 1990.

6. Also see James 1993; Stack 1974; Stack and Burton 1994; Troester 1984.

7. See Giddings 1984; J. Jones 1985; Stack 1974.

8. See, e.g., Daniels 1988; Kaminer 1984.

REFERENCES

Acosta-Belen, Edna, ed. 1986. *The Puerto Rican Woman's Perspectives on Culture, History and Society.* 2d. ed. New York: Praeger Press.

Allen, Paula Gunn. 1986. *The Sacred Hoop: Recovering the Feminism in American Indian Traditions.* Boston: Beacon Press.

———. 1995. "Angry Women Are Building: Issues and Struggles Facing American Indian Women Today." Pp. 32–36 in *Race, Class, and Gender: An Anthology,* ed. Margaret Andersen and Patricia Hill Collins. Belmont, Calif.: Wadsworth Publishing Company.

Apple, R. W., Jr. 1963. "Violence Erupts in Refuse Strike as Owner-Drivers Still Operate." *New York Times* December 3, pp. 1, 46.

Carothers, Suzanne. 1990. "Catching Sense: Learning from Our Mothers to Be Black and Female." Pp. 232–47 in *Uncertain Terms: Negotiating Gender in American Culture,* eds. Faye Ginsburg and Anna Lowenhaupt Tsing. Boston: Beacon Press.

Collins, Patricia Hill. 1990. *Black Feminist Thought: Knowledge, Consciousness, and the Politics of Empowerment.* Boston: Unwin Hyman.

———. 1991a. "Learning From the Outsider Within: The Sociological Significance of Black Feminist Thought." Pp. 35–59 in *Beyond Methodology,* eds. Mary Margaret Fonow and J. A. Cook. Bloomington: Indiana University Press.

Daniels, Arlene Kaplan. 1988. *Invisible Careers: Women Civic Leaders from the Volunteer World.* Chicago: University of Chicago Press.

Essed, Philomena. 1990. *Everyday Racism: Reports from Women of Two Cultures.* Claremont, CA: Hunter House, Inc.

Giddings, Paula. 1984. *When and Where I Enter: The Impact of Black Women on Race and Sex in America.* New York: William Morrow and Company.

Gilkes, Cheryl Townsend. 1988. "Building in Many Places: Multiple Consciousness and Ideologies in Black Women's Community Work." Pp. 53–76 in *Women and the Politics of Empowerment,* eds. Ann Bookman and Sandra Morgen. Philadelphia: Temple University Press.

Glenn, Evelyn Nakano. 1986. *Issei, Nisei, War Bride: Three Generations of Japanese Women in Domestic Service.* Philadelphia: Temple University Press.

Glenn, Evelyn Nakano, Grace Chang, and Linda Rennie Forcey, eds. 1994. *Mothering: Ideology, Experience, and Agency.* New York: Routledge.

Gluck, Sherna Berger, with Maylei Blackwell, Sharon Cotrell, and Karen Harper. 1997. "Whose Feminism, Whose History? Reflections on Excavating the History of (the) US Women's Movement(s)." Pp. 31–56 in *Community Activism and Feminist Politics: Organizing Across Race, Class, and Gender.* New York: Routledge.

Green, Rayna. 1990. "American Indian Women: Diverse Leadership for Social Change." Pp. 61–73 in *Bridges of Power: Women's Multicultural Alliances,* eds. Lisa Albrecht and Rose M. Brewer. Philadelphia: New Society Publishers.

Hewitt, Nancy A. 1990. "Charity or Mutual Aid?: Two Perspectives on Latin Women's Philanthropy in Tampa, Florida." Pp. 55–69 in *Lady Bountiful Revisited: Women, Philanthropy, and Power,* ed. Kathleen D. McCarthy. New Brunswick, NJ: Rutgers University Press.

hooks, bell. 1990. *Yearning: Race, Gender and Cultural Politics.* Boston: South End Press.

James, Stanlie M. 1993. "Mothering: A Possible Black Feminist Link to Social Transformation?" Pp. 44–54 in *Theorizing Black Feminisms: The*

Visionary Pragmatism of Black Women, eds. Stanlie M. James and Abena P. A. Busia. New York: Routledge.

Jones, Jacqueline. 1985. *Labor of Love, Labor of Sorrow: Black Women, Work and the Family, from Slavery to the Present.* New York: Vintage Books.

Kaminer, Wendy. 1984. *Women Volunteering: The Pleasure, Pain and Politics of Unpaid Work from 1830 to the Present.* Garden City, NJ: Doubleday.

Koven, Seth, and Sonya Michel. 1993. "Introduction: 'Mother Worlds.'" Pp. 1–42 in *Mothers of a New World: Maternalist Politics and the Origins of Welfare States.* New York: Routledge.

Ladd-Taylor, Molly. 1994. *Mother-Work: Women, Child Welfare, and the State, 1890–1930.* Urbana: University of Illinois Press.

Mink, Gwendolyn. 1995. *The Wages of Motherhood: Inequality in the Welfare State, 1917–1942.* Ithaca, NY: Cornell University Press.

Moraga, Cherríe. 1981. "La Guerra." Pp. 17–34 in *This Bridge Called My Back: Writings by Radical Women of Color.* Watertown, MA: Persephone Press.

Rollins, Judith. 1995. *All Is Never Said: The Narrative of Odette Harper Hines.* Philadelphia: Temple University Press.

Sanchez-Ayendez, Melba. 1995. "Puerto Rican Elderly Women: Shared Meanings and Informal Supportive Networks." Pp. 172–86 in *All-American Women: Lines That Divide, Ties That Bind,* ed. Johnnetta B. Cole. New York: The Free Press.

Scott, Kisho Y. 1991. *The Habit of Surviving.* New York: Ballantine.

Stack, Carol B. 1974. *All Our Kin: Strategies for Survival in a Black Community.* New York: Harper and Row.

Stack, Carol, and Ling M. Burton. 1994. "Kinscripts: Reflections on Family, Generation, and Culture." Pp. 33–44 in *Mothering: Ideology, Experience, and Agency,* eds. E. Nakano Glenn, G. Chang, and L. Rennie Forcey. New York: Routledge.

Stetson, Damon. 1963. "Strike Is Ended, Refuse Picked Up." *New York Times* December 7, p. 22.

Torres, Lourdes. 1986. "The Construction of the Self in U.S. Latina Autobiographies." Pp. 271–87 in *Third World Women and the Politics of Feminism,* eds. Chandra Talpade Mohanty, Ann Russo, and Lourdes Torres. Bloomington and Indianapolis: Indiana University Press.

Troester, Rosalie Riegle. 1984. "Turbulence and Tenderness: Mothers, Daughters and 'Othermothers' in Paule Marshall's *Brown Girl, Brownstones.*" *Sage: A Scholarly Journal on Black Women* 1(2):13–16.

QUESTIONS FOR DISCUSSION

1. How do the women Naples interviewed expand the concept of "mothering"? Does accepting their new definition require us also to rethink the definition of family?

2. How is it advantageous to understand women's community action as political behavior? Does doing so require us to rethink the common practice of representing the family as a separate, private sphere of action?

3. Did your mother engage in activist mothering? If so, how did it affect you?

4. How does your sense of "home" reflect your race and your class?

5. How does community work conflict with family life? Are the dilemmas of activist mothers similar to the dilemmas of the middle-class workers Hochschild described in Reading 27?

35

DUBIOUS CONCEPTIONS
The Politics of Teenage Pregnancy

KRISTIN LUKER

In the 1970s advocates of a public policy aimed at curbing early childbearing promised a cure for many of America's social ills. They argued that everything from dropout rates to infant mortality to poverty could be reduced if teens just had fewer babies. Back then, reducing early pregnancy and childbearing had political appeal for both conservatives and liberals. Conservatives wanted teens to be less active sexually, to have fewer abortions, and to wind up less often as single mothers on AFDC. Liberals wished to help young women gain control over their reproductive and sexual destinies, thereby ensuring that untimely births would not limit young women's opportunities and chain them to a lifetime of poverty. In achieving these goals, liberals preferred to use a carrot; conservatives, a stick. By the 1970s traditional conservatives, who were worried primarily about the economic dimensions of early childbearing, had been joined by members of the New Right, who were concerned primarily about its moral implications. But in those days, the public did not yet perceive the issue as being an extremely urgent social problem.

Now, some two decades later, the debate over early childbearing has become more heated and widespread. As the economy has slowed and Americans have begun to have a harder time finding and keeping jobs, resentment against certain entitlements has escalated; unwed teenage mothers have been a target of particular scorn. The economy is showing even more of a tendency to bifurcate into an upper, affluent tier and a lower, poorer one—a situation in which workers with high-level skills are reaping more and more rewards. Middle-class people have developed ways of adapting to these pressures: they postpone childbearing until they have gotten enough education to compete for dwindling white-collar jobs, and they form two-earner households so that they can afford a home, live in a safe neighborhood, and send their children to good schools.

Teenagers who have babies don't conform with these middle-class assumptions and expectations. Looked at through middle-class eyes, such teens seem to be closing themselves off from the education that could make them self-supporting and take them off the public dole. They also appear to be limiting their ability to find a husband who could support them, thus making it likely that they will remain unwed and on welfare. As the average incomes of most Americans diminish in real value, the public becomes more restive about welfare and the taxes that support it. All women with dependent children who receive benefits are the targets of public anger these days, but young mothers, who account for a tiny

Reprinted by permission of the publisher from "Teenage Parents and the Future" in *Dubious Conceptions: The Politics of Teenage Pregnancy* by Kristin Luker, pp. 175–183, 191–193, Cambridge, Mass.: Harvard University Press. Copyright © 1996 by the President and Fellows of Harvard College.

portion (about 8 percent) of the women on welfare, provoke special rage.[1] To Americans who are increasingly postponing marriage and childbearing and are limiting the number of children they have, "babies having babies" looks like a recipe for trouble. Worse yet, it's a trouble that young people seem to bring on themselves but that everyone else seems to have to pay for. Not surprisingly, the major political parties have tapped into the public's resentment and now devote special attention to pregnant teenagers.[2]

For most conservatives, early childbearing, especially out of wedlock, is the result of bad values and unwise choices. They see young mothers as inner-city teens who lack stability and guidance, engage in irresponsible behavior, and then expect to be supported by the state. They believe that the welfare system offers what economists call "perverse" incentives—that its mere existence incites young women to get pregnant and live off its bounty. Their remedy: restrict access to welfare, particularly in the case of teenagers. The Republicans' Contract with America, for example, proposes eliminating all welfare payments to children whose mothers were unwed teenagers when they were born, as well as denying them access to food stamps and public housing. The Speaker of the House, Republican Newt Gingrich, has proposed that orphanages be established for children whose mothers cannot take care of them. According to the conservative view, young unwed mothers are rational actors who pursue a course that they see as being in their self-interest; denying teenagers welfare and limiting benefits to older women will reduce the rate of out-of-wedlock births.

Despite a great deal of evidence to the contrary, many people still believe that welfare benefits cause early and out-of-wedlock childbearing. As the Contract with America notes:

Republicans understand one important thing ignored by most Democrats—incentives affect behavior. Currently, the federal government provides young girls the following deal: Have an illegitimate baby and the taxpayers will guarantee you cash, food stamps, and medical care, plus a host of other benefits. As long as you stay single and don't work, we'll continue giving you benefits worth a minimum of $12,000 a year ($3,000 more than a full-time job paying minimum wage). It's time to change the incentives and make responsible parenthood the norm and not the exception.[3]

But although incentives certainly affect behavior, they do so in a moral and social context that shapes how people interpret those incentives. For all women—rich and poor, teenage and older—decisions regarding childbearing and marriage have a great deal to do with feelings, values, beliefs, and commitments. They are rarely governed solely by the availability of a welfare check.

When speaking about their decision to have and raise a child, young mothers use terms that in other contexts would seem praiseworthy. They stress that they are attempting to take responsibility for their actions, sexual and otherwise. They have difficulty accepting abortion and adoption—the ways in which young women have traditionally hidden their shame from society—precisely because these alternatives do permit women to act as if nothing had happened. To be sure, the moral calculus here includes a measure of self-interest: for young women to whom few good things happen, childbearing offers at least the possibility of making a change in life. But the decision to bear and raise a child is not only a selfish one. Many young women describe how morally complex the choice is:

Because his [the baby's] father, he didn't believe in abortion, he said I'm here, you're here, so why can't he come in as well? Don't kill the baby, he's going, we already made it. So we discussed that, too, before I got pregnant, if I got pregnant, that I should keep it because it ain't right to just throw away a life, so I said OK. (Lynn, teenager, black)[4]

I wasn't ready . . . and I thought I should wait a little longer and finish finding pleasure, but my mother didn't want that and she made sure I kept the baby. And afterwards I, like, hey, why not? I started feeling the same, I wanted it, too. It wasn't just like I had it because she wanted me to and stuff. My mother said she wants all her grandchildren. (Liz, sixteen, black, Boston)[5]

You make your bed, you lie in it. (White teenager, living in the rural Northeast)[6]

If I'm responsible enough to be goin' out and doin' these things getting pregnant, then I should be responsible enough to handle what I got myself into. (Sally, seventeen, white, rural Northeast)[7]

A variety of incentives blend together here. Young African American women know that few families want to adopt a minority child. Some young white and black women, like some of their elders, have moral scruples about abortion; and they believe that raising a child gives a young woman an opportunity to be good at something even if she must make sacrifices. In a poor neighborhood squeezed by a declining economy, there are often few opportunities to be responsible. But motherhood provides that opportunity, as well as a spur for a young woman to try make something of herself:

I know I have to go to school because of the responsibility of the baby. It [having the baby] gave me a better outlook on life. I have to be concerned about the baby's future. (Black teenager, Los Angeles area)[8]

Mrs. J. talks about this all the time. She makes us responsible for everything. She says we have two lives to consider now, and she's right.[9]

I think it [having a baby] will press me on to do better and do more, 'cause I want my child to have, you know, basically everything. And it will help me to do better in school and achieving the goals that I want to. I feel I can handle it. I feel that this baby will push me to strive for what I'm looking for, for a better life. I want my child to have a better life. I'm not sayin' my life is bad, I'm sayin' so it will have what it wants. I think that when you have somethin' right there before you, you have a real goal. You see, when I have that baby there, I say, you got to buckle down, you got to get good grades, you got to get the best.[10]

In fact, some young women outright reject the notion that economic considerations should be the primary motive in the decision to have a child:

I know it's hard to try and bring somebody into the world when you're not rich. But that's it, that's just it, everybody around not rich and people who are rich are doin' worse by their kids than the people who don't have. . . . It don't matter if you don't have the money or the know-how, 'cause stuff like that come. . . . Experience, it come with havin' a baby. I know I will never have a lot of money, but what I do have will be for the baby.[11]

The moral reasoning that undergirds the decision to have and raise a child is of course shaped by the larger world, the "incentives" that conservatives like to talk about. But the most visible incentive—

welfare—has been declining in real value at precisely the time that more teenagers are deciding not to marry, and birthrates among teens have been stable or declining for most of the past two decades. Welfare benefits may appear generous ($12,000 a year, according to the Contract with America), but teenagers are likely to receive most of the payments indirectly, as food stamps or, more important, as reimbursed medical care. If one discounts Medicaid, the real value of the average AFDC check is about $7,200 a year, which at $600 a month (or $150 a week) leaves a family below the poverty level.[12]

The problem that confronts poor young people in the 1990s is the dearth of real alternatives to welfare. In the 1950s and 1960s, a young man could support a family on a low-wage job. There are fewer such jobs now, and they pay less: a minimum-wage job no longer allows a man to support a family or a single mother to support a child, even if they work full time and year round. If a woman has to pay for childcare, she earns less working than she would get on welfare.[13] This poses a dilemma for the American public: poor people can't earn enough to support a family, but no one wants to support them on welfare. One solution is the course advocated by policymakers in the nineteenth century: people who cannot afford to have children should simply stay childless. More humane, but ultimately deceptive, is the notion that poor teens should postpone their childbearing until they are emotionally and financially ready. People who identify early childbearing as the core of the poverty problem believe that teenagers are only temporarily unfit for parenthood and that they will mature into it. Alas, many of these young people will never be ready, at least if we define "ready" as having enough money to support themselves and their children. Given the scarcity of decent jobs, a substantial mi-

nority of Americans simply cannot afford to have children without some form of social transfer. A child born to married parents who can fully support it is, like safe neighborhoods and good schools, becoming a luxury accessible only to the wealthy.

Liberal critics of early pregnancy have their own form of myopia about the problem. They realize that the fundamental problem is poverty, but they argue that society should make a greater investment in teenage mothers—that it should create training programs to increase the human capital that young mothers possess and hence increase their long-term self-sufficiency. From the liberal point of view, teenage mothers are disadvantaged people who would be much less likely to stay poor if they did a few simple things: finished their education, postponed childbearing, found a husband, and acquired marketable skills. Although this prescription sounds straightforward and commonsensical, it ignores the fact that most young mothers inherit multiple problems. They were born poor and grew up in poor neighborhoods. Their early lives were often scarred by violence and disorder, including sexual abuse. They attended rundown, underequipped schools in which teachers struggled to discipline and motivate the students, and they were typically not among the lucky and clever few who managed to obtain a little extra attention from their teachers, coaches, or adult neighbors. They were born into families that were at the end of the social and economic queue, and their life experiences rarely moved them any closer to the front. By having babies, such women are manifesting an almost poignant hope—the hope that a better future lies ahead, for their children if not for themselves.

Thus, training programs have very real limits. Even the good ones can only reshuffle people who are standing at the end of the line, not fundamentally transform the nature of the line. If young mothers acquire more training and skills, at best they simply displace others a step or two ahead of them. Most training programs for young women on welfare have a high rate of success, but this success is very specific: such programs raise the income of participants by amounts that exceed the cost of the program. Unfortunately, these women are so poor that this higher income typically raises their financial status only slightly—from desperately poor to miserably poor.[14] If teenagers and their babies represented only poverty in its traditional form—if they were members of poor two-parent families or were worthy widows, as in earlier decades—the public might be more willing to spend resources to bring them and their children into the mainstream. But poverty today brings with it new family structures that many Americans find troubling.

Poor people are more likely to become parents as teenagers than are affluent people, and they are also more likely to have babies out of wedlock. So when conservatives claim, despite all findings to the contrary, that welfare causes early and out-of-wedlock childbearing, they speak to a public worried about two different things—the cost of welfare and changing family structures—in a way that knits these two concerns together. Liberals have been slow to make this distinction: they constantly remind conservatives that AFDC accounts for only a small fraction of federal spending, especially when compared to other federal programs such as the military. They are correct on this point: even the cost of middle-class welfare programs (Social Security, Medicare, deductions for home-mortgage interest) dwarfs the amount spent on AFDC. Social Security in particular, because it is indexed to inflation, has become a significant income-transfer program for middle-class people: most individuals take out far more in benefits than either they or their employ-

ers made in contributions.[15] But liberals have been slow to realize that the public is extremely uneasy about the way family structures have changed, and that this unease has settled on the heads of teenagers and women on welfare. Americans find welfare troubling when it seems to encourage early and out-of-wedlock childbearing, especially among the poor and minorities.

Since the signs of poverty and these new family structures have become more widespread simultaneously, conservatives make a seemingly logical argument when they relate the two. People who believe that welfare is wrong if it creates more single and teenage parents are drawing on a valid intuition: that the more adults there are who are committed to the well-being of a child, the better off that child is. Likewise, they are almost certainly right to suspect that the ties uniting parents with children and husbands with wives have frayed in the last twenty years. They are also right to think that children benefit when their parents have more resources—emotional, spiritual, psychological, financial—to devote to them, and that such resources are becoming ever scarcer.[16] They are wrong, however, in assuming that welfare has had much to do with these unfortunate social trends.

The troubles that teenage parents face today are the same ones that all Americans face: changes in the nature of marriage, in the relations between men and women, in the relations between parents and children. Everyone is having difficulty mustering the emotional, psychological, and financial resources that children need, and many people long for the days when life seemed easier. But Americans are wrong when they assume that teenage parents suffer disproportionately from these problems because they are young; rather, teenage parents are vulnerable parents because they are poor. Society runs the moral risk of scapegoating teenage mothers—symbolically punishing them for trying to solve the problems everyone faces and solve them with more limited resources than most Americans.

Does this mean that people should shrug their shoulders and say that early childbearing is just a fact of modern life? No. The increase in the number of teenage and unwed mothers is an indirect measure of the toll that a bifurcating economy is taking on Americans, especially women of poor and minority backgrounds. It would be better to see early childbearing as a symptom, like infant mortality—not a cause but a marker of events, an indicator of the extent to which many young people have been excluded from the American dream. It is distressing and alarming that early childbearing—like infant mortality—is more common among minorities, the poor, and those who have been failed by the nation's major institutions. In addition, the plight of teenage mothers reveals not only how hard it is to be poor in America, but the special pressures that confront young, poor women. One of the tragedies of early childbearing is that it is one of the few ways in which such women feel they can make a change in their lives, however illusory that change may prove to be. Having a baby can give a young woman permission to be assertive and motivated on her baby's behalf when she has trouble mustering these qualities for herself. For example, a woman disillusioned with education may decide to stay in high school because she doesn't want her baby to have a dropout for a mother. The fact that birthrates among teens have stayed at high levels indicates how discouraged and disadvantaged many young women are—that they have to take the extraordinary step of bearing a child in order to feel they have a meaningful role and mission in society and can make claims on themselves and others.

Having a baby is a lottery ticket for many teenagers: it brings with it at least the dream of something better, and if the dream fails, not much is lost. Some young women say it was the best thing they ever did. In a few cases it leads to marriage or a stable relationship; in many others it motivates a woman to push herself for her baby's sake; and in still other cases it enhances the woman's self-esteem, since it enables her to do something productive, something nurturing and socially responsible. Yet lotteries are by definition unpredictable. To the extent that babies can be ill or impaired, mothers can be unhelpful or unavailable, and boyfriends can be unreliable or punitive, childbearing can be just another risk gone wrong in a life that is filled with failures and losses. Although early childbearing rarely causes a young woman to be poor and discouraged, once she is responsible for a baby a woman may find that she has a harder time taking advantage of lucky breaks and fewer opportunities to make positive changes in her life. What should trouble us when we worry about teenage parents is the fact that poor and minority women feel they risk losing so little by having a child at an early age. American society places great value on individual success, and is remarkably stingy in its support of those who "fail." It is no accident that in the United States—where the penalties for failure are so severe—the birthrate among teenagers is higher than in any other industrialized nation, and 80 percent of babies born to teens are born to poor women. If young men and women felt they had an array of opportunities in life and still chose to become parents as teenagers, their decision would evoke comparatively little concern. But in fact early childbearing is a very constrained choice for poor people who have few other options; for them, being a teenage parent can be much more rewarding and much less costly than is generally supposed. If America cares about its young people, it must make them feel that they have a rich array of choices, so that having a baby is not the only or most attractive one on the horizon.

. . .

The political scientist Hugh Heclo once noted, speaking of antipoverty policies, that what Americans want they can't have, and what they can have they don't want. This dictum seems particularly apt in connection with early pregnancy and childbearing. Americans want teenagers to wait until they are "mature" before they have sex, to wait until they are "ready" before they get pregnant, and to wait until they are married and financially secure before they have children. But there is no consensus on what it means to be "mature," out-of-wedlock births are common throughout the industrialized world, and a great many teenagers will be poor throughout their lives and hence never really "ready" to be parents. Society could conceivably become so punitive and coercive that poor teenagers would be discouraged from ever having babies, but only a few countries such as China have been able to impose this kind of control. It's even doubtful that the draconian welfare-reform policies proposed by the Republicans will make much of a difference. Since teenagers who live in states with generous benefits do not have more out-of-wedlock babies than teens in states with low benefits, and since out-of-wedlock childbearing has been increasing as welfare benefits decline, a radical reduction in welfare benefits for teenagers will probably have a negligible overall effect. As we have seen, myriad factors affect the way in which young people make decisions about sexual activity, relationships, and childbearing; whether or not they are eligible to receive a welfare check is unlikely to alter their behavior. Most will continue to have babies, hoping that things will somehow work out and that their families will rearrange scarce resources to provide for the newcomers.

The more one knows about early pregnancy and childbearing, the more skeptical one becomes that they correlate with poverty in any simple way. Poverty is not exclusively or even primarily limited to single mothers; most single mothers are not teenagers; many teenage mothers have husbands or partners; and many pregnant teenagers do not become mothers. The rates of pregnancy and childbearing among teenagers *are* a serious problem. But early childbearing doesn't make young women poor; rather, poverty makes women bear children at an early age. Society should worry not about some epidemic of "teenage pregnancy" but about the hopeless, discouraged, and empty lives that early childbearing denotes. Teenagers and their children desperately need a better future, one with brighter opportunities and greater rewards. Making the United States the kind of country in which—as in most European countries—early childbearing is rare would entail profound changes in public policy and perhaps even in American society as a whole. Such measures would be costly, and some of them would fail.

Any observer of the current scene would have to conclude that these days Americans seem bent on making the lives of teenage parents and their children even harder than they already are. Society has failed teenage parents all along the line—they are people for whom the schools, the health care system, and the labor market have been painful and unrewarding places. Now, it seems, young parents are being assigned responsibility for society's failures. Michelle and her baby have never needed help more, yet never have Americans been less willing to help and more willing to blame.

NOTES

1. For public opinion on welfare, see Blackside Polls, Inc., for Public Broadcasting System. See also Times Mirror Poll, July 12–25, 1994,

reported in "Compassion for the Poor Is Declining, Poll Finds," *New York Times,* September 21, 1995.

2. The Republican Party has proposed the Personal Responsibility Act, which prohibits AFDC payments to unmarried mothers under eighteen and permits states to withhold AFDC from unmarried mothers under twenty-one. Ed Gillespie and Bob Schellhas, eds., *Contract with America: The Bold Plan by Representative Newt Gingrich, Representative Dick Armey and the House Republicans to Change the Nation* (New York: Times Books, 1994), p. 66. See also House Republican Conference, *Legislative Digest,* September 27, 1994, p. 16. One reading of this proposal ("The Real Welfare Reform Act," H.R. 4566) is that all children born to unmarried mothers under twenty-one (and under twenty-five after 1998) would be barred *forever* from receiving welfare benefits. As I have argued throughout this book, poor women have their babies young, so this is an extraordinarily clever strategy to limit the social safety net by excluding large numbers of children *for life* under the guise of reducing "teenage pregnancy." See also Kathleen Sylvester, *Preventable Calamity: Rolling Back Teen Pregnancy* (Washington, D.C.: Progressive Policy Institute, 1994).

3. Gillespie and Schellhas, eds., *Contract with America,* p. 75.

4. Jill McLean Taylor, "Development of Self, Moral Voice, and the Meaning of Adolescent Motherhood: The Narratives of Fourteen Adolescent Mothers" (Diss., Harvard University, 1989), pp. 79, 130.

5. Constance Willard Williams, "An Acceptable Life: Pregnancy and Childbearing from the Black Teen Mother's Perspective" (Diss., Brandeis University, 1989), pp. 136–37.

6. Brenda Schwab, "Someone to Always Be There: Teenage Childbearing as an Adaptive Strategy in Rural New England" (Diss., Brandeis University, 1983), p. 186.

7. Ibid., p. 188.

8. Virginia Hunter, "Impact of Adolescent Parenthood on Black Teenage Mothers and Their Families" (Diss., UCLA, 1982), p. 134.

9. Kathleen Thornton, "Comprehensive Evaluation of a Teen Pregnancy and Parenting Program" (Diss., University of Pennsylvania, 1992), p. 171.

10. Laurie Ann McDade, "Community Responses to Teenage Pregnancy and Parenting: An Ethnography of a Social Problem" (Diss., Rutgers University, 1987), p. 281.

11. Ibid., p 285.

12. U.S. House of Representatives, Committee on Ways and Means, *Overview of Entitlement Programs,* 103rd Congress, 2nd session (Washington, D.C.: Government Printing Office, 1994), pp. 365–367, Tables 10–11.

13. For an elegant summary of the numbers, see Katherine Edin and Christopher Jencks, "The Real Welfare Problem," *American Prospect* 1, no. 1 (1990).

14. For an overview, see Judith Gueron and Edward Pauly, *From Welfare to Work* (New York: Russell Sage, 1991).

15. Jill Quadagno, *The Transformation of Old Age Security: Class and Politics in the American Welfare State* (Chicago: University of Chicago Press, 1988).

16. For evidence that Americans really have become more "me-centered" (and simultaneously less committed to the notion of "duty" to others, including spouses and children), see Joseph Veroff, *The Inner American: A Self-Portrait from 1957 to 1976* (New York: Basic Books, 1981). For evidence that this may in fact indicate a change in fundamental values across the globe (or at least throughout the First World), see Ronald Inglehart, *Culture Shift in Advanced Industrial Society* (Princeton: Princeton University Press, 1990).

QUESTIONS FOR DISCUSSION

1. According to Luker, the social problem of teenage pregnancy is more closely tied to changing economic conditions than to changes in morality. Given this, what must the government do to reduce teenage pregnancy?

2. Could tapping into teens' desires to be good parents to their children have long-term payoffs? Explain.

THE SOCIAL WEB

- The federal government's ChildStats Web site offers reports on children and their families, including population and family characteristics, economic security, health, behavior and social environment, and education: www.childstats.gov.
- The Alan Guttmacher Institute (AGI) is a nonprofit organization whose mission is to protect women's and men's reproductive choices; and to support an individual's ability to obtain the information and services needed to achieve full human rights, safeguard health, and exercise individual responsibilities in regard to sexual behavior and relationships, reproduction, and family formation. "State Policies in Brief" are a very useful tool: www.agi-usa.org/about/index.html.
- The National Adoption Information Clearinghouse (NAIC) is a service of the Children's Bureau, Administration on Children, Youth and Families, Administration for Children and Families, and Department of Health and Human Services. NAIC is a comprehensive resource on all aspects of adoption for professionals, adoptees, birth relatives, and parents. It supplies statistics, legal information, answers to frequently asked questions, and links to allied agencies: www.calib.com/naic/index.htm.

QUESTIONS FOR DEBATE

1. Why do the myths about the American family that Kain identifies persist?
2. Do we need to consider race as well as class to understand the problems of working families? If so, why? If not, why not?
3. Would Lillian Rubin and Nancy Naples see Gillian Dunne's research as supporting theirs?
4. Is teen pregnancy a social problem?
5. Would we benefit more by changing our perceptions of mothering or fathering?

Chapter 9
Education

Contents

Learning Objectives

By the end of this chapter you should be able to:

- Recognize how these authors use one or more of the major perspectives to analyze education.

- Explore how inequality in education is shaped by the inequalities of race, class, and gender.

- Describe the various ways that people gain a sense of the world and their place in it through education.

- Identify the consequences of educational inequality.

- Analyze how individuals contribute to educational inequality through their everyday behavior.

- Explain how social systems and institutions perpetuate educational inequality.

Defining the Problem

Education is one of the most fundamental institutions in the United States. Schools are vital centers of our communities, and quality education is an important value in American culture. We depend on our schools to give children the skills to become productive citizens. The level of education young people gain frequently determines the employment and economic opportunities available to them for their entire lives. The federal government mandates that states provide children with free primary (grades K through 8) and secondary (grades 9 through 12) education, which is generally funded through state and local taxes. Because tax structures can differ based on economic conditions, poorer areas may not receive the same kinds of resources as wealthier areas. Local school boards control how individual schools operate. They are responsible for hiring teachers, setting teacher pay scales, deciding how funds will be spent, and determining the school curriculum. Local schools also frequently provide government-funded social services, such as health care and nutrition programs. However, our schools are also an arena where social problems are played out every day in the lives of America's children.

Unequal funding can affect the quality of the education a child receives and ultimately can perpetuate existing systems of social and economic inequality. Some sociologists of social problems look at the ways that education is funded in the United States. They would compare what we as a nation spend on education versus what we spend on other major institutions and programs, such as the criminal justice system or corporate welfare. These scholars might also explore the unequal ways that funds for education are distributed.

Researchers also examine the ways that educational experiences shape children's sense of self and the social world around them. Some scholars look at the dynamics within America's classrooms. They examine the ways that inequalities based on race and gender are perpetuated in the interactions of students and teachers. Some social problems scholars look at the significance of education for children's development. They might look at how students interact with one another in classrooms, in cafeterias, on playgrounds, and in extracurricular groups, and the kinds of social messages students receive from one another.

Finally, scholars of social problems may focus on the significance of education as a major American institution. They may examine the ways that our nation's schools are an arena in which political and economic battles are fought. Classrooms are also crucial sites for debates about cultural values and priorities. Because the curriculum is decided by local school boards, politically organized groups can attempt to influence what children are taught. Controversial social issues such as religion, sexuality, patriotism, and cultural diversity are often debated as a public school curriculum is chosen. Finally, education can be a significant source of social change. Some scholars look at the ways that education can contribute to the solutions for major social problems.

The Scope of the Problem

Americans today are better educated than at any time in history. Individuals in the United States have achieved higher levels of education than individuals in any other nation in the world.[1] In 2001, 88 percent of all people 25 to 29 years old had a high school diploma or its equivalent, and 58 percent of these people had completed some college. Twenty-nine percent had completed at least a bachelor's degree, up from 17 percent in 1971.

Education levels in the United States vary according to race. In 2001, 93 percent of Whites had completed high school, compared to 87 percent of Blacks and 63 percent of Hispanics. Sixty-five percent of Whites 25 to 29 years old had completed some college; 51 percent of their Black and 32 percent of their Hispanic counterparts had done so. Inverse patterns appear in dropout rates. Seven percent of Whites 16 to 24 years old were dropouts in 2000; however, dropout rates for Blacks and Hispanics were 13 percent and 28 percent, respectively.

Education drastically affects financial well-being. In 2000, the unemployment rate for high school dropouts was 6.4 percent, compared to unemployment rates for people with some college of 2.9 percent and for people with a bachelor's degree of 1.7 percent. Median annual earnings for males age 25 to 34 who were high school dropouts was $19,225; median annual earnings for their female counterparts was $11,583. Males and females with a high school diploma or its equivalent earned $26,399 and $16,573, respectively; median annual earnings for males with a bachelor's degree was $42,292 and for females, $32,238.

Poverty affects children's education at all levels. In 2001, 15.4 percent of school-age children (5 to 17 years old) were living in poverty. Children whose parents live in poverty are less likely to be in preschool programs (47 percent) than children whose parents live above the poverty level (59 percent). Among children in grades K–12, poverty is associated with lower reading literacy, lower math assessment scores, higher absenteeism, and lower parental involvement. Students living in poverty are also

---

[1]Unless otherwise noted, all data are obtained from "The Condition of Education, 2002" and "Digest of Education Statistics, 2001," both published by the National Center for Education Statistics, U.S. Department of Education.

less likely to report a "very positive" attitude toward educational achievement.

More than 3.6 million elementary and secondary teachers are employed in U.S. public schools. Nationally, this represents a pupil-to-teacher ratio of 16.6. The average public school teacher salary in 2001 was $42,898. This constitutes a 1 percent decline in salaries from the 1990–1991 school year.

Americans are also receiving education at younger ages than ever before. In 2000, 43 percent of 3-year-olds, 66 percent of 4-year-olds, and 73 percent of 5-year-olds were enrolled in preprimary education programs. Although 56 percent of all 3- to 5-year-olds were enrolled in prekindergarten programs, these figures also vary according to race. Sixty-four percent of Black children were enrolled in preschool programs, compared to 59 percent of White children and 40 percent of Hispanic children.

In the 2000–2001 school year, the United States spent $700 billion on education programs, 60 percent of which went to elementary and secondary education. The U.S. spent 1.7 percent of its gross domestic product (GDP) on elementary education. Only three other industrialized nations in the world spent more of their GDP on primary education. However, the U.S. spent 2 percent of its GDP on secondary education, a lower percentage than thirteen other industrialized nations in the world.

The United States also lags behind other industrialized nations in student performance. Fourth graders in the U.S. score above average for science and math among industrialized nations. Yet eighth graders show a drop in their test scores relative to their international peers, while U.S. high school seniors scored below the international average in science and math. According to the United Nations Children's Fund, in 2002 the United States ranks eighteenth among industrialized nations for educa-

tional disadvantage.[2] Sixteen percent of U.S. students fall below the minimum international standard for literacy in reading, math, and science. Eighteen percent of 15-year-olds fall below the international reading literacy standard, and 42 percent of eighth graders in the U.S. are not reaching the international median for math achievement. The gap between the lowest and highest performing students in the nation is very large. The United States ranks twenty-first among industrialized nations for disparity between students. Only three industrialized nations in the world rank worse for such relative educational disadvantage.

Perspectives on the Problem

Sociologists study the social problems associated with education from a variety of perspectives. Sociologists using a *conflict perspective* see education as one of the major social institutions that promote social inequality among our citizenry. They examine the ways that educational policies, funding patterns, curricula, and school practices perpetuate disparity based on social class, race, gender, sexuality, and religion. Sociologists using a *functionalist perspective* explore whether our system of education successfully integrates children into our communities and gives them the practical and moral tools to participate in social life as adults. *Symbolic interactionists* study how administrators, teachers, parents, and students interact with one another and how those interactions can both perpetuate inequality and promote social change. Finally, *social constructionists* look at how education can become a battleground for defining cultural values and interests. They examine how the

---

[2]"A League Table of Educational Disadvantage in Rich Nations." The United Nations Children's Fund, Innocenti Report Card, Issue No. 4, November 2002.

ways that educational problems are defined and discussed reflect larger social issues and conflicts.

Connecting the Perspectives

Jonathan Kozol uses a conflict perspective to examine the plight of children who live in poverty. He argues that patterns of economic inequality are reflected in children's educational experiences. Steven Manning also uses a conflict perspective to examine the ways that large corporations see America's students as potential consumers and are increasingly exerting influence over the nation's schools. Using a symbolic interactionist perspective, Myra Sadker and David Sadker explore the ways that teachers perpetuate patterns of gender inequality in their classrooms. Joe Feagin, Hernán Vera, and Nikitah Imani adopt a social constructionist perspective to look at the ways students define universities as predominantly spaces for White students, a definition that affects the educational experiences of minority students. Finally, James Fraser uses a social constructionist approach to argue that a diverse, multicultural educational experience for students must include attention to religious differences.

Reading Summaries

Kozol turns our attention to the educational consequences of increasing the gap between the Haves and Have-Nots. In "Savage Inequalities," Kozol describes the devastating results of poverty on children's education, arguing that America's schools are segregated according to class divisions in the larger society. He interviews economically disadvantaged students who describe the conditions they encounter in their schools every day: flooded classrooms, rat-infested hallways, and restrooms that don't even have doors on their stalls. These impoverished students must learn their lessons while coping with the added burdens of hunger, drugs, and violence.

Kozol argues that these "savage inequalities" do not just *reflect* economic disparities in the larger society. Our school systems are also a major force for *perpetuating* social inequality. Wealthy parents send their children to private schools where students are immune to the conditions of poverty that poor children in public schools constantly face. Kozol also maintains that elite private schools educate their students in business, political, and leadership skills and give these students ready access to further elite educational opportunities.

In "How Corporations Are Buying Their Way into America's Classrooms," Manning examines the recent trend in elementary and secondary education to obtain funding from the private sector. Many school districts across the country are getting thousands of dollars from corporations in so-called school–business partnerships. Yet Manning argues that there is a heavy price to be paid for this influx of corporate money: America's schools are being turned into a marketplace for advertising and products. Children and teenagers together spend more than $165 billion each year. From a business perspective, schools thus present the ideal forum for influencing these potential buyers. Everything from sports equipment to vending machines to curriculum packages is being used to sell products to schoolchildren, resulting in the corporatization of the American classroom. Manning suggests that, in addition to labor and parents' organizations, students themselves have the power to reverse this trend. Yet as long as other sources of funding for education remain scarce, commercialism will gain a stronghold in school systems across the country.

Our third selection also deals with the ways that social inequalities are played out in America's schools. In "Missing in Interaction," Sadker and Sadker describe the severe gender inequities in our school systems, both within and beyond the classroom. They present the results of their research on gender bias in America's elementary schools, including interactions between teachers and students. Sadker and Sadker find that teachers interact more often with boys than with girls, no matter how the individual student is behaving. Boys who work well at their studies receive more praise than girls, and boys who misbehave receive more teacher attention than any girls. Teachers also tend to allow boys more time to answer questions and are more likely to suspend normal classroom rules—such as raising one's hand for a turn to speak—for boys. All this results in an education that "consists of two worlds: one of boys in action, the other of girls' inaction."

Sadker and Sadker also find that gender inequality extends beyond teacher interaction. School curriculum is heavily gender-biased. Textbooks tend to show women and men in traditionally gender-based occupations. Women are virtually absent from history, science, and math textbooks, and students have a very difficult time even listing the names of significant women in American history. Sadker and Sadker argue that gender bias even extends to the school playground, with boys having a larger play area and greater access to playground equipment. The extreme gender inequality that permeates America's schools affects girls throughout their educational experiences. Sadker and Sadker point out that "every day in America little girls lose independence, achievement, and self-esteem."

In "Confronting White Students: The Whiteness of University Spaces," Feagin and his colleagues examine the ways that social inequality affects the lives of students at American universities. Specifically, these authors focus on how college campuses have become socially constructed "spaces" that reflect racism. They describe how the physical space of college campuses shapes people's relationships according to larger patterns of social inequality, because "those with the greater power and resources ordinarily control the use and meaning of important spaces." Historically, college campuses have been constructed as Whites-only territories, causing many White university students to "assume, consciously or half-consciously, they are in *white* places."

The college spaces that Feagin and colleagues describe can also be symbolic spaces, such as yearbooks, homecoming activities, and school songs. These symbols are all an important part of the college experience and help students to identify with their schools. However, the events and rituals that make students feel an important bond with their college and with one another are highly racialized. According to Feagin and colleagues, these events and rituals are constructed by Whites for Whites and reflect the ways that a typical American college campus becomes an arena for racism in education.

The Whiteness of our university spaces has profound consequences for Black students. They are treated like outsiders on their own campuses. Many Black students interviewed by the authors discuss the alienation and anguish they feel daily. The effects of these White spaces also extend beyond the way students feel about their college experience. The majority of Black students surveyed by Feagin and colleagues indicate they have been victims of racism on their campus. Some students report being subjected to racist epithets or to threats of physical violence. Other students describe how they are confronted with racist stereotypes, such as the assumption by White students that Blacks are in college to play sports. The hostile environment created for Black students can have emotional, social, and academic consequences that permeate their college experience.

In "Religion and Public Education in a Multicultural America," Fraser addresses the most controversial subjects related to religion and public education in American society—school prayer, evolution and creationism, and the general role of religion in our nation's classrooms. He argues that these are major issues that will continue to be controversial and that must be addressed by America's educators, parents, policy makers, and citizens.

One problem, according to Fraser, is that school prayer has become a highly politicized issue for groups that want the power to insert their particular religion into American classrooms. Many parents and educators misunderstand Supreme Court rulings and believe that the act of prayer in public schools has been prohibited. The Constitution only prevents teachers and administrators from requiring students to engage in any religious practice. Most Americans, in fact, support the right of students to be free from religious coercion. Fraser also argues that the teaching of evolution science has needlessly become a controversial issue. He asserts that while teaching the science of evolution, teachers should be receptive to questions about religion and creationism. These can be very productive and educationally enlightening discussions, encouraging students to recognize various models for seeking knowledge and for wrestling with profound questions about human existence.

America's schools cannot afford to ignore the role of religion in social life, nor can America's classrooms become battlegrounds where religions vie to assert the supremacy of their own beliefs. Instead, Fraser argues, educators must be respectful of the many and varied religions—or no religion—of their students. Issues of personal faith are best handled at home, but the study of religion as a significant social institution should be embraced by educators. To do so, Fraser argues, is to recognize the diversity of student populations and of American society as a whole.

FOCUSING QUESTIONS

As you read these selections, think about the ways that education reflects social inequality. How have your own educational experiences demonstrated the patterns described in these articles? Why do you think education is so highly politicized? How does our educational system reinforce power imbalances in our society? How do individuals perpetuate this system?

36

SAVAGE INEQUALITIES
Children in America's Schools

JONATHAN KOZOL

Most academic studies of school finance, sooner or later, ask us to consider the same question: "How can we achieve more equity in education in America?" A variation of the question is a bit more circumspect: "How can we achieve both equity and excellence in education?" Both questions, however, seem to value equity as a desired goal. But, when the recommendations of such studies are examined, and when we look as well at the solutions that innumerable commissions have proposed, we realize that they do not quite mean "equity" and that they have seldom asked for "equity." What they mean, what they prescribe, is *something that resembles equity but never reaches it:* something close enough to equity to silence criticism by approximating justice, but far enough from equity to guarantee the benefits enjoyed by privilege. The differences are justified by telling us that equity must always be "approximate" and cannot possibly be perfect. But the imperfection falls in almost every case to the advantage of the privileged.

In Maryland, for instance, one of several states in which the courts have looked at fiscal inequalities between school districts, an equity suit filed in 1978, although unsuccessful, led the state to reexamine the school funding system. When a task force set up by the governor offered its suggestions five years later, it argued that 100 percent equality was too expensive. The goal, it said, was *75 percent equality*—meaning that the poorest districts should be granted no less than three quarters of the funds at the disposal of the average district. But, as the missing 25 percent translates into differences of input (teacher pay, provision of books, class size, etc.), we discover it is just enough to demarcate the difference between services appropriate to different social classes, and to formalize that difference in their destinies.

"The equalized 75 percent," says an educator in one of the state's low-income districts, "buys just enough to keep all ships afloat. The unequal 25 percent assures that they will sail in opposite directions."

It is a matter of national pride that every child's ship be kept afloat. Otherwise our nation would be subject to the charge that we deny poor children public school. But what is now encompassed by the one word ("school") are two very different kinds of institutions that, in function, finance and intention, serve entirely different roles. Both are needed for our nation's governance. But children in one set of schools are educated to be governors; children in the other set of schools are trained for being governed. The former are given the imaginative range to mobilize ideas for economic growth; the latter are provided with the discipline to do the narrow tasks the first group will prescribe.

Societies cannot be all generals, no soldiers. But, by our schooling patterns, we assure that soldiers' children are more likely to be soldiers and that the offspring of the generals will have at least the option to be generals. If this is not so, if it is just a matter of the difficulty of assuring perfect fairness, why does the unfairness never benefit the children of the poor?

. . .

"Children in a true sense," writes John Coons of Berkeley University, "are all poor" because they are dependent on adults. There is also, he says, "a sameness among children in the sense of [a] substantial uncertainty about their potential role as adults." It could be expressed, he says, "as an equality of innocence." The equality of adults, by comparison, "is always problematical; even social and economic differences among them are plausibly ascribed to their own deserts. . . . In any event, adults as a class enjoy no presumption of homogeneous virtue and their ethical demand for equality of treatment is accordingly attenuated. The differences among children, on the other hand, cannot be ascribed even vaguely to fault without indulging in an attaint of blood uncongenial to our time."

Terms such as "attaint of blood" are rarely used today, and, if they were, they would occasion public indignation; but the rigging of the game and the acceptance, which is nearly universal, of uneven playing fields reflect a dark unspoken sense that other people's children are of less inherent value than our own. Now and then, in private, affluent suburbanites concede that certain aspects of the game may be a trifle rigged to their advantage. "Sure, it's a bit unjust," they may concede, "but that's reality and that's the way the game is played. . . .

"In any case," they sometimes add in a refrain that we have heard now many times,

"there's no real evidence that spending money makes much difference in the outcome of a child's education. We have it. So we spend it. But it's probably a secondary matter. Other factors—family and background—seem to be a great deal more important."

In these ways they fend off dangers of disturbing introspection; and this, in turn, enables them to give their children something far more precious than the simple gift of pedagogic privilege. They give them uncontaminated satisfaction in their victories. Their children learn to shut from mind the possibility that they are winners in an unfair race, and they seldom let themselves lose sleep about the losers. There are, of course, unusual young people who, no matter what their parents tell them, do become aware of the inequities at stake. We have heard the voices of a few such students in this book. But the larger numbers of these favored children live with a remarkable experience of ethical exemption. Cruelty is seldom present in the thinking of such students, but it is contained within insouciance.

Sometimes the residents of affluent school districts point to certain failings in their own suburban schools, as if to say that "all our schools" are "rather unsuccessful" and that "minor differentials" between urban and suburban schools may not therefore be of much significance. "You know," said the father of two children who had gone to school in Great Neck, "it isn't just New York. We have our problems on Long Island too. My daughter had some high school teachers who were utterly inept and uninspired. She has had a devil of a time at Sarah Lawrence. . . ." He added that she had friends who went to private school and who were given a much better preparation. "It just seems terribly unfair," he said.

Defining unfairness as the difficulty that a Great Neck graduate encounters at a top-flight private college, to which any child in the South Bronx would have given her right arm to be admitted, strikes one as a way of rendering the term so large that it means almost nothing. "What is unfair," he is saying in effect, "is what I *determine* to be unfair. What I find unfair is what affects my child, not somebody else's child in New York."

Competition at the local high school, said another Great Neck parent, was "unhealthy." He described the toll it took on certain students. "Children in New York may suffer from too little. Many of our children suffer from too much." The loss of distinctions in these statements serves to blur the differences between the inescapable unhappiness of being human and the needless misery created by injustice. It also frees the wealthy from the obligation to concede the difference between inconvenience and destruction.

. . .

Poor people do not need to be reminded that the contest is unfair. "My children," says Elizabeth, a friend of mine who lives in a black neighborhood of Boston, "know very well the system is unfair. They also know that they are living in a rich society. They see it on TV, and in advertisements, and in the movies. They see the president at his place in Maine, riding around the harbor in his motor boat and playing golf with other wealthy men. They know that men like these did not come out of schools in Roxbury or Harlem. They know that they were given something extra. They don't know exactly what it is, but they have seen enough, and heard enough, to know that men don't speak like that and look like that unless they have been fed with silver spoons—and went to schools that had a lot of silver spoons and other things that cost a lot. . . .

"So they know this other world exists, and, when you tell them that the government can't find the money to provide them with a decent place to go to school, they don't believe it and they know that it's a *choice* that has been made—a choice about how much they matter to society. They see it as a message: 'This is to tell you that you don't much matter. You are ugly to us so we crowd you into ugly places. You are dirty so it will not hurt to pack you into dirty places.' My son says this: 'By doing this to you, we teach you how much you are hated.' I like to listen to the things my children say. They're not sophisticated so they speak out of their hearts."

One of the ideas, heard often in the press, that stirs the greatest sense of anger in a number of black parents that I know is that the obstacles black children face, to the extent that "obstacles" are still conceded, are attributable, at most, to "past injustice"—something dating maybe back to slavery or maybe to the era of official segregation that came to its close during the years from 1954 to 1968—but not, in any case, to something recent or contemporary or ongoing. The nostrum of a "past injustice"—an expression often spoken with sarcasm—is particularly cherished by conservatives because it serves to undercut the claim that young black people living now may have some right to preferential opportunities. Contemporary claims based on a "past injustice," after all, begin to seem implausible if the alleged injustice is believed to be a generation, or six generations, in the past. "We were not alive when these injustices took place," white students say. "Some of us were born to parents who came here as immigrants. None of these things are our responsibility, and we should not be asked to suffer for them."

But the hundreds of classrooms without teachers in Chicago's public schools, the thousands of children without classrooms in the schools of Irvington and Paterson and East Orange, the calculated racial segregation of the children in the skating rink in

District 10 in New York City, and the life-long poisoning of children in the streets and schools of East St. Louis are not matters of anterior injustice. They are injustices of 1991.

Over 30 years ago, the city of Chicago purposely constructed the high-speed Dan Ryan Expressway in such a way as to cut off the section of the city in which housing projects for black people had been built. The Robert Taylor Homes, served by Du Sable High, were subsequently constructed in that isolated area as well; realtors thereafter set aside adjoining neighborhoods for rental only to black people. The expressway is still there. The projects are still there. Black children still grow up in the same neighborhoods. There is nothing "past" about most "past discrimination" in Chicago or in any other northern city.

In seeking to find a metaphor for the unequal contest that takes place in public school, advocates for equal education sometimes use the image of a tainted sports event. We have seen, for instance, the familiar image of the playing field that isn't level. Unlike a tainted sports event, however, a childhood cannot be played again. We are children only once; and, after those few years are gone, there is no second chance to make amends. In this respect, the consequences of unequal education have a terrible finality. Those who are denied cannot be "made whole" by a later act of government. Those who get the unfair edge cannot be later stripped of what they've won. Skills, once attained—no matter how unfairly—take on a compelling aura. Effectiveness seems irrefutable, no matter how acquired. The winners in this race *feel* meritorious. Since they also are, in large part, those who govern the discussion of this issue, they are not disposed to cast a cloud upon the means of their ascent. People like Elizabeth are left disarmed. Their only argument is justice. But justice, poorly argued, is no match

for the acquired ingenuity of the successful. The fruits of inequality, in this respect, are self-confirming.

. . .

There are "two worlds of Washington," the *Wall Street Journal* writes. One is the Washington of "cherry blossoms, the sparkling white monuments, the magisterial buildings of government . . . , of politics and power." In the Rayburn House Office Building, the *Journal* writes, "a harpist is playing Schumann's 'Traumere,' the bartenders are tipping the top brands of Scotch, and two huge salmons sit on mirrored platters." Just over a mile away, the other world is known as Anacostia.

In an elementary school in Anacostia, a little girl in the fifth grade tells me that the first thing she would do if somebody gave money to her school would be to plant a row of flowers by the street. "Blue flowers," she says. "And I'd buy some curtains for my teacher." And she specifies again: "Blue curtains."

I ask her, "Why blue curtains?"

"It's like this," she says. "The school is dirty. There isn't any playground. There's a hole in the wall behind the principal's desk. What we need to do is first rebuild the school. Another color. Build a playground. Plant a lot of flowers. Paint the classrooms. Blue and white. Fix the hole in the principal's office. Buy doors for the toilet stalls in the girls' bathroom. Fix the ceiling in this room. It looks like somebody went up and peed over our heads. Make it a beautiful clean building. Make it *pretty*. Way it is, I feel ashamed."

Her name is Tunisia. She is tall and thin and has big glasses with red frames. "When people come and see our school," she says, "they don't say nothing, but I know what they are thinking."

"Our teachers," says Octavia, who is tiny with red sneakers and two beaded cornrows in her hair, "shouldn't have to eat here in the basement. I would like for them to have a dining room. A nice room with a salad bar. Serve our teachers big thick steaks to give them energy."

A boy named Gregory tells me that he was visiting in Fairfax County on the weekend. "Those neighborhoods are different," Gregory reports. "They got a golf course there. Big houses. Better schools."

I ask him why he thinks they're better schools.

"We don't know why," Tunisia says. "We are too young to have the information."

"You live in certain areas and things are different," Gregory explains.

Not too long ago, the basement cafeteria was flooded. Rain poured into the school and rats appeared. Someone telephoned the mayor: "You've got dead rats here in the cafeteria."

The principal is an aging, slender man. He speaks of generations of black children lost to bitterness and failure. He seems worn down by sorrow and by anger at defeat. He has been the principal since 1959.

"How frustrating it is," he says, "to see so many children going hungry. On Fridays in the cafeteria I see small children putting chicken nuggets in their pockets. They're afraid of being hungry on the weekend."

A teacher looks out at her class: "These children don't smile. Why should they learn when their lives are so hard and so unhappy?"

Seven children meet me in the basement cafeteria. The flood that brought the rats is gone, but other floods have streaked the tiles in the ceiling.

The school is on a road that runs past several boarded buildings. Gregory tells me they are called "pipe" houses. "Go by there one day—it be vacant. Next day, they bring sofas, chairs. Day after that, you see the junkies going in."

I ask the children what they'd do to get rid of the drugs.

"Get the New Yorkers off our streets," Octavia says. "They come here from New York, perturbed, and sell our children drugs."

"Children working for the dealers," Gregory explains.

A teacher sitting with us says, "At eight years old, some of the boys are running drugs and holding money for the dealers. By 28, they're going to be dead."

Tunisia: "It makes me sad to see black people kill black people."

"Four years from now," the principal says when we sit down to talk after the close of school, "one third of the little girls in this fifth grade are going to be pregnant."

I look into the faces of these children. At this moment they seem full of hope and innocence and expectation. The little girls have tiny voices and they squirm about on little chairs and lean way forward with their elbows on the table and their noses just above the table's surface and make faces at each other and seem mischievous and wise and beautiful. Two years from now, in junior high, there may be more toughness in their eyes, a look of lessened expectations and increased cynicism. By the time they are 14, a certain rawness and vulgarity may have set in. Many will be hostile and embittered by that time. Others will coarsen, partly the result of diet, partly self-neglect and self-dislike. Visitors who meet such girls in elementary school feel tenderness; by junior high, they feel more pity or alarm.

But today, in Anacostia, the children are young and whimsical and playful. If you hadn't worked with kids like these for 20 years, you would have no reason to feel sad. You'd think, "They have the world before them."

"The little ones come into school on Monday," says the teacher, "and they're hungry. A five-year-old. Her laces are undone. She says, 'I had to dress myself this morning.' I ask her why. She says, 'They took my mother off to jail.' Their stomachs hurt. They don't know why. We feed them something hot because they're hungry."

I ask the children if they go to church. Most of them say they do. I ask them how they think of God.

"He has a face like ours," Octavia says.

A white face or a black face?

"Mexican," she says.

Tunisia: "I don't know the answer to that question."

"When you go to God," says Gregory, "He'll remind you of everything you did. He adds it up. If you were good, you go to Heaven. If you were selfish, then He makes you stand and wait awhile—over there. Sometimes you get a second chance. You need to wait and see."

We talk about teen-agers who get pregnant. Octavia explains: "They want to be like rock stars. Grow up fast." She mentions a well-known singer. "She left school in junior high, had a baby. Now she got a swimming pool and car."

Tunisia says, "That isn't it. Their lives are sad."

A child named Monique goes back to something we discussed before: "If I had a lot of money, I would give it to poor children."

The statement surprises me. I ask her if the children in this neighborhood are poor. Several children answer, "No."

Tunisia (after a long pause): "We are all poor people in this school."

The bell rings, although it isn't three o'clock. The children get up and say goodbye and start to head off to the stairs that lead up from the basement to the first floor. The principal later tells me he released the children early. He had been advised that there would be a shooting in the street this afternoon.

I tell him how much I liked the children and he's obviously pleased. Tunisia, he tells me, lives in the Capital City Inn—the city's largest homeless shelter. She has been homeless for a year, he says; he thinks that this may be one reason she is so reflective and mature.

QUESTIONS FOR DISCUSSION

1. In what ways has your own class background affected the quality of education that you have thus far received?
2. Ask friends or classmates who may have grown up in a different social class than you how their educational experiences were different from yours.
3. Given the increasing disparity between the "Haves" and "Have Nots," how might our society begin to address class-based inequality in education?

37

HOW CORPORATIONS ARE BUYING THEIR WAY INTO AMERICA'S CLASSROOMS

STEVEN MANNING

When Susan Crockett walked Amy, her 8-year-old daughter, to her school bus stop last September; she was in for a surprise. The school bus that rolled up was covered with advertisements for Burger King, Wendy's and other brand name products. A few weeks later, Amy, a third grader, and Crockett's three older children arrived home toting free book covers and school planners covered with ads for Kellogg's Pop Tarts and Fox TV personalities. Then, in November, came news that local school officials were pushing a year-old contract giving Coca-Cola exclusive permission to sell its products in district schools. That was the last straw for Crockett.

"It really angers me that the school is actively promoting and pushing a product that's not good for kids," says Crockett, whose oldest child was a senior last year in the Colorado Springs, Colorado, school system. "What's next: Will kids be required to wear Nikes before they are allowed to go to school?"

These days, lots of parents are asking that question.

Eager to attract a captive audience of young customers, almost every large corporation sponsors some type of in-school marketing program. Many also sponsor cur-

riculum materials salted with brand names and corporate logos. . . . Throughout the nation, nearly 40 percent of schools begin their day with current events and commercials transmitted by Channel One, the in-school TV news programs for teens. Started in 1989 by controversial entrepreneur Chris Whittle, Channel One is probably the best-known in-school marketing program, but more recent examples are even more alarming:

- An exercise book that purports to teach third graders math by having them count Tootsie Rolls.
- A classroom business course that teaches students the value of work by showing them how McDonald's restaurants are run.
- Multimillion-dollar contracts that have turned some schools into virtual sales agents for Coke and Pepsi.

Why the stampede into the classroom? "That's where the kids are," says Alex Molnar, director of the Center for the Analysis of Commercialism in Education at the University of Wisconsin, Milwaukee. "Companies like to say they are promoting education and school-business partnerships, but what they're really doing is going after the kids' market anywhere they can." Ira Mayer, publisher of *Youth Markets Alert*, an industry newsletter, notes that companies "want to get them started young—and hopefully keep them for life—that's what brand loyalty is all about." In 1997, children 4 to 12

From "How Corporations Are Buying Their Way into America's Classrooms" by Steven Manning in *The Nation,* September 27, 1999: 11–18. Reprinted by permission of The Nation, Inc.

spent an estimated $24.4 billion, according to *American Demographics.* Last year, kids 12 to 19 spent an estimated $141 billion, according to Teenage Research Unlimited. Meanwhile, many cash-strapped public schools find it difficult to resist corporate-sponsored advertising and handouts, especially when they come with free computers or new football stadiums and scoreboards.

Nowhere is the convergence of school-house need and corporate greed more apparent than in Colorado Springs. At Palmer High School, students walk through hall-ways dotted with signs for national brands and local companies, eat in a snack bar sporting brand-new vending machines, use computers with ad-bearing mouse pads and play basketball in a gym decorated with banners of corporate sponsors.

. . .

"This was the first school district in the nation to offer advertising opportunities, and the results have been great for our students," said Kenneth Burnley, superintendent of Colorado Springs School District 11. Burnley dreamed up the district's advertising and corporate-partnership programs in 1993, after years of coping with harsh budget cuts. When Burnley took over in 1989, the school district was $12 million in the red. Although Colorado Springs, located about sixty miles south of Denver, is best known for its beautiful weather and tourist attractions like Pike's Peak, it's also the state's second-largest city, and its schools suffer from ills common to urban school districts: overcrowded classes, lack of extracurricular programs and crumbling school buildings. There's also the problem that until 1996, city voters had not approved a tax increase for education in more than two decades. (In a 1999 survey by *Education Week,* Colorado was ranked forty-ninth in the nation in the adequacy of resources devoted to education.)

"Our taxpayers have challenged us to be more creative and businesslike in how we finance the schools, so we decided to take a page out of business's book," says Burnley. "I realized we could sell for cash something we always had, but never knew we had"—access to students. So far, some fifty companies have signed up as corporate partners, at a cost ranging from $1,500 to $12,000. Top dollar buys advertising rights on school buses, in all schools and four public-address announcements at every basketball and football game, among other benefits. A $1,500 check buys a 2 feet × 5 feet sign in one school and tickets to attend school athletic events. District 11 officials say the advertising packages bring in about $100,000 in revenue annually.

But the district's biggest and most lucrative deal is with Coke. Under a contract signed nearly two years ago, the district will receive $8.4 million over ten years—and more if it exceeds its requirement of selling 70,000 cases of Coke products a year. Along with the contract come other Coke-sponsored sweeteners, like a contest in which a Chevrolet Cavalier was awarded to a senior with perfect attendance.

Last fall, a top District 11 official sent a letter to administrators urging them to increase sales of Coke products in their schools in order to meet their sales goal. In the letter, John Bushey, the official who oversees the contract, instructed principals to allow students virtually unlimited access to Coke machines and to move the machines to where they would be "accessible to the students all day." Wrote Bushey: "Research shows that vendor purchases are closely linked to availability," adding, "location, location, location is the key." The confidential letter, which was first published by the Colorado Springs *Independent,* also urged teachers to allow students to drink Coke in the classroom: "If soda is not allowed in classes, consider allowing juices, water, and teas." Bushey signed the letter "The Coke Dude."

The letter, and the district's policy of establishing school sales quotas—including in elementary schools—has alarmed critics of school commercialism. "This is the first concrete evidence we've had that the soft-drink companies are turning schools into virtual sales agents for their products," says Andrew Hagelshaw, senior program director of the Center for Commercial-free Public Education, a nonprofit group based in Oakland, California. "These kinds of contracts are going to change the priorities from education to soda consumption."

Bushey and other officials deny that the letter was meant to encourage kids to guzzle more Coke. "Our only purpose was to inform people about how the contract works, its incentives and disincentives," said Bob Moore, the district's chief financial officer. A spokesperson for Coca-Cola in Atlanta insisted that the company doesn't have a set quota policy. "It's up to the individual school district," said Coke's Scott Jacobson. "If they want to make more money by selling more product, we'll work with them."

. . .

Most teachers in Colorado Springs are apparently willing to work with Coke as well. "We haven't had a single complaint," says Kathy Glasmann, the president of the Colorado Springs Education Association, the local teachers' union. Superintendent Burnley agrees, attributing lack of protest against the corporate-sponsorship program to the "mores" of a community that is heavily Republican, fiscally conservative and strongly opposed to taxes. Plus, says Nancy Haley, a seventh-grade science teacher at a Colorado Springs middle school, "You just don't turn down a deal that will bring $20,000 a year to your school."

Still, there are pockets of furtive dissent. "Many teachers are quietly opposed to the advertising," says Ed Bailey, a fifth-grade math teacher at Steele Elementary School. "We feel we are being forced into the position of telling students, 'We approve of Coke, we approve of Burger King; we, the school, approve of these products, so they must be good for you.'" Some teachers have taken to hiding ads they've been asked to post in hallways, Bailey says. Others, like John Hawk, a twenty-five-year veteran of Colorado Springs schools, uses them for lessons on propaganda in his social studies classes at Mitchell High School. "Students and teachers need basic training on how to deal with the corporate invasion of every aspect of life," Hawk says. "Schools used to be the one safe haven where kids weren't exposed to a constant barrage of advertising. Now even that's gone."

Yet few students at Mitchell or other area schools seem to know or care what schools used to be like. This doesn't surprise John Crockett, Susan Crockett's oldest child. "Commercials, ads, videos, that's all my generation has known," says Crockett. "The ads [at Doherty High School] are no big topic of hallway conversation, that's for sure. They just seem to fade into the background."

Meanwhile, District 11 is determined not only to attract more corporate sponsors but to spread the Colorado Springs model nationwide. "We get dozens of calls every day from school districts wanting to replicate what we've done," says Bob Moore. "Can they visit here? Can they talk to us? We say, 'Sure, we want to spread the word.'" Already, the Denver, Houston, Newark and Jefferson County, Colorado, school districts have set up soft-drink or marketing programs. Jefferson County even got Pepsi to kick in $1.5 million to help build a new sports stadium, and some county schools tested a new science course, developed in part by Pepsi, titled "The Carbonated Beverage Company," in which students taste-test colas, analyze cola samples, take a video tour of a Pepsi bottling plant and visit a local Pepsi plant.

. . .

In its publicity efforts, District 11 has its own high-powered corporate partner, Dan DeRose, an entrepreneur who has single-handedly invented a brand-new mini-industry: the school-marketing broker. DeRose is the founder and president of DD Marketing, a firm that specializes in putting together exclusive marketing contracts for public schools and colleges. DeRose brought not only Coke to District 11 but also US West—in the first exclusive partnership between a telecommunications company and a school district. (Sign up for phone service or call waiting with US West, and a commission is paid to one's school of choice.) But DeRose has bigger ambitions.

A 37-year-old former professional football player and college athletic director, DeRose is evangelical in his belief that advertising deals are good not only for schools and education but also help level an unfair playing field: "Schools have been opening their doors to corporate America for years," DeRose says, noting that many school districts cut their own marketing deals with big companies, only to wind up with "peanuts" in exchange. "Our philosophy is if you're going to allow corporate America into your schools, maximize your return."

DeRose claims that he and his staff have visited more than 800 school districts nationwide during the past year, of which about 150 have signed exclusive soft-drink contracts, while 600 more are in the negotiating stage. According to published accounts, DD Marketing gets a 25–40 percent cut of each deal. DeRose is known for his imaginative pitches to interested schools and companies. During negotiations for a $3.5 million, ten-year exclusive contract for the Grapevine-Colleyville Independent School District in Texas with Dr. Pepper/7-Up, some school board members expressed unease with having advertisements in classrooms. As an alternative, DeRose helped arrange for Dr. Pepper logos to be painted on the rooftops of two high schools that lie directly under the flight path for Dallas–Fort Worth International Airport.

Critics like Andrew Hagelshaw say the cash being paid out to schools isn't all that impressive. In Colorado Springs, for example, the annual school budget is $165 million. Broken down, the ten-year, $8.4 million Coke contract works out to be a payment of $840,000 per year, or 0.5 percent of the total yearly budget. "On a per pupil basis, that's nothing," says Hagelshaw. "They're selling their kids out cheap."

Indeed, while school officials claim that their main motivation for seeking corporate contracts is money, there is some evidence that in the long run the deals may undermine their ability to obtain more state funds and may reinforce classic financial distinctions between poor and wealthy school districts. Low-income school districts that are desperate for school supplies often are the first and most eager clients of companies that provide free equipment to schools, such as Channel One and ZapMe! . . . The result: Poor schools get their ten or fifteen free televisions or computers (and the advertising that goes along with them), while district and state officials feel less motivated to provide the schools with adequate equipment or an in-school technology plan. Wealthier school districts often turn to corporate cash after being squeezed by local and state funding cutbacks, as was the case with both the Colorado Springs and Grapevine-Colleyville districts. The danger is that school administrators will become dependent on corporate handouts and forget that it was the failure to provide schools with adequate public funding that brought them to the begging bowl in the first place. As

Colorado Springs social studies teacher John Hawk notes, "It says something about our country's social priorities when we have to resort to corporate contracts to fund our schools."

DeRose brushes aside such criticisms. "Every school district of any size in the country wants in on this," he says. Unfortunately, that seems to be the case. Except for the occasional renegade school officials—like the Rhode Island administrator who recently physically removed all the soda machines from his school—most schools seem eager to get on the corporate gravy train. Although a number of educational organizations, including the national PTA and the National Education Association, have endorsed voluntary guidelines to help schools determine which, if any, in-school commercial activities have merit, most educators are unaware of them.

. . .

There are a few school districts, however, where parents and students are fighting back. At Berkeley High School last year, the Pepsi-Cola Company offered the school $90,000 and a fancy new electronic scoreboard for the football stadium in exchange for an exclusive vending deal. Meanwhile, Nike approached the school's athletic director with a proposal to provide athletic equipment and uniforms—as long as all student-athletes wore a Nike swoosh on their back. The deals were ultimately scuttled, in large part because of the efforts of a determined 15-year-old sophomore, Sarah Church. Church organized a student-led forum on whether the school should accept the deals, then inspired her classmates to testify against them at school board meetings. "We took a strong stand against selling out students to advertisers," Church says. Today, she is trying to launch a national student movement against in-school advertising.

In June, in neighboring San Francisco, the school board approved the Commercial Free Schools Act, the first measure of its kind in the country. The act bars the district from signing exclusive beverage contracts or adopting educational materials that contain brand names.

But perhaps the most ambitious and successful anticommercialism campaign has been in Seattle. Three years ago, the Seattle school board proposed a far-reaching corporate-sponsorship program that officials predicted would bring in $1 million a year. The proposal caught the attention of Brita Butler-Wall, a teacher-trainer at the University of Seattle and the mother of two children in Seattle schools. "I thought the idea was wacky, since it seems counter to everything schools are supposed to stand for," she says. Butler-Wall contacted a few other parents, and they decided to "go to the mat on the issue." The group, calling itself the Seattle Citizens' Campaign for Commercial-free Schools (CCC), sponsored a series of public meetings on the issue that drew statewide attention. Then they organized a series of "commercialism walk-throughs" of the city's schools, collecting as many examples of already existing commercial material as they could, sending a copy of their findings to the school board.

The CCC also won support from a group not usually involved in educational battles: organized labor. Mike Miller, a local Teamsters activist and father with a son in the public schools, and David Yao, head of the local postal workers' union, presented a resolution condemning the school board's plan to the King County Labor Council, and to their surprise it passed unanimously. "We are opposed to exposing schoolchildren to corporate values in an educational environment where they assume that whatever is presented to them carries the approval of the educational establishment," the resolution read in part. While the city's teachers' union declined to take a position on the commercialism issue, other local unions played an important role in galvanizing opposition.

In March 1997 the school board rescinded the advertising sponsorship policy. Instead, it appointed a school–community task force—members of the CCC—to study the issue and make policy recommendations. Those recommendations, issued last September, call for sharp restrictions on most forms of commercial activities. The task force's final report, though, is still waiting for official approval. In the meantime, the Seattle school board signed its own exclusive soft-drink contract with Coca-Cola, over the strenuous objections of the CCC and others.

Which raises the question: Are opponents of schoolhouse commercialism fighting a losing battle? For now at least, it seems that the corporations have the upper hand. Unless more parents, teachers and legisla-

tors start paying attention, consumerism may replace learning as the predominant value in American public education.

QUESTIONS FOR DISCUSSION

1. Think about your own educational experiences. Are there additional ways that corporate influence could be found in your schools?
2. What are the consequences of corporate sponsorship of public schools? Are there positive, as well as negative, effects?
3. Manning suggests that the presence of corporations in American schools will only increase. What do you think the long-term effects of this trend will be?

38

MISSING IN INTERACTION
MYRA SADKER • DAVID SADKER

"Candid Camera" would have a field day in elementary school. There would be no need to create embarrassing situations. Just set the camera to take a photograph every sixty seconds. Since classroom action moves so swiftly, snap-

shots slow down the pace and reveal subliminal gender lessons.

Snapshot #1 Tim answers a question.
Snapshot #2 The teacher reprimands Alex.
Snapshot #3 Judy and Alice sit with hands raised while Brad answers a question.
Snapshot #4 Sally answers a question.
Snapshot #5 The teacher praises Marcus for skill in spelling.

Snapshot #6 The teacher helps Sam with a spelling mistake.

Snapshot #7 The teacher compliments Alice on her neat paper.

Snapshot #8 Students are in lines for a spelling bee. Boys are on one side of the room and girls are on the other.

As the snapshots continue, the underlying gender messages become clear. The classroom consists of two worlds: one of boys in action, the other of girls' inaction. Male students control classroom conversation. They ask and answer more questions. They receive more praise for the intellectual quality of their ideas. They get criticized. They get help when they are confused. They are the heart and center of interaction. Watch how boys dominate the discussion in this upper elementary class about presidents.

The fifth-grade class is almost out of control. "Just a minute," the teacher admonishes. "There are too many of us here to all shout out at once. I want you to raise your hands, and then I'll call on you. If you shout out, I'll pick somebody else."

Order is restored. Then Stephen, enthusiastic to make his point, calls out.

Stephen: I think Lincoln was the best president. He held the country together during the war.

Teacher: A lot of historians would agree with you.

Mike (seeing that nothing happened to Stephen, calls out): I don't. Lincoln was okay, but my Dad liked Reagan. He always said Reagan was a great president.

David (calling out): Reagan? Are you kidding?

Teacher: Who do you think our best president was, Dave?

David: FDR. He saved us from the depression.

Max (calling out): I don't think it's right to pick one best president. There were a lot of good ones.

Teacher: That's interesting.

Kimberly (calling out): I don't think the presidents today are as good as the ones we used to have.

Teacher: Okay, Kimberly. But you forgot the rule. You're supposed to raise your hand.

The classroom is the only place in society where so many different, young, and restless individuals are crowded into close quarters for an extended period of time day after day. Teachers sense the undertow of raw energy and restlessness that threatens to engulf the classroom. To preserve order, most teachers use established classroom conventions such as raising your hand if you want to talk.

Intellectually, teachers know they should apply this rule consistently, but when the discussion becomes fast-paced and furious, the rule is often swept aside. When this happens and shouting out beings, it is an open invitation for male dominance. Our research shows that boys call out significantly more often than girls. Sometimes what they say has little or nothing to do with the teacher's questions. Whether male comments are insightful or irrelevant, teachers respond to them. However, when girls call out, there is a fascinating occurrence: Suddenly the teacher remembers the rule about raising your hand before you talk. And then the girl, who is usually not as assertive as the male students, is deftly and swiftly put back in her place.

Not being allowed to call out like her male classmates during the brief conversation about presidents will not psychologically scar Kimberly; however, the system of silencing operates covertly and repeatedly. It occurs several times a day during each school week for twelve years, and even longer if Kimberly goes to college, and, most insidious of all, it happens subliminally. This micro-inequity eventually has a powerful cumulative impact.

On the surface, girls appear to be doing well. They get better grades and receive fewer punishments than boys. Quieter and more conforming, they are the elementary school's ideal students. "If it ain't broke, don't fix it" is the school's operating principle as girls' good behavior frees the teacher to work with the more difficult-to-manage boys. The result is that girls receive less time, less help, and fewer challenges. Reinforced for passivity, their independence and self-esteem suffer. As victims of benign neglect, girls are penalized for doing what they should and lose ground as they go through school. In contrast, boys get reinforced for breaking the rules; they are rewarded for grabbing more than their fair share of the teacher's time and attention.

Even when teachers remember to apply the rules consistently, boys are still the ones who get noticed. When girls raise their hands, it is often at a right angle, arm bent at the elbow, a cautious, tentative, almost insecure gesture. At other times they raise their arms straight and high, but they signal silently. In contrast, when boys raise their hands, they fling them wildly in the air, up and down, up and down, again and again. Sometimes these hand signals are accompanied by strange noises, "Ooh! Ooh! Me! Me! Ooooh!" Occasionally they even stand beside or on top of their seats and wave one or both arms to get attention. "Ooh! Me! Mrs. Smith, call on me." In the social studies class about presidents, we saw boys as a group grabbing attention while girls as a group were left out of the action.

When we videotape classrooms and play back the tapes, most teachers are stunned to see themselves teaching subtle gender lessons along with math and spelling. The teacher in the social studies class about presidents was completely unaware that she gave male students more attention. Only after several viewings of the videotape did she notice how she let boys call out answers but reprimanded girls for similar behavior. Low-achieving boys also get plenty of attention, but more often it's negative. No surprise there. In general, girls receive less attention, but there's another surprise: Unlike the smart boy who flourishes in the classroom, the smart girl is the student who is least likely to be recognized.

When we analyzed the computer printouts for information about gender and race, an intriguing trend emerged. The students most likely to receive teacher attention were white males; the second most likely were minority males; the third, white females; and the least likely, minority females. In elementary school, receiving attention from the teacher is enormously important for a student's achievement and self-esteem. Later in life, in the working world, the salary received is important, and the salary levels parallel the classroom: white males at the top and minority females at the bottom. In her classroom interaction studies, Jacqueline Jordan Irvine found that black girls were active, assertive, and salient in the primary grades, but as they moved up through elementary school, they became the most invisible members of classrooms.

The "Okay" Classroom Is Not

In our studies of sexism in classroom interaction, we have been particularly fascinated by the ways teachers react to student work and comments because this feedback is crucially important to achievement and self-esteem. We found that teachers typically give students four types of responses.

Teacher *praises*:   "Good job." "That was an excellent paper." "I like the way you're thinking."

Teacher *remediates,* encouraging a student to correct a wrong answer or expand and enhance thinking: "Check your addition." "Think about what you've just said and try again."

Teacher *criticizes,* giving an explicit statement that something is not correct: "No, you've missed number four." This category also includes statements that are much harsher: "This is a terrible report."

Teacher *accepts,* offering a brief acknowledgment that an answer is accurate: "Uh-huh." "Okay."

Teachers praise students only 10 percent of the time. Criticism is even rarer—only 5 percent of comments. In many classrooms teachers do not use any praise or criticism at all. About one-third of teacher interactions are comprised of remediation, a dynamic and beneficial form of feedback.

More than half the time, however, teachers slip into the routine of giving the quickest, easiest, and least helpful feedback—a brief nonverbal nod, a quick "Okay." They rely more on acceptance than on praise, remediation, and criticism combined. The bland and neutral "Okay" is so pervasive that we doubt the "Okay Classroom" is, in fact, okay.

In our research in more than one hundred classrooms, we found that while boys received more of all four reactions, the gender gap was greatest in the most precise and valuable feedback. Boys were more likely to be praised, corrected, helped, and criticized—all reactions that foster student achievement. Girls received the more superficial "Okay" reaction, one that packs far less educational punch. In her research, Jacqueline Jordan Irvine found that black females were least likely to receive clear academic feedback.

At first teachers are surprised to see videotapes where girls are "Okay'd" and boys gain clear feedback. Then it begins to make sense. "I don't like to tell a girl anything is wrong because I don't want to upset her," many say. This vision of females as fragile is held most often by male teachers. "What if she cries? I wouldn't know how to handle it."

The "Okay" response is well meaning, but it kills with kindness. If girls don't know when they are wrong, if they don't learn strategies to get it right, then they never will correct their mistakes. And if they rarely receive negative feedback in school, they will be shocked when they are confronted by it in the workplace.

Pretty Is—Handsome Does

Ashley Reiter, National Winner of the 1991 Westinghouse Talent Competition for her sophisticated project on math modeling, remembers winning her first math contest. It happened at the same time that she first wore her contact lenses. Triumphant, Ashley showed up at school the next day without glasses and with a new medal. "Everybody talked about how pretty I looked," Ashley remembers. "Nobody said a word about the math competition."

The one area where girls are recognized more than boys is appearance. Teachers compliment their outfits and hairstyles. We hear it over and over again—not during large academic discussions but in more private moments, in small groups, when a student comes up to the teacher's desk, at recess, in hallways, at lunchtime, when children enter and exit the classroom: "Is that a new dress?" "You look so pretty today." "I love your new haircut. It's so cute." While these comments are most prevalent in the early grades, they continue through professional education: "That's a great outfit." "You look terrific today."

Many teachers do not want to emphasize appearance. "They pull you in," a preschool teacher says. "The little girls come up to you with their frilly dresses and hair ribbons and jewelry. 'Look what I have,' they say and wait for you to respond. What are you supposed to do? Ignore them? Insult them? They look so happy when you tell them they're pretty. It's a way of connecting. I think it's what they're used to hearing, the way they are rewarded at home."

When teachers talk with boys about appearance, the exchanges are brief—quick recognition and then on to something else. Or teachers use appearance incidents to move on to a physical skill or academic topic. In one exchange, a little boy showed the teacher his shiny new belt buckle. Her response: "Cowboys wore buckles like that. They were rough and tough and they rode horses. Did you know that?"

When teachers talk to girls about their appearance, the conversations are usually longer, and the focus stays on how pretty the girl looks. Sometimes the emphasis moves from personal appearance to papers and work. When boys are praised, it is most often for the intellectual quality of their ideas. Girls are twice as likely to be praised for following the rules of form. "I love your margins" is the message.

The Bombing Rate

"How long do you wait for students to answer a question?" When we ask teachers to describe what they do hundreds of times daily in the classroom, their answers are all over the map: One minute. Ten seconds. Five seconds. Twenty-five seconds. Three seconds.

Mary Budd Rowe was the first researcher to frame this question and then try to answer it. Following her lead, many others conducted wait time studies and uncovered an astonishingly hurried classroom. On average, teachers wait only nine-tenths of a second for a student to answer a question. If a student can't answer within that time, teachers call on another student or answer the question themselves.

When questions are hurled at this bombing rate, some students get lost, confused, or rattled, or just drop out of the discussion. "Would you repeat that?" "Say it again." "Give me a minute. I can get it." Requests such as these are really pleas for more time to think. Nobody has enough time in the bombing rate classroom, but boys have more time than girls.

Waiting longer for a student to answer is one of the most powerful and positive things a teacher can do. It is a vote of confidence, a way of saying, "I have high expectations for you, so I will wait a little longer. I know you can get it if I give you a chance." Since boys receive more wait time, they try harder to achieve. As girls struggle to answer under the pressure of time, they may flounder and fail. Watch how it happens:

> "Okay, class, get ready for your next problem. Mr. Warren has four cash registers. Each register weighs thirteen kilograms. How many kilograms do the registers weigh altogether? Linda?"
>
> The teacher waits half a second. Linda looks down at her book and twists her hair. She says nothing in the half-second allotted to her.
>
> "Michael?"
>
> The teacher waits two seconds. Michael is looking down at his book. The teacher waits two more seconds. Michael says, "Fifty-two?"
>
> "Good. Exactly right."

Less assertive in class and more likely to think about their answers and how to respond, girls may need *more* time to think. In the real world of the classroom, they receive less. For female achievement and self-esteem, it is a case of very bad timing.

Boy Bastions—Girl Ghettos

Raphaela Best spent four years as an observer in an elementary school in one of Maryland's most affluent counties. She helped the children with schoolwork, ate lunch with them, and played games with them in class and at recess. As an anthropologist, she also took copious notes. After more than one thousand hours of living with the children, she concluded that elementary school consists of separate and unequal worlds. She watched segregation in action firsthand. Adult women remember it well.

A college student recalled, "When I was in elementary school, boys were able to play basketball and kick ball. They had the side of the playground with the basketball hoops." Another college woman remembers more formal segregation: "I went to a very small grammar school. At recess and gym the boys played football and the girls jumped rope. All except one girl and one boy—they did the opposite. One day they were pulled aside. I'm not exactly sure what they were told, but the next day the school yard was divided in two. The boys got the middle and the girls got the edge, and neither sex was allowed on the other's part."

A third grader described it this way: "Usually we separate ourselves, but my teacher begins recess by handing a jump rope to the girls and a ball to the boys." Like the wave of a magic wand, this gesture creates strict gender lines. "The boys always pick the biggest areas for their games," she says. "We have what's left over, what they don't want."

Every morning at recess in schoolyards across the country, boys fan out over the prime territory to play kick ball, football, or basketball. Sometimes girls join them, but more often it's an all-male ball game. In the typical schoolyard, the boys' area is ten times bigger than the girls'. Boys never ask if it is their right to take over the territory, and it is rarely questioned. Girls huddle along the sidelines, on the fringe, as if in a separate female annex. Recess becomes a spectator sport.

Teachers seldom intervene to divide space and equipment more evenly, and seldom attempt to connect the segregated worlds—not even when they are asked directly by the girls.

"The boys won't let us play," a third grader said, tugging at the arm of the teacher on recess duty. "They have an all-boys club and they won't let any girls play."

"Don't you worry, honey," the teacher said, patting the little girl's hair. "When you get bigger, those boys will pay you all the attention you want. Don't you bother about them now."

As we observed that exchange, we couldn't help but wonder how the teacher would have reacted if the recess group had announced "No Catholics" or if white children had blatantly refused to play with Asians.

Barrie Thorne, a participant observer in elementary schools in California and Michigan whose students are mainly from working-class families, captured the tiny incidents that transform integrated classes into gender-divided worlds: Second-grade girls and boys eat lunch together around a long rectangular table. A popular boy walks by and looks the scene over. "Oooh, too many girls," he says, and takes a place at another table. All the boys immediately pick up their trays and abandon the table with girls, which has now become taboo.

Although sex segregation becomes more pervasive as children get older, contact points remain. School life has its own gender rhythm as girls and boys separate, come together, and separate again. But the points of contact, the together games that girls and boys play, often serve to heighten and solidify the walls of their separate worlds.

"You can't get me!" "Slobber Monster!" With these challenges thrown out, the game begins. It may be called "Girls Chase the Boys" or "Boys Chase the Girls" or "Chase and Kiss." It usually starts out one on one, but then the individual boy and girl enlist same-sex peers. "C'mon, let's get that boy." "Help, a girl's gonna get me!"

Pollution rituals are an important part of these chases. Children treat one another as if they were germ carriers. "You've got cooties" is the cry. (Substitute other terms for different cultures or different parts of the country.) Elaborate systems are developed around the concept of cooties. Transfer occurs when one child touches another. Prepared for such attack, some protect themselves by writing C.V. (cooties vaccination) on their arms.

Sometimes boys give cooties to girls, but far more frequently girls are the polluting gender. Boys fling taunts such as "girl stain" or "girl touch" or "cootie girl." The least-liked girls, the ones who are considered fat or ugly or poor, become "cootie queens," the real untouchables of the class, the most contaminating females of all.

Chasing, polluting, and invasions, where one gender attacks the play area of the other, all function as gender intensifiers, heightening perceived differences between female and male to an extreme degree. The world of children and the world of adults is composed of *different* races, but each gender is socially constructed as so different, so alien that we use the phrase "the *opposite* sex."

It is boys who work hardest at raising the walls of sex segregation and intensifying the difference between genders. They distance themselves, sending the message that girls are not good enough to play with them.

Watch which boys sit next to the girls in informally sex-segregated classrooms and lunchrooms; they are the ones most likely to be rejected by male classmates. Sometimes they are even called "girls." A student at The American University remembers his school lunchroom in Brooklyn:

> At lunch our class all sat together at one long table. All the girls sat on one side, and the boys sat on the other. This was our system. Unfortunately, there were two more boys in my class than seats on the boys' side. There was no greater social embarrassment for a boy in the very hierarchical system we had set up in our class than to have to sit on the girls' side at lunch. It happened to me once, before I moved up the class social ladder. Boys climbed the rungs of that ladder by beating on each other during recess. To this day, twenty years later, I remember that lunch. It was horrible.

Other men speak, also with horror, of school situations when they became "one of the girls." The father of a nine-year-old daughter remembered girls in elementary school as "worse than just different. We considered them a subspecies." Many teachers who were victims of sexist schooling themselves understand this system and collaborate with it; they warn noisy boys of a humiliating punishment: "If you don't behave, I'm going to make you sit with the girls."

Most little girls—five, six, seven, or eight—are much too young to truly understand and challenge their assignment as the lower-caste gender. But without challenge over the course of years, this hidden curriculum in second-class citizenship sinks in. Schools and children need help—intervention by adults who can equalize the playing field.

We have found that sex segregation in the lunchroom and schoolyard spills over into the classroom. In our three-year, multistate study of one hundred classrooms, our raters drew "gender geography" maps of each class they visited. They found that more than half of the classes were segregated by gender. There is more communication across race than across gender in elementary schools.

We have seen how sex segregation occurs when children form self-selected groups. Sometimes the division is even clearer, and so is the impact on instruction.

> The students are seated formally in rows. There are even spaces between the rows, except down the middle of the room where the students have created an aisle large enough for two people standing side by side to walk down. On one side of the aisle, the students are all female; on the other side, all male. Black, white, Hispanic, and Asian students sit all around the room, but no student has broken the gender barrier.
>
> The teacher in the room is conducting a math game, with the right team (boys) against the left team (girls). The problems have been put on the board, and members of each team race to the front of the room to see who can write the answer first. Competition is intense, but eventually the girls fall behind. The teacher keeps score on the board, with two columns headed "Good Girls" and "Brilliant Boys."

The gender segregation was so formal in this class that we asked if the teacher had set it up. "Of course not." She looked offended. "I wouldn't think of doing such a thing. The students do it themselves." It never occurred to the well-meaning teacher to raise the issue or change the seats.

In our research we have found that gender segregation is a major contributor to female invisibility. In sex-segregated classes, teachers are pulled to the more talkative, more disruptive male sections of the classroom or pool. There they stay, teaching boys more actively and directly while the girls fade into the background.

The Character(s) of the Curriculum

At a workshop on sexism in the curriculum, we asked participants, "Have you ever read the book *I'm Glad I'm a Boy! I'm Glad I'm a Girl!?*" Since most of the teachers, principals, and parents had not read it, we showed it to them. *I'm Glad I'm a Boy! I'm Glad I'm a Girl!* is for very young children. One page shows the jobs and activities that boys can do, and the following page shows what is appropriate for girls.

The book announces that boys can be doctors and shows a large male cartoon character with a stethoscope around his neck.

"What do girls do?" we asked the audience.

"They're nurses," the parents and educators chorused as one. They may not have read this book, but they seemed to know the plot line. A little girl nurse pushing a wheelchair is drawn on the page.

"Obviously a case of occupational stereotyping with the girl receiving less of every kind of reward including money, but do you notice anything else?" we asked. Most of the people were puzzled, but a few spotted the subtlety: "Look at how little the girl is." When we showed both pages at once, the boy doctor, a cartoon version of Doogie Howser, towered over the girl pushing the wheelchair.

The next page shows boys as pilots. "What are girls?" we asked.

"Stewardesses," the audience called back. A cartoon girl with a big smile and a short skirt carries a tray of drinks. The audience chuckled as several people remarked, "Look, her underpants are showing." "A little cheesecake for the younger set," someone joked as the next picture emerged, a boy drawn as a policemen.

"What are girls?"

This one had the group confused. "Mommies?" "Criminals?" "Crossing guards?" "Meter maids?" They found it. A tough-looking female figure is shown writing out a ticket for an obviously miserable motorist caught in a parking violation. "She looks as if she's had a steroid treatment," a teacher joked. "She's very big this time." The images continued: boys as those who eat, and girls as the ones who cook; boys as the builders of homes, and girls as the ones who clean them. The picture accompanying the caption about cleaning is that of a smiling cartoon girl pushing a vacuum cleaner. She and the cleaning machine are drawn very large because there is so much work to do. This image upset the audience. "Oh, no," several groaned. Others hissed and booed.

The next caption identified boys as the ones who fix things.

"Girls break things," the audience chorused back. But this time the author had outsmarted them. "Break" was too active. The parents and educators tried other stereotypes: "Girls clean things?" "Play with things?" "Buy things?" "Girls cry over things?"

"These are great responses, but they're all too active."

"Girls watch boys?" an astute parent suggested. She was on to something. Several studies have shown that in basal readers the activity girls are most often engaged in is watching boys in action. They look at boys play baseball, admire them as they perform magic tricks, wave good-bye from behind windows as boys leave for adventure. But in this case even "watch" was too active. The audience was stumped.

"Girls are things!" a young woman burst out. She had actually outdone the author, so we displayed the page: GIRLS NEED THINGS FIXED. The smiling stationary figure

is holding the wheel of her doll carriage in her hand. She isn't doing anything with the wheel, she is just standing there beside her tipped-over vehicle, clearly in need of male help. The audience groaned, but the pictures went on with boys shown as inventing while girls are described as using things boys invent. Accompanying this description is an illustration of a girl lying in a hammock and reading, thanks to a lamp invented by a boy. "Who invented the cotton gin?" we asked. Several people from around the room answered, "Eli Whitney." Like Alexander Graham Bell and Thomas Edison, this name is one of the staples of American education. "Has anyone ever heard of Catherine Littlefield Greene?" The parents and teachers were silent.

We told the story of the woman who, after the death of her husband, Nathaniel, who had been a general in the Revolutionary War, met Eli Whitney. A Yale-educated tutor, Whitney devised a model for the gin while working at Greene's Mulberry Grove Mansion. But his design was flawed; although seeds were pulled from the cotton, they became clogged in the rollers. It was Kitty Greene who came up with the breakthrough idea of using brushes for the seeds. The concept of the machine was so simple that copycat gins sprang up on other plantations. To pay for lawsuits during the fierce battle for patent rights, Kitty Greene sold her estate. It wasn't until seven years later that Eli Whitney won full title to the cotton gin.

"Why wasn't the patent taken out in both names?" a history teacher asked. It was an excellent question, and in the answer is an important lesson for children. At a time when it was unseemly for women to write books (many female authors took male names), it was especially unlikely for a lady to patent an invention. Textbooks tell the story of the names registered in the patent office, but they leave out how sexism and racism denied groups of people access to that registry.

The caricature of gender roles isn't over, and the picture book moves from inventions to politics, showing boys as presidents and girls as their wives.

"Is this some kind of joke?" a teacher asked. "When was it written?"

We threw the question back at the audience.

"The 1920s?" someone called out.

"No, they didn't have stewardesses then. Or meter maids. I think it was the 1950s," another teacher suggested.

Most of the group were stunned to learn that the book was published in 1970 and was in circulation in libraries and schools for years afterward. Few teachers would read a book like this to children today, and if they did, the phone lines would light up in most communities. Twenty-five years ago, books like this were commonplace, and it is a sign of progress that today they are considered outrageous.

"This book is so bad, it's good," a kindergarten teacher said. "I want to show it to my class. A lot of my kids fly on planes and see male flight attendants, and one of my children has a mom who's a doctor."

We agreed that the book with its yester-year sexism was a good teaching tool. We have shown it to students in every grade level. They had often read it critically and identified the stereotypes, but not always.

Balancing the Books

Few things stir up more controversy than the content of the curriculum. Teachers, parents, students—all seem to be aware intuitively that schoolbooks shape what the next generation knows and how it behaves. In this case research supports intuition. When children read about people in nontraditional gender roles, they are less likely to limit themselves to stereotypes. When children read about women and minorities in history, they are more likely to feel these groups have made important contributions to the country. As one sixth grader told us, "I love to read biographies about women. When I learn about what they've done, I feel like a door is opening. If they can do great things, maybe I can, too."

Double Jeopardy

During the spring of 1992 we visited sixteen fourth-, fifth-, and sixth-grade classes in Maryland, Virginia, and Washington, D.C., and gave students this assignment:

> In the next five minutes write down the names of as many famous women and men as you can. They can come from anywhere in the world and they can be alive or dead, but they must be real people. They can't be made up. Also— and this is very important—they can't be entertainers or athletes. See if you can name at least ten men and ten women.

At first the students write furiously, but after about three minutes, most run out of names. On average, students generate eleven male names but only three women's. While the male names are drawn directly from the pages of history books, the female names represent far greater student creativity: Mrs. Fields, Aunt Jemima, Sarah Lee, Princess Di, Fergie, Mrs. Bush, Sally Ride, and children's book authors such as Beverly Cleary and Judy Blume. Few names come from the pages of history. Betsy Ross, Harriet Tubman, Eleanor Roosevelt, Amelia Earhart, Sojourner Truth, Sacajawea, Rosa Parks, Molly Pitcher, and Annie Oakley are sometimes mentioned.

Several students cannot think of a single woman's name. Others have to struggle to come up with a few. In one sixth-grade class, a boy identified as the star history student is stumped by the assignment and obviously frustrated:

"Have you got any girls?" he asks, turning to a classmate.

"Sure. I got lots."

"I have only one."

"Think about the presidents."

"There are no lady presidents."

"Of course not. There's a law against it. But all you gotta do is take the presidents' names and put Mrs. in front of them."

In a fourth-grade class, a girl is drawing a blank. She has no names under her Women column. A female classmate leans over to help. "What about Francis Scott Key? She's famous." The girl immediately writes the name down. "Thanks," she says. "I forgot about her."

As we are leaving this class, one girl stops us. "I don't think we did very well on that list," she says. "It was too bad you didn't let us put in entertainers. We could've put in a lot of women then. I wrote down Madonna anyway."

Given a time line extending from the earliest days of human history to current events, and given no geographic limits whatsoever, these upper-elementary schoolchildren came up with only a handful of women. The most any single child wrote was nine. In one class the total number of women's names given didn't equal ten. We were stunned!

Something was very wrong—was it with the textbooks? We decided to look at them more closely. During the summer of 1992 we analyzed the content of fifteen math, language arts, and history textbooks used in Maryland, Virginia, and the District of Columbia. When we counted pictures of males and females, we were surprised to find that the 1989 language arts textbooks from Macmillan and D.C. Heath had twice as many boys and men as girls and women. In some readers the ratio was three to one. A 1989 upper-elementary history textbook had four times as many males pictured as females. In the 1992 D.C. Heath *Exploring Our World, Past and Present,* a text for sixth graders, only eleven female names were mentioned, and not a single American adult woman was included. In the entire 631 pages of a textbook covering the history of the world, only seven pages related to women, either as famous individuals or as a general group. Two of the seven pages were about Samantha Smith, a fifth-grade Maine student who traveled to the Soviet Union on a peace mission. While we felt that Samantha Smith's story brought an interesting message to other students, we wondered why Susan B. Anthony didn't rate a single line. No wonder students knew so little about women. Given the content of their history books, it was a tribute to their creativity that they could list any female names at all.

Every day in America little girls lose independence, achievement, and self-esteem in classes like this. Subtle and insidious, the gender-biased lessons result in quiet catastrophes and silent losses. But the casualties—tomorrow's women—are very real.

QUESTIONS FOR DISCUSSION

1. Think about your own educational experiences in light of Sadker and Sadker's study. In what ways was traditional gender ideology reflected in your schools? How did your teachers, books, curricular and extracurricular activities reinforce gender bias?

2. What effects did these patterns have on your sense of self?

39

CONFRONTING WHITE STUDENTS
The Whiteness of University Spaces

JOE R. FEAGIN • HERNÁN VERA • NIKITAH IMANI

The Character of Racialized Settings

For the most part, social scientists in Europe and North America have regarded space as a passive container of events, as the environmental vacuum where human lives take place. Yet, space plays a very active role in social life. Social relations are physically structured in material space, and human beings often view space expressively and symbolically.[1] In most societies those with the greater power and resources ordinarily control the use and meaning of important spaces in a society. For example, large amounts of land and other real estate are disproportionately consumed by the higher classes as evidence of their power and monetary position.[2] Indeed, the control of space has often been discussed in terms of a territorial imperative, for individuals and nations.[3]

Humans seek to conquer territory and maintain dominion over territory that can be used to demarcate in-groups and out-groups. The ethnic war in the former Yugoslavia provides one example. The struggles with police officers and the destruction of many city blocks in recent uprisings by African Americans and other people of color in Los Angeles, Miami, and other U.S. cities illustrate the significance of these places as racialized territories. Over the course of U.S. history, whites, from the white slaveholders

and segregationists of yesteryear to many white homeowners, real estate companies, banks, insurers, and law enforcement officers today, have clearly demarcated their territories, usually taking the lack of melanin in the skin as a principal marker for the dominant culture and in-group status. This centrality of territorial demarcation along skin-color lines for Europeans, and their descendants elsewhere, has been underscored by a number of social analysts who have examined the long history of European emergence and development.[4]

Particular places not only contain recurring movements of people and ideas but also are set within larger social contexts which provide additional meanings. The concept of racialized space encompasses the cultural biases that help define specific areas and territories as white or as black, with the consequent feelings of belonging and control. Consider the following interaction in a State University parking lot, a space with a clear campus function, but one not usually thought of as significant in racial terms. One black student made this comment in a focus group interview:

> I was walking to class. . . . It was about twelve noon and I had my backpack. I'm a black student, right. And there was this white girl in the car, and she pulled in the parking space, right. And she's about to get out. And I'm walking up. I'm not even paying attention to her, and the next thing I hear is "click, click." And she's looking at me like I'm going to rape her.

Although he was clearly recognizable as a university student, this young man was subjected to degrading gestures of suspicion by a white student. The white student's actions and look, and the black student's taking offense, can be understood fully if one probes the elaborate biases, fears, and presuppositions that steer racial relations in the United States. The parking lot was not simply a passive container of events but played an active part in what the actors perceived about each other and in the behavior they displayed towards each other. The black man was assumed to be in the wrong place. Many whites at universities like this assume, consciously or half-consciously, they are in *white* places.

In this reading we turn to an in-depth examination of the experiences of courageous black students with whites at one of the nation's major universities. We will see that the African American students suffer at the hands of white students and pay a heavy price for their choice of a white college. The costs include not only personal degradation and mental anguish but also academic costs. These problems are not unique to State University. Recently, for example, researchers at another predominantly white university found that most of the African American students questioned knew of incidents of racial mistreatment on campus. Fifty-nine percent had personally been verbally insulted. Apparently, much of this mistreatment came from other students. The researchers came to the conclusion that "the climate for African American students in this sample, was sufficiently problematic to interfere with academic success."[5]

The Symbolism of College Spaces: "Black Students Aren't Even Represented in the Yearbook"

In a variety of ways, the strong symbolism attached to spaces on college campuses becomes part of the personalities and identities of individuals associated with those spaces. A particular college or university commonly takes on a high level of significance in individuals' lives not only while they are there but also after they graduate. Many college graduates look upon their alma mater with great nostalgia. A diverse assortment of rings, yearbooks, and other paraphernalia emblazoned with college insignia fosters and facilitates the public display of individuals' association with their college. Alumni associations, class meetings, cruises, and various consumer gimmicks designed to build a school's reputation and endowment fund promote the continuation of the graduates' identification with the school.

The college yearbook is a textual and pictorial record of classes of students, their activities, and the campus spaces they have occupied. Yearbook photos are among the campus representations that make different groups of students visible to others on and off campus. This personal and group visibility, or invisibility, is a critical aspect of our idea of racialized space. To be recognized as valued members of the campus community is important to all groups of students, but especially to those who are underrepresented on a large campus like State University. The omission of African American students from the yearbook suggests a general lack of recognition of the black presence and achievements on campus and hints at the low status the whites who prepared the yearbook apparently granted to black students. This kind of neglect encourages black students to congregate in their own groups and plan their own activities and publications, a reaction that may bring white condemnation of this black "segregation."

Most campus activities at majority-white universities reflect white student traditions. In a study of black students at predominantly black and predominantly white colleges Walter Allen found that just under two-thirds of black students on white campuses, but only one-third on black campuses, felt that the campus activities there did not relate to their interests.[6] A 1990s survey of a large national sample of college students by Sylvia Hurtado and her associates found that just over half the African American students felt excluded from certain activities on their campuses because of skin color; the comparable figure for whites was six percent.[7]

Many campus activities become localized, white-dominated rituals in which to display college symbols, promote school solidarity, and spur student, alumni, and public celebration of a college's geographical and educational identities. In one group interview with the black parents, a father reviewed the most important spatial event for alumni, Homecoming ceremonies:

> Homecoming is supposedly what it says: Coming home; coming back to where you're from. I know of no black students who go to State University's homecoming. I know at one point they had separate homecomings, so to speak. There were functions that were set up specifically for the black students, specifically for the white students, because they knew they were not going to mix.

Homecoming events usually include sports activities that have become important rituals involving a display of college spirit and symbols. Yet, at many predominantly white colleges and universities these ceremonial events have long been white-oriented. For example, in 1994 black students at the University of Georgia organized a protest of homecoming activities because an all-white screening board selected an all-white slate of ten finalists for homecoming queen, ignoring seven students of color who were candidates. In recent years two black homecoming queens at the University of North Carolina endured racial harassment and vandalism directed at their cars from whites opposed to their participation in traditionally white ceremonies.[8] Not surprisingly, African American students and alumni often feel uncomfortable at traditional homecoming rituals.

Even the meaning of school traditions and events can be different for black and white students. For example, one of the authors attended Georgetown University as an undergraduate. He and his fellow black students there took great pride in the basketball team as the major black institution on a mostly white campus. At the Georgetown basketball games, the black students sat beside the white students, with all the students yelling "Go Hoyas" (the name of the team) at games. However, in this activity the black students did not feel solidarity with the white students. For most black students, "Go Hoyas" urged on the players as *black* players. It was thus a cry of African American unity in a sea of white faces. For most white students, in contrast, "Go Hoyas" was likely linked to a lofty sports tradition going back many decades. The students were side by side physically, but not joined in their commitments or understandings of the events taking place.

For the most part the black students that we interviewed more or less felt unwelcome. They were asked on an exit questionnaire to assess this statement: "Today State University is a college campus where black students are generally welcomed and nurtured." Eighty-nine percent of the students *disagreed* with the statement. Because of the negative racial messages and racial barriers, black students at SU and similar universities frequently identify the schools as places in which they are not wanted, by white students as well as by other whites on campus. The campuses become sites of daily struggle to survive rather than arenas where educational experiences are savored and where their personal development is central and nurtured.

The Aggressive Defense of White Territory: "Is That a Nigger with a White Girl?"

Ideally, the college experience should represent a special place and time in student lives that enhance in positive ways personal and collective identities. For students who sense that they are not wanted, however, the college campus becomes an unfriendly place and is likely to have a negative impact on both self-esteem and personal identity.

On or near predominantly white college campuses a significant number of white students, as well as other whites, regularly communicate hostile messages to black students, while many other whites stand by and take no action to stop such activity. In the focus groups there were several examples of aggressive white reactions to black intrusions into "white space." A university campus typically has geographical boundaries that blend into a surrounding array of student-oriented stores, restaurants, and night clubs, with students moving between the campus and the surrounding environment. One student gave the following account of an experience walking near the SU campus:

> I was walking down the street with my girlfriend—I guess it was over the summer—and out of the blue comes this guy driving in a van. He had one of those, you know, loudspeakers on the van, and he's like, "Is that a nigger with a white girl?" You do not understand how hard it was for my girlfriend to keep me from running and pulling him from the window of that truck because I knew he had to stop at the stop sign, you know, and I saw him there.

African American students walking on or near predominantly white universities have a heightened visibility for whites, both for students and for non-students. Here an ostensibly neutral space, a public street, was transformed into a place of significant pain and anger for a black student. The white hostility seems to reflect not only the view that the black student is "out of place" but also the deepest of all white-racist preoccupations, a concern about racial miscegenation. Walking on or near campus is an everyday activity that should not be racially threatening. Yet it periodically becomes a stressful act for black students. They are vulnerable to a range of racist acts, including many which can be carried out impersonally and with impunity.

Pain-creating racist epithets, like "nigger," "coon," and "boy," are used by whites as a way of defining certain areas as white spaces. The epithet is frequently meant as an insult and as a warning to a black person: "You should not be in that place" or "Watch your step." The common experience of African Americans is that there is usually a potential for violence when epithets such as these are hurled in public places.

Fear of direct physical attack is not unreasonable. One father in our focus groups noted briefly that he had heard about a racial attack at State University: "I did have one kid tell me that [he was] attacked by other students . . . a black student by some white students." And in a student focus group one young woman gave an account of whites moving from a racial epithet to a physical attack:

> A friend of mine . . . walked me to the bus stop. He was going back to his dorm . . . say three o'clock in the morning or whatever. These kids come by, these three white guys come. And they call him a "boy." He's about five feet ten inches, thin built. He kind of freaks out,

you know. He's like "I ain't nobody's boy." You know, freaks out. And all of a sudden they're kicking his ass. And they beat him down. The next time I'd seen him, he had stitches under his eyes, eyes out to here, and whatever. We had to go to [the] little student court. The [three white students'] old friends, black student athletes, stood up and tried to say their white friends were not racist. It really freaked me out. The case—I mean people saw these . . . three white guys beat one guy down—and the judgment was he could've run. Because he had a cane and he hit them with his cane, and . . . [they] said he could've run. He's just as [much at] fault as the white kids. O.K. [It] freaked me out. I was freaked out from that point on. State University is just so racist.

Some sociologists have suggested that "home territories" are those in which the occupants have a broad freedom to act, which is coupled with a sense of control over the area.[9] The white students' sense of what is home territory appears to underlie this attack. As in the previous incidents, the white words and gestures are ritualized and have well-known, shared meanings going back centuries in U.S. racial relations history. Here the student court (likely run by white students) concluded that because the black target of racial hostility had attempted to defend himself he was as culpable as the whites. Discrimination in white-dominated student justice systems is a complaint as well of black students at other colleges and universities.[10] In the above incident the victim did not suffer alone: at least one other black student shared his suffering. The latter's reaction illustrates again the importance of blacks' collective memories of white hostility.

How widespread are the black students' problems with white students? Their answers to the exit questionnaire indicated that a substantial number of whites on SU's campus were involved in actual instances of discrimination. In reply to the question, "Since you have been on this campus, how often have you had experiences with whites that you thought were racially discriminatory or hostile?" Sixty-nine percent said occasionally, and another fourteen percent said fairly often. Only seventeen percent replied that they never had such experiences. Asked, "How often have you been mistreated by white students at this campus because of your race?" about half said once or twice, while thirty-one percent replied several times or many times. Only nineteen percent said that they had not been mistreated by white students on racial grounds. Clearly, the overwhelming majority have faced some racial discrimination on campus, including mistreatment at the hands of white students. Moreover, one should recognize that these estimates of discrimination are probably on the low side. Past studies have shown that one way for African Americans to cope with everyday racism is not to "see" as much of it as possible, just to be able to survive in traditionally white spaces.[11]

Most white observers of U.S. racial relations, including many in the mass media, are removed from the daily realities of life for African Americans. Whether out of ignorance or intentionally, they usually associated blatant racism, including the hurling of racist epithets and extreme antiblack views, only with intolerant extremists such as segregationists or Ku Klux Klan members.[12] Moreover, some white analysts such as Allan Bloom, Richard Bernstein, and Arthur Schlesinger have claimed that one indicator of major progress in U.S. racial relations is the alleged elimination of blatantly racist discourse in U.S. society.[13] Nevertheless, the hurling of racist epithets and more violent attacks by whites, including white students, on or near a major college campus are by no means extinct.

Several surveys of black students have found that the problems the SU students discuss are common on other campuses. For instance, a 1980 survey of more than two hundred black University of Michigan undergraduates found that most had faced verbal and other racial harassment since their arrival. The most common forms of mistreatment were total avoidance by white students and subtle actions or statements with racial overtones. The black students reported encountering prejudiced statements about African Americans or other minorities, "nigger" epithets, racist "KKK" graffiti on walls, and racially motivated rudeness in social situations.[14] More recent surveys have found similar or worse patterns. A 1988 survey of more than two thousand black students at twenty predominantly white college colleges in Southern and border states found that "black students are still experiencing verbal attacks, written epithets, physical confrontations, and other more subtle, and in some ways more insidious, acts that discourage their participation in and graduation from college."[15]

According to the National Institute Against Prejudice and Violence, there were published reports of at least 250 racial incidents involving physical violence or serious psychological assault on college campuses between 1986 and 1990.[16] Between 1993 and 1996 racist graffiti were reportedly scrawled on dorm doors, on bulletin boards, and in other public places at a number of colleges and universities across the nation, including Harvard University, Yale Law School, Swarthmore College, the University of Colorado (Denver), the University of Wisconsin (River Falls), Antioch University, the Uni-

versity of West Virginia, Central Missouri State University, the Southern College of Technology, Miami University (Ohio), and Heidelberg College. Racist flyers were reportedly posted or handed out at Indiana University, the University of Northern Colorado, and the University of California Law School. Racist effigies were found at the University of Minnesota, and racist cartoons were reportedly published in several campus papers, including one at Princeton. Incidents involving antiblack threats (with "nigger" epithets) were reported at Salisbury State University, the University of Pennsylvania, and Michigan State University.[17]

Other Markers of White Space: "We'll Walk in, and It Seems Like People Just Slowly Disappear"

Not all actions by whites that mark off white spaces involve open hostility in the form of verbal attacks or real or threatened violence. Some antiblack actions are more subtle but still mark off white territory. Even relatively passive behavior can have a destructive impact if it plays a role in reinforcing the racial character of college places. Reflecting on their accumulating experiences, the juniors and seniors in our focus groups cited numerous examples of whites signalling the campus was "home territory" for whites. For many whites, blacks, or black men, are by definition intruders in white territory. A black male presence is frequently seen as a dangerous and threatening anomaly. Negative or hateful glances and actions imply an unspoken question, "Why are you here?" The unfriendly atmosphere is palpable in the way whites even look at blacks. This type of cold glance or "hate stare" on the part of white bystanders is reported by

African Americans in many institutional and street settings.

African American students frequently perceive they are not valued as part of the student body. Many white students, faculty members, and administrators seem to be chronically unable to acknowledge, or to recognize properly, the presence of black students. In settings where they seek services, black students may be avoided, overlooked, or become socially invisible. A number of recent research studies have shown how the white belief that blacks should yield to the white presence, whether on campus, in employment settings, or in restaurants, stores, and other public accommodations, is commonplace and has deep roots in white history and culture.

SU's black students are in an environment filled with racial meanings, meanings that are conveyed by many whites through an amazing variety of actions and reactions. Racial interpretations creep into the most innocent of human interactions. This type of classroom situation is not, as analysts like Bloom and D'Souza have suggested, a matter of white students being too eager to show their liberal credentials and a so-called "political correctness." Instead, it is a matter of racialized spaces that signal to African Americans that they do not really belong.

Sometimes white Americans are hostile to black Americans because of overt bigotry; at other times whites act inappropriately out of ignorance or a lack of experience with African Americans. This last point is very important. It is past experience that guides the black interpretation, and not a shoot-from-the-hip paranoia—the latter view a common misinterpretation by white observers observing this kind of black reaction to a discriminatory event. Black students' individual and collective experience with whites is the foundation on which they base evaluations of recurring white actions and motives. The patronizing behavior toward the black student leaves little doubt as to who is regarded as the anomaly or intruder. The offensiveness of such commonplace actions may be hard even for sympathetic white observers to see. Defining an attitude or action as patronizing involves an understanding of the duplicity involved. While kid-gloves treatment can have the appearance of cordiality, here it is coded in an insincere tone that is picked up by the student's antennae, a tone that signals a condescending diminution of the black person. Ironically, although blacks are often accused of being overly sensitive, it is white hypersensitivity to blacks, rather than the reverse, that is at the heart of most racial difficulties in white "home territories."

Certain incidents recounted by black students and parents suggest that some whites conceal their real feelings about people of color. Much white prejudice is not verbally expressed, at least not within earshot of people of color. Since the 1960s many white Americans have moved from openly expressed prejudices to grudging acknowledgment of, or actual politeness toward, African Americans. Still, many white Americans reveal their negative stereotypes and prejudices privately to friends and relatives, attitudes that play out publicly in the grudging or condescending actions that take the form of subtle discrimination.

White Stereotypes and Images: "You Can Play Basketball, Right?"

Negative or unflattering white images of African Americans are clear in the examples we have so far considered. These interracial incidents are not only about white actions but also about the understandings and stereotypes whites use to justify and interpret discriminatory practices. The educational settings at most predominantly white universities were defined, explicitly and implicitly, as white territories well before any significant number of black students arrived. These definitions include many images of what black students should be able to do:

> This one is kind of dumb, but anyway I'll say it. I was in one of my history classes when I was a freshman, and these white guys were talking about hockey, and I said something about it, and they said, "Oh, what do you know about hockey? You're black." And I said, "Well, just because we don't dominate that sport too doesn't mean I don't know nothing about hockey."

A second example illustrates the opposite white image, the view that black youth can play certain sports well:

> I was in a conditioning class, and we were about to play basketball, and the white girl wanted me on her team. She's like, "We got [says black student's name] on our team." [Then she says] "You can play basketball, right?" You know what I'm saying. . . . I could have not known how to dribble a ball, but just because of the fact that I was black she wanted me on her team.

A white gesture that might be seen as complimentary if it were solely based on achievement criteria is here taken as offensive because of the racial stereotype implied in the white action.

The assumption that African Americans can play certain sports is not unlike other assumptions that white students and professors sometimes make on mostly white campuses. While these assumptions are not as offensive as others the students reported, they nonetheless have a powerful effect in defining the mental model that black students receive about racial relations on campus. Through these white reactions, eloquent messages are given about who the players are in the social field of campus life.

The failure of many whites to recognize the great diversity of interests and inclinations among black students may seem an innocent misunderstanding, yet it nonetheless conveys an eloquent message about white assumptions about social positions on campus.

Well-documented in the student and parental accounts is our point that white racism is a system involving much more than overt and blatant discrimination. Today, racism also encompasses subtle and covert white responses, as well as nonresponses, that make African Americans feel uncomfortable, out of place, or unwanted.

The Injuries of Racism: "It Stifles You"

The accounts of racial hurdles offer much insight into the personal and collective damage that accrues to black students from mistreatment. We have seen the pain brought by hostile epithets and violent attacks, and the pain that comes from being treated as invisible. Reflecting on the suffering caused by a hostile college atmosphere, one mother provided these penetrating insights:

> Prejudice is something that you can't say, "It hurts my finger," or "It hurts in here. Put the bandage here." You know it hurts. You don't know why. Maybe you say, "Well, maybe I shouldn't think that. I should be above this." But you know it hurts. And it has an effect on you, but you can't say, "Well, it's right here. It hurts," or, "It's here. It's right here." But it hurts. It stifles you. . . . It's little things that intimidate you that keep you from being your best.

In the group commentaries, it is clear that to survive in a predominantly white environment, African American students must learn to "read" whites carefully, including white students who may constitute the opposition in particular settings. Frustration and anger are evident in the black student comments, as is the frequency with which black students must endure racial mistreatment without the freedom to give an adequate countering response. Some of the students reported that they confronted barbed comments from whites directly, while others preferred not to challenge the source.

Pain and suffering at the hands of white students is not the only cost of racism on campus. There are academic and personal development costs as well. A study of another predominantly white college campus looked at the experiences of similar groups of white and black students, with a majority of the latter reporting experiences with discrimination on campus. The study also found that the racist campus climate was serious enough to interfere with the academic success of the students.[18] Moreover, another survey of black students at eleven predominantly white universities found they were so concerned about academic survival that they were unable to devote as much attention as they needed to their own social, personal, and cultural development.[19] The consequences of racist barriers on campus are very serious, not only for black individuals' academic success but also for the success and development of black communities—and, ultimately, of the nation as a whole.

White Denial: "There's No Racism on This College Campus"

The denial that there is widespread white racism in U.S. society by a majority of white Americans is a problem for all African Americans, including African American students on mostly white campuses.

Some students in the focus groups noted that the denial of the reality of white racism was shared by some white students on campus:

> It was a creative writing class, and we had to write stories, whatever, and we had to sit in circles. And we had to tell our stories and read them. And mine was on racism, of course, because I'm always bringing that up. And it was just like a tragic mulatto story, and this girl couldn't stand being mixed. . . . So she kills herself, right. So this [white] guy goes, "You guys [have to] make the stories . . . fit reality. You can't make like a fantasy-fiction whatever." And he says, "Why did you do that? Why did you write a story like that?" [I said] "Because the girl also went to this university." And he goes, "There's no racism on this college campus." Freaked everybody out. And I was the only black. But there was a Puerto Rican, and there was a Chinese person in the room, and they just freaked. And I had never heard either one of them speak before. This guy said: "Where the hell do you live?" You know, "Where do you live? Do you live in this state?" And the teacher . . . goes, "Hold up, honey. I don't know what utopia you're living in." This is a white teacher; she said, "But honey you can just, inside of this room, outside of that door, on this campus . . . there is a lot of racism." . . . She's like, "Open your eyes, open your eyes, there's a lot of discrimination and racism on this campus." And that freaked me out.

Then the student added pointedly, "I think white students have the best time at this university. Because I mean, what do they have to go through, what's their biggest problem you know? No beer."

In this poignant incident the intense reaction of the students of color suggests a recurrent experience of maltreatment at this university. Many whites fail to perceive the existence of racism, in part because white privilege is taken for granted and in part because most whites have not experienced being in a subordinate position or have not been educated about the character and impact of racism. Jacqueline Fleming, who has done important research on barriers faced by black students, has suggested that most white students are taught by their elders to ignore the issue of racism. As a result, "the average student does not feel responsible for the racial climate or civil rights."[20] Many whites, both students and nonstudents, participate in subtle and blatant racist actions, or watch while others do, but still deny the reality of widespread discrimination. Moreover, by not educating white students to the reality of everyday racism, the predominantly white faculties at most universities participate as accessories in its maintenance and perpetuation.

Group Cohesion for Survival: "I Kind of Saw More and More Black People, and I Said, 'Okay. This Is Going to Work.'"

In the North and in the South, the system of Jim Crow segregation was a legally enforced system that set aside certain places and arenas for the exclusive use of whites. Today, many white and some neoconservative black observers have attacked the tendency of black college students to "self-segregate." This in-group behavior is frequently lamented and compared with earlier patterns of legal segregation. Black demands for separate dorms and support facilities have been much-discussed issues at major universities such as Brown, Colgate, the University of Virginia, and the University of North Caro-

lina. Many white students there have regularly complained that black groups are a sign of antiwhite hostility and "reverse discrimination."[21] It is significant that most white critics of campus racial relations or of multiculturalism have not collected empirical evidence on the actual experiences of black students on these campuses. If they did so, they would discover a problem that has its roots in institutionalized racism. The creation of distinct social support groups by the black students is *not* in any sense the counterpart of the old Jim Crow segregation.

Long ago, whites invented racial segregation based on their views of and practices toward African Americans, and whites have maintained racial segregation through legal and informal means for many decades. Even today, some white practices of exclusion are common on college campuses. As we noted previously, many black students on a variety of campuses report being excluded from some campus activities because of skin color, yet few whites voice similar complaints. In addition, a survey by Hurtado and her associates found that half the black students reported studying often with those of other racial–ethnic groups, and fifty-five percent reported dining with students from other groups. In contrast, the white figures were much lower, at fifteen percent and twenty-one percent respectively. White students were much more likely to be isolated from students of color than the reverse. In addition, participation in black student groups did not reduce blacks' interaction with students in other groups. In one news story, Hurtado was quoted as concluding that "These basic patterns of interaction suggest that the current concern about whether minority students are promoting and practicing self-segregation is misplaced. In fact, students of color are crossing ethnic/racial lines the most, while white students seem to be segregating themselves."[22]

On white-centered college campuses, most black student groups are defensive and protective, a response to what whites have done to exclude African Americans from white privileges and places. They are typically an attempt at self-determination and cultural maintenance in a sea of whiteness. The ultimate foundation of racial separation on these campuses is the preference of most whites for their own kind and their own culture.

Significantly, research reports on other major campuses have noted that many black students seek out other black students for defensive, social-support, and self-determination reasons. For example, a report on the racial climate at the University of California (Berkeley) campus found much anger over racism among black students, anger that had moved them to seek out the nurturing company of other African Americans.[23] One student there noted that "black students feel alienated on the campus. And if you're not, um, plugged into a support group then chances are, um, you're not going to find the support you need."[24] Similarly, students of color at Princeton reportedly avoid white student hostility there by separating themselves from whites, an action which has led to white criticism of these students as "being overly sensitive, defensive, hostile, angry, and isolationist."[25] In addition, finding supportive black organizations in a local black community can be important for individual survival. A recent survey of black students at mostly white universities found they were so concerned about intellectual survival that they were unable to devote as much attention to their personal, social, and cultural development as they should. Significantly, they reported that external black community involvement was essential for their personal and social development.[26] In addition, numerous research studies done by William Sedlacek at the University of Maryland have shown that black students who become part of a smaller community on campus, usually a group of black students, get higher grades and stay in school longer than those who remain more isolated.[27]

Still, the separation of black and white students on campus creates a dilemma for all concerned with the ideal of educational and societal integration. One student captured the anguish of this unresolved problem:

> Another thing is like when we go in the dining hall and everything. Like if you talk—I feel funny, and I don't know why—but when you talk to white people in the dining hall and everything, black people will look at you funny, and white people look at you funny, too. But we all go to school together. . . . and I don't know if I'm just conscious of that, or how does anybody else feel?

Conclusion

Many white observers of racial relations at predominantly white campuses tend to see black problems in familial, personal, or psychological terms. An array of critics and analysts blame black students or their parents for student problems on white campuses. The black students are faulted for academic troubles, for self-segregation, and for "paranoia" about racism when they should be working harder. Many whites on predominantly white campuses seem to share this point of view. For example, a white student at Stanford told one black analyst that "Blacks do nothing but complain and ask for sympathy when everyone really knows they can't do well because they don't try. If they worked harder, they could do as well as everyone else."[28] Even in those campus situations where some white authorities recognize the need for racial change, there is often an accent on personal changes rather than on structural and institutional changes. A recent Diversity Committee report at Colgate University underscores the different perspectives on change among whites and blacks:

> White students tend to see relationships needing development largely in psychological terms; white students emphasize the need for better 'personal' relationships. Minority students much more often (but not always) see the relationships in need for development also to have important, even primary, 'political' implications.[29]

Clearly, the data in this chapter indicate that both psychological and institutional changes are needed. Viable solutions will entail a consideration of how the campus social structure and campus spaces are racialized. We have examined the ways in which African American students and parents experience mistreatment at the hands of white students in the white home territories of a predominantly white university. In these reports we see the racial meanings that campus spaces have for white and black students. Some of the black experiences involved some whites aggressively expressing their racist attitudes and propensities, while other incidents involved whites engaging in subtle forms of discrimination.

Racialized spaces are part of the daily worlds of African Americans at all predominantly white colleges and universities. From our respondents' accounts we acquire clues as to the character of these spaces: Are they safe places? Are they dangerous? Are black students welcome here? Our data reveal that the black students and parents have been told by white students, in a variety of direct and roundabout ways, that State University is white territory. The students' accounts of the underlying racial hostility, even that hidden beneath superficially friendly gestures, indicate that once whites define campus space racially, the meanings of certain white actions within that space are pervaded with negative racial meanings. Moreover, racial interaction on campus is far more complex than is suggested in the naive views of the white analysts who describe most white students as eager to exhibit "liberal credentials" in interaction with students of color. Most mainstream interpretations of racial relations on college campuses are far from the everyday realities of racism experienced by African American students.

NOTES

1. See Claude Levi-Strauss, *Structural Anthropology* (New York: Doubleday-Anchor, 1967), 282.
2. See Thorstein Veblen, *The Theory of the Leisure Class* (New York: Penguin, 1979), 16.
3. See Stanford M. Lyman and Marvin B. Scott, "Territoriality: A Neglected Sociological Dimension," *Social Problems* 15 (1967): 236–49.
4. See Ani, *Yurugu: An African-Centered Critique of European Cultural Thought and Behavior*; Frances Cress Welsing, *The Isis Papers: Keys to the Colors* (Third World Press: Chicago, 1991).
5. Anthony R. D'Augelli and Scott L. Hershberger, "African American Undergraduates on a Predominantly White Campus: Academic Factors, Social Networks, and Campus Climate," *Journal of Negro Education,* 62 (1993): 67–81.
6. Walter Allen, *Gender and Campus Race Differences in Black Student Academic Performance, Racial Attitudes and College Satisfaction* (Atlanta: Southern Education Foundation, 1986).
7. The data were presented at a New Orleans conference. We draw on the account in Alice Dembner, "Campus Racial Lines May Be Blurring; Study Counters Notion That Minorities Segregate Selves," *Boston Globe* (April 5, 1994): 1.
8. Reported from the *New York Times* (October 10, 1994) in "Racism in Education," *The Race Relations Reporter* (November 15, 1994): 4.
9. Lyman and Scott, "Territoriality: A Neglected Sociological Dimension," 236–49.
10. For example, black students at the University of Florida have periodically made this complaint.

11. See Feagin and Sikes, *Living with Racism.*

12. See Bloom, *The Closing of the American Mind,* 35.

13. See Bloom, *The Closing of the American Mind;* and Arthur Schlesinger, Jr., *The Disuniting of America: Reflections on a Multicultural Society* (New York: Norton, 1991).

14. Walter R. Allen, "Black and Blue: Black Students at the University of Michigan," *LSA Magazine* 6 (Fall, 1982): n.p.

15. Southern Regional Education Board, *Racial Issues on Campus: How Students View Them* (Atlanta: Southern Regional Education Board, 1990), 11.

16. Howard J. Ehrlich, *Campus Ethnoviolence and the Policy Options* (Baltimore: National Institute Against Prejudice and Violence, 1990), iii.

17. Here we draw in part on 1993–95 issues of *The Race Relations Reporter.*

18. D'Augelli and Hershberger, "African American Undergraduates on a Predominantly White Campus," 67–81.

19. Marvalene Styles Hughes, "Black Students' Participation in Higher Education," *Journal of College Student Personnel,* 28 (1987): 532–45.

20. Quoted in Denise K. Magner, "Blacks and Whites on the Campuses: Behind Ugly Racist Incidents, Student Isolation and Insensitivity," *Chronicle of Higher Education,* April 26, 1989, pp. A27–A29.

21. Mary Jordan, "College Dorms Reflect Trend of Self-Segregation," *Washington Post,* March 6, 1994, p. A1.

22. Cited in Dembner, "Campus Racial Lines May Be Blurring," 1.

23. Institute for the Study of Social Change, *The Diversity Project,* 29.

24. Institute for the Study of Social Change, *The Diversity Project,* 29.

25. Ruth J. Simmons, "Report on Campus Race Relations," Princeton University, March 1, 1993, 3.

26. Marvalene Styles Hughes, "Black Students' Participation in Higher Education," *Journal of College Student Personnel* 28 (1987): 532–45.

27. A summary of William Sedlacek's pioneering research, with extensive citations, can be found in William E. Sedlacek, "Using Research to Reduce Racism at a University," Research Report 2–94, Counseling Center, University of Maryland, College Park, Maryland.

28. Shelby Steele, "The Recoloring of Campus Life," *Harper's* (February, 1989): 53.

29. Office of the President, "Report of the Diversity Committee," unpublished report. Colgate University, August 21, 1990, 9.

QUESTIONS FOR DISCUSSION

1. Can you identify ways that racism is spatially structured at your campus?
2. What effects does this have on your college experience?
3. How is the education that all students receive affected by universities being racialized spaces?

40

RELIGION AND PUBLIC EDUCATION
IN A MULTICULTURAL AMERICA

JAMES W. FRASER

Many issues about the proper relationship between religion and the schools are likely to be lively ones for a long time to come. This chapter explores some of the issues that are very much on the horizon at this time and likely to continue for decades—prayer, . . . , evolution and creationism, and finally—and most importantly—the question of how we live together in an increasingly diverse nation.

School Prayer

Alabama's minirebellion against the federal district court and in favor of school prayer in the fall of 1997, and the June 1998 vote by a majority of the members of the U.S. House of Representatives to amend the Constitution to guarantee a right to pray in school both show that the issue of school prayer is going to be a heated one for many years to come. Henry Hyde, chair of the House Judiciary Committee, had gotten to the heart of the Religious Freedom Amendment while it was being debated by the House when he said, "Essentially stripped of all the verbiage, this amendment seeks a couple of things: basically to permit and to guarantee a right to pray in schools and, secondly, to afford equality of treatment between faith-based social service providers and treat them the same as secular ones." An amendment to the Constitution specifically allowing prayer in the schools would have resolved the rebellion in Alabama. It would have legalized the unofficial practices that take place in many classrooms across the country. It would also leave many Americans profoundly uncomfortable. It is clearly both a specific and symbolic issue.[1]

In many ways the Equal Access Law and the federal Department of Education guidelines ought to have resolved the issue. It is ironic that there is such heat on the issue of school prayer when today's federal guidelines support students who wish to pray more clearly than has been the case since the early 1960s. The revised standards for Religious Expression in Public Schools issued in May 1998 by U.S. Secretary of Education Richard W. Riley are clear:

> Generally, students may pray in a nondisruptive manner when not engaged in school activities or instruction, and subject to the rules that normally pertain in the applicable setting. Specifically, students in informal settings, such as cafeterias and hallways, may pray and discuss their religious views with each other, subject to the same rules of order as apply to other student activities and speech. Students may also speak to, and attempt to persuade, their peers about religious topics just as they do with regard to political topics. School officials, however, should intercede to stop

student speech that constitutes harassment aimed at a student or a group of students. Students may also participate in before or after school events with religious content such as "see you at the flag pole" gatherings. . . .

According to these regulations, the kinds of limitations on private prayer of which many conservatives sometimes complain are improper.[2]

In his Saturday radio speech supporting the new regulations and opposing a constitutional amendment, President Clinton noted the same thing:

> [N]othing in the Constitution requires schools to be religion-free zones, where children must leave their faiths at the schoolhouse door. . . . [S]tudents have the right to say grace at lunchtime. They have the right to meet in religious groups on school grounds and to use school facilities, just like any other club. They have the right to read the Bible or any religious text during study hall or free class time. They also have the right to be free from coercion to participate in any kind of religious activity.

Ironically, the freedom to pray, or not pray, free from coercion, is what most people on all sides of the issue say they want.[3]

As Congressman Barney Frank argued during the debate on the constitutional amendment, many of the current complaints about school restrictions on prayer and other religious activity are based on misunderstanding or overzealous cautiousness, or the antireligious bias of teachers. So Frank reminded the House that while some teachers may have limited the rights of students to read the Bible or pray, "[t]hose teachers were wrong." But for others, simply clarifying the issue and maintaining currently existing rights is not enough. . . .

And [their] way to counter the trend . . . seems to be to amend the Constitution . . . and put prayer back as a regular part of the formal exercises of the school day.[4]

Any proposals to formalize prayer in school classrooms, whether done through constitutional amendment or local custom carried on in defiance of the courts, is also going to create resistance. One of the greatest mistakes that advocates of formalized school prayer make is assuming that their opponents are primarily nonbelievers. While there certainly have been atheists and agnostics among those challenging school prayer, . . . they have never been the majority of objectors. In fact it might be easier for a nonbeliever, who viewed the whole exercise as meaningless superstition, to sit through a formal prayer than for a believer whose form of belief was insulted by the prayer.

For most of the nineteenth century, Roman Catholics were insulted by the very Protestant prayers offered in the public schools. Jews have regularly been assaulted by Christian prayers, as were traditional Native Americans forced into Christian missionary schools until well into the twentieth century. Today, a devout Muslim, who believes that prayers should be made facing East and giving praise to Allah, a Buddhist who seeks quiet meditation rather than spoken words to God, or a follower of a modern Wiccan tradition who believes in "relinking, with the divine within and with Her outer manifestations in all of the human and natural world" are all likely to be deeply offended by most school prayers, most especially those seeking Divine intervention for the nation or the local football team.[5]

Those who ask, "What's the harm?" of a generic prayer, or who view it as a way to quiet students down and begin the school day on a reflective note need to hear the experience of Martin Buber, the great Jewish mystic and theologian who remembered the pain he experienced as a Jewish student experiencing Christian rituals in school.

> The obligatory daily standing in the room resounding with the strange service affected me worse than an act of intolerance could have affected me. Compulsory guests, having to participate as a thing in a sacral event in which no dram of my person could or would take part, and this for eight long years morning after morning: that stamped itself upon the life-substance of the boy.

Such use of prayer as cultural imposition should give pause to most people of faith who are serious about their own prayers. In a multicultural nation, such monocultural events are deeply troubling.[6]

Nevertheless, anyone who believes that the debate is closed is seriously out of touch with the main currents of American society. Opponents of formal and organized school prayer may argue, with Nel Noddings, that "Some of us honestly believe that prayer in public school has rightly been declared unconstitutional [and, by implication, that the Constitution should not be changed], others fear that nondenominational exercises will rapidly slide over into overtly denominational ones, and still others simply want to preserve all children from the pain experienced by Buber." On the other hand, advocates of school prayer believe, with equal fervor, that it is an essential means of returning the nation to its religious heritage, of reminding students of the spiritual roots on which life and learning rest, of restoring public morality, and that the court rulings banning formal organized prayer from schools are based on a misreading of the Constitution. It is a difference of opinion not easy to resolve.[7]

. . .

Equal Time: Evolution, Creationism, and the Continuing Debate

When the American Civil Liberties Union submitted its brief to the U.S. Supreme Court in the *Epperson v. Arkansas* case, it began by saying "The Union, having been intimately associated with *Scopes v. Tennessee* 40 years ago, when this issue first arose in the courts, looks forward to its final resolution in this case." Seldom have less accurate predictions been made. . . . The Epperson case did close one phase of the evolution battles—since then few have tried to keep the teaching of evolution out of the schools, at least through the courts—but it opened another surprising chapter. In the wake of the Epperson decision, demands for equal time for alternative views of the origins of life, primarily views based on the Genesis account of creation, have expanded rapidly. As Donald Kennedy of the National Academy of Sciences has noted, "in the United States, religious opposition to teaching evolution is deeply rooted and growing stronger" thirty years after Epperson. Few issues are further from final resolution.[8]

People who are concerned with good science struggle with the kind of openness recommended in the National Academy of Science material that Kennedy supports. Some scientists seem susceptible to a charge of an unbecoming rigidity. Carl Sagan, one of the nation's most famous and respected scientists, published a best-selling book in 1996 titled *The Demon-Haunted World: Science as a Candle in the Dark*. For Sagan, the light of science is needed to drive out what seems to be the gathering darkness of far too much religiosity in the United States today. "Is this worshipping at the altar of science?" Sagan asks. His answer, he says, is based only on evidence. "If something else worked better, I would advocate that something else." But it is pretty clear from reading Sagan's work that he does not think it likely that the "something else" is going to come along any time soon.

To illustrate his discomfort with other worldviews, Sagan creates a story of someone who believes that "a fire-breathing dragon lives in my garage." When the scientist seeks any evidence, the believer insists that the dragon is invisible, floats in air, has fire that is heatless, and is incorporeal. As a scientist, of course, Sagan asks, "what's the difference between an invisible, incorporeal, floating dragon who spits heatless fire and no dragon at all?" The answer is clear: "Claims that cannot be tested, assertions immune to disproof are veridically worthless, whatever value they may have in inspiring us or in exciting our sense of wonder." But for some people, "inspiring us or exciting our sense of wonder" is just the point. When ancient biblical writers defined faith as "the assurance of things hoped for, the conviction of things not seen," perhaps they were talking about realities far more powerful than Sagan's mythical dragon.

Donald Kennedy's approach is more embracing of difference as he reminds his readers "how important it is for scientists to treat religious conviction with respect—in particular, not to suggest, even indirectly, that science and religion are unalterably opposed." After all, many scientists are religious, just as many are not. And what, it must be asked, is wrong with a bit of wonder and inspiration? David Baltimore, also one of the nation's premier scientists, has recently written, "Scientists know that questions are not settled; rather, they are given provisional answers for which it is contingent upon the imagination of followers to find more illuminating solutions. Practitioners of science are different from artists in that they give primacy to logic and evidence, but the most fundamental progress in science is achieved through hunch, anal-

ogy, insight, and creativity." It is not a concession to "creation science" to argue that high school science, like college and the most advanced research-level sciences, must never be taught as dogmatic theology but as a never-ending process of "seeking more illuminating solutions" and doing so not only through sifting the evidence but with "hunch, analogy, insight, and creativity."[9]

In this context, Nel Noddings has argued for a similar approach that includes openness, compassion, and curiosity. She begins with a basic point on which most educators would agree. She reminds high school science teachers that, when faced with a fundamentalist student who rejects evolution, it is important to remember that "Clearly, it is not intelligent to censor or proscribe full discussion of any view passionately held by one or more participant." Indeed, such a debate can become a wonderful "teachable moment" for an informed teacher who is committed to creating a classroom that is safe and engaging for all students.

> To approach questions about our origins intelligently, we should tell the full story as nearly as we can. All cultures have creation stories, and telling them or encouraging students to find and tell them presents a wonderful opportunity for multicultural education. Here our predilection for dichotomies and other rigidly marked categories leads us to insist that, if those stories be told at all, they be included in literature or history classes—not science. . . . [But] intelligent educators must be willing to cross the lines. Science teachers should begin by acknowledging the eternal human quest for solutions to the puzzle of our existence. As science teachers, they have a special obligation to pass on to students the most widely accepted contemporary beliefs in science together with the

evidence used to support them. But as educators, they have an even greater responsibility to acknowledge and present with great sensitivity the full range of solutions explored by their fellow human beings. Again, such discussions do not have to end with, "Now here's the truth." The best teachers will be prepared to present not only the full spectrum of belief but also the variety of plausible ways in which people have tried to reconcile their religious and scientific beliefs.

To do less is to rob our students of the very process of critical inquiry that is fundamental not only to science but to an intelligent approach to all aspects of the universe of learning.[10]

The "Objective" Teaching of Religion

. . . For all of the confusion sown by the Supreme Court's divided and seemingly contradictory opinions, the Court has been clear and consistent in ruling that the study of religion is acceptable in the schools. Justice Tom C. Clark made a point, subsequently reaffirmed by the justices again and again, in the famous 1963 *Abington v. Schemp* decision disallowing official prayers and devotional reading of the Bible. "Nothing we have said here indicates that such study of the Bible or of religion, when presented objectively as part of a secular program of education, may not be effected consistently with the First Amendment." When Justice Abraham Fortas wrote what became his controversial opinion ending any state prohibitions on the teaching of evolution for religious reasons in *Epperson v. Arkansas*, he again went out of his way to reiterate Justice Clark's opinion: "While the study of religions and of the Bible from a literary and

historic viewpoint, presented objectively as part of a secular program of education, need not collide with the First Amendment's prohibition, the State may not adopt programs or practices in its public schools or colleges which 'aid or oppose' any religion." On this point, there should be no confusion. The growing secularization of the school curriculum is thus a result of a secular bias on the part of curriculum developers, fear of controversy over disputed issues, or a clear misreading of the laws and court rulings.[11]

Warren Nord's exhaustive *Religion & American Education: Rethinking a National Dilemma* represents a powerful call for a middle way. Nord begins with the assumption that "We need not make schools Christian or eliminate all religion from public education; there are alternatives." For Nord, an essential starting point is educating educators. "The conventional wisdom among educators is that religion is irrelevant to virtually everything that is taken to be true and important." The result, from an objective view, is that schools thus really do seem to reflect a religion of secularism. "One reason our situation is so difficult is that most educators are not very well educated about religion." In response to this situation, Nord sets out to educate the educators in better and more open ways to view religion, the study of history, science, morality, and the specific field of religious studies. Taking Nord, and others including Hunt, Carper, and more and more new voices appearing on the stage, seriously means a radical rethinking of the textbooks and curriculum of the schools and of the knowledge and attitudes required for effective teachers in those schools.[12]

Where Nord and most of those who seek to expand the teaching of religion in the schools focus on increasing the discussion of religious themes in history, literature, and the sciences, Nel Noddings focuses on perennial human questions that often have religious themes and that certainly cannot be discussed without references to the transcendent. She reminds her readers that most students, whatever their religious or nonreligious background, ask such questions as part of the process of maturing as young people and adults. Just to remind adults of this reality, Noddings quotes a recent comic strip, Calvin and Hobbes, in which the ever inquisitive Calvin raises a question that may not be in the syllabus but is certainly in the minds of many very real children and adults. In this strip, Calvin's teacher, ready to move to a new activity, asks if any of the students has a question:

Calvin: What's the point of human existence?
Teacher: I meant any questions about the subject at hand.
Calvin: Oh. (Staring at his book, he mumbles, "Frankly, I'd like to have the issue resolved before I expend any more energy on this.")

Anyone who has taught school or spent time with children and youth has experienced just this sort of question—often at an awkward moment, or at least at a time when orderly adult minds were preparing to move to the next item on the agenda. As Noddings says so well, failure to attend to such questions, when they arise and in the context in which they arise, is failure to be the kind of open and engaged teacher that most good instructors want to be.[13]

Schools have tended to shy away from the "What's the point of human existence?" questions, however. In part it is a fear of controversy. In part it is an understandable worry about conflict with family and community norms. In part it is worry about "covering the curriculum," especially in our test- and measurement-driven educational atmosphere. In part it is sheer intellectual cowardice. But children are asking the questions. Indeed, as Noddings says, "People of all kinds—of all times and places—have asked questions about gods, existence, and the meaning of life." To put those questions aside is to compartmentalize not only the curriculum but the life of the mind and the life of the human spirit. . . .

For many thoughtful observers, to close schools off from the realm of ultimate questions is to impoverish both schools and children.[14]

At the same time, it is very important to note that the kind of schooling that Noddings and Nord or others talk about is not easy to create. In fact, while nearly every thoughtful observer supports "the objective teaching of religion in the schools," this is not nearly as easy in practice as it is in theory. For one thing, religious faith, by definition, is not objective. Many of us have had the experience of hearing someone else describe our own faith and saying "That's not quite right." After all, Protestants believe many different things and disagree passionately with each other. So do Catholics, Jews, Muslims, Hindus, and atheists. A person so inclined could argue that part of the evidence for considering secular humanism a religion is that its adherents do not agree with each other on many things either. Teaching usually involves generalizing, and generalizing about religion often involves getting it wrong. In addition, as with many fields, it is hard to teach about the topic of religion without providing students with experience with the topic. Science classes without labs are second-rate science classes. But the primary hands-on experience of religion is the worship of believers. School visits to church, synagogue, mosque, or ashram move very close to the fine line of separation between church and state. And many believers are properly wary of simply being observed, as if they are some sort of lab specimen. So—important as the study of religion is, as right as its advocates are in arguing that we cannot understand our culture in any fundamental way without attending to matters of faith—we have not set ourselves an easy task when we seek to move forward on that front.

There are those who argue that we are best served by keeping religion a private matter while the common areas—the public square—is secular. Secular need not be hostile to religion. It can, indeed, be respectful to religion—many *different* religions. But there are things, and personal faith may be one of them, that do not thrive best when receiving the constant exposure of the public arena. Certainly the argument can be made that some matters are best attended to at home, in specifically faith-based communities, in subsets of the society where people who share common assumptions and passions can share them freely, without worry about imposition on others and without needing to explain themselves to others. . . .

Finding New Ways to Respect a Diverse Student Body

In 1966, somewhat facetiously, Supreme Court Justice William O. Douglas reminded Americans that Islam is one of the fastest-growing religions in the world, including in the United States. "In time Moslems will control some of our school boards. In time devout Moslems may want their prayer in our schools; and if Protestant sects can get their prayers past the barriers of the First Amendment, the same passage would be guaranteed for Moslems." Is that really what the advocates of prayer in school wanted? Douglas asked.[15]

A third of a century later, schools in some major urban areas may well have a Muslim majority. There are districts with Buddhist majorities, just as there are districts with Mormon, with Catholic, with Jewish, and with Baptist majorities. The United States is rapidly becoming more and more diverse, far more so than many citizens realize. For some the answer is simple: Let the majority decide. For others who have been in the minority position too long, or fear what it may entail, the issues are much more complex.

Far more than most people have realized, the United States is a very different country at the dawn of a new century from what it was thirty years ago. The last years of the twentieth century [saw] immigration on almost the same scale as the beginning years. And the immigration has been from the farthest reaches of the world: Asia, Latin America, eastern Europe, the Middle East. In addition, many people already in the country are moving frequently. As a result, many assumptions about the ethnic and religious character of the nation's people no longer hold. This is especially true in the nation's major cities.

As Shirley Brice Heath and Milbrey W. McLaughlin have shown in *Identity and Inner-City Youth: Beyond Ethnicity and Gender,* notions of race and ethnicity that motivate many contemporary public policy discussions are far removed from the changing mix of African American, Latino, Asian, and European American youth who are in the housing projects and neighborhoods, the schools, the religious organizations, and human service agencies of many of today's cities. Because of the radical changes in immigration—both from other countries and within the urban areas themselves—housing projects and other institutions are much more racially mixed than they were twenty-five years ago. As a result, "Ethnicity seemed, from the youth perspective, to be more often a label assigned to them by outsiders than an indication of their real sense of self."[16]

Urban turf conflicts in the 1960s and 1970s were often seen as black-white divisions, with most of the blacks coming from a Protestant background and most of the whites coming from Catholic, or in some cases Eastern Orthodox, backgrounds. Today's mix includes youth whose background may be any of the above but may be equally Buddhist, Muslim, Latin American evangelical, Hindu, or others. And for many youth, religion and religious institutions have little bearing on their daily reality. . . .

Looking at a different group that sees itself as marginal to the dominant society, Justin Watson, in *The Christian Coalition,* makes clear that many members of the Coalition and many other conservative religious people are torn between feeling like members of an oppressed minority who simply want the same rights as any other citizens and believing that they are the rightful arbiters of society—the appropriate definers of the dominant culture of what should be a Christian nation—temporarily pushed aside in a secular age. The reality is that a democratic society cannot have one group of citizens who define the culture for others. All citizens must together shape the culture. At the same time, a democratic culture must always respect minority rights—for all minorities.[17]

In this context of minority rights, too many contemporary voices create an unhelpful either/or dichotomy. The usually thoughtful Stephen Carter seriously missed the point when he wrote:

> Consider two examples. Imagine that you are the parent of a child in a public school, and you discover that the school, instead of offering the child a fair and balanced picture of the world—including your lifestyle choice—is teaching things that seem to the child to prove your lifestyle an inferior and perhaps irrational one. If the school's teachings are offensive to you because you are gay or black or disabled the chances are that the school will at least give you a hearing and, if it does not, that many

liberals will flock to your side and you will find a sympathetic ear in the media. But if you do not like the way the school talks about religion, or if you believe that the school is inciting your children to abandon their religion, you will probably find that the media will mock you, the liberal establishment will announce that you are engaged in censorship, and the courts will toss you out on your ear.

Now, Carter must visit different schools from the ones I do. In America at the end of the twentieth century, there are still many schools where the rights of gay students, students of color, and disabled students are far from receiving respect and where those who challenge such practices are also tossed out on their ears.[18]

In supposedly liberal Boston, where I live and work, many school buildings are in violation of the legal requirements for access for disabled students, I have heard gay and lesbian students—and teachers—mocked, and I have heard terrible racist slurs. However, Carter is half right. I also have seen teachers and intellectual leaders who have a seemingly irrational fear of any mention of religion and especially of any religious passion in any form. The question is: Why should Carter, or anyone else, treat one form of discrimination differently from another? Why should Carter assume that some forms of discrimination are solved (when they are not) and then assume that other forms now merit all of our attention? There certainly are schools in America that are sensitive to the rights of students of different sexual orientations or races but not to students of different religions. There are also schools—I suspect many more if we look at the nation as a whole—that are highly sensitive to students' religious orientation but not to diversity in race, gender, or sexual orientation.

The bottom line is simple. Discrimination, in any form, is wrong. An engaged and democratic and yes, multicultural, society must make a place for all of its citizens, not merely as tolerated guests but as citizens—with all the rights, responsibilities, and contributions expected from citizens. Any hierarchy of oppression misses the point. Oppression, in any form, should not be tolerated in the schools of a democracy. To allow it is to cheapen the discussion of democracy and ultimately to impoverish the richness of the dialogue that a democratic classroom ought to sustain.

Where Do We Go from Here, Chaos or Community?

In 1967 Martin Luther King, Jr., issued one of his great challenges to the nation, and to many in the civil rights movement, with a small book, *Where Do We Go from Here, Chaos or Community?* In that book, he told a story that was really a parable for most of his life's work.

> Some years ago a famous novelist died. Among his papers was found a list of suggested plots for future stories, the most prominently underscored being this one: "A widely separated family inherits a house in which they have to live together." This is the great new problem of mankind. We have inherited a large house, a great "world house" in which we have to live together—black and white, Eastern and Western, Gentile and Jew, Catholic and Protestant, Moslem and Hindu—a family unduly separated in ideas, culture and interest, who because we can never again live apart, must learn somehow to live with each other in peace.

Race and religion have long been two great fault lines in American society. In the next century the same challenge King raised is likely to continue to apply in both realms. As King never tired of reminding his generation, we must choose between "chaos and community," in many areas. And religion is far from the least of them.[19]

Justin Watson's brilliant analysis of the Christian Coalition applies to a far wider number of people than the Coalition's members. There is a deep ambivalence within the Coalition, Watson argues, between those demanding a rightful recognition, a respect for their rights as citizens who are also conservative Christians—which every citizen of every persuasion ought to demand—and those wanting something much more far reaching and ominous: a dream of a Protestant restoration, a longing for a past in which Protestant religion and Protestant values dominated all aspects of the nation's life, especially the curriculum and moral tone of the public schools. It is not odd that these two hopes could remain in the same organization, indeed in the same person. Most of those who embraced religious disestablishment at the time of the First Amendment had similar ambivalence. We would prefer an establishment of our particular beliefs, many seemed to say, but if we cannot have that, at least give us tolerance and do not establish someone else's beliefs. How little has changed in 220 years?

Speaking of the religious views of many who are currently most alienated from the schools, Stephen Arons, another scholar who has examined the issue, says: "As expected, the values expressed and fought for by these dissidents are, more often than not, unattractive, wrong-headed, and contrary to the accepted wisdom of the majority. Dissent, by definition, is unpopular. Yet they have acted on conscience, have shown clear commitment to their children, and have expressed fears common to many of us. It is, therefore, inappropriate for the majority to dismiss the dissidents as deranged or to congratulate itself that lack of involvement in school politics is healthy." Democracy, Arons is saying, is by definition messy. It is also a much healthier polity in which to air religious and educational differences than any other.[20]

There is, of course, the old civil liberties saying, "I may disagree with what you have to say, but I'll die for your right to say it." As an educator deeply concerned with the schooling of today's students and with the issues of this volume, I will say it a bit differently: "I may find much to disagree with in many of the claims of the religious Right; I may find creationism to be bad science and wrong-headed; I may find Robertson and Reed and many of their allies mean-spirited and dangerous in their political agenda; but I will fight with all my strength to be sure that their children, and more likely the children of their followers, are treated with as much respect as my own children or any other child in the public schools of this nation." The same, of course, must be said with equal force for the atheist or the agnostic, the Sikh, the Sufi, or the Christian Scientist. Anything less invites a retreat into private schools and ultimately undermines public education. Anything less betrays the best goals of public schools as open and engaging institutions for all of the public. Anything less is fundamentally undemocratic. Many conservative Christians will find what I am saying to be far too little, and many of my closest political and intellectual allies will find that I have engaged in dangerous accommodations with the enemy in this statement. Nevertheless, I believe that at least this degree of openness remains an essential stance for anyone who seriously believes in democracy and in a democratic and multicultural approach to American education.

In a recent essay, Michael Apple has brilliantly stated the case for a more tolerant, open, and welcoming school. Speaking of the growing power of reactionary politics, especially in relation to struggles over schools and their curricula, he writes: "When school bureaucracies do not listen respectfully to criticism, when our definitions of 'professionalism' are used to exclude power-sharing arrangements, when a curriculum seems imposed, when community members feel their voices are ignored—all of this makes rightist arguments seem sensible, even among those people who are not usually sympathetic to such ideological positions." This statement applies with considerable force to the issue of religion in the schools. To the degree religious people have been marginalized and driven into the arms of political conservatives, who are not otherwise their allies, to that degree, educational liberals, secular and not quite so secular have failed. Apple continues: "Thus, the conditions for growth of rightist anti-school and anti-public movements are often created at a local level. Making schools more open and responsive is not 'just' important because it may raise achievement scores or it may get more parents involved in supporting what 'we' want. It is also absolutely crucial for interrupting the growth of rightist social movements."[21]

If we follow Watson's analysis of the Christian Coalition and of the so-called religious right, which extends far beyond membership in the Coalition, the split between those who want to reassert cultural hegemony and those who simply want the right to hold their own beliefs and traditions is very real. And if that split does exist, the latter group need not be driven into the arms of the former. To the degree that the United States allows any return to the cultural hegemony of Protestant or Christian culture in the schools or other institutions, it will be a less humane and democratic society for all of its citizens—including those of us who are Protestant Christians. Tyranny is inhumane for all who are involved in it, even the tyrants. But as Apple notes so well, the way to avoid religious tyranny is not to impose a different, perhaps milder, tyranny of the bureaucrat, the professional, and the curriculum expert.

The way to a better future is through an inclusive and engaging education in which schools encourage all of their citizens—students, teachers, and administrators—to listen respectfully, where power is shared, where all voices are heard and given their due rights. We may not agree with all of the voices; indeed, we *will* not. That is the nature of democratic dialogue. But our education will be richer, our cultural diversity will be strengthened, and our most fundamental democratic sensibilities will be more deeply engaged if we extend a welcoming hand to religious people, to fundamentalists, to believers in creationism, and equally to Native Americans who claim their ancient spirituality, to Muslims of many varieties, to orthodox and not-so-orthodox Jews, to followers of emerging New Age spirituality, and to militant atheists and cautious agnostics. All have a right to a place at the table, all have much to learn from and contribute to the ever-changing American culture, and all are part of the rich tapestry of multicultural America that is emerging in the opening years of a new century.

NOTES

1. *Congressional Record,* June 4, 1998, pp. H4078–H4112. The amendment is discussed in detail in the previous chapter.
2. "Religious Expression in Public Schools," U.S. Department of Education Document, May 1998.
3. "Radio Address of the President to the Nation, May 30, 1998."
4. *Congressional Record,* June 4, 1998, pp. H4088 and H4091.
5. Starhawk, "Witchcraft as Goddess Religion," in C. Spretnak, ed., *The Politics of Women's Spirituality* (Garden City, NY, 1982), p. 51.
6. Martin Buber, "Martin Buber, Autobiographical Fragments," in P. Schilpp and M. Friedman, eds., *The Philosophy of Martin Buber* (LaSalle, IL, 1967), p. 8; Starhawk and Buber are both cited and discussed in Nel Noddings, *Education for Intelligent Belief or Unbelief* (New York, 1993), pp. 72, 140.
7. See Noddings, *Education for Intelligent Belief or Unbelief,* p. 140; *Congressional Record,* June 4, 1998, pp. H4078–H4079.
8. Donald Kennedy, "Helping Schools to Teach Evolution," *Chronicle of Higher Education,* August 7, 1998, p. A48.
9. Carl Sagan, *The Demon-Haunted World: Science as a Candle in the Dark* (New York, 1996), pp. 30, 171–172; Kennedy, "Helping Schools to Teach Evolution"; Hebrews 11:1, Revised Standard Version; David Baltimore, Letter to the Editor, *The New Yorker* (1997).
10. Noddings, *Education for Intelligent Belief or Unbelief,* pp. 143–144.
11. *Abington School District v. Schempp* 374 U.S. 203 (1963); *Epperson v. Arkansas* 393 U.S. 97 (1968).
12. Warren A. Nord, *Religion & American Education: Rethinking a National Dilemma* (Chapel Hill, NC, 1995), pp. xiii–xiv, 1.
13. Noddings, *Education for Intelligent Belief or Unbelief,* pp. 78–79.
14. Noddings, *Education for Intelligent Belief or Unbelief,* p. 11, see also p. 1.
15. William O. Douglas, *The Bible and the Schools* (Boston, 1966), p. 45.
16. Shirley Brice Heath and Milbrey W. McLaughlin, eds., *Identity and Inner-City Youth: Beyond Ethnicity and Gender* (New York, 1993), pp. 6, 214, 222; I reviewed this book in Book Review in *Teachers College Record* 96:2 (Winter 1994), pp. 347–352.
17. Justin Watson, *The Christian Coalition: Dreams of Restoration, Demands for Recognition* (New York, 1997).
18. Stephen L. Carter, *The Culture of Disbelief: How American Law and Politics Trivialize Religious Devotion* (New York, 1993), p. 52.
19. Martin Luther King, Jr., "Where Do We Go from Here: Chaos or Community?" (1967), reprinted in James M. Washington, ed., *A Testament of Hope: The Essential Writings and Speeches of Martin Luther King, Jr.* (San Francisco, 1986), pp. 555–633.
20. Stephen Arons, *Compelling Belief: The Culture of American Schooling* (New York, 1983), pp. vii–ix.
21. Michael W. Apple, "Are Markets and Standards Democratic?" Book review of Geoff Whitty, Sally Power, and David Halpin, *Devolution and Choice in Education: The School,*

the State and the Market (Bristol, PA, 1998), *Educational Researcher* 27:6 (August–September, 1998): 27.

QUESTIONS FOR DISCUSSION

1. Why is there so much misunderstanding about the constitutional limits on prayer in public schools?

2. What are the problems currently associated with addressing religion in America's schools?

3. How can the religious diversity of students be respected while maintaining a secular approach to public education as a whole?

THE SOCIAL WEB

- UNICEF, the United Nations Children's Fund, publishes numerous reports on the problems associated with the global education of children. You can also find comparisons of educational achievement among the world's nations: www.unicef.org.
- The National Education Association offers information on key policies, legislation, and guidelines that affect America's schools. This Web site also provides current comparisons of teachers' salaries: www.nea.org.

QUESTIONS FOR DEBATE

1. Why do America's schools continue to perpetuate inequalities based on class, race, and gender?

2. What are the most significant problems facing our system of public education today?

3. How should America's educators address the needs of an increasingly diverse student population?

4. What solutions do you offer that could remedy the social problems found in education in the United States?

Chapter 10
The Criminal Justice System

Contents

Learning Objectives

By the end of this chapter you should be able to:

- Recognize how the authors use one or more of the major perspectives to explore the criminal justice process.

- Explore how inequalities in the criminal justice process are shaped by inequalities of race, gender, and class.

- Identify the ways that crime and justice are socially constructed.

- Describe various consequences of inequalities in the criminal justice process and criminal policy.

- Analyze how individuals contribute to injustice in the criminal justice process through their everyday behavior.

- Explain how social systems and institutions perpetuate an unjust criminal justice process.

Defining the Problem

In theory, we have a criminal justice system in the United States to protect the lives, liberty, and property of all. But the system was set up by the powerful in society, and we must ask, to what degree does the institution that they created achieve these goals?

One concern sociologists have regarding the criminal justice system is whether, as the official governmental means of determining guilt and dispensing consequences, it improves the safety and well-being of the American public. To explore this concern, some investigators examine what behaviors and conditions are successfully labeled as crimes and become subject to governmental regulation. They study how the success of labeling efforts depends on the political activities undertaken by interest groups, the way claims makers' arguments for greater safety articulate with broader societal concerns, and societal stereotypes and feelings toward the groups targeted for greater social control. Sociologists also examine governmental measures of crime—reports of crime made to police, crimes recorded by police, arrests made by police, and victimization surveys—to determine whether crime rates increase or decrease in relation to particular policy measures. However, some are critical of this approach, because the Federal Bureau of Investigation indexes that many researchers use emphasize individual crimes of violence and property crimes: rape, robbery, aggravated assault, homicide, burglary and larceny. Critics point out that the American public is also affected in material ways by white-collar crimes, corporate crimes, organized crime, and political crime, which go unmeasured.

Another broad concern of sociologists is whether criminal justice practices, to any degree, contribute to racial, gender, or class inequality by valuing the lives, liberty, and property of particular groups of people more than others. Because bias can occur on many levels, research related to this concern is far reaching. One type of investigation examines whether police surveillance practices, prosecutors' decisions about whom and what to charge, judges' decisions regarding bail and sentencing, or parole boards' decisions about release dates are inappropriately guided by extralegal factors like race, class, gender, and sexual orientation. Another type explores whether the personnel of the criminal justice system are representative of the population at large such that the perspectives of all Americans are represented. Sociologists also seek to determine whether formal rights granted to defendants and victims can, in fact, be exercised by them. They ask: Do all defendants regardless of class have the means to secure competent representation? Are all crime victims informed of their rights to weigh in on plea agreements or testify in sentencing hearings? When legislators try to remedy problems of inequality by changing the definitions of crimes or the procedures in the criminal justice system, sociologists study whether their reforms are effective.

The fairness of corrections policies and procedures are also of concern to sociologists. Some investigate whether sanctions such as isolation cells, the death penalty, and frequent body cavity searches meet the prohibition in our federal Constitution against cruel and/or unusual practices. Other sociologists explore whether women and men prisoners have equal access to rehabilitative opportunities, health care, and visitation. Comparing the relative amount of tax dollars that go into jail and prison construction in comparison to education and employment programs is another type of policy investigation that is concerned with social equity.

A review of some current statistics, many from the federal government's Bureau of Justice Statistics, can lead us to see the basis of some of sociologists' concerns.

Scope of the Problem

All governmental measures of serious violent crime have shown declines since 1995.[1] Similarly, the decline in property crime that began in the mid-1970s has continued. Drug arrests, however, have continued to climb since the early 1980s. Whereas 471,200 adults and 109,700 juveniles were arrested for drug abuse violations in 1980, 1,375,600 adults and 203,900 juveniles were arrested for the same in 2000.

Since 1980, Bureau of Justice Statistics records show a significant increase in the number of adults under correctional supervision—probation, jail, prison, parole—in the United States. In 2000, the sentenced corrections population was an estimated 470 inmates per 100,000 U.S. residents, well up from the 1980 figure of 139 per 100,000. The corrections population is disproportionately male and non-White: By the end of 2001, there were 3,535 sentenced Black men inmates in prisons and jails per 100,000 Black men in the population. The comparable figures of sentenced Hispanic and White men inmates were 1,177 and 462. However, the adult probation population is more White: In 2000, the adult male probation population was 64 percent White and 34 percent Black. Sixteen percent of the Black and

---

[1]Unless otherwise noted, statistics in this section are drawn from documents available through the Department of Justice, Bureau of Justice Statistics Web site: www.ojp.usdoj.gov/bjs.

White probation population were Hispanic. We must consider whether these racial/ethnic differences reflect differences in offending and/or in apprehension (surveillance, investigation, and arrest) and prosecution.

Between 1990 and 2000, the largest growth in the state prison population was in the number of violent criminals. During the same time period, the largest growth in the federal prison population was in the number of drug offenders. In 1999, 61 percent of federal inmates were incarcerated for drug offenses. Who are they? Research conducted in 1997 found that only 16 percent of federal drug offenders were importers, growers, or manufacturers, while 25 percent were street-level dealers. Between 1990 and 1999, 35 percent of the increase in the number of women prisoners was due to drug offenses compared to 19 percent of the increase for men.

Direct expenditures for "major criminal justice functions" have increased substantially since 1982. In 1999, police expenditures surpassed $65 billion, corrections expenditures approached $50 billion, and the judicial branch surpassed $32 billion. The percentage changes in expenditures between 1982 and 1999 were 244 percent, 42 percent, and 314 percent, respectively.

Despite continued prison construction, inmates are not in ideal incarceration conditions. State prisons are operating at 1 percent to 16 percent above capacity and federal prisons are operating at 31 percent above capacity. Filling prisons and jails over capacity affects guarding techniques and inmates' access to personal space, recreation, and prison employment opportunities. These are not promising conditions for rehabilitation.

In 2001, 3,581 inmates in the United States were on death row in state and federal prisons. This continued the three-year drop in death row admissions. Sixty-six inmates were executed in 2001, a further drop

from the high of ninety-eight in 1999, but well above the single digits of the early 1980s. Since the death penalty was reinstated in 1976, the majority of inmates executed and on death row have been White. However, blacks are disproportionately represented on death row and among those executed. The sixty-three men and three women executed in 2001 were 72.7 percent White, 25.8 percent Black, and 1.5 percent Native American. The 3,581 individuals under sentence of death at the end of 2001 were 55 percent White, 43 percent Black, and 2.1 percent Native American, Asian, or of unknown race. Multiple studies collected by the NAACP find racial bias in the application of the death penalty at the levels of charging, sentencing, and imposition.[2] Fifty-one women were on death row (1.4 percent of prisoners) at the end of 2001. All executions in 2001 were by lethal injection, although states still allow for execution by firing squad, hanging, electrocution, or lethal gas.

In 1999, a *Chicago Tribune* exposé documented widespread prosecutorial misconduct in death penalty cases, involving concealment of evidence that "suggested innocence" or fabrication of evidence. Ken Armstrong and Maurice Possley reported that nationally between 1963 and 1999, at least 381 defendants had had their convictions for homicide set aside.[3] The set-asides removed sixty-seven of those inmates from death row; half were eventually freed. In 2000, the governor of Illinois responded to the report by halting further implementation of the death penalty pending the

---

[2]"The History of the Death Penalty in the United States Has Been Marked by Racism and Inequality," NAACP Legal Defense and Education Fund, Inc., www.igc.org/africana/archives/eh2/factsheet.html.

[3]Information in this paragraph comes from Ken Armstrong and Maurice Possley, "The Verdict: Dishonor," *Chicago Tribune*, January 10, 1999, C1; and Bureau of Justice Statistics.

outcome of a formal review. Maryland later instituted a similar moratorium. At the end of 2002, the governor of Illinois commuted the sentences of death row inmates to life without parole. Despite the allegations of misconduct that led chief executives to halt executions, the prosecutors in the Illinois cases did not face criminal prosecution or public sanction from the American Bar Association, and the careers of some jumped forward. A handful became district attorneys, congressmen, or government counsel.

Perspectives on the Problem

Sociologists examining the criminal justice system from a *social constructionist perspective* argue that laws reflect people's interests, not some absolute notion of evil and goodness. Thus, they assert that we must examine whether our laws and criminal justice practices are in accord with rates of crime and victimization or with something else, like perceptions of danger. Those looking through the lens of *conflict theory* argue that the criminal justice system is used as a tool by the powerful to control the actions of subordinated groups. Sociologists using *functionalist theory* argue that much of what we define as crime is useful to society, filling needs that would otherwise be ignored. Policy that overlooks this will not achieve its desired outcome. Sociologists adopting a *symbolic interactionist perspective* examine how racial and gender stereotypes and entrenched organizational practices influence legal personnel, affecting their decisions about how to prosecute cases and how to treat defendants and witnesses. They also study how jurors make sense of the evidence and how crime victims negotiate the demands of being a witness.

Connecting the Perspectives

The reading by Steven Donziger directs us to consider the social construction of poli-

cies to control drugs and corporate crime. He calls into question what we generally consider to be the "crime problem." Barry Yeoman adopts a conflict approach in his political-economic analysis of why incarceration and prison construction have increased during a period in which crime is stable or declining. Adopting a social constructionist perspective, Robert Lifton and Greg Mitchell examine how the death penalty is sustained in the United States in spite of international rejection of this sanction. John Lamberth, thinking in conflict terms, asks about the extent of racial bias in traffic apprehensions and demonstrates that one need not be a sociologist to study criminal justice policy. Collectively, these readings highlight the importance of power and inequality in determining what is formally marked as a social problem through legislation and who is targeted by the enforcement of laws. William S. Lofquist uses the lens of symbolic interaction to expose how police and prosecutors rely on culturally typical "crime stories" to build a case for jurors to hear. Also adopting a symbolic interactionist perspective, Amanda Konradi shows how sexual assault survivors who are called to testify manage social expectations in their interactions with others in the courtroom.

Reading Summaries

In "Crime and Policy," Donziger examines the impetus for and impact of two recent trends in criminal justice policy in the United States: the construction of more prisons and the passage of "get tough on crime" legislation to increase the severity of sentences. Donziger argues that these new policies are driven by myths rather than reality. Increases in both the number of prisons and the severity of sentencing cannot be tied to increases in the general amount of crime. Instead, they appear to follow directly from an increasing fear of crime.

Donziger asserts that because the media and politicians tend to quote crime data selectively, many Americans have an inaccurate view of the amount of crime and the most common types of crime that occur in their country. "Crime" and "stranger violence" are synonymous in the minds of many Americans, yet the vast majority of crime in the United States is nonviolent, and violence is most likely to be committed by acquaintances. Donziger argues that the perceptual fusion of crime with violence sets the stage for the funneling of tax money into prison construction and for "get tough" legislation. Average Americans, fearful of becoming crime victims, overwhelmingly support politicians who make "crime" their priority. Donziger evaluates the practical outcome (that is, who serves the time) and fiscal impact of three common forms of "get tough" legislation intended to make us safer from violence. These are "three strikes" laws, which give repeat offenders mandatory long terms; truth-in-sentencing legislation, which requires that defendants serve full sentences; and mandatory minimum sentences, which significantly decrease judicial discretion. Our prison cells have become filled with nonviolent offenders, most often poor minorities, many for selling small amounts of drugs. We pay a great deal to feed and house individuals who would not be a great threat to us on the street. The "get tough" legislation, which prevents judges from exercising discretion in sentencing, could force the release of violent offenders already serving time in order to create more prison space.

Donziger believes that the causes of crime in the United States are largely structural: Blocked economic opportunities lead the economically disenfranchised to commit property offenses and to engage in self-destructive behavior like drug use. For this reason, he argues that continuing a practice of steering money toward incarceration and away from providing educational and economic opportunities is a "plan for social failure."

In "Steel Town Lockdown," Yeoman analyzes the mechanisms underlying the increasing privatization of prisons in the United States, which makes the Corrections Corporation of America (CCA) the "sixth-largest prison system in the country—trailing only California, Texas, the U.S. Bureau of Prisons, New York, and Florida." Although private prisons in deindustrialized urban areas are sold to the community as economic engines, Yeoman argues that state governments save little or no money by contracting out their prison business. Like other corporations, Yeoman points out, CCA relies on corporate welfare, uses funds to drown out the opposing voices of community members directly affected by the siting of private prisons, and limits its investment in infrastructure and employee training for the sake of turning a profit for investors. Yeoman demonstrates that the absence of state regulatory power over private prisons results in no one imposing limits on the extent that private prisons can cut corners to turn a profit. The result is greater danger to the communities in which prisons are located and to the prisoners themselves. The public must deal with the escape of violent criminals. Prisoners must deal with undertrained guards who cannot effectively protect them from other dangerous inmates and who use abuse and humiliation to retain authority.

At the beginning of "Who Owns Death?" Lifton and Mitchell ask why the United States retains the death penalty when most of the world has rejected it as barbaric. Their answer is that America's unique commitment to the death penalty rests on its equally unique ideological association between the right to own guns and conquering the "Wild West," and an absolutist vision of good and evil, wherein killing becomes the only means of fully eliminating evil. However, they argue, there is an inherent contradiction between the death penalty and democracy. We recognize that state killing is total power and, in order to prevent abuse of power, we take pains to allow defendants to appeal their convictions. This appeal process results in extensive and costly litigation.

Lifton and Mitchell argue that necessary, if not completely sufficient, conditions now are in place to lead to the complete ban of the death penalty in the United States. A reasonable alternative to the death penalty, life without parole, now exists in combination with public awareness that errors can be made in prosecution that cannot be remedied through subsequent appeals. Lifton and Mitchell point to recent botched executions and DNA tests that have established the innocence of convicts on death row as proof that the system is flawed. They note as well that state guardians, such as the governor of Illinois, have expressed a lack of faith in the equality of the criminal justice process, and prominent conservatives have publicly called for a moratorium on executions, a position that is usually identified as liberal. Lifton and Mitchell recognize that public attitudes are not strongly in favor of eliminating the death penalty in the United States, but they argue that this was not necessary for the establishment of a ban in France and England. They also argue that Timothy McVeigh's recent execution, following on the heels of publicity about the FBI having withheld evidence, offered a national forum for discussion of fairness in the system and of anti–death penalty views, including those held by survivors of his victims.

In "DWB Is Not a Crime," Lamberth describes how he gathered evidence to determine if police along a particular stretch of the New Jersey Turnpike were using racial profiling in making stops. He explains how he stationed observers to gain an estimate of the racial composition of drivers along the stretch of road in question and how he obtained a measure of drivers' compliance with legal speed limits. Correlating his data with arrest records, Lamberth was able to show that African Americans made up 13.5 percent of the turnpike's drivers, 15 percent of the speeders, but 35 percent of the arrests. Lamberth's analysis was used in a criminal case, and evidence against the suspects was suppressed on the basis of a "de facto policy . . . of targeting blacks for investigation and arrest." Lamberth's methodology has been used in other states, and similar results have been obtained. What do you think you would find if you put it to use in your city or town?

Do innocent people end up serving prison time, even sitting on death row, because individuals who make critical decisions are biased in specific ways or actually corrupt? Or is there another reasonable explanation? Lofquist is interested in why and how our justice system produces wrongful convictions. To investigate this issue, he closely examined the way a particular set of murders in a rural Ohio town was prosecuted. He interviewed key participants and studied the transcripts of the trial and subsequent appeals, which resulted in the appellate judges overturning the guilty verdict. The result of Lofquist's investigation is "Whodunit? An Examination of the Production of Wrongful Convictions."

Lofquist argues that in *Ohio vs. Dale Johnson* a wrongful conviction occurred without malice or intentional misconduct on the part of legal personnel. Rather, police and prosecutors who followed everyday practice within their respective organizations made a premature decision that a particular suspect was guilty and were inattentive to viable alternate scenarios.

Lofquist explains that legal cases are not developed in a vacuum. Legal actors draw on "normal crime" scenarios available in our culture and legal organizations to help them develop investigations and build cases. They put the available evidence into the preexisting narrative that best fits. Once they are committed to a particular story, they seek out additional evidence to fill in gaps. Early commitment to a particular narrative, obviously, closes down a broader investigation.

Lofquist argues that in the case he studied, police responded to statistical patterns of intimate homicide, the fact that the suspect and the victim had a falling out before the murder, and inconsistencies in statements made by the suspect. Based on an admission that the suspect had been naked in the company of the victim, his stepdaughter, the police gravitated to a "sexual molester" crime scenario. Dale Johnson, the defendant, was cast as a sexual molester on the basis of little hard evidence, but the stereotype was so strong that it became the prevailing narrative for the case. The police were also inexperienced with murder investigations, and critical evidence was destroyed during the investigation. In addition, the authority of forensic science was not critically scrutinized in court: A statement made after a witness had undergone hypnosis and a psychological "profile" completed after the expert had given information about the preliminary suspect were admitted as evidence because they were within the realm of normal practice. The defense focused on undermining individual pieces of evidence, but did not challenge the "sexual molester" crime frame and, thus, it stood. Dale Johnson was convicted and sentenced to death. After defense attorneys and the media offered alternative scenarios and he recalled his alibi, the appellate court released him.

Lofquist explains that asking "Who done it?" to find an individual guilty party responsible for a wrongful conviction leads us to look for linearity and rationality in decision making. Rather, he argues, legal actors make decisions in complex contexts with limited information and limited responsibility. Wrongful convictions are unremarkable, in his view; they follow from normal, day-to-day legal practice. Our best bet to minimize them is to foster police professionalism and exploration of a broad range of possibilities; provide effective capital defense attorneys who probe alternate scenarios; and encourage independent investigation by the media.

In "I Don't Have to Be Afraid of You," Amanda Konradi adopts a symbolic interactionist perspective to examine the difficulties that rape survivors have serving as witnesses in courtrooms. She focuses specifically on the emotional impact of testifying and on how survivors manage their feelings both to protect themselves and to advance the case against their alleged assailants. Konradi argues that rape survivors' difficulties stem both from the emotional impact of the rape event and from prosecutors' and defense attorneys' efforts to use their emotions as resources. She reports that rape survivors are frequently overwhelmed with intense feelings from reliving the assault experience in the act of testifying, confronting their attackers, and having problematic interactions with defense attorneys that resemble the dis-empowerment of the rape situation.

Konradi also shows that survivors act to suppress emotional responses that they believe will interfere with their ability to testify, will continue to give their assailant power over them, or will undermine what they perceive to be the state's case. This management effort has its own emotional burden. Konradi argues that survivors' intense feelings could be somewhat mitigated by greater precourt preparation from prosecutors. Prosecutors could diffuse sudden intense emotional responses by giving survivors a chance to see disturbing evidence and practice their testimony before court. Prosecutors could also provide information about rules of interaction in the courtroom and signals to invite their intervention in cross-examination so survivors feel less ma-

nipulated by defense attorneys. However, in order to do this, prosecutors must approach survivors and their emotions as something other than resources for prosecution.

FOCUSING QUESTIONS

The authors presented in this chapter have many overlapping concerns, but each attends to different aspects of the criminal justice process. To focus your reading on these selections, keep the following questions in mind: How is crime a structural problem?

How do laws that define crimes and penalties reinforce the position of the powerful? How do the day-to-day interactions between those who implement the law and those who are suspected of violating it re-create structural inequalities of race, class, and gender?

41

CRIME AND POLICY

STEVEN R. DONZIGER

We are a nation both afraid of and obsessed with crime. Each day, newspapers tell another story of innocence shattered: the Oklahoma City bombing, the drowning of two young boys in a South Carolina lake by their mother, the brutal stabbings of Nicole Brown Simpson and Ronald Goldman. In the evenings, our televisions are saturated with real-crime dramas such as *America's Most Wanted* and *Unsolved Mysteries*. Since the 1960s, hundreds of different crime bills have been passed by Congress and state legislatures.

From *The Real War on Crime* by Steven R. Donziger, editor, pages 1–30. Copyright © 1996 by the National Center on Institutions and Alternatives. Reprinted by permission of HarperCollins Publishers, Inc.

We have fought a war on drugs. Annual expenditures on police have increased from $5 billion to $27 billion over the past two decades. We have built more prisons to lock up more people than almost every country in the world. We are the only country in the West to employ capital punishment and to use the death penalty against teenagers. Yet Americans in record numbers still report that they feel unsafe in their streets and in their homes.

We have leveled our supposedly strongest weapons at crime, to the tune of about $100 billion tax dollars per year, but we have not accomplished much. Crime rates have not gotten worse—as many would have you believe—but neither have they gotten much better. Yet still there is the feeling that the criminal justice system is not doing enough. Many suggest that we need more police, more prisons, harsher sentencing, even a return to the chain gangs. While we continue to take tougher and tougher stances, the underlying problem remains: our criminal justice system is failing to control crime in a way that makes Americans feel safe.

A hoax is afoot. Politicians at every level—federal, state, and local—have measured our obsession, capitalized on our fears, campaigned on "get tough" platforms, and won. Since the Willie Horton advertisement dashed the hopes of Michael Dukakis in the 1988 presidential race, almost every serious candidate has tried to appear tough on crime. But appearances are often deceiving.

We will first review the basic facts about crime in America. It is important to approach the facts with caution because you will see that they rarely tell the whole story. The Commission found that some baseline data about crime are simply untrue or are more complicated than they appear, even though they provide the foundation on which much of our crime policy is constructed.

Crime Rates: The Numbers Do Not Tell the Full Story

There is a widespread perception in this country that crime rates are rising. In most categories, crime rates over the last two decades have remained remarkably stable. What has changed is the nature of criminal violence. Partly because of the prevalence of firearms, one category of the population—young males in the inner city—is at an extremely high risk of being killed. This danger sometimes spills over to the suburbs and rural areas, creating fear throughout the

country. Violence in the inner city is one of the most pressing issues facing our criminal justice system. But it is not the only issue. There are many other criminal justice issues that receive less media attention, but also have devastating implications for public safety—the difference between fear of crime and crime itself, violence, prisons, juvenile crime, domestic violence, policing, and the racial implications of crime policy.

Before delving into these issues, we must keep in mind several basic facts:

- Crime rates are higher today than they were in the 1950s. This is largely because crime increased significantly in the 1960s. But since the early 1970s, crime rates have remained remarkably stable even though they sometimes go up or down from year to year.
- The murder rate in this country dropped 9 percent from 1980 to 1992 and now is almost exactly the same as it was in the 1970s.
- The serious violent crime rate for the United States stands 16 percent below its peak level of the mid-1970s.
- Serious crimes reported to police dropped in 1992, 1993, and 1994.

These statistics tell us only that certain categories of crime have remained remarkably stable over the last two decades. They should not be taken to mean that crime is not a major problem. Crime (particularly homicide) is widespread in this country, and among young people violent crime is expected to increase further in the next few years.

Two Measures of Crime

We have found that there is a huge difference between the public *perception* and the *reality* of crime in the United States. For now, it is important to remember that most people perceive crime to be rising when in

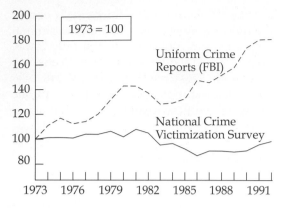

FIGURE 1   Divergent Measures of Violent Crime. *NOTE:* Figures were scaled to 100 in 1973 and have been adjusted to take into account population increases. (*Source:* U.S. Department of Justice, Bureau of Justice Statistics [1994], *Sourcebook of Criminal Justice Statistics—1993,* pp. 247, 352.)

reality it has remained remarkably stable for many years.[1]

One major source of confusion about crime rates in the United States is that there are two major methods by which crime is measured, the Uniform Crime Reports (UCR) and the National Crime Victimization Survey (NCVS) (see Figure 1). It may be startling that these two systems of measurement produce such different numbers. The UCR is tabulated by the FBI, based on arrest information submitted annually by each of the 17,000 different police departments in the United States. Because it is the only survey to provide a state-by-state breakdown of crime rates, the UCR is the measure of crime most cited by the media (who see it as a good local story) and politicians (who talk about it with their constituencies).

However, most criminologists consider UCR figures inaccurate because they tend to exaggerate increases in crime—a fact that is at least partly responsible for the misperception that crime is rising.[2] The UCR overestimates increases in crime for several reasons. First, computers have led to marked improvements in police reporting of crime.

Thus, "increases" in crime reported by police are often the result of improved record-keeping rather than actual increases in criminal activity. For example, in 1973 citizens reported 861,000 aggravated assaults to police, but the police recorded only 421,000.[3] By 1988, citizens reported 940,000 aggravated assaults to the police, and the police recorded 910,000. The number of aggravated assaults did not go up much between 1973 and 1988, but the recording improved dramatically. The same pattern occurred for robbery and rape.

The UCR also is flawed because of the way many police departments tabulate their statistics. If two persons are arrested for a single assault, police usually count the two arrests rather than the one assault. Thus, one crime suddenly turns into two and the total number of crimes becomes inflated. This practice creates the most severe distortions in juvenile crime because juveniles are often arrested in groups.

Moreover, budgetary decisions based on police reports create incentives for police departments to skew their figures upward. The 1994 Federal Crime Control Act, for example, allocates more funds to states with higher levels of crime as recorded by the police. Given these problems, it is not surprising that the UCR reports an increase in violent crime in the last twenty years.

Despite its flaws, the UCR does provide an accurate measure of the homicide rate. This is because murders are rare and serious events that citizens tend to report quickly and accurately to the police, who record them with precision. The UCR indicates that the incidence of murder per capita is lower today than it was in the 1930s, when the rate of incarceration then was about one-fifth what it is today. The current homicide rate of 9.3 per 100,000 population is nearly identical to the rate of 9.4 per 100,000 recorded in 1973. The total number of murders in Boston, for example, was 135 in 1973. In 1993, it was 98.[4] Our national murder rate is not increasing nearly as fast as many might claim.

We believe—as do most criminologists—that the figures produced by the National Crime Victimization Survey are more accurate. To conduct the survey, staff at the Census Bureau telephone a representative sampling of households around the country to determine how many people were victimized by one of seven crimes in the preceding year. The seven crimes are rape, robbery, assault, personal theft, household theft, burglary, and motor vehicle theft. The NCVS generally is considered more reliable because it uses scientific polling techniques similar to those that determine the Nielsen ratings in television. It does not measure murder because the victim cannot be interviewed. The NCVS does not break down crime data for each state, thus making it less interesting to members of the news media who want to find a local angle on crime trends.

The Threat of Violent Crime

It is important to distinguish between crime generally and violent crime specifically. Violent crimes are committed against *people*—murders, rapes, robberies, kidnappings, and assaults. Nonviolent crimes are usually committed against *property*—burglaries, auto thefts, embezzlement, check forgery, fraud, and trespassing. (Burglary, defined as breaking into a dwelling, presents a definitional problem. Though burglary is formally a crime against property, it carries the lurking possibility of violent confrontation and the psychological sense of intrusion associated with violent crime. It is therefore more serious than most nonviolent crimes.) Offenses involving the sale or possession of drugs are also nonviolent, but obviously a violent act associated with the sale or possession of drugs (such as a shooting to protect a drug market) would be a violent crime.

Much violence in our society is not a violation of the criminal law. For example, if someone kills another in self-defense, that person committed an act of violence but not a crime. There is also violence in the media and on television that shapes public perceptions and, according to some experts, actually influences people to commit violent acts. But violence in the media is not a crime. A violent crime is an act of violence that violates a criminal law passed by the Congress or a state legislature.

The vast majority of crime in America is *not* violent. One in ten arrests in the United States is for a violent crime. Only 3 in 100 arrests in the United States are for a violent crime resulting in injury. The distinction between violent and nonviolent crime is critical for understanding why the criminal justice system is not more effective at making Americans safe. When people think of locking up criminals, they usually have an image in mind of a violent offender—a murderer or a rapist. However, the vast majority of people filling our expensive new prisons are nonviolent property and drug offenders.

Violent crime is a major problem in localized areas of the inner city. In those places, firearms violence—especially against young people—has increased dramatically. During the 1980s, teenage boys in all racial and ethnic groups became more likely to die from a bullet than from all natural causes combined. During the time period from 1985 to 1991, annual rates of homicide for males aged 15 to 19 years increased 154 percent.[5] For African-American male youths, the homicide rate is eight times that of white male youths. If you live in the inner city and are young—particularly young and African-American—your chance of being the victim of a violent crime is incredibly high. And if you are not living in the inner city, the localized violence of some communities reverberates nationally, making everybody *feel* less safe even though most people are *more* safe than they were in the 1970s.

The media has focused much of its crime reporting on the tragic phenomenon of youth homicide. As a result, a myth has been created and projected that all Americans have a "realistic" chance of being murdered by a stranger. While it is always good to take precautions to lower the risk of crime, in reality almost all Americans have an extremely remote chance of being killed or victimized by a stranger. Most violent crime is committed by friends and family. The most common homicide is not random but a person shooting someone he or she knows, often in the home. A 1994 government study of 8,000 homicides in urban areas found that eight out of ten murder victims were killed by a family member or someone they knew.[6] Women are far more likely to be assaulted by their husbands or boyfriends than by a stranger in an alley. Children are more likely to be molested by family or friends than by strangers.

While a few neighborhoods are extraordinarily dangerous, most are relatively safe. Males are more at risk of criminal victimization than females (because males commit much more crime than women, they tend to associate more with criminals and therefore run a higher risk of being victimized by them). Young people—particularly adolescents—are much more at risk than elderly people. The risk of being a victim of a serious violent crime is nearly four times higher for a person 16 to 19 years old than it is for a person aged 35 to 49.[7] The chances of a white woman 65 or older becoming a victim of a serious violent crime (e.g., murder, rape, robbery, or assault) are *one-sixtieth* the odds of an African-American male teenager.[8]

U.S. Crime Rates Compared to Other Countries

Although it is often assumed that the United States has a high rate of incarceration because of a high crime rate, in reality the overall rate of crime in this country is not extraordinary. The one exception is murder. Largely because of the prevalence of firearms, we have about 22,000 homicides per year, about 10 times the per capita murder rate of most European countries. Many comparable countries such as Australia and Canada actually have higher rates of victimization than the United States for some crimes. For the crime of assault with force, 2.2 percent of Americans are victimized each year, compared to 2.3 percent of Canadians and 2.8 percent of Australians (see Figure 2). For robbery, 1.7 percent of Americans are victimized annually; in Spain, the number is 2.9 percent. For car theft, the U.S. rate is 2.3 percent; Australia is at 2.7 percent and England is at 2.8 percent.[9] Thus, it is not our higher violent crime rates that lead to our high incarceration rates—the 22,000 homicides per year cannot account for the 1.5 million people behind bars. Rather, American rates of incarceration are higher because of our exceedingly harsh treatment of people convicted of lesser crimes.

The Key to the Problem: Understanding the Difference Between Crime and Violence

We all want to protect ourselves from violent offenders, either by taking the steps necessary to prevent violent crimes or by sending to prison those who commit them. But how do we begin to control violent crime? We must start by understanding the difference between *crime* and *violence*.

We cannot begin to control violent crime until we recognize that *the primary reason most Americans live in fear is not crime but violence.* The United States does not have more crime than other industrialized countries. Rather, it has a *different character of crime.* Criminologists in the Netherlands and the

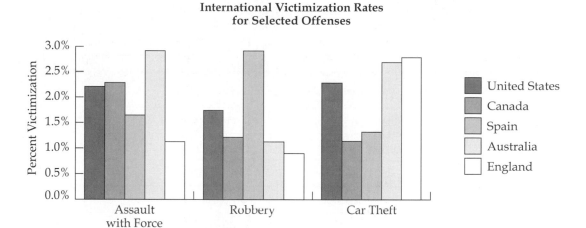

International Victimization Rates for Selected Offenses

Percent Victimization

United States
Canada
Spain
Australia
England

Assault with Force   Robbery   Car Theft

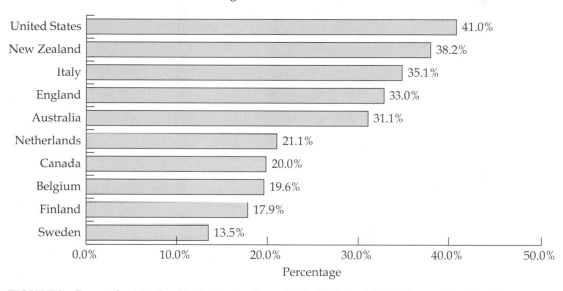

Percentage of the Public Feeling Unsafe When Walking in Their Own Area After Dark

United States	41.0%
New Zealand	38.2%
Italy	35.1%
England	33.0%
Australia	31.1%
Netherlands	21.1%
Canada	20.0%
Belgium	19.6%
Finland	17.9%
Sweden	13.5%

Percentage

FIGURE 2 Except for Murder, Victimization Rates in the U.S. Are Not Higher . . . But Fear Is. (*Source:* Van Dijk, Jan J. M. [November 1992], *Criminal Victimisation in the Industrialized World,* pp. 10, 24, 33, 57, The Netherlands: Ministry of Justice.)

United Kingdom recently compared crime across industrialized countries.[10] With the exception of homicide, the United States had the highest crime rate in only one of the fourteen offenses measured—attempted burglary. Because of the prevalence of firearms on our streets, however, America leads the world in *the proportion of violent crime resulting in injury.* If a person is assaulted with a gun rather than fists, the chances are much higher that injury or death will result. This is why the United States is far and away the world leader in the number of murders.

TABLE 1   How Crime Breaks Down in America

Arrests for Violent Offenses	13.6%	*Arrests for Nonviolent Offenses*	86.4%
Murder	0.2%	Public Order	13.5%
Manslaughter	0.1%	Theft Offenses	13.0%
Forcible Rape	0.3%	Driving Under the Influence	10.9%
Robbery	1.0%	Drug Offenses	8.0%
Aggravated Assault	4.0%	White Collar	3.8%
Other Assaults	8.2%	Liquor Laws	3.7%
		Burglary	2.9%
		All Other	30.8%

NOTE: Totals may not add to 100% due to rounding.

Source: U.S. Department of Justice, Federal Bureau of Investigation (December 1994), *Crime in the United States–1993*, p. 217.

It is not the amount of *crime* but rather the amount of *violence* that adds to our fear. It is the failure to recognize the distinction between crime and violence that diverts attention from finding more effective methods to make our country safer. In order to understand this important distinction, it is necessary to look at crime statistics a little more closely (see Table 1).

Violent Crime Is a Fraction of Overall Crime

We have shown that violent street crime is but a small portion of overall crime. But even within this "violent" category the actual physical violence is often overstated. The vast majority of violent crimes are assaults where one person hits or slaps another or makes a verbal threat. Only about 8 percent of the victims of violent crime nationally went to a hospital emergency room.[11] Most were released immediately or the same day. Of all the victims of violent crime nationally, slightly over 1 percent required a hospital stay of one day or more.[12]

Crime Policy in the United States

Unlike many European countries, there is no cabinet official in charge of national crime policy in the United States. Each of the fifty state legislatures determines its own crime policy separately. Some states refuse to send a person to jail for having a small amount of marijuana, while others impose strict sentences. Some states choose to have the death penalty, while others shun it. Some states have mandatory minimum sentences for drug crimes, while others allow judges unfettered discretion to impose sentences. Though policies vary, most states in recent years have adopted tougher measures—longer sentences and more restrictive bail policies, both of which have led to higher rates of incarceration across the country.

Although it is difficult for these reasons to define the exact parameters of a national crime policy, a national "get tough" trend has been evident over the last fifteen years. Since 1968, six major anticrime bills have passed Congress and been signed into law by presidents. In one way or another, all of these bills have been used by elected officials to convince the public that Washington was getting "tough" on crime by increasing sentences for certain types of offenses. Many of the bills were used to influence crime policy by withholding money from the states unless they adopted certain "get tough" policies favored by the federal government. For example, under the 1994 federal crime bill, a state can receive part of the $9.7 billion set aside for new prison construction only if it requires inmates to serve at least 85 percent of their sentences before parole (in effect doubling sentences for many classes of offenders). The frequency with which Congress passed anti-crime legislation increased in the 1980s, when prisons were expanding most rapidly.

At the time it was signed into law, the 1968 Crime Control and Safe Streets Act was the most extensive anti-crime legislation in history. It provided for emergency wiretapping, tightened controls over interstate firearms transfers, and allocated hundreds of millions of dollars to localities to upgrade their law enforcement capability. The 1984 anti-crime legislation increased penalties for drug offenses, established mandatory sentences for certain firearms offenses, and reformed bail laws to allow for increased pretrial detention of dangerous offenders. In 1986, Congress passed another bill that established stiff mandatory sentences for possession of crack cocaine. The bill made such sentences 100 times greater than those for powder cocaine, even though there was little or no difference between crack and powder except the race of the people using them. A 1988 bill increased funding by billions of dollars for federal drug control efforts. The federal crime bill of 1994—the most expensive in history—added the death penalty to dozens of federal offenses, allocated $23 billion for law enforcement (this includes the $9.7 billion for prisons), and directed another $6.1 billion for crime prevention programs. Although the full impact of the 1994 crime bill has yet to be felt, it will almost certainly contribute to higher rates of incarceration in the federal prison system.

Nonviolent Offenders Fueled the Prison Expansion

Since 1980, the United States has undertaken one of the largest and most rapid expansions of a prison population in the history of the Western world. Between 1980 and 1994, the prison population tripled from 500,000 to 1.5 million. The number of people under some form of correctional supervision (in prison or jail, on probation, or on parole) surpassed 5 million people at the end of 1994, or 2.7 percent of the adult population.

Most of the increase in the prison population during this time was *not* accounted for by violent offenders. Fully 84 percent of the increase in state and federal prison admissions since 1980 was accounted for by *nonviolent* offenders.[13] Legislative changes in sentencing laws in the 1980s made it routine to send nonviolent offenders to prison for long terms. A person arrested for a drug offense in 1992 was five times more likely to go to prison than a person arrested in 1980.[14] In California, people who committed lesser offenses such as car theft and larceny went to prison at much greater rates than those who committed the serious violent crime of robbery.[15] Even for petty offenses, there has been a tendency to enact criminal rather than civil penalties. A county board recently passed legislation imposing thirty days in jail for illegal camping or allowing a dog to run loose.[16]

TABLE 2 Persons Admitted and in Custody—How Many? How Violent?

	Population	Violent	Nonviolent	Annual Admissions	Violent	Nonviolent
Jails	490,442	23%	77%	9,796,000	n/a	n/a
State Prisons	958,704	47%	53%	431,279	27%	73%
Federal Prisons	100,438	11%	89%	38,542	6%	94%
Juvenile	93,851	15%	85%	823,449	n/a	n/a
Total*	1.5 million	35%	65%	11.1 million	n/a	n/a

NOTE: Data are the most recent available. Population figures represent the number of persons under jurisdiction in each category.

*Totals have been adjusted to account for double counting of individuals under more than one jurisdiction.

n/a = not available.

Sources: U.S. Department of Justice, Bureau of Justice Statistics; Federal Bureau of Prisons; Office of Juvenile Justice and Delinquency Prevention.

The state of Texas recently completed an exhaustive study of its felony sentencing patterns and found that 77 percent of all prison admissions were for nonviolent crimes.[17] The most frequent crime resulting in a prison sentence was drug possession. In the federal system, the overwhelming majority of inmates—89 percent—are convicted of nonviolent offenses.[18] We will see shortly that many of these nonviolent offenders do not need to be in prison at all, yet each one may consume tens of thousands of tax dollars per year.

One reason nonviolent offenders are crowding our prisons is because we continue to broaden the definition of crime. Historically, the term applied only to those acts that violated the rules of civilized conduct—murder, theft, and the like. Today, we classify as "criminal" conduct that which is merely undesirable or that which breaks an administrative rule (e.g., laws that ban panhandling). The increasing failure to recognize the distinction between the truly wrong and the minor infraction—and to address minor infractions outside the formal and expensive criminal justice system—at least partly explains why our jails and prisons are overcrowded.

Many state corrections leaders and prison wardens have voiced objections to the fact that nonviolent offenders take up so much space in their facilities. Bishop L. Robinson, Maryland's public safety chief, recently recommended that 32 percent of the prisoners in his state could be paroled immediately or put into alternative programs.[19] James A. Gondles, executive director of the American Correctional Association, agreed with Robinson. "It's not a question of being soft," he said. "It's a question of solving a problem before it eats us alive."[20] One consequence of this policy is that the system occasionally releases violent criminals early because prison space is crammed with new nonviolent offenders.

Table 2 and Figure 3 demonstrate how few people in the system are violent. The chart makes the crucial distinction between the *population* of the system and *admissions* into the system. A facility's *population* is the number of people in that facility on any given day. *Admissions* count the number of people entering the facility during a certain

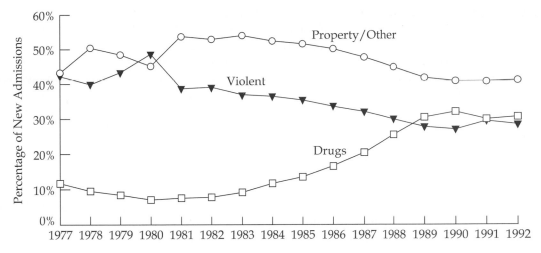

FIGURE 3 Nonviolent Offenders Fueled Prison Expansion: New Court Commitments by Type of Crime to State Prisons, 1977–1992. (*Sources:* U.S. Department of Justice, Bureau of Justice Statistics [May 1993], *Prisoners in 1992*, p. 10, Appendix Table 1; Department of Justice, Bureau of Justice Statistics [June 1994], *Prisoners in 1993*, p. 10, Appendix Table 1.)

period of time, usually a year. Admissions shows the dynamic nature of the system, with people entering and exiting continually. For example, a short-term holding pen in a county jail may hold 10 people on any given day, but admit 2,000 people over the course of a year.

Bait and Switch

A policy that pretends to fight violence by locking up mostly nonviolent offenders is an inefficient use of taxpayer resources. The scam works like the classic "bait and switch" marketing ploy, in which customers are "baited" into a store by an advertisement for an item at an extremely low price. Once in the store, the salesperson "switches" the customer to a higher-priced product that the scheme was designed to promote. In the criminal justice field, the "bait" is citizen fear of violent crime. The "switch" occurs when public officials fight crime by building more prisons *but then fill the new cells with nonviolent offenders.* This

scheme profits those who wish to appear "tough" on crime but in reality are failing to make America safe. One consequence of this policy is that the criminal justice system spends tens of billions of dollars on prisons and then underfunds effective drug treatment, educational programs, and violence prevention programs by asserting that there is not enough money.

Criminologists Franklin Zimring and Gordon Hawkins first applied the term "bait and switch" to this aspect of criminal justice policy. Under the bait and switch, people who commit lesser infractions have borne the brunt of the anti-crime fervor by getting sent to prison at much higher rates and serving much longer sentences. But as the data show, violent crime is undiminished even as we engage in the largest increase in incarceration in American history.

The Bait and Switch in Practice in California

California is a good example of the "bait and switch" in practice and is illustrative of similar trends around the country. In 1980, 60 percent of the 24,569 inmates in the state had been committed to prison for acts of violence—a relatively efficient use of prison space.[21] California increased its prison population by 400 percent between 1980 and 1993 (to 125,605 inmates),[22] *yet only 27 percent of the additional prison space confined people convicted of violent offenses.*[23] The remaining 73 percent were convicted of nonviolent crimes. Today, California has more persons incarcerated for drug offenses than the entire prison population in 1980. If crime policy was intended to combat violence, then its effectiveness in California dropped considerably as the prison population expanded.

"Three Strikes and You're Out"

"Three strikes and you're out" is one of the most popular crime control initiatives. Proposals vary state by state, but the general idea behind "three strikes" is to increase the prison sentence for a second offense and require life in custody without parole for a third offense. Larry Fisher, age thirty-five, recently robbed a sandwich shop near Seattle of $135 by holding a finger in his pocket and pretending it was a gun. In the previous eight years he was responsible for two other minor robberies. Under the traditional sentencing system, Fisher would have spent about two years in prison for the sandwich shop robbery. Under the new "three strikes and you're out" legislation now in effect in Washington state, he faced life in prison with no possibility of parole for this third offense.[24]

Michael Garcia shoplifted a package of meat valued at $5.62 from a grocery store in Los Angeles.[25] At the time, Garcia was temporarily out of work and his mother's Social Security check had failed to arrive. Garcia stuck the package of chuck steak down his pants: one piece for his mother, one for his retarded brother, and one for himself. For this offense, he faces twenty-five years to life in prison under California's "three strikes" legislation. His other "strikes" also involved small sums of money and no physical injury; they were integrally related to a heroin addiction he had never been able to control. In fact, Garcia's parole agent said, "Michael is not a bad guy. He had some problems with dope use, but he's not dangerous."[26] The agent said he would have sent Garcia to a residential drug treatment program, but a slot was not available.

"Three Strikes and You're Out" Is Untested

We all acknowledge that the crime problem in most cities is severe, and that safety is the primary concern. People want tough sentences for repeat offenders, regardless of whether they are violent or nonviolent. But "three strikes and you're out"—though a great slogan—is untested and potentially disastrous. It threatens to drain billions of tax dollars to incarcerate lesser offenders for long periods of time.

The current popularity of "three strikes" legislation is in no way related to its record of success. Cases such as those of Larry Fisher and Michael Garcia appear to be typical. A survey by the legislature in California, the state to pass one of the strictest and broadest "three strikes" provisions, shows that few people sentenced under the new scheme are repeat violent offenders. Fully 70 percent of all second- and third-strike cases filed in California in 1994 were "nonviolent and nonserious offenses."[27] In Los Angeles County, only 4 percent of second and third felony convictions were cases of murder, rape, kidnapping, or carjacking. Although "three strikes" proposals typically arise from fear of violent crime, they often ensnare nonviolent offenders. The "three strikes" proposal is essentially a political ploy. Many voters who are frustrated with violent crime supported the proposal, but as we see again and again in the criminal justice system, it is doubtful they will get their money's worth. "Three strikes" proposals cast a very wide net, and most of the people caught in it do not require the kind of punishment the proposals mandate.

The Costs Run into the Billions

The costs of "three strikes" schemes are staggering. Every year an inmate spends in prison—be it under a "three strikes" law or a regular sentence—costs taxpayers an average of $22,000. As the prisoners get older, the cost of maintenance rises, ultimately reaching an average of $69,000 per year per prisoner for those over the age of fifty-five. In other words, the cost of imprisoning a person under the "three strikes" law will eventually *triple*. A study by a Stanford University professor estimated that the cost of a life term for an average California prisoner is $1.5 million.[28] Multiplied by the expected increase in prison population between now and the year 2020, the study projected total costs to California taxpayers in the hundreds of billions of dollars. While almost every other discretionary line item in the California budget is being slashed—including funds for higher education—the state still ranks first in the country in money spent to build and operate prisons.

The Rand Corporation found that the new "three strikes" law will cost between $4.5 and $6.5 billion every year to implement.[29] This is five times more than the state originally estimated. "Three strikes" will consume every dollar of new money the state expects to receive during the next six to eight years and will drain money from health and education spending. The Rand researchers concluded that the cost of the new legislation is so high that it will be impossible to implement fully. As a result, it is likely that the law will be applied haphazardly across the state. Such partial implementation can lead to dangerous, unplanned results, such as petty offenders spending decades in prison for lesser crimes while dangerous offenders are released early for lack of space.

Other unanticipated consequences already are starting to develop. One report concluded that plea bargaining is down because more felony offenders are opting to go to trial rather than risk getting a strike under the new legislation.[30] The increase in the number of trials is creating massive backlogs in the judicial system and causing court and attorney costs to skyrocket. Moreover, uneven enforcement of the law paves the way for racial and ethnic disparities to develop. Data from the Los Angeles Public Defender's office suggests that minorities with roughly the same criminal history as whites are being charged under "three strikes" at seventeen times the rate of whites.[31]

Truth in Sentencing

Prison populations in many states will increase more rapidly in coming years because of a proliferation of so-called "truth in sentencing" laws. Truth in sentencing requires the prisoner to serve the full sentence without being released early on parole. The laws are the result of public frustration with sentencing systems that do not tell the "truth" about sentence length—certainly a valid concern for all Americans who want to know how their tax dollars are being spent.

Tired of being told one thing and seeing another, the public has supported truth in sentencing enthusiastically without understanding the dramatic impact it will have on prison populations. Such laws take advantage of legitimate public frustration to instantly double and even triple prison sentences for all offenders. What the public is *not* told is that truth in sentencing will dramatically increase the amount of money going into prisons, largely to incarcerate the more numerous nonviolent offenders for longer periods of time.

The Old System of Indeterminate Sentencing

Under the old "indeterminate" sentencing system, a judge could hand down a sentence within a permissible range: Once found guilty, a person might receive a maximum of ten years in prison with the expectation that he would be released after five years if he conformed to the rules of the prison. The prospect of early release was designed to induce good behavior so inmates would be easier to manage and more likely to succeed after release. If inmates violated rules while in prison or on parole, they could be additionally punished by incarceration for the remainder of the original sentence plus any sentences for new charges. Judges usually doubled the maximum potential sentence so that the actual time served was about what the judge wished it to be and the threat of additional sentence was substantial.

This was not a straightforward way to sentence offenders. But it did serve the managerial needs of the prison system by affording parole boards the discretion to release inmates when ready or when conditions became overcrowded.

Two Main Attacks on the Old System

Indeterminate sentencing schemes have been subjected to two attacks in recent years. First, it is said that offenders only spend a portion of their actual sentences behind bars. This makes it appear that the offender gets off easy.

Although it is true that offenders often serve only a portion of the sentence, it does not follow that the offenders get off easy. Judges in indeterminate sentencing systems customarily impose longer sentences, expecting an early release.

Second, if released inmates commit another crime after being paroled, politicians charge that the crime could have been avoided if the inmate had served his full term. While this is a valid point in some cases, under the old sentencing regime the second half of the prison term is not designed to incapacitate because it is not supposed to be served. It is designed only to intimidate the inmate into better behavior. This political attack is often coupled with claims that parolees are running the streets and victimizing innocent citizens. Such claims are usually unwarranted. People paroled from prison or serving probationary sentences commit only 4 percent of offenses known to police each year for the most serious violent crimes of murder, rape, robbery, and assault.[32]

Truth in Sentencing as the Answer

In order to cure these supposed flaws, many politicians wish to require inmates to serve all or almost all (usually 85 percent) of the full sentence no matter how well they behave in prison. Under these truth in sentencing proposals, a person sentenced to ten years in prison would not be eligible for release after the four to six years customary under indeterminate sentencing systems, but would have to serve at least eight and one-half years. This single change in parole policy would effectively double most prison sentences. Although there might be reasons to tighten the old indeterminate system, it does not appear that careful tightening is the purpose of the new proposals. Truth in sentencing tends to mix violent and nonviolent offenders, and particularly for nonviolent offenders, it often increases sentences far beyond what is needed to ensure public safety.

Truth in sentencing has become such a powerful slogan that the federal government is trying to impose it on unwilling states. Most of the $10 billion in federal money available to states for prison construction under the 1994 federal crime bill will only be granted on the condition that states adopt truth in sentencing. This represents a significant shift in the traditional balance between the state and federal governments and a significant federalization of a traditionally local issue.

The Economic Cost of Truth in Sentencing

If the longer sentences are not carefully targeted to reach only the offenders who deserve them, they can be a terrible drain on public funds. Virginia, which is considering adoption of a new truth in sentencing plan, is a case in point. The Virginia plan to abolish parole and establish truth in sentencing originally called for construction of twenty-five new prisons at a cost of nearly $2 billion.[33] The state legislature estimated that the new prisons would cost $500 million per year to operate, double what the state pays for its current system. There was little discussion about how to pay for the plan, although Governor George Allen Jr. pointed toward parks and schools as possible sources of revenue.[34]

Governor Allen claimed that the plan was necessitated by the "rapid rise of violent crime" in the state, even though violent crime fell in the two years preceding introduction of the plan.[35] He claimed that "putting dangerous predators back on the streets" is a leading cause of criminal victimization, despite the fact that only 9 percent of robberies, 4 percent of murders, and 2 percent of rapes and aggravated assaults

in Virginia are committed by people on parole.[36] Most importantly, the governor claimed that the plan targeted "violent career criminals," although his own projections showed that the plan would capture almost four times more nonviolent offenders than violent offenders.

Mandatory Minimum Sentences

Mandatory minimums were a sentencing reform popular among elected officials during the height of the "war" on drugs in the late 1980s. The effect of mandatory minimum sentences on the criminal justice system has been long-term, and is still being felt by thousands of nonviolent drug offenders, many of whom are spending a decade or more behind bars for relatively modest offenses. The Rockefeller drug laws in New York, passed in the 1970s, have been so harsh on drug offenders that current Republican governor George Pataki has sought to repeal some of their provisions.

Mandatory minimums always require offenders to spend time in prison for *at least* a certain number of years. They are similar to truth in sentencing laws in that they increase the length of sentence, but they differ in that they allow parole after the minimum number of years is served. In the federal system, there are currently more than 100 provisions for mandatory minimums. Most states have mandatory minimum sentencing as well. The following illustrates the injustice and waste of tax dollars that can result from mandatory minimum sentences:

• In Mobile, Alabama, Nicole Richardson fell in love at age twenty with a small-time drug dealer who worked out of a local bar. One day, an undercover agent asked her where he could buy some drugs. She told him to talk to her boyfriend. For that degree of involvement, she was sentenced to ten years in prison with no possibility of parole. Her boyfriend had information on other drug dealers to trade. After cooperating with authorities, he received a prison sentence of five years.

• Michael Irish was a carpenter from Portland, Oregon, whose life savings had been wiped out to pay for the medical bills of his cancer-stricken wife.[37] Irish, who had no criminal history, was caught and convicted of unloading boxes of hashish from a boat. Under the mandatory minimum law, he was sentenced to twelve years in prison with no possibility of parole—an incarceration that will cost at least $250,000.

Stories like these are so numerous they have undermined much confidence in mandatory minimum sentences. Ninety percent of federal judges and 75 percent of state judges think mandatory minimum sentences are unsound.[38] On the U.S. Supreme Court, Chief Justice William Rehnquist and Associate Justice Anthony Kennedy are among those who have spoken against mandatory minimums.[39] They have been joined by the United States Sentencing Commission, the American Bar Association, and the National Association of Veteran Police Officers.[40]

Mandatory minimums create a number of problems.[41] First, they apply to everybody regardless of whether the punishment fits the crime or the offender. Second, mandatory minimums create what is known as sentencing "cliffs" for drug offenses. For example, possession of five grams of crack is punished with *no more than* one year in prison; possession of 5.01 grams of crack is punished with *no less than* five years in prison.

Third, mandatory sentences do not produce an equal sentence for everybody who commits the same offense. If a drug defendant decides to cooperate with the prosecution and turns in other people, the prosecutor will often choose not to charge that person with a crime carrying a mandatory minimum sentence, thus allowing the defendant to get out of prison early. Through this process, high-level drug dealers with the most information often get off with light sentences, while low-level dealers receive the longer mandatory minimum sentence.

The Relationship Between Poverty, Family Breakdown, and Criminal Justice

The Commission members feel strongly that crime is an act of personal choice and that an effective criminal justice system holds individuals accountable for their criminal behavior. Nevertheless, those who wish to prevent crime before it occurs cannot ignore the fact that the majority of the people filling our prisons come from impoverished backgrounds and lack a formal education.[42] Research shows that children from low-income families who are placed in early childhood development programs such as Head Start have lower rates of crime and higher rates of marriage than those who are not in the program.[43] We need to recognize that investing money in early childhood development produces a safer and healthier society over the long run. Unfortunately, the United States is the wealthiest nation on earth but has the highest child poverty rates of any industrialized country. More than fifteen million children live in poverty in the United States, and up to twelve million children are malnourished.[44]

Research consistently demonstrates that a disproportionate amount of violent street crime occurs in areas that have the lowest incomes and the most desperate living conditions.[45] Furthermore, medical research suggests that children who are malnourished are more apt to engage in high-risk behavior when they get older.[46] Regardless of what one thinks of our high rates of incarceration, it is also clear that they have had a negative impact on family stability. In some cities, more than half of all young men are under criminal justice supervision on any given day. With so many men in prison, the pool of people available for marriage has dwindled. This is a two-edged sword: while it is good for public safety to take a violent criminal off the streets, it is bad for public safety to incarcerate so many petty offenders that family life is disrupted. It is two-parent families that are least likely to live in poverty and more likely to cushion young people from the temptation to adopt a criminal lifestyle.[47] Eleven percent of children who live in a two-parent family live in poverty, while 60 percent of children who live with a single parent live in poverty.[48]

It troubles the Commission that the size of the American prison population and the number of people living in poverty both increased dramatically in the 1980s. Worse, the growth of each seemed to feed off the growth of the other. This is because funding for prison expansion came largely at the expense of programs designed to alleviate poverty.

Reducing Poverty Can Reduce Levels of Crime

Poverty is not an excuse for crime, nor is crime the exclusive province of low-income persons. But overall, countries with the highest ratio of poverty have the highest rates of crime.[49] The same correlation holds true for cities. It does not follow that an increase in poverty will translate immediately into an increase in crime. It does strongly imply that if overall poverty is reduced, then in the long run the amount of street crime associated with poverty will be reduced as well.

The increase in poverty in the United States during the 1980s was significant. The average rate of poverty in the United States during the decade was 17 percent higher than the average for the 1970s.[50] The poverty rate for African-American children is an astonishing 44 percent. For Latinos it is 38 percent, and for whites it is 16.2 percent.[51] In Sweden, the poverty rate for children is 2.7 percent; in Canada, it is 13.5 percent; and the overall United States rate is 21.0 percent.[52]

The Tradeoff Between Prisons and Opportunity for Youth

The massive prison construction represented a commitment by our nation to *plan for social failure* by spending billions of dollars to lock up hundreds of thousands of people while at the same time cutting billions of dollars for programs that would provide opportunity to young Americans.[53] The result of our social and criminal justice policies is that today among developed countries, the United States has the highest rates of incarceration, the widest spread of income inequality, and the highest levels of poverty. If we are serious about reducing crime, we need to create effective anti-poverty programs and fund them adequately as part of an overall approach to crime policy.

NOTES

1. Boggess, Scott, and John Bounds. July 1993. *Did Criminal Activity Increase During the 1980s? Comparisons Across Data Sources.* Working Paper Series, #4431. Cambridge, MA: National Bureau of Economic Research.
2. See generally Miller, Jerome G. Spring 1996. *Search and Destroy.* Cambridge, MA: Cambridge University Press; Reiss, Albert J., Jr., and Jeffrey A. Roth, eds. 1993. *Understanding and Preventing Violence.* Washington, DC: National Academy Press; Currie, Elliott. 1985. *Confronting Crime: An American Challenge.* New York: Pantheon Books.

3. Reiss, Albert J., Jr., and Jeffrey A. Roth, eds. 1993. *Understanding and Preventing Violence.* Washington, DC: National Academy Press: 414.

4. U.S. Department of Justice, Federal Bureau of Investigation. December 4, 1994. *Crime in the United States—1993;* 1974. *Crime in the United States—1973.* Washington, DC: U.S. Government Printing Office.

5. Centers for Disease Control and Prevention. October 14, 1994. *Morbidity and Mortality Weekly Report:* 726.

6. U.S. Department of Justice, Bureau of Justice Statistics. July 1994. *Murder in Families.* Washington, DC: U.S. Government Printing Office.

7. U.S. Department of Justice, Bureau of Justice Statistics. March 1994. *Criminal Victimization in the United States—1992.* Washington, DC: U.S. Government Printing Office: 23, Table 4.

8. Ibid., p. 28, Table 10.

9. These statistics are from 1988 or 1991, dependent on the country. Van Dijk, Jan J. M., and Pat Mayhew. November 1992. *Criminal Victimisation in the Industrialised World.* The Hague, Netherlands: Ministry of Justice/University of Leyden: 33, 23, 10.

10. Ibid.

11. U.S. Department of Justice, Bureau of Justice Statistics. March 1994. *Criminal Victimization in the United States—1992.* Washington, DC: U.S. Government Printing Office: 91, Table 86.

12. Ibid., p. 91, Table 88.

13. U.S. Department of Justice, Bureau of Justice Statistics. June 1994. *Prisoners in 1993.* Washington, DC: U.S. Government Printing Office: 13, Table 18.

14. U.S. Department of Justice, Bureau of Justice Statistics. August 1995. *Prisoners in 1994.* Washington, DC: U.S. Government Printing Office: 10, Appendix Table 2.

15. Zimring, Franklin, and Gordon Hawkins. 1994. The Growth of Imprisonment in California. *British Journal of Criminology.* Vol 34, special issue: 88.

16. U.S. Advisory Commission on Intergovernmental Relations. May 1993. *The Role of General Government Elected Officials in Criminal Justice.* Washington, DC: U.S. Advisory Commission on Intergovernmental Relations.

17. Fabelo, Tony. January 1993. *Sentencing Dynamics Study.* Austin, TX: Criminal Justice Policy Council: 26.

18. U.S. Department of Justice. February 4, 1994. *An Analysis of Nonviolent Drug Offenders with Minimal Criminal Histories.* Washington, DC: U.S. Government Printing Office.

19. Valentine, Paul. May 24, 1993. "You Can't Build Your Way Out," Maryland Official Says. *Washington Post.*

20. Ibid.

21. Data compiled by Franklin E. Zimring and Gordon Hawkins in Stoff, D. M., J. Breiling, and J. Maser, eds. 1996. *Handbook of Anti-Social Behavior.* New York: John Wiley and Sons.

22. U.S. Department of Justice, Bureau of Justice Statistics Bulletins. *Prisoners* series, 1980-93. Washington, DC: U.S. Government Printing Office.

23. Data compiled by Franklin E. Zimring and Gordon Hawkins in Stoff, D. M., J. Breiling, and J. Maser, eds. 1996. *Handbook of Anti-Social Behavior.* New York: John Wiley and Sons.

24. Egan, Timothy. February 15, 1994. A Three Strikes Penal Law Shows It's Not as Simple as It Seems. *New York Times.*

25. Schiraldi, Vincent, Peter Y. Sussman, and Lanric Hyland. October 1994. *Three Strikes: The Unintended Victims.* San Francisco: Center on Juvenile and Criminal Justice: 15–17.

26. Ibid., p. 17.

27. California Legislative Analyst's Office. January 6, 1995. *The "Three Strikes and You're Out" Law—A Preliminary Assessment.* Sacramento, CA: California Legislative Analyst's Office: 8.

28. Zimbardo, Philip. November 1994. *Transforming California's Prisons into Expensive Old Age Homes for Felons: Enormous Hidden Costs and Consequences for California's Taxpayers.* San Francisco: Center on Juvenile and Criminal Justice.

29. Greenwood, Peter, et al. 1994. *Three Strikes and You're Out—Estimated Benefits and Costs of California's New Mandatory Sentencing Law.* Santa Monica, CA: Rand Corporation.

30. California Legislative Analyst's Office. January 6, 1995. *The "Three Strikes and You're Out" Law—A Preliminary Assessment.* Sacramento, CA: California Legislative Analyst's Office.

31. The data presented by the Los Angeles Public Defender's Office were based on the first six months of actual experience with Assembly Bill 971—the "three strikes" law. Schiraldi, Vincent, and Michael Godfrey. October 1994. *Racial Disparities in the Charging of Los Angeles County's "Third Strike" Cases.* San Francisco: Center on Juvenile and Criminal Justice.

32. U.S. Department of Justice, Bureau of Justice Statistics. August 1995. *Probation and Parole Violators in State Prison, 1991.* Washington, DC: U.S. Government Printing Office: 10; U.S. Department of Justice, Federal Bureau of Investigation. August 30, 1992. *Crime in the United States—1991.* Washington, DC: U.S. Government Printing Office: 10.

33. Virginia House Appropriations Committee. Staff report. September 19, 1994. *Analysis of Potential Costs Under the Governor's Sentencing Reform Plan.* Richmond, VA: Office of the Governor.

34. Baker, Donald P., and Peter Baker. December 21, 1994. Allen's Tax Break Would Force Trade-Offs in N. VA. *Washington Post.*

35. See generally Governor's Commission on Parole Abolition and Sentencing Reform. August 1994. *Final Report.* Richmond, VA: Office of the Governor.

36. Baker, Peter. September 19, 1994. Many Ex-Offenders Succeed After Release. *Washington Post.*

37. Sileo, Chi Chi. December 6, 1993. Sentencing Rules That Shackle Justice. *Insight:* 11.

38. Ibid.

39. Associated Press. March 10, 1994. Justice Kennedy Assails Mandatory Sentences. *Washington Post;* Sileo, Chi Chi. December 6, 1993. Sentencing Rules That Shackle Justice. *Insight.*

40. Families Against Mandatory Minimums. January/February 1993. *FAMM-gram-action kit.* Issue no. 10; Sileo, Chi Chi. December 6, 1993. Sentencing Rules That Shackle Justice. *Insight:* 11.

41. Wilkins, William W. September/October 1993. Testimony of Judge William W. Wilkins Jr., chairman, United States Sentencing Commission: July 28, 1993. *Federal Sentencing Reporter.* Vol. 6, no. 2., p. 68; Campaign for an Effective Crime Policy. October 1993. *Evaluating Mandatory Minimum Sentences.* Washington, DC: Campaign for an Effective Crime Policy; United States Sentencing Commission. 1991. *Mandatory Minimum Penalties in the Federal Criminal Justice System: A Special Report to Congress.* Washington, DC: The Commission; Schulhofer, Stephen. Summer 1993. Rethinking Mandatory Minimums. *Wake Forest Law Review* 28:199; Miller, Marc, and Daniel J. Freed. September/October 1993. The Chasm Between the Judiciary and Congress over Mandatory Minimum Sentences. *Federal Sentencing Reporter.* Vol. 6, no. 2.

42. See generally Currie, Elliott. 1985. *Confronting Crime: An American Challenge.* New York: Pantheon Books.

43. See generally Schweinhart, L. J., H. V. Barnes, and D. P. Weikart. 1993. *Significant Benefits: The High/Scope Perry Preschool Study Through Age 27.* Ypsilanti, MI: High/Scope Press.

44. U.S. Department of Commerce, Bureau of the Census. March 1994. *Current Population Reports.* Washington, DC: U.S. Government Printing Office; Carnegie Task Force on Meeting the Needs of Young Children. April 1994. *Starting Points: Meeting the Needs of Our Youngest Children.* New York: Carnegie Corporation.

45. Reiss, Albert J., Jr., and Jeffrey A. Roth, eds. 1993. *Understanding and Preventing Violence.* Washington, DC: National Academy Press; Currie, Elliott. 1985. *Confronting Crime: An American Challenge.* New York: Pantheon Books.

46. See generally Carnegie Task Force on Meeting the Needs of Young Children. April 1994. *Starting Points: Meeting the Needs of Our Youngest Children.* New York: Carnegie Corporation.

47. Ibid., p. 17.

48. Rainwater, Lee, and Timothy M. Smeeding. August 1995. *Luxembourg Income Study: Working Paper No. 127: Doing Poorly: The Real Income of American Children in a Comparative Perspective.* Syracuse, NY: Maxwell School of Citizenship and Public Affairs, Syracuse University.

49. Currie, Elliott. 1985. *Confronting Crime: An American Challenge.* New York: Pantheon Books: 167–169.

50. U.S. Department of Commerce, Bureau of the Census. March 1994. *Current Population Reports.* Washington, DC: U.S. Government Printing Office.

51. Ibid.

52. These child poverty rates take into account government benefits as a source of income. Rainwater, Lee, and Timothy M. Smeeding. August 1995. *Luxembourg Income Study: Working Paper No. 127: Doing Poorly: The Real Income of American Children in a Comparative Perspective.* Syracuse, NY: Maxwell School of Citizenship and Public Affairs, Syracuse University: Table A-2.

53. For a complete discussion of social trends and their relationship to criminal justice issues, see National Criminal Justice Commission. June 1994. Breakdown of Caregiving

Institutions. Unpublished paper. Alexandria, Va.: National Criminal Justice Commission.

1. Consider Donziger's policy recommendations. Does he make a convincing case that reducing social inequality in the United States will reduce the amount of crime more effectively than longer periods of incarceration?

2. Consider as well Donziger's argument that politicians have engaged in "bait and switch" tactics to get the public behind "get tough" legislation. Could such tactics be effective if the public were better informed? What would it take for the public to become informed about crime?

3. Consider to what extent your perception of crime in the United States is factual or mythic. Give examples of each, if possible.

42

STEEL TOWN LOCKDOWN

BARRY YEOMAN

Bob Hagan was reading his e-mail one July afternoon when the telephone rang at his home in Youngstown, Ohio. "If you have a police radio, turn it on," a friend told the 51-year-old former locomotive engineer. Hagan went down to the basement, hauled out his old scanner, and listened to the news: Six prisoners had escaped in broad daylight from the Northeast Ohio Correctional Center and were still at large. The inmates had cut a four-foot hole in the prison's fence during outdoor recreation, then maneuvered through three rolls of razor ribbon without being detected. No alarm went off, and the officers patrolling the perimeter didn't notice anything amiss.

Hagan, a Democratic state senator who serves on a corrections oversight committee, knew the prison couldn't be trusted to handle the emergency safely. Unlike most prisons, which are government run, the Youngstown facility is managed by Corrections Corporation of America, a multinational company based in Nashville that makes its money running lockups. Since it opened the prison in 1997, CCA had repeatedly demonstrated the dangers of allowing businesses to operate prisons for profit. The company staffed the facility with guards who had little or no experience in corrections—and then imported 1,700 of the most violent inmates from Washington, D.C., to fill what was supposed to be a medium-security prison. CCA left metal equipment everywhere, which the prisoners quickly stripped and fashioned into weapons. During the first year alone, 20 prisoners were

Reprinted with permission from *Mother Jones,* 2000. May/June: 39–47. Copyright © 2000 by the Foundation for National Progress.

stabbed and two were murdered. The inexperienced staff resorted to tear gas and humiliation to keep order. Sick and injured inmates received inadequate medical treatment. "Knowing what I know now," Youngstown mayor George McKelvey later told reporters, "I would never have allowed CCA to build a prison here."

Now, as Hagan listened to the latest crisis on his scanner, he knew someone had to monitor the search for the escapees. He called his son inside from playing baseball, then jumped in his car to drive the seven miles to the prison. "We're in real trouble," he thought, steering past Youngstown's ruined landscape of abandoned steel mills. The city had once led the nation in steel production, but on that summer afternoon, the shuttered industrial buildings seemed like little more than convenient hideouts for escaped convicts. "God, I'm gonna see them," Hagan said to himself, peering into the shadows of buildings.

When Hagan reached the prison, he found local and state police scrambling to make up for lost time. The company, it turned out, had waited at least half an hour before notifying authorities of the escapes, giving the inmates a significant head start. "The warden had his jackbooted Ninja guys, all dressed in black, running through the woods—untrained and unprepared to pursue dangerous criminals—before they notified the police," Hagan recalled later. When CCA finally did call for help, it offered such sketchy information that police didn't know how to respond. Well after the inmates fled, a Youngstown officer radioed the dispatcher, asking if anyone knew when the men had escaped. "Negative," came the response. "Still in a state of mass confusion up there."

The company exhibited no such confusion, however, about how to secure its bottom line. Despite the high-profile escapes and killings in Youngstown, CCA announced last year that it wants to add 500 beds to the private prison—and build two more facilities nearby to incarcerate another 5,000 prisoners. If the expansion is approved, 1 in every 50 residents of Youngstown and the surrounding two-county area would be an out-of-state inmate. The plan suits many elected officials, who are desperate for an economic boost to a region hardened by the loss of its steel industry. But some residents are taking a closer look at what has transpired at the for-profit prison over the past three years—and what will happen if CCA succeeds in making their quiet corner of Ohio the private-prison capital of the world.

Not since slavery has an entire American industry derived its profits exclusively from depriving human beings of their freedom—not, at least, until a handful of corporations and Wall Street investors realized they could make millions from what some critics call "dungeons for dollars." Since the 1980s, when privatization became the rage for many government services, companies like CCA and its rival, Wackenhut Corporation, have been luring elected officials with a worry-free solution to prison overcrowding. Claiming they can lock people up cheaper than government can, the companies build cells on speculation, then peddle the beds to whatever local or state government needs a quick fix for its growing criminal population. "It's a heady cocktail for politicians who are trying to show they're tough on crime and fiscally conservative at the same time," says Judith Greene, a senior justice fellow at the Open Society Institute, a foundation chaired by philanthropist George Soros.

Over the past decade, private prisons have boomed. Corporations now control 122,900 beds for U.S. inmates, up at least eightfold since 1990. The reason is simple: With anti-drug laws and stiffer mandatory sentences pushing the prison population above two million, and governments strapped for capital to build new cells, for-profit prisons seem to offer plenty of cells at below-market prices. "If it could not be done cheaper than the government does it, then we wouldn't be in the business now," says Brian Gardner, warden of the CCA prison in Youngstown. "We believe in giving the taxpayer the best deal."

In fact, research indicates that governments save little or no money by contracting out their prison business. In 1996, the U.S. General Accounting Office reviewed five studies of private prisons and found no "substantial evidence" that for-profit institutions save taxpayer dollars. A more recent report commissioned by the U.S. attorney general notes that private prisons attempt to save money by cutting back on staffing, security, and medical care.

No company has benefited more from this private-prison boom—or been so plagued by understaffing, high turnover, and lax security—than CCA. The company, which controls half of a billion-dollar industry, now operates the sixth-largest prison system in the country—trailing only California, Texas, the U.S. Bureau of Prisons, New York, and Florida. Founded in 1983, CCA has never wanted for business. It now manages 82 prisons with 73,000 beds in 26 states, Puerto Rico, Great Britain, and Australia—raking in $365 million during the first three quarters of 1999.

Yet from the very beginning—when inmates from Texas escaped through the air-conditioner slots of a motel the company used as a makeshift penitentiary—CCA has engaged in cost cutting that jeopardizes the safety of prisoners, guards, and communities. In two Georgia prisons, the company's neglect of medical care and security amounted to "borderline deliberate indifference," according to a 1999 state audit. In Colorado last year, a number of female guards left alone with hundreds of male inmates admitted having sex with prisoners in exchange for protection. And at a South Carolina juvenile facility, children were hog-tied and beaten by an overworked, undertrained staff, according to a lawsuit filed in federal court. "They were grabbing the kids and slamming their heads into walls, slamming them into the floors," says Gaston Fairey, an attorney representing one of the children.

What's more, escapes from CCA prisons have been rampant. According to one survey, at least 79 inmates fled CCA facilities nationwide between 1995 and 1998—compared to nine escapes from California prisons, which have more than twice as many inmates. Many of the breakouts could have been prevented, a report prepared for Attorney General Janet Reno concluded, if CCA had simply learned from its previous mistakes and "implemented preventive measures."

In Youngstown, a class-action lawsuit by prisoners has forced the company to improve conditions. But CCA, which declined to speak with *Mother Jones,* remains unapologetic. When local residents expressed concern after the prison break, the company simply shrugged it off. "It's nice if your community is happy with you—that's an extra," CCA founder Doctor Crants told reports. "But the business is built around providing a valuable service to our customers."

On a snowy morning in January, traffic is light enough on Youngstown's Center Street Bridge that it's possible to park a car in the right-hand lane and look out over the industrial waterfront. In either direction, the Mahoning River is crisscrossed with train tracks and dotted with the occasional crane and ore pile. The hulking horizontal carcass of the Youngstown Sheet & Tube Campbell Works, a steel mill that once employed 5,000 people, dominates the far distance. And there are "brownfields" everywhere: weedy, asbestos-poisoned lots where other mills, and other railroad lines, no longer exist. There's a dark silence to the place—a silence Youngstowners recognize as the sound of economic stagnation.

A quarter-century ago, more trains passed under Center Street than under any other bridge in America. Often, in the dead of night, Bob Hagan would sit at the helm of one of those trains, picking up steel destined for Detroit's auto plants. Coming into Youngstown, he'd see slag pits full of molten metal, so hot that they cast a light bright enough to read by. "When it was good, the graphite floated by and the coke dust followed," he says, "and you knew there was employment."

That sooty prosperity ended September 19, 1977, the day Sheet & Tube announced it would shut down the Campbell Works. The closing triggered a domino effect: In the next few years, mill after mill shut down or announced massive layoffs, eliminating an estimated 60,000 jobs in the metropolitan area. Once-stable neighborhoods crumbled as Youngstown's modest clapboard houses fell into disrepair. Thousands of homes were torn down or put up for sale at rock-bottom prices. The taverns where steelworkers once drank and gambled went belly up, transforming Youngstown's main north-south thoroughfare into a sad strip of payday-loan businesses, discount furniture stores, and abandoned buildings.

By the mid-'90s, with unemployment still in the double digits, Youngstown was desperate for any job it could land. So when the world's largest private-prison company offered to employ 350 people, local officials welcomed it with tax breaks and free water and sewer hookups. As the new prison went up on the edge of town, it looked much like an old steel mill, only surrounded by razor wire. And it held the same promise for the men and women who applied for the $24,600-a-year jobs CCA offered.

But it didn't take long for disillusionment to set in. The day Victoria Wheeler reported for work as a guard, she recalls, the company "explained that these were going to be very, very bad inmates." CCA was negotiating a $182 million contract with the

District of Columbia, which was scrambling to transfer some of its most unmanageable inmates out of a crumbling prison complex in Lorton, Virginia. Margaret Moore, director of the D.C. Department of Corrections, told the local newspaper that Youngstown's newest male residents would be "young, aggressive, and violent."

The first inmates arrived on May 15, 1997—courtesy of a transport company owned by CCA. . . . Many of them were classified as maximum security, in violation of CCA's agreement with the city. Half came without case histories or medical records. And according to the report prepared for the U.S. attorney general's office, they arrived in such large numbers that they completely overwhelmed the prison. Inmates needed bedding and toiletries; they needed health screenings; their property needed to be inventoried and distributed. The prison's skeletal crew couldn't possibly accommodate so many new arrivals—900 in the first 17 days—especially after they discovered that many of the men's possessions hadn't arrived from D.C. "It was chaos," Wheeler said.

Angry and frustrated, some new arrivals refused to return to their cells one day until they received their personal property. When inmates in one unit threatened to "trash the place," prison officials ordered a full-scale teargassing of four cell blocks through a hatch on the roof. The gas, intended for outdoor use, blackened the blocks where it was dropped. "The entire pod was smoked out. You couldn't see through the gas," recalls Anthony Beshara, a former guard. Even after the men returned to their bunks and the prison's security chief gave an "all-clear" signal, court records show, the assault continued. "Three for good measure!" an assistant warden announced as the canisters fell.

Then came the murders. In February 1998, 25-year-old inmate Derrick Davis died in a brawl over a Tupac Shakur tape. He was stabbed a dozen times and bled to death while awaiting attention; the prison was so short-staffed that there was no officer on the floor. Less than three weeks later, 23-year-old Bryson Chisley was stabbed repeatedly while one of Davis' assailants—who had not been separated from other inmates—held him down.

According to the report commissioned by the attorney general, CCA responded to the Chisley murder with a "reign of humiliation directed indiscriminately at the entire inmate population." Clad in helmets and riot gear, the company's Special Operations Response Teams (SORT) burst into living units, forced the inmates to strip, and made them lie or kneel naked on the floor with their legs shackled and their hands cuffed behind their backs. They were ordered not to move or speak for an hour while the riot squad searched and often ransacked their rooms. Men's rectums were probed by employees who had no medical training. When one inmate momentarily looked away from the wall, says an officer's report, "I sprayed pepper spray on my glove and wiped it on his face." Such extreme procedures, the report concluded, "would be uncalled for in any circumstance."

"It seemed like they were trying to take their frustrations out on us," says Tati King, a bearded, broad-shouldered 28-year-old who sports both a tattoo of a pit bull and a knit blue-and-tan Muslim skullcap. "A lot of racial comments were made: niggers this, can't stand you D.C. guys." King later refused to return to his cell to protest not having received a religious meal for four days. "Next thing I know," he says, "maybe 20 or more SORT team members told me to strip down and get naked." After slamming him to the floor, King says, officers took him to a segregation unit in shackles. "They had me walk the distance of a football field and a half, stark naked," he says.

If CCA intended the show of force to make the prison more secure, it didn't work. That summer, six inmates escaped on a bright afternoon and one remained at large for several weeks. According to a report by the D.C. Corrections Trustee responsible for monitoring the private prison, everything that could have gone wrong did. A metal detector broke, a motion detector malfunctioned, and the outside yard went unsupervised for 40 minutes. (One staff member was inside playing Ping-Pong.) At the time of the break, there were 219 prisoners in the yard. "Fortunately," the trustee reported, "large numbers of inmates did not choose to . . . follow the route of these six."

Youngstown residents were alarmed by the escapes, but even those most experienced in community organizing didn't know how to take on a far-flung corporation like CCA. "Once the private prison opened, there didn't seem to be a heck of a lot that one could do to tear it down," says Staughton Lynd, an educator and labor lawyer with four decades of experience as an activist, dating back to his stint as director of the Mississippi Freedom Schools. Some residents put their energy into developing a visitation program to help prisoners' families make the 600-mile round trip from Washington. Senator Hagan pushed a bill through the legislature putting tighter restrictions on for-profit prisons.

Then came the bombshell that sparked a grassroots movement—not just in Youngstown, but for 50 miles up and down Ohio's eastern border. In May 1999, Rep. James Traficant Jr. signed a "memorandum of understanding" with Doctor Crants, CCA's founder, agreeing to help the company site two more prisons in his district. The new lockups would each house at least 2,500 inmates, more than tripling the number of private-prison beds in the valley. The Democratic congressman also promised to push for a 500-bed expansion in Youngstown, saying the plan would generate 1,400 jobs and $200 million in taxes.

Officials in five communities expressed interest in the new prisons, and two immediately became front-runners. In the small city of Campbell, where CCA is eyeing the site of the old Sheet & Tube blast furnace, several hundred people turned out for a meeting at a Catholic church to angrily protest the private prison. Many residents voiced their opposition by supporting the insurgent mayoral candidacy of Juanita Rich, an administrator at an assisted-living center. A staunch CCA critic, Rich missed the runoff by six votes.

But it's in Wellsville, an old manufacturing village of 4,500 where the resistance has been most determined. Located across the Ohio River from the northern panhandle of West Virginia, Wellsville and its environs were once dotted with industrial potteries, including one that, at its peak, churned out 10 million plates of Fiesta dinnerware in a single year. But like Youngstown an hour north, Wellsville declined as factories cut back or went out of business. "It's been a tough go," says Mayor Joseph LaScola. "A lot of our people are working in McDonald's, Wendy's, some of the stores in the outlying areas." At one point village officials declared a fiscal emergency, laid off workers, and shut down a fire station. "There wasn't hardly enough money to close down the town," LaScola says.

So when the mayor learned that CCA needed two more host communities, he made sure Traficant knew that Wellsville had the perfect site: some cleared farmland up a twisting cattle road, on a hill overlooking many of the riverfront industries that have closed down. "This would bring close to $2 million a year to our town," says LaScola. "Most of our residents—a large number—are retirees and low income. Anything that looks like it would be a benefit financially, I have to take a serious look at."

In an area devastated by layoffs, the mere promise of added employment was enough to sway some residents to support the prison. "It's about time for Wellsville to progress," Evelyn Springer, a retired teacher, declared at one public meeting. "You can't stay back in the '50s and '40s."

But others in Wellsville were furious at how quickly their elected officials bought into CCA's lavish promises, despite the company's dismal track record in Youngstown. The lure of jobs and taxes, they felt, was offset by the hidden costs of prison privatization.

Janice Gartland, a 37-year-old office worker at a medical services company, had never been involved in politics before a neighbor told her about Traficant's proposal. But the ideal of a for-profit prison didn't sit well with her. "I have a pretty big problem with using inmates as a commodity," Gartland says. "When you say a person's worth x dollars, and you have to make sure they're fed and medically provided for within that x-dollar range, then something's going to suffer. You're looking at that person as, 'How can I make a profit from them?'"

Gartland and other residents attended a city council meeting to hear Traficant speak—and they didn't like what they heard. The plainspoken congressman defended his alliance with CCA in a long, defensive speech that had council members nodding in agreement. "I would love to bring you Saks Fifth Avenue. I would love to bring you United States Steel," Traficant said. "And this is certainly controversial indeed. But who employs our people? . . . Who pays for our schools? . . . So I'll take your political shots, but I'll bring the opportunity."

Looking for a voice in the decision, Gartland and her neighbors decided to take the fight to the ballot box. Those who opposed the prison campaigned for a referendum prohibiting the village from extending sewer lines to any correctional facility that housed out-of-state inmates. Through last summer and fall, they canvassed door-to-door, warning neighbors about CAA's track record. They met with union leaders, who object to low-paying jobs at for-profit prisons. And they hooked up with Staughton Lynd, who was bringing together CCA opponents from around the region through an organization called the Prison Forum. Meeting in Youngstown, Forum members shared information about privatization, listened to experts from around the country, and offered one another support.

Fired up by the gatherings, Wellsville activists tried to meet with their elected officials, but were repeatedly rebuffed by the mayor and his allies on the council. LaScola acted as if residents weren't in the council chambers, often ignoring their questions. He refused to recognize Bob Hagan during one meeting, ordering the senator bodily ejected for speaking at the microphone during a recess. He told prison opponents that his line of reasoning was "above you, and you would never understand it." At one meeting, when a woman introduced herself as a resident of a neighboring township, the mayor said, "I'm happy for you. I hope you stay there."

The small town never recaptured its civility after that. "HEY ESCAPEES," said a hand-lettered sign posted immediately after one meeting. "TURN RIGHT, 2ND HOUSE DOWN ON LEFT, MAYOR'S HOUSE. GO STEAL HIS CAR, HOLD HIM HOSTAGE . . . AS HE IS US." Wellsville's police chief responded by telling federal authorities that prison opponents had threatened to kill LaScola—a charge that leaders of the anti-prison referendum call ludicrous. "They were making us into this radical, dangerous group," says Diane Dinch, who manages a local video store.

As the election approached, opponents picked up the pace, sponsoring two public forums and continuing their door-to-door campaign. Through Traficant, CCA responded by offering more and more money to Wellsville: a nightly "bed tax" for each inmate, scholarships for local college students, an upgraded sewer system. The company even promised to allow correctional officers to unionize, something it had firmly resisted in Youngstown.

On Election Day, the initiative to block the prison lost by 35 votes. Some opponents blamed the confusing wording on the ballot: Voting "yes" meant opposing the prison. But Janice Gartland also believes that CCA capitalized successfully on the village's desperate financial straits. "We lost support the minute they started throwing dollar figures around," she says.

As residents campaigned to stop CCA, prisoners were also fighting back. In May 1999, inmates at the Youngstown prison won $1.65 million in a class-action lawsuit settlement with the company. Under the terms of the agreement, CCA agreed to pay damages to prisoners, improve security and medical care without cutting back other programs, and pay for an independent monitor to check company abuses. The settlement solves "the worst of the abuse," says Alphonse Gerhardstein, the inmates' attorney. The maximum-security prisoners have been shipped out. Sworn enemies are kept apart. The company has built three new guard towers and put up additional fences. And the prison sponsored more than 50,000 hours of staff training last year, in areas such as conflict resolution and escape prevention.

The Youngstown facility currently appears to enjoy the institutional calm of a well-behaved high school, with murals on the cinderblock walls, monitors in every hallway, and well-stocked classrooms where inmates learn wiring, masonry, and commercial cleaning. And the prison's current leadership tries to distance itself from the earlier debacles. "The past is the past," says assistant chief Jason Medlin. "That was a different administration, a different system altogether."

But Gerhardstein warns that the improved conditions shouldn't be taken as proof that the company—much less the industry—has reformed. After all, he says, it took a lawsuit, new legislation, a renegotiated contract with the city, a monitoring program, and a whole lot of bad publicity just to get CCA to improve conditions at one facility.

For now, negotiations over the proposed expansion have been stalled by CCA's current financial upheaval. Last year, the company merged with a real-estate trust it set up called Prison Realty that was exempt from $50 million in federal income taxes. But the scheme to boost profits even higher wound up backfiring: Prison Realty missed its year-end dividend payment to shareholders last winter, and its stock price has plummeted from $20 to $4 a share.

The cut-rate prices have some heavy hitters on Wall Street hoping to cash in on private prisons. In December, Bank of America teamed up with two high-powered investment firms to offer Prison Realty and CCA an infusion of $350 million—in exchange for as much as 25 percent of the action and four seats on a new 10-member board of directors. The investors are led by the Blackstone Group, a leverage buyout firm with plenty of political connections and annual revenues of $15 billion. Its chairman, former Nixon commerce secretary Peter Peterson, is best known for his recent crusade to privatize Social Security.

Some CCA shareholders have balked at approving the Blackstone deal, which they fear would dilute the value of their shares. But there's no question that some of Wall Street's most respected firms see an opportunity to profit from punishment. "CCA is the market leader in a growing industry," says Thomas Saylak, senior managing director of Blackstone. The infusion of capital, he adds, will enable CCA "to maximize growth prospects."

Investors aren't the only ones who consider the company's current woes a temporary setback in an otherwise lucrative industry. Paul Marcone, chief of staff to Rep. Traficant, insists that negotiations for the proposed expansion in Youngstown will re-open soon. "[CCA] has had some organizational shake-ups," he says, "but now the company is focused more on expanding."

That expansion, many residents fear, would make Youngstown as synonymous with prisons as it was with steel a quarter-century ago. "We may have concentrated the sun's rays somewhat, but it's not clear if we've started a fire," says Lynd, whose Prison Forum is launching a campaign called Schools, Not Jails. Lynd and other opponents want to keep the debate above the level of "not in my backyard"—to convince the public and policymakers that it's both unethical and counterproductive to turn incarceration over to the private sector.

"We can't put somebody in the Black Hole of Calcutta, or the Gulag Archipelago, just because they've done something wrong," says Bob Hagan. "When money's your main motivation, you forget one major lesson: that these people are coming out. If you don't create rehabilitated prisoners, but you only create profit for your shareholders, then you have failed at a system that's supposed to protect society."

1. What is gained by exposing the bureaucratic, political, and economic interests that encourage increased spending on prisons?

2. Weigh the advantages and disadvantages of private prisons. Do they still pass some costs for incarceration on to taxpayers?

43

WHO OWNS DEATH?

ROBERT JAY LIFTON • GREG MITCHELL

A man who seeks revenge digs two graves.

—PROVERB

The American Habit of Violence

However one feels about capital punishment, one must admit that it is almost uniquely ours. The writer David Rieff recently observed that the death penalty is "one of those peculiar American institutions that make citizens of the other developed countries shake their heads with wonder."[1] Indeed, it is so widely disowned that international tribunals seeking to bring the perpetrators of genocide in Bosnia and Rwanda to justice cannot even consider it as an option. Henry LeClerc, president of the Human Rights League in Paris, has said, "For us, what the Americans are doing is completely incomprehensible, that such an advanced country can be involved in such an act of barbarism." The United States is the only nation in the world since 1997 known to have executed inmates who committed crimes while under the age of 18. Even Iran, Nigeria, Pakistan, Saudi Arabia, and Yemen have apparently stopped doing this.

There is no simple answer to the vexing question of why, among western democracies, only America retains the ultimate ownership of death. One could fill many volumes with a consideration of all the relevant factors—historical, psychological, and racial—and still be left with much uncertainty.

We choose here to emphasize one overriding theme, what we call the American habit of violence, as it overlaps with a second important pattern, the sustained polarization of good and evil. America is by no means the only nation of settlers with a history of extreme violence toward the native population; nor are we the only society guilty of centuries of black slavery. But America is special in creating so extreme and long-standing a practice of gun-centered killing, along with a reverence for the gun that has rendered it a sacred object. The overall ideological phenomenon can be given an awkward but revealing name, "gunism." Nothing symbolizes control or ownership of death better than the gun. By holding a loaded gun in one's hand, one takes possession of life and death.

Violence is at the heart of our creation myth. The cultural historian Richard Slotkin tells us that in American mythology the founding fathers were not "those eighteenth-century gentlemen who composed a nation at Philadelphia" but rather "the rogues, the adventurers, and land-boomers; the Indian fighters, traders, missionaries, explorers, and hunters who killed and were killed until they had mastered the wilderness." The mythology was enormously enhanced by romanticized visions of citizens' militias during the American Revolution, and it was racialized from the beginning, bound up with the slaughter by guns of native Americans and with the gun-power that created and sustained the institution of black slavery. It was greatly elaborated in the frontier narratives of Daniel Boone and Davy Crockett, and the flintlock rifle and the Colt .45 revolver were especially sacralized. Both weapons have been lovingly portrayed in generations of western films whose heroes, with only their horses and weapons, create or defend their version of a just society.

Through the flux of people and ideas in our always fragile society, the gun remained entrenched as an essential aspect of our identity—the icon of freedom, power, and the rights of the individual. In that way, the gun has filled some of the psychological vacuum created by the relative absence of traditional American culture. Looked upon as an "equalizer," it became an important

vehicle for our sense of creating a new, egalitarian people. The American reverence for guns became (as a leading proponent put it) "one of the great religions of the world." This suggests how close we have come to being a "gunocracy."

This gunocracy always claimed a religious component, and it came to be bound up with absolutized American visions of good and evil. The gun could be embraced as part of the godly forces of light in the struggle against satanic forces of darkness. Even though the gun, over the years, has been the agent of millions of homicides, we tend to focus more on punishing the gunman (often by sending him to death row) than combating the gun.

Of course, many murders are committed with other weapons, or with bare hands. But the gun, by making murder easy, has had much to do with our astonishing homicide statistics and our large number of convicted killers—and therefore with the widespread American sense of social evil. An early American answer to all such evil was the near-instant death penalty imposed by "frontier justice," whether by means of the gun or by hanging. Evil was to be eliminated by killing. While subsequent forms of execution became more structured and medicalized, the death penalty became an ultimate weapon in this continuing crusade to destroy or "murder" evil.[2]

Executions also became part of a "pornography" of violence and death—a prurient display of grotesque forms of killing and dying. A historian describes a nineteenth-century "taste for body-horror," as displayed in many executions and in most lynchings, as "illicit" and "titillating."[3] In the twentieth century a broader pornography of death (according to the respected anthropologist Geoffrey Gorer) has taken the form of lurid, highly exploitative renditions in the mass media of every variety of killing. Our newest pornography, at the beginning of the twenty-first century, lies in the seemingly opposite direction, a muting of killing—through lethal injections—so that death becomes a "nonevent," deemed necessary for the moral health of American society.

More generally, our many-sided habit of violence feeds our fascination with the death penalty. We can take steps to redirect our imaginations into healthier forms of expression only if we confront that long-standing "habit" which so distorts them.

False Witness

By maintaining the death penalty, we institutionalize our habit of violence. Americans have only now begun to grasp the psychological and moral consequences of this structured state killing which, overtly or indirectly, reverberate throughout our society.

We have seen capital punishment as society's attempt to bear witness to acts of brutal individual murder, but it turns out to be an expression of *false witness*. Other than revenge, it fails to carry out commitments made on behalf of murder victims—to provide solace and "closure" to their families and to the rest of society, to deter other potential murderers, and to diminish homicidal violence in general. And by implementing the death penalty the state assumes ownership of death and thereby claims an ultimate form of omniscience, "the authority of perfect knowledge in final things," as John Leonard put it.[4] That is what Norman Mailer means when he speaks of the prosecutor in capital cases as "an avenging angel" and the judge as "a god."

In that and other ways, the death penalty violates democratic standards. Indeed, the prolonged and excruciating litigation surrounding capital cases can be understood as the desperate efforts of a democracy to deal with a totalistic policy.

The huge costs of that litigation to the state—far exceeding, as many have pointed out, the costs of lifelong imprisonment—have to do with the insistence, within a democracy, upon a detailed search for every possible factor that might prevent what is surely the most extreme abuse of state power: the execution of an innocent man or woman (and by extension, of *any* man or woman). But the overall problem remains the existence in a democratic society of the most antidemocratic of institutions.

To put things differently, by arrogating to itself the ownership of death the state threatens its very democratic structure.

The End of Executions

That institution, however, will not last much longer in America. About half of all Americans, as we've seen, now say they favor an alternative to executions, and we believe that very soon this will become a clear majority, as life without parole, now in wide practice, proves loophole-free and gains credibility. We predict that the number of those opposed, "undecided," or ambivalent about executions will grow so large that the U.S. Supreme Court, or dozens of state legislatures, will move against executions.

Steven Hawkins, longtime director of the National Coalition to Abolish the Death Penalty, recently told us that when capital punishment is abolished in America it will come about "not through one action, but many, over time." In a very real sense, this process, we believe, is already under way.

The year 1999, as we have observed, was a turning point, with a sharp rise in the number of executions forcing the public, the media and religious figures to confront the issue. New opposition from the pope and from Catholic bishops in America provoked debate across the religious and political spectrum, while energizing abolition activists. They held national conferences, circulated petitions, and raised money for full-page ads in the *New York Times*—all aimed at what was politically feasible (a moratorium) over what was, for now, still unlikely (abolition). At the same time, the media widely covered the many emerging cases of innocent men freed from death row (partly because of the rising use of DNA evidence). Finally, late in the year, another botched execution by electric chair in Florida forced an unprecedented outcry in that state, leading to its adoption of lethal injection.

Perhaps the most significant moment of all came on January 31, 2000, when Governor George Ryan of Illinois, a moderate Republican, halted all executions in that state, the first such moratorium in the country. He acted after the *Chicago Tribune* documented the cases of thirteen exonerated prisoners released from death row in the state since 1977 and found, further, that of 260 death sentences appealed in Illinois in recent years, fully half had been reversed (in more than thirty cases, death row inmates had been represented by lawyers who were later disbarred or suspended from practice). "I cannot support a system which, in its administration, has proven so fraught with error, and has come so close to the ultimate nightmare, the state's taking of innocent life," Ryan declared.

Ryan revealed that "the most anguishing period of my life" had occurred the first time he considered, then denied, a stay for a convicted killer, who then went to his death. While remaining a proponent of capital punishment, he clearly felt uncomfortable presiding over such a flawed system, observing, "I am ultimately responsible" and "There is no margin for error when it comes to putting a person to death." Referring to critics of his moratorium, he said, "I'd like to see those people sit in that chair and make the decisions I have to make." He ap-

pointed a panel to study the apparatus that enabled so many flawed convictions, saying, "I believe that a public dialogue must begin on the question of fairness of the application of the death penalty in Illinois."[5]

His action was extremely significant, for it is officials like Ryan—tough-minded but extremely troubled by their personal responsibility—who will ultimately bring an end to executions in this country, much as they did throughout Europe.

And, crucially, Ryan's move met with little public or political opposition. The *Chicago Tribune* poll found that support for the death penalty had fallen off to 58 percent from 76 percent five years earlier, and that two of three Illinoisans supported the moratorium. A Republican state representative named Jim Durkin put it, "Even the most conservative individuals realize that there's a problem."

Later, in an interview, Ryan explained, "When you're the fellow that says, 'We're going to inject this person and put him to death,' you have to be able to live with yourself." Four months after declaring the moratorium, Ryan started sounding like an abolitionist. He said he strongly doubted any inmate would be put to death while he remained governor, unless the panel he appointed gave him "a 100 percent guarantee" against any mistaken convictions (which, of course, is impossible). "I don't know if we'll ever go back to the death penalty as we knew it as long as I am governor," Ryan advised.

As opponents of the death penalty are quick to point out, the possible execution of the innocent is not confined to Illinois. In recent years, over eighty-seven such cases are on record, including nineteen near-misses in Florida alone. In fact, a recent Columbia University study of 4,578 death sentence appeals from 1973 to 1995 found that *two-thirds* were successful in state or federal court, largely due to errors by incompetent defense lawyers or overzealous police and prosecutors who withheld evidence. And in 75 percent of the retrials the defendants were handed sentences less than death. "It's not one state, it's almost all the states," declared James Liebman, the lead author of the June 2000 report. He added that the capital punishment system seemed to be "collapsing under the weight of its own mistakes."

Governor Ryan's widely publicized moratorium marked the zenith of a year of new national soul-searching over the issue, and it set in motion a critical period of political and moral debate. The Roman Catholic archbishop of Los Angeles, for example, has called on the state's Catholic governor, Gray Davis, to impose a moratorium. Richard Dieter, director of the Death Penalty Information Center, said, "It's like snowflakes adding up on the branch may cause the branch to break at some point." Sisten Helen Prejean observed that, at last, she sensed "the waters moving" on this issue. The European Union called on America's other thirty-seven death penalty states to follow the lead of Illinois.

Related actions occurred in many states. Bills to enact statewide moratoriums were introduced by legislators in twelve states, including Oklahoma, Maryland, Alabama, and Kentucky. The state legislature in New Hampshire surprisingly voted to abolish the death penalty, as several conservative lawmakers switched sides expressing concerns about faulty convictions or said they had come to recognize that there was something "unseemly about the state being in the position of executing people," as one senator put it. (The governor later vetoed the bill.)

The Philadelphia city council called for a moratorium in the state until a study could determine that the death penalty was being applied fairly. In Oregon, forces led by former senator Mark Hatfield moved to put a "life for life" measure on the ballot that would end executions and instead provide

for sentences of life without parole. Senator Patrick Leahy, declaring a "growing national crisis in the administration of capital punishment," introduced in Congress a package of death penalty reforms called the Innocence Protection Act. "There hasn't been this kind of discussion questioning the death penalty in decades," U.S. Senator Russ Feingold asserted. "I think you're at the beginning of the wave of public sentiment against the death penalty."

The *St. Petersburg Times, Gainesville Sun,* and *Miami Herald* called for a moratorium in conservative Florida. A wide range of other major newspapers in Maryland, California, Pennsylvania, and Texas demanded halts to (or outright bans on) executions in their states. The *New York Times* called for the abolition of the death penalty *everywhere,* recalling Justice Harry Blackmun's declaration that he wished to dismantle the "machinery of death." The American Bar Association released a report called "A Gathering Momentum," referring to the drive for moratoriums, an idea it had proposed in 1997.

There have been other developments pointing to a profound reconsideration of the entire question of state killings. Shortly after protests caused Florida to practically put its electric chair in mothballs, the U.S. Supreme Court halted an execution by electrocution in Alabama and hinted that the justices might use this opportunity to debate the constitutionality of the method. Meanwhile, Barry Scheck and other attorneys spearheaded a new nationwide drive to study the claims of innocence of hundreds of prisoners on death row, often relying on new DNA results. Indeed, the expanded use of DNA testing dramatically increases the chances of establishing, scientifically, the occurrence of wrongful executions.

Popular culture can be a partial barometer of public and political opinion, and we find it significant that there has been a sharp swing in the number of anti–death penalty dramas on television (even on daytime soap operas) and in movie theaters. The popular film *The Green Mile,* for example, despite its somewhat muddled moral message, exposed millions of Americans to several graphic execution scenes.

Within a few days in February 2000 this sequence of events took place: Senator Feingold, along with the National Conference of Catholic Bishops, called for President Clinton to suspend federal executions (twenty-one prisoners sat on federal death row, including Timothy McVeigh); at a church service attended by Clinton, the president's pastor in Washington called for a "serious reexamination" of capital punishment;[6] Attorney General Reno ordered a new study to determine if racial disparities exist in federal capital cases; and the NBC television program *West Wing* depicted a president agonizing over a federal execution, and after allowing it to proceed, getting down on his knees in the Oval Office, praying, "Forgive me, God, for I have sinned."

In real life, President Clinton ultimately refused to initiate a federal moratorium, but he did voice support for Governor Ryan's "courageous" stand in Illinois and promised to tighten up procedures to decrease the chance of wrongful convictions. Clearly, the image of an innocent man or woman going to the death chamber had put advocates of the death penalty on the defensive, for this is the ultimate denigration of the democratic process Americans revere.

This has caused an increasing number of nationally known conservatives—ranging from Oliver North and Pat Robertson to George Will and William F. Buckley Jr.—to question capital punishment. "The political climate is shifting," Ted Lynch, an authority on criminal justice at the Cato Institute, said recently, adding: "When you consider the foul-ups and mix-ups and incompetence that you often find in government work it gets scary. You realize that the institution that puts people to death is the same one that delivers the mail to the wrong people." Indeed, many longtime anti–death penalty activists now emphasize issues of fairness and innocence, not moral principle. They have discovered that most people "are not going to be opposed to the death penalty just because a few people say they should," Richard Dieter of the Death Penalty Information Center observed.

In addition, some anti-abortion activists are now speaking up against the death penalty, claiming a desire to be "consistent."

Polls continue to drift in the direction of opposition to the death penalty. One of the most interesting came out of Missouri, one of the nation's most active execution states. A poll of 1,000 state residents conducted by the Center for Social Sciences and Public Policy Research of Southwest Missouri State University in November 1999 found that 56 percent said they would support a moratorium on executions for three years to allow a study of sentencing practices. And, equally significantly, only 35 percent said they would be less likely to vote for a legislator if he came out against the death penalty. Indeed, Ron Tabak, a leading anti–death penalty attorney in New York, believes that more politicians will begin speaking out against executions "as they see it no longer means political death to do so."

Indeed, every case of an innocent man freed from death row drives another stake into the heart of capital punishment. The Gallup poll of February 2000 found, rather surprisingly, that the average American estimates that about 10 percent of people sentenced to death "are really innocent." At about the same time, a statewide poll in Connecticut found that 30 percent of the public believed it likely that the state would execute someone later found to be innocent.[7]

While opposition to the death penalty is growing, it is also true that surveys continue to show that most Americans are not philosophically opposed to the notion of state killings. But does that necessarily mean that executions cannot be outlawed in America anytime soon?

Few people know that at the moment when many western nations, such as France and England, abolished the death penalty, polls showed strong public support for capital punishment. In many of these countries, surveys *continue* to find significant support. Yet executions were banned (sometimes quite suddenly) and continue to be outlawed without much protest. In fact, Peter Hodgkinson, director of the Centre for Capital Punishment Studies in London, once said he knew of no country which had abolished executions with clear majority support from its citizens. Today, in Canada, our relatively peaceful neighbor to the north, polls have consistently revealed that three out of four citizens support the death penalty for the most heinous crimes. Yet capital punishment was outlawed in Canada long ago, and there is no strong movement to restore it.[8]

In the final years of "Saint Guillotine" in France, in the 1960s and 1970s, polls showed strong support for the principle of capital punishment, yet little clamor for its widespread use. Many candidates who ran for the National Assembly spoke out against the death penalty and found that this did not prevent their election (the public ranked this issue relatively low in import). Significantly, legislators in France (and England too) tend to claim that they lead public opinion and do not necessarily follow it, unlike their counterparts in America.

In France, the turning point came in 1981, with the election of Francois Mitterand as president. He named as minister of justice a criminal attorney and longtime foe of the death penalty. During his first year in office, riding a wave of popularity, Mitterand endorsed abolition, the assembly complied, and after more than 200 years of decapitations, the reign of the guillotine was over. Although polls show that close to half of the French people support capital punishment, few have pressed for its return.

In England, a long tradition of hangings was challenged repeatedly starting in the 1950s, following a number of controversial cases, including the executions of an innocent man (Timothy Evans), a woman (Ruth Ellis), and a mentally impaired teenager (Derek Bentley). Parliament split on abolition, but in 1965, Prime Minister Harold Wilson freed his Labour party supporters in the House of Commons to vote their conscience on the issue—explaining that while citizens might not like what you stand for, they tend to respect conscience.

This led to two months of Parliamentary debate, culminating in the passage of a bill mandating a five-year moratorium, while the issue was studied further. When the murder rate did not soar, the legislators did away with the hangman permanently in 1969, without much protest from the public, which by then had grown accustomed to the absence of hangings and perhaps felt relief in losing that burden. Since then, bills calling for the return of capital punishment have often been proposed, and they gained some support after IRA terrorist attacks in London. But even the efforts of Prime Minister Margaret Thatcher—and support in the polls—failed to bring back the hangman.

Some of the trends that led these two countries to abolition are already occurring in America: outrage over the possible execution of the innocent; a growing number of legislators speaking their conscience; the imposition of moratoriums. Meanwhile, recognition of the merits and credibility of life without parole expands every year. It became clear in Europe and Canada that most people did not care passionately about this issue; in fact, they felt so ambivalent, even tortured, when the state killed a prisoner that they would just as soon see the practice stopped entirely, and eventually it was. This surely intersects with current attitudes and emotions in our country.

Indeed, William Bowers, the research scientist who has spent years studying attitudes of the public and jurors toward the death penalty, calls capital punishment "a hollow symbol to most who say they favor it." Support, he adds, is abstract, ideological, and nonempirical. The death penalty, he told us, "holds appeal as an expressive symbol, not as a policy preference. It has become a self-perpetuating political myth."

The U.S. Supreme Court could reverse course and, as in the *Furman* case in the early 1970s, suddenly and unexpectedly declare a moratorium—perhaps a lasting one—on executions. This might happen if the Court became persuaded that it is mistaken about the public's view of capital punishment. The tide could turn because, as Bowers declares, "the Eighth Amendment requires the Court to act on its most enlightened interpretation of contemporary values." As Richard Dieter, director of the Death Penalty Information Center, put it, "There are a lot of reasons why the Supreme Court could find that capital punishment is still arbitrary and freakish."

If polls continue to show majority support for life without parole as a preferred alternative to executions, it could change the way judges, lawmakers, and the media respond to this issue on every important level, especially as new cases of innocent men and women on death row emerge, perhaps proliferate in the coming months (as we expect they will). Large numbers of Americans, we feel, will come to believe that if—as nearly everyone agrees—the justice system can never be 100 percent right, then how can it administer punishment that's 100 percent irreversible?

As the *Christian Science Monitor* recently put it, "The best way to resolve the contro-versy would be to put this form of punishment on the shelf of history, as most other modern democracies have. State-sanctioned killing is at odds with the need to reduce the level of violence in society." America would then join most of the modern industrial world, which has abandoned capital punishment "out of some embarrassed sense that it is a barbaric vestige of an archaic culture," as the writer Russell Baker recently observed.[9]

We believe the day will soon come when a clear public desire for an alternative to the death penalty will prompt legislators to convert this preference into law—or they will be replaced by those who will.

Rick Halperin, a historian and director of Amnesty International's Death Penalty Project in Texas, tells us that now, even from the execution capital of the world, he can "clearly see the end of capital punishment in sight. I am much more optimistic now than in recent years. I know we are going to lose many more individuals before it is abolished; but," he adds, "we are reaching the point where abolition is obtainable."

Overcoming Illusions

As always, we have choices. Top officials sometimes find it easier to change their minds later in their careers. This late-life turnabout—what we have called a "retirement syndrome"—exists, as we have seen, among people who have spent much of their careers advocating and carrying out the death penalty. Upon leaving or planning to leave their involvement in that work, they call forth long-suppressed doubts by giving voice to the negative pole of their ambivalence.[10]

. . . Governor Pat Brown's switch late in his final term is a particularly poignant case in point. He went from a deepening doubt to an unsuccessful campaign as an opponent of the death penalty, then wrote a memoir decades later in which he expressed his sense of profound personal cost, of guilt and regret, at having been given such "awesome, ultimate power over the lives of others."

In these ways the "retirement syndrome" permits one to state, and act upon, what one has always known in a part of one's mind: that executions are wrong and profoundly harmful to everyone. But can we, as a society, afford to wait for such retirement wisdom?

A condemned man can be criminally guilty and at the same time an object of human sacrifice. He becomes a target not only for society's justified anger at his crime but for the pain, guilt, and rage having to do with *all* crime—and beyond that, for the overall violence in our society. In the process we fail to confront the broader social conditions that are conducive to destructive behavior of every kind. We also foster the illusion that we are taking bold steps to combat evil.

The death penalty is both a concrete policy—something we can *do* about killing and sin—and a highly abstract symbol. Behind it lies a mystical vision of total evil that can be extirpated to achieve total virtue. Our illusion becomes not only that of controlling crime and killing, but of controlling death itself. We resort to "the most premeditated of murders," as Camus wrote, in order to convert our moral and psychological confusion into an illusory certainty.[11]

. . . There appears to be a psychological need to keep capital punishment in place, for now. Doing so provides a collective vision of toughness and revenge, along with an all-pervasive illusion of control. People can feel that this is the right thing for true justice—until they are exposed to the fact of actual executions and, currently, the alarming rise in the number of executions.

We have seen the widespread moral and psychological ambivalence in prosecutors and all others who implement the death penalty, including judges, jurors, wardens, prison guards, doctors, technicians, and state governors. All make use of distancing mechanisms—forms of psychic numbing—to enable them to carry out their professional duties. Some may embrace the death penalty with particular fierceness as a means of overcoming that ambivalence and of suppressing feelings of guilt. While dealing with the transgressions of convicted murderers, all struggle to fend off a sense of their *own* transgression in assuming the godlike stance of determining whether another human being will live or die. It seems that no one involved can be comfortable with capital punishment.

And what of the ordinary Americans who have nothing to do with actual executions? They may want the death penalty on the books, yet they rarely seem enraged that the vast majority of convicted murderers escape with less than the ultimate penalty. (If they thoroughly believed in violent revenge, they would have to demand thousands of executions every year.) And little widespread celebration greets the instances when the state actually executes someone.

What does this mean? Hugo Bedau wrote a few years ago: "One might hazard the hypothesis that the average person seems convinced the death penalty is an important legal threat, abstractly desirable as part of society's permanent bulwark against crime, but that he or she is relatively indifferent to whether a given convict is executed on a given date as scheduled, or is indeed ever executed." That is, people embrace the principle as a psychological source of security—which turns out to be fragile because it is readily threatened by whatever reminds them that execution is a form of killing.

That fragility has been made clear by the increasing number of Americans—now believed to be a majority—who surrender their support for the death penalty when given the alternative of life without parole. The shift suggests that political support for the death penalty is grounded not in bedrock, as often asserted, but in sand.

Why is that so? We have observed that human beings are constituted so as to resist face-to-face killing of another human being, especially if he is immobilized—a psychological barrier that has to be overcome to carry out the killing. We recall Turgenev's observation at the execution in Paris in 1870 that "not one of us, absolutely no one looked like a man who realized he had been present at the performance of an act of social justice; everyone tried to turn away in spirit and, as it were, shake off the responsibility for the murder." Even those of us far away from an execution can feel glimmers of that disjunction and self-condemnation, whether in connection with the guillotine or the IV drip of the lethal injection. Executioners and bystanders alike have become psychologically vulnerable to the reverberations of the killing many of them endorse—because they feel it to be so deeply wrong.

The Survivor Mission

. . . [F]eelings of vengeance in response to horrible murders are widespread and, in part, understandable. Yet we have observed how such vengeance fails to relieve the terrible pain of grief and loss. At the other end of the continuum we find increasing numbers of Americans who seek to break out of that killing dynamic by rejecting vengeance and by advocating social policies geared to prevent or minimize violence in general.

For this survivor mission on behalf of all society to have genuine power, however, it must also include a visceral sense of the horror of the original crime. That recognition, along with feelings of anger and vengeance,

can then be transmuted into an ethos of enhancing human life. In that way we reject all claims to owning the death of anyone else.

Are we capable of holding a compassionate perception of both the horror of the original murder and the wrongness of legal killing in capital cases? Such an inclusive response requires us to confront rather than fend off difficult issues of death and killing, but this is by no means beyond our psychological capacity. Indeed, we see more and more examples of it occurring today. By sanitizing executions and limiting genuine witness, the state seeks to overcome our inherent revulsion to killing, but that revulsion needs, instead, to be nurtured and mobilized. We can then bear witness to human cruelty in ways that enhance the entire flow of human life.

Afterword

Many troubling questions surrounded the execution of Timothy McVeigh on June 11, 2001. Would the media heed Attorney General John Ashcroft's request that they ignore the condemned man in his final days? Would McVeigh ever express any remorse for his actions? Should the execution be televised or opened up to the general public in a wider way? The answer in all three cases was, of course, no. But a question that received far less attention was the most difficult of all: Should McVeigh be executed at all?

After several years researching and writing this book, we had come to believe the answer to that question was no—even though (to the end) McVeigh expressed no remorse, and even though some of the victims' families felt it would bring them relief, if not "closure." We continued to advocate life in prison with no chance of parole.

As a man who killed 168 people and had shown not a glimmer of contrition since, McVeigh was as strong a candidate for the death penalty as America has ever produced. Moreover, he had decided against any wide-ranging appeals, in a sense taking the matter into his own hands. Carrying out his execution seemed to most in the media a no-brainer. But was it?

Despite its apparent logic, many people were surprisingly uneasy about the execution. Some family members of people killed by his Oklahoma City bomb wanted McVeigh to linger longer and suffer more; a quick, relatively painless death was "too easy" for him. Other observers wished to give him additional time to demonstrate a measure of repentance. Still others expressed the concern that by executing him, on the date of his choosing, we were simply doing what he wanted us to do, and we should naturally resist any of this murderer's wishes. . . .

Although anti–death penalty activists failed to halt the McVeigh execution, the event nevertheless provided a national forum for their views. Revelations that the FBI had withheld evidence from the McVeigh defense team intensified awareness of the human fallibility in the death penalty system. While media coverage was often exploitative and hysterical, anyone paying minimal attention to reports in the press and on television was exposed to questions . . . about the entire death penalty regime. Bud Welch, the father of one of the Oklahoma City victims . . . received a good deal of sympathetic attention . . . and there was other nuanced coverage. In some measure, the media tempered its blatant support for the execution of McVeigh by repeatedly pointing out that support for capital punishment in the United States was fading.

Indeed, taken as a whole, the year 2001 continued the trends we noted. . . . Several more inmates were released from death row after DNA tests or other evidence indicated that they were innocent. Polls continued to

drift in a direction far away from what was once referred to as "overwhelming" support for executions. The option of life with no chance for parole continued to gain more confidence, as suggested by new polls which showed that more than half of all Americans now support that as sufficient penalty for murder. Calls for a moratorium on executions came from more and more legislators and editorial pages. Several journalists, most memorably Sara Rimer in the *New York Times* and David Isay on National Public Radio, explored the conflicted feelings of prison guards, wardens, chaplains, and others involved in carrying out executions.

And while still small, the number of high-ranking public officials willing to question or attack the death penalty continued to grow. Probably the most significant statement in this regard came from U.S. Supreme Court Justice Sandra Day O'Connor, a longtime proponent of capital punishment who, shortly after the McVeigh execution; expressed strong concerns about the current system, especially in light of revelations about innocent men on death row. The terrorist attacks of September 11 may have temporarily heightened feelings of anger and vengeance, but it still seems likely to us that even a conservative Court will one day in the not distant future issue a ruling that will halt, if not abolish, capital punishment in our land. Or perhaps some combination of judicial, political, and ethical actions will bring about the end of executions.

To do that we must absorb the lessons from both the early and recent history of capital punishment in our country, and take the necessary steps as individuals to eradicate this deep stain on our democracy.

NOTES

1. "one of those peculiar": *Los Angeles Times,* January 13, 2000. Henry LeClerc: *New York*

Times, January 25, 2000. the only nation in the world: *U.S. News,* January 17, 2000.

2. American habit of violence . . . destroy or "murder" evil: See Lifton, *Destroying the World,* 327–28; Robert Jay Lifton, *The Protean Self: Human Resilience in an Age of Fragmentation* (University of Chicago Press, 1993, 1999), 34–36; Lifton, *Home from the War,* 137–59; and "The psyche of a 'gunocracy,' " *Newsweek,* August 23, 1999. "the rogues, the adventurers, and land-boomers": Richard Slotkin, *Regeneration Through Violence: The Mythology of the American Frontier, 1600–1860:* (Wesleyan, Conn.: Wesleyan University Press, 1973), 83–84.

3. "taste for body-horror"/"illicit"/"titillating": Karen Halttunen, *Murder Most Foul: The Killer and the American Gothic Imagination* (Cambridge: Harvard University Press, 1998), 60–90. pornography of death: Geoffrey Gorer, "The Pornography of Death," in *Death, Grief, and Mourning* (New York: Doubleday, 1965).

4. false witness: For concept, see Lifton, *Home from the War,* 392–93. "the authority of perfect knowledge and final things": John Leonard quoted in Mello, *Dead Wrong,* 44.

5. "I'd like to see those people": *Chicago Tribune,* February 19, 2000. The *Chicago Tribune* poll: Reported in *Chicago Tribune,* March 7, 2000.

6. the president's pastor: Reuters, February 15, 2000.

7. Ron Tabak: Associated Press, February 14, 2000. poll in Connecticut: *The Economist,* May 15, 1999.

8. Today, in Canada: *Montreal Gazette,* December 31, 1998.

9. "There are a lot": *USA Today,* November 14, 1999. "The best way to resolve": *Christian Science Monitor,* November 17, 1999. "out of some embarrassed": From *New York Review of Books,* January 20, 2000.

10. "retirement syndrome": Pattern discussed in Robert Jay Lifton, "Nuclear Fundamentalism," in Robert Jay Lifton and Richard Falk, *Indefensible Weapons* (New York: Basic Books, 1982), 96–99.

11. "the most premeditated of murders": Camus, *Resistance, Rebellion and Death,* 143.

QUESTIONS FOR DISCUSSION

1. Do you agree with Lifton and Mitchell's assessment that the current conditions in the United States are similar to the conditions in Britain before the repeal of the death penalty there?

2. Lifton and Mitchell argue that the new technology of DNA analysis has lent support to anti–death penalty advocates. Do you agree? Are there other new technologies that might support pro–death penalty advocates?

3. Where do you draw the line between reasonable and unreasonable punishments?

4. How are Lifton and Mitchell involved in the social construction of social problems?

44

DWB IS NOT A CRIME
The Numbers Show That Police Unfairly and Unconstitutionally Pull Over More Cars Driven by Blacks

JOHN LAMBERTH

In 1993, I was contacted by attorneys whose clients had been arrested on the New Jersey Turnpike for possession of drugs. They told me they had come across 25 African American defendants over a three-year period all arrested on the same stretch of turnpike in Gloucester County, but not a single white defendant. I was asked whether, and how much, this pattern reflected unfair treatment of blacks.

They wanted to know what a professional statistician would make of these numbers. What were the probabilities that this pattern could occur naturally, that is, by chance? Since arrests for drug offenses occurred after traffic stops on the highway, was it possible that so many blacks were arrested because the police were disproportionately stopping them?

I decided to try to answer their questions and embarked on one of the most intriguing statistical studies of my career: a census of traffic and traffic violators by race on Interstate 95 in New Jersey. It would require a careful design, teams of researchers with binoculars and a rolling survey.

To relieve your suspense, the answer was that the rate at which blacks were stopped was greatly disproportionate to

their numbers on the road and to their propensity to violate traffic laws. Those findings were central to a March 1996 ruling by Judge Robert E. Francis of the Superior Court of New Jersey that the state police were de facto targeting blacks, in violation of their rights under the U.S. and New Jersey constitutions. The judge suppressed the evidence gathered in the stops. New Jersey is now appealing the case.

The New Jersey litigation is part of a broad attack in a number of states on what has been dubbed the offense of "DWB"—driving while black. Although this problem has been familiar anecdotally to African Americans and civil rights advocates for years, there is now evidence that highway patrols are singling out blacks for stops on the illegal and incorrect theory that the practice, known as racial profiling, is the most likely to yield drug arrests. Statistical techniques are proving extremely helpful in proving targeting, just as they have been in proving systemic discrimination in employment.

This was not my first contact with the disparate treatment of blacks in the criminal justice system. My academic research over the past 25 years had led me from an interest in small group decision-making to jury selection, jury composition and the application of the death penalty. I became aware that blacks were disproportionately charged with crimes, particularly serious ones; that they were underrepresented on jury panels and thus on juries; and that they were sentenced to death at a much greater rate than their numbers could justify.

As I began the New Jersey study, I knew from experience that any research that questioned police procedures was sensitive. I knew that what I did must stand the test of a court hearing in which every move I made would be challenged by experts.

First, I had to decide what I needed to know. What was the black "population" of the road—that is, how many of the people traveling on the turnpike over a given period of time were African American? This task is a far cry from determining the population of a town, city or state. There are no Census Bureau figures. The population of a roadway changes all day, every day. By sampling the population of the roadway over a given period, I could make an accurate determination of the average number of blacks on the road.

I designed and implemented two surveys. We stationed observers by the side of the road, with the assignment of counting the number of cars and the race of the occupants in randomly selected three-hour blocks of time over a two-week period. The New Jersey Turnpike has four lanes at its southern end, two in each direction. By the side of the road, we placed an observer for each lane, equipped with binoculars to observe and note the number of cars and the race of occupants, along with a person to write down what the observers said. The team observed for an hour and a half, took a 30-minute break while moving to another observation point and repeated the process.

In total, we conducted more than 21 sessions between 8 A.M. and 8 P.M. from June 11 to June 24, 1993, at four sites between Exits 1 and 3 of the turnpike, among the busiest highway segments in the nation. We counted roughly 43,000 cars, of which 13.5 percent had one or more black occupants. This was consistent with the population figures for the 11 states from which most of the vehicles observed were registered.

For the rolling survey, Fred Last, a public defender, drove at a constant 60 mph (5 mph above the speed limit at the time). He counted all cars that passed him as violators and all cars he passed as nonviolators. Speaking into a tape recorder, he also noted the race of the driver of each car. At the end of each day, he collated his results and faxed them to me.

Last counted 2,096 cars. More than 98 percent were speeding and thus subject to being stopped by police. African Americans made up about 15 percent of those drivers on the turnpike violating traffic laws.

Utilizing data from the New Jersey State Police, I determined that about 35 percent of those who were stopped on this part of the turnpike were African Americans.

To summarize: African Americans made up 13.5 percent of the turnpike's population and 15 percent of the speeders. But they represented 35 percent of those pulled over. In stark numbers, it works out that blacks were 4.85 times as likely to be stopped as were others.

We did not obtain data on the race of drivers and passengers searched after being stopped or on the rate at which vehicles were searched. But we know from police records that 73.2 percent of those arrested along the turnpike over a 3½ year period by troopers from the area's Moorestown barracks were black—making them 16.5 times more likely to be arrested than others.

Attorneys for the 25 African Americans who had been arrested on the turnpike and charged with possessing drugs or guns filed motions to suppress evidence seized when they were stopped, arguing that police stopped them because of their race. Their motions were consolidated and heard by Judge Francis between November 1994 and May 1995.

. . .

My statistical study, bolstered by an analysis of its validity by Joseph B. Kadane, professor of statistics at Carnegie Mellon University, was the primary exhibit in support of the motions.

But Francis also heard testimony from two former New Jersey troopers who said they had been coached to make race-based "profile" stops to increase their criminal arrests. And the judge reviewed police in-service training aids such as videos that disproportionately portrayed minorities as perpetrators.

The statistical disparities, Francis wrote, are "indeed stark. . . . Defendants have proven at least a de facto policy on the part of the State Police . . . of targeting blacks for investigation and arrest." The judge ordered that the state's evidence be suppressed.

My own work in this field continues. In 1992, Robert L. Wilkins was riding in a rented car with family members when Maryland State Police stopped them, ordered them out and conducted a search for drugs, which were not found. Wilkins happened to be a Harvard Law School–trained public defender in Washington, D.C. With the support of the Maryland ACLU, he sued the state police, who settled the case with, among other things, an agreement to provide highway-stop data to the organization.

I was asked by the ACLU to evaluate the Maryland data in 1996 and again in 1997. I conducted a rolling survey in Maryland similar to the one I had done before and found a similar result. While 17.5 percent of the traffic violators on I-95 north of Baltimore were African American, 28.8 percent of those stopped and 71.3 percent of those searched by the Maryland State Police were African American. U.S. District Judge Catherine Blake ultimately ruled in 1997 that the ACLU made a "reasonable showing" that Maryland troopers on I-95 were continuing to engage in a "pattern and practice" of racial discrimination.

Other legal actions have been filed in Pennsylvania, Florida, Indiana and North Carolina. Police officials everywhere deny racial profiling.

Why, then, are so many more African American motorists stopped than would be expected by their frequency on the road and their violation of the law? It seems clear to me that drugs are the issue.

The notion that African Americans and other minorities are more likely than whites to be carrying drugs—a notion that is perpetuated by some police training films—seems to be especially prevalent among the police. They believe that if they are to interdict drugs, then it makes sense to stop minorities, especially young men. State police are rewarded and promoted at least partially on the basis of their "criminal programs," which means the number of arrests they make. Testimony in the New Jersey case pointed out that troopers would be considered deficient if they did not make enough arrests. Because, as Judge Francis found, training points to minorities as likely drug dealers, it makes a certain sort of distorted sense to stop minorities more than whites.

But there is no untainted evidence that minorities are more likely to possess or sell drugs. There is evidence to the contrary. Indirect evidence in statistics from the National Institute of Drug Abuse indicates that 12 percent to 14 percent of those who abuse drugs are African American, a percentage that is proportionate to their numbers in the general population.

. . .

More telling are the numbers of those people who are stopped and searched by the Maryland State Police who have drugs. The data, which has been unobtainable from other states, indicate that of those drivers and passengers searched in Maryland, about 28 percent have contraband, whether they are black or white. The same percentage of contraband is found no matter the race.

The Maryland data may shed some light on the tendency of some troopers to believe that blacks are somehow more likely to possess contraband. The data show that for every 1,000 searches by the Maryland State Police, 200 blacks and only 80 non-blacks are arrested. This could lead one to believe that more blacks are breaking the law—until you know that the sample is deeply skewed. Of those searched, 713 were black and only 287 were non-black.

We do not have comparable figures on contraband possession or arrests from New Jersey. But if the traffic along I-95 there is at all similar to I-95 in Maryland—and there is a strong numerical basis to believe it is—it is possible to speculate that black travelers in New Jersey also were no more likely than non-blacks to be carrying contraband.

That a black was 16.5 times more likely than a non-black to be arrested on the New Jersey Turnpike now takes on added meaning. Making only the assumption that was shown accurate in Maryland, it is possible to say even more conclusively that racial profiling is prevalent there and that there is no benefit to police in singling out blacks.

More important, even if there were a benefit, it would violate fundamental rights. The Constitution does not permit law enforcement authorities to target groups by race.

Fundamental fairness demands that steps be taken to prohibit profiling in theory and in practice. There is legislation pending at the federal level and in at least two states, Rhode Island and Pennsylvania, that would require authorities to keep statistics on this issue. This is crucial legislation and should be passed.

Only when the data are made available and strong steps are taken to monitor and curtail profiling, will we be able to assure minorities, and all of us who care about fundamental rights, that this practice will cease.

QUESTIONS FOR DISCUSSION

1. Why does it matter if police decisions regarding the relatively minor offense of speeding are made on the basis of race?
2. How might you design a study to determine if arrests for underage alcohol consumption in your city or town are based on race or on gender?
3. From a social constructionist perspective, what is the importance of this chapter first appearing in the *Washington Post Weekly* and not in an academic journal?

45

WHODUNIT?

An Examination of the Production of Wrongful Convictions

WILLIAM S. LOFQUIST

The Scene of the Crime

On 4 October 1982, Annette Cooper Johnston, age eighteen, and her fiancé, Todd Schultz, age nineteen, went for a walk in the small town of Logan, in rural southeastern Ohio. They were never again seen alive. Ten days later, police found their torsos floating in a river on the edge of town. Two days after that, their heads, arms, and legs were found buried in a cornfield on the river's edge. Their genitals had been removed and were never conclusively identified. The public was shocked. Gun sales surged. Halloween was canceled. The police were under tremendous pressure to solve these murders. In the days leading up to and in the months immediately following the discovery of the bodies, the specter of drugs, satanism, and sexual abuse loomed over Logan.

Police questioned parents, friends, neighbors, and others who were somehow tied to Annette and Todd. Although no one was arrested for more than eleven months, within a matter of days police focused their investigation on Dale Nolan Johnston, Annette's stepfather. Under police interro-

gation just after the bodies were found, Johnston confessed to having had sexual contact with his stepdaughter a number of years earlier. He also admitted to a strained relationship with Annette due to her connection to Todd. Further, he consented to a search that produced evidence used to place him in the cornfield. In addition, the FBI's Behavioral Sciences Unit—the now famous "Mindhunters"—developed a profile of the likely killer, who bore an uncanny resemblance to Johnston. With this information, the police obtained warrants for further searches of Johnston's property and, with the evidence collected there, obtained an indictment of him. Johnston was arrested in September 1983. After a two-week trial in January 1984, he was convicted and sentenced to death.

On appeal, however, Johnston's conviction and death sentence were reversed. Critical evidence was deemed inadmissible: (1) a coerced confession regarding his sexual contact with Annette and (2) witness testimony placing him with the two victims near the crime scene—testimony that had been "strengthened" after a police-conducted hypnosis session with the witness. Without this evidence, prosecutors decided not to retry Johnston; he was released from death row in 1990, an innocent man. No one else was ever investigated or arrested for the murders, which remain unsolved. The case is a classic whodunit: a grisly double murder in a small town; the victims young, attractive, and about to be-

William S. Lofquist, "Whodunit? An Examination of the Production of Wrongful Convictions" in *Wrongly Convicted: Perspectives on Failed Justice,* ed. by Saundra A. Westervelt and John A. Humphrey. Copyright © 2000 by William Lofquist. Reprinted with permission of Rutgers University Press.

gin their lives together; a sexually abusive stepfather; rumors of drugs and police corruption. The whodunit examined in this chapter, however, concerns not the killer of Todd and Annette but the wrongful prosecution and conviction of Dale Johnston.

Theorizing Organizational Wrongdoing

Despite existing research and public scrutiny of wrongful conviction cases, the causes of such cases are undertheorized. If we recognize wrongful convictions as organizational products produced by police and prosecutorial agencies in a manner analogous to corporations' manufacture of unsafe products, we can theorize these cases using the growing and sophisticated literature on organizational wrongdoing (see Ermann and Lundman 1996; Ermann and Rabe 1997; Fisse and Braithwaite 1993; Kelman and Hamilton 1989; Lofquist et al. 1997). Through detailed reconstruction of the Johnston case, this chapter takes on that task. . . .

Organizational process or structure theories approach organizational outcomes as emergent, shaped by the complex interactions of numerous decision makers and their larger environments (see Perrow 1984, 1986). When examining organizational outcomes, one must substantially recontextualize their occurrence and, in so doing, consider how macrolevel forces and microlevel rationality are mediated by the mesolevel organizational contexts in which they are expressed. In this view, wrongful convictions are organizational outcomes linked to premature commitment to a particular suspect, inattention to alternative scenarios due to the operation of "normal science" among investigators, the organizational and legal structures of the criminal

justice system, and the lack of resources available to the defense (see also Parloff 1996; Tucker 1997). . . .

The research presented in this chapter fits squarely within this structural approach. Challenging the conventional, rationalistic view that identifiable misconduct serves as a starting point for wrongful convictions, I contend that wrongful convictions are more likely to be produced through the routine operations of flawed systems of police investigations, prosecutorial case making, and death penalty jurisprudence operating within larger social and cultural contexts. Although this vantage point does not deny the existence of bad faith or malicious prosecution, it seeks to present a more comprehensive alternative explanation.

Particularly important are a host of arguments rooted in the dense ethnographic traditions of symbolic interactionism: that the meaning imposed on behavior viewed in hindsight is insensitive to the reality that such meaning is best discerned within the context in which it occurred; that the direction of behavior is highly contingent on factors often deemed irrelevant, if even visible, in hindsight; and that actors impose preexisting frameworks on emergent scenarios. This final point is especially significant. It suggests that legal actors adopt narrative frameworks into which particular crime scenarios are fitted more or less well. These "normal crime" frameworks (Sudnow 1965) shape investigations, assessments of evidence, interpretations of legal rules, and the entire range of decisions in the same way that "normal science" shapes the conduct of engineers (Vaughan 1996).

Before moving on, we should note the significance of this study as it relates to the current death penalty controversy. The death penalty is the most procedurally encumbered area of American criminal law. Its use necessarily involves a bifurcated trial and multiple appeals, rarities in other areas of criminal law. It therefore involves prosecutors, judges, and defense lawyers in active and open presentation of evidence, police and defense investigators, and expert witnesses, all operating under the watchful gaze of the media (at least in those times and places where capital prosecutions are deemed newsworthy). This enormous scope of law and the great number of legal actors involved may lead one to conclude that arrests, prosecutions, and convictions in these cases are particularly "good" in a legal sense—that is, less influenced by social conditions, financial considerations, cultural concerns, or the whole host of extralegal factors that otherwise affect legal decision making. To the contrary, however, a compelling argument has been made for precisely the opposite conclusion (Gross 1996): that capital-case processing has features that are likely to increase the occurrence of wrongful convictions.

In this chapter, I focus on explaining how the police, prosecutors, and judges involved in investigating and trying Dale Johnston's case produced a wrongful conviction despite, or perhaps because of, these legal, social, and cultural contexts. Although the argument that wrongful convictions and executions are so infrequent as to be freakish once relegated such research to the margins of the death penalty debate, a growing body of empirical evidence showing the frequency of wrongful convictions has led many to reconsider this position (Bedau and Radelet 1987; Dieter 1997; Huff et al. 1996; Radelet et al. 1992, 1996). Even death penalty advocates have conceded the importance of wrongful convictions in the debate (Markman and Cassell 1988). A recent national conference on the subject, followed in quick succession by a series of nationally profiled wrongful convictions, has made this issue central to contemporary discussions of the death penalty.[1]

Methodology: Reconstructing the Scene of the "Crime"

Research of the sort undertaken in this chapter requires careful reconstruction of the contexts in which decisions were made, which in turn requires examination of numerous sources of information. I scrutinized newspaper accounts of the crime and case as well as newspaper reports relevant to the broader social, cultural, and criminal justice contexts of the case.[2] I also examined the entire official record of the case, including the trial transcript, each written judicial opinion, and dozens of pre- and post-trial motions and affidavits.[3] It was notably more difficult to discuss the case with the involved parties—attorneys, judges, police, witnesses, reporters. Events such as this one, which divide and even disgrace a small town and call into question the job performance of the entire range of criminal justice professionals, make those involved in the case reluctant to talk. This reluctance is compounded by the fact that the case remains unresolved and that Dale Johnston was never formally exonerated. (Formal exoneration by criminal justice officials is a rare occurrence among wrongful conviction cases.) This legal limbo means that parties to the case may refuse to discuss a formally ongoing investigation.

Despite these problems, some individuals were quite forthcoming in their discussions with me and have provided essential insights into the case and its larger contexts. Although their names and contributions are openly acknowledged in some places, more often these individuals asked that their identities be protected. It remains important to acknowledge that the picture drawn here is incomplete. Nevertheless, I believe that my inferences are warranted by information available in the written record and from the numerous interviews I was able to conduct. All conclusions drawn from outside the written record are based on corroboration from at least two sources.

What Happened? Searching for Clues

The search for Annette Cooper Johnston and Todd Schultz was slowed by the fact that they were adults, known to be contemplating marriage, and known to have an interest in leaving Logan. Although they were reported missing to police only hours after they were last seen leaving Todd's mother's house on 4 October, a police investigation did not begin until 14 October; and police found their torsos several hours later. By then, friends and neighbors had been searching for days; police undertook the search only under pressure from the victims' families. The torsos were found floating in the Hocking River within the town of Logan. Two days later, their arms, legs, and heads were found buried in the cornfield bordering the river, just outside the town limits.[4] The coroner concluded that the cause of death in each case was gunshot wounds; multiple stab wounds were also found and were determined to have occurred after death. Todd's body experienced considerably more violence than did Annette's.

The Investigation: Forensic Science and Escalating Commitment

Initially, police believed that the killings occurred in the cornfield. Preliminary speculation focused on a "psychopathic loner." Within days, however, both Todd's parents and Annette's friends reported to police that Annette had told them she had been sexually molested by her stepfather, and attention turned to Dale Johnston. Over the course of the next several months, this version of events, portraying Johnston as a sexually abusive and jealous stepfather, was bolstered by a series of contributions from forensic science. Three pieces of evidence— hypnotically refreshed witness statements placing Johnston near the cornfield, a boot-print placing Johnston in the cornfield, and a profile of the likely offender—formed the core of the state's case against him, despite the fact that each piece of evidence turned out to be seriously flawed. Discerning the circumstances and motives surrounding the development of these items of evidence lies at the core of theorizing this wrongful conviction. Was the evidence manufactured to create guilt, or was it "discovered" as part of a thorough, albeit cumulatively misdirected, police investigation?

After going to the police station on 21 October 1982 to provide evidence he thought might be helpful in the investigation, Dale Johnston was held by police and interrogated for more than six hours. Reports from Sandra Schultz, Todd's mother, that Annette had confided to her about the sexual relationship with her stepfather and her fear of him, precipitated the interrogation. During this interrogation, which became so heated and coercive that investigator Herman Henry of the Ohio Bureau of Investigation and Identification left in protest of police tactics, Johnston is alleged to have confessed to sexual contact with Annette when she was younger and to the possession of nude photos of her. He also expressed his dislike for Todd Schultz and Todd's relationship with Annette. Further, he consented to a search of his property. This search was conducted immediately, in the last hours of that evening, and led to the seizure of several items of evidence— notably, Dale Johnston's cowboy boots.

This "confession" provided a strong boost to the state's case; it served as a kernel of truth, offered by the primary suspect himself, around which a larger case could be built. Because there are no audio or video recordings, we cannot know precisely what was said. In his subsequent statements, as well as in his wife's statements, Johnston admitted that his family practiced nudism, that he possessed nude photos of Annette, and that he sometimes became aroused in her presence. Nevertheless, he denied sexual contact with her, stating that his earlier confession was coerced. Yet within the highly charged environment of Logan and broader cultural concern about the sexual abuse of children, many interpreted these statements as an admission to an ongoing abusive sexual relationship—as if Johnston had confessed to the allegations of Sandy Schultz and others.

During this same period, as part of a routine canvass of the area, police interviewed Steven R. Rine, a Logan resident and a Schultz family friend. In a series of interviews between 23 October and 3 November, Rine related to police that on the afternoon of 4 October he had seen a vehicle bearing some similarity to one owned by Dale Johnston in Logan within easy walking distance of the cornfield. Johnston denied having been in Logan that afternoon. Rine also related having seen a middle-aged man driving this car yelling at a younger man and woman and forcing them into the car. This initial, very tentative, report to police was followed by police-conducted hypnotic sessions on 11 and 16 November, during which Rine identified the car as a perfect match for Johnston's, the man as a perfect match for Johnston, and the younger people as Todd and Annette, whom he had met briefly a week before their deaths.

Reports from a forensic anthropologist further strengthened the state's case by matching Johnston's boot to bootprints

found in the cornfield. Reports from a forensic meteorologist corroborated this finding by suggesting that the condition of the boot-print matched the weather conditions with respect to rainfall and fallen leaves between the time of the murders and the discovery of the bootprint more than two weeks later. These reports supported the state's theory, placing Johnston in the cornfield very near the time of Todd and Annette's disappearance.

Throughout the winter and spring of 1983, the investigation proceeded with surprisingly few developments or disclosures beyond those of October 1982. Although their investigation clearly focused on Johnston, the police told reporters they had no suspects or major clues. In May 1983, the FBI profile of the likely suspect, which Logan police had requested in late October 1982, was given to investigators. It suggested that the offender knew the victims, "had a long term sexual involvement with the female, and also a resentment of a possible sexual relationship which may have existed between the victims," and "killed them at a location some distance from the final location of burial." More specifically, the offender was described as a "white male in his mid to late forties . . . who prefers outdoor work and self-employment." The profile suggested that he had "been divorced and remarried." Finally, the offender was described as underachieving and antisocial, with little formal education and a history of personal and job failures. At the time of the murders, Johnston was a forty-nine-year-old self-employed contractor living on a farm with his second wife and two stepdaughters.

With this information and evidence, the police came to believe that the murders and dismemberments occurred some miles away, on Johnston's farm. Evidence to the contrary did exist at this time, including eyewitness testimony that Todd and Annette were alive in Logan after being sighted by Rine, that gunshots were heard in the cornfield that evening, and that a man other than Johnston was seen following Todd and Annette, as well as problems with the state's theory of the case.[5] This evidence, however, was overwhelmed by the strength of the sexual history evidence, the narrative power attached to it, and the evidence developed pursuant to it. Contradictory evidence was normalized, witnesses were deemed unreliable, and gunshots in a rural area were deemed unremarkable.

Within weeks, police obtained warrants for two more searches of Johnston's property, including all buildings and a strip mine. These searches produced blood-stained building materials and carpets, feedbags, bullets, shoes matching those worn by Annette on the day of the murders, and a personal check. This evidence was used to elaborate the official version of events: Dale Johnston went to Logan on 4 October (as confirmed by the personal check to a Logan business) with his wife and other stepdaughter, Michelle; forced Todd and Annette into his car (as witnessed by Steven Rine); returned to his farm; shot, stabbed, and dismembered Todd and Annette (as confirmed by the bloody carpets and building materials and the matching-caliber bullets); stuffed them into feedbags; and returned to Logan to dispose of their bodies.

A grand jury was convened in September 1983. Over the course of several days of witness testimony, the state portrayed Johnston as a pathologically jealous stepfather engaged in long-term sexual abuse of his stepdaughter. He was indicted by a nine-to-zero vote on two counts of aggravated murder with death penalty specifications and was arrested later that same day, 29 September. With little likelihood of gaining a change of venue from a town in which his arrest was met with jubilant celebration and a special edition of the *Logan Daily News*,

Johnston opted for a bench trial by a three-judge panel.[6] At the forthcoming trial, Hocking County prosecutor Christopher Veidt and assistant prosecutor Frederick Mong would try Johnston. For his defense, he retained the services of Columbus attorneys Thomas Tyack and Robert Suhr, both experienced capital defense attorneys. The judges were James Stilwell, Joseph Cirigliano, and Michael Corrigan. In the meantime, as a result of threats to his safety, Johnston was relocated to the Pickaway County Jail to await trial.

The Trial: Constructing a Compelling Narrative

Without an unambiguous confession or corroborated eyewitness testimony, legal wrongdoing is not the product of factual certainty. Rather, it is the product of narrative constructions: efforts by various people to construct a highly credible narrative account. This process of storytelling or narrative construction inevitably relies on popular images, assumptions, and inferences. Factually unique stories are fitted into particular narrative frames ("normal crime" scenarios) in a manner that diminishes their distinctiveness. The trial is a particularly significant location of narrative construction; "the struggle of attorneys to find the best accounts for their clients turns courtroom transcripts into excellent barometers of what is said and thought in a culture at any given moment of time" (Ferguson 1996: 87). In this forum, the power, resonance, and effectiveness of a narrative can overwhelm the facts or logic of a particular case, leading legal decision makers to ratify a narrative that results in a wrongful conviction.

The three-judge panel hearing the case *State v. Johnston* (1984) convened in Hocking County Common Pleas Court on 11 January 1984. The trial lasted for nine days. The primary evidence against Johnston, most of which was admittedly circumstantial, was the bootprint found in the cornfield, the hypnotically refreshed accounts of eyewitness Steven Rine, and accounts by Todd's mother and several of Annette's friends concerning Johnston's sexual improprieties with Annette. Anthropologist Dr. Louise Robbins testified that the bootprint found on the riverbank matched the cowboy boots taken from Johnston's home. Meteorologist Jym Ganahl testified that weather conditions in Logan at the time were consistent with the condition of the bootprint. Steven Rine testified that on 4 October 1982 he observed Johnston arguing with Todd and Annette before forcing them into his car on a Logan street corner. Also significant to the prosecution's case were police accounts of Johnston's interrogation, focusing on his sexual contact with Annette and his anger at Annette's relationship with Todd. All of this evidence was woven together by a narrative depicting Johnston as a jealous, incestuous stepfather.

Before and during the trial, the defense did little to offer an alibi for Johnston or a narrative alternative to the state's version of events. Rather, because there was neither a weapon nor a reliable eyewitness, the defense believed that the state's case was too circumstantial to meet the burden of proof, and focused on challenging this case. More specifically, the defense offered evidence from state police investigator Herman Henry that the crime scene had not been properly preserved and that Johnston had been coerced during his October 1982 interrogation. State criminalists also testified that none of the physical evidence removed from Johnston's property in the two June 1983 searches, including bullets, carpets, clothing fibers, and bloodstains, could be conclusively linked to the crime.

The defense was able to elicit testimony that the footprint so central to the state's case had not been cast until 19 October, fifteen days after the murders and three days after the body parts were discovered. The defense also argued that Dr. Robbins was not an expert in footprint identification, thereby disqualifying her testimony. A defense footprint expert argued that the impression in question was not only not Johnston's bootprint but the print of a bare foot. Most important, defense experts challenged the reliability of hypnotically refreshed testimony, arguing that such a procedure inevitably and irreversibly contaminates memory, making it impossible to distinguish pre- and post-hypnosis memories. The defense also challenged the methodology used in hypnotizing Rine, arguing that it was done by an untrained and biased police officer.

Because the defense did not point toward alternative stories, the media covered the case as a straightforward, although ghastly, murder, suggesting little doubt as to Dale Johnston's guilt until well after the verdict and sentencing. Even though the formal, legal burden of proof rests with the state, the absence of a credible alternative narrative can be viewed as strengthening the state's case. Research suggests that legal decision makers, including prosecutors, judges, and juries, use a story frame (a kind of "normal crime" scenario) to organize information (Greene 1989; Pennington and Hastie 1986). Here, the cultural availability of a stepfather–sexual predator framework served to strengthen the state's case, particularly without an alternative frame. After brief and collegial deliberations among the unanimous judges, Johnston was convicted on 28 January 1984. The verdict was met with public celebration. The sentencing phase of his trial was held in March, and he was sentenced to death after a brief trial on 23 March 1984. His execution was scheduled for 4 October 1984, the second anniversary of the murders.

Post-Conviction Proceedings: Constructing an Alternative Narrative

In the immediate aftermath of the conviction, Johnston's attorneys professed shock and aggressively challenged the prosecution's case and methods. In doing so, they proceeded along two paths: filing the customary appeal of the verdict, while filing a separate appeal for a new trial based on newly discovered evidence. The first appeal challenged the admission of Rine's testimony and other elements of the trial. The second appeal took a more affirmative tack, offering alternative accounts of the events of 4 October 1982. The first alternative, offered in the first of a series of motions for a new trial filed throughout the summer of 1984, appealed to another popular narrative construction of the time—that the murders had been committed by a satanic cult. Subsequent motions presented the affidavits of witnesses able to offer exculpatory testimony and argued that the prosecution had violated discovery rules by withholding the names or statements of these witnesses. With these later motions, the defense quickly abandoned its satanic cult theory and focused on a second alternative scenario—that local resident Kevin "Tex" Meyer had committed the murders. Meyer was a drifter and an experienced butcher and was alleged to be enamored of Annette.

The trial judges heard and denied the first series of motions for a new trial, ruling that the state had complied with discovery requests and that the defense had failed to present any evidence warranting a new trial (*State of Ohio v. Dale Johnston* 1984). The defense then appealed to the Hocking County Court of Appeals, which heard and ruled on each of the two lines of appeal (*State of Ohio v. Dale Johnston* 1986). While upholding the state in its reliance on the expertise of Dr. Louise Robbins and on minor points re-

lating to the search warrants and the grand jury proceedings, the court ruled that Rine's testimony was improper, that discovery rules had been violated, and that sentencing procedures were violated. With these rulings, the court ordered a new trial.

As the cases were working through Ohio's appellate courts, two important developments occurred outside the courtroom. First, while on death row, Dale Johnston recalled what he had been doing in the late afternoon of 4 October 1982; he had heretofore been unable to remember. By looking at a calendar and reconstructing events, he remembered that he had been talking to three men—Ralph Cherry, John Cherry, and John Johnson—who had come to the area to work on the property across the street from his farm. Defense investigators pursued this lead and were able to corroborate this alibi, placing Johnston on his farm eleven miles from Logan at the same time Rine had placed him in Logan. Second, *Akron Beacon Journal* reporter Bill Osinski, who had covered the trial and been troubled by the verdict, conducted an independent investigation, the results of which were published in a series of articles beginning on 27 October 1985. In addition to alleging police and prosecutorial misconduct, Osinski argued that the likely killer was William Wickline, who by then was on death row in Ohio for the August 1982 murder and dismemberment of a couple from Columbus. These murders were six weeks and forty miles removed from the Logan killings.

At the same time, continuing defense investigation further weakened the state's case. The defense produced affidavits of witnesses placing Todd and Annette in the cornfield in the late afternoon of 4 October; these witnesses further reported seeing a man following them in the cornfield and hearing shots and screaming from the direction of the cornfield soon after. The defense also further deposed meteorologist Ganahl, who reversed his earlier testimony and expressed considerable doubt that the footprint in the cornfield was made in early October. Rather, the condition of the print suggested that someone searching for Todd and Annette had made it.

In its appeal, the prosecution countered by challenging the veracity and timing of these new defense disclosures and presenting additional witnesses of its own. Most notable was Kevin Scudder, a former cellmate of Johnston's in the Pickaway County Jail, who stated that Johnston had confessed to him that he had killed Todd and Annette.

On 5 October 1988, the Ohio Supreme Court affirmed the appellate court decision in support of a new trial (*State v. Johnston* 1988). More specifically, the Supreme Court used this case to establish guidelines for hypnotically induced testimony and held that Rine's testimony met none of these guidelines. The court also ruled that the prosecution had withheld exculpatory information from the defense. The case was then remanded to Hocking County and granted a change of venue to Franklin County. The presiding judge then ruled that Rine's testimony would be inadmissible at the second trial and that the interrogation of Johnston was inadmissible due to police violations of Johnston's rights under the Fifth and Fourteenth Amendments.

Although the prosecution appealed these rulings, the Franklin County Court of Appeals upheld the rulings on 10 May 1990 (*State v. Johnston* 1990). On 11 May, the prosecution announced that it lacked the evidence to proceed with a second trial; all charges against Johnston were withdrawn, and he was released from custody that same day.

. . .

Structure Perspective: "Throwing Pebbles on a Pond"

. . . The structure perspective is not amenable to [a] concise and neat summary. Quite the opposite, it requires an elaborate reconstruction of the many contexts in which the case occurred so as to gain an understanding of the meaning and significance of decisions at the time they were made. Dale Johnston described this complexity aptly. When I asked him to explain his wrongful conviction, he analogized it to "throwing pebbles on a pond" (Johnston 1998). There is no clear starting point or orderly sequence of events; rather, each pebble creates ripples, and the ripples intersect and interact in a manner too complex to anticipate or fully understand.

Although the evidence can be marshaled to suggest that Johnston was framed, a more contextualized reconstruction suggests that he was a viable suspect around whom an adequate case could be constructed and into which evidence could be fitted by straining, but not breaking, credulity, law, science, and standards of practice. Dale Johnston was the most likely suspect in the murders of Todd and Annette. Police attention to him was consistent with the statistical reality that family members or acquaintances perpetrate most homicides. This statistical truth was reinforced by specific exigencies: reports from Annette's associates as well as from Johnston himself of sexual contact between stepfather and stepdaughter, Annette's decision to leave home in the months before her death, conflict between Dale and Todd, Annette and Todd's intentions to marry and possibly leave Logan, and inconsistencies and inaccuracies in Johnston's version of events leading up to the deaths.

Initial police investigation of the murders was compromised—partly for reasons beyond anyone's control, partly due to serious police errors.[7] By the time the bodies were discovered, the crime scene had been trampled by scores of people, destroying important evidence. This was unavoidable: no strong impetus to search for two missing adults existed, and the cornfield was, of course, not recognized as a crime scene until the bodies were discovered. This problem was aggravated by the several-day delay in casting footprints and collecting other evidence. The police also failed to collect and analyze evidence that was available in the cornfield. These latter problems are more troubling. It is important to recognize, however, that the Logan police had little experience in murder or violent crime investigations; the town's most recent previous murder took place in 1976.

Compounding these problems, the lead investigator in the case, Logan police detective James Thompson, was an overzealous, highly moralistic, somewhat unstable figure said to have been adversely affected by his service in Vietnam. Those with whom I spoke portrayed him as a small-town police officer who viewed Logan as beset by big-city crime problems. He believed that the crimes of popular imagination—rampant drug use and trafficking, child sexual abuse, and child pornography—were active threats in Logan. Quite plausibly, once Thompson was persuaded of Johnston's guilt, a result probably easily accomplished through adoption of the sexual abuse narrative of the case, he became single-minded in his focus.

Police and prosecutorial reliance on hypnotically refreshed testimony was not inconsistent with practice at the time.[8] The same can be said for reliance on the testimony of Louise Robbins, a widely used witness, certified by judges as an expert in courts across the country.[9] The FBI profile implicating Johnston, perceived in hindsight as crafted with Johnston's picture and

biography in hand, was more likely the product of the sometimes careless and unsystematic manner in which profiles were constructed.[10]

The failure of the police to pursue leads provided by various witnesses, particularly those who saw people resembling Todd and Annette and heard gunshots near the cornfield in the late afternoon of 4 October, is consistent with their comfort level with Dale Johnston as a suspect. Although in hindsight it may appear that the police went to insupportable lengths to discredit these witnesses, within the context of the time, the witnesses were some among many that brought forth evidence evaluated as immaterial. We now know that these witnesses were probably correct in their identifications and supporting versions of events, but at the time their reports were not remarkable. As information retrospectively recognized as exculpatory emerged in the course of the investigation, it was easily and routinely rationalized and realigned, or ignored, particularly as the case against Johnston strengthened.

It is also important to recognize the extent to which existing investigative rules and practices serve as structural advantages to the state, producing a tendency toward wrongful convictions independent of the practices of particular officers. The police function as the de facto investigative arm of the prosecutor's office. Although criminal proceedings are ideally a search for truth by competing parties, the agency empowered to represent the public in investigating crimes has an open relationship with only one party in these proceedings (Fisher 1988, 1993; "Toward a Constitutional Right," 1978).

Efforts to require police and prosecutorial cooperation with the defense have been inadequate. Most notably, the *Brady* rule, created by the Warren Court in *Brady v.*

Maryland (1963), requires the prosecution to provide the defense with evidence that is material and exculpatory. Nevertheless, it allows the prosecution the discretion to define these standards, provides few inducements for cooperation, and, as established in a later related case, requires the defense to ask specifically for what it may not know exists.[11] This last requirement is especially problematic because it reinforces the initial problem that evidence collected by police is the property of the prosecution. These rulings are of additional significance in that they occur within a larger legal culture that treats cases as battles to be won or lost and a larger social context that views policing as the central source of public safety and social order.

Police and prosecutorial reliance on Kevin Scudder was routine. Jailhouse snitches serve as a common law enforcement means to strengthen cases by providing what is otherwise lacking: a confession (Winograde 1990). Although this practice is one of the most glaring faults in capital prosecutions and is frequently the subject of calls for reform (Zimmerman 1994), it is a normal feature of prosecutorial practice. As such, it reveals more about prosecutorial culture and the "win at all costs" ethic of prosecutors than it does about the practice of the Hocking County District Attorney's Office in particular.

As for the judges, careful review of the trial transcript and other written records of the case, as well as appellate reviews of the trial, suggests that their rulings were even-handed and in keeping with existing statutory and case law. Although their decisions regarding hypnotically induced testimony and discovery rules were reversed on appeal, the appellate courts made no suggestion of grievous error. The use of hypnosis in legal proceedings had been an issue for at least fifty years before the Johnston trial (see Diamond 1980; McDonald 1987; Sies and Wester 1985). While the failure of the judges to scrutinize closely the recordings of hypnotic sessions with Steven Rine was unfortunate, it leaves us no reason to believe it was designed to avoid knowledge of the inadequacies of the hypnosis.[12] Further, my interviews with two of the judges revealed an apparently sincere and continuing belief in Johnston's guilt and in the veracity of hypnotically induced testimony. More notably, in these interviews, the judges appeared genuinely unaware of the numerous controversies relating to alternative theories of the case, suggesting the implausibility of their complicity in any effort to frame Johnston.[13]

Conclusion: Beyond Whodunit

The cultural power of the whodunit framework distorts our understanding of organizational wrongdoing by emphasizing the rationality, linearity, and individuality of wrongdoing within organizational settings characterized by powerful opposing forces: complexity, routines, multiple decision makers, and limitations on individual information and responsibility.

Working within the framework provided by Vaughan (1996), the foregoing analysis has directed attention toward the environments (structural and cultural) within which organizations operate and that mediate macro and micro agency. In this view, individual decision making is nested within organizational structures and cultures, which are themselves nested within larger institutional and societal environments. Carefully reconstructing and closely examining these contexts makes it possible to understand the knowledge and policies that guide decisions and the meaning assigned to decisions by those making them.

Seen from this perspective, the wrongful conviction of Dale Nolan Johnston was the product of the normal, day-to-day, routine operations of decision makers acting free of conspiratorial intent or wrongdoing; the outcome was generated by the structures and routines in which actors act. Such actors are engaged in a kind of "normal science" (Kuhn 1962; Vaughan 1996) in which assumptions of normality and regularity lead actors to follow prescribed practices. . . .

Perhaps most disturbing is the implication that wrongful convictions are essentially unremarkable and much more difficult to guard against than by simply controlling against bias and wrongdoing. More specifically, the foregoing suggests that the occurrence of wrongful convictions is limited first and foremost by the large number of capital murder cases in which the factual involvement of the defendant is not in question. Beyond that, police professionalism, effective capital defense, and independent and investigative media are important sources of protection against wrongful convictions. Conversely, the use of law to improve the implementation of the death penalty may make matters worse (by increasing the complexity of structures as well as our confidence in the process itself). There is little reason to believe that the complex legal framework constructed around the death penalty has reduced the number of wrongful convictions or that further movement in this direction will produce a better result.

NOTES

1. The National Conference on Wrongful Convictions and the Death Penalty was held in Chicago, 13–15 November 1998.
2. The crime and the trial were given substantial coverage by the local paper, the *Logan Daily News,* as well as by several urban papers: the *Columbus Dispatch,* the *Akron Beacon Journal,* and the *Dayton Daily News.* I examined each of these papers.
3. All of the newspapers and legal materials used in reconstructing this case are on file with the author and available on request.
4. This is relevant in that the torsos and limbs were found in different police jurisdictions. The cornfield is in the jurisdiction of the Hocking County Sheriff's Department. The river is in the jurisdiction of the Logan Police Department.
5. It strains credulity to believe that Johnston would abduct Todd and Annette in Logan, return them to his secluded farm to kill them, and then return to more populated Logan to dispose of their bodies. This is particularly true considering the presence of a strip mine on his property, where the bodies could have been disposed of fairly easily.
6. As a measure of the intensity of local interest in the case, this was the first special edition of the *Logan Daily News* since the end of World War II. A special edition was also printed to mark Johnston's conviction.
7. One well-known consultant to police departments who has direct knowledge of this case described the investigation as the "sloppiest piece of police work" he had ever seen. He rejected the suggestion of a conspiracy against Johnston (Griffis 1997).
8. Only through this case and other contemporaneous higher-profile cases (notably, the Bundy and Spaziano cases in Florida) was hypnotically induced testimony barred.
9. In an interview years after Johnston's conviction was reversed and Robbins's reputation tarnished, Judge Corrigan described her as "very, very impressive" and a central figure in Johnston's conviction (Corrigan 1997).
10. As far as I can determine, the FBI never visited the crime scene or conducted an independent investigation. Rather, their profile was based on materials given to them by local law enforcement and therefore reproduced the bias toward Johnston found in these materials.
11. *United States v. Agurs* (1976) established a high standard for defense efforts to argue that exculpatory material was wrongly withheld by the prosecution.
12. Because capital cases present judges with enormous volumes of material, it would be naïve to deny that much of this material is underscrutinized.
13. It is also interesting, and perhaps significant, to note that Judge Michael Corrigan from Cuyahoga County, who came to the case

with the reputation of being hard-nosed and punitive, is the son of Thomas Corrigan, the prosecutor in the infamous Sam Sheppard wrongful conviction case. This raises questions about Corrigan's response to claims of wrongful prosecution and conviction.

REFERENCES

Bedau, Hugo Adam, and Michael L. Radelet. 1987. "Miscarriages of Justice in Potentially Capital Cases." *Stanford Law Review* 40: 21–179.

Corrigan, Michael. 1997. Interview with author, 15 October.

Diamond, Bernard L. 1980. "Inherent Problems in the Use of Pretrial Hypnosis on a Prospective Witness." *California Law Review* 68: 313–49.

Dieter, Richard C. 1997. *Innocence and the Death Penalty.* Washington, D.C.: Death Penalty Information Center.

Ermann, M. David, and Richard J. Lundman, eds. 1996. *Corporate and Governmental Deviance.* 5th ed. New York: Oxford University Press.

Ermann, M. David, and Gary A. Rabe. 1997. "Organizational Processes (Not Rational Choices) Produce Most Corporate Crimes." In *Debating Corporate Crime: An Interdisciplinary Examination of the Causes and Control of Corporate Misconduct,* edited by William S. Lofquist, Mark A. Cohen, and Gary A. Rabe, 53–67. Cincinnati: Anderson.

Ferguson, Robert A. 1996. "Untold Stories in the Law." In *Law's Stories: Narrative and Rhetoric in the Law,* edited by Peter Brooks and Paul Gewirtz, 84–98. New Haven: Yale University Press.

Fisher, Stanley Z. 1988. "In Search of the Virtuous Prosecutor: A Conceptual Framework." *American Journal of Criminal Law* 15: 197–261.

———. 1993. " 'Just the Facts, Ma'am': Lying and the Omission of Exculpatory Evidence in Police Reports." *New England Law Review* 28: 1–62.

Fisse, Brent, and John Braithwaite. 1993. *Corporations, Crime and Accountability.* New York: Cambridge University Press.

Greene, Edith. 1989. "On Juries and Damage Awards: The Process of Decisionmaking." *Law and Contemporary Problems* 52: 225–46.

Griffis, Dale. 1997. Interview with author, 14 October.

Gross, Samuel R. 1996. "The Risks of Death: Why Erroneous Convictions Are Common in Capital Cases." *Buffalo Law Review* 44: 469–500.

Huff, C. Ronald, Arye Rattner, and Edward Sagarin. 1996. *Convicted but Innocent: Wrongful Conviction and Public Policy.* Thousand Oaks, Calif.: Sage.

Johnston, Dale N. 1998. Interview with author, 14 November.

Kelman, Herbert C., and V. Lee Hamilton. 1989. *Crimes of Obedience.* New Haven: Yale University Press.

Kuhn, Thomas S. 1962. *The Structure of Scientific Revolutions.* Chicago: University of Chicago Press.

Lofquist, William S., Mark A. Cohen, and Gary A. Rabe, eds. 1997. *Debating Corporate Crime: An Interdisciplinary Examination of the Causes and Control of Corporate Misconduct.* Cincinnati: Anderson.

Markman, Stephen J., and Paul G. Cassell. 1988. "Protecting the Innocent: A Response to the Bedau-Radelet Study." *Stanford Law Review* 41: 121–60.

McDonald, David S. 1987. "The Admissibility of Hypnotically Refreshed Testimony." *Ohio Northern University Law Review* 14: 361–78.

Parloff, Roger. 1996. *Triple Jeopardy.* Boston: Little, Brown.

Pennington, N., and Reid Hastie. 1986. "Evidence Evaluation in Complex Decision Making." *Journal of Personality and Social Psychology* 51: 242–58.

Perrow, Charles. 1984. *Normal Accidents: Living with High-Risk Technologies.* New York: Basic Books.

———. 1986. *Complex Organizations: A Critical Essay.* 3d ed. New York: McGraw-Hill.

Radelet, Michael L., Hugo Adam Bedau, and Constance E. Putnam. 1992. *In Spite of Innocence.* Boston: Northeastern University Press.

Radelet, Michael L., Williams S. Lofquist, and Hugo Adam Bedau. 1996. "Prisoners Released from Death Rows Since 1970 Because of Doubts about Their Guilt." *Thomas M. Cooley Law Review* 13: 907–66.

Sies, Dennis Ellsworth, and William C. Wester, II. 1985. "Judicial Approaches to the Question of Admissibility of Hypnotically Refreshed Testimony: A History and Analysis." *DePaul Law Review* 35: 77–124.

Sudnow, David. 1965. "Normal Crimes: Sociological Features of the Penal Code in a Public Defender Office." *Social Problems* (Winter): 255–76.

"Toward a Constitutional Right to an Adequate Police Investigation: A Step Beyond *Brady.*" 1978. *New York University Law Review* 53: 835–74.

Tucker, John C. 1997. *May God Have Mercy.* New York: Norton.

Vaughan, Diane. 1996. *The Challenger Launch Decision.* Chicago: University of Chicago Press.

Winograde, Jana. 1990. "Jailhouse Informants and the Need for Judicial Use Immunity in Habeas Corpus Proceedings." *California Law Review* 78: 755–85.

Zimmerman, Clifford S. 1994. "Toward a New Vision of Informants: A History of Abuses and Suggestions for Reform." *Hastings Constitutional Law Quarterly* 22: 81–178.

CASES CITED

Brady v. Maryland, 363 U.S. 83 (1963).

State v. Johnston, 83–CR-54 (1984).

State v. Johnston, 529 N.E.2d 898 (1988).

State v. Johnston, 580 N.E.2d 1162 (1990).

State of Ohio v. Dale Johnston, Memorandum opinion, Oct. 25 (1984).

State of Ohio v. Dale Johnston, No. 425, Aug. 6 (1986).

United States v. Agurs, 427 U.S. 97 (1976).

QUESTIONS FOR DISCUSSION

1. Lofquist discusses how the "child molester" crime scenario shaped the way legal personnel collected and interpreted evidence. Can you think of other crime scenarios that are common in our culture?
2. Do false convictions that result from personal bias and normal approaches suggest different solutions? Why or why not?
3. Do you agree with Lofquist that increased professionalism of legal personnel will minimize the conviction of innocent individuals?
4. Do you agree that false convictions are a serious social problem? Why or why not?

46

"I DON'T HAVE TO BE AFRAID OF YOU"

Rape Survivors' Emotion Management in Court

AMANDA KONRADI

Introduction

Research indicates that women are not passive in the face of rape attempts (Bart and O'Brien 1985; Caignon and Groves 1987; Kleck and Sayles 1990), and

Reprinted from Amanda Konradi, "I Don't Have to Be Afraid of You": Rape Survivors' Emotion Management in Court," *Symbolic Interaction* (1): 45–77. Copyright © 1999 with permission from Elsevier Science.

they selectively bring assaults to the attention of the legal system (Greenberg and Ruback 1992; Williams 1984). Yet rape survivors' active involvement in the process of prosecuting their assailants has not been extensively examined. Research on rape survivors' experiences in courtrooms, where they make an essential contribution to the justice process, has emphasized their emotional trauma. Researchers have emphasized that rape survivors are frustrated and pained when blamed in cross-examination, they are fearful to confront their assailants, and they experience distress when relating the rape event during direct-examination (Bohmer and Blumberg 1975; Holmstrom and Burgess 1983; Lurigio and Resnick 1990; Madigan and Gambel 1989). Yet little has been done to analyze the sources of rape survivors' discomfort and no one has sought to understand what rape survivors *do* with and about their feelings. To fully understand how the courts operate as sites of resistance as well as domination it is essential that the emotional aspect of courtroom interaction be examined. This research begins to fill that gap.

This article, based on semi-structured "life history" interviews with thirty-two rape survivors conducted between 1990 and 1992, explores why and how rape survivors' emotions are managed during court events. I examine their accounts to identify the factors that contribute to intense feelings in the courtroom, incentives or motivations rape survivors have to manage their feelings and expressions of specific emotions, survivors' individualized strategies for deflecting, suppressing, and cultivating emotion, and interpersonal strategies for achieving emotional control that involve others in the courtroom. . . .

. . .

In American criminal justice, the truth or "facts" of a disputed situation are believed to emerge from an adversarial encounter. Legal agents for the state and the defendant focus on presenting a consistent line and on exposing the weaknesses in each others' arguments. Their efforts to diminish the opposing argument include challenging the credibility of witnesses called by the opposing side. I propose that, in addition to challenging the content of testimony, this takes the form of opposing counsel seeking to provoke negative emotions in witnesses, obstructing witnesses' efforts to remain in

face, and seeking, specifically, to expose them in wrong face to the jury (i.e., to evoke shame in them). . . .

Most rape survivors are lay witnesses and are transient participants in the courtroom. As such, they lack experience with the protocols of courtroom interaction and are unaware of how the adversarial process plays out. In addition, the witness role structurally limits their interactional options. They are not in a position to initiate interaction and, thus, cannot keep away from topics that make them uncomfortable, a typical face-saving defensive measure (Goffman 1967). It seems likely that rape survivors who confront interactions in which threats to their face and place are willfully made by opposing counsel (the defense attorney) will experience discomfort due to loss of face, a continued experience of being one down (Clark 1990), and the violation of rules of tact. An empirical investigation of this possibility is necessary. . . .

. . . To what extent are emotions in the courtroom "manufactured" for audience consumption? Toward what audience do rape survivors orient in court? Toward what feeling rules and display rules do survivors orient in court? How do feeling rules and display rules communicated to rape survivors by prosecutors reflect broader organizational needs? What efforts do rape survivors make to evoke or suppress feelings? Yet perhaps this is an overly calculated and rational conceptualization of emotion in a situation that research shows is highly charged. Perhaps, as well, it is wrong to assume that one set of feeling rules can be identified in the courtroom and that it universally guides rape survivors' emotional performances. . . .

. . . [I]t is reasonable to ask to which courtroom participants (prosecutor, judge, defense attorney, defendant, and friends) rape survivors' emotions are a resource (O'Brien 1994) and what specific investments these others have in how rape survivors emote. . . . [D]efense attorneys may seek to provoke negative emotions in rape survivors in order to protect defendants. Obtaining convictions is essential for prosecutors' career advancement (Frohmann 1991, 1997); they must convince jurors and judge that the defendant perpetrated rape on their prime witness. Thus, prosecutors have incentives to approach rape survivors' emotions as a resource for making their case to the jury and to ensure that rape survivors have enough control over their emotions to complete their testifying responsibilities. It is essential to investigate several questions: Do prosecutors communicate organizationally specific feeling and display rules to survivors? Do prosecutors act as team members to assist rape survivors in managing face during cross-examination? How do rape survivors respond to management efforts undertaken by others? . . .

. . . [O]n the basis of a variety of evidence, . . . like divorced people, the ill, the unemployed, and those who have lost loved ones, crime victims are worthy of sympathy. If this is indeed a cultural norm, then crime victims called to be witnesses in court will expect to be extended the sympathy consistent with their status. Yet it is hard to imagine that being treated as an adversary and undermined in one's efforts to maintain face and place will be perceived as consistent with a broad sympathy margin. Whether *victim*-witnesses conceptualize their treatment in court in terms of sympathy needs to be explored.

. . .

Findings

Sources of Emotion in the Courtroom

Three-fourths of the rape survivors I interviewed described testifying as an intensely emotional experience. At some point in their court appearances they said that they felt extreme fear, anger, embarrassment, frustration, anxiety, or unspecified pain. The most frequently reported sources of intense emotion for survivors were, in declining order, recalling the rape experience, encountering the defendant, and having the defense attorney make interaction difficult. Powerful, but less often mentioned contributors were waiting, observing the pain of supporters, speaking before a public audience, and feeling a lack of knowledge about the legal process.

Recalling the Rape Experience Through the Act of Testifying. A few survivors in this study did not achieve control over the fears that followed from their rapes before they were called to appear in court. Thus, their emotional memory of the assault was in their conscious mind or close to the surface of consciousness. Talking about the rape in the courtroom or elsewhere was not easily done, as it might mean remaining seated while shaking and experiencing an intense desire to cower or flee. However, the majority of survivors I interviewed had gained emotional distance from their assaults, and their personal safety in the courtroom was not their greatest concern. Nevertheless, as they gave accounts of their assault experiences in direct-examination, many survivors recalled feeling at some point as though the sexual assault was recurring. When they described the defendant overpowering them, threatening them, and abusing them, they indicated that they actually re-experienced a lack of control and terror. When this emotional recall occurred, it was vivid and extremely frightening. Why did this happen?

Some of the survivors who were more distanced from their rape experience felt that to convey their rape experience clearly, to give details that would be necessary to convince a judge or jury that an assault took place, they needed to get close to their memories. Thus, they tried to recall aspects of the assault that they had successfully repressed. This entailed letting down their emotional guard. When they finally did remember forgotten aspects of the assault, they often also reconnected with their emotional experiences of it. Thus, retelling the rape event functioned to produce feelings much as re-enactments function in psychodrama (Thoits 1996). Such emotional reconnections were abrupt. Unlike the survivors who entered the courtroom with intense feelings, these survivors unpredictably experienced rushes of pain, anger, hatred, disgust, and fear. These feelings were not easily ignored or suppressed, coming as a rush and without warning.

The introduction of tangible evidence of the sexual assault was another trigger for recall and sudden intense emotion. Survivors who described their assaults without experiencing rushes of emotion were sometimes overcome when presented with police photographs of their bloodied and bruised bodies or the clothes they had worn. Seeing these items provoked feelings (Thoits 1996); they brought back the horror of the assault experience.[1]

Encountering the Defendant and Re-Experiencing Disempowerment.

Between a third and a half of the survivors in this sample said that they had feelings of *great* fear of, anger at, or betrayal by the defendant. Thus, many of them had intense emotional responses when they encountered him in the courtroom. For Natalie, a white 26-year-old raped by a stranger, the physical presence of the stranger who assaulted her was a visual reminder of what he forced upon her and the injuries she suffered. Testifying about being raped in his presence was, for her, tantamount to re-experiencing the assault, and it was emotionally overwhelming. She described her intense fear and the pain of reliving the assault as follows:

I was crying because of fear from him, seeing him again for the first time brought all those memories back, and goin' through the story with him in the room um, it just brought it all back to life again, it was so real, it was happenin' all over again and also havin'. . . . I think, my family and my brothers listenin' to all that again and seein' them upset, but. . . . but mainly it was just fear of him and . . . and . . . and just goin' through the whole thing again, and I . . . I think that's why I was cryin' so much.

Other fearful survivors did not report flashbacks, but nonetheless felt irrationally paralyzed in the defendant's presence. From Clark's perspective (1990), these survivors' inferior place relative to their assailants was marked by the emotions they experienced. These women may have experienced their lack of power in the courtroom as the defendants' continued violation of them through institutional means. This perception would be consistent with Sue Lees's (1996) assertion that the criminal justice system is a mechanism for shaming women who dare challenge men's collective power. Survivors who were acquainted with their assailants, particularly those who had had intimate relationships, confronted the betrayal of their trust in the persons of their assailants.

Although some readers may have difficulty with conceptualizing the defendant as an interactant when he and the survivor exchange no words, his object status for survivors is quite apparent when it gets in the way of their interactions with others. Two survivors found that their emotional involvement with the defendant pulled their attention toward him and away from their interaction with the questioning attorney. Specifically, Cindy's anger led her to attempt to stare her assailant down, while Connie's gratitude for being allowed to live led her to look to her assailant for confirmation of her recollections of the assault.[2] Focused on their assailants, both women were less attentive to their interaction with the questioning attorney. This had serious consequences for Cindy, who was involved in cross-examination when it happened. Focusing on meeting her assailant's gaze, she concentrated less on formulating answers to the defense attorney's questions. This tripped her up eventually. She gave an imprecise justification of her identification of the defendant.

Problematic Interaction with the Defense Attorney. The third most significant contributor to intense feelings, particularly frustration and anger, was survivors' interactions with the defense attorney. Survivors experienced different kinds of cross-examination depending on whether they were testifying at a preliminary hearing or trial, the defense strategy, the defense attorney's personality, and the prosecuting attorney's efforts to protect them. Some survivors experienced no problems, but most reported having some kind of difficulty dealing with the defense attorney. Most often, survivors were frustrated and angered by the defense attorney's attempts to make interaction difficult for them or to inappropriately blame them.

Survivors reported that rapid delivery styles undermined their ability to formulate good answers. Their ability to formulate responses were further disturbed by defense attorneys' interruptions and efforts to limit them to one-word responses. Survivors identified some questions as illogical or illogically placed within a sequence of questions. This raised concerns about the ability to provide a "right" answer, and anxiety about becoming trapped into giving an answer they would later regret. For example, Isabel, a white 21-year-old raped by a stranger, told me, "I remember sitting there being questioned by the defense [attorney, and] a little flag kept coming up that they're trying to trap me. I felt like a victim again, they're trying to trap me."[3] Survivors also reported a belief that some questions were repeated to wear them out or to confuse them, and minute details of the assault event or assault location were focused on only to prolong the length of time they were on the stand. They indicated that this angered them as it wore on them mentally and physically. A few survivors stated that they were asked personal questions that embarrassed and angered them. They believed that these questions were unrelated to the assault, and they should not have had to answer them. Some also reported that the defense attorney appeared to be emotionally invested in the interaction and seemed to enjoy making them uncomfortable. Such investment breached the decorum they expected from a legal actor, and they were not sure how to deal with it. Moreover, it left them feeling that the interaction had no limits.

Rachel, a white 26-year-old, was angry enough to want to slap the man defending her ex-husband—an attorney who appeared to enjoy making her uncomfortable. Rosanne, a white 30-year-old raped by a stranger, was pushed to hysteria and became physically incapable of continuing to testify:

> I mean it got totally out of control, I got hysterical, I mean I was shaking so bad that I couldn't even answer him [the defense attorney] because I was so angry and I couldn't believe all this was happening and the judge finally said, "I think that's enough."

In sum, rape survivors were frustrated and angered by defense attorneys' gamesmanship—efforts to fluster them, pull them out of face, and show them in wrong face (Goffman 1967), and leave them emotionally one down (Clark 1990)—and failures to extend them an appropriate margin of sympathy (Clark 1987).

Additional Sources of Intense Feeling. Some survivors with little knowledge of the criminal justice system, and thus little knowledge of the "rules of the game" (Mills and Kleinman 1988, p. 1014), reported a generalized fear of the unknown that made them anxious. A few survivors described feeling grief as they observed the pain of family members who sat listening to them speak about the details of the assaults. The public audience observing the court event raised the stress level of other survivors who felt embarrassed to discuss the sexual activity in which they were forced to participate. Like wheelchair users, they feared "being an embarrassing and embarrassed public spectacle" (Cahill and Eggleston 1994, p. 302). Finally, Rachel, who reported being angry enough at the defense attorney to want to slap him, explained that the stress of waiting was more emotionally taxing than answering questions. Like a few others, she described reaching a state of mental turmoil that caused her to become physically ill:

> But the courtroom itself, I had such knots in my stomach. I mean, I was just sick over it. I actually went down to the ladies' room several times and got sick, because I was just so upset. And every time they would call break, even though I was tired, I would just dread these breaks. [On] one hand I was looking forward to them, but towards the end I was beginning to realize that these breaks were killing me. [. . .] I'm like waiting in this room for me to be called back into the courtroom, and that time that I'm waiting, it's like waiting for the guillotine. And my stomach is just tied up in knots and I just want to get this

thing over with. So that was, I think, that was the hardest part about the court, you know.

In sum, rape survivors confronted feelings in the courtroom that emerged from recollections of past interaction, from interaction with the defense attorneys (in which they were explicitly engaged), and from interactions with the defendants, their families, and the public (in which they were tacitly engaged). Most survivors reported more than one source of intense emotion during their testimony. Sometimes multiple causes and multiple emotions overlapped in the manner described by Clark (1990). Emotions "from another time and setting mix with or even fuel 'current' emotion" (Clark 1990, p. 329). For example, a survivor might experience fear as a result of seeing the defendant and recalling the rape. Alternatively, she might painfully view her parents' misery as they listen to her story and experience anger at the defense attorney's efforts to blame her for the rape. The intense feelings brought on by testifying were in themselves problematic for the study participants because they were negative emotions and they caused them physical discomfort. The feelings aroused in the courtroom also interfered with rape survivors' ability to concentrate on testifying and maintaining their faces. The feelings created "self doubt and stagefright" (Clark 1990, p. 312) which undermined rape survivors' claims of place, and they conflicted with successful performance of the witness role.

A number of incentives to control emotional expression were layered on top of the immediate problems posed by the intensity of rape survivors' feelings. In the section that follows, I describe the reasoning rape survivors gave to suppress or evoke specific emotions and to control the amplitude of their emotional expression.

Incentives to Suppress or Evoke Specific Emotions and to Control the Amplitude of Emotional Expression

First, survivors sought to produce emotional demeanors consistent with feeling rules for rape victims and for witnesses in courts of law. Second, survivors sought to craft emotional representations that resisted reaffirming the dominance their rapist established in the rape event. Third, rape survivors sought to achieve an emotional intensity that allowed them to maintain their position in interaction with the defense attorney.

Achieving Consistency with Feeling Rules. Rape survivors were attentive to two sets of feeling rules: those for the courtroom and those for victims of rape. Survivors' awareness of feeling rules came from their general awareness of cultural ideas concerning rape and the legal system and their contacts with supporters and legal personnel. Many survivors stated that television was a source of information about the legal system.[4]

Typically, the study participants perceived the courtroom to be a rational domain which called for a neutral, controlled, and polite demeanor. This emotional neutrality reflected both respect for the authority of the court and a commitment to the search for truth in the facts presented to the court. Some survivors believed that remaining emotionally neutral would indicate their lack of investment in the case, thereby undermining their credibility. In addition, some survivors indicated that they felt expressions of hostility violated the implied social contract of the court event. In a situation they defined as rational and dispassionate, they felt obliged to provide information in a calm, business-like way. To express anger was to be irrational and impolite, and it was counter to the court's decorum and

the court's mission of fact finding. Gabriella, a white self-supporting college student raped by a stranger, indicated that she "knew" she could not openly display the negative feelings she had for the defense attorney:

> But [the defense attorney] was an asshole. I mean, I wanted to kill him. I was so angry with him. . . . [Gabriella goes on about being cross examined] I just wanted to say, "Fuck you, you fucking asshole!" But, I knew that I couldn't say that in court.

Similarly, Anna, a black 28-year-old, described thinking about swearing at the defendant, her ex-boyfriend, rather than doing so audibly.

Many study participants were aware of cultural stereotypes that implied women make up allegations of rape in order to get revenge, lead men to aggressively pursue intercourse by dressing in revealing clothing, and are not "really" injured by forced sexual contact.[5] Study participants were also aware of the fact (and were warned by legal personnel) that some demeanors are viewed as consistent with these stereotypes and others are viewed as consistent with "real" sexual victimization. The false rape victim is angry, deceptive, or hard (i.e., unmoved and inexpressive). The demeanor of the "real" victim is consistent with someone who was damaged by the rape event; she displays fear and embarrassment and is subject to emotional breakdown. In this regard, several survivors mentioned the televised and tearful testimony of Patricia Bowman, who was involved in prosecuting William Kennedy Smith in Florida.

Some rape survivors explained that prosecutors actually directed them to hide any feelings of anger at the defendant or defense attorney from view. These prosecutors appeared to worry that short answers, a rising voice, and other signs of irritation might be misinterpreted as a lying woman's efforts to avoid answering questions. They said that angry displays would harm their witnesses' credibility. Prosecutors also expressed concerns to survivors that displays of anger would contradict the image of a weak and fearful rape victim that they believed jurors expected. . . .

The concerns that rape survivors attributed to prosecutors were echoed in my interviews with prosecutors. Together, the roles of witness and rape victim framed a narrow band of appropriate emotional expression that excluded anger, frustration, boredom, or disgust. However, the display rules that accompanied these two ideal images were somewhat contradictory with respect to an appropriate emotional intensity, calling for emotional suppression on the one hand (the rational witness) and evocation on the other (the traumatized rape victim). Each woman handled this contradiction in her own way depending on her assessment of competing incentives to manage emotions: the prosecutor's specific framing of the situation, her desire to regain emotional status relative to the defendant and defense attorney, and her desire to perform her role.

Resisting Domination. Some survivors wanted to suppress what they were feeling when the defendant was present. They believed that to reveal their recalled terror of the assault, their discomfort with the defense attorney's questions, and particularly their fear of him, was to again lose control to him. Displaying discomfort would allow their assailants to see continued success in dominating their lives, even as survivors sought to assert themselves and use the legal system against them. This was of greatest concern to survivors like Jennifer, a while 31-year-old raped by an acquaintance, who lost emotional control and became hysterical during the assault. At some length,

she discussed the problem of showing her vulnerability to the defendant by crying on the witness stand:

> I started crying. [. . .] I hated it. [. . .] And at that point everything came back. All the emotions and stuff I had pushed aside, all the memories, just flooded the whole time. And I realized how long I had been pushing them back and I hadn't realized it. And I also can't stand losing control. And I wasn't going to give him the satisfaction. [. . .] 'Cause I cried through the entire night. When I was in the truck with him. And that was the first time I'd ever done something like that. First time I'd actually had a break that *deep* in my control. And I wasn't gonna let him do that to me again.

Limiting Threats to Ability to Perform the Witness Role. When survivors were intent on formulating answers to questions, they perceived and experienced intense emotions as a general threat to their ability to testify. Unpredictable physical responses that accompanied feelings intruded on their efforts to give the accounts they desired the court to hear. Nausea, as described above by Rachel, inhibited concentration. Unbidden, breath-stealing sobs or tears, running down their faces, smearing their makeup, and dripping onto their clothes, broke their lines of thought. Tears and involuntary gestures also impeded survivors' efforts to exert control over the questioning behavior of defense attorneys. These expressions "given off" let the defense attorney know that his or her line of action was having an emotional impact (Goffman 1959).

Given rape survivors' expression of incentives to manage emotions, it was logical to examine their efforts to do so. In the next section, I will discuss how they achieved desired emotional control and how they handled any failure at that control.

Strategies for Management of Emotions

Survivors managed the expression of emotions in three ways. First, rape survivors sought to control the courtroom situation to avoid triggering undesirable emotions and to minimize their intensity, once present. They did this through avoidance of interaction with specific individuals and by focusing on the question-answer task before them. Second, survivors engaged in surface and deep acting in order to achieve demeanors and emotions that were consistent with courtroom feeling rules or those of a credible victim, or to achieve an alternative emotion that allowed them to maximize their ability to fulfill their testifying obligations. Third, survivors engaged in interactions with the audience in the courtroom and the prosecuting attorney to decrease the intensity of felt emotions and to recover when overcome by their physical manifestations.

Limiting Conditions of Discomfort.   Many survivors attempted to minimize the intensity of their emotions, whether or not they were desirable from the standpoint of feeling rules. That is, the survivors made efforts to limit conditions that would initiate or intensify their anger, embarrassment, fear, and so forth. Most of the women who made this effort directed their energy at avoiding interaction with the people who would make them most uncomfortable (Goffman 1967). This is not surprising, given that survivor-witnesses have little choice about being in a courtroom and sitting in the witness stand. Some survivors asked would-be supporters who might add to their unease not to come to court. This group included parents as well as friends. Three survivors who felt very uncomfortable about a public presence in the courtroom asked the prosecuting attorney if the court could be closed or the audience limited. They sought to avoid having

to deal with a known source of anxiety and embarrassment by initiating the elimination of persons they viewed as intimidating.[6]

When survivors could not eliminate persons in the courtroom they found troublesome, some described efforts to limit the extent to which they interacted with them. A prime candidate for this strategy was the defendant. The U.S. Constitution grants a defendant the opportunity to face his or her accuser, and, in all but one court event described by the survivors in this study, the defendants exercised their right to be in the courtroom. Survivors for whom the defendant's presence posed an emotion management problem described two ways of avoiding interaction with him: putting him out of sight and putting him out of mind. The tactic most survivors described was to avoid looking in the defendant's direction. They averted their eyes except when it was absolutely necessary to look at him, as when making an in-court identification. One survivor reported sitting back in the witness stand and using the judge's name plate to block her view of the defendant. However, the small size and layout of the courtrooms in which preliminary hearings are commonly held precluded this avoidance strategy for many survivors. For example, Julianne, a white college student, described herself sitting directly in front of and about six feet from the boyfriend who raped her. She had to step in front of him to take the witness stand and said that his gaze was not something she could easily avoid.

Looking away from one's assailant in order to avoid experiencing fear can, however, be a double-edged sword. It can cut off a survivor from others with whom eye contact would be a comfort and support. For example, Natalie, who was brutally raped and beaten by a stranger, described giving up eye contact with her family, who had attended the trial en masse to support her, after she realized that to do so would have required her to look at the defendant.

Putting the defendant out of mind, and thus figuratively out of sight, is a more difficult mental task than looking away, but it is not limited by the physical environment of the courtroom. Isabel, a white 21-year-old raped by a stranger, did this successfully. She attended to the defendant enough to be aware of this demeanor, then rationalized him out of the scope of her concern. She did not acknowledge the defendant as "being a person" in the courtroom. Intellectually, she erased him and the emotions associated with him and focused her energies on the people who would be making a decision— the judge and jury:

> Oh, that was terrible, he sat there through the whole thing and just glowered at me or whatever, just . . . and he would have this little smirk on his face like . . . I did it, and I'm gonna get away with it. [. . .] I don't believe I ever even acknowledged him as being a person in that courtroom, my state of mind was he wasn't worth it, it was the other people in that room I had to convince because he already knew the truth and he wasn't worth it.

Survivors also described avoiding eye contact with spectators in the courtroom who aroused feelings of fear—usually the defendant's supporters and family.

Some survivors, like Sandra, a white 21-year-old who was raped by an acquaintance, also feared the judgment of the jury and avoided their gaze. She recalled, "I was scared to look at the jury. I was wondering what they were thinking of me, do they believe me? . . . I tried not to look at the jury because I was afraid of them." Natalie, a white 26-year-old, who said that she generally tried to direct her answers to the jury as the prosecutor had instructed her, tuned them out when the content of her testimony

required her to minimize strong feelings of embarrassment:

> That day . . . I . . . I was very . . . I was very embarrassed, I was embarrassed with some of the things that I did have to say about um, you know, the oral sex, and . . . and the things that he had told me, um, but for those parts, I would just . . . I would close my eyes and I would just say it and . . . I . . . I couldn't look at the jurors when I was sayin' those things, um, the very personal things I . . . I'd just either look down or . . . or close my eyes and . . . and got through it and then when I was finished and I . . . and I would be able to look at them again.[7]

Sandra and Natalie's statements support Shott's (1979) argument that the capacity to evaluate oneself from the standpoint of the other—in this case the jury—leads individuals to minimize interactions that are expected to produce negative emotions of shame and embarrassment.

Three survivors said that, at some point during cross-examination, they tried to avoid eye contact with defense attorneys who aroused their anger. It is possible that others tried this as well. However, it would not be surprising if they did not. Avoiding the defense attorney during interrogation goes against the social convention that one looks at the person with whom one is conversing. In addition, as it is harder for defense attorneys to manipulate a survivor who refuses to look at them, they probably will challenge witnesses who do this. For example, in one preliminary hearing that I observed, the defense attorney tried to intimidate a rape survivor into looking at him. The survivor, a white woman in her late teens, had seated herself at right angles to the prosecutor during direct-examination and had directed her testimony toward a victim-witness advocate seated a few feet away. It appeared that she intended to remain in this position during cross-examination. My field notes show that the defense attorney's first comments to her made an issue of her potential lack of attention to him:

> I am B———M———, I want to make some comments. You don't have to look at me, but it might be easier. I want to point out for the record that *the witness is not looking at me.* Try to remember please not to guess. . . .

The young woman held her ground despite this effort to intimidate her. She remained positioned as she was through most of the cross-examination. She also maintained a very controlled, neutral demeanor in spite of continued needling by the defense attorney. By privatizing her emotion (Zurcher 1985) and exhibiting no outward response to a clearly provoking statement, this survivor elevated her moral status relative to the defense attorney (Clark 1990). She came out ahead in the game.

Many survivors experience embarrassment and find it difficult to put forward a timely answer when a defense attorney initiates a topic that they believe to be illegitimate. Their embarrassment is usually exacerbated if they believe that the attorney is trying to place blame for the assault on them. Likewise, survivors find that feelings of anger or frustration develop as a result of excessive questioning about details or the repetition of questions during cross-examination. In order to counteract these negative feelings, some study participants reported disengaging from interaction with the defense attorney and focusing on individual questions to reduce their emotional involvement in cross-examination. Survivors who employed this technique ignored the argument being built by the defense attorney. They interpreted and answered each question without thinking about the broader meaningful context within which it was asked. . . . Through this strategy, survivors felt that they protected themselves from becoming confused or pulled into a trap. Monica, 16 at the time of the assault and legal proceedings, explained her perception that the defense attorney was trying to make answering, and thus fulfilling her witness role, difficult for her.[8] She assessed this as "stupid" and described how she solved her problem:

Monica: And . . . and I felt in the trial that they were insulting my intelligence quite a bit, you know, the way the defense attorney was trying to confuse me and say all these really dumb things.
Author: How did you deal with that?
Monica: Hmmm? Oh, I just answered, [focused on the questions] really simply . . . instead of getting confused, 'cause [what] I'm supposed to do is get confused, I don't know. It's really (pause) stupid.

Answering the questions "really simply," Monica was able to focus on describing what she recalled to have happened. She avoided becoming emotionally involved in defending herself against the defense attorney's assertion that she accepted a ride from the defendant because she was a prostitute. . . .

While focusing on questions may not appear to entail active negotiation of interaction, the cognitive control exerted to carry out this strategy should not be underestimated. Survivors are invested in the way they are represented to the friends, family members, jurors, and judges who sit and listen in the courtroom. Not addressing the overarching picture painted by a defense attorney means letting it stand unaltered before them. It also requires effort for survivors to disattend the context of questions, because doing so is so central to making sense of utterances in regular social interaction. . . .

Maintaining Control Over Emotions and the Physical Manifestations of Feeling. When some survivors experienced the growing intensity of their feelings, but did not perceive them as threatening to erupt, they focused on maintaining a calm outward appearance, hoping that it would help them keep their cool. By representing themselves in a way that was consistent with ideal notions of witnesses, survivors tried to alter *what* they were feeling. They engaged in deep acting (Hochschild 1979, 1983). For example, Anna, a black 28-year-old raped by her ex-boyfriend, swallowed her profanity and gritted her teeth in an attempt to turn her anger into something else. . . .

In some cases, survivors' efforts worked and the intensity of their unwanted feelings did not increase before the immediate irritant dissipated. However, many survivors eventually found themselves fighting against an intense urge to yell, cry, vomit, and shake—physical manifestations of their intense feelings. . . .

Joanna, a white college student raped by a faculty member, provides a good example of someone who held emotions at bay until the circumstances changed so that she no longer felt the need to present a particular demeanor in the courtroom. Toward the end of a strenuous cross-examination she was very angry, frustrated, and nauseous with emotional discomfort. However, she fought back tears (which would make her true feelings apparent) until the defendant walked out of the courtroom in order to deny him continued power over her. At the point she allowed her self-control to dissolve, no observers who had any bearing on the outcome of the case were present:

> I felt like it was very demeaning the entire time um, and I felt awful on top of it, but I told myself that I wasn't gonna let myself break down in front of them [the defendant and his attorney]. [. . .] I felt like um, I guess I felt like he had seen me vulnerable too much before and I was vulnerable before and he hurt me and that I wasn't gonna let this attorney intimidate me to the point that I would break down and cry. [. . . .] [After the judge ordered the courtroom cleared] I turned to my attorney who just said stay there, stay seated, I was still in the witness chair, um, and then as soon as of course he [the defendant] walked out the courtroom I lost it (laughs).

. . . Despite survivors' talk about needing to meet cultural expectations that real victims are distraught there was very little indication that survivors cultivated such displays once testimony was underway. Most were more concerned about the difficulties of recovering from a complete loss of composure associated with their feelings of pain, anger, and fear. However, two survivors in the study recalled actually making their feelings available to the court audience in order to enhance their credibility.

Donna, a white 30-year-old raped by an acquaintance, went to trial twice. The first trial ended in a hung jury. During that trial, Donna maintained full control over her emotions and testified in a calm, almost stoic manner. After her assailant was released, Donna became concerned that her stoicism during her testimony in the first trial was not believable in the eyes of the jury. She concluded that her fear of the defendant and the pain of the rape needed to be visible if the case went to trial again. Thus, Donna decided that she would "have to lose it" when testifying again. With this in mind, before going to court, she prepared herself psychologically to allow her emotions free rein. Her testimony in the second trial was very tearful:

Donna: I cried on the stand and told them what he had said, and [I] broke down every time I had to say "fuck."

Author: Now was that calculated on your part?

Donna: No, I had gone over the testimony that I knew I was gonna give, and I figured that I was . . . there was a part I was just gonna have to lose it on, and I figured that was gonna be it and that's about the part that I did start to cry, and they called a recess and . . . and handed me some water and calmed me down and then went on from there. But I figured that I was gonna have to 'cause otherwise they weren't gonna believe anything.

When Jennifer, a white 31-year-old raped by an acquaintance, testified at trial, she recalled that on one occasion she deliberately tried to perform her fear of the defendant for the jury. It is striking to consider her differentiation of the honest part of her emotion, that which was responsive to the defendant, from that which was a conscious extension:

Jennifer: I had dressed real prim and proper again as they would put it, and I just [tried] not to look at anyone. I didn't want to look at Mr. T. [the defendant], but at the same time I was aware that if I called him *Mr. T.* they would take it wrong. [I] just basically [was] trying to radiate the personality that you can believe me. I wasn't aware of how I was doing it, I [thought] if I continue telling the truth they'll believe me.

Author: Why did you not want to look at him?

Jennifer: Because at that point I was feeling a slip on my control of my emotions, and I also felt that if I didn't look at him, that was also conveying that I can't stand to look at this guy 'cause of what he did to me. So there was [an] honest part of it

'cause I didn't want to look at him, and also the conscious decision that if I could convey that by not looking at him that'll help the case.

. . . While there were no cultural incentives to express anger openly in the courtroom, there were certainly personal reasons for survivors to allow the intensity of this emotion to develop. Engaging in deep acting and becoming pro-actively angry helped some survivors concentrate on the business of the court in the face of other feelings. Nurturing anger displaced fear, anxiety, and embarrassment. However, nurturing the emotion did not necessarily mean allowing it full public expression, which would conflict with cultural ideals of credible victims and witnesses and possibly interfere with a survivor's ability to testify.

Below, Arlene, a white 34-year-old raped by a stranger, describes how she created an emotional space in which she had control. She chose to let herself feel her rage to avoid being nervous and to keep other feelings at bay. Note the distinction she makes between feeling the emotion in a controlled way and displaying it to the court— that is, being "enraged":

> I had a good idea of how to create a . . . that kind of space for myself. Not only by what I did, but how (fades out). I was very nervous and um, found what it was to like [to] let my rage take over. I wasn't like enraged at all, on the stand, I was very clear. A couple of times I got angry, but um, I was able to stay very focused on why I was there and very clear about what I was doing and not let my feelings get in the way.

. . . Those who chose to be angry, or let themselves become angry, were shielded from defense efforts to arouse different types of emotion in them and to break their flow (Clark 1990). . . .

Two other survivors in this sample also reported that becoming angry allowed them to bring themselves under emotional control when it otherwise seemed quite impossible. Below, in a lengthy passage, Lauren, a white law student raped by a stranger, describes falling apart when she was asked to identify her clothes, then moving to a still intense but more even emotional keel. In anger, she overcame her fear of the defendant, which brought on her uncontrollable tears. She found this emotional transformation exhilarating:

> . . . And finally just kind of just fell in on me just what all this stuff meant, and I finally got the courage up and was getting mad at this point. I stopped crying and started gettin' mad, and [I] wanted to look at [the defendant] so I did. There was a desk that they were sitting at, there was like a stack of files or whatever, and he was trying to slump down in his chair and hide behind those files. They asked me to identify him in court, and asked me if I was sure that was him. And I was able to look at him, and say yes it was, I felt that it was him. Then it started feeling exhilarating, 'cause I saw that I'd won the jurors over um, that they believed me. [. . .] Knowing that I was in control, I think that was where it went exhilarating. I didn't have to be afraid of him, and all that went through my head. It's like, "I don't have to be afraid of you!" I saw that he was cowering, trying to hide, and then I finished up and I walked out of the courtroom and I was jumping up and down and screaming. It was just, "Yeah!" outside. . . . It was like going to Disneyworld ten times over to feel everything like that. It's the best thing I've ever had in my life, I think, at the end.

Essentially, Lauren's cultivation of feelings of anger allowed her to overcome the feel-ings associated with the assault which led to her breakdown on the witness stand, thereby threatening her ability to testify. However, her description also highlights the fact that for some survivors, testifying is part of the healing process, in spite of its draining properties. In facing her assailant, Lauren was able to hold him up against the terrifying image she recalled and reject it. This shift from fear to anger underscores the social construction of emotion (Shott 1979). In Goffman's (1967) terms, the court event gave Lauren the opportunity to witness the defendant in wrong face. This gave her the upper hand in their tacit interaction and led her to reject feelings associated with being dominated. Cowering and trying to hide from her, the defendant was not behaving like a rapist and was not worthy of her fear and tears. Through her anger, Lauren is asserting her position relative to the defendant, conveying her evaluation of his moral worth and her own (Clark 1990). Without the opportunity to testify, it would have been a very long time before Lauren felt like "going to Disneyworld ten times over." Several other survivors discussed the need to confront their assailant. For them, testifying was a necessary hardship on the road to mental health. For them, the potential costs of expressing anger are far outweighed by the personal satisfaction of doing so (Cahill and Eggleston 1994).

Interpersonal Emotion Management. Several survivors who had supporters in the courtroom engaged in interactions with them to bring negative emotions under control. These supporters formed a team (Goffman 1959; Konradi 1996a, 1996b) invested in maintaining the survivor's face in her ongoing interaction with the prosecutor and defense attorney. Interactions between survivors and teammates were completely nonverbal and initiated with eye contact. They did not appear to be noticed by others present. . . . Interactions with family members, friends, and legal personnel, all of whom believed the survivor, assisted her in remaining in face and were a source of positive emotions.

During direct-examination, and specifically while giving their descriptions of the assault, interactions with supporters helped survivors keep at bay embarrassment associated with testifying publicly about details of the assault and fear associated with relating their rape experience and seeing the defendant. . . .

During cross-examination, nonverbal interaction with supporters provided an opportunity for survivors to momentarily disengage from their troubling interaction with the defense attorney, which aroused frustration and anger. . . .

Sandra's courtroom team, her sister and two rape crisis counselors/friends, were more expressive than most. When the badgering of the defense attorney made Sandra, a white college student raped by an acquaintance, feel that her loss of composure was imminent, she turned her eyes to them. Her sister demonstrated her encouragement with a hand signal as well as through eye contact. This helped Sandra re-focus, suppress her frustration with the interaction, her fear of the jury, her anger at the attorney, and proceed with her testifying task. When Sandra was unable to suppress these emotions and lost her composure, she again looked to her supporters to regain control and recover her face. By following the nonverbal cues they gave her, she was able to modulate her emotional expression—suppressing her tears and returning to a normal breathing pattern—and pull herself together:

> [During cross-examination] I was looking at [the DA]. I kept eye contact with [the DA], and when I started to get a little upset, I would look at [Sister], and

[Sister] would like do this (making a fist with one hand over her stomach area). You know, like "Right on Sandra!" and stuff like that. And so when I started crying, I looked up at [Sister]. And then [two rape crisis counselors/friends] were there [sitting near her], and they were going, you know, doing the breathing thing (breathing slowly and deeply in an exaggerated manner). And they're doing that, so I started to do that.

Thus, Sandra modulated her emotion through direct coaching. . . .

As these examples show, many survivors were overcome by undesired emotions despite their best efforts to shape what they were feeling and suppress the intensity of their feelings. For the reasons described above, they attempted to recover themselves as quickly as possible when this happened. They looked to their supporters and asked the court for tissues, water, or breaks from questioning. Prosecutors and judges met survivors requests, and occasionally judges offered survivors access to back rooms where they might retreat for a few minutes. Thus, they supplied survivors with "time-outs during which they had an opportunity for role release, specifically release from formal display rules" (Rafaeli and Sutton 1989, p. 13). On most occasions, survivors were able to gather themselves and resume testimony in a short period of time.

Survivors generally perceived the behavior of legal personnel to be displays of kindness in the face of their obvious discomfort. The greatest number of unsolicited references to the role of judges in the legal proceedings were made in connection to their efforts to help survivors who were in distress. That is, survivors perceived the behavior of judges and prosecutors to be consistent with the margin of sympathy to which they were entitled (Clark 1987).

However, a close examination of two cases in this study demonstrate that rape survivors' emotion management is essential to the smooth functioning of court. . . .

Judges and prosecutors need to believe that survivors are in control of their faculties in order to believe that the mission of the court is being met. Thus, they facilitate survivor's efforts to manage the intensity of their emotions. Prosecutors must believe that survivors can understand what is asked and have the capacity to respond. Despite their interest in tearful victim-like performances from survivors, prosecutors also must have confidence that a survivor can, where appropriate, support the prosecution's case. This becomes questionable when a survivor is in tears and breathing irregularly. Judges further need to avoid lengthy delays that will prolong legal proceedings in backlogged court facilities. They need witnesses to recognize and act within a legal-rational framing of the situation rather than a therapeutic-emotive framing (Goffman 1974). Thus, judges and prosecutors monitor survivors' emotional displays and facilitate recovery from breakdowns that threaten the continuation of interaction. Most of the time, the survivor's own focus on maintaining face and success with suppressing the expression of emotions meets the needs of prosecutors and judges. When intense feelings lead to losses of control, small acts of assistance follow. I suggest that when a survivor is unable to achieve control, prosecutors and judges will do more. . . .

Discussion and Policy Recommendations

. . .

Policy Recommendations

Within the context of the courtroom, prosecutors appear to be primarily concerned with surface expressions of emotion—such as tears, tones of voice, and facial expressions—that are available to the judge and jury and give the appearance of feelings of pain, terror, and anger. Likewise, they appear to be interested in controlled emotional displays: tears without convulsive weeping and tears that can be brought to a halt through the application of tissues, water, and minor time-outs. A desire for surface-level expression of emotion is inconsistent with the emotional intensity of much testimony as it is recounted by most survivors in this study. The pain, anger, and terror associated with seeing one's assailant, reliving the assault, seeing one's parents' pain, and so forth, are intensely felt. Rape survivors report expending a great deal of energy to manage deep-seated feelings in order to carry out the responsibilities of their witness role. Their apparent "rationality" and calm demeanor (which is at odds with prosecutors' expectations for "victims of rape") is *achieved* in order to protect their selves and is not a dispassionate emotional state (Pierce 1996). Their anger, which likewise is inappropriate from a feeling rule standpoint, may be what stands between their coherent testimony and incoherent sobbing.

Prosecutors must accept the fact that while they can inform survivors of the emotional displays that are most likely to convince a jury, they cannot script survivors' emotions (Zurcher 1985). Survivors will, out of necessity, work to protect their selves. As Thoits points out, "research has long shown that uncontrolled venting of emotion is not beneficial to individuals" (1996, p. 98). Prosecutors can either work with or against this reality. I believe that prosecutors will secure the best performances from their witnesses by assisting them with their perceived needs (Martin and Powell 1994; Konradi 1997). If prosecutors would reconceptualize the nature of emotions in the courtroom in accordance with these findings, it would have three important effects. First, by helping mitigate emotional threats, prosecutors might encourage the cooperation of rape survivors with their efforts to present a particular emotional display. Second, survivors' cooperation might increase the success of prosecution. Third, prosecutors might enhance the legitimacy of the criminal justice system by working to reduce the perception of the "second assault" among rape survivors.

There are several aspects to the process of mitigating emotional threats. By virtue of their organizational roles, prosecutors are positioned to define the courtroom situation for witnesses called by the state. Through pre-court interaction with witnesses, prosecutors can depict the witness role and the roles of others with whom the witness will interact, the formal and informal rules of interaction, and identify the audiences for the witness's court performances and what will influence them. Sometimes prosecutors prepare rape survivors well ahead of court events, but many times . . . this information is only provided when court events are in process (Konradi 1997). In addition, information about influencing the audience is often given at the expense of information about the survivors' place in interaction and her ability to shape its development (Konradi 1997). When prosecutors do not thoroughly inform rape survivors, they contribute to the survivors' dis-ease (Mills and Kleinman 1988) and anger as well as their efforts to regain a superior position relative to the defendant and defense attorney (Clark 1990). From the standpoint of securing convictions, this is counterproductive. It works against the key witness's desire to accommodate display and feeling rules that are consistent with what prosecutors' believe jurors expect from rape victims. Prosecutors could facilitate rape survivors' cooperation with their emotional agenda by educating them thoroughly before court events.

In cross-examination, defense attorneys typically do not follow face-saving rituals and, moreover, employ emotion-provoking language and questioning patterns. Disabusing rape survivors of any expectation that cross-examination will have the "normal" ritual qualities of conversation or that they will be extended sympathy by the defense attorney should assist them in avoiding or at least anticipating feelings of shame, embarrassment, and hurt.

Clearly, the defendant and the defense attorney are sources of intense feeling which compete for survivors' attention whether or not they are in conversation with her. To lessen their impact, prosecutors can alert survivors to strategies for avoiding their gaze. Prosecutors can ensure that the survivor has someone who will provide friendly eye contact by assisting supporters in finding seats that are out of the line of sight of the defendant. Prosecutors can also introduce an alternative audience toward whom the rape survivor can direct her responses (such as an advocate) if she wishes to turn away from the defendant or defense attorney. In the event that a survivor does not have a support network, it is in the prosecutor's best interest to assist her in securing an advocate through local agencies. If prosecutors are aware that survivors are in counseling, they can encourage them to work on mentally erasing or diminishing the defendant (Vacchs 1993). Prosecutors can also avoid contributing to sudden rushes of emotion by showing survivors photographs and other physical evidence before they introduce them into the courtroom. Moreover, prosecutors could give survivors a great deal of confidence by formalizing "organizational tolerance of 'time-out' emotional expression" (Zurcher 1985, p. 201). In concrete terms, prosecutors could give survivors a nonverbal cue that they can use when they are in trouble, are close to losing emotional control, and desperately need a break. It is very doubtful that these three mitigation tactics will eliminate the surface expression of emotions from the courtroom; however, they should make the management of interaction somewhat less difficult for survivors and make it easier for them to align with prosecutorial concerns about emotional expression. . . .

ACKNOWLEDGMENTS

I thank the women who shared their experiences of prosecuting their assailants with me and Laura Meizel for her excellent transcription of their accounts. In addition to three anonymous reviewers, the following people provided invaluable feedback on various drafts of this paper: Martha Copp, Mary Beth Krouse, Christine Mattley, Josie Mendez Negrete, Barry Ochrach, Pamela Roby, Steve Rubenstein, Nancy Stoller, and Norma Wikler. Funding which supported this study was provided by the Society for the Psychological Study of Social Issues, the Hattie M. Strong Foundation, TDK Electronics, the Social Sciences Division and Feminist Studies FRA at the University of California—Santa Cruz, and the Ohio University College of Arts and Sciences and Department of Sociology & Anthropology.

NOTES

1. All the survivors who reported this type of response to photographs and clothing said that they had not seen these materials prior to court.
2. Cindy is a white 37-year-old raped by a stranger. Connie is a white woman in her fifties raped by a stranger.
3. It is possible that "they" in this quotation refers to the defendant as well as the defense attorney. That is, the defense attorney traps and continues to torment the rape survivor for the defendant. This would be consistent with survivors' experience of paralysis when seeing the defendant, described earlier.
4. I discuss the influence of television on survivors' legal consciousness elsewhere at greater length (Konradi 1996b).
5. See Sanday (1996) and Schafran (1985) for a discussion of these stereotypes.
6. However, the success of this particular effort was limited by standard legal practice. Only one survivor, whom the prosecuting attorney felt was legally due protection from retaliation, was successful in this effort.

7. The hesitation in the quotation indicates her continued discomfort discussing oral sex.
8. Monica is white and was raped by a stranger.

REFERENCES

Bart, Pauline and Patricia O'Brien. 1985. *Stopping Rape: Successful Survivor Strategies.* New York: Pergamon Press.

Bohmer, Carol and A. Blumberg. 1975. "Twice Traumatized: The Rape Victim and the Court." *Judicature* 58: 391–99.

Cahill, Spencer E. and Robin Eggleston. 1994. "Managing Emotions in Public: The Case of Wheelchair Users." *Social Psychology Quarterly* 57: 300–12.

Caignon, Denise and Gail Groves (eds.). 1987. *Her Wits about Her: Self-defense Success Stories by Women.* New York: Harper and Row.

Clark, Candace. 1990. "Emotions and Micropolitics in Everyday Life: Some Patterns and Paradoxes of Place." Pp. 305–33 in *Research Agendas in the Sociology of Emotions,* edited by Theodore Kemper. Buffalo: State University of New York Press.

———. 1987. "Sympathy, Biography, and Sympathy Margin." *American Journal of Sociology* 93: 290–321.

Frohmann, Lisa. 1991. "Discrediting Victims' Allegations of Sexual Assault: Prosecutorial Accounts of Case Rejections." *Social Problems* 38: 213–26.

———. 1997. "Complaint Filing Interviews and the Constitution of the Organizational Structure: Understanding the Limitations of Rape Reform." *Hastings Women's Law Journal* 8: 365–400.

Goffman, Erving. 1974. *Frame Analysis: An Essay on the Organization of Experience.* Boston: Northeastern University Press.

———. 1967. *Interaction Ritual: Essays on Face-to-Face Behavior.* New York: Pantheon Books.

———. 1959. *The Presentation of Self in Everyday Life.* Garden City, NY: Doubleday.

Greenberg, M. and R. B. Ruback. 1992. *After the Crime: Victim Decision Making.* New York: Plenum Press.

Hochschild, Arlie. 1983. *The Managed Heart: Commercialization of Human Feeling.* Berkeley: University of California Press.

———. 1979. "Emotion Work, Feeling Rules, and Social Structure." *American Journal of Sociology* 85: 551–75.

Holmstrom, Lynda L. and Ann W. Burgess. 1983. *The Victim of Rape: Institutional Reactions.* New Brunswick, NJ: Transaction.

Kleck, Gary and S. Sayles. 1990. "Rape and Resistance." *Social Problems* 37: 149–62.

Konradi, Amanda. 1996a. "Preparing to Testify: Rape Survivors Negotiating the Criminal Justice Process." *Gender & Society* 10: 404–32.

———. 1996b. "Understanding Rape Survivors' Preparations for Court: Accounting for the Influence of Legal Knowledge, Cultural Stereotypes, and Prosecutor Contact." *Violence Against Women* 2: 25–62.

———. 1997. "Too Little, Too Late: Prosecutors' Pre-court Preparation of Rape Survivors." *Law & Social Inquiry* 22: 1101–54.

Lees, Sue. 1996. *Ruling Passions: Sexual Violence, Reputation, and the Law.* Philadelphia: Open University Press.

Lurigio, A. and P. Resnick. 1990. "Healing the Psychological Wounds of Criminal Victimization: Predicting Postcrime Distress and Recovery." Pp. 50–68 in *Victims of Crime: Problems, Policies, and Programs,* edited by A. Lurigio, W. Skogan, and R. Davis. Newbury Park, CA: Sage.

Madigan, Lee and Nancy Gambel. 1989. *The Second Rape: Society's Continued Betrayal of the Victim.* New York: Lexington Books.

Martin, Patricia Yancey and Marlene Powell. 1994. "Accounting for the 'Second Assault': Legal Organizations and Rape Victims." *Law and Social Inquiry* 19: 853–90.

Mills, Trudy and Sherryl Kleinman. 1988. "Emotions, Reflexivity, and Action: An Interactionist Analysis." *Social Forces* 66: 1009–27.

O'Brien, Martin. 1994. "The Managed Heart Revisited: Health and Social Control." *Sociological Review* 42: 393–413.

Rafaeli, Anat and Robert I. Sutton. 1989. "The Expression of Emotion in Organizational Life." *Research on Organizational Behavior* 11: 1–42.

Sanday, Peggy R. 1996. *A Woman Scorned: Acquaintance Rape on Trial.* New York: Doubleday.

Schafran, Lynn Hecht. 1985. "Mary, Eve, and Superwoman: How Stereotypes About Women Influence Judges." *Judges Journal* 24: 12–17, 48–53.

Shott, Susan. 1979. "Emotion and Social Life: A Symbolic Interactionist Analysis." *American Journal of Sociology* 84: 1317–34.

Thoits, Peggy. 1996. "Managing the Emotions of Others." *Symbolic Interaction* 19: 85–109.

Vacchs, Alice. 1993. *Sex Crimes: Ten Years in the Front Lines Prosecuting Rapists and Confronting Their Collaborators.* New York: Random House.

Williams, L. 1984. "The Classic Rape: What Do Victims Report?" *Social Problems* 31: 459–67.

Zurcher, Louis A. 1985. "The War Game: Organizational Scripting and the Expression of Emotion." *Symbolic Interaction* 8: 191–206.

QUESTIONS FOR DISCUSSION

1. Does the U.S. court system fail raped women? Are rape survivors' difficulties in court an example of gender bias?
2. What do we gain by recognizing the full scope of victims' participation in the criminal justice process?
3. Do you agree with Konradi's policy recommendations?

THE SOCIAL WEB

- The Bureau of Justice Statistics is a comprehensive resource for information about current crime trends and crime-related expenditures: www.ojp.usdoj.gov/bis.
- Prison Activist Resource Center (PARC) is committed to exposing and challenging the institutionalized racism of the criminal justice system. PARC provides support for educators, activists, prisoners, and prisoners' families. PARC's work includes building networks for action and producing materials that expose human rights violations while fundamentally challenging the rapid expansion of the prison industrial complex: www.prisonactivist.org.
- A useful interactive flowchart showing the process of prosecution has been posted by Cecil Greek at Florida State University: www.fsu.edu/~crimdo/cj-flowchart.html.

- The Keck Center Clearinghouse at Stanford University makes available electronic versions of numerous reports concerning women's access to and representation in the profession of law. These include reports produced by the Commission on Women in the Profession of the American Bar Association: www.womenlaw.stanford.edu.

QUESTIONS FOR DEBATE

1. Would Litton and Mitchell agree with Donziger's argument that fear motivates criminal justice policy?

2. Konradi and Lofquist both explore the role of cultural narratives in shaping the behavior of prosecutors. Can they successfully prosecute crime without paying attention to the frameworks used by potential jurors?

3. Does Lamberth supply empirical evidence to support Lofquist's argument that normal policing is driven by stereotypes?

4. Lifton and Mitchell and Konradi consider whether victims' perspectives should guide criminal justice policy in their analyses of the death penalty and sexual assault prosecution. To what degree do you think the system should be responsive to crime victims?

5. Would Donziger support the growth of Corrections Corporation of America and other private prison companies described by Yeoman? Why or why not?

6. Are problems of racial and gender bias likely to be greater or smaller in privatized corrections situations?

Chapter 11
Illness and Health Care

Contents

Learning Objectives

By the end of this chapter you should be able to:

- Recognize how the authors use one or more of the major perspectives to explore illness and health care.
- Explore how inequalities in the health care system are shaped by inequalities of race, gender, and class.
- Identify ways that illness and health care are socially constructed.
- Describe various consequences of inequalities in the health care system.
- Analyze how individuals contribute to injustice in the health care system through their everyday behavior.
- Explain how social systems and institutions perpetuate an unequal distribution of health care.

Defining the Problem

More than a century ago, the famous German sociologist Max Weber argued that a society's level of social equality should be assessed in terms of the "life chances" of its people, that is, the opportunities available to an individual to obtain such basic human needs as adequate nutrition, education, and housing. It is hard to imagine a life chance more significant than the ability to obtain health care. Yet illness is not distributed evenly across American society. Patterns of disease, as well as the availability of health care services, reflect larger social patterns of inequality. Health care costs have never been greater. They pose a serious threat to the economic stability of many of our nation's businesses, families, and individuals. Issues related to illness and health care are increasingly gaining the attention of scholars of social problems.

Some social problems researchers focus on the cultural context in which illness and health care occur. They are interested in how defining problems increases the power of the medical field in our lives. They look at the ways that specific human behaviors and physical conditions become "medicalized" —that is, they study the social processes through which behaviors and conditions are identified as problems that can be fixed through medical treatment. These researchers show that the definition of a medical issue is historically specific. For example, anxiety, drug use, obesity, gambling, poor school performance, and children's bad behavior are all seen as problems for which medical science can offer "treatments" or "cures." In the past, these problems were seen as individual human failures. Today, there are even medical solutions to the "problem" of unattractiveness, such as cosmetic surgery, treatments for baldness, and systems for removing unwanted hair.

Other social problems investigators focus on the ways that health care reflects major economic disparities. Medical resources are not evenly distributed across the globe. Wealthy nations have greater power to decide how funds, technology, personnel, and medicines are distributed. These countries have the ability to define research and treatment priorities. In addition, capitalism plays a central role in how health care services are developed and managed. Major corporations, especially pharmaceutical and biotechnology companies, serve as a significant source of funding for medical research and treatment options. They are most likely to fund the development of treatments that are highly profitable. The distribution of health care resources does not occur on the basis of global medical needs. Instead, it reflects the economic interests of the world's wealthiest countries and medical corporations.

Another major area of concern to sociologists is the effectiveness of the health care delivery system in the United States. They focus on the implications of operating in a for-profit model. The costs of health care that must be borne by employers, the government, and individuals are enormous, while certain corporations, especially pharmaceutical and biotechnology companies, make tremendous profits. Researchers concerned with health care delivery are also likely to examine the inequalities in how health care is distributed in the United States, especially whether it varies according to class and race. What are the barriers that prevent all people from receiving the same level of health care? Do these barriers affect people's ability to be healthy? Other sociologists look at the efficacy of our current model of health care. They investigate whether the patients' well-being is being adequately addressed within the institutional structures of medical systems. Do the policies and procedures of health care organiza-

tions promote the patients' interests? Has the current system of medical care become so highly bureaucratized that the original goals of health care have been lost?

Finally, many social problems researchers take a micro approach when studying illness and health care. They may examine the various roles that people assume in a medical care setting along with their accompanying set of norms for behavior, demeanor, and emotions. Patients are required to play the "sick role," which includes losing independence, obeying authority, exhibiting gratitude, and being compliant. Researchers often explore what happens when patients step out of the sick role to assert their own knowledge, competencies, and rights. They may emphasize the ways that the doctor-patient interaction is constructed to assert the ultimate authority of the physician. Still others focus on the issues and needs of nurses, looking at the often conflicting and overwhelming demands placed on nurses by physicians and hospital administrators. The conditions in which hospital nurses must operate lead to a high rate of job burnout and account for the nationwide shortage of nurses, which has reached crisis-level proportions.

Scope of the Problem

Americans are living longer than ever before in history.[1] In 2000, life expectancy at birth was 76.9 years. White females have the highest life expectancy (79.9 years), followed by Black females (74.7 years). The life expectancy for White males is 74.6 years, and for Black males, 67.8 years.

The racial disparity seen in other institutions in the United States is especially

---

[1]Unless otherwise noted, all data are derived from "Health, United States, 2002." National Center for Health Statistics, Centers for Disease Control and Prevention, U.S. Department of Health and Human Services.

apparent in basic indicators of health and well-being. In 1998, 7.6 percent of infants born in the United States suffered from low birthweight, the highest rate since 1973. Although the low birthweight rates were comparable for Whites and Hispanics (6.6 and 6.4 percent, respectively), the low birthweight rate for Blacks was 13.2 percent. In 1998, the national infant mortality rate was 7.2 deaths per 1,000 live births. For Whites and Hispanics, the infant mortality rate was 6 per 1,000 live births, while the rate for Blacks was 13.7 per 1,000 live births. The national death rate for children age one to four years was 34 per 100,000 children. For Whites and Hispanics, this death rate was 30 per 100,000, and for Blacks the death rate for young children was 61 per 100,000. A similar pattern is evident for maternal mortality rates.[2] Between 1991 and 1997, the pregnancy-related mortality ratio (PRMR) for the United States was 11.5 per 100,000. For Whites and Hispanics, the PRMR was 7.3 and 10.3, respectively. The maternal mortality rate for Blacks during that same time period was 29.6 per 100,000.

Economic status also profoundly affects people's health. Those families who live in poverty or near poverty are more likely to have health care risk factors, such as having no regular source of medical care, delaying medical care, being uninsured, and having unmet medical needs.[3] More children from families living above the poverty threshold are in excellent health (63 percent) than children from poor families (40 percent).

---

[2]"Fact Sheet, 5/11/2001." National Center for Chronic Disease Prevention and Health Promotion, Centers for Disease Control and Prevention, U.S. Department of Health and Human Services.

[3]"Summary Health Statistics for U.S. Children: National Health Interview Survey, 1977." Vital and Health Statistics, Series 10, Number 203. National Center for Health Statistics, Centers for Disease Control and Prevention, U.S. Department of Health and Human Services.

Americans do not have equal access to the health care system. In 2000, 17 percent of the nonelderly population of the United States—40.5 million people—had no health insurance coverage. Twelve percent of children under age 18 had no health insurance coverage, while 26 percent of children from poor families lacked coverage. Differences in health insurance are also greatly based on race. While 15.2 percent of Whites live without health coverage, 20 percent of Blacks, 35.4 percent of Hispanics, and 38 percent of American Indians do not have health care insurance coverage. Between 1995 and 2000, only about 70 percent of the U.S. population had some form of private health insurance. Ninety percent of those people were covered by workplace-related insurance plans.

Medicare is the federal program designed to cover health care costs for the elderly and disabled. In 2000, the federal government spent $222 billion to cover the 40 million people enrolled in Medicare. Although the elderly are the highest consumers of prescription drugs, Medicare paid only 2 percent of prescription drug costs in 2000. Medicaid is the program jointly funded by federal and state governments that is designed to cover the health care costs of the poorest Americans. Nearly half (47 percent) of the people enrolled in Medicaid are under 21. The disabled and elderly, while constituting only one-quarter of Medicaid recipients, are responsible for 71 percent of all Medicaid expenditures.

Despite the absence of a comprehensive public health insurance program, the United States spends a larger share of its gross domestic product (GDP) on health care costs than any other industrialized nation in the world. In 2000, the United States spent 13.2 percent of its GDP on health care, amounting to $1.3 trillion. This represents a 7 percent increase in just one year. The federal government spent 22.5 percent of its total expenditures on health care costs; states spent an additional 14.8 percent of their budgets on health care.

Expenditures on hospital care accounted for nearly one-third of all medical expenditures in 2000. Physician care accounted for 22 percent of total expenditures; prescription drugs and nursing home services accounted for 9 and 7 percent of total expenditures, respectively. Between 1995 and 2000, the average annual rate of increase for prescription drug expenditures was 15 percent, constituting the highest increase in all health care costs.

Perspectives on the Problem

Sociologists studying health care from a *conflict perspective* would look at the implications of capitalism on the funding structures, research priorities, and quality of services provided by our health care system. They would argue that patterns of inequality based on class, race, and gender can be seen in how health care is provided. Sociologists using a *functionalist perspective* would look at the ways that disease causes disruption in social life, undermining families, business, and other social networks. They would examine how the strengths of the current health care system can be maximized to improve the delivery of health care. Sociologists using a *constructionist perspective* would look at the cultural ways we view disease and illness. They would explore the processes by which certain conditions come to be seen as medical problems and how the ways that we define diseases affect our responses to them. Finally, sociologists using an *interactionist perspective* look at the multiple roles and interactions that take place in medical situations, including the ways that patients and physicians define and respond to one another.

Connecting the Perspectives

Robert Hanneman uses a conflict perspective to argue that, as long as private employment–based health insurance determines our access to quality care, the health care system in the United States will remain inefficient, ineffective, and expensive. Ken Silverstein also uses a conflict perspective to further explore the relationship between business interests and health care research in the United States. Focusing specifically on the multi-billion-dollar pharmacology industry, he argues that the profit motive comes before all other considerations in the research and development of new medicines. Using a social constructionist perspective, Joshua Wolf Shenk looks at the ways that social problems can be constructed as medical problems. He explores the implications of defining drug abuse as a medical problem, rather than as a criminal or moral one. David Chambliss takes an interactionist perspective to examine how health care professionals exert their authority in their daily interactions with their patients. Finally, Carol Heimer and Lisa Staffen use an interactionist approach to look at the ways that parents make difficult decisions regarding the health care needs of their children. They argue that gender profoundly affects the ways that we define our responsibilities as they relate to meeting others' needs.

Reading Summaries

In "Your Money or Your Life," Hanneman argues that, although health care has drastically improved in general, the quality of health care given in the United States lags far behind that in other industrialized nations. It is not the state of medical knowledge or lack of technology that creates this problem. Instead, Hanneman claims, it is the state of the business of health care that creates such a disadvantage for so many Americans. As a nation, we spend more on health care costs than do all European countries, yet our health care system is inefficient in meeting the needs of the poor. It is insurance companies, he argues, that determine who will be helped with what kind of help. Health insurance in the United States is primarily private plans that are offered through large employers of full-time, usually middle-class, workers. This leaves millions of Americans, including children, without health insurance. Private insurance companies thus establish health care policies that are designed to meet the needs of the healthiest citizens. Those people who are most likely to require medical care—the nation's poor and low-wage workers—have the least access to health care and the least amount of power to determine what kind of health care system we will all share.

The crucial role of money in determining access to health care is also addressed in "Millions for Viagra, Pennies for Diseases of the Poor." In this reading, Silverstein explores the world of pharmacological research. This is not simply a business, Silverstein argues—it is BIG business, with corporate profits in the billions of dollars annually. The goal of pharmacological research is not to develop new drugs to fight disease, but to make money developing new drugs. Silverstein reminds us that profit does not simply provide research funds; it provides the direction that pharmacological research will take, determining which research will be conducted and which new drugs will be developed. Thus more resources go into researching so-called lifestyle drugs for the problems of middle-class people, such as impotence, baldness, obesity, and toenail fungus. Meanwhile, diseases such as malaria and tuberculosis cause millions of deaths each year, yet receive little research attention from drug companies who are reluctant to develop medicines for poor Third World countries.

Our next reading also examines the interplay between social construction, social problems, and medicine. "An Old City Seeks a New Model" explores different ways of viewing drug use and abuse. Within the past two decades, drug use has been defined by policy makers as a criminal problem, especially when abuse involves the urban poor and minority communities. Such approaches, Shenk argues, are ineffective at curbing drug use and are tremendously expensive to enforce. America's prison population is at an all-time high, and new prisons need to be built across the nation. Mandatory sentencing and other criminal policies to deal with drug abuse accomplish little except clogging the judicial system and costing taxpayers billions of dollars. Shenk discusses a different approach; he presents Baltimore as a city that has found a new and effective way to address drug use. Instead of seeing drug abuse as a *criminal* problem, Baltimore officials are redefining drug abuse as a *medical* problem. Programs and policies seek to treat drug abusers rather than to punish them. This approach has received severe criticism from the federal government because it contradicts current popular views of drug abuse. Shenk's reading is important not only for what it says about drug use, but for demonstrating the significance of social construction in dealing with social problems.

Our fourth reading in this section focuses on the role of health care providers. In "The Patient as Object," Chambliss uses a micro-level symbolic interaction approach to understand interactions between patients and health care providers. He describes the numerous ways that patients become objects to the doctors and nurses in hospital settings. Patients are defined as their diseases ("the colon cancer in room 8"), privacy is nonexistent, and complaints that cannot be clinically explained or controlled are dismissed. On one hand, Chambliss surmises, such objectification is seen as necessary for allowing health care professionals to detach from the suffering of their patients. On the other hand, he argues, being turned into an object strips away patients' dignity and ultimately represents a loss of control over their bodies, their health care, and their eventual recovery (or death). Chambliss calls for redefining patients' rights in such a way as to increase the power of those suffering the effects of injury and disease.

In "The Social Organization of Responsibility in the Hospital and the Home," Heimer and Staffen examine how individuals accept responsibility within the organizational context of the health care system. They begin with the story of Sue and Will, young parents who have an ill, premature baby requiring significant care. Sue and Will take on the responsibility of caring for their infant daughter and completely adjust their lives to make her medical care their central focus. Yet they find that hospital staff are frequently resistant to acknowledge the responsibility that the couple feels for the care of their baby. Doctors and nurses often refuse to recognize the skills that Sue has developed in providing care to the child. Sue, on the other hand, is horrified to see the lack of care and concern on the part of the health care providers and refuses to tolerate their incompetence as an acceptable standard of care for her daughter.

Heimer and Staffen argue that the norms that govern the organization of the health care system either support or undermine individuals' acceptance of personal responsibility. What kinds of messages do doctors and nurses communicate to Sue and Will about their proper place in the care of their daughter? To what degree do they make it possible for the couple to act on their perceived obligations to their daughter? Do Sue and Will feel competent or incompetent as a result of their efforts? Heimer and Staffen use the couple's experiences with the health care system to examine how institutional conditions affect the ways that individuals define their own responsibilities. They believe that we must understand the organizational constraints and opportunities that govern how people make decisions about responsibility before we can discuss the morality of the choices people make.

Heimer and Staffen also argue that responsibilities are allocated differently to different members of the population. Some responsibilities are defined as "fates," as obligations that people cannot escape and that often deplete their personal resources. Other responsibilities are seen as "opportunities." Individuals can choose to take on such responsibilities and are often rewarded for doing so. Heimer and Staffen maintain that gender is often the significant determinant of which responsibility one is given. As a result of social expectations about caregiving, women are more likely than men to have fate-like responsibilities that cannot be denied without raising serious questions about their moral character. Men, on the other hand, have the uncertainties of life greatly absorbed by women's caregiving and are more free to take on responsibilities that bring status and financial rewards.

FOCUSING QUESTIONS

As you read these selections, think about the ways that illness and health care can be seen as social conditions. So-called medical problems are not just issues for physicians, researchers, and insurance executives. What are the social consequences of the ways we think about illness and disease? What are the implications of a health care system that operates according to the principles of capitalism? How do illness and good health reflect social inequality?

47

YOUR MONEY OR YOUR LIFE
Access to Medical Care as a Social Problem

ROBERT A. HANNEMAN

During 1994, the President of the United States proposed that Congress pass legislation that would result in all Americans being covered by medical insurance. Supporters of "universal coverage" argued that access to medical care is a basic social right, but that the high cost of medical care, in effect, denied this right to citizens who did not have medical insurance. Even opponents of the President's proposal agreed that the American medical care system was an "institution in trouble" and that reform was needed. But there were sharp disagreements about how to reform the medical care system. Opponents of the President's proposals raised objections to government intervention into medical care and worried that the cost of providing universal coverage would be too great and would result in higher taxes and federal deficits. Many different proposals were considered, but none were adopted.

Why is it that something as uninteresting as medical insurance has come to be regarded as a national social problem to be debated in Congress? Is the American medical care system really in trouble? If there are serious problems, what are their causes? What can we do about reforming

medical care, and why are there such strong disagreements about what we should do about it?

Public debates about social problems are often complex, emotional, and filled with contradictory truths, half-truths, and outright lies from interested parties. Social scientists need to take a "step back" from the debates and try to see social problems in a broader perspective. The social scientist must seek to understand why social institutions, like medicine, perform the way they do. That is, before we can examine possible solutions, we must try to understand the causes of the problem. To gain a broader perspective on contemporary social problems, it is helpful to make comparisons. What are the problems with American medicine, and what are the trends? Are the problems of American medical care unique, or are they similar to those in other similar societies?

The State of American Medicine: Effectiveness

In part, the problems of contemporary American medical care are the result of its own past success. Over the last 100 years, advances in medicine have been part of the cause of dramatic declines in mortality and disease in the United States and elsewhere. As medical care has become more effective, people have come to believe in it and to expect continuing progress. But, making rapid

Hanneman, Robert. 1999. "Your Money or Your Life: Access to Medical Care as a Social Problem." Pp. 43–47 in *Analyzing Social Problems: Essays and Exercises,* Second Edition, edited by Dana Dunn and David Waller. Saddle River, NJ: Prentice-Hall. Copyright © 1999 by Robert Hanneman. Reprinted with permission from the author.

progress in overcoming health problems is becoming more difficult. In a sense, the "easy" medical problems have already been solved, leaving the difficult ones. We have learned to prevent death and disability from many diseases that used to be major killers. Most of the technologies for dealing with these "old" problems (e.g., smallpox, cholera, polio, tuberculosis) are relatively simple and inexpensive. But, as we have conquered these health problems, we have changed the nature of the health care problems in our population. Medical knowledge, along with other factors, has dramatically reduced the number of people who die very young and has all but eliminated death from many major infectious diseases. As a result, people live much longer now than they did a century ago, and have very different medical problems. Far more of our efforts today go toward the treatment of conditions for which we have only "halfway" technologies. That is, some treatments prolong life and reduce suffering, but do not cure such major killers as heart disease, cancer, pulmonary disease, and other "age-related" conditions.

The health of the American population is excellent by world standards but unexceptional compared to the other advanced nations. Americans do not live quite as long, on average, as people in many European countries (though Americans who do live to be age 65 can expect to live as long as those who do in most European nations). Infant mortality is believed to be a sensitive measure of societal health, because it reflects the health and medical care of both mothers and infants. Infant mortality rates (deaths of persons in the first year of life after a live birth) are higher in the United States than in many European nations. Some comparisons are shown in Figures 1 and 2.

Because of past successes in improving societal health in both the United States and the other wealthy nations, the rate of im-

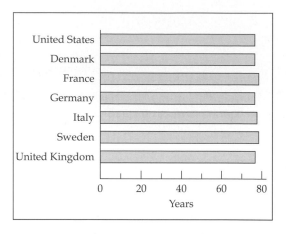

FIGURE 1   Life Expectancy at Birth, 1993. (*Source: Statistical Abstract of the United States, 1993.*)

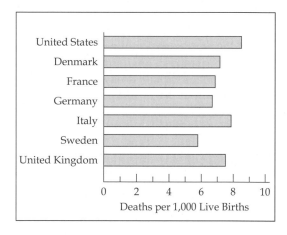

FIGURE 2   Infant Mortality Rates, 1993. (*Source: Statistical Abstract of the United States, 1993.*)

provement in life expectancy and infant mortality have slowed markedly in recent decades. And, in all of the wealthy nations, the average age of the population has been increasing rapidly. As a result, improving population health overall is becoming more difficult, and this trend can be expected to continue into the next millennium.

The State of American Medicine: Cost

One of the major reasons that medical insurance and access to medical care has become a social problem in the United States is financial; many people are questioning if we, as a society, can afford to continue to provide medical care in the same way as our medical problems change and our population ages. Again, to get perspective on the situation, it is useful to make some comparisons. In Figure 3, we can see that the United States spends significantly more of its wealth on medical care than many (actually, all) of the European countries (primarily medical insurance for people with low incomes). But, compared to the European countries, private out-of-pocket payments and private insurance are higher in the United States. In most other wealthy nations, about three quarters of the costs of medical care are paid by government—almost twice as much as in the United States. In 1960, over half of the medical expenditures in the United States came directly from individuals and families. By 1990, only 21.7 percent of the bill was paid directly, and almost 80 percent was paid by insurance, either governmental or private. To understand who gets what medical care in the United States, and why the United States appears to make socially inefficient choices in medical care, we need to understand medical insurance.

Paying the Bill and Making Choices: "She or He Who Pays the Piper, Calls the Tune"

In 1992, we spent an average of $3,094 on medical care for each man, woman, and child in the United States. [See Figure 4.] For a family of four, this amounts to about $12,000; more than one-half the official

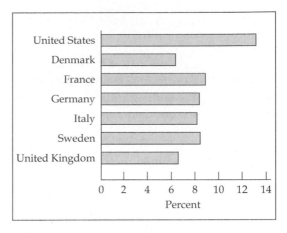

FIGURE 3   Medical Expenditures as a Percentage of GDP, 1993. (*Source: Statistical Abstract of the United States, 1993.*)

poverty line. The average cost of spending a day in the hospital that same year approached $1,000 (U.S. Bureau of the Census, 1993). Without adequate medical insurance, a major accident, illness, or chronic disability is a financial disaster that can place a severe strain on any family. Of course, these figures are only averages. Most young people and people who did not have insurance or high incomes spent less; many people who were older, had the misfortunes of chronic disability, severe accidents or illnesses, and who had good medical insurance spent a great deal more.

Medicare insurance pays much of the bill for older and chronically disabled Americans, who are major consumers of medical care. Medicaid pays much of the bill for persons and families receiving welfare. Persons who do not fall in these categories rely on private medical insurance (usually provided through an employer) and on payments out of pocket. As our population ages and the technology of medicine continues to increase, the costs of Medicare have increased and can be expected to continue to do so. Throughout the 1980s the

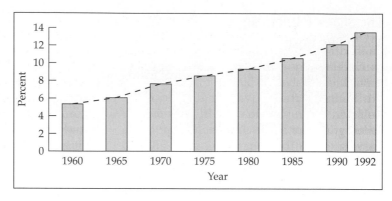

FIGURE 4 U.S. Medical Expenditures as a Percentage of GDP, 1960–1992. (*Source: Statistical Abstract of the United States, 1993.*)

proportion of families living in poverty (and particularly families with young children) in the United States increased, increasing the costs of Medicaid.

For those "in the middle" who rely on private insurance, the 1980s and early 1990s were a difficult time. Large employers have cut back on middle management and permanent employees—in part to avoid the high cost of providing medical insurance. Small employers, particularly in the rapidly growing service industries, provide either limited or no medical benefits. As a result, the proportion of Americans who have no medical insurance (public or private) has been rising rapidly. In 1987, about 31 million Americans (12.9 percent of the population) had no insurance; by 1993, nearly 40 million persons (15.3 percent) had no coverage (U.S. Bureau of the Census, 1993). These Americans at risk of catastrophic medical costs are more likely to be younger working families with children. Those at risk are also disproportionately composed of the less-well-educated and ethnic minorities who are less likely to have permanent and stable employment that provides medical insurance coverage. These patterns of allocation of medical coverage have consequences for the social efficiency of medical care delivery:

getting the largest amount of the kinds of care that preserve life to the people who need it most.

Good medical insurance for older Americans means that they are able to make effective demands on the delivery system. However, the medical conditions of older persons are more likely to be chronic, and difficult and expensive to treat. While effective treatment of age-related conditions may have very important effects on the quality of life, it does not result in dramatic improvements in the length of life. Therefore, these high and rapidly growing expenditures for medical treatment of the aged are reducing the social efficiency of American medicine. But the aged are a growing and politically powerful group, and reform of Medicare will be difficult. Changing the prevailing pattern of treatment for the aged, such as rationing health care, is also a difficult moral issue that raises fundamental questions about our social values.

Government medical insurance for those in poverty clearly does provide services where it is most efficiently consumed: to younger persons, and particularly women and children who are at greater risk for medical problems because of their poverty. However, medical treatment of persons in poverty is severely limited, and it cannot solve the problems of poor education, poor nutrition, and dangerous living conditions. In contrast to the aged, the poor are a politically weak group. Efforts to balance budgets and reduce the size of the government have slowed the growth of Medicaid expenditures, and even further cuts in Medicaid are a possibility in the coming years. But reducing medical aid for the poor may be socially inefficient; the poor are mostly young (almost 30 percent of all children are raised in poverty) and expenditures on the young and poor can improve the overall health of the population at relatively low cost.

Ironically, our best medical insurance coverage (plans provided by private employers) assures that the best and most services are available to those who need them least: persons who have reasonably well-paying jobs, have relatively secure incomes, are well educated and middle aged, and who have lower levels of severe medical problems. Those who fall in the middle— who do not have good jobs but are not officially in poverty—have limited access to either governmental or private insurance. As a result, they consume less medical care than they need. The burden of this inadequate care falls on relatively younger persons and children, where good care can cure effectively and cheaply, and prevent long-term disability. Absence of any medical insurance for this growing group of Americans is also socially inefficient in that failure to provide preventive care will result in even greater and more costly demands on the Medicare system over time.

Looking for Answers

Are American medical care institutions "in crisis"? The answer depends on your perspective. American medicine is among the most technologically advanced in the world and offers remarkable choice and resources to those who can afford it. Yet the trends we have discovered and the comparisons we have made are quite disturbing: American medicine is much more expensive than European systems, and produces little difference in overall societal health. We have seen that the main reason for this is that our medical institutions do a relatively poor job of allocating the most beneficial kinds of care to the people who most need them. The total cost of the system is increasing rapidly with technology and the aging of the population; these increasing costs are leaving more and more middle- and working-class Americans without effective access to medical treatment.

Policy makers in the medical industry and government are searching for answers, and many changes are already occurring that are fundamentally transforming medical institutions in the United States. Government-sponsored medical insurance for the aged and disabled has been one of the most rapid areas of growth in medical expenditure. Attempts are being made to control these cost increases in a number of ways. Insurance premiums charged to covered persons have been increased, and there are proposals to make the benefits received by the insured subject to income taxation. The goal of this plan is to place a greater cost burden on those among the aged and disabled who have high enough incomes to pay more. Government-sponsored medical care and medical insurance for the poor has also been an area of rapid growth in expenditure (Hollingsworth, Hage, and Hanneman, 1990). Here too, efforts are being made to control costs—primarily by limiting the availability of services and making it more difficult to qualify to receive coverage. Private employers are also acting to hold down costs indirectly by providing limited or no medical benefits for temporary and part-time workers, and by excluding from coverage "preexisting" medical conditions (i.e., medical problems that existed when an employee changes jobs).

Both government and industry have moved toward *managed care* and *health maintenance organizations* (HMOs) as a way of organizing medical coverage. These types of plans make specific contracts about what insurance will pay for specific services, and they place restrictions and conditions on certain expensive types of treatments. HMO plans pay the medical care providers specific amounts per person per year, rather than the actual costs of treatments delivered. As a result, the organizations that deliver medical treatments have strong financial incentives to emphasize preventive and basic medical services, and to deemphasize expensive specialty care.

These changes in who pays the bill and how they do it are rapidly changing the way that medical care is organized in the United States. Hospital-based high-technology care based on the use of specialist physicians is becoming a smaller part of our medical care delivery system. Hospitals are increasingly becoming parts of large "chains" managed by medical care corporations. Fewer and fewer physicians operate in private practice, and more and more are basically employees of HMOs and medical corporations. As a result, American consumers of medical care often find that they have fewer choices about their medical treatment and physician. Maintaining access to medical insurance can also be a deciding factor when people compare employment opportunities.

Whether the changes that are already occurring will solve the "crisis" in American medical care institutions is far from certain. What is certain is that changes will continue to occur. You have an important role to play in the direction that these changes take through your choices as a consumer of medical care and as a politically active citizen. The choices that you make are important, because it is "your money or your life."

REFERENCES

Hollingsworth, J. Rogers, Jerald Hage, and Robert A. Hanneman. 1990. *State Intervention in Medical Care: Consequences for Britain, France, Sweden, and the United States, 1890–1970.* Ithaca, NY: Cornell University Press.

U.S. Bureau of the Census. 1993. *Statistical Abstract of the United States: 1993.* Washington, DC: U.S. Government Printing Office.

QUESTIONS FOR DISCUSSION

1. Do you think that the health care system in the United States is in a state of crisis? Why or why not?
2. According to Hanneman, what are the challenges currently faced by the health care system? Are these likely to get worse as time goes on?
3. What do you think are possible solutions to the problems in the U.S. health care system? Can you identify the various stakeholders who would play a role in your solutions? What would be their likely responses to your proposal?

48
_____

MILLIONS FOR VIAGRA,
PENNIES FOR DISEASES OF THE POOR
KEN SILVERSTEIN

Almost three times as many people, most of them in tropical countries of the Third World, die of preventable, curable diseases as die of AIDS. Malaria, tuberculosis, acute lower-respiratory infections—in 1998, these claimed 6.1 million lives. People died because the drugs to treat those illnesses are nonexistent or are no longer effective. They died because it doesn't pay to keep them alive.

Only 1 percent of all new medicines brought to market by multinational pharmaceutical companies between 1975 and 1997 were designed specifically to treat tropical diseases plaguing the Third World. In numbers, that means thirteen out of 1,223 medications. Only four of those thirteen resulted from research by the industry that was designed specifically to combat tropical ailments. The others, according to a study by the French group Doctors Without Borders, were either updated versions of existing drugs, products of military research, accidental discoveries made during veterinary research or, in one case, a medical breakthrough in China.

Certainly, the majority of the other 1,210 new drugs help relieve suffering and prevent premature death, but some of the hottest preparations, the ones that, as the *New York Times* put it, drug companies "can't seem to roll. . . . out fast enough," have absolutely nothing to do with matters of life and death. They are what have come to be called lifestyle drugs—remedies that may one day free the world from the scourge of toenail fungus, obesity, baldness, face wrinkles and impotence. The market for such drugs is worth billions of dollars a year and is one of the fastest-growing product lines in the industry.

The drug industry's calculus in apportioning its resources is cold-blooded, but there's no disputing that one old, fat, bald, fungus-ridden rich man who can't get it up counts for more than half a billion people who are vulnerable to malaria but too poor to buy the remedies they need.

. . .

Western interest in tropical diseases was historically linked to colonization and war, specifically the desire to protect settlers and soldiers. Yellow fever became a target of biomedical research only after it began interfering with European attempts to control parts of Africa. "So obvious was this deterrence . . . that it was celebrated in song and verse by people from Sudan to Senegal," Laurie Garrett recounts in her extraordinary book *The Coming Plague*. "Well into the 1980s schoolchildren in Ibo areas of Nigeria still sang the praises of mosquitoes and the diseases they gave to French and British colonialists."

U.S. military researchers have discovered virtually all important malaria drugs. Chloroquine was synthesized in 1941 after quinine, until then the primary drug to treat the disease, became scarce following Japan's occupation of Indonesia. The discovery of

Ken Silverstein, "Millions for Viagra, Pennies for Diseases of the Poor." Reprinted with permission from the July 19, 1999 issue of *The Nation*.

Mefloquine, the next advance, came about during the Vietnam War, in which malaria was second only to combat wounds in sending U.S. troops to the hospital. With the end of a ground-based U.S. military strategy came the end of innovation in malaria medicine.

The Pharmaceutical Research and Manufacturers of America (PhRMA) claimed in newspaper ads early this year that its goal is to "set every last disease on the path to extinction." Jeff Trewhitt, a PhRMA spokesman, says U.S. drug companies will spend $24 billion on research this year and that a number of firms are looking for cures for tropical diseases. Some companies also provide existing drugs free to poor countries, he says. "Our members are involved. There's not an absolute void."

The void is certainly at hand. Neither PhRMA nor individual firms will reveal how much money the companies spend on any given disease—that's proprietary information, they say—but on malaria alone, a recent survey of the twenty-four biggest drug companies found that not a single one maintains an in-house research program, and only two expressed even minimal interest in primary research on the disease. "The pipeline of available drugs is almost empty," says Dyann Wirth of the Harvard School of Public Health, who conducted the study. "It takes five to ten years to develop a new drug, so we could soon face [a strain of] malaria resistant to every drug in the world." A 1996 study presented in *Cahiers Santé,* a French scientific journal, found that of forty-one important medicines used to treat major tropical diseases, none were discovered in the nineties and all but six were discovered before 1985.

Contributing to this trend is the wave of mergers that has swept the industry over the past decade. Merck alone now controls almost 10 percent of the world market. "The bigger they grow, the more they decide that their research should be focused on the most profitable diseases and conditions," one industry watcher says. "The only thing the companies think about on a daily basis is the price of their stocks; and announcing that you've discovered a drug [for a tropical disease] won't do much for your share price."

That comment came from a public health advocate, but it's essentially seconded by industry. "A corporation with stockholders can't stoke up a laboratory that will focus on Third World diseases, because it will go broke," says Roy Vagelos, the former head of Merck. "That's a social problem, and industry shouldn't be expected to solve it."

Drug companies, however, are hardly struggling to beat back the wolves of bankruptcy. The pharmaceutical sector racks up the largest legal profits of any industry, and it is expected to grow by an average of 16 to 18 percent over the next four years, about three times more than the average for the Fortune 500. . . . Profits are especially high in the United States, which alone among First World nations does not control drug prices. As a result, prices here are about twice as high as they are in the European Union and nearly four times higher than in Japan.

"It's obvious that some of the industry's surplus profits could be going into research for tropical diseases," says a retired drug company executive, who wishes to remain anonymous. "Instead, it's going to stockholders." Also to promotion: In 1998, the industry unbuckled $10.8 billion on advertising. And to politics: In 1997, American drug companies spent $74.8 million to lobby the federal government, more than any other industry; last year they spent nearly $12 million on campaign contributions.

. . .

Just forty-five years ago, the discovery of new drugs and pesticides led the World Health Organization (WHO) to predict that malaria would soon be eradicated. By 1959, Garrett writes in *The Coming Plague,* the Harvard School of Public Health was so certain that the disease was passè that its curriculum didn't offer a single course on the subject.

Resistance to existing medicines—along with cutbacks in healthcare budgets, civil war and the breakdown of the state—has led to a revival of malaria in Africa, Latin America, Southeast Asia and, most recently, Armenia and Tajikistan. The WHO describes the disease as a leading cause of global suffering and says that by "undermining the health and capacity to work of hundreds of millions of people, it is closely linked to poverty and contributes significantly to stunting social and economic development."

Total global expenditures for malaria research in 1993, including government programs, came to $84 million. That's paltry when you consider that one B-2 bomber costs $2 billion, the equivalent of what, at current levels, will be spent on all malaria research over twenty years. In that period, some 40 million Africans alone will die from the disease. In the United States, the Pentagon budgets $9 million per year for malaria programs, about one-fifth the amount it set aside this year to supply the troops with Viagra. For the drug companies, the meager purchasing power of malaria's victims leaves the disease off the radar screen. As Neil Sweig, an industry analyst at Southeast Research Partners, puts it wearily, "It's not worth the effort or the while of the large pharmaceutical companies to get involved in enormously expensive research to conquer the Anopheles mosquito."

The same companies that are indifferent to malaria are enormously troubled by the plight of dysfunctional First World pets. John Keeling, a spokesman for the Washington, DC–based Animal Health Institute, says the "companion animal" drug market is exploding, with U.S. sales for 1998 estimated at about $1 billion. On January 5, the FDA approved the use of Clomicalm, produced by Novartis, to treat dogs that suffer from separation anxiety (warning signs: barking or whining, "excessive greeting" and chewing on furniture). "At Last, Hope for Millions of Suffering Canines Worldwide," reads the company's press release announcing the drug's rollout. "I can't emphasize enough how dogs are suffering and that their behavior is not tolerable to owners," says Guy Tebbitt, vice president for research and development for Novartis Animal Health.

Also on January 5 the FDA gave the thumbs up to Pfizer's Anipryl, the first drug approved for doggie Alzheimer's. Pfizer sells a canine pain reliever and arthritis treatment as well, and late last year it announced an R&D program for medications that help pets with anxiety and dementia.

Another big player in the companion-animal field is Heska, a biotechnology firm based in Colorado that strives to increase the "quality of life" for cats and dogs. Its products include medicines for allergies and anxiety, as well as an antibiotic that fights periodontal disease. The company's Web site features a "spokesdog" named Perio Pooch and, like old "shock" movies from high school driver's-ed classes, a photograph of a diseased doggie mouth to demonstrate what can happen if teeth and gums are not treated carefully. No one wants pets to be in pain, and Heska also makes drugs for animal cancer, but it is a measure of priorities that U.S. companies and their subsidiaries spend almost nothing on tropical diseases while, according to an industry source, they spend about half a billion dollars for R&D on animal health.

· · ·

Although "companion animal" treatments are an extreme case—that half-billion-dollar figure covers "food animals" as well, and most veterinary drugs emerge from research on human medications—consider a few examples from the brave new world of human lifestyle drugs. Here, the pharmaceutical companies are scrambling to eradicate:

- *Impotence.* Pfizer invested vast sums to find a cure for what Bob Dole and other industry spokesmen delicately refer to as "erectile dysfunction." The company hit the jackpot with Viagra, which racked up more than $1 billion in sales in its first year on the market. Two other companies, Schering-Plough and Abbott Laboratories, are already rushing out competing drugs.

- *Baldness.* The top two drugs in the field, Merck's Propecia and Pharmacia & Upjohn's Rogaine (the latter sold over the counter), had combined sales of about $180 million in 1998. "Some lifestyle drugs are used for relatively serious problems, but even in the best cases we're talking about very different products from penicillin," says the retired drug company executive. "In cases like baldness therapy, we're not even talking about healthcare."

- *Toenail fungus.* With the slogan "Let your feet get naked!" as its battle cry, pharmaceutical giant Novartis recently unveiled a lavish advertising campaign for Lamisil, a drug that promises relief for sufferers of this unsightly malady. It's a hot one, the war against fungus, pitting Lamisil against Janssen Pharmaceutical's Sporanox and Pfizer's Diflucan for shares in a market estimated to be worth hundreds of millions of dollars a year.

- *Face wrinkles.* Allergan earned $90 million in 1997 from sales of its "miracle" drug Botox. Injected between the eyebrows at a cost of about $1,000 for three annual treatments, Botox makes crow's feet and wrinkles disappear. "Every 7½ seconds someone is turning 50," a wrinkle expert told the *Dallas Morning News* in an article about Botox last year. "You're looking at

this vast population that doesn't want frown lines."

Meanwhile, acute lower respiratory infections go untreated, claiming about 3.5 million victims per year, overwhelmingly children in poor nations. Such infections are third on the chart of the biggest killers in the world; the number of lives they take is almost half the total reaped by the number-one killer, heart disease, which usually strikes the elderly. "The development of new antibiotics," wrote drug company researcher A.J. Slater in a 1989 paper published in the Royal Society of Tropical Medicine and Hygiene's *Transactions,* "is very costly and their provision to Third World countries alone can never be financially rewarding."

In some cases, older medications thought to be unnecessary in the First World and commercially unviable in the Third have simply been pulled from the market. This created a crisis recently when TB re-emerged with a vengeance in U.S. inner cities, since not a single company was still manufacturing Streptomycin after mid-1991. The FDA set up a task force to deal with the situation, but it was two years before it prodded Pfizer back into the field.

In 1990 Marion Merrell Dow (which was bought by German giant Hoechst in 1995) announced that it would manufacture Ornidyl, the first new medicine in forty years that was effective in treating African sleeping sickness. Despite the benign sounding name, the disease leads to coma and death, and kills about 40,000 people a year. Unlike earlier remedies for sleeping sickness, Ornidyl had few side effects. In field trials, it saved the lives of more than 600 patients, most of whom were near death. Yet Ornidyl was pulled from production; apparently company bean-counters determined that saving lives offered no return.

Because AIDS also plagues the First World, it is the one disease ravaging Third

World countries that is the object of substantial drug company research. In many African countries, AIDS has wiped out a half-century of gains in child survival rates. In Botswana—a country that is not at war and has a relatively stable society—life expectancy rates fell by twenty years over a period of just five. In South Africa, the Health Ministry recently issued a report saying that 1,500 of the country's people are infected with HIV every day and predicting that the annual deathrate will climb to 500,000 within the next decade.

Yet available treatments and research initiatives offer little hope for poor people. A year's supply of the highly recommended multidrug cocktail of three AIDS medicines costs about $15,000 year. That's exorbitant in any part of the world, but prohibitive in countries like Uganda, where per capita income stands at $330. Moreover, different viral "families" of AIDS, with distinct immunological properties, appear in different parts of the world. About 85 percent of people with HIV live in the Third World, but industry research to develop an AIDS vaccine focuses only on the First World. "Without research dedicated to the specific viral strains that are prevalent in developing countries, vaccines for those countries will be very slow in coming," says Dr. Amir Attaran, an international expert who directs the Washington-based Malaria Project.

All the blame for the neglect of tropical diseases can't be laid at the feet of industry. Many Third World governments invest little in healthcare, and First World countries have slashed both foreign aid and domestic research programs. Meanwhile, the U.S. government aggressively champions the interests of the drug industry abroad, a stance that often undermines healthcare needs in developing countries. . . .

In one case where a drug company put Third World health before profit—Merck's manufacture of Ivermectin—governmental inertia nearly scuttled the good deed. It was the early eighties, and a Pakistani researcher at Merck discovered that the drug, until then used only in veterinary medicine, performed miracles in combating river blindness disease. With one dose per year of Ivermectin, people were fully protected from river blindness, which is carried by flies and, at the time, threatened hundreds of millions of people in West Africa.

Merck soon found that it would be impossible to market Ivermectin profitably, so in an unprecedented action the company decided to provide it free of charge to the WHO. (Vagelos, then chairman of Merck, said the company was worried about taking the step, "as we feared it would discourage companies from doing research relevant to the Third World since they might be expected to follow suit.") Even then, the program nearly failed. The WHO claimed it didn't have the money needed to cover distribution costs, and Vagelos was unable to win financial support from the Reagan Administration. A decade after Ivermectin's discovery, only 3 million of 120 million people at risk of river blindness had received the drug. During the past few years, the WHO, the World Bank and private philanthropists have finally put up the money for the program, and it now appears that river blindness will become the second disease, after smallpox, to be eradicated.

. . .

Given the industry's profitability, it's clear that the companies could do far more. It's equally clear that they won't unless they are forced to. The success of ACT UP in pushing drug companies to respond to the AIDS crisis in America is emblematic of how crucial but also how difficult it is to get the industry to budge. In late 1997, a coalition of public health organizations approached a group of major drug companies, including Glaxo-Wellcome and Roche, and asked them to fund a project that would dedicate itself to developing new treatments for major tropical diseases. Although the companies would have been required to put up no more than $2 million a year, they walked away from the table. Since there's no organized pressure—either from the grassroots or from governments—they haven't come back. "There [were] a number of problems at the business level," Harvey Bale, director of the Geneva-based International Federation of Pharmaceutical Manufacturers' Association, told *Science* magazine. "The cost of the project is high for some companies."

While the industry's political clout currently insures against any radical government action, even minor reforms could go a long way. The retired drug company executive points to public hospitals, which historically were guaranteed relatively high profit margins but were obligated to provide free care to the poor in return. There's also the example of phone companies, which charge businesses higher rates in order to subsidize universal service. "Society has tolerated high profit levels up until now, but society has the right to expect something back," he says. "Right now, it's not getting it."

. . .

The U.S. government already lavishly subsidizes industry research and allows companies to market discoveries made by the National Institutes of Health and other federal agencies. "All the government needs to do is start attaching some strings," says the Malaria Project's Attaran. "If a company wants to market another billion-dollar blockbuster, fine, but in exchange it will have to push through a new malaria drug. It will cost them some money, but it's not going to bankrupt them."

Another type of "string" would be a "reasonable pricing" provision for drugs developed at federal laboratories. By way of explanation, Attaran recounted that the vac-

cine for hepatitis A was largely developed by researchers at the Walter Reed Army Institute. At the end of the day, the government gave the marketing rights to SmithKline Beecham and Merck. The current market for the vaccine, which sells for about $60 per person, is $300 million a year. The only thing Walter Reed's researchers got in exchange for their efforts was a plaque that hangs in their offices. "I'll say one thing for the companies," says Attaran. "They didn't skimp on the plaque; it's a nice one. But either the companies should have paid for part of the government's research, or they should have been required to sell the vaccine at a much lower price."

At the beginning of this year, Doctors Without Borders unveiled a campaign calling for increased access to drugs needed in Third World countries. The group is exploring ideas ranging from tax breaks for smaller firms engaged in research in the field, to creative use of international trade agreements, to increased donations of drugs from the multinational companies. Dr. Bernard Pécoul, an organizer of the campaign, says that different approaches are required for different diseases. In the case of those plaguing only the Southern Hemisphere—sleeping sickness, for example—market mechanisms won't work because there simply is no market to speak of. Hence, he suggests that if multinational firms are not willing to manufacture a given drug, they transfer the relevant technology to a Third World producer that is.

Drugs already exist for diseases that ravage the North as well as the South—AIDS and TB, for example—but they are often too expensive for people in the Third World. For twenty-five years, the WHO has used funding from member governments to purchase and distribute vaccines to poor countries; Pécoul proposes a similar model for drugs for tropical diseases. Another solution he points to: In the event of a major health emergency, state or private producers in the South would be allowed to produce generic versions of needed medications in exchange for a small royalty paid to the multinational license holder. "If we can't change the markets, we have to humanize them," Pécoul says. "Drugs save lives. They can't be treated as normal products."

1. According to Silverstein, why do pharmaceutical companies pay such attention to so-called "lifestyle" drugs?

2. How are the research and development decisions made by multinational pharmaceutical companies affecting people in less developed nations?
3. Silverstein argues that human health care needs are being ignored in favor of corporate profit needs. What are other ways that profit determines the health care people can obtain, both in the United States and globally?

49

AN OLD CITY SEEKS A NEW MODEL
JOSHUA WOLF SHENK

In early December 1984, an undercover police officer named Marcellus Ward met with a pair of heroin dealers above a candy store in southwest Baltimore. Ward had planned to make a buy, then an arrest. But when Drug Enforcement Administration agents stormed into the building, one of the dealers panicked and shot Ward to death. The next day, Kurt Schmoke listened to the recording from Ward's body wire. A friend of the slain detective, Schmoke was then Baltimore's 35-year-old chief prosecu-

tor. The incident, he would say later, prompted him to rethink the drug laws he had spent six years enforcing: Setups and stings and jail terms hadn't curbed the violence associated with the drug trade, let alone reduced drug use.

In 1988, soon after his election as Baltimore's mayor, Schmoke proposed easing many drug laws and repealing others—in part to undercut the black market, in part to focus resources on reducing demand. It was startling talk from a big-city mayor, and Schmoke's call for decriminalization got him on *Nightline* and on the front page of the *New York Times*. But of course no mayor can decriminalize drugs. Schmoke was soon overshadowed by national drug czar

Joshua Wolf Shenk, "An Old City Seeks a New Model: Baltimore Moves Toward Medicalization." Reprinted with permission from the July 19, 1999, issue of *The Nation*.

William Bennett, who preferred escalation of the drug war, not reform.

In 1992 Schmoke returned to the drug issue—this time with a strategy that went beyond rhetoric. That year he appointed Peter Beilenson, then 32, a young and relatively inexperienced doctor, as health commissioner. The two officials then set about increasing capacity for drug treatment, pledging to continue until they reached "treatment on demand." In the past three years, the city's treatment slots have doubled, making Baltimore a case study for the promise—and problems—of universal drug treatment. . . .

The soft-spoken Beilenson quickly shook up a system that had grown lethargic. Two years ago he spent an afternoon calling the city's public treatment centers, telling them he was "Todd Jackson," a three-times-a-day heroin user for four years, and asking "When can I start treatment?" Only one of the twenty-three programs he called would even put him on the waiting list; the others insisted he call later or come in person. He visited three other treatment centers but none would let him through the doors—telling him, via intercom, to come back when they were open for intake. So Beilenson ordered the programs to coordinate their intake, and he created a citywide referral line.

Far more important is the added treatment capacity. The waiting list for outpatient counseling—which is least in demand—has dropped to zero. Waits for methadone and inpatient programs, which account for two-thirds of slots, still range from about a week for some clinics to as much as a month for others. (Despite the citywide referral line, many people still contact programs directly.) When Beilenson makes the case for more slots, he always returns to the bottom line: The cost of treatment ranges from $3,500 a year for a methadone slot to about $35,000 a year for an inpatient slot (with a twenty-eight-day program, this would serve twelve people). Meanwhile, a drug user supporting a $50 habit might easily need to steal $300 worth of property each day. (Baltimore police estimate that fenced goods sell for one-sixth of their retail value.) That, plus the costs ranging from broken car windows to security guards to AIDS treatment to prison cells, adds up. In a finding that has been repeated elsewhere, the California Department of Health under Governor Pete Wilson followed addicts before, during and after treatment and found that every dollar spent on treatment yielded seven dollars in savings.

Which is not to say that treatment yields permanent abstinence—from either drugs or crime. University of Maryland studies have found that people in outpatient treatment programs commit crimes, on average, forty-one days a year, which seems high until it's compared with the addict population not in treatment—for whom the average is 248 days.

Schmoke says he now prefers the word "medicalization" to "decriminalization" but that his goal is still to treat "drug abuse primarily as a public health problem and not primarily as a criminal justice problem." And the refrain of the city's police commissioner, Thomas Frazier, is that "we can't arrest our way out of this problem." Still, Baltimore police have hardly laid down their arms. From 1988 to 1998, Maryland's prison population climbed from about 13,000 to more than 22,000; a significant percentage of the increase was the result of drug arrests in Baltimore. Last year city police made 90,000 arrests, 85 percent of which were for drug possession, sales or some offshoot of the drug trade.

Hundreds of those arrests came near the corner of Monroe and Fayette in West Baltimore. . . . A city-run needle-exchange van comes to Monroe and Fayette each week. When Beilenson took me to visit the program, we met a woman who embodied his wish for drug treatment—and his frustration. Wearing a vacant look and moving in jerk-steps, she pushed a handful of needles into a canister and picked up a package of new ones. I followed her onto the street, where Beilenson joined us. Jackie, who wanted to be known only by her first name, is 37 years old and looks twenty years older. She has five children and uses between $50 and $200 worth of heroin and cocaine a day. She's been in jail five times, for soliciting prostitution and for "boosting" (shoplifting). She spoke with evident anguish about this—about the jobs she had lost, about "what I put my parents through."

"Have you thought about getting into treatment?" I asked.

"Oh yes," she said "If I could right this minute, yes I would. Yes I would. Next time I get the chance to get into treatment . . ." She trailed off. The meaning of "right this minute" was clear enough. At that moment, Jackie was in withdrawal—the low point of the addiction cycle and a time when treatment referrals can be most successful. Beilenson gave her a phone number to call, but her interest in treatment seemed unlikely to last beyond the next score.

As we drove away, Beilenson made his diagnosis: "This is the typical addict in Baltimore. In and out of jobs. Boosting. Prostituting. Did you see the yellow in her eyes? She has serious liver issues—and if she doesn't get taken care of she's going to end up very sick. What I would have liked to do is say, 'Look, we've got treatment for you. Right now. This afternoon. Here's where to go, and here's a token for a cab.'" But Baltimore can't even offer immediate care to people who are begging for treatment. Despite shorter wait lists, psychiatric hospitals report that addicts regularly feign threats of suicide or violence to gain entry. When the city added a twenty-four-hour staff to its treatment hotline, it turned out that 80 per-

cent of after-hours calls came between 7:30 and 8 A.M. The morning's slots are dispensed beginning at 8 A.M., and the callers were trying to be first in line.

People who already want treatment, Beilenson argues, shouldn't have to compete for slots. Everyone benefits if they get off the streets as quickly as possible. But the real advantage with immediate treatment would apply to people like Jackie—people who struggle with an addiction but, in the five or ten or thirty days it takes for a slot to open, are likely to have a change of heart, switch addresses, lose their phone or even land in jail. And an ideal treatment system would go even further, cajoling people who might be amenable to treatment but who would never seek it out.

Just how much will Beilenson need to make treatment-on-request a reality? He suggests $30 million to $35 million, on top of the current budget of $32 million. But a precise figure is impossible because no one knows how many people would seek treatment if it were easily, immediately available. Even the total number of addicts is unknown—60,000 is just the best guess. Finally, adding capacity to the existing system is only the beginning. At the Glenwood Life Counseling Center, which offers methadone and therapy for addicts, three positions went unfilled for months. The reason, says executive director Frank Satterfield, is that the starting salary for a job that requires a bachelor's degree and offers a slim chance of raises is only $21,000. Satterfield says he would need to pay $27,000 to be minimally competitive. Applied to treatment programs across the city, such salary increases would require $2.4 million. Even fully staffed, Glenwood can barely stay on top of administering 340 patients, soon to increase to about 500. With rare exceptions, therapy is done in groups. Vocational training, family counseling, good psychiatric care—these services, which Satterfield says he took for granted when he first entered the field in the early seventies, are not possible with his budget.

. . .

The irony is that these deeper needs will only become apparent once the first steps are taken. In other words, the further Baltimore moves down the path to "medicalization," the longer the path seems. And though political obstacles have so far been few—there is no Republican Party to speak of in Baltimore—that may change.

A hint of future conflict came . . . when Beilenson expressed interest in a plan by Johns Hopkins researchers to conduct a trial in heroin maintenance. The idea was to replicate a now-legendary Switzerland study in which heroin addicts who had failed in repeated treatments were given injections of the drug in a clinical setting. The results were impressive (though not necessarily definitive): Many in the test group found housing and employment, and the percentage committing crimes went from 59 percent to 10 percent. In casual conversation about such a study in Baltimore, Beilenson told a *Sun* reporter—while they watched their kids play soccer—"It will be politically difficult, but I think it's going to happen." The *Sun* printed these remarks, and sharp criticism came quickly—from Governor Parris Glendening, City Council members and even the Mayor. "This administration has no intention of initiating a heroin maintenance program," Schmoke told the *Sun*. But in a recent interview, Schmoke struck a different tone. He had to rebuke Beilenson, he explained, because the commissioner floated a radical idea without building consensus. But, Schmoke continued, "if you ask me what should be a part of a good public health system to combat substance abuse, many different treatment options should be part of that system—plus this last one, medical distribution of certain drugs."

This puts Schmoke and Beilenson on a collision course with state officials, most notably Lieut. Gov. Kathleen Kennedy Townsend, who said such an idea "undermines [the] whole effort" of convincing young people that "heroin is bad."

Indeed, while city officials try to build a model program of treatment on demand, Townsend is staking her reputation on a different model: coerced treatment. Last year the legislature approved Townsend's proposal to administer twice-a-week drug tests to 25,000 people on probation or parole. Under the $2.9 million program, positive tests for cocaine, heroin or marijuana would trigger a series of escalating sanctions—for a midlevel offender, for example, the first failed test would lead to two days in jail, then five, ten, thirty, forty-five and finally a return to court for parole violation. "You don't have to want treatment for it to work," says Adam Gelb, Townsend's policy director.

Researchers and treatment providers have mixed opinions on coerced treatment. "If you have leverage, you ought to use it," says Dr. Robert Schwartz, who directs the University of Maryland School of Medicine's division of alcohol and drug abuse. . . . Still, Schwartz urges that coerced treatment not squeeze out voluntary programs—which seems a real possibility were Townsend to get her way. Beilenson urges the state to spend more on both forms of treatment, arguing that the big savings will come from keeping people out of the criminal justice system in the first place.

. . .

The idea that drug users belong in prison has in the past few decades been carved deeply into U.S. politics and won't be easy to change. In New York, for example, a recent study found that the state spends $680 million a year to lock up nonviolent drug offenders, and yet the legislature has stalled on even modest reforms of its draconian Rockefeller drug laws. Those laws, adopted in the early seventies, were quickly adopted by other states and by federal officials. Now, the damage is apparent even to many hawks. "We have a failed social policy, and it has to be reevaluated," national drug policy director Gen. Barry McCaffrey said this year. "Otherwise, we're going to bankrupt ourselves."

Of course McCaffrey won't propose the next logical step, which would be to eliminate mandatory minimums and other harsh measures and redirect that money into treatment. During his 1992 campaign, Bill Clinton pledged to enact "treatment on demand." He quickly abandoned the promise, not just because it would be expensive but because it runs contrary to a winning political formula: more arrests, longer sentences, more jails.

The experiment in Baltimore challenges that formula. Officials there are driven by the basic instinct that drug users need help, not punishment. But they also believe the policy makes fiscal sense. And they know they'll have to support that view with hard numbers. That's why Beilenson contracted with a team of independent social scientists (from Johns Hopkins and two other universities) to measure the crime, health and income of three groups of addicts in Baltimore: those who get treatment immediately, those who have to wait and those who get no treatment at all. The results of the $2.8 million study are expected in 2001. If it con-firms Beilenson's argument that "treatment saves money and treatment on request will save more," the study could turn an iconoclastic experiment into a model for other cities and states. Today, the idea of universal, immediate treatment on a national scale is hard to imagine. But then, so was Governor Nelson Rockefeller's idea that possession of two grams of cocaine deserved fifteen years in prison.

QUESTIONS FOR DISCUSSION

1. Why is the new model of drug abuse being used in Baltimore so controversial?
2. What are the social and economic implications of defining drug abuse as a medical problem? How are these effects different from defining drug abuse as a criminal justice problem?
3. There are other behaviors that traditionally have been seen as either medical or criminal problems, but that have been constructed differently as social norms have changed (think, for example, about sexuality, abortion, alcohol use, or cigarette smoking). What are the implications of constructing a social problem as a medical issue?

50

THE PATIENT AS OBJECT
DANIEL F. CHAMBLISS

. . .

Nurses' most persistent challenges, though, arise in their dealings with a relatively weak and apparently almost defenseless party: patients. In particular, disputes arise over what a patient is—one might say, over the patients' ontological status. For a medical institution, the patient is an object to be processed in institutionalized ways and to be treated as a biomechanical entity. Patients are institutionally objectified: detached from their own lives and life stories, physically taken from their home settings, behaviorally managed as a conglomerate of discrete parts to be treated by different specialists. But patients often resist this treatment in a number of ways, and nurses and doctors try to overcome the institutional habit. But the habit remains nonetheless. In these cases, moral problems result not from the contingent structure of the hospital but from the prevalent style of scientific medical treatment. Contemporary medicine, almost by its nature, treats patients as medical objects. Patients resist, and the resulting conflicts express themselves as "ethical problems."

The Gap Between Patients and Staff

Staff and patients often begin their relationship separated by a huge cultural gap. Certain people work in the health professions; certain other people are most in need of their services. Even apart from health conditions, the two groups are dramatically different. Especially in large hospitals, the staff is young while the patients are old. Head nurses twenty-seven years of age run floors filled with eighty-year-old patients; residents of thirty perform surgery on patients who could be their own grandparents. The staff is highly educated, holding college and graduate degrees; patients are often uneducated, even illiterate. Add to this the ethnic differences as well, with predominantly white doctors and nurses caring for a disproportionate number of minority patients, or Jewish doctors and Catholic nurses treating Protestant patients.[1] . . .

Patients and staff also differ in social class. Doctors are often wealthy, and nurses are fairly well off (and steadily employed). Patients, in contrast, are disproportionately poor and suffer misfortunes which compound each other. Malnutrition weakens the immune system. Without medical insurance, patients struggle to find a willing physician. The family car—if there is one—is often broken down and can't make the long drive to the clinic; there's no one to stay home and watch the baby. The poor are more often crime victims. When their diseases are left untreated, one ailment leads to another: diabetes to kidney failure, an infection to gangrene, despair to drugs to AIDS. Seeing poor people in hospitals, a middle-class observer is astonished by the huge array of problems they suffer and bring with them, like dirty clothes and barefoot children, to sit for 6 hours in an emergency room. Many patients are society's undesirables; in a Neurosurgery Unit, a third of all patients are young men who've been in motorcycle crashes, often more than once, many wearing tattoos. ("Tattoos are a risk factor for neuro problems," jokes one nurse.) Or prisoners in the state penal system, given free care by law, generating new resentments among staff. ("They come in here wanting nose jobs!" claims one nurse. "That's our money paying for that.") . . .

A few patients are young, educated, white, and well-off, and thus somewhat like the staff. Most, though, are quite different. But all are, crucially, patients, and this by itself may prove the greatest difference of all. By definition, patients are different; here begins their creation as medical objects.

. . . What is the conception of disease, and of patienthood, that is imposed on patients? Basically, the hospital projects a quasi-scientific vision of reality. This includes many elements of the scientific style: reliance on chemistry and biology, reliance on quantitative measures, and a belief in the primacy of a physiological view of reality. At the same time, it accepts the validity of empirical "clinical judgment." Medicine has a somewhat de-personalized vision, in which, as Renée Anspach says, staff actions "both reflect and create a world view in which biological processes exist apart from persons, observations can be separated from those who make them, and the knowledge obtained from measurement instruments has a validity independent of the persons who use and interpret this diagnostic technology."[2]

From such a perspective, detachment is a reasonable way to deal with patients. When illness is defined biologically, it's professionally reasonable for a gastroenterologist to say that "a colonoscopy's not a bad procedure," just a matter of inserting a long flexible tube up the rectum and into the colon for a careful inspection. Colonoscopy is useful for removing polyps and detecting early colon cancer, which is very curable in the early stages. "Not bad." (One is reminded of "the old clinical saw that a minor operation is an operation being performed on someone else.")[3] And it's reasonable for a medical manual's lengthy description of a Swan-Ganz pulmonary artery catheterization to make no mention whatsoever of the patient's experience. . . .

From the medical viewpoint, it is reasonable to believe that technical problems have technical solutions.[4] . . . But for the patient, the technical definition of illness is all a giant mistake. "[P]atients do not experience illness as symptoms that can be mapped empirically onto a medically diagnosed syndrome (unless they are medically oversocialized or hypochondriacal) . . . curing of the disease does not automatically cure the illness (that is, the human response to the symptom)."[5] Patients may feel, "I don't belong here; why am I walking into a cancer clinic?" "To the layman, [the body] is a sacred thing," not to be handled and used lightly; it is, though, "a different sort of object" to the physician.[6]

So when patients' complaints are irrelevant to the medically defined problem they are, well, just irrelevant. One nurse tells of a patient, long unconscious, waking up and saying. "My feet hurt." The nurse laughed as she recounted this example of patients' concern with "little things." When patients complain of the room being cold, or a needle hurting, some staff will label them "whiners" (and I've seen a number of nurses in one hospital wearing buttons that say "whiners," with a circle and cross-line drawn on it). From the medical view, patients' complaints—gowns open in the back, too many blood samples drawn, crowds of doctors going in and out of the room at all hours—are often seen as trivial. Such complaints are *not* about disease but about how the hospital treats its patients. When treated well, when the "small" things are handled, patients can lavish praise on staff, doctors, and nurses. (Zussman, I think, in this respect accepts the medical view, saying nurses offer only "small" kindnesses. Patients, like children, have little control over their lives in the hospital, and what appear to those in the "healthy" world as small kindnesses are, to those benefiting from them, quite substantial indeed.)[7] What the doctor treats, that is, is not what the patient suffers.

The Patient Created as Object

The patient's transformation into an object of medical scrutiny begins with his or her removal to the hospital, and not only in the physical sense. To be treated, the patient must accept the medical world's view of disease and treatment.[8] On leaving home and entering the hospital, the patient relinquishes the right to decide what bothers him or her. Professionals now diagnose "the problem" and decide what's wrong—or, indeed, that perhaps there's "really" nothing wrong at all.[9]

The patient is first separated from home, work, and even from biography. For most, illness is abnormal; it is a pathology, an unusual breakdown in an otherwise healthy daily routine. "I'm not usually like this," patients may feel. Families, too, suffer because their loved one has a normal life outside; they see the suffering against a background of a (relatively) healthy life. But the staff have only a hazy picture of this background. Nurses are not surprised that Mr. Jones has a Foley catheter in his penis, or that Ms. Jackson has a nasogastric tube in her nose, or that all patients are punctured with needles a half-dozen times a day. It's part of "being a patient." Once admitted to the hospital, the "patient" is dressed in a gown and laid in a bed with a chart outside on the door. All else is set aside. It's normal from then on for "patients" to be examined by teams of physicians, injected, given enemas, catheterized, and discussed in rounds. . . .

One becomes an object of looking and talking. Examples are familiar: the written history, the chart detailing everything done to the patient, the physicians' and nurses' notes, and the endless physical exams (sometimes several times in a day). Then there are the more invasive lookings: endoscopies, bronchoscopies, colonoscopies, eye, ear, and nose exams; the blood tests, X-rays, CAT scans, MRIs, and the cardiac catheterizations. Hospital life for patients is an endless round of being looked at, listened to, touched and poked and prodded. . . .

The patient forfeits other rights, for instance, that of privacy, and by virtue of patienthood seems to become *less*, not more, morally protected from others. . . .

> From a chair in the ICU, I can look right into the rooms of 4 sick people—a violation of their privacy. The double doors are usually wide open, with nurses going in and out. When I'm sick, I want more privacy, not less—but they get less. [Field Notes]

. . .

Of course, patients can benefit from becoming a standardized object of medical attention. For instance, despite occasional charges to the contrary,[10] I saw little evidence anywhere in my research that social "undesirables"—criminals, drug abusers, unpleasant people—were individually given lesser treatment than the respectable.[11] I say "individually" because, as a class, the poor receive much less solicitous care than those with full insurance, and are sometimes totally rejected by some physicians and hospitals. At the same time, many nurses I spoke with and watched in nonprofit teaching hospitals were deeply committed to giving full care, the best technical care possible, to even the most indigent of their patients; the same held, I think, for criminals. The nurses sometimes resented such work, but at the same time they took great professional pride in doing it. Zussman makes the point well: "If contemporary medicine is less personal, it is also more tolerant. It is prepared to offer help not only to the solid citizen or the blameless victim but also to those of more often questioned character. It is prepared to treat the drug user, the drinker, the diabetic who fails to take her insulin, the man with kidney disease who misses his appointments for dialysis, with the same principled indifference that is, in other circumstances, a source of strident criticism."[12]

Surgery provides a clear example of how patients are treated as objects. In the operating room the patient is ritualistically transformed from living person to medical object, making even the most grisly invasions routine. Typically, the patient is unconscious for the operation, save for an initial greeting by the anesthesiologist before he or she gives the patient the general anesthetic. ("What is your name?" "Grace." "OK, Grace, I'm Dr. Rodriguez. I'll be here the whole time. Now just breathe deeply.") And so the patient really is little more than a piece of living flesh. (When the patient is awake, on a spinal anesthetic, a sign will usually be on the door into the operating room, "Patient Awake," to warn staff who may come in to be on their best behavior.) Objectification is heightened by the initial preparation in which the area to be operated on is clearly separated from the rest of the patient's body. The patient's body is first covered by sheets save for the area to be cut open (say, the lower right abdomen for an appendectomy). That area is left bare; is shaved of hair; is cleansed thoroughly with a disinfectant solution; and is finally covered with a thin tight sheet of plastic, like you would use to cover leftover food. A drapery is put down between the patient's head (where the anesthesiologist sits) and the rest of the body, thus furthering the

sense that "this is not a person." Even when a patient is awake, much can happen at the far end of the body—such as toes being amputated—while the patient chats away amiably with the anesthesiologist up at the head. Thus, there is little sense that the target tissue is fully human.

. . . Once the patient is anesthetized, the surgeons treat flesh as a careful chef might treat a piece of turkey being prepared for a Thanksgiving dinner. They slice, cut, sever; they pull on skin, muscles, sinews. They encounter fat, which looks just like it does in a turkey—yellow and greasy, it's the same stuff; they push fingers and hands deep into the viscera, dig around with fingers (say, to find different organs, all packed in there together); they sometimes pry and heave to move intestines, pressing and prodding with no evident hesitation. The "person," the patient, at this point certainly looks like no person you've ever seen or known, and it's hard to think of this body as a human being. "The body is meat," as Anne Sexton said.[13] Surgery is a violent procedure, and no wonder that when the anesthesia wears off the patient is sore. And surgery is profoundly intimate, though conducted with little evident sense of that. For the patient, the prospect of it can be terrifying:

> Big guy (6'4", well over 200 lbs.)—[state prison system inmate] strapped onto the operating table, cruciform [arms on boards straight out to sides, for IV lines], about to be intubated by wimpy little anesthesiology resident with glasses. Patient looks very scared, visibly trembling. Seems to me I'm watching the neighborhood bully's worse nightmare. [Field Notes]

In two other functions of the hospital, patients are quite explicitly objectified and used in pursuit of goals other than their own restored health. These goals are the teaching of young doctors and nurses, and medical research. The use of current patients for teaching is justified as helping future patients. "The doctors are here to learn," nurses often say in teaching hospitals. The phrase shifts attention from what is happening now to an indefinite future. The good of the immediate patient is not the goal, then, but is a constraint on other work which seeks to train doctors to help future patients. In the meanwhile, some patients are obviously used:

> I've seen a pt have a pneumothorax because an intern went to put in a subclavian, and would cause a spontaneous pneumothorax. They gave it to him again, and let him try again on the other side, and he caused *another* pneumothorax. Now this pt has bilateral chest tubes, because the intern was practicing . . . [Interview]

Similar cases occur frequently, where interns try multiple times to start an arterial line (putting a needle into an artery to measure blood pressure) or carry out other difficult and, for the patient, painful procedures. Some procedures can be learned on the recently deceased—for instance, intubation, the insertion of an endotracheal tube into the throat for mechanical ventilation of the lungs. Perhaps a harsher example is provided by a nurse who reported that her worst ethical problems were in a medical ICU:

> A guy bleeding out of his eyes and ears, hopeless, and in the code they'd say, "Let's try 5 compressions and see what happens." Or "Look at what this drug does to the heart." They did codes for no reason, on patients who were going to die anyway. Just experimenting. [Interview]

The patient here is clearly being treated as an object for another's purpose.

In clinical research, too, patients are used. A nurse may find that after giving an experimental drug to five of the thirty patients chosen for a study, the drug is actually doing harm. But new patients keep coming in, and, says one such nurse, the nurses think, "My God, we're going to have to use that drug again . . . it won't help the patient, just test the drugs." But "you have to give the drug anyway, even if it isn't working well, because you're a research nurse." . . . True, patients are required by law to give their "informed consent" before participating in a research project. But do patients understand what they have signed in an "informed consent" form? The form says that the patient has been told the risks and benefits of the operation or research, yet it is the staff that chooses how much to tell and how optimistically to tell it.[14] Patients are possibly intimidated, probably in desperate condition, and certainly dependent on nurses and doctors. They have good reason to avoid angering the staff. So they are easily pressured to sign. . . .

Limitations on Objectification

Still, we should not overstate the objectification of patients. Even in the highly technicized ICUs, staff know personal information about their patients and form judgments of them as human beings. One evening two ICU nurses, Maggie and Ken, sat and shared their thoughts on the difficulty in this setting of recognizing patients as persons:

> "We chemically restrain a lot of 'em," says Ken, "so they don't give us a hard time. Just conk 'em out."
>
> "It's good to have a photo of them outside the hospital," says Maggie, "just to know they have other lives." [Field Notes]

Efforts to remember patients as people take many forms. In the unit just mentioned, one nurse, known widely as being excellent both in technique (starting IVs, for instance) and in attitude, habitually attends to "little things." She makes symbolic statements of respect for her patients, giving them a bit of ice when they're thirsty, for instance, or protecting their fragile modesty. . . .

Staff members can try to respect the person when the person is hardly there. In a Newborn Unit, where nurses care for premature infants—tiny creatures, some born as many as ten weeks early—many of the bassinets are decorated with little baby things:

> A yellow Winnie the Pooh, a little pink lamb with a white face . . . ; a plastic-painted balloon over another, with "Get Well Soon" on it; "I'm a Boy" card or "I'm a Girl" card over each bassinet, hospital provided, with name. Often the surnames have been changed, crossed out and revised—mother's or father's name, they aren't sure, etc., ambiguous family relations a common phenomenon here. The little baby toys, lots of them in some cribs, none in others. One now has a musical mobile of plastic rings and balls that plays "Brahm's Lullaby"; this baby, on a ventilator, is very active and stimulated. Others, tiny little overgrown fetuses almost, lie on vent[ilator] asleep, curled up, tiny, with a little stuffed animal in the corner. [Field Notes]

In many other ways a patient's "real life" may become evident. Sometimes a patient will dress in street clothes and walk about the floor, part of the civilian world again. Or a terminal patient will refuse the standard "heroic" treatment, and a nurse finds, as one put it, that

> it's harder to watch someone die when they are just *there,* breathing, talking, awake, instead of with lots of lines and tubes, intubated . . . they look like a real

person from the street . . . it's like a regular person is dying. [Interview]

. . .

So from a number of causes—a deliberate effort, close long-term contact, some kind of personal identification—staff do often see their patients in less objectified ways. . . .

Controlling the Patient

Because patients resist being treated like objects, the staff must work at controlling them. Control techniques range from gentle suggestions that "this will only hurt a little" to restraints put on violent patients who try to hurt themselves or other people (some psychiatric patients are suicidal; some neurology patients are hallucinatory and try to jump out of windows). Often nurses must negotiate between what patients want and what patients should get, making the sort of deals parents make with their children ("If you're good now, you can go for a walk later"). They persuade patients to stop smoking, to report symptoms promptly, to take their medications, to respect their prescribed dietary limits, to stay in the hospital until properly discharged, and not to pull out their IV lines. Nurses are responsible for maintaining such patient discipline. Doctors may talk angrily about patients' "noncompliance," but face-to-face it is a nurse who has to get Mrs. Jones to take her medication.

Some common elements of hospital care are designed to control difficult patients, protecting them from hurting themselves and others. Standard devices include "Posey belts," for preventing patients from falling out of bed, or leather restraints for patients who are badly disoriented or violent. Pain-killing drugs are also part of the regimen; a patient's suffering can disrupt the work flow and thus needs controlling.[15]

In ICUs, patients are also controlled with amnesiac drugs such as Versed. "You'll hear a lot of ICU nurses say—and this sounds terrible—sometimes it's a real hassle to have a patient who can talk . . . you've got somebody who's really sick, and you've been doing all this stuff, and all of a sudden they wake up and say, 'My feet hurt,' or something . . . Sometimes you just want a patient who's on Versed and is not going to talk to you" [Interview].

Staff can also control patients by limiting patients' information about their medical condition. Northern General Hospital is a spinal cord injury center for the state, and many of the patients are young male victims of motorcycle and diving accidents. They are angry at being in the hospital; they are also often paralyzed. The doctor sometimes won't say, "You can never walk." But the nurse knows, and the patient asks. "They know when they're not being told."[16] One nurse tells of avoiding a patient, or spending her brief visits in the room talking nonstop, hoping to escape being asked the question she doesn't want to answer. When she finishes up with the patient, she says hurriedly, "if you need anything, just let me know," and runs out. But she says, "The patient knows something is wrong if you aren't talking with him." . . .

Sometimes patients are told only "what the doctors feel like they can handle"; the staff sometimes lies to the patients.[17] Because of specialization in medicine, such lies may involve several doctors and nurses.

> One patient, a boy 16 years old, came into Northern General with a brain tumor. Three different attending physicians were on the case—a neurosurgeon, a pediatrician, and a hematologist. The boy didn't know he had cancer until the hematologist, unaware that the boy didn't know, said something about chemotherapy. The boy and his family were devastated.[18] [Interview]

. . .

Perhaps controlling patients by these means (restraints, drugs, limiting information) is justified. Many patients are genuinely incompetent and in no position to decide on their own appropriate treatment. As one physician, director of an ICU, says,

> What do you do: a patient comes in, septic, seizing like a maniac, can barely breathe, incoherent—how can we ever get his "informed consent" to anything? [Field Notes]

Even when patients are coherent, control efforts may be used for the patient's own protection. One geriatric nurse explained that many attending physicians don't like using restraints on their elderly patients, but

> they aren't here to see what we deal with. Patients get out of bed, fall and break hips, ribs—then the family sues! Or the family complains about the restraints when patient is tied to prevent his/her pulling out lines, catheters, to stay in bed—so restraints come off, patient gets hurt, or leaves, walks out, gets hit by a car on the street—and the family sues! You can't win. [Field Notes]

In these cases, it's easy to see the staff's point of view. In others, it's more debatable. . . .

Patients' Rights

At this point, the skeptical or dismayed reader may ask, "But don't patients have rights? And aren't these recognized by hospitals?"

Yes, in recent years many hospitals have adopted (and posted prominently) a "Patient's Bill of Rights." But one should recognize that such rights are *granted* to patients, not taken by them. Even here the organization maintains an upper hand. Indeed, the very idea of a "Patient's Bill of Rights" is peculiarly revealing of the system's inherent paternalism:[19]

- First, a Bill of Rights given by the hospital can be revoked by the hospital; it is presented as a gesture of good will, not a statement of legally enforced rights. If anything, such gestures put the weaker party that much more in the debt of the powerful.
- Second, like a consent decree in law, the Patient's Bill of Rights has about it the faint odor of guilt. It seems to say: "We will never do these things which we didn't really do in the first place," such as operating on unconsenting patients.
- Third, this beneficent giving of rights to the patient may only heighten the patient's sense of powerlessness, a reminder of what *could* happen.

It is interesting that in cases where patients have won the legal power to accept or reject medical judgment, they often go ahead and accept it. To some M.D.s I spoke with, this shows patients' "irrationality"; but perhaps, instead, it reveals that the patients' argument is not over the value of scientific medicine but over the control of it.

So even what appear as efforts for "patient's rights" can subtly reinforce the status of medicine. Consider the case of Dr. Jack Kevorkian, who in 1990 invented a device for helping willing patients commit suicide. A lively public debate ensued around whether this was appropriate medical (or even human) behavior. I would note here that Kevorkian's device, a metal frame with a series of IV bottles controlled by the "patient" pushing a button, is visibly a medical/technological machine. As a suicide method, it is obviously unlike the tradi-

tional revolver or carbon monoxide in a closed garage. The machine is designed, and prepared for the patient, by a licensed M.D.—Dr. Kevorkian, in the famous case. Presented as enhancing patient's control over when to die, Kevorkian's device, I suggest, in fact reinforces the medicalized vision and control of death. Even suicide, it says, can be medically managed. You just need the right doctor.[20]

The hospital, then, has its own priorities and habits, some of which may directly conflict with those of the patient. Patients entering a hospital—with thousands of employees, with a long and distinguished tradition of medical science, a training center for the nation's finest young physicians—have little hope that their opinions will count for much. They can expect to be treated as objects—valuable ones, certainly—for processing, something like a car on an assembly line. One person admits them, another decides what they will eat, still another serves their meals, another tries to cure their sicknesses, and another, perhaps, comforts them in their grief. The extensive division of labor subjects patients to "process production" in which each member of the staff has some particular job to do on them. This is entirely apart from the motivations or personal beliefs of any particular doctor or nurse.

Reform efforts, as expressed in a Patient's Bill of Rights, fail to address the fundamental issue: the powerful staff can impose its view that the patient is a kind of object. And if the patient is sick enough to wind up in Intensive Care, the levels of abstraction from commonsense perception of problems grow. The patient may say, "I can't walk without becoming exhausted," but the "real" problem—as diagnosed by experts—becomes abnormal blood gas values, or pH levels, or inadequate blood volumes in an artery from the heart. This physiological reality becomes the medically recognized problem, and the patient's "personal" difficulties become "precipitating factors." Medical doctors, by training, believe in physical reality at the biological level; that's where disease for them really exists, and that is where it can be treated.

Conclusion

Sometimes it seems that the hospital as an organization wants to know everything it can about this physical object, the patient. Perhaps this results from "defensive medicine," in which doctors try to prevent any malpractice suits by covering every possible contingency. Perhaps it results in part from a technological imperative, in which expensive machinery must be frequently used to justify its purchase. The sources of this effort at "total knowledge" are multiple, and the effort itself is evident in the endless quest for information on patients: tests, exams, X-rays, MRIs, CAT scans, and catheterizations; in the monitors hooked up, temperatures taken, blood pressures, urine and stool output measured, food and water intake recorded; in the yearly checkup, the monthly breast self-exam, the hearing and vision tests, dentists checking over and under tongues for signs of cancer, blood tests, cholesterol tests, the routine chest X-ray, the six-month dental X-rays, not to mention routine notings of height and weight. All of this searching is conducted through an endless and seemingly increasing array of "lookings-in"—in search of some diagnosis, perhaps, or in the hope of finding something. The computerization of records has only expedited the effort. The goal of all this looking seems to be an idealized "total viewing" of the patient, in which everything is seen, recorded, and classified. . . .

Patients' very first encounters with physicians typically begin with a nurse saying, "The doctor will see you now." That phrase, we now realize, is more true than we knew.[21] The ailing person, in becoming a patient, enters a world in which seeing, in the broad and deep senses, is the key to understanding; and in which perhaps even the rounds of examinations, tests, and recordings serve to keep the patient in his or her place, as an object of medical scrutiny.[22] Medical observation then becomes a ritual of power in which roles are recurrently played out. . . . The patient becomes, as we have seen, a person *defined* as sick, regarded as open for inspection as needed, and treated with procedures appropriate for a delicate living organism but not for a sacred creature.

NOTES

1. Robert Zussman also deals with this issue in *Intensive Care.* Chicago: University of Chicago Press, 1992, pp. 65–66.
2. Renée Anspach. "Notes on the Sociology of Medical Discourse: The Language of Case Presentation," *Journal of Health and Social Behavior* 29, no. 4 (1988), p. 373.
3. David J. Rothman. *Strangers at the Bedside: A History of How Law and Bioethics Transformed Medical Decision Making.* New York: Basic Books, 1991, p. 80.
4. Andrew Jameton. *Nursing Practice: The Ethical Issues.* Englewood Cliffs, NJ: Prentice-Hall, 1984, p. 254.
5. Patricia Benner and Judith Wrubel. *The Primacy of Caring: Stress and Coping in Health and Illness.* New York: Addison-Wesley, 1989, p. 8.
6. Everett C. Hughes. *Men and Their Work.* Westport, CT: Greenwood Press [1958] 1981, p. 35.
7. Zussman, *Intensive Care,* chap. 5.
8. See Rothman, *Strangers at the Bedside,* for the history of how this state of affairs came about.
9. For an excellent description, see S. Kay Toombs, "Disability and the Self: A Matter of Embodiment," unpublished paper, October 1990.
10. See David Sudnow. *Passing On: The Social Organization of Dying.* Englewood Cliffs, NJ: Prentice-Hall, 1967.
11. Diane Crane agrees. See Crane, *The Sanctity of Social Life: Physicians' Treatment of Critically Ill Patients.* New Brunswick: Transaction Books, 1977, p. 96 and chap. 3.

12. Zussman, *Intensive Care*, p. 30.
13. See Anne Sexton, *All My Pretty Ones*. Cambridge, MA: Riverside Press, 1961, p. 13.
14. See the excellent discussions in both Charles Bosk, *All God's Mistakes: Genetic Counseling in a Pediatric Hospital* (Chicago: University of Chicago Press, 1992); and Anspach, *Deciding Who Lives*.
15. Barney Glaser and Anselm Strauss. *Awareness of Dying*. New York: Aldine Publishing Co., 1965, p. 208.
16. This puts special strain on nurses: "[T]he closed context instituted by the physician permits him to avoid the potentially distressing scene that may follow an announcement to his patient, but subjects nurses to strain, for they must spend the most time with the unaware patient, guarding constantly against disclosure." Ibid., p. 45.
17. See Sissela Bok, *Lying*. New York: Vintage, 1979, chap. 15.
18. For further details on this issue, see Glaser and Strauss, *Awareness of Dying*, p. 31.
19. See Rothman, *Strangers at the Bedside*, p. 146; and Jameton, *Intensive Care*, pp. 202–203.
20. Lisa Belkin. "Doctor Tells of First Death Using Suicide Device." *New York Times,* June 6, 1990.
21. The idea was suggested to me by Dan Ryan, Jr.
22. The classic work on medical observation is Stanley Reiser, *Medicine and the Reign of Technology.* Cambridge: Cambridge University Press, 1978.

QUESTIONS FOR DISCUSSION

1. What are the factors that influence the ways medical personnel objectify their patients?
2. Why would many health care professionals argue that such a process is a necessary and unavoidable part of their work?
3. Think about your own experiences as a medical patient. What are ways you have felt like an object? Did this affect your assertiveness as a patient or the overall quality of care that you received?

51

THE SOCIAL ORGANIZATION OF RESPONSIBILITY IN THE HOSPITAL AND THE HOME

CAROL A. HEIMER • LISA R. STAFFEN

I just want to get to be a normal family," Sue said quietly. "You know, other people get to take their babies here and there

From Carol A. Heimer and Lisa Staffen, "Why We Need a Sociology of Responsibility" in *For the Sake of the Children: The Social Organization of Responsibility in the Hospital and the Home.* Copyright © 1998 University of Chicago Press. Reprinted with permission.

or hear them talk. . . . Everybody says just wait, just wait until she starts screaming. I'd be so happy, you know" (1009F, p. 49).[1] Sue and Will had been married for only a few months when Sue became pregnant. It was a planned pregnancy, they both stressed; they didn't think it was right to bring a child into the world inadvertently. They also shared a strong conviction that once a child was born, the parents had an obligation to care for the child, adjusting in whatever way the situation required. As Sue put it, parents "should switch their lives around for the baby," because they "should take care of it no matter what" (1009F, p. 39).

Sue and Will's plans changed abruptly one day sixteen months before our interviews with them, when their daughter was born prematurely. Tiffany spent the next four-and-a-half months in hospitals, overcoming difficulties associated with her prematurity or created by the medical staff's attempts to help her. As many "premies" do, Tiffany had difficulty breathing and was placed on a ventilator. But the fragile tissue of tiny lungs is easily scarred through forced expansion by a ventilator, and infants who spend more than a brief period on a ventilator are likely to suffer permanent damage to their lungs. In addition, their tracheas may be scarred by the endotracheal tube through which air flows from the ventilator into the lungs. Tiffany experienced both problems and as a result had a serious bout of pneumonia, which led to a second hospitalization and numerous surgeries to remove scar tissue and increase the size of her airway. When corrective surgery failed, Tiffany's parents were crushed to learn their daughter would require a tracheostomy. A surgical opening was made in her trachea, and the ventilator was attached to a tracheostomy tube. As a result of these complications, Sue and Will faced great uncertainty about what their daughter's future would be like.

Serious problems such as these often lead to other, more minor problems, which may not be life threatening, but nevertheless wear parents down. For much of her life Tiffany was an extremely reluctant eater. Sue was particularly distressed about this, because it was she who had to organize her day around coaxing her daughter to eat. She also had to explain to physicians and nurses that the problem was not that Tiffany was

being held in an uncomfortable position or being fed ineptly or any number of other explanations that they came up with as they laid the blame at Sue's feet.

Over the months of Tiffany's early life, Sue and Will became quite skilled at caring for their child, at training the nurses who were supposed to relieve them for a few hours a day, and at confronting medical staff if they did their jobs ineptly. Sue was particularly galled by incompetence or inattentiveness. Though she was quick to recognize that the hospital staff had skills she lacked, she was infuriated when they failed to recognize that she also had skills and that she was in some ways their supervisor (though she did not describe the problem in quite this way). She complained bitterly that they were unwilling to take her seriously because she was so young. Despite her youth (she was only nineteen when Tiffany was born), she was the one responsible for ensuring that her child received good care.

Sue took her job very seriously, even insisting that Tiffany be transferred from one hospital to another when she became dissatisfied with the quality of care. Sue believed that the nurses did not change the tracheostomy tube that connected Tiffany to the ventilator frequently enough or clean the area around the tube as well as she thought necessary; she also charged them with neglecting to cushion the connection between the tracheostomy tube and the child's skin, failing to tie the tube in place properly to prevent it from becoming dislodged, and leaving soiled diapers on Tiffany so long that she developed severe diaper rash. In addition to arranging for her daughter's transfer, Sue's achievements included successfully resuscitating Tiffany after she stopped breathing one night at home, confronting medical equipment suppliers who brought the wrong parts or who failed to keep machinery in good repair, and detecting signs of illness in Tiffany before the home nurses did (and indeed before the illness could be confirmed by anything other than X rays or ultrasounds).

These young parents had become formidable advocates for their child—they had mastered the intricacies of hospital systems and medical hierarchies, had worked out the arcane details of how to arrange funding through the Katie Beckett program, had figured out how to cope (though unhappily) with a large staff of home nurses, and had reorganized their household by moving in with Will's parents so that they could manage on one working-class salary.[2] And throughout this experience, they retained a sense of what all this effort was for—to raise a child. Sue described her attempts to teach Tiffany to crawl, happily talked about Tiffany blowing kisses to them and clucking her tongue (important evidence that Tiffany was learning the skills necessary for speech even though her tracheostomy prevented her from making much sound), and longed for the day when they would be able to do ordinary things like taking a trip to the zoo, unencumbered by medical equipment.[3]

Sue and Will had risen to the challenges presented by Tiffany's fragile health but nevertheless looked forward to the time when their lives would not be ruled by their daughter's demanding health-care needs. Though neither seemed to have had elaborate plans for his or her own life before Tiffany's birth, they both felt their lives had been put on hold by her prematurity and subsequent medical problems. "We want to go to school, start getting on with our lives, and start doing something" (1009F, p. 17), Sue said. Quite simply, though, Tiffany's needs had to come first. "Tiffany's my involvement until she gets her 'trach' out," Sue explained (1009F, p. 59). Plans for both parents to go back to school, to buy a house, and to have another child all were deferred. Sue left her job as a sales clerk in a local discount store when she went into labor and

was never able to return to work after Tiffany's birth, as she had planned. And Will continued to work as a manual laborer, because they relied on his income, even though he desperately wanted to escape the physically demanding and mind-numbing work. As he put it, though, "The big trauma's over. Now it's just a waiting game" (1009M, p. 36).

As tales of premature births go, this one is not particularly dramatic. But its very mundanity makes it a good starting point for our discussion of what it means to take responsibility. Sue and Will experienced an unexpected event, followed by a long period of considerable uncertainty. The chronicle of their adjustment to Tiffany's birth can be told as a story about a series of unprovoked shocks from the external world or as a tale of a couple's reactions, adjustments, and thoughtful initiatives to improve their daughter's life. Both versions contain a measure of truth, of course—Sue and Will often either had no control over the course of events or only learned about how they might have intervened after the fact. But rather than be passive passengers on a roller-coaster ride (to use a metaphor often invoked by such parents) they had never wished to take, these young parents looked for ways to influence events, to improve the situation even marginally, and to prevent what further disasters they could.

By focusing on what Will and Sue, and others like them, do when confronted with unexpected events with potentially grave consequences, we can learn a great deal about the conditions under which people embrace or reject responsibility. To start with, we learn that there is variability in the people themselves and in the extent to which they accept responsibility. While Will and Sue felt that they had primary responsibility for Tiffany's welfare, not all parents feel that way. Some, for instance, feel that the child only becomes their responsibility after discharge home, and others continue to feel that health professionals have the primary responsibility for some aspects of the child's development. But not all of the variation resides in the people who confront questions about whether to take on responsibilities. Just as a division of labor between professionals and parents may shape parents' sense of what their responsibilities are, so organizational contexts also transform people's views about their responsibilities and their capacity to shoulder them. For those (like physicians and nurses) who are regular participants in an organization, the division of labor may make responsibilities much more manageable. For those who are outsiders (like parents), drawing only briefly on the expertise or resources of organizational members, organizational divisions of labor and boundaries may pose obstacles. Parents who feel, as Will and Sue did, that parental responsibility is not left at the doorstep of the hospital may still have difficulty acting on their views. It may be far from clear how to be a responsible parent on someone else's turf. When contacts with professionals leave some people feeling enlightened and empowered and others demoralized and incompetent, we can be sure that some of the variability is coming from professionals and the organizations in which they work. Some organizations are easy to penetrate, but others are not. Some organizational staff members see outsiders as intruders to be kept at bay while the real work is done by insiders, whereas other staff members see outsiders as potential contributors who must be quickly inducted into the group.

By scrutinizing people's responses to life-altering circumstances, we try to show how responsibility arises and how the acceptance of responsibility can be either undermined or supported by the way that institutions are designed and the way that normative systems (including the informal rules of family life, the rules of professional conduct, the routines and procedures of particular organizations, the administrative regulations of state and federal bureaucracies, and state and federal law) work together. Although we here examine parents' acceptance of responsibility for children, we argue that such an example can tell us much about the general process by which high-quality compliance with norms (what we here call responsibility) comes about.

Situations such as that faced by Sue and Will provide us with the raw materials for studying two fundamental aspects of social life: agency and responsibility. We learn about human agency—the capacity of people to make meaningful choices rather than just do what they have been programmed to do—and what happens when people confront situations for which they have not been prepared either by anticipatory socialization for a particular role or by being supplied with an appropriate "script:" It is not that social structure ceases to be important, only that it plays a somewhat different role when extreme uncertainty makes the scripting of activity difficult and when the consequential nature of the events motivates reflection rather than unthinking compliance.

By examining situations like that faced by Will and Sue, we are also able to ask how responsibility arises. Although much of social science is concerned with questions about when people abide by rules rather than violate them, here we instead ask about a different aspect of compliance. We ask how it happens that people actively attempt to figure out what they should do, try to determine which means are most appropriate to the ends, adjust their own behavior and enlist the help of others in a valiant attempt to produce a desired outcome. We turn now to a more formal presentation of the questions that motivated this research and an explanation of why we believe a study of people like Sue and Will is a good way to answer these questions.

Responsibility and Moral Hazard as Concerns of Social Control Systems

Three ubiquitous problems for social systems are how to get people not to violate norms, how to get them to meet minimum standards (e.g., not to shirk on the job), and how to get at least some people to perform at a higher level, providing the flexible adjustment to changing conditions that is the hallmark of responsibility. The first of these problems, the outright violation of norms, or deviance, has been a central concern of sociology since its earliest days. . . . The second problem, shirking, or moral hazard as it is often called in the social science literature, has received considerable attention in recent years, though until recently most of this attention has come from economists rather than from sociologists (Arrow 1971, 1991; Fama 1980; Fama and Jensen 1983; Heimer 1985; Holmstrøm 1979, 1982). The third problem, which we here call responsibility, has received much less attention.[4] By responsibility, we mean high-quality compliance with norms—thoughtful compliance oriented toward achieving the objective of the norm or meeting one's obligations to others rather than toward avoidance of blame or superficial conformity. What's crucial here is that people are actively choosing how best to conform to norms, altering their own contributions of labor and other resources as necessary, and monitoring to ensure that the outcomes are what they intended. . . . We are explicitly concerned then with how normative systems foster responsibility. We argue that Will and Sue's reaction to their daughter's plight can only be understood when we analyze it as an attempt to take responsibility—to comply thoughtfully and wholeheartedly with their normative obligations to Tiffany.

Though responsibility has received scant attention from social scientists, it has become a buzzword in politics and public discourse on issues ranging from the decline of the American family to the escalation of corporate greed. Legislators often debate how welfare recipients can be induced to take responsibility for their own lives rather than rely on the public purse (although scholars like Luker [1996] point out that such discussions are plagued by deep misconceptions about teenage pregnancy and unwed motherhood and their relation to poverty). At the same time, given that children now make up a larger percentage of the nation's poor than at any time since we began keeping statistics (Coltrane 1996: 124), legislative debate about welfare cannot completely ignore questions about societal as well as parental responsibilities for children. Juvenile crime has also been a focus of national concern, and questions about responsibility have been raised in that discussion as well. If parents would take more responsibility for their children, some suggest, juvenile crime rates would fall. Concerns about responsibility are pervasive. Teachers are accused of failing to take responsibility for their students' learning. Corporate managers, we are told, have conceived themselves as beholden only to shareholders and have neglected their responsibilities to other stakeholders. Responsibility was also the rallying cry of the controversial and closely watched Million Man March, of African-American men, in Washington, D.C., in 1995. The refrains are familiar: If individuals, groups, and large organizations took more responsibility, the world would be a better place. But what exactly does it mean to take more responsibility? Who should take responsibility? How is responsibility encouraged? And alternately, how is it undermined?

Responsibility, as it is commonly understood, has a multiplicity of meanings. But whether they are onerous obligations or rewards for past achievements, and whether they are individual or collective ones, responsibilities carry with them an obligation to achieve some desired, but perhaps ambiguously defined, objective. In analyzing responsibilities, we need to make understanding the nature of the obligation our first task. Here we are interested in how widely shared the obligation is, asking whether it falls on the shoulders of one person or is shared with others. We are also interested in how compulsory the obligation is and ask whether one is drafted or volunteers. In addition, we are interested in how the desired outcome is defined, whether by those who must meet it or by other authorities, in how closely compliance is monitored, and in how rewards and punishments are distributed for meeting, exceeding, or falling short of expectations. Responsibility implies some social group. We must therefore ask: Responsible to whom? For what? And with what consequences?

Responsibilities as Fates or Opportunities

We can distinguish between two different ways that people come to have particular responsibilities and their correspondingly different experiences with them. Briefly, responsibilities can be either opportunities or fates; they can be more strongly associated with positions or with persons. People may come to have particular responsibilities because they choose them, for instance by volunteering for one task rather than another at work, or by deciding on a line of employment. The physicians who cared for Tiffany during her hospitalization acquired a responsibility for her (and other patients) when they chose to become neonatologists; one or more of her nurses might have requested to care for her in particular and to act as her "primary nurse." In choosing one

responsibility rather than another, a person might be driven by the chance to do an interesting task, to get credit for a job well done, to avoid an onerous alternative task, or to win the opportunity to undertake an especially attractive job later. Reactions to this first type of responsibility are tapped by survey questions that ask whether respondents would like to take more responsibility at work or whether they already have as much responsibility as they want. Evidence from surveys suggests that people like their jobs better when those jobs carry more responsibility.[5]

But not all responsibilities are so freely chosen. Some responsibilities are received as accidents of fate and experienced as burdens rather than opportunities, though a person may still be able to refuse a responsibility or to limit his or her obligations. A premature birth, such as Tiffany's, or the illness of an aging parent does not lead to fantasies of credit for a job well done or future opportunities to care for disabled relatives.[6] Instead people worry about how to balance the new responsibility with preexisting commitments and how to husband their resources or find new ones. Rather than seek rewards, people strive to avoid guilt and blame. The best they can hope for is credit for having "done their duty" despite the unfairness of being dealt a hand of inescapable obligations.

Though in some senses a responsibility is a "fate" whenever one does not freely choose the responsibility and cannot escape it (and so exercises agency more in deciding how to meet the obligation rather than in whether to meet it), the potential disproportion between obligations and resources is fundamental to the consequential character of fatelike responsibilities. When a responsibility is a fate, one must dip into or even deplete one's own resources even though others do not pitch in. A responsibility is a fate, then, whenever one might be stuck in a permanently losing situation, in which a responsibility can be discharged only by exhausting one's resources. It is even more a fate if such a permanently losing position does not leave one with sufficient resources to discharge the responsibility adequately. But fatelike responsibilities are not limited to personal life. One is confronted with property ownership as a fate when one's business goes bankrupt with unlimited liability, especially if one then feels an obligation to pay all the creditors even after the bankruptcy. And in social systems, such as caste systems, in which occupations are ascriptively assigned (on the basis of such immutable traits as gender, race, and ethnicity), occupational responsibilities are more likely to be experienced as fates.

Two aspects of responsibility—the inescapability of the obligations and the relation between resources and obligations—predict being stuck in a situation similar to bankruptcy. When resources do vary with the magnitude of an obligation, and when one can escape burdens that have become intolerable or just unattractive in comparison with other responsibilities one might shoulder, a person retains the flexibility to strategize about which package of obligations to accept. In contrast, when resources cannot be adjusted in response to contingencies, and when one retains responsibility "come hell or high water," one's capacity to maneuver is decreased, and previous obligations act as rigid constraints on one's ability to respond to other opportunities that might arise. It is this constraining aspect of fatelike responsibility that so deeply shapes women's experience of responsibility. As we discuss below, women and men are not equally exposed to the burdens of fatelike responsibilities. There is a central irony here: though fate implies inevitability, fatelike responsibilities are more inevitable for women that for men. Fate, in short, is quite an elaborate social achievement. . . .

Gender: A Strategic Resource

Because responsibilities carry contingent obligations, assuming one responsibility tends to limit one's capacity to accept others. The conflict is more acute for responsibilities that are fates than for those that are opportunities, because fates cannot as easily be shed or reduced to accommodate new possibilities and because they are more likely to be associated with the shallower pockets of families than the deeper pockets of organizations. Characteristics that are associated with taking on fatelike responsibilities are therefore key subjects in an empirical study of responsibility. We argue that women are disproportionately likely to shoulder such fatelike responsibilities as the care of children and the elderly and that this gender inequality is a deep and abiding constraint on the capacity of women to seek or accept more highly rewarded responsibilities. While gender is clearly not the only variable that affects the likelihood that a person will take on such responsibilities, we believe that we cannot understand either how acceptance of responsibility affects gender stratification or how responsibilities are allocated without taking a close look at this piece of the puzzle. . . . Our concern is more with how such gender inequalities come about than with the consequences of such inequalities. But because inequalities tend to reproduce themselves, we will necessarily focus on both causes and consequences.

We need not dig very deep to find evidence that women disproportionately shoulder the burdens of caring for small children or aged, ailing, or disabled family members. Clearly, maternal responsibilities are less often shed than paternal ones.[7] In 1995, 23% of children under eighteen lived with their mother only, 69% with both parents, 4% with their father only, and 4% with neither parent (U.S. Bureau of the Census 1996: 65; people under eighteen who maintained their own households or family groups were excluded). Indeed, McMahon (1995) argues that shirking parental responsibilities is almost unthinkable for women, because motherhood is so central to their identities. In consonance with our argument that some responsibilities come to be associated more with the person rather than with a position, McMahon finds that for mothers "the feeling of responsibility for their children is more than the expectation of a social role; it becomes constitutive of the self, making the denial of such responsibility almost unthinkable. Thus for a woman to be remiss in feeling responsible for her child would implicate her whole moral character. Being responsible for her child is about being moral as a person . . . motherhood [is] associated with female morality" (270).

Over the life course, women's ties with kin are stronger than men's, and their sense of normative obligation to kin is also stronger (Rossi and Rossi 1990). Women spend more hours per day on child care and household work whether or not they are employed, and women with children at home have fewer hours of leisure than men. Daughters are more likely than sons to assist aging parents (Spitze and Logan 1990). Women also do the kinwork of maintaining ties across households (DiLeonardo 1987). And women shoulder obligations to others even when it hurts—Simmons, Klein, and Simmons (1977) found that, controlling for the type of relationship (parenthood, sibling, etc.), women are more likely than men to donate kidneys.

To understand apparent gender differences in the extent to which responsibilities are inescapable and constraining personal obligations, we need to look at three sets of conditions. First, concerning how responsibilities are assigned, we need to ask whether women are more likely than men to define obligations as theirs rather than as someone else's. We also must ask whether others see

obligations as belonging to particular women but not to particular men. Second, concerning the conditions under which obligations are incurred, we need to ask whether women are more likely than men to believe that a relationship is at stake and that they might jeopardize the relationship if they failed to take responsibility. Do gender differences in expressivity (e.g., awareness and discussion of their own and others' feelings) shape the sense of obligation? Are women more likely than men to be embedded in ongoing exchange relations, and do these relations create different obligations for the two sexes? Third, concerning whether other resources give relief from obligation, we need to ask whether men and women differ in their access to resources such as money with which to meet obligations. When are substitutions, for instance money for one's own labor, acceptable? Are others (e.g., neighbors or the state) more likely to provide assistance to men than to women, so that familial obligations can be met without substantial changes in a care provider's life? Although questions about how responsibilities are assigned to individuals, about the extent to which obligations are incurred in the context of ongoing relationships, and about how other resources substitute for contributions of one's own labor are analytically separable, they are not empirically independent. In particular, often it is through relationships that obligations come to feel and be defined as personal, and relationships arise and are sustained through repeated exchange.

To say that women are disproportionately saddled with the burdens of fatelike responsibilities says little about how these "personal" responsibilities shape men's and women's capacities to take on responsibilities outside the home. Pleck (1977) long ago suggested that the boundary between work and home was asymmetrically permeable for men and women—that for men work intruded into the time and space allocated to family life, while for women family life intruded on work time and space. Men then use the resources of the home to provide the flexibility needed to make a go of their careers—working weekends when necessary, entertaining a customer or colleague for the evening, working an extra shift because a coworker is ill. In contrast, women are more likely to use whatever flexibility can be wrung from a job to handle the uncertainties of family life—they make deals with bosses about making up hours so they can stay home with a sick child, rank potential jobs by how tolerant the supervisor is of obligations to children, and refuse offers of extra hours or chances to entertain business associates because such tasks are incompatible with household obligations (Freeman 1982). Working men tend to work longer hours than working women, and men are more likely to be employed in the sorts of occupations that require them to work especially long hours. But even when both spouses are employed, women spend more time than men on housework and child care (Hochschild 1989; Szalai 1972; Robinson 1977).

For both men and women these statistical differences in hours spent on household versus employment obligations are produced by processes that are often uncomfortably constraining. Although both sexes are constrained, we must not overlook the differences both in how behavior is shaped and in the long-term consequences of these patterns. For men and women, hours of labor very likely go up in response to increases in the demand for their labor. For both sexes, increases in hours are at least partly an attempt to reduce costs—for instance by providing more attention for a troubled child at home or by placating an angry supervisor at work. But when men placate angry supervisors or put in extra hours because of a bulge in the flow of work, they anticipate that such investments will yield returns in stability of employment, increases in wages, or opportunities for advancement. Women have no similar expectations about changes in returns at home, although they may expect some gratitude (and Hochschild [1989] discusses the family economy of gratitude) and hope that their children will benefit from the attention.[8] Because some family obligations are accepted almost unconditionally, the economy of family life does not require as close a tie between investment and return.

As one rises in an organization, whether it be a firm, political party, religious group, or voluntary association, the variability of demands increases. People who have other responsibilities are less able to adapt quickly to new demands unless a staff of assistants can carry much of the load. But fatelike responsibilities typically must be met with resources from the flexibility of small groups of people and the shallow pockets of families and friends rather than the large staffs and deep pockets of organizations. Further, family work is more constraining than many commitments at work. Family life is more variable in its demands—only really exceptional employment situations call for round-the-clock work, as sick children occasionally do in every family—and therefore calls for more adaptability than most other occupations. Anyone assigned the primary responsibility for a home and family will have little capacity to take on responsibilities in other settings. As long as such responsibilities are perceived as *personal* and women lack the resources to decrease the burden, they will be unable to invest equally with men in the world of positional responsibilities. The fateful consequence of being the gender that shoulders fatelike responsibilities is that women are less able to invest strategically in responsibilities that are also opportunities.

The facts are not new, and indeed they have been pithily presented before: wives provide their husbands with continuous flexibility (Hertz 1986); the boundary between work and family life is asymmetrically permeable for men and women (Pleck 1977); because of gender differences in the "second shift," employed women with children in effect work an extra month of twenty-four hour days (Hochschild 1989); women are more likely than men to be assigned the high-periodicity household tasks that preclude their joining the councils of state or business (Douglas and Isherwood 1978). As Hochschild (1989, 1997), Hertz (1986), and Gerson (1985) argue, changes in the workplace have outstripped changes in the home.[9] Women continue to do more than their share at home despite participation in the labor force, and this inequality in both labor and responsibility stunts or distorts women's careers. The link between the domestic sphere and the public sphere, between the more complete revolution at work and the stalled one at home (Hochschild 1989), continues to pose a puzzle.

We argue . . . that in whatever setting they occur, roles that carry a lot of responsibility differ from other roles in requiring a person to look out for the interests and needs of others, to define obligations diffusely, to think about both long- and short-term consequences, to use discretion in adapting to contingencies, and to accept the consequences "come hell or high water." But when responsibilities are tied to persons (as family obligations are especially tied to mothers, daughters, wives, and sisters) rather than to positions (as responsibilities at work often are), it is difficult to escape responsibilities that have become losing propositions.[10] Further, one is more likely to have to meet personal obligations with one's own time, skill, and money. Because one must meet whatever obligations life brings from one's own reserves and because the responsibilities of family life are quite variable compared with the demands im-

posed by the world of paid work, women cannot as easily invest their reserves in high-powered careers. Neither family life nor high-powered careers come packaged in limited-liability, forty-hour weeks with specified tasks. But having a wife makes family life more like a "job" for men; the bulk of the uncertainty is absorbed by a woman, leaving the man free to make strategic investments in his career. The complaint that husbands are willing to "help out" at home but don't accept responsibility is then not a petty gripe but a key element of the persistence of gender inequality.

Gender is, in short, not just a variable, but a resource for men. . . . Though we wish to acknowledge women's agency in their decisions about taking responsibility, we also cannot deny that people face constraints that vary with gender. Women lack some of the resources that allow men to escape some of the most burdensome familial responsibilities. Gender is thus important for understanding the variation between parents in their acceptance of the responsibilities of caring for a sick child, but there are other important variables as well. There are no simple explanations as we try to account for variations among families in their willingness and ability to shoulder a burdensome responsibility. But richer families can more easily accommodate the additional burden by hiring extra help and seeking the opinions of experts. Likewise, parents with more education can more easily understand the arcane medical details, master the necessary care routines, arrange complicated schedules, and coordinate the efforts of many participants. However, we must emphasize that wealth and education do not necessarily produce responsibility and are certainly not the only routes to a desired outcome. Gender works somewhat differently from these other resources, then. It determines whether one will be expected (both by others and by oneself) to shoulder a burdensome responsibility. These other resources help to lighten the load.

Of course, noting that women are disproportionately likely to shoulder burdensome familial responsibilities or that parents with more money and more education may have an easier time of it is nothing new. However, when we recast these all-too-familiar facts in a new light, we learn something new about responsibility. When we look closely, . . . we see variations among parents and among families that elucidate the process by which incumbents of roles come to define their obligations so differently. We begin to see how it is that some parents come to embrace an onerous responsibility and others reject it. By then comparing this case with other settings, we begin to understand the general process through which responsibility is produced or undermined well beyond the infant intensive care units where we begin our investigation.

NOTES

1. To protect confidentiality, we refer to all people and places by pseudonyms. Throughout this reading, we refer to the families we interviewed with case and page numbers from those interviews.
2. The Katie Beckett program provides federal funding so that chronically ill or disabled children who would otherwise have to be cared for in a hospital or other institution can instead be cared for at home. The program was signed into law by President Ford, and named after the child whose family had pressed for funding so that they could care for their daughter at home.
3. Will and Sue were fully aware of the importance of these indicators. Will commented on hearing Tiffany's first cry, a particularly welcome sound given the distinct possibility that she might have been stillborn: "It was a real nice first cry because, you know, we didn't expect to hear anything, you know" (1009M, p. 12). He was eager to hear her voice again: "We haven't heard her but make that one noise. That's a little hard, you know, but we're almost to the end, thank God"

(1009M, p. 19). The next surgery would remove the "trach;" and "she'll be ready to make noise" (p. 36).
4. Two notable exceptions are Selznick (1992) and Wuthnow (1991). Selznick, whose work is cited later in this chapter, discusses both the responsible self and the responsible enterprise, and Wuthnow contributes an empirical study of compassion. Wuthnow argues that the distinction between compassion and corruption is a distinction between two forms of overcommitment (1991: 279–80). Both entail exercising discretion in the application of rules, going beyond a job description, the letter of the law, or the fine print of a contract. But while corruption entails bending the rules for personal benefit, compassion involves going beyond what is required in the opposite direction—overconforming, overperforming for the benefit of others.
5. These surveys do not usually measure actual responsibility. Instead they ask about numbers of superiors and subordinates, ownership of the business, frequency of supervision, and sometimes whether the respondent is happy with current responsibilities or would like to have more or fewer. As one example, Jencks, Perman, and Rainwater's (1988) index of job desirability includes some items that could be construed as measures of responsibility.
6. Although people do not think of "opportunities" to care for sick or disabled relatives or to take on other similar fates as "investments;" they may nevertheless subsequently choose to make use of the skills and knowledge acquired in the course of meeting such obligations. People might, for instance, be called on to offer advice and solace to others experiencing similar events. Sue and Will's decision to build on their experiences with Tiffany by enrolling in a nursing curriculum, and so to use their new empathy and skills in a professional capacity, is rather unusual. We suspect that the likelihood of treating the new knowledge and skills as "human capital" is greater when people experience these crises before having made major decisions about careers.
7. It may be somewhat easier to give up motherhood by refusing the role at the start, for instance by relinquishing a child for adoption or having an abortion. Still, the lore about "birth mothers" (but not "birth fathers") needing to compensate for having given up babies or worrying about how their

children have fared, and about the lingering guilt felt by women years after having abortions, suggests some residual sense of personal obligation.

8. Research, however, suggests that mothers' expectations of gratitude may not be fulfilled. Because children expect their mothers to care for them, they are not grateful to their mothers for providing care, but only to their fathers (Maccoby and Mnookin 1992: 36).

9. Coltrane (1996) presents evidence that over the last three decades fathers in intact families have become more involved in family work, although he concedes that most men still avoid doing routine child care and housework. Although this increased involvement by some men is good news, we must keep in mind that it is evidence about intact families and that a lower proportion of families are "intact" than in the past.

10. In arguing that responsibilities associated with persons are different from those associated with positions, we do not wish to minimize the importance of variations among families and among jobs. How much familial responsibilities are personal rather than positional varies with family structure and with one's position in the family. And the work-related obligations of professionals sometimes become associated with the person, particularly when the professional possesses rare expertise or has special information about interaction partners, as occurs in the relationship between faculty and long-term student, physician and chronically ill patient, lawyer and client, or therapist and patient.

REFERENCES

Arrow, Kenneth J. 1971. *Essays in the Theory of Risk Bearing.* Chicago: Markham.

Coltrane, Scott. 1996. *Family Man: Fatherhood, Housework, and Gender Equity.* New York: Oxford University Press.

DiLeonardo, Micaela. 1987. "The Female World of Cards and Holidays: Women, Families, and the Work of Kinship." *Signs* 12:440–53.

Douglas, Mary and Baron Isherwood. 1978. *The World of Goods.* New York: Basic.

Fama, Eugene F. 1980. "Agency Problems and the Theory of the Firm." *Journal of Political Economy* 88:288–307.

Fama, Eugene F. and Michael C. Jensen. 1983. "Agency Problems and Residual Claims." *Journal of Law and Economics* 26:327–49.

Freeman, Caroline. 1982. "The 'Understanding Employer.'" Pp. 135–53 in Jackie West, ed., *Women, Work, and the Labour Market.* London: Routledge and Kegan Paul.

Gerson, Kathleen. 1985. *Hard Choices: How Women Decide about Work, Career, and Motherhood.* Berkeley: University of California Press.

Heimer, Carol A. 1985. *Reactive Risk and Rational Action: Managing Moral Hazard In Insurance Contracts.* Berkeley: University of California Press.

Hertz, Rosanna. 1986. *More Equal than Others.* Berkeley: University of California Press.

Hochschild, Arlie Russell. 1997. *The Time Bind: When Work Becomes Home and Home Becomes Work.* New York: Metropolitan.

———, with Anne Machung. 1989. *The Second Shift.* New York: Viking.

Holmstrøm, Bengt. 1979. "Moral Hazard and Observability." *Bell Journal of Economics* 10:74–91.

———. 1982. "Moral Hazard in Teams." *Bell Journal of Economics* 13:324–40.

Jencks, Christopher, Lauri Perman, and Lee Rainwater. 1988. "What Is a Good Job? A New Measure of Labor Market Success." *American Journal of Sociology* 93:1322–57.

Luker, Kristin. 1996. *Dubious Conceptions: The Politics of Teenage Pregnancy.* Cambridge: Harvard University Press.

Maccoby, Eleanor E. and Robert H. Mnookin. 1992. *Dividing the Child: Social and Legal Dilemmas of Custody.* Cambridge: Harvard University Press.

McMahon, Martha. 1995. *Engendering Motherhood: Identity and Self-Transformation in Women's Lives.* New York: Guilford Press.

Pleck, Joseph H. 1977. "The Work-Family System." *Social Problems* 26:417–27.

Robinson, J. P. 1977. *How Americans Use Time.* New York: Praeger Press.

Rossi, Alice S. and Peter H. Rossi. 1990. *Of Human Bonding.* New York: Aldine de Gruyter.

Selznick, Philip. 1992. *The Moral Commonwealth: Social Theory and the Promise of Community.* Berkeley: University of California Press.

Simmons, Roberta G., Susan D. Klein, and Richard L. Simmons. 1977. *Gift of Life.* New York: Wiley.

Spitze, Glenna and John R. Logan. 1990. "Sons, Daughters, and Intergenerational Social Support." *Journal of Marriage and the Family* 52:420–30.

Szalai, Alexander, ed. 1972. *The Use of Time.* The Hague: Mouton.

U.S. Bureau of the Census. 1996. *Statistical Abstract of the United States: 1993.* 116th ed. Washington, DC: Government Printing Office.

Wuthrow, Robert 1991. *Acts of Compassion.* Princeton, NJ: Princeton University Press.

QUESTIONS FOR DISCUSSION

1. What are the ways that the organization of our health care system defines responsibility for illness and recovery?
2. Are there ways that individuals are discouraged from taking on responsibility for their own health? From offering care to others?
3. Do you agree with Heimer and Staffen's assertion that "women are disproportionately saddled with the burdens of fatelike responsibilities"?
4. Do we have different social expectations for women and men regarding the care of children, the sick, and the elderly? What are the social and financial costs and rewards of these different expectations?

THE SOCIAL WEB

- The Centers for Disease Control and Prevention presents the latest statistical information on health care and disease in the United States. The CDC Web site also offers guidelines for employers and health care professionals, as well as health tips for the general public about numerous health-related issues: www.cdc.gov.
- The World Health Organization is the agency of the United Nations whose primary concern is related to the global promotion of health and wellness. The WHO defines health not merely in terms of the absence of disease, but as the physical, mental, and social well-being of all individuals in the world: www.who.int.
- The American Association of Retired Persons is dedicated to promoting the interests of Americans over the age of 49. AARP provides information and advocacy for a variety of health-related issues, including the rising costs of prescription drugs, the availability of quality home health care, and standards of affordable nursing home care: www.aarp.org.

QUESTIONS FOR DEBATE

1. What are the ways that our current health care system reflects larger patterns of social inequality?
2. What are the implications of medicalizing social problems? What happens when we define certain social conditions—for example, drug and alcohol abuse—as medical problems?
3. How should priorities for medical funding and research be determined? Who should be making such decisions?
4. Can the problems in our health care system be fixed with the current system in place? Do we need to dismantle the current system? How do we make health less of a financial burden for individuals and for our society as a whole?

Chapter 12
The Environment

Learning Objectives

By the end of this chapter you should be able to:

- Recognize how the authors use one or more of the major perspectives to explore environmental issues.
- Explore how environmental problems are shaped by inequalities of race, gender, and class.
- Identify the ways that environmental issues are socially constructed.
- Describe various consequences of environmental policies and problems.
- Explain how social systems and institutions perpetuate environmental problems.

Defining the Problem

Scholars of social problems who study the environment believe that the inequalities that plague the global economy are central to environmental problems as well. The desire of powerful multinational corporations to maximize short-term profits can cause them to define the earth's natural environment as an exploitable resource. Little regard is given to the consequences of massive industrialization either in terms of the consumption of natural resources necessary for production or in terms of the polluting by-products of industry. Individuals who live in wealthy nations typically presume the right to consume goods and resources, with little regard for the effects of overconsumption on poorer nations or on the environment. The most severe consequences of overconsumption—the depletion of vital resources, the degradation of the land, air, and water, and the increase in health risks produced by toxic waste products—tend to occur in poorer, less developed nations.

Social problems investigators are also likely to look at the relationship between environmental degradation and economic and racial inequality in the United States. The patterns of environmental racism demonstrate the ways that common environmental problems like pollution and hazardous wastes reflect larger issues of social injustice. Some researchers examine why the most polluted areas are also most likely to be populated by the poor and racial minorities. Other scholars analyze data suggesting that facilities for dealing with environmental problems, such as hazardous waste incinerators, nuclear waste storage sites, or water treatment plants, tend to be located in areas where residents do not have economic or political power.

Finally, many sociologists look at local environmental issues and debates to learn how individuals become social activists. Some researchers study how new citizens' organizations are formed and the ways that people are able to mobilize important resources for changing the environmentally hazardous procedures of corporations or municipalities. Other researchers study what kinds of organizations, tactics, and strategies are effective for creating new environmentally sound social policies.

Scope of the Problem

Current human patterns of consumption represent a serious and growing threat to the world's ecosystems. The expanding global economy and global population have caused a drastic increase in the consumption of the major commodities produced by our ecosystems in the past forty years.[1] Since 1961, global wood consumption has increased by almost two-thirds, grain consumption has more than doubled, and meat consumption has tripled. The consumption of fish has increased more than six times since 1950. There is tremendous disparity in patterns of consumption between rich and poor nations. Individuals living in developed countries consume, on average, twice as much fish and grain, three times as much meat, and eleven times as much gasoline as people living in developing nations. In 1997, people in the wealthiest nations—16 percent of the world's population—accounted for 80 percent of the total amount of money spent on private consumption, while those in low-income countries—35 percent of the total population—accounted for only 2 percent of such expenditures.

Land use and availability are major concerns around the world. Twenty-nine percent of the world's lands have been converted to agricultural and urban areas.[2] Agriculture alone accounts for the loss of one-third of forests and one-fourth of natural grasslands. The United Nations projects that an additional one-third of undeveloped land worldwide will be converted within the next 100 years.

One of the major problems associated with current global agricultural practices is the increasing desertification of land. Land is overcultivated and poorly managed, resulting in the loss of topsoil and the reduction of water quality. It becomes unusable for agriculture or grazing, which threatens the capacity of countries to produce food.[3] Land is being lost to desertification at astonishing rates, representing, according to the United Nations, "an urgent global problem."[4] Desertification is a major concern for 110 countries, affecting 20 percent of the planet's drylands and placing one billion people at risk.

Farmland is not the only kind of land experiencing significant degradation. The world's forests are also diminishing. Eighty percent of the Earth's original forests are gone.[5] Because of logging, mining, warfare, agricultural cultivation, and large-scale development projects, 39 percent of remaining forests are threatened. The consequences of deforestation are far reaching. Many species of plants and animals are disappearing with the forests. Tropical rain forests contain more than 90 percent of the world's species and are the richest areas in biodiversity. The United Nations estimates that 25 percent of the world's mammal species and 11 percent of bird species are threatened with extinction.

Marine and coastal habitats are also being diminished. One-third of the planet's coastlines are threatened due to land degradation, erosion, oil spills, and pollution. In the United States alone, nearly 100,000 acres

---

[1]Gregory Mock, "How Much Do We Consume?" *World Resources 2000–2001*, World Resources Institute.

[2]Gregory Mock, "Domesticating the World: Conversion of Natural Ecosystems," *World Resources 2000–2001*, World Resources Institute.

[3]"Fact Sheet," United Nations Convention to Combat Desertification, 2002.

[4]"Global State of the Environment Report, 1997," United Nations Environment Programme.

[5]Unless otherwise indicated, data are obtained from "GEO-2000: Global Environment Outlook," United Nations Environment Programme.

of wetlands are being lost every year.[6] Wetlands provide a natural barrier between large bodies of water and land. They help to prevent land erosion and are home to significant numbers of marine and plant life. Overfishing is also becoming a severe problem, with more than 60 percent of fisheries worldwide being heavily exploited. It is important to remember that the majority of the world's population lives within a short distance of a coastline, and more than 3 billion people are in some way dependent on coastal habitats.

Freshwater contamination is another significant global problem. According to the United Nations, 20 percent of the world's population does not have access to safe drinking water, and one-half of the world's population lacks access to adequate sanitation facilities. In developing nations, 90 percent of wastewater runs directly into rivers and streams without any treatment.[7] Sewage pollution is a major public health crisis. It is estimated that 1.2 billion people suffer ill health and 15 million children under five die each year as a result of polluted water.

Worldwide pollution is increasing as a result of agricultural and industrial expansion. In the 1990s 400 million tons of hazardous waste were produced, 300 million of which were by industrialized nations. Annual carbon dioxide emissions were four times the 1950 level. Air pollution in developing urban areas has reached crisis levels around the world, according to the United Nations. It is estimated that 50 percent of all chronic respiratory illnesses are associated with air pollution.

In the United States alone industrial factories released 7.1 billion pounds of toxic chemicals into the environment in 2000.[8] An estimated 450,000 areas are so polluted by hazardous industrial contaminants as to make them unusable for any human activity. These so-called "brownfields" are often found in poor urban neighborhoods near minority populations.[9]

Rapid urbanization only compounds the problems associated with environmental degradation. One-half of the world's population—3 billion people—live in urban areas and 160,000 people are added to the world's cities every day. It is projected that an additional one billion people will join the world's cities by the year 2010. More than 600 million people live in such urban squalor that their health and lives are continuously threatened. Cities have a profound impact on the entire global environment. According to the United Nations, "their ecological footprints can be enormous because of their huge demands for energy, food and other resources, and the regional and global impacts of their wastes and emissions to soil, air, and water."[10]

Perspectives on the Problem

Sociologists looking at environmental issues from a *conflict perspective* would examine the ways that corporations and individuals with vested economic interests influence environmental policies and the use of worldwide resources. They would explore how specific environmental problems, such as pollution and hazardous material disposal,

---

[6]"Profile," *1998 National Water Quality Inventory Report to Congress,* U.S. Environmental Protection Agency.

[7]Carmen Revenga and Greg Mock, "Dirty Water: Pollution Problems Persist," World Resources Institute, October 2000.

[8]From "Pollution" on the Sierra Club Web site: www.sierraclub.org.

[9]From "Brownfields" on the Environmental Literacy Council Web site: www.enviroliteracy.org.

[10]From "Urban Areas, The State of the Environment—Regional Synthesis," *GEO-2000: Global Environment Outlook,* United Nations Environment Programme.

disproportionately affect individuals based on class, race, and gender inequalities. Sociologists using a *functionalist approach* would emphasize the interplay of population growth, industrial development, and environmental issues and would examine how the depletion of valuable resources results in environmental degradation and social disruption. They would argue that societies need to change the way they relate to their ecosystems in order to minimize environmental problems. Sociologists examining the environment from a *social constructionist perspective* would focus on the ways that the cause of, nature of, and solutions to environmental problems are defined by governments, environmental groups, and individuals. They would look at how corporations, policy makers, and environmental activists compete to construct the ways that we culturally view and behave toward the environment and how we decide what constitutes legitimate problems for governmental intervention. Finally, sociologists using a *symbolic interactionist approach* would look at the effects of environmental problems on individuals. They would explore the lives of people who have been personally affected by environmental degradation, as well as the experiences of those individuals who have become involved in environmental activism.

Connecting the Perspectives

Michael T. Klare uses a conflict perspective to examine global struggles over the availability and use of the world's natural resources. Bob Burtman also uses a conflict perspective to analyze current land use policies in the United States. He argues that oil interests have been given a higher priority by the federal government than the protection and preservation of fragile public lands. Valerie Kuletz takes a social constructionist approach to examine the U.S. government's decisions to store nuclear waste on American Indian lands. She looks at how the federal government successfully labeled lands that are sacred to Native Americans as wastelands and ideal disposal sites. Finally, using a functionalist perspective, Paul Hawken proposes that corporations redefine natural resources as a form of capitalism. Hawken believes that protecting the environment can contribute to the well-being of capitalism, while capitalism can advance the interests of environmental preservation.

Reading Summaries

In "Resource Wars: The New Landscape of Global Conflict," Klare examines the increasing significance of conflict over valuable resources for international relationships and for world peace and security. He argues that the September 11, 2001, Al Qaeda attacks against the United States are best understood in the context of America's global oil policies. Since World War II the United States has been the major ally of Saudi Arabia, giving the United States access to one-fourth of the world's remaining oil supply. Al Qaeda and other Middle East organizations view Saudi Arabia as a principle focal point in the struggle over world petroleum resources and, thus, wealth and worldwide power. Because of these oil and natural gas supplies, the United States is increasingly enmeshed in the politics of the Gulf region, putting it at the center of what Klare terms "resource wars."

Conflicts over the world's valuable resources have become the arena in which struggles for wealth and power are played out. According to Klare, the resource wars have become a central feature of global politics because of several major factors. During the last half of the twentieth century, world population more than doubled. This population explosion created a huge demand for the basic requirements of human life—water, food, shelter, and clothing. There has also been an accompanying rise in global industrialization, making the demand for basic industrial commodities such as automobiles, televisions, and personal computers higher than ever before. While the demands of the global economy continue to expand, the available supplies of basic resources that are necessary for industrialization, especially water and oil, are diminishing. Increasing industrialization also means increasing pollution and environmental degradation. Finally, there are growing conflicts between adjoining nations over ownership of important natural resources, such as water and oil field reserves.

Klare argues that these factors are interrelated and contribute to one another. They also promote conflict and competition between nations and regions. The gap between rich and poor is not only increasing within countries; it is also growing between nations. Although the majority of these conflicts will be solved without violence, they nevertheless contribute to an international climate of instability and hostility. The resource wars, Klare argues, provide a global backdrop for disputes, economic injustice, and the threat of warfare.

In "Open Season on Open Space," Burtman examines the consequences of the Bush administration's policies on oil and gas drilling on public lands in the American West. Since taking office in 2001, George W. Bush's administration declared that the development of energy resources in the West takes priority over environmental concerns throughout the Rocky Mountain states. Oil companies have received leases to drill for oil and natural gas reserves on unspoiled national parkland. This drilling activity includes building tens of thousands of miles of roads, pipelines, and power lines. In addition, the drilling sites are located in delicate habitat areas for many species, including eagles, falcons, antelope, cougars, and bighorn sheep. They also include some

of the most visually spectacular scenes in the American landscape, such as Utah's Arches and Canyonlands. Much of this land had been declared off-limits by the Clinton administration, which proposed making some of these sites federal wilderness protection areas. Burtman argues that the drastic change in federal policy can be explained by the increasing political power of the oil industry. Both President Bush and Vice President Dick Cheney became multimillionaires as oil company executives. As a result, the Bush administration has proposed offering even more federal subsidies and tax cuts to oil companies as an incentive to drill in the West. Burtman maintains that current land use policies will only slightly decrease the United States' dependence on foreign oil sources. They will, however, damage the local tourist economies of these scenic areas and cause irreparable environmental harm to some of the nation's most unusual and beautiful public lands.

In "Mapping the Nuclear Landscape," Kuletz examines the consequences of nuclear testing in the Southwest region of the United States during the latter half of the twentieth century. Most of the sites of such tests were on or near land inhabited by various Native American tribes, resulting in severe health consequences for their people. Kuletz argues that looking at a map of nuclear test sites and nuclear waste disposal sites reveals more than simply U.S. nuclear and environmental policies. Instead, such mapping also tells the story of economic and racial inequality, especially among America's native peoples. Just as native tribes were not regarded seriously by federal and state governments in the nineteenth century, the land needs and health concerns of Native Americans in the twentieth century were disregarded in favor of the loosely controlled development of nuclear technology. Ultimately, Kuletz asserts, such environmental maps of the nuclear landscape point not to location so much as to power, wealth, and economic disadvantage.

Like the other readings in this part, our final selection focuses on the interconnections between environmental problems and social inequality. In "Natural Capitalism," Hawken describes how "social and environmental decay" are interwoven in our highly industrialized society. Hawken argues that we need to redefine what constitutes "capital" in a capitalist system. Capital is currently seen as economic materials and assets. The "natural capital" that Hawken describes are the renewable and nonrenewable materials of the earth—coal, oil, forests, grasslands—and the "services" they provide—clean air, fresh water, natural waste decomposition.

Hawken maintains that companies currently resist recognizing the central importance of natural capital, primarily because they have not had to pay attention to the declining state of the earth's resources. Yet corporate policies have not just harmed the environment; they have also hurt capitalism. Current business practices are highly wasteful and inefficient and have harmed both industry and the earth. Shrinking fish harvests, declining forests, and diminishing fresh water supplies are all environmental problems and business problems. Capitalism must make environmental changes for its own survival, as well as for the good of the earth.

Hawken also challenges businesses to change the ways they think about growth. Indicators of growth currently measure the level of monetary exchange. Yet the true measure of growth is what happens with that money. Does it improve the quality of life for people around the world? Hawken argues that a great deal of money is invested in projects that do not enhance the long-term quality of life and therefore do not contribute to true growth. The technology that displaces people from their jobs is also wasteful, inefficient, and destructive to the environment. Hawken calls for a major restructuring of the tax system that can reform capitalism to be environmentally friendly, which will benefit business as well as the earth's population.

FOCUSING QUESTIONS

As you read the selections in this chapter, think about environmental concerns in your own community. Can they be explained by the conflict between large corporations and the needs of private citizens? Do you think that in the United States we tend to define environmental problems as someone else's problems? What solutions can you offer for the environmental problems in your own community that do not contribute to existing patterns of social inequality?

52

RESOURCE WARS
The New Landscape of Global Conflict

MICHAEL T. KLARE

Introduction

Conflict over valuable resources—and the power and wealth they confer—has become an increasingly prominent feature of the global landscape. Often intermixed with ethnic, religious, and tribal antagonisms, such conflict has posed a significant and growing threat to peace and stability in many areas of the world. With the September 11, 2001, attacks on the World Trade Center and the Pentagon, the United States, too, became the victim of resource-related conflict. Motivated though they may have been by religious zeal, the September 11 hijackers were part of a global network whose ultimate objective—the overthrow of the pro-Western Saudi monarchy and the installation of a doctrinaire Islamic regime—would give it control over one-fourth of the world's remaining supply of petroleum. Success in this campaign would also deprive the United States of a major source of wealth and power—and it is precisely to avert this peril that Washington has long endeavored to protect the Saudi regime against its various enemies, including Osama bin Laden. In this and other ways, U.S. efforts to secure the flow of oil have led to ever increasing involvement in the region's ongoing power struggles.

These struggles were under way, of course, long before oil was discovered in the region. For centuries, local tribes and kingdoms fought over the rivers, ports, and oases of the greater Gulf area. Typically, these conflicts combined religious antagonisms with more worldly concerns, such as access to vital streams and wells. But the discovery of oil in the late nineteenth century added a new dimension to this violent panorama: from that point on, major outside powers acquired interests of their own in the region and periodically employed military force to protect these new interests. First to spar were Great Britain and czarist Russia, later joined by France, Germany, and the United States. By the end of the twentieth century, safeguarding the flow of oil from the Persian Gulf had become one of the most important functions of the U.S. military establishment.

Osama bin Laden and his associates were not directly engaged in the pursuit of oil when they launched a jihad against the United States and the Saudi government, but oil was central to their strategic calculations. . . . [T]he Saudi royal family has for decades permitted U.S. companies to extract vast quantities of petroleum from the kingdom, thus helping to sustain the long economic growth spurt of the second half of the twentieth century. The close relationship between the United States and the royal family was forged in the final months of World War II, when U.S. leaders sought to ensure favored access to Saudi petroleum. In one of the most extraordinary episodes in modern American history, President Franklin D. Roosevelt met with King Abdel-Aziz ibn Saud, the founder of the modern Saudi dynasty, while returning from the Allied summit conference in Yalta. Although the details of this meeting have never been made public, it is widely believed that Abdel-Aziz offered Roosevelt unlimited access to Saudi oil in return for a U.S. pledge to protect the royal family against internal and external attack. And whatever the exact nature of this agreement, the United States has served as Saudi Arabia's principal defender ever since.

The U.S. link with Saudi Arabia has been of considerable benefit to both parties concerned, but it has also led to ever deepening U.S. involvement in regional politics. And it has made Washington the enemy of those who, like Osama bin Laden, seek to overthrow the monarchy and replace it with a different sort of government. As a result, the United States has become embroiled in a series of what can best be termed "resource wars" in the greater Gulf area. . . .

Why have resources become so important? . . . [T]he adoption of an econocentric security policy almost always leads to an increased emphasis on resource protection— at least for those states that depend on raw material imports for their industrial prowess. The almost complete disappearance of ideological conflicts in today's world has also contributed to the centrality of resource issues, in that the pursuit and protection of critical materials is viewed as one of the state's primary security functions. In addition, certain resources are worth an immense amount of money . . . and so their possession is widely seen as something worth fighting over.

But these factors alone do not explain the current centrality of resource concerns: several features of resources themselves fig-

ure in this equation. These include the escalating worldwide demand for commodities of all types, the likely emergence of resource scarcities, and disputes over the ownership of valuable sources of critical materials.

Insatiable Demand

Global demand for many key materials is growing at an unsustainable rate. As the human population grows, societies require more of everything (food, water, energy, timber, minerals, fibers, and so on) to satisfy the basic material requirements of their individual members. Some nations may consume more than others—the United States alone consumes approximately 30 percent of all raw materials used by the human population in any given year[1]—but almost every society is increasing its utilization of basic materials.

The growing demand for resources is driven, to a considerable degree, by the dramatic increase in human numbers. During the past fifty years alone, the world population grew by over 3 billion people, jumping from 2.6 billion people in 1950 to just over 6 billion in 1999. The rise in population naturally entails an increased requirement for food, clothing, shelter, and the other basic necessities of life. This, alone, explains the growth in demand for many materials. But population increase accounts for only part of the explosion in demand; of equal importance is the spread of industrialization to more and more areas of the globe and the steady worldwide increase in personal wealth, producing an insatiable appetite for energy, private automobiles, building materials, household appliances, and other resource-intensive commodities.

Between 1950 and 1999, gross world product (GWP) soared by 583 percent, from approximately $6 trillion to $41 trillion (in constant 1998 dollars). Even when translated into per capita GWP, the increase has been substantial, jumping from \$2,500 in 1950 to \$6,750 in 1999.[2] While not all individuals have experienced the benefits of this impressive statistical gain—many millions, in fact, remained trapped in poverty—large numbers of people around the world can now afford items that were previously inaccessible to them. Private automobile ownership, for example, jumped from about 53 million cars in 1950 to an estimated 520 million in 1999.[3] The ownership of refrigerators, television sets, air conditioners, personal computers, and other such items has grown to a similar degree. Because the production and utilization of these products entails the consumption of vast amounts of energy, minerals, and other materials, the global requirement for many basic commodities has consistently exceeded the rate of population growth.[4] . . .

It is sometimes argued that the rising demand for resources in the developing world will be offset by a declining demand in the older industrialized nations, as computers and other high-tech devices take over the tasks once performed by less efficient, resource-consuming systems. And, to some degree, this is true: the use of copper in electrical wiring, for example, has been substantially diminished through the introduction of fiber-optic cables, which are made from cheap and plentiful silicon. On the whole, however, the introduction of computers has been accompanied not by a decline in overall resource consumption but an increase. This is so because technological innovation in the advanced economies has generated a considerable increase in personal wealth, and this, in turn, has led to a huge increase in personal consumption. In the United States, for example, automobile owners are driving greater distances every year—from 1.5 trillion miles in 1982 to 2.5 trillion in 1995—in larger and less fuel-efficient vehi-

cles; the average American home, moreover, has grown in size by one-third since the early 1970s.[5] As a result, net resource consumption in the United States has steadily risen over the past few decades, and a similar pattern is evident in Western Europe and other computer-rich areas.[6]

It is safe to conclude, therefore, that the global demand for basic resources will continue to grow in the decades ahead. Such growth will be driven, as before, by a combination of population increase and economic expansion. The human community is expanding by roughly 80 million people per year; at this rate, total world population will reach 6.8 billion people by 2010 and close to 8 billion by 2020.[7] On top of this, global per capita income is expected to rise by about 2 percent per year over the next few decades, nearly twice the rate of population growth.[8] If this added wealth is used for the continuing procurement of cars, trucks, appliances, large homes, and other such amenities, the worldwide demand for most basic materials will be substantially greater in 2020 than it was in the 1990s.

The Looming Risk of Shortages

Growing demand for basic materials is colliding with another key aspect of the global resource equation: the fact that the world supply of some substances is quite limited. While the earth is blessed with vast quantities of most vital materials—water, arable land, minerals, timber, and fossil fuels—there are practical limits to what can be extracted from the global environment. According to one recent study, the earth lost nearly one-third of its available natural wealth between 1970 and 1995 as a result of human activity, more than in any other period in history. This study, released by the World Wildlife Fund (WWF) in 1998, revealed a significant decline in the availability or quality of many critical resources, including forest cover, marine fisheries, freshwater systems, and fossil fuels. Although the WWF study did not cover all resources of concern, it did suggest that humanity could face significant shortages of many vital materials.[9]

When, or if, particular resources will reach the point of severe exhaustion is not something that can be predicted with any degree of certainty. Many minerals, for instance, are widely dispersed across the surface of the planet, and so new supplies are discovered all the time. Other resources, like timber, are theoretically "renewable," in the sense that new trees can be planted to replace those that have been cut down. Substitutes are also available (or can be developed) for many of the materials that are likely to experience future shortages. Nevertheless, it is evident that the world supply of certain key resources is being diminished at a rapid pace—in some cases, exceeding the world's capacity to exploit new sources or develop substitute materials.

Of the various materials that fall into this sensitive category, the most significant are oil and water. Both are critical for the functioning of modern industrial society, are being used in ever-increasing amounts, and most importantly are likely to be in insufficient supply to meet global requirements by the middle of the twenty-first century. At the beginning of 2000, the world's proven reserves of petroleum stood at 1,033 billion barrels, or sufficient oil to sustain global consumption (at the then-current rate of 73 million barrels per day) for another forty years.[10] If, however, oil consumption rises by 2 percent per year—as predicted by the U.S. Department of Energy—the existing supply will disappear in twenty-five to thirty years, not forty. Future oil discoveries will, of course, augment the global supply of oil,

while the introduction of new technologies will permit the extraction of untapped supplies now considered too remote or too difficult to exploit (such as those in northern Siberia and the deep waters of the Atlantic Ocean). Even so, it is likely that the world will begin to experience significant shortages of conventional petroleum by the second or third decade of the twenty-first century.[11] . . .

The global water equation is roughly similar. Although the earth possesses vast amounts of salt water, the global supply of fresh water is relatively limited: less than 3 percent of the planet's total water supply is fresh water, and much of this amount is locked up in the polar ice caps and glaciers. Of the amount that is readily available (approximately 12,000 cubic kilometers per year), half is already being appropriated for human use.[12] As in the case of oil, population growth and higher standards of living are constantly boosting the global demand for water. If this pattern persists, total human usage will approach 100 percent of the available supply by the mid-twenty-first century, producing severe shortages in some areas and intensified competition for access to important sources of supply. . . .

Significant shortages of other vital materials can also be expected in the decades to come. The world's natural forest cover, for example, is disappearing at the rate of about 0.5 percent per year—equivalent to the loss of a forest the size of England and Wales—and many individual tree species are at risk of disappearing altogether. Already, approximately 70 percent of the world's tropical dry forest has been obliterated, along with 60 percent of temperate forest and 45 percent of tropical moist forest.[13] Some of these forests are being replaced with tree plantations, but not at a rate fast enough to compensate for the annual loss of forest cover.

The future availability of certain key commodities will also be affected by changes in the global environment. The growing accumulation of carbon dioxide and other heat-trapping "greenhouse" gases in the environment—itself a product of accelerated fossil fuel consumption—is contributing to a gradual rise in average annual temperatures, producing drought in some regions and threatening the survival of many plant and animal species. Climate change of this sort could also reduce rainfall and/or increase evaporation rates in dry inland areas, reducing the flow of water into vital river systems like the Nile and the Indus. As suggested by Professor Thomas Homer-Dixon of the University of Toronto, "environmental scarcities" of this sort will further inflame the competition between groups and societies over access to vital raw materials.[14]

As global consumption rises and environmental conditions deteriorate, the total available supply of many key materials will diminish and the price of whatever remains will rise. In many cases, this will lead to the development of new sources of supply and/or the introduction of substitute materials, thereby alleviating worldwide shortages. Also, those societies with the means to do so will simply pay higher prices for whatever they need or desire. But market forces will not be able to solve every resource problem, nor avert all future conflicts over scarce materials. Some commodities, such as water, cannot be replaced by other substances, and many poor societies cannot afford to pay higher prices for essential goods. In these circumstances, conflict may arise between states over access to vital sources of supply, and within states over the distribution of the limited materials available. As prices rise, moreover, contending groups and elites in resource-producing countries will have greater incentive to seize and retain control of valuable mines, oil fields, and timber stands. The result, inevitably, will be increasing conflict over critical materials.

Contested Sources of Supply

The risk of conflict over diminishing supplies of vital materials is all the more worrisome because of another key feature of the global resource equation: the fact that many key sources or deposits of these materials are shared by two or more nations, or lie in contested border areas or offshore economic zones. Normally, states prefer to rely on materials lying entirely within their borders for their requirements of essential materials; as these supplies become exhausted governments will naturally seek to maximize their access to contested and offshore deposits, thereby producing an increased risk of conflict with neighboring states. This situation is potentially disruptive even under the best of circumstances, when the states involved are relatively friendly with one another; when this sort of competition occurs against a backdrop of preexisting hostility, as is the case in many parts of Africa and the Middle East, disputes over contested supplies of vital materials could prove explosive.

Disorder can arise from several types of resource contests. Disputes may occur over the allocation of a particular source of supply that extends across international boundaries, such as a large river system or an underground oil basin. The Nile River, for example, carries water through nine countries, the Mekong River through five, and the Euphrates three. Because these rivers arise in one set of countries and travel through others before reaching their egress to the sea, the upstream countries in the system are always in a position to control the flow of water to the downstream states; when the upstream states actually use this power to increase their water allocations at the expense of those lying downstream, conflict can arise. . . .

Similarly, when two states sit astride a large underground oil basin and one of the two extracts a disproportionate share of the total petroleum supply, this could diminish the oil revenues of the second state and lead to conflict. This was, in fact, one of the key irritants in the Iraq-Kuwait relationship in the late 1980s: Baghdad claimed that the Kuwaitis were extracting more than their rightful share of oil from the shared Rumaila field, thereby impeding its recovery from the Iran-Iraq war of 1980–88.[15] Conflict over shared oil supplies has also broken out between Saudi Arabia and Yemen, which share a poorly defined border in the Rub' al-Khaili (the "Empty Quarter").

A second type of conflict arises over contested claims to offshore areas that harbor significant energy or mineral resources. . . . [T]he U.N. Convention on the Law of the Sea allows ocean-bordering states to claim an exclusive economic zone extending offshore for up to two hundred miles, within which they have the sole right to exploit marine life and undersea resource deposits. This system works smoothly enough in large, open bodies of water, but it generates enormous friction in situations where several states border on an inland sea (such as the Caspian) or a relatively confined body of water. In these circumstances, claims to maritime EEZs often overlap, producing disputes over the location of offshore boundaries. A prime example is the South China Sea, where a total of seven states—Brunei, China, Indonesia, Malaysia, the Philippines, Taiwan, and Vietnam—have laid claim to large areas of water. . . .

Finally, disputes can arise over access to bodies of water considered essential for the transportation of vital materials, such as the Persian Gulf and the Suez Canal. A very large proportion of the world's daily oil intake travels by ship from the Gulf to ports in Europe, the Americas, and Japan. In many cases, these ships must pass through narrow and circumscribed bodies of water, such as the Strait of Hormuz (at the mouth of the Persian Gulf), the Strait of Malacca (between Indonesia and Malaysia), or the Red Sea. Because the free passage of ships through these waters is considered essential for the uninterrupted flow of materials, major importing states have always resisted efforts by local powers to block or constrict them.[16] In 1986, for instance, the United States "reflagged" Kuwaiti ships with the American flag and escorted them through the Persian Gulf, then the site of naval clashes between Iran and Iraq. Concern over the safe transportation of vital materials can also extend to oil and gas pipelines, particularly those that travel through areas of recurring disorder.

The Emerging Landscape of Conflict

Each of these three factors—the relentless expansion in worldwide demand, the emergence of significant resource shortages, and the proliferation of ownership contests—is likely to introduce new stresses into the international system. The first two will inevitably intensify competition between states over access to vital materials; the third will generate new sources of friction and conflict. Each factor, moreover, will reinforce the destabilizing tendencies of the others: as resource consumption grows, shortages will emerge more rapidly and governments will come under mounting pressure to solve the problem at any cost; this, in turn, will heighten the tendency of states to seek maximum control over contested sources of supply, thereby increasing the risk of conflict between the countries that share or jointly claim a given resource deposit.

In most cases, these conflicts will be resolved without recourse to violence, as the nations involved arrive at a negotiated solution to their predicament. Global market forces will tend to encourage such an outcome: the perceived economic benefits of compromise are generally much greater than the likely costs of war, and so most states will choose to pull back from their maximum demands if they can be assured of a reasonable slice of the resource pie. But negotiations and market forces will not work in every instance. In some cases, the materials at stake will be viewed as so essential to national survival or economic well-being that compromise is unthinkable. It is difficult, for example, to imagine that the United States will ever allow the Persian Gulf to fall under the control of a hostile power, or that Egypt will allow Sudan or Ethiopia to gain control over the flow of the Nile River. In such situations, national security considerations will always prevail over negotiated settlements that could be perceived as entailing the surrender of vital national interests.

Global market forces can also increase the likelihood of conflict, most notably when a contested resource is seen as being so valuable in monetary terms that none of the claimants involved is willing to accept its loss. This appears to be the case in the Democratic Republic of Congo (formerly Zaire), where several internal factions and foreign powers have been fighting for control over the lucrative gold and copper fields of the south and west.[17] A similar situation has long prevailed in Sierra Leone—in this case, involving internal conflict over the country's valuable diamond fields. Typically, contests of this sort arise in poor and underdeveloped countries where possession of a mineral deposit or oil field is seen as the only viable route to the accumulation of wealth.

The risk of internal conflict over resources is further heightened by the growing divide between the rich and the poor in many developing countries—a phenomenon widely ascribed to globalization. While those at the top of the economic ladder are able to procure the basic necessities of life, those at the bottom are finding themselves increasingly barred from access to such vital commodities as food, land, shelter, and safe drinking water. As supplies contract and the price of many materials rises, the poor will find themselves in an increasingly desperate situation—and thus more inclined to heed the exhortations of demagogues, fundamentalists, and extremists who promise to relieve their suffering through revolt or ethnic partition.

"The distribution of [economic] competitiveness is now uneven," the Institute for National Security Studies observed in 1999. "This pattern raises the disturbing prospect of a 'globalization gap' between winners and losers. . . . Leaders of the losers often blame outsiders or unpopular insiders for economic hardship. Some foment crises to distract domestic attention from joblessness and hunger."[18]

This danger will only grow more acute as increased economic competition and pressure from international lending agencies force the governments of developing nations to eliminate subsidies on food and other basic commodities and to privatize such essential services as water delivery. A foretaste of this was provided in April 2000, when Bolivia's major cities were paralyzed by protests against a government plan to privatize municipal utilities and impose fees on drinking water. At least five people died in skirmishes with the police, and many more were injured. Order was restored only after President Hugo Banzer declared a state of emergency and ordered army troops to clear major thoroughfares.[19]

Thus, while market forces and globalization can help avert violence in many instances of resource scarcity, there are situations in which they are likely to fail. When this occurs, disputes over access to critical (or extremely valuable) resources may lead to armed conflict. Such encounters can take the form of an internal struggle for control over a particular resource, a territorial dispute over contested border zones or EEZs, a naval contest over critical waterways, or a regional power struggle in areas holding large supplies of critical resources, such as the Persian Gulf and Caspian Sea regions. Whatever form these engagements take, they are best described as *resource wars*—conflicts that revolve, to a significant degree, over the pursuit or possession of critical materials.[20]

Human history has been marked by a long succession of resource wars—stretching all the way back to the earliest agrarian civilizations. After World War II, the relentless pursuit of resources was overshadowed by the political and ideological exigencies of the U.S.-Soviet rivalry; but it has resurfaced with fresh intensity in the current era. Given the growing importance ascribed to economic vigor in the security policy of states, the rising worldwide demand for resources, the likelihood of significant shortages, and the existence of numerous ownership disputes, the incidence of conflict over vital materials is sure to grow.

Resource competition will not, of course, prove the sole source of conflict in the twenty-first century. Other factors—ethnic hostility, economic injustice, political competition, and so on—will also lead to periodic outbreaks of violence. Increasingly, however, these factors will be linked to disputes over the possession of (or access to) vital materials. However divided two states or societies may be over matters of politics or religion, the likelihood of their engaging in mutual combat becomes considerably greater when one side believes that its essential supply of water, food, or energy is threatened by the other. And with the worldwide availability of many key resources facing eventual decline, the danger of resource disputes intruding into other areas of disagreement can only increase.

NOTES

1. Gary Gardner and Payal Sampat, *Mind over Matter: Recasting the Role of Materials in Our Lives,* Worldwatch Paper no. 144 (Washington, D.C.: Worldwatch Institute, December 1998), p. 15.
2. Lester R. Brown, Michael Renner, and Brian Halweil, *Vital Signs 2000* (New York: W. W. Norton and the Worldwatch Institute, 2000), p. 71. Hereinafter cited as WWI, *Vital Signs 2000.*
3. Ibid., p. 87.
4. For discussion, see Gardner and Sampat, *Mind over Matter.*
5. Allen R. Myerson, "U.S. Splurging on Energy After Falling off Its Diet," *New York Times,* October 22, 1998. See also Carlos Tejada and Patrick Barta, "Big Footprints: Hey, Baby Boomers Need Their Space, OK? Look at All Their Stuff," *Wall Street Journal,* January 7, 2000.
6. See the data provided in Albert Adriaanse, et al., *Resource Flows: The Material Basis of Industrial Economies* (Washington, D.C.: World Resources Institute, 1997).
7. World Resources Institute (WRI), *World Resources 1998–99* (Oxford and New York: Oxford University Press, 1998), pp. 141–45, 244–45. Hereinafter cited as WRI *World Resources 1998–99.*
8. U.S. National Intelligence Council (NIC), *Global Trends 2010* (Washington, D.C.: NIC, November 1997), p. 2.
9. World Wildlife Fund (WWF), *Living Planet Report 1998* (Gland, Switzerland: WWF, 1998).
10. BP Amoco, *Statistical Review of World Energy 2000* (London: BP Amoco, 2000), p. 4.
11. For discussion, see Colin J. Campbell and Jean H. Laherrère, "The End of Cheap Oil," *Scientific American,* March 1998, p. 78–83, and James J. MacKenzie, "Heading Off the Permanent Oil Crisis," *Issues in Science and Technology,* Summer 1996, pp. 48–54.
12. See J. W. Maurits la Rivière, "Threats to the World's Water," *Scientific American,* September 1989, pp. 80–94.
13. WWF, *Living Planet Report 1998,* p. 6.
14. See Thomas F. Homer-Dixon, "On the Threshold: Environmental Changes as Causes of Acute Conflict," *International Security,* vol. 16, no. 2 (Fall 1991), pp. 76–116; Homer-Dixon, "Environmental Scarcities and

Violent Conflict," *International Security,* vol. 19, no. 1 (Summer 1994), pp. 5–40.

15. See Lawrence Freedman and Efraim Karsh, *The Gulf Conflict, 1990–1991* (Princeton: Princeton University Press, 1993), pp. 48, 57, 59–60.
16. For discussion, see DoE, EIA, "World Oil Transit Chokepoints," May 1998, electronic document accessed at www.eia.doe.gov/emeu/cabs/choke.html on May 26, 1998.
17. For discussion, see Ian Fisher and Norimitsu Onishi, "Many Armies Ravage Rich Land in the 'First World War' of Africa," *New York Times,* February 6, 2000.
18. NDU/INSS, *Strategic Assessment 1999,* p. 29.
19. "Bolivia Calls an Emergency After Protest over Water," *New York Times,* April 9, 2000.
20. I first used this term in "Resource Wars," *Harper's,* January 1980, pp. 20–23. The term was also used at that time by General Alexander M. Haig Jr., former commander in chief of NATO, in testimony before the Mines and Mining Subcommittee of the House Committee on Interior and Insular Affairs. Suggesting that aggressive Soviet moves in Afghanistan, the Middle East, and Africa were designed to impede U.S. access to vital raw materials, Haig declared that "the era of 'resource wars' has arrived." Prepared statement (xerox copy), September 18, 1980.

QUESTIONS FOR DISCUSSION

1. What are the most important factors contributing to global resource wars?
2. Do resource wars represent a larger source of conflict between nations than struggles over religion or ideology?
3. Do you agree with Klare's argument that the Sept. 11, 2001, terrorist attacks against the United States can best be understood in terms of resource wars?

53

OPEN SEASON ON OPEN SPACE

BOB BURTMAN

The view from Dead Horse Point reveals a sweeping panorama of red sandstone buttes, sheer cliffs, and deep gorges carved into shapes at once familiar and grotesque. Located 32 miles from the Utah desert town of Moab, the narrow rock peninsula juts jaggedly into canyon country, 2,000 feet above the Colorado River. The vista draws more than 250,000 visitors to the state park at Dead

Horse each year, and the unspoiled landscape has been featured prominently in movies like *Thelma and Louise* and *Mission: Impossible 2.* Modest by the standards of two nearby national parks, the vast Arches and Canyonlands, Dead Horse makes up in grandeur what it lacks in size. "It's amazing," says ranger Dan Dranginis. "I probably have the best backyard of anybody."

Though it took 300 million years to create, the wilderness around Dead Horse Point could change in short order. A Denver-based company called Intrepid Oil and Gas has filed plans to drill two wells on

Reprinted with permission from *Mother Jones,* July/August 2002. Copyright © 2002 Foundation for National Progress.

park grounds, including one right next to the visitors center. Another firm, Aviara Energy, has permits for three wells on 23,000 acres of high desert between the park and nearby Canyonlands. Other oil companies have received leases in the neighboring Lockhart Basin and the sprawling Dome Plateau near Arches, both of which have been proposed as national wilderness areas. "Pretty much wherever people hike, they're going to see oil wells," says Dranginis.

Even before the Senate blocked proposals to drill in the Arctic National Wildlife Refuge in April, the Bush administration was moving to accelerate energy production across the West—often targeting highly sensitive areas that have remained largely closed to exploration and drilling. In Utah, the proposed drilling would do more than spoil scenic views—it also threatens crucial habitat for desert bighorn sheep and cougars, as well as eagles and other raptors. . . . [T]he federal Bureau of Land Management (BLM), which controls mineral rights on much of the public land in the region, allowed 52,000-pound "thumper" trucks to pound the ground near Dead Horse Point and Canyonlands, searching for oil with seismic measuring equipment. The trucks crushed ancient stands of juniper, left fragile desert soil vulnerable to erosion, and cut 176 miles of new roads. . . . [A] federal review board halted similar exploration in the Dome Plateau, saying the BLM had failed to conduct environmental reviews mandated by federal law.

"With oil and gas development you get roads, you get drill pads, you get trucks driving out there, you get air and water pollution," says Pamela Eaton, who directs the Four Corners office of the Wilderness Society, a research and advocacy organization based in Washington, D.C. "It will harm the soil, fragment wildlife habitat, damage plants, and erode the land."

Four months after former oil executives George W. Bush and Dick Cheney took of-

fice, the administration issued an executive order calling on all federal agencies to "expedite energy-related projects." Since then, officials have been speeding approval of oil and gas wells throughout the Rocky Mountain states. In Colorado, the BLM is revising land-use plans on 77,000 undeveloped acres in Vermillion Basin, the first step before drilling can be approved on land the agency previously recommended for wilderness status. In New Mexico, similar revisions could open up 160,000 acres of grasslands in the Otero Mesa region, threatening the habitat of pronghorn antelope, falcons, hawks, and bobcats. And in Wyoming and Montana, the administration supports plans to develop 51,000 wells to extract methane gas from shallow coal beds in the Powder River Basin—a process that even the BLM's own studies conclude could poison wildlife, kill vegetation, and crisscross the area with 20,000 miles of pipeline, 5,300 miles of power lines, and 17,000 miles of roads.

"The president, vice president, and their corporate friends are trying to drill into everything," says Ken Sleight, a longtime environmental activist who runs a guest ranch in the foothills of the snow-capped La Sal Mountains outside Moab. "They don't care about the value of wildlands. Bush has zeroed in on southern Utah, but he has no idea what he will destroy."

The drilling proposals have sparked opposition not only from environmentalists, but also from some cattle ranchers and most of the nation's major hunting and sportsfishing organizations. Yet the administration remains undeterred, claiming that increased exploration on public lands is essential to curb dependence on foreign oil. "The additional reserves we have domestically could help bolster America's energy security," says BLM spokesman Rem Hawes. To make sure energy development gets the green light, the newly created White House Task Force on Energy Project Streamlining is removing environmental protections that industry considers a roadblock to domestic production. And . . . the BLM issued an internal memo to its Utah field offices making clear that energy, not the environment, is now the top concern for federal land managers. "Utah needs to ensure that existing staff understand that when an oil and gas lease parcel or when an application for permission to drill comes in the door, that this work is their No. 1 priority," the memo concluded.

If he's under pressure to approve every energy proposal that comes his way, Bill Stringer shows no sign of it. Relaxed and rugged in his polo shirt and faded jeans, Stringer looks like he prefers a day on the range to eight hours at his desk. The assistant field manager for resources in BLM's Moab office, Stringer handles all issues related to energy production, including exploration permits, drilling applications, and wilderness designations. Like many federal officials, he shrugs off the heated debate surrounding the push to open up areas previously considered off-limits to energy exploration. "Moab has been at the center of controversy for a long time," he says. "It's not new."

What *is* new is the kind of public lands that the Bush administration wants to see populated with oil rigs. The proposed drilling around Moab would take place within view of Arches and Canyonlands, two national parks that encompass some of the West's most spectacular landscapes. Edward Abbey, who worked as a park ranger in Arches during the 1950s, began his classic *Desert Solitaire* by declaring, "This is the most beautiful place on Earth." The park is home to scores of unique sandstone monoliths, including the graceful Delicate Arch that is featured on Utah's license plate. The surrounding canyons, immense and arid, left Abbey "gaping at this monstrous and inhuman spectacle of rock and cloud and sky and space."

Many of the areas targeted for drilling, including the Dome Plateau and Lockhart Basin, were considered off-limits to development by the Clinton administration, which launched studies to determine whether the land should be designated as federally protected wilderness areas. But under Bush, the BLM is speeding up such reviews, and then often recommending that the land be opened to drilling. According to Heidi McIntosh, conservation director of the Southern Utah Wilderness Alliance, the agency's recent verdicts have been distressingly consistent: "The BLM always says, 'Nope, no wilderness qualities here.'"

In other areas, the agency is simply ignoring provisions designed to protect the environment. In May 2001, Cheney's energy task force directed officials to review any "impediments" to oil and gas drilling and to "modify those where opportunities exist." On many federal lands, one such "impediment" stipulates that drilling must be halted during periods of wildlife migration. But last year the BLM proposed waiving the restriction in the Upper Green River Basin in Wyoming, allowing one gas company to drill during the winter even though the work threatened to disrupt the migration of one of the world's largest populations of pronghorn antelope and mule deer. In proposing the waiver, the agency suggested that it would actually benefit wildlife: By interrupting migration, drilling would enable scientists to study the effects of habitat disruption on the deer. . . .

Nowhere is the Western energy boom more pronounced—or the environmental damage more evident—than in the Powder River Basin, which spans 8 million acres of Montana and Wyoming. Since Bush took office, nearly 5,400 wells have already been drilled to extract methane gas from coal seams, and the administration wants to increase the number fivefold, transforming the area into what it calls "the major natural gas-producing region in the United States by 2015." But releasing the trapped gas also involves pumping up an estimated 1.4 trillion gallons of water laden with salt and minerals, a process that already has drained local wells, flooded farms and ranches, and covered the arid land with waste lagoons. In many areas, drill pads will be located every 80 acres, each with diesel-powered compressors running day and night and a maze of access roads for heavy machinery.

"We're going to be witnessing massive environmental degradation," says David Alberswerth, the Wilderness Society's director of BLM programs. . . .

When officials do try to protect the environment—by denying drilling permits, closing roads, or designating historic trails—they find themselves under fire from Washington. In a . . . memo, the Interior Department ordered BLM personnel to justify their actions in writing whenever their decisions have "a direct or adverse impact on energy development, production, supply and/or distribution." In some cases, the White House has stepped in to make sure industry gets what it wants. After Texaco waited five months for permission to drill near a historic trail in Lincoln County, Wyoming, the Petroleum Association of Wyoming lodged a complaint with the White House energy streamlining task force. . . . Approval was quickly granted, and a BLM directive that barred drilling near other national historic trails in Wyoming was also withdrawn.

Take a trip into the desert around Moab these days, and the biggest oil rigs you're likely to see are SUVs. The town is a recreation mecca that takes in $100 million a year from tourists eager to experience the area's desolate beauty. Mountain-bike and river-rafting outfitters line Moab's one main drag, sharing space with motels and souvenir shops. Following old drilling roads—and often going off-road—hundreds of four-wheel-drive vehicles roam the territory each day, kicking up dust clouds visible from park overlooks. . . .

But beyond the town, much of this vast red-rock canyon country remains as unspoiled as it was decades ago, often accessible only on foot or horseback. Many in Moab who depend on tourism for their livelihood worry about the prospects of oil wells dotting their routes, especially in areas that have remained off-limits to energy exploration. "It's disturbing from a business standpoint, because people come to get away from that," says Judy Nichols, who offers tours to mountain bikers. "I don't know that my customers would still want a tour through Lockhart Basin if they're going to see heavy machinery." Nichols favors restrictions on drilling—even if it means closing some land to the four-wheel-drive vehicles that accompany her tours. "That's fine with me," she says.

Even some ranchers and others in the area who traditionally clash with environmentalists over issues of land use and growth are concerned about the Bush administration's push to pave the way for drilling. "This county is not all environmentalist to say the least," says Susie Harrington, who lives in Moab and serves on the Grand County Planning Commission. "But it's a point of agreement that the quality of the open space is important. It's the general impression that degrading our open space is going to affect tourism."

Some in southern Utah have already gotten a glimpse of how much damage oil wells can do. In neighboring counties, hundreds of wells have been drilled on Navajo land, raising concerns about pollution. "They've cut roads into the reservation, disrupted people's lives, and left them worried about water quality," says Mark Maryboy, a San Juan County commissioner and member of the Navajo Tribal Council. "The people who are trying to sell us another oil and gas boom don't look down the road."

In Emery County to the west, dozens of gas wells have sprouted since Bush took office. "It looks like Texas," says Tom Bunn, whose ranch is located a few miles from Convulsion Canyon, where Native Americans covered cliff walls with pictographs depicting bighorn sheep and the night sky. Under the new administration, the U.S. Forest Service is developing plans to destroy the rock art to make way for a coal-mining road through the canyon. "I asked the Forest Service what would be left in 15 to 20 years after the coal is all played out and the canyon is beaten up," says Bunn. "They said the new road could be used for recreation. That's a new one: You mine for coal, and you end up with hikers."

The canyons and mesas surrounding Moab experienced an energy boom once before. In the years after World War II, prospectors went looking for oil across southeastern Utah, hoping for a gusher. Most of the wells went bust, producing fewer than 60,000 barrels, and dozens of small vertical pipes are still visible from the road leading to Dead Horse Point, a silent testament to all the dry holes the drill bits found. In the surrounding desert known as Big Flat, only five wells are still pumping. Intrepid's Long Canyon #1 stands at the end of a dirt road near the lip of the canyon, the pump jack noisily bobbing and grinding 24 hours a day.

Just how much oil could be recovered in the area remains a matter of speculation. The industry insists that companies won't drill unless they're certain to hit pay dirt. "If somebody wants to go after it, then it's by definition worthwhile," says Mike Shanahan, spokesman for the American Petroleum Institute. Modern technologies such as horizontal drilling and new seismic techniques have increased the chances of striking a deposit, but the risks of coming up dry are still high. So are the costs—exploratory wells run as much as $2.2 million each, not counting the expense of hauling equipment and building roads in rugged terrain.

To prime the pumps, the administration has proposed offering industry more incentives for energy production in the form of tax breaks and government subsidies. But even if companies are paid to drill, untapped lands in the West aren't expected to yield enough oil to significantly reduce the nation's dependence on foreign petroleum. According to Pete Morton, an economist with the Wilderness Society, the government's own figures show that a proposal to open 15 national monuments in the West to drilling would produce enough oil to meet U.S. consumption for only 15 days.

Studies show that the amount of gas on Western lands is far more plentiful than oil: As one industry scientist puts it, "The Rocky Mountains are a Persian Gulf of gas." But fewer than 1 in 10 acres of public land is currently closed to gas drilling—and enough gas exists in the remainder, according to data from the National Petroleum Council, to supply consumer needs for 40 years. "You don't have to develop every square inch of public lands—especially when it's not going to make any difference whatsoever to our energy independence," says Jim Baca, who served as director of the BLM under Clinton.

In the long run, drilling near national parks and monuments may not produce much oil—but it will effectively remove millions of acres in the West from consideration as wilderness areas. Once an area is approved for energy production, it opens up the land to other development, even if a single well is never drilled. "For the extractive industries, it's one last time at the trough," says Morton, the Wilderness Society economist. "They've got oilmen in the White House. If you put in roads and construct drill pads and cut trees, you eliminate areas from wilderness consideration."

Environmental groups stress that they aren't opposed to all oil and gas development. The Southern Utah Wilderness Alliance, which is leading the fight to block drilling around Moab, supports production in the Uinta Basin in northeastern Utah, which holds most of the state's energy resources. What the organization objects to, says Liz Thomas, staff attorney in the group's Moab office, is the effort to encroach on what's left of the nation's wilderness. "We should step back and evaluate what the benefits are if we drill, and what they are if we don't drill," she says. "There's just some places that deserve to be protected as they are."

> ## QUESTIONS FOR DISCUSSION
>
> 1. Should federal land, including national parks, be opened to energy exploration?
> 2. What are the environmental and economic impacts of the current Bush administration's land drilling policies?
> 3. Do you agree with Burtman's argument that there is a connection between the new drilling policies and the oil interests of the Bush administration?

54

MAPPING THE NUCLEAR LANDSCAPE
VALERIE L. KULETZ

Mapping the Invisible Nuclear Landscape

In April 1995, while visiting a group of Southern Paiute women elders on the Moapa reservation in the desert 45 miles northeast of Las Vegas, Nevada, I was told how tribal members used to drive up into the mountains that separated the reservation from the Nevada Test Site and watch tests of atomic bombs. As one woman recalled:

> They didn't tell us how dangerous it was. They just said in the news media

and the papers that there was going to be a test. So naturally, you know, a whole bunch of us after we got off work, away we'd go headed right toward that place. And we'd get on the road there, and there'd be miles and miles and miles of cars just going to see it. We'd all get out and get on the little hills, you know, all around there and we could see right across there where it was, this big beautiful cloud! Just all white and fiery, you know, and just gorgeous! They didn't tell us how dangerous it was. They just told us they were going to have it at such and such a time. And now I think, I think personally, that we're suffering—almost all of us have something wrong with us. I've had thyroid problems.

No one at the time, or in the years that followed, thought to warn them that exposing themselves to fallout might prove dangerous to their health. The Moapa women told me stories about how they foraged for wild plants near the Test Site, ate rabbit and deer that roamed the Test Site, and, as was their custom during the hot summers, moved their beds outside to sleep in the cool night air:

> So in the summertime in the fifties . . . the reservation wasn't really that well established. Some of us didn't have electricities. So in the summertime when it got hot we moved everything outdoors into now what we call the little arbors. And every family made one of those in the summertime, and they took out the stove, table, and chairs. And we'd even take our beds out and sleep outside underneath the trees. All of our activities were outside during those times, during times that they were having the tests. And at that time we didn't have indoor plumbing or indoor water. Our water ran down in ditches along in front of the homes, so that was our water. I mean, like I say, we lived outdoors in the summertime. We never moved back in until the fall when it got cold. Everything went outdoors, and that's where we were in the summertime. So during the nuclear tests, well, we were still outside.

These domestic activities were common long before the time of the nuclear testing, but they take on new meaning when we recognize how nuclear contamination moves through the food chain and water supply, and through the air in the form of radiation fallout. With their greater reliance on obtaining sustenance from the land, Indian communities may have been far more exposed than, for instance, people in nearby Las Vegas, or even other downwinders in Utah

and Arizona. In recent years the 250-member tribe claims to have suffered from increased incidence of cancers. As eight of us were seated around a fold-up table in the tribal council hall, one Moapa elder woman said she had lost three nephews to cancer. Another described her own struggles with thyroid disease, and another with ovarian cancer. Others had similar stories.

With incomplete and inaccessible health records to rely on, no official epidemiological study has been undertaken of the tribe's past exposure to radiation. The extent of official disregard for the health of Moapa tribal members was brought strikingly home to me when one of the elders told me that I had been one of the few people from outside the tribal community to ask about possible links between their health and the community's exposure to nuclear tests conducted on the Nevada Test Site—less than 60 miles from their homes. As noted by a Department of Energy publication: "Through 1992, when the President halted underground nuclear testing, the United States conducted 1,054 nuclear tests, of which 928 occurred at the Nevada Test Site. The remaining 126 nuclear tests were conducted at other sites in and outside Nevada." From 1951, when a B-50 bomber dropped the first atomic bomb on the Nevada desert, to 1963 the U.S. government detonated more than 120 atomic bombs into the atmosphere over the Nevada Test Site.

The plight of "downwinders" in southern Utah, the use of soldiers in nuclear tests, and the recent Department of Energy revelations that civilians were used as subjects in nuclear medical experiments have received, if not extensive, at least partial media coverage. Such reports only partly tell the story of the human cost of nuclear weapons development in the United States. Curiously, the vulnerability of Native Americans living near sites of nuclear weapons research, development, and testing has gone virtually unnoticed. Western Shoshone and Southern Paiute individuals, as well as individuals from other Indian tribes, have reported increased incidences of cancer on their reservations and "colonies." Increased numbers of birth defects have also been noted.

Most historians and government officials have ignored the presence of certain populations at risk in areas of nuclear weapons development and testing—populations whose subsistence economies depend heavily on land resources, including its flora, fauna, and water. This neglect is not accidental. When not deliberately part of official secrecy, it reveals an all-too-familiar pattern of disregard for the people that inhabit these desert areas, masking an exploitation of their land that goes back to the beginning of the so-called westward expansion. This is a landscape—a nuclear landscape—too often ripened by sacrifice, for sacrifice, shrouded in secrecy, and plundered of its wealth.

One method for piercing the veil of secrecy cloaking these landscapes is to listen to the stories of those who live on the land (those who are often invisible to Euroamericans) and to examine their "unofficial" maps that identify where and how nuclearism has affected them. This methodology relies on and uses local knowledge to make visible geographies of sacrifice—areas of the United States set aside for weapons testing and development, uranium mining, and military training that reveal a pattern of what several commentators have termed nuclear colonialism. My use of the term "nuclear colonialism" attempts to situate the emergent nuclear landscape in the arid regions of the American Southwest within a larger history of U.S. internal colonialism, that is, within the expropriation of native lands and the displacement of North America's indigenous population by their European conquerors.

. . . Fifty years of the unbridled pursuit of nuclear power have obscured a geography of sacrifice that, when mapped, shows how racism, militarism, and economic imperialism have combined to marginalize a people and a land that many within government and industry, consciously or not, regard as expendable. Many of the same lands that have been used for weapons testing and development are currently being designated as waste repositories for the byproducts of America's headlong pursuit of nuclear power. For instance, if Yucca Mountain in Nevada is designated the United States's high-level nuclear waste repository, most of the waste from commercial reactors destined for this site will be transported by truck and by rail only a few miles from the Moapa reservation. Yucca Mountain is partially within the Nevada Test Site, on land claimed as traditional homeland by both Western Shoshone and Southern Paiute people. Thus, a tribe such as the Moapa Paiutes, or the Yomba band of the Western Shoshone, or the Timbisha Shoshone, encounter nuclearism at various stages of its life cycle (in both testing and waste disposal). Like radiation itself, nuclearism doesn't simply disappear once the combatants have called off the dogs of war.

Seeing and Deterritoriality

Naming and mapping the nuclear landscape opens a space for other critical narratives to emerge: narratives about science (and what constitutes objectivity), power (and the representations used to legitimate it), racism, and cultural marginalization. It provides an avenue to explore some of the ways human culture and politics transform place and "nature." Most importantly, mapping the nuclear landscape employs the political practice of *seeing* purposefully unmarked and secret landscapes; it makes visible those who have been obscured and silenced within those landscapes.

Once made visible, the zones of sacrifice that comprise these local landscapes can begin to be pieced together to reveal regional, national, and even global patterns of *deterritoriality*—the loss of commitment by modern nation-states (and even the international community) to particular lands or regions. Deterritoriality is a term used to explain the construction of national and international sacrifice zones. It is a phenomenon that is becoming an increasingly common feature of . . . industrialized societies, where extensive zones of sacrifice are allowed to emerge as the price for, and inevitable result of, a particular set of power requirements. As such, deterritoriality is a particularly dramatic form of disembodiment—the perceived separation between self and nature. This pattern of land use, on such a massive scale, indicates one of the cultural differences between capitalist, late-industrial Euroamerican societies and many Native American and indigenous societies for whom land is linked not only more immediately to economic subsistence but also to their cultural viability and religious identity. With such cultural differences in mind, the practice of deterritoriality can be seen as a form of cultural imperialism. . . .

The nuclear landscapes in this region began to emerge in the 1940s and have included many aspects of nuclear activity—from uranium mining and milling to the development, manufacture, and testing of weapons to the present activity of siting nuclear waste repositories. Uranium mining, nuclear weapons testing, and nuclear waste dumps are not the only activities that have transformed the West and Southwest over the last fifty years, but they comprise significant activities that demonstrate how nuclearism can be understood as a form of internal colonialism. The concept of internal colonialism has been used by political scholars . . . to describe political and economic inequalities between regions within a given

society. Like colonialism, where "core" countries in the "first world" exploit "peripheral" countries for their natural resources, internal colonialism is characterized by one region—usually a metropolis that is closely associated with state power—exploiting a colonylike peripheral region. In the case of nuclear colonialism, what is seen as usable, sparsely populated, arid geographic space is used as a dumping ground or a testing field to allow more powerful regions to continue their present form of energy production or to continue to exert military power globally. The relationship between core and periphery is typically one of exploitation, where the human populations in the periphery usually consist of people with a different cultural, racial, or class background. The presence of internal colonialism argues against the myth of an integrated and truly democratic society, and it argues that such regional inequalities are not temporary but necessary features of industrial society—features we choose not to see in order to maintain the myth of American equality and democracy. . . .

The Emerging Landscape

Science and the military meet in the deserts of the Southwest literally to transform the landscape. While militarization plays a large part in the creation of the nuclear landscape, this landscape is the product of an even larger social and technological transformation that emerged most forcefully in the second half of the twentieth century. The emergence of nuclear culture occurred simultaneously with an escalation in technological knowledge and practices—nuclear power, commercial air travel, television, computers—that has profoundly changed our lives and our environment. The technological transformations of the postwar era are themselves part of a process of rationalization—a particular kind of rationalization—

that is hundreds of years old and that has always resulted in hardship for Native peoples:

> [I]t may be the central assumption of technological society that there is virtue in overpowering nature and native peoples. The Indian problem today, as it always has been, is directly related to the needs of technological societies to find and obtain remotely located resources, in order to fuel an incessant and intrinsic demand for growth and technological fulfillment. The process began in our country hundreds of years ago when we wanted land and gold. Today it continues because we want coal, oil, uranium, fish, and more land. . . . All these acts were and are made possible by one fundamental rationalization: that our society represents the ultimate expression of evolution, its final flowering. It is this attitude and its corresponding belief that native societies represent an earlier, lower form on the evolutionary ladder, upon which we occupy the highest rung, that seem to unify all modern political perspectives.

Having emerged piece by piece over the last fifty years, the nuclear landscape constitutes as much a social and political geography as it does an environmental region. Because it is a rather recent phenomenon and has taken time to emerge in a recognizable form, because it exists in desert lands, and because it is the child of secret operations hidden behind the veil of national security, the nuclear landscape is to a large extent an invisible landscape. One could argue that it exists in many places throughout the continental United States, including Oak Ridge, Tennessee; nuclear processing centers in Kentucky and Ohio; Hanford, Washington; Rocky Flats, Colorado; and the Pantex plant in Amarillo, Texas. Indeed, as a result of the Cold War, the soil of the North American Great Plains has been seeded with a thousand intercontinental ballistic missiles—sentinels of the nuclear age. And the eastern United States contains a dense constellation of nuclear facilities of all kinds, including the majority of nuclear power plants in the country. With cooling ponds overflowing, these facilities have reached the limits of their storage capacity for the byproducts of nuclear-power generation. Thus, in order to continue production, utility companies must now find repositories for waste that remains dangerous for more than 240,000 years.

Though the nuclear landscape can be said to exist throughout the United States, nowhere has it emerged as extensively as in the Southwest interdesert region. This is because the nuclear landscape is much more than a collection of weapons stockpiles and production facilities; it includes large land masses for uranium mining and milling, the testing of high-tech weaponry, and waste repositories—all found in the Southwest.

Originally chosen for its inaccessibility and inhospitable character—making secrecy easier to maintain—the interdesert region now stands as a testament to our entry into the nuclear age and to the dominance of the military-industrial complex in the late twentieth century. Encompassing most of the Southwest, the nuclear landscape covers a swath of land that includes much of New Mexico, Nevada, southeastern California, and parts of Arizona, Utah, Colorado, and Texas. (To the north, in the West, we can also add parts of the state[s] of Washington and Idaho.) This region . . . includes all five of the major North American deserts: the lower Great Basin desert in Nevada and the southeastern margins of California, the Navajoan desert in the Four Corners area, the upper Chihuahuan desert in New Mexico, the upper Sonoran desert in California and Arizona, and the Mojave Desert in California, Nevada, and Arizona.

Within this region stand thousands of abandoned and unreclaimed open-pit and underground uranium mines and mills, two proposed national sites for deep geologic nuclear waste repositories of monumental proportions, all potential sites for the nation's above-ground temporary nuclear waste containment facilities, a constellation of other nuclear pollution points such as "unofficial" waste holding stations, and secret testing sites. The nation's largest nuclear accident—known as the Rio Puerco accident—took place in northern New Mexico. Home to "downwinders," or victims of airborne radiation, this region also includes the site where the U.S. government has detonated more than 928 above-ground and below-ground nuclear bombs, as well as hundreds of secret and previously undisclosed nuclear tests. This region contains important nuclear research and development centers, with their own "private" on-site nuclear waste disposal areas of significant size. The region has seen more military land withdrawals than any other region in the United States, eliminating many millions of acres of land from public access, transforming whole mountain ranges and desert valleys into massive weapons testing theaters. Finally, it contains a site where shallow burial of "low-level" nuclear waste is scheduled to occur. Significantly, this region is home to the majority of *land-based* American Indians alive today on the North American continent.

The Indian Landscape

In this Indian country two landscapes—Indian and nuclear—meet at nearly every point of the nuclear cycle, from uranium mining to weapons testing to the disposal of nuclear waste. . . .

Today, the only above-ground, temporary nuclear waste storage facilities under consideration have been on the Nevada Test Site and the Mescalero Apache, Skull Valley Goshute, and Fort McDermitt Paiute Shoshone reservations. The nation's moderate-level nuclear waste storage facility, called WIPP (for Waste Isolation Pilot Project), is in the same general region as the Mescalero Apache reservation in the Chihuahuan desert. Radioactive waste from research at Los Alamos National Laboratory is now stored at "Area G," which borders the San Ildefonso Pueblo and is near the Santa Clara Pueblo's lands. Low-level nuclear waste is targeted for disposal in the Mojave Desert's Ward Valley, home of the Fort Mojave Indians and the Chemehuevi of the Colorado River Indian tribes. Finally, the proposed premiere site for the nation's high-level nuclear waste repository is Yucca Mountain—"holy land" to the Western Shoshone, Southern Paiute, and Owens Valley Paiute.

This discursive map demonstrates how the development, testing, and waste storage of nuclear materials in the highly militarized landscapes of the western United States might be understood as a form of environmental racism. At the very least, it sets the stage for asking how land use, racism, power, and internal colonialism intersect in this region. This mapping not only makes *visible* the millions of acres that were removed from access for weapons testing and development in the postwar years, it also reveals the peoples affected and displaced by these activities. Once revealed, the nuclear landscape can be perceived and experienced differently; it can be seen as one landscape superimposed upon another: a *landscape of national sacrifice,* an *expendable landscape,* over what many North American Indians understand as a *geography of the sacred,* a geography where spiritual and cultural life are woven directly into the landscape itself.

The Wasteland Discourse

Along with their Indian inhabitants, these dry, arid regions are perceived and discursively interpreted as marginal within the dominant Euroamerican perspective. Environmental science discourse often supports the preexisting settler discourse about desert lands as barren wastelands by organizing bioregions within hierarchies of value according to productive capacity. In this scheme, deserts are placed at the bottom of the ladder. They become marginal lands. Similarly, American Indians in these regions tend to be placed at the bottom of the ladder of economic productivity. For example: Indians have the lowest per capita income of any population group in the United States, the highest rates of malnutrition, the highest rates of infant mortality, the highest rates of plague disease, death by exposure, and so on.

These desert lands commonly referred to as wastelands, or badlands, are, ironically, very rich in energy resources. Indian reservations alone account for two-thirds of all U.S. "domestic" uranium reserves, one-quarter of oil and natural gas reserves in the United States, and one-third of U.S. low-sulfur coal reserves, not to mention substantial reserves of minerals such as gold, silver, copper, bauxite, and others. The ironic and continuing designation of this resource-rich terrain as wasteland in fact represents a very important means of justifying the relentless plunder of the region through highly environmentally destructive extractive technologies. The wasteland designation also supports the region's use as a large-scale waste dump and weapons testing range in the minds of policy makers, government bureaucrats, and military officials. The wasteland discourse remains useful for private corporate energy and waste management industries as well. Bolstering this wasteland perspective are a variety of scientific discourses that serve to legitimate these industrial practices. The "logical" outcome of such practices renders not only the land but the people who live on it expendable.

Indeed, today's version of the wasteland discourse has serious implications for the very real bodies that inhabit the zones of sacrifice within the nuclear landscape. Within the context of a nuclear society that produces deadly byproducts that alter and transform the earth and living organisms, those paying the highest price for advanced technologies are often those for whom technology offers the least benefits.

Virtually unknown to the public at large, an alternative narrative exists about these dry desert places. Rather than a no man's land, or wasteland, many Indians describe these deserts as places of origin and emergence, as holy places, and sacred geographies. Much controversy surrounds these alternative discourses. Whether they represent resurgent Indian cultural identity or political postures stemming from an ingenuous "higher" moral understanding, or whether they articulate genuine, long-sustained indigenous wisdom founded on an earth-based, animistic cosmology—these alternative stories about this landscape are as much a part of the region's cultural history as any of those that have emerged in the past 500 years of European and American occupation and dominance. (The co-optation of such views by "New Age" sympathizers—largely white and middle class—demonstrates their power over the imagination.) To counterbalance the powerful wasteland discourse, these alternative Indian discourses on sacred geographies must be made continually visible, that is, discursively mapped in conjunction with the nuclear landscape. At the very least they provide a perspective from which to view the Euroamerican "frontier," "pioneer," and even scientific narratives about place in this region. They underscore the diversity of cultural constructions of place and nature and reinforce the view that ethnic groups, including whites, are often bound by their own cultural lenses, that different cultures create very different landscapes, both narratively and materially. While the Euroamerican narrative in this instance results in the nuclear landscape, these preexisting and continuing indigenous representations of nature and place refuse to remain silent, refuse to acquiesce to the wasteland discourse. . . .

Interlocking Desires: Science, Industry, and the Military

Behind the sacrificial geography of the nuclear landscape lie the Cold War and the development of nuclear power, those who manipulated these events, and those who prospered by them.

The United States has paid a high price for "winning" the Cold War and for its use of nuclear energy in the pursuit of global economic and military superiority. But the actual price of the Cold War, and of "national competitiveness," hasn't even begun to be tallied. An exploration of the nuclear waste crisis reveals the inequitable distribution of payment, weighing most heavily on the disenfranchised, and thus contributes to a more accurate assessment of what "collateral" damage has been inflicted in the pursuit of capitalist political hegemony. The so-called "price" for "freedom" is paid for by those with the least power, the least chance to benefit from U.S. control of global order and the wealth it brings. If we look beneath the rhetoric of progress so common in the postwar twentieth century—a rhetoric that equates nuclear technology with unlimited clean power—we find a familiar triad: the military, science, and industry. These comprise the institutions that have most benefited from nuclearism and whose interlocking desires have resulted in, among other things, the emergence of a nuclear wasteland in the interdesert region populated by communities with far less prestige, privilege, and power.

QUESTIONS FOR DISCUSSION

1. In what ways do environmental policies and practices reflect larger patterns of social inequality?
2. Think about environmental practices in your community. Where are the high-polluting factories, landfills, and hazardous waste facilities located? What are the economic and racial characteristics of the people who live in those areas?
3. How does the social mapping technique that Kuletz uses help to identify racism in U.S. nuclear policies and practices? What policy changes should occur to remedy this problem?

55

NATURAL CAPITALISM

PAUL HAWKEN

Somewhere along the way to free-market capitalism, the United States became the most wasteful society on the planet. Most of us know it. There is the waste we can see: traffic jams, irreparable VCRs, Styrofoam coffee cups, landfills; the waste we can't see: Superfund sites, greenhouse gases, radioactive waste, vagrant chemicals; and the social waste we don't want to think about: homelessness, crime, drug addiction, our forgotten infirm and elderly.

Nationally and globally, we perceive social and environmental decay as distinct and unconnected. In fact, a humbling design flaw deeply embedded in industrial logic links the two problems. Toto, pull back the curtain: The efficient dynamo of industrialism isn't there. Even by its own standards, industrialism is extraordinarily inefficient.

Modern industrialism came into being in a world very different from the one we live in today: fewer people, less material well-being, plentiful natural resources. As a result of the successes of industry and capitalism, these conditions have now reversed. Today, more people are chasing fewer natural resources.

But industry still operates by the same rules, using more resources to make fewer people more productive. The consequence: massive waste—of both resources and people.

Decades from now, we may look back at the end of the 20th century and ponder why business and society ignored these trends for so long—how one species thought it could flourish while nature ebbed. Historians will show, perhaps, how politics, the media, economics, and commerce created an industrial regime that wasted our social and natural environment and called it growth. As author Bill McKibben put it, "The laws of Congress and the laws of physics have grown increasingly divergent, and the laws of physics are not likely to yield."

The laws we're ignoring determine how life sustains itself. Commerce requires living systems for its welfare—it is emblematic of the times that this even needs to be said. Because of our industrial prowess, we emphasize what people can do but tend to ignore what nature does. Commercial institutions, proud of their achievements, do not see that healthy living systems—clean air and water, healthy soil, stable climates—are integral to a functioning economy. As our living systems deteriorate, traditional forecasting and business economics become the equivalent of house rules on a sinking cruise ship.

One is tempted to say that there is nothing wrong with capitalism except that it has never been tried. Our current industrial system is based on accounting principles that would bankrupt any company.

Conventional economic theories will not guide our future for a simple reason: They have never placed "natural capital" on the balance sheet. When it is included, not as a free amenity or as a putative infinite supply, but as an integral and valuable part of the production process, everything

Reprinted with permission from *Mother Jones,* March/April 1997. Copyright © 1997 Foundation for National Progress.

changes. Prices, costs, and what is and isn't economically sound change dramatically.

Industries destroy natural capital because they have historically benefited from doing so. As businesses successfully created more goods and jobs, consumer demand soared, compounding the destruction of natural capital. All that is about to change.

Natural Capital

Everyone is familiar with the traditional definition of capital as accumulated wealth in the form of investments, factories, and equipment. "Natural capital," on the other hand, comprises the resources we use, both nonrenewable (oil, coal, metal ore) and renewable (forests, fisheries, grasslands). Although we usually think of renewable resources in terms of desired materials, such as wood, their most important value lies in the services they provide. These services are related to, but distinct from, the resources themselves. They are not pulpwood but forest cover, not food but topsoil. Living systems feed us, protect us, heal us, clean the nest, let us breathe. They are the "income" derived from a healthy environment: clean air and water, climate stabilization, rainfall, ocean productivity, fertile soil, watersheds, and the less-appreciated functions of the environment, such as processing waste—both natural and industrial.

For anyone who doubts the innate value of ecosystem services, the $200 million Biosphere II experiment stands as a reality check. In 1991, eight people entered a sealed, glass-enclosed, 3-acre living system, where they expected to remain alive and healthy for two years. Instead, air quality plummeted, carbon dioxide levels rose, and oxygen had to be pumped in from the outside to keep the inhabitants healthy. Nitrous oxide levels inhibited brain function. Cock-roaches flourished while insect pollinators died, vines choked out crops and trees, and nutrients polluted the water so much that the residents had to filter it by hand before they could drink it. Of the original 25 small animal species in Biosphere II, 19 became extinct.

At the end of 17 months, the humans showed signs of oxygen starvation from living at the equivalent of an altitude of 17,500 feet. Of course, design flaws are inherent in any prototype, but the fact remains that $200 million could not maintain a functioning ecosystem for eight people for 17 months. We add eight people to the planet every three seconds.

The lesson of Biosphere II is that there are no man-made substitutes for essential natural services. We have not come up with an economical way to manufacture watersheds, gene pools, topsoil, wetlands, river systems, pollinators, or fisheries. Technological fixes can't solve problems with soil fertility or guarantee clean air, biological diversity, pure water, and climatic stability; nor can they increase the capacity of the environment to absorb 25 billion tons of waste created annually in America alone.

Natural Capital as a Limiting Factor

Until the 1970s, the concept of natural capital was largely irrelevant to business planning, and it still is in most companies. Throughout the industrial era, economists considered manufactured capital—money, factories, etc.—the principal factor in industrial production, and perceived natural capital as a marginal contributor. The exclusion of natural capital from balance sheets was an understandable omission. There was so much of it, it didn't seem worth counting. Not any longer.

Historically, economic development has faced a number of limiting factors, including the availability of labor, energy resources, machinery, and financial capital. The absence or depletion of a limiting factor can prevent a system from growing. If marooned in a snowstorm, you need water, food, and warmth to survive. Having more of one factor cannot compensate for the absence of the other. Drinking more water will not make up for lack of clothing if you are freezing.

In the past, by increasing the limiting factor, industrial societies continued to develop economically. It wasn't always pretty: Slavery "satisfied" labor shortages, as did immigration and high birthrates. Mining companies exploited coal, oil, and gas to meet increased energy demands. The need for labor-saving devices provoked the invention of steam engines, spinning jennies, cotton gins, and telegraphs. Financial capital became universally accessible through central banks, credit, stock exchanges, and currency exchange mechanisms.

Because economies grow and change, new limiting factors occasionally emerge. When they do, massive restructuring occurs. Nothing works as before. Behavior that used to be economically sound becomes unsound, even destructive.

Economist Herman E. Daly cautions that we are facing a historic juncture in which, for the first time, the limits to increased prosperity are not the lack of man-made capital but the lack of natural capital. The limits to increased fish harvest are not boats, but productive fisheries; the limits to irrigation are not pumps or electricity, but viable aquifers; the limits to pulp and lumber production are not sawmills, but plentiful forests.

Like all previous limiting factors, the emergence of natural capital as an economic force will pose a problem for reactionary institutions. For those willing to embrace the challenges of a new era, however, it presents an enormous opportunity.

The High Price of Bad Information

The value of natural capital is masked by a financial system that gives us improper information—a classic case of "garbage in, garbage out." Money and prices and markets don't give us exact information about how much our suburbs, freeways, and spandex cost. Instead, *everything else* is giving us accurate information: our beleaguered air and watersheds, our overworked soils, our decimated inner cities. All of these provide information our prices should be giving us but do not.

Let's begin with a startling possibility: The U.S. economy may not be growing at all, and may have ceased growing nearly 25 years ago. Obviously, we are not talking about the gross domestic product (GDP), measured in dollars, which has grown at 2.5 percent per year since 1973. Despite this growth, there is little evidence of improved lives, better infrastructure, higher real wages, more leisure and family time, and greater economic security.

The logic here is simple, although unorthodox. We don't know if our economy is growing because the indices we rely upon, such as the GDP, don't measure growth. The GDP measures money transactions on the assumption that when a dollar changes hands, economic growth occurs. But there is a world of difference between financial exchanges and growth. Compare an addition to your home to a two-month stay in the hospital for injuries you suffered during a mugging. Say both cost the same. Which is growth? The GDP makes no distinction. Or suppose the president announces he will authorize $10 billion for new prisons to help combat crime. Is the $10 billion growth? Or what if a train overturns next to the Sacramento River and spills 10,000 gallons of atrazine, poisoning all the fish for 30 miles downstream? Money pours into cleanups, hatchery releases, announcements warning people about tainted fish, and lawsuits against the railroad and the chemical company. Growth? Or loss?

Currently, economists count most industrial, environmental, and social waste as GDP, right along with bananas, cars, and Barbie dolls. Growth includes *all* expenditures, regardless of whether society benefits or loses. This includes the cost of emergency room services, prisons, toxic cleanups, homeless shelters, lawsuits, cancer treatments, divorces, and every piece of litter along the side of every highway.

Instead of counting decay as economic growth, we need to subtract decline from revenue to see if we are getting ahead or falling behind. Unfortunately, where economic growth is concerned, the government uses a calculator with no minus sign.

Wasting Resources Means Wasting People

Industry has always sought to increase the productivity of workers, not resources. And for good reason. Most resource prices have fallen for 200 years—due in no small part to the extraordinary increases in our ability to extract, harvest, ship, mine, and exploit resources. If the competitive advantage goes to the low-cost provider, and resources are cheap, then business will naturally use more and more resources in order to maximize worker productivity.

Such a strategy was eminently sensible when the population was smaller and resources were plentiful. But with respect to meeting the needs of the future, contemporary business economics is pre-Copernican. We cannot heal the country's social wounds or "save" the environment as long as we cling to the outdated industrial assumptions that the *summum bonum* of commercial enterprise is to use more stuff and fewer peo-

ple. Our thinking is backward: We shouldn't use more of what we have less of (natural capital) to use less of what we have more of (people). While the need to maintain high labor productivity is critical to income and economic well-being, labor productivity that corrodes society is like burning the furniture to heat the house.

Our pursuit of increased labor productivity at all costs not only depletes the environment, it also depletes labor. Just as overproduction can exhaust topsoil, overproductivity can exhaust a workforce. The underlying assumption that greater productivity would lead to greater leisure and well-being, while true for many decades, has become a bad joke. In the United States, those who are employed, and presumably becoming more productive, find they are working 100 to 200 hours more per year than 20 years ago. Yet real wages haven't increased for more than 20 years.

In 1994, I asked a roomful of senior executives from Fortune 500 companies the following questions: Do you want to work harder in five years than you do today? Do you know anyone in your office who is a slacker? Do you know any parents in your company who are spending too much time with their kids? The only response was a few embarrassed laughs. Then it was quiet—perhaps numb is a better word.

Meanwhile, people whose jobs have been downsized, re-engineered, or restructured out of existence are being told—as are millions of youths around the world—that we have created an economic system so ingenious that it doesn't need them, except perhaps to do menial service jobs.

In parts of the industrialized world, unemployment and underemployment have risen faster than employment for more than 25 years. Nearly one-third of the world's workers sense that they have no value in the present economic scheme.

Clearly, when 1 billion willing workers can't find a decent job or any employment at all, we need to make fundamental changes. We can't—whether through monetary means, government programs, or charity—create a sense of value and dignity in people's lives when we're simultaneously developing a society that doesn't need them. If people don't feel valued, they will act out society's verdict in sometimes shocking ways. William Strickland, a pioneer in working with inner-city children, once said that "you can't teach algebra to someone who doesn't want to be here." He meant that urban kids don't want to be here at all, alive, anywhere on earth. They try to tell us, but we don't listen. So they engage in increasingly risky behavior—unprotected sex, drugs, violence—until we notice. By that time, their conduct has usually reached criminal proportions—and then we blame the victims, build more jails, and lump the costs into the GDP.

The theologian Matthew Fox has pointed out that we are the only species without full employment. Yet we doggedly pursue technologies that will make that ever more so. Today we fire people, perfectly capable people, to wring out one more wave of profits. Some of the restructuring is necessary and overdue. But, as physicists Amory Lovins and Ernst von Weizsacker have repeatedly advised, what we *should* do is fire the unproductive kilowatts, barrels of oil, tons of material, and pulp from old-growth forests—and hire more people to do so.

In fact, reducing resource use creates jobs and lessens the impact we have on the environment. We can grow, use fewer resources, lower taxes, increase per capita spending on the needy, end federal deficits, reduce the size of government, and begin to restore damaged environments, both natural and social.

At this point, you may well be skeptical. The last summary is too hopeful and promises too much. If economic alternatives are this attractive, why aren't we doing them now? A good question. I will try to answer it. But, lest you think these proposals are Pollyannaish, know that my optimism arises from the magnitude of the problem, not from the ease of the solutions. Waste is too expensive: it's cheaper to do the right thing.

Resource Productivity

Economists argue that rational markets make this the most efficient of all possible economies. But that theory works only as long as you use financial efficiency as the sole metric and ignore physics, biology, and common sense. The physics of energy and mass conservation, along with the laws of entropy, are the arbiters of efficiency, not *Forbes* or the Dow Jones or the Federal Reserve. The economic issue is: How much work (value) does society get from its materials and energy? This is a very different question than asking how much return it can get out of its money.

If we already deployed materials or energy efficiently, it would support the contention that a radical increase in resource productivity is unrealistic. But the molecular trail leads to the opposite conclusion. For example, cars are barely 1 percent efficient in the sense that, for every 100 gallons of gasoline, only one gallon actually moves the passengers. Likewise, only 8 to 10 percent of the energy used in heating the filament of an incandescent lightbulb actually becomes visible light. (Some describe it as a space heater disguised as a lightbulb.) Modern carpeting remains on the floor for up to 12 years, after which it remains in landfills for as long as 20,000 years or more—less than .06 percent efficiency.

According to Robert Ayres, a leader in studying industrial metabolism, about 94 percent of the materials extracted for use in manufacturing durable products become waste before the product is even manufactured. More waste is generated in production, and most of that is lost unless the product is reused or recycled. Overall, America's material and energy efficiency is no more than 1 or 2 percent. In other words, American industry uses as much as 100 times more material and energy than theoretically required to deliver consumer services.

State-of-the-shelf technologies—fans, lights, pumps, superefficient windows, motors, and other products with proven track records—combined with intelligent mechanical and building design, could reduce energy consumption in American buildings by 90 percent. State-of-the-art technologies that are just being introduced could reduce consumption still further. In some cases—wind power, for example—the technologies not only operate more efficiently and pollute less, they also are more labor-intensive. Wind energy requires more labor than coal-generated electricity but has become competitive with it on a real-cost basis.

The resource revolution is starting to show up in all areas of business. In the forest products industry, clearinghouses now identify hundreds of techniques that can reduce the use of timber and pulpwood by nearly 75 percent without diminishing the quality of housing, the "services" provided by books and paper, or the convenience of a tissue. In the housing industry, builders can use dozens of local or composite materials, including those made from rice and wheat straw, wastepaper, and earth, instead of studs, plywood, and concrete.

Although a new "hypercar" is now in development, "new urbanist" architects, such as Peter Calthorpe, Andres Duany, Elizabeth Plater-Zyberk, and others, are designing communities that could eliminate 40 to 60 percent of driving needs. (A recent San Francisco study showed that communities can decrease car use by 30 percent when they double population density.) Internet-based transactions may render many shopping malls obsolete. Down the road we'll have quantum semiconductors that store vast amounts of information on chips no bigger than a dot; diodes that emit light for 20 years without bulbs; ultrasound washing machines that use no water, heat, or soap; hyperlight materials stronger than steel; deprintable and reprintable paper; biological technologies that reduce or eliminate the need for insecticides and fertilizers; plastics that are both reusable and compostable; piezoelectric polymers that can generate electricity from the heel of your shoe or the force of a wave; and roofs and roads that do double duty as solar energy collectors. Some of these technologies, of course, may turn out to be impractical or have unwanted side effects. Nevertheless, these and thousands more are lining up like salmon to swim upstream toward greater resource productivity.

Resource Politics

How can government help speed these entrepreneurial "salmon" along? The most fundamental policy implication is simple to envision, but difficult to execute: We have to revise the tax system to stop subsidizing behaviors we don't want (resource depletion and pollution) and to stop taxing behaviors we do want (income and work). We need to transform, incrementally but firmly, the sticks and carrots that guide business.

Taxes and subsidies are information. Everybody, whether rich or poor, acts on that information every day. Taxes make something more expensive to buy; subsidies artificially lower prices. In the United States, we generally like to subsidize environmental exploitation, cars, big corporations, and technological boondoggles. We don't like to subsidize clean technologies that will lead to more jobs and innovation because that is supposed to be left to the "market." Specifically, we subsidize carbon-based energy production, particularly oil and coal; we massively subsidize a transportation system that has led to suburban sprawl and urban decay; we subsidize risky technologies like nuclear fission and pie-in-the-sky weapons systems like Star Wars. (Between 1946 and 1961 the Atomic Energy Commission spent $1 billion to develop a nuclear-powered airplane. But it was such a lemon that the plane could not get off the ground. History's dustbin also includes a nuclear-powered ship, the Savannah, that was retired after the Maritime Administration found she cost $2 million more per year than other ships.)

We subsidize the disposal of waste in all its myriad forms—from landfills, to Superfund cleanups, to deep-well injection, to storage of nuclear waste. In the process, we encourage an economy where 80 percent of what we consume gets thrown away after one use.

As for farming, the U.S. government covers all the bases: We subsidize agricultural production, agricultural nonproduction, agricultural destruction, and agricultural restoration. We provide price supports to sugarcane growers, and we subsidize the restoration of the Everglades (which sugarcane growers are destroying). We subsidize cattle grazing on public lands, and we pay for soil conservation. We subsidize energy costs so that farmers can deplete aquifers to grow alfalfa to feed cows that make milk that we store in warehouses as surplus cheese that does not get to the hungry.

Then there is the money we donate to dying industries: federal insurance provided to floodplain developers, cheap land leases to ski resorts, deposit insurance given to people who looted U.S. savings and loans, payments to build roads into wilderness areas so that privately held forest product companies can buy wood at a fraction of replacement cost, and monies to defense suppliers who have provided the Pentagon with billions of dollars in unnecessary inventory and parts.

To create a policy that supports resource productivity will require a shift away from taxing the social "good" of labor, toward taxing the social "bads" of resource exploitation, pollution, fossil fuels, and waste. This tax shift should be "revenue neutral"—meaning that for every dollar of taxation added to resources or waste, one dollar would be removed from labor taxes. As the cost of waste and resources increases, business would save money by hiring less-expensive labor to save more-expensive resources. The eventual goal would be to achieve zero taxation on labor and income.

Of course, a tax shift alone will not change the way business operates: a broad array of policy changes on issues of global trade, education, economic development, econometrics (including measures of growth and well-being), and scientific research must accompany it. For the tax shift to succeed, we must also reverse the wrenching breakdown of our democracy, which means addressing campaign finance reform and media concentration.

It is easier, as the saying goes, to ride a horse in the direction it is going. Because the costs of natural capital will inevitably increase, we should start changing the tax system now and get ahead of the curve. Shifting taxes to resources won't—as some in industry will doubtless claim—mean diminishing standards of living. It will mean an explosion of innovation that will create products, techniques, and processes that are far more effective than what they replace.

Some economists will naturally counter that we should let the markets dictate costs and that using taxation to promote particular outcomes is interventionist. But *all* tax systems are interventionist; the question is not whether to intervene but *how* to intervene.

The Future

In 1750, few could imagine the outcome of industrialization. Today, the prospect of a resource productivity revolution in the next century is equally hard to fathom. But this is what it promises: an economy that uses progressively less material and energy each year and where the quality of consumer services continues to improve; an economy where environmental deterioration stops and gets reversed as we invest in increasing our natural capital; and, finally, a society where we have more useful and worthy work available than people to do it.

A utopian vision? No. The human condition will remain. We will still be improvident and wise, foolish and just. No economic system is a panacea, nor can any create a better person. But as the 20th century has painfully taught us, a bad system can certainly destroy good people.

Natural capitalism is not about making sudden changes, uprooting institutions, or fomenting upheaval for a new social order. (In fact, these consequences are more likely if we don't address fundamental problems.) Natural capitalism is about making small, critical choices that can tip economic and social factors in positive ways.

Natural capitalism may not guarantee particular outcomes, but it *will* ensure that economic systems more closely mimic biological systems, which have successfully adapted to dynamic changes over millennia. After all, this analogy is at the heart of capitalism, the idea that markets have a power that mimics life and evolution. We should expand this logic, not retract it.

For business, the opportunities are clear and enormous. With the population doubling sometime in the next century, and re-source availability per capita dropping by one-half to three-fourths over that same period, which factor in production do you think will go up in value—and which do you think will go down? This basic shift in capital availability is inexorable.

Ironically, organizations like Earth First!, Rainforest Action Network, and Greenpeace have now become the *real* capitalists. By addressing such issues as greenhouse gases, chemical contamination, and the loss of fisheries, wildlife corridors, and primary forests, they are doing more to preserve a viable business future than are all the chambers of commerce put together. While business leaders hotly contest the idea of resource shortages, there are few credible scientists or corporations who argue that we are not losing the living systems that provide us with trillions of dollars of natural capital: our soil, forest cover, aquifers, oceans, grasslands, and rivers. Moreover, these systems are diminishing at a time when the world's population and the demand for services are growing exponentially.

Looking ahead, if living standards and population double over the next 50 years as some predict, and if we assume the developing world shared the same living standard we do, we would have to increase our resource use (and attendant waste) by a factor of 16 in five decades. Publicly, governments, the United Nations, and industries all work toward this end. Privately, no one believes that we can increase industrial throughput by a factor anywhere near 16, considering the earth's limited and now fraying life-support systems.

It is difficult for economists, whose important theories originated during a time of resource abundance, to understand how the decline in ecosystem services is laying the groundwork for the next stage in economic evolution. This next stage, whatever it may be called, is being brought about by powerful and much-delayed feedback from living systems. As we surrender our living systems, social stability, fiscal soundness, and personal health to outmoded economic assumptions, we are hoping that conventional economic growth will save us. But if economic "growth" does save us, it will be anything but conventional.

So why be hopeful? Because the solution is profitable, creative, and eminently possible. Societies may act stupidly for a period of time, but eventually they move to the path of least economic resistance. The loss of natural capital services, lamentable as it is in environmental terms, also affects costs. So far, we have created convoluted economic theories and accounting systems to work around the problem.

You can win a Nobel Prize in economics and travel to the royal palace in Stockholm in a gilded, horse-drawn brougham believing that ancient forests are more valuable in liquidation—as fruit crates and Yellow Pages—than as a going and growing concern. But soon, I would estimate within a few decades, we will realize collectively what each of us already knows individually: It's cheaper to take care of something—a roof, a car, a planet—than to let it decay and try to fix it later.

While there may be no "right" way to value a forest or a river, there is a wrong way, which is to give it no value at all. How do we decide the value of a 700-year-old tree? We need only ask how much it would cost to make a new one. Or a new river, or even a new atmosphere.

Despite the shrill divisiveness in media and politics, Americans remain remarkably consistent in what kind of country they envision for their children and grandchildren. The benefits of resource productivity align almost perfectly with what American voters say they want: better schools, a better environment, safer communities, more economic security, stronger families and family support, freer markets, less regulation, fewer taxes, smaller government, and more local control.

The future belongs to those who understand that doing more with less is compassionate, prosperous, and enduring, and thus more intelligent, even competitive.

QUESTIONS FOR DISCUSSION

1. Do you think the restructuring of the tax system that Hawken calls for will help to alleviate environmental problems?
2. Should the environment be seen as another form of capital?
3. Is Hawken's solution possible on a global level?
4. Can capitalism be truly earth-friendly, or do the demands of maximizing profits prevent corporations from adopting policies that place the needs of the environment first?

THE SOCIAL WEB

- The Natural Resources Defense Council is one of the leading environmental organizations in the United States. Its Web site offers a wealth of information on a wide variety of environmental issues, as well as current environmental legislation: www.nrdc.org.
- The Environmental Literacy Council is an independent nonprofit organization dedicated to advancing environmental education. Its Web site contains numerous resources for teachers and students of environmental science: www.enviroliteracy.org.

- The Environmental Protection Agency Web site enables you to find the most recent environmental statistics related to your community: www.epa.gov/enviro.

QUESTIONS FOR DEBATE

1. How do environmental problems reflect and perpetuate social and economic inequalities?
2. Does the growth of global capitalism contribute to the increase of environmental problems?
3. How should our social policies balance the often competing demands of industrial growth and natural resource preservation?
4. Does the United States share in the responsibility for global environmental degradation? What economic and social price should we, individually, be willing to pay to solve global environmental problems?

Chapter 13
Global Politics, Terrorism, and War

Learning Objectives

By the end of this chapter you should be able to:

- Recognize how the authors use one or more of the major perspectives to explore global politics, terrorism, and war.
- Explore how global politics and war are shaped by inequalities.
- Identify ways that national security, patriotism, terrorism, and warfare are socially constructed.
- Describe various consequences of war and nationalism.
- Analyze how individuals cope with war and help to build a global community in their everyday behavior.

Defining the Problem

Scholars of social problems recognize that global politics and war are interrelated with the other problems we have presented in this book. Some researchers look at the relationship between armed conflict and global economic disparity. Maintaining a military is expensive during both wartime and peacetime and is a major factor contributing to global poverty. War is also a major contributor to environmental degradation and causes famine, disease, and the displacement of large numbers of people.

Some social problems investigators explore the ways that concepts and issues related to global politics, war, and terrorism are culturally defined. What constitutes a "threat" to national security? How do we decide what kinds of military machinery and strategies are "defensive" and what kinds are "offensive"? How do we define what is in our "national interest?" What do global "strength" and "leadership" really mean? The twenty-first century began with a national and international focus on terrorism. Yet terrorism is a concept filled with cultural meaning. "Terrorism" is typically defined in the United States as illegitimate violent activities on the part of individuals targeting civilians. "War" is constructed as a legitimate violent activity engaged in by nations with state-sanctioned military organizations. Despite the notion that war is committed by militaries against other militaries, most of the people killed in the major wars of the twentieth century were civilians. Many revolutions (including the American revolution) began as actions taken by individuals operating outside the realm of a government. What is the difference between a "freedom fighter" and a "terrorist"? Sociologists do not deny the very devastating consequences that terrorist attacks, such as the one that occurred in the United States on September 11, 2001, have on people's lives. These investigators do, however, attempt to understand such actions within their own cultural context.

Some sociologists examine the ways that the arms race, high levels of military spending, and the increasing threat of military action maintain the global economic and political power of a few nations. Many scholars argue that the United States benefits economically and politically from promoting military build-up and war as the ultimate solutions to global problems. The U.S. far outspends every other nation in the world on its military and has refused to sign major treaties developed by the United Nations to promote global peace and the reduction of nuclear weapons. Weapons are a major commodity for the United States, and the U.S. government is the largest arms dealer in the world. How much of the U.S. economy is dependent on military production and spending? What effects does U.S. military build-up have on other nations? How do powerful multinational corporations owe their wealth to contracts with the U.S. military?

Some sociologists examine the military as a social organization. They examine the normative relationships, behaviors, and attitudes that comprise military culture. They also may explore the ways that patterns of racial inequality are perpetuated in the military system. Other researchers focus on gender and the military. What are the ways that traditional gender norms are reinforced and perpetuated in the military? Does the military also provide individuals with the opportunities to challenge traditional gender assumptions? Some social problems investigators address the problems encountered by individuals and families who operate within the military system. They may research such issues as domestic violence, children's behavioral problems, difficulties in educating children, the social isolation of military families, the financial difficulties faced by military families, or the transition of families out of the military system.

Finally, social problems researchers look at the effects of war on individuals. They may explore the consequences that war has on combat personnel. They may examine the impact of war on civilians. They look at the problems encountered by refugees of war or the long-term impact that war has on social relationships and communities. What kinds of effects does war have on the children who witness it? What kinds of social consequences occur when children are injured, orphaned, or fall ill as a result of war? Still other researchers may look at the short-term and long-term consequences of terrorism on the individuals who experience it. Do people respond to terrorist attacks in the same ways they respond to other disasters? Does terrorism represent a new and unique human experience?

Scope of the Problem

The twentieth century was the bloodiest hundred years in human history, with more per capita deaths due to war than in any other century. In the 1990s alone, war claimed the lives of more than 5 million people.[1]

The preparations for warfare represent a significant expense for the world's nations. In 1987, worldwide military spending reached an all-time high of $1.2 trillion. Following the end of the Cold War, global military spending declined, although it began to increase again in 1997. Worldwide spending is now approximately $800 billion, 70 percent of which is spent by the most advanced industrialized countries. Wealthy nations are also responsible for more than 90 percent of military arms sales, amounting to $296 billion between 1992 and 1999. Seventy percent of these sales were to poorer countries.

According to the United Nations, there is a strong relationship between war and

---

[1]Nitin Desai and Jayantha Dhanapala, "A Peace Dividend for Developing Countries Would Pay Off," *International Herald Tribune*, December 22, 2000.

global poverty. Nations currently spend an average of 10 percent of their total budgets on military expenditures. Active warfare causes great economic strain, social upheaval, and environmental degradation in the countries in which war occurs. Even in peacetime, defense spending diverts significant funds that could be used to fight poverty. The U.N. has proposed that developing nations can experience a "peace dividend" by reducing military spending, thereby increasing the resources available to them for education, public health, and economic development. At the same time, the U.N. calls on developed nations to increase their subsidies to developing nations and to reduce their sales of weaponry to poorer countries.

In 1961, President Dwight D. Eisenhower warned of the dangers of what he called the "military-industrial complex." He believed that true national security is compromised when a country's economy becomes increasingly dependent on military production and spending. In 2001, total U.S. military spending was nearly $330 billion.[2] The United States far outspends any other nation in the world on its military. Its military budget is six times larger than that of Russia, the world's second largest spender, and twenty-six times larger than the combined military spending of the seven nations identified by the Pentagon as its most likely enemies (Cuba, Iraq, Iran, North Korea, Sudan, Libya, and Syria).[3] U.S. military spending comprises 36 percent of total worldwide military expenditures. This enormous amount of spending has greatly benefited a few military industrial giants.

Since the end of the Cold War, major U.S. military contractors have merged, giving a few corporations tremendous economic and political power.[4] For example, General Dynamics Corporation now owns one-half of the shipyards where Navy vessels are manufactured. Three corporate giants—Lockheed Martin, Boeing, and Raytheon—received 26 percent of all defense contracts awarded in 1999.

Between 1940 and 1995, the United States spent $3.5 trillion in preparation to fight a nuclear war.[5] Today, the U.S. spends $27 billion annually on nuclear arms. There are currently 20,000 nuclear weapons in the world, 5,000 of which are on "hair-trigger alert," meaning they are ready to be launched within minutes.[6] There may be as many as 10,000 additional Russian warheads of indeterminate status. More than 95 percent of the world's nuclear stockpile is in the hands of the United States or Russia.[7] The United States alone has produced 55 percent of the world's supplies of nuclear weapons and currently accounts for more than 10,000 intact nuclear warheads. A total of ten nations in the world currently have nuclear weapons—the United States, Russia, Great Britain, France, China, India, Pakistan, North Korea, Israel, and Iran.

Despite the global destructive capabilities of nuclear arsenals, most of the world's wars are fought with small arms and light weapons. According to the United Nations, more than 600 million small arms and light

[2]"Objective Information on Military Matters, Including Transparency of Military Expenditures, 2001," Report of the Secretary-General, United Nations General Assembly.

[3]"World Military Expenditures: U.S. vs. World," Center for Defense Information, December 16, 2002.

[4]"Military Industrial Complex," Center for Defense Information, December 16, 2002.

[5]"Nuclear Issues: Facts at a Glance," Center for Defense Information, April 12, 2002.

[6]"Nuclear Weapons and World Security," Non-Governmental Organizations Committee on Disarmament, Peace, and Security Web site, www.disarm.igc.org.

[7]"Global Nuclear Stockpiles, 1945–2002," NRDC Nuclear Notebook, Bulletin of the Atomic Scientists, Vol. 58, No. 6, pp. 103–104.

weapons (SALW) are available for use worldwide.[8] During the 1990s, forty-seven of the forty-nine armed conflicts around the world were fought with these weapons. The United States supplies one-half of the annual $53.4 billion market in these weapons.[9] The Middle East is the world's largest market for small arms and light weapons. Because these weapons cost relatively little and are easy to use, the United Nations proclaims that they undermine peace initiatives, foster human rights abuses, and create a culture of violence in unstable nations.

One of the most persistent, enduring, and devastating consequences of global warfare has been the proliferation of landmines. It is estimated that between 60 and 70 million landmines exist in at least 70 different countries.[10] Each year, landmines kill or injure an estimated 26,000 people, the vast majority of whom are civilians. Landmines have been produced by fifty-four countries, increasingly as offensive weapons. They are also inexpensive, costing as little as $3 each to deploy. Yet the financial as well as human price of abandoned landmines is high. The cost of removing an unexploded landmine ranges from $300 to $1,000, while the cost of providing artificial limbs to the people who are maimed by landmines ranges from $100 to $3,000. Survivors of landmine explosions can be found in nearly two-thirds of the countries in the world, making landmine survivor assistance a major global health issue.[11] In De-

cember 1997, 122 nations met at the Ottawa Convention on Anti-Personnel Land Mines and adopted a treaty to ban the production and use of these weapons. The United States refused to sign this treaty.

Perhaps the most deplorable consequence of war is its devastating effects on the world's children. The United Nations Children's Fund estimates that between 1986 and 1996, more than two million children were killed and more than six million injured in armed conflicts.[12] Another one million children were orphaned as a result of warfare and ten million children suffered severe or permanent emotional trauma. Armed conflict is responsible for giving more than four million children physical disabilities and is the leading cause of injury to children worldwide. Children are also frequently used as support labor by armed groups and are subject to sexual abuse by soldiers. During armed conflicts, children are frequently forced into battles. It is estimated that currently more than 300,000 children serve as soldiers; the common use of light weapons only encourages the use of children as combat personnel.

Perspectives on the Problem

Sociologists using a *conflict perspective* to examine global politics and war would examine the ways that our national policies regarding international relationships promote the economic interests of major industrial powers. Scholars using a *functionalist perspective* would explore how global policies, including the build-up of a military threat, contribute to national stability and unity. Sociologists using a *social constructionist*

[8]"Conventional Arms: Small Arms and Light Weapons," United Nations Department for Disarmament Affairs.

[9]"Small Arms and Light Weapons," Non-Governmental Organizations Committee on Disarmament, Peace, and Security Web site, www.disarm.igc.org.

[10]"Fact Sheet: Landmines," Center for Global Health & Security, Physicians for Social Responsibility, 2002.

[11]"Fact Sheet—September, 2002: Landmine/UXO Casualties and Survivor Assistance," Landmine Monitor, International Campaign to Ban Landmines.

[12]Barbara Fae Feldstein, "Child Soldiers: Armed to Die. The Impact of War on Children," Cardozo School of Law International Law Practicum. Published by the Non-Governmental Organizations Committee on Disarmament, Peace, and Security Web site, www.disarm.igc.org.

approach would look at the ways that politics, war, and terrorism are defined by a nation to promote its own interests. They would explore how notions of the enemy, evil, and righteousness are constructed by national leaders to support their own military actions and policies. *Symbolic interactionists* would examine the consequences of warfare on individuals. They would investigate how leaders make decisions to go to war and how military training turns citizens into soldiers who can kill when ordered. They would also explore the meanings of war and peace for individuals in their everyday lives.

Connecting the Perspectives

Joseph S. Nye uses a functionalist perspective to argue that the United States must see itself as part of an interdependent global community. He contends that it is in our national interest to include human rights considerations in making foreign policy. Chip Pitts and Jennifer Holmes take a social constructionist approach to examine the conflicting interests of promoting national security while protecting fundamental civil rights. Joshua S. Goldstein uses a conflict perspective to look at the ways that military operations promote traditional notions of masculinity and contribute to the violent sexual exploitation of women. Finally, David Lamb takes a symbolic interactionist approach to look at the process of healing that soldiers who were once sworn enemies can find with one another.

Reading Summaries

In "Why the World's Only Superpower Can't Go It Alone," Nye explores the unprecedented power of the United States in world politics and the global economy. He also addresses the limits of that power and argues that our foreign policies need to recognize the importance of participating in a true global community. Traditionally, U.S.

foreign policies have been based exclusively on what serves our national interest. National interests have been narrowly defined in terms of protecting our borders, promoting military power, and containing the power of our enemies, most notably the Soviet Union. Yet Nye argues that the very nature of power and national interest are shifting in this post–Cold War, global information age. Power is distributed along three different planes—military, economic, and "transnational relations"—that cut across the control of individual governments. Although the U.S. clearly stands alone in terms of military might, the arenas of global economics and transnational issues are much more complex and diverse. The "hard power" of military capability is still important, but the United States must recognize the increasing significance of "soft power"—the cultural influence that we have worldwide as an open, democratic society.

Nye argues that, when developing foreign policy, the United States must realize that it is in our national interest to be involved in international issues. Events that occur in other lands, such as the development of terrorist groups, environmental damage, the increasing violence of the global drug trade, and the proliferation of weapons of mass destruction, can threaten our own national stability. If the United States places its own "narrow domestic interests before global needs" the amount of soft power we have will be diminished. The needs of a global community will require us to place a greater emphasis on diplomacy and on international economic development. It is also in our national interest, Nye contends, to develop foreign policies that are based on promoting democracy and human rights. This does not mean that the United States should be heavy-handed in insisting that the rest of the world adopt American values. True humanitarian-based policies involve basic human rights such as eliminating famine, assisting political refugees, or preventing genocide. It is ultimately in our own national interest, Nye argues, that we develop policies that support global peace, freedom, and stability.

In "Liberty vs. PATRIOTism," Pitts and Holmes explore the implications of U.S. antiterrorism policies for civil rights in the United States. Following the September 11, 2001, al Qaeda attacks against the World Trade Center and the Pentagon, Congress passed the "USA PATRIOT" Act. Pitts and Holmes maintain the act was rushed into law and was not read by most of the members of Congress. It gives the federal government unprecedented rights to access a tremendous amount of information about individuals (citizens and non-citizens alike) without the need to provide any evidence of criminal activity. It allows the government to search private homes without warrants and permits the indefinite detention or deportation of individuals based on "association" with questionable organizations. The law also blurs the distinction between domestic law enforcement and international intelligence gathering.

Pitts and Holmes argue that the USA PATRIOT Act raises serious questions about the power of the federal government to fight terrorism and the role of civil liberties. In the 1960s the FBI abused its power to illegally infiltrate and wiretap politically active civil rights, women's rights, and antiwar groups. Pitts and Holmes worry that law enforcement is now being given the legal power to target unpopular organizations, all in the name of fighting "terrorism." One of the problems with this is that terrorism is an inherently politicized, controversial, and hard-to-define term; they point out that even different federal agencies have different definitions of terrorism. Moreover, concepts of patriotism and national unity can be used to squelch free speech and other basic American rights and values. Pitts and

Holmes argue that as a nation we must grapple with the fundamental tensions between national security on one hand and principles of liberty and democracy on the other.

In "Conquests: Sex and Rape in Wartime," Goldstein examines the highly gendered experience of war. He argues that the sexual exploitation and abuse of women increases during times of war. In war-torn countries with few economic resources, women are more likely to be drawn into exploitive sex work, especially prostitution. The social organization of the military tends to be gender segregated, and combat situations generally isolate large groups of post-adolescent men. Conventional social and sexual norms and relationships are disrupted. Goldstein asserts that sex becomes a primary preoccupation for these men. Sexual promiscuity on the part of male soldiers tends to be viewed as a normal part of the experience of being a soldier. Military commanders frequently encourage the use of prostitutes, and organized prostitution rings become located around military establishments. The widespread use of prostitution contributes to the rampant spread of sexually transmitted diseases and the sexual and physical abuse of large numbers of women and girls.

Goldstein further argues that gender becomes a code for expressing domination, power, and control in combat situations. Male sexual aggression becomes a metaphor for violent confrontation. Weapons, especially bombs, are frequently portrayed as phallic symbols, distinctly male tools for asserting dominance. Military targets are explicitly portrayed as female, the object to receive the bomb's power. The "enemy" is typically constructed as a female entity, and the metaphoric rape of the enemy represents the ability to conquer, dominate, and control. Yet rape is not used only in symbolic form in wartime. Goldstein maintains that the rape of women is widespread during war. Rape is often used as a military tactic, as an instrument of spreading fear and powerlessness. The systematic rape of women and girls in Kosovo, Rwanda, Kashmir, Indonesia, and many other warring regions has been a deliberate strategy for asserting control over the defeated. Gang rape is frequently used as a method of torture and as a means to destroy the social fabric of an enemy's culture. Thus misogyny is more than a symbol of male aggression in war; it becomes a tool for asserting violent domination over large groups of people, both men and women.

In "The Painful Art of Reconciliation," Lamb explains how former soldiers can find healing from the pain and trauma of war. Lamb accompanies a group of American Vietnam veterans on their first trip back to Vietnam since the end of the war. These men are not only returning to the site of their armed conflict. They are also scheduled to meet with a group of former Viet Cong—the soldiers of the National Liberation Front who were the enemy of the South Vietnamese and American armies. The first meeting between these two groups of aging former soldiers begins awkwardly. After all, Lamb asks, "What do you say when you meet a man whom thirty years ago you would have shot dead on the spot?" As the men begin to relax with one another, they swap photographs of their families and laugh over how much weight the American veterans have gained. Eventually, they begin to talk over their war experiences. They find they had respect for one another as soldiers. They also find they had shared a great deal in common as teenage soldiers, overwhelmed by the terror, responsibility, and camaraderie that each had experienced. Through conversation and reflection, the Vietnam veterans could give meaning to their experiences and could make sense of how they occupied their dual combat roles of killers and targets.

Lamb argues that the American soldiers who served in the Vietnam War do not fit Hollywood stereotypes of drug abusers, losers, and war-hungry psychotics. He maintains that they fought "for the same reason soldiers fight in any war—to survive and go home." Yet America's ambivalence about the war meant that the reception these soldiers received when they went home was lukewarm at best. This prevented many soldiers from getting support to emotionally heal from their traumatic experiences. Lamb documents the ways that war veterans can come to terms with their experiences when they have the opportunity to find peace with their former enemies. He believes that there can be tremendous power for healing when enemies who were once sworn to kill one another work to understand their commonalities despite large cultural differences.

FOCUSING QUESTIONS

As you read through these selections, consider the following issues. In the wake of the September 11, 2001, terrorist attacks against the United States, how have notions of patriotism been defined? What does it mean to be an American? How should we determine what actions are in the best interest of national security? What kind of role should America play in global politics? Consider your assumptions about the role of the military in maintaining social stability. What are the ways that the military promotes social and economic inequality worldwide?

56

WHY THE WORLD'S ONLY SUPERPOWER CAN'T GO IT ALONE
JOSEPH S. NYE JR.

Redefining the National Interest

How should the United States define its interests in this global information age? How shall we decide how much and when to join with others? What should we do with our unprecedented power? Isolationists who think we can avoid vulnerability to terrorism by drawing inward fail to understand the realities of a global information age. At the same time, the new unilateralists who urge us to unashamedly deploy it on behalf of self-defined global ends are offering a recipe for undermining our soft power and encouraging others to create the coalitions that will eventually limit our hard power. We must do better than that.

When Condoleezza Rice, now the national security advisor, wrote during the 2000 campaign that we should "proceed from the firm ground of the national interest and not from the interest of an illusory international community," what disturbed our European allies was "the assumption that a conflict between the pursuit of national interest and commitment to the interests of a far-from-illusory international community necessarily exists."[1] The ties that bind the international community may be weak, but they matter. Failure to pay proper respect to the opinion of others and to incorporate a broad conception of justice into our national interest will eventually come to hurt us. As our allies frequently remind us, even well-intentioned American champions of benign hegemony do not have all the answers. While our friends welcomed the multilateralism of the Bush administration's approach after September 2001, they remained concerned about a return to unilateralism.

Democratic leaders who fail to reflect their nation's interest are unlikely to be re-elected, and it is in our interest to preserve our preeminent position. But global interests can be incorporated into a broad and farsighted concept of the national interest. After all, terrorism is a threat to all societies; international trade benefits us as well as others; global warming will raise sea levels along all our coasts as well as those of other countries; infectious diseases can arrive anywhere by ship or plane; and financial instability can hurt the whole world economy. In addition to such concrete interests, many Americans want global values incorporated into our national interest. There are strong indications that Americans' values operate in a highly global context—that our sphere of concern extends well beyond national boundaries. Seventy-three percent agreed with the poll statement "I regard myself as a citizen of the world as well as a citizen of the United States," and 44 percent agreed strongly.[2] We need a broad definition of our national interest that takes account of the interests of others, and it is the role of our leaders to bring this into popular discussions. An enlightened national interest need not be myopic—as September 2001 reminded us.

Traditionalists distinguish between a foreign policy based on values and a foreign policy based on interests. They describe as vital those interests that would directly affect our safety and thus merit the use of force—for example, to prevent attacks on the United States, to prevent the emergence of hostile hegemons in Asia or Europe, to prevent hostile powers on our borders or in control of the seas, and to ensure the survival of U.S. allies.[3] Promoting human rights, encouraging democracy, or developing specific economic sectors is relegated to a lower priority.

I find this approach too narrow, as I believe that humanitarian interests are also important to our lives and our foreign policy. Certainly national strategic interests are vital and deserve priority, because if we fail to protect them, our very survival would be at stake. For example, today countering and suppressing catastrophic terrorism will deserve the priority that was devoted to containing Soviet power during the Cold War.[4] Survival is the necessary condition of foreign policy, but it is not all there is to foreign policy. Moreover, the connection between some events (for example, Iraq's invasion of Kuwait, or a North Korean missile test) and a threat to our national survival may involve a long chain of causes. People can disagree about how probable any link in the chain is and thus about the degree of the threat to our survival. Consequently, reasonable people can disagree about how much "insurance" they want our foreign policy to provide against remote threats to a vital interest before we pursue other values such as human rights.

In my view, in a democracy, the national interest is simply what citizens, after proper deliberation, say it is. It is broader than vital strategic interests, though they are a crucial part. It can include values such as human rights and democracy, particularly if the American public feels that those values are so important to our identity or sense of who we are that people are willing to pay a price to promote them. Values are simply an intangible national interest. If the American people think that our long-term shared interests include certain values and their promotion abroad, then they become part of the national interest. Leaders and experts may point out the costs of indulging certain values, but if an informed public disagrees, experts cannot deny the legitimacy of their opinion.

Determining the national interest involves more than just poll results. It is opinion after public discussion and deliberation. That is why it is so important that our leaders do a better job of discussing a broad formulation of our national interest. Democratic debate is often messy and does not always come up with the "right" answers. Nonetheless, it is difficult to see a better way to decide on the national interest in a democracy. A better-informed political debate is the only way for our people to determine how broadly or narrowly to define our interests.

The Limits of American Power

Even when we agree that values matter, the hard job is figuring out how to bring them to bear in particular instances. Many Americans find Russia's war in Chechnya disturbing, but there are limits to what we can do because Russia remains a nuclear power and we seek its help on terrorism. As our parents reminded us, "Don't let your eyes get bigger than your stomach, and don't bite off more than you can chew." Given our size, the United States has more margin of choice than most countries do. But as we have seen . . . , power is changing, and it is not always clear how much we can chew. The danger posed by the outright champions of hegemony is that their foreign policy is all accelerator and no brakes. Their focus on unipolarity and hegemony exaggerates the degree to which the United States is able to get the outcomes it wants in a changing world.

I argue . . . that power in a global information age is distributed like a three-dimensional chess game. The top military board is unipolar, with the United States far outstripping all other states, but the middle economic board is multipolar, with the United States, Europe, and Japan accounting for two-thirds of world product, and the bottom board of transnational relations that cross borders outside the control of governments has a widely dispersed structure of power. While it is important not to ignore the continuing importance of military force for some purposes, particularly in relation to the preindustrial and industrial parts of the world, the hegemonists' focus on military power can blind us to the limits of our power. As we have seen, American power is not equally great in the economic and transnational dimensions. Not only are there new actors to consider in these domains, but many of the transnational issues—whether financial flows, the spread of AIDS, or terrorism—cannot be resolved without the cooperation of others. Where collective action is a necessary part of obtaining the outcomes we want, our power is by definition limited and the United States is bound to share.

We must also remember the growing role of soft power in this global information age. It matters that half a million foreign students want to study in the United States each year, that Europeans and Asians want to watch American films and TV, that American liberties are attractive in many parts of the world, and that others respect us and want to follow our lead when we are not too arrogant. Our values are significant sources of soft power. Both hard and soft power are important, but in a global information age, . . . soft power is becoming even more so

than in the past. Massive flows of cheap information have expanded the number of transnational channels of contacts across national borders. As we also noted earlier, global markets and nongovernmental groups—including terrorists—play a larger role, and many possess soft power resources. States are more easily penetrated and less like the classic military model of sovereign billiard balls bouncing off each other.

The United States, with its open democratic society, will benefit from the rapidly developing global information age if we develop a better understanding of the nature and limits of our power. Our institutions will continue to be attractive to many and the openness of our society will continue to enhance our credibility. Thus as a country, we will be well placed to benefit from soft power. But since much of this soft power is the unintended by-product of social forces, the government will often find it difficult to manipulate.

The good news is that the social trends of the global information age are helping to shape a world that will be more congenial to American values in the long run. But the soft power that comes from being a shining "city upon a hill" (as the Puritan leader John Winthrop first put it) does not provide the coercive capability that hard power does. Soft power is crucial, but alone it is not sufficient. Both hard and soft power will be necessary for successful foreign policy in a global information age. Our leaders must make sure that they exercise our hard power in a manner that does not undercut our soft power.

Grand Strategy and Global Public Goods

How should Americans set our priorities in a global information age? What grand strategy would allow us to steer between the "imperial overstretch" that would arise out of the role of global policeman while avoiding the mistake of thinking the country can be isolated in this global information age? The place to start is by understanding the relationship of American power to global public goods. On one hand, for reasons given above, American power is less effective than it might first appear. We cannot do everything. On the other hand, the United States is likely to remain the most powerful country well into this century, and this gives us an interest in maintaining a degree of international order. More concretely, there is a simple reason why Americans have a national interest beyond our borders. Events out there can hurt us, and we want to influence distant governments and organizations on a variety of issues such as proliferation of weapons of mass destruction, terrorism, drugs, trade, resources, and ecological damage. After the Cold War, we ignored Afghanistan, but we discovered that even a poor, remote country can harbor forces that can harm us.

To a large extent, international order is a public good—something everyone can consume without diminishing its availability to others.[5] A small country can benefit from peace in its region, freedom of the seas, suppression of terrorism, open trade, control of infectious diseases, or stability in financial markets at the same time that the United States does without diminishing the benefits to the United States or others. Of course, pure public goods are rare. And sometimes things that look good in our eyes may look bad in the eyes of others. Too narrow an appeal to public goods can become a self-serving ideology for the powerful. But these caveats are a reminder to consult with others, not a reason to discard an important strategic principle that helps us set priorities and reconcile our national interests with a broader global perspective.

If the largest beneficiary of a public good (like the United States) does not take the lead in providing disproportionate resources toward its provision, the smaller beneficiaries are unlikely to be able to produce it because of the difficulties of organizing collective action when large numbers are involved.[6] While this responsibility of the largest often lets others become "free riders," the alternative is that the collective bus does not move at all. (And our compensation is that the largest tends to have more control of the steering wheel.)

This puts a different twist on former secretary of state Madeleine Albright's frequent phrase that the United States is "the indispensable nation." We do not get a free ride. To play a leading role in producing public goods, the United States will need to invest in both hard power resources and the soft power resources of setting a good example. The latter will require more self-restraint on the part of Congress as well as putting our own house in order in economics, environment, criminal justice, and so forth. The rest of the world likes to see the United States lead by example, but when "America is seen, as with emission standards, to put narrow domestic interests before global needs, respect can easily turn to disappointment and contempt."[7]

Increasing hard power will require an investment of resources in the nonmilitary aspects of foreign affairs, including better intelligence, that Americans have recently been unwilling to make. While Congress has been willing to spend 16 percent of the national budget on defense, the percentage devoted to international affairs has shrunk from 4 percent in the 1960s to just 1 percent today.[8] Our military strength is important, but it is not sixteen times more important than our diplomacy. Over a thousand people work on the staff of the smallest regional military command headquarters, far more than the total assigned to the Americas at the Departments of State, Commerce, Treasury, and Agriculture.[9] The military rightly plays a role in our diplomacy, but we are investing in our hard power in overly militarized terms.

As Secretary of State Colin Powell has pleaded to Congress, we need to put more resources into the State Department, including its information services and the Agency for International Development (AID), if we are going to get our messages across. A bipartisan report on the situation of the State Department recently warned that "if the 'downward spiral' is not reversed, the prospect of relying on military force to protect U.S. national interests will increase because Washington will be less capable of avoiding, managing or resolving crises through the use of statecraft."[10] Moreover, the abolition of the United States Information Agency (which promoted American government views abroad) as a separate entity and its absorption into the State Department reduced the effectiveness of one of our government's important instruments of soft power.[11] It is difficult to be a superpower on the cheap—or through military means alone.

In addition to better means, we need a strategy for their use. Our grand strategy must first ensure our survival, but then it must focus on providing *global* public goods. We gain doubly from such a strategy: from the public goods themselves, and from the way they legitimize our power in the eyes of others. That means we should give top priority to those aspects of the international system that, if not attended to properly, would have profound effects on the basic international order and therefore on the lives of large numbers of Americans as well as others. The United States can learn from the lesson of Great Britain in the nineteenth century, when it was also a preponderant power. Three public goods that Britain attended to were (1) maintaining the balance of power among the major states in Europe, (2) promoting an open international economic system, and (3) maintaining open

international commons such as the freedom of the seas and the suppression of piracy.

All three translate relatively well to the current American situation. Maintaining regional balances of power and dampening local incentives to use force to change borders provides a public good for many (but not all) countries. The United States helps to "shape the environment" (in the words of the Pentagon's quadrennial defense review) in various regions, and that is why even in normal times we keep roughly a hundred thousand troops forward-based in Europe, the same number in Asia, and some twenty thousand near the Persian Gulf. The American role as a stabilizer and reassurance against aggression by aspiring hegemons in key regions is a blue chip issue. We should not abandon these regions, as some have recently suggested, though our presence in the Gulf could be handled more subtly.

Promoting an open international economic system is good for American economic growth and is good for other countries as well. . . . [O]penness of global markets is a necessary (though not sufficient) condition for alleviating poverty in poor countries even as it benefits the United States. In addition, in the long term, economic growth is also more likely to foster stable, democratic middle-class societies in other countries, though the time scale may be quite lengthy. To keep the system open, the United States must resist protectionism at home and support international economic institutions such as the World Trade Organization, the International Monetary Fund, and the Organization for Economic Cooperation and Development that provide a framework of rules for the world economy.

The United States, like nineteenth-century Britain, has an interest in keeping international commons, such as the oceans, open to all. Here our record is mixed. It is good on traditional freedom of the seas. For example, in 1995, when Chinese claims to the Spratly Islands in the South China Sea sparked concern in Southeast Asia, the United States avoided the conflicting claims of various states to the islets and rocks, but issued a statement reaffirming that the sea should remain open to all countries. China then agreed to deal with the issue under the Law of the Seas Treaty. Today, however, the international commons include new issues such as global climate change, preservation of endangered species, and the uses of outer space, as well as the virtual commons of cyberspace. But on some issues, such as the global climate, the United States has taken less of a lead than is necessary. The establishment of rules that preserve access for all remains as much a public good today as in the nineteenth century, even though some of the issues are more complex and difficult than freedom of the seas.

These three classic public goods enjoy a reasonable consensus in American public opinion, and some can be provided in part through unilateral actions. But there are also three new dimensions of global public goods in today's world. First, the United States should help develop and maintain international regimes of laws and institutions that organize international action in various domains—not just trade and environment, but weapons proliferation, peacekeeping, human rights, terrorism, and other concerns. Terrorism is to the twenty-first century what piracy was to an earlier era. Some governments gave pirates and privateers safe harbor to earn revenues or to harass their enemies. As Britain became the dominant naval power in the nineteenth century, it suppressed piracy, and most countries benefited from that situation. Today, some states harbor terrorists in order to attack their enemies or because they are too weak to control powerful groups. If our current campaign against terrorism is seen as unilateral or biased, it is likely to fail, but if we continue to maintain broad coalitions to suppress terrorism, we have a good prospect of success. While our antiterrorism campaign will not be seen as a global public good by the groups that attack us, our objective should be to isolate them and diminish the minority of states that give them harbor.

We should also make international development a higher priority, for it is an important global public good as well. Much of the poor majority of the world is in turmoil, mired in vicious circles of disease, poverty, and political instability. Large-scale financial and scientific help from rich countries is important not only for humanitarian reasons but also, as Harvard economist Jeffrey Sachs has argued, "because even remote countries become outposts of disorder for the rest of the world."[12] Here our record is less impressive. Our foreign aid has shrunk to 0.1 percent of our GNP, roughly one-third of European levels, and our protectionist trade measures often hurt poor countries most. Foreign assistance is generally unpopular with the American public, in part (as polls show) because they think we spend fifteen to twenty times more on it than we do. If our political leaders appealed more directly to our humanitarian instinct as well as our interest in stability, our record might improve. As President Bush said in July 2001, "This is a great moral challenge."[13] To be sure, aid is not sufficient for development, and opening our markets, strengthening accountable institutions, and discouraging corruption are even more important.[14] Development will take a long time, and we need to explore better ways to make sure that our help actually reaches the poor, but both prudence and a concern for our soft power suggest that we should make development a higher priority.

As a preponderant power, the United States can provide an important public good by acting as a mediator. By using our good offices to mediate conflicts in places such as Northern Ireland, the Middle East, or the

TABLE 1   A Strategy Based on Global Public Goods

1. Maintain the balance of power in important regions
2. Promote an open international economy
3. Preserve international commons
4. Maintain international rules and institutions
5. Assist economic development
6. Act as convenor of coalitions and mediator of disputes

Aegean Sea, the United States can help in shaping international order in ways that are beneficial to us as well as to other nations. It is sometimes tempting to let intractable conflicts fester, and there are some situations where other countries can more effectively play the mediator's role. Even when we do not want to take the lead, our participation can be essential—witness our work with Europe to try to prevent civil war in Macedonia. But often the United States is the only country that can bring together mortal enemies as in the Middle East peace process. And when we are successful, we enhance our reputation and increase our soft power at the same time that we reduce a source of instability.

Human Rights and Democracy

A grand strategy for protecting our traditional vital interests and promoting global public goods addresses two-thirds of our national interest. Human rights and democracy are the third element, but they are not easily integrated with the others. Other countries and cultures often interpret these values differently and resent our intervention in their sovereign affairs as self-righteous unilateralism. As Malaysian prime minister Mahathir Mohamed complained of the Clinton administration: "No one conferred this right on this crusading presi-

dent." Or in the words of a Republican critic (now a high official in the Pentagon): "America is genuinely puzzled by the idea that American assertiveness in the name of universal principles could sometimes be seen by others as a form of American unilateralism." Yet this charge is levied by many countries, including some of our friends. "Wilsonian presidents drive them crazy—and have done ever since the days of Woodrow Wilson."[15]

Americans have wrestled with how to incorporate our values with our other interests since the early days of the republic, and the four main views cut across party lines. Isolationists hark back to John Quincy Adams's famous 1821 assertion that the United States "goes not abroad in search of monsters to destroy," while realists focus on his pragmatic advice that we should not involve ourselves "beyond the power of extrication in all the wars of interest and intrigue."[16] At least since the days of Woodrow Wilson, liberals have stressed democracy and human rights as foreign policy objectives, and Jimmy Carter reestablished them as a priority. Even Ronald Reagan, certainly a conservative, resorted to the language of human rights, and today's neoconservatives "represent, in fact, a Reaganite variant of Wilsonianism."[17] President George W. Bush frequently reiterated the realist warning that the United States "cannot become the world's 911," but two dozen leading neoconservatives, including William Bennett and Norman Podhoretz, have urged him to make human rights, religious freedom, and democracy priorities for American foreign policy and "not to adopt a narrow view of U.S. national interests."[18]

Geopolitical realists deplore Wilsonian idealism as dangerous. As Robert Frost ironically noted, good fences can help to make good neighbors. While the erosion of sovereignty may help advance human rights in repressive regimes, it also portends considerable disorder. The Peace of Westphalia in the seventeenth century created a system of sovereign states to curtail vicious civil wars over religion. The fact that sovereignty is changing is generally a constraint for policy, not an objective of policy. But whether the realist strategists like it or not, humanitarian cases such as Somalia, Bosnia, Rwanda, Haiti, Kosovo, and East Timor will force themselves to the foreground because of their ability to command attention in a global information age. And their number will continue to burgeon. . . . Globalization is disrupting traditional lifestyles, and the weak states left in the aftermath of the collapse of the Soviet empire and old European empires in Africa are particularly vulnerable. If there are clashes of civilizations, they occur more often within countries or regions over what Freud called the narcissism of small differences rather than a grand clash between "the West and the rest."[19] This in turn leads to increased violence and violation of human rights—all in the presence of television cameras and the Internet. The result puts a difficult set of issues on our foreign policy agenda and presents a challenge to our values. And, of course, our values are an important source of our soft power.

So where do human rights and democracy fit in the strategy? Human rights is an important *part* of foreign policy, but it is not foreign policy itself, because foreign policy is an effort to accomplish several objectives: security and economic benefits as well as humanitarian results. During the Cold War, this often meant that we reluctantly had to tolerate human rights abuses by regimes that were crucial to balancing Soviet power, such as in South Korea before its transition to democracy. Similar problems persist in the current period—witness the absence of an American policy to promote democracy in Saudi Arabia, or the need to balance human rights in Russia with our interest in forming an anti-terrorist coalition.

Former Clinton administration officials William Perry and Ashton Carter have suggested a scheme to evaluate risks to U.S. security and help reassert national priorities in cases that might involve the use of force. At the top of their hierarchy are A-list threats, of the scale that the Soviet Union presented to our survival. A threatening China or the spread of nuclear materials would also fit this category. The B list of imminent threats to our interests (but not to our survival) includes situations such as those on the Korean Peninsula and in the Persian Gulf. Their C list of important "contingencies that indirectly affect U.S. security but do not directly threaten U.S. interests" includes "the Kosovos, Bosnias, Somalias, Rwandas, and Haitis."[20]

What is striking, however, is that their C list of humanitarian interventions often dominates the foreign policy agenda. Carter and Perry speculated that this was because of the absence of A-list threats after the end of the Cold War. To some extent this is true, but another reason is the ability of C-list issues to dominate media attention in the global information age. Dramatic visual portrayals of immediate human conflict and suffering are far easier to convey to the public than A-list abstractions such as the possibility of a "Weimar Russia," the importance of our alliance with Japan, or the potential collapse of the international system of trade and investment. Few Americans can look at television pictures of starving people or miserable refugees on the evening news just before dinner and not feel that we should do something about it if we can. Some cases are quite easy, such as hurricane relief to Central America or the early stages of famine relief in Somalia. But as with Somalia, apparently simple cases can turn out to be extremely difficult, and others, such as Kosovo, are difficult from the start.

The problem with such cases is that the humanitarian interest that instigates the action often turns out to be quite shallow when it encounters significant costs in lives or money. The impulse to help starving Somalis (whose food supply was being interrupted by various warlords) vanished in the face of an image of a dead American being dragged through the streets of Mogadishu. This is sometimes attributed to popular reluctance to accept casualties. That is too simple. Americans went into the Gulf War expecting more than ten thousand casualties. More properly expressed, Americans are reluctant to accept casualties when their *only* interests are unreciprocated humanitarian interests. Ironically, the reaction against such cases may not only divert attention and limit willingness to support A-list interests but also interfere with action in more serious humanitarian crises. One of the direct effects of the Somalia disaster was an American failure (along with other countries) to support and reinforce the United Nations peacekeeping force in Rwanda, which could have limited a true genocide in 1994.[21]

There are no easy answers for such cases. We could not simply turn off the television or unplug our computers even if we wanted to. We cannot simply ignore the C list, nor should we. But there are certain rules of prudence for humanitarian interventions that may help us integrate our values and our security interests, to steer a path between the dangers of unfettered Wilsonianism and the narrow realism that George W. Bush articulated in his 2000 campaign.

First, there are many degrees of humanitarian concern and many degrees of intervention, such as condemnation, sanctions targeted on individuals, broad sanctions, and various uses of force. We should save the violent end of the spectrum for only the most egregious cases discussed below. Second, when we do use force, it is worth remembering some principles of just war: having a just cause in the eyes of others, dis-

crimination in means so that we do not unduly punish the innocent, proportionality of our means to our ends, and a high probability (rather than wishful thinking) of good consequences. Such considerations would keep us from sending troops into civil wars in Congo or Chechnya, where the difficulty and costs of achieving our ends would exceed our means.

Third, we should generally (except in cases of genocide) avoid the use of force unless our humanitarian interests are reinforced by the existence of other national interests, because we are unlikely to have the necessary staying power. This was the case in the Gulf War, where we were concerned not only with the aggression against Kuwait but also with energy supplies and regional allies. This was not the case in Somalia, where, as we have seen, the absence of other interests made the intervention unsustainable when costs mounted. In the former Yugoslavia (Bosnia and Kosovo), our other interests flowed from our European allies and NATO.

Fourth, we should try to involve other regional actors, letting them lead where possible. In East Timor, Australia took the lead, while the United States offered support in logistics and intelligence. In Sierra Leone, Britain took the lead. After our failure in Rwanda, the United States belatedly offered to help African countries with training, intelligence, logistics, and transportation if they would provide the troops for a peacekeeping force. If regional states are unwilling to do their part, we should be wary of going it alone. In Europe, we should welcome the idea of combined joint task forces, including the planned European Rapid Reaction Force, that would be able to act in lesser contingencies where we did not need to be involved. We should encourage a greater European willingness and ability to take the lead on such issues as keeping the peace in the Balkans.

Fifth, the American people have a real humanitarian interest in not letting another holocaust occur, as we did in Rwanda in 1994. We need to do more to organize prevention and response to real cases of genocide. Unfortunately, the genocide convention is written so loosely and the word is so abused for political purposes that there is danger of the term becoming trivialized by being applied to any hate crimes. We should follow the recommendations of a 1985 UN study that recommended that "in order that the concept of genocide should not be devalued or diluted by the inflation of cases . . . considerations both of proportionate scale and of total numbers are relevant."[22] Regardless of the wording of the convention and the efforts of partisans in particular cases, we should focus our military responses on instances of intent to destroy large numbers of a people.

Finally, we should be very wary about intervention in civil wars over self-determination, such as demands for secession by groups in Indonesia, Central Asia, or in many African countries. Sometimes we will be drawn in for other reasons as in the cases mentioned above, but we should avoid taking sides among ethnic groups as much as possible. Albanians killing Serb civilians after the Kosovo war is no more justifiable than Serbs killing Albanian civilians before the war. In a world of nearly ten thousand ethnic and linguistic groups and only about two hundred states, the principle of self-determination presents the threat of enormous violence. It is dangerously ambiguous in moral terms. Atrocities are often committed by activists on both sides (reciprocal genocide), and the precedent we would create by endorsing a general right of self-determination could have disastrous consequences.

None of these rules will solve all the problems of determining our national interest in hard cases. They would have led to

TABLE 2   Rules of Prudence for Humanitarian Interventions

1. Distinguish degrees of intervention and proportionality
2. Determine that there is just cause and probable success
3. Reinforce humanitarian interests with other interests
4. Give priority to other regional actors
5. Be clear about genocide
6. Be wary of civil wars over self-determination

intervention in former Yugoslavia and stronger action in Rwanda, but greater caution in Somalia and many African civil wars. Somewhere between being the world's 911 and sitting on the sidelines, we will need some such prudential rules to help us meld our strategic, economic, and human rights interests into a sustainable foreign policy.

Finding a formula for deciding when humanitarian intervention is justified is necessary but not sufficient for the integration of human rights into foreign policy. How we behave at home also matters. Amnesty International is overly harsh in its declaration that "today the United States is as frequently an impediment to human rights as it is an advocate," but by ignoring or refusing to ratify human rights treaties (such as those concerning economic, social, and cultural rights and discrimination against women), the United States undercuts our soft power on these issues.[23] Sometimes the causes of our reluctance are minor while the costs to our reputation are considerable. For instance, it took six years for the United States to sign the Protocol on Involvement of Children in Armed Conflict because the Pentagon wanted to recruit seventeen-year-olds (with parental consent). It turned out that this affected fewer than 3,000 of the 1.4 million Americans in uniform.[24]

The promotion of democracy is also a national interest and a source of soft power, though here the role of force is usually less central and the process is of a longer-term nature. The United States has both an ideological and a pragmatic interest in the promotion of democracy. While the argument that democracies never go to war with each other is too simple, it is hard to find cases of *liberal* democracies doing so.[25] Illiberal populist democracies such as Peru, Ecuador, Venezuela, or Iran, or countries going through the early stages of democratization, may become dangerous, but liberal democracies are less likely to produce refugees or engage in terrorism.[26] President Clinton's 1995 statement that "ultimately the best strategy to ensure our security and to build a durable peace is to support the advance of democracy elsewhere" has a core of truth if approached with the caveats just described.[27] The key is to follow tactics that are likely to succeed over the long term without imposing inordinate costs on other foreign policy objectives in the near term.

NOTES

1. Peter Ludlow, "Wanted: A Global Partner," *The Washington Quarterly,* summer 2001, 167.
2. Program on International Policy Attitudes, "Americans on Globalization: A Study of US Public Attitudes," University of Maryland, 1999, 8.
3. *America's National Interests: A Report from the Commission on America's National Interests* (cochairs Robert Ellworth, Andrew Goodpaster, and Rita Hauser, 1996), 13.
4. See Ashton Carter, John Deutch, and Philip Zelikow, *Catastrophic Terrorism: Elements of a National Policy* (Cambridge, MA: Belfer Center for Science and International Affairs, Harvard University, 1998). See also Joseph S. Nye Jr. and R. James Woolsey, "Perspective on Terrorism," *Los Angeles Times,* June 1, 1997, M-5.
5. For a full discussion of the complexity and problems of definition, see Inge Kaul, Isabelle Grunberg, and Marc A. Stern, eds., *Global Public Goods: International Cooperation in the 21st Century* (New York: Oxford University Press, 1999). Strictly defined, public goods are nonrivalrous and nonexclusionary.
6. Mancur Olson, *The Logic of Collective Action: Public Goods and the Theory of Groups* (Cambridge, MA: Harvard University Press, 1965).
7. Philip Bowring, "Bush's America Is Developing an Image Problem," *International Herald Tribune,* May 31, 2001, 8.
8. Richard N. Gardner, "The One Percent Solution," *Foreign Affairs,* July–August 2000, 3.
9. Dana Priest, "A Four Star Foreign Policy?" *Washington Post,* September 28, 2000, 1.
10. Robin Wright, "State Dept. Mismanaged, Report Says," *Los Angeles Times,* January 30, 2001, 10.
11. The United States Advisory Commission on Public Diplomacy, *Consolidation of USIA into the State Department: An Assessment After One Year* (Washington, D.C.: October 2000).
12. Jeffrey Sachs, "What's Good for the Poor Is Good for America," *The Economist,* July 14, 2001, 32–33.
13. "Bush Proposes Aid Shift to Grants for Poor Nations," *New York Times,* July 18, 2001, A1.
14. William Esterly, "The Failure of Development," *Financial Times* (London), July 4, 2001, 32; Dani Rodrik, *The New Global Economy and Developing Countries: Making Openness Work* (Washington, D.C.: Overseas Development Council, 1999).
15. Peter Rodman, *Uneasy Giant: The Challenges to American Predominance* (Washington: The Nixon Center, 2000), 3, 15, 44.
16. Richard Bernstein, "To Butt In or Not in Human Rights: The Gap Narrows," *New York Times,* August 4, 2001, 15.
17. Rodman, *Uneasy Giant,* 40.
18. Steven Mufson, "Bush Nudged by the Right over Rights," *International Herald Tribune,* January 27–28, 2001, 3. See also "American Power—For What? A Symposium," *Commentary,* January 2000, 21n.
19. G. Pascal Zachary, "Market Forces Add Ammunition to Civil Wars," *Wall Street Journal,* June 12, 2000, 21. From 1989 to 1998, 108 armed conflicts broke out in seventy-three places around the world; 92 of them took place within a country rather than between countries.
20. Ashton B. Carter and William J. Perry, *Preventive Defense: A New Security Strategy for America* (Washington, D.C.: Brookings Institution Press, 1999), 11–15.
21. Samantha Power, "Bystanders to Genocide," *Atlantic Monthly,* September 2001, 84–108.

22. Samantha Power, *"A Problem from Hell":
    America's Failure to Prevent Genocide* (New
    York: Basic Books, 2002), chapter 5.
23. Norman Kempster, "US Is Sharply Criticized
    on Human Rights Issues," *International Her-
    ald Tribune,* May 31, 2001, 3.
24. Barbara Crossette, "Clinton Signs Agree-
    ments to Help Protect Children," *New York
    Times,* July 6, 2000, A7.
25. John M. Owen, "How Liberalism Produces
    Democratic Peace," *International Security,* fall
    1994; John R. Oneal and Bruce Russett, "As-
    sessing the Liberal Peace with Alternative
    Specifications: Trade Still Reduces Conflict,"
    Journal of Peace Research (Oslo), July 1999;
    Fareed Zakaria, "The Rise of Illiberal Democ-
    racy," *Foreign Affairs,* November–December
    1997. For a critical monographic look at the
    "liberal peace" thesis, see Joanne Gowa, *Bal-
    lots and Bullets: The Elusive Democratic Peace*
    (Princeton: Princeton University Press, 1999);
    for a favorable monographic assessment, see
    Spencer R. Weart, *Never at War: Why De-
    mocracies Will Not Fight One Another* (New
    Haven: Yale University Press, 1998).
26. See Edward D. Mansfield and Jack Snyder,
    "Democratization and War," *Foreign Affairs,*
    May 1995.
27. Thomas Carothers, *Aiding Democracy Abroad:
    The Learning Curve* (Washington, D.C.: Car-
    negie Endowment, 1999), 5.

QUESTIONS FOR DISCUSSION

1. How are national interests currently defined in U.S. policy?
2. What kinds of soft power does the
   United States have in global relations?
3. What kinds of policy changes would
   have to take place in order for the U.S.
   to view global humanitarian concerns
   as important for domestic stability?

57

LIBERTY VS. patriotISM
CHIP PITTS • JENNIFER HOLMES

Given the unprecedented sense of national vulnerability in the wake of
Sept. 11, we undoubtedly need to
correct gaps in our security. In so doing,
however, we should not needlessly erode
civil liberties. The balance between security
and liberty now clearly tilts too much in the
direction of government control and away
from liberty.

Even before the current crisis, our
government had garnered extensive new
powers to combat terrorism. These powers
themselves go too far. With the carnage of
the Twin Towers and the Pentagon attacks,
the balance between security and liberty
now clearly tilts too much in the direction of
government control and away from liberty.

The measures enacted in the wake of
Sept. 11 are not our nation's first responses
to terrorism. In response to the Oklahoma
City bombing, 1995's Omnibus Counter-
terrorism Act and 1996's Antiterrorism and
Effective Death Penalty Act became law. The

first law granted government the authority to subject suspected terrorists to greater electronic surveillance, including access to telephone, motel, and travel records; to expedite the deportation of aliens even on secret evidence; and to prohibit members of foreign groups designated as terrorist organizations from raising funds in the United States. The second law allows the United States to prevent presumed terrorists from entering the country and gives the government the power to deport aliens with ties to terrorist groups. People who contribute to or raise funds for suspected terrorist groups can also be prosecuted.

After the attacks of Sept. 11, Congress passed the "USA PATRIOT" Act. The USA PATRIOT Act was rushed through Congress with unseemly haste, and admittedly wasn't read by most members of Congress. The haste was facilitated by including provisions that had been on law enforcement and intelligence "wish lists" for many years but which had been resisted in the more deliberative pre-Sept. 11 environment. The cute acronym stands for "Uniting and Strengthening America by Providing Appropriate Tools Required to Intercept and Obstruct Terrorism," but it would be more accurate if the "A" stood for "Alarming" rather than "Appropriate."

The law includes some much-needed updates to take into account modern technology (such as resources to enhance shared databases for border enforcement, and providing for a personal wiretap order so that terrorists cannot circumvent the order by using varied or even disposable mobile phones).

But it also includes several provisions that appear to be clearly unconstitutional and a violation of our nation's human rights treaty obligations. Among these are the new requirements that:

- allow government to access personal consumer credit, health, or other data from businesses maintaining such data, and student data from universities (all without proving any crime);
- expand government ability to monitor your email and Internet habits without your knowledge;
- allow government to search your house or premises without the warrant or probable cause traditionally required by the Fourth Amendment, without even needing to notify you in advance;
- expand government's ability to detain indefinitely and deport aliens by lowering the standard to mere "reason to believe" that the alien has engaged in "any activity that endangers national security";
- explicitly allow indefinite detention or deportation or mere "association" with any organization that ever used weapons (Would the Daughters of the American Revolution qualify? Surely contributions to peaceful branches of the African National Congress, or the political branch of the IRA, would.);
- diminish the key distinction, built up over years, between domestic law enforcement (traditionally subject to a higher standard) and foreign intelligence gathering (traditionally a lower standard), effectively putting the CIA back in the domestic surveillance business;
- in general, increase government discretion to act without the "individualized suspicion" usually required as a constitutional minimum.

Why should law-abiding citizens fear these laws? Recent history demonstrates the danger in expanding the FBI's power without proper oversight. Beginning in the 1950s, the FBI counterintelligence group, Cointelpro, actively investigated and infiltrated "seditious" groups. The vast intelligence operation was generally aimed at the left, targeting the Socialist Workers Party, the Black Panthers, anti-war activists, civil rights groups, and women's liberation groups in the 1960s. In addition, the FBI admitted that in the 1970s it wiretapped federal offices, members of Congress, their aides, and journalists. The agency used unapproved wiretaps, made illegal break-ins, and infiltrated suspected groups. In the 1980s, the FBI actively investigated the Committee in Solidarity with the People of El Salvador (CISPES), which opposed U.S. military aid to El Salvador. The group did not fund leftist guerrillas in El Salvador and was not active in terrorist activities in the United States. Its only "crime" was to oppose U.S. policy. The FBI used surveillance, informants, undercover operatives, and extensive gathering of bank records, trash, telephone records, and more, creating files on almost 2,400 citizens. More groups that support unpopular policies are likely to be targeted.

Unfortunately, suspected groups are not merely scrutinized. The government attacked the Black Panthers and the Symbionese Liberation Army. At the infamous Ruby Ridge siege, the FBI approved rules of engagement allowing the use of lethal force, without warning, against any armed individual. Normally, there must be imminent mortal danger before deadly force can be used. These are examples of an overzealous agency, or, at least, overzealous agents within the agency without sufficient oversight.

What about non-citizens? The president's executive order of Nov. 13 regarding military tribunals and detention is very broad and vague, applying to *any* non-U.S. citizen—not even limiting it to those fighting against us. Under this executive order, non-citizens would not be treated with the same rights and liberties as citizens. Yet according to long-standing constitutional law precedent, alienage is a "suspect class" justifying enhanced ("strict") scrutiny of discriminatory laws affecting this vulnerable group. In the words of U.S. Supreme Court Justice Hugo Black, "classifications based on alienage, like those of race or ethnicity, are inherently suspect." Moreover, the definition of terrorism leaves to presidential discretion who is subject to this executive order. The net is cast wide: Non-citizens whom the president has "reason to believe" are members of al Qaeda, or engage in, conspire for, or prepare for "acts of international terrorism" are subject to detention and military trial. This broad definition can be stretched to include resident aliens who exercise political speech in a purely peaceful, humanitarian way. For example, an Irish-American permanent resident who contributes to a fund for the widows and orphans of those killed in Belfast, or a Muslim permanent resident who contributes to a Palestinian relief fund, could be covered by the order.

The executive order exemplifies the problem that "terrorism" is a nebulous term that can be easily abused. Different agencies of the United States government can't even agree on a definition. Terrorism is an inherently political term, because it can be subjectively interpreted by those in power to support their own purposes. It is often difficult to distinguish between a terrorist group and a legitimate national liberation movement, especially among those in the establishment. Governing elites have easy resort to the terrorist label to justify the status quo. This definitional ambiguity poses a particular problem in that the 1996 Antiterrorism and Effective Death Penalty Act allows the secretary of state and attorney general to designate which groups are terrorist and to restrict their fundraising and other activities. The word "terrorism" in other words, can clearly be politically manipulated.

The problem is that, in moving toward a national security state, we're moving toward a Kafkaesque universe in which the mere suspicion that someone may be a terrorist means that he is then presumed to be one and is treated like one. This inverts the presumption of innocence that is at the heart of our criminal justice system. Though most of us are unlikely to be subject to this prejudicial treatment, many—or any—of us could be. Even in peaceful times, the definition of terrorism is political, problematic, and open to abuse. In times of national crisis, this definitional problem combined with enhanced executive discretion becomes extremely dangerous. Attorney General John Ashcroft recently said, "To those . . . who scare peace-loving people with phantoms of lost liberty, my message is this: your tactics only aid terrorism, for they erode our national unity and diminish our resolve. They give ammunition to America's enemies and pause to America's friends." Recently, Senate Majority Leader Tom Daschle criticized President Bush's proposed expansion of the war against terror. In response, Senate Minority Leader Trent Lott accused him of undermining the unity of the nation.

Patriotism and unity are important in times of crisis, but they should not be a substitute for the democratic process that produces good policy. Of course, there is always tension between order and liberty: Some order is necessary to create the conditions for liberty, but too much order can endanger liberty and even order itself. Before Sept. 11, traditionally leftist groups, like the ACLU, aligned themselves with traditionally rightist groups, like the NRA, to oppose versions of the 1995 and 1996 legislation. Ominously, since Sept. 11, fewer voices of dissent, constructive criticism, and honest questioning have been heard (with the ACLU being a notable exception).

Dissent is a fundamental value of this country—one the terrorists hate. We must be careful to uphold the value of free speech, especially in times of crisis. Even conservative columnist William Safire, and Republicans such as Georgia Congressman Bob Barr and Pennsylvania Senator Arlen Specter objected to the military tribunals. Criticism of U.S. policy is necessary, healthy,

and desirable. Now our own government is promulgating secrecy of names of detainees, of evidence against aliens detained, in withdrawing government documents from libraries, in secret searches of homes or your Internet activity. The chief weapon against such secrecy is the disinfectant light of dissent.

The issue transcends proper balance between order and liberty. Our policies must also be effective. The dismal reality is that none of these new measures would have prevented the attacks on Sept. 11. To the extent that the measures alienate those best situated to provide intelligence on al Qaeda, or provide too much information to effectively sift through, they will be counterproductive. "Feel-good" measures play to politicians' desires to be seen as "doing something." But can any measure that upsets the balance between security and liberty by going so far that it undercuts our core values and societal identity truly be considered "effective"?

A closed and repressive society, intolerant of "alien" people and ideas, is precisely what the al Qaeda terrorists want us to become. By thoughtlessly moving our society in that direction, especially without clear corresponding benefits, we give the terrorists the most significant victory they are likely to achieve in this war. Strong dissent aimed at preserving and restoring liberty is the best route to victory for freedom and democracy.

·QUESTIONS FOR DISCUSSION

1. What are the difficulties in defining terrorism?
2. How do national security and civil liberties exist in opposition to each other?
3. What are the implications of blurring the distinction between domestic law enforcement practices and foreign intelligence gathering?

58

CONQUESTS
Sex and Rape in Wartime

JOSHUA S. GOLDSTEIN

Men and women in virtually all human cultures occupy dominant and subordinate status ranks. Men often exploit women's work, with and without pay—including sex work, domestic work, child care, nursing, and the array of low-wage jobs in modern industrial economies. Overall, though not everywhere, men enforce women's subordinate condition with widespread threats and uses of "hidden violence . . . [r]ape, battery, and other forms of sexual and domestic violence."[1]

In the context of an exploitive dominance relationship, and especially in wartime when that relationship intensifies, keeping weapons out of the hands of the exploited-subordinate class makes sense. Letting women become warriors could threaten men's dominance over women. Therefore patriarchal cultures (i.e., all cultures) limit women's participation in combat. In this view, the armed male soldier faces both outward to meet dangers and opportunities beyond the border, and inward to maintain the gendered hierarchy of domestic society. Some conservative opponents of women in combat today connect war roles with the domestic gender order. According to a 1998 Southern Baptist resolution, the idea of women in combat "rejects gender-based distinctions established by God," negates "the unique gender-based responsibility of men to protect women and children," and implies a "shameful failure of male leadership." For these reasons, it "undermines male headship in the family."[2] . . .

I will explore . . . the premise that in wartime the exploitation of women intensifies, although this does not apply to every individual or category of woman in every war. First, war (which disrupts social relationships and norms) brings more women into sex work on more exploitive terms (although this sexuality covers a range that includes reciprocity at one end and slavery at the other). Is heightened male sexuality (reflected by women's wartime sex work) necessary for participation in combat? Second, war borrows gender as a code for domination–submission relationships. . . . Enemies and subordinates are gendered feminine. As a result, recurrently, victorious soldiers express domination by raping conquered women. Does the tendency of male soldiers to feminize enemies explain the absence of women in their ranks? . . .

Sex in Wartime

Soldiers show an "almost universal preoccupation with sex"—an "obsession with sex in a community of men . . . deprived of usual social and emotional outlets." A British officer in World War I concluded that "[m]ost soldiers were ready to have sexual intercourse with almost any woman whenever they could." As one US soldier in

World War II wrote: "army conversation has a beautiful simplicity and directness. It is all on one solid, everlasting subject . . . Women, Women, Women." Or, another: "Anyone entering military service for the first time can only be astonished by soldiers' concentration upon the subject of women and, more especially, upon the sexual act. The most common word in [their] mouths . . . does duty as adjective, adverb, verb, noun, and in any other form it can possibly be used."[3]

US and British military culture in World War II promoted this preoccupation with sex. Over 5 million copies of *Life* magazine's 1941 photo of Rita Hayworth (captioned the "Goddess of Love") were sent out to US soldiers. Such "pin-ups" were ubiquitous among US forces. They were published not only in men's magazines but in service publications like *Stars and Stripes* (or for Britain, *Reveille*). The appeal of the "undisputed leader," Betty Grable, "was less erotic than as a wholesome symbol of American womanhood," based on a "carefully groomed exploitation of her good-natured hominess by 20th Century-Fox." Hayworth, however, the "runner-up" to Grable, "exuded the sultry sex appeal of a mature woman" whose "appeal was more erotic than wholesome." Jane Russell's "flamboyant sex appeal made her pin-ups wildly popular with GIs overseas." Her large breasts were shamelessly exploited by movie producers as "the two great reasons for [her] rise to stardom." Moralists at home opposed the pin-up craze. In 1944, the Postmaster General banned *Esquire* with its Vargas Girl fantasies, and Congressional hearings ensued. However, officers decided that pin-ups contributed to soldiers' morale. In Britain, meanwhile, the cartoon heroine "Jane" boosted morale during the Blitz and thereafter by taking her clothes off during periods of bad news. "It was said that the first armored vehicle ashore on D-Day carried a large representation of naked Jane." The comic-strip Jane "finally lost the last vestiges of her modesty during the Normandy campaign" in 1944, and soldiers said, "Jane gives her all."[4]

Disruption of Social Norms Whatever other roles male sexuality may play, armies segregate large numbers of post-adolescent males for extended periods, thereby creating a kind of critical mass of pent-up sexual desire. In wartime, social norms are disrupted and soldiers often operate far from home, with new sexual opportunities and motives. The disruption of normal sexual patterns was noted empirically by a New Orleans "madam" whose business increased when America entered World War I: "I've noticed it before, the way the idea of war and dying makes a man raunchy . . . It wasn't really pleasure at times, but a kind of nervous breakdown that could only be treated with a girl and a set to."[5]

Wars lift social taboos, disrupt relationships, and send large groups of young men far from home. Sociological explanations "fasten upon the uprooting character of war experience . . . [and the] artificial separation of the sexes." The men see prostitutes, with and without military blessing, and sometimes form relationships with local women (whose relationships may also have been disrupted). Promiscuity increases as people are less focused on the long-term future. . . . None of this means that increased sexuality underlies male soldiers' aggressiveness in the war, however. Rather, war may simply disrupt social norms, with sexual changes as a result. . . .[6]

Uncoerced Sex Sex in wartime covers a range of contexts, with women's voluntary participation at one end (sometimes becoming "war brides"), their implicit or explicit trading of sex for money or food in the middle, and rape at the other extreme. On this continuum, most war-related sex occurs in the middle, but I will begin at the voluntary end. By some reports, "war aphrodisia"—common among soldiers in many wars—extended into many segments of society during "total war." Thus, among not only soldiers but civilians, "sexual restraint . . . [was] suspended for the duration." As one British housewife put it, "We were not really immoral, there was a war on."[7] . . .

Back in the United States, "Victory Girls" gave free sex to soldiers as their "patriotic duty." A 1942 conference of the American Social Hygiene Association concluded that these promiscuous adolescents (most were under 21 and many under 19) practiced "sexual delinquency of a non-commercial character . . . [seeking] adventure and sociability." An Army doctor blamed these young women for troops' high VD rates: "While mothers are winning the war in the factories, their daughters are losing it on the streets." The ill-defined " 'victory girl' was usually assumed to be a woman who pursued sexual relations with servicemen out of a misplaced patriotism or a desire for excitement. She could also, however, be a girl or woman who, without actually engaging in sexual relations, was testing the perimeters of social freedom in wartime America." A "surprising number were young married women." One study of 210 women detained on morals charges in Seattle showed that only one-third were single.[8] . . .

Drawbacks of Sex   Male soldiers' sexuality creates three particular challenges for commanders. First, prostitutes and lovers can serve as enemy intelligence sources. . . . US soldiers in Vietnam sometimes first learned about their next mission not from their officers but from prostitutes (who presumably also told the Vietcong). British troops in North Africa in World War II sang of a legendary seductress working for Germany, who boasted, "The order of the battle, I obtained from last night's rattle." Meanwhile, French prostitutes, whose establishments were taken over intact by occupying German troops, worked with the French Resistance to pass along vital intelligence and to harbor Allied pilots trying to escape occupied France (police generally did not intrude in houses of prostitution frequented by German officers). In occupied French ports where prostitutes might reveal the missions of U-boats, German commanders quarantined their crews for weeks before departure, and brought in German women to staff "rest-camps" with dance halls and hotel-style rooms.[9]

Second, male sexuality that runs amok—especially when it leads to rape—can generate resentments and reactions contrary to the military's mission. For example, the huge US bases in Okinawa, Japan, are central to US military operations in East Asia. In 1995, relations with local residents plummeted after US Marines raped a local schoolgirl. This incident, which contributed to a climate where the United States began scaling back the Okinawa bases, clearly worked directly against the effectiveness of the US military. Male soldiers' rambunctious and aggressive sexuality did not contribute to morale, or male bonding, or any military goal, but the opposite. . . .

The third and most important challenge created by wartime sexuality is the spread of various debilitating sexually transmitted diseases, collectively known as venereal disease (VD), which have taken a serious toll on armies throughout history. (In turn, armies have used VD as a "stalking horse for a far more expansive military misogyny"—an excuse to tighten control on women—as with Britain's 1864 Contagious Diseases Act.) In the present-day AIDS epidemic, the long-standing problem of VD has new salience.[10]

VD apparently spreads more rapidly when an army stays in one position than when it is mobile. Thus, in World War I it was the shift to static warfare after the battles of 1914 that sharply increased VD rates. During the German Occupation of part of France in 1870, French prostitutes were urged to deliberately infect masses of German troops. In one German corps during the 1870–71 war with France, an initial 3 percent VD rate increased only to 10 percent during the war but then to 78 percent when the corps had been encamped in France for five months.[11] . . .

Military Prostitution

To bring these dangers under control while providing for male soldiers' morale, military commanders have often encouraged, or directly organized, prostitution to service their armies. . . . The word "hooker" comes from US Civil War general Joseph Hooker, whose Army of the Potomac was accompanied by "Hooker's girls." In World Wars I and II, French and German armies set up systems of military-supervised brothels. Cynthia Enloe writes that "many men will not stay in the military if they cannot marry and/or otherwise have ready sexual access to women. Women, therefore, must somehow be brought under sufficient military control."[12]

UN peacekeeping troops in Bosnia during the war allegedly used Muslim prostitutes controlled by Serbian forces. After the war, a number of UN police and SFOR troops in Bosnia participated in both local prostitution and trafficking in Eastern European sex slaves. Similarly, international troops in Kosovo in 1999 fueled a prostitution boom. Catherine MacKinnon writes: "Each layer of protection adds a layer of violence against women. Perhaps intervention by a force of armed women should be considered."[13]

A recent study of 500 prostitutes worldwide found that two-thirds had PTSD, a higher percentage than found for combat veterans. The vast majority had suffered repeated physical and sexual assaults. More than 90 percent wanted to get out of prostitution but were unable to do so. In wartime, conditions are even worse.[14] . . .

Comfort Women   Japan's own army in World War II developed an extensive system of so-called "comfort women." Thousands of women in occupied countries were forced into the sexual service of Japanese soldiers under conditions much harsher than those of the European prostitutes just described. It was "a large-scale, officially-organised system of rape by the Imperial Japanese Forces." The women had sex with as many as 30 men per day, working in stations of about 15 women. The total number of women is unknown. Where documented, the ratio of soldiers to women was typically about 50:1. Applying this ratio to all 7 million Japanese soldiers yields a *maximum* size of over 100,000 women in the comfort system. Service near the front was harsh, especially when units in transit passed through a station, or when comfort women were sent with a supply run to service a garrison in a forward pillbox, or when women had to follow military units on marches.[15] . . .

Asian Prostitution Since the Vietnam War   During the Vietnam War, US soldiers received R&R leave as a reward. Having sex was often a major component of these leaves. "Married men typically rendezvoused with their wives in Hawaii; the unattached headed for various liberty towns in Southeast Asia . . . [including] Bangkok for the sex." Locally, Vietnamese prostitutes and girlfriends were widely visited by US soldiers. US Green Berets had over 25 contacts with prostitutes per man, on average. By 1973, 300,000–500,000 women worked as prostitutes in South Vietnam, the "precise number" being "impossible to calculate because thousands . . . worked as cleaners and servants for American troops and thousands more were raped by American soldiers."[16]

Although prostitution has long been institutionalized in Thailand and some other Asian societies, it was during the Vietnam War that Bangkok "first came to prominence as a centre for commercial sex . . . Servicemen on R&R created the tourist infrastructure—the bars, nightclubs and massage parlors—that continue to service the tourist industry." Filipina activist Mary Perpinan describes the role of US military bases in generating the sex industry in Southeast Asia in the late 1960s. In Thailand, "[e]ntertainment centres were established around [US] air bases" and Thai women learned "the art of servicing the foreigner with 'exotic pleasures'"—leading to the establishment of Bangkok as the "sex capital of Asia" within a decade. By the end of the 1970s, as militarized prostitution led to sex tourism, "an estimated 100,000 women in Bangkok were working as prostitutes; 70 percent of them suffered from venereal disease."[17]

In the Philippines, as many as 100,000 women and girls worked in the sex/entertainment industry serving US bases at Subic Bay and Clark, in the Olongapo and Angeles districts. In the 1960s, local businessmen convinced "wary town officials" in Olongapo that "instead of endangering our decent and respectable women to the possibility of rape and other forms of sexual abuse, better provide an outlet for the soldiers' sexual urge and at the same time make money out of it." When US soldiers were based in the Philippines, US commanders supported compulsory medical examinations of local prostitutes and received reports from local authorities with the names of sex workers who had contracted sexually transmitted diseases. Base commanders then ordered pictures of these women "pinned upside down on the public notice board as a warning to the American men." US authorities refused, however, to

help pay for treatment of these women. Overall, "the girls [we]re recruited from depressed provinces and given false promises of high pay." They lost their freedom, were mistreated by the men they worked for, and, in the late 1980s, began dying from AIDS. The bases closed in 1992 but the effects linger.[18]

The largest US military presence in Asia is now in Japan and South Korea. The South Korean government worked hard to control and "clean up" (i.e., improve) prostitution around US military bases, in order to help keep the bases open despite US force reductions in Asia in the 1970s. Despite their strategic value both in "supplying" US bases and acting as "unofficial ambassadors" to the United States, these prostitutes are marginalized in Korean society.[19]

Currently, prostitution in Asia is highly internationalized, but the military plays a less and less central role in it. A thorough recent study sponsored by the International Labor Organization (ILO) concludes that although US military personnel on leave during the Vietnam War era played a role in catalyzing the growth of a foreign-oriented sector of the Thai sex industry, this sector has since been sustained by tourists (especially from Japan and Germany)—notwithstanding periodic visits of US Navy ships. (US Navy ships returning from the Gulf War in 1991 made a sex stop in Thailand.) The transformation of Thailand's economy from agriculture to export-oriented industry (sharpening urban–rural disparities, and providing men more opportunities and women fewer ones) was a "more important influence" in the development of the Thai sex sector than was the foreign military and tourist presence. Although the investment brought in by foreign men helped stimulate the industry, the increasing disposable income of Thai men was more important. "Numerically . . . foreigners are probably only a small proportion of the customers of the commercial sex market . . . Most clients of prostitutes in Thailand are Thai men."[20] . . .

Does Sex Affect Aggression?

Thus far, the association of sex with war could plausibly result from war's disruption of social norms. What about the other direction of causality, with sexuality as cause and war as effect? The "conflation of sexuality and violence" is a strong element in popular notions of masculinity. In many animals, "[s]ome of the brain's neural circuitry for aggression seems dangerously cheek by jowl with the neural circuitry for sex." If male sexuality made soldiers aggressive, that could help explain the absence of women in the ranks.[21]

Some soldiers, but apparently a minority, have described combat as sexually gratifying. For them, "the procreative act and the destructive act are inextricably interlinked." One US soldier in Vietnam said, "I was literally turned on when I saw a gook shot." Another said that in combat, like in sex, "the space . . . between subject and object . . . banged shut in a fast wash of adrenalin." The feeling of a firefight, difficult to recall afterwards, "was the feeling you'd had when you were much, much younger and undressing a girl for the first time." One US Marine captain confessed to disappointment that Iraqi forces in the Gulf War "surrendered too fast to kill a lot of them . . . If you've ever got close to a girl hoping to get it and you didn't, it was about the same.[22] . . .

Phallic Symbolism of Weapons According to some writers "squeezing the trigger—releasing a hail of bullets—gives enormous pleasure and satisfaction. These are the pleasures of combat . . . the primal aggression, the release, and the orgasmic discharge." One US Vietnam veteran said that "[t]o some people carrying a gun was like having a permanent hard-on. It was a pure sexual trip every time you got to pull the trigger." "Many men who have carried and fired a gun—especially a full automatic weapon—must confess in their hearts that the power and pleasure of explosively spewing a stream of bullets is akin to the emotions felt when explosively spewing a stream of semen."[23]

However, phallic imagery hardly requires automatic weapons. Colonel Dave Grossman suggests that "[t]hrusting the sexual appendage (the penis) deep into the body of the victim can be perversely linked to thrusting the killing appendage (a bayonet or knife) deep into the body of the victim." The phallic character of weapons has seemingly persisted even as technology has evolved—from spears to guns to missiles. The latest nuclear weapon drills deep into the earth before exploding. Each weapon makes sense tactically and aerodynamically, yet the phallic theme still seems surprisingly pervasive.[24]

In US basic training, men chant: "This is my rifle [holding up rifle], this is my gun [pointing to penis]; one's for killing, the other's for fun." In World War II, and the Gulf War, the US military ordered large numbers of condoms to place over gun barrels to keep dirt and sand out (and also as an excuse to distribute them to the men for other uses). A sensible solution to a real problem, this practice nonetheless underscores the gun's phallic nature. Robin Morgan argues that men receive "an orgasmic thrill in violent domination" and that "maleness itself becomes the weapon of destruction." It has been argued that a "man is only a man in so far as he is capable of using his penis as an instrument of power."[25]

Carol Cohn analyzes the gender-laden vocabulary of American "defense intellectuals," whom she worked with and observed for a year. Concepts and terminology employed by those who design and implement weapons policies contained a blatant "sexual subtext." "[L]ectures were filled with discussions of vertical erector launchers, thrust-to-weight ratios, soft lay-downs, deep penetration, and the comparative advantages of protracted versus spasm attacks—. . . 'releasing . . . our megatonnage in one orgasmic whump.'" On a submarine tour, official visitors were given a chance to reach through a hole to "pat the missile" (a nuclear ballistic missile). A lecture mentioned that new nuclear missiles were deployed in Europe "so that our allies can pat them." "What are men doing when they 'pat' these high-tech phalluses? Patting is an assertion of intimacy, sexual possession . . . the proximity of all that phallic power, the possibility of vicariously appropriating it as one's own."[26]

Helen Caldicott reports in *Missile Envy* that Pentagon officials got Congress to approve bigger military budgets during the Cold War by bringing scale models of missiles—red for the Soviets and blue for the Americans—to Congressional hearings. The smaller and more accurate US missiles were superior (US bombs were smaller, relative to explosive power). But the painted scale models carried a subtext: their "great big red missiles" threaten our "small blue missiles." Caldicott notes that the Pentagon always got its money.[27]

Nuclear weapons carry masculine gender. The bombs dropped on Japan in 1945 were named "little boy" and "fat man." Nuclear weapons scientists referred to bombs as "babies" being born, and expressed hope that their bomb would not be born a girl, i.e., a dud. Edward Teller's coded telegram informing Washington, DC, that a test hydrogen bomb had worked said simply, "It's a boy." "The nuclear scientists gave birth to male progeny with the ultimate power of violent domination over female Nature."[28]

Since bombs are male, their containers, vehicles, and targets are female. For example, the plane that dropped the atomic bomb on Hiroshima (the "Enola Gay") was named after the pilot's mother. Ships are always "she," and the first practical British tank

built in World War I was named "Mother." [A] US Army poster from World War II . . . tells male soldiers that their military equipment is like a pin-up girl that "won't let you down." During World War II, US soldiers pasted or painted "pin-ups" onto tanks and planes throughout the US military forces, as in naked Jane on D-Day. . . . Commanders also used pin-ups to teach recruits to read grids on maps. . . . The "target" was thus explicitly feminized and objectified.[29]

Pilots and ground crews have also often pasted "pin-up" photos of women onto conventional bombs before dropping them. That way the male bomb has a symbolic female target (for orgasmic destruction) when it gets there. The famous pin-up photo of Rita Hayworth was pasted to the first US nuclear weapon exploded over Bikini atoll in 1946, presumably to enhance its potency. Bombing an actual target feminizes it as well. Thus a World War II era *Life* magazine article calls the bombing of German sites "emasculation." The French atom bomb test sites in the South Pacific were all given women's names.[30] . . .

War and Voyeurism The home consumption of distant bombing in recent wars can be seen as a form of violent and voyeuristic pornography. Judith Butler argues that the Gulf War bombing—consumed euphorically on American TV sets—served to "champion a masculinized Western subject . . . who determines its world unilaterally." The war conflated "the television screen and the lens of the bomber pilot" through rebroadcasting of images recorded by "smart bombs" as they approached their targets ("a kind of optical phallus"). The viewer is thus constituted as part of the bomber and bomb, identified with the distant action "yet securely wedged in the couch in one's own living room." The kill itself produces no blood since the optical link destroys itself in the process of destroying the target. The viewer thus gains a "radical impermeability," both proximate and distant from the enactment of violence, an embodiment of imperial power. The viewer becomes, like a sniper, "the disembodied killer who can never be killed . . . securing a fantasy of transcendence . . . infinitely protected from a reverse-strike through the guarantee of electronic distance." McBride similarly argues that the televised Gulf War "was deeply satisfying to most viewers."[31]

McBride connects war with both battering and male sports (football) in contemporary Western society, arguing that "misogynist violence—either figuratively or literally expressed— . . . embod[ies] a culturally constructed psychological need to abuse women for the sake of a male identity . . . Castration anxiety and the imagery of phallic penetration seem to play obsessive compulsive roles in male activities like war and competitive sports." The incidence of woman-battering reportedly increased during both the Gulf War and the Super Bowl. Football, like war, allows males to enter an "adversarial mentality that seeks to dominate, humiliate, and vanquish the foe and restore wholeness." War is exciting to participants and observers alike because it "marks the eruption of ecstatic time into everyday life," a kind of "holy madness" in which desires are "consummated in an ecstatic expulsion of bodily fluids, for example, vomit, urine, semen, blood, and excrement." As for male sexuality itself, however, overall, little evidence suggests that it is a key component of male soldiers' aggressiveness, notwithstanding the temporary dislocation of sexual norms during wartime.[32]

Feminization of Enemies as Symbolic Domination

. . . [M]en's participation in combat depends on feminizing the enemy and enacting rape symbolically (and sometimes literally), thereby using gender to symbolize domination. "In war's coding, the inferior and hated enemy is feminine." For example, a US pilot, after shooting down a male Iraqi pilot, reportedly said he "cold smoked the bitch" (not the "bastard"). Men who feminize enemies in this way might be confused by having women warriors in their own ranks.[33]

Male soldiers use gender to represent domination. Psychologically, they assume a masculine and dominant position relative to a feminine and subordinate enemy. Within armies, by the same principle, subordinates are coded as feminine. One US soldier in Vietnam said of his officers that "[w]e are their women." Thus, the feminization not only of enemy troops and civilians, but of subordinates and nonsoldiers, plays into soldiers' militarized masculinity. In war films, the feminine is a "purely symbolic presence" for boys. In an all-male environment, the subordinate males take on feminine gender (as "girls," "pussies," etc.). The absence of actual females frees up the gender category to encode domination. In war films, "the feminine . . . is something to be conquered."[34]

Means of Feminization

Historian Richard Trexler documents the "inveterate male habit of gendering enemies female or effeminate" throughout the ancient world. Several methods accomplish this regendering of male enemies in ancient and modern cultures.[35]

Gendered Massacre The most common pattern in warfare in the ancient Middle East and Greece was to literally feminize a conquered population by executing male captives, raping the women, then taking women and children as slaves. . . . Kidnapped females have been called the first form of private property. The pattern of gendered massacre recurs even today. In 1995, after conquering the town of Srebrenica in Bosnia (a UN-designated safe haven), Serb forces sorted out the 7,000 men and adolescent boys, executed them all, and buried them in mass graves. The women and younger children they put on busses and deported from Serb-controlled territory, except some young women pulled out, evidently, to be raped. In the Kosovo war, "young men were . . . by far the most targeted" group, and "[m]any were executed on the spot."[36]

Castration   Another way to feminize conquered enemies is to castrate prisoners—or to castrate men before or after killing them. The castration of both male prisoners and dead enemies was widespread in the ancient world, practiced by Chinese, Persian, Amalekite, Egyptian, and Norse armies. The type of castration varied by culture, from mere circumcision (symbolic castration, rendering men as boys) to cutting off testicles, to cutting off both testicles and penises.[37] . . .

Such attitudes continue in modern times. President Lyndon Johnson said of the damage inflicted on Vietnamese communists during the 1968 Tet offensive: "I didn't just screw Ho Chi Minh. I cut his pecker off!" McBride sees an "underlying discourse of castration" in the 1991 Gulf War. US General Colin Powell's famous strategy towards the Iraqi Army was to first "cut it off" and then "kill it." Richard Nixon called Saddam Hussein "militarily castrated" by the war, and reporter Sam Donaldson said that Saddam "folded like a banana" under the attack.[38]

In the hyper-masculinized context of war, with manhood on the line, soldiers show widespread castration fear. After World War I, sexual wounds became a common theme of postwar literature, reflecting "symbolic disorders of powerlessness." US pilots in World War II, "[l]ike all men at war . . . feared above all getting hit in the testi-

cles." Ambrose refers obliquely to "the wound that above all others terrified the soldiers"—apparently so scary it should not be named. The theme resurfaced for US soldiers in Vietnam, notably in the best-selling country-western song, *Ruby, Don't Take Your Love to Town*, about a paraplegic veteran who's "not the man I used to be" but still needs his wife's love. Australian soldiers in Vietnam expressed castration fear more often than warranted by the real dangers of land mines, reflecting a "maimed self-image" among the veterans. (The Vietnam War, for some analysts, represented the failure of a Western "Orientalist fantasy" of sexual conquest in Asia.) During the Cold War, the superpower missile race led some observers to conclude that men in power feared losing phallic weapons. "If disarmament is emasculation, how could any real man even consider it?"[39]

Homosexual Rape   A third method of feminizing enemy soldiers in the ancient world was anal rape, with the victor in the dominant/active position and the vanquished in the subordinate/passive one. . . .

. . . Among the messages inscribed on US bombs in the Gulf War was the theme, "Bend Over, Saddam." Saddam's promised "mother of all battles" would be engaged by American "motherfuckers," and one US Congressman invoked the phrase, "slam, bam, thank you ma'am," substituting Saddam for ma'am. These constructions "were frequently complemented by allusions to both oral and anal violation." The Bosnia and Kosovo wars also saw sexual abuse of men (perhaps intensified because Muslim but not Christian men there were circumcised).[40] . . .

Rape in War

As for the rape of women, it is "a 'normal' accompaniment to war." In contexts where war atrocities occur, rape usually is among them. In seventeenth-century Europe, Spanish troops in the Netherlands committed "countless cases of rape, murder, robbery and arson." During the US Civil War, members of the California Volunteers (militia) in Utah perpetrated the Bear River Massacre against Shoshone Indians, and raped surviving women. Massive atrocities including rapes followed the partition of India and Pakistan in 1948. In Central America in the 1980s, brutal guerrilla and counterinsurgency warfare was accompanied by widespread sexual assault.[41] . . .

Rape arises from different specific motivations in various wars—revenge for Russian soldiers in Berlin in 1945, frustration for US soldiers in Vietnam, ethnic cleansing in Bosnia. Historically, the main point of rape in war seems to be to humiliate enemy males by despoiling their valued property—"the ultimate humiliation . . . the stamp of total conquest." A raped woman "is devalued property, and she signals defeat for the man who fails in his role as protector." Rape is thus "a means of establishing jurisdiction and conquest." "Rape at once pollutes and occupies the territory of the nation, transgresses its boundaries, defeats its protectors." For its victims, rape as a "violent invasion into the interior of one's body represents the most severe attack imaginable upon the intimate self and the dignity of a human being," constituting "severe torture."[42]

Rape is a crime of domination, and war has everything to do with domination. "[T]he rapist's sexuality is not at the center of his act; it is placed instrumentally at the service of the violent act." Rapes in wartime apparently bear no relationship to the presence of prostitutes or other available women—showing that rape is not driven by sexual desire.[43] . . .

In Bosnia, rape was an instrument of ethnic cleansing—used to humiliate and terrorize a population from one ethnic group in order to induce it to abandon desirable territory. The number of women raped (mostly Muslims raped by Serbian forces) has been estimated at 20,000 (by a European Union commission) to 50,000 (by the Bosnian government). "Rape occurs in nearly every war, but in this one . . . degradation and molestation of women was central to the conquest." Some rapes were peculiarly oriented towards forced impregnation as a part of ethnic cleansing. The Bosnia war resulted in the inclusion of rape for the first time in an international tribunal's indictments for war crimes.[44]

The Bosnia case "is not an exceptional case" in magnitude. Systematic mass rape during conquest occurred in the Pakistani war against Bangladesh's independence in 1971 (200,000 women), the Berlin area after World War II (over 100,000), the Japanese "rape of Nanking" [Nanjing] in 1937–38 (over 20,000), and Japan's "comfort women" system. . . . The international women's movement from the late nineteenth century through World War II took steps to organize against rape in wartime. At the 1915 Hague Congress, Jane Addams said: "Worse than death . . . is the defenselessness of women in warfare and their violation by the invading soldier."[45]

Rape as an instrument of territorial control and domination seems to have spread in the 1990s. A "new style of warfare is often aimed specifically at women," using "organized sexual assault as a tactic in terrorizing and humiliating a civilian population." Simultaneously with Bosnia, rape played a role in the genocide in Rwanda and in the Haitian military's suppression of resistance. In one town in Mozambique in 1991 (during a little-noticed war that took a million lives), "every woman and girl in the town had been sexually assaulted" while the town was occupied by right-wing guerrillas. In the "ethnic cleansing" of Kosovo by Serb forces in 1999, rapes were again common, though apparently less systematic than in Bosnia. Other recent reports come from Liberia, Sierra Leone, Burundi, Uganda, Algeria, Indonesia, Kashmir, and Burma. At UN refugee camps, workers now regularly provide "morning-after" contraceptive pills to women raped in, or just before arriving at, the camps.[46]

Latin American military governments in the 1980s "developed patterns of punishment specifically designed for women" who opposed the regime. In Central America, governments meted out sexual torture as part of a generalized, day-to-day pattern of violence against villages thought to sympathize with rebels. In Chile, Argentina, and Uruguay, by contrast, individual women were identified by the government as enemies, then jailed and sexually tortured. Gang rape was "the standard torture mechanism." The military sought to break the spirit of these women by arresting them in front of their families and then destroying their sense of self, which was rooted in their identities as mothers, i.e., "morally superior and spiritually stronger than men." Thus, misogynist military states have used female sexual slavery and torture to control women.[47]

Similarly, "women have become central targets" in the Mexican government's counterinsurgency warfare against Zapatista guerrillas. "Rape has become a central tactic" to intimidate women and dominate communities. Furthermore, women are "doubly affected as they often become targets of the frustrations of their husbands and fathers" under the stress of wartime.[48]

Motives and Opportunities   Rape in wartime may arise from different motivations than in peacetime. Among other reasons, a male soldier rapes because "war . . . has awakened his aggressiveness, and he directs it at those who play a subordinate role in the world of war." Wartime also offers different opportunities. One US soldier in Vietnam said "They are in an all-male environment. . . . There are women available. Those women are of another culture, another colour, another society . . . You've got an M-16. What do you need to pay a lady for? You go down to the village and you take what you want." Some said that having sex and then killing the woman made the soldier a "double veteran."[49]

In one view, raping by soldiers in wartime results from the weakening of social norms—parallel with increased sex, swearing, looting, cruelty, and other such behaviors. Some see a "return to nature" in war. The *US Infantry Journal* in 1943 referred to soldiers as "a society of men, frequently unwashed, who have been dedicated to the rugged task of killing other men, and whose training has emphasized that a certain reversion to the primitive is not undesirable." Romantic or forced sexual conquests reflect "the rapist in every man." "Copulation under such circumstances is an act of aggression; the girl is the victim and her conquest the victor's triumph. Preliminary resistance on her part always increases his satisfaction."[50]

One function of gang rape is to promote cohesion within groups of men soldiers. Men who would not rape individually do so as part of a display within the male group, to avoid becoming an outcast. "There is male bonding in the violence of massive criminal rape—performed in succession, by 3 to 27 men in some cases—against women political prisoners" under Latin American military regimes. Gang rapes may serve to relieve individual men of responsibility, just as groups absolve soldiers in killing. . . . "Rape is obviously not an exclusive preserve of military men. But . . . aspects of the military institution and ideology" may increase pressure on men to participate in gang rape—to control a chaotic and fearsome external world while proving manhood and toughness to one's buddies within the military "family."[51]

War rapes frequently go unreported, because of backlash against rape victims in traditional societies. The problems of shame associated with being the victim of rape (e.g., in Kosovo) are connected with certain cultural traditions in which family honor is stained by *any* violation of sexual property norms. In Egypt until very recently, a rapist could receive a pardon by agreeing to marry his victim. In some places, adultery or premarital sex are considered the woman's fault by definition, and her male relatives receive taunts impugning their manhood until they kill her to restore family honor (and serve as an example to other women who might stray sexually). These "honor killings" apparently accounted for around one-quarter of homicides in Egypt and Jordan in recent years. Killers typically receive light sentences. A Jordanian chief judge explained: "Nobody can really want to kill his wife or daughter or sister. But sometimes circumstances force him to do this." (The United States ruled in 1999 that women who face threats of this nature are not eligible for refugee status.)[52]

Thus, rape in wartime is both a violation of men's cherished property rights, and an extension of everyday misogyny by other means. Susan Brownmiller writes: "Sexual trespass on the enemy's women is one of the satisfactions of conquest . . . [reflecting] submerged rage against all women who belong to other men."[53] . . .

Defending "Our" Women Gender plays a role in ethnonationalism. The nation is often gendered female, and the state male. Women in some sense embody the nation, and the political inclusion of women and the masses of men (democratization) seemed to accompany the rise of nationalism in Europe a century ago. . . . The process of redrawing territorial borders to unite some people and exclude others sometimes uses women's bodies as symbols of the nation, markers of the in-group, and national "property" to be defended and protected by men.[54]

Rape of "our" women sometimes becomes a dominant metaphor of the danger to the nation from enemy males. An ethnic group's perceived "vulnerability or porousness of national boundaries" is embodied in songs and legends about the abduction or seduction of young women by the enemy. These constructions also provide "opportunities for heroism." During the US Civil War and Reconstruction, the symbolism of sex between white Southern women and black men served to mobilize white Southern men. Invasions, such as the German conquest of Poland and France at the outset of World War II or Iraq's conquest of Kuwait, are frequently described as "rape."[55]

Propaganda in the World Wars used the theme of rape to rally patriotism. . . . In World War I, British propaganda played up German gang rapes, so that "the rape and sexual mutilation of women dominated contemporaries' imaginings and representations of the war." Italy dropped leaflets to Austrian soldiers warning that while they were fighting Italy, Russians could occupy their homes and rape their women. In World War II, Japanese forces warned Australian soldiers that Americans were consorting with their women back home. Germany informed British soldiers likewise. German propaganda played up the humiliation implied by French women having sex with black African troops from French colonies, and British women having sex with black US soldiers. In the former Yugoslavia, rape across ethnic lines became an "ethnomarker" and sharpened intergroup boundaries around the propagandistic promotion of images of the other group as rapists to be feared.[56]

These constructions limit all women's (not just rape victims') gender mobility, reinforcing traditional sexism. Croatian women in the 1990s were scolded by the government for having too few babies, and especially for having abortions (since, as the ruling party put it, a "fetus is also Croat"). Meanwhile the Serbian Orthodox Patriarch told women who had lost their only children in the war that they should have had more children. Beyond their reproductive roles, women are keepers of a group's culture, expected to "preserve tradition in the home . . . [and] reflect the virtue of the nation."

The symbolism of an enemy danger to "our" women can become bizarre. In 1997, the Palestinian Authority claimed that Israeli chewing gum sold in Palestinian areas was spiked with progesterone as a plot to drive Arab women into a sexual frenzy (undermining Islamic morals and, in one version, setting them up to be prostitute-informants), while sterilizing both girls and boys to reduce the Arab birth rate. The story gained wide credence even though the gum was made in Spain, it contained no progesterone according to an independent analysis, and progesterone tends to slightly reduce rather than increase women's sexual desires (nor would the method have worked as a contraceptive).[57]

War and Misogyny

If symbolic and actual rape encode domination, then misogyny serves as an important motor of male aggression in war. Rape is "the ultimate metaphor for the war system," according to Betty Reardon. As a symbolic form of rape, armed violence genders the victor as male and the vanquished as female. Symbolic rape is acted out in various ways in different cultures and contexts, but key themes repeat across time and space.[58] . . .

Whatever the mix of male and female victims in various wars, one thing is clear.

Neither men nor women benefit from war at the expense of the other gender. Women do not get a good deal, on balance, when men bear the burden of protecting them, nor do men get a good deal when they run around playing war while women bear the costs. Rather, *both genders lose in war,* although they lose in somewhat different ways. . . .

NOTES

About the footnotes: The footnotes, grouped by paragraph of text, provide work and page citations for quotes and specific claims, indicated by an identifier word before the page number. A subject word followed by a colon applies to subsequent citations until the next colon. A citation without identifier or subject word refers to a discussion relevant to the paragraph but not to any particular claim or quote in it. Some authors cited for a paragraph may be dissenting arguments from the paragraph's point. Some of the footnotes encapsulate running conversations, which the interested reader can reconstruct from the sequence of page citations given.

1. Herman 1992, violence 32; Mies 1986, 153–67.
2. Resolution 3, June 9–11, 1998, Salt Lake City; Korea: Moon 1998.
3. Holmes 1985, almost 93, ready 93; Hicks 1995, outlets 28–29; Costello 1985, subject 78; Gray 1959, 59–70, duty 61.
4. Griffin 1992, sent 76; Costello 1985, wholesome–vestiges 149–55; Koppes 1995; Parry 1996, vii.
5. Costello 1985, set 211.
6. Gray 1959, Uprooting, 62–63.
7. Costello 1985, 3, 7–9.
8. Costello 1985, sociability–streets 207; Enloe 1983, 29–31; Anderson 1981, perimeters 104, married 110.
9. Goldman and Fuller 1983, Viet 126; Costello 1985, rattle 79, French 218–19.
10. Enloe 1983, stalking 23–26.
11. Hirschfeld 1934, 93–94.
12. De Pauw 1998, European 96–100, Civil 165–67, WWI 219–20; Levine 1993; Enloe 1993, 142–60; Hicks 1995, mounted 29; Costello 1985, French 81–82; Enloe 1983, access 4, 6, 18–45; Gray 1959, 65.
13. Bosnia: Reuters 2000; Kosovo: Agence France-Presse 2000; layer: MacKinnon 1994b, 192.
14. Zuger 1998b.

15. Hicks 1995, rape 11, 18, ratio 19, marches 73–74; De Pauw 1998, 259–62.
16. Goldman and Fuller 1983, liberty 141–42; Holmes 1985, contacts 93–94; Enloe 1983, precise 33.
17. Gerster 1995, first 228; Yayori 1997, 148–52; Chizuko 1997, 294; Perpinan 1994, 149–50; Enloe 1983, estimated 43.
18. Enloe 1993, industry 149, warning 149–51, linger 149–51; Enloe 1983, money 39–42; Perpinan 1994, pay 149–53.
19. Moon 1997.
20. Study: Boonchalaksi and Guest 1998, 133–36, men 137; Lim ed. 1998; Navy: Enloe 1993, 183.
21. Brittan 1989, conflation 11; Sagan and Druyan 1992, jowl 191; Harris 1974, 106.
22. Grossman 1995, procreative 134; Keegan and Holmes 1985, shot 267; Michael Herr, in Kinney 1991, wash–undressing 39; McBride 1995, same 58; Costello 1985, 80, 94.
23. Grossman 1995, semen 136.
24. Grossman 1995, 137; Mosse 1990, 166.
25. McBride 1995, condoms 56; Morgan 1988, thrill 70, maleness 69; Brittan 1989, instrument 47, 46.
26. Cohn 1987, 692–93, 695.
27. Caldicott 1986, 297.
28. Easlea 1983, 3; Cohn 1987, progeny 701.
29. Keegan and Holmes 1985, tank 121.
30. Griffin 1992, pin-up 76, emasculation 13; Cohn 1987, names 701.
31. Butler 1992, 10–12; McBride 1995, 107–9, 112, deeply 60.
32. McBride 1995, xvi, xvii, 3, 77–106, eruption 147, 149; Ehrenreich 1997a.
33. Gray 1997, coding 43, bitch 43.
34. Gray 1997, women 175; Simpson 1994, presence 217, conquered 234; Trexler 1995, 2, 174; Krauss and Chiu 1998, 70; Jeffords 1989, xi.
35. Trexler 1995, 1, 12–37.
36. Ancient: Trexler 1995; Property: Mies 1986, 62; Bosnia: Sudetic 1998; Holbrooke 1998, 70; A. Jones 1994; Kosovo: OSCE 1999, chapter 15; A. Jones 2000.
37. Trexler 1995, 16–19, 66.
38. Kimmel and Messner eds. 1995, pecker xiii; Gulf: McBride 1995, 43–44.
39. Showalter 1987, symbolic 62; Ambrose 1997, testicles 47, terrified 143; Ulman and Brothers 1988, 182; Goldman and Fuller 1983, song 10, 78; Gerster 1995, maimed–fantasy 225–28; Cohn 1990, disarmament 35; Ashworth and Swatuk 1998; de Waal 1989, 73–75.
40. Trexler 1995, passive 71, prisoners 71, insult 65; Parker et al. 1992, bend 6; McBride 1995, mother–violation 56–57; Bosnia: Rieff 1995, 107; Kosovo: A. Jones 2000.
41. Stiglmayer 1994b, normal 84; Keegan and Holmes 1985, 267, arson 280; Shoshone: Madsen 1985, 180–200, 231–38, 233; brutal: Enloe 1993, 121–22.
42. Wilden 1987, stamp 179; Mostov 1995, devalued–boundaries 524, 526; Seifert 1994, 55–66, torture 55; Seifert 1996; MacKinnon 1994a; Rejali 1996; Copelon 1994, 206–8; Pettman 1996a, 100–4; Reardon 1985, 38–40; Rorty 1993, 112; Warren and Cady 1996, 6–7; Nikolić-Ristanović 1996, 361.
43. Seifert 1994, act 56, presence 58; Lorber 1994, 76–78; Wilden 1987, 163–88.
44. Brownmiller 1994; Stiglmayer ed. 1994; Bowery Productions 1996; Enloe 1994; Stiglmayer 1994b, number 85; Gutman 1993, central ix–x; Copelon 1994, 207; Nikolić-Ristanović 1996, 361; Drakulić 1994; tribunal: Socolovsky 2000.
45. Stiglmayer 1994b, case 85; Bangladesh: Brownmiller 1975, 78–86; Berlin: Seifert 1994, 54; Nanking: Copelon 1994, 197, 205; Addams: Rupp 1996, 345.
46. Style: Crossette 1998; Human Rights Watch 1995; Haiti: Human Rights Watch 1994; Mozambique: Nordstrom 1998, 82; Kosovo: Human Rights Watch 2000; Smith 1999; Rohde 1999; Liberia: Human Rights Watch 1997; Sierra Leone: Human Rights Watch 1998b; Farah 2000; Burundi: Human Rights Watch 1998a; Kashmir: Human Rights Watch 1993.
47. Bunster-Burotto 1994, patterns 156, standard 166, morally 163–64; Davies ed. 1994; Enloe 1993, 60–61.
48. Mora 1998, 172–73.
49. Stiglmayer 1994b awakened 84, Enloe 1983, 32–36, want 321, double 208–9; cf. Turner 1996, 30.
50. Keegan and Holmes 1985, looting 53; Gray 1959, 63–70, nature 63, rapist 66, triumph 67; Costello 1985, primitive 73.
51. Jeffords 1989, gang 69–71; Lomnitz 1986, 19; May and Strikwerda 1996; Bunster-Burotto 1994, bonding 168; Enloe 1983, preserve 35.
52. Jehl 1999.
53. Brownmiller in Rejali 1996, 366; Higonnet and Higonnet 1987, 42.
54. Pettman 1996a, 45–63, gendered 49; Chatterjee 1993, formations 68, 137, 135–40; Halliday 1991, 165; Peterson 1996b; Stiglmayer 1994a; Gioseffi ed. 1988, 119; Pettman 1996a, 45, 64; Williams and Best 1982, 130; Smith 1991, 44,

4; Kristof 1998; Bloom 1990; Gurr 1993; Gurr and Harff 1994.

55. Mostov 1995, 516–23, metaphor 523, porousness 517; Seifert 1996; Civil: Hodes 1992; invasions: McBride 1995, 41, 49; Sasson 1991; Parker et al. 1992, 6.

56. British: Kent 1993, 24–26; Italy: Hirschfeld 1934, 321; Japanese: Gubar 1987, 239; Yugoslavia: Rejali 1996, 370.

57. Gellman 1997.

58. Reardon 1985, metaphor 40.

REFERENCES

Ambrose, Stephen E. 1997. *Citizen Soldiers: The US Army from the Normandy Beaches to the Bulge to the Surrender of Germany June 7, 1944–May 7, 1945.* New York: Simon & Schuster.

Anderson, Karen. 1981. *Wartime Women: Sex Roles, Family Relations, and the Status of Women during World War II.* Westport, CT: Greenwood.

Ashworth, Lucian M. and Larry A. Swatuk. 1998. "Masculinity and the Fear of Emasculation in International Relations Theory." In Zalewski and Parpart eds.: 73–92.

Bloom, William. 1990. *Personal Identity, National Identity, and International Relations.* Cambridge: Cambridge University Press.

Boonchalaksi, Wathinee and Philip Guest, 1998. "Prostitution in Thailand." In Lim ed. 130–69.

Bowery Productions. 1996. *Calling the Ghosts* [videorecording]; written and directed by Mandy Jacobson and Karmen Jelinci, in association with Julia Ormond and Indican Productions. New York: [distributed by] Women Make Movies.

Brittan, Arthur. 1989. *Masculinity and Power.* New York: Basil Blackwell.

Brownmiller, Susan. 1975. *Against Our Will: Men, Women, and Rape.* New York: Simon & Schuster.

——— 1994. "Making Female Bodies the Battlefield." In Stiglmayer ed.: 180–82 [reprinted from *Newsweek,* January 4, 1993: 37].

Bunster-Burotto, Ximena. 1994. "Surviving beyond Fear: Women and Torture in Latin America." In Davies ed.: 156–75.

Butler, Judith. 1990a. *Gender Trouble: Feminism and the Subversion of Identity.* New York: Routledge.

——— 1992. "Contingent Foundations: Feminism and the Question of 'Postmodernism.'" In Butler and Scott eds.: 3–21.

Caldicott, Helen. 1986. *Missile Envy: The Arms Race and Nuclear War.* Revised edition. New York: Bantam.

Chatterjee, Partha. 1993. *The Nation and Its Fragments: Colonial and Postcolonial Histories.* Princeton, NJ: Princeton University Press.

Chizuko, Ueno. 1997. "Are the Japanese Feminine? Some Problems of Japanese Feminism in Its Cultural Context." In Sandra Buckley, ed., *Broken Silence: Voices of Japanese Feminism.* Berkeley: University of California Press: 293–300.

Cohn, Carol. 1987. "Sex and Death in the Rational World of Defense Intellectuals." *Signs: Journal of Women in Culture and Society* 12, 4: 687–718.

——— 1990. "'Clean Bombs' and Clean Language." In Elshtain and Tobias eds.: 33–56.

Copelon, Rhonda. 1994. "Surfacing Gender: Reconceptualizing Crimes Against Women in Time of War." In Stiglmayer ed.: 197–218.

Costello, John. 1985. *Virtue under Fire: How World War II Changed Our Social and Sexual Attitudes.* Boston: Little, Brown.

Crossette, Barbara. 1998. "An Old Scourge of War Becomes Its Latest Crime." *The New York Times,* June 14: D1.

Davies, Miranda, ed. 1994. *Women and Violence.* London: Zed.

De Pauw, Linda Grant. 1998. *Battle Cries and Lullabies: Women in War from Prehistory to the Present.* Norman: University of Oklahoma Press.

De Waal, Frans. 1989. *Peacemaking Among Primates.* Cambridge, MA: Harvard University Press.

Drakulić, Slavenka. 1994. "The Rape of Women in Bosnia." In Davies ed.: 176–81.

Easlea, Brian. 1983. *Fathering the Unthinkable: Masculinity, Scientists and the Nuclear Arms Race.* London: Pluto.

Ehrenreich, Barbara. 1997a. *Blood Rites: Origins and History of the Passions of War.* New York: Metropolitan.

Enloe, Cynthia H. 1983. *Does Khaki Become You? The Militarization of Women's Lives.* Boston: South End Press.

——— 1993. *The Morning After: Sexual Politics at the End of the Cold War.* Berkeley: University of California Press.

——— 1994. "Afterword." In Stiglmayer ed.: 219–30.

Farah, Douglas. 2000. "A War Against Women: Sierra Leone Rebels Practiced Systematic Sexual Terror." *The Washington Post,* February 11: A1, A19.

Gellman, Barton. 1997. "Pop! Went the Tale of the Bubble Gum Spiked with Sex Hormones." *The Washington Post,* July 28: A14.

Gerster, Robin. 1995. "A Bit of the Other: Touring Vietnam." In Damousi and Lake eds.: 223–38.

Gioseffi, Daniela, ed. 1988. *Women on War: Essential Voices for the Nuclear Age.* New York: Simon & Schuster.

Goldman, Peter and Tony Fuller, with Richard Manning, Stryker McGuire, Wally McNamee, and Vern E. Smith. 1983. *Charlie Company: What Vietnam Did to Us.* New York: William Morrow.

Gray, Chris Hables. 1997. *Postmodern War: The New Politics of Conflict.* New York: Guilford.

Gray, J. Glenn. 1959. *The Warriors: Reflections of Men in Battle.* New York: Harper & Row.

Griffin, Susan. 1992. *A Chorus of Stones: The Private Life of War.* New York: Anchor.

Grossman, Dave. 1995. *On Killing: The Psychological Cost of Learning to Kill in War and Society.* Boston: Little Brown.

Gubar, Susan. 1987. " 'This Is My Rifle, This Is My Gun': World War II and the Blitz on Women." In Higonnet et al. eds.: 227–59.

Gurr, Ted Robert. 1993. *Minorities at Risk: A Global View of Ethnopolitical Conflicts.* Washington, DC: United States Institute of Peace Press.

Gurr, Ted Robert and Barbara Harff. 1994. *Ethnic Conflict in World Politics.* Boulder, CO: Westview.

Gutman, Roy. 1993. *A Witness to Genocide: The 1993 Pulitzer Prize-Winning Dispatches on the "Ethnic Cleansing" of Bosnia.* New York: Macmillan.

Halliday, Fred. 1991. "Hidden from International Relations: Women and the International Arena." In Grant and Newland eds.: 158–69.

Harris, Marvin. 1974. *Cows, Pigs, Wars and Witches: The Riddles of Culture.* New York: Random House.

Herman, Judith Lewis. 1992. *Trauma and Recovery.* New York: Basic.

Hicks, George. 1995. *The Comfort Women: Japan's Brutal Regime of Enforced Prostitution in the Second World War.* New York: W. W. Norton.

Higonnet, Margaret R. and Patrice L.-R. Higonnet. 1987. "The Double Helix." In Higonnet et al. eds.: 31–50.

Hirschfeld, Magnus. 1934. *The Sexual History of the World War.* New York: Panurge Press.

Hodes, Martha. 1992. "Wartime Dialogues on Illicit Sex: White Women and Black Men." In Clinton and Silber eds.: 230–46.

Holbrooke, Richard. 1998. *To End a War.* New York: Random House.

Holmes, Richard. 1985. *Acts of War: The Behavior of Men in Battle.* New York: Free Press.

Human Rights Watch. 1993. *Rape in Kashmir: A Crime of War* [C509]. New York: Human Rights Watch, May.

———— 1994. *Rape in Haiti: A Weapon of Terror* [B608]. New York: Human Rights Watch, July.

———— 1995. *The Human Rights Watch Global Report on Women's Human Rights* [5469]. New York: Human Rights Watch, August.

———— 1997. *Liberia: Emerging from the Destruction* [A907]. New York: Human Rights Watch, November.

———— 1998a. *Proxy Targets: Civilians in the War in Burundi* [1797]. New York: Human Rights Watch, March.

———— 1998b. *Sowing Terror: Atrocities Against Civilians in Sierra Leone* [1003A]. New York: Human Rights Watch, August.

———— 2000. *Kosovo: Rape as a Weapon of "Ethnic Cleansing"* [Yugoslavia, D1203]. New York: Human Rights Watch, March.

Jeffords, Susan. 1989. *The Remasculinization of America: Gender and the Vietnam War.* Bloomington: Indiana University Press.

Jehl, Douglas. 1999. "Arab Honor's Price: A Woman's Blood." *The New York Times,* June 20: A1.

Jones, Adam. 1994. "Gender and Ethnic Conflict in ex-Yugoslavia." *Ethnic and Racial Studies* 17, 1: 115–34.

———— 2000. "Gendercide and Genocide." *Journal of Genocide Research* 2, 2: 185–211.

Keegan, John and Richard Holmes, with John Gau. 1985. *Soldiers: A History of Men in Battle.* London: Hamish Hamilton.

Kent, Susan Kingsley. 1993. *Making Peace: The Reconstruction of Gender in Interwar Britain.* Princeton, NJ: Princeton University Press.

Kimmel, Michael S. and Michael A. Messner, eds. 1995. *Men's Lives,* 3rd edition. Boston: Allyn & Bacon.

Koppes, Clayton R. 1995. "Hollywood and the Politics of Representation: Women, Workers, and African Americans in World War II Movies." In O'Brien and Parsons eds.: 25–40.

Krauss, Robert M. and Chi-Yue Chiu. 1998. "Language and Social Behavior." In Gilbert, Fiske, and Lindzey eds.: 41–88.

Kristof, Nicholas D. 1998. "Casanovas, Beware! It's Risky for Non-Koreans." *The New York Times,* February 2: A4.

Levine, Philippa. 1993. "Women and Prostitution: Metaphor, Reality, History." *Canadian Journal of History* (December): 479–94.

Lim, Lin Lean, ed. 1998. *The Sex Sector: The Economic and Social Bases of Prostitution in Southeast Asia.* Geneva: International Labour Office.

Lomnitz, Larissa. 1986. "The Uses of Fear: Porro Gangs in Mexico." In Foster and Rubinstein eds.: 15–24.

Lorber, Judith. 1994. *Paradoxes of Gender.* New Haven, CT: Yale University Press.

McBride, James. 1995. *War, Battering, and Other Sports: The Gulf Between American Men and Women.* Atlantic Highlands, NJ: Humanities Press.

MacKinnon, Catherine A. 1994a. "Turning Rape into Pornography: Postmodern Genocide." In Stiglmayer ed.: 73–81.

———— 1994b. "Rape, Genocide, and Women's Human Rights." In Stiglmayer ed.: 183–96.

Madsen, Brigham D. 1985. *The Shoshoni Frontier and the Bear River Massacre.* Salt Lake City: University of Utah Press.

May, Larry and Robert Strikwerda. 1996. "Men in Groups: Collective Responsibility for Rape." In Warren and Cady eds.: 175–91.

Mies, Maria. 1986. *Patriarchy and Accumulation on a World Scale: Women in the International Division of Labour.* London: Zed.

Moon, Katharine H. 1997. *Sex Among Allies: Military Prostitution in US–Korea Relations.* New York: Columbia University Press.

Mora, Mariana. 1998. "Zapatismo: Gender, Power, and Social Transformation." In Lorentzen and Turpin eds.: 164–76.

Morgan, Robin. 1988. *The Demon Lover: On the Sexuality of Terrorism.* New York: W. W. Norton. [Pages refer to excerpts in *Ms.,* March 1989.]

Mosse, George L. 1990. *Fallen Soldiers: Reshaping the Memory of the World Wars.* Oxford University Press.

Mostov, Julie. 1995. " 'Our Women'/'Their Women': Symbolic Boundaries, Territorial Markers, and Violence in the Balkans." *Peace & Change* 20, 4 (October): 515–29.

Nikolić-Ristanović, Vesna. 1996. "War, Nationalism and Mothers." *Peace Review* 8, 3: 359–64.

Nordstrom, Carolyn. 1998. "Girls Behind the (Front) Lines." In Lorentzen and Turpin eds.: 80–89.

OSCE [Organization for Security and Cooperation in Europe]. 1999. *Kosovo/Kosova As Seen, As Told.* Vienna: OSCE.

Parker, Andrew, Mary Russo, Doris Sommer, and Patricia Yaeger. 1992. "Introduction." In Andrew Parker, Mary Russo, Doris Sommer, and Patricia Yaeger, eds., *Nationalisms and Sexualities.* New York: Routledge: 1–20.

Parry, Sally E. 1996. "So Proudly They Serve: American Women in World War II Films." Presented at the American Political Science Association Annual Meeting, San Francisco, August 29–September 1.

Perpinan, Sister Mary Soledad. 1994. "Militarism and the Sex Industry in the Philippines." In Davies ed.: 149–52.

Peterson, V. Spike. 1996b. "Women and Gender in Power/Politics, Nationalism and Revolution." *Journal of Politics* 58, 3 (August): 870–78.

Pettman, Jan Jindy. 1996a. *Worlding Women: A Feminist International Politics.* New York: Routledge.

Reardon, Betty A. 1985. *Sexism and the War System.* New York: Teachers College Press.

Rejali, Darius M. 1996. "After Feminist Analysis of Bosnian Violence." *Peace Review* 8, 3: 365–71.

Rieff, David. 1995. *Slaughterhouse: Bosnia and the Failure of the West.* New York: Simon & Schuster.

Rohde, David. 1999. "Albanian Tells How Serbs Chose Her, 'the Most Beautiful One,' for Rape." *The New York Times,* May 1: A8.

Rorty, Richard. 1993. "Human Rights, Rationality, and Sentimentality." In Stephen Shute and Susan Hurley, eds. *On Human Rights: The Oxford Amnesty Lectures.* New York: Basic: 111–34.

Rupp, Leila J. 1996. "Wartime Violence Against Women and Solidarity." *Peace Review* 8, 3: 343–46.

Sagan, Carl and Ann Druyan. 1992. *Shadows of Forgotten Ancestors: A Search for Who We Are.* New York: Random House.

Sasson, Jean. 1991. *The Rape of Kuwait: The True Story of Iraqi Atrocities Against a Civilian Population.* New York: Knightsbridge.

Seifert, Ruth. 1994. "War and Rape: A Preliminary Analysis." In Stiglmayer ed.: 54–72.

———— 1996. "Der weibliche Koerper als Symbol und Zeichen: Geschlechtsspezifische Gewalt und die Kulturelle Konstruktion des Krieges" [The Female Body as a Symbol and a Sign: Gender-Specific Violence and the Cultural Construction of War.] In Andreas Gestrich, ed., *Gewalt im Krieg.* Münster: Jahrbuch für Historische Friedensforschung.

Showalter, Elaine. 1987. "Rivers and Sassoon: The Inscription of Male Gender Anxieties." In Higonnet et al. eds.: 61–69.

Simpson, Mark. 1994. *Male Impersonators: Men Performing Masculinity.* New York: Cassell.

Smith, Anthony D. 1991. *National Identity.* London: Penguin.

Smith, R. Jeffrey. 1999. "Rape as a Weapon of War: Refugees Tell of Gang Assaults by Troops." *The Washington Post,* April 13: A1, A17.

Socolovsky, Jerome. 2000. "War Crimes Panel Examines Sex Case." The Hague: Associated Press, March 19.

Stiglmayer, Alexandra. 1994a. "The War in the Former Yugoslavia." In Stiglmayer ed.: 1–34.

——— 1994b. "Rape in Bosnia-Herzegovina." In Stiglmayer ed.: 82–169.

——— ed. 1994. *Mass Rape: The War Against Women in Bosnia-Herzegovina.* Lincoln: University of Nebraska Press.

Sudetic, Chuck, 1998. *Blood and Vengeance: One Family's Story of the War in Bosnia.* New York: W. W. Norton.

Trexler, Richard C. 1995. *Sex and Conquest: Gendered Violence, Political Order, and the European Conquest of the Americas.* Ithaca, NY: Cornell University Press.

Turner, Fred. 1996. *Echoes of Combat: The Vietnam War in American Memory.* New York: Doubleday.

Ulman, Richard B. and Doris Brothers. 1988. *The Shattered Self: A Psychoanalytic Study of Trauma.* Hillsdale, NJ: Analytic Press.

Warren, Karen J. and Duane L. Cady. 1996. "Feminism and Peace: Seeing Connections." In Warren and Cady eds.: 1–15.

Wilden, Anthony. 1987. *Man and Woman, War and Peace: The Strategist's Companion.* New York: Routledge & Kegan Paul.

Williams, John E. and Deborah L. Best. 1981. *Measuring Sex Stereotypes: A Thirty-Nation Study.* Beverly Hills, CA: Sage.

Yayori, Matsui. 1997. "Asian Migrant Women in Japan." In Sandra Buckley, ed., *Broken Silence: Voices of Japanese Feminism.* Berkeley: University of California Press: 143–54.

Zuger, Abigail. 1998. "Many Prostitutes Suffer Combat Disorders, Study Finds." *The New York Times,* August 18: C8.

QUESTIONS FOR DISCUSSION

1. How does the military reinforce traditional notions of masculinity and femininity?
2. In what ways is gender used as a code for systems of domination?
3. How are women and girls uniquely affected by war?

59

THE PAINFUL ART OF RECONCILIATION

DAVID LAMB

The dirt road to Pho Vinh was narrow and rutted and, in the monsoons, all but impassable. It jutted off Highway 1, south of Danang, and headed toward the hills, through lowland rice paddies and past little villages whose occupants had not seen a foreigner in nearly thirty years. People here moved by bicycle and on foot. They worked their crops by hand. Occasionally we would see a water buffalo in the fields, but that was rare. The sun was hard and steady and sweat came quickly. We humped, eleven out-of-shape, middle-aged former GIs and me. My companions were men on the mend. Behind me was Steve Lemire, and it had been seven years since he had slept with a loaded .44 on one side of the pillow and a bottle of whiskey on the other. Next to him was Buck Anderson. He was on his eighth marriage, and this one was working. Chuck Owens was in the pack, and he was 110 percent sober. Walt Bacak hadn't thought of suicide in a long time.

"I feel like I've been walking guard duty for thirty years," Mike Farquhar said to me, his eyes sweeping the road ahead. I knew we both had the same irrational thought: Did Charley plant any mines last night? "Up at night every two hours, smoke a couple of cigarettes, then try to sleep. Can't. If I get anything out of this trip, if there's something I'd pray for, it'd be to go home and get some sleep. The funny thing is, being back in 'Nam, I've slept really good every night."

Except for Bacak, this was the first time the men had set foot in Vietnam since the war, and returning had been very unnerving. Now they were headed toward a meeting with their former Viet Cong enemies—the very men some of the GIs had fought in this very spot—and what they hoped was that somewhere out here among the jungle-covered hills—or perhaps in the meeting itself—they would find the secret to finally come to grips with one simple fact: The war was over.

Bacak was nearly sixty, a three-tour, once-wounded vet. He was Airborne, an army lifer. He had first returned, alone, in 1997, bogged down in drugs, and he found the trip such a healthy antidote that he set up a nonprofit organization, A Quest for Healing, back home in Lakewood, Washington, and ran two trips a year for former veterans who wanted to return to Vietnam and lay the past to rest.

"I've never brought anyone back that didn't find the trip positive," said Bacak, who had spent a year fighting in the hills and paddies around Pho Vinh. "It doesn't eradicate all the problems, but it allows the vets to change the mental black-and-white photos. It lets them put a face on the men they fought. Over weeks, maybe months, they go home and find the nightmares diminish. They start sleeping better. They don't get angry so easily. Before my first trip back I was seriously into drugs. The only reason I didn't try suicide was because I'd spent so much time in 'Nam trying to stay alive. When I got back to Washington my wife, Joyce, says to me, 'Walter, this is like having a new husband come home.'"

This was Bacak's eighth trip to postwar Vietnam, and he had mastered the protocol. So at lunch in Quang Ngai earlier that day, he had tried to ease the Americans' apprehension about the meeting. "When you meet them," he said, "just keep it light at first. They won't speak English, but we've got a good translator. Be polite. Ask about their families. Don't ask, 'How many people did you kill?' or any shit like that. Then play it by ear. If they want to talk about the war, OK. Let them bring it up. You're going to find they're very gracious."

Pho Vinh wasn't much more than a cluster of shops and bamboo homes strung out on a dusty stretch of the road. In the small one-room building used by the Communist Party, three former Viet Cong guerrillas waited. The Americans entered warily, wearing baseball caps emblazoned with the words "Vietnam: I Came Back." An electric fan groaned overhead. A portrait of Ho Chi Minh hung on the blue wall. Outside, by the open door, villagers stood ten deep, trying to get a good look at these broad-shouldered strangers who towered over their hosts. The crowd kept growing until an old man in a frayed security guard's shirt arrived to shoo everyone away.

Doan Vinh Quay, who was sixty-two, spoke first. He wore a fedora, and over his best shirt he had pinned a black medal commemorating his parents, killed just up the road by U.S. artillery in 1967. He said he was honored to welcome the Americans as friends. He showed them scars where a bullet had shattered his hand. He asked what unit each had fought with and when each had served. A chorus came back: "First Mar Div, '65 . . . 1970, Eleventh Cav. . . . 101st Airborne, Second Brigade, '66. . . ."

"Ah, the 101st. They were good, very tough," Quay replied. He smiled when someone asked how long a tour of duty had been for the Viet Cong. For the duration, he replied. Quay had fought for fifteen years, some of his friends much longer.

Conversation did not come easily at first. What do you say when you meet a man whom thirty years ago you would have shot dead on the spot? But some of the men on both sides had brought scrapbooks and photos. Everyone laughed that the Americans had grown hefty and the Vietnamese were still skinny. "That was your wife?" an American asked, pointing to one of the album photos. "Wow. Very beautiful. You lucky man." Tea was served, and the Vietnamese stood willingly among the Americans for group pictures. Before long, amid jokes and banter, the ice melted, the anxiety faded, and it was apparent to both sides that this was not a gathering of enemies. "I just want to say that, during the war, we had a lot of respect for the VC," Steve Lemire said. "You were good soldiers."

VC, or Viet Cong, was a contraction of Viet Nam Cong San, Vietnamese communists, used derogatorily by the Saigon regime but never by the insurgents themselves. They preferred National Liberation Front. Still, Quay nodded in appreciation, and one could hear him thinking, "I know."

Later, with Bacak walking point, the fourteen men—eleven Americans and three Vietnamese—set off for the old headquarters of the 101st's First Brigade, in the hills a mile away. It was, in a manner of speaking, a joint GI-VC patrol, a sight I never thought I'd live to see. During the war, I'd been just about everywhere in South Vietnam that U.S. units were based, including all three of the 101st's brigade camps. So I must have been in Pho Vinh before. But after a while the camps and fire support bases all looked pretty much alike, and any memory I might once have had of this place had faded with time. We reached the long, high empty plateau. Crumbling asphalt covered the chopper landing pads. Jungle scrub had reclaimed most of the hill. Not a trace remained of the sandbagged barracks where a thousand Americans once lived. One GI pointed to a head-high rock overlooking the valley and said a soldier nicknamed Wolfman used to howl at the moon there after coming back from long-range patrols.

"That's where we slept, right over there," one former grunt said. Former VC guerrilla Nguyen Minh Duc replied, "I know. And your command bunker was just over by the tree." He went on to recall exactly how many choppers were at the camp, where the mess hall was, what time patrols were likely to go out. "We were never far away," Duc said. He recalled how GIs used to search the villagers hired to do menial chores when they passed through the barbed-wire perimeter at the end of every workday. But what they stole wasn't some commodity hidden under skirts and shirts. It was intelligence.

So with darkness settling in on the abandoned hilltop base, the GIs and VC pulled up shirts and rolled up pant legs to show one another their wounds. They roasted seven chickens and drank beer. They shared more photographs and joked about building a veterans meeting hall for Americans and Vietnamese over by the old command post. One GI asked how much an acre of land would cost because this looked like a beautiful place for a retirement home, and the VC answered that in exchange for a visa to the United States he could provide an acre very reasonably. Everyone laughed.

"When I heard about this trip," Bob Garrison said, "I said, 'Man, I'd like to go, but we can't afford it.' And my wife says, 'Like hell we can't. You're going if I have to eat beans for a month.' She paid for me and Mike to come over. And you know, I'm feeling a little softer inside already."

One American swapped his sneakers for a Vietnamese's sandals. Two vets gave Duc their unit medals. He fingered them with interest and slipped them into his breast pocket. "Boom-boom," he laughed, his forefinger extended like a gun barrel. "I shoot you. You shoot me."

The Americans grew quiet after a while. When night came, they made a circle of rocks by the edge of the plateau, and one by one they entered it, sitting alone in the silent, peaceful darkness. The Americans had come of age as teenagers on hills like this. They remembered the adrenaline rush of combat, the dreamy calm of postbattle fatigue. Never had life been so terrible—or so exhilarating. Never had they known such camaraderie or had so much authority and responsibility. For many, all that lay ahead would be a mere footnote.

Don Harris left the rock circle. At first, until he drew close to the group by the flaming barbecue, he appeared as only a shadow, making its way out of the darkness. He had a rare heart disease, and his doctor in Tennessee had told him it was too risky to make the trip to Vietnam. But he had insisted on going, choosing to spend "some of my last days" with the people he truly cared about—Vietnam vets.

"Vietnam," he mused. "This is the one place I really felt like somebody."

More and more American vets are making the journey back to Vietnam, though the total of those returning is only a small fraction of the 2.5 million who served. Clearly, Walt Bacak and his colleagues had led troubled lives; maybe they would have even if there had been no war. Of that I had no idea. But—and I don't think I was imagining this—I saw a change in them during the few days we spent together. After the Pho Vinh trip, they seemed less edgy. I saw Steve Lemire smile for the first time. One infantryman who had looked trampish when I saw him in Pho Vinh showed up for breakfast at the hotel in Danang bathed, shaved, and groomed, and I was surprised to see that he was quite handsome. Everyone was taken aback to discover that a people they had hated—Henry Kissinger had called North Vietnam's leaders "just a bunch of shits; tawdry, filthy shits"—were gracious, friendly, and decent. They had names. They had faces. They had families. They had their dreams and they had their sorrows.

As Bobby Muller, the paraplegic former Marine with whom I had toured the cemetery for North Vietnamese veterans, put it: "You could probably shut down a lot of VA psychiatric clinics in the States simply by bringing the vets back to Vietnam. It's better than any medication, and the angrier the veteran is, the more powerful the experience seems to be."

By the time I went to Pho Vinh with Bacak's group, I had been in Vietnam for more than three years. The country seemed so hospitable, felt so much like home, I could no longer quite fathom why so many Americans lived with its ghosts, why Vietnam kept playing games with our national psyche, opening wounds we thought had healed and forcing us to remember all that we had tried to forget. Perhaps it was that for my generation—including the 2.5 million Americans who went to Vietnam and the 13 million who were eligible but did not—Vietnam was not a country as much as a state of mind. It was where our childhood ended and the long, dark shadows of the Ashau Valley began.

Of the eleven wars the United States has fought on foreign soil, at the cost of 600,000 dead, none lasted as long. Only the Civil War was more divisive. And somewhere between Dong Ha near the DMZ and Ca Mau in the Mekong Delta, the character of an American era was defined. That era challenged the standards of World War II—the yardstick against which we had judged heroism and the rightness of battle—and turned society topsy-turvy in a social and political upheaval of drugs, free love, political scandals and assassinations, interracial strife, protest demonstrations, and the cry: "Hell, no! We won't go!"

Six U.S. presidents, from Harry Truman to Gerald Ford, felt the Vietnam War was worth fighting. Although revisionists believe John F. Kennedy would have extracted the United States from Vietnam, he said just weeks before his assassination: "I don't agree with those who say we should withdraw. That would be a great mistake. I know people don't like Americans to be engaged in this kind of an effort. Forty-seven Americans have been killed in combat with the enemy, but this is a very important struggle."

The problem was that Vietnam left Americans with nothing to celebrate. We didn't lose a battle, yet we remained emotionally stuck at a besieged fire base with no American flag to plant firmly in the ground. And if there is nothing to celebrate, what do you do? You continue to mourn. You go back to the Vietnam Veterans Memorial over and over again. But everything that helped heal, like the wall, also ensured that the wounds kept festering and denied us closure.

"We want a president to be commander in chief, not commander in chicken," U.S. Senator Bob Kerrey—one of 238 Americans who earned the Medal of Honor in Vietnam—said during Bill Clinton's presidential campaign in 1992. We were still trapped at the wall, grieving and groping, unable to move beyond it. Why were we still talking about Vietnam in our political campaigns, nearly twenty years after the war ended?

If the war was so widely regarded as a misadventure, why should Clinton have been penalized for deciding not to rush off to the jungles of Vietnam? After all, John Wayne—deferred from the World War II draft because of his age (thirty-four) and a football shoulder injury—and U.S. Army Captain Ronald Reagan—who spent the war making movies in Hollywood—were viewed as genuine patriots. Vice President Dick Cheney used his draft deferments to avoid Vietnam. Former Vice President Dan Quayle and President George W. Bush joined the National Guard, widely regarded as a dodge. Republican superhawk Newt Gingrich took a pass on Vietnam, too. Politician-journalist Patrick J. Buchanan, a fervent supporter of the war, stayed home with a bum knee. Twenty-seven million Americans came of age during the Vietnam War era, and the vast majority ducked the war through legal or illegal means. It was a huge voting bloc. Why didn't a candidate declare, "Hell, yes, I ducked it. I'm one of you." Because, I suppose, we still heard a voice whispering that all American wars are honorable and that one's duty, when called upon, is simply to go. It's part of punching the clock to adulthood, as every president from Truman to George Bush did. . . .

We couldn't even decide in those days if the real Americans were Jane Fonda and Father Philip Berrigan or John Wayne and Cardinal Richard Cushing. There we were destroying a country in a distant war we chose not to win, being deceived by our leaders and given bloated body counts by our generals, so no wonder we were confused. "This used to be a hell of a good country," the drunken lawyer played by Jack Nicholson said in *Easy Rider*. "I can't understand what's gone wrong with it."

Kennedy's idealism, Johnson's Great Society—had they been just illusions?

Most people in my wartime generation were keenly aware of what they *didn't* do, the road not taken. The grunt under fire in Tay Ninh was aware of the choice he didn't make—to go AWOL or dodge the draft. Those who fled to Canada or stayed in the United States, having found any one of a hundred ways to avoid Vietnam—straights became gay for a day at induction centers, old leg injuries started hurting again for the first time in years, feet suddenly went flat, colleges were swamped with applications— were aware of the innuendo of cowardice and knew there might be a price to pay for their decision down the road. . . .

My recollection of the GIs I knew and saw in combat during the war bore little resemblance to what Hollywood producers would have us believe. They weren't a collective bunch of losers or a gang of psychopaths. They fought well and bravely and for the same reason soldiers fight in any war—to survive and go home. On operations I covered, most commanders went to extraordinary lengths to avoid civilian casualties. If there were shameful incidents for the Americans, such as the massacre of nearly 500 civilians at My Lai in 1968, there were just as many for the North Vietnamese, such as the execution of as many as 3,000 civilians in Hue during the Tet Offensive. I was in Hue in 1969 when the victims' bodies were exhumed from mass graves. There were men and women, many of them teachers, merchants, low-level civil servants. Their hands had been bound behind their backs with wire. Neither in My Lai nor in Hue, I feel certain, was any official order given to kill civilians. In each case, an individual unit under bad leadership had run amok. The results were tragic but were not an accurate reflection of either nation's army as a whole.

Nearly 9 million men and women served in the U.S. armed forces during the Vietnam War era, including 2,594,000 men and 7,484 women in Vietnam and another 600,000 on the offshore fleet and at air bases in Thailand and Guam. As research by MIT professor Arnold Barnett and others, published in 1992, and the book *Stolen Valor,* written by B. G. Burkett and Glenna Whitley in 1998, have shown, they were neither undereducated and ill-disciplined nor disproportionately minority in racial makeup. Nor as a group were they unable to readjust to postwar life even though society gave them the cold shoulder instead of a warm welcome home and no particular benefits. By any criteria the negative image they had to bear as Vietnam vets was a bum rap.

Ninety-seven percent of Americans who served in Vietnam between 1965 and 1975 received honorable discharges—exactly the same percentage as for the ten-year period before the war. The use of drugs was no greater in Vietnam than it was among the same age group in the United States (and it was many joints less than in San Francisco's flower-child Haight-Ashbury neighborhood where I lived before heading off to the war). Only 249 men deserted in Vietnam. As Burkett and Whitley point out, no U.S. platoon ever surrendered as a unit to the NVA or VC; in World War II, several thousand Americans not only surrendered, they ended up fighting for Germany.

The average soldier in Vietnam was nineteen years old—seven years younger than his World War II counterpart. In Vietnam 80 percent of the GIs had completed high school and 14 percent had attended college. In World War II, 35 percent had not gone beyond grammar school. Blacks made up 12.5 percent of the combat deaths in the Vietnam War at a time when blacks of draft age represented 13.5 percent of the U.S. population. Eighty-six percent of the men killed in action were Caucasian. After a statistical analysis of economic levels of ZIP codes where GIs had lived before entering the military, Barnett concluded that variations by income among Vietnam's casualties were minimal.

After the war, most Vietnam vets got on with their lives. Many became leaders in Congress, industry, and the media. In 1994, the unemployment rate for veterans was 3 percent, well below the national average of 4.9 percent. The Centers for Disease Control in Atlanta reported that suicide rates were within the normal range for the general population. In 1999, the *Vietnam Economic Times* reported that in an earlier U.S. poll 71 percent of vets said they were "glad to have served in Vietnam" and 74 percent said they "enjoyed" their tour of duty. A survey by the Veterans of Foreign Wars said 87 percent of the public held Vietnam veterans in high esteem.

A few days after Saigon fell in 1975, communist cadres went from embassy to abandoned embassy, raising the National Liberation Front flag. The only embassy they bypassed was that of the United States. Nayan Chanda, the *Far Eastern Economic Review*'s Saigon bureau chief, one of a handful of journalists who stayed behind after the helicopter evacuation, asked a soldier guarding the U.S. Embassy why no Viet Cong flag was flying overhead. "We are not authorized to raise one," he told Chanda. "We do not want to humiliate the Americans. They will come back."

The response perhaps reflected more pragmatism than magnanimity. Indeed, the United States had economic and technological resources the Soviet Union lacked, and tapping into them would have provided a huge boost to Vietnam's development. But first Washington wanted to ensure Hanoi was punished for its victory: Washington froze Vietnam's assets in the United States ($260 million) and prohibited Americans

from sending money to Vietnam; severed mail and telephone links between the two nations; refused to consider diplomatic relations with the newly reunited state; reneged on Nixon and Kissinger's promise to supply Vietnam with $3.3 billion in reconstruction aid; vetoed Vietnam's requests to join the United Nations; blocked credits and loans from the World Bank and the Asian Development Bank; and instituted a trade embargo that Japan and other allies were pressured into observing.

Washington's punitive policies pushed Vietnam toward the precipice of disaster. And Hanoi's doctrinaire rulers gave the country the final shove over the edge with an agenda that was both vindictive and ill-conceived. When Bui Tin of the North Vietnamese Army accepted South Vietnam's surrender on April 30, 1975—he was a journalist but, as a colonel, was the senior officer present—he told Saigon's nervous cabinet ministers: "You have nothing to fear. Between Vietnamese, there are no victors and no vanquished. Only the Americans have been beaten. If you are patriots, consider this a moment of joy. The war for our country is over."

But if the war was over, the Dark Years were just beginning: the reeducation camps and forced resettlement of peasants in so-called economic zones; the collectivization of farming and near famine; the confiscation of wealth and loss of civil liberties; the wars against Cambodia and China; paranoia, isolation, and deprivation. Never had anyone imagined peace could bring such deep suffering.

The anguish and misery of the people, however, did not stir much response from former antiwar protestors who had expressed such sympathy for the Vietnamese when they themselves had been in danger of going off to war. Tom Hayden had cheered the fall of Saigon, saying it would lead to the "rise of Indochina." Huh? A thousand University of California students had marched through Berkeley on April 30 in celebration. But in celebration of themselves or the Vietnamese? Where was Jane Fonda after the war was over? There was silence, I suppose, because the protests never had anything to do with the ultimate well-being of the Vietnamese people. They were about self-interests and ending U.S. involvement. Once those goals had been met, what the Vietnamese did to the Vietnamese didn't matter. Reconciliation could wait for another day.

Japan and the United States normalized diplomatic relations six years after the end of World War II. It took Vietnam and the United States twenty years to take the same step. But if the war was characterized by missed opportunities for peace on both sides, so was the peace defined by lost chances to chart a new and constructive direction in U.S.-Vietnamese relations. . . .

Among the many strange twists along the rapprochement road Hanoi and Washington traveled was that the reconciliation process was started by the men who fought the war and concluded by a man, President Clinton, who avoided it. It began with the small group of vets Bobby Muller, the paraplegic Marine, had taken back to Hanoi in 1981. When he returned to Washington, he went to see then–U.S. Representative (and now Senator) John McCain, the former Navy pilot who had been shot down and taken prisoner within spitting distance of my Hanoi apartment. McCain shook with anger and pounded on his desk, "God damn it, Bobby! What are you going back and talking to the enemy for?" But McCain gradually softened. He came to believe the anger and hatred inside him only served to keep the past alive, and although he continued to refer to his torturers in Hoa Lo Prison as "gooks," he became a leading advocate of reconciliation. He was joined by other veter-

ans, Republicans and Democrats, on Capitol Hill: Senators Bob Kerrey of Nebraska, John Kerry of Massachusetts, Max Cleland of Georgia, and Chuck Robb of Virginia; Representatives Jay Rhodes and Jim Kolbe of Arizona, Tom Carper of Delaware, Lane Evans of Illinois, David Skaggs of Colorado, Wayne Gilchrist of Maryland, and fellow POW Pete Peterson of Florida.

Clinton formalized the reconciliation process. He lifted the trade embargo and established diplomatic relations in 1995. He sent Peterson to Hanoi in 1997 as the first U.S. ambassador to Vietnam since Saigon fell. In 2000 Clinton signed a bilateral trade agreement with Vietnam and visited Hanoi and Ho Chi Minh City. He was the first U.S. president to set foot on Vietnamese soil since 1969, when in a muddy field twelve miles north of Saigon Richard Nixon told two rifle companies of the 1st Infantry Division: "Out here in this dreary difficult war, I think history will record that this may have been one of America's finest hours, because we took on a difficult task and succeeded." He went on to note: "This is the first time in our history when we have had a lack of understanding of why we are here, what the war is all about."

Two men who had both everything and nothing in common found themselves seated next to each other at a dinner party in Hanoi, struggling to find common ground for conversation. One was Do Muoi, a one-time house painter who had joined the Communist Party in 1939 and become a revolutionary. French authorities had sentenced him to ten years in prison at the onset of World War II, but he escaped after serving less than half his time. He rose steadily in the Party's hierarchy, always the conservative ideologue, and now was one of Vietnam's most powerful figures. The other man was Pete Peterson, eighteen years Do Muoi's junior. He was a retired career U.S.

Air Force colonel and Vietnam vet, a fresh-man Democratic congressman from Florida who knew more than his share of tragedy after the war ended: His teenage son, Doug, had died in a car crash in 1983; his wife, Carlotta, would die of cancer in 1995.

Do Muoi leaned close to Peterson and asked, "Were you ever tortured?" Such bluntness is unusual in Vietnam, and Peterson wasn't sure what to say. Had he wanted to, Peterson could have told him about his six years in Hoa Lo Prison—the Hanoi Hilton as American POWs called it—and other wartime prisons with nicknames like Heartbreak Hotel, the Zoo, the Pigsty, Dogpatch, and Camp Unity. He could have told him about the beatings that left him unconscious; about the leg irons and the elbows manacled so tightly behind the back that it felt his chest would explode at any moment; about solitary confinement and a diet of grass soup and pumpkin; about the ropes that curled his body into the shape of a rocking horse and the guards who sat on his contorted body and, smiling, bounced him up and down like a toy; about being forced to kneel for days, arms extended overhead, until swollen limbs went numb with pain and the mind went dead. He could have said all this, but he didn't. That chapter of his life was over. Peterson dismissed the question with a wave of the hand. "I'd rather talk about the future, about what we can do to move relations between the United States and Vietnam forward," he said.

But Do Muoi was insistent. "No, I want to know. Were you tortured?"

"Yes," Peterson said. He rolled back his shirtsleeves. Rope burns still scarred his elbows. He held up the hand that sometimes went so numb he momentarily wondered if it had fallen off his body. Do Muoi said nothing at first. Then he pulled up one trouser leg. The long scar he revealed was ugly and jagged. "I was tortured, too," Do

Muoi said, "in the same prison as you, Hoa Lo. By the French, a good many years before you got there."

That exchange occurred in 1991, during Peterson's first trip to Vietnam since being released from Hoa Lo with other American POWs in 1973. He had come back to grapple with a question Americans were just beginning to ask: Was it time for the United States and Vietnam to exorcise the past and reconcile their differences? Peterson found the answer in the streets of Hanoi—in the faces of the students he passed, in the eyes of the street kids who hawked pirated reprints of Graham Greene's *The Quiet American* and Bao Ninh's *The Sorrow of War,* in the enthusiasm and graciousness of the young people with whom he stopped to chat—and the answer was a resounding yes.

"Only a small percentage of the people I saw had had any involvement with the war," Peterson said. "Most were born after we'd left. And I said to myself, 'Why should we disallow them the better life they want and deserve? Why should we disallow them the well-being of Vietnam?'"

Peterson was shot down by antiaircraft fire in 1966 on his sixty-seventh mission, a nighttime bombing run against the rail line just north of Hanoi. His arm and leg fractured, his plane in flames, Peterson parachuted into the village of An Doai east of Hanoi. He heard the voices of angry villagers approaching through the rice paddies. He took his .38 revolver from its holster and considered blowing his brains out. "Everyone mobilize," yelled militiaman Do The Dong, who was in charge of the village loudspeaker that day. "Find the American!" His eyes unfocused, squinting, Peterson could see the outline of a peasant mob pushing close, armed with rifles, sticks, knives. Enemies everywhere, not a friendly for a million miles. Never had he felt—or been—so alone. Many of the villagers wanted to beat or kill the American, Dong later recalled, but did not because Ho Chi Minh had said many times that captured Americans were to be turned over to the authorities, not killed. After a night in An Doai, Peterson was dumped into a motorcycle sidecar and paraded through villages where peasants pelted him with rocks. It took several hours to get to Hanoi. There in the old French-built prison on Hai Ba Trung Street Peterson would begin the "most terrible, disgusting, sad event of my life"—six years as a POW.

Thirty-one years to the day of being shot down, Peterson returned to An Doai. I went to meet him, but I got lost on the ninety-minute drive from Hanoi. I stopped at villages along the way to ask directions, and smiling farmers would point this way and that, usually giving entirely contradictory instructions. Finally I happened upon a town where local officials had gathered in the dirt courtyard of the People's Committee headquarters, and I knew I'd arrived at the right place. The new U.S. ambassador pulled into An Doai an hour later, in a Toyota Land Cruiser that flew an American flag. He stepped from the vehicle, smiling, right hand extended, and greeted his former enemies in Vietnamese. If the event wasn't exactly a homecoming, it was at least a symbol of the reconciliation that would become Peterson's trademark as ambassador.

Peterson walked out along an earthen dike and stood by the mango tree where he and his copilot, Bernard Talley (who was captured, uninjured, the day after Peterson and now flew DC-10s for American Airlines), had landed by parachute. He didn't say much at first. Most of the village had gathered around him, and he asked if anyone had found the revolver he had ditched in the paddies as the militia approached. "I did," said seventy-year-old Nguyen Danh Xinh. "I found it and turned it over to the People's Committee. It had all six bullets in it."

"And my necklace. Did you find the necklace?" he asked, referring to the Christ medallion he had worn since he and Carlotta had purchased it at a church shop in Florida years earlier. That too had been found, Xinh said, but no one knew where it was any more. Peterson, clearly disappointed, let the matter drop.

One of the first militiamen to reach the downed Air Force captain, Nguyen Viet Chop (*chop* means "seize" in Vietnamese), had assembled his three daughters and four grandchildren for Peterson's return. Now seventy and a shopkeeper, Chop wrapped both his hands around the ambassador's right hand in greeting. He led him past a shed where a water buffalo was tethered and into his one-room home. Grapes and tea were on the table, and incense burned on the altar. The air was heavy with heat and humidity. Chop and Peterson came from such different worlds that there wasn't a great deal to talk about or many memories to share. But Chop said Peterson was the most important foreign visitor to ever come to An Doai; he would always welcome him in his home. Peterson spoke about progress toward reconciliation and told Chop to drop by the U.S. Embassy and say hello if he were ever in Hanoi. (One imagined Mr. Chop was not a man who left his village often. But a few months later, a puzzled U.S. Marine guard at the embassy called Peterson's secretary and said, "There's a Mr. Chop down here. He says he knows the ambassador and wants to say hello." Peterson came down to the lobby, and they chatted for fifteen minutes.)

During his more than four years in Vietnam, Peterson became a walking billboard for reconciliation. He could have harbored anger but didn't. He could have been a career POW but wasn't. He never apologized for the war or his involvement in it—Vietnamese officials never asked him to—but he never stopped thinking that a firm and lasting friendship was within Vietnam and the United States' reach.

Peterson became such a popular figure that ordinary Vietnamese would stop him on the streets and ask to have their picture taken with him. A popular expat restaurant, the Red Onion, located next to the Hanoi Hilton, printed a line on its menu stating that in deference to Ambassador Peterson it did not serve pumpkin soup. Peterson rode through Hanoi on weekends, unescorted, on his motor scooter, got his hair cut at a local barber shop for half a buck, and enjoyed slurping *pho,* the traditional noodle broth, in sidewalk cafés for lunch. At a diplomatic reception, he met a beautiful Vietnamese businesswoman, Vi Le, who had left Saigon as a child and become an Australian citizen, and in 1998 they were married in Hanoi's Catholic Cathedral. Their marriage, he said, wasn't about reconciliation—just love.

"I went back to Vietnam not because I had to," Peterson said. "I went back because I wanted to. I saw the Vietnamese at their very worst, and they saw me at my very worst as well. And it's a rare opportunity for someone to go back to a country like this in which there was so much pain, and to then focus on the future. I can't do anything about what happened yesterday, but I can help move forward positively and constructively on what happens tomorrow."

My time in Hanoi overlapped with Peterson's assignment as ambassador, and we became friends. I poked around, looking for a soft spot in his shield. He delivered his reconciliation message with the zeal of a warrior-turned-missionary, but surely he carried some animosity. He couldn't have laid all the demons to rest. Surely some monster images rattled around his head when he passed Hoa Lo Prison a couple of times a day en route to or from work. He denied it, and I came to believe him without understanding where he had found the capacity to separate past and present. Perhaps

part of the explanation was that he was a religious man, which I assume gave him strength, but this was not something he talked about. He had known great personal loss with the deaths of his son and wife, and that probably reminded him of the value of filling Kipling's unforgiving minute with sixty seconds of distance run. The military had taught him discipline; prison, how to survive; war, that it was easier to destroy than to build.

My wife spent months shadowing Peterson for a documentary profile of him broadcast by PBS. Sandy and I both reached the same conclusion: He was who and what he said he was. Like the Vietnamese themselves, he had forgiven if not forgotten. He had channeled his pain into constructive energy. He did not let memories take control of him or what he did. "If I'd let them," he said, "I couldn't have functioned."

On Vietnam's National Day in 1997, his first in Hanoi as U.S. ambassador, Peterson walked in ceremonial procession up the red-carpeted stairs of Ho Chi Minh's mausoleum with other members of the diplomatic corps. At the open casket, each ambassador was to execute a left-face and make a respectful bow. Every eye was on Peterson. Would the former POW bow as he once had to do, in a sign of forced respect, before his sadistic prison torturers? Would the new ambassador show reverence to the man who had been his country's mortal enemy for a generation?

Inside the mausoleum the temperature was a controlled sixty-eight degrees. The light was dim, almost eerily so. At the coffin, Peterson did a smart left-face, paused with his arms extended at his side, and bent forward slightly from the waist. "I really had no trouble doing it," he later recalled. "Especially when I remembered Ho's policy that prisoners not be killed on the spot. If it wasn't for that, I might not be here today."

QUESTIONS FOR DISCUSSION

1. How does the actual profile of Vietnam veterans differ from popular stereotypes?
2. How were the veterans of both sides of the war able to experience reconciliation?

3. What are the implications of this reading for other forms of conflict between nations and groups? Does this provide useful insights for conflict resolution?

THE SOCIAL WEB

- The International Campaign to Ban Landmines was awarded the Nobel Peace Prize in 1997. This organization monitors the location of landmines, the removal of landmines, and the casualties resulting from landmine explosions. It also addresses key issues in assisting survivors of landmine explosions: www.icbl.org.
- The *Bulletin of Atomic Scientists* has been publishing its famous "Doomsday Clock" every year since 1947. The clock represents the degree of danger the world faces from the threat of nuclear annihilation. For a history of the clock and to compare what "time" it has been in various years, log onto: www.thebulletin.org/media/current.html.
- The United Nations Department for Disarmament Affairs maintains a Web site offering the latest information on disarmament research, treaties and programs. It also offers links to a comprehensive list of peace-related Web sites around the world: www.disarmament.un.org.

QUESTIONS FOR DEBATE

1. Does the threat of terrorism demand that certain civil liberties be contained or suspended altogether? How far should we go to promote national security within our own borders?
2. How should our national interests be defined? Do we have a responsibility to develop foreign policies that promote humanitarian concerns? Are we willing to pay the economic and military costs to promote human rights worldwide?
3. Does the U.S. military need to achieve greater gender equity? What changes would be required in both military structure and culture to achieve gender parity?
4. What are the circumstances under which you think it is appropriate for the United States to go to war?
5. What are the benefits of global peace? What are the factors that must be addressed in order to achieve global peace? What role could the United States play in that process?

READING BETW